D0556255

EMORY UNIVERSITY STUDIES IN LAW AND RELIGION

John Witte Jr., General Editor

BOOKS IN THE SERIES

Religious Liberty in Western Thought
Noel B. Reynolds and W. Cole Durham Jr., eds.

Political Order and the Plural Structure of Society
James W. Skillen and Rockne M. McCarthy

The Idea of Natural Rights:
Studies on Natural Rights, Natural Law, and Church Law, 1150-1625
Brian Tierney

The Fabric of Hope: An Essay
Glenn Tinder

Liberty: Rethinking an Imperiled Ideal
Glenn Tinder

Religious Human Rights in Global Perspective: Legal Perspectives
Johan D. van der Vyver and John Witte Jr., eds.

Natural Law and the Two Kingdoms:
A Study in the Development of Reformed Social Thought
David VanDrunen

Early New England: A Covenanted Society
David A. Weir

God's Joust, God's Justice: Law and Religion in the Western Tradition
John Witte Jr.

Religious Human Rights in Global Perspective: Religious Perspectives
John Witte Jr. and Johan D. van der Vyver, eds.

RELIGIOUS LIBERTY

VOLUME 1

Overviews and History

Douglas Laycock

Yale Kamisar Collegiate Professor of Law,
The University of Michigan

Alice McKean Young Regents Chair in Law Emeritus,
The University of Texas

WILLIAM B. EERDMANS PUBLISHING COMPANY
GRAND RAPIDS, MICHIGAN / CAMBRIDGE, U.K.

Published 2010 by
Wm. B. Eerdmans Publishing Co.
2140 Oak Industrial Drive N.E., Grand Rapids, Michigan 49505 /
P.O. Box 163, Cambridge CB3 9PU U.K.
www.eerdmans.com

Printed in the United States of America

15 14 13 12 11 10   7 6 5 4 3 2 1

Library of Congress Cataloging-in-Publication Data

Laycock, Douglas.
   Religious liberty: overviews and history / Douglas Laycock.
         p.   cm.   — (Emory University studies in law and religion)
   Includes index.
   ISBN 978-0-8028-6465-9 (pbk.: alk. paper)
   1. Freedom of religion — United States.
   2. Church and state — United States.   I. Title.

   KF4783.L39   2010
   342.7308′52 — dc22

                                             2009042567

"Religious Liberty as Liberty." Copyright 1996 *Journal of Contemporary Legal Issues.* Reprinted with the permission of the Journal of Contemporary Legal Issues.

"Religious Liberty: The Legal Rights of Religious Belief and Ministry" originally appeared in the January 1988 issue of *Concern,* published by Presbyterian Women. For more information on Presbyterian Women and their current magazine, *Horizons,* visit www.pcusa.org/pw or www.pcusa.org/horizons.

"Forging Ideological Compromise." © 2002, The New York Times. Reprinted by permission.

"Injudicious: Liberals Should Get Tough on Bush's Conservative Judicial Nominees — Stop Opposing Michael McConnell." Reprinted from *The American Prospect Online:* October 30, 2002. www.prospect.org. The American Prospect, 1710 Rhode Island Avenue NW, 12th Floor, Washington, DC 20036. All rights reserved.

In memory of

REV. DEAN M. KELLEY

trained as a pastor,

self-taught in law,

long-time executive and counselor for religious liberty

at the National Council of Churches,

a strong and effective voice

who defended the religious liberty of all

Contents

Foreword

It is a special privilege for the Emory University Studies in Law and Religion Series to publish the collected writings of Douglas Laycock on religious liberty. Professor Laycock has been one of the world's leading scholars of religious liberty for the past three decades and has written briefs and argued in a number of Supreme Court and Court of Appeals cases. He has crafted federal and state legislation on religious liberty, testified before countless Congressional committees, and appeared regularly in televised and print media. He has stood at distinguished lecterns throughout North America, including two memorable keynote appearances at Emory Law School. Currently the Yale Kamisar Professor of Law at the University of Michigan Law School, he was formerly chaired professor of law at the University of Texas at Austin and before that professor of law at the University of Chicago Law School.

It is his work as a scholar of religious liberty, however, that has set Professor Laycock apart from virtually every other person now working in the field of religious liberty. Laycock's work has shaped a number of major religious liberty doctrines in America. Building on the writings of Paul Kauper and Arlin Adams, for example, he developed the concept of "church autonomy" in a path-breaking 1981 article in the *Columbia Law Review*. The phrase is now commonly used, as he advocated, to describe a church's right to manage its own internal affairs, as distinguished from the right of a church or believer to refrain from violating their religious teachings. This understanding is also now common currency in European jurisprudence of "religious autonomy." He wrote a path-breaking article on "non-preferential aid" in the 1986 *William & Mary Law Review* that exposed a number of the false historical claims being pressed by judges and jurists alike in their attempts to weaken the First Amendment Establishment clause. He helped create the idea of equal access for religious and secular speakers by writing the seminal article on that idea in a 1986 *Northwestern Law Review,* an article which has convinced secular liberals and religious conservatives alike to support equal access for religious speech. That concept has driven a dozen major Supreme Court cases. He coined the phrase "substantive neutrality," distinguishing it from "formal neutrality," in a memorable lecture at the DePaul Center for Church/State Studies. He was the first to explain how exempting religiously motivated behavior from regulation could be substantively neutral — and therefore consistent with neutrality understandings of the First Amendment religion clauses — even if it looked like special treatment for religion and thus was not formally neutral. Formal and substantive neutrality is now a widespread usage in the literature and case law. He was also one of the principal champions of the 1993 Religious Freedom Restoration Act and the 2000 Religious Land Use and Institutionalized Persons Act, two federal statutes which, among others, have provided some measure of protection for vulnerable religious minorities.

His writing is consistently crisp, concise, and cogent. He is not given to ponderous academic prose or arcane legalese, yet he finds a way of capturing complex legal issues artfully and comprehensively. Most of his work is readily accessible to scholars and students of law, theology, ethics, political science, history, and American studies alike. The chapters gathered in this volume and its sequels are goldmines of information and meet gold standards of erudition. Here are a few choice phrases you will encounter in the pages that follow:

- "Suppression of a faith is no less suppression when the victims go quietly."
- "Reliance on post-ratification practice leads to such absurd consequences because it proceeds backwards. It lets the behavior of government officials control the meaning of the Constitution, when the whole point is for the Constitution to control the behavior of government officials."
- "Nor is it the case that tax exemption, considered alone, is a subsidy. Government does not subsidize a church by leaving it alone."
- "Religion is not free when the government charges for its exercise."
- "Proponents of landmarking seem genuinely unable to comprehend why churches object to maintaining their houses of worship as permanent architectural museums, at the expense of those who worship there, for the aesthetic pleasure of those who do not."
- "The judicial role is defined by the Constitution; the Constitution is not defined by changing conceptions of the judicial role."

In all his writing, Professor Laycock's perspective is not pro-religion or anti-religion, but pro-religious liberty. In his writing and advocacy, he has defended religious liberty for believers and nonbelievers alike. He has worked closely with groups from across the religious and political spectrum — Evangelicals, Catholics, Mormons, Mainline Protestants, Seventh-day Adventists, Jews (including Orthodox, Conservative, and Reform), the ACLU, People for the American Way, Americans United for Separation of Church and State, liberal Democrats and conservative Republicans. Hanging on his office wall at the University of Texas when I visited him (and no doubt now at the University of Michigan, too) are pictures with him and Bill Clinton and a framed thank you note from George W. Bush. All serious sides of the perennial culture wars surrounding religion and religious liberty respect him, regardless of whether they agree or disagree with him.

It is a great boon to the field of religious liberty — and American religion and culture more generally — to have Professor Laycock's wise writings, currently scattered in multiple forums and formats, gathered in one thematically organized collection. It is fitting to have his work appear in a book series that has included entries from several other scholarly titans on law and religion, including Harold J. Berman, Brian Tierney, and Glenn Tinder, with further volumes forthcoming from Michael McConnell, David Little, and others.

This effort to publish the collected writings of leading scholars of religious liberty is part and product of a major project on "Law, Religion, and Human Rights," generously sponsored by the Henry Luce Foundation in New York City. My colleagues and I in the Center for the Study of Law and Religion at Emory University would like to express our deep appreciation to Luce President Michael Gilligan and Senior Program Officer, Terry Lautz, for their uncommonly kind and keen project guidance and support. We would also to thank the University of Michigan Law School and the University of Texas Law School for their generous subvention in support of this collected works projects. We also express our deep gratitude to Amy Wheeler, Associate Editor of the Emory University Studies in Law and Religion Series, for her hard work on the preparation of this manuscript. And we express our deep gratitude to Jon Pott and his colleagues at Eerdmans for taking on this important collection and for publishing it with their usual efficiency, sharp editing, and handsome production.

We reserve our deepest thanks and praise to Douglas Laycock for his exemplary scholarship and advocacy on issues of religious liberty, religion and human rights, and church-state relations. May it long continue!

> JOHN WITTE, JR.
> *General Editor,*
> *Emory University Studies in Law and Religion*

Preface to the Collected Works

It was both a surprise and an honor when the Center for the Study of Law and Religion at Emory University invited me to help compile a comprehensive collection of my work on religious liberty. At least, it will be comprehensive up to the date of publication; I do not intend to quit thinking and writing about these issues when these volumes are sent to the printer.

In 2007, I finished my first thirty years of studying, defending, and writing about religious liberty. For reasons having nothing to do with me, it has been a remarkable thirty years, a time of great religious fervor and substantial religious conflict in the United States. Some commentators describe this time as a culture war. It is quite possible that historians will call it the fourth Great Awakening — one of a series of periods of intense evangelical Christian revival that have swept through the United States at long intervals since the first Great Awakening, which peaked in the 1740s. However we characterize the last thirty years, this period has produced serious debate and reexamination of every aspect of religious liberty.

I have participated in these debates from a position of relative neutrality in the putative culture wars. Of course I have taken strong positions on individual issues, but I have sometimes defended conservative Christians, sometimes their secular opponents, sometimes believers in other faiths. My perspective has never been for religion or against religion, but for religious liberty — for believers of all kinds and for nonbelievers as well. From that perspective, each of the publicly perceived sides in the culture wars is right on some issues and wrong on others. There is a simple reason why each side is right on some issues and wrong on others: it is because their positions are too often dictated by their own self-interest, by what is good for religion or bad for religion, or sometimes, by what is good for evangelical Christians or bad for evangelical Christians.

I have argued for maximizing the religious freedom of all sides and letting the chips fall where they may. I have strongly defended the right of individuals and of organized groups to believe what they will about religion, to speak about those beliefs and attempt to persuade others, and to act on those beliefs. I have strongly opposed all efforts to get government to take sides with respect to beliefs about religion, to impose religious exercises on audiences assembled for other purposes, or to encourage or discourage any religious belief or practice. I have tried to think systematically about what it means to encourage or discourage religion and what it means for government to minimize its influence on religious choices and commitments.

This fundamental perspective led to a series of theoretical and policy principles that are prominently associated with my work (although none of them is entirely unique to me). One such principle, prominent in this volume, is substantive neutrality as distinguished from formal neutrality. Formal neutrality means religiously neutral categories — religion-blind government. Substantive neutrality means religiously neutral incentives — government conduct that insofar as possible neither encourages nor discourages religion. This theme is pervasive in my work, often explicit, sometimes implicit and simply assumed. *Formal, Substantive, and Disaggregated Neutrality toward Religion* (1990) is my original statement of substantive neutrality; *Substantive Neutrality Revisited* (2007) is a mature summary and review.

Another premise fundamental in my work is that religious believers should be free to act on religious teachings or religiously informed conscience, except where the state must intervene to prevent significant harms to others. This right to "exercise" one's religion, in the language of the Constitution's Free Exercise Clause, sometimes requires that religiously motivated conduct be exempted from generally applicable laws, as when some faiths refuse to employ women as clergy, or when they give sacramental wine to children and adolescents. In a pervasively regulated society, such exemptions are essential to religious liberty. That view is by no means unique to me; it is very widely shared among defenders of religious liberty. But it has been controversial in the last generation, and it has been the subject of extensive legislation and litigation as well as academic debate. The Supreme Court of the United States interpreted the Constitution not to include any right to religious exemption from general regulation; Congress, many state legislatures, and many state supreme courts have disagreed.

This claim of a right to regulatory exemptions under the Constitution will be the focus of much of volume 2; multiple attempts to create a right to regulatory exemptions by legislation will be the focus of most of volume 3. My most basic statement on the right to religious exemption from regulation is *The Remnants of Free Exercise* (1990), projected to appear in volume 2. In volume 1, the issue gets significant treatment in articles overviewing the entire field, especially *Religious Liberty as Liberty* (1996), *The Supreme Court and Religious Liberty* (2000), and *Theology Scholarships, the Pledge of Allegiance, and Religious Liberty* (2004). *Religious Liberty as Liberty* is also my most basic statement of why we protect religious liberty in the first place.

The original impetus for my theory of substantive neutrality was to reconcile the claim to religious exemption from generally applicable laws, which seems axiomatic to religious liberty, with the widely shared intuition that government should be neutral towards religion. An exemption from regulation is a form of special treatment, and thus a departure from religiously neutral categories, but because it removes the threat that government will penalize religious observance, the exemption often creates religiously neutral incentives. So the right to regulatory exemptions is prominent in articles on substantive neutrality.

A principle more specifically associated with my work is church autonomy — that religious organizations are entitled to manage their own internal affairs free of government interference. Church autonomy is distinct from, and independent of, the more widely understood claim of a right to regulatory exemptions on the basis of specific religious doctrines or conscientiously held beliefs. A church's right to select its own clergy, define its own governing structure, and resolve its own internal disputes should not depend on whether it can show in every case that its decisions are based on some specific church teaching. Rather, the right to make such inherently religious decisions is inherent in religious liberty. Sometimes the courts agree; sometimes they seem not to understand the argument.

Church autonomy will be prominent in volume 2. I did not coin the phrase "church autonomy," but I seem to have brought it to the attention of religious liberty scholars. The original article in which I defined and promoted the concept is *Towards a General Theory of the Religion Clauses* (1981). Volume 2 will also contain numerous applications of church autonomy to religious governance, religious employment, religious schools, and religious counseling, including the limits of church autonomy in such controversial contexts as the sex-abuse cases.

Another principle, widely shared but also prominently associated with my work, is that religious speech by citizens speaking in their private capacity is constitutionally protected, while the same religious speech by government employees speaking in their governmental capacity is constitutionally prohibited or very tightly restricted. This basic distinction and its many applications is projected to be the subject of much of volume 4. The original article in which I first promoted the idea is *Equal Access and Moments of Silence* (1986). The idea gets prominent treatment in overview articles in this volume, especially *Religious Liberty as Liberty* (1996), and *Theology Scholarships, The Pledge of Allegiance, and Religious Liberty* (2004).

Still another basic principle, especially in my later work, is that government cannot fund religious activities, but that when a religious organization provides a secular service in a religious environment, government can fund the secular service to the same extent that it funds similar services by secular providers. I came to the second half of this position by a long slow evolution over the course of my career; many others had promoted the idea before me. Specific treatments of this idea will appear in volume 4. But my most complete statements of the theory appear in parts of overview articles in volume 1: *Theology Scholarships, the Pledge of Allegiance, and Religious Liberty* (2004), and *Substantive Neutrality Revisited* (2007).

Constitutional debates over religious liberty are much informed by history — the history of religious conflict and persecution in Europe and the American colonies, the debate in the Founding Era of the United States over religious liberty and especially over disestablishing the established churches in New England and the southern colonies, and the history of Catholic-Protestant conflict in the United States, especially in the nineteenth century. I have investigated each of these historical conflicts, and this historical work appears in volume 1. The history article that has had the greatest influence is probably *"Nonpreferential" Aid to Religion* (1986), which refutes the claim that the American Founders intended to permit government to aid religion so long as it aided all religions without showing any preference among them.

Each of these broad principles and each of these historical investigations has many applications, most of them disputed. Much of my work has been inductive in a sense, developing and elaborating broader principles in the course of proposing solutions to specific controversies. These treatments of specific applications appear throughout these volumes, in a variety of genres.

Some of these specific applications involve distinctly contemporary disputes. But the underlying disagreements have had a remarkable staying power. The argument over whether to regulate religious practices, or to exempt them from regulation where possible, goes back to colonial times. The argument over government speech promoting or endorsing religion goes back to the creation of the public schools in the second quarter of the nineteenth century. The argument about government funding of religious institutions goes back to the same period, in substantially its modern form, and back to colonial times in a rather different form, when the debate was about funding the church itself. The persistence of these issues implies that they will be with us long into the future, and that the discussions here will remain relevant to live controversies, both theoretical and practical.

The principles set forth here align me with different groups on different issues. Consequently, I have worked closely with groups from across the religious and political spectrum — mainline Protestants, evangelicals, the Catholic bishops, Jews (including Orthodox, Conservative, and Reform), Mormons, Seventh-day Adventists, small religions far outside the mainstream (Hare Krishna, Scientology, Santeria, Uniao do Vegetal), the American Civil Liberties Union, People for the American Way, Americans United for Separation of Church and State, liberal Democrats, conservative Republicans, the Clinton Administration, and the Bush Administration. Hanging on my office wall are photographs with Bill Clinton and a thank-you note from George W. Bush. I have worked closely with all these groups when we agreed, and they have generally respected my integrity when we disagreed.

I have participated in these debates in the law reviews, in the religious and secular press, in the courts, and in legislative hearings, producing scholarly articles, popular articles, written and oral arguments to courts, and formal and informal statements to legislators. These different genres slice the material in different ways and may be useful to different readers. Some readers will prefer a fully elaborated, fully footnoted scholarly treatment; others will find it easier to get the main ideas from a short popular treatment. Each form is included here. And while there is overlap, each entry says something at least somewhat different from all the others. The editors and I have decided to omit only those writings that are almost entirely duplicative of earlier work. I will have more to say about the inclusion of briefs and legislative testimony in later volumes where those genres appear.

Most of this work is available only in major law libraries or subscription-based legal databases. These sources are accessible to lawyers but seriously inconvenient or wholly inaccessible to non-lawyers. Some of this work was circulated in limited quantities to select audiences and is not publicly available anywhere except in this collection. We hope that this collection will make this work available to religious leaders and religious scholars and to scholars studying these issues from the perspective of political science, sociology, or other disciplines, and that it will make the entire corpus more readily accessible to lawyers and law students.

We anticipate that the work will appear in four volumes. The law of religious liberty is dominated by three broad sets of disputes, over regulation of religious practice, regulation and sponsorship of religious speech, and funding of religious institutions. Volume 1, *Overviews and History,* includes overview articles that address at least two — often all three — of these broad areas. Volume 1 also includes my historical work, book reviews not focused on a specific issue addressed in a later volume, and some work on judicial nominations, where disagreements over religious liberty have played a large role.

Volume 2, *The Free Exercise Clause,* will collect my work on the constitutional right to free exercise of religion. Volume 3, *Religious Liberty Legislation,* will collect work on statutory guarantees of religious liberty. Volume 4, *The Free Speech and Establishment Clauses,* will collect work on freedom of religious speech and on the disestablishment of religion, including disputes over government speech about religion and government funding of religious institutions.

Each entry is accompanied by a short introduction that places it in context. Each section of related entries has a similar introduction that explains the theme of the section and very briefly describes each entry. These introductions also contain cross-references to related entries that appear elsewhere because their dominant theme placed them in a different organizational category. Readers can use these introductions to find the pieces that most interest them. Within each section, the pieces are arranged chronologically.

Many of the entries have a second explanatory paragraph, which appears in an unnumbered footnote at the bottom of the first page. This is the author's note from the original publication, slightly amended because it is no longer necessary to identify the author.

Readers without legal training should not be intimidated by the footnotes. If you wish, you can ignore them and miss very little. I have always viewed textual footnotes as a burdensome distraction, and I try to write as few of them as possible. I see that I have succumbed to the temptation to write more of them than I like to remember, but even so, the great bulk of what you will find in the footnotes is extensive citations to other scholarly articles, court decisions, statutes, and regulations, usually with brief parenthetical explanations of what those sources say. If you are not interested in the details of my sources, you can skip those citations.

Legal writing is so voluminously footnoted because law is an adversary discipline. Practicing lawyers are paid to make arguments, they are tempted to exaggerate, and they don't entirely trust each other. So when a lawyer wants to show that he's telling the truth, he includes a footnote for every detail of his argument. The practice carried over to scholarly legal writing, which has absorbed some of the same adversary characteristics, and it was exaggerated by the tradition of entrusting the leading journals to student editors, who are understandably insecure about their role and compensate in part by strictly enforcing excessively detailed rules about footnoting. All this footnoting can be annoying, but much more so for authors than for readers. The advantage is that when a reader wants to know where some assertion comes from, she can generally get a very precise answer by taking a peek at the footnotes. The main thing for readers from other disciplines to remember is that lawyers put the volume number *before* the title of the book or journal article, not after.

Because they footnote so heavily, lawyers developed a compact system of citation that conveys a lot of information about the cited source. Most of that information is surprisingly easy to extract. For any readers who are interested, Appendix 2 is a decoder ring — a short and simple readers' guide to the basics of legal citation form and the information encapsulated in citations. To reduce the number of citation forms and thus simplify the decoding process, citations have generally been conformed to current practice. Subsequent developments in cases cited while they were still pending are generally noted in brackets. Other minor editorial corrections have been made without notation.

Cross-references to my own work of course generally refer to the page number of the original publication. To enable readers to find the referenced passages in these volumes, we have added a parenthetical reference to the footnote number or numbers nearest to the cited passage.

It has been my good fortune to teach at three great law schools — The University of Chicago from 1976 to 1981, The University of Texas from 1981 to 2006 (where I still hold an emeritus appointment), and The University of Michigan since 2006. The great bulk of this work was done during my long stay at Texas, but some of it was written at Chicago, and some of it was written at Michigan. None of it could have been done as well without the intellectual support of my colleagues in those places and the recurring financial support of my deans in those places. Nor could it have been done as well without the intellectual community of many other fine lawyers and scholars toiling in these same vineyards. Some of these people hold academic appointments, some work for public interest organizations, a few are in private practice; all those I am thinking of have made issues of religious liberty in our time and place a central part of their work. I am grateful to all who supported this work, in many different ways, over the decades.

Douglas Laycock
Ann Arbor
November 2009

Preface to Volume 1

The law of religious liberty is dominated by three broad sets of disputes: over regulation of religious practice, regulation and sponsorship of religious speech, and funding of religious institutions. Of course there are some smaller areas of controversy that do not fit neatly into these three broad divisions.

The overview articles in Part One of this volume address at least two of these broad areas; most address all three. There is a continuing market for explanations of how it all fits together. For the nonspecialist, the law of religious liberty is often experienced as a series of incomplete news reports about particular controversies, received at irregular intervals and rarely placing the dispute in any more helpful context than that of secularists and religious conservatives at it again. So there can be real value in an overview that organizes these discrete controversies into a few broad issues and identifies larger patterns in judicial decisions.

These overviews do not necessarily give equal treatment to all three areas of religious liberty. Written at different times and for different purposes, they have different emphases. Some of these overviews contain my most extensive treatment of particular issues, and those treatments are identified by cross-references in the introductions to more focused treatments of the same or related issues.

The division between Normative Overviews, and Analytic and Descriptive Overviews, is of course not a bright line. But the basic division is this. In Section A, Normative Overviews, the emphasis is on what I think the law of religious liberty should be. In Section B, Analytic and Descriptive Overviews, the emphasis is on making sense of what the law of religious liberty actually is, according to the Supreme Court of the United States and other authoritative sources of law.

Section C, Book Reviews, reviews books that are themselves broad overviews of the field. Other book reviews, more focused on specific issues, will appear in later volumes.

Section D, on Judicial Nominations, is included because the cluster of issues that have polarized the process of nominating and confirming federal judges has prominently included religious liberty and culture war issues such as abortion, and the two nominations that provoked these writings were of considerable interest to religious conservatives and their opponents.

Part Two of this volume, on History, is largely self-explanatory. Some of these articles are investigations into the original understanding of the Constitution on particular issues, and might plausibly have gone in a later volume that includes that issue. But it seemed to make the most sense to gather in one place all the work that was primarily historical.

This volume also contains two Appendices. Appendix I is a report for the Presbyterian Church (U.S.A.), a collaborative work that speaks in the church's voice and not mine, even though I drafted substantial parts of it. Appendix II is a short and simple explanation of legal citation form for non-legal readers.

DOUGLAS LAYCOCK

PART ONE

Overviews

A. Normative Overviews

Four of the eight articles in this Section are major scholarly works; they set out the basic principles that underlie all my work in the field. There are also four short pieces here, three written for scholarly outlets and one for law school alumni.

The Long . . .

Formal, Substantive, and Disaggregated Neutrality toward Religion (1990) was the first clear development of the distinction between formal and substantive neutrality. That distinction, and that vocabulary, is now widely used in the academic community. Both conceptions of neutrality appear in Supreme Court cases, but without the vocabulary and rarely with any attention to the difference. Substantive neutrality was and is an attempt to reconcile the lawyer's instinct for neutrality with a robust conception of religious liberty, and to escape the implication that neutrality requires that churches be regulated to the same extent as commercial businesses.

Substantive Neutrality Revisited (2007) is a more mature elaboration of the same distinction, written nearly two decades later, responding to some of the ways in which substantive neutrality had been criticized or misunderstood. This article also provided an occasion to compare my approach with those of the centrist Noah Feldman at Harvard and the strict separationist Steven Gey at Florida State.

Religious Liberty as Liberty (1996) attempts to set out a religion-neutral case for religious liberty. We protect religious liberty not because religion is a good thing or a bad thing, but because individual liberty with respect to religious choices and commitments is a good thing. This piece also contains my most complete elaboration of why nonbelievers should be protected by the Religion Clauses.

Theology Scholarships, the Pledge of Allegiance, and Religious Liberty (2004) is organized around two Supreme Court decisions in 2004. The Court held that Washington does not have to provide state scholarships to theology majors, and it ducked on the constitutionality of "under God" in the Pledge of Allegiance. This article places those decisions in larger context and uses them to survey the whole field, although of course the most detailed attention is devoted to the bodies of law that most directly controlled those two cases.

. . . and the Short

Religious Liberty: Not for Religion or against Religion, but for Individual Choice (2004) is a 1,000-word summary of the themes in the larger pieces. There is not much detail or nuance, but if you want a five-minute introduction to what I think, this is the place to start.

Remarks on Acceptance of National Award from the Council for America's First Freedom (2009) is even shorter and draws the moral more pointedly. We must protect the religious liberty of those we disagree with as vigorously as we would protect religious liberty for ourselves.

Free Exercise Clause and Establishment Clause: General Theories (2000) is a brief summary of all the important competing theories of the Religion Clauses. They say you can't tell the players without a scorecard; this short encyclopedia entry offers a scorecard.

The Benefits of the Establishment Clause (1992) is a talk on what the Establishment Clause adds to the Free Exercise Clause. Because of that comparative focus, and because the talk was delivered during the period of greatest concern about the Supreme Court's contraction of the Free Exercise Clause, the talk and the questions and answers that follow the talk address both clauses.

Formal, Substantive, and Disaggregated Neutrality toward Religion

39 DePaul Law Review 993 (1990)

This was the Sixth Annual Lecture at the Center for Church/State Studies at DePaul University in Chicago. It is the first elaboration of "substantive neutrality," a concept that has been foundational to much of my subsequent work. The core of the conceptual problem addressed in the lecture is this. Religious liberty sometimes requires that religiously motivated conduct be exempted from government regulation, so that believers can actually practice their faith. But regulatory exemptions on religious grounds look like special treatment for religion, and that seems inconsistent with another widely shared intuition, important in other religious liberty controversies: that government should be neutral toward religion. Is there a coherent understanding of neutrality that is consistent with full religious liberty?

This article is adapted from the Sixth Annual Lecture of the Center for Church/State Studies, delivered in Chicago, Illinois, on April 6, 1989. Much of the argument speaks as of that date. In the interim, the Supreme Court has announced sweeping changes in the relevant law. Initial reaction to those changes is largely confined to inserts.

I am grateful to the DePaul University Law School and the Center for Church/State Studies for their invitation, support, and helpful reactions to this lecture; to Jay Westbrook and Sanford Levinson for helpful comments on an earlier written draft; and to the University Research Institute at the University of Texas for a research leave that made it possible for me to accept DePaul's invitation.

I should disclose that I wrote and filed amicus briefs in the Supreme Court in the following cases cited or discussed in this Article: George v. International Soc'y for Krishna Consciousness, 499 U.S. 914 (1991); Board of Educ. v. Mergens, 496 U.S. 226 (1990); Jimmy Swaggart Ministries v. Board of Equalization, 493 U.S. 378 (1990), and that I was of counsel on the petition for rehearing in Employment Div. v. Smith, 494 U.S. 872 (1990).

Introduction

A wide range of courts and commentators commonly say that government must be neutral toward religion.[1] There are dissenters in both directions — those who think that government can support religion, and those who pursue separation to the point of hostility. In this Article, I will largely ignore those dissenters. I will assume that neutrality is an important part of the meaning of the Religion Clauses.

This Article is about the meaning of neutrality. My goal is to clarify the concept, or at least to clarify our disagreements over its meaning. In the course of doing that, I will address a third group of dissenters — those who think that neutrality is meaningless and should be dropped from our discourse.[2]

Those who think neutrality is meaningless have a point. We can agree on the principle of neutrality without having agreed on anything at all. From benevolent neutrality[3] to separate but equal,[4] people with a vast range of views on church and state have all claimed to be neutral.

Consider *Texas Monthly, Inc. v. Bullock*.[5] The Supreme Court said that Texas can not exempt the sale of religious publications from a sales tax that applies to all other publications. Justice Brennan and Justice Scalia fundamentally disagreed on almost every issue in the case, but they both claimed to be neutral.[6] Both of them used the word "neutrality," but neither of them defined it.

Most of us think of ourselves as fairminded, and so we tend to assume that our instinctive preferences are fair, and therefore neutral. Some scholars

---

1. County of Allegheny v. American Civil Liberties Union Greater Pittsburgh Chapter, 492 U.S. 573, 589-94 (1989). Earlier cases are collected in Laycock, *Equal Access and Moments of Silence: The Equal Status of Religious Speech by Private Speakers,* 81 Nw. U.L. Rev. 1, 2 n.6 (1986). Commentators are collected in Steven D. Smith, *Symbols, Perceptions, and Doctrinal Illusions: Establishment Neutrality and the "No Endorsement" Test,* 86 Mich. L. Rev. 266, 314 n.183 (1987).

2. For a clear statement of this position, *see* Smith, *supra* note 1, at 313-32. *Cf.* John T. Valauri, *The Concept of Neutrality in Establishment Clause Doctrine,* 48 U. Pitt. L. Rev. 83 (1986). Valauri would keep the concept of neutrality because its appeal is "compelling," but would restrict the Supreme Court's power to enforce it because it is "multiply and irresolvably ambiguous." *Id.* at 149, 151.

3. *See, e.g.,* Robert Miller & Ronald Flowers, Toward Benevolent Neutrality: Church, State, and the Supreme Court (3d ed. 1987).

4. Ruti Teitel, *When Separate Is Equal: Why Organized Religious Exercises, Unlike Chess, Do Not Belong in the Public Schools,* 81 Nw. U.L. Rev. 174 (1986).

5. 489 U.S. 1 (1989).

6. *Id.* at 13 (Brennan, J.) (plurality opinion); *id.* at 40 (Scalia, J., dissenting).

have tried to define neutrality more carefully, but they have produced quite inconsistent definitions.

Both of these points — the power of our instincts and the inconsistency of formal definitions — were brought home to me when I presented a paper[7] on the Equal Access Act.[8] The Act tries to guarantee the right of student religious groups to meet in empty classrooms on the same terms as other extracurricular student groups. The Supreme Court has finally upheld the statute,[9] ending six years of debate over its constitutionality. This seemed to me an easy case to resolve with the neutrality principle. I argued that government could not discriminate against religious speech by private speakers.

A distinguished panel of commentators attacked me from all directions. Ruti Teitel insisted that the only neutral course was to exclude the religious speakers. She thought that my error was to treat as alike things that were different.[10] Geoffrey Stone argued that neutrality permitted my solution, but certainly did not require it. He thought it was neutral to exclude the religion club if the school board also promised to exclude the atheist club, if there ever were one.[11] Michael McConnell agreed with my solution, but he said my definition of neutrality was "heterodox."[12] He insisted that neutrality is not a reliable principle, because properly defined, it is often at odds with religious liberty.

It was McConnell's attack that troubled me the most. I believe that neutrality is consistent with religious liberty — indeed, essential to its preservation. Our miscommunication did not seem to flow from any underlying policy disagreement. As a result of that exchange, I feared that other meanings of neutrality had so captured our vocabulary that I could not use the term to communicate, even to sympathetic audiences and even when I defined it. McConnell's comment on my definition of neutrality made it inevitable that I would explore the definition in greater depth. I take considerable comfort from McConnell's move toward a somewhat similar definition in the intervening four years.[13]

---

7. Laycock, *supra* note 1.

8. 20 U.S.C. §§ 4071-4074 (1988).

9. Board of Educ. v. Mergens, 496 U.S. 226 (1990).

10. Teitel, *supra* note 4, at 183-89.

11. Geoffrey Stone, *The Equal Access Controversy: The Religion Clauses and the Meaning of "Neutrality."* 81 Nw. U.L. Rev. 168, 170-71 (1986).

12. Michael McConnell, *Neutrality Under the Religion Clauses,* 81 Nw. U.L. Rev. 146, 149 n.17 (1986).

13. *See* Michael McConnell & Richard Posner, *An Economic Approach to Issues of Religious Freedom,* 56 U. Chi. L. Rev. 1, 14 (1989) (proposing requirement of neutrality toward

I. Is Neutrality Worth Defining?

Maybe these conflicting uses of "neutrality" prove that we should abandon the concept. A few years ago, Peter Westen stirred up a great fuss by claiming that equality is an empty concept.[14] Neutrality and equality are near cousins; they have most of the same attractions and most of the same inadequacies. If Westen were right, then neutrality would also be empty.

I am quite sure that Westen was wrong, but he highlighted something important that we too often ignore. Equality and neutrality are not empty concepts, but neither are they self-defining. They are insufficient concepts — insufficient to decide cases without supplemental principles. Let me briefly explain this point, with apologies to those who are familiar with the debate.

A claim to equal or neutral treatment is very different from an outright claim of entitlement. If I go to court claiming a constitutional right to a monthly check from the government, the court will laugh at me. It is up to Congress, and not the courts, to create government benefit programs. But if I go to court claiming a constitutional right to a check on the same terms as someone similarly situated, I may have a serious claim. If Congress has given social security benefits to women in my situation but not to men, I will probably win.[15] My claim to an equal entitlement to benefits is very different from my claim to an outright entitlement to benefits.

Nor is it the case that once we have fully specified the entitlement, equality drops out. Westen would say that once we decide that sex is not one of the

---

religion, conceived not as "treating religion just like other activities," but as minimizing effects on religious practice); Michael McConnell, *Unconstitutional Conditions: Unrecognized Implications for the Establishment Clause*, 26 SAN DIEGO L. REV. 255, 260 (1989) (government "may not redistribute wealth on the basis of an individual's, or group's, exercise of a constitutionally protected right, unless it can show that it has a legitimate justification for doing so"). I have learned much from what he has written. Of course, he is not responsible for anything I say in this Article.

14. Peter Westen, *The Empty Idea of Equality*, 95 HARV. L. REV. 537 (1982). For critical commentary, see Steven J. Burton, *Comment on "Empty Ideas": Logical Positivist Analyses of Equality and Rules*, 91 YALE L.J. 1136 (1982); Anthony D'Amato, *Comment: Is Equality a Totally Empty Idea?*, 81 MICH. L. REV. 600 (1983); Kent Greenawalt, *How Empty Is the Idea of Equality?*, 83 COLUM. L. REV. 1167 (1983); Kenneth W. Simons, *Equality as a Comparative Right*, 65 B.U.L. REV. 387 (1985). For Westen's responses, see Peter Westen, *To Lure the Tarantula from Its Hole: A Response*, 83 COLUM. L. REV. 1186 (1983); Peter Westen, *The Meaning of Equality in Law, Science, Math & Morals: A Reply*, 81 MICH. L. REV. 604 (1983); Peter Westen, *On "Confusing Ideas": Reply*, 91 YALE L.J. 1153 (1982).

15. *See, e.g.,* Califano v. Goldfarb, 430 U.S. 199 (1977) (invalidating different eligibility standards for widows and widowers); Weinberger v. Wiesenfeld, 420 U.S. 636 (1975) (same).

eligibility criteria, we no longer need equality to decide my case. That is descriptively true, but it is not true until after we have decided. It begs the question of how we decide that sex is not one of the eligibility criteria. The elimination of sex as a criterion will depend in part on our understanding of sexual equality, and not merely on the policy of the social security program.

This separation in theory is greatly reinforced in practice by the constitutional separation of powers. Congress first specifies the eligibility criteria, and has sole responsibility for social security policy. But the Court reviews those criteria to see if they violate its understanding of constitutional rights to equality. This separation of responsibility for policy definition is critical to the debate over Westen, and it has received too little attention. It means that equality claims can never be collapsed into the initial specification of the entitlement. So equality is not an empty concept.

But equality is an insufficient concept. No one claims that all five billion humans must be given precisely equal treatment in all matters. Some inequalities are considered fair and just, like punishing the guilty but not the innocent. Some are considered unfair but lawful, like homelessness in the midst of wealth.

Only a few inequalities violate legal rights to equality. Claims about equality, or neutrality, always require further specification: equality with respect to what classification, for what purpose, in what sense, and to what extent? Let me briefly consider these four variables.

First, there is the classification at issue. Those who are similarly situated should be treated equally, but what does it mean to be similarly situated? If Congress grants benefits to 40-year-old women but not to 40-year-old men, my claim will specify equality with respect to sex, and I will probably win. But if I specify equality with respect to age — if I claim that 40-year-old men are similar to 65-year-old men — I will surely lose.[16] Our law embodies a fairly strong and general commitment to sexual equality, but only a weak and narrow commitment to age equality.

Second, there is the purpose of the classification. What it means to be similarly situated depends on why we are asking. If I claim that my employer fired me because of my age, then I have a claim under the age discrimination laws.[17] Forty-year-old men are similar to 65-year-old men for purposes of hiring and firing, but not for purposes of social security. Third, there are dif-

---

16. *Cf.* Massachusetts Bd. of Retirement v. Murgia, 427 U.S. 307 (1976) (upholding mandatory retirement law); McCarthy v. Sheriff of Suffolk County, 322 N.E.2d 758 (Mass. 1975) (same).

17. Age Discrimination in Employment Act, 29 U.S.C. §§ 621-634 (1988).

ferent senses of equality. Two sharply different meanings are inherent in the concepts of equality and neutrality. These different meanings are familiar from the great national debate over affirmative action.[18] Americans believe in equal opportunity and equal treatment, but in some contexts, we also believe in equal impact and equal outcomes. This is not an all-or-nothing universal choice; our choices vary with context. Few people would argue that equal impact is never the relevant measure, but we often disagree over when equal impact is the relevant measure.

Fourth, there is the extent of the claim. Is it sufficient for government to treat people equally when it imposes penalties and distributes benefits — to treat people equally in all tangible ways? Or do we also require government to be neutral in intangible ways as well — to be neutral in its speech and symbolic conduct? This distinction is critical to debates about religious neutrality. I will call it the difference between equality and neutrality. When I say government should be neutral towards religion, I mean to include the claim that it should not express an opinion about religion. But this is a controversial claim. Nothing in the concepts themselves will tell us whether the Religion Clauses commit government to neutrality in this sense, or only to equal treatment.

---

18. *See, e.g.,* Stephen Carter, *The Best Black, and Other Tales,* 1 RECONSTRUCTION 6 (1990); Drew Days, *Turning Back the Clock: The Reagan Administration and Civil Rights,* 19 HARV. C.R.-C.L. L. REV. 309 (1984); Charles Fried, *Affirmative Action After* City of Richmond v. J. A. Croson Co.: *A Response to the Scholars' Statement,* 99 YALE L.J. 155 (1989); Randall Kennedy, *Persuasion and Distrust: A Comment on the Affirmative Action Debate,* 99 HARV. L. REV. 1327 (1987); David L. Kirp & Nancy A. Weston, *The Political Jurisprudence of Affirmative Action,* 5 SOC. PHIL. & POL'Y 223 (1987); Douglas Laycock, *Taking Constitutions Seriously: A Theory of Judicial Review* (Book Review), 59 TEX. L. REV. 343, 376-85 (1981); Glenn Loury, *Why Should We Care About Group Inequality,* 5 SOC. PHIL. & POL'Y 249 (1987); Bernard Meltzer, *The Weber Case: The Judicial Abrogation of the Antidiscrimination Standard in Employment,* 47 U. CHI. L. REV. 423 (1980); Charles E. Mitchell, *Race-Conscious Remedies: Pursuing Equal Employment Opportunity or Equal Employment Results?,* 38 LAB. L.J. 781 (1987); George Rutherglen & Daniel Ortiz, *Affirmative Action Under the Constitution and Title VII: From Confusion to Convergence,* 35 UCLA L. REV. 467 (1988); Martin Schiff, *Reverse Discrimination Redefined as Equal Protection: The Orwellian Nightmare in the Enforcement of Civil Rights Laws,* 8 HARV. J.L. & PUB. POL'Y 627 (1985); David A. Strauss, *The Myth of Colorblindness,* 1986 SUP. CT. REV. 99; Laurence Tribe, *"In What Vision of the Constitution Must the Law Be Color-Blind?",* 20 J. MARSHALL L. REV. 201 (1986); William Van Alstyne, *Rites of Passage: Race, the Supreme Court, and the Constitution,* 46 U. CHI. L. REV. 775 (1979); J. Skelly Wright, *Color Blind Theories and Color-Conscious Remedies,* 47 U. CHI. L. REV. 213 (1980); *Affirmative Action,* 72 IOWA L. REV. 255 (symposium featuring Jesse Choper, Rex Lee, and Paul Brest); Joint Statement, *Constitutional Scholars' Statement on Affirmative Action After* City of Richmond v. J.A. Croson Co., 98 YALE L.J. 1711 (1989); *Scholars' Reply to Professor Fried,* 99 YALE L.J. 163 (1989).

The first three variables are also controversial and insufficiently specified. Equality with respect to religion does not even sufficiently specify the classification. Religion may refer to status, to belief, to speech, or to conduct. The principal line of disagreement is different for each of these.

Most of our serious disagreements are about religious conduct, and not about religious status or belief. It is therefore religious conduct that is the principal subject of our inquiry into religious neutrality. Americans have very different intuitions about what it means to say that religious conduct is similarly situated to secular conduct, or what it means to treat religious conduct equally.

In religion as elsewhere, the answers sometimes depend on the second variable — the purpose of the classification. Whether we think religious conduct is similarly situated may depend on whether we are talking about direct regulation of conduct, resolution of private disputes, expenditures of government funds, taxation and tax exemption, and so on through the whole range of ways in which religion and government interact.

The debate over religious conduct also triggers sharp disagreement over the choice between equal treatment and equal impact. This may be the most fundamental source of disagreement about the meaning of neutrality toward religion.

Because neutrality requires so much further specification, it cannot be the only principle in the Religion Clauses. Nor can it be the most fundamental. We must specify the content of neutrality by looking to other principles in the Religion Clauses. When we have done that, neutrality should be defined in a way that makes it largely congruent with those other principles. We will often be able to explain the objection to a law by saying either that it restricts the autonomy of religious belief or practice, or that it threatens religious voluntarism, or that it deviates from religious neutrality, and so on.

This variety of explanations is important, and the neutrality explanation should not be omitted. In a nation of immense religious diversity, it is of great symbolic value that government views all manner of religious belief neutrally. That the government aspires to religious neutrality, and that the courts stand ready to hold government to its aspiration, is an important reassurance to religious minorities. We should not abandon or de-emphasize that reassurance. We should not omit neutrality from our set of explanations, even if we also offer other explanations, and even if some readers believe that those other explanations are more fundamental. Neutrality has great explanatory importance.

Neutrality also continues to have operational importance. If neutrality properly understood is largely congruent with other principles of the Religion Clauses, then any of these principles can be the warning flag that calls attention to a threat to religious liberty. Sometimes the deviation from neutrality will be the most obvious explanation of the danger, and even the most fundamental.

For example, I think neutrality is the most straightforward explanation in the equal access controversy. There is no general right to demand that the government make its property available for religious observance: there is not even such a right in narrow and especially appealing circumstances. The lack of such a right is implicit in *Lyng v. Northwest Indian Cemetery Protective Association*,[19] where the Court refused to stop the government from building a useless road on land owned by the government but sacred to Native Americans. There is no entitlement to special access to government property for religious exercise.

Nevertheless, if the government makes its property available for meetings of nonreligious private groups, then it must make that property equally available to religious groups.[20] This is a classic equality right. The equality or neutrality explanation is the one that best and most directly fits the case. Neutrality is the easiest way to recognize the problem, to decide the case, and to explain the result.

More generally, I doubt that there is any single foundational principle from which all the others can be derived. The Religion Clauses embody several principles, which are largely congruent, but occasionally in tension. The search for solutions is rarely a matter of deciding which principle is more fundamental. The search for solutions is more like an iteration in mathematics. In an iteration, you solve a problem by a series of approximations, each building on the one before, until you have as close an approximation as you need or as close as you can get with reasonable effort. We iterate Religion Clause problems by considering them in light of each of the relevant principles, including neutrality.

For all these reasons, I think that neutrality is worth defining. To that end, I will sketch the principal conceptions of neutrality toward religion in the cases and the literature, illustrating the differences with examples.

---

19. 485 U.S. 439 (1988).

20. Widmar v. Vincent, 454 U.S. 263 (1981); Equal Access Act, 20 U.S.C. § 4071-4074 (1988).

II. Formal Neutrality

By far the best-known definition of religious neutrality is Philip Kurland's. In 1961, he tendered the following principle:

> The [free exercise and establishment] clauses should be read as stating a single precept: that government cannot utilize religion as a standard for action or inaction because these clauses, read together as they should be, prohibit classification in terms of religion either to confer a benefit or to impose a burden.[21]

This standard of no religious classifications is closely akin to the equal treatment and equal opportunity side of the affirmative action debate. But the shift of context has enough implications so that a different label is required. I will call this standard "formal neutrality." I will not call it Kurland's Rule, because I am not sure he intended it in the way it has come to be understood. But I suspect that if you say "neutrality" to most religious liberty scholars, the first thing that they think of is Philip Kurland and a ban on religious classifications.

Formal neutrality sounds highly plausible until you think through its implications. Its simplicity and apparent even-handedness are appealing. It can explain some important cases, including my argument for the constitutionality of the Equal Access Act.

Yet formal neutrality has been almost universally rejected.[22] No major commentator endorsed it for a generation, and no case has adopted it, although many cases and commentators have applied part of it to particular problems. Now an endorsement has come from a most unlikely source, Professor Mark Tushnet.[23] Hardly anyone else has been willing to apply it universally, because it produces surprising results that are inconsistent with strong intuitions.

The most striking example is historical. The National Prohibition Act forbad the sale or consumption of alcoholic beverages in the United States, but it exempted the use of sacramental wine.[24] Under formal neutrality, the

21. Philip Kurland, *Of Church and State and the Supreme Court*, 29 U. CHI. L. REV. 1, 96 (1961).

22. See Philip Kurland, *The Irrelevance of the Constitution: The Religion Clauses of the First Amendment and the Supreme Court*, 24 VILL. L. REV. 3, 24 (1978).

23. Mark Tushnet, *"Of Church and State and the Supreme Court": Kurland Revisited*, 1989 SUP. CT. REV. 373. It is surprising to find a leader of the critical legal studies movement endorsing a rule of formal neutrality, implicitly assuming that the government is not responsible for the unequal impact of its actions, and urging the virtues of clear legal doctrine.

24. An Act to Prohibit Intoxicating Beverages, ch. 85 § 6, 41 Stat. 305, 311 (1919).

exemption was unconstitutional. The exemption undeniably classified on the basis of religion. It was lawful to consume alcohol in religious ceremonies, but not otherwise.

Now consider Prohibition without the exemption. There would be no violation of formal neutrality; religion would not even be mentioned in the statute. But it would be a crime to celebrate the Eucharist or the Seder. If the free exercise of religion includes anything beyond bare belief, it must be the right to perform the sacred rituals of the faith. A law enacted largely at the behest of Protestants that barred the sacred rites of Catholics and Jews, a law that changed the way these rites had been performed for millennia, could not be reconciled with any concept of religious liberty worthy of the name. That the law was formally neutral and enacted for a secular purpose would be no comfort to the victims.

But facial neutrality would be dispositive to the Supreme Court of the United States. In a stunning opinion handed down after this lecture was delivered, the Court said that government may regulate the Mass for good reasons, bad reasons, or no reasons at all, so long as the regulation is facially neutral and does not single out religion.[25] The Court held that criminal punishment of the central religious ritual of an ancient faith raises no issue under the Free Exercise Clause and requires no governmental justification whatever! The example that I chose because I thought it was beyond reasonable argument has now been decided the other way.

Prohibition as applied to sacramental wine is the exemplar of a large class of cases, in which the exercise of religion requires exemption from laws of general applicability. Such exemptions are now a matter of legislative grace. The Court did not go all the way to Professor Kurland's ban on exemptions for religious exercise. Rather, it said that the Constitution is indifferent to such exemptions — that legislatures may grant or refuse exemptions as they choose.

I will return to the problem of exemptions for religious conduct. For now, I note only that formal neutrality would permit a state to ban the Mass. If it produces such an implausible result in a case at the core of religious exercise, the principle is not off to a good start.

In the Prohibition example, formal neutrality seems to trample religion. But formal neutrality also produces results that many Americans find unacceptably favorable to religion. Consider the case of financial aid to private education. Under formal neutrality, government can give unlimited amounts of

---

25. Employment Div. v. Smith, 494 U.S. 872 (1990). For analysis of this case, see Douglas Laycock, *Peyote, Wine, and the First Amendment*, 106 CHRISTIAN CENTURY 876 (1989).

unrestricted aid to religious schools, so long as the aid goes to all schools and not to religious schools alone. But formal neutrality does not stop there. Any aid to secular private schools must be given to religious schools, on exactly the same terms. To exclude religious schools from the aid program, or to impose restrictions on religious uses of the money, would be to classify on the basis of religion. That would violate formal neutrality.

I do not think that this implication of formal neutrality is beyond the range of reasonable debate. Indeed, I think it captures an important insight. But I also believe that at least some of its results would be unconstitutional.

Stricter separationists react much more strongly. To many American separationists, the possibility that government could fully fund religious education must seem as preposterous as the banning of the Mass. This implication of formal neutrality is wildly inconsistent with the Supreme Court's cases and with dominant understandings of the Establishment Clause.[26]

As these two examples make clear, formal neutrality has something to offend everybody. As a general standard, it appeals to none of the competing factions in Religion Clause litigation. But it has had disproportionate influence on our understanding of what it means to be neutral.

III. Substantive Neutrality

My understanding of neutrality is quite different. Again because we need a label, I will call my proposal "substantive neutrality."

My basic formulation of substantive neutrality is this: the Religion Clauses require government to minimize the extent to which it either encourages or discourages religious belief or disbelief, practice or nonpractice, observance or nonobservance.[27] If I have to stand or fall on a single formulation of neutrality, I will stand or fall on that one. But I must elaborate on what I mean by minimizing encouragement and discouragement. I mean that religion is to

26. *See, e.g.,* Aguilar v. Felton, 473 U.S. 402 (1985); Lemon v. Kurtzman, 403 U.S. 602 (1971).

27. This is a modest elaboration of the definition I offered in 1986:

> I do not mean neutrality in the sense of a ban on religious classifications. Instead, I mean neutrality in the sense of government conduct that insofar as possible neither encourages nor discourages religious belief or practice. This requires identification of a base line from which to measure encouragement and discouragement.

Laycock, *supra* note 1, at 3 (text at note 10).

be left as wholly to private choice as anything can be. It should proceed as unaffected by government as possible. Government should not interfere with our beliefs about religion either by coercion or by persuasion. Religion may flourish or wither; it may change or stay the same. What happens to religion is up to the people acting severally and voluntarily; it is not up to the people acting collectively through government.

This elaboration highlights the connections among religious neutrality, religious autonomy, and religious voluntarism.[28] Government must be neutral so that religious belief and practice can be free. The autonomy of religious belief and disbelief is maximized when government encouragement and discouragement is minimized. The same is true of religious practice and refusal to practice. The goal of maximum religious liberty can help identify the baseline from which to measure encouragement and discouragement.

My conception of religious neutrality includes a neutral conception of religion. That is, any belief about God, the supernatural, or the transcendent, is a religious belief. For constitutional purposes, the belief that there is no God, or no afterlife, is as much a religious belief as the belief that there is a God or an afterlife. It is a belief about the traditional subject matter of religion, and it is a belief that must be accepted on faith, because it is not subject to empirical investigation. Serious believers and serious disbelievers are sometimes troubled by this equation of their belief systems, but we cannot make sense of the Religion Clauses without it. This constitutional conception of religious belief as any belief about religion explains why atheists are protected from persecution,[29] and why the government cannot establish atheism.

Similarly, the deeply held conscientious objection of a non-theist must be treated equally with a similar objection rooted in a more traditional faith. As a plurality of the Supreme Court put it in a statutory context, the relevant category is "all those whose consciences . . . would give them no rest or peace" if they were compelled to comply with government policy.[30] To be sure, there are difficulties in applying that standard to non-traditional sources of conscience. But in a nation with millions of non-believers, no other conception of conscientious objection is even plausibly neutral.

28. *Cf.* Smith, *supra* note 1, at 316 n.192 (listing commentators who argue that neutrality, voluntarism, and separation are not consistent values).

29. *See* Torcaso v. Watkins, 367 U.S. 488, 496 (1961) (requiring atheist to affirm belief in God violates his "freedom of belief and religion"); *cf.* EEOC v. Townley Eng. & Mfg. Co., 859 F.2d 610, 613 (9th Cir. 1988) (requiring atheist employee to attend religious services at work discriminates against him on basis of religion).

30. Welsh v. United States, 398 U.S. 333, 344 (1970).

That is a bare sketch of substantive neutrality. The next step is to compare and contrast formal and substantive neutrality. Sometimes the two types of neutrality produce the same result. That is, sometimes we can minimize encouragement or discouragement to religion by ignoring the religious aspects of some behavior and treating it just like some analogous secular behavior.

But often the two understandings of neutrality diverge. Government routinely encourages and discourages all sorts of private behavior. Under substantive neutrality, these encouragements and discouragements are not to be applied to religion. Thus, a standard of minimizing both encouragement and discouragement will often require that religion be singled out for special treatment.

Consider two of the examples I have mentioned so far. To prohibit the consumption of alcohol, without an exception for religious rituals, is to flatly prohibit important religious practices. Such a prohibition would discourage religious practice in the most coercive possible way — by criminalizing it. Many believers would abandon their religious practice; some would defy the law; some of those would go to jail. Such a law would be a massive departure from substantive neutrality.

To *exempt* sacramental wine is not perfectly neutral either. Religious observers would get to do something that is forbidden to the rest of the population, but that observation goes to formal neutrality. Would this special treatment encourage religion? It is conceivable that the prospect of a tiny nip would encourage some desperate folks to join a church that uses real wine, or to attend Mass daily instead of weekly or only at Easter. It is conceivable, but only to a law professor or an economist. Such an exemption would have only an infinitesimal tendency to encourage religious activity. In contrast, withholding the exemption would severely discourage religious activity. The course that most nearly approaches substantive neutrality — the course that minimizes both encouragement and discouragement — is to single out religious uses for an exemption. In this and similar applications, substantive neutrality is akin to the equal impact, equal outcome side of the affirmative action debate.

Prohibition is an easy case under formal neutrality, and an easy case under substantive neutrality. The difference is that substantive neutrality gets the right answer. Formal neutrality, as applied to Prohibition, would lead directly to religious persecution.

Sometimes the two concepts of neutrality seem to converge. In the equal access controversy, I argued that substantive neutrality was best achieved by something close to formal neutrality — that student religious groups should be treated like any other student extracurricular group.[31] To give them special privileges would encourage religion; to exclude them would discourage religion.

But even in that example, some deviations from formal neutrality were required. Most student extracurricular groups have a faculty sponsor, but it is widely agreed that a student religious group should not have a faculty sponsor.[32] To say that the school will sponsor any student group except a religious group is to classify on the basis of religion. Withholding the faculty sponsor violates formal neutrality.

The school prayer cases[33] are the most obvious source of our intuition that public schools should not provide faculty sponsors to student religious groups. But substantive neutrality can explain that intuition. School sponsorship of a religious group commits the government to the success of a religious group, thus encouraging religion and violating substantive neutrality. Moreover, the faculty sponsor will inevitably influence the group's conduct, thus encouraging some forms of religious practice and discouraging others.

It is true that religious groups are in some sense discouraged by being forced to organize and function without the school sponsorship available to all other student groups. But withholding the sponsor does not actively harm religious groups; it does not reduce or divert their own resources, or create obstacles for them to overcome. It merely withholds an intrusive benefit that is widely available to other groups that are in some ways analogous. The hoped-for benefit may turn out to be seriously harmful if the government sponsor changes the course of the religious organization. Withholding this risky benefit is not perfectly neutral, but the deviation from neutrality is considerably smaller than the deviations inherent in sponsorship. Thus, the closest the schools can come to substantive neutrality is to leave such groups alone.

Prohibition and equal access are simple examples. I have not yet gotten to the hard cases, like public aid to religious schools. But even these simple cases illustrate some important points about substantive neutrality.

---

31. Laycock, *supra* note 1, at 10-11 (text at notes 47-56).

32. *See id.* at 28-31 (text at notes 142-50). The Equal Access Act somewhat ineptly provides that schools should not sponsor student religious groups. 20 U.S.C. § 4071(c)(2) & (3) (1988).

33. *E.g.*, Wallace v. Jaffree, 472 U.S. 38 (1985) (striking down statute authorizing moment of silence "for meditation or voluntary prayer" where legislative history showed intent to return prayer to public schools); School Dist. of Abington Township v. Schempp, 374 U.S. 203 (1963) (state cannot require daily Bible reading and recitation of Lord's Prayer in public schools); Engel v. Vitale, 370 U.S. 421 (1962) (state may not compose or require recitation of official state prayer).

Most obviously, substantive neutrality is harder to apply than formal neutrality. It requires judgments about the relative significance of various encouragements and discouragements to religion. Absolute zero is no more attainable in encouragement and discouragement than in temperature. We can aspire only to minimize encouragement and discouragement. Because substantive neutrality requires more judgment than formal neutrality, substantive neutrality is more subject to manipulation by advocates and result-oriented judges and law professors.

More important, substantive neutrality requires a baseline from which to measure encouragement and discouragement. What state of affairs is the background norm from which to judge whether religion has been encouraged or discouraged? This question also requires judgment; there is no simple test that can be mechanically applied to yield sensible answers.

A conceivable mechanical standard is to treat religion as though government did not exist. If religion is better off than if government did not exist, it has been encouraged; if it is worse off, it has been discouraged. The only thing to recommend this standard is its intellectual purity; I doubt that it appeals to anyone in the real world.

To take the most obvious example, no one suggests that churches be denied police and fire protection. Police and fire protection are sometimes explained as merely incidental benefits.[34] But to what are they incidental? I am not at all sure that police and fire protection arise as an incident of something else. These services are not incidental; they are provided outright and for their own sake. One might say that police and fire protection for churches is incidental to police and fire protection for everybody else, or for all property in the community. But it is easy to imagine either isolated or concentrated religious properties that would strain that rationale to the breaking point. That rationale also fails to explain why we protect churches against vandalism, embezzlement, and other property crimes that pose no threat to the neighbors.

One of the Supreme Court's better opinions on incidental benefits answers the question I have posed. A permissible benefit is one that is incidental to a larger policy of neutrality.[35] The benefits of police and fire protection are such an incident of neutrality. Police and fire protection are such a universal part of our lives that they have become part of the baseline. To deny police and fire protection would be to outlaw religion in the original sense of that word — to put religion outside the protection of the law. To demand that

34. Roemer v. Board of Public Works, 426 U.S. 736, 747 (1976).
35. *Id.* at 746-47.

churches provide their own police and fire protection in a modern society would be to place an extraordinary obstacle in their way — a discouragement that would make religion a hazardous enterprise indeed. To provide such services does not make religion attractive to anyone who is not attracted on the merits. As a practical matter, any encouragement is tiny. The discouraging effect of cutting off basic services greatly exceeds the encouraging effect of providing them.

Similar judgments about the baseline level of government activity are at the heart of the equal access controversy. To deny religious groups a faculty sponsor is neutral in the sense of leaving such groups where they would be if government did not exist. But if government did not exist, there would be no public schools and no classrooms in which groups could meet. The opponents of equal access argued that use of the classroom was a benefit — an encouragement in the terms I have been using — that violated the Establishment Clause.[36] The supporters of equal access argued that once classrooms were made available to other extracurricular groups, the use of the room was part of the baseline — a background norm that both religious and secular groups could take for granted.[37] Most of the opponents seemed to concede that religious groups could use the streets and parks on an equal basis.[38] Streets and parks are in the baseline by common consent; faculty sponsors are not in the baseline; classrooms are controversial.

The proper background norm about public facilities is related to the background norm about student behavior. If the norm is that students can generally do what they want on their own time, subject only to restraints on harmful or disruptive behavior, then banning religious groups is discouragement. But if the norm is that high school students can do nothing without school sponsorship, then allowing meetings looks like sponsorship, and even endorsement, and excluding them from campus can be characterized as the neutral course of simply declining to sponsor them. Opponents of equal access have seriously made this argument.[39] Supporters of equal access have looked to basic First Amendment principles, and to student free speech cases not involving religion — to cases involving war protest and underground newspapers. They argued that the relevant

---

36. Ruti Teitel, *The Unconstitutionality of Equal Access Policies and Legislation Allowing Organized Student-Initiated Religious Activities in the Public High Schools: A Proposal for a Unitary First Amendment Forum Analysis.* 12 HASTINGS CONST. L.Q. 529, 562-65 (1985).

37. *See, e.g.,* Laycock, *supra* note 1, at 10 (text at notes 47-48).

38. *See, e.g.,* Teitel, *supra* note 36, at 582.

39. *See* Bender v. Williamsport Area School Dist., 741 F.2d 538, 554-55 (3d Cir. 1984), *vacated on other grounds,* 475 U.S. 534 (1986); Teitel, *supra* note 36, at 579-90.

constitutional norm was that unsponsored students could say what they wanted on school premises.[40]

Unless we carefully think through such issues, we will tend to select our baselines by intuition, and we will give free rein to our political preferences and our prejudices. Our preferences can operate freely because the principle of neutrality by itself is insufficient to define the baseline. Judgments about the state of the world must be brought to bear. Equally important, the other principles of the Religion Clauses must be brought to bear. We must keep in mind what neutrality is supposed to accomplish. Our goal is not to leave religion in a Hobbesian state of nature, nor to leave it regulated exactly to the extent that commercial businesses are regulated, with no extra burdens and no exemptions. Our goal is to maximize the religious liberty of both believers and nonbelievers.

I will return to the difficult problems of justifying and implementing substantive neutrality. But first, I want to briefly introduce a third way in which neutrality has been invoked.

IV. Disaggregated Neutrality

The Supreme Court is rarely content with a broad principle if it can substitute a three-part test.[41] Its most famous formulation of the neutrality requirement is the second part of the *Lemon* test, which says that a law violates the Establishment Clause if one of its substantial effects is either to advance or inhibit religion.[42] This formulation began simply as an elaboration of neutrality,[43] but is often disaggregated into a test of no advancement and a separate test of no inhibition. If a law has some substantial effect that advances religion, that may be the end of the case. And there is sometimes a very low threshold for finding effects to be substantial.

In the extreme case of *Aguilar v. Felton*,[44] the Supreme Court invalidated a federal program to provide remedial instruction in math and reading to low income children in private schools. Congress enacted this program in

40. *See* Laycock, *supra* note 1, at 16-17, 28, 47-51 (text at notes 79-92, 141, 225-42).

41. *See generally* Robert Nagel, *The Formulaic Constitution*, 84 MICH. L. REV. 165 (1985).

42. Lemon v. Kurtzman, 403 U.S. 602, 612 (1971), *as modified in* Committee for Pub. Educ. & Religious Liberty v. Nyquist, 413 U.S. 756, 783-84 n.39 (1973).

43. The antecedents of the test are traced in Douglas Laycock, *Towards a General Theory of the Religion Clauses: The Case of Church Labor Relations and the Right to Church Autonomy*, 81 COLUM. L. REV. 1373, 1380-81 (1981) (text at notes 70-74).

44. 473 U.S. 402 (1985).

pursuit of neutrality — to provide the same remedial program to disadvantaged children without regard to their religious choices. Why did the Court strike it down? Because the public employees who provided the remedial instruction might be influenced by the religious environment of parochial schools, and under that hypnotic influence, might encourage the children to religious belief.[45] That possibility created a risk of a substantial effect of advancing religion; that risk could be avoided only by close supervision that would excessively entangle church and state.[46] That was the end of the case.

I call this disaggregated neutrality, because it looks only at one side of the balance of advancing or inhibiting. Because absolute zero is not achievable, it is always possible to find some effect of advancing or inhibiting religion. Thus, if you look only at one side of the balance, you can always find a constitutional violation. Some of those who would have government sponsor their faith play the same game on the inhibits side of the balance: if government does not lead school children in prayer, or display religious symbols on major holidays, the public may infer that government is hostile to religion.[47] Therefore, these critics conclude, silence is not neutral.

Substantive neutrality always requires that the encouragement of one policy be compared to the discouragement of alternative policies. The principal effect of *Aguilar* was to greatly increase the cost of providing remedial programs to children in private schools.[48] After *Aguilar,* the government or the school must provide separate off-campus facilities and the children must travel to those facilities and back again. The effect of increasing the cost was to reduce the number of children who could be served. So thousands of our least advantaged citizens are now forced to choose: forfeit their right to remedial instruction in math and reading, or forfeit their right to education in a religious environment. That effect discourages religion, and dwarfs the risk that the government's remedial math or reading teacher might suddenly start

45. *Id.* at 411-12.

46. *Id.* at 412-14.

47. County of Allegheny v. American Civil Liberties Union Greater Pittsburgh Chapter, 492 U.S. 573, 657-58 (1989) (Kennedy, J., dissenting); W. H. MOBERLY, THE CRISIS IN THE UNIVERSITY 55-56 (1949); RICHARD JOHN NEUHAUS, THE NAKED PUBLIC SQUARE (1984); James Hitchcock, *Church, State and Moral Values: The Limits of American Pluralism,* 44 LAW & CONTEMP. PROBS. 3 (Spring 1981); Andrew Woodbridge Hull, Note, *A Moment of Silence: A Permissible Accommodation Protecting the Capacity to Form Religious Belief,* 61 IND. L.J. 429, 431-33 (1986).

48. The costs of implementing *Aguilar* are carefully assessed in T. VITULLO-MARTIN & B. COOPER, SEPARATION OF CHURCH AND CHILD: THE CONSTITUTION AND FEDERAL AID TO RELIGIOUS SCHOOLS 41-66 (1987).

proselytizing. By disaggregating neutrality, the Court has lost sight of its original objective.

Another way to disaggregate neutrality is to shift back and forth among different versions of neutrality without explanation. If you think that neutrality with respect to government-imposed burdens means that churches and believers never get an exemption (formal neutrality), but that neutrality with respect to government benefits means that churches can never participate (disaggregated substantive neutrality), you had better have a good explanation. The most obvious explanation is simply hostility to religion. If you have the opposite preferences, you are equally in need of a good explanation.

Voting patterns in the Supreme Court are often disaggregated, sometimes in suspicious ways. Justice Brennan applied formal neutrality to strike down a legislative tax exemption in *Texas Monthly, Inc.*,[49] and he applied disaggregated neutrality to strike down the remedial education program in *Aguilar.*[50] But he believes the Constitution *requires* exemptions from laws that violate religious conscience, a position consistent with substantive neutrality.[51] Justice Rehnquist takes the opposite position on all three of these issues.[52] Justice Stevens agrees with Brennan on tax exemptions[53] and aid to religious schools,[54] but with Rehnquist on exemptions for conscience.[55] Stevens votes against traditional religions on all three issues, an odd interpretation of religious liberty.

In the Term since this lecture was delivered, the Court has dramatically embraced formal neutrality to uphold taxation and regulation of churches and believers.[56] In *Jimmy Swaggart Ministries,* the Court unanimously held that churches can be taxed, so long as the tax laws do not single out churches for discriminatory rates or incidents of taxation. The Court in dictum suggested that it would apply the same standard to regulation of churches, ex-

---

49. Texas Monthly, Inc. v. Bullock, 489 U.S. 1, 10-17 (1989) (plurality opinion).

50. Aguilar v. Felton, 473 U.S. 402 (1985) (opinion of the Court by Brennan, J.).

51. *See* Goldman v. Weinberger, 475 U.S. 503, 520-24 (1986) (Brennan, J., dissenting); Wisconsin v. Yoder, 406 U.S. 205 (1972) (Brennan, J., joining opinion of the Court).

52. *Texas Monthly, Inc.,* 489 U.S. 1, 29-45 (Rehnquist, C.J., joining dissent of Scalia, J.); *Aguilar,* 473 U.S. at 420-21 (Rehnquist, C.J., dissenting); *Goldman,* 475 U.S. 503 (opinion of the Court); Thomas v. Review Bd., 450 U.S. 707, 720 (1981) (Rehnquist, C.J., dissenting).

53. *Texas Monthly, Inc.,* 489 U.S. 1, 10-17 (Stevens, J., joining plurality opinion).

54. *Aguilar,* 473 U.S. 402 (Stevens, J., joining opinion of the Court).

55. Goldman v. Weinberger, 475 U.S. 503, 510-13 (1986) (Stevens, J., concurring); United States v. Lee, 455 U.S. 252, 261-64 (1982) (Stevens, J., concurring).

56. Employment Div. v. Smith, 494 U.S. 872 (1990); Jimmy Swaggart Ministries v. Board of Equalization, 493 U.S. 378 (1990).

cept where compliance with the regulation would require the church to violate its "sincere religious beliefs."[57] In *Employment Division v. Smith,* the exception for sincere religious belief disappeared by a vote of five to four.[58] The free exercise of religion now means that churches cannot be taxed or regulated any more heavily than General Motors. The only remaining protection is that provided by formal neutrality; religious conduct cannot be singled out for facially discriminatory regulation.

The Court recognized that these holdings burdened the exercise of religion. The *Smith* opinion acknowledged that the conduct at issue was "the 'exercise of religion,'"[59] and that Oregon had subjected this conduct to "an across-the-board criminal prohibition,"[60] but it insisted that this prohibition of an exercise of religion did not mean that Oregon was "prohibiting the free exercise of religion."[61] In *Swaggart,* the Court said that the economic burden of paying the tax, and "substantial administrative burdens" of collecting the tax or complying with other regulations, were "not constitutionally significant."[62] The Court found it "undeniable that a generally applicable tax has a secular purpose and neither advances nor inhibits religion, for the very essence of such a tax is that it is neutral and nondiscriminatory on questions of religious belief."[63]

This conception of neutrality is irreconcilable with *Aguilar* and the other cases striking down government payments to religiously affiliated schools. In *Aguilar,* the federally-funded instruction in remedial math and reading was directed on equal terms to poor children in all schools, public and private, secular and religious. But the Court did not say that this "neutral and nondiscriminatory" instruction "neither advances nor inhibits religion." Instead, it found that the government money conferred obvious benefits on religion, and did not say that those benefits were of no constitutional significance.

The Court's current position comes to this: when government demands money or obedience *from* churches, neutrality consists of treating churches just like other subjects of taxation or regulation, and it is irrelevant that the church is worse off than it would be without the tax or the regulation. But when government pays money *to* churches, neutrality consists of not making the churches any better off than they would be without the payment, and it is

---

57. *Swaggart,* 493 U.S. at 391-92.
58. 494 U.S. 872.
59. *Id.* at 877 (quoting U.S. CONST. amend. I).
60. *Id.* at 884.
61. *Id.* at 878.
62. Jimmy Swaggart Ministries v. Board of Equalization, 493 U.S. 378, 391, 394 (1990).
63. *Id.* at 394.

irrelevant that the churches are treated just like other beneficiaries of the same program.

Whatever explains these results, it is not a consistent understanding of neutrality. I suspect that the Justices are not deciding on the basis of neutrality at all, although they invoke it in their opinions. If they are deciding on the basis of neutrality, they have not defined it in any consistent way. But the inconsistency of the current rules may be only a transitional step on the way to widespread application of formal neutrality as the rule of judicial decision.

The current rules may result from a temporary voting paradox. Justices Brennan, Marshall, and Blackmun would restrict both regulation of religion and government support of religion. Justices Rehnquist, White, Scalia, and Kennedy would generally permit both regulation and support of religion. Justice O'Connor is a swing vote on both regulation and support. For all eight of these Justices, their votes in Religion Clause cases are best explained by their general attitudes toward judicial enforcement of constitutional rights.

Justice Stevens is the exception. He votes with the judicial activists on most issues, including the Establishment Clause, but he joins the judicial minimalists in free exercise cases. The apparent explanation for his voting pattern is hostility to religion. Religion in his view is subject to all the burdens of government, but entitled to few of the benefits. And because the Court has been closely divided between activist and minimalist judges, he has been a swing vote on religion issues. His hostility to religion is reflected in the Court's rules, even though he has but one vote.

Aguilar, the decision striking down federally-funded remedial instruction in religious schools, was a five-four decision in 1985. Justices Scalia and Kennedy have replaced Burger and Powell, and it is a reasonable guess that if it came up today, *Aguilar* would be five-four the other way. We may soon see a formal neutrality opinion upholding government aid to religious education.

That hypothetical development would greatly reduce the inconsistencies in the Court's opinions. But it would not be a triumph for neutrality. Legislatures would be free to practice disaggregated formal neutrality. They could support religion or burden it, support some religions and burden others, as long as they stated their rules in facially neutral terms. The Court in *Smith* acknowledged somewhat euphemistically that its decision "will place at a relative disadvantage those religious practices that are not widely engaged in."[64] In plain English, this means that churches without political clout may be suppressed, that more powerful churches may be accommo-

---

64. *Smith,* 494 U.S. at 890.

dated, and if the principle is extended to the financial aid cases, they may be supported. If the Court's decisions are eventually reconciled in this way, the explanatory principle will not be neutrality, but statism. The majority will be permitted to do anything it can achieve by facially neutral rules, however gerrymandered, and the Court will have largely abdicated its role of protecting religious minorities.

V. Applying Substantive Neutrality

Formal and substantive neutrality are broad categories. But as I noted earlier, religious liberty controversies present a succession of specific problems. It is necessary to search out the most neutral course with respect to each problem. That process will at least clarify our disagreements, and it might provide some basis for principled argument to legislatures and state courts.

Recall my distinction between equality and neutrality: equality refers only to tangible penalties and rewards; neutrality also includes expression of government opinion. It seems to me that we have widespread consensus on both equality and neutrality with respect to religious status, consensus on equality but not on neutrality with respect to religious belief, consensus except for a few exceptional cases with respect to religious speech, and no consensus at all with respect to religious conduct.

That is a glib set of categories; what do I mean by them? First, consensus with respect to status: almost no one any longer openly claims that non-believers, or non-Christians, or non-Protestants, should be discriminated against because of their religious affiliation. There are occasional exceptions, such as the recent attacks on Father Healy's appointment to head the New York Public Library.[65] But these attacks are nearly always disguised with

---

65. For news stories, see James Barron, *Georgetown's President Named Head of Public Library,* New York Times, Feb. 24, 1989, at B1, col. 2; Dena Kleiman, *Jesuits See Library Post as Part of Their Mission,* New York Times, Feb. 25, 1989, at A33, col. 1; Peter Steinfels, *Priest Picked for Library Post Responds to Critics,* New York Times, Apr. 2, 1989, at A29, col. 1. For editorials, one on each side, see *The Librarian Priest,* New York Times, Mar. 21, 1989, at A24, col. 1 (opposed); *Father Healy as Public Man,* New York Times, Apr. 9, 1989, at A26, col. 1 (supporting). For letters to the editor, see New York Times, Mar. 1, 1989, at A24, col. 3 (Gay Talese, opposed); New York Times, Mar. 16, 1989, at A30, col. 4 (Garry Wills, supporting); New York Times, Mar. 31, 1989, at A34, col. 3 (Joseph Heller, opposed: Albert H. Bowker & Joseph S. Murphy, supporting; Andrew Humm, Eleanor Cooper, and Tom Smith, opposed); New York Times, Apr. 13, 1989, at A26, col. 3 (Sen. Daniel Patrick Moynihan, supporting; Paul Halsall, supporting); New York Times, Apr. 21, 1989, at A30, col. 3 (Andrew M. Greeley, supporting); New York Times, May 8, 1989, at A18, col. 3 (Peter G. Finn, supporting).

pretextual justifications. Moreover, hardly anyone thinks it a proper function of government to denounce the adherents of some religious faiths and laud the adherents of others.

Second, partial consensus with respect to religious belief: we have consensus on equality; no one argues that government should actively penalize some religious beliefs and reward others. But we do not have consensus on neutrality. A vocal minority of lawyers and scholars,[66] and perhaps a majority of the public,[67] believe that government may endorse a preferred religious belief. Some urge generic theism, some the Judeo-Christian tradition, some Christianity. Whatever their preferred teaching, these people reject the Supreme Court's holdings that government should be neutral with respect to religious belief. And of course, the Supreme Court itself does not seem to take those holdings very seriously.[68]

Third, partial consensus with respect to religious speech: religious speech and political speech are the two core cases of highly protected speech, and they should be treated equally. A long line of Supreme Court cases are consistent with that proposition,[69] and I think there is widespread agreement with those results, although not necessarily with my formulation of the principle. Religious speech in and around public schools is an exceptional case where consensus breaks down. Consensus also breaks down when money is involved, as in the *Texas Monthly* case, in the campaign finance and disclosure laws,[70] and in the restrictions on political speech in the

66. *See, e.g.*, County of Allegheny v. American Civil Liberties Union Greater Pittsburgh Chapter, 492 U.S. 573, 668-77 (1989) (Kennedy, J., dissenting); Wallace v. Jaffree, 472 U.S. 38, 114 (1985) (Rehnquist, J., dissenting); Edwin Meese, *The Supreme Court of the United States: Bulwark of a Limited Constitution*, 27 S. Tex. L. Rev. 455, 464 (1986) (argument that Religion Clauses require neutrality between religion and nonreligion "would have struck the founding generation as bizarre"); John Whitehead & John Conlan, *The Establishment of the Religion of Secular Humanism and Its First Amendment Implications*, 10 Tex. Tech. L. Rev. 1, 21-25 (1978) (Supreme Court rulings have replaced theism with secular humanism as an established faith).

67. *See, e.g.*, Herbert McClosky & Alida Brill, The Dimensions of Tolerance: What Americans Think About Civil Liberties 133 (1983).

68. *See* Lynch v. Donnelly, 465 U.S. 668 (1984) (upholding municipal creche); Marsh v. Chambers, 463 U.S. 783 (1983) (upholding legislative chaplain who opens daily sessions with prayer).

69. *See, e.g.*, Widmar v. Vincent, 454 U.S. 263 (1981); Heffron v. International Soc'y for Krishna Consciousness, Inc., 452 U.S. 640 (1981); Poulos v. New Hampshire, 345 U.S. 395 (1953); West Virginia State Bd. of Educ. v. Barnette, 319 U.S. 624 (1943); Largent v. Texas, 318 U.S. 418 (1943); Cantwell v. Connecticut, 310 U.S. 296 (1940); Lovell v. City of Griffin, 303 U.S. 444 (1938).

70. *See, e.g.*, Buckley v. Valeo, 424 U.S. 1 (1976); L.A. Powe, *Mass Speech*, 1982 Sup. Ct. Rev. 243.

Internal Revenue Code.[71] My principle that religious and political speech should be treated equally could have explained the *Texas Monthly* case, and my principle had some relation to the discordant and troublesome combination of opinions that made up the majority. The more recent decision in *Jimmy Swaggart Ministries*[72] makes it harder to sustain benign readings of *Texas Monthly*. But it remains open to the Court to uphold a tax exemption that includes religious speech in some broader category, such as not-for-profit speech, or religious, anti-religious, and political speech. The relationship between constitutional protections for religious and political speech is now before the Court in the quite different context of judgments against churches for such speech torts as defamation and intentional infliction of emotional distress.[73]

Finally, dissensus with respect to religious conduct. What does it mean to be neutral with respect to conscientious objection to government policy, or religious education, or religious charities, or the management of religious institutions? I am not sure we have consensus that either equality or neutrality is required with respect to religious conduct; we certainly have no consensus on what that means.

Allow me to consider just one of these examples, exemption from facially neutral laws that forbid religious conduct or require people to violate deeply held conscientious beliefs. The Supreme Court repeatedly announced the constitutional right to such exemptions, but enforced it half-heartedly.[74] The

71. 26 U.S.C. § 501(c)(3) (1982). For criticism of the use of tax exemptions to restrict religious speech, see Wilfred Caron & Deidre Dessingue, *IRC § 501(c)(3): Practical and Constitutional Implications of "Political" Activity Restrictions*, 2 J.L. & POL. 169 (1985); Edward Gaffney, *On Not Rendering to Caesar: The Unconstitutionality of Tax Regulation of Activities of Religious Organizations Relating to Politics*, 40 DePAUL L. REV. 1 (1990) (forthcoming).

72. Jimmy Swaggart Ministries v. Board of Equalization, 493 U.S. 378 (1990), discussed in text *supra* notes 56-63.

73. George v. International Soc'y for Krishna Consciousness, No. D007153 (Cal. App. 4th Dist. 1989), *vacated*, 499 U.S. 914 (1991).

74. *Compare* Frazee v. Illinois Dept. of Employment Sec., 489 U.S. 829 (1989) (employee who loses his job for religious reasons is entitled to unemployment compensation); Hobbie v. Unemployment Appeals Comm'n, 480 U.S. 136 (1987) (same); Thomas v. Review Bd., 450 U.S. 707 (1981) (same); Wisconsin v. Yoder, 406 U.S. 205 (1972) (Amish parents who conscientiously object to public high school exempted from compulsory education laws); Sherbert v. Verner, 374 U.S. 398 (1963) (another unemployment compensation case) *with* Goldman v. Weinberger, 475 U.S. 503 (1986) (military can discipline officer for wearing *yarmulke* with uniform); Bob Jones Univ. v. United States, 461 U.S. 574, 602-04 (1983) (pervasively religious school that conscientiously forbids interracial dating by students has no constitutional right to retain its charitable tax exemption); United States v. Lee, 455 U.S. 252 (1982) (conscientious objectors to social security have no constitutional right to refuse to pay social security

Reagan Administration quietly hammered at that right for eight years.[75] Now the Court has wholly repudiated the right.[76]

Scholars are also attacking the right to exemption, often in the name of neutrality. Two major scholars have recently offered all-out attacks on the constitutional right to such exemptions. One is Ellis West, a political scientist at the University of Richmond;[77] the other is William Marshall, a lawyer at Case Western Reserve.[78]

Neither the scholars or the Court goes as far as requiring formal neutrality.[79] Neither claims that exemptions for religion are unconstitutional when the legislature voluntarily grants them. Both rely on the formal conception of neutrality, but both draw back from its full implications, or at least from the claim that it is constitutionally required.

They do not appear to flinch from the full implications of their claim that the Constitution requires no exemptions for religious exercise. I assume that they would permit a state to enact Prohibition without an exception for the Mass or the Seder. The Court says as much in its opinion,[80] and Professor West said as much in response to a question.[81] He also said that if a law forbidding ethnic and religious discrimination in employment had no excep-

taxes); Gillette v. United States, 401 U.S. 437 (1971) (conscientious objectors to unjust wars have no constitutional right to exemption from serving in such wars).

75. *See* Brief of the United States as Amicus Curiae Supporting Appellees at 7-10, Hobbie v. Florida Unemployment Comm'n, 480 U.S. 136 (1987) (No. 85-993) (arguing that government may *restrict or penalize* free exercise of religion as long as it does not *prohibit* free exercise of religion); Brief for the Appellants at 27-30, Bowen v. Roy, 476 U.S. 693 (1986) (No. 84-780) (arguing that government's interest in denying constitutional exemption to conscientious objector must be measured by the cost of repealing the challenged law entirely, and not by the cost of exempting conscientious objectors); Brief for the Respondents, Goldman v. Weinberger, 475 U.S. 503 (1986) (No. 84-1097) (arguing against right to wear *yarmulke* with military uniform); Brief of the United States as Amicus Curiae at 5-15, Jensen v. Quaring, 472 U.S. 478 (1985) (No. 83-1944) (arguing that Constitution does not require exemption from photograph required for driver's license); Brief for the United States at 15-18, United States v. Lee, 455 U.S. 252 (1982) (No. 80-767) (arguing that Constitution does not protect against indirect burdens on exercise of religion).

76. Employment Div. v. Smith, 494 U.S. 872 (1990).

77. Ellis West, *The Case Against a Right to Religion-Based Exemptions,* 4 NOTRE DAME J.L. ETHICS, & PUB. POL'Y 591 (1990).

78. William Marshall, *The Case Against the Constitutionally Compelled Free Exercise Exemption,* 40 CASE W. RES. 357 (1989-90).

79. *But see* Tushnet, *supra* note 23, at 384, 402.

80. *Smith,* 494 U.S. at 877 (using example of "sacramental use of bread and wine").

81. Oral exchange at Notre Dame conference on religious liberty, South Bend, Indiana, March 1989.

tion for rabbis, then a synagogue might have to hire a Baptist rabbi. He defended himself on the ground that no state would pass such a law, and that probably the Baptist would be unqualified on some other ground.[82]

The hope that no state would pass such a law is insufficient protection for religious minorities. It is true that Americans are more tolerant than many other populations, in part because of the teachings of the Religion Clauses. Many religious minorities have assimilated into the general culture and into the political process, and the legislature is unlikely to knowingly victimize these minorities in ways that go to the heart of their faith. That is why Jews and Catholics were protected by an exception to Prohibition.

But the precondition of assimilation and respectability is why Oregon has failed to protect Native Americans' ritual use of peyote.[83] This social precondition is why in the nineteenth century we denied Mormons the right to vote,[84] imprisoned some of their leaders,[85] confiscated all the property of their church,[86] and dissolved its legal existence,[87] until the church changed its practice, its teaching, and its belief on plural marriage.[88] This social precondition is why multi-million-dollar tort judgments threaten the very existence of the Hare Krishnas, the Scientologists, and other so-called "cults."[89] I am not much comforted by the prospect that only small and unfamiliar religions will be persecuted.

Nor am I willing to assume that larger religious minorities are always safe. The Church of Christ is hardly a fringe group in Collinsville, Oklahoma, but it too is threatened with destruction from a huge tort judgment for in-

---

82. *Id.*

83. *See* Employment Div. v. Smith, 494 U.S. 872 (1990).

84. *See* Davis v. Beason, 133 U.S. 333 (1890).

85. *See* Reynolds v. United States, 98 U.S. 145 (1878).

86. *See* Late Corp. of the Church of Jesus Christ of Latter Day Saints v. United States, 136 U.S. 1 (1890).

87. *Id.*

88. See JOHN NOONAN, THE BELIEVER AND THE POWERS THAT ARE 207 (1987).

89. *See* George v. International Soc'y for Krishna Consciousness, No. D007153 (Cal. App. 4th Dist. 1989) ($32.7 million verdict reduced to $3 million), *vacated,* 499 U.S. 914 (1991); Wollersheim v. Church of Scientology, 260 Cal. Rptr. 331 (Cal. App. 1989) ($30 million verdict remitted to $2.5 million), *vacated,* 499 U.S. 914 (1991); Church Universal & Triumphant, Inc. v. Witt, No. B021187 (Cal. App. 2d Dist. 1989) ($1.5 million); O'Neil v. Schuckardt, 733 P.2d 693 (Idaho 1986) ($1 million); Christofferson v. Church of Scientology, 5 Religious Freedom Rptr. 126 (Or. Cir. Ct. Multnomah County 1985) ($39 million). For earlier proceedings in *Christofferson,* see 644 P.2d 577 (Or. App. 1982). The California courts appear not to believe that judicial destruction of a minority faith even requires a published opinion.

tangible harm to a disgruntled former member.[90] In this decade, the military attempted to eliminate Jewish officers who wore their yarmulke while in uniform. In what appeared to be a fit of unthinking deference, the Supreme Court upheld that practice.[91] Congress intervened with protective legislation,[92] but much harm had been done in the meantime. In retrospect, the Court's refusal to protect yarmulkes was a precursor to its refusal in *Smith* to protect any religious conduct at all.

In times of political excitement, of xenophobia, of outbursts of anti-Catholic or anti-Semitic feeling, almost any kind of law is possible, especially at the state and local level. The question is not merely what the federal government might do in such times, although that is scary enough. It was Congress that persecuted the Mormons, and the federal executive that tried to purge observant Jewish military officers. But we must also consider what state and local jurisdictions with religiously homogeneous populations might do to small and unfamiliar minorities. The point is not that such populations are any less enlightened than other Americans, but simply that the forces of pluralism are more attenuated in homogenous communities. What might Utah, or Arkansas, or Yalobusha County do in times of excitement? We have a bill of rights to be enforced by an independent judiciary in part to get us through such times with minimal damage. To claim that the worst horror stories are unlikely to happen is to miss the point of a bill of rights.

I start with overt hostility because it would be a mistake to assume it away. But hostility is not the only source of law forbidding people to practice their religions, and probably not even the most important. The practice of a small faith may be forbidden just because the legislature did not know about it and never considered its needs. Then the bureaucracy will grind forward, enforcing the rule without regard to exceptional circumstance. This may be what happened to Frances Quaring, who thought the picture on her driver's license was a graven image forbidden by the second commandment.[93] The Frances Quarings of the world may or may not be organized enough to get the attention of the legislature, but a court is required to listen to their complaint and to rule one way or the other.

Of course, inadvertence can interact with hostility, or with an insensitivity that borders on hostility. Consider what might happen when Frances

90. Guinn v. Church of Christ, 775 P.2d 766 (Okla. 1989) ($390,000 against local congregation).

91. Goldman v. Weinberger, 475 U.S. 503 (1986).

92. 10 U.S.C. § 774 (1988).

93. Quaring v. Peterson, 728 F.2d 1121 (8th Cir. 1984), *aff'd by equally divided Court, sub nom.* Jensen v. Quaring, 472 U.S. 478 (1985).

Quaring writes her legislator. She may get a sympathetic response and a legislated exemption. But her legislator may find it so impossible to empathize with her belief that he never seriously considers whether an exemption would be workable. Even if he empathizes, the legislative calendar is crowded, and the original statute having been enacted, all the burdens of legislative inertia now work against an exemption.

For a variety of reasons, therefore, we cannot always rely on legislatures to protect minority religious conduct. Courts are not always better, but they give religious liberty claims a second chance to be heard.[94] If we take seriously the constitutional right to freely exercise religion, we must restore a judicially enforceable right to religious exemption in appropriate cases.

The right to exemptions for religious conduct is more easily explained in terms of religious liberty than in terms of neutrality. But the right is consistent with substantive neutrality, and it can be explained in those terms as well.

As I have already noted with respect to Prohibition, a law that penalizes religious conduct discourages religion. The discouragement is often severe, as when the penalty is criminal punishment or Frances Quaring's loss of the right to drive. But in many of the cases, an exemption for conscientious objectors has only a de minimis tendency to encourage any aspect of religion. The exemption is substantively neutral; the lack of an exemption is not.

Another way to state this is that equal impact comes closer to the proper sense of neutrality with respect to conscientious objection. People with a deeply held conscientious objection to a law are not similarly situated to people without such an objection. To insist on formally equal treatment of objectors and non-objectors is to pursue the same majestic equality that forbids the rich and the poor alike to sleep under bridges.[95]

Substantive equality and equal impact are not wholly equivalent. The difference between them appears in cases where religious belief coincides too closely with self-interest, as in conscientious objection to military service or payment of taxes. The distorting effects of self-interest do not make sincere conscientious objectors similarly situated with non-objectors; denying the exemption still has severe and unequal impact on objectors. The equal impact sense of neutrality would focus on the objectors and presumptively

94. I elaborate on the second-chance rationale for judicial review in Douglas Laycock, *Notes on the Role of Judicial Review, the Expansion of Federal Power, and the Structure of Constitutional Rights* (Book Review), 99 YALE L.J. 1711, 1727-30 (1990).

95. See BARTLETT'S FAMILIAR QUOTATIONS 802a (14th ed. 1968) ("The law, in its majestic equality, forbids the rich as well as the poor to sleep under bridges, to beg in the streets, and to steal bread") (quoting ANATOLE FRANCE, LE LYS ROUGE (1894)).

grant the exemption, subject only to the government's proof of a compelling reason to deny it.

But substantive neutrality as I have defined it must also consider the non-objectors. If we grant exemptions from military service or general taxation, on the basis of conscientious objection, we will inevitably encourage religion. I do not refer to the people willing to feign religious belief in order to claim an exemption. There may be millions of these people, and the difficulty of adjudicating their false claims is relevant to the government's claim of compelling interest,[96] but these false claimants are only incidentally relevant to neutrality.

I refer instead to the people who honestly persuade themselves that they have come to hold the religious belief that entitles them to the exemption, or who feel pressured to adopt that belief. Human nature being what it is, there may be millions of these people as well. The lure of exemption creates cognitive dissonance between the individual's desire for the exemption and the belief that makes him ineligible for it. The psychological effort to reduce this dissonance can move his actual belief into conformity with the belief that serves his self-interest.[97]

The problem for religious neutrality is that denying the exemption discourages religious belief in one set of people, and granting the exemption encourages religious belief in another, overlapping, set of people. It is no longer clear that exemption is the more nearly neutral course. If we suspect that the original number of conscientious objectors is small, and that the number of non-objectors seriously tempted by the exemption is large, then denying the exemption appears to be more nearly neutral than granting it. If we have no plausible estimate of which effect is larger, then there may be no basis in substantive neutrality for the courts to second-guess the legislature.

Whatever we do in these difficult cases, the deviation from neutrality is large. Either we will deny the exemption, with severe and unequal impact on the original objectors, devastating to their religious liberty, or we will grant the exemption, and greatly encourage religious belief in the objectors induced by the exemption. The case is hard, and the most nearly neutral course will not be very neutral.

Legislatures can sometimes solve these problems by imposing an alternative burden, designed to accommodate conscience while reducing the self-

96. *See* Mayer Freed & Daniel Polsby, *Race, Religion, and Public Policy:* Bob Jones University v. United States, 1983 SUP. CT. REV. 1, 20-30; Marshall, *supra* note 78; West, *supra* note 77.

97. *See generally* LEON FESTINGER, A THEORY OF COGNITIVE DISSONANCE 1-31, 84-122 (1957).

interested reasons for claiming the exemption. That is part of the logic of the alternative service requirement for objectors to military service,[98] and of the requirement that workers who object to union dues make an equivalent contribution to a charity other than their church.[99] These legislative solutions are not perfect — thousands of Jehovah's Witnesses spent World War II in prison because they objected even to alternative service[100] — but they permit a closer approximation to substantive neutrality. They come from thoughtful legislatures; it is harder to see how courts could create them.

VI. Conclusion

I hope I have at least persuaded you that the meaning of neutrality is not self-evident, and that substantive neutrality is a possible alternative to formal neutrality. Beyond that, I hope I have persuaded you that substantive neutrality is more consistent with religious liberty than is formal neutrality. I have much more work to do to show that a neutral baseline can usually be identified in a principled way across the whole range of interactions between religion and government. But I hope I have persuaded you that the work is worth doing. For that is the path toward maximum religious liberty, neutrally distributed among all kinds of believers and non-believers. And that multifarious formulation is as close as I can come to a single principle that summarizes the Religion Clauses.

---

98. 50 U.S.C. App. § 456(j) (1982).

99. 29 U.S.C. § 169 (Supp. V. 1987).

100. MULFORD SIBLEY & PHILIP JACOB, CONSCRIPTION OF CONSCIENCE: THE AMERICAN STATE AND THE CONSCIENTIOUS OBJECTOR, 1940-1947, at 84 (1952).

The Benefits of the Establishment Clause

42 DePaul Law Review 373 (1992)

This was presented at a conference at the DePaul Center for Church/State Studies. I was part of a panel asked to respond to the question, "Does the United States need an Establishment Clause?" To answer that question, I focused on what the Establishment Clause adds to the Free Exercise Clause. The published version closely tracks the oral presentation, and exchanges with the audience are included. Footnotes have been renumbered in the Question and Answer segment.

∗   ∗   ∗

I must begin by briefly discussing both the Free Exercise Clause and the Establishment Clause and the relationship between them. In my view, they are both clauses to protect religious liberty. Together, they protect both believers and nonbelievers. Indeed, each clause considered separately protects both believers and nonbelievers, or each would if it were properly interpreted. The shortest summary I can offer is that the clauses together are designed to minimize government influence on religious belief and practice. By minimizing government influence, they maximize religious liberty. Much more than with respect to any of our other liberties, the Religion Clauses are designed to make religious practice and nonpractice, belief and nonbelief, wholly matters of private choice insulated from government influence or control.

Much of the contribution of the Establishment Clause is that religious

---

This paper is based on oral remarks delivered at a conference sponsored by the Center for Church/State Studies, DePaul University College of Law, held on December 6 and 7, 1991.

belief and practice are insulated even from government persuasion. There is no other area of our life where we say that government cannot even try to persuade you. On political issues, persuasion is a large part of what government does. Government leads; government tries to mold opinion. But with respect to religious opinion, we say that molding opinion is precisely what government should not do.

In too many discussions of the Religion Clauses, including at least occasionally at this conference, you get a sense that each Religion Clause is one side's club to beat the other with. Among some aggressively proselytizing religious groups you occasionally hear the Free Exercise Clause explained as their way to maximize their religious influence, and the Establishment Clause as an unfortunate inconvenience. On the other side, and far more often in academic life, you hear the Establishment Clause pointed to as the clause by which we keep these troublesome religious folks under control and out of the public sphere. Each of these views is nonsense. These two clauses, which are found in the same sentence, are not in opposition to one another. At the big picture level, they are not even in tension with one another, although I concede that in applying the clauses in close cases, the hard cases, there is sometimes tension.

It is important to remember that the votes for disestablishment came from evangelicals.[1] The votes came from Baptists, Presbyterians, Methodists, and Quakers. I do not mean to underestimate the contribution of James Madison, but he alone did not have the votes. The necessary political pressure, the demand for disestablishment, the threat not to ratify the Constitution unless something were done about religious liberty, came from the evangelical dissenting churches.

I am sure about where the votes came from. I am less sure about this next point, but I think it is more probable than not: but for the evangelicals, Madison would not have had the motivation to pursue religious liberty. He was influenced by the specter and the occasional reality of persecution of Baptist preachers in Virginia. Without that experience, I am not at all sure there would be *The Memorial and the Remonstrance*[2] or any of the rest that

1. See, e.g., Thomas J. Curry, The First Freedoms: Church and State in America to the Passage of the First Amendment 134-37, 141, 143-46, 148-51, 156-57, 163-77, 179-83, 185-89, 195, 198-99, 216-17 (1986); Michael W. McConnell, *The Origins and Historical Understanding of Free Exercise of Religion,* 103 Harv. L. Rev. 1409, 1436-43 (1990).

2. Madison's *Memorial and Remonstrance Against Religious Assessments* was circulated in 1785 in response to the general assessment bill then pending in the Virginia legislature. The bill and *Memorial and Remonstrance* are reprinted in an appendix to *Everson v. Board of Education,* 330 U.S. 1, 63-74 (1990).

we credit to Madison. In fact, Madison was nearly defeated for election to the First Congress, partly because of an Anti-Federalist gerrymander, but also because he was dragging his feet on a federal bill of rights, and religious dissenters in his district were demanding an explicit guarantee of religious liberty.[3]

Under the Religion Clauses, as I understand them and as the Supreme Court has understood them, all religions are protected. But that commitment itself entails one choice about types of religion. There is one type of religion that cannot be fully protected. That is the religion of those people who believe that their religious exercise requires the use of the instruments of government, either to directly impose their belief on others or to use government in their own worship services. This choice among types of religion is also a choice among types of liberty. I believe it is not simply a raw choice. It is a principled choice, based on the view that the best you can do to maximize religious liberty for all citizens is to prevent anyone from using the government for religious purposes.

What then is the role of the Establishment Clause as one of this pair of clauses to protect religious liberty? One way to view this question is in practical lawyer terms. What does the Establishment Clause add to the Free Exercise Clause? What abuses are forbidden by the Establishment Clause that would not be forbidden if we had the Free Exercise Clause alone?

Susan Gilles[4] and Richard Kay[5] have outlined what an established church can look like in a tolerant society under the most favorable conditions for liberty. One can decide for oneself whether the results are satisfactory. I tend to approach the question from the opposite perspective. Constitutional rights do not exist to protect us against the times when things are going well. Rather, we have constitutional rights to ameliorate the times when things are going very badly. Constitutional rights are aimed at abuses. The question then becomes: What abuses are forbidden by the Establishment Clause that are not forbidden by the Free Exercise Clause?

It is certainly true that constitutional clauses and judicial review are very thin reeds to rely on. When a society is bent on abuse or persecution, there is a great danger that judges will go along. A sufficiently determined political majority can appoint judges who promise not to enforce much of the Bill of

---

3. ROBERT A. RUTLAND, JAMES MADISON: THE FOUNDING FATHER 44-49 (1987); CURRY, *supra* note 1, at 198-99.

4. Susan M. Gilles, *"Worldly Corruptions" and "Ecclesiastical Depredations": How Bad Is An Established Church*, 42 DEPAUL L. REV. 349 (1992).

5. Richard S. Kay, *The Canadian Constitution and the Dangers of Establishment*, 42 DEPAUL L. REV. 361 (1992).

Rights. Our mechanisms for preserving minority rights and majority rule are ingenious but fragile.

The claim that constitutional clauses do some good is not a claim that judges are inherently better than legislators at protecting liberty. Sometimes they are better; sometimes they are worse. Usually they are about the same. The claim that the Constitution does some good is simply the claim that two chances are better than one. Unlike legislators, judges have to at least go through the motions of listening to every complaint that is presented to them and of giving principled reasons for each decision. They have some incentives to do so, incentives in judicial tradition and in insulation from political pressure. Some of the time, judicial review will do some good. The judges did nothing for the Mormons,[6] but they may have saved the Jehovah's Witnesses[7] and the Amish.[8] If judges can save one religious minority a century, I consider that ample justification for judicial review in religious liberty cases.

I come at last to the question of what abuses might be forbidden by the Establishment Clause that may not be forbidden by the Free Exercise Clause. The first, and most obvious, is taxation to support religion as religion. In Virginia by 1776, there were still some licensing provisions, and Baptist ministers were occasionally hassled, but Virginians were very close to general free exercise.[9] The dissenting churches were already allowed to function. It would have been very easy to enact a Free Exercise Clause with no Establishment Clause.

In fact, that is what they did. The Virginia Free Exercise Clause was enacted in 1776, and disestablishment came some time later.[10] The general assessment proposal that Madison resisted would have continued free exercise for all but required each citizen to pay taxes to support the religion of his choice.[11] The historian Thomas Curry thinks that many at the time believed that taxation to support the church violated free exercise.[12] He may be right,

6. *See* Late Corp. of the Church of Jesus Christ of Latter-Day Saints v. United States, 136 U.S. 1 (1890); Davis v. Beason, 133 U.S. 333 (1890); Reynolds v. United States, 98 U.S. 145 (1878).

7. The Jehovah's Witness cases are collected in Douglas Laycock, *A Survey of Religious Liberty in the United States,* 42 Ohio St. L. Rev. 409, 419-20 (1986).

8. *See* Wisconsin v. Yoder, 406 U.S. 205 (1972).

9. Thomas E. Buckley, Church and State in Revolutionary Virginia, 1776-87, at 36 (1977).

10. Curry, *supra* note 1, at 135-36.

11. *Id.* at 136.

12. *Id.* at 147, 217.

although there is no support in the case law for that claim today.[13] Certainly it is easier to explain to a judge why taxation to support the church violates the Establishment Clause than to explain why it would violate the Free Exercise Clause.

Taxation to support education and social services delivered by churches may or may not be distinguishable from taxation to support religion as religion.[14] If church-sponsored education and social services are distinguishable from the church itself, then tax support violates neither Religion Clause. If church-sponsored education and social services are indistinguishable from the church itself, then the tax support violates the Establishment Clause. A free exercise claim is much harder to make out. The analysis of whether the Establishment Clause adds anything to the Free Exercise Clause with respect to education and social services is analogous to the analysis of which clause forbids taxation to support religion as religion.

A second abuse forbidden by the Establishment Clause is coerced worship. Just as the general assessment proposal would have required everybody to pay a tax to some church, it is easy to imagine a law that required everybody to attend some church. Such a law might let the individual choose the church, but would require attendance somewhere. In fact, that is a rule at military academies today.* Coerced worship is one way to understand school prayer: all the students are required to participate in this little worship service. I am assuming that in our pluralistic society, such a requirement would at least have some aspect of nonpreferentialism about it. But one can even

---

13. See Tilton v. Richardson, 403 U.S. 672, 689 (1971) (rejecting a free exercise challenge to tax support for religious schools, on ground that paying taxes to support another religion did not violate any practice or exercise of plaintiff's religion); cf. United States v. Lee, 455 U.S. 252 (1982) (rejecting a free exercise challenge to use of tax money to support the Social Security system, which *did* violate the Amish plaintiffs' religious tenets against participation in public insurance programs, on the ground that the government's interest in collecting taxes was compelling); Flast v. Cohen, 392 U.S. 83, 103-04 (1968) (holding that the Establishment Clause is exception to the general rule of no standing for taxpayers to challenge government expenditures, and that this clause operates as a specific constitutional limitation upon Congressional taxing and spending powers; there is no similar holding under the Free Exercise Clause).

14. For an analysis of this possible distinction, see Michael W. McConnell, *The Selective Funding Problem: Abortion and Religious Schools,* 104 HARV. L. REV. 989 (1991).

[*I did not know it at the time, but that rule had been held unconstitutional in *Anderson v. Laird,* 466 F.2d 283 (D.C. Cir. 1972). Students at the academies may feel some pressure to attend services, but I am not aware of allegations that any of the academies have openly violated this decision. My information was seriously out of date, and for a collateral illustration in an informal talk, I made the mistake of not checking.]

imagine a rule that says every church can continue to function, and you can go to your own church, as long as you also show up at the established or preferred church once a week.

A requirement that everyone worship would violate the Free Exercise Clause, if properly interpreted. Just as the Speech Clause protects one's right not to speak, the Free Exercise Clause protects one's right not to worship. I am not at all convinced, however, that the current Supreme Court would have agreed with this, even before *Employment Division v. Smith*.[15] The Court says there is no free exercise claim unless a person is required to violate a specific and obligatory tenet of her religious belief.[16]

Consider what the Court's rule implies for coerced worship. Suppose I say: "I am a traditional Roman Catholic and I have a specific tenet against worshiping with anyone else. And I still believe that, even though the rest of the Catholic Church has become considerably more liberal as to this tenet." If I sincerely believe this, then I may have a free exercise claim of coerced worship at another faith's service. But suppose I say: "I'm just a non-believer. I do not care about any of this stuff." Or suppose I say: "I am a post–Vatican II Catholic. I have no objection in principle to worshiping with other faiths. But except on special occasions, I do not get much out of it. I am certainly not going to give up the Mass, and it is a burden to also attend someone else's worship service every week."

In either of the latter scenarios, the current judicial response is likely to be: "You have no specific religious tenet that says you cannot show up and worship in someone else's church once a week as the law requires. You have no free exercise claim. The burden of two worship services every week is irrelevant, or in any event is much less onerous than the burden of closing a store two days a week in *Braunfeld v. Brown*."[17] That may be the wrong interpretation of the Free Exercise Clause but, again, protection against coerced worship is much more easily explained in terms of the Establishment Clause.

Neither coerced worship, nor coerced tax support for religion as religion, seems very likely in the current political environment. A third and more real

15. Employment Div. v. Smith, 494 U.S. 872 (1990) (holding that there is no constitutional right to exemption from facially neutral and generally applicable laws that prohibit religious practices).

16. Jimmy Swaggart Ministries v. Board of Equalization, 493 U.S. 378, 391-92 (1990). *See also* Douglas Laycock, *The Remnants of Free Exercise*, 1990 Sup. Ct. Rev. 1, 23-28 (analyzing this part of the *Swaggart* opinion).

17. 366 U.S. 599 (1961) (holding that a Sunday closing law did not violate the free exercise rights of an Orthodox Jewish merchant where religion required him to close on Saturday and law required him to close on Sunday).

concern, as raised here by Daniel Conkle, is noncoercive religious observances by government.[18] What about government-sponsored worship that no one has to attend but anyone may attend? What about government crosses, creches, menorahs, Christmas pageants, and the like? This is where much of the real issue exists today. If the Establishment Clause were cut back to only a rule against coercive impositions of religion by government, and if coercion were interpreted to mean only physical force or formal sanctions,[19] then there would be much less political controversy.

So, what are the benefits of a rule against all government-sponsored religious observances? What are the reasons for a rule that government cannot even persuade about religion, cannot engage in religious observances, and cannot put up religious symbols, even if it's not coercing anybody?

I will begin my response by saying that if I had to give up one of the rights in the First Amendment, this is the one I would give up. A rule against government persuasion or influence is less critical than a rule against government coercion. In terms of history, in terms of comparative law, and in terms of what the rest of the world does, the Establishment Clause is an extraordinary protection. We would probably still be a free society without it. But I at least would mourn the loss. Repeal of our protection against religious persuasion by government would be a serious loss for reasons that have already been mentioned by other speakers at this conference. I review those reasons briefly.

First is the harm it would bring to religious minorities, those whose faith will not be the one that the government observes and whose symbols will not be displayed. These minorities include nonbelievers — atheists, agnostics, and the wholly indifferent — but also believers in the extraordinary array of minority faiths in this country. Justice O'Connor described this harm in principle, although she can never recognize it when she sees it.[20] Government observance of the majority religion does indeed tell religious minorities that they are outsiders and not fully accepted members of the community.

---

18. Daniel O. Conkle, *God Loveth Adverbs*, 42 DePaul L. Rev. 339, 346 (1992).

19. *Compare* Lee v. Weisman, 505 U.S. 577, 592-96 (1992) (recognizing coercive pressure to participate in prayer at graduation ceremony), *with id.* at 640 (Scalia, J., dissenting) (recognizing coercion only if imposed "by force of law and threat of penalty"). For an analysis of why the majority has the more realistic understanding of coercion, see Douglas Laycock, *"Noncoercive" Support for Religion: Another False Claim About the Establishment Clause*, 26 Val. U.L. Rev. 37, 67-68 (1991).

20. See Lynch v. Donnelly, 465 U.S. 668, 688 (1984) (O'Connor, J., concurring) (concluding that a government endorsement of one religion sends a message of exclusion to others, but that a government display of a creche does not endorse Christianity).

Those who think government ought to be able to engage in religious rituals and display religious symbols might ask: "What is the problem? We see ideas that offend us all the time. Political dissenters who are seriously alienated from the policies of the Bush Administration are told that they are second class citizens in the same sense as offended religious minorities. If no one thinks it unconstitutional that the government lets political dissenters know it does not care about their views, what is so different about religion?" What's different is that on matters of governmental policy, somebody has to decide. This polity has decided that it should be the majority, but it must inevitably be someone. The government *must* make decisions about political matters.

In the case of religion, no one has to rule. There is no need for the government to make decisions about Christian rituals versus Jewish rituals versus no religious rituals at all. For government to make that choice is simply a gratuitous statement about the kind of people we really are. By making such statements, the government says the real American religion is watered-down Christianity, and everybody else is a little bit un-American.

It is also relevant here that people suffer more when you take away something they have come to think of as their own than if you never give it to them in the first place. After forty years of telling religious minorities in this country that it is part of their rights that the government will not engage in school prayer and in public religious observance, the harm of overruling all those cases at this point would be more severe than if the issue had been decided the other way from the beginning.

The other set of harms from noncoercive establishments is to the religious majority. It is not good for religion to have government engaged in religious rituals. Government by its sheer size and prominence will have a disproportionate influence on the kinds of rituals that are exercised and on public perception of what are appropriate rituals. The result will not be pretty. Government-sponsored religion is theologically and liturgically thin. It is politically compliant. It is supportive of incumbent administrations. In intolerant communities, it inevitably tends to impose the majority's forms, rituals, and terminology on everybody. In tolerant communities, efforts to be all-inclusive inevitably lead to desacralization, to the least common denominator, to a secular Incarnation with plastic reindeer, to Christmas and Chanukah mushed together as the Winter Holidays.[21] By stripping all the

---

21. See County of Allegheny v. ACLU, Greater Pittsburgh Chapter, 492 U.S. 573, 616 (1990) ("[B]oth Christmas and Chanukah are part of the same winter-holiday season, which has attained a secular status in our society."). For further analysis of the harm to religion, see Laycock, *supra* note 19, at 61-65 (text at notes 154-64).

specific elements of different faiths and denominations and attempting to keep only the common elements that all faiths share, tolerant governments produce a mishmash that no faith can accept or believe in. It has always been a great puzzle to me why certain elements of the religious community invest so much effort in demanding that government model bad religion in this way. There are serious costs to these government religious observances.

Finally, it is occasionally suggested that the Establishment Clause helps keep religion out of politics. Simply put, that is nonsense. As history clearly demonstrates, religion is always a part of politics. I think Daniel Conkle offered more or less the right distinction.[22] What the Establishment Clause separates from government is theology, worship, and ritual, the aspects of religion that relate only to things outside the jurisdiction of government. Questions of morality, of right conduct, of proper treatment of our fellow humans, are questions to which both church and state have historically spoken. They are questions within the jurisdiction of both. In a democratic society, the state will ultimately decide these questions at least to the extent of deciding what conduct will be subject to legal sanctions. But these are also questions on which churches are absolutely entitled to speak.

For better or worse, churches always have spoken on these issues. Those who think that religion and religious believers should be kept out of politics should reflect on abolition. Those who think that there are no risks of religion intruding into politics should meditate on Prohibition. There are good stories and bad stories about religious views and about religious participation in politics. The bad stories are about intolerance and failure to accommodate differing views in a pluralistic society; but there are equally bad stories about secular movements of all sorts. In a society where David Duke can be taken seriously as a candidate for President, I am not uniquely or especially worried about religious participation in politics.

Questions and Answers to Panel 5

Mary Mitchell (Indiana University Law School): I am extremely interested in Professor Kay's list of noncoercive injuries. And I would like to pick up Professor Laycock's point and be sure that his point gets added to your list; there is a very important kind of noncoercive injury that comes when government tries to persuade people. I don't look on that as a lightweight kind of harm, because another way of saying "persuasion" is "indoctrination." And, espe-

---

22. Conkle, *supra* note 18, at 345-46.

cially in the arena of the public schools, I believe that type of injury becomes a very serious kind of injury.

In *Engel*[23] and *Schempp*,[24] the Supreme Court cases dealing with prayer and Bible reading in the schools, the Supreme Court justices made a point of saying that they did not consider this kind of activity coercive. So presumably there would not be a Free Exercise Clause issue there. And if coercion is also required to show an Establishment Clause violation, then there would not be protection against this kind of harm.

I think we keep assuming, when we talk about injuries that the Establishment Clause can cause, that we have two kinds of people: we have the people whose religion is favored and those whose religion is disfavored. And those whose religion is favored, the harm to them is maybe dilution or weakening of their religion; for others, the harm is offense to them or humiliation or the communication of a message that they're outsiders. But it seems to me that we have another class of people, and those are the uncommitted. And especially children who have not yet made their decision. And in our society where religious choices are so fluid, people do change opinions. So it seems to me there is harm in government attempting to influence the religious decision at all.

And if we do not call that coercive, it is the kind of harm that is hard to detect; it is one of those harms that the more severe it is, the harder it is to detect. How do parents know how their children are being indoctrinated? How do you measure that? And that is another reason why, when you say: "Well, maybe it's not so bad in England; we just have this little problem in the schools," to me it looms very large. I just want to be sure that gets added to the list of noncoercive injuries. You might even want to call that a form of coercion; and that may bear on what we mean by religious freedom: we mean freedom to influence our own children, not let the government do that.

Richard Kay (University of Connecticut Law School): There is little to disagree with in what you said. If we have a difference, I suppose it is a classification question; it is just a quibble. As to the kind of harm that arises when government attempts to persuade, I think we can, I can break it down into two different kinds of injuries. On the one hand there is, as you said, the persuasion which becomes indoctrination, which I would then essentially assimilate under the idea of coercion. And I think the prayer cases really could very easily be understood as coercion. And I have not read the cases in a while but I

---

23. Engel v. Vitale, 370 U.S. 421 (1962).
24. Abington School Dist. v. Schempp, 374 U.S. 203 (1963).

thought that, in discussing the effect of the opting out part of the laws in those cases, that coercion — indirect coercion — was an element of the decisions. And, insofar as we find no coercive influence, then I think it would fall under one of the other categories that I mentioned and that Professor Laycock mentioned about the other affronts which that kind of a speech can effect. But as I say, this is just a question of your category and mine; in substance, I agree.

Mark Tushnet (then of Georgetown University Law School, later of Harvard University Law School): This picks up on something Professor Laycock said, and also that came up earlier. It is something I have been campaigning unsuccessfully about; but I should try it again. It is the argument that: "Why not try it twice rather than once?" Or in Professor Hartigan's version: "I give up on one of the branches of government." The presentations of that argument are always one-sided in giving the necessary cost/benefit analysis. The analysis goes, the cost of giving judicial review up is that you are relinquishing the chance of getting another institution to consider this. What harm can come from that? And occasionally benefit can come.

There is a harm that can come from having judicial review. As my comment indicates, legislatures can act mindlessly; courts have to explain what they're doing. In Oregon, the imposition of the requirement on the Native Americans was mindless; it communicated nothing about the society's view of their practice. Justice O'Connor writes an opinion explaining why, while we sort of regret that we have to do this to you, the imperatives of the war on drugs are so great as to overcome this burden that we are placing on your religion.[25] Or even worse in *Lyng*,[26] where the acknowledgement of the harm to the religious interests is even more direct.

Similarly, it seems to me not irrelevant that Professor Laycock says: "Justice O'Connor has the right test, but she never knows it when she sees it." The origins of the endorsement test are in her opinion in *Lynch v. Donnelly*.[27] I do not need a Supreme Court Justice to get up there, using the authority of my government, to say I am unreasonable in believing that a nativity scene communicates a message of exclusion. She makes us think that a reasonable Jew would not regard the communication as a message of exclusion. But who is she to tell me that sort of thing? Given who the Justices are likely to be, the chance of their articulating bad things about religion when they do the bal-

---

25. Employment Div. v. Smith, 494 U.S. 872, 903-07 (1990) (O'Connor, J., concurring).
26. Lyng v. Northwest Indian Cemetery Protective Ass'n, 485 U.S. 439 (1988).
27. 465 U.S. 668, 688, 690-94 (1984).

ancing is pretty high, and that is a cost that has to be factored into this overall balance of the costs and benefits of judicial review.

Douglas Laycock: I agree that some of the things the Court says are outrageous, and its opinions can sometimes do real harm by giving prominence and legitimacy to repressive or offensive views on these issues. I am not sure you can eliminate that. You can make that cost greater or smaller, but you can not get rid of it by simply saying: Let's get the Court out of this business. Cases are going to be filed; and then, in the cases where they get out of the business, they are going to say some outrageous things. And then in subsequent cases looking for exceptions and loopholes and trying to chip away at it, they are going to say some more outrageous things. Trying to get out of these cases in *Smith,* the Court in effect said it is open season on religious minorities, and a lot of lawyers for political actors are reading it exactly that way. Nothing they could say in the course of entertaining a claim and then rejecting it would hurt worse than that.

I do not have a whole lot of confidence in courts. But I have considerably more confidence in courts than in local legislators and city councils. There have been religious persecutions in this country. There are localized persecutions right now. I am representing some of those people. We have not gotten any of them off yet, although we have gotten some judgments delayed, and we may accomplish something more permanent. I can at least say the Hare Krishnas are going to have a temple to worship in for two years longer than they would have if we had not had a federal appeal to take.[28] Some of these cases will be won, but many of them will be lost. There have been periods in the past when a larger percentage of these cases were won.

Even if the record of the courts is not all that good, there is no reason whatever in my view to think that, on average, unpopular minorities will do better with legislators than they will do with courts. That may just be an empirical disagreement between the two of us.

Daniel O. Conkle (Indiana University Law School): If I could add one comment. There are not just legislators and there are not just federal courts; there are state courts. And although the state courts are not overwhelmingly — for

---

28. *See* International Soc'y for Krishna Consciousness v. George, 499 U.S. 914 (1991), *vacating and remanding* 262 Cal. Rptr. 217 (Cal. App. 1989) (awarding a judgment of more than three million dollars, more than five million dollars with interest added, that would have been collected by judicial sale of all Krishna temples and monasteries. For the initial judgment on remand, see 4 Cal. Rptr. 2d 473 (Cal. App. 1992) (remanding for a new trial on punitive damages, and reinstating a judgment for $1,837,500 in compensatory damages).

example, on the *Smith* free exercise issues — moving away from the United States Supreme Court, some are.[29] So there is a path where you have — depending on the way that they are elected or whether they are appointed — at least somewhat politically detached judges at the state court level who may have different views from the current Supreme Court.

William P. Marshall (then of Case Western University Law School, later of the University of North Carolina Law School): Professor Laycock, not surprisingly my question is to you. I want to make my position clear if I did not before, that I do not believe the Establishment Clause stands for the proposition that religion can not get involved in political issues. If in fact it did, it would come in conflict with the Free Speech Clause which would demand that the religious values be infused by whoever wants to infuse them into the public dialogue. What I see the Establishment Clause standing for — or actually not the Establishment Clause but this privatization theory — is that there should be a legitimate rhetorical objection to be made when religion comes into the public square. Now, if religion wants to recognize this objection and then say: "Okay, we recognize this but we really need to come in here because this is important!" as it frequently has in our political history, then so be it. I was not going to comment on this, because I thought it was fairly obvious what our differences were, but you brought up the David Duke campaign, and as long as you did, that is the perfect example. The man ran on the idea of bringing Christian principles back into government. And he did not mask that; he masked his racism, but he said outwardly: "This is just putting Christian values back into government." I want the rhetorical response still to be available when that kind of campaigning takes place. I do not want this objection eliminated as a matter of constitutional theory. In short, I think it is appropriate that, when religion is used in that sort of way, that it is a legitimate criticism to say that religion has got no place coming into the public square through this kind of interplay. And I just want your response to that.

Douglas Laycock: "Religion has no place coming into the public square," and "Religion has no place coming into the public square in this kind of interplay," are profoundly different statements. I do not know what you mean by "this kind of interplay." And I suspect it would take us a lot of exchanges to work that all out. But what "in this kind of interplay" adds is: There can be

29. *See, e.g.,* Donahue v. Fair Empl. & Housing Comm'n, 2 Cal. Rptr. 2d 32 (Cal. App. 1991), *review granted,* 825 P.2d 766 (Cal. 1992); State v. Hershberger, 462 N.W.2d 393 (Minn. 1990). [Supreme Court review in *Donahue* was later dismissed.]

good ways and bad ways, and we have to do something about the bad ways. I do not disagree with that.

But when you say, "Religion has no business coming into the public square," I hear you making the Bruce Ackerman argument that this is a state in which religious values cannot be considered and should not be spoken out loud.[30] I think that is preposterous. You say you do not mean that, but that is what I hear without the qualifier.

With respect to the particular example of Duke, I think the response that he drew from many religious leaders is far more effective as a political matter than your response: "This isn't Christianity. You are a racist, Nazi phony trying to invoke the symbols and language of Christianity; and that is not what our religion teaches. This is not real Christianity." Simply as a political matter, you're going to persuade more people with the religious response than with the secularist response.

William P. Marshall: Maybe, if you are fortunate enough to be able to get that response in those particular circumstances. Now, you have pointed out the supposed inconsistency in what I seem to be saying. But if I may point back, if you admit that there is some legitimate concern with religious involvement in the public square, then you must recognize that there is a problem.

Douglas Laycock: I think there are good arguments and bad arguments, right. And there are good and bad religious arguments, and there are good and bad secular arguments. When the Catholic bishops teach on social justice, I like what I hear although I think they may go a little too far; when they teach on abortion, I say I disagree. But I do not think their arguments are any more or less acceptable in the public sector depending on whether I agree with them or not.

Now, it may be that what you were principally thinking about is something I am hardly thinking about at all, which is people who say: "Everyone should vote for candidate X or you'll go to hell." Right? All right, if that's what you're concerned about, I agree with you. That is an inappropriate form of argument; it is not an argument we hear much; it is not an argument that is very effective in a pluralistic society. I don't disagree, but I think it is such a

---

30. *See* Bruce A. Ackerman, Social Justice in the Liberal State (1980). I had thought that Kathleen Sullivan took this position, but she disclaims it in the published version of her paper. Kathleen M. Sullivan, *Religion and Liberal Democracy,* 59 U. Chi. L. Rev. 195, 196 (1992). Her position is far from clear; I think she says that religious believers can make their arguments but government can never act on them.

tiny slice of religious arguments that I . . . if you are confined to that, then I think you have to single that out and say that is what you mean.

What I hear you saying and Ackerman saying is that it is illegitimate to appeal to the religious basis of moral values. It is illegitimate to say: "One reason for putting more money into welfare programs is the Sermon on the Mount and the values that are expressed there." No, that argument I find preposterous. And no caution flag goes up for me when I hear somebody make that argument from the Sermon on the Mount.

Keith Pavlischek: I wanted to get at an Establishment Clause hypothetical by addressing the education issue. As Professor Gilles said, on the one hand, you have the English situation in which there is direct funding of religious schools, which clearly would not — and, I think, should not — pass the establishment test. But on the other hand, in our country we have a situation in which many people argue the educational system has, in effect, served the sociological purpose that the church once did; so now it is the focal point of unity. To the point that, now, many evangelicals and fundamentalists feel the way Catholics did in the 1840s and 1850s when Protestants told them they were having a neutral public educational system.[31]

And so on the one hand, you have the idea of direct funding of private education, which wouldn't work. On the other hand, you have a situation in which many people cannot feel comfortable in putting their kids into the public school system because it promotes an ethos which is contrary to some of their deepest religious convictions or sometimes perceived as an antagonistic ethos to their deepest convictions.

Now, the alternatives that are increasingly gaining currency are voucher-type schemes in which the arguments are: "Well, funding will go not to the schools, as in England, and they won't go directly into a governmental school system; but rather they'll go to the parents of the school children, who can opt for the type of education they wish." And the argument would be that that would go to Jewish parents and fundamentalist parents and Missouri Synod Lutheran parents and Catholic parents.

Now, my question is: Do you believe that that type of funding — and I think we're going to see it within the next ten or fifteen years; I mean, it is going to happen, and I would expect it is going to be litigated, perhaps under the Establishment Clause — do any of you have any beliefs about whether that type of scheme would be a violation of the Establishment Clause? Because, although it is nondiscriminatory, nevertheless I guess Jewish people

31. *See, e.g.,* Diane Ravitch, The Great School Wars (1974).

would set up Jewish schools and Marxists perhaps — if they can get together — would set up Marxist schools and fundamentalists would set up their fundamentalist schools.

Daniel O. Conkle: If you're asking what the United States Supreme Court would rule, my belief would be that the Supreme Court — depending on how the program was structured — would probably approve it. It is not entirely clear from what the Supreme Court has previously decided. But I think it is likely, given the direction the Court has taken in previous cases — particularly *Bowen v. Kendrick*[32] and some of the earlier parochial aid cases that approved tax deductions and credits for parents, primarily for parents, who sent their kids to religious schools. It seems to me that the Court probably would approve it. Whether it would run into state constitutional problems would be a separate issue, and the policy wisdom of vouchers, I think, is a separate issue that I am not really prepared to comment on.

Douglas Laycock: It would run into state constitutional problems because nearly all the state constitutions have much more explicit provisions, enacted during a wave of nineteenth-century anti-Catholicism, that expressly talk about funds to sectarian schools while preserving Protestant devotional services in the public schools.[33] So it might not be sufficient for the United States Supreme Court to say vouchers are okay. It might also have to say vouchers are constitutionally required, which no court is likely to say.

On the underlying policy matter, I part with most other separationists here. I would not allow the Christmas tree; I think it is an establishment. But I would allow a voucher scheme if it were implemented in a way that avoids the kinds of unfairness that Professor Gilles described in the English system.

The existing system is a classic unconstitutional condition. The state says to these people: "You have a constitutional right to a private, religiously-affiliated education or you have a state constitutional right to a free education, but you can't have both. You have to choose. And if you want the religious education, you forfeit the $2000 or the $4000 that the state is otherwise willing to spend on educating your child."

If you want to think through the arguments about that, read Professor

---

32. 487 U.S. 589 (1988).

33. For the history of these provisions, see 2 ANSON P. STOKES, CHURCH AND STATE IN THE UNITED STATES 69-70 (1950); CARL ZOLLMAN, AMERICAN CHURCH LAW §§ 62-66 at 75-80 (2d ed. 1933). For typical state provisions, *see, e.g.,* CAL. CONST. art. IX, § 8; IDAHO CONST., art. IX, § 5; MASS. CONST., art. XVIII, § 2; MINN. CONST. art. XIII, § 2; N.H. CONST. pt. 2, art. 83; N.Y. CONST. art. XI, § 3.

McConnell's article on school funding and abortion funding.[34] There is hardly anybody in the country with a consistent position on those two issues. The pro-choice people tell us it is an unconstitutional condition not to fund abortions for poor women, but it would be an establishment to fund religious education for poor children. Those two positions do not fit together. Funding cannot be a forbidden subsidy for education but a required part of the constitutional right for abortion. The political right is equally inconsistent. These issues are very hard, and few of us have thought through them all the way.

Susan Gilles (Capital University Law School): I would like to address this issue from an English point of view. I think you described two different schemes. One is an opt-out scheme for those with (I presume you would say) conscientious objections, as well as religious-based objections.

Keith Pavlischek: I would say for any reason whatever.

Susan Gilles: For any ideological reason.

Keith Pavlischek: Yes.

Susan Gilles: If you do that, I do not think you walk into establishment problems and you avoid the British problem of defining what qualifies as a religion. But I do want to emphasize, having grown up in a system which does separate school children based on religion, you would have a cost there. You would have a loss of understanding of other religions. And one way to fix it, which is part of the British idea, is to have compulsory religious education so everybody understands everybody else's religion. If you are going to opt everyone out, are you going to require people to understand others' religion as part of the tolerance which we expect in the United States?

Stanley Ingber (Drake University Law School): I would like to pick up on something that Professor Laycock said at the very beginning of his talk, in which he mentioned that the two clauses, the two Religion Clauses, should be interpreted as mutually supporting and interrelating. I would like to then deal with that in terms of some of the things that Professor Bradley said in the panel before, and the implications for the Establishment Clause of the

---

34. Michael W. McConnell, *The Selective Funding Problem: Abortions and Religious Schools,* 104 Harv. L. Rev. 989 (1991).

Smith decision and what happened in the free exercise scenario. And I would be pleased if someone could show me how the scenario that I am about to describe is wrong, because this is how I see it progressing.

We have Justice Scalia fairly adamantly decrying the confusion in the religion field — the seeming schizophrenia, the uncertainty of doctrine, the confusion in this area. And there is an attempt to sort of simplify this all, partially, in *Smith.* At the same time, we see him joining Justice Rehnquist's decision in *Jaffree*[35] on the Establishment Clause, trying to, in essence, simplify the history of the Establishment Clause and holding it to that history. And he says — this is Rehnquist — in its most simplified form, as we infuse meaning into the Establishment Clause, it means that there should not be a single national established church or there shall not be political discrimination among the sects.

Then you see *Smith,* which says, "No constitutionally compelled accommodations, but individual legislators can make separate accommodations as they see fit." And if it affects some religions differently than others, that is the way the political cookie crumbles. And so you would have a situation, for example, where there would be an exemption for the use of wine for ritual sacraments, but maybe not for the use of peyote for religious sacraments. That would seem to me to fall into the very limited description, the historical description, of the Establishment Clause set up in the *Jaffree* decision — discrimination between sects.

Consequently, what I find is that even to avoid the schizophrenia and the confusion, the simple historical description of the Establishment Clause needs to be rejected for *Smith* to be able to be sustained. Otherwise, we continue with the same confusion that Scalia was talking about. No preference among sects must be rejected; and we need to move to a situation where coercion — which is basically the same type of thing as the Free Exercise Clause — coercion becomes the rule for the Establishment Clause. Because otherwise, even in this very limited historical perspective of the Establishment Clause, *Smith* becomes just as subject to the difficulties that Scalia is trying to avoid as the earlier jurisprudence was.

Douglas Laycock: I think you're clearly right that, under the regime of *Smith,* some religions will be allowed to practice either because their practices are

---

35. Wallace v. Jaffree, 472 U.S. 38, 91-114 (1985) (Rehnquist, J., dissenting). Justice Scalia was not on the Court at the time of *Jaffree,* but he appears to have endorsed at least the general thrust of Rehnquist's dissent in that case. *See* Edwards v. Aguillard, 482 U.S. 578, 636 (Scalia, J., dissenting).

not forbidden by a majoritarian legislature in the first place or because they secure exemptions. You are right that other religions with seemingly analogous and indistinguishable practices will fall within the statute and will not get exemptions and will not be allowed to practice. The Court is going to have to deal with that and it is going to be messy.

The realist in me says they will deal with it largely by denying the problem; they will always find that the two cases are distinguishable and there really isn't any discrimination. But they've got that problem under free exercise and under equal protection as well as under establishment. And certainly the victimized religion whose practice is prohibited is being coerced; so cutting the Establishment Clause back to coercion does not help solve the Court's problem. So I guess I do not see how the Establishment Clause plays into your question.

But I think the problem is a very real one; and there are going to be cases about it. One of the cases I am involved in at the moment is one of the ones I had in mind when I said there are localized persecutions going on: the set of ordinances in Hialeah that are carefully drafted to protect Kosher ritual slaughter but to outlaw Santeria ritual sacrifice of small animals. The lower courts were wholly uninterested in the rather obvious discrimination; I was surprised when the Supreme Court said it might be interested.[36] But *Smith* produces that kind of problem: accepted groups get exemptions and unaccepted groups do not.

Steve Green (then at Vermont Law School, now at Willamette Law School): I guess this question is probably for Professor Laycock, too. To what extent are you concerned about the expropriation of government by religious organizations and then the acquiescence of the governmental entity to that expropriation under the noncoercive level that you were talking about?

Douglas Laycock: "Expropriation" meaning what?

Steve Green: The expropriation of governmental symbols or governmental approval. The claims by religious entities that they have certain governmental blessings, either subtly or explicitly. And then the concomitant actions or inaction by government against that. And that could be in the form of what Jerry Falwell used to do. It could be in the form of a religious entity attempt-

---

36. Church of the Lukumi Babalu Aye, Inc. v. City of Hialeah, 723 F. Supp. 1467 (S.D. Fla. 1989), *aff'd mem.*, 936 F.2d 586 (11th Cir. 1991), *cert. granted*, 503 U.S. 935 (1992). [The Supreme Court later struck down the ordinances. 508 U.S. 520 (1993).]

ing to put up a symbol on a public forum in front of a governmental office or whatever. And then the government not doing anything to counter the impression that may come about by that.

Douglas Laycock: Okay. One question that I have never thought about, and one that I have. So let me talk about the second one.

The private placement of religious symbols on the public square seems to me a fairly straightforward public forum problem, although it has not been treated that way. If the government lets lots of groups put up symbols there, then certainly religious groups ought to be included. And I think the better policy is, the government ought to let lots of groups set up symbols in some appropriate place in the community. And I think if we did that, a whole lot of this creche litigation would be solved. There is no reason for the city government to put it up if the association of churches can put it up.

The other problem — the televangelist flying the flag and interweaving patriotism and religion — is not one I have ever thought about. Although I guess my instinct is: it is demeaning to religion, but there are a lot of bad religions out there and there is not much the government can or should do about it. Lots of secular groups do the same sort of thing. It is probably protected by the Speech Clause and the Free Exercise Clause.

Jeanne Swantko: I'm not sure if this rises to the level of a question or just an expression of a concern. But I will state it, and I guess anyone on the panel can respond if they want to. It is related to what the previous questioner asked about the standard in *Smith* where Justice Scalia says, "If the locals pass a law and it incidentally infringes on your religion, basically it's too bad for you because that wasn't the intent of it." So you have that standard emerging from the Court on the one hand.

And then, I will use for an example something that Dean Gaffney said earlier, when he described the law school association that passed a regulation that said you had to not discriminate in hiring against anyone because of their sexual preference; and this impacted on religious law schools who see homosexuality as a violation of a basic tenet of their faith.

Now, I guess I'm trying to see how those two things can be reconciled. And from my own perspective as a parent in a community in a minority religion, I have concerns as to how the oftentimes state-sponsored legislation — which has a sort of common denominator element to it — impacts on me and the way that I want to raise my children when the defense that can be given is: "The state legislature passed it; so if it impacts on your religion, it's too bad," even when it goes to something fundamental. But I want to issue to lawyers a challenge. When preparing briefs and doing litigation, I think there has to be some foresight to suggest remedies to judges and courts that somehow make common sense and provide a right way of reasoning to go forward from here. That makes a way for the court to — if you want to say — do the right thing. Violating one side against the other as little as possible. But I guess I would like to know if anybody has any response to my concern.

Daniel O. Conkle: I share your concern. And I guess that my only point is to state again that I think, at least for the United States Supreme Court and other federal courts, I am very pessimistic as to whether these kinds of claims will be taken seriously in the foreseeable future. The other avenues of appeal are state courts and trying to sensitize and educate legislators and local decisionmakers. I do not know that that will be successful.

Douglas Laycock: Scalia's quite clear: it does not matter how central or fundamental the religious obligation is. And keep in mind the facts in *Smith*. This is a worship service. Suppression of a worship service raises no issue under the Constitution of the United States and requires no justification. That is the law of the land at the moment.

Richard Kay: I would like to add to that, so that we do not leave with the wrong impression, that the result of that decision is not that there can be no religious exemptions. As Professor Conkle just pointed out, there are alternative avenues to pursue, both constitutional in terms of state systems, and in terms of political redress. Now, that might not avoid what we regard as an injustice in every case. But it is not the situation that, by this opinion, all religious exemption was eliminated.

Religious Liberty as Liberty

7 Journal of Contemporary Legal Issues 313 (1996)

This article was part of a symposium in which leading church-state scholars were invited to set out their theory of how and why the Constitution protects religious liberty. It addresses such questions as why religious liberty is singled out for special constitutional protection, why nonbelievers must be included in that protection, and what the content of that protection should be. The theme is that the point of the Religion Clauses is not to protect religion as such, but rather, to protect liberty in matters of religion. This piece also tries to explain how different applications of substantive neutrality fit together, without falling into the trap of disaggregating neutrality or pleading for special interests. And it contains a rare discussion of my personal views on religion.

*   *   *

I. The Fundamentals

Religious liberty is first and foremost a guarantee of liberty. To be sure, the guarantee is of liberty within a specified domain; it is liberty with respect to religious choices and commitments. But religion is not guaranteed, and nei-

---

I am grateful to the participants in this symposium for provoking a clear statement of the ideas in this paper. With respect to our disagreements, I had the quite unfair advantage of seeing substantially complete drafts of their papers while providing no reasonable draft of my paper. I regret that conflicting commitments made it impossible to attend to this paper sooner. I am also grateful to Sanford Levinson and L. A. Powe for remarkably quick and helpful reads of an earlier draft.

ther is secularism — only liberty is guaranteed. Within the liberty guaranteed by the Religion Clauses, the free human beings who make up the sovereign People may experience a Great Awakening of Christianity, a mass conversion to Islam or New Age mysticism or any other faith, or an overwhelming swing to atheism. In the Supreme Court's inelegant but accurate phrase, the state should neither advance nor inhibit religion.[1]

Religious liberty does not presuppose that God is good,[2] nor that faith is bad or subordinate to reason.[3] These are equal and opposite errors. Religious liberty guarantees instead that each citizen in a free country may believe as he will about the existence and characteristics of God and about the role of faith.

Religious liberty does not constitute America as a Christian nation,[4] nor does it establish a "secular public moral order."[5] These too are equal and opposite errors. Each assumes that on the most fundamental religious questions, the Constitution has taken a position. But the core point of religious liberty is that the government does not take positions on religious questions — not in its daily administration, not in its laws, and not in its Constitution either.

Religious liberty does not view religion as a good thing to be promoted, nor as a dangerous force to be contained. But people who view religion in each of these ways struggle to capture the Religion Clauses for their side. Each side claims that it won the late-twentieth-century culture wars and took over the government — two hundred years ago.[6] These too are equal and opposite errors. What happened two hundred years ago is that conflict over theology, liturgy, and church governance was confined to the private sector, the federal government was declared a permanent neutral, and all factions were

---

1. Lemon v. Kurtzman, 403 U.S. 602, 612 (1971).

2. *Contra*, John H. Garvey, *An Anti-Liberal Argument for Religious Freedom*, 7 J. CONTEMP. LEGAL ISSUES 275, 291 (1996). For another argument that religious liberty can be explained only by a commitment to theistic religion (perhaps only by a commitment to true religion, but this is not clear), see Steven D. Smith, *The Rise and Fall of Religious Freedom in Constitutional Discourse*, 140 U. PA. L. REV. 149 (1991).

3. *Contra*, Suzanna Sherry, *Enlightening the Religion Clauses*, 7 J. CONTEMP. LEGAL ISSUES 473 (1996).

4. *Contra*, Church of the Holy Trinity v. United States, 143 U.S. 457, 471 (1892).

5. *Contra*, Kathleen M. Sullivan, *Religion and Liberal Democracy*, 59 U. CHI. L. REV. 195, 198 (1992).

6. *Compare, e.g.*, Smith, *supra* note 2 (arguing that eighteenth-century America was pervasively Protestant, and that the Constitution reflects Protestant views), *with, e.g.*, Sherry, *supra* note 3 (arguing that eighteenth-century America was pervasively committed to reason, and that the Constitution reflects rationalist views).

given equal political rights and a guarantee of religious liberty no matter what faction took over the government. In 1868, these guarantees were extended to the states.

II. Why *Religious* Liberty?

A. *The Problem of Reasons*

Contemporary scholars have puzzled over why the Constitution would specially protect religious liberty, as distinguished from liberty in other domains.[7] If one views religion as a silly superstition of no importance, or as a dangerous force that requires tight regulation, or as containing one fundamental and binding truth competing with many falsehoods that lead to individual and collective ruin — *and* if one fails to learn from history — then constitutional guarantees of religious liberty might indeed seem puzzling or even wrongheaded.

Even so, the why of religious liberty may not matter as much as is sometimes supposed. For whatever reason, the Constitution does give special protection to liberty in the domain of religion, and we cannot repudiate that decision without rejecting an essential feature of constitutionalism, rendering all constitutional rights vulnerable to repudiation if they go out of favor. "Because the Constitution says so, and because all our liberties depend on maintaining the authority of the Constitution's guarantees," should be sufficient reason to vigorously protect religious liberty.[8] We can work out the regime that maximizes liberty with respect to religious choices and commitments without agreeing on why our Constitution specially protects liberty in that domain.

Of course it is more satisfying, and sometimes clarifying, to have a reason. And unfortunately, "because the Constitution says so" does not appear to be a sufficient reason to persuade many Americans to support a constitutional right unless they are also persuaded of the wisdom of the right at issue. But the search for underlying reasons is not easy. As great as are the difficul-

---

7. *See, e.g.* Mark Tushnet, *The Constitution of Religion*, 18 CONN. L. REV. 701, 729 (1986) ("Constitutionalists today are committed to developing a law of religion even though they do not understand why they have to do so.").

8. Yes, and the Second Amendment too, although the preamble's recital that the holders of this right are to be "well-regulated" implies a very different sort of right from the textually absolute rights created in the First Amendment. For further insightful comparison of the First and Second Amendments, see L. A. Powe, *Guns, Words, and Constitutional Interpretation*, 38 WM. & MARY L. REV. 1311 (1997).

ties of identifying the originally intended *meaning* of a provision, it is even more difficult to identify the original *reasons,* because supporters who agree on what a provision means can support it for quite different reasons.

The incredible diversity of views represented in this symposium highlights the danger. If we are each permitted to characterize in global terms the dominant themes of the eighteenth century, or the dominant themes of the Constitution generally, or sound general policy toward religion, and then impose the resulting analysis on the Religion Clauses, anything can happen. Suzanna Sherry concludes that secular rationalists won the eighteenth-century political battles and dominated the drafting of the Constitution;[9] Steven Smith concludes that the Protestants won;[10] John Garvey concludes that at least those who believe in a benevolent God won.[11] Professor Smith concludes that the clauses are only about federalism and are incoherent if applied to religious liberty;[12] Professor Sherry concludes that the Religion Clauses are about religious liberty but are incoherent because contradictory, and that the Free Exercise Clause must be subordinated to the Establishment Clause.[13] William Marshall proposes that the Free Exercise Clause is just a special case of the Free Speech Clause,[14] leaving us to wonder whether any cases would be decided differently if the Free Exercise Clause were repealed; Abner Greene and Michael Perry struggle with the contrasting possibility that the Establishment Clause is an exception to the Free Speech Clause, so that religious speakers might have less free speech than secular speakers.[15] Only Greene, Perry, and Ira Lupu give sufficient attention to liberty and neutrality to get inside my conception of the ballpark.[16]

If I could confine all these people to the literal text of the Constitution, I suppose that they would somehow reach the same astonishing conclusions;

9. Sherry, *supra* note 3.

10. Steven D. Smith, *Unprincipled Religious Freedom,* 7 J. CONTEMP. LEGAL ISSUES 497, 503-04 (1996).

11. Garvey, *supra* note 2.

12. STEVEN D. SMITH, FOREORDAINED FAILURE: THE QUEST FOR A CONSTITUTIONAL PRINCIPLE OF RELIGIOUS FREEDOM (1995).

13. Susanna Sherry, *Lee v. Weisman: Paradox Redux,* 1992 SUP. CT. REV. 123.

14. William P. Marshall, *Religion as Ideas: Religion as Identity,* 7 J. CONTEMP. LEGAL ISSUES 385, 392-94 (1996).

15. Michael J. Perry, *Religion, Politics, and the Constitution,* 7 J. CONTEMP. LEGAL ISSUES 407, 437-46 (1996); Abner Greene, *The Irreducible Constitution,* 7 J. CONTEMP. LEGAL ISSUES 293, 303-05 (1996).

16. Greene, *supra* note 15; Ira C. Lupu, *To Protect Religious Liberty and Control Religious Faction: A General Theory of the Religion Clauses,* 7 J. CONTEMP. LEGAL ISSUES 357 (1996); Perry, *supra* note 15.

Maimon Schwarzschild's paper implies as much.[17] But at least if we were confined to the text, readers could check authors' claims without learning most of sociology, political science, epistemology, and religious and political history. Interpretations that obliterated or deeply discounted one of the two clauses would be immediately suspect, and there would be less material available to rationalize these suspicious results. If searching for reasons leads to this symposium, literalism is looking better.

Searching for "the reason" has an extra difficulty with respect to religious liberty, because many people support religious liberty for reasons based in their views about religion. These conflicting views about religion cannot be imputed to the Constitution without abandoning the widely held intuition that part of the core content of religious liberty is that government may not adopt some religious beliefs and reject others. The Constitution cannot adopt a Baptist or Deist or Episcopal conception of religious liberty, at least not without deep paradox. Nor can the Constitution adopt a view of religion as idea or religion as identity;[18] religion plainly includes both.

Moreover, explanations of religious liberty based on beliefs about religion cannot possibly persuade persons who do not hold the same religious beliefs, and so these explanations have little ability to explain or maintain support for religious liberty. To those who do not share the relevant religious belief, "because my religion says so," or "because the Founders' religion said so," is even less persuasive than "because the Constitution says so." To explain the Religion Clauses as a Baptist or Deist or Episcopalian capture is to forfeit their credibility.

B. The Religion-Neutral Case for Religious Liberty

An acceptable explanation of the Religion Clauses must make sense of the ratified text. For the reasons just given, the strongest such explanation would make sense of the ratified text without entailing commitments to any proposition about religious belief. On what theory would the Founders single out the domain of religious choice and commitment for a special guarantee of liberty? The answer seems to me obvious, and while it is not at all illogical, it depends far more on history than on logic. Three secular propositions are sufficient to justify a strong commitment to religious liberty.

17. Maimon Schwarzschild, *Pluralism, Interpretation, Religion, and the First Amendment*, 7 J. CONTEMP. LEGAL ISSUES 447 (1996).

18. *Contra*, Marshall, *supra* note 14.

First, in history that was recent to the American Founders, governmental attempts to suppress disapproved religious views had caused vast human suffering in Europe and in England[19] and similar suffering on a smaller scale in the colonies that became the United States.[20] The conflict had continued for centuries without producing a victor capable of restoring peace by suppressing all opposition. This is prima facie reason to forever ban all such governmental efforts. Madison argued:

> Torrents of blood have been spilt in the old world, by vain attempts of the secular arm to extinguish Religious discord, by proscribing all difference in Religious opinions. Time has at length revealed the true remedy. Every relaxation of narrow and rigorous policy, wherever it has been tried, has been found to assuage the disease. The American Theatre has exhibited proofs, that equal and complete liberty, if it does not wholly eradicate it, sufficiently destroys its malignant influence on the health and prosperity of the state.[21]

The negative goal is to minimize this conflict; the affirmative goal is to create a regime in which people of fundamentally different views about religion can live together in a peaceful and self-governing society.

Second, beliefs about religion are often of extraordinary importance to the individual — important enough to die for, to suffer for, to rebel for, to emigrate for, to fight to control the government for. This is why governmental efforts to impose religious uniformity had been such bloody failures. But this is also an independent reason to leave religion to the people who care about it most, which is to say, to each individual and to the groups that individuals voluntarily form or join.

Third, beliefs at the heart of religion — beliefs about theology, liturgy, and church governance — are of little importance to the civil government. Failure to achieve religious uniformity had not led to failure of the state. By the time of the American founding, experience had revealed that people of quite different religious beliefs could be loyal citizens or subjects. The claim here is not that religious beliefs are *wholly* irrelevant to the government; it

19. For an overview that collects historical sources, see Douglas Laycock, *Continuity and Change in the Threat to Religious Liberty: The Reformation Era and the Late Twentieth Century*, 80 Minn. L. Rev. 1047, 1049-66 (1996) (text at notes 3-142).

20. *See generally* Thomas Curry, The First Freedoms: Church and State in America to the Passage of the First Amendment (1986).

21. James Madison, Memorial and Remonstrance Against Religious Establishments ¶11 (1785), reprinted in Everson v. Board of Educ., 330 U.S. 1, 69 (appendix to opinion of Rutledge, J., dissenting).

may be that some religious beliefs are more conducive than others to behaviors the government legitimately seeks to encourage or require.[22] But this indirect and always debatable government interest in religious beliefs will never make religious beliefs as important to the government as to the individual (the second proposition), and experience showed that government could not impose the religious beliefs it wanted anyway (the first proposition).

This third proposition was the most controversial of the three, and some in the founding generation were not sure it applied to Catholics,[23] or to the hypothetical atheists that occasionally appeared in their rhetoric.[24] Some citizens today continue to believe that atheists are unreliable citizens and that decent government cannot survive without a critical mass of believers. But with increasing religious pluralism, longer experience, and the universalizing logic of legal principle, the law at least has made the point general. It is enough for the state to regulate behavior, not belief; to regulate conduct, not theology or liturgy or church governance. The state could enforce the murder laws in 1791 without agreeing on the proper mode of worship or the proper form of church governance; it can enforce the murder laws today without agreeing on the Ten Commandments, the Sermon on the Mount, the Kantian imperative, or the utilitarian calculus as the best explanation for those laws. It is a sufficient explanation that the People have enacted such a law through constitutional processes and that it violates no limitation on governmental authority enacted by the People through a more authoritative process.

These three propositions are readily inferable from the history of failed governmental attempts to achieve religious uniformity. They are in no sense religious claims; they are testable against the facts of history and the experience of governments and citizens. They are equally accessible to believers and nonbelievers; they are consistent with the most profound belief and with the most profound skepticism.

These three propositions are entirely neutral about the truth or value of any religious belief save one: the third proposition necessarily rejects any belief that the State should or must support religion. But that belief is rejected in the Establishment Clause itself, so it must necessarily be rejected in any justification for the Establishment Clause. Those who believe that religious

22. *See, e.g.,* Joseph Fagan, Why Religion Matters: The Impact of Religious Practice on Social Stability (1995) (collecting studies).

23. *See* Douglas Laycock, *"Nonpreferential" Aid to Religion: A False Claim About Original Intent,* 27 Wm. & Mary L. Rev. 875, 918 & nn.223-26 (1986) (collecting historical sources).

24. *See* James Turner, Without God, Without Creed: The Origins of Unbelief in America 44-47 (1985).

exercise requires the instruments of government, or that state support is essential or important to continued religious belief, are really arguing for repeal of the Establishment Clause or for its minimalist interpretation.[25]

These three propositions are entirely adequate to explain a special guarantee of religious liberty, in which religion is to be left as wholly to private choice and private commitment as anything can be.[26] Once it is understood that government efforts to control religious belief create conflict and suffering, that they cannot succeed without the most extraordinary tyranny (and often not even then), any government will abandon such attempts if it is committed to liberty or even if it is committed only to utilitarian avoidance of human suffering. Once it is understood that religion is far more important to individuals than to the government, the same considerations of liberty and utility argue for leaving religion entirely to individuals and their voluntary groups.

C. Some Implications of These Reasons

Most obviously and most powerfully, these three propositions argue for separating the coercive power of government from all questions of religion, so that no religion can invoke government's coercive power and no government can coerce any religious act or belief.

These three propositions argue for presumptively extending this protection to religiously motivated behavior, because attempts to suppress religious behavior will lead to all the problems of conflict and suffering that religious liberty is designed to avoid, and because religious behavior is as likely as religious belief to be of extraordinary importance to individuals.[27] This protection can be only presumptive; sometimes religiously motivated behavior will

---

25. *See* Douglas Laycock, *The Benefits of the Establishment Clause*, 42 DePaul L. Rev. 373, 374-75 (1992) (text at notes 3-4) (conceding that constitutional protection of religious liberty "entails one choice about types of religion," but arguing that this "is a principled choice, based on the view that the best you can do to maximize religious liberty for all citizens is to prevent anyone from using the government for religious purposes.").

26. An earlier version of this formulation appears in Douglas Laycock, *Formal, Substantive, and Disaggregated Neutrality Toward Religion*, 39 DePaul L. Rev. 993, 1002 (1990) (text at notes 27-28). I have added the phrase "and private commitment" after "private choice," to avoid the unintentional exclusion of believers who feel bound by religious commitments with no sense of having chosen them. See text at note 47 *infra*.

27. For further argument, see Douglas Laycock, *The Remnants of Free Exercise*, 1990 Sup. Ct. Rev. 1; Michael W. McConnell, *Free Exercise Revisionism and the Smith Decision*, 57 U. Chi. L. Rev. 1109 (1990).

be sufficiently important to the government to justify suppression. But that is a reason for something like the compelling interest exception; it is not a reason to tell people that they are free to believe their religions but not to practice them.

The coercive powers of government include its powers to allocate money, licenses, privileges, and the like in discriminatory ways. The principle that government should not coerce religious beliefs or behaviors necessarily entails the proposition that government should not create incentives to change religious beliefs or behaviors — that government should be neutral with respect to religion in all its regulation, taxation, and spending. I have argued elsewhere that this goal is best achieved by substantive neutrality, defined in terms of minimizing government incentives to change religious behavior, and not by formal neutrality, defined as the mere absence of religious classifications:[28]

> The Religion Clauses require government to minimize the extent to which it either encourages or discourages religious belief or disbelief, practice or nonpractice, observance or nonobservance.[29]

In this formulation, autonomy and neutrality are mutually reinforcing elements of religious liberty:

> Government must be neutral so that religious belief and practice can be free. The autonomy of religious belief and disbelief is maximized when government encouragement and discouragement is minimized.[30]

The case for extending this guarantee of neutrality to the noncoercive powers of government — for separating those powers too from all questions of religion — is weaker than the case for separating the coercive powers,[31] but I think the case is easily strong enough. Government should be entirely neutral in matters of religion even when it coerces no one. That is, government should not sponsor or endorse a church or any set of beliefs about religious questions, and it should not resolve or seek to influence disputes about religion.

My three propositions suggest several reasons for this commitment to neutrality. First, because beliefs about religion are so much more important

---

28. Laycock, *supra* note 26; *see also* Church of the Lukumi Babalu Aye, Inc. v. City of Hialeah, 508 U.S. 520, 562 (Souter, J., concurring) (distinguishing substantive and formal neutrality in similar terms).

29. Laycock, *supra* note 26, at 1001 (text at note 27).

30. *Id.* at 1002 (text at note 28).

31. See Laycock, *supra* note 25, at 379 (text at notes 19-20) ("[I]f I had to give up one of the rights in the First Amendment, this is the one I would give up.").

to individuals than to the government, individuals and their voluntary groups should be free to develop their own beliefs about religion without the distorting influence of government. Government influence interferes with a matter important to individuals, a matter that many individuals believe is sacred and to be ordered by God, with little gain to government if religious choices and commitments are generally unimportant to government.

Second, because religious choices and commitments are so important to so many individuals, and because of the history of government efforts to suppress disapproved religions, many citizens will be highly sensitive to any hint that government disapproves of their religious beliefs or even that it prefers some other set of religious beliefs. This sensitivity is illustrated by fights over creches, public prayers, and conscientious objection today,[32] and by Baptist and Presbyterian complaints about remnants of recognition for the formally disestablished Episcopal Church in eighteenth-century Virginia.[33] Individuals and groups will fear that what starts with mere preference or disapproval will escalate to discrimination, suppression, or coerced participation in observances of the dominant religion. These fears gain substance from history, and also because the line between coercion and mere influence is easily crossed and hard to monitor or even define, as illustrated by Justice Kennedy's unsuccessful struggle to articulate a coherent coercion standard.[34] Government attempts to influence religious choices and commitments cause some of the harms of government coercion and threaten the rest.

Third, these direct harms of noncoercive government influence have a corollary. If government is permitted to attempt to influence religious beliefs and commitments, each religious faction must necessarily seek to control or at least influence the government so that the faction's members will be more benefited than harmed. Even if government is permitted only to express views about religion, religious factions will seek to control or influence the government so that they can control or influence the religious views that it

32. *See, e.g.,* Sherry, *supra* note 13, at 149 ("[G]ranting an exemption sends a message of endorsement of religious over secular beliefs and relegates nonbelievers to the status of outsiders.").

33. *See* Douglas Laycock, *"Noncoercive" Support for Religion: Another False Claim About the Establishment Clause*, 26 VAL. L. REV. 37, 43-44 (1991) (text at notes 38-40) (reviewing complaints that incorporation of Episcopal Church gave it "the Honour of an important name" and "the particular sanction" of the legislature).

34. *See* Lee v. Weisman, 505 U.S. 577, 593-99 (1992) (opinion of the Court by Kennedy, J.) (finding coercion in "public pressure, as well as peer pressure . . . though subtle and indirect"); County of Allegheny v. ACLU, 492 U.S. 573, 660-61 (1989) (Kennedy, J., dissenting in part) (arguing that coercion may be "indirect," and implying that "the permanent erection of a large Latin cross on the roof of city hall" would be coercive).

expresses. Individuals and groups will compete over which religions are respected and which are disrespected, over which can feel safe and which must fear more serious government hostility in the future. Even if this conflict is confined to peaceful political processes, it is an unnecessary source of conflict over a matter of little legitimate importance to government; it diverts politics into unproductive issues and perpetuates religious conflict. Justice O'Connor captures a small part of this explanation with her recognition that government endorsements of religious beliefs make citizens of other faiths feel like outsiders or second-class citizens.[35]

It is a plausible response that the dominant religious faction will so strongly demand government endorsement and practice of that faction's religion that the pursuit of neutrality will cause even more religious conflict than letting the dominant faction have its way. This necessarily entails the proposition that religious minorities should suffer in silence and hope things get no worse; it comes close to arguing that "the vitality of these constitutional principles [must] yield simply because of disagreement with them."[36] Which interpretation will minimize religious conflict is unanswerable empirically; all we can say is that a regime of religious liberty has dramatically reduced but not wholly eliminated religious conflict, and there is little reason to expect that to change.

But there is an answer in principle; only one of these interpretations has at least the potential to minimize religious conflict. If we could all agree on the principle of government neutrality toward religion, we could all abandon our efforts to influence government on religious matters, and devote all that energy to religious practice and proselytizing in the private sector. Conflict over the government's role in religion could, in theory, end. But if we interpret the Religion Clauses to mean that government may promote the religious views of the dominant religious faction so long as it refrains from coercion, we ensure perpetual battles for dominance, perpetual battles to control or influence the government's religious message. That interpretation abandons in principle the goal of eliminating conflict over the government's role in religion.

Secular intellectuals skeptical of religious liberty may argue that other strong personal commitments should have been protected as well. But they were not, for the sufficient reason that other strong personal commitments had not produced the same history. The protected liberty is religious liberty, and although the word "religion" must be construed in light of continuing

---

35. Lynch v. Donnelly, 465 U.S. 668, 688 (1984) (O'Connor, J., concurring).
36. Brown v. Board of Educ., 349 U.S. 294, 300 (1955).

developments in beliefs about religion, we cannot rewrite the Constitution to say that religious liberty should not receive special protection.

Professors Garvey and Smith make similar claims from the other side of the religious spectrum.[37] They say that concern for autonomy alone cannot explain religious liberty, because autonomy claims extend to all aspects of human existence, and Professor Smith adds that other issues have been more disruptive of American social peace than religion. But the Founders gave special protection to *religious* liberty, and they had good historical reason for that choice. That protection remains in the Constitution even if the problem that made it necessary has receded. And certainly the problem has not disappeared. The Constitution has not been able to prevent intermittent episodes of religious violence, most notably against Mormons, Catholics, and Jehovah's Witnesses.[38] And we can only speculate about the possible results of the contemporary culture wars if both sides were not imbued with a two-hundred-year-old tradition of at least some core concept of religious liberty.

Professor Garvey also says that peace alone cannot explain religious liberty, because peace might be achieved by suppressing all religious dissent, or at least by suppressing all dissent from groups small enough to be suppressed. But my claim is that the autonomy and peace arguments work together and in light of history. Pursuing peace by suppressing dissent is historically a failed policy, and even if it could succeed, it would be utterly inconsistent with the protection of autonomy in a domain that is extraordinarily important to individuals. Professor Garvey considers autonomy and peace separately and finds the argument wanting, but he does not consider the argument whole.[39]

Reading free exercise and disestablishment in light of my three historical propositions, it is possible to generate the full range of modern religious liberty protections — separating church and state, maximizing religious liberty in individuals and their voluntary groups, minimizing government influence on religion, and forbidding government to take positions on religious questions. Believers and nonbelievers may each find more emotional resonance in their separate theistic and anti-theistic perspectives, but they can have no hope of persuading each other from those perspectives. My account may seem thin to some, although I do not find it so. But thin or thick, its great advantage is that it is not dependent on beliefs about religion.

---

37. Garvey, *supra* note 2, at 275-82; Smith, *supra* note 2, at 202-04, 207-10.

38. For a summary with citations to sources, see Douglas Laycock, *A Survey of Religious Liberty in the United States,* 47 Ohio St. L.J. 409, 416-20 (1986) (text at notes 38-76).

39. That may be my fault. See the unnumbered note p. 54 *supra*.

III. Other Explanations

Of course my three propositions were not the only important propositions in the intellectual milieu that led to the American guarantees of religious liberty, nor are they an exhaustive list of the reasons for protecting religious liberty today.[40] Other explanations are not necessarily wrong, and they often reinforce or enrich the basic argument. But other explanations are not necessary, and to the extent that they depend on particular views about religion, they must be reformulated to have any persuasive force for those with different views about religion.

As in all political debates, self-interest played an important role in the decision to commit to religious liberty. The groups most fearful of government persecution were the most aggressive in demanding the broadest guarantees of religious liberty. That is why the established Anglicans and Congregationalists offered free exercise and resisted disestablishment, and why the dissenting evangelical sects insisted on both.[41] But these sects protected themselves by protecting everyone; no one suggests that we construe the Religion Clauses to prefer evangelical sects over Episcopalians and Congregationalists.

Self-interest promoted the recognition that a government that oppresses one faith today might turn on another tomorrow. The point is most directly illustrated by the Massachusetts establishment, which ended when its principal defenders started losing parish elections to Unitarians.[42] It was in everyone's interest to agree that government would not interfere with anyone's beliefs about religion.

Fear of the new federal government played an important role, but the Religion Clauses were not just federalism provisions.[43] The brief Congressional debate over the Religion Clauses focused on religious liberty issues, not federalism issues.[44] The battle for religious liberty was also fought out state by state, and the various state and federal debates informed the similar debates that came later. All the states eventually did disestablish their churches, and

---

40. For a longer but still not exhaustive list of reasons gathered from recent literature, see William P. Marshall, *Truth and the Religion Clauses*, 43 DePaul L. Rev. 243 (1994).

41. *See, e.g.*, Curry, *supra* note 20, at 134-40, 163-73; Leonard W. Levy, The Establishment Clause: Religion and the First Amendment 30-34, 63-67 (2d ed. 1994); *infra* text accompanying notes 132-62.

42. For accounts, see Levy, *supra* note 41, at 36-52; John T. Noonan, The Believer and the Powers That Are 159-60 (1987).

43. *Contra*, Smith, *supra* note 12.

44. *See* Laycock, *supra* note 23, at 879-81, 906-08 (text at notes 26-37, 166-72).

the federal guarantee of religious liberty was eventually extended to and enforced against the states.[45] Federalism and religious liberty were separate issues, interacting but independent.

Theological developments played an important role, perhaps an indispensable one. These religious beliefs are consistent with the Constitution, and they are among the multiplicitous reasons that motivated a broad coalition to enact constitutional guarantees of religious liberty. But these religious beliefs cannot be imputed to the Constitution without abandoning governmental neutrality on religious questions. Theistic arguments for religious liberty can neither persuade nontheists nor speak equally to all the varieties of theistic religious experience. Religious reasons have to be recast in the form of a statement about what some people believe.

Many Christians came to believe that religious belief and practice are efficacious only when voluntary.[46] This belief eliminated the principal religious reason for opposing religious liberty; if coerced belief could not save souls, there was no reason to pay the terrible temporal costs of struggling to maintain uniformity. But the theological point is neither unambiguous nor uncontroversial: Christianity rejected it for a long time, Protestants came to it sooner than Catholics, and fundamentalist Islam appears to reject it today. Atheists and agnostics can have no informed opinion on what makes theistic religious belief efficacious. Believers committed to an inherited religious tradition take understandable offense at overly enthusiastic statements of the value of voluntariness, which judges sometimes mistakenly equate with the value of individual religious choice.[47] Believers who are offended by judicial rhetoric about individual choice should see the threat of serious discrimination between faiths in Professor Marshall's suggestion that religious ideas should be protected but religious identities constrained.[48] None of these con-

45. *See* Kurt T. Lash, *The Second Adoption of the Establishment Clause: The Rise of the Nonestablishment Principle*, 27 Ariz. St. L.J. 1085 (1995); Kurt T. Lash, *The Second Adoption of the Free Exercise Clause: Religious Exemptions Under the Fourteenth Amendment*, 88 Nw. U.L. Rev. 1106 (1994).

46. *See, e.g.,* Madison, *supra* note 21, ¶ 1 at 64 ("Religion or the duty which we owe to our Creator and the Manner of discharging it, can be directed only by reason and conviction, not by force or violence") (quoting Va. Declaration of Rights art. 16); Garvey, *supra* note 2; Smith, *supra* note 2, at 154-55.

47. *See* Mary Ann Glendon, *Law, Communities, and the Religious Freedom Language of the Constitution*, 60 Geo. Wash. L. Rev. 672, 678-79 (1992); Michael J. Sandel, *Freedom of Conscience or Freedom of Choice?*, in Articles of Faith, Articles of Peace: The Religious Liberty Clauses and the American Public Philosophy 74, 85-89 (James Davison Hunter & Os Guinness, eds., 1990).

48. Marshall, *supra* note 14.

flicting views about the nature of religious belief can be imputed to the Constitution. What we can say on behalf of the Constitution is that government should not impose beliefs about religion, whatever the various faiths teach about the efficacy of the attempt.

Another important religious argument, traceable to Roger Williams, is that religion is sacred and the state is corrupt, so that separation of church and state is necessary to protect religion from corruption by the state.[49] This is as much an argument for disestablishment as for free exercise; the state may corrupt the church even when it tries to help. There was and is substantial evidence, both in the Founders' time and in ours, that establishment reduces the appeal of the established church.[50] But here too nonbelievers are likely to disagree with the claim that religion is sacred in its private form and faces only corruption from the state, and some particularistic believers are likely to think that their own religion is sacred but that many others are false or corrupt and might benefit from state intervention were it not for all the other reasons for keeping the state out of religion. The argument that religious liberty protects the sacred is best understood as a particularized version of the claim that religion is of extraordinary importance to many individuals. Individuals and their voluntary groups are entitled to keep their religion in what *they* believe to be its pure form; any government interference changes it from what the religion would have been on its own.

Still another religious argument is that each citizen's duties to God are superior to his duties to the civil society; by respecting religious liberty, the state defers to this prior duty.[51] Undoubtedly many religious citizens at the founding and today have supported religious liberty partly on this ground.

---

49. *See* Mark DeWolfe Howe, The Garden and the Wilderness 5-6 (1965) (quoting Roger Williams, *Mr. Cotton's Letter Lately Printed, Examined and Answered*); *see generally* Howe, *supra;* Edwin S. Gaustad, Liberty of Conscience: Roger Williams in America (1991).

50. *See, e.g.,* Andrew M. Greeley, Religious Change in America 126-27 (1989) (reporting survey data showing that difference in religious participation between United States and Great Britain is entirely explained by lower participation of members of established Church of England); Madison, *supra* note 21, ¶ 7 at 68 (arguing that fruits of establishment had been "pride and indolence in the Clergy; ignorance and servility in the laity; in both, superstition, bigotry and persecution"); *see also* R. Stephen Warner, *Work in Progress Toward a New Paradigm for the Sociological Study of Religion in the United States,* 98 Am. J. Soc. 1044, 1048-58 (1993) (exploring the relationship between disestablishment and measures of religious vitality).

51. Madison, *supra* note 21, ¶ 1 at 64 ("This duty [to the Creator] is precedent both in order of time and degree of obligation, to the claims of Civil Society."); McConnell, *supra* note 27, at 1150-52; Smith, *supra* note 2, at 154.

But again, those who do not believe that God exists cannot believe that God imposes binding obligations superior to those imposed by civil society, and certainly not that the Constitution of the United States writes such a theistic proposition into the fundamental law of the land. And although each believer may believe that God imposes binding obligations, only radical theistic pluralists really believe that God imposes inconsistent but equally binding obligations on adherents of different faiths.[52]

But this argument too can be reworked consistently with the three fundamental propositions set out above. It is irrelevant whether God *really* imposes a bewildering variety of inconsistent obligations, all superior to the claims of civil society, on persons of different faiths. It is sufficient that many individuals *believe* themselves subject to such God-imposed obligations, that these beliefs are usually far more important to the individual than to the state, and that state attempts to override these beliefs will cause unnecessary conflict and human suffering.

IV. Defining "Religion"

I have said that the domain of religious liberty is liberty with respect to religious choices and commitments. This seemingly simple formulation conceals a fundamental and largely unexamined disagreement. What is "religion" within the meaning of the Religion Clauses? To avoid incoherence the answer must be that "religion" is any set of answers to religious questions, including the negative and skeptical answers of atheists, agnostics, and secularists.

I have argued that the most fundamental reason for religious liberty is to avoid conflict over the answers to religious questions, to enable people of fundamentally different views about religion to live together in peace and self-governance. It is utterly irrelevant to that purpose which answers to religious questions are in conflict. "What is the nature of God and what does He/She want for us?" is the fundamental religious question, and any answer to that question is inherently a religious proposition. "No God exists and this imaginary construct wants nothing for us" is a belief about religion. It is not merely a descriptive statement about religion, such as an anthropologist might make, or a scholar of comparative religion. Rather, it is an affirmation

---

52. *See* Book Note, First Things No. 63 at 66 (May 1996) (deriding the claim that a single Ultimate "lies behind each of the great religious traditions") (reviewing More Than One Way? Four Views on Salvation in a Pluralistic World (Dennis L. Okholm & Timothy R. Phillips, eds.).

of belief, capable of generating commitment and even lifelong activism on behalf of the cause.

The emergence of a vocal nontheistic minority in a predominantly theistic society causes serious social conflict. If the government is allowed to take sides, the two sides will fight to control the government, and the government will disapprove of, discriminate against, or suppress the losers. The most fundamental religious conflict in the United States today is between those who have abandoned theistic belief or accommodated their theism to contemporary secular values, and those who have not. This conflict has multiple axes that are not quite parallel. James Davison Hunter emphasizes the conflict between orthodox believers, who believe that God laid down unchangeable moral laws, and progressives, who believe that human understanding of truth, including religious and moral truth, is changeable and ever unfolding.[53] Phillip Johnson emphasizes the conflict between modernists or naturalists, who have excluded the possibility of supernatural events and explanations from their working worldview, and believers to whom the world is incomprehensible without creation and the continuing presence of God.[54]

Each side has its passionate advocates. Many traditional theists genuinely believe that morality can have no secure basis unless founded on God's law;[55] many nontheists are equally certain that religious faith is like reading entrails[56] or denying the Holocaust[57] and that morality can have no secure basis unless founded on reason. Suzanna Sherry vigorously attacks the destructive effects of faith,[58] while Peter Kreeft calls for an "ecumenical jihad" by believers of all faiths against modernism and relativism.[59] These are the sides in the much discussed culture wars. Any interpretation is wrong if it amounts to a claim that the Religion Clauses award victory to one side or the other.[60]

The second and third historical points are also applicable to nontheists.

---

53. *See generally* JAMES DAVISON HUNTER, CULTURE WARS (1990).

54. *See generally* PHILLIP JOHNSON, REASON IN THE BALANCE: THE CASE AGAINST NATURALISM IN SCIENCE, LAW AND EDUCATION (1995).

55. *See, e.g.,* PETER KREEFT, ECUMENICAL JIHAD 17-21 (1996) ("The abolition of God entails the abolition of man, the abolition of the specifically human faculty of conscience, God's prophet in the soul. The authority of conscience, like that of any prophet, depends on the authority of God."); R. C. SPROUL, ETHICS AND THE CHRISTIAN 28 (1986) ("Without God the only possible end of ethical reflection is chaos.").

56. *See* BRUCE ACKERMAN, SOCIAL JUSTICE IN THE LIBERAL STATE 280-81 (1980).

57. Sherry, *supra* note 3, at 491, 493.

58. *See id.;* Suzanna Sherry, *The Sleep of Reason,* 84 GEO. L.J. 453 (1996).

59. *See generally* KREEFT, *supra* note 55.

60. For further analysis, see Laycock, *supra* note 19, at 1069-89 (text at notes 166-248).

Atheistic and agnostic beliefs will be very important to many of the individuals who hold such beliefs; these people will define themselves partly in reaction to the strongly held theistic beliefs of others. And these beliefs are of little importance to government if both theists and nontheists can be loyal citizens. Thus, "the core purpose of the Religion Clauses applies to nonbelievers as well as to believers."[61]

The resistance to this conclusion seems to me partly linguistic and partly strategic. The linguistic argument is that the word "religion" has traditionally been used to refer only to affirmative answers to the great religious questions; atheism, agnosticism, and secularism have been thought of not as religion, but as the opposite of religion. This description of usage is accurate so far as I know in the Founders' time, when the question could hardly have arisen; this description of usage is mostly accurate in this century, but not entirely so.

John Dewey and the first *Humanist Manifesto* presented humanism as a new religion to supersede traditional religions thought to have become unconvincing.[62] The *Manifesto* opened with the statement that "the time has come for widespread recognition of the radical changes in religious beliefs through the modern world."[63] The second paragraph warned that "There is a great danger of a final, and we believe fatal, identification of the word *religion* with doctrines and methods which have lost their significance and which are powerless to solve the problem of human living in the Twentieth Century."[64] The third paragraph proclaimed the need for "a new statement of the means and purposes of religion."[65] The Manifesto then set out fifteen "theses of religious humanism";[66] these theses included explicit rejection of creation, theism, and "supernatural guarantees of human values."[67] Searching for a new definition of religion, the drafters came up with the wholly unworkable proposition that "Religion consists of those actions, purposes, and experiences which are humanly significant."[68]

This work by a handful of intellectuals is evidence of some usage, obvi-

61. Norman Dorsen, *The Religion Clauses and Nonbelievers*, 27 Wm. & Mary L. Rev. 863, 868 (1986).

62. *See* John Dewey, A Common Faith (1934) (proposing a religion based on faith in the accumulated values of human civilization); *Humanist Manifesto I*, 6 New Humanist No. 3 (1933), *reprinted in* Corliss Lamont, The Philosophy of Humanism 285 (7th ed. 1990).

63. *Humanist Manifesto I, supra* note 62, at 285.

64. *Id.*

65. *Id.* at 286.

66. *Id.* at 288.

67. *Id.* at 286-87.

68. *Id.* at 287.

ously not of general usage. The drafters' usage may have been strategic; they might have thought that they were more likely to win converts with this formulation than if they repudiated all religion. But their usage also reflects a genuine and steady evolution through "theism, deism, modernism, and the several varieties of 'new thought.'"[69] *Humanist Manifesto II* dropped the talk of religion, although it continued to recognize religious humanism as one branch of humanism.[70] *The Encyclopedia of American Religions* lists a "liberal family" of religions that includes the Unitarian Universalist Association, the American Humanist Association, the American Ethical Union, American Atheists, and others.[71]

Eventually the religious right began to argue that secular humanism is a religion and that it is established in the schools, and the organized humanist movement began to respond that it is not a religion after all. In 1980, the Council for Democratic and Secular Humanism (now the Council on Secular Humanism) split off from the American Humanist Association, and published its own statement, *A Secular Humanist Declaration.*[72] The leading founder of this new organization later explained that "the term *secular* humanism has thus been introduced to distinguish it from *religious* humanism."[73] The core beliefs do not appear to have changed, but the characterization has.

Assume that this is all epiphenomenon, and that in the dominant American usage, disbelief is the opposite of religion. So what? Where neutrality, equality, and nondiscrimination are part of the central purpose of a clause, it is no anomaly that the clause applies to opposites. The whole point of neutrality, equality, and nondiscrimination is to give equal treatment to categories that are opposite in some way that has been socially significant. To prefer one set of answers to religious questions over other answers to the same questions is to violate the core of the Religion Clauses. The only way to avoid that violation is to recognize that for constitutional purposes, any answer to religious questions is religion.

As the history of organized humanism illustrates, actual usage in this

---

69. *Id.* at 287; *see generally* TURNER, *supra* note 24 (documenting the historic intellectual path from traditional Christianity though deism and modernism to agnosticism and atheism).

70. *Humanist Manifesto II,* HUMANIST (Sept./Oct. 1973), reprinted in LAMONT, *supra* note 62, at 290, 291.

71. J. GORDON MELTON, THE ENCYCLOPEDIA OF AMERICAN RELIGIONS 145-58 (1978).

72. PAUL KURTZ, A SECULAR HUMANIST DECLARATION (1980).

73. PAUL KURTZ, LIVING WITHOUT RELIGION: EUPRAXOPHY 8 (1994). I have to doubt that the word "eupraxophy" is going to catch on.

century has been driven in part by strategic considerations. The strategic temptations lie on both sides. Some believers insist that nonbelief is not a religion, so that theistic religion gets special constitutional recognition, so that the government can endorse generic theism or give "nonpreferential" aid to religion without departing from neutrality, or so that regulatory exemptions under the Free Exercise Clause or the Religious Freedom Restoration Act are available only to those whose conscientious objection is rooted in theism. Nontheists typically insist that their nontheistic views are not religious, so that government is free to promote them and act on them, and so that they can dismiss without analysis the claim that secular humanism has been established. Thus Paul Kurtz argues that the most immediate reason not to consider secular humanism a religion is that it would then follow that secular humanism "cannot be taught to the young, using public funds and in the guise of neutrality."[74]

For reasons I have explained at somewhat greater length elsewhere, I do not believe that secular humanism has been established in the schools.[75] Secular humanism offers explicit negative answers to the basic theological questions, but I know of no case in which schools have taught those answers. But certainly we can imagine a school that did teach those answers. We can imagine a government that established atheism, and even think of real examples; the Soviet Union did it.

If atheism is not a religion for constitutional purposes, such an establishment would be perfectly constitutional. The Free Speech Clause would protect citizens from being forced to affirm atheistic beliefs,[76] and the Free Exercise Clause would protect believers from persecution or discrimination, but there is no Establishment Clause with respect to secular ideas. If atheism is just a secular idea, government would be free to promote atheism to the same extent that it has ever promoted any other secular idea — say the war effort in World War II, or civil rights during the Second Reconstruction. Government could teach atheism in the schools, promote atheism in the mass media, subsidize the American Atheists and a network of local chapters, and ridicule God as the opiate of the masses. The only sensible interpretation is that this would be an establishment of religion — an establishment of a certain set of views about religion, of a certain set of answers to the fundamental religious questions.[77]

74. *Id.* at 9-10.
75. Laycock, *supra* note 19, at 1081-82 (text at notes 216-19).
76. *See, e.g.,* Wooley v. Maynard, 430 U.S. 705, 713-17 (1977); West Virginia Board of Education v. Barnette, 319 U.S. 624 (1943).
77. For a much more fully developed but essentially consistent argument that secular

73

The consequences of excluding nontheists from the Free Exercise Clause would be less dramatic, because the Free Speech Clause and the Test Oath Clause would fill much of the gap. The most important residual gap would be the protection for religiously motivated conduct — either the substantive protection argued for here and provided in the Religious Freedom Restoration Act,[78] or the nondiscrimination protection recognized in *Church of the Lukumi Babalu Aye v. City of Hialeah*[79] and *Employment Division v. Smith*.[80]

The law should recognize nontheistic answers to religious questions as religion for constitutional purposes and for RFRA purposes. And the law should provide parallel protections for theistic and nontheistic beliefs about religion for as far as the parallels can be reasonably extended. Government should be neutral among these beliefs, endorsing none of them and taking no position on the truth or value of any of them. Private speech from any of these perspectives should be protected as high-value speech, doubly protected by both the Free Speech and Free Exercise Clause.[81] The Constitution and RFRA should protect the autonomy of atheist, agnostic, and humanist organizations, just as they protect the autonomy of churches;[82] they should protect conduct motivated by disbelief in God, if any there be, just as they protect conduct motivated by more traditional religious beliefs.[83]

Most controversial, but essential to the pursuit of religious neutrality, the law should protect nontheists' deeply held conscientious objection to compliance with civil law to the same extent that it protects the theistically motivated conscientious objection of traditional believers. *United States v.*

---

humanism must be treated as a religion for constitutional purposes, see Mary Harter Mitchell, *Secularism in Public Education: The Constitutional Issues,* 67 B.U. L. Rev. 603, 627-63 (1987).

78. 42 U.S.C. §§ 2000bb to 2000bb-4 (1994).

79. 508 U.S. 520 (1993).

80. 494 U.S. 872 (1990).

81. For the proposition that religious speech is protected by both clauses, see Capitol Square Review & Advisory Bd. v. Pinette, 515 U.S. 753, 767 (1995) (plurality opinion); Board of Educ. v. Mergens, 496 U.S. 226, 250 (1990) (plurality opinion); Largent v. Texas, 318 U.S. 418, 422 (1943); Douglas Laycock, *Freedom of Speech That Is Both Religious and Political,* 29 U.C. Davis L. Rev. 793 (1996).

82. *See, e.g.,* Serbian E. Orthodox Diocese v. Milivojevich, 426 U.S. 696, 723 (1976) (holding that Constitution precludes "searching and therefore impermissible inquiry" into questions of religious doctrine or administration); EEOC v. Catholic Univ., 83 F.3d 455, 460-62 (D.C. Cir. 1996) (holding that constitutional protection for internal management of religious organization survived *Employment Div. v. Smith,* 484 U.S. 872 (1990)).

83. In re Young, 82 F.3d 1407, 1418 (8th Cir. 1996) (interpreting RFRA to protect "religiously motivated as well as religiously compelled conduct"); Mack v. O'Leary, 80 F.3d 1175, 1179 (7th Cir. 1996) (interpreting RFRA to protect "religiously motivated conduct").

Seeger[84] and *Welsh v. United States*[85] were rightly decided; they implement policies at the core of religious liberty.[86] The law cannot protect the pursuit of all personal commitments or obligations, or all disagreements with the policy or prudence of political decisions. Unlike religious disagreements, political disagreements are committed to the political process; my third reason for religious liberty does not apply when the disagreement is essentially political. What the law can do is protect those moral obligations of nontheists that are functionally equivalent to the protected moral obligations of theists.

Some commentators seem to assume that this interpretation takes unacceptable liberties with the constitutional text. The full elaboration of this argument runs that nontheism is not religion, so nontheistic conscientious objectors cannot be protected. Because it would be discriminatory to protect theistic conscientious objectors without protecting nontheistic conscientious objectors, whatever we might think the underlying policy of free exercise would be otherwise, the pursuit of religious neutrality requires that we repudiate regulatory exemptions for theistic objectors. Variations on this argument may be the longest standing modern objection to recognizing regulatory exemptions at all.[87] I should therefore note before continuing that the Supreme Court has unanimously rejected the claim that regulatory exemptions for religion violate the Establishment Clause.[88] That decision is clearly right; one does not establish a religion by leaving it alone.[89]

Consider on the merits the argument that nontheistic objectors cannot be protected and so it is discriminatory to protect theistic objectors. This argument accepts my claim that neutrality is a central purpose of the Religion Clauses, and it accepts my claim that theistic and nontheistic answers to religious questions are essentially parallel and entitled to equal treatment. But it pursues neutrality at the expense of liberty; it repudiates everyone's substan-

---

84. 380 U.S. 163 (1965).

85. 398 U.S. 333 (1970).

86. For a less complete statement of this position, see Laycock, *supra* note 26, at 1002 (text at notes 29-30).

87. *See, e.g.,* PHILIP B. KURLAND, RELIGION AND THE LAW: OF CHURCH AND STATE AND THE SUPREME COURT 40-41 (1962); William P. Marshall, *The Case Against Free Exercise Exemptions,* 40 CASE W.L. REV. 357, 388-94 (1990); William P. Marshall, *The Religious Freedom Restoration Act: Establishment, Equal Protection and Free Speech Concerns,* 56 MONT. L. REV. 227, 229-44 (1995); Sherry, *supra* note 13, at 135-43.

88. Corporation of the Presiding Bishop v. Amos, 483 U.S. 327 (1987).

89. Douglas Laycock, *Towards a General Theory of the Religion Clauses: The Case of Church Labor Relations and the Right to Church Autonomy,* 81 COLUM. L. REV. 1373, 1416 (1981) (text at notes 316-17). Even Professor Marshall reluctantly concedes some force to this point. Marshall, *supra* note 87, at 240.

tive liberty to exercise a religion rather than extend that liberty from the more familiar case of theistic conscientious objectors to the parallel case of nontheistic conscientious objectors.

This repudiation of the substantive right to exercise a religion is perverse in terms of liberty and perverse in terms of human suffering. A principal argument for the repudiation is to avoid the intangible indignity to nontheists of knowing that they are ineligible for exemptions available to some theists.[90] (This resentment of exemptions available only to theists is of course an example of my point that religious groups are highly sensitive to any indication that government likes some other religious group best.) If exemptions were eliminated, the nontheistic conscientious objectors would still have to comply with the laws to which they object. They would be no better off, except that they would no longer feel slighted. The proposed cost of eliminating this intangible indignity is tangible and vastly disproportionate to the gain: believers whose religion forbids compliance with certain laws would have to abandon religious behaviors of profound importance to them, or go to jail, or expatriate, or rebel against the government — even if the burdensome law serves no particularly important government interest. On the free exercise side, the argument that nontheistic answers to religious questions are not religion sacrifices liberty in pursuit of a dog-in-the-manger version of neutrality.

The argument becomes even more perverse on the establishment side where, as we have seen, it would permit nontheistic views about religion to be established. Thus, any gains to neutrality on the free exercise side would be offset by the total abandonment of neutrality on the establishment side. There would be a major loss to liberty on the free exercise side, and no gain whatever to liberty on the establishment side; indeed, there would be a loss to liberty on the establishment side too if you accept my view that government expression of religious views interferes with the free development of beliefs about religion.

This perverse combination of results cannot be justified on the mere ground that the Founders did not think to consider atheism a religion. We do know that in the case where they thought most explicitly about disbelief, they protected it — in the Test Oath Clause. This protection did not go unnoticed; it was a point of some controversy in the state ratifying conventions.[91] Other models were available in state constitutions; South Carolina provided that there could be no oaths except for monotheism and belief in a future state of

---

90. Sherry, *supra* note 13, at 149.

91. For an account, see Edwin S. Gaustad, *Religion and Ratification,* in THE FIRST FREE-
DOMS: RELIGION AND THE BILL OF RIGHTS 41, 46-53 (James E. Wood, Jr., ed., 1990).

rewards and punishments.[92] But the federal Constitution's prohibition on test oaths is absolute.

More fundamentally, the Founders knew that the principal antagonists in religious conflicts varied from time to time and place to place. They knew about Christians and Muslims in the Crusades, Christians and Jews in the Spanish Inquisition, Catholics and Protestants in Reformation Europe, Anglicans and Puritans in the English Civil War, Episcopalians and Baptists in Virginia, Congregationalists and Baptists in Massachusetts. They knew that the immediate combatants were typically a religious movement on one side and a government on the other; Madison noted that it was "the secular arm" that had spilled "torrents of blood" in the effort to eliminate religious differences.[93] They knew, if they thought about it, that the secular arm often acted for secular reasons of its own.[94] Certainly they knew about Henry II and Thomas à Becket, and about Henry VIII taking over the English Church. The identity of the factions did not change the central problem; the Founders' principle had to cover future religious conflicts whatever the factional alignment.

The Founders may not have predicted that the central conflict in early nineteenth-century Massachusetts would be between Trinitarians and Unitarians, but the Religion Clauses applied to any federal manifestations of that unforeseen conflict, and that conflict forced Massachusetts to rewrite its religious liberty provisions and join the rest of the country in disestablishment.[95] The Founders greatly feared Catholicism, and they probably did not foresee the massive Catholic immigration beginning in the mid-nineteenth century. The Founders undoubtedly did not anticipate the current alignment of forces, in which traditional Protestants, Catholics, and Jews maintain their distinct traditions while making common cause against the forces of secularism. But the Religion Clauses speak to this conflict and can still serve to mediate it, helping these antagonists like others before them to live together in a peaceful and self-governing society. The clauses cannot serve this function if one side in the central conflict is defined as a religion and the other side is not.

Michael McConnell has offered a somewhat different argument for refusing protection to nontheistic conscientious objectors. He agrees that

92. S.C. Const. of 1778, art. XXXVIII, in Francis N. Thorpe, 6 The Federal and State Constitutions, Colonial Charters, and Other Organic Laws of the States, Territories, and Colonies Now or Heretofore Forming the United States of America 3255-57 (1906).

93. Madison, *supra* note 21, ¶ 1 at 64.

94. *See* Laycock, *supra* note 19.

95. *See supra* note 42.

"[u]nbelief is, after all, a system of opinions regarding the existence of God and thus regarding ultimate religious questions of life and value."[96] And he agrees that "[t]he protection of religious opinion will equally benefit religion and unbelief."[97] But he insists that conscientious objection is different:

> [U]nbelief entails no obligations and no observances. Unbelief may be coupled with various sorts of moral conviction. . . . But these convictions must necessarily be derived from some source other than unbelief itself; belief in the nonexistence of God does not in itself generate a moral code. Accordingly, to the extent that religious *actions* are protected under the Religion Clauses, there will be an asymmetry in the treatment of religion and unbelief.[98]

This is true in a sense, but largely irrelevant. In the case of theistic conscientious objectors, and in common usage, we understand "religion" to include a cluster of associated beliefs, and we rarely if ever undertake close examination of the causal connections among them. Theology and liturgy are at the core; church governance is plainly included though not very salient for most people today; moral obligations associated with religious belief are both included and more salient. The path of derivation within the cluster is not, and should not be, dispositive of exemption claims. Consider four cases, not entirely hypothetical.

First, consider a Catholic pacifist. He has moral beliefs not derived from his Church's teaching on the subject, possibly derived from other teachings of his Church or from his understanding of God's will, but quite possibly derived from reading the moral arguments of nontheistic pacifists. Courts can inquire into his sincerity, but I think that they cannot inquire into whether his pacifism is "derived from" his belief in God.

Second, consider a person who becomes a pacifist out of secular moral conviction, and then becomes a Quaker because his pacifism leads him to a pacifist church. He is not disqualified from exemption on the ground that his religion is "derived from" his moral conviction instead of the other way around.

Third, consider a secular Jew who doubts or denies the existence of God, but who observes the Sabbath and the dietary laws out of loyalty to the faith of his fathers. His observances are "derived from" somebody's religion, although perhaps not from "his" religion, and certainly not from a belief in the

96. Michael W. McConnell, *Accommodation of Religion*, 1985 Sup. Ct. Rev. 1, 10.
97. *Id.* at 11.
98. *Id.* at 10-11.

existence of God. But surely the state must recognize his observances as religious; he is entitled to Sabbath accommodation under the employment discrimination laws and to Kosher food if he lands in prison.

Fourth, consider a modernist Christian who thinks the essence of Christianity is the Sermon on the Mount, who is therefore committed to serving his fellow humans, and who thinks that killing is inconsistent with that obligation. He is active in his church, but he thinks that Jesus was just a great teacher, and he doubts the existence of God. For him, Christianity is a powerful symbol system that he "resymbolize[s]" in modern terms.[99]

I think that each of these claimants must be treated as having religious claims. To do otherwise would be inconsistent with common usage and understanding of what is religious behavior, and would inquire far too deeply into the workings of religious belief systems. Variations in the content and derivation of religious beliefs cannot be the basis for differences in legal treatment. Yet it is not clear that any of the moral beliefs in these four cases meet McConnell's standard of being "derived from" a belief in the existence of God.

With respect to the nontheistic objector, the challenge is to identify that cluster of beliefs that are analogous to the cluster of beliefs we recognize as religious in the case of adherents to traditions that we can all agree are religions. Beliefs about the nonexistence of God are plainly analogous to the theist's belief in God's existence. Professors Sherry, Marshall, McConnell, and I all agree on that.

The nontheist's belief in transcendent moral obligations — in obligations that transcend his self-interest and his personal preferences and which he experiences as so strong that he has no choice but to comply — are analogous to the transcendent moral obligations that are part of the cluster of theistic beliefs that we recognize as religious. The derivation of these beliefs may be murky, as in the four cases just considered, but these beliefs and the sources from which the nontheist derived them are serving the same functions in his life as the equivalent moral beliefs and sources of derivation serve for theists. The nontheist may experience natural law or the equality of all humans as "a transcendent authority prior to and beyond the authority of civil government,"[100] just as the theist experiences divine command or religious tradition. An individual's religious beliefs may evolve from theism to deism to modernism to resymbolized Christianity to humanism to agnosti-

99. The word in quotation marks is from James Davison Hunter's description of religious progressives. HUNTER, *supra* 53, at 144-45.

100. The phrase is from Michael W. McConnell, *The Origins and Historical Understanding of Free Exercise of Religion,* 103 HARV. L. REV. 1409, 1500 (1990). But he would reject the application.

cism to atheism. This evolution is itself an exercise of religion; it is a series of religious choices or of shifting religious commitments. The state should not draw a line across this evolutionary path; it should not decree that anyone who crosses the line forfeits his right to conscientious objection and loses protection for his deepest moral commitments. Such a line would not be consistent with either liberty or neutrality.

Of course judges may draw such a line despite its incoherence. All that should follow is that nontheism would be outside the Religion Clauses and outside RFRA. The scope of protection for religions inside the Clauses and inside RFRA should not be changed, lest the core of religious liberty be determined by anomalous cases at the margin.

Consistently for decades, 95% of Americans have said they believe in God or a Universal Spirit.[101] This number includes people whose beliefs are modernist, attenuated, or unconventional; it includes most people on both sides of the culture wars. It includes all sorts of minorities, many of them tiny; the fact that 95% have theism in common does not mean that the enormous range of religious views that make up the 95% can protect themselves through the political process. These 95% will be able to state any conscientious objection to government policy in theistic terms, so their moral beliefs will qualify as religious under theistic definitions.

The problem of avowed nontheists is statistically marginal; judicial refusal to protect the 5% should not become the excuse for withdrawing protection from the 95%. A judge who says that "religion" in the First Amendment means theism cannot then say that special protection for theism violates the Establishment Clause because it discriminates against the 5% he refuses to protect. I would prefer liberty and neutrality for all, but if forced to choose between liberty and neutrality for 95%, or liberty for none and neutrality for all, the constitutional choice is easy. The neutrality of universal suppression is not the constitutional vision.

V. Constitutional Text and History

My argument so far has been based on history and function at the very largest scale. I have asked what we can infer about religious liberty from centuries of religious conflict. I turn now to more specific sources of constitutional meaning — to constitutional text, to the political debate that led to that text, and to the history of our national effort to implement that text.

---

101. *See* GEORGE BARNA, VIRTUAL AMERICA 107 (1994); Greeley, *supra* note 50, at 14.

The Constitution consists of the ratified text; the People's representatives voted on nothing else. All inferences from history, structure, and policy must be tested for consistency with that text. I think that the text is consistent with the views expressed so far, and that to the extent possible in so brief a formulation, the text affirmatively supports the interpretation of guaranteeing as much liberty as possible to holders of all views about religion.

The Free Exercise Clause guarantees a substantive right to exercise one's religion. "Exercise" means activity or practice, both now and in the Founders' time;[102] it is not confined to belief or to speech. The right is not stated as a mere right to nondiscrimination. It is common ground that religious conduct is the exercise of religion;[103] otherwise, the Free Exercise Clause would not protect such conduct even from discrimination. But once that is conceded, a law prohibiting religious conduct is quite literally a law "prohibiting the free exercise thereof" — a law prohibiting the exercise of religion. This is the most straightforward, plain-meaning interpretation of the text, and only this reading can satisfy the religion-neutral rationales for religious liberty.[104]

The phrase "free exercise of religion" was deliberately substituted for a guarantee of "toleration" in drafting the Virginia Declaration of Rights.[105] "Toleration" might have suggested a mere right of religious minorities to live within our boundaries. Indeed, "toleration" might have been consistent with Professor Sherry's view that believers are a dangerous, superstitious faction whose epistemology is rejected in our founding documents, but whose liberty must unfortunately be protected to prevent their becoming angry and resentful.[106] Whatever "toleration" might have meant, the word would have been less probative on the right to "exercise" one's religion. The more protective phrase was the one written into the federal bill of rights.

The constitutional text lends indirect support to the argument that nontheistic views about religion must be recognized as religion, although the argument is hardly free of difficulty. The principal argument against such recognition is also textual — that nontheistic views simply are not "religion" in common usage or in the Founders' usage, and worse, that the First Congress considered and rejected drafts that would have protected "liberty of

---

102. McConnell, *supra* note 100, at 1488-89.

103. Employment Div. v. Smith, 494 U.S. 872, 877 (1990) ("But the 'exercise of religion' often involves not only belief and profession but the performance of (or abstention from) physical acts;").

104. *See supra* text accompanying note 27.

105. *See* CURRY, *supra* note 20, at 135.

106. Sherry, *supra* note 3, at 485.

conscience" instead of, or in addition to, "free exercise of religion."[107] But there was no recorded controversy in the First Congress or elsewhere over the supposed distinction between religion and conscience,[108] and speakers and state constitutions of the time used the two phrases interchangeably.[109] The great Calvinist teaching that "God alone is Lord of the conscience"[110] plainly referred to religion and not to something different. Nontheistic conscientious objection was simply not a significant issue in the Founders' time. One speaker on a proposal to constitutionalize a specific right to exemptions from militia service was able to envision the possibility of nontheistic conscientious objectors, but he did not describe that possibility in terms of a distinction between religion and conscience.[111] Professor McConnell identifies two other distinctions that might be read into the choice between "free exercise of religion" and "liberty of conscience."[112] With three possible explanations of what the choice of language might have meant if it meant anything, no record of an actual dispute, and no record of a consistent difference in usage, it is hard to draw much meaning from the failure to include a conscience clause. But I do agree that when the Founders thought of religion, they thought of theism.

Assuming some force to the argument that the Founders' common understanding of religion excluded nontheistic views, we are faced with a new situation that creates serious tension within the constitutional text. We now have significant numbers of citizens with nontheistic beliefs; we now have new axes of religious conflict that the Founders could not foresee. Either we must expand the textual meaning of "religion" to include the new answers to religious questions, or we must shrink the textual meaning of "exercise" to avoid preferring theistic beliefs with respect to conscientious objection, or we

107. *See* McConnell, *supra* note 100, at 1488-500. Each successive draft also changed the more controversial Establishment Clause. The successive drafts are set out in sequence in Laycock, *supra* note 23, at 879-81 (text at notes 27-36).

108. McConnell, *supra* note 100, at 1495.

109. *Id.* at 1493-94.

110. *The Westminster Confession of Faith* (1647), reprinted in 3 THE CREEDS OF CHRISTENDOM 600 (Philip Schaff, ed., 1919); *Principles of Church Order,* adopted by the 1st General Assembly of the Presbyterian Church in the United States (1788), quoted in *"God Alone Is Lord of the Conscience": Policy Statement and Recommendations Regarding Religious Liberty Adopted by the 200th General Assembly, Presbyterian Church (U.S.A.)* (1988), reprinted in 8 J.L. & RELIGION 331, 331 (1990) [and in Appendix I of this volume].

111. 1 ANNALS OF CONG. 796 (J. Gales ed. 1834) (Aug. 20, 1789) (remarks of Mr. Scott).

112. McConnell, *supra* note 100, at 1489-91 (suggesting that the difference between the two words might have been between exercise as action and conscience as belief, or between religion as institutional religion and conscience as individual belief).

must exclude nontheists from the goal of government neutrality on religious questions. The purely textual argument becomes at worst a draw.

In fact, the textual argument for protecting nontheistic beliefs about religion is better than a draw. I would expand the traditional meaning of "religion" to include beliefs that secularists agree cannot be discriminated against relative to the traditional religious beliefs that are most explicitly protected. That is, I read the constitutional term to include newly emerged beliefs that were not socially significant in the Founders' time but that fall easily into a category — beliefs about the nature of God — that we know the Founders meant to protect. By contrast, those who would deny protection to conscientious objectors must shrink the meaning of "exercise" so dramatically that any substantive right to practice a religion disappears. And, as argued above, this dispute is not even close in terms of constitutional purposes. Shrinking the meaning of "exercise" and refusing to recognize nontheistic views as "religion" abandons both the liberty and neutrality policies of the clauses and permits the government to take sides in a core religious conflict.

The constitutional text is absolute; there is no textual exception in either of the Religion Clauses. Of course we know from experience that absolute religious liberty is unacceptable. But a strong burden of persuasion rests on those who would imply exceptions to an expressly absolute constitutional text. This is the textual basis for inferring the compelling interest exception and construing it narrowly[113] — for minimizing the exception and maximizing the protected liberty.

Speakers of English do not use "establishment" in quite the same sense with respect to anything but religion; the word really has no plain English meaning. It takes its meaning from its historical usage, of which the core case is the "the Church of England as by law established."[114] An established church was supported by the government in multiple ways;[115] in my view, any of these forms of support is a law respecting an establishment of religion.

Coercing citizens to support a religion in which they do not believe will often, and arguably always, violate the Free Exercise Clause. If the Establishment Clause were also confined to coercion, it would be redundant. This re-

---

113. Douglas Laycock, *Notes on Judicial Review, the Growth of Federal Power, and the Structure of Constitutional Rights* (Book Review), 99 YALE L.J. 1711, 1744-46 (1990).

114. *The Church of England Canons of 1604*, quoted in GUY MAYFIELD, THE CHURCH OF ENGLAND: ITS MEMBERS AND ITS BUSINESS 5 (1963). Eighteenth-century American statutes used similar constructions. *See, e.g.,* An Act for Exempting the Different Societies of Dissenters (1776), in 9 Hening's Stat. 164-67 ("the church established by law"); Curry, *supra* note 20, at 173 (quoting Massachusetts provisions for the "ministers established by law").

115. Laycock, *supra* note 33, at 41-42 (text at notes 22-28).

dundancy in the coercion interpretation is textual support for the belief that the Establishment Clause goes beyond coercion, and therefore that noncoercive support of religion is an establishment. This reading is consistent with the fact that endorsements of the established church were part of the package of support that government gave to the established church, and in some cases in the period just before the First Amendment, endorsements were all or nearly all that the established church got.[116]

This prohibition on endorsements makes Religion Clause neutrality an extraordinary kind of neutrality. Unlike political matters, government is forbidden to influence opinion even by persuasion. Religion is to be as free of government influence as anything can be in a society with a large government.

In general terms, the Free Exercise Clause prohibits government suppression of religion; the Establishment Clause forbids government support of religion. This balance between the clauses is further evidence for believing that government must be neutral toward religion, although the text is not specific enough to define neutrality without further inquiry.[117] It is at least clear that each clause must be construed in light of the other, and in light of the rest of the First Amendment.

I reject Professor Sherry's view that this contrast between the clauses renders them inconsistent.[118] That would be a last resort interpretation, after exhausting all attempts to reconcile the clauses.[119] In fact, the reconciliation is not difficult, especially in the light of history. Both disestablishment and free exercise protect the liberty of individuals and their voluntary groups with respect to choices and commitments about religion. Government support of established churches had harmed the religious liberty of persons who did not believe in the teachings of the established church; in different ways, government support had harmed the religious liberty of the established church and its members. The two clauses together are complementary guarantees of religious liberty for both the majority (if any) and the various minorities, including nontheists.

I think it is of some significance that the Establishment Clause prohibits laws "respecting an establishment of religion," and not merely establishment of a church or establishment of a particular religion. The reference seems to

116. *Id.* at 43-45 (text at notes 32-45).

117. For elaborations of my understanding of neutrality, see Laycock, *supra* note 26; Douglas Laycock, *Equal Access and Moments of Silence: The Equal Status of Private Speech by Private Speakers*, 81 Nw. U.L. Rev. 1 (1986).

118. *See* Sherry, *supra* note 13.

119. *Cf., e.g.*, Marbury v. Madison, 5 U.S. (1 Cranch) 137, 174 (1803) ("It cannot be presumed that any clause in the constitution is intended to be without effect;").

be to religion generally; the clause includes generic support for theism.[120] Particularly given the drafting history and the then-recent debates over the meaning of disestablishment, this is strong evidence against the claim that government can support religion if it does so nonpreferentially.[121]

The principal alternative to the policy eventually ratified in the Religion Clauses had been nonpreferential establishments. The defenders of the established churches tried to make establishment acceptable by converting it into nonpreferential support for all Christian denominations. The effort to be nonpreferential was mostly sham in New England, more genuine in Maryland and Virginia, but in both regions, nonpreferentialism was the last strategy to save the establishment. Nonpreferential establishment was rejected in the drafting of the Religion Clauses, and eventually in all the states.[122] I think history is clearer on this than history usually is on most things.

This prohibition on nonpreferential support for generic theism is further indirect evidence for the claim that both theistic and nontheistic beliefs are protected by the clauses. The Founders opposed nonpreferential establishments partly for fear that they would be preferential in practice, partly out of genuine commitment to religious voluntarism. They were not thinking about unanticipated conflict between generic theism and nontheism, but their rejection of nonpreferential support for theistic churches left their Religion Clauses open to that application when the axes of religious conflict changed.

Another central issue in the founding generation was the financing of churches. The Founders clearly rejected the view that government should pay for churches as such. There is no evidence that they considered the principal modern controversy, which is funding for secular health, educational, or welfare services provided by churches.[123] They sent missionaries to the Indians, but it is not clear that anyone thought about whether that raised Establishment Clause issues.

The Protestant Bible controversy in the nineteenth century is a formative national experience that has gotten insufficient attention in the interpretation of the Religion Clauses.[124] That controversy demonstrates that conflict

---

120. *See* Lee v. Weisman, 505 U.S. 577, 614 n.2 (Souter, J., joined by Stevens and O'Connor, JJ., concurring).

121. *See* Laycock, *supra* note 23.

122. *Id.;* Lee v. Weisman, 505 U.S. 577, 615 (1992) (Souter, J., joined by Stevens and O'Connor, JJ., concurring).

123. For discussion, see Douglas Laycock, *Text, Intent, and the Religion Clauses,* 4 Notre Dame J.L. Ethics, & Pub. Pol'y 683, 695 (1990) (text at notes 30-36).

124. For a brief review, collecting historical sources, see Laycock, *supra* note 33, at 50-53 (text at notes 65-79).

over government-sponsored religious observances can lead to violence. It is powerful confirmation of the wisdom of the school prayer decisions, and more generally, of the view that government should take no position on religious questions. This controversy is also the source of the widespread belief that government payments to religiously affiliated schools violate the Establishment Clause. Thirty-two states amended their Constitutions in this period to prohibit public funding of religious schools.[125] Democrats in the Senate narrowly defeated the Blaine Amendment to the federal Constitution, which would have codified the Protestant position by authorizing Bible reading in the public schools and forbidding any use of state or federal funds to support religious schools.[126]

It is important that the Religion Clauses restrict Congress, a branch of government; they do not restrict churches or religious believers. Restricting the power of Congress restricts the entire federal government in most contexts, because most of the work of the other branches is to execute or interpret Congressional legislation;[127] in any event, the Court has interpreted "Congress" to mean the whole federal government without attending to the problem.[128] Slavery and the Civil War confirmed Madison's view that the states were an equal or greater threat to liberty, and the Privileges or Immunities Clause makes the Religion Clauses binding on state and local governments.[129] The Supreme Court's explanation is less textually plausible, but it works, and it has fewer ambiguities about the scope of coverage.[130]

125. For a list, see CARL ZOLLMAN, AMERICAN CHURCH LAW §§ 65-66 at 78-80 (2d ed. 1933). For additional background, see CHARLES GLENN, THE MYTH OF THE COMMON SCHOOL 251-53 (1988).

126. For the text of the amendment with discussion, see GLENN, *supra* note 125, at 251-53; ANSON PHELPS STOKES, 2 CHURCH AND STATE IN THE UNITED STATES 68-69, 722-28 (1950); ZOLLMAN, *supra* note 125, § 62 at 75-76.

127. *See* Douglas Laycock, *Taking Constitutions Seriously: A Theory of Judicial Review,* 59 TEX. L. REV. 343, 366 n.203 (1981) (Book Review). For the drafting history, and the view that the First Amendment does not restrict the judiciary in the exercise of its common law and equitable powers, see Mark P. Denbeaux, *The First Word of the First Amendment,* 80 NW. U.L. REV. 1156 (1986).

128. Denbeaux, *supra* note 127, at 1157-61, 1201-10.

129. *See* Laycock, *supra* note 127, at 348; Lash, *Establishment, supra* note 45; Lash, *Free Exercise, supra* note 45.

130. The Due Process Clause applies to "persons," which includes aliens and artificial legal persons such as churches. The Privileges or Immunities Clause arguably applies only to "citizens," although the difficulty is not textually insurmountable. *See* JOHN HART ELY, DEMOCRACY AND DISTRUST 24-25 (1980) (arguing that the clause forbids any state to deprive any person of any of that class of entitlements described as "the privileges and immunities of citizens of the United States"); Douglas Laycock, *Equal Citizens of Equal and Territorial*

Each of these extensions of the original textual constraint on Congress extended the constraint to other branches and levels of government. Of course this tracks the whole constitutional structure; the Bill of Rights is a set of constraints on government, and only the Thirteenth Amendment directly restricts the conduct of private persons not engaged in state action. It is breathtaking to assert — without even acknowledging the existence of contrary constitutional text and structure — that the primary purpose of the Religion Clauses was to protect the state from the church and not to protect churches from the state.[131]

This is not the place for an intellectual history of attitudes toward religion in the founding generation. But I cannot pass without comment Professor Sherry's remarkable claim that the Religion Clauses must be interpreted to subordinate religious faith because the Founders were committed to reason.[132] She and I at least agree on this much: most of the Founders saw no conflict between faith and reason. She says that "[t]he question of whether to privilege faith or reason would not have occurred to the founders for the simple reason that they did not see them as in conflict."[133] Professor Smith's statement that "the founding generation was deeply and pervasively influenced by Protestant thought and practice"[134] is irrelevant, according to Professor Sherry, because "the founding generation did not draw the same distinction between faith and reason that we do."[135] But of course, if the lack of conflict between faith and reason makes the pervasive commitment to Protestantism irrelevant, it makes the commitment to reason equally irrelevant.

Yet Professor Sherry says that somehow the Founders addressed this unrecognized conflict and resolved it in the Constitution. Her preferred resolution is not in the constitutional text, which singles out religion rather than reason. And it could not be in any conscious intention if the Founders did not see the issue. The appeal to unexamined practice in the absence of a real controversy is the most worthless form of intentionalist argument.[136] To say the Founders enshrined reason because they reasoned is like saying they enshrined prayer because they prayed. It is considerably weaker than saying

---

States: The Constitutional Foundations of Choice of Law, 92 COLUM. L. REV. 249, 268-70 (1992) (arguing that clauses that apply only to citizens might protect organizations by protecting the right of their members or shareholders to form and control organizations).

131. Sherry, *supra* note 3, at 487.

132. *Id.; see also* Sherry, *supra* note 58, at 464-72.

133. Sherry, *supra* note 58, at 468.

134. Smith, *supra* note 2, at 157.

135. Sherry, *supra* note 3, at 487.

136. *See* Laycock, *supra* note 123, at 689 (text at notes 16-17).

they enshrined seditious libel because they passed the Sedition Act; they at least had a real argument about the Sedition Act, an argument that surfaced the constitutional issues.

Professor Sherry attempts to deny that the evangelicals were a major force behind the Religion Clauses. This is, quite simply, preposterous; it is as absurd and inconsistent with the evidence as any belief held by people she accuses of irrationally relying on faith alone. She cites no sources for this proposition, and no responsible historian would support the claim. She does cite legal scholars who disagree with the much more specific and controversial claim that the original intention supports free exercise exemptions for religious objectors.[137] These citations are accurate but irrelevant; they imply nothing about the role of evangelicals in enacting the Religion Clauses.

Of course the Enlightenment was an important intellectual influence in eighteenth-century America, especially but not exclusively among the elites who led the Constitutional Convention and the First Congress. But the Great Awakening was an equally important intellectual influence. A great religious revival swept through the colonies in the 1740s — through most of the western world in the eighteenth century[138] — partly in reaction to the Enlightenment's rationalizing of religion.[139] The Great Awakening invigorated the Baptists, Presbyterians, and other evangelical sects and greatly expanded their numbers. And there is simply no doubt that it was these dissenting sects who made religious liberty a central issue of the time. "The chief political demand of Radical Evangelicals was religious toleration."[140] It was the evangelicals who provided the political muscle behind the legislative leadership "of a few liberally minded individuals" such as Madison.[141] These few individuals "could have accomplished little without the support they received from religious groups opposed to any Church-State connection. The Baptists, the Quakers, and the Presbyterians were specially prominent in this effort."[142] "[C]hronologically, the effective efforts of the philosopher-statesmen came only after the ground had been well cleared by the dissenting ministers."[143]

Scholars of unimpeachable strict separationist credentials agree on the

137. Sherry, *supra* note 3, at 485 n.62.

138. Perry Miller, *Jonathan Edwards and the Great Awakening*, in AMERICA IN CRISIS 5 (Daniel Aaron, ed., 1952).

139. *Id.*

140. STEPHEN A. MARINI, RADICAL SECTS OF REVOLUTIONARY NEW ENGLAND 23 (1982).

141. 1 STOKES, *supra* note 126, at 243.

142. *Id.* at 244.

143. *Id.* at 379.

basic outlines of this story. Thus Leonard Levy writes that the Great Awakening "proliferated sects, mainly Separates, Baptist, and New Side Presbyterian, whose dissenter experiences led them to oppose establishments of religion and advance the cause of religious liberty."[144] Levy's history of disestablishment in America starts not with James Madison, but with Isaac Backus and the Baptists.[145] Leo Pfeffer wrote that "the ardent revivalist groups which formed the movement [the Great Awakening] became staunch partisans of the separation of church and state."[146] In considering why the complete separation of church and state first occurred in Virginia, the first reason Pfeffer offers is that "[t]he dissenting sects, particularly the Baptists and Presbyterians, were numerous and well organized; from half to two-thirds of the population were dissenters."[147]

Madison himself was educated at Princeton from 1769 to 1771, then a New Light Presbyterian college, founded in 1746 as a direct product of the Great Awakening.[148] Some of his friends and classmates became itinerant preachers, and in 1773-74, we find Madison protesting the imprisonment of unlicensed Baptist preachers in Virginia.[149] By 1776, he was in the legislature, successfully substituting a guarantee of "free exercise" for a proposed guarantee of "toleration," and unsuccessfully moving to disestablish the Anglican Church.[150] We can only speculate whether Madison would have eventually become committed to religious liberty for rationalist reasons; it seems clear that in fact he became committed to religious liberty out of sympathy for and persuasion by the evangelicals.

Whatever his motivation, it is clear that Madison depended on the evangelicals for votes. He failed in his efforts to defeat the general assessment bill in the Virginia legislature; it passed on two readings and passed again on a vote to engross a bill.[151] But he prevailed on a vote to postpone final reading to the next session, so that members could consult their constituents.[152] In

144. Leonard W. Levy & Alfred Young, Foreword to THE GREAT AWAKENING: DOCUMENTS ILLUSTRATING THE CRISIS AND ITS CONSEQUENCES v-vi (Alan Heimert & Perry Miller, eds., 1967).

145. LEVY, *supra* note 41, at 2-4.

146. LEO PFEFFER, CHURCH, STATE, AND FREEDOM 92 (1953).

147. *Id.* at 93-94.

148. *See* RALPH KETCHAM, JAMES MADISON: A BIOGRAPHY 28-29 (1971); Levy & Young, *supra* note 144, at vi.

149. KETCHAM, *supra* note 148, at 54-58.

150. *Id.* at 72-73.

151. THOMAS E. BUCKLEY, CHURCH AND STATE IN REVOLUTIONARY VIRGINIA, 1776-1787, at 105-08 (1977).

152. *Id.* at 108.

the ensuing public debate, a great outpouring of evangelical opposition swamped the bill. Madison's *Memorial and Remonstrance,* which combined religious and rationalist arguments, attracted well under two thousand signatures,[153] compared with just over one thousand signatures supporting the assessment.[154] Other petitions, overwhelmingly from the dissenting sects, attracted some *ten* thousand signatures.[155] Many petitions came from Baptist, Presbyterian, and Quaker churches; the single most common petition, with more than twice as many signatures as the *Memorial and Remonstrance,* came from evangelical Christians of unidentified affiliation.[156] The *Memorial and Remonstrance* is a brilliant synthesis of many arguments, and Madison's legislative maneuvering secured the critical opportunity for expression of public opinion, but "to contemporary observers, the work of the evangelicals and particularly the Presbyterians appeared ever more decisive for the outcome."[157]

The record is most fully developed in Virginia, but there is no doubt that in the other states as well, it was the evangelicals who led the fight for disestablishment. "It was naturally everywhere the nonestablished churches, and particularly the Baptists, who led the movement for disestablishment, which they favored both from reasons of religious conviction and practical advantage."[158] Indeed, one of the ironies is that the elites on whom Professor

153. The historian Forrest McDonald says 1,552. FORREST MCDONALD, NOVUS ORDO SECLORUM: THE INTELLECTUAL ORIGINS OF THE CONSTITUTION 45 (1984). Thomas Buckley, whose investigations were concentrated on religious liberty issues in Virginia, and so were probably more thorough, says "approximately seventeen hundred." BUCKLEY, *supra* note 151, at 147.

154. BUCKLEY, *supra* note 151, at 147.

155. *See* MCDONALD, *supra* note 153, at 45 (9,337 signatures on petitions other than the *Memorial and Remonstrance*); BUCKLEY, *supra* note 151, at 147 (more than twelve thousand signatures opposed, of whom only about seventeen hundred signed the *Memorial and Remonstrance* and about three hundred signed a somewhat similar petition by Madison's protege John Breckenridge).

156. BUCKLEY, *supra* note 151, at 148-49; CURRY, *supra* note 20, at 141-42; LEVY, *supra* note 41, at 63-64. Levy appears to have examined the petitions independently. *See id.* at 64 n.36.

157. BUCKLEY, *supra* note 151, at 143. To similar effect, see CURRY, *supra* note 20, at 143 (noting that the *Memorial and Remonstrance* "did not in its contemporary setting enjoy the preeminence it would acquire over time"); LEVY, *supra* note 41, at 63-67 (reviewing the evangelical contribution to the fight); STOKES, *supra* note 126, at 366-97 (separately reviewing the contributions of the Baptists, the Presbyterians, and the "political philosophers").

158. STOKES, *supra* note 126, at 426. For further detail, *see, e.g., id.* at 240-44, 306-10, 353-58, 364-65, 410-11, 418-26; and see the index entries for Baptists, Presbyterians, and Quakers in CURRY, *supra* note 20, and LEVY, *supra* note 41.

Sherry relies to show the dominance of reason were disproportionately members of the established Congregational and Episcopal Churches.

Throughout the ratification process, and into the elections to the First Congress, Madison remained firmly opposed to adding a Bill of Rights or any other amendments to the new Constitution.[159] In the elections to the Virginia ratifying convention, Madison was forced to campaign for the first time in his life, and Paul Finkelman concludes that a meeting with the Baptist leader John Leland, two days before the election, was "critical" to Madison's election.[160] In the elections to the First Congress, Madison encountered both an anti-Federalist gerrymander and organized opposition from Baptists on the ground of his continued opposition to amendments. To secure the Baptist vote, Madison reminded them of his long service to their cause, and he repeatedly and unequivocally committed himself to work for amendments.[161] It is familiar history that in the First Congress he successfully honored this commitment.[162] But for the Virginia Baptists, we might not have a Bill of Rights.

I have no strong view on the relative overall influence of the Enlightenment and the Great Awakening in eighteenth-century America. On religious liberty issues, the evangelicals appear to have been more important than the Deists. Certainly the evangelicals were necessary; perhaps they would have been sufficient if the Deists had not been available to help. But relative importance or counterfactual speculation is not my point. What is clear is that as history actually developed, there were important roles for both the evangelicals and for sympathetic Episcopalians such as Madison and Jefferson. Religious liberty was the product of an alliance, and neither side in today's culture wars can claim it as exclusively their own.

VI. The Principal Contemporary Issues

I see three major clusters of contemporary issues, and one large question of how to integrate responses to these issues.

---

159. *See* Paul Finkelman, *James Madison and the Bill of Rights: A Reluctant Paternity*, 1990 SUP. CT. REV. 301, 313-33.

160. *Id.* at 323-24.

161. *See* CURRY, *supra* note 20, at 198-99; Finkelman, *supra* note 159, at 334-36; KETCHAM, *supra* note 148, at 276; ROBERT A. RUTLAND, JAMES MADISON: THE FOUNDING FATHER 44-49 (1987).

162. For a detailed account, see Finkelman, *supra* note 159.

A. Exemptions for Religious Conduct and Religious Organizations

Laws that restrict religiously motivated conduct or interfere with the autonomy of religious organizations prima facie violate the Free Exercise Clause.[163] The Religious Freedom Restoration Act was an appropriate response to the Supreme Court's unwillingness to enforce the clause.[164]

It is common ground that exemptions expand religious liberty. Exemptions are also consistent with substantive neutrality so long as they do not encourage religious belief or practice. Refusal to exempt is not consistent with neutrality, because government regulation is a powerful incentive not to practice one's religion, or to conform it to the government's preferences. Claims for exemption that align with self-interest are problematic because they create incentives to join the exempted faith, and in practice such claims have not been recognized.[165]

As argued above, nontheists subject to moral compulsion based on their own belief system should be entitled to exemption on the same basis as theists. This is the only neutral solution. It remains the case that exemptions cannot be extended to political disagreement or personal needs whose only analogy to religion is that they may be deeply felt. Just where to draw the line here is difficult, but the nature of the problem is the familiar one of applying old principles to new conditions. The Religion Clauses guarantee government neutrality with respect to answers to religious questions; a new set of answers has become important in our time, and those who give such answers must be treated neutrally. To the extent that they present issues that are analogous to the issues presented by those who give older, more familiar answers, they should be treated under the same rules.

---

163. *See* Laycock, *supra* note 27; Laycock, *supra* note 89; McConnell, *supra* note 27.

164. *See* Thomas C. Berg, *What Hath Congress Wrought? An Interpretive Guide to the Religious Freedom Restoration Act*, 39 VILL. L. REV. 1 (1994); Douglas Laycock & Oliver S. Thomas, *Interpreting the Religious Freedom Restoration Act*, 73 TEX. L. REV. 209 (1994); Douglas Laycock, *RFRA, Congress, and the Ratchet*, 56 MONT. L. REV. 145 (1995); Douglas Laycock, *The Religious Freedom Restoration Act*, 1993 B.Y.U. L. REV. 221; Douglas Laycock, *Summary and Synthesis: The Crisis in Religious Liberty*, 60 GEO. WASH. L. REV. 841, 846-56 (1992) (text at notes 28-75); Michael Stokes Paulsen, *A RFRA Runs Through It: Religious Freedom and the U.S. Code*, 56 MONT. L. REV. 249 (1995); Rex E. Lee, *The Religious Freedom Restoration Act: Legislative Choice and Judicial Review*, 1993 B.Y.U. L. REV. 73; Matt Pawa, Comment, *When the Supreme Court Restricts Constitutional Rights, Can Congress Save Us? An Examination of Section 5 of the Fourteenth Amendment*, 141 U. PA. L. REV. 1029 (1993).

165. *See* Laycock, *supra* note 26, at 1016-18 (text at notes 95-99).

B. Religious Speech

There have been vast amounts of litigation over religious speech, where I think the rules should be quite simple.[166] Private speakers have freedom of speech; religious speech is high value speech (a reasonable textual inference from the Free Exercise Clause); private religious speakers should be as fully protected as though they were discussing politics. With qualifications confined to dictum, that is what the Supreme Court has held.[167] Religious speakers are free to use public forums and to speak in places where they have a right to be. They are free to make religious arguments in political debates; any other rule would be transparent viewpoint discrimination.[168]

By contrast, government speech about religion is tightly circumscribed by the Establishment Clause. Government should not conduct religious observances, and it should not take a position on religious questions. Usually the best course is for government to remain silent and provide ample public forums.

Sometimes government must speak about religion, most obviously in public school curricula. It must teach about the role of religion in history and in contemporary society. It must teach about society's moral expectations, and it is cannot do that honestly without noting that for many citizens, morality has a religious base. In such situations, government must be scrupulously even-handed, treating the range of religious and nonreligious views as neutrally as possible.

C. Funding

The third great cluster of issues is funding. It is clear that government cannot give preferential funding to churches or religious activities. After a long evolution of views, I have finally come to the conclusion that government generally should fund religious organizations that fall within the scope of secular programs for funding private activity.[169]

166. *See generally* Laycock, *supra* note 117.

167. *See, e.g.,* Rosenberger v. Rector of the Univ. of Va., 515 U.S. 819 (1995); Capitol Square Review & Advisory Bd. v. Pinette, 515 U.S. 753 (1995); Board of Educ. v. Mergens, 496 U.S. 226 (1990); Widmar v. Vincent, 454 U.S. 263 (1981); Cantwell v. Connecticut, 310 U.S. 296 (1940).

168. Laycock, *supra* note 81.

169. For a thorough analysis, see Michael W. McConnell, *The Selective Funding Problem: Abortions and Religious Schools,* 104 HARV. L. REV. 989 (1991).

The easier case is secular services delivered by religious organizations. The neutral course is to fund the secular service without regard to the religious or secular nature of the organization providing the service. We may need to devise accounting rules that separate the cost of the secular from the cost of the religious with as little intrusion into internal church affairs as possible.

The harder case is illustrated by *Rosenberger v. Rector of the University of Virginia*,[170] where a religious magazine fell within the scope of a program for subsidizing student activities, including publications. Here the activity was clearly religious; the secular benefit was a broad debate that included all views on campus. Perhaps government should not be in the business of funding publications, but if it is there, it should not skew the debate. The more neutral course is to fund everybody.

D. Reintegrating Disaggregated Neutrality

I have wondered in earlier work about an arguable contradiction that appears in much work in this area, on all sides of most questions.[171] I will illustrate principally with my own positions.

With respect to the exemptions issue, I say that the most neutral course is usually exemptions. Religion is different from other human activities, and the neutral course is to treat it differently. With respect to government speech, I say government should generally refrain from religious speech; once again, religion is different and the neutral course is to treat it differently. But with respect to the private speech issues and the funding issues, I say that the most neutral course is to treat religion like other private speech and other funded activities. Religion is not so different after all. Am I guilty of wanting substantive neutrality with respect to exemptions and government speech, and formal neutrality with respect to funding and private speech?

I think not. I am arguing for substantive neutrality in all four contexts, but substantive neutrality is sometimes achieved by special treatment for religion and sometimes by identical treatment. Recall that substantive neutrality is about incentives. The goal is to minimize government influence, to avoid distorting private religious choices and commitments. So look at the incentives that are created.

Restrictions on private religious speech discourage religion. They say that speakers can have access to the public forum (a desirable thing from the

170. 515 U.S. 819 (1995).
171. Laycock, *supra* note 26, at 1008 (text at notes 48-55).

perspective of most speakers) if they omit the religious content from their speech. A worship service cannot comply and will abandon the public forum, suffering a penalty for religious speech. But at the margins, speakers can adjust their message. Religious articles can be dropped from magazines; religious references can be dropped from political arguments or public appeals.

The University of Virginia unwittingly provided a clear example in *Rosenberger.*[172] In an effort to show that the Muslim students' publication was cultural and therefore eligible for funding, the University reported that the publication had previously published articles that were "specifically religious," that the Student Activities Committee had challenged this content when the magazine's funding came up for renewal, that the Muslim students had given "adequate reassurance on this point," and that they then "published a second and very different issue of *Al-Salam.*" The plaintiffs could not have imagined a clearer demonstration of how the power to fund or refuse funding was used to limit the content of student publications. Restricting religious speech skews the marketplace of ideas; in this example, secular viewpoints were amplified and religious viewpoints were restricted. Equal access is substantively neutral; censoring speech is not.

The same analysis applies to funding. If I am running a school, or a homeless shelter, or a child welfare agency, and the government says it will fund the social services if I completely segregate them from any church and exclude all religious references, that is a powerful incentive to do what the government asks. Once again government would skew the market; secular social service agencies would expand and religious agencies would contract. Government must be sure that it gets its secular service, which probably justifies nondiscrimination rules, but the neutral course is to fund whoever will provide the service and to not interfere with the religious environment in which some providers deliver the service.

With respect to self-interested exemptions, the analysis is the same as for private speech and funding. If religious objectors to paying taxes do not have to pay, there is an incentive to adopt the faith that gives rise to the objection. That is why I carved self-interested exemptions out of my general analysis of exemptions.

But with respect to most exemptions, exemptions minimize the incentive effects. Most religious behavior is meaningless or burdensome to nonbelievers. I do not want to have a driver's license without a picture; I would have a harder time cashing checks or proving my identity in other contexts. I do not want to refrain from work on the Sabbath; I am too far behind as it is. I do

172. See Respondent's Brief, 1995 Westlaw 16452 at n.3.

not want to eat peyote; I would almost certainly throw up. Most exemptions do very little to draw adherents to a faith. But criminal liability or loss of government benefits is a powerful incentive to abandon a faith. Exemptions — treating religion differently — are generally more neutral because they generally minimize government influence on religion.

With respect to government speech, neutrality requires treating religion differently. Certainly religion must be treated differently from the myriad of political issues on which government takes positions and tries to lead opinion. More fundamentally, in many contexts government silence is more neutral than attempts at even-handed speech. It is very hard to discuss religion in a way that is neutral and fair to the myriad of competing views. When government prays, it models a particular form of prayer. It puts its influence behind that form as opposed to all others, and behind prayer as opposed to no prayer at all. When government celebrates Christmas, it puts its influence behind a particular version of how to celebrate Christmas — usually a secularized version, sometimes a devout version, always a public version — but a particular version, whatever it chooses. Government influence on religion is generally minimized by government silence and a public forum that is wide open to the broad range of views about religion that compete in the private sector.

Michael McConnell has argued that when government is large, government silence on matters of religion is itself a distortion of public discourse and a departure from neutrality.[173] He has proposed a different measure of neutrality with respect to government speech:

> If the aspects of culture controlled by the government (public spaces, public institutions) exactly mirrored the culture as a whole, then the influence and effect of government involvement would be nil; the religious life of the people would be precisely the way it would be if the government were absent from the cultural sphere.[174]

This is logically perfect and practically disastrous. Government has no way to "exactly mirror[] the culture as a whole," or even to get in the ballpark. It has only the vaguest notion of how many Christians, Jews, Muslims, atheists, etc., are in the population, and no idea whatever of the distribution of views over how to celebrate Christmas, whether and how to take public note of Hanukkah, Passover, or Purim, or what are the means of salvation. In practice, Pro-

---

173. Michael W. McConnell, *Religious Freedom at a Crossroads*, 59 U. Chi. L. Rev. 115, 188-94 (1992).
174. *Id.* at 193.

fessor McConnell's approach would lead to predominant government expression of majoritarian religious views, diluted to appeal to the largest possible coalition, with occasional nods to influential minorities. In short, government statements on religion would be indistinguishable from those of a relatively tolerant government with an established church.

A far better way to make the public sphere mirror the culture is to open public forums to religious speech and to clearly provide that the responsibility for religious speech in those forums lies exclusively with the private sector. Religion is vibrant in the private sector; in such a regime, the public square would not remain naked for a single season. Those people who cared enough to say anything would say what they wanted, and we would get some sense of the distribution of views in the culture. Thus, with respect to government speech, I adhere to the view that the most nearly neutral course is for government to be quiet and let the private sector do it.

VII. Conclusion: A Personal Note

Almost twenty years ago, I circulated the manuscript of my first article on religious liberty, a comment on the Seventh Circuit's decision in *Catholic Bishop v. NLRB*.[175] The first footnote said that I was not a Catholic and had never been one. Professor (now Justice) Scalia, then my colleague, crossed out the footnote and wrote in the margins, "Never give the bastards any comfort."

We never discussed this marginal note, but I took "the bastards" to be anti-Catholic bigots, and I decided he was right, at least in part. He may have over-estimated the number of anti-Catholic bigots, but he had correctly inferred the reason for the footnote. The article showed familiarity with Catholic sources, it would be a reasonable inference from that familiarity that I might be Catholic, and I was embarrassed by the possibility that anyone might draw that inference about me. Especially in an academic environment, I did not want anyone to think that I held beliefs that seemed to me so untestable and implausible. I was not worried about tenure, or discrimination, or even that anyone would ever say anything to me. I was projecting my own inability to comprehend belief; I did not want anyone to think that I was gullible enough to be a Catholic. From Scalia's perspective, to disclaim Catholicism might give the bastards comfort because it implied these attitudes

---

175. Douglas Laycock, *Civil Rights and Civil Liberties,* 54 CHI.-KENT L. REV. 390, 415-35 (1977) (text at notes 146-265) (analyzing Catholic Bishop v. NLRB, 559 F.2d 1112 (7th Cir. 1977), *aff'd on other grounds,* 440 U.S. 490 (1979)).

and put them in print. The footnote implied that Catholicism is the sort of movement that requires a disclaimer or disassociation, in the same way a scholar might disclaim any sympathy with the Ku Klux Klan in an article defending the Klan's free speech rights.

More generally, I decided that my views on religion were and should be irrelevant to my views on religious liberty. The whole point of religious liberty, it seemed to me, was that people from across the whole range of views about religion agree to respect the religious liberty of everyone else across the whole range of views about religion. Religious liberty only or principally for people of one's own views would not be religious liberty at all; that was the Puritan mistake in seventeenth-century Massachusetts.

So I took out the footnote, and I have since worked in this field without referring to my own views about religion. I have never concealed anything, but only very rarely have I volunteered anything. I have been disappointed at the widespread tendency to assume that I must share the religious views of whatever client I am representing at the moment. People have explicitly assumed over the years that I must be Catholic, Jewish, Presbyterian, or evangelical; I do not know what people thought about the Christian Scientists, the Hare Krishnas, and the Santeria. The underlying assumption must be that I am most likely to defend religious liberty for my own faith group, or at least for some group in strategic or tactical alliance with my own faith group. This is the Puritan mistake.

I break silence now, after all these years, because the Puritan mistake has taken on new significance as I come to better understand the new axes of religious conflict. I have gradually come to realize that one of the more serious threats to religious liberty is from people who think very much like me about religion, and who, because their commitment to winning their religious disputes exceeds their commitment to religious liberty, want to subordinate or marginalize religious views. Consequently, I now see a new cost to letting people make false assumptions about my religious beliefs — not that I might be embarrassed, but that my arguments about liberty might be discounted as mere special pleading on behalf of my presumed religious commitments. I have some concern that once I go public, believers will discount my arguments instead. That too would be the Puritan mistake, and I hope I have enough accumulated credibility with that side that the risk is small. So here goes. Whatever mistakes I may have made, I at least have not made the Puritan mistake.

I am agnostic about matters of religion. None of the claims of the world's religions seem to me either plausible or falsifiable. A Creator God who set the universe in motion is hard to imagine, but so are all the other explanations for the origins of the universe. Assuming there might be such a God, I find all claims about the details of His/Her nature and intentions to be wildly implausible. No God has given me the slightest hint of His/Her existence; if there is a God Who wants me to believe in Him/Her, He/She should quit being so secretive. I am inclined to think that humans create God in their own images — that knowing nothing whatever of God, most people impute to God those traits they think an attractive God should have.

All my early sympathies were with the nonbelieving minority. As a high school sophomore, flush with adolescent excitement from reading Thomas Paine,[176] I walked out of the school Christmas assembly in constitutional protest. The principal was not interested in my explanation of the Establishment Clause, and I felt victimized.

As a law student, I was outraged at *Walz v. Tax Commission*.[177] I entered the field of religious liberty enthusiastic about the Establishment Clause and eager to defend the rights of nonbelievers. But from the very beginning, I at least recognized the central premise that religious liberty must protect people of all views about religion. And as it turned out, I have had many more occasions to defend the rights of believers than of nonbelievers. Lawyers for theists with viable claims call me continuously; only once in twenty years have I gotten a call from a lawyer for an atheist with a viable claim. I have had occasion to challenge establishments of religion[178] and to challenge broad arguments for why some kinds of establishments should be permitted.[179] But the dominant forces of regulation are more at odds with traditional believers than with nonbelievers; my experience has been that believers' rights are violated more often than nonbelievers' rights. And over the years, I have come to realize that some of my early conceptions of the Establishment Clause reflected special pleading for my own religious views rather than neutrality toward all religious views. I now think that *Walz* was right and that the mistake came in *Jimmy Swaggart Ministries v. Board of Equalization*.[180]

176. THOMAS PAINE, THE AGE OF REASON (1793).

177. 397 U.S. 664 (1970) (rejecting an Establishment Clause challenge to exempting church property from taxation).

178. *See* Brief of National Council of Churches of Christ in the U.S.A. et al., as Amici Curiae in Support of Respondents, Board of Educ. v. Grumet, 512 U.S. 687 (1994) (arguing that Establishment Clause precludes deliberate creation of public school district with population all of the same religion); Brief Amici Curiae of the American Jewish Congress et al., Lee v. Weisman, 505 U.S. 577 (1992) (arguing that Establishment Clause precludes prayer as part of official program at public school graduation).

179. *See* Laycock, *supra* note 23 (arguing against nonpreferential aid to religion); Laycock, *supra* note 33 (arguing against noncoercive aid to religion).

180. 493 U.S. 378 (1990) (holding that application of general sales and use tax to distri-

My epistemological views are largely those of Professor Sherry.[181] In my own decision making, I am a rationalist, a reasoner, an empiricist. I got extreme scores on the "Thinker" variable when I once had to take the Myers-Briggs Personality Inventory. Personal feelings and claims of personal revelation are important facts about human beings, never safely ignored, but they are not in my view a method of making judgments. In terms of the fundamental religious split in the culture, I am firmly on Professor Sherry's side.

But hostility to theistic religion need not follow from this worldview. I went through my period of hostility to theistic religion, went through my period of stick figure caricatures of believers, and I learned better. I learned that highly intelligent and accomplished people are devout believers — indeed, that they believe that they have personally experienced the presence of God. I learned that believers reason just as well as nonbelievers on average, and that most believers do not see the conflict between faith and reason that Professor Sherry posits. I learned that religious faith is a powerful force for good in the lives of many believers. I learned that the great religious traditions often embody accumulated wisdom, whatever its sources and whatever the accumulated baggage of positions that seem to me mistaken.

I believed as a sophomore, and I believe now, that organized religion has done great harm in the world. But in the interim I have attended to the rather obvious fact that this does not distinguish organized religion from any other human institution. Reason is prone to its own set of excesses; reasoners often carry out ideas to the limits of their logic, without regard to competing values or common sense or accumulated wisdom. Stephen Jay Gould, as secular a reasoner as one could wish for, often writes about the mistakes of scientists who reason from a mistaken premise or a cultural prejudice, or who reason beyond the limits of data or common sense.[182] Paul Johnson, a less sympa-

---

bution of religious literature is not a cognizable burden on the free exercise of religion). For commentary, see Laycock, *supra* note 27, at 4-7, 23-28, 39-41 (text at notes 17-31, 99-118, 156-58).

181. See Sherry, *supra* note 3; Sherry, *supra* note 58.

182. *See, e.g.,* Stephen Jay Gould, Bully for Brontosaurus 215, 225 (1991). Reviewing the work of a naturalist who convinced himself that flamingos are pink so they will be camouflaged when seen against the sunset, Gould wrote:

> Thayer's pathway from insight to ridicule followed a distressingly common route among intellectuals. . . . Little by little, plausibly at first, but grading slowly to red wings in the sunset . . . Thayer progressively invaded the categories of mimicry and revealing coloration to gain, or so he thought, more cases for concealment. . . .
>
> The *idée fixe* is a common intellectual fault of all professions. . . . I have often written about scientists as single-mindedly committed to absurd unities and false

thetic witness, has blamed the influence of reasoning intellectuals for many of the policy disasters of modern history.[183] He exaggerates; his book is an example of the excessive pursuit of a single idea that he criticizes in others. But he supplies ample illustrations of my point: like organized religion, secular reasoning has also done great harm in the world. I am a direct intellectual descendant of the Enlightenment, comfortable with Enlightenment methodologies and with no other. But I recognize that among the Enlightenment's first fruits were the Terror, the persecution of the Catholic Church in France, and the Napoleonic Wars.

The preceding two paragraphs are a statement of tolerance and respect for beliefs that I cannot begin to share. But this renewed respect for religion is not the source of my commitment to religious liberty. Both chronology and causation are clear: the source of my respect for religion was frequent contact with sophisticated believers, and one of the sources of those contacts was my work on behalf of religious liberty.

It probably is the case that my agnostic view of religion predisposes me to an agnostic explanation for religious liberty. But as I have written before, this equation of different levels or kinds of agnosticism is "misleading in an important way."[184]

> An agnostic has no opinion on whether God exists, and neither should the government. But an agnostic also believes that humans are incapable of knowing whether God exists. If the government believed that, it would prefer agnostics over theists and atheists. Agnostics have no opinion for epistemological reasons; the government must have no opinion for constitutional reasons. The government must have no opinion because it is not the government's role to have an opinion.[185]

Excluding the government from religious opinions entails interpreting the Constitution in a way that is free of religious opinions. And this commitment to a government free of religious opinions should be part of religious liberty whatever one's views about religion. To explain religious liberty on either theistic or anti-theistic grounds is to make a diluted form of the Puritan mistake. It is to say that religious liberty is principally for the benefit of people on

---

simplifications as Thayer was devoted to the exclusivity of concealing coloration in nature. Some are charming and a bit dotty. . . . Others are devious and more than a bit dangerous. . . .

183. PAUL JOHNSON, INTELLECTUALS (1988).
184. Laycock, *supra* note 117, at 7 (text at notes 32-33).
185. *Id.* at 7-8 (text at notes 32-33).

only one side of a great dividing line on the religious spectrum. But in my view of religious liberty, the goal is to enable people on both sides of such divides to live together in peace and equality and without surrender of religious autonomy.

Free Exercise Clause and Establishment Clause: General Theories

in Religion and American Law: An Encyclopedia 516
(Paul Finkelman, ed., 2000)

This encyclopedia entry succinctly summarizes the principal competing theories about the meaning of the Religion Clauses of the Constitution in their principal applications. It also contains a substantial bibliography.

*　　　*　　　*

Judges, scholars, and religious and political movements have offered many competing interpretations of the Religion Clauses. These interpretations cannot be neatly distinguished and categorized. Different theories overlap or combine similar elements in different combinations; some people would apply different theories in different contexts. Some theories stated in general terms actually grew out of particular controversies and could not plausibly be applied generally. Still, it is possible to identify several principal approaches, each with quite different implications.

I. Free Exercise of Religion

A. Absolute Protection of Religious Belief.

Almost everyone agrees that the Free Exercise Clause guarantees the right to believe any religion whatever. But even this bedrock principle has been violated on occasion. In *Davis v. Beason* (1890), the Supreme Court upheld a test oath that excluded Mormons from voting in federal territories. The decision has never been formally repudiated, but it was implicitly overruled in *Torcaso v. Watkins* (1961), which struck down a Maryland requirement that holders of public office declare their belief in God.

B. Protection of Religious Speech.

There is similar consensus about the right to teach almost any religion one chooses, although some scholars would insist that this right is guaranteed only by the Free Speech Clause. The better view would seem to be that it is guaranteed by both the Free Speech and Free Exercise Clauses, and that it is the Free Exercise Clause that tells us that religious speech is of special constitutional value and entitled to the highest level of constitutional protection, generally analogous to the protection for political speech. Important affirmations of the sweeping scope of freedom of speech in religious contexts include *United States v. Ballard* (1944) and *West Virginia State Board of Education v. Barnette* (1943).

Religious speech is not absolutely protected. It is subject to content-neutral time, place, and manner regulations; and government presumably may punish deliberate incitement to inflict immediate and serious harm, although the Supreme Court has never had occasion to say so in the context of religious speech. Some contend that the Establishment Clause requires that religious speech be excluded from some public properties or from the political process. This view, which has no support in the Supreme Court's cases, is considered below.

C. Protection of Religiously Motivated Conduct.

The principal controversy over free exercise relates to religious conduct, including worship services and ritual acts, refusal to comply with law because of religious objections, and the operation and management of religious institutions. The central question is whether religious institutions or believers should ever be exempted from generally applicable laws that interfere with the exercise of their religion.

Four major solutions to these issues have been proposed: (1) exemptions are forbidden, (2) exemptions are permitted but not required, (3) exemptions are required for matters of conscience, and (4) exemptions are required for matters of conscience and also for matters of religious autonomy.

1. Exemptions Are Forbidden (Mandatory Formal Neutrality).

The view that exemptions are forbidden is associated with formal neutrality interpretations of the Religion Clauses. It is helpful to call this theory "mandatory formal neutrality" (although that term is not in common use), to distinguish it from the variation to be discussed next. Mandatory formal neutrality theorists read the two Religion Clauses together to mean that religion should not be singled out for discriminatory benefits or burdens. It follows that religious conduct is fully subject to all generally applicable regulatory laws and criminal prohibitions, and that religious conduct must be treated the same as analogous secular conduct.

Thus, a law forbidding the Catholic Mass or Jewish Seder would violate the Free Exercise Clause, and a law forbidding the use of wine at the Mass or Seder would violate the Free Exercise Clause. But a law forbidding the consumption of wine anywhere within a jurisdiction may and must be applied to wine at the Mass or Seder, and a law against serving wine to minors may and must be applied to First Communion or to children attending the Mass or Seder. A law permitting children to consume wine at the Mass or Seder would violate the Establishment Clause unless the state permitted children to consume equivalent amounts of wine in secular contexts. Exemptions for religiously motivated conduct are said to be a preference for religion over nonreligion.

The principal academic defender of mandatory formal neutrality was the late Philip Kurland. In *Corporation of the Presiding Bishop v. Amos* (1987), the Court unanimously rejected Kurland's claim that *regulatory* exemptions establish religion. But the Court appeared to adopt Kurland's claim with respect to *tax* exemptions in *Texas Monthly, Inc. v. Bullock* (1989). A divided set of opinions with no majority may be read to hold that religious institutions and activities cannot be singled out for tax exemption, although they can be included in broader tax-exempt categories, such as not-for-profit organizations, or religious, charitable, and educational organizations.

2. Exemptions Are Permitted but Not Required (Permissive Formal Neutrality).

Others argue that formal neutrality satisfies the Constitution but is not required by the Constitution. That is, generally applicable laws may be applied to religious practices, and the Free Exercise Clause does not require exemptions, but legislatures may exempt religious practices if they choose. On this view, the Constitution does not protect wine at the Mass, Seder, or First Communion, but legislatures may exempt sacramental wine from liquor laws, or prosecutors may simply look the other way and allow a de facto exemption. This view may be labeled "permissive formal neutrality" (although again, that phrase is not in common use).

This understanding of religious liberty predates the Constitution; it appears prominently in John Locke's *Letter Concerning Toleration* (1689). Important academic defenders today include Mark Tushnet and William Marshall. The Supreme Court adopted permissive formal neutrality as its interpretation of the Free Exercise Clause in *Employment Division v. Smith* (1990). Permissive formal neutrality arguably explains many of the Court's decisions prior to 1963; it plainly was not the Court's interpretation from 1963 to 1990.

It is an important corollary of formal neutrality that religious conduct cannot be regulated when similar secular conduct is not, and religious conduct of one faith cannot be regulated when the similar conduct of another faith is not. The leading application of this principle in the Supreme Court is *Church of the Lukumi Babalu Aye, Inc. v. City of Hialeah* (1993), holding that a city could not ban religious sacrifice of animals while permitting secular killings of animals for food, sport, and human convenience. The value of this protection for religious minorities depends on the willingness of courts to investigate government's claims that the regulated and unregulated conduct differ in some way other than religion.

3. Exemptions Are Required for Matters of Conscience.

A third view is that religious institutions and believers are presumptively exempt from laws that burden or prohibit compliance with conscientiously held tenets of their faith. Almost no one claims that this right to exemptions is absolute; nearly everyone concedes that government may burden or prohibit religious observances for sufficiently important reasons.

a. Positivist Arguments. The positivist argument for exemptions proceeds straightforwardly from the Free Exercise Clause. The Constitution says that there shall be no law "prohibiting the free exercise" of religion. If consumption of wine at the Mass or Seder or First Communion is the exercise of religion, the state cannot prohibit it, even if the state has prohibited consumption of wine in other contexts. Supporters of exemptions argue that the Free Exercise Clause on its face creates a substantive right to practice one's religion, and not merely to believe in it or be protected from discrimination because of it. From this perspective, the defect of the formal neutrality interpretations of free exercise is that they eliminate this substantive right to exercise religion, leaving a mere equality right not to be discriminated against. In a pervasively regulated society, formal equality means that religion too can be pervasively regulated, and pervasively regulated religion is not the free exercise of religion.

Supporters of formal neutrality respond that a law is not a law prohibiting the free exercise of religion unless it prohibits religious exercise deliberately, or perhaps principally, or perhaps discriminatorily. A law that also does other things, and that incidentally prohibits the exercise of religion in some of its applications, is not in their view a law prohibiting the free exercise of religion.

b. Religious Arguments. The theoretical arguments for the right to exemptions are varied. The principal religious argument, most prominently attributable to James Madison, is that one's duties to God are superior to one's duties to the civil society. It follows, under American theories of government, that when the people form a government and consent to be governed, they cannot delegate to government any power to regulate their duties to God.

c. Secular Variations. A secular version of this argument holds that the Constitution takes no view on whether humans owe duties to God or even on whether God exists. But many Americans believe they owe prior duties to God, and so in the Free Exercise Clause they reserved the right to perform those perceived duties. More generally, the secular argument for exemptions holds that exemptions are inherent in the concept of religious liberty. Religion includes religious conduct, and so religious liberty includes liberty for religious conduct. Any attempt to punish religious conduct will lead to religious conflict and persecution as surely as attempts to punish religious belief or teaching.

d. Substantive Neutrality. Some supporters of exemptions agree with their opponents that the two Religion Clauses together require government to be neutral toward religion. But supporters of exemptions understand neutrality very differently; they say the Constitution requires substantive neutrality rather than formal neutrality.

Substantive neutrality consists of neither encouraging nor discouraging religious belief or practice. If government minimizes the extent to which it either encourages or discourages religion, government neutrality will be maximized, government influence on religion will be minimized, and religious liberty will be maximized for both believers and non-believers. The goal of minimizing both encouragement and discouragement requires that any challenged government policy be compared to the available alternatives. A policy may seem to benefit or encourage religion when considered in isolation, but the alternative policy may burden or discourage religion. The Constitution requires the alternative that departs least from the hypothetical baseline of neither encouraging nor discouraging religion.

Because government encourages and discourages many types of secular activities, treating religion like analogous secular activities will rarely be substantively neutral. Thus, formal neutrality and substantive neutrality have very different implications.

Substantive neutrality generally requires exemptions for religiously motivated conduct. If the state threatens to send people to jail for consuming wine at a Mass or Seder, that threat of punishment severely discourages the exercise of religion. But permitting religious use of wine in a dry district would rarely encourage anyone to become Catholic or Jewish, or even to practice their Catholic or Jewish rituals more faithfully. The small quantities of wine consumed in religious services — set in the lengthy ritual surrounding their consumption — would be little inducement to one attracted by the wine but not by religion.

When religious obligation aligns with secular self-interest, as in religious objections to military service or to taxation for military spending, the substantive neutrality rationale for exemptions fails. Requiring conscientious objectors to serve in the military or pay taxes, on pain of punishment if they refuse, severely discourages their religious exercise. But exempting religious objectors from such burdens encourages people to accept the religious beliefs that would make them eligible for the exemption. It remains the case that a law requiring religious objectors to violate their conscience with respect to military service or taxes prohibits them from freely exercising their religion, but government may have compelling reasons not to exempt such self-interested behavior. Congress has sometimes dealt with dilemmas of this sort by enacting alternative service requirements that attempt to impose some equivalent burden on conscientious objectors.

Opponents of substantive neutrality deny that it is neutral even in the routine cases where religious observance does not align with self-interest. Opponents do not claim that exemptions for religious behavior often encourage religious behavior; instead, they usually deny the relevance of that standard. They view exemptions from generally applicable laws as special treatment that the Constitution does not require. Some of them view exemptions as a symbolic endorsement of religious believers and a denigration of the motives of those who would engage in analogous conduct for secular reasons.

e. Accommodation. Many supporters of a right to exemptions do not subscribe to substantive neutrality, principally because of its implications for the Establishment Clause, described below. These supporters of exemptions make one or more of the other arguments described above — that duties to

God are superior to duties to the state, or that religious liberty requires exemptions because the exercise of religion includes conduct. Exemptions from regulation are sometimes described as "accommodations" of religion, a vague phrase that has been used to describe everything from regulatory exemptions to school prayer. Michael McConnell has written the principal scholarly attempt to give content to the concept of accommodation.

f. Compelling Government Interests. Supporters of exemptions concede that the right to exemptions can be overridden where the need is great enough. The usual formulation is that government may limit or burden the exercise of religion if the limit or burden serves a compelling interest by the least restrictive means. But there is little consensus on what constitutes a compelling interest. Civil libertarians tend to argue that a compelling interest must be an interest of extraordinary importance, such as protecting identifiable individuals from tangible and significant harm, or preventing the wholesale evasion of an important government program. They note that the constitutional text states an absolute right, and that the compelling interest exception is indeed an exception, implied by necessity. Lawyers for government agencies tend to argue that most laws serve compelling interests and that every incremental violation defeats that interest. The government lawyers' understanding of compelling interest tends to eliminate the right to exemptions. That is, deference to government agencies on the issue of compelling interest tends to erode substantive neutrality back to the level of formal neutrality. The Supreme Court cases are mixed; neither courts nor scholars have developed any consistent and widely accepted understanding of compelling government interest.

g. Supporters of Exemptions. Supporters of a right to exemptions for matters of conscience include virtually the entire religious leadership in the United States, the major civil liberties organizations, an apparent majority of constitutional law scholars, and the Congress of the United States. In 1993 Congress enacted a statutory right to religious exemptions from all state and federal law, subject to the compelling interest test, in the Religious Freedom Restoration Act. Douglas Laycock and Michael McConnell have written the most extensive defenses of a right to exemptions. However, the Supreme Court invalidated RFRA as applied to state and local governments in *City of Boerne v. Flores* (1997), holding that it was outside the scope of Congress's enumerated powers. Congressional leaders have indicated their desire to pass more limited legislation in response.

4. Exemptions Are Required for Matters of Conscience and Also for Matters of Religious Autonomy.

Those who support a right to exemptions are divided over the scope of the right. A few would confine exemptions to conduct that is religiously mandated. This approach has led at least one federal court, in *Brandon v. Board of Education* (2d Cir. 1980), to distinguish between mandatory prayers and voluntary prayers. A more common approach is to protect conduct that is motivated by a doctrinal tenet of the claimant's religion, without inquiring whether the conduct is mandated or merely encouraged.

Some supporters of exemptions believe that religious institutions should be exempt from regulation, subject to the compelling interest test, without regard to whether the conduct at issue flows from a specific doctrinal tenet. The claim is that religious liberty protects the autonomy of religious institutions. To protect only conformity to specific doctrinal tenets is to reduce religion to a set of rules that must be obeyed — and to deny protection to all other varieties of religious experience.

Supporters of religious autonomy would presumptively exempt religious organizations from regulation of their internal affairs, such as regulation of church labor relations. Regulation of internal affairs can insert the state into the development of religious ideas and the resolution of religious disputes. Most supporters of church autonomy would also presumptively exempt religious organizations from regulation that imposes physical limits or economic burdens, such as zoning or taxation. Such regulation can limit the level of religious activity, divert resources from missions chosen by the church to missions chosen by the state, and, occasionally, may drive religious organizations out of existence. Claims to religious autonomy follow from substantive neutrality; regulation that burdens or interferes with religion is a way of discouraging religion. Scholars who have argued extensively for religious autonomy include Carl Esbeck and Douglas Laycock.

Scholars who have argued against exemptions for religious autonomy are generally those who have argued against exemptions for conscience as well; Mark Tushnet, and William Marshall and Douglas C. Blomgren, are principal examples. Ira Lupu supports exemptions for individual claims of conscience, but opposes any exemption for religious institutions, whether for conscience or autonomy.

The Supreme Court has protected religious autonomy in certain contexts where the religious significance is especially apparent, such as the employment of ministers and parochial-school teachers and in the resolution of disputes over religious doctrine. In other contexts the Court has generally failed to protect religious autonomy, even during the period when it was requiring exemptions for matters of conscience. The leading case is *Jimmy Swaggart Ministries v. Board of Equalization* (1990), upholding the application of a sales tax to the dissemination of religious messages, and commenting that economic burdens on churches have no constitutional significance. The comment seems to have been based on an intuitive and largely unexamined understanding of religion.

The Religious Freedom Restoration Act does not specify whether it reaches religious autonomy claims. But senators and representatives repeatedly used zoning cases as one example of the problems that made the Act necessary, and the Act can affect these cases only if it protects against economic and regulatory burdens unrelated to religious doctrine. In *Corporation of the Presiding Bishop v. Amos* (1987), the Supreme Court upheld statutory exemptions that extended to matters of religious autonomy.

II. Establishment of Religion

It is more difficult to distinguish competing theories of the Establishment Clause and to array them on a single continuum. There are more controversial issues, more axes of disagreement, and fewer sharp divisions. Some of the theories summarized below overlap or differ in degree rather than in kind; some commentators subscribe to more than one of them.

A. Institutional Separation.

Almost everyone agrees that the Establishment Clause requires at least institutional separation. That is, the institutions of the state should be separate from the institutions of the various religions, and neither set of institutions should control the other nor exercise the authority of the other. Religious organizations as such should have no formal role in the selection of political leaders, although they may — like any other association of citizens — attempt to persuade voters and policymakers. Similarly, government should have no role in the selection of religious leaders. No church can invoke the coercive power of the state to enforce compliance with religious norms, and the state cannot invoke the moral or theological authority of a church to demand compliance with government policy.

But institutional separation would not necessarily preclude voluntary cooperation between church and state. It would not preclude government from encouraging religious belief or providing financial support to projects with religious sponsorship or management, and it would not preclude religious organizations from voluntarily supporting or endorsing government policies. Steven Smith has published the leading academic statement of the view that the Establishment Clause requires merely institutional separation; this is also the position of some conservative Christian denominations.

B. Voluntarism.

A widely accepted corollary of the Religion Clauses is that religious activity should be voluntary. Few offer voluntarism as a general theory of the Religion Clauses, but nearly all accept voluntarism as consistent with their preferred theory or occasionally as limiting their preferred theory. Voluntarism is principally a function of the right to freely exercise any religion one chooses. But voluntarism is also a policy of the Establishment Clause; religious institutions are to be supported voluntarily, and not through government taxation, coerced contributions, or coerced participation. There is consensus that purely religious institutions — the church itself — should be supported voluntarily. There is sharp disagreement about financial support of religious institutions that also serve secular functions, and most especially about church-affiliated elementary and secondary schools.

C. Noncoercion.

"Noncoercion" is almost a synonym for "voluntarism," but in practice the two terms have been used in different ways. Many agree that voluntarism is one policy of the Religion Clauses, but insist that it is not the only policy. Noncoercion theory might be understood as arguing that voluntarism is the only policy; the phrase has been associated with the claim that there can be no violation of the Religion Clauses without coercion. Noncoercionists believe that government may give symbolic, rhetorical, or political support to religion in general, or to preferred religions in particular, so long as it does not coerce anyone. Noncoercion theory emerged to political prominence in response to *Lynch v. Donnelly* (1984), in which the Court narrowly upheld a municipally sponsored Nativity scene, and it has been focused on the narrow set of issues arising out of government-sponsored prayer and religious displays.

Noncoercion has sometimes been offered as though it were a complete theory of the Establishment Clause, but it is doubtful that its proponents so intend it. Collection of taxes is coercive, so a rule of no coercion would seem to preclude all forms of government expenditures that benefit religious institutions. It seems likely that most noncoercion theorists subscribe to some other theory to justify some of these expenditures.

The principal academic statement of noncoercion theory is by Michael Paulsen. The Bush Administration unsuccessfully urged the Supreme Court to adopt noncoercion theory in *Lee v. Weisman* (1992). The principal judicial statement is Justice Kennedy's dissent in *County of Allegheny v. American Civil Liberties Union* (1989). Justice Kennedy would add a requirement that government not proselytize, and he apparently assumes a background requirement of institutional separation.

D. The Endorsement Test.

Justice O'Connor has repeatedly offered the endorsement test as a general theory for all Establishment Clause cases; the Supreme Court has applied it principally in cases of government prayer or government religious displays. Taken literally, the endorsement test would seem to state a clear principle that is the direct opposite of the noncoercion theory. The endorsement test says that government should be neutral, taking no position for or against religion; the noncoercion theory responds that government may endorse religion so long as it does not coerce anyone to believe or participate.

But the endorsement test lacks this clarity in practice. Justice O'Connor proposed the test in her concurring opinion in *Lynch,* arguing that a municipal Nativity scene does not endorse Christianity. This made it impossible from the beginning to predict when she would find an endorsement, even in a case where the government was deliberately communicating.

The endorsement test is not even potentially clear in other contexts. In considering an exemption for religiously motivated conduct, or government-funded math books for a religious school, or any other law or program challenged as an establishment of religion, Justice O'Connor has asked whether the program implicitly endorses religion. Endorsement has been inferred or not inferred from functional characteristics of the challenged law, from legislative history, or from both. Except in the rare case where the legislature has said it is enacting the bill because it will help a good religion, results have turned on specification of the functional characteristics from which Justice O'Connor would infer endorsement. In practice, lawyers and commentators from many schools of thought tend to find implied endorsements whenever they object to a government program on the basis of their own preferred theory of the Establishment Clause. Justice O'Connor and the Court would surely do better to drop talk of endorsement outside the context of religious displays and observances, and state a test directly in terms of the underlying functional characteristics. There was some suggestion in her concurring opinion in *Board of Education of Kiryas Joel School District v. Grumet* (1994) that she had come to view the endorsement test as limited to, or at least principally concerned with, "cases involving government speech on religious topics."

Leading academic commentators on the endorsement test are William Marshall, who attempted to give it meaningful content while recognizing its subjectivity, and Steven Smith, who rejected it as incoherent.

E. Nonpreferentialism.

Nonpreferentialism is the view that government may support religion so long as it does not prefer one religion over others, that is, so long as it supports all religions equally. During the debates on disestablishment in the revolutionary and early national periods, defenders of the old establishments unsuccessfully offered various compromises under which government would provide tax support for all churches in proportion to their support among the taxpayers. In current terminology, these proposals were nonpreferential.

Nonpreferentialism reemerged in modern times in response to the Supreme Court's decisions in *Everson v. Board of Education* (1947), announcing in unanimous dictum that government could not aid religion financially, and *Illinois ex rel. McCollum v. Board of Education* (1948), striking down a public school program that set aside time for religious instruction by the various denominations. Nonpreferentialism has been a persistent theme in criticisms of the Court ever since; the leading academic statement of nonpreferentialism is by Robert Cord.

Nonpreferentialism is a straightforward theory with respect to financial aid: Government can give money to any religious school or to any other religious program or institution, so long as it applies the same nondiscriminatory funding formula to similar programs and institutions of all faiths. Nonpreferentialism also made sense in the context of *McCollum;* any denomination could offer a class on school premises during the period set aside for religious instruction.

But nonpreferentialism also figured prominently in the argument against the Supreme Court's school prayer decisions, where the theory seems incoherent. It is impossible to pray in a form that is equally appropriate for all faiths; in this context, nonpreferentialists seem to support forms of prayer that are generically Protestant, or vaguely Judeo-Christian and without references to Christ.

Taken literally, nonpreferentialism would permit government to fund the church itself, including cathedrals, synagogues, mosques, and temples; the salaries of priests, ministers, rabbis, imams, and santeros; and publication of Bibles, Talmuds, Korans, and other holy books, so long as all such programs were nonpreferential. Similarly, nonpreferentialism would permit a law requiring every person to attend religious services in the faith of his or her choice. It is doubtful that any nonpreferentialist actually supports such laws. Nonpreferentialists may believe that such laws would be constitutional but unwise. Or, nonpreferentialism may be an incomplete theory that assumes some background principles, such as institutional separation or noncoercion.

F. Formal Neutrality.

Neutrality theories differ from nonpreferentialism in one essential respect: Neutrality theories require government to be neutral as between religion and nonreligion; nonpreferentialism requires government to be neutral among religions, although it can act on the view that religion generally is a good thing.

Formal neutrality holds that government may not use religion as a basis for classification, either to confer a benefit or impose a burden. In free exercise cases, that has the consequence that religion may not be, or at least need not be, exempted from generally applicable laws. In establishment cases, formal neutrality has the consequence that religion may participate in the full range of government-funded programs.

The principal policy consequence of adopting formal neutrality would be that government aid to religious schools would become constitutionally unproblematic. Government could aid public education only and private education not at all, or government could aid all education, public and private, religious and secular. The only clearly unconstitutional alternatives would be to aid secular private education without aiding religious private education, or vice versa. Philip Kurland was the principal supporter of formal neutrality. Most other supporters of financial aid to religious schools have invoked nonpreferentialism or substantive neutrality rather than formal neutrality, presumably because they do not want to endorse formal neutrality's prohibition on religious exemptions from regulation and taxation.

G. Substantive Neutrality.

Substantive neutrality holds that government should neither encourage nor discourage religious belief or practice. Thus, most supporters of substantive neutrality believe that government should not be allowed to engage in speech that is either religious or overtly anti-religious; government should not sponsor prayers, or Nativity scenes, or attacks on religious belief. But religious speech by private speakers should be fully protected on public property and in public debates; student prayer groups can meet on campuses without school sponsorship, and private groups can put up Nativity scenes in public forums. Difficult cases for this theory sometimes arise when government speaks on a range of topics such that religion falls naturally within the range, or when government subsidizes private speech with cash, or when government creates a forum with limited capacity and then picks and chooses among potential private speakers. Such arrangements blur the line between government and private speech; sometimes silence about religion may be less neutral than including competing religious views.

Supporters of substantive neutrality generally believe that individual citizens may participate in all government programs and receive all government benefits to which they are entitled, without limiting their religious or anti-religious speech or conduct. Most supporters of substantive neutrality believe that government may disburse money to or through religious institutions that perform secular functions and are not principally involved in the transmission of faith, such as hospitals and social service agencies.

This consensus breaks down with respect to schools. Some supporters of substantive neutrality believe that the same principle applies to schools, and that government may fund religious schools to the extent that these schools provide education in secular subjects. Parents have a constitutionally protected choice between secular schools and religious schools; some believe that it is a classic unconstitutional condition for government to finance one of these choices and refuse to finance the alternative. The principal exploration of this argument is by Michael McConnell, who compares the debate over funding religious schools with the debate over funding abortions.

Others believe that the support of schools is a special case, where substantive neutrality conflicts with principles of institutional separation and voluntarism, or where instruction in religious and secular subjects is so commingled that it is meaningless to speak of substantively neutral financial support. Substantive neutrality theorists who believe that schools are a special case are divided. Some believe that religious schools should get no government money; some are searching for a line that will permit nondiscriminatory use at religious schools of funds appropriated for special purposes distinct from the general support of education, such as aid to the disabled, without swallowing the general rule that government should not finance religious institutions.

The National Council of Churches, the Baptist Joint Committee on Public Affairs, and the Presbyterian Church (U.S.A.) are major participants in church-state debates whose positions are generally consistent with substantive neutrality but who oppose government financial support for religious schools. Leading academic defenses of substantive neutrality have been written by Douglas Laycock and by Michael McConnell and Richard Posner.

H. Strict Separation.

"Strict separation" is a vague phrase that connotes a vigorous commitment to separation of church and state that is not confined to institutional separation. In contrast to neutrality theories, the defining characteristic of strict separationists may be a willingness to discriminate against religion if necessary to avoid government aid and to achieve complete separation.

Thus, strict separationists generally oppose any use of public funds to support programs sponsored or managed by religious institutions. They especially oppose any use of public funds to directly or indirectly support religiously affiliated elementary or secondary schools, even if the money is earmarked for a part of the program that would be secular if considered in isolation. For example, strict separationists have generally opposed programs for supplying math books and other secular equipment or supplies to religious schools. They generally opposed allowing disabled students to use state educational assistance in religious schools.

Strict separationists also tend to believe that some restrictions on private religious speech are necessary to preserve separation. Thus, many strict separationists oppose any organized meeting for religious purposes on the premises of any public school or university, even if the meeting is student-initiated and not sponsored by the school. Many strict separationists oppose privately-sponsored Nativity scenes or menorahs on public premises, even in a public forum open to wide range of secular speech. Some strict separationists believe that religious speech should be excluded from debates on public policy questions, or alternatively, that religious speech is inappropriate in such debates and that good religious citizens will limit their own speech and speak only in secular terms.

Strict separation is most prominently associated with the secular civil liberties organizations, such as the American Civil Liberties Union, People for the American Way, and Americans United for Separation of Church and State, and the major reform and conservative Jewish organizations, such as the American Jewish Congress, the American Jewish Committee, and the Anti-Defamation League. But none of these organizations goes so far as to claim that religious speech is legally barred from public policy debates. An academic who has attempted to clearly distinguish strict separation from substantive neutrality is Ira Lupu.

Most supporters of substantive neutrality share the strict separationist belief that government should not sponsor or subsidize religion, and some supporters of substantive neutrality are as stringent as the strictest separationist in their opposition to government-sponsored prayer and religious displays. But supporters of substantive neutrality understand the no-aid principle in light of the equal and opposite principle that government should not burden religion. Consequently, they find mere neutrality in many programs where strict separationists find aid.

I. No Aid or Preference to Religion.

Some who call themselves strict separationists oppose regulatory exemptions for religiously motivated conduct, on the ground that exemptions are a form of aid or preference to religion. "Separation" seems an especially inapt label for this view, because government regulation of religion involves more church-state contact, and hence less separation, than exempting religion. The dominant principle here is not separation, but something else — sometimes formal neutrality, sometimes a belief that no government decision should give any benefit to religion. Steven Gey has stated the case against exemptions in the rhetoric of strict separation. None of the major organizations associated with strict separation interpret strict separation to preclude exemptions for religious conduct.

J. The Lemon Test.

The Supreme Court's most general explanation of the Establishment Clause is the three-part test of *Lemon v. Kurtzman* (1971): "First, the statute must have a secular legislative purpose; second, its principal or primary effect must be one that neither advances nor inhibits religion; finally, the statute must not foster an excessive government entanglement with religion."

The first two parts of this test are derived from an attempt to explain neutrality in a school prayer case, *School District of Abington Township v. Schempp* (1963). The facts of *Schempp* did not require the Court to distinguish formal neutrality from substantive neutrality, and inadvertent linguistic substitutions shifted the emphasis away from any form of neutrality. Thus, the first part of the *Lemon* test has shifted from asking whether the legislative purpose was neutral to asking whether the legislative purpose was secular or religious; this question is fatally ambiguous with respect to the purpose of laws that lift burdens from churches, such as religious exemptions from regulation or laws against religious discrimination.

The second part of the *Lemon* test literally asks whether the challenged law departs from neutrality. For emphasis, the Court specified that government could not depart from neutrality in either direction; it could neither advance nor inhibit religion. Lower courts and advocates have read that formulation to disaggregate the search for the most nearly neutral course into two separate inquiries: (1) Has government advanced religion? (2) Has government inhibited religion? It is possible to ask these two questions separately, and it is therefore possible to ask either without asking the other. And so many courts now ask whether government has advanced religion — the no-benefit-to-religion theory — instead of asking whether government has departed from neutrality.

A series of reversals in the Supreme Court suggest that the Court has never read the primary-effect test to preclude exemptions for religious conduct, or to preclude religious applications of generally available government benefits. In these contexts, the Court's understanding of primary effect seems generally consistent with substantive neutrality theory, and the Court has never adopted a no-benefit-to-religion position. But the Court has never clarified the language of the *Lemon* test. And the same verbal formula is used as the basis for many of the Court's tangled limitations on financial aid to religious schools.

The third part of the *Lemon* test prohibits excessive entanglement. This use of "entanglement" first appeared in *Walz v. Tax Commission of the City of New York* (1970), as an antonym for "separation." In context, it was clear that the Court did not mean strict separation; neither did it seem to mean only institutional separation. In *Walz*, the Court seemed to mean general separation partially achieved; separation and entanglement were matters of degree, with the acceptable degree of entanglement to be assessed in light of practicalities and an unspecified form of neutrality. This vague aspiration was not clearly defined, but it took context from the opinion's examples and repetitive explanations. It became vaguer still when the isolated phrase "excessive government entanglement" was removed from context and inserted into the *Lemon* test.

The derivation of its three prongs helps explain why the *Lemon* test has been so unsatisfactory to so many, and why the Court seems capable of reaching almost any result without abandoning its "test." The *Lemon* test is a confused amalgam of unspecified neutrality theories, unspecified separation theories, and no-benefit-to-religion theory. Its final linguistic formulation does not reflect its origins and probably does not reflect the Court's actual understanding. In the context of financial aid to religious schools, the Court often measured advancement of religion from the baseline of government inactivity, so that any aid was an unconstitutional advancement. But in all other contexts, and sometimes even in the context of religious schools, the Court measured advancement from the baseline of how government treated analogous secular activities. Efforts to reconcile cases derived from these two inconsistent definitions of neutrality account for much of the inconsistency in the Court's cases. But it appears that until quite recently, the Court did not see the inconsistency. And unlike many academic commentators, the Court did not view neutrality toward religion, however defined, as inconsistent with separationism.

The *Lemon* test's principal defenders have been strict separationists, who give it a strict separationist interpretation by arguing that any incidental benefit to religion is an advancement in violation of the second prong, and that any contact between religion and government is an excessive entanglement in violation of the third prong. They sometimes win and sometimes lose with these arguments, but they fear that any change or clarification from the current Court will be less helpful to their cause.

BIBLIOGRAPHY

Articles

1996 JCLI Symposium on Religion and the Constitution, 7 Journal of Contemporary Legal Issues 275 (1996).

Cord, Robert, *Separation of Church and State: Historical Fact and Current Fiction* (1982).

Esbeck, Carl H., *Establishment Clause Limits on Governmental Interference with Religious Organizations,* 41 Washington & Lee Law Review 347 (1984).

Esbeck, Carl H., *Five Views of Church-State Relations in Contemporary American Thought,* 1986 Brigham Young University Law Review 371.

Gey, Steven, *Why Is Religion Special?: Reconsidering the Accommodation of Reli-*

gion Under the Religion Clauses of the First Amendment, 52 University of Pittsburgh Law Review 75 (1990).

Kurland, Philip B., *Of Church and State and the Supreme Court,* 29 University of Chicago Law Review 1 (1961).

Laycock, Douglas, *Formal, Substantive, and Disaggregated Neutrality Toward Religion,* 39 DePaul Law Review 993 (1990).

Laycock, Douglas, *Noncoercive Support for Religion: Another False Claim About the Establishment Clause,* 26 Valparaiso Law Review 37 (1991).

Laycock, Douglas, *"Nonpreferential" Aid to Religion: A False Claim About Original Intent,* 27 William & Mary Law Review 875 (1986).

Laycock, Douglas, *The Remnants of Free Exercise,* 1990 Supreme Court Review 1.

Laycock, Douglas, *The Underlying Unity of Separation and Neutrality,* 46 Emory Law Journal 43 (1997).

Laycock, Douglas, *Towards a General Theory of the Religion Clauses: The Case of Church Labor Relations and the Right to Church Autonomy,* 81 Columbia Law Review 1373 (1981).

Lupu, Ira C., *Free Exercise Exemptions and Religious Institutions: The Case of Employment Discrimination,* 67 Boston University Law Review 391 (1987).

Lupu, Ira C., *The Lingering Death of Separationism,* 62 George Washington Law Review 230 (1994).

Marshall, William P., *The Case Against the Constitutionally Compelled Free Exercise Exemption,* 40 Case Western Reserve Law Review 357 (1990).

Marshall, William P., *"We Know It When We See It": The Supreme Court and Establishment,* 59 Southern California Law Review (1986).

Marshall, William P., & Blomgren, Douglas C., *Regulating Religious Organizations Under the Establishment Clause,* 47 Ohio State Law Journal 293 (1986).

McConnell, Michael W., *Accommodation of Religion,* 1985 Supreme Court Review 1.

McConnell, Michael W., *Free Exercise Revisionism and the Smith Decision,* 57 University of Chicago Law Review 1109 (1990).

McConnell, Michael W., *Religious Freedom at a Crossroads,* 59 University of Chicago Law Review 115 (1992).

McConnell, Michael W., *The Selective Funding Problem: Abortions and Religious Schools,* 104 Harvard Law Review 989 (1991).

McConnell, Michael W., & Posner, Richard A., *An Economic Approach to Issues of Religious Freedom,* 56 University of Chicago Law Review 1 (1989).

Paulsen, Michael, *Lemon Is Dead,* 43 Case Western Reserve Law Review 795 (1993).

Smith, Steven D., *Separation and the "Secular": Reconstructing the Disestablishment Decision,* 67 Texas Law Review 955 (1989).

Smith, Steven D., *Symbols, Perceptions, and Doctrinal Illusions: Establishment Neutrality and the "No Endorsement" Test,* 86 Michigan Law Review 266 (1987).

Tushnet, Mark V., *"Of Church and State and the Supreme Court": Kurland Revisited,* 1989 Supreme Court Review 373.

Cases

Board of Education of Kiryas Joel School District v. Grumet, 512 U.S. 687 (1994).

Brandon v. Board of Education, 635 F.2d 971 (2d Cir. 1980).

Church of the Lukumi Babalu Aye, Inc. v. City of Hialeah, 508 U.S. 520 (1993).

City of Boerne v. Flores, 521 U.S. 507 (1997).

Corporation of the Presiding Bishop v. Amos, 483 U.S. 327 (1987).

County of Allegheny v. American Civil Liberties Union, 492 U.S. 573 (1989).

Davis v. Beason, 133 U.S. 333 (1890).

Employment Division, Department of Human Resources of Oregon v. Smith, 494 U.S. 872 (1990).

Everson v. Board of Education, 330 U.S. 1 (1947).

Illinois ex rel. McCollum v. Board of Education, 333 U.S. 203 (1948).

Jimmy Swaggart Ministries v. Board of Equalization, 493 U.S. 378 (1990).

Lee v. Weisman, 505 U.S. 577 (1992).

Lemon v. Kurtzman, 403 U.S. 602 (1971).

Lynch v. Donnelly, 465 U.S. 668 (1984).

School District of Abington Township v. Schempp, 374 U.S. 203 (1963).

Texas Monthly, Inc. v. Bullock, 489 U.S. 1 (1989).

Torcaso v. Watkins, 367 U.S. 488 (1961).

Walz v. Tax Commission of the City of New York, 397 U.S. 664 (1970).

West Virginia State Board of Education v. Barnette, 319 U.S. 624 (1943).

Religious Liberty: Not for Religion or against Religion, but for Individual Choice

3 UT Law 42 (No. 1, Spring 2004)

This was one of a series of very short pieces in the alumni magazine of The University of Texas Law School, showcasing the work of various members of the faculty. It succinctly states my view of what the Religion Clauses are supposed to accomplish.

*   *   *

I work on a broad range of issues in constitutional law and in remedies (damages, injunctions, restitution, etc.). I rarely see a legal problem that doesn't interest me. But what I find most interesting, and most rewarding, is my work on religious liberty. The American experiment in religious liberty is a way for people with deeply incompatible views on some of the most fundamental questions to live together in peace and equality in the same society.

Some scholars in this field, and nearly all the activists, come to the field because of their religious commitments or their anti-religious commitments. Some of these folks seem to think that religious liberty means whatever is good for religion or whatever is good for secularism.

I call this the Puritan mistake. The Puritans came to Massachusetts for religious liberty, but they meant religious liberty only for themselves. Quakers, Baptists, and Catholics had only the liberty to go somewhere outside Massachusetts. We are not so blatant today; nearly all Americans defend the religious liberty of others in principle. But on both the religious side and the secular side, many Americans think their side should win all the cases that are the least bit arguable, and that the other side should bear all the costs of living in a pluralistic society.

My own approach is different. Religious liberty is a guarantee of *liberty,* not a guarantee of religion or of secularism. Religious liberty does not view religion as a good thing to be promoted, nor as a dangerous force to be contained. Within the liberty guaranteed by our Religion Clauses, the American people may experience a Great Awakening of Christianity, a total loss of religious faith, a diffusion into cafeteria religion (picking beliefs from diverse traditions around the world), or any other possibility you can imagine. The reality is that some Americans will do each of these things.

The Religion Clauses do not guarantee either side a win, or even an advantage, in this competition of ideas about religion. Anyone who claims that his side won the contemporary culture wars 200 years ago, when his views about religion were conveniently written into the First Amendment, is engaged in self-delusion.

The long-running battle over religion in schools illustrates the different approaches. The Supreme Court holds that school officials may not sponsor any religious observance in the public schools. Many religious Americans object to this rule, but the Court has recognized no exceptions in more than fifty years.

The Court also holds that student prayer clubs can meet on school premises on the same terms as other clubs, and that students have full rights of religious free speech on campus (as long as they are not speaking at an official school function to an audience captured by the school itself). Many secularists object to religious free speech, fearing that their children will be pressured by student proselytizers in the public schools. But the Court has never allowed schools to censor private speech on the ground that it is religious.

There is a separate but related issue of government funding for private religious schools. Here the Court gradually changed its mind; it now permits government to issue vouchers that can be used to pay tuition at a broad range of private schools and unconventional public schools, including private religious schools.

From the perspective of who's winning, the secular side is winning the school-sponsored prayer cases and the religious side is winning the private speech cases and the voucher cases. But from a perspective of religious liberty, all these cases are consistent. In the view of the swing votes, Justices Kennedy and O'Connor, all these cases are about individualizing religious choice.

School-sponsored prayer commits a whole set of religious questions to the government — whether to pray, when to pray, how long to pray, in what religious tradition to pray. Should we pray in Jesus' name, or not? These choices are imposed on everyone at the school event where the prayer is offered. Permitting after-school prayer clubs leaves all these choices to the individuals who choose to attend, and their choices are not imposed on anyone else.

Similarly with vouchers. Vouchers go to parents, and parents decide whether to use them at a religious school or a secular school. If they choose a religious school, they can choose which religious tradition and how intensely religious. Their choice is not imposed on others who choose to go elsewhere.

This year we might get the first-ever exception to the ban on school-sponsored religion. The Court might uphold "under God" in the Pledge of Allegiance, even though that phrase represents government's choice for a brief religious affirmation every morning. The residual protection for individual choice would be each child's right not to say the Pledge, or not to say the parts he doesn't believe.

We also got an exception to individual choice on the funding question. The Court recently considered state scholarships that could be used at any college in any major — except theology. The Court held that the state could have included theology — each student would choose a major individually — but the state could also choose to exclude theology. Funding any major except theology was open discrimination against religion, which would normally be unconstitutional. But funding the training of clergy was special, in the Court's view, because of long tradition and because no one has a right to government funding.

This decision, and a possible decision upholding the Pledge, illustrate a dose of legal realism. The Court's center will not carry its principle of individual choice to what it considers extreme results. But individual choice explains a lot of cases. The religious liberty question is not whether religion is winning or losing, or whether church and state should be more separate or less. True religious liberty means minimizing government's influence on the religious choices and commitments of the American people. The more religious choices that are left to individuals, the healthier the state of religious liberty.

Theology Scholarships, the Pledge of Allegiance, and Religious Liberty: Avoiding the Extremes but Missing the Liberty

118 Harvard Law Review 156 (2004)

The Harvard Law Review *publishes an annual review of the Supreme Court's Term, and the editors invited this review of the two religious liberty cases the Court decided in 2004. The two cases implicated all three major areas of controversy over religious liberty: funding religious institutions, regulating religious practice, and government-sponsored religious speech. I placed the two cases in this larger context and took the occasion to survey the entire field. In some ways, this is my most ambitious attempt to synthesize the law of religious liberty. But of course the issues in the two 2004 cases get primary attention.*

While I work out the implications of the Court's brief opinions, I also criticize the Court's work and explain how I think the cases should have been decided. I argue from a perspective of religious liberty (as opposed to the more common perspectives of supporting or opposing religion) that Washington should have been required to fund theology scholarships and that "under God" should have been removed from the Pledge of Allegiance. I conclude that the Court's result — government discretion to include religious institutions in broader funding programs, or to exclude them, or to include them subject to conditions — is worse than either an absolute rule of funding or an absolute rule of no funding, because government discretion maximizes government's ability to use its funding power to control religious institutions. This is my most extensive treatment of the government funding cases.

On the Pledge, I take its words seriously. Either we are asking every child in

---

I am grateful to Mark Gergen, Sanford Levinson, and Ernest Young, and to my colleagues at the University of Texas Law School's Faculty Colloquium series, for helpful comments on earlier drafts, and to Sachin Gandhi for research assistance.

public school for a brief affirmation of faith, or we are taking the name of the Lord in vain. Government should not be doing either of those things.

*   *   *

The Supreme Court heard two important religious liberty cases this Term; it decided one and produced revealing separate opinions in the other. *Locke v. Davey*[1] asked whether the State of Washington could exclude students majoring in theology, taught from a believing perspective, from a generally available scholarship program.[2] In *Elk Grove Unified School District v. Newdow*,[3] the question was whether the state can ask school children to recite the religious affirmation — "one Nation under God" — in the Pledge of Allegiance.[4]

This Comment places these cases in a larger context and reviews them from a perspective of substantive neutrality, concluding that the theology scholarships should have been constitutionally required and that the current Pledge ceremony is constitutionally forbidden. These are not the Court's views, and they do not appear to be the views of any organized interest group. But for reasons to be explained, these are the results that would best serve religious liberty.

Together, *Davey* and *Newdow* implicated all three major lines of religious liberty cases: funding of religious organizations, regulation of religious practice, and sponsorship and regulation of religious speech. Two of these fields have recently seen dramatic doctrinal change. Federal constitutional restrictions on funding religious institutions have collapsed.[5] Protections for religious practice abruptly changed from a substantive liberty, triggered by a burden on religious practice, to a form of nondiscrimination right, triggered by a burden that is not neutral or not generally applicable.[6] These two changes set up the plaintiff's claim in *Davey:* if funding is permitted and discrimination is forbidden, it seemed to follow that a discriminatory refusal to fund is forbidden.

These changes have not touched the religious speech cases.[7] The Court has long protected private religious speech to the same extent as other pro-

---

1. 540 U.S. 712 (2004).
2. *See id.* at 715-18.
3. 542 U.S. 1 (2004).
4. *See id.* at 7-10.
5. *See* text at notes 58-71 *infra*.
6. *See* text at notes 271-361 *infra*.
7. *See* text at notes 405-39 *infra*.

tected speech.[8] The Court has prohibited government sponsorship of religious speech for more than forty years, without exception in the public schools and with few exceptions elsewhere.[9] The issue in *Newdow* was whether to create an arguably de minimis exception in the public schools.

Why have the speech cases not moved in unison with the funding cases? If it were a simple function of the Court's swing to the right, or of the religious and separationist interest groups that file amicus briefs, we might expect the two principal lines of Establishment Clause cases to move together. Seven Justices seem to view the cases this way: three consistently vote to permit religious funding and protect religious speech, even if government sponsored, while four consistently vote to prohibit religious funding and often to prohibit religious speech in government-sponsored forums, even by private speakers. But to Justices Kennedy and O'Connor, the speech and funding cases are very different. What reconciles the speech and funding cases is the principle of minimizing government influence and maximizing individual choice.

Financial aid can be distributed in a way consistent with individual choice; the inelegant catch phrase in the recent voucher case is "true private choice."[10] Each family receiving a government voucher can choose the school that it prefers among all the options available. In a metropolitan area with many choices, each family can choose religious or secular, which religious tradition, and how intensely religious. Choice may be constrained by poverty, the inadequacy of the voucher, or the inadequacy of choices in some educational markets. But even where the choices are inadequate, there are more choices with the voucher than without it.[11] Nondiscriminatory funding expands individual choice.

The Court's protection of private religious speech also fits this theory of individual choice. When a student prayer club meets in an empty classroom, its audience is only those who choose to attend the prayer club, not all those assembled for some other school event. Those who choose to participate can decide whether the club will be religious or secular, in what religious tradition, and how intensely religious. If an individual dislikes the direction in which the group is moving, he can stop attending.

8. *E.g.*, Capitol Square Review & Advisory Bd. v. Pinette, 515 U.S. 753, 760 (1995).

9. *See* Engel v. Vitale, 370 U.S. 421, 430-36 (1962).

10. *See* Zelman v. Simmons-Harris, 536 U.S. 639, 649-50, 653, 662 (2002) (upholding a program that permitted the general population to redeem publicly funded tuition vouchers at secular or religious private schools).

11. Eugene Volokh, *Equal Treatment Is Not Establishment,* 13 Notre Dame J.L. Ethics & Pub. Pol'y 341, 349-50 (1999).

But individual choice is impossible in cases of government-sponsored religious speech. Any religious observance at a public event necessarily requires a collective decision. *Government* must decide whether the content of the speech will be religious or secular, in which religious tradition, and how intensely religious, or it must delegate these choices to a selected citizen who becomes a government agent for this purpose. The frequent result is prayer that can hold a majority in the school board or prayer by a student who can win a student election.

The speech and funding cases are thus united by a principled commitment to government neutrality and individual choice in religious matters.[12] The Court's decisions reflect that commitment, but it is actually the commitment of only two Justices. Seven Justices seem to vote — in speech and funding cases — for or against religion instead of for or against religious liberty. That voting lineup is mostly scrambled in the religious practice cases; votes on regulation of religious practice (except for those of Justice Stevens) appear to be better explained by views about the proper role of the judiciary.

To some extent, these voting patterns broke down in *Davey* and *Newdow*. The plaintiff's claim in each case was a straightforward application of recent precedents. But Davey involved an important competing principle: there is very little that the government is constitutionally required to fund. In *Newdow*, many holdings pointed one way, but many dicta pointed the other. And in different ways, each claim was extreme. Joshua Davey claimed not only that government may fund his theology major, but that it *must* — that what had long been constitutionally prohibited, and had only just been constitutionally permitted,[13] was now constitutionally required. In *Newdow*, politicians and the general public overwhelmingly condemned the Ninth Circuit's invalidation of the Pledge of Allegiance. From a realist perspective, neither claim seemed likely to prevail in the Supreme Court. Neither claim did.

In *Davey*, the gravitational pull of the no-aid tradition overrode the rule prohibiting discrimination against religion.[14] *Newdow* went off on standing grounds,[15] but three Justices would have reached the merits and

---

12. For a basically compatible analysis, with somewhat different emphasis, see Ira C. Lupu, *Government Messages and Government Money: Santa Fe, Mitchell v. Helms, and the Arc of the Establishment Clause*, 42 Wm. & Mary L. Rev. 771, 815-17 (2001). For an account of this distinction in terms of larger social forces, see John C. Jeffries, Jr. & James E. Ryan, *A Political History of the Establishment Clause*, 100 Mich. L. Rev. 279, 358-68 (2001).

13. *See Zelman*, 536 U.S. at 648-63.

14. *See Davey*, 540 U.S. at 721-25.

15. For analysis of the standing issues, see *The Supreme Court, 2003 Term — Leading Cases*, 118 Harv. L. Rev. 248, 426 (2004).

would have upheld "under God" in the Pledge — for three radically different reasons.[16]

Interest groups lined up in predictable ways. Some of these groups have more nuanced positions across the full range of religious liberty issues, but in this Term, those who filed amicus briefs in both cases appeared to support religion, oppose religion, or support government discretion. Religious conservatives and their allies supported theology scholarships in *Davey* and "under God" in the Pledge of Allegiance,[17] as did Justices Thomas[18] and Scalia.[19] Most separationist groups who filed in both cases took the opposite positions, opposing theology scholarships and also opposing "under God" in the Pledge.[20]

16. See *Newdow*, 542 U.S. at 25-33 (Rehnquist, C.J., concurring in the judgment); *id.* at 33-45 (O'Connor, J., concurring in the judgment); *id.* at 45-54 (Thomas, J., concurring in the judgment).

17. *See, e.g.,* Brief for the United States as Amicus Curiae Supporting Respondent, *Davey* (No. 02-1315), *available in* 2003 WL 22087613; Brief for the United States as Respondent Supporting Petitioners, *Newdow* (No. 02-1624), *available in* 2003 WL 23051994 [hereinafter U.S. *Newdow* Brief]; Brief of the States of Texas et al. as Amicus Curiae in Support of Respondent, *Davey* (No. 02-1315), *available in* 2003 WL 22118862; Brief of Texas et al. as Amici Curiae in Support of Petitioners, *Newdow* (No. 02-1624), *available in* 2003 WL 23011472 [hereinafter Fifty-State Brief]; Brief of Liberty Counsel as Amicus Curiae in Support of Respondent, *Davey* (No. 02-1315), *available in* 2003 WL 22118860; Brief of Liberty Counsel et al. as Amicus Curiae in Support of Petitioners, *Newdow* (No. 02-1624), *available in* 2003 WL 23051982; Brief Amici Curiae of Common Good Legal Defense Fund et al. in Support of Respondent, *Davey* (No. 02-1315), *available in* 2003 WL 22220105; Brief Amici Curiae of Common Good Foundation et al. in Support of Petitioner, *Newdow* (No. 02-1624), *available in* 2003 WL 23010744; Brief of the National Jewish Commission on Law and Public Affairs as Amicus Curiae in Support of Respondent, *Davey* (No. 02-1315), *available in* 2003 WL 22087608; Brief of the National Jewish Commission on Law and Public Affairs as Amicus Curiae in Support of Petitioners, *Newdow* (No. 02-1624), *available in* 2003 WL 23011476.

18. See *Davey*, 540 U.S. at 734 (Thomas, J., dissenting); *Newdow*, 542 U.S. at 45 (Thomas, J., concurring in the judgment).

19. See *Davey*, 540 U.S. at 726 (Scalia, J., dissenting). In *Newdow*, Scalia announced his views on the case before receiving the briefs. *See* Jacqueline L. Salmon, *Scalia Defends Public Expression of Faith: Recent Rulings Have Gone Too Far, Justice Says During Tribute to Va. Gathering,* WASH. POST, Jan. 13, 2003, at B3, *available at* 2003 WL 2367996. These comments became the basis of a motion to recuse, *see* Charles Lane & David Von Drehle, *Is Scalia Too Blunt to Be Effective? Justice Out of Case About Which He Cares,* WASH. POST, Oct. 17, 2003, at A27, *available at* 2003 WL 62223514, and Scalia did not participate in *Newdow, see* 542 U.S. at 3 (noting Scalia's recusal).

20. *See, e.g.,* Brief of Amici Curiae Anti-Defamation League et al. in Support of Petitioners, *Davey* (No. 02-1315), *available in* 2003 WL 21692828; Brief Amicus Curiae of Anti-Defamation League in Support of Respondent, *Newdow* (No. 02-1624), *available in* 2004 WL 314092; Brief Amicus Curiae of Historians and Law Scholars on Behalf of Petitioners Gary Locke et al., *Davey* (No. 02-1315), *available in* 2003 WL 21697729 [hereinafter Scholars Brief];

Education groups[21] and five states[22] opposed mandatory theology scholarships but supported "under God" in the Pledge. This religiously mixed position supports the educational establishment and governmental discretion, but is also consistent with a separationist opposition to government funding of religious education and a realist recognition that the Pledge has overwhelming popular support. Popular support for "under God" in the Pledge is presumably the reason the American Jewish Congress supported it,[23] and the reason other prominent separationist organizations filed no brief in *Newdow*.[24]

Only one amicus or attorney who filed in both cases supported theology scholarships in *Davey* and opposed the Pledge in *Newdow*: the author of this Comment. Representing two very different groups of amici, I took what I believe to have been a consistent position in favor of minimizing government's influence on the religious beliefs and practices of the American people.[25] The discriminatory funding scheme discouraged a religious practice — actually paid students not to major in theology. The Pledge encouraged a religious practice — actually imposed a short profession of faith on millions of children. I have long argued that government should be substantively neutral to-

Brief Amicus Curiae of Historians and Law Scholars in Support of Respondent, *Newdow* (No. 02-1624), *available in* 2004 WL 298112.

21. *See* Brief for the National Education Association as Amicus Curiae Supporting Petitioners, *Davey* (No. 02-1315), *available in* 2003 WL 21697737; Brief Amicus Curiae of the National Education Association in Support of Petitioners, *Newdow* (No. 02-1624), *available in* 2003 WL 23011470; Amicus Curiae Brief of National School Boards Association et al. in Support of Petitioners, *Davey* (No. 02-1315), *available in* 2003 WL 21697733; Brief of Amicus Curiae National School Boards Association in Support of Petitioners, *Newdow* (No. 02-1624), *available in* 2003 WL 23011475.

22. *See* Brief of the States of Vermont et al., Amici Curiae in Support of Petitioners, *Davey* (No. 02-1315), *available in* 2003 WL 21715036; Fifty-State Brief, *supra* note 17.

23. *See* Brief Amicus Curiae of the American Jewish Congress in Support of Neither Party, *Newdow* (No. 02-1624), *available in* 2003 WL 23144816 [hereinafter AJC *Newdow* Brief] (concluding that "under God" in the context of the Pledge is basically secular and should be upheld).

24. People for the American Way Foundation, the Baptist Joint Committee on Public Affairs, and the American Jewish Committee did not file in *Newdow*.

25. *See* Brief Amici Curiae of the Council for Christian Colleges & Universities et al. in Support of Respondent, *Davey* (No. 02-1315), *available in* 2003 WL 22176102; Brief of Rev. Dr. Betty Jane Bailey et al. as Amici Curiae Supporting Respondent Michael A. Newdow, *Newdow* (No. 02-1624), *available in* 2004 WL 314150 [hereinafter Clergy Brief]. Seeing little prospect of success, I also devoted a third of the Clergy Brief in *Newdow* to suggesting a way to uphold the Pledge that would do the least damage to religious liberty. *See id.* at *20–30; note 529 and accompanying text *infra*. Professor Thomas Berg at St. Thomas University (Minnesota) was the principal author of the Christian Colleges Brief. I participated actively and take full responsibility, but much less than full credit.

ward religion, meaning that government should "minimize the extent to which it either encourages or discourages religious belief or disbelief, practice or nonpractice, observance or nonobservance."[26] Minimizing the influence of government maximizes the freedom to make religious choices or to act on existing religious commitments. The government's conduct failed this neutrality test in both *Davey* and *Newdow.*

I describe these positions here, partly in the interest of full disclosure, but mostly to highlight the difference between promoting religious *liberty* and promoting or opposing *religion.* A strong commitment to religious liberty necessarily requires equal concern for the rights of believers and nonbelievers. One's views on religious liberty should be independent of one's views on religion. To support religious liberty only or mostly for people with views more or less like one's own would be to repeat, in diluted form, the Puritan mistake in seventeenth-century Massachusetts.[27]

This Comment is organized around the three principal sets of religious liberty issues. Part I considers *Davey's* implications for funding programs. As so often happens in constitutional litigation, each side's clear and simple principle leads to results that the Court considers unacceptably extreme. But nine independent minds trying to define a position in the middle are likely to appear unprincipled, illogical, and inconsistent.[28]

The Court struggled for decades to find a middle ground that would permit some funding for religious institutions but not too much. Its new middle ground is to permit most funding but to require hardly any. This position maximizes government discretion and judicial deference, but it threatens religious liberty. The Court has quite possibly come to the worst solution for religious liberty, maximizing government power over religious institutions.

---

26. Douglas Laycock, *Formal, Substantive, and Disaggregated Neutrality Toward Religion,* 39 DePaul L. Rev. 993, 1001 (1990) (text at note 27). For broadly similar approaches to religious liberty, see, for example, Thomas C. Berg, *Religion Clause Anti-Theories,* 72 Notre Dame L. Rev. 693 (1997), arguing that government should "minimize the effect it has on the voluntary, independent religious decisions of the people as individuals and in voluntary groups," *id.* at 703-04; and Michael W. McConnell & Richard A. Posner, *An Economic Approach to Issues of Religious Freedom,* 56 U. Chi. L. Rev. 1 (1989), arguing that economic measure of neutrality toward religion requires that "[e]ffects on religious practice must be minimized," *id.* at 14.

27. *See* Douglas Laycock, *Religious Liberty as Liberty,* 7 J. Contemp. Legal Issues 313, 313-23, 352-53 (1996) (text at notes 1-39, 175-76) (elaborating on the Puritan mistake and on defending religious liberty without regard to views about religion).

28. *See* Frank H. Easterbrook, *Ways of Criticizing the Court,* 95 Harv. L. Rev. 802, 811-31 (1982) (showing how voting paradoxes inevitably yield inconsistent decisions when a court has more than two choices).

Davey also poses important questions about the boundaries of its holding. As written, it applies only to funding the training of clergy, but it may well be extended to all funding decisions, including discriminatory refusals to fund secular services or instruction delivered by religious institutions. There are exceptions for government-funded forums for speech, for badly motivated refusals to fund, and for withholding government funds for secular activities in ways that penalize religious activities, but these exceptions are narrowly conceived and may be illusory. Important questions remain open, but *Davey* is a major win for the opponents of funding.

Part II considers *Davey's* implications for disputes over government regulation of religious practice. At least some of those who would narrowly construe the Free Exercise Clause claim that *Davey* authorizes facially discriminatory regulation of religion and requires proof of bad motive for any successful free exercise claim.[29] This is wishful thinking on their part. *Davey's* holding has one clear limit, dictated by the facts of the case and the scope of the dispute: *Davey* is a funding case. It authorizes discriminatory funding, but it does not authorize discriminatory regulation, and it does little to clarify the regulation cases.

Part III considers *Newdow* and the religious speech cases. Once past the phony argument that "under God" is not a religious statement, *Newdow* posed a longstanding question about the limits of the rule against government-sponsored religious observances. The logic of the Court's rule leads to an absolute ban on any government endorsement of a religious viewpoint, and the Court has carried that principle further than it carries most principles. But the Court's aversion to extreme results sometimes overrides doctrinal logic. Repeated dicta have disclaimed absolutism and asserted the permissibility of some de minimis government expressions of religious faith. *Newdow* required the Court to define the de minimis exception and decide whether it encompassed the Pledge of Allegiance. The Court postponed the problem by finding that the plaintiff lacked standing.

Three Justices addressed the merits in separate opinions. Justice O'Connor attempted to define a reasonably objective boundary to the de minimis exception; her opinion is a substantial improvement over all previous judicial comments on this issue. Chief Justice Rehnquist offered fuzzy euphemisms with no prospect of leading to a workable solution. Justice Thomas would have eliminated this issue and many others by holding that

29. *See* Marci Hamilton, *The Supreme Court Issues a Monumental Decision: Equal State Scholarship Access for Theology Students Is Not Required by the Free Exercise Clause,* FINDLAW (Feb. 27, 2004), *at* http://writ.news.findlaw.com/hamilton/20040227.html.

the Establishment Clause creates no individual rights. Fortunately, this position is far too extreme to attract five votes.

I. *Davey* and the Funding Cases

A. *The Doctrinal Context: Funding of Religious Institutions*

The case law on funding religious institutions has changed dramatically over the last twenty years. These changes are rooted in tensions that go back to the very beginnings of modern Establishment Clause doctrine.

From 1947 on, the Court struggled to reconcile two competing intuitions, announced in consecutive paragraphs in *Everson v. Board of Education*.[30] On one hand was the no-aid principle: "No tax in any amount, large or small, can be levied to support any religious activities or institutions, whatever they may be called, or whatever form they may adopt to teach or practice religion."[31] On the other was the nondiscrimination principle: the state "cannot exclude individual Catholics, Lutherans, Mohammedans, Baptists, Jews, Methodists, Non-believers, Presbyterians, or the members of any other faith, *because of their faith, or lack of it,* from receiving the benefits of public welfare legislation."[32]

The no-aid principle derived from eighteenth-century debates over earmarked taxes levied exclusively for the funding of churches.[33] In an era with few public welfare benefits, these taxes funded purely religious programs and funded those programs preferentially. As applied to that dispute, the two principles did not conflict, and the no-aid principle served religious liberty. No-aid protected citizens from being forced to contribute to churches, it protected the churches from financial dependence on the government, it prevented discrimination in favor of religion, and it did not discriminate against religion.

But all the modern cases involved equal funding of religious and secular alternatives. And in all the modern cases, government money funded secular services in a religious environment, not purely religious programs. In that context, the Court had to choose: either government money would flow through to religious institutions, or students in religious schools and patients

30. 330 U.S. 1 (1947).

31. *Id.* at 16.

32. *Id.*

33. *See* Douglas Laycock, *The Underlying Unity of Separation and Neutrality,* 46 EMORY L.J. 43, 48-53 (1997) (text at notes 32-53) (comparing the eighteenth-century proposals to disputes in the nineteenth century and later).

in religious hospitals would forfeit instruction or services that the state would have paid for if they had chosen a secular school or hospital.

This difficulty was apparent in *Everson* itself and produced a 5-4 split. Free bus rides to school were a public welfare benefit. Free bus rides to Catholic school supported the religious activity of attending Catholic school. Refusing free bus rides to students attending Catholic school excluded individual Catholics from the public welfare benefit because of a choice that, for most of them, was based squarely on their faith.

The nondiscrimination principle prevailed in *Everson,* which upheld the government-funded bus rides to a Catholic high school,[34] and again in *Board of Education v. Allen*[35] in 1968, which allowed states to provide secular textbooks for use in religious schools.[36] These cases applied the weak form of the nondiscrimination principle; they permitted equal funding, but did not require it. Few judges took seriously the possibility that equal funding might be constitutionally required.[37]

In *Lemon v. Kurtzman*[38] in 1971, the Court struck down a funding program for the first time, holding that states could not subsidize teachers' salaries in religious schools.[39] The no-aid principle predominated from then until its highwater mark in *Aguilar v. Felton*[40] in 1985. *Aguilar* invalidated the use of federal Title I funds[41] to pay public school teachers to provide remedial instruction in secular subjects to educationally deprived children in low-income neighborhoods, on the campuses of religious schools.[42]

Even so, the no-aid principle never completely triumphed; the *Lemon* era was also the era of much-ridiculed distinctions.[43] The state could provide

34. *See Everson,* 330 U.S. at 17-19.

35. 392 U.S. 236 (1968).

36. *Id.* at 243-49.

37. *See* Luetkemeyer v. Kaufmann, 364 F. Supp. 376, 381-87 (W.D. Mo. 1973), *aff'd mem.,* 419 U.S. 888 (1974) (holding that state was not required to provide bus rides to private schools); *cf.* Sloan v. Lemon, 413 U.S. 825, 834 (1973) (rejecting claim that if state aided private schools, equal protection required aid to religious schools that would otherwise have been prohibited by the Establishment Clause).

38. 403 U.S. 602 (1971).

39. *Id.* at 615-25.

40. 473 U.S. 402 (1985), *overruled by* Agostini v. Felton, 521 U.S. 203, 235 (1997).

41. *See* Elementary and Secondary Education Act of 1965, tit. I, Pub. L. No. 89-10, 79 Stat. 27, 27 (codified as amended in 20 U.S.C. §§ 6301-6578 (2000 & Supp. 2001)).

42. *See Aguilar,* 473 U.S. at 404-07 (describing the program); *id.* at 408-14 (invalidating the program).

43. *See, e.g.,* Wallace v. Jaffree, 472 U.S. 38, 110-11 (1985) (Rehnquist, J., dissenting) (ridiculing a lengthy list of such distinctions).

books, but not maps;[44] it could provide bus rides to school, but not bus rides to field trips.[45] Perhaps most absurd, after *Aguilar* the government provided remedial instruction in vans parked near religious schools.[46] The cost of vans, and of dressing children to go back and forth in all weathers between the school building and the vans, was a deadweight economic and educational loss for a symbolic change that completely failed to satisfy the objections of those who thought there should be no funding at all.

The awkward distinctions persisted partly because the swing votes were unwilling to overrule the earlier cases, and partly because they were still trying to leave some scope for the two competing principles of no-aid and non-discrimination.[47] Even the *Lemon* test, the very symbol of strict separationism, took its first two elements almost verbatim from the Court's earlier elaborations of "wholesome neutrality" toward religion.[48] *Lemon* formally prohibited government actions that inhibit religion as well as government actions that advance religion.[49]

The Court implicitly reconciled its commitment to no-aid with its lingering sense of neutrality in part by manipulating baselines,[50] and in part by

44. *Compare* Bd. of Educ. v. Allen, 392 U.S. 236, 243-49 (1968), *with* Meek v. Pittenger, 421 U.S. 349, 362-66 (1975), *overruled in part by* Mitchell v. Helms, 530 U.S. 793, 835-37 (2000) (plurality and concurring opinions).

45. *Compare* Everson v. Bd. of Educ., 330 U.S. 1, 17-18 (1947), *with* Wolman v. Walter, 433 U.S. 229, 252-55 (1977), *overruled in part by Mitchell,* 530 U.S. at 835-37 (plurality and concurring opinions).

46. *See* Walker v. San Francisco Unified Sch. Dist., 46 F.3d 1449, 1455-61 (9th Cir. 1995) (describing and upholding the van program).

47. *See* Laycock, *supra* note 33, at 53-65 (text at notes 53-133) (reviewing the conflicting pressures on the Court, including the influence of the school desegregation cases); *see also* LAURENCE TRIBE, AMERICAN CONSTITUTIONAL LAW § 14-10, at 1219-21 (2d ed. 1988) (offering a more sympathetic analysis and imposing order and some rationale on the Court's distinctions); Douglas Laycock, *A Survey of Religious Liberty in the United States,* 47 OHIO ST. L.J. 409, 443-49 (1986) (text at notes 208-50) (documenting frequent changes of theory in this period); Richard E. Morgan, *The Establishment Clause and Sectarian Schools: A Final Installment?,* 1973 SUP. CT. REV. 57, 67-97 (assessing the apparently definitive decisions of 1971 and 1973); Eric J. Segall, *Parochial School Aid Revisited: The* Lemon *Test, the Endorsement Test and Religious Liberty,* 28 SAN DIEGO L. REV. 263, 267-88 (1991) (subdividing the *Lemon* era into two shorter periods).

48. *Lemon,* 403 U.S. 602, 612 (1971), cites *Board of Education v. Allen,* 392 U.S. 236, 243 (1968). *Allen* quotes *School District v. Schempp,* 374 U.S. 203, 222 (1963). In *Schempp,* the words that became the first two elements of the *Lemon* test were offered as a test for identifying "[t]he wholesome 'neutrality' of which this Court's cases speak." *Id.*

49. *Lemon,* 403 U.S. at 612.

50. *See* Laycock, *supra* note 33, at 48 (text at notes 32-33) (explaining the choice of baselines).

disaggregating the measure of neutrality into separate inquiries into effects that advanced religion and effects that inhibited religion.[51] This made it possible to characterize any benefit to religion as an advancement, without considering the relative magnitude of advancement and inhibition under alternative policies.

Manipulating the baseline and disaggregating the neutrality inquiry sharply limited government aid to religious schools in the period after *Lemon*. But as the ridiculed distinctions illustrate, these techniques never fully captured the field for the no-aid principle. Even at the height of the *Lemon* era, the Court let government provide bus transportation,[52] textbooks,[53] standardized testing,[54] diagnostic services,[55] state income-tax deductions,[56] and remedial instruction and therapeutic services delivered off the property of the religious school.[57] Because the Court manipulated neutrality instead of repudiating it, because it never squarely repudiated the nondiscrimination principle, and because the resulting body of law seemed incoherent, the no-aid decisions remained vulnerable to new Justices measuring neutrality from a different baseline.

Beginning in 1986, the Court progressively elevated the nondiscrimination principle and subordinated the no-aid principle.[58] Since 1986, the Court has upheld six programs that permitted government funds to reach religious institutions;[59] it has invalidated none. Four decisions from the *Lemon* era

51. *See* Laycock, *supra* note 26, at 1007-11 (text at notes 41-64) (explaining disaggregated neutrality).

52. *See* Everson v. Bd. of Educ., 330 U.S. 1, 17-19 (1947).

53. *See* Meek v. Pittenger, 421 U.S. 349, 359-62 (1975) (plurality opinion); *id.* at 385 (Burger, C.J., concurring); *id.* at 396 (Rehnquist, J., concurring); *Allen*, 392 U.S. at 243-49.

54. *See* Comm. for Pub. Educ. & Religious Liberty v. Regan, 444 U.S. 646, 654-62 (1980); Wolman v. Walter, 433 U.S. 229, 238-41 (1977).

55. *See Wolman*, 433 U.S. at 241-44.

56. *See* Mueller v. Allen, 463 U.S. 388, 394-403 (1983).

57. *See Wolman*, 433 U.S. at 244-48.

58. Charles Fried dates the change to *Mueller*. Charles Fried, *The Supreme Court, 2001 Term — Comment: Five to Four: Reflections on the School Voucher Case*, 116 HARV. L. REV. 163, 173 (2002). Justice Powell provided the fifth vote to uphold state income-tax deductions for private school tuition in *Mueller* and to strike down remedial instruction in *Aguilar v. Felton*, 473 U.S. 402, 408-14 (1985), *overruled by* Agostini v. Felton, 521 U.S. 203, 235 (1997). In 1986, Justice Scalia replaced Justice Powell, providing a much more reliable fifth vote. For a good account of the doctrinal transition after 1985, written while that transition was still in progress, see Ira C. Lupu, *The Lingering Death of Separationism*, 62 GEO. WASH. L. REV. 230 (1994).

59. *See* Zelman v. Simmons-Harris, 536 U.S. 639 (2002); Mitchell v. Helms, 530 U.S. 793 (2000); *Agostini*, 521 U.S. 203; Zobrest v. Catalina Foothills Sch. Dist., 509 U.S. 1 (1993);

have been overruled in whole or in part.[60] The Court has upheld vouchers that can be used to pay tuition at any public or private school, including religious schools,[61] and it has upheld long-term loans of equipment to private schools, including religious schools, where the equipment is distributed to all schools on the basis of enrollment.[62] *Lemon's* ban on direct cash grants to religious institutions remains,[63] but at least in the school context, there is no reason for state legislatures to test that limit. They can deliver as much money as they are willing to spend in the form of grants or vouchers to students and their families.[64]

Some of the cases in this transition were decided on narrow facts[65] or in

---

Bowen v. Kendrick, 487 U.S. 589 (1988); Witters v. Wash. Dep't of Servs. for the Blind, 474 U.S. 481 (1986).

60. *See Mitchell,* 530 U.S. at 835-37 (plurality and concurring opinions) (overruling invalidations of aid to religious schools in *Wolman,* 433 U.S. at 248-55, and *Meek v. Pittenger,* 421 U.S. 349, 362-73 (1975)); *Agostini,* 521 U.S. at 235 (overruling invalidations of aid to religious schools in *Aguilar v. Felton,* 473 U.S. 402 (1985), and of a "shared time" education program in *Grand Rapids School District v. Ball,* 473 U.S. 373, 384-98 (1985)).

61. *See Zelman,* 536 U.S. 639.

62. *See Mitchell,* 530 U.S. 793.

63. *See* Am. Jewish Cong. v. Corp. for Nat'l & Cmty. Serv., 323 F. Supp. 2d 44, 58-64 (D.D.C. 2004) (invalidating direct grants to religious agencies to support small stipends for volunteer teachers).

64. The Bush Administration's initiatives for faith-based social services might be different in practice from vouchers for schools. Legislators and judges might doubt the capacity for private choice among the mentally ill, the drug addicted, and other beneficiaries suffering severe social problems. And while government funds secular schools for all, it has not funded secular programs for all who need these other services. But direct cash grants to religiously affiliated social service providers were rarely controversial until the Bush proposals. The real issues in that controversy are over the rules for delivering and administering the money: whether the church-affiliated provider must be separately incorporated from the church, whether it must separate religious and secular components of the program, whether it must forfeit its right to hire employees of its own faith, and whether granting agencies will be forbidden to discriminate between religious and secular providers. This last issue parallels the issue in *Davey:* are grants to religious providers merely permitted, or should they be required (by statute if not by the Constitution) on equal terms with secular providers? For pre-*Davey* analyses of faith-based social services, see Ira C. Lupu & Robert W. Tuttle, The State of the Law 2003: Developments in the Law Concerning Government Partnerships with Religious Organizations 2-28 (2003), *available at* http://www.religionandsocialpolicy.org/publications/publication.cfm?id=60.0; Ira C. Lupu & Robert W. Tuttle, Zelman's *Future: Vouchers, Sectarian Providers, and the Next Round of Constitutional Battles,* 78 Notre Dame L. Rev. 917, 982-83 (2003); and Symposium, *Public Values in an Era of Privatization,* 116 Harv. L. Rev. 1211 (2003).

65. *See* Zobrest v. Catalina Foothills Sch. Dist., 509 U.S. 1, 3-4 (1993) (upholding state-paid translator for deaf student at Catholic high school); Witters v. Wash. Dep't of Servs. for

narrow opinions;[66] others were decided with no majority opinion.[67] But in *Zelman v. Simmons-Harris*,[68] the voucher case, the opinion had sweeping implications and there were five votes throughout.[69] Unless the dissenters persist and acquire a fifth vote from new appointments, the Establishment Clause part of this fight is over.[70] There is a long political tradition of no aid to Catholic or other "sectarian" schools,[71] but Supreme Court decisions restricting such aid are confined to a remarkably brief period, from 1971 to 1985. The no-aid principle never dominated constitutionally to the extent it once dominated politically, and *Zelman* appears to be a huge consolidating win for the proponents of nondiscriminatory funding.

B. *What the State* May *Fund*

Washington State Promise Scholarships were available to any student with a certain level of academic achievement and a family income below 135% of the state median.[72] A Promise Scholarship could be used at any accredited school in Washington, for any college-related expense (including room and board), and for the study of any major — except that it could not be used for any expense, however secular, incurred by a student majoring in theology.[73] By uncontroversial stipulation, although not on the face of the statute, "theology" meant theology taught from a perspective that is "devotional in nature or designed to induce religious faith."[74] So a Promise Scholarship *could* be used to major in theology from a neutral academic perspective, as in the typical academic religion department.

Joshua Davey claimed that excluding devotional theology majors was un-

---

the Blind, 474 U.S. 481, 482-83 (1986) (upholding a blind student's use of a scholarship to attend seminary).

66. *See* Bowen v. Kendrick, 487 U.S. 589, 593, 620-22 (1988) (leaving open the possibility of as-applied challenges).

67. *See Mitchell,* 530 U.S. at 801.

68. 536 U.S. 639 (2002).

69. *See* Thomas C. Berg, *Vouchers and Religious Schools: The New Constitutional Questions,* 72 U. Cin. L. Rev. 151, 153-64 (2003) (exploring the reach of *Zelman*); Mark Tushnet, *Vouchers After* Zelman, 2002 Sup. Ct. Rev. 1, 2-14 (same).

70. The dissenters' persistence and the possibility of their acquiring a fifth vote is the theme of Fried, *supra* note 58.

71. *See* Jeffries & Ryan, *supra* note 12, at 300-02, 306-07, 312-18.

72. *Davey,* 542 U.S. at 716.

73. *See id.*

74. *Id.*

constitutional discrimination against religion.[75] Washington did not even argue an Establishment Clause defense.[76] The state might have argued that there is something special about training clergy — that funding the training of clergy is decisively different from subsidizing attendance at a church-affiliated elementary or secondary school that satisfies the state's secular compulsory education requirements. *Witters v. Washington Department of Services for the Blind,*[77] which allowed a student to attend seminary with his scholarship for the blind, would have been an obstacle to that argument.[78] But *Witters* might have been distinguished as a special case about aid to the disabled.

The bigger obstacle to an Establishment Clause defense, even for state funds for training the clergy, was the Court's reasoning in upholding financial aid delivered through programs of "true private choice." At bottom, the Court has held that there is no state action in a student's choice of a school or a major. As *Davey* summarizes:

> Under our Establishment Clause precedent, the link between government funds and religious training is broken by the independent and private choice of recipients. As such, there is no doubt that the State could, consistent with the Federal Constitution, permit Promise Scholars to pursue a degree in devotional theology, and the State does not contend otherwise.[79]

This statement is dictum, but it accurately describes the Court's reasoning.

This private-choice reasoning implies the irrelevance of an argument that has long been central to the funding debate. Supporters of the constitutionality of modern funding programs have argued not just that the programs are nondiscriminatory, but also that the state gets full secular value for its money.[80] The state pays for math, reading, and history, or it pays for medi-

---

75. *See id.* at 718.

76. *Id.* at 719.

77. 474 U.S. 481 (1986).

78. *See id.* at 485-90.

79. *Davey,* 540 U.S. at 719 (citations omitted).

80. *See, e.g.,* JESSE H. CHOPER, SECURING RELIGIOUS LIBERTY: PRINCIPLES FOR JUDICIAL INTERPRETATION OF THE RELIGION CLAUSES 176-88 (1995); Berg, *supra* note 69, at 176-79; Michael W. McConnell, *The Selective Funding Problem: Abortions and Religious Schools,* 104 HARV. L. REV. 989, 1018-20 (1991); *see also* Lemon v. Kurtzman, 403 U.S. 602, 664 (1971) (White, J., concurring) (arguing that states were "financing a separable secular function of overriding importance"); Chittenden Town Sch. Dist. v. Dep't of Educ., 738 A.2d 539, 545-46, 562-63 (Vt. 1999) (holding, under the state constitution, that a tuition-payment plan could not pay for the religious portion of instruction at religious schools, but implying that it could pay for the secular portion).

cal care, or for food and shelter for the homeless; it does not pay for the clergy or the training of clergy. But this secular-value distinction no longer matters.

If "true private choice" breaks the link to state action, then there are no constitutional constraints on how the money can be spent. And that should mean that there is no need to allocate the cost of a church-affiliated school between the secular portion of the instruction and the religious portion. If the state can pay for seminarians, it can surely pay for middle-schoolers' religion classes, so long as the money is routed through "true private choice." If its voters can be persuaded to support the expenditure, a state can provide vouchers that pay the full cost of attending church-affiliated schools.

Rosenberger v. Rector & Visitors of University of Virginia[81] also supports the inference that the religious intensity of the program is irrelevant to the constitutionality of funding. *Rosenberger* held that where a state university used student fees to pay for a broad forum of student publications, it could not refuse to pay for a student religious publication.[82] *Rosenberger* was a free speech case, distinguished as such in *Davey*.[83] But in rejecting the university's Establishment Clause defense, *Rosenberger* relied on neutral funding of the students' independent publications.[84] This reasoning is a variant on the private-choice and no-state-action rationale that culminated in *Zelman: Rosenberger* emphasized neutrality rather than individual choice, because the money did not pass through the hands of an individual before benefiting the magazine.[85] But individual choice was still at work; the Court required the program to be viewpoint neutral, and small groups of students chose the content of each publication.[86] And while the Court implausibly said that the money in *Rosenberger* benefited only a publication and not a religious institution,[87] it was undisputed that much of that publication's content was core proselytizing speech.[88] The religious intensity of the program did not matter in *Rosenberger* or *Witters*, and the dictum in *Davey* treats it as settled that religious intensity does not matter if funds are administered through "true private choice."

---

81. 515 U.S. 819 (1995).

82. *See id.* at 828-46.

83. *See Davey*, 540 U.S. at 720 n.3. This dubious distinction is considered *infra* section I.C.3.c, text at notes 217-39.

84. *See Rosenberger*, 515 U.S. at 839-40, 843-44.

85. *See id.* at 825 (describing procedures for payment from the student council to creditors of the funded organization).

86. *See id.* at 825-26 (describing the founder, editors, and content of the magazine founded by the lead plaintiff).

87. *Id.* at 844.

88. *See id.* at 826; *id.* at 865-68 (Souter, J., dissenting).

There probably will still be a ban on gerrymandered categories that fund purely religious programs and little else. Examples might be a subsidy for all groups that meet once a week to consider issues pertaining to the meaning of life, or a Utah subsidy for the costs of traveling and living away from home while working without pay for a tax-exempt organization for up to two years.[89] But so long as the funding *category* includes substantial secular content, there appears to be no constitutional limit on the religious intensity of individual choices within the category.

This emerging rule may plausibly be viewed as an exception to the generalization that the Court avoids pursuing its logic to extreme results. No doubt this clear rule avoids difficult problems of apportionment and line-drawing. And avoiding such line-drawing promotes religious liberty, by eliminating incentives for programs to stay just on the secular side of the line. But refusing to draw lines also overrides the core religious liberty claim of the opponents of funding — that they should not be forced to pay taxes for other people's religious instruction. That claim was weak and attenuated as applied to instruction in secular subjects; the longstanding objection to funds for secular subjects in religious schools is a category mistake.[90]

The objection to government funds for instruction in religious subjects is far more plausible but still not obviously correct. Government financial incentives to choose secular over religious instruction directly discourage individual religious choices, whereas taxpayers' knowledge that a tiny fraction of the government's tax revenues goes to nondiscriminatory funding of education in religious subjects does not influence any person's religious choices. Even so, there is much to recommend a rule that although government may or must pay for secular value delivered, churches or individuals must pay for religious components of the program. The case for such a limit on funding is strongest in programs for the delivery of social services, where the service plainly could be delivered without the religious message accompanying it or supporting it. It is considerably weaker where the government is funding pri-

---

89. This hypothetical program would exactly fit the practice of young Mormons to go "on mission" for two years, seeking to spread the faith. *See* RICHARD N. OSTLING & JOAN K. OSTLING, MORMON AMERICA: THE POWER AND THE PROMISE 203-20 (1999). Where the state is funding secular content, as in elementary and secondary education, the Court has not cared that most of the private institutions in the program were offering that secular content in a religious environment. *See, e.g.,* Zelman v. Simmons-Harris, 536 U.S. 639, 656-60 (2002). But the Court might react differently in the unlikely event of a program that funded overwhelmingly religious content.

90. *See* Ira C. Lupu, *To Control Faction and Protect Liberty: A General Theory of the Religion Clauses,* 7 J. CONTEMP. LEGAL ISSUES 357, 373 (1996); text at notes 33-42 *supra.*

vate speech, including secular and anti-religious speech. However this balance should be struck, there is not much evidence that either wing of the Court saw two competing claims to religious liberty. The no-state-action rationale resolved the may-fund cases without reference to religious liberty.

C. What the State Must Fund

The holding in *Locke* v. *Davey* concerns what the state must fund. The answer appears to be very little, perhaps nothing. *Davey* held that when the state elects to fund a category of private-sector programs, it may facially discriminate against religious programs within the category.[91] From the perspective of the Court's cases on claims of a right to government funding, this holding is not surprising. From the perspective of the Court's cases on discrimination against religion, it is remarkable. The Court had never before held that the state can discriminate against religion.

The plaintiff's claim in *Davey* attempted to apply to a funding program the nondiscrimination principle that is newly prominent in the cases on regulation of religious practice. The two most recent Supreme Court cases in that line — *Employment Division v. Smith*[92] *and Church of the Lukumi Babalu Aye, Inc. v. City of Hialeah*[93] — converted the right to free exercise of religion into some kind of nondiscrimination right. For now I fudge with "some kind," because there is a large debate about the precise nature of this right. We will have to explore the full complexity of that debate to understand *Davey's* implications for the regulation cases.[94] But little of that complexity is necessary to understand either the claim in *Davey* or *Davey's* disputed implications for the funding cases.

There was no subtlety to the discrimination in the Washington State Promise Scholarships. The scholarships could be used to study in any accredited program except theology taught from a perspective designed to induce or reinforce belief.[95] So Davey filed a very simple claim: barring his theology major was discrimination against religion, on the face of the statute, in open and obvious violation of the *Smith-Lukumi* rules. *Lukumi* had said: "[T]he minimum requirement of neutrality is that a law not discriminate on its face. A law lacks facial neutrality if it refers to a religious practice without a secular

91. *See Davey,* 540 U.S. at 718-25.
92. 494 U.S. 872 (1990).
93. 508 U.S. 520 (1993).
94. *See infra* Part II, text at notes 271-404.
95. *See Davey,* 540 U.S. at 716.

meaning discernible from the language or context."[96] The statute creating the Promise Scholarships referred to theology on its face,[97] and no one claimed that the reference to theology included any secular meaning. The law treated the believing study of theology worse than it treated any other accredited major; theology majors were excluded, because of their faith-based choice of major, "from receiving the benefits of public welfare legislation."[98] This was discrimination under any understanding of discrimination. Moreover, the Establishment Clause was not a defense, because the money went to the student and the student's decision to major in theology was a "true private choice."[99]

To be clear on the scope of this free exercise claim, note that virtually everyone agrees that the state can distinguish between funding its own schools and funding private schools.[100] There is no plausible claim of a constitutional right to have the state contract out its services. Public and private schools may or may not differ in their treatment of religion, but they differ fundamentally in their ownership, and there is nothing constitutionally suspect about the state discriminating on the basis of public or private ownership. Religious minorities who find unacceptable secularism in public schools chafe under the burden of paying taxes for public schools and tuition for private schools, but an attack on that burden would not be a simple discrimination claim. It would require a far more robust claim: that the secularism of public education is so burdensome to some families' exercise of religion that they have no choice but to forgo their right to a free public education, and that the only remedy for that burden is for the state to pay for education in a religiously acceptable environment. It is easy to imagine such a claim, but it is impossible to imagine a court taking it seri-

---

96. *Lukumi,* 508 U.S. at 533.

97. *See* WASH. REV. CODE § 28B.10.814 (1997) ("No aid shall be awarded to any student who is pursuing a degree in theology.").

98. Everson v. Bd. of Educ., 330 U.S. 1, 16 (1947).

99. *See* text at notes 75-88 *supra.*

100. *See* Norwood v. Harrison, 413 U.S. 455, 461-63 (1973) (rejecting claim that the right to attend private schools implies a right to funding for those schools); Brusca v. Missouri *ex rel.* State Bd. of Educ., 332 F. Supp. 275, 279-80 (E.D. Mo. 1971), *aff'd mem.,* 405 U.S. 1050 (1972) (rejecting claim of free exercise right to funding for private religious schools); Gary S. v. Manchester Sch. Dist., 374 F.3d 15, 19-22 (1st Cir. 2004) (rejecting claim that disabled students in private schools are entitled to the same government-funded services as are disabled students in public schools); *Davey,* 540 U.S. at 729 (Scalia, J., dissenting) (conceding that the state "could make the scholarships redeemable only at public universities," which "would replace a program that facially discriminates against religion with one that just happens not to subsidize it").

ously. The courts have rejected claims merely to be exempted from small parts of the curriculum — claims that were much less sweeping and much simpler to remedy.[101]

Discrimination claims like the one in *Davey* arise only after the state makes a voluntary decision to fund attendance at private institutions. Then the question is whether it can fund attendance at secular institutions but not religious ones,[102] or as in *Davey,* fund secular courses of study but not religious ones. Prohibiting such discrimination would not require the state to fund religious institutions. A decision not to fund private schools at all would eliminate any argument about discrimination *among* private schools. Davey's claim depended on a prior political decision to fund private schools; once the state did that, he argued, it could not discriminate between secular and religious schools or majors.[103]

Davey's claim appeared to be a slam dunk under *Lukumi.* And yet it lost, 7-2. The Court held that *Lukumi's* ban on discriminatory regulation did not apply to a discriminatory refusal to fund the training of the clergy, at least absent antireligious motive. The Court cited a long national tradition against government funding of the clergy, reflected in "popular uprisings"[104] and made explicit in state constitutions from the founding era.[105] The state's interest in adhering to this tradition was "historic and substantial."[106] In a strangely structured opinion, the Court relied on this interest to conclude that the discriminatory refusal to fund was not presumptively unconstitu-

---

101. *See, e.g.,* Swanson *ex rel.* Swanson v. Guthrie Indep. Sch. Dist. No. I-L, 135 F.3d 694, 696-702 (10th Cir. 1998) (rejecting home-school student's claim of right to take selected classes at public school); Brown v. Hot, Sexy & Safer Prods., Inc., 68 F.3d 525, 537-39 (1st Cir. 1995) (refusing to exempt students from attending a salacious student assembly); Mozert v. Hawkins County Bd. of Educ., 827 F.2d 1058, 1063-70 (6th Cir. 1987) (refusing to exempt students from using a particular reader). For extensive criticism of such cases, see Nomi Maya Stolzenberg, *"He Drew a Circle That Shut Me Out": Assimilation, Indoctrination, and the Paradox of a Liberal Education,* 106 HARV. L. REV. 581 (1993).

102. *See* Strout v. Albanese, 178 F.3d 57, 60-66 (1st Cir. 1999) (upholding such a plan where the money was paid directly to the schools); Bagley v. Raymond Sch. Dep't, 728 A.2d 127, 133-36, 143-47 (Me. 1999) (upholding the same plan); Chittenden Town Sch. Dist. v. Dep't of Educ., 738 A.2d 539, 563-64 (Vt. 1999) (reserving the question).

103. Not all commentators have realized that Davey's claim was self-limiting in this way. *See* Richard C. Schragger, *The Role of the Local in the Doctrine and Discourse of Religious Liberty,* 117 HARV. L. REV. 1810, 1864 (2004) (arguing that under Davey's theory, funding of secular *public* schools would require funding of religious *private* schools). For the reasons explained in the text, this claim would not follow from Davey's theory.

104. *Davey,* 540 U.S. at 722.

105. *See id.* at 723 (collecting provisions from early state constitutions).

106. *Id.* at 725.

tional or inherently suspect,[107] and then relied on the same interest to justify the discrimination under the unspecified but apparently more deferential standard that applied in the absence of such a presumption or such suspicions.[108] These points were the entirety of the holding.

The terse opinion implies more than it states. The remainder of this section teases out and evaluates what the Court has done. Section I.C.1 reviews the Justices' inconsistent voting patterns in cases about what the state must fund. Section I.C.2 shows that the Court relied on earlier cases distinguishing financial penalties from "mere refusals to fund," and that deference to government definitions of "mere refusal to fund" has led the Court to uphold what are in fact financial penalties on the exercise of constitutional rights. Section I.C.3 explores other limits to *Davey's* holding and finds that these limits are likely to be illusory. Section I.C.4 assesses the regime that *Davey* creates: unchecked government discretion to either fund religion or not — with or without conditions — thus maximizing government power to interfere with religious liberty.

1. A Realist Introduction to the Discriminatory Funding Cases.

Joshua Davey was not the first litigant to complain that a state funding program discriminated against the exercise of a constitutional right. Usually, the Court rejects such claims; occasionally, it grants them. There are principled distinctions to be drawn among some of these cases, but it is clear that the votes of individual Justices are influenced by their sympathy or lack of sympathy for the underlying constitutional right. Michael McConnell demonstrated such inconsistencies on the Burger and early Rehnquist Courts.[109] This pattern has continued and perhaps gotten worse.

Only two recent discriminatory funding claims were unambiguously successful. *Rosenberger v. Rector & Visitors of University of Virginia*[110] required the university to fund a religious magazine so long as it maintained a forum of subsidized student publications.[111] *Legal Services Corp. v. Velazquez*[112] required the government to fund lawsuits seeking to "reform a Federal or State welfare system"[113] so long as it funded lawsuits seeking bene-

---

107. *See id.*
108. *See id.*
109. *See* McConnell, *supra* note 80, at 989-91.
110. 515 U.S. 819 (1995).
111. *See id.* at 828-46.
112. 531 U.S. 533 (2001).
113. *Id.* at 538 (quoting Omnibus Consolidated Rescissions and Appropriations Act of 1996, Pub. L. No. 104-134, § 504(a)(16), 110 Stat. 1321-55).

fits under an existing and unreformed welfare system.[114] Chief Justice Rehnquist and Justices O'Connor, Scalia, and Thomas voted to require funding for religious magazines but not for law-reform litigation; Justices Stevens, Souter, Ginsburg, and Breyer voted to require funding for law-reform litigation but not for religious magazines. Only Justice Kennedy voted to require funding in both cases. Part of the disagreement between the two blocs of four was based on the Establishment Clause.[115] But quite independently of the Establishment Clause, the Stevens-Souter-Ginsburg-Breyer bloc thought that there was no free speech claim in *Rosenberger*,[116] where the university funded a broad range of publications, but that there was a free speech claim in *Velazquez*,[117] where the government paid lawyers for the poor but limited the lawsuits it was willing to pay for.

Rosenberger and *Velazquez* are not the only examples of such apparent inconsistency. Chief Justice Rehnquist and Justices Scalia and Kennedy, who voted to require equal funding of religious magazines in *Rosenberger,* voted not to require equal funding of abortion information in *Rust v. Sullivan*.[118] Justice Stevens cast the opposite vote in each case.[119] Justices Stevens, Souter, and Ginsburg, who voted to require equal funding of law-reform litigation but not of religious magazines, also voted to require equal funding of computers without pornography filters in *United States v. American Library Ass'n*.[120] Chief Justice Rehnquist and Justices O'Connor, Scalia, and Thomas cast the opposite votes in each case, voting to require equal funding of religious magazines but not of law-reform litigation or computers without pornography filters. Some of these votes can no doubt be reconciled. But it is hard to resist the inference that in *Rosenberger,* Justices were voting for and against religion more than they were interpreting liberty.

114. *See id.* at 540-49.

115. *See Rosenberger,* 515 U.S. at 864-92 (Souter, J., dissenting) (relying on the Establishment Clause).

116. *See id.* at 892-99 (finding subject-matter exclusion, which is permissible, instead of viewpoint discrimination, which is forbidden).

117. *See Velazquez,* 531 U.S. at 540-49.

118. 500 U.S. 173 (1991).

119. Not everyone was inconsistent. Justice Souter voted not to require funding in either case, and Justice O'Connor voted to require funding in both cases, but on statutory rather than constitutional grounds in *Rust*.

120. *See* 539 U.S. 194, 220 (2003) (Stevens, J., dissenting); *id.* at 231 (Souter, J., dissenting).

2. *Penalties Versus Refusals to Fund.*

One distinction from these earlier cases was central to the Court's reasoning in *Davey*. The Court often says that when the government refuses to fund a constitutionally protected activity, it imposes no cognizable burden on the exercise of the unfunded constitutional right. It also says that the government cannot respond to an exercise of a constitutional right by withholding money for *other* activities eligible for government funding; this would penalize the exercise of the right. The no-penalty side of this distinction is an application of the much-debated rule against unconstitutional conditions.[121] But the Court places most funding cases on the other side of the line, as "mere" failures to fund.

Invoking this body of law without citation or elaboration, the Court denied that Washington had pressured Davey to abandon his theology major.[122] Rather, "[t]he State has merely chosen not to fund a distinct category of instruction."[123] This is a close paraphrase of *Rust v. Sullivan*,[124] where the government paid doctors to advise patients about contraception but forbade them to mention abortion. *Rust* said that "the Government has not discriminated on the basis of viewpoint; it has merely chosen to fund one activity to the exclusion of the other."[125] With or without citation, *Davey's* paraphrase of *Rust* is unmistakable.

Similarly, when the Court upheld government programs that paid for live birth but not for abortion, it said that refusal to fund did not pressure indigent women to surrender their right to abortion. Cutting off other benefits, instead of merely refusing to fund the abortion, would have penalized the choice to abort, a consequence the Court recognized as raising "[a] substantial constitutional question."[126] But "[a]n indigent woman who desires an abortion suf-

---

121. For an introduction to the voluminous literature on unconstitutional conditions, see Mitchell N. Berman, *Coercion Without Baselines: Unconstitutional Conditions in Three Dimensions*, 90 GEO. L.J. 1, 2-6 & nn.1-22 (2001). For promising steps toward a general solution, see *id.* at 6-112.

122. *See Davey*, 540 U.S. at 720-21.

123. *Id.* at 721.

124. 500 U.S. 173 (1991).

125. *Id.* at 193.

126. *See* Harris v. McRae, 448 U.S. 297, 317 n.19 (1980) ("A substantial constitutional question would arise if Congress had attempted to withhold all Medicaid benefits from an otherwise eligible candidate simply because that candidate had exercised her constitutionally protected freedom to terminate her pregnancy by abortion."); Maher v. Roe, 432 U.S. 464, 474–75 n.8 (1977) ("If Connecticut denied general welfare benefits to all women who had obtained abortions and who were otherwise entitled to the benefits, . . . strict scrutiny might be appropriate. . . .").

fers no disadvantage as a consequence of Connecticut's decision to fund child-birth; she continues as before to be dependent on private sources for the service she desires."[127] And the state "has imposed no restriction on access to abortions that was not already there" in the form of the woman's indigency.[128]

There are two substantial problems with *Davey's* reliance on this argument. First, because the Court has never required government to be neutral toward abortion, the implicit analogy to abortion is fundamentally flawed. Second, taking the argument on its own terms, the Court's rule against penalizing constitutional rights has been seriously eroded by a collateral rule: the government can insist that funded activities be kept rigorously separate from activities it refuses to fund.

(a) The Error in the Abortion Analogy: Burden Rights and Neutrality Rights.

Davey's model for analyzing discriminatory funding programs unmistakably originated in the abortion cases. But there are fundamental differences between religion and abortion: The Court has never said that government must be neutral toward abortion. Government can attempt "to persuade the woman to choose childbirth over abortion";[129] what it cannot do is impose undue burdens on the right to choose abortion.[130] Religious liberty is different; the Court has "often stated the principle that the First Amendment forbids an official purpose to disapprove of a particular religion or of religion in general."[131] The Court's endorsement test equally prohibits statements that "endorse or disapprove of religion."[132] The right to choose abortion is a right to be free of undue burdens; the right to religious liberty is a right to government neutrality. That is why litigants can object to government-sponsored religious symbols even though plaintiffs in such cases are *not* "unduly burdened."

In the first abortion-funding case, *Maher v. Roe*,[133] the Court squarely re-

127. *Maher*, 432 U.S. at 474.

128. *Id.*

129. Planned Parenthood of Southeastern Pa. v. Casey, 505 U.S. 833, 878 (1992) (plurality opinion).

130. *See, e.g., id.* at 874-79 (adopting the undue burden standard and reviewing its evolution in abortion cases); Bellotti v. Baird, 428 U.S. 132, 147 (1976) ("[A] requirement of written consent on the part of a pregnant adult is not unconstitutional unless it unduly burdens the right to seek an abortion.").

131. Church of the Lukumi Babalu Aye, Inc. v. City of Hialeah, 508 U.S. 520, 532 (1993) (collecting cases); *see also* Volokh, *supra* note 11, at 365-73 & nn.46-66 (collecting many cases requiring government neutrality toward religion).

132. Wallace v. Jaffree, 472 U.S. 38, 56 (1985) (quoting *Lynch v. Donnelly*, 465 U.S. 668, 690 (1984) (O'Connor, J., concurring)) (internal quotation mark omitted).

133. 432 U.S. 464 (1977).

lied on this distinction between burden rights and neutrality rights. A key precedent for the women seeking funding was *Sherbert v. Verner*,[134] which had held that the state could not refuse unemployment compensation to a Seventh-day Adventist who was unavailable for work on Saturdays.[135] *Sherbert* was the first holding to enforce the Court's earlier dictum that no person could be denied "the benefits of public welfare legislation" because of her faith.[136] But in *Maher* the Court said that abortion was different. The right to abortion "protects the woman from unduly burdensome interference with her freedom to decide whether to terminate her pregnancy. It implies no limitation on the authority of a State to make a value judgment favoring childbirth over abortion. . . ."[137] *Sherbert* "was decided in the significantly different context of a constitutionally imposed 'governmental obligation of neutrality.'"[138] So government can make "a value judgment" that live birth is preferable to abortion, but it cannot make a value judgment that secularism is better than religious faith.[139]

Pornography that falls short of obscenity is another example of a constitutional right that government can refuse to fund.[140] And as with abortion, the right to pornography does not include a right to government neutrality. Government could teach children in public schools that pornography is bad for them; it certainly could not teach children in public schools that religion is bad for them. Government could refuse to fund abortion because it could make a value judgment in favor of live birth, but that reasoning cannot be applied to religion.

The Court ignored this distinction in *Davey*. Instead, the Court said that government had a different reason for not funding religion — not that it disapproved of religion, but that there was a long tradition of no government funding.[141] Funding is now an exception to the rule of government neutrality toward religion.

134. 374 U.S. 398 (1963).

135. *See id.* at 403-10.

136. Everson v. Bd. of Educ., 330 U.S. 1, 16 (1947), *quoted in Sherbert*, 374 U.S. at 410.

137. *Maher*, 432 U.S. at 473–74.

138. *Id.* at 475 n.8 (quoting *Sherbert*, 374 U.S. at 409).

139. *See* Church of the Lukumi Babalu Aye, Inc. v. City of Hialeah, 508 U.S. 520, 537-38 (1993) (condemning ordinance that "devalues religious reasons for killing [animals] by judging them to be of lesser import than nonreligious reasons"); Fraternal Order of Police Newark Lodge No. 12 v. City of Newark, 170 F.3d 359, 366 (3d Cir. 1999) (condemning "a value judgment" that medical reasons for not shaving were more important than religious reasons for not shaving).

140. *See* United States v. Am. Library Ass'n, 539 U.S. 194 (2003).

141. *See Davey*, 540 U.S. at 724.

(b) Separating Funded and Unfunded Activities. Even assuming that funding theology majors should be subject to the same rules as funding abortions, it remains to explore those rules. The most important part of those rules is neither the rule permitting mere refusals to fund, nor the rule prohibiting penalties on the exercise of constitutional rights, but the collateral rule that marks the boundary between those two more visible rules. Here too the story begins with how the abortion-funding cases distinguished *Sherbert v. Verner.*

When *Sherbert* was decided, the Court had not yet introduced its distinction between refusing to fund and withholding other benefits. The Court in *Sherbert* conceived of unemployment compensation as a generally available benefit, withheld from Sherbert because of her religious practice, and thus imposing "the same kind of burden upon the free exercise of religion as would a fine imposed against appellant for her Saturday worship."[142] The Court did not conceive of the unemployment benefits as paying for her religious practice, which would have made *Sherbert* a mere refusal-to-fund case under the distinction developed later. Rather, these payments "reflect[ed] nothing more than the governmental obligation of neutrality in the face of religious differences."[143]

In the abortion-funding cases, the Court said that the facts of *Sherbert* were analogous to withholding all Medicaid benefits from women who chose an abortion, because in *Sherbert* the state had withheld "*all* unemployment compensation benefits from a claimant who would otherwise be eligible for such benefits but for the fact that she is unwilling to work one day per week on her Sabbath."[144] This characterization of the case overlooks the causal sequence from refusing work on the Sabbath to losing one's job to needing unemployment compensation for the whole week. A closer analogy to *Sherbert* would be a state that refused Medicaid benefits for injuries or medical complications caused by privately funded abortions. It is not clear that *Sherbert* would come out the same way if it first arose today, but the Court continues to treat *Sherbert* and its progeny as good law.[145]

---

142. *Sherbert,* 374 U.S. at 404.

143. *Id.* at 409.

144. Harris v. McRae, 448 U.S. 297, 317 n.19 (1980); *see also* Maher v. Roe, 432 U.S. 464, 475 n.8 (1977) (briefly distinguishing *Sherbert* on similar grounds). *Maher* distinguishes *Sherbert* on two grounds, separated by "[i]n addition." The first ground is that *Sherbert* involved a penalty on the constitutional right; the opinion distinguishes other penalty cases, and then says that *Sherbert* "similarly is inapplicable here." The second ground is the ground discussed *supra* in text at notes 129-37.

145. *See Davey,* 540 U.S. at 720-21; City of Boerne v. Flores, 521 U.S. 507, 514 (1997); Church of the Lukumi Babalu Aye, Inc. v. City of Hialeah, 508 U.S. 520, 537-38 (1993). The

The rule against withholding other benefits became a holding in *FCC v. League of Women Voters*,[146] where Congress had prohibited editorials on public television stations that received federal funds.[147] The majority reasoned that Congress had not merely prohibited editorializing with federal grant money, which would have been a mere failure to fund. Congress had also prohibited the stations from editorializing with their own money if they accepted *any* federal money. From the stations' perspective, if they editorialized with their own money, they forfeited all federal money. That forfeiture, the Court held, was an unconstitutional penalty on political speech.[148] But Justice Rehnquist dissented. He thought the distinction between editorializing with federal money and with private money "ignore[d] economic reality,"[149] because both sources of funds supported the same staff and facilities, and therefore everything done by that staff or in those facilities.

Rehnquist's reasoning underlay the Reagan Administration's regulations at issue in *Rust v. Sullivan*. Under these regulations, a federal grant recipient could use federal funds to provide information on contraception and use its own funds to provide abortions or information about abortion.[150] But the regulations required the two programs to be "physically and financially separate," with separateness measured not just by separate accounting, but by separate personnel and separate space as well.[151] These rules were highly burdensome to the grantees, their doctors, and their patients,[152] but the Court upheld the rules as necessary to ensure that no federal money for contraception subsidized abortion.[153] In effect, the Court permitted the government to

---

strongest reason for preserving the result in *Sherbert* itself is that the calendar does not yield a neutral set of rules. Government and most of secular society operate on a Christian calendar that best accommodates the largest denominations. *See* Douglas Laycock, *The Remnants of Free Exercise*, 1990 SUP. CT. REV. 1, 51 (text at note 209).

146. 468 U.S. 364 (1984).

147. *See id.* at 366; *see also* Regan v. Taxation with Representation, 461 U.S. 540, 544-45 (1983) (elaborating the distinction between penalizing and refusing to subsidize, in an opinion upholding the loss of tax benefits for charities that spent substantial funds on lobbying); *id.* at 552-54 (Blackmun, J., concurring) (same); McConnell, *supra* note 80, at 1015-22 (reviewing the development of the distinction and applying it to abortion and to religious schools).

148. *See* League of Women Voters, 468 U.S. at 399-401.

149. *Id.* at 406 (Rehnquist, J., dissenting).

150. *See* Rust v. Sullivan, 500 U.S. 173, 178-81, 196 (1991) (describing the regulations).

151. *Id.* at 180-81.

152. *See* New York v. Bowen, 690 F. Supp. 1261, 1271 (S.D.N.Y. 1988) (reviewing evidence of financial burdens and interference with medical care), *aff'd on other grounds sub nom.* New York v. Sullivan, 889 F.2d 401 (2d Cir. 1989), *aff'd sub nom.* Rust v. Sullivan, 500 U.S. 173 (1991).

153. *See* Rust, 500 U.S. at 196-99.

require prophylactic degrees of separation, to avoid any possibility of indirect subsidy through shared overhead and the like.

Davey did not cite this line of cases either, but Chief Justice Rehnquist tried to bring *Davey* within it. He said that Washington's program "does not require students to choose between their religious beliefs and receiving a government benefit."[154] As a factual matter, that statement was false. All Davey's general education courses, and all his electives — even including theology electives[155] — were eligible for support from a Promise Scholarship. He could claim that scholarship if he declared a different major, or presumably if he delayed declaring his major for as long as possible, but he forfeited the scholarship for his secular courses as soon as he declared a theology major. He was indeed required to choose between his religious beliefs and a government benefit for his secular courses.

As it happened, Joshua Davey was a double major in theology and business administration.[156] It was perfectly clear that in his case, he forfeited a scholarship for his business administration major as a consequence of declaring his theology major. The Court addressed that problem in a footnote, arguing that "Promise Scholars may still use their scholarship to pursue a secular degree at a different institution from where they are studying devotional theology."[157] By focusing on the unusual case of a dual-degree candidate, the Court entirely avoided the more common problem of forfeiting scholarship funds for electives and general education requirements. Even for a dual-degree candidate, taking the two degrees at two separate schools is impractical, at least requiring much commuting, quite likely requiring extra courses and extra semesters, and certainly depriving him of his first choice of school, faculty, and curriculum for the second degree. There is no doubt that these difficulties would be cognizable burdens on a constitutional right in any context except government funding.[158]

But the convenience of taking secular courses and a theology major at the same school is like the savings of overhead in *Rust v. Sullivan*. And allocating the scholarship to the secular courses looks like a bookkeeping entry

---

154. *Davey*, 540 U.S. at 720-21.

155. *See id.* at 725 n.9. The state professed doubts about this rule but had not changed it. *Id.*

156. *Id.* at 717.

157. *Id.* at 721 n.4.

158. The Court relied on similar inconveniences to explain why a male student was burdened by exclusion from the nursing program at a state university even though the state offered other nursing programs that were open to him. *See* Miss. Univ. for Women v. Hogan, 458 U.S. 718, 723 n.8 (1982).

with no real-world consequences. So although it is false to say that Davey was not penalized, that is not the point. The rule of *Davey* and *Rust* is that the state can impose prophylactic rules to minimize the chances for cross-subsidization, and that the resulting burdens on recipients of government funds are constitutionally irrelevant. The Court's tolerance for such prophylactic rules means that the rule permitting mere refusals to fund is swallowing the rule against penalizing a constitutionally protected activity by withholding other related benefits. None of this paragraph is spelled out in the opinion, but this is undoubtedly what it means.

Similar arguments about how to allocate or account for the flow of government funds have arisen in other contexts, with varied implications for religious liberty. For a time, the Court held that states could give religious schools only secular goods and services that were incapable of diversion to religious uses.[159] The heart of the *Lemon* test in operation was a dilemma built on the divertibility of aid: any aid diverted to religious uses advanced religion, and any government monitoring to prevent such diversion caused excessive entanglement.[160] Later, the Court said that any substantial benefit to a religious school advanced religion, basically because money is fungible.[161] Even if the state provided only math books, the school would save the cost of buying math books, and the money saved might be spent on religion. The Court eventually rejected the legal relevance of these economic realities with respect to goods and services, but it has not yet done so with respect to cash. Even the plurality opinion in *Mitchell v. Helms,* the opinion that would go furthest to uphold direct aid, reserved the issue of direct cash grants to religious schools.[162] *Zelman v. Simmons-Harris*[163] avoids the whole problem; because "true private choice"[164] is said to break the link between the government giving the money and the religious school receiving it, the possible uses of the money are irrelevant to the permissibility of voucher programs. But *Davey* held that government may *choose* to be concerned with how the money might be spent, even in programs of "true private choice," and that it can act on that concern by adopting prophylactic rules requiring stringent separation of funded and unfunded activities.

159. *See* Mitchell v. Helms, 530 U.S. 793, 890-95 (2000) (Souter, J., dissenting) (reviewing the cases).

160. *See* Lemon v. Kurtzman, 403 U.S. 602, 619 (1971); *id.* at 668 (White, J., concurring).

161. *See* Wolman v. Walter, 433 U.S. 229, 248-51 (1977) (invalidating loans of educational equipment); *see also Lemon,* 403 U.S. at 641 (Douglas, J., concurring).

162. *See Mitchell,* 530 U.S. at 818-19 & n.8.

163. 536 U.S. 639 (2002).

164. *Id.* at 649, 650, 653, 662.

Similar issues about the fungibility of cash arise with respect to the scope of the federal spending power. The United States can attach conditions to its grants of money, and it has historically applied those conditions to the entire program or activity that receives the money, even if the United States supplies only a small part of the budget.[165] Within the assisted program, Congress can assume that "[m]oney is fungible," and that "money can be drained off here because a federal grant is pouring in there."[166]

Title VI of the Civil Rights Act of 1964,[167] which prohibits racial discrimination in programs or activities receiving federal funds, defines "program or activity" broadly.[168] Title VI has long been at the core of federal civil rights policy, and many other civil rights statutes borrow its definition.[169] One of these is the Spending Clause provisions of the Religious Land Use and Institutionalized Persons Act (RLUIPA),[170] which requires compelling justification for substantial burdens on religious exercise in federally assisted prisons.[171] Courts have so far rejected claims that the Act exceeds the scope of the spending power.[172] The broad reach of the spending power in RLUIPA depends on the view that money is fungible, the same view that underlies Washington's requirement that Davey attend two colleges if he wants a scholarship for his secular courses.

If one accepts the Court's view that states have a constitutional right not to be held to Congress's understanding of individual liberties,[173] then *Davey* and the challenges to RLUIPA are parallel. Washington was permitted to withhold all funds for Davey's education to avoid any risk of subsidizing theology, and Congress may similarly withhold all funds for state prisons to avoid any risk of subsidizing unjustified restrictions on the prisoners' religious liberty. If the Court acts on its view of permissible rules for tracing the

---

165. *See, e.g.*, South Dakota v. Dole, 483 U.S. 203, 206-12 (1987).

166. Sabri v. United States, 541 U.S. 600, 606 (2004) (upholding an indictment for bribery in a federally assisted program, and rejecting a defense that the indictment did not allege a connection between the bribe and the federal funds). *Sabri* reserves the possibility that a state grant recipient might have a valid objection where a briber would not. *Id.* at 608.

167. 42 U.S.C. §§ 2000d to 2000d-7 (2000).

168. *See* 42 U.S.C. § 2000d-4a (2000) (defining the aided "program or activity" to include the entire department, agency, university, or "public system of higher education" that receives the money).

169. *See* 20 U.S.C. § 1687 (2000) (sex discrimination in education); 29 U.S.C. § 794(b) (2000) (disability discrimination); 42 U.S.C. § 6107(4) (2000) (age discrimination).

170. 42 U.S.C. §§ 2000cc to 2000cc-5 (2000).

171. *Id.* § 2000cc-1(b)(1).

172. *See infra* note 379 and accompanying text.

173. *See* City of Boerne v. Flores, 521 U.S. 507, 516-29 (1997).

flow of funds — and not on its policy views about the challenged funding condition — RLUIPA's Spending Clause provisions are constitutional and *Davey* is one more precedent supporting that conclusion.[174]

My own view is that the Spending Clause cases are about interpreting the scope of legislative power expressly delegated to Congress, where that power is not limited by a countervailing guarantee of individual rights. In that context it is perfectly sensible to assume that money is fungible. The same assumption is much more troubling where government uses it to override an express constitutional right. But that is not the Court's view.

The Court has so far given total deference to government's desire to avoid any risk of indirectly subsidizing something it chooses not to subsidize, and it has given no weight to the resulting practical penalty on the exercise of constitutional rights. Plainly, there must be some limit to this approach. In the full logic of fungibility, separate schools or separate facilities are not enough. Davey would be more able to afford his theology degree if the state had paid for his business administration degree elsewhere, or if the government had subsidized his student loan, or if it had paid social security benefits to his mother. Of course the Court will not go to that extreme. But it has gone far already: under *Davey* and *Rust*, government's power to withhold funding can be leveraged into substantial power to penalize religious liberty or any other constitutional right. Assuming that money is fungible has enabled the Court to avoid facing the problems of the unconstitutional conditions doctrine, but drawing boundaries to that assumption will eventually add another layer of complexity to those problems.

3. Other Limits to the Holding.

The most important limit to *Davey*'s holding is that it applies only to funding, not to regulation.[175] That limit is real and important; it is separately discussed in section II.B.[176]

Within the universe of funding cases, serious limits are harder to find. The rule against penalties is a limit, although judicial deference to prophylactic rules of physical separation will often make that limit illusory. The *Davey* opinion suggests at least three more distinct limits to the holding. On its face,

174. Marty Lederman first pointed out the parallel between *Davey* and RLUIPA. Posting of Marty Lederman to religionlaw.lists.ucla.edu (May 27, 2004), *available at* http://lists.ucla.edu/pipermail/religionlaw/2004-May/016822.html.

175. *See Davey*, 540 U.S. at 722 n.5 ("[T]he only interest at issue here is the state's interest in not funding the religious training of clergy.").

176. *See infra* section II.B, text at notes 381-404.

the holding is confined to the training of clergy, to refusals to fund that are not based on hostility to religion, and to cases that do not involve forums for speech. Like the rule against penalties, each of these limitations may well turn out to be illusory.

(a) **Religious Intensity of the Program Where Funds Are Used.** There is much to suggest, beginning with the Court's discussion of tradition and its collection of early state constitutions, that the opinion is confined to the training of clergy. The Court says that "[t]raining someone to lead a congregation is an essentially religious endeavor," and that "majoring in devotional theology is akin to a religious calling as well as an academic pursuit."[177] The Court insists that "the *only* interest at issue here is the State's interest in not funding the religious training of clergy."[178] And the Court concludes: "We need not venture further into this difficult area to uphold the [program] as currently operated. . . ."[179]

The Court is certainly right that the training of clergy is an "essentially religious endeavor." The well-established "clergy exception" in employment law holds that the relationship between a church and its clergy is immune from state interference,[180] and this doctrine has also been applied to employment disputes arising in the seminaries that train clergy.[181] In a case now pending in the Texas Supreme Court, unaccredited seminaries are arguing that the state has no constitutional power to license the training of clergy or to regulate the content of their education. That claim should prevail, although the lower courts have so far held that the state is not regulating content.[182] But if training the clergy is especially sensitive on the regulation side, it may be equally sensitive on the funding side.

None of the *Davey* opinion's comments about the training of clergy

---

177. *Davey*, 540 U.S. at 721.

178. *Id.* at 722 n.5 (emphasis added).

179. *Id.* at 725.

180. *See, e.g.,* Serbian E. Orthodox Diocese v. Milivojevich, 426 U.S. 696, 715-20 (1976) (reversing a judgment purporting to reinstate a deposed bishop); EEOC v. Roman Catholic Diocese, 213 F.3d 795, 800 & n.* (4th Cir. 2000) (collecting cases).

181. *See, e.g.,* EEOC v. Catholic Univ., 83 F.3d 455, 460-65 (D.C. Cir. 1996) (dismissing sex discrimination claim by professor of canon law); EEOC v. Southwestern Baptist Theological Seminary, 651 F.2d 277, 282-85 (5th Cir. 1981) (holding that a seminary is a church, and its faculty are clergy, for purposes of the ministerial exception).

182. *See* HEB Ministries, Inc. v. Tex. Higher Educ. Coordinating Bd., 114 S.W.3d 617, 628-34 (Tex. App. 2003), *review granted,* No. 03-0995 (Tex. Dec. 3, 2004). [After this article was published, the Texas Supreme Court struck down the state's regulation of unaccredited seminaries. 235 S.W.3d 627 (Tex. 2007).]

would apply to other discriminatory refusals to fund services delivered by religious institutions. A state that will pay for secular private schools but not religious private schools, or secular charter schools but not religious charter schools, is not refusing to pay for the training of clergy. Such a state is refusing to pay for education that satisfies the state's compulsory education requirements in math, reading, and other secular subjects.

There is some national tradition of not paying for such instruction in religious schools, but that tradition does not go back to the Founding and is not reflected in early state constitutions. The strongest and most persistent version of that tradition goes back to the mid-nineteenth century, and is reflected in many state constitutions, but that version consisted principally of a refusal to fund Catholic education in private schools while Protestant education flourished in public schools.[183] It is hard to make a case for a *general* reluctance to fund education in a religious environment before prayers and religious instruction were removed from the public schools, a change that began in the late-nineteenth century in a few states,[184] spread broadly in the third quarter of the twentieth century in states that complied with the Supreme Court's decisions on school-sponsored prayer,[185] and remains contested even today in some states.[186] As applied to elementary and secondary schools, the no-funding tradition is a misinterpretation of the Establishment Clause, deeply rooted in historic anti-Catholicism. And there is no sustained national tradition of any kind that refuses to fund religious delivery of social services. Billions of government dollars have flowed through religious charities over the decades.[187]

---

183. *See* Jeffries & Ryan, *supra* note 12, at 297-305; David B. Tyack, *Onward Christian Soldiers: Religion in the American Common School,* in History and Education: The Educational Uses of the Past 212, 212-33 (Paul Nash ed., 1970).

184. *See* State *ex rel.* Weiss v. Dist. Bd., 44 N.W. 967, 973-76 (Wis. 1890) (prohibiting Bible reading in public schools); Steven K. Green, *The Blaine Amendment Reconsidered,* 36 Am. J. Legal Hist. 38, 45-47 (1992) (reviewing voluntary decisions to eliminate religious observances in public schools).

185. *See* Sch. Dist. v. Schempp, 374 U.S. 203 (1963) (invalidating school-sponsored prayer and Bible reading); Engel v. Vitale, 370 U.S. 421 (1962) (invalidating school-sponsored prayer). Compliance was slow. *See, e.g.,* Kenneth M. Dolbeare & Phillip E. Hammond, The School Prayer Decisions: From Court Policy to Local Practice (1971) (examining compliance in an unnamed midwestern state).

186. *See* Santa Fe Indep. Sch. Dist. v. Doe, 530 U.S. 290, 295 (2000) (describing multiple ways in which the school district supported religion); Wallace v. Jaffree, 472 U.S. 38, 40 & n.3, 44 & n.23 (1985) (describing daily classroom prayers); Ingebretsen v. Jackson Pub. Sch. Dist., 88 F.3d 274, 278-81 (5th Cir. 1996) (enjoining newly enacted "School Prayer Statute").

187. *See* Steven V. Monsma, When Sacred and Secular Mix: Religious Non-

The tradition-based interest on which the Court relied is thus at its maximum in *Davey* itself; it is considerably weaker in other contexts. Distinctions along these lines would be perfectly sound. But *Davey* is likely to lead to a more general principle that all religious programs and institutions can be excluded from funding programs. There is first the magnitude of the vote. Seven Justices voted to uphold the discriminatory refusal to fund, and four of them probably believe that nondiscriminatory funding would be unconstitutional even if the state volunteered to provide it.[188] If only three votes are in play, all three would have to distinguish refusing to provide tuition at religious elementary schools from refusing to provide tuition for theology majors. That could and should happen, but for supporters of nondiscriminatory funding, it is a bit like drawing to an inside straight. New Justices could of course change the odds.

A second reason for thinking that religious intensity will not matter to what the state must fund is that, as already noted, religious intensity has dropped out of the debate over what the state may fund.[189] On the question of what the state *may* fund, there is no difference between soup kitchens, math classes, and training clergy. This doctrinal development makes it harder to reintroduce that distinction and make it central to the question of what the state *must* fund. There would be no logical inconsistency: In the may-fund cases, religious intensity is irrelevant to the issue of state action, and the finding of no state action disposes of the case. In the must-fund cases, there is obviously state action; the question is the strength of the state's interest in not funding, and religious intensity may be relevant to the weight of that interest without being relevant to the presence of state action. The case for symmetry is thus more impressionistic and aesthetic than logical or doctrinal. The distinction may yet be drawn, but the Court's reasoning on what the state may fund makes it less likely to rely heavily on degrees of religious intensity with respect to what the state must fund.

The Court's willingness to uphold prophylactic rules requiring physical separation of functions is another obstacle to distinguishing funding of educa-

---

PROFIT ORGANIZATIONS AND PUBLIC MONEY 63-80, 104-05 (1996) (reporting that most charities surveyed, religious or secular, received substantial government funds); David Saperstein, *Public Accountability and Faith-Based Organizations: A Problem Best Avoided*, 116 HARV. L. REV. 1353, 1359 & n.15 (2003) (reporting dollar amounts for selected religious charities).

188. *See* Zelman v. Simmons-Harris, 536 U.S. 639, 686-717 (2002) (Souter, J., dissenting, joined by Stevens, Ginsburg, and Breyer, JJ.); Agostini v. Felton, 521 U.S. 203, 240-53 (1997) (Souter, J., dissenting, joined in whole or in part by Stevens, Ginsburg, and Breyer, JJ.).

189. *See supra* section I.B, text at notes 80-88.

tion in secular subjects from funding the training of clergy. If the Court were to say that states funding private schools can refuse to fund religion courses, but cannot refuse to fund secular courses in religious schools, states could respond that the religious and secular instruction must be rigorously separated to avoid any risk of cross-subsidies. A state could apparently insist that religion classes be offered in a separate building, staffed by separate personnel.

Such a requirement of physical separation would not be entirely unprecedented. In the twelve years between *Aguilar v. Felton*[190] and *Agostini v. Felton*,[191] when the Court prohibited federally funded remedial instruction in the buildings of religious schools, that instruction was moved to nearby vans.[192] One can imagine, in a state that wanted to fund secular private education but not religious private education, the religious schools moving their *religious* instruction to vans and staffing it with personnel paid by the local church instead of by the school. But while one can imagine that result, it is hard to imagine the political process that would lead to it.

Refusing state funding for math and reading, because the school also teaches religion, is clearly a penalty on teaching religion and on attending a school that does so. If religious liberty consists of minimizing government influence on religious choices, such a penalty restricts religious liberty. But states choosing to impose that penalty seem likely to prevail after *Davey*. Early decisions applying *Davey* have extended it to elementary and secondary education without even noting that this was an extension or that it presented a substantial choice.[193]

(b) **Bad Motive.** Bad motive is a clearer doctrinal limit to the holding in *Davey*. The Court emphasized that Washington had a legitimate reason for refusing to fund the training of clergy, and that that reason suggested no hostility or animus against religion.[194] The Court implied that discriminatory refusal to fund religious education *would* be constitutionally suspect if it were motivated by hostility to religion.[195] The question is whether support-

---

190. 473 U.S. 402 (1985).

191. 521 U.S. 203 (1997).

192. *See supra* text at notes 40-47.

193. *See* Am. Jewish Cong. v. Corp. for Nat'l & Cmty. Serv., 323 F. Supp. 2d 44, 64-65 (D.D.C. 2004); Bush v. Holmes, No. 1D02-3160, 2004 WL 1809821, at *17-19 (Fla. Dist. Ct. App. 2004), *superseding opinion en banc*, 886 So.2d 340, 362-66 (Fla. Dist. Ct. App. 2004), *aff'd in part, on other grounds*, 919 So.2d 392 (Fla. 2006). [This case was pending in the District Court of Appeal, en banc, when this article was published.]

194. *See Davey*, 540 U.S. at 723-24.

195. *See infra* text at notes 390-95.

ers of funding can prove bad motive in any significant range of cases. They think they can.

Much of the American tradition of refusing to fund private schools is derived from nineteenth-century anti-Catholicism.[196] The proposed Blaine Amendment to the federal Constitution would have codified the nineteenth-century Protestant position, permitting government-sponsored Bible reading in the public schools and prohibiting government money for "sectarian" schools.[197] "Sectarian" initially meant something like denominational; the term arose in early-nineteenth-century battles between liberal and conservative Protestants.[198] But Protestants closed ranks in response to Catholic immigration,[199] and for most of the nineteenth century, "sectarian" was a code word for Catholic.[200] The Blaine Amendment failed in the Senate, but state Blaine Amendments addressed to the funding issue were added to about three-quarters of the state constitutions.[201] These amendments come in many varia-

---

196. *See* PHILIP HAMBURGER, SEPARATION OF CHURCH AND STATE 191-478 (2002) (detailing virulent anti-Catholicism in this and other church-state issues); Jeffries & Ryan, *supra* note 12, at 297-318 (reviewing Protestant-Catholic school battles from the mid-nineteenth to mid-twentieth centuries); Douglas Laycock, *The Many Meanings of Separation,* 70 U. CHI. L. REV. 1667, 1678-82 (2003) (text at notes 20-26) (summarizing scattered passages from Hamburger). I cite Hamburger for his detailed factual history and do not accept his tendentious conception of separation of church and state, which persistently gets in the way of his history. *See id.* at 1667-72.

197. For the text of the proposed amendments, see H.R. Res. 1, 44th Cong. (1876), as amended by the Senate Committee on the Judiciary, 4 CONG. REC. 5453 (1876), *reprinted in* Green, *supra* note 184, at 60.

198. *See* CHARLES LESLIE GLENN, JR., THE MYTH OF THE COMMON SCHOOL 131-32, 179-96 (1988); CARL F. KAESTLE, PILLARS OF THE REPUBLIC: COMMON SCHOOLS AND AMERICAN SOCIETY, 1780-1860, at 98-99 (1983); Jeffries & Ryan, *supra* note 12, at 298.

199. *See* GLENN, *supra* note 198, at 179; KAESTLE, *supra* note 198, at 98; Jeffries & Ryan, *supra* note 12, at 301.

200. For the anti-Catholic politics of the Blaine Amendment, see Green, *supra* note 184 *passim;* and HAMBURGER, *supra* note 196, at 324-26. For explicit contemporary acknowledgement of the code meaning of "sectarian," see *id.* at 325 n.99 (quoting the September 7, 1878 edition of the *Index,* a separationist newspaper).

201. For efforts to categorize these provisions, see Berg, *supra* note 69, at 167-68; Mark Edward DeForrest, *An Overview and Evaluation of State Blaine Amendments: Origins, Scope, and First Amendment Concerns,* 26 HARV. J.L. & PUB. POL'Y 551, 576-602 (2003); and Linda S. Wendtland, Note, *Beyond the Establishment Clause: Enforcing Separation of Church and State Through State Constitutional Provisions,* 71 VA. L. REV. 625, 631-42 (1985). The Becket Fund for Religious Liberty has compiled links to thirty-nine state Blaine Amendments at http://www.blaineamendments.org/states/states.html (last visited Oct. 10, 2004). Most other states have provisions that ban "compelled support" for places of worship. *See* Wendtland, *supra,* at 631-32.

tions; they are generally more detailed than the federal Establishment Clause. Some of them have been read to permit nondiscriminatory funding of religious and secular schools,[202] others to prohibit funding of religious schools by any mechanism.[203] Many have not been interpreted in recent years. Contemporary supporters of aid to religious schools argue that these amendments are invalid because they were motivated by anti-Catholic bigotry.[204] Opponents have argued that there were other, more legitimate motives,[205] or even that papal resistance to democracy justified anti-Catholicism at the time.[206]

Judges are notoriously reluctant to find bad motive, but seven Justices have already taken note of this history;[207] good litigators might be able to prove it to judicial satisfaction in many states. And ancient bad motive is sufficient grounds to invalidate current applications of a badly motivated provision. In 1985, the Court invalidated a facially neutral provision of the Alabama Constitution because of bad motive at the Constitutional Convention of 1901.[208]

The problem with this litigation strategy is that states need not rely on their Blaine Amendments. Scholars of bad motive have long worried about the harmful law being struck down for bad motive and then reenacted without any bad motive apparent on the legislative record.[209] A legislature could enact a discriminatory funding scheme that excludes religious institutions

---

202. *See* Kotterman v. Killian, 972 P.2d 606, 616-25 (Ariz. 1999) (upholding tax credits for gifts to scholarship funds for private schools); Simmons-Harris v. Goff, 711 N.E.2d 203, 211-12 (Ohio 1999) (concluding that Cleveland voucher plan could include religious schools); Jackson v. Benson, 578 N.W.2d 602, 620-23 (Wis. 1998) (upholding Milwaukee voucher plan).

203. *See* Bush v. Holmes, No. 1D02-3160, 2004 WL 1809821, at *4-16 (Fla. Dist. Ct. App. 2004) (invalidating Florida's voucher plan), *superseding opinion en banc,* 886 So.2d 340, 347-61 (Fla. Dist. Ct. App. 2004), *aff'd in part, on other grounds,* 919 So.2d 392 (Fla. 2006); Witters v. State Comm'n for the Blind, 771 P.2d 1119, 1121-22 (Wash. 1989) (upholding state's refusal to grant scholarship for the blind to student attending seminary).

204. *See* Berg, *supra* note 69, at 199-208 (summarizing the argument); LUPU & TUTTLE, *supra* note 64, at 959-60, 967-70 (assessing the strengths and difficulties of the argument).

205. *See* Scholars Brief, *supra* note 20 (citing support for public schools and noting early disagreements among Protestants).

206. *See* Brief Amici Curiae of the American Jewish Congress et al., *Davey* (No. 02-1315), *available in* 2003 WL 21697726, at *25-30.

207. *See* Zelman v. Simmons-Harris, 536 U.S. 639, 720-21 (2002) (Breyer, J., dissenting, joined by Stevens and Souter, JJ.); Mitchell v. Helms, 530 U.S. 793, 828-29 (2000) (plurality opinion by Thomas, J., joined by Rehnquist, C.J., and Scalia and Kennedy, JJ.).

208. *See* Hunter v. Underwood, 471 U.S. 222, 227-33 (1985).

209. *See, e.g.,* John Hart Ely, *Legislative and Administrative Motivation in Constitutional Law,* 79 YALE L.J. 1205, 1214-15 (1970) (suggesting the "[f]utility" of invalidating for bad motive).

and rely simply on a "tradition" of not funding religious institutions. Or a legislature could refuse to enact any private funding plan at all. Surely it is not required to do so, no matter what badly motivated provisions lurk in the state constitution.

To invalidate a modern program on the basis of a state's Blaine Amendment, a litigant would have to show some causal connection between the state Blaine Amendment and the modern provision at issue. *Davey* suggests that that will be difficult. Washington argued that the religious exclusion in its Promise Scholarship Program was designed to implement Article I, Section 11 of the state constitution. Section 11 is a detailed provision, combining strong guarantees of free exercise with a strong guarantee against establishment, and specifying that "[n]o public money or property shall be appropriated for or applied to any religious worship, exercise or instruction, or the support of any religious establishment."[210] The apparent reason for asserting the statute's connection to this provision was the doubtful hope that a state constitutional provision might get more judicial deference than a state statute. But states need not assert such connections; Washington could have argued that the religious exclusion was a modern legislative provision, untainted by any bad history attaching to the state constitutional provision.

The Washington Constitution contains another provision, Article IX, Section 4, providing that "[a]ll schools maintained or supported wholly or in part by the public funds shall be forever free from sectarian control or influence."[211] The Court identified this provision as Washington's Blaine Amendment.[212] Then it said that "[n]either Davey nor *amici* have established a credible connection between the Blaine Amendment and Article I, [S]ection 11, the relevant constitutional provision. Accordingly, the Blaine Amendment's history is simply not before us."[213]

It is not clear whether this conclusion means that there is no connection between the federal Blaine Amendment and Article I, Section 11, or no connection between the two sections of Washington's constitution. Either way, the Court implies a very narrow view of what would count as "a credible connection." The two sections were both drafted at the Constitutional Convention of 1889, a convention of seventy-five delegates who met for twenty-nine days in Olympia.[214] If those few delegates in that short time in that small

210. WASH. CONST. art. I, § 11.

211. *Id.* art. IX, § 4.

212. *Davey,* 540 U.S. at 723 n.7.

213. *Id.*

214. WASH. CONST. constitutional convention note. For the original 1889 text, see *id.* art. I, § 11 historical note; and *id.* art. IX, § 4.

town[215] wrote two provisions restricting the flow of state money to religious institutions, it beggars the imagination to suppose that one provision was tainted by anti-Catholicism but not the other. If the Court could not find a credible connection between the funding provision of Section 11 and either the state or federal Blaine Amendment, it is unlikely to find a connection between nineteenth-century Blaine Amendments and any twenty-first-century enactment.

If courts invalidate an enacted program under a state's Blaine Amendment, the Supreme Court could presumably reverse that judgment on the ground that the state Blaine Amendment, as applied in that case, violated the federal Constitution. But if the Court denies certiorari when the question first arises, how could anyone create a new case or controversy that would present the question? There would be no state program, the lack of a state program would not be unconstitutional, and federal courts would not order a new spending program to be enacted.

All that said, *Davey* expressly held the issue open.[216] Good lawyers believe that supporters of funding will ultimately prevail on these motive claims. But *Davey* also seems to erect a very large obstacle to ever reaching the issue.

(c) **Speech.** The two recent cases in which the Court invalidated discriminatory funding programs were both decided on free speech grounds.[217] For *Davey,* the most obviously relevant precedent was *Rosenberger v. Rector & Visitors of University of Virginia.*[218] In *Rosenberger,* where the university funded a limited forum for student publications, the Court held that excluding a student religious magazine was unconstitutional viewpoint discrimination.[219] Evangelical Christianity offered viewpoints on many issues important to college students, including issues addressed from secular viewpoints in other student publications funded by the university. Joshua Davey sought to apply this reasoning to Washington's exclusion of theology majors.

Education consists largely of speech.[220] That statement surely seems

---

215. Olympia had a population of 4698 in 1890. CENSUS OFFICE, DEP'T OF THE INTERIOR, REPORT ON POPULATION OF THE U.S. AT THE ELEVENTH CENSUS: 1890, pt. 1, at 353 tbl.5 (1895).

216. *See Davey,* 540 U.S. at 723 n.7 ("[T]he Blaine Amendment's history is simply not before us.").

217. *See* Legal Servs. Corp. v. Velazquez, 531 U.S. 533, 540-49 (2001); Rosenberger v. Rector & Visitors of Univ. of Va., 515 U.S. 819, 828-37 (1995).

218. 515 U.S. 819 (1995).

219. *See id.* at 828-37.

220. *See* Volokh, *supra* note 11, at 366.

more sensible to law professors than to chemistry professors. But in any discipline, education consists largely of the transmission and exchange of information and viewpoints, and at more advanced levels, of the discovery or creation of new knowledge. These are central concerns of the First Amendment;[221] education is not an activity to which speech is merely incidental. Theology and other disciplines are likely to yield different viewpoints on a variety of issues. More obviously, the difference between studying theology from a believing perspective and studying it from a detached or skeptical perspective is purely a difference of viewpoint. So Davey alleged viewpoint discrimination in violation of *Rosenberger*.

The Court rejected this claim in a conclusory footnote, saying that "the Promise Scholarship Program is not a forum for speech."[222] The program's purpose was to assist students with their education, not to "encourage a diversity of views from private speakers."[223] The Court did not elaborate this intuition, but it made similar points at greater length in *United States v. American Library Ass'n*:[224]

> A public library does not acquire Internet terminals in order to create a public forum for Web publishers to express themselves, any more than it collects books in order to provide a public forum for the authors of books to speak. It provides Internet access, not to "encourage a diversity of views from private speakers," but for the same reasons it offers other library resources: to facilitate research, learning, and recreational pursuits by furnishing materials of requisite and appropriate quality.[225]

It is true enough that the scholarship program was not designed to "encourage a diversity of views from private speakers," and certainly there is no forum for the general public to offer courses at public or private universities. Such a claim of access for private speakers is what the Court seemed to be worried about when it said that a library is not a forum for authors of books. But it is equally certain that Davey made no such claim. He sought access only to the existing

---

221. *See* Grutter v. Bollinger, 539 U.S. 306, 328-29 (2003) (relying on "the expansive freedoms of speech and thought associated with the university environment"); *Rosenberger*, 515 U.S. at 835-36 (relying on a "tradition of thought and experiment that is at the center of our intellectual and philosophical tradition"); Bd. of Regents of the Univ. of Wis. Sys. v. Southworth, 529 U.S. 217, 237-39 (2000) (Souter, J., concurring) (collecting cases).

222. *Davey*, 540 U.S. at 720 n.3.

223. *Id.* (quoting *United States v. American Library Ass'n*, 539 U.S. 194, 206 (2003) (plurality opinion) (quoting *Rosenberger*, 515 U.S. at 834)).

224. 539 U.S. 194 (2003).

225. *Id.* at 206 (plurality opinion) (quoting *Rosenberger*, 515 U.S. at 834).

"diversity of views" within the existing array of courses and majors, and he claimed viewpoint discrimination within that array. The set of speakers offering these courses — some public, some private, all subject to some degree of institutional control, and all available only to limited audiences pursuing specified programs — fits oddly into forum analysis. But forum analysis was a distraction, because Davey showed viewpoint discrimination. Viewpoint discrimination is presumptively unconstitutional even in nonpublic forums,[226] and even if the speech is not on government property and there is no forum of any kind. If a new Huey Long attempted to suppress opposition newspapers,[227] it would not be a defense that the state had not created a forum for newspapers.

Another way to read the Court's free speech footnote is that the Promise Scholarship Program was intended to benefit the students, not the universities or their faculties, and that the students are more in the role of audience than of speaker. That debatable characterization of students should not change the analysis; the Free Speech Clause protects audiences as well as speakers.[228] We may likewise assume that the legislature did not view Promise Scholarships as a means of expanding the diversity of courses and majors that students might study. But except for devotional theology majors, it intended to assist students in studying whatever they chose to study from the existing offerings. The state excluded the viewpoint Davey wished to study, even though that viewpoint was already available within the class of speech that Promise Scholarships subsidized.

The only way to make sense of the Court's footnote is to reduce it to a special rule about funding: viewpoint discrimination in funding is permitted unless the purpose of the funding program is to "encourage a diversity of views from private speakers."[229] But the Court had already rejected that very formulation in *Legal Services Corp. v. Velazquez*,[230] which required the government to fund law-reform suits for indigents:

> Although the LSC program differs from the program at issue in *Rosenberger* in that its purpose is not to "encourage a diversity of views," the

---

226. *See* Cornelius v. NAACP Legal Def. & Educ. Fund, Inc., 473 U.S. 788, 806 (1985); Perry Educ. Ass'n v. Perry Local Educators' Ass'n, 460 U.S. 37, 46, 48-49 (1983).

227. *See* Grosjean v. Am. Press Co., 297 U.S. 233, 249-51 (1936) (invalidating Louisiana tax on large-circulation newspapers, most of which opposed the governor).

228. *See* Bd. of Educ. v. Pico, 457 U.S. 853, 866-69 (1982) (plurality opinion) (protecting students' right to receive information in the school library, and collecting cases supporting the right to receive information and ideas).

229. *Davey*, 540 U.S. at 720 n.3.

230. 531 U.S. 533 (2001).

salient point is that, like the program in *Rosenberger,* the LSC program was designed to facilitate private speech, not to promote a governmental message.[231]

This distinction — between the government's own messages and the government's subsidies of private messages that it is unwilling to endorse — has had some persistence in the cases. In *Rust v. Sullivan,*[232] the government wanted to spread information about contraception. It was willing to pay private doctors to do that, but it was not willing to pay for other messages of which it disapproved.[233] In *Rosenberger,* the university wanted to encourage student speakers, but it certainly was not willing to be responsible for what they said.[234] So it had to say it was subsidizing private speech, and that meant it could not discriminate among viewpoints. In *Velazquez,* the United States wanted to pay lawyers to represent indigents, without promising to agree with the indigent clients when they sued private defendants or state and local governments and certainly without conceding anything when they sued federal agencies.[235] So although there was nothing remotely like a forum in *Velazquez,* it was clear that the government was funding private speech and not sending a message of its own.

This intuitively sensible distinction breaks down in a range of cases in the middle, where the government makes some choices itself and leaves other choices to private speakers, as in grants to artists based on judgments about artistic excellence,[236] or grants to scientists based on promising lines of research. The government has its own purposes in these programs, and does not want to subsidize everybody, but neither does it want to be responsible for what grantees do with their awards. The state universities are such a middle case. Legislators, regents, and educational administrators may decide which disciplines or programs they are willing to fund, but there is a long tradition of academic freedom for individual professors within those programs, and universities are quite willing to disclaim responsibility when a professor says something politically embarrassing.

231. *Id.* at 542.

232. 500 U.S. 173 (1991).

233. *See id.* at 193 (characterizing the program as one "to encourage certain activities" and not others).

234. *See* Rosenberger v. Rector & Visitors of Univ. of Va., 515 U.S. 819, 824 (1995) (describing university's efforts to disclaim all responsibility).

235. *See Velazquez,* 531 U.S. at 542-44.

236. *See* Nat'l Endowment for the Arts v. Finley, 524 U.S. 569, 583-87 (1998) (narrowly construing, and upholding, statutory restrictions on funding for indecent or disrespectful art).

This distinction between government and private messages, whatever its attractions and its problems, cannot explain the result in *Davey*. The scholarships in *Davey* were available to all within a very broad category; no one would claim they supported any government message more specific than that young people should aspire to attend college. The program was not designed to steer students into a few disciplines selected by the state as especially important, like a scholarship for education majors. Nor was it designed to subsidize the speech of the faculty at state universities. Student choices of major were plainly private choices about what to study. The subsidized speech was private for purposes of this distinction for the same reason that funding would have been permissible:[237] Davey's choice of major was not state action.

The distinction between the government sending its own message and subsidizing diverse private messages is related to two other suggested distinctions. The first is between funding (or permitting) one or a few speakers or messages and excluding most, as opposed to funding (or permitting) nearly all speakers or messages within a broad category and excluding one or a few. The latter is much more suspect, in part because it prima facie appears to be censorship of the excluded speaker or message, rather than promotion of any affirmative message or government purpose. Of course, *Davey* is an example of the latter. A second refinement is Robert Post's distinction between public discourse and managerial speech, by which he means speech that is part of the government's effort "to achieve specified ends."[238] In this useful formulation, the government may not be sending a message when it speaks; it may just be getting its work done.[239] But that does not describe *Davey* either. The rules of managerial speech could explain why a professor has to teach contracts instead of his latest research, but they do not explain why Davey can choose any major except devotional theology.

Davey's free speech claim does not appear to have received much thought. The Court had already concluded that funding was not required, and alternative theories were not going to change that. In theory, there remains a range of cases in which discriminatory refusals to fund religious speech would violate the Free Speech Clause. But those cases may have to look exactly like *Rosenberger:* explicit, self-conscious government efforts to promote a forum for private speech.

---

237. *See Davey,* 540 U.S. at 719.
238. Robert C. Post, *Subsidized Speech,* 106 Yale L.J. 151, 164 (1996).
239. *Id.*

4. The Hazards of Governmental Discretion.

At least with respect to funding, the rule now appears to be that government may treat religion neutrally, but it is not required to. This is not the only doctrinal area where the Court has increased government discretion over religion. Government may exempt religious organizations and practices from neutral and generally applicable laws,[240] but it is not required to.[241] Government may exempt churches from tax[242] (so long as the exemption is not too narrow[243]), but it is not required to.[244] In church property disputes, state courts may defer to the highest church authority recognized by both sides before the dispute arose,[245] but they are not required to.[246]

This discretion minimizes judicial interference with majoritarian political decisions. But all this discretion threatens religious liberty. The discretion — and the problem — is greatest with respect to funding. *Davey* relied on the traditional view that "state-supported clergy undermined liberty of conscience."[247] The state can control a state-funded clergy by threatening to take the money away. That risk is minimized if the state funds nothing; the Court seems to have seen that. The risk is greatly reduced if the state's funding is controlled by stringent rules that tie the flow of funds to some external standard and prevent the state from dictating policies or views to the groups or activities it funds.[248] The Court did not see that. And the risk to religious liberty is maximized if the state has broad discretion to fund, not to fund, or to

240. *See* Bd. of Educ. v. Grumet, 512 U.S. 687, 705-06 (1994) (collecting cases); Employment Div. v. Smith, 494 U.S. 872, 890 (1990) (saying that "nondiscriminatory religious-practice exemption[s]" are the responsibility of legislators, not courts); Corp. of the Presiding Bishop v. Amos, 483 U.S. 327, 334-40 (1987) (unanimously upholding exemption of religious institutions from statutory ban on religious discrimination in employment).

241. *See Smith*, 494 U.S. at 876-90.

242. *See* Walz v. Tax Comm'n, 397 U.S. 664, 672-80 (1970).

243. *See* Tex. Monthly, Inc. v. Bullock, 489 U.S. 1, 8-17 (1989) (plurality opinion); *id.* at 26-29 (Blackmun, J., concurring).

244. *See* Jimmy Swaggart Ministries v. Bd. of Equalization, 493 U.S. 378, 384-97 (1990).

245. *See* Presbyterian Church v. Mary Elizabeth Blue Hull Mem'l Presbyterian Church, 393 U.S. 440, 445-49 (1969).

246. *See* Jones v. Wolf, 443 U.S. 595, 602-06 (1979).

247. *Davey*, 540 U.S. at 722 (quoting FRANK LAMBERT, THE FOUNDING FATHERS AND THE PLACE OF RELIGION IN AMERICA 188 (2003)).

248. *See* Michael W. McConnell, *The Problem of Singling Out Religion*, 50 DEPAUL L. REV. 1, 39-40 (2000) ("[T]he great dangers arise from the government's discretion to engage in selective subsidy: the power to create incentives for individuals to alter their conduct by providing financial support to one choice and not to a substitute.").

fund with conditions. The Court clearly did not see that, because that is the situation it created.

What the Court has created is for some important purposes the worst of all worlds. When the state chooses to fund private education, it can freely make a second choice: to fund religious and secular education alike, to fund secular education only, or to fund some forms of religious education and not other forms. The Court in *Davey* emphasized how much religious higher education Washington was willing to pay for, including secular courses at pervasively religious schools and devotional courses so long as the student did not major in devotional theology.[249] This suggests significant power for the state to pick and choose.

Maryland for many years funded secular colleges and some church-affiliated colleges, but not "pervasively sectarian" colleges. The Fourth Circuit struck down this discrimination,[250] but that holding is in jeopardy after *Davey*. If Washington can draw the line between devotional electives and devotional majors, it is hard to see why Maryland cannot draw the line between somewhat religious schools and pervasively religious schools. (But perhaps Maryland's rule is still invalid because of the "shameful pedigree" of "hostility to aid to pervasively sectarian schools."[251]) If discriminatory funding imposes only a "minor burden"[252] that can be justified by tradition, and if *Davey's* holding expands beyond the training of clergy to the full range of secular services offered by religious institutions, there would seem to be few enforceable limits on government discretion in funding decisions. Funding once granted could be taken away at any time, or the scope of funded programs could expand and contract, without regard to any claim of discrimination between religious and secular education. Political movements opposed to funding religious programs could attack that funding without having to take on analogous secular programs.

Davey also strengthens government's claim of power to put conditions on the money, without regard to the possible conscientious objections of recipients or of the institutions where recipients spend the money.[253] The rule

---

249. *See Davey,* 540 U.S. at 724-25.

250. *See* Columbia Union College v. Oliver, 254 F.3d 496, 504-08 (4th Cir. 2001).

251. Mitchell v. Helms, 530 U.S. 793, 828 (2000) (plurality opinion). Or perhaps, because the money goes to the college and not the students, the college's free speech claim will survive. *See supra* text at note 228.

252. *Davey,* 540 U.S. at 725.

253. For pre-*Davey* analyses of the problem, which were more optimistic about limiting conditions on money, see Berg, *supra* note 69, at 194-96, 208-20; Lupu & Tuttle, *supra* note 64, at 972-82; and Tushnet, *supra* note 69, at 22-29.

of *Rust* and *Davey* — that government can choose what it wants to fund and confine its money to that program — is far more threatening from the perspective of grantees. *Rust* and *Davey* mean that if you take money from the government, the government acquires full power to prohibit any other activity, including the exercise of constitutional rights, performed by subsidized staff or conducted on the property where the government money is spent. Any regulation imposed as a funding condition can be described as defining what the government is willing to subsidize, or as taking care to avoid indirect subsidies of an activity the government is not willing to subsidize.[254] Opponents of funding who are unable to defeat the program outright can attach poison-pill conditions that make the funding unacceptable. For example, the most vigorous debate about the Bush Administration's proposals for nondiscriminatory funding of faith-based social services has been the debate over whether recipients of government funds must surrender their existing right, under an exemption from the employment discrimination laws, to hire employees who share their faith commitments.[255]

At least there is a firm rule against denominational discrimination.[256] But even that rule is of limited value. Of course no state could fund Catholic seminary students and not Protestant seminary students. But a state may impose a funding condition offensive only, or primarily, to one or a few faiths with strong views on a particular issue. Suppose California provided that vouchers could be used only at schools that offer contraception and abortion services to students and staff. This example is not entirely hypothetical.[257] *Larson v. Valente*[258] found denominational discrimination in a rule that mentioned no particular faith but affected only a few.[259] But that was because the Court found the denominational discrimination to be deliberate. It distinguished *Gillette v. United States,*[260] which had upheld discrimination between

---

254. For an analysis of the range of conditions commonly attached to government funds, see CARL H. ESBECK, THE REGULATION OF RELIGIOUS ORGANIZATIONS AS RECIPIENTS OF GOVERNMENTAL ASSISTANCE 11-42 (1996).

255. *See* 42 U.S.C. § 2000e-1(a) (2000). For analysis, see Saperstein, *supra* note 187, at 1389-94.

256. *See* Larson v. Valente, 456 U.S. 228, 244 (1982).

257. *See* Catholic Charities v. Super. Ct., 85 P.3d 67, 76-94 (Cal. 2004) (upholding a provision requiring employer-sponsored health insurance to cover prescription contraceptives); St. Agnes Hosp. v. Riddick, 748 F. Supp. 319, 324-32 (D. Md. 1990) (upholding a requirement that hospitals with residency programs in obstetrics and gynecology must perform abortions).

258. 456 U.S. 228.

259. *See id.* at 246 n.23, 255.

260. 401 U.S. 437 (1971).

conscientious objectors who objected to war in any form and those who objected on the basis of just-war theory, describing that distinction as merely having "disparate impact" on the denominations that teach just-war theory.[261] Legislatures should have little difficulty excluding religious institutions with commitments on faith and morals that are unpopular with competing interest groups.

There was some protection against such discriminatory or conditional funding in the cases requiring laws that burden religion to be neutral and generally applicable,[262] but *Davey* appears to hold those cases inapplicable to funding decisions. There was also some protection in the nondiscrimination rule in *Rosenberger.*[263] To the extent that activities or institutions that did and did not qualify for funding could be described as offering different viewpoints, funding discrimination could be characterized as viewpoint discrimination. At best this would have offered limited protection, but now that protection is mostly gone.[264] There may be some protection in the right of expressive association, most recently illustrated by *Boy Scouts v. Dale,*[265] but the expressive association cases have invalidated outright regulation, not funding conditions.

Of course it will always be true that grant programs can come and go. A state may fund private education for a time and then reduce or eliminate that funding to concentrate on public education or some new political priority. Similarly, any funding program must insist that grantees achieve the program's secular goals. A voucher plan could not exclude Islamic schools that taught the Koran and the secular curriculum, but it could exclude schools that taught only the Koran and not the secular curriculum. And even if the Court prohibited discriminatory refusals to fund and seriously scrutinized conditions on funding, its aversion to extreme results would ensure that the burden on government to justify withholding funds would be less stringent than the burden to justify a criminal prohibition on the same conduct. For example, there would inevitably be a range of hate speech that government

261. *See Larson,* 456 U.S. at 246 n.23. In the same footnote, the Court distinguished on similar grounds *McGowan v. Maryland,* 366 U.S. 420 (1961), which upheld Sunday-closing laws over the objection that they promoted the views of certain faiths, *id.* at 442. *See Larson,* 456 U.S. at 246 n.23.

262. *See infra* Part II, text at notes 271-404.

263. *See* Rosenberger v. Rector & Visitors of Univ. of Va., 515 U.S. 819 (1995).

264. *See Davey,* 540 U.S. at 720 n.3; *see also supra* section I.C.3.c, text at notes 217-39.

265. 530 U.S. 640 (2000) (holding that the Boy Scouts could not be required to retain an openly gay scout leader). Mark Tushnet suggested this argument before *Davey* was decided. *See* Tushnet, *supra* note 69, at 24–25.

could refuse to fund but could not ban. It is impossible to protect funded groups against all risk of the loss of funds.

But it is possible to protect against unrestrained government discretion. Under a strong neutrality rule, the state could not cut funds to religious private education without also cutting funds to secular private education. And it could not cut off a particular program alleged to be harmful or dangerous without judicial review and a burden of justification.

The line of decisions culminating in *Zelman v. Simmons-Harris*[266] gave a green light to indirect government funding of religion, and thus eliminated the constitutional protection that opponents of funding cared about most. But *Davey* seems to give a green light to attaching strings to that money. The worst case would be government offering broad conditional subsidies and buying up the right to free exercise of religion. That is not likely to happen apart from isolated incidents. And it is not too late to create doctrine to address the worst case if it begins to happen on a larger scale. But the current doctrinal combination — few limits on funding, few limits on discrimination in funding programs, and few limits on conditions attached to funding — maximizes government power over religion.

Religious organizations may or may not have thought through these risks.[267] The rosy scenario is that they will get the money with few strings attached in states where they are politically strong, they will get no money in states where they are politically weak, and the offer of money with ruinous conditions will be a rare political outcome. The pessimistic scenario is that in some states they will get enough money to become dependent on it. And then, when some financial abuse or unpopular practice is reported, or when political power shifts, the conditions and distinctions among recipients will proliferate. And there will be no basis in judicial doctrine to protect the free exercise of religion. Religious communities will have to surrender the money or surrender control of their institutions. Of course, religious strict separationists have long been warning of such an outcome.[268]

Funding secular programs, but not religious equivalents that provide the same secular benefit, is rank discrimination, with the immediate and obvious effect of discouraging or penalizing the free exercise of religion. It is hard to accept such discrimination out of fear that correcting it will make

266. 536 U.S. 639 (2002).

267. For a careful and equivocal analysis from a scholar sympathetic to religious organizations, see CHARLES L. GLENN, THE AMBIGUOUS EMBRACE: GOVERNMENT AND FAITH-BASED SCHOOLS AND SOCIAL AGENCIES (2000).

268. *See, e.g.,* Berg, *supra* note 69, at 194 & nn.205-08 (collecting sources); Saperstein, *supra* note 187, at 1365-69.

things worse in the long run. Moreover, some scholars argue that religious organizations are better off with equal access to money and the risk of regulation than with no money[269] and the risk of being regulated anyway.[270] But permitting nondiscriminatory government funding to include secular services at religious institutions is clear progress for religious liberty only if the Court is willing to provide strong protection against attaching unconstitutional conditions to that money. It now seems clear that this is not going to happen.

II. *Davey* and the Regulation Cases

There are few firm limits to *Davey's* reach within the universe of funding cases. But that universe is itself the clearest and most important limit: *Davey* is a funding case. Davey's claim to equal funding relied on the Free Exercise Clause and on *Church of the Lukumi Babalu Aye, Inc. v. City of Hialeah,*[271] the leading case on government regulation of religious practices. Inevitably, *Davey* is a major interpretation of *Lukumi. Davey* holds that *Lukumi's* complex nondiscrimination rules do not apply to discriminatory funding. But *Davey* does not change those rules as applied to regulation.

A. *The Doctrinal Context: Regulation of Religious Practice*

The most direct and forceful way for government to interfere with individual choice in religious matters is to prohibit a religious practice. It is a hollow assurance of religious liberty to tell people they can believe their faith but cannot practice their faith. The threat of criminal penalties powerfully discourages the regulated religious practice, but deregulating such a practice (or exempting it from regulation that would otherwise apply) normally does little to encourage it. This comparison of discouragement and encouragement works out differently for religious practices that serve some secular self-interest, so that exemption would encourage people to adopt the religious practice for reasons other than religious conviction. Consider a religious objection to paying taxes. And some religious practices must be regulated or

---

269. *See* Berg, *supra* note 69, at 195 (emphasizing the difficulty of competing with cultural and ideological opponents who are funded by the government).

270. *See* Glenn, *supra* note 267, at 42-61 (discussing strings without money).

271. 508 U.S. 520 (1993).

prohibited to prevent some significant temporal harm to others. So no simple and universal rule is possible. But from the view that religious liberty consists of minimizing government influence and maximizing individual choice, government best protects religious liberty in the usual case by exempting religious practices from regulation.

The Supreme Court shared this view from 1963 to 1990. The Court's rule was that government-imposed burdens on religious practice presumptively violated the Free Exercise Clause, and that government could justify such a burden only by showing that it served a compelling government interest by the least restrictive means.[272] The best-known cases in this line were *Sherbert v. Verner,*[273] holding that a state could not refuse unemployment compensation to a Sabbatarian who was unavailable for work on Saturdays,[274] and *Wisconsin v. Yoder,*[275] holding that a state could not require Amish children to attend high school.[276] But results were mixed. Prison and military regulations were subject to a much more deferential standard,[277] and many commentators thought the compelling interest test was relaxed in some of the cases that the government won.[278]

The Court famously amended the *Sherbert-Yoder* test in 1990, in *Employment Division v. Smith.*[279] Under *Smith,* the threshold question is whether the law that burdens religious exercise is "neutral" and "generally applicable."[280] If so, the burden on religion requires no justification whatever. If not, the burden on religion is subject to the compelling interest test as before. The meaning of *Smith's* threshold test remains disputed, but *Smith* undoubtedly provides less protection for religious liberty — and less protection for religion — than the *Sherbert-Yoder* rule. Filing rates for free exercise claims

---

272. *See, e.g.,* Bowen v. Roy, 476 U.S. 693, 728 (1986) (plurality opinion); Bob Jones Univ. v. United States, 461 U.S. 574, 603-04 (1983); Thomas v. Review Bd., 450 U.S. 707, 718 (1981).

273. 374 U.S. 398 (1963).

274. *See id.* at 403-06.

275. 406 U.S. 205 (1972).

276. *See id.* at 213-36.

277. *See* O'Lone v. Estate of Shabazz, 482 U.S. 342, 348-53 (1987) (prisons); Goldman v. Weinberger, 475 U.S. 503, 506-10 (1986) (military).

278. *See, e.g.,* Ira C. Lupu, *Of Time and the RFRA: A Lawyer's Guide to the Religious Freedom Restoration Act,* 56 MONT. L. REV. 171, 182-85 (1995); Michael W. McConnell, *Free Exercise Revisionism and the* Smith *Decision,* 57 U. CHI. L. REV. 1109, 1110, 1127-28 (1990).

279. 494 U.S. 872 (1990). For accounts of the *Smith* litigation and its aftermath, see GARRETT EPPS, TO AN UNKNOWN GOD: RELIGIOUS FREEDOM ON TRIAL (2001); CAROLYN N. LONG, RELIGIOUS FREEDOM AND INDIAN RIGHTS: THE CASE OF *OREGON V. SMITH* (2000).

280. *Smith,* 494 U.S. at 881.

plummeted after *Smith*,[281] and these claims had lower success rates than the larger number of claims decided before *Smith*.[282]

The Justices' views on *Smith* confound any simple model of voting for or against religion. Justices Souter and Breyer, who have generally appeared to vote against religion in the funding and speech cases, have called for the reconsideration of *Smith*.[283] Justices Rehnquist and Scalia, who have generally appeared to vote for religion in the funding and speech cases, were in the majority in *Smith*; Scalia wrote the opinion. Justices Kennedy and O'Connor, who have been the swing votes in the funding and speech cases, are divided over *Smith*: Kennedy was in the majority and O'Connor has persistently rejected its central holding.[284] Only Justice Stevens generally appears to vote against religion in the funding, speech, *and* regulation cases, and even he has found important exceptions.[285] Justices Thomas and Ginsburg have not spoken to the choice between *Smith* and *Sherbert-Yoder*. Except for Justice Stevens, votes on *Smith* are better explained by views about the scope of individual liberty and the proper role of judges than by views about religion. *Smith* conceded that leaving regulation of religious practice to the political process would advantage large religions and disadvantage small ones, but it said that that consequence must be preferred to a system "in which judges weigh the social importance of all laws against the centrality of all religious beliefs."[286]

Smith changed free exercise from a substantive liberty — a rebuttable

281. *See* Amy Adamczyk, John Wybraniec, & Roger Finke, *Religious Regulation and the Courts: Documenting the Effects of* Smith *and RFRA,* 46 J. CHURCH & STATE 237, 250 tbl.1 (2004) (reporting 310 claims decided in the nine-and-a-quarter years before *Smith*, compared to thirty-eight claims decided in three-and-a-half years after *Smith*).

282. *Id.* (reporting success rates of 39.5% and 28.4%, respectively, for the periods described *supra* note 281). Under the Religious Freedom Restoration Act, 42 U.S.C. § 2000bb (2000), a statute that temporarily restored the *Sherbert-Yoder* rule, filing rates approached, and success rates exceeded, pre-*Smith* levels. *See* Adamczyk, Wybraniec, & Finke, *supra* note 281, at 250 tbl.1.

283. *See* City of Boerne v. Flores, 521 U.S. 507, 565 (1997) (Souter, J., dissenting); *id.* at 566 (Breyer, J., dissenting); Church of the Lukumi Babalu Aye, Inc. v. City of Hialeah, 508 U.S. 520, 559 (1993) (Souter, J., concurring).

284. *Compare Smith,* 494 U.S. 872, *with Boerne,* 521 U.S. at 544-65 (O'Connor, J., dissenting), *and Lukumi,* 508 U.S. at 577-80 (Blackmun, J., concurring, joined by O'Connor, J.), *and Smith,* 494 U.S. at 891-903 (O'Connor, J., concurring).

285. *See Lukumi,* 508 U.S. 520; Frazee v. Ill. Dep't of Employment Sec., 489 U.S. 829 (1989); Corp. of the Presiding Bishop v. Amos, 483 U.S. 327 (1987); Witters v. Wash. Dep't of Servs. For the Blind, 474 U.S. 481 (1986); McDaniel v. Paty, 435 U.S. 618 (1978). These five decisions were unanimous.

286. *Smith,* 494 U.S. at 890.

guarantee of freedom to act within the domain of religiously motivated behavior — to a comparative right,[287] in which the constitutionally required treatment of religious practices depends on the treatment of some comparable set of secular practices.[288] A prohibition on discriminating against religion was not new; it was implicit in the earlier substantive liberty, and there were cases invalidating discrimination against religious conduct,[289] discrimination against atheists,[290] and discrimination among religious faiths.[291] But free exercise claims before *Smith* had not required proof of discrimination, and when discrimination was subtle, there had been little incentive to look for it. A burden on religious practice was a prima facie violation; discrimination was just an aggravating factor. Thus in *Sherbert,* where the state protected the jobs of workers unavailable to work on Sunday, but refused even unemployment compensation to workers who lost their jobs for their religiously motivated refusal to work on Saturday, the Court said that this religious discrimination "compounded" the "unconstitutionality of the disqualification of the Sabbatarian."[292]

Smith changed all this. Eliminating the substantive liberty put the focus on the comparative right. And thus the challenge to discriminatory funding in *Davey* was based squarely on *Church of the Lukumi Babalu Aye, Inc. v. City of Hialeah,*[293] the leading case interpreting *Smith.*

Although it was immediately clear that *Smith* created a comparative right, the precise nature of that right was unclear. Many commentators gave *Smith* a worst-case reading, fearing that the Court might treat all or most laws as neutral and generally applicable.[294] I joined in pointing out that

---

287. On the concept of comparative rights, see Kenneth W. Simons, *Equality as a Comparative Right,* 65 B.U. L. REV. 387 (1985).

288. *See id.* at 391 (defining a comparative right as one that is triggered by the treatment of some other person). For the argument that it is irrational to make the free exercise of a religious practice depend on whether some significant population does the same thing for secular reasons, see Christopher C. Lund, *A Matter of Constitutional Luck: The General Applicability Requirement in Free Exercise Jurisprudence,* 26 HARV. J.L. & PUB. POL'Y 627 (2003).

289. *See McDaniel,* 435 U.S. 618 (invalidating the exclusion of clergy from the state legislature).

290. *See* Torcaso v. Watkins, 367 U.S. 488, 495-96 (1961) (invalidating the exclusion of atheists from public office).

291. *See* Larson v. Valente, 456 U.S. 228, 244 (1982) ("The clearest command of the Establishment Clause is that one religious denomination cannot be officially preferred over another.").

292. Sherbert v. Verner, 374 U.S. 398, 406 (1963).

293. 508 U.S. 520 (1993).

294. *See, e.g.,* James D. Gordon III, *Free Exercise on the Mountaintop,* 79 CAL. L. REV. 91,

worst-case scenario,[295] but I also argued from the beginning that *Smith* "may be sweeping or limited, depending on how the Court interprets all the boundaries and exceptions to its opinion."[296] Those ambiguities are still not entirely resolved, but *Lukumi* and the trend of lower court opinions read *Smith* in a way that provides substantial protection to religious liberty.

One source of ambiguity is that *Smith* is written not in terms of what the Free Exercise Clause requires, but rather in terms of what it does not require. Another is *Smith's* novel formulation of the comparative right. Nothing in the opinion tracks the conventional language of discrimination laws; *Smith* does not mention laws that discriminate against, because of, or on the basis of, religion. Forms of the word "discriminate" appear only twice in the opinion, and neither instance refers to the kind of laws the Court deems suspect under the Free Exercise Clause.[297] Nor is there any reference to bad motive, anti-religious animus, or religious bigotry. Instead, *Smith* is written in terms of a new category: the "generally applicable law." The Court refers to generally applicable laws at least twelve times: four times in combination with the word "neutral,"[298] and eight times without that addition.[299]

---

115 (1991) ("*Smith* essentially rendered the free exercise clause a dead letter."); McConnell, *supra* note 278, at 1153 (characterizing the Free Exercise Clause under *Smith* as "a largely redundant equal protection clause for religion"); Mark Tushnet, *The Redundant Free Exercise Clause?*, 33 Loy. U. Chi. L.J. 71 (2001) (title says it all). For the reasons for this rhetorical strategy among *Smith's* critics, see Douglas Laycock, *Conceptual Gulfs in* City of Boerne v. Flores, 39 Wm. & Mary L. Rev. 743, 774-78 (1998) (text at notes 175-89). For defenses of *Smith* (with varying degrees of enthusiasm), see, for example, Christopher L. Eisgruber & Lawrence G. Sager, *The Vulnerability of Conscience: The Constitutional Basis for Protecting Religious Conduct*, 61 U. Chi. L. Rev. 1245 (1994); and William P. Marshall, *In Defense of* Smith *and Free Exercise Revisionism*, 58 U. Chi. L. Rev. 308 (1991).

295. *See* Laycock, *supra* note 145, at 54–68 (text at notes 217-74) (exploring the consequences of *not* enforcing the protective portions of *Smith*).

296. *Id.* at 41 (text at notes 158-59); *see also id.* at 41-54 (text at notes 159-217) (exploring the consequences of *enforcing* the protective portions of *Smith*).

297. *See* Employment Div. v. Smith, 494 U.S. 872, 886 n.3 (1990) (quoting Justice O'Connor's reference to "race discrimination"); *id.* at 890 (referring to "nondiscriminatory religious-practice exemption[s]" — that is, to laws exempting religious practice from regulation, not to laws imposing regulation). Footnote 3 does analogize religious classifications to racial classifications, and neutral, generally applicable laws burdening religion to neutral laws with uneven effects on different racial groups. *See id.* at 886 n.3.

298. *Id.* at 879 ("valid and neutral law of general applicability" (quoting *United States v. Lee*, 455 U.S. 252, 263 n.3 (1982) (Stevens, J., concurring) (internal quotation mark omitted)); *id.* at 880 ("neutral, generally applicable regulatory law"); *id.* at 881 ("neutral, generally applicable law"); *id.* at 886 n.3 ("generally applicable, religion-neutral laws").

299. *Id.* at 878 ("generally applicable law"); *id.* ("generally applicable and otherwise valid provision"); *id.* at 882 ("generally applicable criminal laws"); *id.* at 884 ("generally ap-

Smith's explanation of the Court's prior cases implies that one or a few exceptions or gaps in coverage can prevent a law from being "generally applicable." The Court distinguished generally applicable laws from the unemployment compensation laws at issue in *Sherbert v. Verner* and its progeny.[300] The unemployment compensation laws required "individualized governmental assessment of the reasons for the relevant conduct"[301] — in those cases, the claimant's reasons for refusing a proffered job. The unemployment cases thus "stand for the proposition that where the State has in place a system of individual exemptions, it may not refuse to extend that system to cases of 'religious hardship' without compelling reason."[302]

A law that permits individualized exemptions lends itself to discrimination in administration, and because the allowance of such exemptions is likely to be dispersed in time and place, such discrimination will often be difficult to detect and prove.[303] It is an effective protection against this risk of unverifiable discrimination to apply the compelling interest test to laws that burden religious practice and that require or permit "individualized governmental assessment of the reasons for the relevant conduct,"[304] "consideration of the particular circumstances,"[305] or "individual exemptions"[306] for personal hardships of a secular kind. A law with individualized exemptions might be thought "generally applicable" in the weaker sense of applying to most cases of the regulated conduct, but such a law is not "generally applicable" in the stronger sense of applying to *all* cases of the regulated conduct. In the law of unemployment compensation, the general rule is that beneficiaries must be available for work,[307] and acceptable reasons for refusing work are obviously exceptional.[308] The Court's treatment of individualized assess-

---

plicable criminal law"); *id.* at 885 ("generally applicable prohibitions"); *id.* at 886, 886 n.3, 887 n.4 ("generally applicable laws").

300. *See* Frazee v. Ill. Dep't of Employment Sec., 489 U.S. 829 (1989); Hobbie v. Unemployment Appeals Comm'n, 480 U.S. 136 (1987); Thomas v. Review Bd., 450 U.S. 707 (1981); Sherbert v. Verner, 374 U.S. 398 (1963).

301. *Smith,* 494 U.S. at 884.

302. *Id.* (quoting *Bowen v. Roy,* 476 U.S. 693, 708 (1986) (opinion of Burger, C.J.)).

303. *Cf.* Bd. of Educ. v. Grumet, 512 U.S. 687, 702-05 (1994) (invalidating law accommodating a single religious group, because there was no way to ensure that other religious groups would receive comparable accommodations over time).

304. *Smith,* 494 U.S. at 884.

305. *Id.*

306. *Id.*

307. Mark A. Rothstein et al., Employment Law § 9.10, at 768 (2d ed. 1999).

308. *See id.* §§ 9.10-9.14, at 768-96 (reviewing decisions on the acceptability of proffered reasons for losing or refusing work).

ments, especially in the unemployment cases, thus implies a strong requirement of general applicability.

The *Smith* opinion also contains one reference to a hypothetical law with the "object" of prohibiting the free exercise of religion,[309] one quotation referring to hypothetical laws "aimed at the promotion or restriction of religious beliefs,"[310] one example of a hypothetical law that prohibits certain acts "only when they are engaged in for religious reasons,"[311] and one hypothetical example of a law that prohibits acts that would usually be done for religious reasons if done at all — "bowing down before a golden calf."[312] These examples are another source of ambiguity. Government attorneys of course claim that these examples are exhaustive — that all other laws are neutral and generally applicable.[313] But that interpretation would nullify the whole discussion of individualized assessments and individualized exemptions. These examples are thus best understood as polar types — the obviously unconstitutional exact opposites of generally applicable laws. Between a law that applies generally and a law that applies only to religion, there is a large middle ground. The discussion of individualized exemptions implies that most of these laws in the middle, applicable to some cases of the regulated conduct but not to others, are less than generally applicable.

The Court elaborated further in *Church of the Lukumi Babalu Aye, Inc. v. City of Hialeah*.[314] *Lukumi* was a challenge to a set of local ordinances that prohibited animal sacrifices. As defined by the ordinances, to "sacrifice" was "to unnecessarily kill, torment, torture, or mutilate an animal in a public or private ritual or ceremony not for the primary purpose of food consumption."[315] The city argued that this was a generally applicable ban on sacrifice.[316] The church argued that it was a ban on killing animals for religious reasons, carefully drafted so as not to prohibit any killings of animals for sec-

---

309. *See Smith*, 494 U.S. at 878 ("[I]f prohibiting the exercise of religion . . . is not the object of the tax but merely the incidental effect of a generally applicable and otherwise valid provision, the First Amendment has not been offended.").

310. *Id.* at 879 (quoting *Minersville School District v. Gobitis*, 310 U.S. 586, 594 (1940)).

311. *Id.* at 877. The example is a law "to ban the casting of 'statues that are to be used for worship purposes.'" *Id.* at 877-78.

312. *Id.* at 878.

313. *See infra* notes 316, 336, and 347 and accompanying text.

314. 508 U.S. 520 (1993). For an account of the *Lukumi* litigation, see DAVID M. O'BRIEN, ANIMAL SACRIFICE AND RELIGIOUS FREEDOM: CHURCH OF THE LUKUMI BABALU AYE V. CITY OF HIALEAH (2004).

315. *Lukumi*, 508 U.S. at 527 (quoting Hialeah, Fla., Ordinance 87-52 (Sept. 8, 1987), *reprinted in* 508 U.S. at 550-52).

316. *See* Brief of Respondent, *Lukumi* (No. 91-948), *available in* 1992 WL 541282, *12-27.

ular reasons.[317] The Court unanimously agreed with the church. *Lukumi* gives substance to *Smith's* requirements of neutrality and general applicability, but it does not entirely eliminate the ambiguity.

The opinion in *Lukumi* treats "neutrality" and "general applicability" as two "interrelated"[318] but separate requirements,[319] and it illustrates a variety of ways to show that a law fails to meet them. "At a minimum," the Free Exercise Clause requires heightened justification of a law that "discriminates against" religious beliefs or regulates conduct "because it is undertaken for religious reasons."[320] A law is facially discriminatory "if it *refers to* a religious practice without a secular meaning discernible from the language or context."[321] To discriminate "against" or "because of" religion is the conventional language of nondiscrimination laws. If these are "minimum" requirements, then the full meaning of neutrality and general applicability must require something more than the usual model of non-discrimination.

The neutrality requirement prohibits any "[o]fficial action that targets religious conduct for distinctive treatment,"[322] or laws with "the object" of suppressing a religious practice.[323] These inquiries into targets and objects are objective; that the Hialeah ordinances prohibited religious but not secular killings of animals constituted objective evidence of such targeting.[324]

Lukumi invalidated some of the ordinances under *Smith's* rule for individualized assessments. It was an element of the offense of sacrifice that the animals were killed "unnecessarily."[325] This required "an evaluation of the particular justification for the killing," and thus represented a system of individualized assessments.[326] The Court said that the city's "application of the ordinance's test of necessity devalues religious reasons for killing by judging them to be of lesser import than nonreligious reasons."[327]

Smith had spoken only of "individualized" exceptions,[328] but *Lukumi*

---

317. *See* Petitioners' Brief, *Lukumi* (No. 91-948), *available in* 1992 WL 541280, *8-27.

318. *Lukumi*, 508 U.S. at 531.

319. *See id.* at 532-42 (neutrality); *id.* at 542-46 (general applicability).

320. *Id.* at 532.

321. *Id.* at 533 (emphasis added).

322. *Id.* at 534.

323. *See id.*

324. *See id.* at 535-36. Justice Scalia joined this part of the opinion, which further shows that these inquiries are objective. *See id.* at 558-59 (Scalia, J., concurring) (denouncing reliance on motive); *see also* text at notes 342-46 *infra*.

325. *See supra* note 315 and accompanying text (quoting the ordinance).

326. *Lukumi*, 508 U.S. at 537; *see also* Employment Div. v. Smith, 494 U.S. 872, 884 (1990).

327. *Lukumi*, 508 U.S. at 537-38.

328. *Smith*, 494 U.S. at 884.

also relied heavily on the ordinances' categorical exceptions. There were exceptions (or a lack of any prohibition) for "licensed [food] establishment[s],"[329] fishing,[330] extermination of pests,[331] medical research,[332] animals without commercial value,[333] and so on. Both the narrow prohibitions and the existence of categorical exceptions tended to show that the ordinances were not generally applicable.[334] The Court said that "[a]ll laws are selective to some extent, but categories of selection are of paramount concern when a law has the incidental effect of burdening religious practice."[335]

The city argued, as government lawyers are prone to do, that the ordinances applied to everything within their scope.[336] In that sense, every law is generally applicable to whatever it applies to, but that tautology would render the requirement of general applicability entirely vacuous. The Court refused to confine its analysis to the four corners of the challenged ordinances,[337] and its opinion ranged over the entire body of state and local law on the killing of animals.[338] The ordinances' lack of general applicability was shown by their collective failure to prohibit secular killings of animals[339] — analogous secular conduct outside the scope of the ordinances — and also by their failure to prohibit other secular conduct, not analogous as conduct, that caused analogous harmful *consequences*.[340] For example, garbage from restaurants caused the same public health problems as those the city attributed to improper disposal of sacrificed animals.[341]

Finally, Justice Kennedy included in the lead opinion a section, joined only by Justice Stevens,[342] marshalling evidence of the city's hostility to reli-

---

329. *Lukumi,* 508 U.S. at 536 (first alteration in original).

330. *Id.* at 543.

331. *Id.*

332. *Id.* at 544.

333. *Id.*

334. *See id.* at 537, 543.

335. *Id.* at 542.

336. For a discussion of the government's general-applicability argument in the less obvious context of a narrow exception to the general policy of the Bankruptcy Code, see Douglas Laycock, *The Supreme Court and Religious Liberty,* 40 CATH. LAW. 25, 29-32 & nn.21-22 (2000).

337. *See Lukumi,* 508 U.S. at 544.

338. *See id.* at 537, 539, 543-45.

339. *See id.* at 543 ("[M]any types of animal deaths or kills for nonreligious reasons are either not prohibited or approved by express provision.").

340. *See id.* ("They fail to prohibit nonreligious conduct that endangers these interests in a similar or greater degree. . . .").

341. *Id.* at 544-45.

342. *Id.* at 522; *see also* Midrash Sephardi, Inc. v. Town of Surfside, 366 F.3d 1214, 1234

gious sacrifice.[343] He concluded that "the ordinances were enacted 'because of,' not merely 'in spite of,' their suppression of Santeria religious practice."[344] He offered this evidence as among the "objective factors" that "bear on the question of discriminatory object."[345] Nothing in the opinion suggests that this evidence was essential rather than cumulative, even for Justice Kennedy. And it had only two votes. Nine Justices voted to hold the ordinances unconstitutional, but only two found bad motive; whatever else it is, *Lukumi* is not a holding about motive.

The facts of *Lukumi* were extreme; when carefully analyzed, the ordinances applied to almost nothing but religious killings of animals. So opponents of exemptions argue that *Lukumi* implies nothing about any facts less extreme.[346] Governments argue that *Lukumi* was really a bad motive case even though most Justices refused to say so.[347] Less implausibly, opponents of exemptions say that *Lukumi* applies only if religion is singled out for unique disadvantages.[348] But the Court also disavowed that reading. The Court said it did not need to "define with precision the standard used to evaluate whether a prohibition is of general application," because the ordinances in question "fall *well below* the minimum standard necessary to protect First Amendment rights."[349]

Subsequent lower court cases have addressed the location of that boundary. The leading case is *Fraternal Order of Police v. City of Newark*,[350] which

---

n.16 (11th Cir. 2004) ("Under *Lukumi*, it is unnecessary to identify an invidious intent in enacting a law — only Justices Kennedy and Stevens attached significance to evidence of the lawmakers' subjective motivation.").

343. *Lukumi*, 508 U.S. at 540-42 (opinion of Kennedy, J.).

344. *Id.* at 540 (quoting *Personnel Administrator v. Feeney*, 442 U.S. 256, 279 (1979)).

345. *Id.*

346. *See* Am. Family Ass'n v. FCC, 365 F.3d 1156, 1171 (D.C. Cir. 2004) (stating that facially neutral laws violate the Free Exercise Clause if "they target religious faith or speech to an extreme degree, and if those extreme burdens are not related to . . . legitimate government interests"). This formulation misstates all three elements that it purports to summarize — generally applicable law, substantial burden, and compelling government interests.

347. *See* Brief of the Defendants-Appellants at *16-17, Murphy v. Zoning Comm'n, 402 F.3d 342 (2d Cir. 2005) (arguing that *Lukumi* requires proof of "animus or hostility") (available at 2004 WL 589542).

348. *See* Am. *Family Ass'n*, 365 F.3d at 1171 (reading *Lukumi* to apply only where regulatory burden falls on religion and "almost no others" (quoting *Lukumi*, 508 U.S. at 536)).

349. *Lukumi*, 508 U.S. at 543 (emphasis added). For further analysis of the implications of *Lukumi*, see Richard F. Duncan, *Free Exercise Is Dead, Long Live Free Exercise: Smith, Lukumi and the General Applicability Requirement*, 3 U. PA. J. CONST. L. 850 (2001); and Laycock, *supra* note 336, at 25-39 (text at notes 1-50).

350. 170 F.3d 359 (3d Cir. 1999).

reviewed a regulation requiring police officers to be clean-shaven.[351] The regulation contained exceptions for officers with medical conditions and for undercover officers, but not for officers with religious restrictions.[352] The court of appeals held the exception for undercover officers irrelevant, because it did not undermine the rule's stated purpose of maintaining a uniform appearance among persons recognizable as police officers.[353] But the medical exception undermined that interest in the same way as a religious exception.[354] The city had "made a value judgment" that medical reasons were more important than religious reasons, and such value judgments require compelling justification.[355] A single secular exception that undermined the rule's purpose made the rule less than generally applicable.[356]

The persistent effort to read a bad motive requirement into the *Smith-Lukumi* rules distorts the structure of those rules. Bad motive may be one way to prove a violation, but first and foremost, *Smith-Lukumi* is about objectively unequal treatment of religion and analogous secular activities. The protection for religious liberty under the *Smith-Lukumi* rules lies in their effect on the political process. Legislatures can impose on religious minorities

351. *Id.* at 360.

352. *Id.* at 360, 365-66.

353. *See id.* at 366.

354. *Id.*

355. *Id.*

356. *See also* Blackhawk v. Pennsylvania, 381 F.3d 202, 206-12 (3d Cir. 2004) (holding that a permit fee for keeping wild animals, with exceptions for zoos, circuses, hardship, and extraordinary circumstances, was not neutral and generally applicable); Midrash Sephardi, Inc. v. Town of Surfside, 366 F.3d 1214, 1235 (11th Cir. 2004) (holding that a zoning law was not generally applicable where it prohibited religious institutions but permitted private clubs and lodges); Axson-Flynn v. Johnson, 356 F.3d 1277, 1297-99 (10th Cir. 2004) (holding that one exception given to student of another faith, and earlier exceptions given to plaintiff, gave rise to triable issue of fact on whether defendant maintained a system of individualized exceptions); Tenafly Eruv Ass'n v. Borough of Tenafly, 309 F.3d 144, 167-68 (3d Cir. 2002) (holding that a ban on attaching "any sign or advertisement, or other matter" on utility poles was not neutral where, in practice, authorities had not disturbed house number signs, directional signs, lost animal signs, orange ribbons, and other signs); Keeler v. Mayor of Cumberland, 940 F. Supp. 879, 885–86 (D. Md. 1996) (holding that a landmarking ordinance was not neutral and generally applicable where it had exceptions for substantial benefit to city, financial hardship to owner, and best interests of a majority of the community); Rader v. Johnston, 924 F. Supp. 1540, 1551-53 (D. Neb. 1996) (holding that a rule applicable to college freshmen was not generally applicable where a variety of individual and categorical exceptions exempted about one-third of freshman class); Horen v. Commonwealth, 479 S.E.2d 553, 556-57 (Va. Ct. App. 1997) (holding that a ban on possession of certain bird feathers was not neutral, when it contained exceptions for taxidermists, academics, researchers, museums, and educational institutions).

only those laws that they are willing to impose on all their constituents. *Smith-Lukumi* makes sense, if at all, as an application of Justice Jackson's observation that "there is no more effective practical guaranty against arbitrary and unreasonable government than to require that the principles of law which officials would impose upon a minority must be imposed generally."[357] Regulation that "society is prepared to impose upon [religious groups] but not upon itself"[358] is the "precise evil [that] the requirement of general applicability is designed to prevent."[359]

Even narrow secular exceptions rapidly undermine this interest. If the legislature can exempt those secular groups with the greatest motivation or ability to resist a proposed law, then the effective secular opposition would be left with no reason to continue its opposition, and the religious minority would be left without political protection in the legislature. And if these secular exceptions do not trigger strict scrutiny under *Smith-Lukumi,* the religious minority would also be left without the protection of judicial review. The focus on secular exceptions is thus an integral part of the *Smith-Lukumi* rules.

When unequal treatment of religious and secular activity imposes a burden on religion, the *reasons* for the unequal treatment are evaluated under the compelling interest test.[360] Insistence on proof of bad motive assumes that the treatment is not really unequal unless badly motivated, or if there is a reason for it. But such assumptions would fundamentally rearrange the *Smith-Lukumi* burdens of justification. Such arguments attempt to move the inquiry into the state's reasons out of the compelling interest test and into the threshold determination of neutrality and general applicability. They attempt to substitute a rational-basis inquiry, in which a not-terrible reason is sufficient to uphold the unequal treatment, for strict scrutiny, in which the state must prove a compelling justification for the unequal treatment. Requiring the religious claimant to prove bad motive goes even further, attempting to change the state's burden to prove a compelling interest into the religious claimant's inherently difficult burden to prove the government's motive.

Interpreted most generously to religious liberty, the comparative right of *Smith* and *Lukumi* still provides protection that is less inclusive, more compli-

---

357. Ry. Express Agency v. City of New York, 336 U.S. 106, 112 (1949) (Jackson, J., concurring), *quoted with approval in* Larson v. Valente, 456 U.S. 228, 245-46 (1982), *and in* Eisenstadt v. Baird, 405 U.S. 438, 454 (1972).

358. Church of the Lukumi Babalu Aye, Inc. v. City of Hialeah, 508 U.S. 520, 545 (1993) (quoting *Florida Star v. B.J.F.,* 491 U.S. 524, 542 (1989) (Scalia, J., concurring)).

359. *Id.* at 546.

360. *See id.* at 533; Employment Div. v. Smith, 494 U.S. 872, 883 (1990).

cated, and harder to invoke than the substantive liberty of *Sherbert* and *Yoder*. The shift away from substantive liberty provoked widespread disagreement among other branches and levels of government. Congress enacted first the Religious Freedom Restoration Act (RFRA),[361] then the American Indian Religious Freedom Act Amendments,[362] then the Religious Liberty and Charitable Donation Protection Act,[363] and then the Religious Land Use and Institutionalized Persons Act (RLUIPA).[364] RFRA attempted to restore the *Sherbert-Yoder* test as a matter of statutory right.[365] The Court invalidated RFRA as applied to the states,[366] but Congress strengthened RFRA as applied to the federal government, broadening the definition of protected "religious exercise."[367] Twelve state legislatures passed state RFRAs,[368] and Alabama put a similar provision in its state constitution.[369] At least ten state courts have considered *Smith* and adopted a more protective standard under their own constitutions.[370] At least

361. Pub. L. No. 103-141, 107 Stat. 1488 (1993) (codified as amended at 42 U.S.C. §§ 2000bb to 2000bb-4 (2000)).

362. Pub. L. No. 103-344, 108 Stat. 3125 (1994) (codified at 42 U.S.C. § 1996a (2000)) (protecting religious use of peyote by Native Americans).

363. Pub. L. No. 105-183, 112 Stat. 517 (1998) (amending 11 U.S.C. §§ 544, 546, 548, 707, 1325 (1994)) (protecting charities from claims of creditors of bankrupt contributors).

364. Pub. L. No. 106-274, 114 Stat. 803 (2000) (codified at 42 U.S.C. §§ 2000cc to 2000cc-5 (2000)).

365. *See* 42 U.S.C. § 2000bb-1 (codifying the *Sherbert-Yoder* compelling interest test). For accounts of the legislative and judicial battles over RFRA, see Epps, *supra* note 279, at 225-41; and Long, *supra* note 279, at 227-76.

366. *See* City of Boerne v. Flores, 521 U.S. 507, 529-36 (1997).

367. *See* 42 U.S.C. § 2000bb-2(4) (incorporating into RFRA the definition from RLUIPA). The biggest win for a religious minority burdened by federal law is *O Centro Espirita Beneficente Uniao Do Vegetal v. Ashcroft*, 342 F.3d 1170 (10th Cir. 2003), in which the panel affirmed a preliminary injunction prohibiting the government from enforcing drug laws against religious use of hoasca, a mild hallucinogenic. *Id.* at 1176-87. [Since this article was published, the Court of Appeals en banc and then the Supreme Court also affirmed the preliminary injunction. 389 F.3d 973 (10th Cir. 2004), *aff'd*, 546 U.S. 418 (2006).]

368. *See* Ariz. Rev. Stat. Ann. §§ 41-1493 to -1493.02 (West 2004); Conn. Gen. Stat. Ann. § 52-571b (West Supp. 2004); Fla. Stat. Ann. §§ 761.01–.05 (West Supp. 2004); Idaho Code §§ 73-401 to -404 (Michie Supp. 2004); 775 Ill. Comp. Stat. Ann. 35/1–99 (West 2001 & Supp. 2004); Mo. Ann. Stat. §§ 1.302–.307 (West Supp. 2004); N.M. Stat. Ann. §§ 28-22-1 to 28-22-5 (Michie Supp. 2000); Okla. Stat. Ann. tit. 51, §§ 251–258 (West Supp. 2004); 71 Pa. Cons. Stat. Ann. §§ 2401–2407 (West Supp. 2004); R.I. Gen. Laws §§ 42-80.1-1 to -4 (1998); S.C. Code Ann. §§ 1-32-10 to -60 (West Supp. 2003); Tex. Civ. Prac. & Rem. Code Ann. §§ 110.001–.012 (West Supp. 2004).

369. Ala. Const. amend. 622.

370. *See* Larson v. Cooper, 90 P.3d 125, 131 & n.31 (Alaska 2004) ("substantial threat to public safety, peace or order or where there are competing state interests of the highest or-

three other state courts followed more protective precedents and simply ignored *Smith*.[371] Another has applied pre-*Smith* law and reserved the question whether to adopt *Smith*.[372] Three states have more protective pre-*Smith* precedents expressly decided under their state constitutions.[373] In all, more than half the states appear to have adopted some version of the *Sherbert-Yoder* test.

RLUIPA requires compelling justification for land use regulations that substantially burden the exercise of religion, if the burden is imposed in implementation of a system of regulation that permits "individualized assessments of the proposed uses for the property involved."[374] This is a direct ap-

---

der"); City Chapel Evangelical Free Inc. v. City of South Bend, 744 N.E.2d 443, 445-51 (Ind. 2001) (protecting religious conduct against material burdens, but not formulating a standard for justifying such burdens); Attorney Gen. v. Desilets, 636 N.E.2d 233, 235-41 (Mass. 1994) (state "interest sufficiently compelling to justify" burden on religious exercise); State v. Hershberger, 462 N.W.2d 393, 396-99 (Minn. 1990) (compelling interest and least restrictive means); Rourke v. N.Y. State Dep't of Corr. Servs., 603 N.Y.S.2d 647, 649-50 (N.Y. Sup. Ct. 1993) ("least restrictive compelling interest test"), *aff'd*, 615 N.Y.S.2d 470, 472-73 (N.Y. App. Div. 1994) ("legitimate state interest which outweighs the negative impact upon his religious freedom"); Humphrey v. Lane, 728 N.E.2d 1039, 1043-45 (Ohio 2000) (compelling interest and least restrictive means); Hunt v. Hunt, 648 A.2d 843, 852-53 (Vt. 1994) ("[T]he Vermont Constitution protects religious liberty to the same extent that the Religious Freedom Restoration Act restricts governmental interference with free exercise. . . ."); First Covenant Church v. City of Seattle, 840 P.2d 174, 185-89 (Wash. 1992) (compelling interest and least restrictive means); State v. Miller, 549 N.W.2d 235, 238-42 (Wis. 1996) (compelling interest and least restrictive alternative); *see also* McCready v. Hoffius, 586 N.W.2d 723, 729 (Mich. 1998) (compelling interest), *vacated on other grounds,* 593 N.W.2d 545 (Mich. 1999). The first *McCready* opinion found a compelling interest. See 586 N.W.2d at 729. The religious claimant sought rehearing on the basis of new authority elsewhere holding that a similar state interest was not compelling. *See* 593 N.W.2d at 546 (Cavanagh, J., dissenting) (describing the petition's reliance on *Thomas v. Anchorage Equal Rights Commission,* 165 F.3d 692, 714-17 (9th Cir. 1999), *vacated on other grounds,* 220 F.3d 1134 (9th Cir. 2000)). *But see In re* Petition of Smith, 652 A.2d 154, 160-61 (N.H. 1994) (adopting the *Smith* standard).

371. *See* State v. Evans, 796 P.2d 178 (Kan. App. 1990); St. John's Lutheran Church v. State Comp. Ins. Fund, 830 P.2d 1271 (Mont. 1992); *In re* Browning, 476 N.E.2d 465 (N.C. App. 1996); *see also* Lower v. Bd. of Dirs., 56 P.3d 235, 244-46 (Kan. 2002) (quoting the *Smith* standard but applying pre-*Smith* standard).

372. *See* Rupert v. City of Portland, 605 A.2d 63, 65-66 & n.3 (Me. 1992); *see also* Catholic Charities, Inc. v. Super. Ct., 85 P.3d 67, 90-91 (Cal. 2004) (finding state law unsettled and reserving issue).

373. *See* Ky. State Bd. for Elementary & Secondary Educ. v. Rudasill, 589 S.W.2d 877 (Ky. 1979); *In re* Brown, 478 So.2d 1033, 1037-39 & n.5 (Miss. 1985); State *ex rel.* Swann v. Pack, 527 S.W.2d 99, 107, 111 (Tenn. 1975). *But see* State v. Loudon, 857 S.W.2d 878, 882-83 (Tenn. Crim. App. 1993) (applying the *Smith* standard without noting how it differed from the *Pack* standard).

374. 42 U.S.C. § 2000cc(a)(2)(C) (2000).

plication of the individualized assessment portion of the *Smith-Lukumi* rules. RLUIPA also prohibits other forms of discrimination against religious land use[375] and restores the *Sherbert-Yoder* test to land-use regulations and prison practices within the reach of the commerce power[376] or the spending power.[377] The constitutionality of the land-use provisions has been upheld by all but one of the district courts that have considered their validity.[378] The prison provisions have been upheld in three circuits,[379] but invalidated on Establishment Clause grounds in another.[380]

All of these issues are interconnected. Lawyers, judges, and legislators most inclined to protect individual choice in religious practice want the *Sherbert-Yoder* rule restored where possible, and where that is not possible, they want the *Smith-Lukumi* rules interpreted broadly, consistent with a sophisticated understanding of the risks of subtle and not-so-subtle discrimination in a pervasively regulated society. Those lawyers, judges, and legislators most hostile to the unregulated free exercise of religion want the *Smith-Lukumi* rules to be applied universally and interpreted very narrowly, so that the compelling interest test hardly ever applies and the Free Exercise Clause protects only against the most hostile and least disguised government efforts to restrict religious practice.

---

375. *Id.* § 2000cc(b); *see also* Midrash Sephardi, Inc. v. Town of Surfside, 366 F.3d 1214, 1235-43 (11th Cir. 2004) (upholding key parts of this section).

376. 42 U.S.C. § 2000cc(a)(2)(B) (land use); *id.* § 2000cc-1(b)(2) (prisons).

377. *See id.* § 2000cc(a)(2)(A) (land use); *id.* § 2000cc-1(b)(4) (prisons).

378. *See* Congregation Kol Ami v. Abington Township, No. Civ. A. 01-1919, 2004 WL 1837037, at *9-15 (E.D. Pa. Aug. 17, 2004), *amended on other grounds on denial of reh'g*, 2004 WL 2137819 (E.D. Pa. Sept. 21, 2004); Castle Hills First Baptist Church v. City of Castle Hills, No. SA-01-CA-1149-RF, 2004 WL 546792, at *17-19 (W.D. Tex. Mar. 17, 2004); United States v. Maui County, 298 F. Supp. 2d 1010, 1014-17 (D. Haw. 2003); Murphy v. Zoning Comm'n, 289 F. Supp. 2d 87, 115-24 (D. Conn. 2003), *vacated on other grounds*, 402 F.3d 342 (2d Cir. 2005); Westchester Day Sch. v. Vill. of Mamaroneck, 280 F. Supp. 2d 230, 233-39 (S.D.N.Y. 2003), *vacated on other grounds*, 386 F.3d 183 (2d Cir. 2004); Freedom Baptist Church v. Township of Middletown, 204 F. Supp. 2d 857 (E.D. Pa. 2002). *Contra* Elsinore Christian Ctr. v. City of Lake Elsinore, 291 F. Supp. 2d 1083, 1096-1104 (C.D. Cal. 2003), *rev'd*, 197 Fed. Appx. 718 (9th Cir. 2006). [None of the appeals in these cases had been decided when this article was originally published.]

379. *See* Madison v. Riter, 355 F.3d 310 (4th Cir. 2003); Charles v. Verhagen, 348 F.3d 601 (7th Cir. 2003); Mayweathers v. Newland, 314 F.3d 1062 (9th Cir. 2002).

380. Cutter v. Wilkinson, 349 F.3d 257 (6th Cir. 2003), *rev'd*, 544 U.S. 709 (2005). [The Supreme Court's decision came after the original publication of this article.] The Sixth Circuit holding was contrary to the great weight of authority upholding RFRA and RLUIPA against Establishment Clause challenges. *See Kol Ami*, 2004 WL 1837037, at *13 (collecting cases); *see also* Corp. of the Presiding Bishop v. Amos, 483 U.S. 327 (1987) (unanimously upholding a regulatory exemption for religious institutions).

B. The Impact of Davey

The *Smith-Lukumi* rules ban facial discrimination against religion as part of "the minimum requirement of neutrality."[381] Yet *Davey* upholds facial discrimination against religion, without requiring a compelling justification. An exception to the ban on facial discrimination is surely also an exception to the ban on more subtle forms of discrimination manifested in laws that are less than generally applicable. *Davey* is thus an important exception to the remaining protection for religious practice, and it is important to define the scope of that exception.

Those who sought from the beginning to confine *Smith-Lukumi* to cases of bad motive now claim that *Davey* confirms their view. Most prominently, Marci Hamilton argues that *Davey* requires a showing of anti-religious motive in every case.[382] But whether on close reading or on simple examination of the facts at issue, that is not what the opinion says.

The heart of the opinion is a response to Davey's claim that the Washington program "is presumptively unconstitutional because it is not facially neutral with respect to religion."[383] The opinion accepts the premise of facial discrimination but concludes that the consequence of presumptive unconstitutionality does not follow. The unifying theme is that facial discrimination against religion is presumptively unconstitutional if, and only if, the discrimination burdens a religious practice. There are multiple ways to show such a burden, but none of them were present in *Davey;* a mere refusal to fund does not impose a substantial burden.

First, the Court says that the state "imposes neither criminal nor civil sanctions on any type of religious service or rite."[384] That is, this case is not about regulation of conduct. A regulatory prohibition on a religious practice, with penalties for violation, unambiguously burdens that religious practice. But the Court has often said that a mere refusal to fund does not burden the unfunded practice, and as we have already seen, the Court put Davey's funding claim in that line of cases.[385] It is an essential part of the holding that the law at issue in this case carries no sanctions.

Second, the Court says that Washington "does not deny to ministers the

---

381. Church of the Lukumi Babalu Aye, Inc. v. City of Hialeah, 508 U.S. 520, 533 (1993).

382. Hamilton, *supra* note 29 ("There are few instances where strict scrutiny is justified under the Free Exercise Clause. In Free Exercise challenges, *hostility to religion must be shown* for strict scrutiny to apply.").

383. *Davey,* 540 U.S. at 720.

384. *Id.*

385. *See supra* text at notes 121-28, 150-59.

right to participate in the political affairs of the community."[386] This observation distinguishes *McDaniel v. Paty*,[387] which struck down restrictions on political participation. A law that required the surrender of political First Amendment rights as the cost of exercising religious First Amendment rights would of course be "presumptively unconstitutional."

These two points are alternative grounds of presumptive unconstitutionality. A discriminatory law is presumptively unconstitutional if it imposes civil or criminal penalties, *or* if it requires surrender of political rights. It would make no sense to require claimants to prove both conditions in every case. Nor could the Court possibly mean that proving one of these conditions yields presumptive unconstitutionality, but proving the other one does not; in that case, the Court's discussion of one of these alternatives would be meaningless. Rather, these are alternate grounds that, when combined with a form of discrimination cognizable under *Smith-Lukumi*, result in presumptive unconstitutionality.

Third, the Court says that the law "does not require students to choose between their religious beliefs and receiving a government benefit. The State has merely chosen not to fund a distinct category of instruction."[388] This alternative is more complicated, as we saw in the discussion of what the state must fund.[389] What amounts to a mere refusal to fund theology majors, and what amounts to withholding other benefits from theology majors, becomes a complicated question once the state is allowed to require prophylactic separation of funded and unfunded programs. But for purposes of interpreting *Smith* and *Lukumi*, there is no change in the relationship among the points the Court listed. A discriminatory law is presumptively unconstitutional if it imposes penalties, or if it restricts rights of political participation, or if it forces people to choose between their religious practice and other government benefits for which they are eligible. Any of these three alternatives would impose a burden. But a mere failure to fund does not impose a burden.

At this point, the Court begins a lengthy response to Justice Scalia, who suggests a fourth way to show a burden. Scalia argues that Promise Scholarships are so generally available that they are part of the baseline for measuring burdens; withholding such a generally available public welfare benefit burdens the religious exercise of devotional theology majors.[390] The Court responds that funding theology is different from funding other majors, and

386. *Davey*, 540 U.S. at 720.
387. 435 U.S. 618 (1978).
388. *Davey*, 540 U.S. at 720-21 (citations omitted).
389. *See supra* text at notes 121-59.
390. *See Davey*, 540 U.S. at 726-27 (Scalia, J., dissenting).

that Washington has legitimate reasons for its distinction.[391] This response to Scalia is the exclusive context for the Court's discussion of motive. The Court says that facial discrimination with respect to the funding of clergy is readily explained by the long tradition of not funding the clergy, and thus is "not evidence of hostility toward religion."[392] Washington has been solicitous of free exercise rights in other contexts, squarely rejecting the *Smith-Lukumi* test and retaining a state version of *Sherbert-Yoder*,[393] and it has voluntarily funded a substantial quantity of religious higher education, drawing the line only at devotional theology majors.[394] Finding no evidence of animus toward religion, and finding a substantial state interest in not funding the clergy, the Court says that it "cannot conclude that the denial of funding for vocational religious instruction alone is inherently constitutionally suspect."[395]

Anti-religious motive is thus a fourth reason for finding presumptive unconstitutionality, and like the third reason, it applies even to funding programs. If a discriminatory refusal to fund is based on a bad motive, that refusal to fund is presumptively unconstitutional. But nothing in this opinion implies that a bad motive requirement now applies to the first three sources of presumptive unconstitutionality. The Court does not say that the state can impose discriminatory penalties on religion if it does so without bad motive; the single sentence distinguishing laws that impose civil or criminal sanctions stands on its own. The state cannot condition political participation on forgoing religious exercise even if it somehow does so without bad motive; allowing that would overrule *McDaniel v. Paty*,[396] a decision that found no bad motive[397] and that *Davey* clearly preserves. Nor does the Court suggest an inquiry into motive when a state withholds secular benefits from claim-

---

391. *Id.* at 721-23 (citing tradition of not funding clergy).

392. *Id.* at 721.

393. *Id.* at 724 n.8 (describing Washington's free exercise rule as "more protective" than the federal rule). For the content of Washington's free exercise rule, see *First Covenant Church v. City of Seattle*, 840 P.2d 174, 185-88 (Wash. 1992).

394. *Davey*, 540 U.S. at 724-25.

395. *Id.* at 725.

396. 435 U.S. 618 (1978).

397. The provision at issue in *McDaniel* dated to 1796. *Id.* at 621 (plurality opinion). The plurality accepted that the original purpose had been to protect the new and possibly fragile experiment of disestablishment. *See id.* at 622-25. The plaintiff suggested that the true purpose was to codify a Presbyterian belief that it was sinful for a minister to become involved in politics. *Id.* at 636 n.9 (Brennan, J., concurring). No one appears to have believed that the provision arose from subjective hostility to religion, although Justice Brennan said that the state's Establishment Clause rationale inherently "manifests patent hostility toward, not neutrality respecting, religion." *Id.* at 636.

ants who used their own funds for some religious practice. The discussion of motive is in the context of mere refusals to fund; it does not introduce a new and universal requirement.

This close analysis of the opinion merely confirms what should be obvious from the larger context: *Davey* is a funding case. Davey's claim relied on *Lukumi,* the leading regulation case, but his goal was to extend the *Lukumi* rules from regulation to funding. That effort failed; *Lukumi* does not apply to funding. But neither was *Lukumi* rolled back as applied to regulation. The central dispute about the meaning of "generally applicable laws" was not clarified. The only thing the Court said about regulation of religious practice is that *Davey* is not such a case: the state "imposes neither criminal nor civil sanctions on any type of religious service or rite."[398]

In the Court's view, *Davey* was a case of unequal treatment but not a case of significant burden on religion, because the Court has repeatedly said that failure to fund is not a burden.[399] As the *Davey* Court concluded, "the exclusion of such funding places a relatively minor burden on Promise Scholars."[400]

The Court's initial discussion of *Lukumi* and the sources of presumptive unconstitutionality also makes sense in terms of burden. When the Court says that "the State's disfavor of religion" in *Davey* "is of a far milder kind,"[401] it is referring to the mildness of the burden, not to the nature or magnitude of the discrimination — express discrimination on the face of the statute is rarely thought to be a mild form of discrimination. The sentence about "a far milder kind" of disfavor is immediately followed, in the same paragraph, by the listing of the three burdens this case does not involve — criminal or civil penalties, loss of political rights, or loss of government benefits beyond the state's refusal to pay for the one activity it will not fund for anybody[402] — and then by the Court's response to Justice Scalia's suggestion that there is a fourth source of burden.[403]

In responding to Scalia's broader conception of burden, the Court considers the state's reason for discriminating as part of its analysis of why the

---

398. *Davey,* 540 U.S. at 720.

399. *See* Rust v. Sullivan, 500 U.S. 173, 192-93 (1991); Harris v. McRae, 448 U.S. 297, 317 n.19 (1980).

400. *Davey,* 540 U.S. at 725. Professor Schragger, whose views on religious liberty are very different from mine, and who is generally much less disposed to protect religious liberty from local political majorities, also reads *Davey* as a holding that failure to fund is not a burden. *See* Schragger, *supra* note 103, at 1858-64.

401. *Davey,* 540 U.S. at 720.

402. *Id.* at 720-21.

403. *Id.* at 721-25.

law is not *burdensome* — not as part of its consideration of whether the law is neutral and generally applicable. The law was not neutral, and the Court did not claim otherwise. But *Davey* does stand for the proposition that in the absence of any other burden, bad motive may suffice to show that discrimination is burdensome. And to that extent, the inquiry into reasons for discrimination can be taken out of the compelling interest test and moved to the threshold inquiry into whether the compelling interest test applies.[404] Stated affirmatively, *Smith-Lukumi* requires a showing that the challenged law is less than generally applicable *and* that it burdens the exercise of religion. That dual requirement is not a surprise, but *Davey* clarifies it; *Smith* and *Lukumi* focused on general applicability because burden was obvious.

Davey lies at the intersection of the funding and regulation cases, but fundamentally, it distinguishes the two lines and maintains their separation. The Court rejects the attempt to transport *Lukumi* wholesale from the regulation cases to the funding cases. But it does not rewrite the regulation cases.

III. *Newdow* and the Religious Speech Cases

A. The Doctrinal Context: Religious Speech With and Without Government Sponsorship

The religious speech cases include cases of religious speech by government and cases of religious speech by private speakers; these two subsets are separated by a much-litigated border. Most of these cases, on both sides of that border, have arisen in public schools. And for more than forty years, the Court has decided cases on religious speech in public schools with remarkable consistency: without a single exception in all that time, these cases are explained by the "crucial difference between *government* speech endorsing religion, which the Establishment Clause forbids, and *private* speech endorsing religion, which the Free Speech and Free Exercise Clauses protect."[405] Put more fundamentally, the difference between establishment and free exercise is the presence or absence of state action.

Neither side in the culture wars much likes this rule. From the perspective of either promoting or restricting religion, state action is beside the

---

404. Compare this exception for funding cases with the discussion *supra* text at note 360, which explains why the inquiry into the state's reasons for unequal treatment generally cannot be taken out of the compelling interest test.

405. Bd. of Educ. v. Mergens, 496 U.S. 226, 250 (1990) (plurality opinion).

point. One side would restore school-sponsored prayer; the other side would censor much private religious speech in public schools and sometimes in other public places as well.[406] But the Court is plainly right to draw the line; the religious speech cases are its most successful sustained effort to protect religious liberty. Protecting the religious speech of individuals and voluntary groups prevents government from suppressing or discouraging an important set of religious practices. This protection enables religious communities to form and function, to explore and develop their faith, to spread their message, and to seek to persuade or convert others. Prohibiting government speech that takes positions on religious questions prevents these private speakers from bringing government power to bear in their efforts to persuade or convert; protects all views about religion from having to compete with the power of government promoting some other view; protects everyone from being coerced or manipulated into attending religious observances they would not freely choose to attend; and in general, prevents government from either encouraging or discouraging any religious belief or practice.[407]

When speaking to the Court, litigants no longer challenge the basic distinction between private and governmental speech about religion. Instead, they struggle to move or manipulate the boundary. Those who would restrict religious speech in public schools claim to find government sponsorship everywhere; those who would expand religious speech in public schools claim to find student free speech everywhere. But identifying government sponsorship is not so difficult or manipulable as it is made out to be by litigants unhappy with the underlying rule.

Justices have disagreed about nuances in the formulation of a test for government sponsorship,[408] but all of the Court's *judgments* are consistent with the simple rule that if persons are speaking in their private capacities, government cannot discriminate for or against them based on the religious content of their speech. Religious speech is attributable to the government if government gives it any assistance not equally available to other private

---

406. *See, e.g.,* DeBoer v. Vill. of Oak Park, 267 F.3d 558, 561-62 (7th Cir. 2001) (meeting rooms in village hall); Church on the Rock v. City of Albuquerque, 84 F.3d 1273, 1276-77 (10th Cir. 1996) (city senior centers).

407. For an extended defense of this approach to religious speech, see Douglas Laycock, *Equal Access and Moments of Silence: The Equal Status of Religious Speech by Private Speakers,* 81 Nw. U.L. Rev. 1 (1986).

408. *See, e.g.,* Capitol Square Review & Advisory Bd. v. Pinette, 515 U.S. 753, 763-70 (1995) (plurality opinion) (favoritism test); *id.* at 772-83 (O'Connor, J., concurring) (endorsement test).

speech — that is, if government employees select the religious message,[409] deliver or lead a recitation of the religious message,[410] encourage students to deliver or reflect on their own religious thoughts or message,[411] arrange for a third party to deliver the religious message,[412] or give an otherwise private speaker preferential access to a school forum, program, audience, or facility.[413] The Court has recognized no exception to these rules in a school case since 1952, when it upheld a program that gave churches offering religious education preferential and mildly coercive access to school children.[414] The Court has recognized two more recent exceptions outside the school context, permitting legislative sessions to open with prayer[415] and permitting a municipal Christmas display that included Santa Claus and candy canes as well as a Nativity scene.[416] "Under God" in the Pledge of Allegiance would likely have become another school exception if the Court had reached the merits; realistically, the question was how to define the scope of that exception.

If government has not endorsed religious speech by one of the means just listed, that speech is private and constitutionally protected, even on government property or in a public school. If a private speaker selects and delivers his own message, and if government employees do not express an opinion about that message, do not invite or arrange for the message, do not give the speaker preferential access to government forums, programs, audiences, or facilities, and in general, if they treat the religious speaker like similarly situated secular speakers, the religious speech is attributable to the private

409. *See* Engel v. Vitale, 370 U.S. 421, 422-23 (1962).

410. *See* Sch. Dist. v. Schempp, 374 U.S. 203, 206-08, 211-12 (1963).

411. *See* Wallace v. Jaffree, 472 U.S. 38, 40 & n.2 (1985); Karen B. v. Treen, 653 F.2d 897, 899 (5th Cir. 1981), *aff'd mem.*, 455 U.S. 913 (1982).

412. *See* Santa Fe Indep. Sch. Dist. v. Doe, 530 U.S. 290, 305-06 (2000); Lee v. Weisman, 505 U.S. 577, 581, 587-88 (1992).

413. *See Santa Fe,* 530 U.S. at 303; *Weisman,* 505 U.S. at 581; Stone v. Graham, 449 U.S. 39, 39 & n.1 (1980).

414. *See* Zorach v. Clauson, 343 U.S. 306, 308-10 (1952) (describing a program in which the only choices were religious instruction at a local church or custodial care by the school). In such programs, the school "serves as a temporary jail for a pupil who will not go to Church." *Id.* at 324 (Jackson, J., dissenting). The Court denied that this arrangement was coercive, *Zorach,* 343 U.S. at 311-12, and upheld the program, *id.* at 311-15. For a first-person account of how one such program embarrassed participants and burdened nonparticipants, see Ira C. Lupu, *The Trouble with Accommodation,* 60 GEO. WASH. L. REV. 743, 743-45 & nn.3, 10 (1992).

415. *See* Marsh v. Chambers, 463 U.S. 783, 792-95 (1983).

416. *See* Lynch v. Donnelly, 465 U.S. 668, 678-87 (1984); *cf.* County of Allegheny v. ACLU, 492 U.S. 573, 598-602 (1989) (invalidating a prominently displayed Nativity scene not accompanied by any "secular" Christmas displays).

speaker. This is the rule in public schools,[417] in higher education,[418] and on other government property.[419] The rule is broader than speech on government property; the Court has never doubted the right to make religious arguments in political debate,[420] and it has upheld the right of clergy to hold political office.[421] These rules are not a product of any recent swing to the right; protection of religious speech on public property goes back to the Jehovah's Witness cases in the Vinson Court and before.[422] Indeed, prior to *Locke v. Davey,* the Court had *never* held in any context that government may or must discriminate against a private speaker based on the religious content of his speech. *Davey* creates a funding exception to the rule prohibiting discrimination against religious speech.[423]

Having repeatedly lost on their claim that equal access to a government forum would violate the Establishment Clause, litigants seeking to limit private religious speech have increasingly shifted strategies. They now give greater emphasis to the claim that government controls the scope of the forums it creates, so that access is not guaranteed under the Free Speech Clause.[424]

It is familiar doctrine that the Court's free speech cases recognize three

417. *See* Good News Club v. Milford Cent. Sch., 533 U.S. 98, 107-20 (2001); Lamb's Chapel v. Ctr. Moriches Union Free Sch. Dist., 508 U.S. 384, 392-97 (1993); Bd. of Educ. v. Mergens, 496 U.S. 226, 247-53 (1990) (plurality opinion).

418. *See* Rosenberger v. Rector & Visitors of Univ. of Va., 515 U.S. 819, 828-46 (1995); Widmar v. Vincent, 454 U.S. 263, 267-76 (1981).

419. The Court has long protected religious speech on public property — simply as speech. *See, e.g.,* Capitol Square Review & Advisory Bd. v. Pinette, 515 U.S. 753, 761-63 (1995); Bd. of Airport Comm'rs v. Jews for Jesus, Inc., 482 U.S. 569 (1987); Poulos v. New Hampshire, 345 U.S. 395, 402-08 (1953); Fowler v. Rhode Island, 345 U.S. 67 (1953); Kunz v. New York, 340 U.S. 290, 290-95 (1951); Niemotko v. Maryland, 340 U.S. 268, 269-73 (1951); Cantwell v. Connecticut, 310 U.S. 296, 300-11 (1940). The early cases generally assumed the equal status of religious speech, but the issue was raised at least twice. *See* Laycock, *supra* note 407, at 11-12 & n.59.

420. *See* Walz v. Tax Comm'n, 397 U.S. 664, 670 (1970); Douglas Laycock, *Freedom of Speech That Is Both Religious and Political,* 29 U.C. Davis L. Rev. 793 (1996) (defending the legal and moral right to make religious arguments in political debate).

421. *See* McDaniel v. Paty, 435 U.S. 618 (1978).

422. *See* cases cited *supra* note 419.

423. *See supra* section I.C.3.c, text at notes 217-39.

424. The most dramatic example arose in *Rosenberger,* when Professor (now Dean) John Jeffries made only a Free Speech Clause argument, and no Establishment Clause argument. *See* Brief for the Respondents, Rosenberger v. Rector & Visitors of Univ. of Va., 515 U.S. 819 (1995) (No. 94-329), *available in* 1995 WL 16452. Even before that, a New York school district had devoted twenty pages to its Free Speech Clause argument and only four pages to its affirmative Establishment Clause argument. *See* Brief for Respondents, Lamb's Chapel v. Ctr. Moriches Union Free Sch. Dist., 508 U.S. 384 (1993) (No. 91-2024), *available in* 1992 WL 512049, at *7-27 (Free Speech Clause); *id.* at *27-31 (Establishment Clause).

kinds of forums. The first, perhaps confined to streets and parks, is "property that has traditionally been available for public expression."[425] Second is "the designated public forum," property that is a forum because the government said so.[426] Third is the nonpublic forum on "all remaining public property."[427] Designated and nonpublic forums can be open to private speakers but may be limited by subject matter or speaker identity.[428] The difference between a nonpublic forum and a designated forum with limitations has never been expressly defined, but it is a reasonable inference that limits on a designated forum must be imposed by category;[429] in a nonpublic forum, speakers may be admitted or excluded individually.[430] The important point for present purposes is that in both designated and nonpublic forums, government has substantial power to pick and choose who will be permitted to speak and what they will be permitted to discuss.

Of course this power is not unlimited. Viewpoint discrimination is forbidden in any kind of forum.[431] And so long as a designated forum remains open, government must have a compelling reason for excluding a speaker who falls within the forum's designated limits.[432] But government can exclude unwanted speakers by further restricting the designated subject matters or classes of permitted speakers, or by closing the designated forum entirely.[433] These rules have been criticized on the ground that in nontraditional forums, free speech depends on government fiat[434] and censorship is self-justifying.[435] But the rules survived an attack by four Justices in *ISKCON v. Lee*,[436] and the Court continues to work within them.

425. Int'l Soc'y for Krishna Consciousness, Inc. (ISKCON) v. Lee, 505 U.S. 672, 678 (1992).

426. *Id.*

427. *Id.* at 678-79.

428. *See* Cornelius v. NAACP Legal Def. & Educ. Fund, Inc., 473 U.S. 788, 802-03, 806 (1985).

429. *See* Perry Educ. Ass'n v. Perry Local Educators' Ass'n, 460 U.S. 37, 48 (1983) (noting that if admission of selected speakers "has created a 'limited' public forum, the constitutional right of access would in any event extend only to other entities of similar character").

430. *See Cornelius,* 473 U.S. at 804-05 (describing admission of "appropriate" speakers on criteria that were not "merely ministerial"); *Perry,* 460 U.S. at 47 (describing practice of "selective access").

431. *See ISKCON,* 505 U.S. at 678-79.

432. *See* Ark. Educ. Television Comm'n v. Forbes, 523 U.S. 666, 677 (1998).

433. *See Cornelius,* 473 U.S. at 802; *Perry,* 460 U.S. at 46.

434. *See ISKCON,* 505 U.S. at 693-94 (Kennedy, J., concurring).

435. *See* Laycock, *supra* note 407, at 45-51 (text at notes 213-42).

436. *See ISKCON,* 505 U.S. at 693 (Kennedy, J., concurring).

The distinction between viewpoint discrimination and subject-matter exclusions is far more important than the difference between designated and nonpublic forums. Governments argue that religion is a subject matter, permissibly excluded from either kind of forum, and speakers argue that excluding their religious speech is viewpoint discrimination. The speakers have been winning; the Court has consistently held that government exclusion of religious speech is viewpoint discrimination.[437]

The distinction between government and private speech, and the characterization of religious speech as an expression of viewpoints, have been remarkably stable and persistent, but these two rules actually have the full support of only two Justices, Kennedy and O'Connor. Justices Rehnquist, Scalia, and Thomas would permit significant government sponsorship of religious speech,[438] and Justices Stevens, Souter, Ginsburg, and Breyer would impose significant restrictions on private religious speech in public places.[439] This persistent 4-3-2 split has enabled Kennedy and O'Connor to prevail; they generally have six votes to prohibit government sponsorship of religious speech, and at least five votes to invalidate government discrimination against private religious speech.

B. The Pledge of Allegiance

The Pledge of Allegiance in *Newdow* was clearly government-sponsored speech. Congress enacted the text of the Pledge by statute;[440] teachers led the Pledge in public school classrooms. The question was whether the religious

---

437. *See* Good News Club v. Milford Cent. Sch., 533 U.S. 98, 107-12 (2001); Rosenberger v. Rector & Visitors of Univ. of Va., 515 U.S. 819, 830-32 (1995); Lamb's Chapel v. Ctr. Moriches Union Free Sch. Dist., 508 U.S. 384, 393-94 (1993); *see also* Widmar v. Vincent, 454 U.S. 263, 267-70 (1981) (applying the compelling interest test to content discrimination against religious speech).

438. *See, e.g.*, Santa Fe Indep. Sch. Dist. v. Doe, 530 U.S. 290, 318 (2000) (Rehnquist, C.J., dissenting); Lee v. Weisman, 505 U.S. 577, 631 (1992) (Scalia, J., dissenting); Wallace v. Jaffree, 472 U.S. 38, 113-14 (1985) (Rehnquist, J., dissenting) ("Nothing in the Establishment Clause of the First Amendment, properly understood, prohibits any such generalized 'endorsement' of prayer.").

439. *See, e.g.*, *Good News Club*, 533 U.S. at 127 (Breyer, J., concurring in part); *id.* at 130 (Stevens, J., dissenting); *id.* at 134 (Souter, J., dissenting); *Rosenberger*, 515 U.S. at 863 (Souter, J., dissenting).

440. 4 U.S.C. § 4 (2000). For uncodified Congressional findings, see 4 U.S.C.A. § 4 (Supp. 2004).

portion of the Pledge could somehow be rationalized, treated as secular, or fit within a de minimis exception that had a long history in dicta.

Despite the Court's repeated holdings that government may not endorse any view about religion, the Justices have always assumed that some modest degree of government-sponsored religious observance is permissible. Repeated dicta suggested that the Court would not invalidate "In God We Trust" on the currency, presidential Thanksgiving Day proclamations, or the opening invocation at the Court's own sessions: "God save the United States and this honorable Court."[441] At least one opinion of the Court, and many separate opinions, offered "under God" in the Pledge of Allegiance as an example of the minimal religious references permitted by the Constitution.[442] "Ceremonial deism" has been another label for this de minimis exception.[443]

But the Court had never been required to define the boundary between these tolerated manifestations of government-sponsored religion and all the others that are unconstitutional. Lower courts had always upheld references that might have fallen within the de minimis exception,[444] thus sparing the Court the difficulty of writing an opinion either defending it or defining it. The opinion would be difficult to write because the implicit exception is at best a matter of judgment rather than principle. It is easy to explain why government can never say anything about religion, and equally easy (though less convincing) to explain why government can say anything it wants about religion so long as it does not coerce or penalize those who disagree. Avoiding either extreme requires the Court to pick and choose, to explain why govern-

441. *See, e.g.,* County of Allegheny v. ACLU, 492 U.S. 573, 630-31 (1989) (O'Connor, J., concurring in part and concurring in the judgment); Sch. Dist. v. Schempp, 374 U.S. 203, 303-04 (1963) (Brennan, J., concurring).

442. *See* Lynch v. Donnelly, 465 U.S. 668, 676 (1984); *id.* at 716-17 (Brennan, J., dissenting); *Weisman,* 505 U.S. at 638-39 (Scalia, J., dissenting); *County of Allegheny,* 492 U.S. at 674 n.10 (Kennedy, J., concurring in the judgment in part and dissenting in part); *Jaffree,* 472 U.S. at 78 n.5 (O'Connor, J., concurring); *id.* at 88 (Burger, C.J., dissenting); Engel v. Vitale, 370 U.S. 421, 449 (1962) (Stewart, J., dissenting); *see also County of Allegheny,* 492 U.S. at 602-03 (reserving the issue).

443. For a well-developed attack on the exception, see Steven B. Epstein, *Rethinking the Constitutionality of Ceremonial Deism,* 96 Colum. L. Rev. 2083 (1996).

444. *See, e.g.,* ACLU v. Capitol Square Review & Advisory Bd., 243 F.3d 289, 293-310 (6th Cir. 2001) (en banc) (upholding "With God All Things Are Possible," the state motto of Ohio); Gaylor v. United States, 74 F.3d 214 (10th Cir. 1996) (upholding "In God We Trust"); Sherman v. Cmty. Consol. Sch. Dist. No. 21, 980 F.2d 437 (7th Cir. 1992) (upholding Pledge of Allegiance); Myers v. Loudoun County Sch. Bd., 251 F. Supp. 2d 1262 (E.D. Va. 2003) (upholding Pledge of Allegiance), *aff'd,* 418 F.3d 395 (4th Cir. 2005).

ment can endorse some religious propositions but not others, with no clear principle to guide the choices.

No matter how the Court defines a de minimis exception, it would be hard to fit the Pledge of Allegiance within it. In *Newdow,* it may have been politically impossible to affirm and legally impossible to reverse.

1. The Religious Content of the Pledge.

To recite that the nation is "under God" is inherently a religious affirmation. In theistic faiths, the existence of God is perhaps the most fundamental religious proposition. The politicians who added "under God" to the Pledge openly announced their religious purposes, including religious indoctrination of the nation's children.[445] Yet as so often happens in religious speech cases, defenders of the Pledge attempted to deny its obvious religious meaning.[446] The United States argued that "under God" in the Pledge is a permissible reference to historic and demographic facts about the nation's religious and mostly Christian population.[447] Chief Justice Rehnquist seemed to agree, arguing that the Pledge "is a patriotic exercise, not a religious one," and that "[t]he phrase 'under God' is in no sense a prayer, nor an endorsement of any religion, but a simple recognition of the fact" that the nation was founded on a belief in God.[448]

No nonbeliever can take these claims seriously. Michael Newdow could readily tell the difference between his daughter writing on a history exam that religious movements have been important to political developments, or that most Americans have believed in God — which would indeed be statements of fact — and his daughter personally affirming that the nation is "under God." The Pledge has no statement about what many Americans believe, or about what the Founders believed. There is only a profession of what each person taking the Pledge believes: "*I* pledge allegiance to . . . one Nation under God."[449]

---

445. *See* Epstein, *supra* note 443, at 2118-22. For the argument that the Pledge is unconstitutional under existing precedent, see *id.* at 2151-53.

446. *See* U.S. *Newdow* Brief, *supra* note 17, at *45 ("It is not a religious exercise at all. . . ."); Petitioners' Brief on the Merits, *Newdow* (No. 02-1624), *available in* 2003 WL 23051996, at *30 ("The Pledge Is Not a Religious Act or a Profession of Religious Belief. . . .").

447. *See* U.S. *Newdow* Brief, *supra* note 17, at *20-23 & n.18; *id.* at *31-33.

448. *Newdow,* 542 U.S. at 31 (Rehnquist, C.J., concurring in the judgment).

449. "One Nation" is an appositive phrase, an alternate name for the preceding noun phrase ("Republic for which it stands"), and stands in the same relation to the rest of the sentence. *See, e.g.,* BRYAN A. GARNER, A DICTIONARY OF MODERN LEGAL USAGE 68 (1995).

The secularized interpretation of the Pledge is equally unacceptable to serious believers. From the religious right, Father Richard John Neuhaus twice condemned such arguments, claiming "widespread agreement that the government botched its case for keeping 'under God' in the Pledge," and that "most Americans . . . agree . . . with Mr. Newdow . . . that a reference to God is a reference to God, the government's brief notwithstanding."[450] In an earlier comment, condemning similar arguments from the American Jewish Congress,[451] Neuhaus said: "In other words, such references to God in public are permissible because nobody really believes what they say. . . . Maybe the Court will next rule that pigs can fly."[452]

From the religious left, thirty-two Christian and Jewish clergy whom I represented argued that "[e]ither government is asking school children to make a sincere statement of belief in the one true God Whom the Nation is under, or it is asking children to take the name of the Lord in vain."[453] Neither request is consistent with government's duty of neutrality toward and among religions. If the Pledge means what it says, it is a short profession of faith; if it does not, it is an insincere statement of religious faith that has been redirected — misappropriated — to secular and political purposes.

Of course, the government's secular interpretation of the Pledge was a polite lie, told only to the Court. Perhaps the government hoped the Court would repeat the lie, but surely it did not expect that the Court would *believe* the lie. The United States interpreted the Pledge very differently in the President's letter to citizens who wrote the White House about the Pledge case:

> As citizens recite the Pledge of Allegiance, we help define our Nation. In one sentence, we affirm our form of government, our belief in human dignity, our unity as a people, and our reliance on God. . . . When we pledge allegiance to One nation under God, our citizens participate in an important American tradition of humbly seeking the wisdom and blessing of Divine Providence.[454]

---

450. Richard John Neuhaus, *The Public Square*, FIRST THINGS, June/July 2004, at 64, 83.

451. *See* AJC *Newdow* Brief, *supra* note 23, at *1-20.

452. Richard John Neuhaus, *The Public Square*, FIRST THINGS, March 2004, at 55, 70.

453. Clergy Brief, *supra* note 25, at *8.

454. Letter from George W. Bush, President of the United States, to Mitsuo Murashige, President of the Hawaii State Federation of Honpa Hongwanji Lay Associations (Nov. 13, 2002), *reprinted in* Amicus Curiae Brief of Americans United for Separation of Church and State et al. in Support of Affirmance, *Newdow* (No. 02-1624), *available in* 2004 WL 298118, at *3a [hereinafter Americans United Brief]. This letter responded to a Buddhist resolution *opposing* "under God" in the Pledge. Letter from Mitsuo Murashige, President of the Hawaii

The President's claim that the Pledge seeks God's wisdom and blessing also goes beyond the literal language of the Pledge, but at least it elaborates that language without negating its primary meaning, and it may be that many believers think of themselves as seeking God's blessing whenever they invoke His name. Certainly the White House letter was more honest than the government's brief.

Once we get past the polite lie and agree that "under God" is religious, it is common to assume that "under God" is so generic that it includes all believers, and that only atheists and agnostics could dissent. The legal relevance of this assumption is unclear; atheists and agnostics have as much right as anyone else to invoke the Establishment Clause. But the assumption matters politically, and it may also matter to whether the Pledge falls within a de minimis exception. In any event, it is false to assume that only nonbelievers dissent from the Pledge; a range of religious believers dissent as well. On careful analysis, "under God" implies a succinct religious creed, less specific than most creeds, but carrying substantial religious meaning.

Most obviously, the Pledge affirms that God exists. Further, as the court of appeals emphasized,[455] the Pledge affirms that there is only one God. The Pledge does not recite that the nation is under "the Gods," or that it is under "our God," "a God," "some God," or "one of the Gods," but simply that the nation is "under God." The lack of any article or modifier necessarily implies that there is no other possible meaning or referent in the category mentioned; the Pledge does not speak for either nontheistic or polytheistic religions. If there is only one God, worshipers of other alleged gods are mistaken. They are worshiping false gods; the God of the Pledge is the one true God.

The Pledge also affirms an important characteristic of the one true God. God exercises some sort of broad superintending authority that an entire nation can be "under." The nature of this authority is not further specified — it might be judgmental, protective, or triumphant, or it might reflect some other understanding of divine authority — but some conceptions of God are excluded. A "Nation *under* God" does not plausibly refer to God as First Cause, starting the universe in motion and then withdrawing, nor to God as a name or metaphor for all the goodness immanent in the universe.

State Federation of Honpa Hongwanji Lay Associations, to George W. Bush, President of the United States (Sept. 2002), *reprinted in* Americans United Brief, *supra*, at *1a. The obvious mismatch between the original letter and the White House response implies that this was the form letter for all who wrote about the Pledge. The workload has increased unmanageably, and standards have declined, since Jefferson's reply to the Danbury Baptists.

455. *See* Newdow v. U.S. Cong., 328 F.3d 466, 487 (9th Cir. 2003), *rev'd on other grounds sub nom.* Elk Grove Unified Sch. Dist. v. Newdow, 542 U.S. 1 (2004).

Some Americans read "under God" in much more specific ways than I have read it. Father Neuhaus reads the Pledge to mean that the nation is "under judgment" by a higher authority.[456] Thomas Berg expands on this theme, reading "under God" to imply "that government is a limited institution, subject to standards of authority higher than itself," and that individual rights are derived from "a source higher than the nation or any other human authority."[457] A questioner at a Pew Forum discussion read "under" God to imply a Calvinist conception of God.[458] For both Neuhaus and Berg, their reading of the Pledge states a truth that they believe; for the questioner at the Pew Forum, her reading states a belief that she appeared to reject.

School children do not carefully parse the language of the Pledge; children who believe are likely to casually equate the God of the Pledge with their own conception of God. Children who do not believe likely hear only a bald and literal assertion of God's existence. Whether read carefully or casually, the religious content is definitely not secular. And it is not so generic as one might think on a cursory recital.

2. The Intrusiveness of the Pledge.

The religious affirmation in the Pledge is very brief; it is reasonably, although imperfectly, generic. These are the obvious reasons for thinking it might fit within a de minimis exception. But in other ways, the Pledge is an unlikely candidate: it is most frequently used in public schools, it asks for a personal statement of belief in God, and it links that request to a profession of loyalty to the nation.

Nowhere has the Court been more sensitive to departures from religious neutrality than in public schools. Public schools have been a battleground over religious instruction since their origins in the early nineteenth century.[459] Parents reasonably believe they should be able to send their children

456. Richard John Neuhaus, *The Public Square,* FIRST THINGS, Oct. 1999, at 78, 89-90.

457. Thomas C. Berg, *The Pledge of Allegiance and the Limited State,* 8 TEX. REV. L. & POL. 41, 52 (2003).

458. *See* Lee McAuliffe Rambo, Comment at *Discussion: Under God? Pledge of Allegiance Constitutionality* (March 19, 2004) (transcript available at http://pewforum.org/events/index.php?EventD=R53). On the record, Ms. Rambo said: "[O]ne of those words is a preposition, which, to at least some ears, implies a particular type of God, one that we are under, one that is transcendent." *Id.* In one-on-one questioning at the end of the event, she said that the connotations of authority attaching to "under," emphasized by Neuhaus and Berg, connoted Calvinism.

459. *See* GLENN, *supra* note 198, at 146-206; KAESTLE, *supra* note 198, at 98-99, 167-71; Jeffries & Ryan, *supra* note 12, at 297-305.

to public school without the state taking advantage of the opportunity to teach someone else's religion. The other examples of permitted ceremonial deism are religious observances directed to audiences consisting principally of adults — as in prayers at the opening of legislative sessions and the marshal's cry at sittings of the Supreme Court — or to no one in particular, as in Thanksgiving proclamations and the motto on the currency. In contrast, public schools, with a captive audience of children subject to compulsory education laws, are the most sensitive place to recognize an exception for government-sponsored religious observances.

More fundamentally, only the Pledge asks each student for a personal commitment to the propositions it contains. In the Court's first prayer cases, students were asked to join in reciting the prayer,[460] but no subsequent case presented such facts until *Newdow*. In the intervening cases, students at most had to stand or "maintain respectful silence";[461] they did not have to overtly join in. No other common example of ceremonial deism, in or out of the public schools, asks citizens to recite either a prayer or a religious proposition.[462]

The Pledge is different. However briefly and generically, the Pledge ceremony asks for a personal profession of faith. As the Court observed long ago, "the compulsory flag salute and pledge requires affirmation of a belief and an attitude of mind."[463] Speaking of the wholly secular Pledge as it existed in 1943, the Court said that "[i]t requires the individual to communicate by word and sign his acceptance of the political ideas it thus bespeaks,"[464] including the truth of "liberty and justice for all" and the other descriptive characteristics attributed to the nation.[465] Moreover, the Court recognized that one reason for refusing to recite the Pledge might be disagreement with one or more of these descriptive claims.[466]

It is equally true today that recitation of the Pledge in a solemn ceremony affirms the truth of its description of the nation, including the additional be-

---

460. *See* Sch. Dist. v. Schempp, 374 U.S. 203, 207 (1963); Engel v. Vitale, 370 U.S. 421, 422 (1962).

461. Lee v. Weisman, 505 U.S. 577, 593 (1992). The Court's other prayer cases involved prayers before an assembled audience, *see* Santa Fe Indep. Sch. Dist. v. Doe, 530 U.S. 290, 297 (2000), or a moment of silence, *see* Wallace v. Jaffree, 472 U.S. 38, 40, 48 (1985).

462. *See* County of Allegheny v. ACLU, 492 U.S. 573, 603 n.52 (1989) (distinguishing religious observances that "urge citizens to engage in religious practices" from those that do not).

463. W. Va. State Bd. of Educ. v. Barnette, 319 U.S. 624, 633 (1943).

464. *Id.*

465. *Id.* at 634 n.14.

466. *Id.* at 634 & n.14.

lief, inserted in 1954,[467] that the nation is "under God." To affirm this description necessarily affirms the propositions included in that description: that there is a God, and only one, of such a nature that a nation can be under that God.

In a single sentence, the Pledge links this profession of religious faith to a profession of national allegiance. The Court has repeatedly expressed its concern that government endorsements of religious viewpoints tend to exclude from the political community citizens who do not share those viewpoints.[468] That implication is more direct in the Pledge than when a government agent leads an audience in prayer. The Pledge expressly links not just religion and government, but also religion and loyalty. Students who cannot in good conscience affirm that the nation is "under God" cannot recite the officially prescribed pledge of their allegiance to the nation. They might not recite the Pledge at all, or they might drop out for two words in the middle. Either way, the message of exclusion is unmistakable. What kind of citizen cannot even recite in good faith the Pledge of Allegiance?

3. The Remedy for Government-Sponsored Religious Observances.

This combination of religious and political sentiments evades the Court's long-standing rules on the proper remedy for those who conscientiously object to government ceremonies. No one may be required to affirm a political sentiment.[469] But this rule does not preclude the state from asking citizens to pledge their allegiance. In *West Virginia State Board of Education v. Barnette*,[470] which

467. *Compare* Act of June 14, 1954, Pub. L. No. 83-396, 68 Stat. 249 (enacting Pledge including "under God"), *with* 36 U.S.C. § 172 (1952) (repealed in 1998) (Pledge without "under God"). In 1998, the Pledge was recodified at 4 U.S.C. § 4. *See* Pub. L. No. 105-225 § 2, 112 Stat. 1257, 1494 (1998).

468. *See, e.g.,* Santa Fe Indep. Sch. Dist. v. Doe, 530 U.S. 290, 309-10 (2000) ("School sponsorship of a religious message is impermissible because it sends the ancillary message to members of the audience who are nonadherents 'that they are outsiders, not full members of the political community, and an accompanying message to adherents that they are insiders, favored members of the political community.'" (quoting *Lynch v. Donnelly,* 465 U.S. 668, 688 (1984) (O'Connor, J., concurring))); County of Allegheny v. ACLU, 492 U.S. 573, 593-94 (1989); Tex. Monthly, Inc. v. Bullock, 489 U.S. 1, 9 & n.1 (1989) (plurality opinion); *see also* Lee v. Weisman, 505 U.S. 577, 627 (1992) (Souter, J., concurring); Wallace v. Jaffree, 472 U.S. 38, 69 (1985) (O'Connor, J., concurring).

469. *See* Wooley v. Maynard, 430 U.S. 705, 713-17 (1977) ("Live Free or Die" on license plate); *Barnette,* 319 U.S. at 635-42 (secular Pledge of Allegiance, before the addition of "under God").

470. 319 U.S. 624 (1943).

struck down compulsory recital of the secular Pledge of Allegiance as it then existed, the only remedy sought or granted was to enjoin enforcement "as to the plaintiffs" and "others similarly situated."[471]

The rule is fundamentally different with respect to government sponsored religious statements. The Court's first school-sponsored prayer case held that it was not enough to excuse objecting children from participating in the brief government-sponsored prayer.[472] The only adequate remedy was to prohibit school employees from leading *any* students in prayer, willing or otherwise. The Court has adhered to this rule ever since. If a religious practice violates the Establishment Clause, the government sponsorship is enjoined; allowing individuals to opt out does not avoid the constitutional violation.

The reason for this distinction between political and religious speech lies deep in constitutional structure and the legitimate functions of government. On political matters, government may lead public opinion to the best of its ability. It can encourage patriotism and civic duty; it can rally support for the war effort, the tax cuts, or the civil rights movement. It can discourage drug abuse, encourage physical fitness, or urge the populace to "Whip Inflation Now."[473] Constitutional structure implies some limits on government propaganda efforts,[474] but those limits are very broad and enforced more by the political system than by any prospect of judicial review.[475] Citizens remain free to agree or disagree, to rally in support of the government or in protest, to support the incumbent administration or to vote the rascals out. But on political matters, electoral losers must accept the results of the election.

None of these political practices apply to religion. On religious matters, citizens do not vote and government does not lead. The government has no legitimate role in shaping the religious opinions of the American people; that is what it means to say that government may not endorse any position on a religious question.[476] Conceding government power to lead religious opinion implies the legitimacy of voting and campaigning on religious proposi-

471. *Id.* at 629, 630.

472. *See* Engel v. Vitale, 370 U.S. 421, 430 (1962).

473. The Ford Administration produced buttons bearing this helpful message. Inflation did not appear to be intimidated.

474. *See* MARK G. YUDOF, WHEN GOVERNMENT SPEAKS: POLITICS, LAW, AND GOVERNMENT EXPRESSION IN AMERICA 51-66 (1983).

475. *See id.* at 111-38.

476. For the no-endorsement rule, see Santa Fe Indep. Sch. Dist. v. Doe, 530 U.S. 290, 308 (2000); County of Allegheny v. ACLU, 492 U.S. 573, 592-94 (1989); Wallace v. Jaffree, 472 U.S. 38, 56, 60-61 (1985).

tions, because voting and campaigning are how democracies choose positions for their governments to take. But voting on the truth of religious propositions is utterly inconsistent with committing religious faith to individual choices and commitments. The Court has correctly said that a referendum on religion is unconstitutional: "Simply by establishing this school-related procedure, which entrusts the inherently nongovernmental subject of religion to a majoritarian vote, a constitutional violation has occurred."[477] Government statements on religion seem harmless only when a vote seems unnecessary because the statement is bland enough to have overwhelming support. But government has no more legitimate power to lead religious opinion on the basis of an implicit vote than on the basis of an explicit vote.

The Court explained the essence of this distinction in *Lee v. Weisman*:[478]

> The First Amendment protects speech and religion by quite different mechanisms. Speech is protected by ensuring its full expression even when the government participates, for the very object of some of our most important speech is to persuade the government to adopt an idea as its own. The method for protecting freedom of worship and freedom of conscience in religious matters is quite the reverse. In religious debate or expression the government is not a prime participant, for the Framers deemed religious establishment antithetical to the freedom of all. . . . A state-created orthodoxy puts at grave risk that freedom of belief and conscience which are the sole assurance that religious faith is real, not imposed.[479]

I would delete the word "prime" and simply say that government may not participate in religious debates. But the qualification leaves open the long-acknowledged de minimis exception.

By combining religious and patriotic affirmations in a single sentence, the Pledge straddles both sides of the distinction between government's roles in the shaping of religious and political opinions. The only remedy for the religious portion of the Pledge was the Establishment Clause remedy, forbidding government to lead or sponsor the recitation. But supporters of the Pledge argued that its patriotic elements determined the character of the Pledge as a whole, so that the existing right to opt out was a sufficient remedy. If accepted, that argument would lead to a regime in which government could freely sponsor religious observances, so long as each religious observance was combined with a sufficient quantity of political observance to bring the combined whole

---

477. *Santa Fe*, 530 U.S. at 317.
478. 505 U.S. 577 (1992).
479. *Id.* at 591-92 (citations omitted).

under the rule for government-sponsored *political* speech instead of the quite different rule for government-sponsored *religious* speech.

Under principles that had been consistently applied over forty years, the court of appeals properly invalidated "under God" in the Pledge.[480] This brief recital is a government-sponsored religious observance, and prohibiting such observances is the settled remedy. The only plausible alternative would be to define a de minimis exception that somehow includes this uniquely intrusive, but very brief and relatively generic, religious observance.

C. The Court's Response

The Court did not reach the merits of the Pledge, because it held that Michael Newdow, an unmarried father with disputed custody rights,[481] lacked standing to sue.[482] But three Justices would have found standing and reached the merits. Not surprisingly, all three would have upheld the Pledge. Also not surprisingly, they could not agree on a reason. Justice O'Connor offered the first serious effort by any Justice to define the de minimis exception. Justices Rehnquist and Thomas would have given government broad or unlimited discretion.

1. Defining a De Minimis Exception.

Justice O'Connor begins unpromisingly, joining in full Chief Justice Rehnquist's opinion,[483] which says both that the Pledge is secular and that government can often endorse religious sentiments.[484] She says more in the same vein, concluding that the Pledge is, in a sense, secular. But she does not deny that language means what it means. She writes that "these references speak in the language of religious belief,"[485] thus nodding to reality, but she adds that "they are more properly understood as employing the idiom for essentially secular purposes."[486]

---

480. See Newdow v. U.S. Cong., 328 F.3d 466, 485-90 (9th Cir. 2003), *rev'd on other grounds sub nom.* Elk Grove Unified Sch. Dist. v. Newdow, 542 U.S. 1 (2004).

481. See *Newdow*, 542 U.S. at 14-18.

482. See *id.* at 11-18. For analysis, see *Leading Cases, supra* note 15, at 426-36.

483. *Newdow*, 542 U.S. at 33 (O'Connor, J., concurring in the judgment).

484. See *infra* text at notes 532-34.

485. *Newdow*, 542 U.S. at 35 (O'Connor, J., concurring in the judgment).

486. *Id.; see also id.* at 36 (arguing that "[f]acially religious references" can serve secular purposes).

To this point, she has added only the nod to reality. Justice O'Connor's contribution is to offer relatively objective criteria for identifying religious statements that can be treated as secular. She offers four factors to be considered in assessing whether the government has endorsed religion, plus a requirement that must be separately satisfied.

Her first factor is "History and Ubiquity."[487] A finding of secular purpose requires "a shared understanding" of that purpose, which "can exist only when a given practice has been in place for a significant portion of the Nation's history."[488] "[N]ovel or uncommon references to religion" are unlikely to qualify, because reasonable observers will not know their origins.[489] This factor insures that a decision upholding one traditional recitation does not become the basis for an endless round of new experiments in government imposition of religion. It confines her opinion to a rather short list of existing practices that have long gone unchallenged. With regard to the Pledge, Justice O'Connor says that fifty years as "our most routine ceremonial act of patriotism" is long enough.[490] One lesson is that separationist groups should sue immediately when they encounter any religious practice newly sponsored by the government.

Justice O'Connor's second factor is "Absence of worship or prayer."[491] She quite plausibly found the Pledge to be neither. Passive religious symbols, such as crosses, Nativity scenes, and the Ten Commandments, would also pass this factor. To me, this factor relies on a mere difference in form. Leading students in a brief profession of faith is no more defensible than leading them in worship or prayer. Even so, this factor does substantial work, because government-sponsored prayer has been the most common form of government-sponsored religious observance. Government requests for a profession of faith have been confined to the Pledge. Any new practice of government-sponsored creeds would satisfy this factor, but not the History-and-Ubiquity factor.

Justice O'Connor saw more in this Absence-of-worship factor than a mere difference in form. She knew of no religion "that would count the Pledge as a meaningful expression of religious faith."[492] That statement is surely wrong,[493] but it approximates something important.

487. *Id.* at 37.
488. *Id.*
489. *Id.*
490. *Id.* at 38.
491. *Id.* at 39.
492. *Id.* at 40.
493. *See supra* text at notes 445-58.

No religion would draft a meaningful religious statement in the sparse language of the Pledge *if the religious community were free to write the statement for itself.* Brief, generic, least-common-denominator formulations are the inevitable result of drafting professions of faith to appeal to a national supermajority. Despite its inadequacies from a religious perspective, the Pledge retains sufficient religious meaning for millions of Americans to get angry at the prospect of removing its religious content. Father Neuhaus and Professor Berg, coming from different faith traditions and different places on the political spectrum, each read into the Pledge serious propositions of religious faith.[494] Professor Berg goes further, predicting that if "under God" is removed, many Americans will refuse to recite the Pledge, viewing it as a pledge of loyalty to an absolute government that acknowledges no higher limits on its authority.[495] The most committed believers and the most committed nonbelievers are thus united in taking the religious language of the Pledge seriously.

"In matters of religious liberty, we must give substantial attention to the prickly people; it is their rights that are most often at stake."[496] For the "reasonable observer" in the middle of the political spectrum, it may be hard to imagine the full range of religious views in this country. But these strongly held views about religion go to why there should not be a de minimis exception at all. If we assume that there will be such an exception and that the task is to carefully define it, then Justice O'Connor is on the right track, and her view that no religion would count the Pledge as religiously meaningful is a pardonable overstatement.

Justice O'Connor's third factor is "Absence of reference to particular religion."[497] Here she borrows a line from Justice Scalia, who once conceded that our constitutional tradition rules out "government sponsored endorsement of religion . . . where the endorsement is sectarian, in the sense of specifying details upon which men and women who believe in a benevolent, omnipotent Creator and Ruler of the world are known to differ (for example, the divinity of Christ)."[498] Some of Justice Scalia's other votes cast doubt on the depth of his commitment to this concession,[499] but in Justice O'Connor's

---

494. *See supra* text at notes 450-52, 456-58.

495. *See* Berg, *supra* note 457, at 69-70.

496. *Id.* at 70.

497. *Newdow,* 542 U.S. at 42 (O'Connor, J., concurring in the judgment).

498. Lee v. Weisman, 505 U.S. 577, 641 (1992) (Scalia, J., dissenting), *quoted in part in Newdow,* 542 U.S. at 42 (O'Connor, J., concurring in the judgment).

499. *See* Santa Fe Indep. Sch. Dist. v. Doe, 530 U.S. 290, 318 (2000) (joining Chief Justice Rehnquist's dissent); County of Allegheny v. ACLU, 492 U.S. 573, 655 (1989) (joining Justice

hands, this no-particular-religion factor is a significant limitation on government. This factor excludes references to particular Gods or names for God, such as Jesus or Vishnu.[500] She recognizes that it is impossible to be neutral with respect to nontheistic religions such as Buddhism,[501] and she might have added polytheistic religions and nonbelievers. But she says that "under God" comes as close as language permits,[502] and if the goal is to avoid an absolute rule, that is the best we can do.[503]

Justice O'Connor's fourth factor is "Minimal religious content."[504] She contrasts the two words of the Pledge with the "repeated thanks to God and requests for blessings"[505] in the prayers in *Lee v. Weisman*,[506] which were a little more than one hundred words each.[507] She says that brevity "tends to confirm" secular purpose, makes it easier for dissenters to "opt out" by omitting the religious passage, and limits government's ability "to express a preference for one religious sect over another."[508]

In Justice O'Connor's view, a statement that survives review under her four factors does not actually endorse the religious sentiments asserted on its face:

> Such references can serve to solemnize an occasion instead of to invoke divine provenance. The reasonable observer discussed above, fully aware of our national history and the origins of such practices, would not perceive these acknowledgements as signifying a government endorsement of any specific religion, or even of religion over non-religion.[509]

This rationale is unconvincing both to serious nonbelievers and to serious believers. Justice O'Connor cannot solve the problem for nonbelievers, who

---

Kennedy's dissent). The *Santa Fe* dissent would have permitted a student to open football games with Christian prayer; the *Allegheny* dissent would have upheld a Christian Nativity scene.

500. *See Newdow,* 542 U.S. at 42 (O'Connor, J., concurring in the judgment).

501. *Id.*

502. *See id.*

503. For a proposal that government religious observances should be constrained only by a tradition of nonsectarianism — defined as no reference to particular religious traditions — and that this limit should be judicially enforceable only in extreme cases, see Steven D. Smith, *Nonestablishment "Under God?" The Nonsectarian Principle,* 50 Vill. L. Rev. 1 (2004).

504. *Newdow,* 542 U.S. at 42 (O'Connor, J., concurring in the judgment).

505. *Id.* at 43 (characterizing the prayers in *Lee v. Weisman,* 505 U.S. 577 (1992)).

506. 505 U.S. 577 (1992).

507. *See id.* at 581-82 (reprinting the prayers verbatim).

508. *Newdow,* 542 U.S. at 43 (O'Connor, J., concurring in the judgment).

509. *Id.* at 36.

will experience the government's "language of religious belief" as a singularly inappropriate and exclusionary means of achieving secular purposes. Nor can she solve the problem for thoughtful believers, who see their religious language and images explained away and appropriated for purposes deemed secular.[510] The attempt to secularize religious language is a collective choice, overriding individual choices on both sides.

Justice O'Connor would surely have done better to concede that observances within the de minimis exception are religious, and to simply say that she viewed them as so nearly harmless that the Court should not interfere. The de minimis exception makes sense as a prudential judgment not to pay the costs of absolutist enforcement of an unpopular rule, but it is hard to make the line appear principled.

Justice O'Connor also adds a fifth criterion, confirming that government may not "*overtly* coerce a person to participate in an act of ceremonial deism."[511] In other words, *West Virginia v. Barnette*[512] is still good law; no one can be required to say the Pledge of Allegiance or the portion of it that is "facially religious."[513] This is a bright-line rule about coercion of any involuntary statement, whether religious, political, or other. It is not merely a factor to be considered in assessing endorsement.[514]

It appears that for Justice O'Connor, the government need not satisfy all four of the endorsement factors in every case. She says that prayer could be upheld "only in the most extraordinary circumstances,"[515] which implies that her second factor is not quite an absolute rule. She acknowledges *Marsh v. Chambers,*[516] which upheld prayers in state legislatures on the basis of long tradition. *Marsh* made no effort to fit within any of the tests announced before it was decided, and it probably will not fit within Justice O'Connor's test either. For *Marsh* to fit within her four factors, it must be the case that an un-

---

510. *See* Smith, *supra* note 503, at 13 & n.58 (criticizing Justice O'Connor's *Newdow* opinion as "probably the leading example" of judicial statements that "lose all credibility" in their efforts to explain the religious as secular). Another conservative scholar also harshly condemned Justice O'Connor's effort to give the Pledge a secular reading. *See* Michael M. Uhlmann, *The Supreme Court Rules: 2004,* FIRST THINGS, Oct. 2004, at 17, 22–25. Yet he reported without comment Chief Justice Rehnquist's equally implausible claim that "under God" in the Pledge merely recites a historical fact about the Founding. *See id.* at 22.

511. *Newdow,* 542 U.S. at 44 (O'Connor, J., concurring in the judgment).

512. 319 U.S. 624 (1943).

513. *Newdow,* 542 U.S. at 36 (O'Connor, J., concurring in the judgment).

514. *See id.* at 43-44.

515. *Id.* at 40.

516. *Id.* (citing *Marsh,* 463 U.S. 783 (1983)).

usually strong showing on two factors (or one and a half) can make up for failure to satisfy the others. *Marsh* was decided on the basis of an unbroken tradition of legislative prayer going back to the First Congress,[517] so it was very strong on history. But these prayers were not a rote recitation; each day's prayer had new content,[518] so they did not satisfy the "ubiquity" half of the History-and-Ubiquity factor. The prayers in *Marsh* omitted all references to Christ after a Jewish legislator complained,[519] and a later opinion treated that fact as essential to the holding.[520] So the prayers in *Marsh* satisfied the no-particular religion factor. But they could never satisfy the factors of minimal religious content or absence of worship or prayer.

Justice O'Connor says that the Pledge itself "is a close question,"[521] even though it satisfies all four factors. Her treatment of the Pledge is a better guide to her approach than the sui generis opinion in *Marsh*. The purpose of her factors is to mark a relatively objective boundary for those modest religious references that she will treat as secular in purpose and effect. The factors will not serve their purpose if government generally needs to satisfy only one and a half of the four factors. On the other hand, the Pledge is a close case in part because of factors not mentioned in her list of four: that it is used in public schools, that it asks for a personal affirmation, and that it links religious faith to political loyalty.

An impending test of her four factors is large government-sponsored monuments displaying the text of the Ten Commandments.[522] These monuments clearly satisfy only one of the four factors; they do not ask for worship

517. *See Marsh,* 463 U.S. at 786-92.

518. The Court neglected to state this fact, but it is implicit in the opinion. *See id.* at 785 n.1 (describing how the "prayers" were "collected from time to time into prayer books").

519. *See id.* at 793 n.14.

520. *See* County of Allegheny v. ACLU, 492 U.S. 573, 603 (1989).

521. *Newdow,* 542 U.S. at 37 (O'Connor, J., concurring in the judgment).

522. Three circuits have upheld such monuments. *See* Van Orden v. Perry, 351 F.3d 173 (5th Cir. 2003), *aff'd,* 545 U.S. 677 (2005); Freethought Soc'y v. Chester County, 334 F.3d 247 (3d Cir. 2003); Anderson v. Salt Lake City Corp., 475 F.2d 29 (10th Cir. 1973). Four circuits have ordered them removed. *See* ACLU Neb. Found. v. City of Plattsmouth, 358 F.3d 1020 (8th Cir. 2004), *vacated en banc and monument allowed to stay,* 419 F.3d 772 (8th Cir. 2005); ACLU v. McCreary County, 354 F.3d 438 (6th Cir. 2003), *aff'd,* 545 U.S. 844 (2005); Glassroth v. Moore, 335 F.3d 1282 (11th Cir. 2003); Ind. Civil Liberties Union v. O'Bannon, 259 F.3d 766 (7th Cir. 2001); Baker v. Adams County/Ohio Valley Sch. Bd., 86 Fed. Appx. 104 (6th Cir. 2004). The decision in *Freethought Society* was based in part on the monument's obscure location and long history, *see* 334 F.3d at 253-54, 265-67, 269-70, which somewhat reduces the conflict between this decision and those of other circuits. [The Supreme Court's decisions in *Van Orden* and *McCreary County,* and the en banc decision in *City of Plattsmouth,* were announced after the original publication of this article.]

or prayer. There is no long and ubiquitous history of large monuments displaying the text of the Commandments. Many of these monuments were donated by the Fraternal Order of Eagles in conjunction with promotions of Cecil B. DeMille's 1956 movie, *The Ten Commandments*.[523] So they have as long a history as "under God" in the Pledge, but they are not nearly so ubiquitous. A few hundred monuments scattered about the country does not compare to "our most routine ceremonial act of patriotism," repeated daily in more than a million classrooms. The "Ten Commandments" are well known as a phrase and as a concept, but no version of the text is well known; I am confident that most Americans could not list the Ten Commandments.[524] The reasonable observer is not familiar with the text, let alone with any ubiquitous secular use of the text.

The Eagles version devotes sixty-six words to the five commandments with explicitly religious content.[525] Supporters of such displays commonly claim that the Ten Commandments are the basis of secular law, but counting generously, only four of the Commandments are any part of current law.[526] The Commandments are in fact predominantly religious, but predominance

---

523. *See* Books v. City of Elkhart, 235 F.3d 292, 294-95 (7th Cir. 2000).

524. I could not find polling data on this question, but I did find a poll on a much easier question about religious knowledge. In 1990, fifty percent of the population could name at least *one* of the four Gospels (Matthew, Mark, Luke, and John). GEORGE GALLUP, JR., THE GALLUP POLL: PUBLIC OPINION 1990, at 158 (1991). Surely a much smaller percentage could list all ten of the Ten Commandments.

525. The Eagles monuments begin as follows:

> [T]he Ten Commandments
> I AM the LORD thy God.
> Thou shalt have no other gods before me.
> Thou shalt not make to thyself any graven images.
> Thou shalt not take the Name of the Lord thy God in vain.
> Remember the Sabbath day, to keep it holy.
> Honor thy father and thy mother that thy days may be long upon the land
>   which the Lord thy God giveth thee.

Books, 235 F.3d at 309. The first two lines are in larger type. For a photograph of a typical Eagles monument, see *id.*

526. The commandments not to kill, steal, or bear false witness are embodied in the law of murder, theft, perjury, and defamation. Adultery lingers in the law vestigially; it is an unenforced criminal offense in a few states, repealed in most, and a possible ground for divorce, rarely used now that divorces are awarded without fault. *See* Jonathan Turley, Editorial, *Of Lust and the Law*, WASH. POST, Sept. 5, 2004, at B1 (arguing that adultery laws are widely violated, rarely enforced, unconstitutional, and archaic). Coveting was never an offense in Anglo-American law, and with the health of the economy dependent on consumer spending, national economic policy now seems to affirmatively encourage it.

is far more than Justice O'Connor requires. Her factor is "minimal religious content," and certainly the religious content of the Commandments is more than minimal.

Finally, the Commandments' religious content is from a specific religious tradition. "Thou shalt have no other Gods before me" is unambiguously a claim of religious exclusivity. The God making this demand is not identified in typical displays of the Commandments, but that missing fact is certainly known to the reasonable observer. Large textual displays of the Ten Commandments should be an easy case under Justice O'Connor's four factors; if not, the factors will fail to accomplish their purpose.

Symbolic representations of the Commandments in art or architecture, without visible text, are a closer case.[527] Such representations have minimal religious content and a longer history in a relatively defined context. They do not call for worship or prayer. Their allusion to a specific religious tradition is unmistakable, but less pointed and less substantial. These cases could be decided either way, but a reasonable observer of Justice O'Connor must predict that she would vote to uphold them.

For now, Justice O'Connor has only her own vote for her four factors. But she is the swing vote; her opinions tend to control results.[528] And even if she has left the Court when the issue returns, her factors have much to recommend them. I am awkwardly situated to comment, because I proposed substantially the same five points as five requirements to be satisfied, rather than as four factors and one requirement.[529] Factors to be considered are less stringent and more manipulable than requirements to be satisfied; neither her opinion applying the factors to the Pledge, nor my attempt to apply them to the Ten Commandments, reads like a bright-line rule. Moreover, these fac-

---

527. *See* King v. Richmond County, 331 F.3d 1271, 1283-86 (11th Cir. 2003) (upholding such a symbol in a county seal).

528. On the particular issue of religious speech in public schools, Justices Kennedy and O'Connor have been the controlling swing votes. *See supra* text at notes 438-39. In 5-4 decisions across the range of issues, Justice O'Connor has been the most frequent swing vote by a large margin. *See The Supreme Court, 2003 Term — Nine Justices, Ten Years: A Statistical Retrospective,* 118 HARV. L. REV. 510, 520-21 tbl. V (2004).

529. *See* Clergy Brief, *supra* note 25, at *24-30. That brief proposed that if the Pledge were to be upheld, the grounds should be that "1) the Pledge is not in form a prayer; 2) the Pledge does not refer to Christianity or to any other particular religion; 3) the religious portion of the Pledge is only two words; 4) the Pledge was recited unchanged for fifty years before this Court considered the question; 5) no one can be required to say the Pledge. . . ." *Id.* at 29-30. That brief also proposed that "all these factors are essential to the decision." *Id.* at 30. That brief may have had some influence, but Justice O'Connor plainly made these five points her own and modified them substantially.

tors do not capture all the important considerations; they were designed to uphold the Pledge, so they omit the strongest reasons for invalidating it. They are imperfect, but the problem does not admit of a principled solution. If the Court will not enforce an absolute rule against government-led religious exercises, then it sorely needs an objective and judicially administrable boundary for the exception. Justice O'Connor's factors are a great advance over the Court's previous efforts to explain the de minimis exception.[530]

2. Efforts to Unleash Government-Sponsored Religion.

The other separate opinions would have given government much more freedom to endorse religious sentiments and lead religious observances. Chief Justice Rehnquist took the familiar approach of blurring all lines between the religious and the secular. Justice Thomas proposed to get the Court out of the business of enforcing the Establishment Clause.

The broad implications of the Rehnquist and Thomas opinions are not surprising, because these two Justices have been persistent dissenters in the cases on school-sponsored prayer.[531] But these opinions do not address the Court's problem. They may explain why government officials can lead the public in prayer whenever they choose. But they do not point the way to a rule that generally prohibits government endorsement of religion while permitting a narrow exception for modest, relatively harmless religious references. That is the problem raised by current doctrine, and the persistent dissenters do not address it.

(a) **The Rehnquist Opinion.** Chief Justice Rehnquist first argued that the Pledge is secular, a patriotic rather than religious exercise, and not an endorsement of any religion.[532] He devoted more space to the claim that government has made religious statements throughout our history, quoting Presidents Washington, Lincoln, Wilson, Franklin Roosevelt, and Eisenhower; "In God We Trust"; "God Save the United States and this honorable

---

530. For a powerful argument against any de minimis exception, see Epstein, *supra* note 443, at 2166-69. Epstein effectively quotes some of my own earlier work. *See id.* at 2168-69 & nn.476-478. I agree with Epstein in principle, but if a de minimis exception is politically inevitable, it is better to have clearly defined boundaries than a slippery slope.

531. *See, e.g.,* Santa Fe Indep. Sch. Dist. v. Doe, 530 U.S. 290, 318-26 (2000) (Rehnquist, C.J., joined by Scalia and Thomas, JJ., dissenting); Lee v. Weisman, 505 U.S. 577, 631-46 (1992) (Scalia, J., joined by Rehnquist, C.J., and Thomas, J., dissenting); Stone v. Graham, 449 U.S. 39, 43-47 (1980) (Rehnquist, J., dissenting).

532. *See Newdow,* 542 U.S. at 31 (Rehnquist, C.J., concurring).

Court"; and the fourth verse of the National Anthem.[533] The implicit premise of this second argument is not that the Pledge is secular, but that it is permissible for it to be religious. None of his examples arose in public schools, and in none of his examples were individual citizens asked to personally affirm the religious sentiment. Most of his examples were political speeches, occupying the murky ground at the border between the President's official capacity and his free speech rights as political leader and candidate for reelection. Those examples probably are protected free speech, but they tell us nothing about government employees unambiguously using their offices to lead citizens in religious observances.

Chief Justice Burger wrote a similar opinion in *Lynch v. Donnelly*,[534] upholding a Nativity scene on the ground that it "depicts the historical origins of this traditional event long recognized as a National Holiday."[535] Of course, for most non-Christians, the events depicted were not "historical," because they never happened. For many Christians, the central event happened, but much of what is depicted in the conventional Nativity scene is not "historical" because it is nonessential embellishment and quite possibly metaphorical. And for most Christians, the central event depicted was one of the two most important miracles in the history of the universe — the Incarnation of God in human form — and not merely the "historical origin" of a "traditional event" and a "National Holiday."

These Burger and Rehnquist opinions fail to identify any boundaries. If the Court simply decrees the religious to be secular, instead of conceding that it is religious and then carefully defining a permitted subset of religious references or observances, then any religious statement can be labeled secular in the same essentially arbitrary way. The same problem follows from saying that government has said many religious things, so it can say some more. Either there are no limits, so that government can offer the Mass or a full-length worship service of any other faith, or the limits are undefined and standardless. If the limits are undefined, then every case must be appealed to the Supreme Court. And of course, such a standardless rule is more than usually subject to manipulation. This approach enabled the Fifth Circuit to hold a Ten Commandments monument secular in purpose and effect, with only the most abstract allusions to its religious content.[536]

Quite possibly, the Chief Justice has some limit in mind, but he said

533. *See id.* at 26-29.

534. 465 U.S. 668 (1984).

535. *See id.* at 680.

536. *See* Van Orden v. Perry, 351 F.3d 173, 178-82 (5th Cir. 2003), *aff'd*, 545 U.S. 677 (2005). [The Supreme Court's decision was announced after the original publication of this article.]

nothing to help public officials, lawyers, or trial judges identify that limit. With no attention to line drawing, the opinion appears to be another effort to undermine the endorsement rule and roll back the cases on school-sponsored prayer.

(b) The Thomas Opinion. Justice Thomas wrote the most sweeping opinion. He conceded that the Pledge is unconstitutional under *Lee v. Weisman* (the graduation prayer case),[537] but he argued that *Weisman* was wrongly decided.[538] Not only that, he appears to believe that every decision in the Court's history giving any content to the Establishment Clause was also wrongly decided. Justice Thomas argued that "it makes little sense to incorporate the establishment Clause,"[539] and more fundamentally, that the Establishment Clause "does not protect any individual right."[540]

Justice Thomas is a notable exception to the Court's aversion to extreme results. Perhaps he would feel or behave differently if he were the fifth vote. As long as he writes only for himself, his occasional extreme opinions have little consequence; his *Newdow* opinion appears to be one more example. But the opinion is intellectually important and deserving of comment.

Justice Thomas candidly acknowledged that the Pledge ceremony asks students to affirm a religious belief.[541] But he said the states are free to do this. If the Establishment Clause protects any individual right, he said, it is against coercion imposed *"by force of law and threat of penalty,"*[542] not coercion by government-induced social pressure in the classroom. *Weisman* relied on such social pressure, and *Weisman* was therefore wrong in his view.

His larger argument — that the Establishment Clause is a federalism provision that protects no individual right and cannot be coherently incorporated — appears to be offered in the alternative.[543] I addressed that argument nearly twenty years ago and concluded that it was mistaken.[544] Subsequent work by other scholars marshals additional evidence and analysis for the fed-

---

537. *Newdow,* 542 U.S. at 46-49 (Thomas, J., concurring) (applying *Lee v. Weisman,* 505 U.S. 577 (1992)).

538. *Id.* at 49.

539. *Id.*

540. *Id.* at 50.

541. *See id.* at 48.

542. *Id.* at 49, 52 (quoting *Weisman,* 505 U.S. at 640 (Scalia, J., dissenting)).

543. *See id.* at 49-52.

544. *See* Douglas Laycock, *"Nonpreferential" Aid to Religion: A False Claim About Original Intent,* 27 WM. & MARY L. REV. 875, 885–94 (1986) (text at notes 52-96) (reviewing the debate in the First Congress); *id.* at 906–10 (text at notes 166-76) (reviewing early versions of the federalism interpretation).

eralism interpretation[545] and requires a more serious response than the few paragraphs that are possible here. But I have not changed my position.

It is true that the Establishment Clause left states free to decide whether to maintain established churches. But that is not significantly different from any other provision of the Bill of Rights, which left all state-level liberty questions to the states. There was not yet a consensus for disestablishment, which suggests that the Founders might not have been able to agree on a substantive understanding of the Establishment Clause. But they did not have to agree on disestablishment; they had to agree only on what powers they were denying to the federal government.[546]

The Bill of Rights was debated on the *assumption* that without it, Congress could use its delegated powers in ways that interfered with the rights to be protected. Read against that assumption, the Establishment Clause had to impose some substantive restriction on the federal government. The brief recorded debate focused on the substantive bounds of what would be forbidden to the federal government, not on any federalism implications.[547] At the very least, the Establishment Clause forbids Congress to use its taxing and spending powers to impose an earmarked tax on every citizen to support the clergy — a live issue at the state level in the late-eighteenth century.[548] A taxpayer objecting to such a tax would be asserting a claim of individual right under the Establishment Clause. That right is a privilege or immunity of citizens of the United States, as readily incorporated as any other provision of the Bill of Rights.[549] We can certainly debate what else the Establishment

---

545. *See* AKHIL REED AMAR, THE BILL OF RIGHTS: CREATION AND RECONSTRUCTION 20-45 (1998); STEVEN D. SMITH, FOREORDAINED FAILURE: THE QUEST FOR A CONSTITUTIONAL PRINCIPLE OF RELIGIOUS FREEDOM 17-54 (1995); Kurt T. Lash, *The Second Adoption of the Establishment Clause: The Rise of the Nonestablishment Principle*, 27 ARIZ. ST. L.J. 1085, 1089-1100 (1995).

546. There is also the intriguing coincidence that the states most committed to established churches did not ratify the First Amendment until 1939. *See* LEONARD W. LEVY, THE ESTABLISHMENT CLAUSE: RELIGION AND THE FIRST AMENDMENT 106-07 (2d ed. 1994) (discussing the failures to ratify in Massachusetts, Connecticut, and Georgia). But these failures might in fact have had more to do with federalism than with disestablishment; these states did not ratify the other amendments either. *See id.*

547. *See* Laycock, *supra* note 544, at 908-09 (text at notes 171-75).

548. *See id.* at 896-97, 899-901 (text at notes 106-13, 124-43) (describing proposals in Virginia and Maryland and laws in Massachusetts, Connecticut, and Georgia).

549. *See* MICHAEL KENT CURTIS, NO STATE SHALL ABRIDGE: THE FOURTEENTH AMENDMENT AND THE BILL OF RIGHTS 1–170 (2d ed. 1994) (marshaling evidence for incorporation through the Privileges or Immunities Clause); Lash, *supra* note 545, at 1100-54 (marshaling evidence for incorporation of the Establishment Clause as a substantive protection for religious liberty even if, as he believes, the Clause was originally a federalism provision).

Clause protects against; some of its important applications derive more from applying its principles to subsequent developments than from any specific practice or intention of the Founders.[550] But the claim that it protects no individual rights is, in my judgment, false to constitutional text and structure.

The no-individual-right view also greatly underestimates the importance of the Establishment Clause in protecting individual religious liberty. A central feature of the old formal establishment was the requirement that all persons attend services of the religion sponsored by the state.[551] Only a radical fringe would defend such a requirement today; the right not to attend a religious service is an undoubted individual liberty. When the service is very short and the penalty is reduced to exclusion from a public meeting or ceremony, the thing has changed greatly in degree but not at all in principle. Religious liberty includes the right to attend school or participate in governmental affairs without having to sit through a prayer service of the state-sponsored religion, however brief that service may be.

The Pledge of Allegiance could be conceived in such terms, but a two-word service stretches the concept to the limit. The Pledge has more in common with another feature of formal establishments: the test oath. Englishmen were required, on pain of civil disabilities, to affirm their belief in various doctrines of the Church of England or, after 1689, of Protestantism more generally.[552] Again the changes in degree are enormous but the principle is the same. In the Pledge as in the test oath, government tries to secure from every citizen an affirmation of religious conformity. The affirmation in the Pledge is far more generic, it is not under oath, and dissenters can refuse to say it (although this right seems little known outside the legal community). These important differences are partly offset by other differences: government requests the Pledge daily from children instead of occasionally from adults.

The modern remnants of establishment are less severe than those in the

---

550. *See* Laycock, *supra* note 544, at 913-23 (text at notes 193-243) (arguing that the founding generation rejected government aid to churches in forms that were controversial among the Protestant population of the time, and that this principle applies to other forms of aid that soon became controversial as the nation became more religiously pluralistic); Douglas Laycock, *"Noncoercive" Support for Religion: Another False Claim About the Establishment Clause*, 26 VAL. U.L. REV. 37, 41-53 (1991) (text at notes 52-79) (extending the argument).

551. *See* 4 WILLIAM BLACKSTONE, COMMENTARIES ON THE LAW OF ENGLAND *51–52, *55–58 (1769) (listing the fines and civil disabilities for failure to attend services of the Church of England).

552. *See id.* at *53, *57–58 (summarizing these laws).

memory of the Founders, but that observation is true of most constitutional rights. Modern violations of the Establishment Clause, like their more severe seventeenth-century analogs, impose majoritarian religious observances on individual dissenters, and some of those dissenters experience these impositions as acute violations of their own religious liberty. The Establishment Clause protects against such religious imposition, and this protection is as much an individual right as any other in the Bill of Rights.

IV. Conclusion

Religious liberty is maximized when government influence on religion is minimized. Minimizing government influence provides a criterion for defining neutrality: government departs from neutrality when it does things that tend to influence private religious choice. If government requires or prohibits religious practices, if it offers incentives that reward or penalize religious practices, or if it makes statements that encourage or discourage religious belief or practice, it is influencing religious choices and commitments and thus interfering with religious liberty.

Because government is very large, its influence will rarely be zero. Often we must accept some modest government influence on religious belief and practice — sometimes even a large influence — because the only alternate policy would have greater influence. Promise Scholarships for theology majors no doubt make it easier to major in theology. Scholarships reduce the net cost, and reduced cost should increase demand. But the effect is very small if Promise Scholarships are available for every academic major, so that cost is reduced across the board. Students of modest means are encouraged to attend college, and that is a necessary prerequisite to majoring in theology. But students are not encouraged to choose theology over any other major.

Promise Scholarships for every major except theology have a much bigger effect; they reduce the cost for all the direct alternatives and thus increase the relative cost of studying theology. This policy does not discourage students from attending college; it discourages them from studying theology. At the margin, some students will choose a secular major to get the scholarship; those who continue in theology will suffer a financial loss. A Promise Scholarship for secular courses, if and only if the student does not major in theology, is like a fine on theology majors.[553]

---

553. *Cf.* Sherbert v. Verner, 374 U.S. 398, 403-04 (1963) (treating the burden of forfeiting unemployment compensation as equivalent to the burden of a fine).

Protecting individual choice from government influence requires different operational rules in different contexts. In the funding cases, religious liberty is best protected from government influence by nondiscriminatory funding for both religious and secular providers of whatever secular goods or services government is willing to subsidize, and by tight limits on government discretion. In the regulation cases, religious liberty is best protected from government influence by exempting religious practices from regulation where possible. In the speech cases, religious liberty is best protected from government influence by nondiscriminatory protection of religious and secular private speech, and by government making no statements that depend on views about religious truth.[554]

The Court has approached this ideal in the speech cases; private religious speech is fully protected and government religious speech is almost fully prohibited. These rules have been stable for more than forty years, a remarkable achievement sustained by many Justices. But at the moment, this achievement depends on just two Justices, who are able to control the Court on religious speech issues because the other seven Justices are deeply divided.

In the funding cases, nondiscriminatory funding is again permissible after a long doctrinal battle. But *Davey* holds that discriminatory refusal to fund is also permissible. The Court is thus far from the ideal of minimizing government influence on religion. Four Justices have a very different vision of the ideal; they believe that all or most funding of religious providers should be prohibited even if it is perfectly nondiscriminatory. In *Davey,* this alternative vision still influenced Justices Kennedy and O'Connor, and perhaps Chief Justice Rehnquist, even though they say that this vision is not constitutionally required.

The funding cases implicate not just religious liberty, but also budget responsibility. All the Justices, but especially the Chief, believe that it is rarely a judicial function to expand the scope of spending programs. That premise is no doubt sound, but it competes with the equally sound premise that government should not be allowed to penalize the exercise of constitutional rights. *Davey* and the cases on which it implicitly relies fail to balance or reconcile these two premises. The Court defers to rules requiring prophylactic separation of functions, and this deference leaves few limits on government's power to offer funding in exchange for a surrender of constitutional rights, at least when the money flows to institutions that conduct multiple activities with the same staff or on the same property.

---

554. The conclusions in this paragraph are elaborated in Laycock, *supra* note 27, at 347-52 (text at notes 163-75).

In the regulation cases, protecting individual religious choice is not a goal the majority feels free to pursue. But most of the argument in these cases is not about religion or even about *religious* liberty. It is about the limits of liberty generally and about the proper role of the judiciary. For some of the Justices, an individual right to sometimes engage in legally prohibited conduct is a scary prospect, and judicial balancing of the government's regulatory interest against the individual's religious interest is another scary prospect. But government regulating religion in the same unrestrained way it regulates the commercial sector is also a scary prospect. The alternate vision of substantive liberty to practice one's faith lingers and may influence some Justices in the majority, just as the abandoned rule against funding influenced some of the majority in *Davey*. With respect to regulation of religious practice, the Court appears to be creating an unusually strong nondiscrimination right. *Davey* does nothing to change or undermine that emerging right.

The Court's aversion to extreme results influenced both of this Term's cases, but especially *Newdow*. This aversion is often frustrating to advocates and analysts alike, and it is no doubt overdone on occasion, but it is not a bad thing. Avoiding extreme results generally avoids extreme blunders: it reduces the stakes at doctrinal turning points and reduces the costs of judicial error. And it reduces the risk of Pyrrhic victories. A decision to invalidate the Pledge would have galvanized supporters of government-sponsored religious observances and quite possibly provoked a constitutional amendment. Perhaps that cost is worth paying over the Pledge, with its intrusive demands for personal professions of faith, but probably it is not. A ratified constitutional amendment would mean that the Court and the cause of religious liberty would have paid all the cost and retained none of the benefit. Whatever the right judgment with respect to the Pledge, it is not worth paying such a price to eliminate every vestige of ceremonial deism from government functions and every religious place name from the map of the United States. At some point, the Court must recognize either a substantive de minimis exception or a category of cases where the harm to individuals is too slight to justify standing. *Newdow* is not that case; the standing holding is confined to the facts. But Justice O'Connor's opinion is a start.

Davey is a much bigger decision. Its deference to prophylactic rules of physical separation to avoid confronting an unconstitutional conditions issue has implications for all constitutional liberties. With respect to religious liberty, *Davey* is the bookend to *Zelman v. Simmons-Harris*.[555] Together, the

---

555. 536 U.S. 639 (2002).

two cases may mark the end of an era. For more than 150 years, Americans have argued in constitutional terms about the funding of religious schools. But under *Davey* and *Zelman,* the Constitution may have remarkably little to say about that question. *Davey* appears likely to mean that funding is never required; *Zelman* means that if the money follows the right path, funding is never limited.

These decisions will not resolve the underlying controversy. There will at least be mopping-up cases, and if the limits on *Davey* are not as illusory as I fear, the Court will have to work out their boundaries. Having held that money can be granted with strings, the Court will have to decide whether money can be granted to religious institutions with fewer strings than are attached to secular institutions. Some new political initiative or doctrinal turn will eventually open up whole new lines of battle. But for now, the Court appears to be moving to the sidelines. If *Davey* is extended to the funding of elementary and secondary education, then the basic issue of whether to fund religious institutions will have been returned to Congress, to state legislatures and state supreme courts, and to the processes for amending state constitutions.

Substantive Neutrality Revisited

110 West Virginia Law Review 51 (2007)

This address to a conference at West Virginia University reviews and clarifies my proposal for substantive neutrality after two decades of experience. It shows that substantive neutrality has been one thread in the Supreme Court's more intuitive treatment of neutrality. And it explores my disagreements with Noah Feldman at Harvard, who seems to share my centrist predilections but comes to precisely opposed solutions on questions of government religious speech and government funding. He would permit government speech but not funding; I would permit funding but not speech. This article also explores my disagreements with Steven Gey, the other keynote speaker at the conference and the leading academic spokesperson for "strict" separation of church and state stringently conceived.

*   *   *

I. Introduction

Twenty-one years ago, in the course of an article mostly devoted to the Equal Access Act,[1] I distinguished two meanings of government "neutrality" to-

---

1. 20 U.S.C. §§ 4071-74 (2000).

This article was a Keynote Address at the Conference on The Religion Clauses in the 21st Century at the West Virginia University College of Law. The other keynote speaker was Steven Gey, whose work is addressed in Part IV of this Article. I am grateful to the conference participants for helpful comments and questions. I also presented this paper at Harvard Law School in October 2007, with Noah Feldman as a commentator. I am grateful to Professor Feldman for a very helpful exchange, which is now reflected in the text.

ward religion. I explained that I did not mean neutrality "in the sense of a ban on religious classifications," but rather neutrality "in the sense of government conduct that insofar as possible neither encourages nor discourages religious belief or practice."[2] That definition seemed straightforward enough to me, but both the definition and its application were controversial to those who commented on my paper.[3]

Four years later, returning to the point in a more general way, I distinguished formal neutrality, substantive neutrality, and disaggregated neutrality toward religion, and I urged substantive neutrality as the best understanding of religious liberty.[4] Since then, substantive neutrality has been a unifying theme of my work on the Religion Clauses.[5]

Over the years, substantive neutrality has been praised,[6] defend-

2. Douglas Laycock, *Equal Access and Moments of Silence: The Equal Status of Religious Speech by Private Speakers*, 81 Nw. U. L. Rev. 1, 3 (1986) (text at notes 10-11). I published a nearly identical formulation about the same time in Douglas Laycock, *"Nonpreferential" Aid to Religion: A False Claim About Original Intent*, 27 Wm. & Mary L. Rev. 875, 922 (1986) (text at notes 241-42) [hereinafter Laycock, *"Nonpreferential" Aid*].

3. *See* Michael W. McConnell, *Neutrality Under the Religion Clauses*, 81 Nw. U. L. Rev. 146, 149 n.17 (1986) ("commend[ing]" my "somewhat heterodox formulation of neutrality"); Geoffrey R. Stone, *The Equal Access Controversy: The Religion Clauses and the Meaning of "Neutrality,"* 81 Nw. U. L. Rev. 168, 169-71 (1986) (arguing that the Constitution requires only neutrality among religions, and not neutrality between religious and nonreligious speech, where there is substantial government interest in excluding religious speech); Ruti Teitel, *When Separate Is Equal: Why Organized Religious Exercises, Unlike Chess, Do Not Belong in the Public Schools*, 81 Nw. U. L. Rev. 174, 174-76 (1986) (arguing that in context of public schools, religious and nonreligious speech are different, and that it is therefore discriminatory to treat them the same).

4. *See* Douglas Laycock, *Formal, Substantive, and Disaggregated Neutrality Toward Religion*, 39 DePaul L. Rev. 993 (1990).

5. *See, e.g.*, Thomas C. Berg & Douglas Laycock, *The Mistakes in* Locke v. Davey *and the Future of State Payments for Services Provided by Religious Institutions*, 40 Tulsa L. Rev. 227, 232-36 (2004) (text at notes 36-62) (using substantive neutrality to analyze a state program of scholarships for all majors except theology); Douglas Laycock, *Theology Scholarships, the Pledge of Allegiance, and Religious Liberty: Avoiding the Extremes but Missing the Liberty*, 118 Harv. L. Rev. 155, 156 (2004) (text at notes 4-5) [hereinafter Laycock, *Theology Scholarships*] (undertaking to review cases of theology scholarships and the Pledge of Allegiance "from a perspective of substantive neutrality"); Douglas Laycock, *The Underlying Unity of Separation and Neutrality*, 46 Emory L.J. 43, 68-73 (1997) (text at notes 151-73) [hereinafter Laycock, *Underlying Unity*] (offering substantive neutrality as a way of uniting separation and neutrality); Douglas Laycock, *Religious Liberty as Liberty*, 7 J. Contemp. Legal Issues 313, 319-20, 347-51 (1996) (text at notes 27-31, 163-74) [hereinafter Laycock, *Liberty*] (urging substantive neutrality and responding to a misunderstanding of the concept).

6. *See* Abner S. Greene, *Kiryas Joel and Two Mistakes About Equality*, 96 Colum. L. Rev. 1,

ed,[7] and even more or less adopted.[8] It has been independently invented under other names.[9] It has been adopted analytically by authors who rejected it normatively,[10] and adopted normatively, more or less, by authors who rejected it analytically.[11] It has been noted,[12] analyzed,[13] criticized,[14] ridi-

---

67 n.275 (1996) (saying that I have "cogently" criticized formal neutrality and proposed substantive neutrality); Ira C. Lupu, *The Lingering Death of Separationism,* 62 GEO. WASH. L. REV. 230, 263 n.248 (1994) ("best work on the general idea of religious neutrality").

7. *See* Thomas C. Berg, *Can Religious Liberty Be Protected As Equality?,* 85 TEX. L. REV. 1185, 1211-15 (2007) (defending substantive neutrality against attacks in CHRISTOPHER L. EISGRUBER & LAWRENCE G. SAGER, RELIGIOUS FREEDOM AND THE CONSTITUTION (Harvard Univ. Press 2007)).

8. *See* Thomas C. Berg, *Religion Clause Anti-Theories,* 72 NOTRE DAME L. REV. 693, 703-07 (1997) (arguing that government should "minimize the effect it has on the voluntary, independent religious decisions of the people as individuals and in voluntary groups").

9. *See infra* notes 24-27 and accompanying text.

10. *See* Robin Charlow, *The Elusive Meaning of Religious Equality,* 83 WASH. U. L.Q. 1529, 1536-37, 1563-66 (2005) (accepting the difference between formal and substantive neutrality, but ultimately seeming to reject any commitment to neutrality or equality as unworkable); Keith Werhan, *Navigating the New Neutrality: School Vouchers, the Pledge, and the Limits of a Purposive Establishment Clause,* 41 BRANDEIS L.J. 603, 608-09, 612, 628 (2003) (using formal and substantive neutrality to analyze the Court's reasoning, but concluding that results generated by substantive neutrality are counterintuitive).

11. *See* Carl H. Esbeck, *The Establishment Clause as a Structural Restraint on Governmental Power,* 84 IOWA L. REV. 1, 112 n.477 (1998) ("It is a view I share, but it is not neutral."); Frank S. Ravitch, *A Funny Thing Happened on the Way to Neutrality: Broad Principles, Formalism, and the Establishment Clause,* 38 GA. L. REV. 489, 505 (2004) ("Professor Laycock's substantive neutrality has a lot to recommend it. . . . [H]is approach has a lot of substantive value, but no neutrality.").

12. *See* Daniel O. Conkle, *The Path of American Religious Liberty: From the Original Theology to Formal Neutrality and an Uncertain Future,* 75 IND. L.J. 1, 9-10 (2000) (finding substantive neutrality "attractive," but difficult to apply, and a clear trend to formal equality in the Supreme Court's cases).

13. *See* John H. Garvey, *All Things Being Equal,* 1996 BYU L. REV. 587, 595-97, 601-04, 609 (1996) (arguing that the case for substantive neutrality depends on a prior normative judgment that religious faith is a good thing); *see generally* Hugh J. Breyer, *Laycock's Substantive Neutrality and Neuchterlein's Free Exercise Test: Implications of Their Convergence for the Religion Clauses,* 10 J.L. & RELIGION 467 (1994) (generally adopting substantive neutrality but arguing that it is incomplete). For my attempt to justify substantive neutrality without making any judgments about the value of religion, see Laycock, *Liberty, supra* note 5, at 314-23 (text at notes 7-40).

14. STEVEN D. SMITH, FOREORDAINED FAILURE 81 (1995) (arguing that substantive neutrality depends on certain contested assumptions about the value and sources of religious belief, and thus is not neutral); Steven K. Green, *Locke v. Davey and the Limits to Neutrality Theory,* 77 TEMP. L. REV. 913, 947-48 (2004) (arguing that neutral awards of grants to religious and secular providers alike do not ameliorate the problems of government funding

culed,[15] and ignored.[16] Nearly all the attention, for good and ill, has come from other academics. Of all the thousands of judges in America, only Justice Souter has ever cited my account of substantive neutrality in reported opinions, and of course he did it only when it suited his purposes.[17]

My purpose here is to briefly review substantive neutrality, perhaps refreshing the recollections of some readers and introducing an unfamiliar concept to others, to clarify what I mean, and to compare and contrast substantive neutrality with prominent proposals from Noah Feldman and Steven Gey. Professor Feldman and I have similar centrist instincts, yet come to

---

of religious institutions); Toni M. Massaro, *Religious Freedom and "Accommodationist Neutrality": A Non-Neutral Critique*, 84 OR. L. REV. 935, 995-96 & n.267 (2005) (arguing that neutrality toward religion is appropriate in some domains but not others, and certainly not with respect to funding); *see generally* Paul E. Salamanca, *Quo Vadis: The Continuing Metamorphosis of the Establishment Clause Toward Realistic Substantive Neutrality*, 41 BRANDEIS L.J. 575 (2003) (arguing that substantive neutrality is a marginal criterion because people's religious beliefs are largely immune to government pressure or discrimination); Steven D. Smith, *Separation as a Tradition*, 18 J.L. & POL. 215, 227-28 (2002) [hereinafter Smith, *Separation*] (treating substantive neutrality as an example of the implausible claim that new legal conclusions have been developed from fixed underlying principles); Nelson Tebbe, *Free Exercise and the Problem of Symmetry*, 56 HASTINGS L.J. 699, 710-23 (2005) (arguing that substantive neutrality is not neutral, and that its goals would be better supported by arguing for "substantive liberty").

15. *See* Christopher L. Eisgruber & Lawrence G. Sager, *Congressional Power and Religious Liberty After* City of Boerne v. Flores, 1997 SUP. CT. REV. 79, 119 (1997) (arguing that if religion were unaffected by government, "the life of a religious institution [would be] nasty, brutish, and short"); Lino A. Graglia, City of Boerne v. Flores: *An Essay on the Invalidation of the Religious Freedom Restoration Act*, 68 MISS. L.J. 675, 675-77 (1998) ("Neutrality is still the requirement, there is no quarreling with that, it's just that it now means discrimination. Nothing better illustrates the essence of the lawyerly arts."). I anticipated Eisgruber and Sager's state-of-nature argument, without providing an equally bright-line alternative baseline, in Laycock, *supra* note 4, at 1005-06 (text at notes 33-41).

16. *See, e.g.,* NOAH FELDMAN, DIVIDED BY GOD: AMERICA'S CHURCH-STATE PROBLEM — AND WHAT WE SHOULD DO ABOUT IT (2005) (never mentioning "substantive neutrality").

17. Church of the Lukumi Babalu Aye, Inc. v. City of Hialeah, 508 U.S. 520, 561-62 (1993) (Souter, J., concurring); Lee v. Weisman, 505 U.S. 577, 627 (1992) (Souter, J., concurring). Justice Scalia has used the phrase in a religious liberty case, without attribution and without indicating what he thought it meant or whether he approved. *See* Locke v. Davey, 540 U.S. 712, 730 (2004). Other judges have used the phrase in unrelated contexts. *See, e.g.,* Free Speech Coal. v. Reno, 198 F.3d 1083, 1092 (9th Cir. 1999), *quoting* United States v. Hilton, 167 F.3d 61, 68-69 (1st Cir. 1999) (using the phrase in a child pornography case arising under the Free Speech Clause); Atkins v. Schmutz Mfg. Co., 435 F.2d 527, 537 (4th Cir. 1970) (using the phrase to describe the proper attitude of federal courts toward state law under *Erie R.R. v. Tompkins*, 304 U.S. 64 (1938)).

proposed solutions that are almost diametrically opposed on important issues.[18] That seems to be a phenomenon worth investigating. Professor Gey, who is academia's most able and most prominent defender of absolutely no aid to religion, views substantive neutrality with a despairing and mystified air — as if to say: what's a nice guy like you, who sometimes sounds like a separationist, doing with a proposal like that?[19] I will try to answer.

II. Substantive Neutrality

A. *Vocabulary*

I distinguished three measures of neutrality — two intellectually coherent measures, plus one incoherent measure that courts had stumbled into by inadvertence. For better or worse, I called these measures formal neutrality, substantive neutrality, and disaggregated neutrality.[20]

Formal neutrality requires neutral *categories.* A law is formally neutral if it does not use religion as a category — if religious and secular examples of the same phenomenon are treated exactly the same.

Substantive neutrality requires neutral *incentives.* A law is substantively neutral if it neither "encourages [n]or discourages religious belief or disbelief, practice or nonpractice, observance or nonobservance."[21] I will return to disaggregated neutrality in due course.

To illustrate formal and substantive neutrality with a very simple and clear-cut example, forbidding children to take communion wine is formally neutral. Children cannot consume alcoholic beverages in any amount for any purpose. Religion is not a category in the formulation or application of this rule; alcohol is forbidden to children whether for religious purposes or secular purposes.

---

18. *Compare* FELDMAN, *supra* note 16, at 237 (proposing "greater latitude for public religious discourse and religious symbolism, and at the same time . . . a stricter ban on state funding of religious institutions and activities"), *with* Laycock, *Theology Scholarships, supra* note 5, at 160 (text at notes 25-26) (arguing that broadly inclusive scholarship program should have been required to include theology majors, and that "under God" should be removed from the Pledge of Allegiance).

19. *See* Steven G. Gey, *Reconciling the Supreme Court's Four Establishment Clauses*, 8 U. PA. J. CONST. L. 725, 786-88 (2006) (puzzling over recent work by me and others that he views as abandoning separationism and as mischaracterizing the debate).

20. Laycock, *supra* note 4, at 999, 1001, 1007 (text at notes 21, 27, 41).

21. *Id.* at 1001 (text at note 27).

But an exception that permits children to take communion wine is substantively neutral. Exempting communion wine from the ban on under-age consumption of alcohol is extraordinarily unlikely to induce anyone to become a Christian, to join a denomination that uses real wine in its communion service, or to attend communion services more often — unless that person already desired to do these things but had been deterred by the threat of government-imposed penalties. Consuming communion wine is a desirable activity only to those who already believe in the religious teaching that gives meaning to the act. Forbidding children to take communion wine, or criminally punishing their parents and the priest who gives them the sacrament, powerfully discourages an act of worship. But exemption does not encourage any child to take communion, or any parent to take his child to a communion service, who is not already religiously motivated do so. An exemption does not change anyone's religious incentives; criminalization changes those incentives profoundly.

Some critics reject this explanation out of hand. To them, neutrality simply *is* what I have called formal neutrality. No other kind of neutrality is imaginable, and substantive neutrality is not neutrality at all. An exemption from a generally applicable law is special treatment, and to claim that exemption is a form of neutrality is mere verbal wordplay.[22]

I have learned to explain that formal neutrality requires neutral categories, and substantive neutrality requires neutral incentives.[23] So perhaps I should have called these two standards "category neutrality" and "incentive neutrality." Category neutrality and incentive neutrality may better emphasize that each is a real measure of neutrality and that each focuses on a specific criterion that must be kept neutral. Judge Posner and then-Professor McConnell did use the phrases "category neutrality" and "incentive neutrality" to describe a very similar idea[24] in an article published while my elaboration of neutrality was in the editorial process.[25] But it is too late now. Cate-

---

22. *See* Graglia, *supra* note 15, at 676; Tebbe, *supra* note 14, at 714-23.

23. *See* Douglas Laycock, *Regulatory Exemptions of Religious Behavior and the Original Understanding of the Establishment Clause*, 81 NOTRE DAME L. REV. 1793, 1797-98 (2006) (text at note 15) (making the point clearly and succinctly); Laycock, *Liberty, supra* note 5, at 319-20 (text at notes 27-28) (making the point a little less clearly).

24. Michael W. McConnell & Richard A. Posner, *An Economic Approach to Issues of Religious Freedom*, 56 U. CHI. L. REV. 1, 37 (1989).

25. My article was based on a lecture delivered in April 1989, and for the most part, it spoke "as of that date." Laycock, *supra* note 4, at 993 n.*. Professor McConnell attended the lecture. I read and commented on the McConnell and Posner article in manuscript, McConnell & Posner, *supra* note 24, at n.1, and cited it in my article, Laycock, *supra* note 4, at

gory neutrality and incentive neutrality have gotten almost no attention, probably because McConnell and Posner mentioned their proposed labels only briefly, deep in an article with a title promising an economic analysis of religious liberty. Formal and substantive neutrality were part of my title and the centerpiece of my article, with the result that these labels have been cited far more often.[26] For better or worse, formal neutrality and substantive neutrality have become the labels for the distinction that McConnell, Posner, and I tried to draw.

Stephen Monsma, a political scientist at Pepperdine, proposed a similar idea in 1993 and called it "positive neutrality."[27] That label has not caught on either. To that large part of our culture that fears or mistrusts organized religion, I fear that "positive neutrality" may sound like neutrality with some measure of favoritism.

B. Neutrality in the Supreme Court

The Supreme Court has been notoriously inconsistent in its uses of the idea of neutrality. It sometimes talks about "benevolent neutrality,"[28] or "wholesome neutrality,"[29] but neither of these modifiers was ever used consistently to mean a specific theory of neutrality. And "benevolent neutrality" may have the same problem as "positive neutrality"; to some people, it sounds like neutrality with favoritism included.

---

995 n.13. Neither McConnell nor I had the foresight to suggest that we settle on a common vocabulary. It is possible that distinguishing the two forms of neutrality was a late addition to the McConnell and Posner manuscript, so that I did not see their proposed vocabulary when I read the draft.

26. A search in Westlaw's "Text and Periodicals — All" database, as of September 3, 2007, yielded four hits for "McConnell" in the same paragraph as "incentive neutrality," but 118 hits for "Laycock" in the same paragraph as "substantive neutrality."

27. *See* STEPHEN V. MONSMA, POSITIVE NEUTRALITY: LETTING RELIGIOUS FREEDOM RING 188 (Greenwood Press 1993) (proposing "to assure that religious associations and communities, and their individual members, are not constricted or disadvantaged in the living-out of their religious beliefs," and that they "not transgress on the rights and prerogatives of the other spheres and that one religious structure does not transgress on those of another or of nonbelievers").

28. Bd. of Educ. v. Grumet, 512 U.S. 687, 705 (1994); Corp. of Presiding Bishop v. Amos, 483 U.S. 327, 334 (1987); Comm. for Pub. Educ. & Religious Liberty v. Nyquist, 413 U.S. 756, 792 (1973); Walz v. Tax Comm'n, 397 U.S. 664, 669, 676 (1970).

29. Bd. of Educ. v. Grumet, 512 U.S. 687, 696 (1994); Sch. Dist. v. Schempp, 374 U.S. 203, 222 (1963).

The Court often equates neutrality with formal neutrality, with no analysis or explanation,[30] but many of its classic formulations of religious neutrality read as statements of substantive neutrality. Thus, in *Everson v. Board of Education*,[31] the Court said that "[n]either [a state nor the federal government] can force [or] influence a person to go to or to remain away from church against his will[.]"[32] This speaks not to categories of classification, but to government conduct that may change, or "influence," private religious behavior. Other parts of that famous paragraph, and the equally important but neglected paragraph that follows (the one that says no person can be deprived of a social welfare benefit because of his faith or lack of faith[33]) are equally consistent with either formal or substantive neutrality. To say that no person can be punished[34] or deprived of a social welfare benefit[35] because of his religious views implements formal neutrality (because punishment or loss of benefits on the basis of religious belief would create rules and categories based on religion), and it also implements substantive neutrality (because punishment or loss of benefits would discourage the religious belief). Some sentences are written in terms of no-aid to religion,[36] a position that is a principal alternative to neutrality of any kind, although the Court appeared to think in 1947 that the two approaches were consistent. I do not claim that *Everson* adopted substantive neutrality; I do claim that substantive neutrality was one of the multiple meanings of neutrality that the Court jumbled together and failed to distinguish.

In *Sherbert v. Verner*,[37] and again in *Wisconsin v. Yoder*,[38] the Court relied on "neutrality" to strike down rules that were defended as formally neutral and which the Court seemed to view as formally neutral.[39] The Court said

---

30. See, most famously, Employment Div. v. Smith, 494 U.S. 872, 876-90 (1990), which held that burdens on religious practice require no justification if imposed by laws that are neutral and generally applicable.

31. 330 U.S. 1 (1947).

32. *Id.* at 15.

33. *Id.* at 16.

34. *Id.*

35. *Id.*

36. *Id.* at 15 ("Neither can pass laws which aid one religion, [or] aid all religions[.]").

37. 374 U.S. 398, 409 (1963) (holding that the state cannot refuse unemployment compensation to employee who loses her job because of religious refusal to work on her Sabbath).

38. 406 U.S. 205, 220 (1972) (holding that Amish parents cannot be required to send their children to public high school).

39. The Court might have said that the South Carolina law in *Sherbert* was not even formally neutral, but that was not the holding. In *Employment Div. v. Smith*, 494 U.S. 872

that accommodation or exemption from regulation "reflects nothing more than the governmental obligation of neutrality in the face of religious differences[.]"[40] And more specifically, "[a] regulation neutral on its face may, in its application, nonetheless offend the constitutional requirement for governmental neutrality if it unduly burdens the free exercise of religion."[41] The Court did not explain its understanding of neutrality in these passages, but it can only have meant what I have called substantive neutrality.

In *School District v. Schempp,*[42] the Court offered a "test" to define "[t]he wholesome 'neutrality' of which this Court's cases speak":[43]

> The test may be stated as follows: what are the purpose and primary effect of the enactment? If either is the advancement or inhibition of religion then the enactment exceeds the scope of legislative power as circumscribed by the Constitution. That is to say that to withstand the strictures of the Establishment Clause there must be a secular legislative purpose and a primary effect that neither advances nor inhibits religion.[44]

"That is to say" implies that these two formulations were intended to be equivalent — that a "secular" purpose is simply any purpose other than a purpose to advance or inhibit religion. But that equivalence was hidden when the Court quoted the requirement of "secular legislative purpose"

(1990), the Court said that the requirement of "good cause" for refusing work means that unemployment compensation laws allow secular exceptions, so that it is discriminatory to refuse religious exceptions. *Id.* at 884. But there is no suggestion of that theory in *Sherbert,* and the only South Carolina cases cited in *Sherbert* held that the proffered secular reasons for refusing work were not good cause. 374 U.S. at 401 n.4. The state's entire economy was organized around the mainstream Christian observance of Sunday, but the Court has never understood the discrimination inherent in that. *See* Ansonia Bd. of Educ. v. Philbrook, 479 U.S. 60 (1986) (treating a school teacher's request for days off for religious observance as an "accommodation" under 42 U.S.C. § 2000e(j), even though school's entire calendar was set up so that school never met on Sunday, Easter, or Christmas, and except for extracurricular activities, never met on Saturday); Braunfeld v. Brown, 366 U.S. 599, 605 (1961) (treating Sunday closing law as "simply regulat[ing] a secular activity" and refusing exemption to Saturday Sabbath observer); McGowan v. Maryland, 366 U.S. 420 (1961) (upholding Sunday-closing laws against Establishment Clause challenge). The Court in *Sherbert* did note that South Carolina law protected Sunday observers from job loss, but it viewed this discrimination as merely "compound[ing]" a constitutional violation that was already complete when the state refused unemployment compensation to Saturday observers. 398 U.S. at 406.

40. Wisconsin v. Yoder, 406 U.S. 205, 235 n.22 (1972) (quoting *Sherbert,* 374 U.S. at 409).
41. *Yoder,* 406 U.S. at 220.
42. 374 U.S. 203 (1963).
43. *Id.* at 222.
44. *Id.*

without the two sentences that preceded it. Only the "secular purpose" formulation was incorporated into the famous *Lemon* test: "First, the statute must have a secular legislative purpose; second, its principal or primary effect must be one that neither advances nor inhibits religion[.]"[45] Secular purpose thereafter took on a life of its own, but it was only very occasionally the basis for a judgment.[46]

The Court's description of the prohibited effect did not suffer the same ambiguity. The Court's rule that government must neither advance nor inhibit religion appears to be equivalent to my proposed rule that government neither encourage nor discourage religion. No advancing or inhibiting is a neutrality standard, but the word "neutrality" does not appear in the canonical formulation of the *Lemon* test. And of course the doctrine did not work out to be either formally neutral or substantively neutral in practice. In part this was because the justices who administered the *Lemon* test had goals not fully captured in its wording. In part it was because these justices did not attend to the question of the baseline from which to measure advancing or inhibiting. And in part it was because the second prong of the *Lemon* test could be read to state two separate requirements: no effect of advancing religion, and, independently, no effect of inhibiting religion.

It was this verbal accident that I described as "disaggregated neutrality."[47]

---

45. Lemon v. Kurtzman, 403 U.S. 602, 612 (1971). The third prong of the *Lemon* test is avoiding "excessive government entanglement with religion." *Id.* at 613.

46. Government actions were invalidated for lack of secular purpose in *McCreary County v. ACLU*, 545 U.S. 844, 859-74, 881 (2005) (Ten Commandments display); *Santa Fe Indep. Sch. Dist. v. Doe*, 530 U.S. 290, 308-09 (2000) (prayer at high school football games); *Edwards v. Aguillard*, 482 U.S. 578, 586-93 (1987) (teaching of creation science); *Wallace v. Jaffree*, 472 U.S. 38, 56-61 (1985) (moment of silence with legislative encouragement to pray); *Stone v. Graham*, 449 U.S. 39, 41 (1980) (Ten Commandments display); and *Epperson v. Arkansas*, 393 U.S. 97, 107-09 (1968) (ban on teaching evolution). The Court also found an effect of advancing religion in *Santa Fe*, 530 U.S. at 312, and it would have been easy enough to find such effects in *McCreary*, *Stone*, and probably *Jaffree*. Purpose may have mattered only in *Aguillard* and *Epperson*, the two cases on evolution in the public schools, and I suspect that even there, the same justices would have reached the same result with or without the secular-purpose requirement.

Even if we count all six of these cases as turning on a purpose to advance religion, there were far more cases that found or assumed a secular purpose. In all the cases on financial aid to religious schools, there was a secular purpose to aid education. *See, e.g., Lemon*, 403 U.S. at 613. Alleviating regulatory burdens on religion is a secular purpose. Corp. of the Presiding Bishop v. Amos, 483 U.S. 327, 335-36 (1987). More dubiously, the Court held that Sunday closing laws had a secular purpose, *McGowan v. Maryland*, 366 U.S. 420 (1961), and that municipal nativity scenes had a secular purpose, *Lynch v. Donnelly*, 465 U.S. 668, 680-81 (1984).

47. Laycock, *supra* note 4, at 1007-08 (text at notes 41-49).

Instead of asking directly whether a statute was as neutral as could be under the circumstances, or more nearly neutral than any available alternative, courts asked simply whether a statute had an effect that "advanc[ed]" religion.[48] The "inhibits" part of the test became a mere recital, undeveloped and without content, and the Court ignored the possibility that its own judgments inhibited religion. So far as I am aware, the Court has never struck down any law on the ground that it has a primary effect that inhibits religion. But from 1971 to 1985, ever smaller and more attenuated effects were held to have a primary effect of advancing religion. The risk that public school teachers, and employees delivering "auxiliary services" such as counseling, testing, speech and hearing therapy, and remedial instruction, might be overcome by the religious environment and begin teaching religion, was held to be a primary effect that advanced religion.[49] The risk that secular public services delivered in religious schools would be perceived as a "symbolic union" of church and state was held to be a primary effect that advanced religion.[50] In the lower courts, turning on the lights for an after-school religion club was held to be a primary effect that advanced religion.[51]

But this form of disaggregated neutrality is mostly of historical interest. The *Lemon* test has been fundamentally reinterpreted, most dramatically in *Zelman v. Simmons-Harris*,[52] to focus directly on neutrality. *Zelman* is in principle both formally and substantively neutral, but let me postpone that question for now.[53]

With increasing frequency, the Court has held that formal neutrality is constitutionally sufficient but not constitutionally required. Thus, the Court holds that legislatures may apply neutral and generally applicable regulation

---

48. *See id.* (analyzing Aguilar v. Felton, 473 U.S. 402 (1985), *overruled by* Agostini v. Felton, 521 U.S. 203, 235 (1997)).

49. Sch. Dist. v. Ball, 473 U.S. 373, 385-89 (1985) (invalidating local funding of remedial and enrichment courses taught by public school teachers in religious schools); Meek v. Pittenger, 421 U.S. 349, 367-72 (1975) (invalidating federal funding for such auxiliary services). This holding in *Ball* was partly overruled in *Agostini*, 521 U.S. at 235. This holding in *Meek* was not expressly overruled, but it was the precedential basis for *Ball* and it is impossible to see how it can survive *Agostini*.

50. *Ball*, 473 U.S. at 389-92.

51. Johnson v. Huntington Beach Union High Sch. Dist., 137 Cal. Rptr. 43, 49 (Cal. Ct. App. 1977) ("It would be entitled to use classroom space rent free, receive heat and light and would be monitored by a paid faculty sponsor.").

52. 536 U.S. 639, 648-63 (2002) (upholding state-funded vouchers that could be used to pay for educational services at a wide variety of schools, including public schools, secular private schools, and religious private schools).

53. *See infra* text accompanying notes 108-109.

to the exercise of religion[54] (formal neutrality is permitted), or, within limits that preclude discrimination among faiths and burdens on third parties,[55] legislatures may grant regulatory exemptions[56] (an alternative to formal neutrality is also permitted). Courts may apply "neutral principles of law" to church property disputes[57] (formal neutrality is permitted), or they may defer to the highest church authority recognized by both sides before the dispute arose[58] (an alternative is also permitted). Legislatures may impose neutral and generally applicable taxes on religious organizations[59] (formal

54. Employment Div. v. Smith, 494 U.S. 872, 876-90 (1990).

55. Texas Monthly, Inc. v. Bullock, 489 U.S. 1, 8-25 (1989) (plurality opinion) (invalidating sales tax exemption exclusively for publications that promote a religion, at least where that exemption is not found necessary to relieve a burden on the exercise of religion); Estate of Thornton v. Caldor, Inc., 472 U.S. 703, 708-11 (1985) (invalidating a law that gave employees an absolute right to not work on their Sabbath and left no ability to consider any resulting burdens on the employer or co-workers).

56. Cutter v. Wilkinson, 544 U.S. 709, 719-26 (2005) (rejecting Establishment Clause challenge to the prison provisions of the Religious Land Use and Institutionalized Persons Act, 42 U.S.C. § 2000cc-1(a) (2000)); Bd. of Educ. v. Grumet, 512 U.S. 687, 705-06 (1994) (quoting and reaffirming cases holding that governments may exempt religious practices from regulation); *Smith*, 494 U.S. at 890 (stating that legislatures may exempt religious practices from regulation when not constitutionally required to do so); Corp. of the Presiding Bishop v. Amos, 483 U.S. 327, 334-40 (1987) (rejecting Establishment Clause challenge to provision exempting religious institutions from statutory ban on employment discrimination on the basis of religion); *see also* Wisconsin v. Yoder, 406 U.S. 205, 234 n.22 (1972) (rejecting Establishment Clause challenge to exemption from truancy laws); Sherbert v. Verner, 374 U.S. 398, 409 (1963) (rejecting Establishment Clause challenge to exemption from requirement that workers seeking unemployment compensation be available for Saturday work); Jones v. Butz, 374 F. Supp. 1284, 1289-93 (S.D.N.Y. 1974) (upholding exemption of kosher slaughter from general requirements of Federal Humane Slaughter Act), *aff'd mem.*, 419 U.S. 806 (1974); Commonwealth v. Arlan's Dep't Store, 357 S.W.2d 708, 710 (Ky. 1962) (upholding exemption from Sunday-closing laws of persons who observed a Sabbath other than Sunday), *appeal dismissed for want of substantial federal question*, 371 U.S. 218 (1962).

57. Jones v. Wolf, 443 U.S. 595, 602-06 (1979).

58. *Id.* at 602 ("[A] State may adopt *any* one of various approaches for settling church property disputes so long as it involves no consideration of doctrinal matters. . . ."), quoting Md. & Va. Eldership of the Churches of God v. Church of God, 396 U.S. 367, 368 (1970) (Brennan, J., concurring) (emphasis by Justice Brennan); Kedroff v. Saint Nicholas Cathedral, 344 U.S. 94, 113-16 (1952) (constitutionalizing the common-law rule of deference to the highest church authority); *see also* Serbian E. Orthodox Diocese v. Milivojevich, 426 U.S. 696, 708-20 (1976) (requiring rule of deference to highest church authority in cases of church personnel disputes).

59. Jimmy Swaggart Ministries v. Bd. of Equalization, 493 U.S. 378 (1990) (upholding sales tax as applied to sale of religious literature).

neutrality is permitted), or, within limits,[60] they may grant tax exemptions[61] (an alternative is also permitted). States may provide equal funding to secular and religious educational programs[62] (formal neutrality is permitted), or, at least sometimes, they may fund private secular education and refuse to fund private religious education[63] (an alternative is also permitted).

These optional rules may be described as permissive formal neutrality — formal neutrality is permitted but some alternative is also permitted. Permissive formal neutrality may be contrasted with mandatory formal neutrality, in which Congress and the states would be required to implement formal neutrality with no alternatives permitted. Mandatory formal neutrality would prohibit regulatory exemptions, prohibit tax exemptions, prohibit deference to internal resolutions of church disputes, and require equal funding for religious institutions. Prominent academics have argued for mandatory formal neutrality,[64] but it is hardly surprising that the Court has shown no interest in a rule with such controversial consequences.

The Court's permissive neutrality rules are some protection for religious liberty, because the Court usually permits government to depart from formal neutrality in only one direction. Religion cannot be singled out for discriminatory regulation, taxation, or dispute resolution, and it cannot be singled out for preferential funding. But these permissive neutrality rules also contain a large measure of judicial minimalism and deference to majoritarian political processes: if two rules seem plausible to the Court, the legislature can choose.

I have noted four sets of rules in which formal neutrality is permitted but not required. Three of these sets of rules may be restated somewhat differently: with respect to regulation, taxation, and resolution of church property disputes, Congress and the states may choose either formal or substantive

---

60. Texas Monthly, Inc. v. Bullock, 489 U.S. 1, 8-20 (1989) (plurality opinion) (invalidating sales tax exemption exclusively for publications that promote a religion, at least where that exemption is not found necessary to relieve a burden on the exercise of religion).

61. Walz v. Tax Comm'n, 397 U.S. 664, 672-80 (1970) (upholding broadly inclusive property-tax exemption for churches and other not-for-profit charitable organizations).

62. Zelman v. Simmons-Harris, 536 U.S. 639, 648-63 (2002) (upholding state-funded vouchers that could be used to pay for educational services at a wide variety of schools, including public schools, secular private schools, and religious private schools).

63. Locke v. Davey, 540 U.S. 712 (2004) (permitting Washington to exclude devotional theology majors from a scholarship program available to any other accredited major).

64. Philip B. Kurland, *Of Church and State and the Supreme Court*, 29 U. Chi. L. Rev. 1, 96 (1961); Mark Tushnet, *"Of Church and State and the Supreme Court": Kurland Revisited*, 1989 Sup. Ct. Rev. 373, 402 (concluding, after exploring pros and cons, that Supreme Court should adopt Kurland's formal neutrality approach).

neutrality. Regulatory exemptions for religiously motivated behavior are generally (not universally) substantively neutral for the reasons illustrated by the example of children taking Communion wine[65] and discussed at length in my earlier work:[66] penalizing a religious practice is a substantial discouragement, but permitting a religious practice does not encourage anyone not independently attracted to it. So the Court's rule — that the legislature may grant or refuse exemptions from neutral and generally applicable laws — means that the legislature may choose between the two versions of neutrality.

Deference to the highest religious authority previously recognized by both sides is substantively neutral, because it avoids government resolution of internal religious disputes — and thus avoids a judgment that rewards one side and rejects or penalizes the other — and it leaves these decisions in the religious hands to which both sides originally committed them. Of course the rule of deference also ends with a winner and a loser, but if the court simply identifies the highest church authority and refrains from interpreting the church documents at the heart of the dispute, the decision for the secular court is usually much simpler and much less substantive, and it presents much less opportunity for manipulating the result. I think the Court's rule that secular courts may either defer to the highest church authority or decide church disputes themselves under neutral principles of law means that state courts may choose either substantive or formal neutrality.

Tax exemptions are generally substantively neutral, at least as currently implemented in most American jurisdictions, which exempt a broad range of nonprofit organizations, including churches, schools, and charities. The incentive to convert from for-profit status (taxed) to nonprofit status (tax exempt) is balanced by a strong counter-incentive: conversion to nonprofit status forever surrenders the right to distribute profits or return capital to the owners of the enterprise.[67] Within the set of nonprofits, there might be substantial effect on religious incentives if secular schools and charities were ex-

---

65. *See supra* text accompanying notes 21-22.

66. *See* Douglas Laycock, *The Remnants of Free Exercise*, 1990 SUP. CT. REV. 1, 10-21 (text at notes 49-91); Laycock, *supra* note 4, at 1013-18 (text at notes 73-100).

67. *See* 26 U.S.C. § 501(c)(3) (2000) (requiring that tax-exempt organizations be "organized and operated exclusively" for one or more tax-exempt purposes). An organization is not "organized . . . exclusively" for exempt purposes unless its articles of incorporation provide that no assets can ever be distributed to members or shareholders and that, on dissolution, its assets will be distributed exclusively to another tax-exempt organization or to a government agency. 26 C.F.R. § 1.501(c)(3)-1(b)(4). *See also* 26 U.S.C. § 501(c)(3) (2000) (requiring that "no part of the net earnings of [the organization] inure[] to the benefit of any private shareholder or individual . . .").

empt and religious schools and charities were not (or vice versa). It would often be tempting to increase or decrease the religious content in a school's curriculum or a charity's program in an effort to qualify for the exemption. This would have been the proper rationale for the Court's decision in *Texas Monthly v. Bullock*.[68] Tax exemption only for publications that "consist wholly" of religious teachings[69] discriminated among speakers on the basis of their viewpoint,[70] and at the margin, it encouraged publications with small amounts of secular content to eliminate it and become "wholly" religious. Exempting both religious and secular nonprofits creates no such incentive.

The Court's fourth set of alternatives is very different. Equal funding for religious and secular schools is formally neutral, and for reasons to be explained, I believe that it is also substantively neutral. Funding secular private education but not religious private education is not neutral in either sense, but the Court permits it anyway.[71] Funding secular private education but not religious private education creates a religious category (thus not formally neutral), and it creates incentives to secularize religious education (thus not substantively neutral). Joshua Davey could have gotten a state Promise Scholarship if he had studied theology from a secular perspective instead of a religious perspective.[72] Some states offer state funding to colleges that become merely "sectarian," instead of "pervasively sectarian."[73] In a state such as Maine, which pays tuition for some students to attend secular private high schools but not religious private high schools,[74] a religious high school could

---

68. 489 U.S. 1 (1989) (invalidating, in splintered opinions, sales tax exemption that applied only to religious publications).

69. Tex. Tax Code Ann. § 151.312 (1982), quoted *id.* at 5.

70. *See Texas Monthly*, 489 U.S. at 25-26 (White, J., concurring) (arguing that this was content discrimination that violated the Free Press Clause). *See generally* Rosenberger v. Rector and Visitors of Univ. of Va., 515 U.S. 819, 828-37 (1995) (reviewing and applying the rule that discrimination between different viewpoints is presumptively unconstitutional).

71. *See* Locke v. Davey, 540 U.S. 712 (2004) (permitting Washington to exclude devotional theology majors from a scholarship program available to any other accredited major).

72. *See id.* at 716 (noting that ban on scholarships for theology majors applied only to "degrees that are 'devotional in nature or designed to induce religious faith,'" quoting briefs of both parties).

73. *Compare* Columbia Union Coll. v. Oliver, 254 F.3d 496, 498 (4th Cir. 2001) (summarizing and rejecting the state's position), *with* Colorado Christian Univ. v. Baker, 2007 WL 1489801 (D. Colo., May 18, 2007), *appeal pending* (reaching the opposite result on the basis of the intervening decision in *Locke v. Davey*, 540 U.S. 712 (2004)). [The district court's decision in *Colorado Christian* was later reversed, because the "pervasively sectarian" rule discriminated among religions. 534 F.3d 1245 (10th Cir. 2008).]

74. *See* Eulitt v. Maine, 386 F.3d 344, 353-57 (1st Cir. 2004) (upholding this discrimination); Strout v. Albanese, 178 F.3d 57, 60-66 (1st Cir. 1999) (same).

qualify for funding if it would drop its religious instruction. These incentive effects are strong, because students are entirely free to respond to them by choosing another school, and schools are also relatively free to respond to them: once an institution is running a school, it is not difficult to augment or reduce the religious content in the curriculum.

The Court's first three sets of permissive neutrality rules, on regulation, taxation, and dispute resolution, can thus be described as permitting states to choose between formal and substantive neutrality. *Locke v. Davey*[75] is the outlier; it permits states to choose between neutrality and discrimination against religion. That is not how the Court has thought about its rules, but that is what it has done.

C. Neutrality, Liberty, Voluntarism, and Separation

I never claimed or intended that substantive neutrality should be the single explanation or only value of the Religion Clauses. To the contrary, my whole purpose was to reconcile or unify distinct but tangled threads of explanation for the Religion Clauses. I said that:

> Because neutrality requires so much further specification, it cannot be the only principle in the Religion Clauses. Nor can it be the most fundamental. We must specify the content of neutrality by looking to other principles in the Religion Clauses. When we have done that, neutrality should be defined in a way that makes it largely congruent with those other principles. We will often be able to explain the objection to a law by saying either that it restricts the autonomy of religious belief or practice, or that it threatens religious voluntarism, or that it deviates from religious neutrality, and so on.[76]

Obviously the Religion Clauses are about religious liberty. We also say that government should be neutral among religions and between religion and nonreligion. We say religion should be voluntary. We say church and state should be separate. We say that government should not aid religion. Sometimes these different formulations point in the same direction; sometimes they seem to point in opposite directions. Most importantly, regulation of re-

---

75. 540 U.S. 712 (2004) (holding that state can award scholarships to students in every accredited major but refuse scholarships to students majoring in theology taught from a believing perspective).

76. Laycock, *supra* note 4, at 998 (text at notes 18-19).

ligious practice often restricts religious liberty, yet regulatory exemptions for religious practice are often attacked as departures from neutrality. Do we have to choose between liberty and neutrality, or is there an understanding of liberty and neutrality that reconciles the two approaches?

I offered substantive neutrality as that reconciliation. Neutral incentives, neither encouraging nor discouraging religion, is a coherent conception of neutrality that is consistent with religious liberty and consistent with regulatory exemptions for religious behavior. At the conceptual level, substantive neutrality insists on minimizing government influence on religion. Minimizing government influence leaves religion maximally subject to private choice, thus maximizing religious liberty. Carl Esbeck, whose work has emphasized the importance of religious voluntarism,[77] has noted that voluntarism bears the same relationship to government influence. "Voluntarism is not merely the absence of official coercion. It is also the absence of the government's influence concerning inherently religious beliefs and practices."[78] Substantive neutrality — minimizing government influence on religious incentives — is thus an understanding of neutrality that is more consistent with religious liberty and religious voluntarism than formal neutrality is. It was no doubt an oversimplification, but in one early article I simply equated "substantive neutrality" with "liberty."[79]

Later, I undertook to unite substantive neutrality with separation, and more audaciously, to do so in the context of what was then called charitable choice — government payments for social services delivered by religious providers.[80] Of course that provoked objections;[81] maybe it was a bridge too far.[82] I agree that neutrality of any kind — either formal or substantive — is inconsistent with the goals of the legal and political movement that has most

77. *See* Carl H. Esbeck, *Dissent and Disestablishment: The Church-State Settlement in the Early American Republic,* 2004 BYU L. Rev. 1385, 1395-1401; Esbeck, *supra* note 11, at 63-67.

78. Esbeck, *supra* note 11, at 64.

79. Douglas Laycock, *Summary and Synthesis: The Crisis in Religious Liberty,* 60 Geo. Wash. L. Rev. 841, 848 (1992) (text at notes 41-42).

80. *See* Laycock, *Underlying Unity, supra* note 5.

81. *See, e.g.,* Frederick Mark Gedicks, *A Two-Track Theory of the Establishment Clause,* 43 B.C. L. Rev. 1071, 1073 & n.7 (2002) ("Laycock eliminates the tension between separation and neutrality only by begging the question whether religious belief and activity merit special constitutional protection."); Smith, *Separation, supra* note 14, at 227 (calling the argument "ingenious (and perhaps too clever)").

82. *See* Cornelius Ryan, A Bridge Too Far (1974) (recounting the unsuccessful Allied attempt to capture the bridge over the Rhine at Arnhem, in the Netherlands, at a time when several major streams, and thus several bridges, still lay between the Allied front lines and the bridge at Arnhem).

emphatically claimed the banner of separationism.[83] I did not mean to claim otherwise.

What I did claim was that the Supreme Court had never set up separationism in opposition to neutrality. It had always talked of both, and in its own not-very-theoretical way, it had assumed that separation and neutrality were consistent.[84] Recall that the *Lemon* test, the very symbol of strict separationism, incorporates verbatim an earlier definition of "wholesome neutrality."[85] The assumption that neutrality and separation are opposites is a product of the last twenty years, a time when conservative justices used the language of neutrality to uphold government financial aid to religious schools, a result that most separationists opposed. Where *Lemon* had found a departure from neutrality in any aid that might benefit a school's religious mission,[86] the Court's new majority found neutrality in the fact that aid flowed on similar terms to religious and secular schools alike.[87] This argument over neutrality versus separation has extended to arguments over free

83. *See* John C. Jeffries, Jr. & James E. Ryan, *A Political History of the Establishment Clause*, 100 Mich. L. Rev. 279, 281 (2001) (equating separationism with two propositions: "that public aid should not go to religious schools and that public schools should not be religious. . . ."); Ira C. Lupu, *The Lingering Death of Separationism*, 62 Geo. Wash. L. Rev. 230, 230-31 (1994) (offering these two propositions as the "most concrete, operational meaning" of a somewhat more complex underlying idea of separationism); *see also* Douglas Laycock, *The Many Meanings of Separation*, 70 U. Chi. L. Rev. 1667, 1687-94 (2003) (text at notes 35-80) (surveying competing meanings of separation).

84. *See* Laycock, *Underlying Unity*, *supra* note 5, at 53-65 (text at notes 53-134) (reviewing the cases and the conflicting pressures on the Court).

85. Lemon v. Kurtzman, 403 U.S. 602, 612 (1971) (paraphrasing *School District v. Schempp*, 374 U.S. 203, 222 (1963)). *Lemon* cites *Bd. of Educ. v. Allen*, 392 U.S. 236, 243 (1968), but the cited passage in *Allen* is a quotation from *Schempp*, where the formulation originated.

86. *See Lemon*, 403 U.S. at 619 ("The State must be *certain*, given the Religion Clauses, that subsidized teachers do not inculcate religion. . . .") (emphasis added).

87. *See* Zelman v. Simmons-Harris, 536 U.S. 639, 648-63 (2002) (upholding state-funded vouchers that could be used to pay for educational services at a wide variety of schools, including public schools, secular private schools, and religious private schools); Mitchell v. Helms, 530 U.S. 793, 829-36 (plurality opinion) (upholding loans of educational equipment on per capita basis to all schools that chose to participate, including religious schools); Agostini v. Felton, 521 U.S. 203, 222-35 (1997) (upholding federal program that provided remedial instruction to low income students in both secular and religious schools); Zobrest v. Catalina Foothills Sch. Dist., 509 U.S. 1, 8-14 (1993) (rejecting argument that Establishment Clause prohibits government-paid sign-language interpreter for deaf student in Catholic high school); Mueller v. Allen, 463 U.S. 388, 396-404 (1983) (upholding state income-tax deductions for educational expenses, including tuition paid to religious schools).

speech, with separationists losing their argument that private religious speech may be or must be excluded from public forums.[88] But even over the last twenty years, Justice O'Connor's endorsement test was a measure of neutrality — government should not endorse any position either pro or con about religion[89] — that produced separationist results with respect to government speech endorsing religious views.[90]

Back when the Court talked about separation, it assumed that separation protects religious liberty. On what understanding of separation would that make any sense? In setting the question up in this way, I was of course reflecting my own separationist history and my reluctance to give up the label. I have been inconsistent over the years about separation.[91] When thinking about how I would use separation, I like it. When thinking about how some folks have misused the same word, I tend to find "separation" fatally ambiguous.

Once when I was focused on my own view of separation, I suggested that on one plausible understanding, the fundamental purpose of separation is to separate private religious choices and commitments from governmental

88. Good News Club v. Milford Cent. Sch., 533 U.S. 98, 107-20 (2001) (protecting right of student religion club to meet in elementary school on equal terms with secular clubs); Rosenberger v. Rector & Visitors of Univ. of Va., 515 U.S. 819, 828-46 (1995) (protecting right of religious magazine to receive funding from student activity fees on equal terms with secular publications); Capitol Square Rev. & Advisory Bd. v. Pinette, 515 U.S. 753, 763-70 (1995) (protecting right to erect cross in public forum on capitol grounds); Lamb's Chapel v. Center Moriches Union Free Sch. Dist., 508 U.S. 384, 390-97 (1993) (protecting right of church to meet in public school on equal terms with other community groups); Widmar v. Vincent, 454 U.S. 263, 267-77 (1981) (protecting right of student religion club to meet on university campus on equal terms with secular clubs).

89. See Lynch v. Donnelly, 465 U.S. 668, 692 (1984) (O'Connor, J., concurring) ("What is crucial is that a government practice not have the effect of communicating a message of government endorsement or disapproval of religion.").

90. See McCreary County v. ACLU, 545 U.S. 844, 859-81 (2005) (invalidating Ten Commandments display in county courthouse on grounds that county's purpose in mounting the display was inconsistent with the government's obligation of neutrality toward religion); Santa Fe Indep. Sch. Dist. v. Doe, 530 U.S. 290, 306-08 (2000) (holding that prayer as part of official program at high school football games unconstitutionally endorses religion); Lee v. Weisman, 505 U.S. 577, 627, 631 (1992) (Souter, J., concurring) (arguing that school-sponsored prayer at high school graduation, invalidated by Court on grounds that school coerced students to participate, was also invalid on ground that it endorsed religion); County of Allegheny v. ACLU, 492 U.S. 573, 592-94, 598-602 (1989) (holding that nativity scene in courthouse unconstitutionally endorsed religion); Wallace v. Jaffree, 472 U.S. 38, 56-61 (1985) (holding that moment-of-silence law unconstitutionally endorsed religion).

91. See Laycock, *supra* note 83, at 1700 (text at notes 109-10) (collecting my own inconsistent statements about whether separation is a usable concept).

power.[92] On that understanding, separation is congruent with religious liberty, because it leaves religious choices to individuals. It is consistent with voluntarism for the same reason: people will participate in religious activities only when they voluntarily choose to do so. And it is consistent with substantive neutrality: separating religious choice from government influence minimizes government influence on religious choice.

At a conceptual level, this is a perfectly sensible understanding of separation. But it is different from lack of contact between church and state as an end in itself, and different from separation as no aid to religion. That difference leaves two possibilities for the dispute over financial aid to education and social services provided by religious institutions. Either one side or the other has made a mistaken judgment about how the unified principle of liberty, voluntarism, separation, and substantive neutrality applies to the funding issue, or both sides are right about their own principles and separation is ultimately at odds with religious liberty and voluntarism understood in terms of substantive neutrality.

One could continue this march of conceptual unification and try to make the principle of no aid to religion fit with all the rest. The claim would have to be that the aid we are talking about when we say no aid to religion is aid that is preferentially directed to religion, and that the no-aid principle does not include aid that is neutrally distributed to religious and nonreligious providers of the same services. Or we might say that so long as the government gets full secular value for its money, from religious and secular providers on equal terms, its activity is more akin to a purchase of services than to a distribution of aid. If the government can buy a case of wine from a monastery on competitive terms, why can it not buy a math course or the services of a homeless shelter from a religious organization? To fold no-aid into neutrality in this way would not be objectively wrong, and it might conceivably help a few folks who were changing their minds anyway to reconcile their old no-aid principles with their new tolerance for government funding, but I think it would be a mistake. It would leave us with no vocabulary to describe a position with a long and important history in American debates. Some people believe that no government should aid religion in any way, and that this principle trumps all competing principles, including nondiscrimination principles. "No aid" is a sensible way to talk about that idea, and we should preserve the phrase for that use.

---

92. Laycock, *Underlying Unity,* supra note 5, at 46 (text at note 21).

III. Laycock and Feldman

Noah Feldman and I did not start out from the same point analytically, but we started out from about the same place on the political spectrum concerning these issues. We are both centrists in important but somewhat different senses.

I am a centrist in the sense that I am equally concerned for the religious liberty of all, believers and nonbelievers. Many activists and judges, and some scholars, address these issues only with a view to helping or opposing the religious side in general, or helping or opposing conservative Christians in particular.[93] My ideal is that one's views on religion should not predict one's views on religious liberty, and that every American, of every shade of religious belief and disbelief, is entitled to the same protection from government interfering with, or attempting to influence, his views about religion.

Professor Feldman may well share the view that every American of whatever belief is equally entitled to religious liberty. I do not know, but I would be surprised if he disagreed with that. But fundamentally, he is a centrist in the quite different sense of looking for compromise. He is trying to pull a divided nation together.[94] I would like to do that too, but we proceeded in quite different ways.

My approach has been to try to figure out what each side in the culture wars is justly entitled to in principle. Feldman's approach is more political. He identifies two large social movements, which he calls legal secularists and values evangelicals.[95] He is explicitly trying to broker a deal between them.[96]

Steven Gey is not a centrist in my judgment, although he has told me orally that I am wrong about that. Professor Gey is a strong legal secularist in terms of Feldman's categories, a strict no-aid separationist, staunchly opposed to any form of government support for religion.[97] Unlike Feldman, Gey is not looking for compromise. He wants his side to win and the other side to lose.

93. *See* Laycock, *Theology Scholarships, supra* note 5, at 159-61 (text at notes 17-27) (reviewing positions of interest groups, and some justices, and contrasting support for religious *liberty* with support or opposition to *religion*).

94. *See* FELDMAN, *supra* note 16, at 16 ("I undertook this book in the spirit of seeking reconciliation between the warring factions that define the church-state debate. . . .").

95. *See id.* at 150-85 (describing legal secularists); *id.* at 186-219 (describing values evangelicals).

96. *See id.* at 235-36 ("[A] workable solution to our church-state problem must reconcile secularists and evangelicals by making both sides feel included in the experiment of American government and nationhood.").

97. *See* Steven G. Gey, *Vestiges of the Establishment Clause,* 5 FIRST AMDT. L. REV. 1, 5-12 (2006) (summarizing his understanding of church-state separation).

But Gey and Feldman agree with each other, and disagree with me, on one important point. They both think that current Establishment Clause law is an unprincipled contradiction. The current case law in the Supreme Court continues to sharply restrict government speech endorsing religion, especially in public schools.[98] Indeed, the formal doctrine is still that government must be neutral between religion and nonreligion, even in its speech.[99] There are exceptions in which the Court has applied a different rule,[100] or in which the Court's swing voter found that a plainly religious statement did not endorse religion.[101] But the big picture, until and unless new justices change the rules, is one of substantial restrictions on government speech endorsing or attacking religion.

In sharp contrast, at least from a culture wars perspective, government can send apparently unlimited amounts of money to religious schools through voucher programs.[102] This is so obviously a contradiction to Feldman and Gey that they mostly just assert it.[103] Unless I missed it in another article somewhere else, Feldman sees no possible argument for reconciling these two positions that is worth taking time to rebut. Gey explores a little further, but never actually considers the one argument that might reconcile these two positions.[104]

98. *See* cases cited *supra* note 90.

99. *See* McCreary County v. ACLU, 545 U.S. 844, 860 (2005) (stating, in a case about a passive religious display, that "[t]he touchstone for our analysis is the principle that the 'First Amendment mandates government neutrality between religion and religion, and between religion and nonreligion.'") (quoting Epperson v. Arkansas, 393 U.S. 97, 104 (1968)).

100. Marsh v. Chambers, 463 U.S 783, 786-95 (1983) (permitting legislative chaplain to open daily sessions with prayer because the First Congress had the same practice).

101. Van Orden v. Perry, 545 U.S. 677, 698-705 (2005) (Breyer, J., concurring) (finding that the Ten Commandments display on the grounds of the Texas capitol conveyed a mixed religious and secular message and that the historic lack of controversy suggested that the secular message had dominated in public perception); Lynch v. Donnelly, 465 U.S. 668, 687-94 (1984) (O'Connor, J., concurring) (finding that a nativity scene accompanied by Santa Claus, reindeer, candy-striped poles, and more did not endorse Christianity).

102. Zelman v. Simmons-Harris, 536 U.S. 639, 648-63 (2002) (upholding state-funded vouchers that could be used to pay for educational services at a wide variety of schools, including public schools, secular private schools, and religious private schools).

103. FELDMAN, *supra* note 16, at 215-16 ("What we have, then, is a contradiction. . . . [N]o single, unified theory or logical reason can explain the arrangements we now have."); Gey, *supra* note 19, at 774 ("The problem is that the bodies of doctrine that underlie these two Establishment Clauses — the separationist clause governing endorsement and the neutrality clause governing financing — are intrinsically and comprehensively inconsistent.")

104. *See* Gey, *supra* note 19, at 774-76. Gey considers the argument that school prayer with student elections is neutral in the sense that all viewpoints can compete, but he never considers the argument that the resulting prayer imposes a collective choice on everyone

The Court took this combination of positions because Justices Kennedy and O'Connor took this combination of positions.[105] They never saw any contradiction, so they never explained how their positions fit together. But it is not difficult to make sense of their intuitions. With respect to the Establishment Clause, substantive neutrality and the protection of individual choice in religious matters can explain their votes. I confine this claim to the Establishment Clause, because with respect to the Free Exercise Clause, Justice Kennedy went off in a very different direction.[106]

Consider first the Court's voucher decision, *Zelman v. Simmons-Harris*.[107] The details of Cleveland's program were messy, and details matter. A choice program can be implemented well or badly, and if implemented badly, it may not provide the choice it promises. I will take up a few of these details below,[108] but for now, let us assume reasonable implementation.

The principle of the voucher decision is both formally neutral and substantively neutral. The state pays for education that satisfies the compulsory education requirements — math, reading, science, history, etc. — and it pays for that education at any school the parents choose, public or private, religious or secular. This law is formally neutral, because there are no religious categories in the program. It is also substantively neutral, because it creates no incentives to choose religious or secular education. You get the same government subsidy either way. As always, substantive neutrality protects individual choice; each family can choose for itself which school to attend.

In terms of minimizing government interference with private religious choices, this is a huge improvement over the traditional public school monopoly. Traditionally, the states have said that here is five, eight, even ten thousand dollars a year that we will spend on your child's education — *if* you choose a thoroughly secular education in a public school. You also have a

---

while each use of a voucher implements an individual choice. I suppose he would say taxation to fund the voucher imposes a collective choice on everyone. For my view of the grievance of taxpayers paying for educational choices that include religious choices, see *infra* text following note 178.

105. *Compare Zelman*, 536 U.S. at 641 (O'Connor & Kennedy, JJ., joining opinion of the Court upholding vouchers), *and id.* at 663-76 (O'Connor, J., concurring), *with* Santa Fe Indep. Sch. Dist. v. Doe, 530 U.S. 290, 292 (2000) (O'Connor & Kennedy, JJ., joining opinion of the Court striking down school-sponsored prayer at high school football games).

106. *Compare* Employment Div. v. Smith, 494 U.S. 872, 873 (1990) (Kennedy, J., joining opinion of the Court holding that burdens on religious practice require no justification if imposed by laws that are neutral and generally applicable), *with id.* at 891-903 (O'Connor, J., concurring) (emphatically rejecting that view).

107. 536 U.S. 639 (2002).

108. *See infra* text accompanying notes 181-191.

constitutional right to choose a religious education,[109] but if you choose that, you forfeit all this money. That threatened forfeiture vigorously discourages any parent inclined to choose the religious alternative; it creates a huge distortion of the constitutionally protected choice between religious and secular education. A program that offered the same state funding no matter what school a family chooses would be substantively neutral and would protect private choice in religious matters.

Now consider a school-sponsored prayer at the opening of every class, or at every meeting of the school board, or at every graduation ceremony. This is not substantively neutral. Government is taking a whole series of positions on religion: that there is a God, that praying to God is a good thing, that all students are encouraged to join in prayer, that the form of prayer offered at the school is a good or efficacious way to pray — maybe the best way to pray. There are many forms and styles of prayer, but each school-sponsored prayer will be a particular form and in a particular style. The odds are that over the course of a year, all or most of the school's prayers will be in the same form and style. The government endorses all these positions, both general and specific, and encourages all to participate.

And there is no individual choice. The school makes a series of collective decisions and imposes those decisions on everyone. Whether to pray, how to pray, whom to pray to — in Jesus' name or not? — all these choices are made by state actors and their choices are imposed on everyone in the room. Everyone in the room will either participate in the particular prayer the school or its appointed agent selected, or they will conspicuously not participate while everyone else prays, or they will conspicuously leave the room and return when the prayer is over. Everyone is pushed to join in a particular form of prayer, and effective individual choice is eliminated.

The short version of this extended comparison is that money can be delivered in a way that is consistent with individual choice. Prayers cannot. Neither can scriptures, creeds, Christmas displays, or any other government speech promoting or denigrating religion.[110]

A second important difference between money and prayer is relevant here, although the Court has neglected the point.[111] When the government

109. *See* Pierce v. Soc'y of Sisters, 268 U.S. 510 (1925) (invalidating law requiring all children to attend public schools).

110. *See* Laycock, *Theology Scholarships, supra* note 5, at 156-58 (text at notes 5-12) (elaborating this distinction).

111. The Court's theory is that the choice of a religious school or major is an "independent and private choice" that breaks "the link" to government funds. Locke v. Davey, 540 U.S. 712, 719 (2004). This theory implies that the religious content of the student's choice is no

pays for education, it gets full secular value for its money. It pays for courses that satisfy the compulsory education requirements. When it supports a broad range of schools, it supports education in secular subjects and lets parents choose whether to add religion to the curriculum. But when government adds a religious observance to a meeting or ceremony, there is no secular value added. Government is verbally supporting religion as religion.

So what does Professor Feldman say about this comparison between financial support for education in religious schools, on the one hand, and government-sponsored religious speech on the other? As I said, Feldman has almost exactly the opposite proposal. He would have the Court tighten up on financial support for religiously-affiliated institutions, including for religious schools.[112] And he would have the Court loosen up on verbal support for religion, letting government endorse religious teachings and sponsor religious displays.[113] I frankly cannot tell how far he would go with this. He says he would abandon the secular purpose requirement and the endorsement test, and substitute the simple principle of "no coercion and no money."[114]

But he never explains his understanding of coercion. Does he accept something like the Court's view that religious ceremonies at public events inherently coerce those in attendance?[115] Or Justice Scalia's view that coercion means only "coercion of religious orthodoxy and of financial support *by force of law and threat of penalty*"?[116] He never says. Would he permit school-sponsored prayer in classrooms? Or only at special events like graduations? Or would he permit only passive displays like Nativity scenes and Ten Com-

---

longer relevant. Surely there are some limits to this reasoning, but the Court has not yet found any. For analysis, see Laycock, *Theology Scholarships, supra* note 5, at 167-71 (text at notes 72-90).

112. *See* FELDMAN, *supra* note 16, at 237, 244-48.

113. *See id.* at 237-44.

114. *Id.* at 238.

115. *See* Santa Fe Indep. Sch. Dist. v. Doe, 530 U.S. 290, 312 (2000) ("Even if we regard every high school student's decision to attend a home football game as purely voluntary, we are nevertheless persuaded that the delivery of a pregame prayer has the improper effect of coercing those present to participate in an act of religious worship."); Lee v. Weisman, 505 U.S 577, 593 (1992) ("[P]ublic pressure, as well as peer pressure, . . . though subtle and indirect, can be as real as any overt compulsion."); Sch. Dist. v. Schempp, 374 U.S. 203, 221 (1963) ("When the power, prestige and financial support of government is placed behind a particular religious belief, the indirect coercive pressure upon religious minorities to conform to the prevailing officially approved plan is plain." (quoting *Engel v. Vitale,* 370 U.S. 421, 431 (1962))).

116. *Lee,* 505 U.S. at 640 (Scalia, J., dissenting).

mandments monuments? I don't know. But on the central thrust, his proposal is the opposite of mine.

On what grounds? So far as I can tell, Feldman has no legal principle that generates both of these results. He says money for religious schools but no verbal support for religious belief is a contradiction,[117] apparently because the issue in both contexts is whether government can support religion. When he reverses both results, permitting verbal support but prohibiting financial support, presumably he still thinks it is a contradiction. So what is he doing?

Actually, Feldman appears to be doing two rather different things, or perhaps acting on two different motivations. First, he is trying to broker a political compromise, and second, independent of whether it leads to compromise, he seems to think that pushing both sides to moderate their positions is a good thing.

Feldman's argument for compromise is also two-fold. One argument for his compromise is that he thinks it gives each side what it cares about most, or at least what each side *should* care about most. He thinks that secularists are simply *choosing* to feel excluded by government endorsements of religion; they should *choose* to feel differently.[118] There is an echo here of the Supreme Court's old view that African-Americans were simply choosing to feel stigmatized by segregation.[119] The tangible harm of segregation was of course much greater than the tangible harm of Christian prayers at government events,[120] but the government's declaration of preference for one race over others in segregation was no more real or unambiguous than the government's declaration of preference for one religious belief over others in a government-sponsored religious ceremony.

On the voucher issue, Feldman says that evangelicals have made little use of educational vouchers so far, because they have not been able to enact generally applicable voucher plans.[121] He also predicts, no doubt correctly, that

---

117. FELDMAN, *supra* note 16, at 215-16.

118. *See id.* at 238-39 ("Talk can always be reinterpreted, and more talk can always be added, so religious speech and symbols need not exclude.").

119. *See id.* at 242 ("[I]t is largely an interpretive choice to feel excluded by the fact of other people's faith," even when — this is the context of his statement — the government is promoting that faith). *Cf.* Plessy v. Ferguson, 163 U.S. 537, 551 (1896) (arguing that if segregation be a badge of inferiority, "it is not by reason of anything found in the act, but solely because the colored race chooses to put that construction upon it.").

120. *See generally* GARY S. BECKER, THE ECONOMICS OF DISCRIMINATION (1957) (analyzing the economic consequences of discrimination); Charles L. Black, Jr., *The Lawfulness of the Segregation Decisions*, 69 YALE L.J. 421 (1960) (describing the consequences of the system of racial segregation in the American South).

121. *See* FELDMAN, *supra* note 16, at 248 ("Given that voucher programs are widely

evangelicals would not like some of the other schools that would get money under a voucher plan[122] — think Islamic schools, Hare Krishna schools, or left-wing anti-American schools. For both these reasons, he thinks that evangelicals should be able to give up vouchers.

He does not put it this way, but a reader might reasonably infer that he thinks that legal secularists care most about money and that values evangelicals care most about symbolism. I frankly do not know what each side cares about most. But I suspect that each side cares so deeply about both issues that no compromise is going to be acceptable until and unless imposed on both sides and established by long usage.

Feldman's failure to specify what he means by coercion creates fatal ambiguity at the heart of his proposed compromise. If he is putting school-sponsored prayer or religious instruction back in public-school classrooms, coercion is inevitable. Children will be forced — by teachers who do not know the rules or dislike the rules they know, by intense social pressure from other children, and sometimes by direct intimidation[123] — to join in religious observances or to at least go through all the outwardly visible motions of religious observances. And parents who object to their children being subjected to somebody else's prayer service feel very strongly about that objection.

Alternatively, if Feldman is permitting only passive displays and no government-led religious ceremonies, he is not giving the values evangelicals more than a few crumbs. They are not going to take a deal in which they get no money for their private schools, a public school system as secular as ever, but a free hand on Nativity scenes and Ten Commandments monuments. A major part of his argument is that he offers a grand deal that is actually achievable, but this egregiously one-sided version is obviously a non-starter.

Feldman emphasizes that by abolishing *Lemon*'s secular purpose requirement,[124] he also would give values evangelicals a free hand to make their religious arguments in the political process.[125] I fully agree that no law should be

---

underused and have not spread widely, it should be relatively easy for values evangelicals to abandon them.").

122. *See id.* at 245-46 ("[W]hile values evangelicalism claims to advocate national unity and inclusion through shared values, school voucher programs cut exactly the other way, promoting difference and nonengagement.").

123. *See* Walter v. W. Va. Bd. of Educ., 610 F. Supp. 1169, 1170-73 (S.D. W. Va. 1985) (quoting testimony of Jewish child accosted for not appearing to pray during moment of silence, who was told that he would go to hell and that the Jews killed Christ, and of Catholic child who feared that if he did not stand and pray, he would get in trouble with his teacher).

124. *See* FELDMAN, *supra* note 16, at 237.

125. *See id.* at 222-27.

held unconstitutional because its supporters made a religious argument.[126] But clarifying this point would give the evangelicals little that they don't already have. They have the right to make their religious arguments in the political process;[127] the political arena is full of religious arguments and full of appeals to religious voters. As far as the law is concerned, churches can even create political affiliates and political action committees,[128] although they choose not do so, probably for good religious and political reasons.

"The Court has never accepted in any context the view that religious arguments are excluded from or restricted in political debate."[129] The secular purpose requirement does *not* lead to invalidation of laws to promote sexual morality,[130] restrict abortions,[131] close stores on Sunday,[132] or any other religiously-motivated law that falls short of promoting or mandating a religious ritual or observance. That a law coincides with some religious group's moral teachings does not make it unconstitutional.[133] The Court has relied on the secular purpose requirement in only a handful of cases, most of which — quite possibly all of which — could have been decided the same way on other grounds.[134] The claim that religious arguments have no place in politics is mostly an academic argument, occasionally a political argument, but it is not the law and never has been the law. Clarifying the point might reassure some evangelicals, but this is another crumb, not a substantial gain.

Feldman's second argument for his compromise is that it would return us to the solution that prevailed through much of our history.[135] There is

126. *See* Douglas Laycock, *Freedom of Speech That Is Both Religious and Political*, 29 U.C. DAVIS L. REV. 793, 811-12 (1996) (text at notes 70-71) (urging that judicial review focus on political outputs — the content and consequences of legislation — and not political inputs — the arguments made in support of that legislation).

127. *See* McDaniel v. Paty, 435 U.S. 618 (1978) (invalidating provision that excluded members of the clergy from the legislature); Walz v. Tax Comm'n, 397 U.S. 664, 670 (1970) ("Of course, churches as much as secular bodies and private citizens have [the] right" to "take strong positions on public issues.").

128. *See* Branch Ministries v. Rossotti, 211 F.3d 137, 143 (D.C. Cir. 2000) (holding that these alternatives eliminate any burden on free exercise from the restrictions on political speech by charities organized under 26 U.S.C. § 501(c)(3)).

129. Laycock, *supra* note 126, at 797 (text at notes 22-23).

130. Bowen v. Kendrick, 487 U.S. 589 (1988) (upholding Adolescent Family Life Act).

131. Harris v. McRae, 448 U.S. 297 (1980) (upholding restrictions on public funding of abortions).

132. McGowan v. Maryland, 366 U.S. 420 (1961) (upholding Sunday closing laws).

133. *Bowen*, 487 U.S. at 604 n.8; *Harris*, 448 U.S. at 319-20; *McGowan*, 366 U.S. at 442.

134. *See supra* note 46 (collecting cases).

135. *See* FELDMAN, *supra* note 16, at 236-37 ("I believe that the history of church and state in America that I have offered in these pages does point toward an answer.").

some truth to this claim, but the history to which it appeals is not very attractive. It is certainly true that at the founding, the controversy was over financial support for churches and the salaries of clergy.[136] Prayer and religious ceremonies at government events did not become controversial until the nineteenth century.[137] For most of the nineteenth and much of the twentieth centuries, there were Protestant religious ceremonies in the public schools;[138] children were coerced to participate, by corporal punishment if necessary;[139] and there was no money for private alternatives for children of other faiths.[140] The Protestants argued that their religious observances in public schools were "nonsectarian," because they simply read the Bible "without note or comment," and thus they took no position on issues that divided different Christian denominations.[141] Non-Christians did not count, and the Catholic view — that the Bible should be read only in a translation approved by the hierarchy and only when accompanied by the official interpretations of the magisterium — didn't count either.[142]

Feldman is proposing some version of this nineteenth-century Protestant practice — majoritarian religious observances at government events, and no money for private schools. He does not appear to require a pretense or fig leaf of nonsectarianism. His rejection of coercion means he is not really going back to the nineteenth-century practice. His failure to define coercion affects his historical argument, too. If he would permit only

136. *See* Laycock, *"Nonpreferential" Aid, supra* note 2, at 913-19 (text at notes 193-229) (contrasting the founding generation's treatment of financial and nonfinancial aid to religion).

137. *See* FELDMAN, *supra* note 16, at 57-92 (reviewing the nineteenth-century battles over religion in public schools); Jeffries & Ryan, *supra* note 83, at 297-305 (describing "The Protestant Establishment" and its nineteenth-century conflict with Catholic immigrants); Douglas Laycock, *"Noncoercive" Support for Religion: Another False Claim About the Establishment Clause,* 26 VAL. U. L. REV. 37, 50-53 (1991) (text at notes 65-79) (summarizing the same developments and collecting additional sources).

138. *See* FELDMAN, *supra* note 16, at 61-65, 87-88; Jeffries & Ryan, *supra* note 83, at 298-99.

139. *See* Donahoe v. Richards, 38 Me. 376 (1854) (dismissing, without reaching the merits of the underlying controversy, father's claim for damages caused by child being expelled from public school for refusing to read the King James Bible); Commonwealth v. Cooke, 7 Am. L. Reg. 417 (Boston Police Ct. 1859) (dismissing prosecution of a teacher who beat a Catholic student with a stick for thirty minutes until he agreed to read or recite from the King James translation of the Bible); CARL F. KAESTLE, PILLARS OF THE REPUBLIC: COMMON SCHOOLS AND AMERICAN SOCIETY 1760-1860, at 171 (1983) (reporting a similar case in Oswego, New York).

140. *See* FELDMAN, *supra* note 16, at 66, 86-87; Jeffries & Ryan, *supra* note 83, at 300-02.

141. *See* FELDMAN, *supra* note 16, at 61-62; Jeffries & Ryan, *supra* note 83, at 298-99, 301.

142. *See* FELDMAN, *supra* note 16, at 63-67; Jeffries & Ryan, *supra* note 83, at 299-300.

passive religious displays, but not religious exercises in classrooms, he is not even approximating any practice from the American past. If he would restore religious exercise to public school classrooms, then the difference between his proposal and the nineteenth-century practice would be in the degree of coercion.

The corollary of moving back toward practices that prevailed through much of our history is that his proposal seeks to reverse the historical trend of the last generation on both issues. I do not think the changes of the last generation were just mistakes or random variations in doctrine. The nineteenth-century Protestant practice was appalling, and we abandoned it for good reason.

I have already explained why the Kennedy-O'Connor position — prohibiting government speech observing or endorsing religion but permitting government to fund programs of private choice that include religiously-affiliated providers of education, social services, medical care, and the like — is consistent with substantive neutrality and individual choice.[143] The two halves of that position emerged at somewhat different times and coincided with important changes in American attitudes toward religious minorities. The first Supreme Court decisions prohibiting school-sponsored prayer,[144] in 1962 and 1963, came at a time of growing religious pluralism and full assimilation of Catholics and Jews into the American mainstream.[145] When the Court began to take religious minorities seriously after World War II, majoritarian religious ceremonies at public events, and especially in public schools, looked less and less tolerable.

The shift to permitting funding of religious schools began in the 1980s, gathered momentum in the 1990s, and came to fruition at the turn of the millennium.[146] In the 1980s, the evangelicals switched sides on this issue, moving from intense opposition to intense support.[147] Free marketeers making economic arguments for school choice became much more numerous and got more attention in a political environment more interested in market

---

143. *See supra* text accompanying notes 105-110.

144. Sch. Dist. v. Schempp, 374 U.S. 203 (1963); Engel v. Vitale, 370 U.S. 421 (1962).

145. *See generally* WILL HERBERG, PROTESTANT-CATHOLIC-JEW (1955) (arguing that by the 1950s, these three religions had come to constitute three accepted branches of the American civil religion). The first Catholic President was elected in 1960.

146. *See* Laycock, *Theology Scholarships, supra* note 5, at 166 (text at notes 58-64) (collecting cases).

147. *See* Laycock, *Underlying Unity, supra* note 5, at 58-59 (text at notes 92-96) (describing evangelical opposition to funding for religious schools in *Lemon v. Kurtzman*, 403 U.S. 602 (1971), and continuing up to 1980).

solutions.[148] In the 1960s and 1970s, religious schools had been actual or potential refuges from desegregation,[149] but by the 1990s, frustrated black parents in inner cities were demanding school choice.[150] As this broad coalition joined Catholics in demanding money for private schools, and as Protestant hostility to Catholics faded further into the past, aid to private schools looked less like a special interest demand for Catholics; it became much easier to see the issue in terms of neutrality and private choice.

Feldman's nineteenth-century model was a Protestant model that imposed Protestant preferences on both issues — on government speech and on government money.[151] Both halves of the nineteenth-century Protestant model were deeply rooted in anti-Catholicism. Anti-Catholic feeling has faded, but the problem with the nineteenth-century model is more general. The Protestant model served a nineteenth-century anti-Catholic agenda because — precisely because — both halves of that solution catered to the religious majority and overrode the needs and views of religious minorities. The changes of the past sixty years on these two issues represent progress toward greater tolerance and equality; it would be a mistake to roll back the clock on either issue.

Feldman's second reason for his proposal, his desire to push all sides toward the middle, is more subtly stated. Only on rereading Feldman did I realize that this was part of his argument. But I think it is a more fundamental source of our disagreement. Feldman and I come to opposite solutions on both sets of concrete issues because we make opposite judgments on a more fundamental question: how can Americans live together in peace and equality despite our deep religious differences? My answer to that question is to

---

148. In the online catalog of the main libraries of the University of Michigan, http://mirlyn.lib.umich.edu, there were 195 entries when I searched for "school choice" as a phrase in the subject matter index on September 24, 2007. The earliest entry was published in 1976. Four were published in the 1970s, 14 in the 1980s, 90 in the 1990s, and 87 between 2000 and 2007.

149. *See* Laycock, *Underlying Unity, supra* note 5, at 61-62 (text at notes 111-17) (briefly describing the segregation academies and the desegregation claim in *Lemon v. Kurtzman,* 403 U.S. 602 (1971)).

150. *See* William G. Howell et al., *What Americans Think About Their Schools: The 2007 Education Next–PEPG Survey,* EDUC. NEXT, Fall 2007, at 12. This article reports a survey in which 68% of African-Americans completely or somewhat favored the use of "government funds to pay the tuition of low-income students who choose to attend private schools." *Id.* at 17. *See also* THOMAS C. PEDRONI, MARKET MOVEMENTS: AFRICAN AMERICAN INVOLVEMENT IN SCHOOL VOUCHER REFORM (2007) (reviewing the participation of African-American activists in the campaign for vouchers in Milwaukee).

151. *See supra* text accompanying notes 135-142.

maximize religious liberty for each American. I want to minimize government influence on religious choices and commitments — this is the very definition of substantive neutrality — and let each American live his life as freely as possible in accord with his own beliefs and commitments. Feldman does not. His solution is to push us all to take more moderate positions, reducing the scope of liberty or leaning on us not to fully exercise the liberties we have.

Values evangelicals very much want government sponsorship for religion, so Feldman says that legal secularists should swallow their objections.[152] It is not so bad to see religious displays on government walls, and although he is ambiguous on this, he may think it is not so bad to have to sit quietly through someone else's prayer service. The public school monopoly encourages a "cohesive national identity that evangelicals have wanted to restore or re-create";[153] vouchers are bad because they empower groups that want to teach other traditions or other identities, and they will inevitably provoke political battles about whether some schools are too radical or un-American to be funded.[154] He thinks we will get along better if we all moderate our views and reduce our differences.

I think that is unlikely to happen. We always will have an extraordinary diversity of religious opinions, including fire-breathing believers and fire-breathing nonbelievers. Given that reality, we will get along better if we agree to leave each other alone with respect to our beliefs and commitments about religion. The virtues of leaving each other alone are nicely illustrated by the difference between classroom prayer, which was deeply polarizing, and the Equal Access Act,[155] which enables thousands of student prayer clubs (and gay rights clubs) to meet on their own time without imposing on their classmates. Whatever the relative merits of competing empirical predictions about the possibility of moderating religious conflict, I think that liberty with respect to religious matters is both intrinsically valuable[156] and a deeply rooted constitutional commitment. My solution seeks to maximize liberty; Feldman's solution seeks to constrain the exercise of liberty and to encourage moderation.

Professor Feldman and I recently had an exchange at Harvard that clarified our differences and clarified some of the positions in his book. Of course

---

152. *See* FELDMAN, *supra* note 16, at 238-42.

153. *Id.* at 244.

154. *See id.* at 245-46.

155. 20 U.S.C. § 4071-74 (2000).

156. *See* Laycock, *Liberty, supra* note 5, at 316-23 (text at notes 18-40) (arguing that religious liberty reduces conflict and human suffering, and that reasons for keeping government out of religion extend to noncoercive intrusions).

he should not be held responsible for my attempts to summarize his informal oral remarks. But the exchange was sufficiently revealing to deserve summary here.

He agrees that he failed to specify what he meant by coercion. He now says that, for everyone who is not an elementary school student, he means Justice Scalia's understanding of coercion. So after elementary school, people would indeed have to sit through other people's religious exercises at government events. Many people complain to him about having been subjected to government-sponsored prayers, but none of the complainers was ever converted and many report being strengthened in their own faith in reaction to the unpleasant experience. He thinks that government-sponsored religious exercises deliver no message about the truth or value of any religion, but simply a message that one religion is the choice of a local majority — an uncontroversial fact that everyone already knows.

More fundamentally, he sees no difference between a majority exercising its religion privately or through the organs of government, because he thinks the state action doctrine is a laughable fetish. By contrast, I think that state action is definitional in the Religion Clauses: the difference between protected free exercise and prohibited establishment is precisely the presence or absence of state action in a religious ritual or activity. The difference is as clear as day and night — including cases of dusk, where the presence of state action is debatable and cases on either side of the line do not seem very different from each other. But we must draw the line as best we can, in close cases as well as easy cases, or the Religion Clauses become incoherent.

Feldman's definition of coercion clarifies what evangelicals would get from his proposed compromise. They would get prayer at football games, Christmas carols without a legal cloud, more religion-friendly perceptions from administrators, and the like. Presumably they would get prayer in classrooms as well, at least after elementary school. He does not want a quarter of the population to feel that the public schools are a hostile environment.

Feldman also emphasizes that evangelicals would get intelligent design and creationism in public schools, taught not as science but as a theological belief widely held in the American population. Feldman and I agree that under existing law, schools could do much more than they do to accommodate religious objections to evolution. They could teach more about the boundaries of science and the difference between naturalism as a method of inquiry (a method that defines the reach of science) and naturalism as an ultimate truth (a question for religion or philosophy), thus making clear that science simply does not address any question about the role of God in causing or directing evolution or in creating the evidence that supports evolution. Per-

257

haps schools would feel freer to take these steps if they were free to teach religion. But if schools were free to teach religion, they could teach intelligent design and creationism as true. If not — if Feldman means only that schools could teach that many people believe in intelligent design or creationism — then again he has changed nothing, because schools clearly can teach sociological or demographic facts about what many Americans believe. Whatever schools might teach about intelligent design and creationism under Feldman's proposal, he thought that it should not be taught in a science class. But that would seem to be merely a pedagogical preference; if schools are constitutionally free to teach something, it is hard to see any constitutional reason why they can teach it in one class but not in another.

With respect to money, he thinks politics is about money and not symbolism, and that the wars of religion and lesser forms of religious conflict were about money and institutional control, not about symbolism. The point here seemed to be that if money goes to religious institutions, we will fight about it. This formulation is also open to the interpretation that he proposes victory for the secularists on what is important — money — and victory for the evangelicals on what is not important — symbolism.

My exchange with Professor Feldman was friendly and clarifying for both of us, but neither of us made much progress toward persuading the other. For me, the fundamental fact continues to be that money can be distributed to individuals and used consistently with individual choice, but that a religious exercise at a government event imposes on everyone present the religious exercise and all the religious choices inevitably contained within it.

IV. Laycock and Gey

Professor Gey has a more traditional objection. He wants neither financial nor verbal support for anything connected to religion. To him, separation means no government aid to any religiously-affiliated organization and a completely secular environment in any place even touching on the governmental sphere.[157] He would go further, "prohibiting accommodation of religiously mandated behavior beyond the scope of religious expression,"[158] refusing to allow regulatory exemptions even when an exemption would

---

157. *See* Gey, *supra* note 97, at 5-12.
158. Steven G. Gey, *Why Is Religion Special?: Reconsidering the Accommodation of Religion Under the Religion Clauses of the First Amendment*, 52 U. PITT. L. REV. 75, 182 (1990).

permit believers to practice their faith and would impose no cost on those around them.[159] He believes that the Establishment Clause limits the free speech rights of religious speakers.[160] He may be the only American religious liberty scholar to defend the French decision to prohibit students from wearing conspicuous religious dress or symbols in public schools.[161] The sum of these positions is why I do not think of him as a centrist.

It is no surprise that he opposes government money flowing to religious schools, even if they teach all the secular subjects and even if the money is routed through parents who choose from a broad array of schools.[162] He is concerned about the conscience of taxpayers who object to these religious schools. In his view, if I do not like the religious views being taught in evangelical or Catholic schools, I should not have to pay tax money for their support.[163] And, of course, he appeals to the American founding; he thinks that this is precisely the issue the Establishment Clause was intended to resolve.[164]

I would agree with him 100% if we were giving money to support the religious functions of churches. How to finance the church was *the* central issue of church-state relations in late-eighteenth century America, and the issue was resolved in favor of purely private funding.[165] It is still the law, although almost never litigated, and thus little noticed, that government may not subsidize the religious functions of a church. That rule creates a special category consisting only of religion, so it is not a formally neutral rule. Government is

159. *See id.* at 182-84 (arguing that schools may not constitutionally exempt a religious student from a requirement to wear shorts in gym class).

160. *See* Steven G. Gey, *When Is Religious Speech Not "Free Speech"?*, 2000 U. ILL. L. REV. 379, 381 ("[T]he First Amendment itself limits the extension of free speech protection to religious speech whenever that protection would undermine the separation of church and state.").

161. *See* Steven G. Gey, *Free Will, Religious Liberty, and a Partial Defense of the French Approach to Religious Expression in Public Schools*, 42 HOUS. L. REV. 1 (2005).

162. *See* Gey, *supra* note 19, at 739 (arguing that in the voucher cases, "the government is not only actively touting the virtues of one religion over another; it is also using its coercive taxing authority to force one person to support another person's faith").

163. *See, e.g., id.* at 776 (arguing, in the context of the school funding cases, that "[f]orcing one set of adherents to pay for the sectarian activities of their religious adversaries is quintessentially coercive").

164. *See, e.g., id.* at 745 (arguing that the theory of the voucher cases "leads to the conclusion that Patrick Henry was correct and James Madison was wrong about the basic requisites of religious liberty").

165. *Compare* Laycock, *"Nonpreferential" Aid, supra* note 2, at 894-902 (text at notes 97-146) (reviewing founding-era debates over government-paid clergy), *with id.* at 913-19 (text at notes 193-229) (reviewing lack of debate about nonfinancial support of religion).

free to subsidize anything else it chooses — education,[166] farmers,[167] etha-nol,[168] bridges to nowhere,[169] you name it. For decades we subsidized to-bacco farmers[170] while simultaneously subsidizing medical care for smok-ers.[171] Every other interest group is free to seek subsidies for its core func-tions. But churches are not.

That rule is not formally neutral, but it is as close as we can come to sub-stantively neutral. No subsidies to churches and no taxes from churches is the best we can do to prevent the fiscal operations of the government from either encouraging or discouraging churches. And if the substantively-neutral course is a little murky here, it is clarified by the cognate principle of volunta-rism — religious people should fund their own churches in their own way — and by the history of the founding.

I said above that if I could link substantive neutrality with separation, then one side or the other had made a mistaken judgment about the meaning of neutrality or the meaning of separation. I think that is in fact what hap-

166. Every state operates a system of free public schools.

167. *See, e.g.,* David M. Herszenhorn, *Farm Subsidies Seem Immune to an Overhaul — Crop Prices Are Good, but Lobby Is Strong,* N.Y. TIMES, July 26, 2007, at A1 (reporting sub-stantial failure of political effort to limit farm subsidies); Andrew Martin, *Making Waves in Dairyland: Lawmaker Raises Hackles with Plan for Deep Cuts in Subsidies to Farmers,* N.Y. TIMES, June 22, 2007, at C1 (reporting that federal government paid $16 billion in farm sub-sidies in 2006).

168. *See, e.g.,* Alexei Barrioneuvo, *6 Get Grants From U.S. to Support Bio-Refineries,* N.Y. TIMES, Mar. 1, 2007, at C3 (reporting that "corn-based ethanol . . . has relied for many years on a 51-cent-a-gallon subsidy to be competitive with gasoline," and that government "would provide up to $385 million in six bio-refinery projects that would produce cellu-losic ethanol").

169. The "bridge to nowhere," made famous in 2005 debates about earmarked Congres-sional appropriations, would have gone from Ketchikan, Alaska, on the mainland, to the city's airport on Gravina Island, population 50. Congress appropriated the money to the state of Alaska and let the state choose whether to use it for this bridge. *See, e.g.,* William Yardley, *Alaska Bridge Projects Resist Earmarks Purge,* N.Y. TIMES, Mar. 6, 2007, at A13. The Governor of Alaska, however, decided that "the bridge really was going nowhere" and offi-cially abandoned the project. *Alaska Seeks Alternative to Bridge Plan,* N.Y. TIMES, Sept. 23, 2007. Of course, this was a political decision not to build the bridge, not a decision about lack of government authority to build the bridge.

170. *See, e.g.,* Simon Romero, *In Tobacco Country, Growers Keep Their Fingers Crossed for a Windfall,* N.Y. TIMES, July 26, 2004, at A10 (describing plan to buy out "tobacco produc-tion quotas created by a Depression-era subsidy program").

171. State payments for medical care for diseases caused by tobacco, under programs such as Medicaid, were the basis for the state claims that led to the large settlements between states and tobacco companies. *See* Doug Rendleman, *Common Law Restitution in the Missis-sippi Tobacco Settlement: Did the Smoke Get in Their Eyes?,* 33 GA. L. REV. 847, 852-55 (1999).

pened. I think it happened in the nineteenth century, when the Protestant majority equated funding of schools with the funding of churches. Certainly there is overlap: religious instruction goes on in churches, and religious instruction goes on in religious schools. Even worship goes on in both places. And if government pays the entire cost of a religious school, it will pay for the school's religious instruction.

But secular instruction also goes on in these schools. They satisfy the compulsory education requirements. They teach skills and knowledge that government also teaches in its public schools. To refuse to pay for a child's education because of her parents' religious choices is very different from refusing to pay the salary of the clergy.

The problem, of course, is that religious and secular education are combined in these schools. The government is forbidden to pay for one and obliged to pay for the other, but the two courses of instruction share facilities and staff and sometimes may be commingled in textbooks and lesson plans, though my impression is that usually they are not. No solution is perfect, but that is hardly unusual. It is very difficult for government to have no effect on people's religious incentives; government is the 800-pound gorilla in the society. Government spends a third of gross domestic product;[172] it also has the power to regulate behavior and to throw people in jail. In a regime of substantive neutrality, the magnitude of effects matters; we must sometimes choose a small degree of support for religion to avoid a very large penalty on religion, or vice versa.[173] This is such a case. It is more nearly neutral, and allows more private choice — more liberty — for government to pay the cost of education in secular subjects, offered in a religious environment, than to offer large education subsidies only to those families willing to abandon the religious environment.

I am inclined to add, although the Court apparently is not, that government can never pay the full cost of a religious school.[174] The rationale that the

---

172. *See* UNITED STATES CENSUS BUREAU, STATISTICAL ABSTRACT OF THE UNITED STATES: 2007, at 266 tbl. 420 (126th ed., 2007), *available at* http://www.census.gov/compendia/statab/ (total current expenditures of state and local governments in 2005 were $1,686,400,000,000); *id.* at 307 tbl. 458 (total federal outlays in 2005 were $2,472,200,000,000); *id.* at 428 tbl. 648 (gross domestic product in 2005 was $12,487,100,000,000).

173. *See* Laycock, *supra* note 4, at 1008 (text at notes 47-48) ("Substantive neutrality always requires that the encouragement of one policy be compared to the discouragement of alternative policies.").

174. *See* Laycock, *Theology Scholarships, supra* note 5, at 169-71 (text at notes 80-90) (noting that the Court's "true private choice" theory implies that the religious content of the instruction purchased with the voucher is irrelevant).

state is paying for secular courses, whether delivered in a secular or religious environment, implies that some reasonable portion of the cost should be allocated to the religious function, and the school should pay that part itself. But there are counterarguments. This allocation requires someone to investigate the school's curriculum to determine the percentage of cost allocable to religious instruction. Ideally, government would do that allocation in round numbers and in a minimally intrusive way, but ideals are hard to achieve. If the number thus determined is never reviewed, a school could increase its proportion of religious instruction and still collect the same government funds. If the number is reviewed at frequent intervals, there is persistent pressure on schools to reduce their religious instruction and collect more government funds. Maybe it would be better to think of vouchers as a purchase of services at a fixed price; if the government gets the secular value it bargained for, the school's cost of delivering those services should be irrelevant. I have waffled before on the choice between these two rules, and suggested that the choice might depend on context,[175] and I am no closer to a confident judgment now.

Even if the private school must pay for religious instruction itself, it is enormously easier for churches to run these schools if government pays for the secular part of the program. But it is enormously more difficult to run these schools if government offers a free secular education to all children and withholds that support from anyone who chooses a religious education.

My view that subsidizing secular subjects in a school is fundamentally different from subsidizing religious functions in a church is one of the central points on which Professor Gey and I disagree. Subsidizing a religiously-affiliated school aids religion, and for him, that makes schools the equivalent of churches. Assessing the Court's recent decisions, he says that "government can provide financial assistance for religious education, which is one of the primary mechanisms by which churches cultivate their young members and attract new adherents."[176] I suspect that these schools do much better at cultivating young members than at attracting new adherents,[177] but I do not

175. *See id.* at 170-71 (text at notes 90-91).

176. Gey, *supra* note 19, at 776.

177. I put this question to Rev. Andrew Greeley, the Chicago priest and sociologist. He was not aware of any data on conversion rates for students enrolled in religious schools. Anecdotally, he recalled that in the early years of black Protestant enrollment in Catholic schools in Chicago, some priests pressured families to convert. The resulting conversions rarely lasted, wiser heads prevailed within the church, and the effort was abandoned. Interview with Andrew M. Greeley, in Grand Beach, Michigan, August 4, 2007. The practice might be different among evangelical schools, and the result may be that families of other faiths or of none are less willing to enroll in such schools.

disagree with his basic point. Religion benefits when government helps fund church-affiliated schools. For Gey, that is the end of the analysis; for me, it is only half the analysis. We must compare that benefit to the consequences of any alternative policy, and the alternative is for government to offer up to $10,000 for education to those families, and only those families, who surrender their constitutional right to get that education in a religious environment. The coercive effect of that conditional offer dwarfs the benefit to religion of making the money available on equal terms.

This disagreement also can be thought of as a baseline question. Gey would measure the impact on religion from a baseline of the government doing nothing — or at least, doing nothing relevant to a decision on whether to fund religious schools. If government did nothing, these schools would have to fully fund themselves, in secular and religious subjects alike; compared to that, any government money is aid.

I would measure the impact on religion from a baseline of what the government is already doing, or, to put it another way, from a baseline of how government treats the same activity — education in reading, math, etc. — in a wholly secular environment. These two baselines were the same in 1785, when there were no public schools and when government funded almost nothing in the private sector. But they are not the same today. From the perspective of what government is already doing, government offers to spend money for education, and one who chooses religious education forfeits that money.

More fundamentally, the choice of baseline depends on the practical incentives that will ensue. If government money is equally available for any school, then the family's choice can be made on the educational and religious merits of the schools, and the government money will have no effect on the choice. Generalizing this point, the equal treatment baseline minimizes the government's effect on incentives in government spending programs, so long as all the funded institutions offer a genuine secular service that government can fund in either a religious or a secular context.[178] Of course government

---

178. In the free exercise cases, where government prohibits conduct that is the exercise of religion for some people, the baseline of government doing nothing usually minimizes the effect on incentives. Regulation and threat of penalty discourage religion; exemption usually does little to encourage religion. *See supra* text accompanying notes 21-22. But the problem becomes much more difficult if religious behavior aligns with self-interest, as in conscientious objection to serving in the military or paying taxes. Then exemptions must be denied or conditioned on the imposition of some alternative burden. *See* Laycock, *supra* note 4, at 1016-18 (text at notes 95-99). For a more extensive analysis of the problem of choosing baselines, see Laycock, *Liberty, supra* note 5, at 349-52 (text at notes 171-75).

has to monitor enough to confirm that the secular service is really being delivered. But at least for schools, that monitoring is already in place: government has to confirm that a private school satisfies the compulsory education laws.

As to the taxpayers who object to funding religious education, I would explain that they are paying for secular education, and the church is paying for the religious instruction. Probably this would mollify very few of them. But any effect on them is just too small and too attenuated to outweigh the effect, on families choosing schools, of funding some options and not others. Each taxpayer's money goes into an enormous pool, making an infinitesimal fraction of the government's budget, and government then spends a small fraction of that budget to support secular education in religious institutions, and that expenditure makes it easier for those institutions to teach religion with their own funds. This is not nearly a big enough effect to outweigh the large penalty we traditionally impose on the choice to be educated in a religious environment.

Any grievance on behalf of the taxpayer is further ameliorated by the fact that his money is spread, on an equal opportunity basis, across schools teaching a wide range of views. His money goes to schools he supports as well as to those he opposes, and the schools he supports also get taxes from his ideological enemies. The ideological benefit and burden to each taxpayer is small to begin with, and it tends to balance out. The Court has emphasized the balancing-out effect of viewpoint neutrality in its cases on using state-authorized dues and fees to support private political speech. Dissenters have a right to withhold the part of their dues and fees that goes to such uses,[179] but not if the money is distributed on a viewpoint-neutral basis.[180]

I have been analyzing an ideal program in which government provides equal funding for any school a family chooses, subject only to the constraint that government cannot pay for that part of a school's cost that is reasonably allocated to the religious part of the education it offers. Of course, this does not describe any actual program. Programs enacted by the political process depart from this ideal in multiple ways.

In Cleveland, as in most such programs, the financial incentives still tipped toward the secular public schools. Students got a bigger government subsidy if they chose a secular public school,[181] although many of those who

179. *See, e.g.,* Keller v. State Bar, 496 U.S. 1, 9-16 (1990) (bar dues); Abood v. Detroit Bd. of Educ., 431 U.S. 209, 232-37 (1977) (union dues).

180. *See* Bd. of Regents v. Southworth, 529 U.S. 217, 233-34 (2000) (holding that viewpoint neutral distribution adequately protects the First Amendment interest in not paying for private political speech with which one disagrees).

181. *See* Zelman v. Simmons-Harris, 536 U.S. 639, 646-48, 654 (2002). Ohio spent far more

chose a private school got a second subsidy from the private school. The opinions give little information about the size of the two subsidies combined, but the subsidy from private schools appears to generally be small.[182] More important, families paid less if they chose a public school. Private schools could charge low-income students $250 in cash in addition to the voucher,[183] and could charge other students the full difference between the school's tuition and the state's voucher.[184] Public schools were free.[185] This is considerably less than full substantive neutrality, but because the discrimination is *against* religion, it in no way suggests a violation of the Establishment Clause.

Nor do I argue that this discrimination is unconstitutional, which is to say, I do not argue that voucher programs are constitutionally required. Government may discriminate between public schools and private schools, even if that discrimination has disparate impact on religion. It is difficult or impossible to construct a plausible doctrinal argument that government must create privatized options for the services it provides.[186] I do think it is unconstitutional for government to discriminate between secular private schools and religious private schools,[187] but the only Supreme Court decision so far upholds such discrimination,[188] in an ambiguous opinion of unclear scope.[189]

---

per student on public schools than it paid in vouchers. Compare *id.* at 646 (voucher for private school capped at $2250), *with id.* at 647-48 (per student spending of $7746 in public schools).

182. Justice Souter cites average tuition figures from a variety of sources, ranging from well below the voucher amount at the average Catholic elementary school to "about $4,000" at nonreligious schools. *Zelman,* 536 U.S. at 705-06 & n.14 (Souter, J., dissenting). He also cites data suggesting that part of the reason religious schools can charge lower tuition is that they get subsidies from their church and secular private schools do not. *Id.* at n.14. If we take his $4000 figure for tuition at secular private schools as a reasonable measure of the cost of a private education, then the combined public and private subsidy to a low-income voucher student would still be well below the subsidy of more than $7000 available to that student in free public schools. It should be emphasized that all these numbers are from the 1990s, so they would be higher now, and that there is wide variation around these averages.

183. *See id.* at 646 (opinion of the Court).

184. *Id.*

185. *Id.* at 654.

186. *See* Laycock, *Theology Scholarships, supra* note 5, at 173 (text at notes 101-02) (noting that claims to discrimination against religion "arise only after the state makes a voluntary decision to fund attendance at private institutions").

187. *See id.* at 195-200 (text at notes 241-70) (arguing that government discretion to include or exclude religious institutions from funding programs is the worst of all possible worlds).

188. Locke v. Davey, 540 U.S. 712 (2004).

189. On the fundamental ambiguity of *Davey,* see Laycock, *Theology Scholarships, supra* note 5, at 184-87 (text at notes 187-93) (noting that opinion may be confined to the training

Other features of real-world voucher programs arguably encourage families to choose religious schools. In most cities, there are more religious private schools than secular private schools, so the newly available choices are disproportionately religious. In Cleveland, the suburban public schools refused to participate; the state lacked the political will to require them to participate; and the political conditions that generated these results are likely to be quite common. The Cleveland public schools were dysfunctional, so that pursuit of educational quality might lead some families to choose religious schools even if they objected to the religious content. The vouchers were small, more attractive to a school operating on a shoestring budget, and therefore, on average more attractive to religious private schools than to secular private schools. Because the political party that supports vouchers opposes taxes to fund government programs, the political conditions that generated such a small voucher also are likely to be quite general.

This is not the forum to consider all the issues relevant to ideal or reasonable or minimally acceptable implementation of a voucher plan. But a few points can be made in general terms. The encouragement to choose a religious school suggested by these factors is partially or entirely counterbalanced by the financial incentive still running the other way: vouchers in Cleveland required a copayment, and the political conditions that led to that requirement are likely to be quite general, but the public schools are always free. To say that religious schools are disqualified if they provide too good an education would create bizarre and perverse incentives.[190] An offer of better quality does not constrain choice; it expands choice. More generally, substantive neutrality is designed to implement liberty, and offering additional choices increases liberty. Students in Cleveland are better off with a choice of weak public schools and better private schools than with weak public schools only, even if they are not entirely happy with either choice.

---

of clergy or expanded to cover all funding programs); Berg & Laycock, *supra* note 5, at 229-30 (text at notes 12-26) (explaining that the opinion has two independent rationales, one of which would be confined to the training of clergy and one of which would reach all funding programs).

190. In the context of halfway houses for parolees, Judge Posner hyperbolically predicted a race to the bottom. If religious providers were disqualified whenever they offered higher quality programs than their secular competitors, Posner feared that they would reduce quality to remain eligible for vouchers, and secular private providers would reduce their quality to make their religious competition ineligible. *See* Freedom from Religion Found. v. McCallum, 324 F.3d 880, 884 (7th Cir. 2003). The fallacy here was to implicitly assume that providers care about nothing except the eligibility of religious providers. One need not go that far to reject a rule that vouchers can be used at bad religious schools but not at religious schools good enough to attract students on the basis of educational quality.

Even if you find these points utterly unpersuasive and remain convinced that the Cleveland plan steered students toward religious schools, you have to consider the alternative. Any encouragement to choose religious education would be a considerably smaller departure from substantive neutrality than the enormous encouragement to choose secular schools inherent in offering to spend thousands of dollars on each child who chooses a secular school but zero on each child who chooses a religious school.

Choice would be eliminated, and students would be forced into religious schools, if there were not enough seats in secular schools to meet the demand. This is not a problem in primary and secondary education, where the public schools guarantee a seat to all comers, but it is a problem in social services. I have testified that the Bush Administration's faith-based initiative is "a fraud" unless accompanied by enough funds to actually implement the original commitment to guarantee a secular alternative to every program beneficiary who requests one.[191] And a gerrymandered program that deliberately steered students to religious schools might well be unconstitutional, although there may be insuperable problems in creating a judicially-administrable rule to implement that intuition. This and other problems of implementing voucher plans require further analysis.

V. Conclusion

I doubt that I have persuaded many readers to abandon long-held positions on either funding religious schools or government-sponsored religious observances. I do hope that I have induced a bit of doubt and expanded lines of thought, and that I have helped clarify the source of disagreements among me, Professor Feldman, Professor Gey, and the Supreme Court. Getting government out of the way of religious choices, and minimizing the pressure that government brings to bear on either believers or nonbelievers, is an attractive goal. Achieving that goal may require rethinking some old assumptions.

---

191. *Constitutional Role of Faith-Based Organizations in Competitions for Federal Social Service Funds, Hearing Before the Subcommittee on the Constitution of the House Comm. on the Judiciary*, 107th Cong., Serial No. 17, at 48 (2001) (statement by Douglas Laycock) (early in questions and answers) ("[W]e will protect the beneficiary by really making available an alternate provider. You have got to really do that or this program is a fraud."); *see also id.* at 25 (part IV.C) (emphasizing in written statement that ready availability of secular providers is essential but difficult to provide in social service programs); *id.* at 55 ("If funding continues to shrink, this thing will not work at all.") (near end of questions and answers).

Remarks on Acceptance of National First Freedom Award from the Council for America's First Freedom

January 15, 2009

It is a pleasure and an honor to be recognized tonight. And it is very special to be recognized with Cole Durham and Sam Ericsson. They have done great work for many years, and I have had fruitful collaborations with each of them.

If I am remembered for anything after my career is over, I hope it will be that I avoided the Puritan mistake, and that I warned others against it. The Puritans came to Massachusetts for religious liberty, but they meant religious liberty only for themselves. Everyone else had the liberty to go anywhere in the world outside Massachusetts, and in the Puritan view, that was quite enough liberty for the likes of them.

We are not so transparent today about protecting liberty only for ourselves. We do not criminalize belief or expel dissenters from the jurisdiction. But most Americans still care far more about liberty for themselves than about liberty for those they disagree with. And this unfortunate bias is especially pronounced with respect to religious liberty.

For too many Americans, their view of religious liberty is driven by their view of religion. For some Americans, religion is a good thing, the most important and transcendent of all things, so religious liberty should be protected and religious observance should be promoted. For other Americans, religion is a bad thing, a source of repression and social conflict and even violence, so religion should be carefully contained and the rights of nonbelievers should be vigorously protected. Whether or not they put it so bluntly, many Americans resolve all debatable religious liberty questions either in favor of promoting religion or in favor of constraining religion. And some questions that really aren't debatable — they resolve some of those in the same biased way.

For other Americans, religious liberty should be protected with exceptions. John Locke had an exception for Catholics and atheists; many Americans today would have an exception for atheists and Muslims. And neo-pagans. And Santerians. And any religion that discriminates. And anybody else whose religion is too threatening to a favored secular interest.

Some of these errors come from unsophisticated people in the pews. Too often, they come from people who should know better — from activists and politicians and even religious liberty organizations.

I have devoted much of my career to defending the rights of religious believers to exercise their various religions free of all but essential government regulation. I have supported equal government funding for religious providers of education and social services, but I have opposed government funding for religion as such. I have supported freedom of religious speech, including in governmental buildings and in the public schools. But I have opposed government-sponsored prayers and government-sponsored religious displays, and I have opposed government asking school children to affirm that the nation is "under God."

Public opinion would say that some of these positions are pro-religion and some are anti-religion. In my view, public opinion would be mistaken. These positions are consistent; they are united by a commitment to minimizing government influence on the religious choices and commitments of the American people. No government pressure to believe, no government pressure to disbelieve, no government pressure *what* to believe — liberty for all in matters of religion.

Religious liberty is for everyone — for believers and nonbelievers of every stripe. If my career stands for anything, I hope it stands for that. The value of religious liberty is not religion, and the value of religious liberty is not secularism. The value of religious liberty is liberty — liberty with respect to choices and commitments that are of profound importance to many humans, and usually of much less importance to the state.

I hope that is why I have been honored tonight, and I hope that the many organizations active on religious liberty issues will think more carefully about the Puritan mistake, and whether they are maybe, just possibly, on some occasions, slipping into it.

B. Analytic and Descriptive Overviews

The articles in this Section try to assess what the legal situation with respect to religion actually is, as distinguished from what I think it ought to be. There are six scholarly works of various descriptions and three short popular accounts. The most ambitious attempt to survey the whole field is *Church and State in the United States* (2006).

The Long . . .

A Survey of Religious Liberty in the United States (1986) reviews the development of the law of religious liberty, with emphasis on the period after 1963 and with a brief history of developments before then. This is my most complete treatment of the era when the Supreme Court protected religious behavior from regulation (or at least claimed to) and sharply restricted financial aid to religious schools. The Court has since changed its mind about each of those issues.

Religious Freedom and International Human Rights in the United States Today (1998) reviews the principal sources of restrictions on religious liberty in the United States and the extent to which the United States does or does not comply with its obligations under international human rights agreements — recognizing that most of the world either flouts the religious liberty provisions of those agreements or interprets them very narrowly. The principal audience for this talk was the United Nations Special Rapporteur on Human Rights.

Round Table Discussion on International Human Rights Standards in the United States (1998) is a discussion immediately following the talk for the Special Rapporteur.

The Supreme Court and Religious Liberty (2000) reviews the Supreme Court cases for a group of practicing lawyers. This is my most complete treatment on how to argue for constitutional protection for free exercise under the Court's restrictive decision in *Employment Division v. Smith* (1990).

Church and State in the United States (2006) is a survey of the entire field, originally written for a French audience and limited to 10,000 words. For the French audience, I tried to assume nothing and explain everything; this is a review of American church-state law from the foundations. We have printed the English version and omitted the French translation.

A Conscripted Prophet's Guesses about the Future of Religious Liberty in America (2007) is an attempt, as of late 2007, to predict developments in religious liberty over the next twenty-five years. Of course this is a fool's errand, but the task was assigned, and I made some guesses that seemed reasonable at the time.

. . . and the Short

Religious Liberty: The Legal Rights of Religious Belief and Ministry (1988) is a short summary of the field written for Presbyterian women.

Vouching Towards Bethlehem (2002) is a short explanation of Establishment Clause issues, written principally for journalists.

Religious Liberty in America (2006) is a 3,000-word summary of the whole field, written principally for civil liberties lawyers who are not religion specialists. The tight word limit and broad scope combine to make this article terse and abrupt.

A Survey of Religious Liberty in the United States

47 Ohio State Law Journal 409 (1986)

This is a full survey of the field, divided into a short historical section that covers the founding to 1963, with emphasis on the persecutions of Mormons, Catholics, and Jehovah's Witnesses, and a longer section on legal doctrine that covers 1963 to 1986 in much more detail. 1986 turned out to be the turning point toward a dramatic change in the law of financial aid to religiously affiliated schools, and 1990 saw a dramatic change in the law of free exercise. So the rules have changed since this was written, and new rules generate new questions about how to implement those rules. The principal value of this article today is as a survey of how the law actually worked before these dramatic changes, back when Lemon v. Kurtzman *and* Wisconsin v. Yoder *were the leading cases. This is information that has gradually dropped out of books and articles written more recently.*

This article divides the field into seven major areas rather than the three highlighted in most of my more recent work. The seven divisions in this article identify real and sensible distinctions, and I did not yet have sufficient insight to see that some of them were simply subdivisions of more fundamental divisions.

As explained in the author's footnote, this grew out of my work for the Presbyterian Church (U.S.A.). The church's official statement from that project, which I helped to draft, is in Appendix I. This article is my own.

An earlier version of this Article was published in *Church and Society,* a publication of the Presbyterian Church (U.S.A.). That version was a background paper prepared for that church's Advisory Committee on Religious Liberty and Church-State Relations. I am grateful to the Committee and its staff for helpful suggestions on many earlier drafts. Neither the Committee nor any other organ of the Presbyterian Church (U.S.A.) was asked to adopt the background paper, and the views expressed are my own.

*　　　*　　　*

This is a brief survey of a large field. I have attempted to summarize the current law of religious liberty and how it developed. I hope that scholars in the field will find some new insights, but I am also writing for students and non-specialists who need a thorough overview. Professor Kurland completed the last such survey in 1961.[1] Much of the law of conscientious objection, much of the law of government aid to church schools, and virtually all the law of school prayer is more recent than that. Expanding church activities have collided with expanding government regulation, producing new issues of church autonomy. Another wave of new and unpopular religions has renewed controversy over limits on the right to proselytize. Politically active fundamentalists have steadily attacked the Supreme Court's Establishment Clause jurisprudence, and a new generation of scholars has attacked the historical foundations of that jurisprudence. The Reagan Administration has endorsed these attacks with gusto. The cumulative result is that the Supreme Court now is deciding several religious liberty cases each Term, and the great bulk of its religious liberty cases have been decided since 1961. Every time I teach my seminar on religious liberty, I am struck by the lack of any introductory overview to assign or recommend to students. This is an attempt to fill that gap.

Unlike Professor Kurland, I offer no single theory to answer all religious liberty questions.[2] I begin with a strong commitment to religious liberty and a belief that constitutional text should be mined for all the meaning it can yield.[3] It follows that I take the Free Exercise and Establishment Clauses with equal seriousness, and I therefore believe that government neutrality towards religion is a good first approximation for the meaning of the two clauses.[4] But

1. Philip Kurland, *Of Church and State and the Supreme Court*, 29 U. Chi. L. Rev. 1 (1961).

2. Kurland proposed the following "simple" principle: "the freedom and separation clauses [by which he means the Free Exercise and Establishment Clauses] should be read as stating a single precept: that government cannot utilize religion as a standard for action or inaction because these clauses, read together as they should be, prohibit classification in terms of religion either to confer a benefit or to impose a burden." *Id.* at 96. "That proposition met with almost uniform rejection." Philip Kurland, *The Irrelevance of the Constitution: The Religion Clauses of the First Amendment and the Supreme Court*, 24 Vill. L. Rev. 3, 24 (1978).

3. For a defense of textualism, see Douglas Laycock, *Taking Constitutions Seriously: A Theory of Judicial Review*, 59 Tex. L. Rev. 343 (1981).

4. *See generally* Douglas Laycock, *Equal Access and Moments of Silence: The Equal Status of Religious Speech by Private Speakers*, 81 Nw. L. Rev. 1 (1986); Douglas Laycock, *Towards a General Theory of the Religion Clauses: The Case of Church Labor Relations and the Right to Church Autonomy*, 81 Colum. L. Rev. 1373 (1981).

neutrality is not self-defining, and to work out the detailed applications of those clauses is a complex task. I do provide an analytic framework for each major issue or group of decisions. Sometimes my analytic framework closely tracks the Supreme Court's own explanations of its work. On other issues, when the Court's decisions do not fit together well, my analytic framework is largely independent of anything the Court actually has said. I hope that these analytic frameworks will be useful even after the decisions discussed here are superseded by subsequent decisions. Parts I and II carry the story up to 1963, with topics arranged in roughly chronological order. Part III reviews developments since 1963 in much greater detail and is organized topically.

I. Origins

By the end of the Revolution, Americans were approaching consensus in support of religious toleration. There was also substantial support for disestablishment, but that was more controversial, and some states still had formally established churches. Several state constitutions written in the revolutionary and immediate post-revolutionary period contained bills of rights that guaranteed free exercise, nonestablishment, or both.[5]

A. The Debates in Virginia

The most significant developments prior to the Federal constitution occurred in Virginia, where disestablishment of the Anglican church was a recurring legislative issue from 1776 to 1786.[6] James Madison and Thomas Jefferson were the most prominent proponents of disestablishment. In the winter of 1785-86, after Jefferson became the American ambassador to France, Madison won a complete victory. Three years later, in 1789, Madison was the principal drafter and sponsor of the Religion Clauses of the First Amendment. Thus, the Supreme Court has often looked to Madison's views, as expressed in the debates in Virginia, to inform its understanding of those clauses, particularly the Establishment Clause. Therefore, a brief review of the dispute in Virginia is necessary.

5. For a generally excellent overview of the colonial and constitution-making periods, see THOMAS CURRY, THE FIRST FREEDOM: CHURCH AND STATE IN AMERICA TO THE PASSAGE OF THE FIRST AMENDMENT (1986).

6. These developments are reviewed in detail in THOMAS BUCKLEY, CHURCH AND STATE IN REVOLUTIONARY VIRGINIA, 1776-1787 (1977).

Before 1777, all Virginians were taxed to support Anglican ministers' salaries, although only half the population was Anglican. In 1776 the legislature voted to suspend the tax. Subsequent debates centered on bills to reinstate it. In 1784, establishment supporters introduced a bill that was not limited to Anglicans. It would have imposed a tax to support all Christian ministers, and it would have allowed each taxpayer to designate the church that would receive his tax. This approach won support from some non-Anglican denominations, and the bill passed second reading in the fall.

Madison was able to delay the bill's final consideration until the new legislature convened in the fall of 1785. In the meantime, he published his *Memorial and Remonstrance Against Religious Assessments,*[7] articulating his argument against any form of establishment. Many other petitions also opposed the bill, and all the large non-Anglican denominations now opposed it. When the legislature reconvened, the bill to tax for the support of ministers died without a vote. In its place, the legislature enacted the Bill for Establishing Religious Freedom — first introduced by Thomas Jefferson in 1779 and unsuccessfully introduced in each intervening legislature. The Bill for Establishing Religious Freedom enacted both free exercise and disestablishment in Virginia.

B. The Framing of the First Amendment

In contrast to the lengthy battle in Virginia, the debates about religion during the drafting of the federal constitution were brief and uninformative. The Constitution was proposed in 1787 without a bill of rights. The only religious reference was the Test Oath Clause: "No religious Test shall ever be required as a Qualification to any Office of public Trust under the United States."[8]

The lack of a bill of rights was a principal source of opposition to the proposed Constitution. Some of the Constitution's supporters promised to add a bill of rights by amendment. By July of 1788 eleven states had ratified the new Constitution, but five had appended requests for amendments to their ratifications. Three of the five proposed freedom-of-religion clauses.

The First Congress was elected that fall and met for the first time in the spring of 1789. Madison promptly moved to consolidate support for the new Constitution by proposing the promised amendments. The Religion Clauses were included in what became the First Amendment. The clauses went

---

7. Reprinted in THE COMPLETE MADISON 299-306 (Saul K. Padover ed. 1953).
8. U.S. CONST. art. VI, cl. 3.

through several drafts, with little or no explanation for various wording changes. Some of the changes appear to have been matters of style without substantive significance. Others reflected infighting between federalists and antifederalists about whether the new government was a nation or a federation. But some reflect clear differences in meaning, and it is possible to draw inferences about the drafters' intent by analyzing the versions that were rejected.

Some supporters of government aid to religion argue that the Supreme Court's decisions interpreting the Establishment Clause are fundamentally wrong. In the view of these critics the Establishment Clause had a narrow and specific purpose: to prevent government from favoring one religion over another, while permitting nonpreferential government support for religion generally.[9] A lawyer trying to draft that view of the Establishment Clause might write something like this: "Congress shall make no law establishing one Religious Sect or Society in preference to others, nor shall the rights of conscience be infringed."

In fact, that is exactly how it was written in 1789 by members of the First Senate. The Senate tentatively adopted that version on September 3.[10] But later in the day the Senators thought better of it and adopted a draft that spoke of religion generically: "Congress shall make no law establishing Religion, or prohibiting the free exercise thereof."[11]

The Senate rejected two other drafts that were unambiguously limited to preferential aid.[12] But on September 9 the Senate changed its mind again and adopted the narrowest version of the Establishment Clause considered by either House: "Congress shall make no law establishing articles of faith or a mode of worship, or prohibiting the free exercise of religion."[13]

The House rejected that version. It appointed Madison and two others to a

9. Wallace v. Jaffree, 472 U.S. 38, 94-100 (1985) (Rehnquist, J., dissenting); ROBERT CORD, SEPARATION OF CHURCH AND STATE: HISTORICAL FACT AND CURRENT FICTION 8-12 (1982); MICHAEL MALBIN, RELIGION AND POLITICS: THE INTENTIONS OF THE AUTHORS OF THE FIRST AMENDMENT (1978). For a more detailed response to these critics, see Douglas Laycock, *"Non-Preferential" Aid to Religion: A False Claim About Original Intent*, 27 WM. & MARY L. REV. 875 (1986).

10. 1 DOCUMENTARY HISTORY OF THE FIRST FEDERAL CONGRESS OF THE UNITED STATES OF AMERICA 136, 151 (Linda Grant De Pauw ed. 1972) (Senate Legislative Journal).

11. *Id.*

12. *Id.* at 151. ("Congress shall not make any law, infringing the rights of conscience, or establishing any Religious Sect or Society." "Congress shall make no law establishing any particular denomination of religion in preference to another, or prohibiting the free exercise thereof, nor shall the rights of conscience be infringed.").

13. *Id.* at 166.

conference committee[14] that produced the version ultimately ratified as the first two clauses of the First Amendment: "Congress shall make no law respecting an establishment of religion, or prohibiting the free exercise thereof."[15]

The amendment actually adopted is one of the broadest versions considered by either House. It speaks generically of "religion," not "a religion," "a national religion," "one sect or society," or "any particular denomination of religion," another phrase appearing in a rejected Senate draft. Read in light of the alternatives that Congress considered and rejected, the textual inference is plain. The language rejected would have permitted government to support religion generically while trying to be neutral among religions; the adopted language does not. The adopted language appears to require the government to be entirely neutral towards religion.

The legislative history does not add much to our understanding. The Senate met in secret and its debates were not recorded; we have only the Journal entries recording its votes. There was only one recorded debate in the House. There is no verbatim record and the reporter's notes take slightly less than two columns in the Annals of Congress.[16] This debate was before any of the events in the Senate and at the very beginning of consideration in the House. The debate concerned a committee draft that was somewhat narrower than the amendment ultimately adopted. The draft provided: "No religion shall be established by law, nor shall the equal rights of conscience be infringed."[17]

In debate, Mr. Sylvester expressed concern that the amendment "might have a tendency to abolish religion altogether."[18] Mr. Huntington feared the amendment would make it impossible for federal courts to enforce state taxes for the support of churches.[19] Huntington also hoped the amendment would not "patronize those who professed no religion at all."[20] Madison tried to reassure the doubters by saying the amendment meant that "Congress should not establish a religion, and enforce the legal observation of it by law."[21]

Some who favor nonpreferential aid to religion have sought support for their position from Madison's brief description of this preliminary draft in the

14. *Id.* at 181.

15. 3 Documentary History of the First Federal Congress of the United States of America 228 (House Legislative Journal).

16. 1 Annals of Congress 757-59 (Aug. 15, 1789).

17. *Id.* at 57.

18. *Id.*

19. *Id.* at 758.

20. *Id.*

21. *Id.*

House. But even they concede that the Establishment Clause means more than he mentioned. If Congress appropriated one million dollars to support the Presbyterian Church (U.S.A.), it would not be enforcing the "observation" of Presbyterianism by law. But the appropriation would be preferential aid, unconstitutional even under the view that nonpreferential aid to religion is permitted. If Madison's statement described the entire meaning of the clause, the Senate draft forbidding uniform "articles of faith or a mode of worship" would have captured the meaning perfectly. But that draft was rejected.

An important new book by Reverend Curry argues that the Framers did not understand the difference between preferential and nonpreferential aid to religion and that their choice among competing drafts of the Establishment Clause reflected choices about style rather than principle.[22] Curry supports this position with various quotations in which politicians opposed to schemes of nonpreferential aid denounced them as preferential.

My own sense of the evidence is that Curry's examples show only that political rhetoric was as loose then as it is now.[23] The debates in Virginia in 1785-86 focused squarely on the choice between banning all state aid to religion and banning only preferential aid. It is hard to believe the First Congress could not understand that distinction three years later. I see no sufficient reason to presume that the Framers did not understand what they were doing when they repeatedly rejected drafts that would have permitted nonpreferential aid. Rejecting those drafts was consistent with Madison's successful fight against government support for all churches in Virginia three years before. Nothing in the brief recorded debate is inconsistent with the natural inference that those drafts were rejected because they did not express the intention of a majority of the First Congress.

It is important to understand that Curry's argument does little to support the attack on the Supreme Court decisions that invalidate nonpreferential aid. The Court's critics argue that the Framers specifically intended to permit nonpreferential aid. If they didn't understand the difference between preferential and nonpreferential aid they can hardly have intended to forbid one and permit the other. The most Curry shows is that the choice was left to a later generation. If the Framers did understand the distinction, which seems likely, the clear difference between the draft they adopted and the drafts they rejected shows that they intended to forbid both preferential and nonpreferential aid.

---

22. CURRY, *supra* note 5, at 207-15.

23. For a more thorough response to Curry, see Laycock, *supra* note 9, at 902-10 (text at notes 148-75).

C. The Early Practice of the Government

Government practice during the Framers' generation provides another source for understanding the meaning of the Religion Clauses. The government did things in that period that supported religion.[24] The First Congress appointed chaplains, and even Madison acquiesced. Presidents Washington, Adams, and Madison issued Thanksgiving proclamations, although Madison did so only in time of war and at the request of Congress, and his proclamations merely invited citizens so disposed to unite their prayers on a single day. President Jefferson refused to issue Thanksgiving proclamations, believing them to be an establishment of religion. In retirement, Madison concluded that both the congressional chaplains and the Thanksgiving proclamations had violated the Establishment Clause.

Congress also subsidized missionary work among the Indians. Even President Jefferson signed a treaty agreeing to provide a church building and a Catholic priest to the Kaskaskia Indians. Those missionaries were expected to provide secular as well as religious teaching, but there is no doubt that religious teaching was an accepted part of their mission. Congress continued to support sectarian education on Indian reservations until 1898. These practices were uncontroversial in a homogeneous Protestant society, and there is little evidence the Framers thought about their relationship to the Establishment Clause.[25]

D. The Fourteenth Amendment

As originally adopted the Religion Clauses did not bind the states. The First Amendment refers only to Congress. In *Barron v. Mayor of Baltimore,*[26] the Supreme Court decided that the protections of the whole Bill of Rights were good only against the United States and not against state or local governments. Some states guaranteed free exercise and disestablishment in their own constitutions, but some did not. Formally established churches persisted in Massachusetts and South Carolina until the 1830s. In 1842 the city of New Orleans made it unlawful to expose dead bodies to public view. A Roman Catholic priest was convicted of violating the ordinance when he blessed the deceased at a funeral mass. The Supreme Court upheld his conviction in

24. These events are reviewed in great detail in CORD, *supra* note 9, at 20-80.
25. See Laycock, *supra* note 9, at 913-19 (text at notes 193-228).
26. 32 U.S. (7 Pet.) 243 (1833).

Permoli v. City of New Orleans.[27] The First Amendment applied only to the federal government; Father Permoli had to look to Louisiana law for protection against New Orleans.

At the end of the Civil War Congress proposed and the states ratified the Fourteenth Amendment. Section 1 of that amendment provides in part as follows:

> No state shall make or enforce any law which shall abridge the privileges or immunities of citizens of the United States; nor shall any State deprive any person of life, liberty, or property, without due process of law; nor deny to any person within its jurisdiction the equal protection of the laws.[28]

This amendment was intended to do what the Bill of Rights had not done — to give individual citizens federally enforceable constitutional rights against the states. The Supreme Court has held that those rights include all the rights protected against the federal government by the Free Exercise and Establishment Clauses.[29] The most plausible way to reach that conclusion would be to say that free exercise and nonestablishment are privileges and immunities protected by the first clause of the Fourteenth Amendment,[30] but that was not the Court's way. It held instead that state actions establishing religion or interfering with its free exercise infringe upon liberty without due process of law.

A persistent minority has criticized the Court's interpretation of the Fourteenth Amendment. This minority argues that Congress did not intend to change *Barron v. Baltimore* or *Permoli v. New Orleans* and that there is still no federal protection against state interference with religious liberty.[31] Edwin Meese, the incumbent Attorney General of the United States, takes this view.[32] It is occasionally claimed that the legislative history of the Fourteenth Amendment provides absolutely no support for the Court's view. That claim is simply false: On the floor of the Senate, the amendment's principal sponsor said that the Privileges and Immunities Clause would make the Bill of

27. 44 U.S. (3 How.) 589 (1845).

28. U.S. Const. amend. XIV, § 1.

29. Everson v. Board of Educ., 330 U.S. 1, 8 (1947); Cantwell v. Connecticut, 310 U.S. 296, 303-04 (1940).

30. See John Ely, Democracy and Distrust 22-30 (1980); Laycock, *supra* note 3, at 347-49.

31. The most prominent statement of the view that the Bill of Rights does not apply to the states is Raoul Berger, Government by Judiciary: The Transformation of the Fourteenth Amendment (1977).

32. Ed Meese, *Toward a Jurisprudence of Original Intention*, 2 Benchmark 1, 4-5 (1986).

Rights binding on the states.[33] But the legislative history may not be conclusive because there is also conflicting evidence.[34]

What is conclusive, in my view, is the combined effect of the amendment's language, the sponsor's explanation, the lessons of the Civil War, and the resulting understanding of our governmental structure. In 1789 the federal government was new and fearsome; the Framers perceived it as the principal threat to liberty. The Civil War and its aftermath made clear that state governments can be as much a threat to liberty as the federal government. It would be intolerable to allow individual states the choice to respect religious liberty or not; that right must be guaranteed throughout the land and against government intrusion at all levels. It is textually implausible to suggest that free exercise of religion and freedom from establishment are not privileges and immunities of citizens of the United States. Whether the Supreme Court uses the Due Process Clause or the Privileges and Immunities Clause, the result is the same.

Prohibiting state religious establishments presents one question not raised by other liberties now protected against the states. The Establishment Clause prohibits any law "respecting an establishment of religion" and not merely any law "establishing religion." The chosen language appears to forbid not just formal establishments, but any law tending toward an establishment.[35] But it is likely that this language also had another purpose. Probably one of the original purposes of the Establishment Clause was to prevent the federal government from interfering with the formal religious establishments that still existed in some states. Thus the Establishment Clause affirmatively protected state establishments of religion even as it prohibited such action to Congress. This aspect of the clause implemented the 1789 view of federalism, but it cannot survive the 1868 view of federalism. Protecting state establishments would be wholly inconsistent with the premise of the Fourteenth Amendment — to protect individual rights against state violations. As it applies to the states through the Fourteenth Amendment, the Establishment Clause can mean only that the states may not establish religion. It is logically impossible to apply the federalism aspect of the clause to the states.

Whatever the theoretical questions, it is firmly settled in the case law that both free exercise and nonestablishment are protected from violations by state and local governments. The Supreme Court has persistently rejected all attacks on this conclusion.[36] There is no prospect that it will change its mind.

33. Cong. Globe, 39th Cong., 1st Sess. 2765-66 (1866) (remarks of Sen. Howard).
34. The legislative history and subsequent debate are briefly reviewed in Ely, *supra* note 30, at 24-30.
35. Lemon v. Kurtzman, 403 U.S. 602, 612 (1971).
36. Wallace v. Jaffree, 472 U.S. 38, 49-55 (1985).

II. Developments to 1963

A. *The Mormon Cases*

The Supreme Court's first serious encounter with the Religion Clauses arose out of the nineteenth-century persecution of the Mormons. The early Mormons in the east and midwest encountered hostility from both government and private citizens. Their prophet, Joseph Smith, was murdered by a mob while imprisoned in an Illinois jail.[37] In 1847, the Mormons fled to Utah. They hoped that, isolated and surrounded by desert, they would be left alone.[38]

In 1848, the treaty ending the war with Mexico made Utah a territory of the United States, subject to the power of Congress. In the 1860s, Congress enacted a series of laws against polygamy, obviously directed at the Mormons.[39] *Reynolds v. United States*[40] was a criminal prosecution under those laws. The Supreme Court affirmed Reynolds' conviction, rejecting his claim that polygamy was an exercise of his religion protected from congressional interference by the First Amendment. The Court said that the Free Exercise Clause protected his right to believe, but not his right to act on those beliefs.

Unfortunately for the Mormons, the Court would not protect even their right to believe. In *Davis v. Beason,*[41] the Court upheld an Idaho territorial statute that required all voters to sign an oath swearing that they were not a member of any organization that taught polygamy or celestial marriage. In effect, voters had to swear that they were not Mormons. The law was indistinguishable from Stuart test oaths imposing civil disabilities on English Catholics.[42] In *Late Corporation of the Church of Jesus Christ of Latter-Day Saints v. United*

---

37. LEONARD ARRINGTON, BRIGHAM YOUNG: AMERICAN MOSES 111 (1985).

38. *Id.* at 128.

39. Act of July 1, 1862, 37th Cong., 2d Sess., ch. 126, 12 Stat. 501 (1862). For a variety of reasons, legislation and enforcement did not promptly follow American acquisition of Utah. The Mormons proclaimed the Kingdom of Deseret and did not recognize American authority until threatened with military force in 1858. PAGE SMITH, THE NATION COMES OF AGE 562-66 (1981). By then, Congressional power to ban polygamy had become entangled in the bitter debate over slavery in the territories. The Republican platform linked slavery and polygamy as "twin relics of barbarism," asserting Congressional power to ban both in the territories. DON FEHRENBACHER, THE DRED SCOTT CASE 202 (1978). But no polygamy legislation was passed until the representatives of seceding states had withdrawn from Congress. Serious efforts at enforcement then had to await the end of the Civil War.

40. 98 U.S. 145 (1878).

41. 133 U.S. 333 (1890).

42. Test Act, 1673, 25 Car. II, ch. 2.

States,[43] the Court also upheld government confiscation of all the church's property. The Religion Clauses had failed at their most fundamental task: they had failed to prevent government persecution of a religious minority.

The Court upheld a conviction of a religiously motivated polygamist as recently as 1946.[44] Presumably it would do so today,[45] although the result would be difficult to reconcile with the modern law of conscientious objection[46] and of constitutional protection for autonomy in matters of sex and the family.[47]

Davis v. Beason, the test oath case, was presumably overruled in *Torcaso v. Watkins.*[48] The Maryland law in *Torcaso* required all public office holders to swear that they believed in God. Torcaso refused, and the Supreme Court held the requirement unconstitutional. *Davis* was not mentioned, and it could conceivably be distinguished, but not on any intellectually respectable ground.

B. The Catholic Experience

Roman Catholics have experienced hostility throughout our history, although little important constitutional litigation has resulted. Nineteenth-century hostility toward Catholics was partly religious, partly ethnic, and partly hostility to recent immigrants.[49] Catholicism was viewed as a threat to American liberties. The mid-nineteenth century was marked by violence between Protestant and Catholic mobs. Protestant mobs in Philadelphia burned Catholic churches in 1844.[50] The "Know Nothing" party, the political expression of the Protestant nativist movement, was explicitly anti-Catholic and anti-immigrant. It swept elections in eight states in the 1850s.[51]

43. 136 U.S. 1 (1890).

44. Cleveland v. United States, 329 U.S. 14 (1946).

45. A court of appeals rejected a renewed challenge to polygamy laws in Potter v. Murray City, 760 F.2d 1065 (10th Cir. 1985).

46. The modern law of conscientious objection is reviewed in part III, section A, *infra.*

47. The right to autonomy in matters of sex and family is developed in such cases as Moore v. City of East Cleveland, 431 U.S. 494 (1977) (upholding the right of cousins to live together with their grandmother); Roe v. Wade, 410 U.S. 113 (1973) (upholding a right to abortion); Eisenstadt v. Baird, 405 U.S. 438 (1972) (upholding a right to contraception for unmarried individuals); and Griswold v. Connecticut, 381 U.S. 479 (1965) (upholding a right to contraception for married couples).

48. 367 U.S. 488 (1961).

49. The Catholic experience in this country is reviewed in ANSON STOKES, CHURCH AND STATE IN THE UNITED STATES 784-853 (1950).

50. *Id.* at 830-35.

51. *Id.* at 836-37.

Catholics also were victimized by a de facto Protestant establishment. When the states began to create public schools in the nineteenth century, many of those schools openly taught Protestant Christianity and read from the King James version of the Bible. The King James version omits some books included in the Catholic canon. Perhaps more important, it is a Protestant translation, and differences in translations were keenly felt. Catholics viewed the public schools and the "Protestant Bible" as a threat to their children's faith and responded by creating their own schools, many more than any other denomination.[52]

Anti-Catholicism did not end with the turn of the century. Oregon banned private schools in the wake of World War I, a move with enormous impact on Catholics. The Oregon law was invalidated in *Pierce v. Society of Sisters of the Holy Names of Jesus & Mary*,[53] a case that also involved secular schools and was not decided on religious liberty grounds. A minority of Protestants openly opposed John F. Kennedy in 1960 because of his Catholicism. The 1963 Presbyterian policy statement on church-state relations found it necessary to consider whether Presbyterians should evaluate the "fitness of candidates for public office on the basis of religious affiliation," a roundabout way of asking whether Presbyterians could vote for Catholic candidates.[54] The answer was yes, but with a caveat that Presbyterians should not vote for any candidate who supported government financial aid to religious schools. Thus, that mainstream and generally liberal[55] Protestant denomination had no objection to Catholic candidates in principle, but it encouraged single-issue voting that disqualified most of them in practice.

At approximately the same time, a fundamentalist press published a five-hundred page hate tract proposing that Catholics be barred from teaching in the public schools or holding high public office.[56] The book described Catholicism as a "totalitarian system" that threatened American freedoms and was more dangerous than Communism because "it covers its real nature with a

52. *Id.* at 822-25.

53. 268 U.S. 510 (1925).

54. THE UNITED PRESBYTERIAN CHURCH IN THE UNITED STATES OF AMERICA, RELATIONS BETWEEN CHURCH AND STATE IN THE UNITED STATES OF AMERICA 8-9 (1963).

55. The same policy statement took positions opposing school prayer, *id.* at 6-7, opposing municipal Christmas displays, *id.* at 7-8, opposing censorship of books and movies, *id.* at 13, supporting no-fault divorce, *id.* at 14, opposing special privileges for the clergy, including draft exemption, *id.* at 16-17, and questioning government pay for military chaplains, *id.* at 18.

56. LORRAINE BOETTNER, ROMAN CATHOLICISM 372, 421 (1962). A similar and influential book is PAUL BLANSHARD, AMERICAN FREEDOM AND CATHOLIC POWER (1949). Blanshard's book is described in Phillip E. Johnson, *Concepts and Compromise in First Amendment Religious Doctrine*, 72 CAL. L. REV. 817, 843-44 (1984).

cloak of religion."[57] Justice Douglas quoted this book in a 1971 opinion,[58] and a court of appeals quoted the book again in 1977.[59] The Ku Klux Klan and similar hate groups continue to attack Catholics and Jews as well as blacks.

C. The Jehovah's Witness Cases and the Right to Proselytize

Like the Mormons, the Jehovah's Witnesses in the 1930s and 1940s were an intensely unpopular new religion. Their own doctrines were intolerant, especially of Catholics, and they preached those doctrines aggressively. They proselytized on street corners and door-to-door. All over the country, cities tried to stop the Jehovah's Witnesses from proselytizing. Many cities invoked ordinances requiring a license to solicit. The cities had no intention of granting licenses to Jehovah's Witnesses. Moreover, the Witnesses conscientiously objected to applying for a license; they thought the state had no right to license religious teaching. The cities tried many other tactics as well, prosecuting Jehovah's Witnesses under a wide variety of statutes. The Witnesses aggressively litigated these prosecutions, producing a large number of cases in the Supreme Court. For the most part, the Witnesses won. Many of these cases were decided under the Free Speech Clause instead of the Free Exercise Clause; religious speech is protected by both.[60]

The Court struck down licensing laws that gave public officials any discretion to decide who could solicit door-to-door and who could not.[61] It struck down outright bans on door-to-door distribution of literature.[62] It struck down taxes on the sale of Witness literature.[63] It struck down bans on the use of loudspeakers.[64] It struck down prohibitions on proselytizing or holding religious services in public parks.[65] It overturned breach of peace convictions of Witnesses who promulgated anti-Catholic propaganda in a Catholic neighborhood.[66]

57. BOETTNER, *supra* note 56, at 3.

58. Lemon v. Kurtzman, 403 U.S. 602, 635 n.20 (1971) (Douglas, J., concurring).

59. Catholic Bishop v. NLRB, 559 F.2d 1112, 1122 n.12 (7th Cir. 1977), *aff'd on other grounds,* 440 U.S. 490 (1979).

60. Largent v. Texas, 318 U.S. 418, 422 (1943).

61. Lovell v. City of Griffin, 303 U.S. 444 (1938).

62. Martin v. City of Struthers, 319 U.S. 141 (1943).

63. Murdock v. Pennsylvania, 319 U.S. 105 (1943).

64. Saia v. New York, 334 U.S. 558 (1948).

65. Fowler v. Rhode Island, 345 U.S. 67 (1953).

66. Cantwell v. Connecticut, 310 U.S. 296 (1940).

However, the Court upheld some regulation of proselytizing. It affirmed the conviction of a Jehovah's Witness who cursed a police officer, denying First Amendment protection to "fighting words" that tended to provoke an immediate retaliatory response.[67] It upheld application of the child labor laws to Witnesses who allowed their children to help distribute religious literature.[68] It upheld restrictions on the sound level produced by loudspeakers.[69] And it upheld a nondiscriminatory licensing requirement for religious services in public parks.[70]

Another controversy involving Jehovah's Witnesses in this period turned on compulsory flag salutes in public schools. The witnesses believed that saluting the flag and pledging allegiance to it violated the scriptural commandment not to worship graven images. In 1940, the Court held that the Free Exercise Clause did not exempt religiously motivated conscientious objectors from schoolroom flag salutes.[71] In 1943, after a change in personnel and some changes of mind, the Court invalidated compulsory flag salutes on free speech grounds. The Court held that no one can be forced to affirm views he does not believe, whether or not the objection is religiously based.[72]

Perhaps the most difficult case in this period was *United States v. Ballard*,[73] a criminal prosecution for fraud. The Ballards claimed to have received divine revelations and miraculous powers. Sometimes they claimed to be the reincarnation of Christ, St. Germain, Joan of Arc, George Washington, and other figures. They claimed to have performed miraculous cures. They solicited contributions on the strength of these representations and sold books and records alleged to have supernatural powers. In their own defense, they noted that other religions made similar claims, including Christianity. They argued that if it is legal to solicit money on the strength of ancient miracles, it can not be illegal to solicit money on the strength of contemporary miracles.

The trial judge instructed the jury not to consider whether the Ballards' claims were true, but to consider only whether the Ballards really believed their own claims. So instructed, the jury found them guilty. The court of appeals reversed, holding that the jury should have been instructed to find

67. Chaplinsky v. New Hampshire, 315 U.S. 568 (1942).

68. Prince v. Massachusetts, 321 U.S. 158 (1944).

69. Kovacs v. Cooper, 336 U.S. 77 (1949).

70. Poulos v. New Hampshire, 345 U.S. 395 (1953).

71. Minersville School Dist. v. Gobitis, 310 U.S. 586 (1940).

72. West Virginia Bd. of Educ. v. Barnette, 319 U.S. 624 (1943).

73. 322 U.S. 78 (1944). For an insightful analysis, see John Mansfield, *The Religion Clauses of the First Amendment and the Philosophy of the Constitution*, 72 CAL. L. REV. 847, 869-77 (1984).

whether the claims were true. The Supreme Court reversed again, holding that no secular court could pass on the truth of religious claims. But the Court did not decide whether the trial court had properly instructed the jury to consider whether defendants really believed their own claims. Instead, it sent the case back to the court of appeals for further consideration.

Justices Stone, Roberts, and Frankfurter would have sustained the convictions and the trial court's original instruction. Justice Jackson would have dismissed the prosecution. He thought it impossible to determine whether defendants really believed their claims without determining whether they were true, that literal truth was often not the point of religion, and that such prosecutions could easily degenerate into persecution of minority religions. He "would have done with this business of examining other people's faiths."[74] But he conceded that any immunity from fraud prosecutions was limited to matters of faith; the Ballards could not solicit money to build a church and spend it on high living for themselves.

The underlying issue in *Ballard* remains unresolved. The convictions eventually were reversed on the ground that women had been excluded from the jury,[75] and the Court has never decided whether jurors can decide whether religious solicitors really believe their own claims. But Justice Jackson's view seems to have prevailed in practice. Entrepreneurial preachers continue to solicit money and promise miracles, but prosecutions have been rare. Civil fraud suits against the Church of Scientology are the most notable exceptions.[76]

D. The Beginnings of Establishment Clause Doctrine

1. Financial Aid

The first significant Establishment Clause case in the Supreme Court was *Bradfield v. Roberts*,[77] upholding federal payments to a Catholic hospital for the care of indigents. The Court reasoned that the government was entitled to purchase medical care for its wards and that the religion of those who ran the hospital was wholly irrelevant.

In 1908 the Court approved the use of Indian trust funds to support

---

74. 322 U.S. at 95.

75. Ballard v. United States, 329 U.S. 187 (1946).

76. *E.g.*, Christofferson v. Church of Scientology, 5 Religious Freedom Rep. 126 (Multnomah County Cir. Ct., Or. 1985).

77. 175 U.S. 291 (1899).

Catholic schools for Sioux Indians.[78] The decision's main premise was that the trust funds belonged to the Indians and were merely managed by the federal government; the Indians were entitled to pick their own schools and teachers. Citing *Bradfield,* the Court also said that the payments clearly were constitutional. The implication seems to be that even government money could have been spent — that when the government purchases services, the religious affiliation of the provider is irrelevant and that educational services are no different than medical services.

The most important Establishment Clause case is *Everson v. Board of Education,* decided in 1947.[79] A closely divided Court upheld a program under which state-funded buses transported students to their schools. The program covered both public and parochial schools. The majority viewed transportation to schools as a secular public service that the state could provide to all; the dissenters thought the program gave an impermissible state subsidy to religious education.

The holding in *Everson* is still good law. But the case is more important for its general approach. *Everson* was the first case to hold that the Establishment Clause is binding on the states, and the first case to explore the history of the Establishment Clause. All nine justices agreed that the Establishment Clause embodies Madison's approach to disestablishment, and thus all nine agreed that the clause forbids government aid to religion, even though they divided on the application of these principles to the facts in *Everson.* Despite many doctrinal twists and turns, the Court has adhered to those basic principles ever since.

2. Released Time

The next problem before the Court was "released-time" programs: programs under which public schools released students for religious education by their own churches during regular school hours. Students who chose not to participate were not free to leave, but neither could their secular education continue. In 1948, the Court struck down such programs in *Illinois ex rel. McCollum v. Board of Education.*[80] The Court reasoned that the program invoked the power of the truant officer to coerce students to go to church.

The Court's reasoning would not have invalidated programs known as

---

78. Quick Bear v. Leupp, 210 U.S. 50 (1908).
79. 330 U.S. 1 (1947).
80. 333 U.S. 203 (1948).

"dismissed-time," in which the school let students out early one day each week to accommodate religious instruction. Under dismissed-time programs, students who chose not to participate in religious instruction could go about their business; they would not be detained at school. The sponsors of released-time programs argued that dismissed-time was inadequate because it did not incorporate religious instruction into the children's regular working day. Their argument made the Court's point — released-time programs used the coercive power of the compulsory school attendance laws to increase attendance at religious instruction. Released-time plans worked better than dismissed-time plans precisely to the extent that marginal believers or nonbelievers found religious education more attractive than sitting in school with little or nothing to do. Thus, the widespread protest against *McCollum* largely vindicated the Court's judgment.

Even so, the Court retreated in *Zorach v. Clauson.*[81] *Zorach* was identical to *McCollum* in every way but one. In *McCollum,* the ministers came to the school and gave religious instruction on school property; in *Zorach,* the students were released to go to their separate churches. That had nothing to do with the rationale of *McCollum;* in each case, students were detained without purpose unless they went to church. But the majority seized on the incidental distinction to rewrite *McCollum.* The Court said that the only problem in *McCollum* was that religious instruction took place on public property; released-time programs were permissible if the religious instruction took place on private property.

3. Sunday Closing Laws

In 1961 the Court upheld several states' Sunday closing laws.[82] The Court reasoned that Sunday closing laws had come to serve secular as well as religious purposes by providing a uniform day of rest when families could be together. It seemed irrelevant to the Court that this purpose coincided with the doctrines of some religions. The Court also held that the Sunday closing laws did not violate the rights of Orthodox Jews whose religion compelled them to close on Saturday as well.[83]

---

81. 343 U.S. 306 (1952).
82. McGowan v. Maryland, 366 U.S. 420 (1961); Two Guys, Inc. v. McGinley, 366 U.S. 582 (1961); Braunfeld v. Brown, 366 U.S. 599 (1961); Gallagher v. Crown Kosher Super Mkt., 366 U.S. 617 (1961).
83. Braunfeld v. Brown, 366 U.S. 599 (1961).

4. School Prayer

The Court had its first encounter with school prayer the following year. The case was *Engel v. Vitale.*[84] The New York Board of Regents wrote a prayer and recommended its use in every public school classroom in the state. Local school boards adopted the prayer, but individual students who objected to it could be excused from the room while it was recited. The Court noted the inherently coercive effect on religious minorities but insisted that coercion was not essential to its decision. Rather, the Court held that for the state to promulgate and encourage prayer was wholly inconsistent with the Establishment Clause.

Engel produced a storm of public protest, but this time the Court did not back down. It reaffirmed *Engel* in *School District v. Schempp.*[85] The Establishment Clause violations in *Schempp* were even more egregious than in *Engel.* The prayer at issue in *Engel* had been as nonsectarian as the Regents could make it, although it plainly sounded in Judeo-Christian theology and King James syntax. The cases consolidated for decision in *Schempp* involved no nonsectarian pretense. Pennsylvania required all public schools to begin the day by reading ten verses from the Bible; Maryland required them to begin either by reading a chapter from the Bible or by reciting the Lord's Prayer. Both states distributed the King James version of the Bible to school teachers, but permitted students to bring other versions if they wished. A Jewish theologian testified that the concept of Christ as the Son of God was "practically blasphemous" to Jews and that parts of the New Testament "tended to bring Jews into ridicule and scorn."[86]

The Court could have summarily held these practices unconstitutional under *Engel.* Instead, it undertook to respond to the protest, explaining once again, in more than a hundred pages of majority and concurring opinions, why states could not conduct religious exercises consistently with the Establishment Clause. The protesters were unconvinced. The controversy continues to this day, generating unsuccessful efforts to amend the Constitution and attempts to develop a form of school prayer that will pass constitutional muster.

84. 370 U.S. 421 (1962).
85. 374 U.S. 203 (1963).
86. *Id.* at 209.

E. The Beginnings of Modern Conscientious Objection Doctrine

In the Mormon cases, the Supreme Court had said that the Free Exercise Clause protects only belief and never action. The implication seemed to be that there is no constitutional right to exemption from governmental policies that violate one's religion. The Jehovah's Witness cases made some inroads into that view, but all of them could be explained on free speech grounds as well as on free exercise grounds.

The only area in which there was any significant development of conscientious objection law before 1963 was the military draft. That law derived from statute, not from the Constitution. Congress has made some provision for conscientious objectors in each major war. But the provisions were often narrow. The World War I exemption for conscientious objectors was limited to members of historic peace churches.[87] The Court saw no problem in this discrimination against conscientious objectors from other religions.[88]

The first Supreme Court case squarely requiring a religious exemption from a law of general application was *Sherbert v. Verner,*[89] decided in 1963 on the same day as *School District v. Schempp.* Sherbert was a Sabbatarian who lost her job because she refused to work on Saturday. The state held that she had been discharged for cause and refused to pay unemployment compensation. The Supreme Court disagreed. It held that the state could not penalize her religious belief without a compelling reason, and that denying unemployment compensation because she refused to work on Saturday was a penalty.

Justices Harlan and White dissented. They thought the Court established religion by requiring payments to those who refused Saturday work for religious reasons without requiring payments to those who refused Saturday work for secular reasons. The Court rejected that argument in rather conclusory fashion.

Justices Harlan, White, and Stewart also thought the decision was inconsistent with *Braunfeld v. Brown.*[90] *Braunfeld* had rejected an Orthodox Jew's request to be exempted from the Sunday closing laws. His religion compelled him to close on Saturday, and he feared that if he also closed on Sunday, eventually he would be forced out of business. The dissenting Justices thought per-

---

87. Act of May 18, 1917, ch. 15, § 4, 40 Stat. 78 (1919).
88. Selective Draft Law Cases, 245 U.S. 366, 389-90 (1918).
89. 374 U.S. 398 (1963).
90. 366 U.S. 599 (1961).

manent Sunday closing laws imposed a greater burden on Sabbatarians than denying twenty-two weeks of unemployment compensation.

The majority responded that the *Braunfeld* burden was less direct and that the state's interest in denying exemption was much greater. They argued that allowing Sabbatarian merchants to remain open on Sunday might give them such a competitive advantage that it would make Sunday closing laws unworkable. The competitive advantage of an exemption to Sabbatarians would invite spurious claims and encourage conversions to Sabbatarian religions. The majority thought that unemployment compensation benefits presented neither of these problems.

F. The Beginnings of Modern Church Autonomy Doctrine

Submitting internal church disputes to secular courts is another recurring source of religious liberty litigation. The Supreme Court has imposed substantial restrictions on suits of this type.

The first case was *Watson v. Jones*.[91] *Watson* arose out of the schism between the northern and southern branches of the Presbyterian church, a schism produced by fundamental disagreement over slavery. The particular dispute in *Watson* was between two factions of the Walnut Street Presbyterian Church in Louisville, Kentucky. One faction adhered to the northern church, one to the southern. Both claimed the Walnut Street church building.

Several members of the northern faction moved to Indiana so they could sue in federal court, invoking the federal court's jurisdiction over suits between citizens of different states. The case was consequently decided as a matter of federal common law, not as a matter of constitutional right.[92] But the Court said its decision was "founded in a broad and sound view of the relation of church and state under our system of laws."[93] The Court held that federal courts were bound by the decision of the highest church authority recognized by both sides before the dispute began. It feared that any other rule would involve secular courts in theological controversies.

The Court constitutionalized these principles in *Kedroff v. Saint Nicholas Cathedral of the Russian Orthodox Church*.[94] The Court held that the Free Ex-

---

91. 80 U.S. (13 Wall.) 679 (1871).

92. This was in the days when federal courts asserted power to declare the general law in diversity cases. See Swift v. Tyson, 41 U.S. (16 Pet.) 1 (1842).

93. Watson v. Jones, 80 U.S. (13 Wall.) 679, 727 (1871).

94. 344 U.S. 94 (1952).

ercise Clause protects the right of churches to resolve disputes internally. The Court reaffirmed this holding in 1960.[95]

III. Developments since 1963

By 1963 the Supreme Court had laid the groundwork for its modern Religion Clause jurisprudence, but it had done little more than that. It had adopted Madison's view of the Establishment Clause. It had recognized the right to proselytize and at least some right to conscientious objection under the Free Exercise Clause. And it had recognized a right to church autonomy at least with respect to resolving internal church disputes. But except for the right to proselytize, there had been no opportunity to work out the details of any of these rights. Since 1963 the Court has had many occasions to elaborate on these basic principles. Whole new doctrines have developed, doctrines that could not have been predicted from any materials extant in 1963. The rest of this Article reviews those developments.

A. Conscientious Objection

Judicial recognition of the right to conscientious objection to public policy has its roots in the Jehovah's Witness cases of the 1940s. But those cases all involved speech, and they were largely based on the Free Speech Clause. *Sherbert v. Verner*,[96] the 1963 unemployment compensation case, was the first time the Supreme Court clearly held that the Free Exercise Clause protects religiously motivated conduct. *Sherbert* said that the Free Exercise Clause exempts conscientious objectors from government policy unless the government has a "compelling interest" in denying the exemption.

1. Conscientious Objection to Military Service

The Vietnam War produced a large number of cases involving conscientious objection to military service. Most conscientious objection claims were based on the Selective Service Act. The Act exempted from the draft any person who, "by reason of religious training and belief, is conscientiously opposed

---

95. Kreshik v. Saint Nicholas Cathedral of the Russian Orthodox Church, 363 U.S. 190 (1960).

96. 374 U.S. 203 (1963).

to participation in war in any form."[97] At the beginning of the Vietnam War the statute defined religious training and belief as follows:

> Religious training and belief in this connection means an individual's belief in relation to a Supreme Being involving duties superior to those arising from any human relation, but does not include essentially political, sociological, or philosophical views, or a merely personal moral code.[98]

This definition posed problems analogous to those raised by the World War I exemption for members of the historic peace churches. To exempt conscientious objectors only if they held theistic beliefs discriminated against conscientious objectors with less orthodox beliefs. The Court avoided the constitutional problem by construing the definition of religious belief quite broadly, virtually ignoring the reference to a Supreme Being. In *United States v. Seeger,* the Court exempted conscientious objectors who did not believe in God if their objection was based on a "sincere and meaningful" belief that "occupies in the life of its possessor a place parallel to that filled by the God of those admittedly qualifying for the exemption."[99]

Congress then amended the statute, deleting the reference to a Supreme Being but retaining the requirement of religious training and belief and the exclusion of "essentially political, sociological, or philosophical views, or a merely personal moral code." Even so, in 1970 the Court construed the exemption to cover "all those whose consciences, spurred by deeply held moral, ethical, *or* religious beliefs, would give them no rest or peace if they allowed themselves to become a part of an instrument of war."[100]

Another provision in the statute limited exemption to those who objected to "war in any form." Those who objected to some wars but not all wars were not exempt. Thus, all those who subscribed to just war doctrine were denied exemption, no matter how deeply held their conscientious belief that a particular was unjust. Just war doctrine has ancient roots; it was elaborated by pre-Reformation theologians, and it is now taught by many mainstream Christian Churches.[101]

97. 50 U.S.C. App. § 456(j) (1982).

98. *Id.* (1964).

99. 380 U.S. 163, 176 (1965).

100. Welsh v. United States, 398 U.S. 333, 334 (1970) (emphasis added).

101. *See generally* JAMES JOHNSON, JUST WAR TRADITION AND THE RESTRAINT OF WAR (1981); JUST WAR THEORY IN THE NUCLEAR AGE (John Jones & Mark Griesbach, eds., 1985); UNITED STATES CONFERENCE OF CATHOLIC BISHOPS, THE CHALLENGE OF PEACE: GOD'S PROMISE AND OUR RESPONSE (1983).

In *Gillette v. United States,*[102] the Court upheld the requirement that objectors object to war in any form. The Court rejected challenges under both the Establishment and Free Exercise Clauses. It thought that the greater difficulty of adjudicating claims of conscientious objection to particular wars was a compelling interest that justified both the discrimination between religious beliefs and the burden on the selective conscientious objector's exercise of religion.

2. Other Conscientious Objection Cases

The constitutional law of conscientious objection has continued to develop in contexts other than the military draft. But there are only a few cases at the Supreme Court level and it is hard to generalize about them.[103]

The Supreme Court first upheld a conscientious objection challenge to a criminal statute in 1972, in *Wisconsin v. Yoder.*[104] Yoder was an Amish father who refused to send his children to public school beyond the eighth grade. Wisconsin prosecuted him under the truancy laws. The Court found that the Amish continued to train the children for life in the Amish community and that the state's interest in two more years of public education was insufficiently compelling to justify the severe burden on the Amish religion. The Amish feared that their children would abandon the religion completely if they were exposed to the temptations in a public high school. *Yoder* reaffirmed the approach taken in *Sherbert v. Verner* that only state interests "of the highest order" can justify denying a right to conscientious objection. But the Court also emphasized that the balance of government and religious interests in *Yoder* was "close" and that few religions could qualify for the exemption granted to the Amish.

In *Thomas v. Review Board of the Indiana Employment Security Division,* the Court required Indiana to pay unemployment compensation to a Jehovah's Witness who quit his job in a defense plant for reasons of conscience.[105] The Court found it irrelevant that other Witnesses worked in the plant. The test of individual conscience is what the individual believes, not what his denomination believes.

In *United States v. Lee,*[106] the Court refused to exempt Amish employers from the Social Security tax on their Amish employees, although self-

---

102. 401 U.S. 437 (1971). *See generally* Kent Greenawalt, *All or Nothing at All: The Defeat of Selective Conscientious Objection,* 1971 Sup. Ct. Rev. 31.

103. For another review of these cases, see Mansfield, *supra* note 73, at 896-903.

104. 406 U.S. 205 (1972).

105. 450 U.S. 707 (1981).

106. United States v. Lee, 455 U.S. 252 (1982).

employed Amish are exempted by statute. The Court found the Social Security tax indistinguishable from any other tax and found the government interest in collecting its revenues to be compelling. The Court used the example of war tax resisters to illustrate how unworkable it would be to let people refuse to pay taxes for programs to which they had religiously motivated objection.

The Court also rejected a conscientious objection claim in *Bob Jones University v. United States.*[107] The university, on grounds of religious belief, refused to allow interracial dating among its students. The Court held that the government's interest in eliminating racial discrimination in education substantially outweighed the university's free exercise rights. Thus, the Court upheld the Internal Revenue Service revocation of Bob Jones' tax-exempt status.

More recently, in *Jensen v. Quaring,* the Court was presented with a woman's claim that she conscientiously objected to having her picture on her driver's license.[108] Frances Quaring took literally the commandment to make no graven images. The court of appeals held that the Constitution protected her right to a driver's license without a photograph.[109] The Supreme Court was unable to decide the case. Four Justices would have allowed her claim; four would have rejected it; Justice Powell did not participate. That split affirmed the lower court decision in favor of Quaring, but it did not establish a rule for anyone else.

The Court's sharp division continued in the 1985 Term's conscientious objection cases. In *Goldman v. Weinberger,*[110] the Court refused to invalidate military rules that precluded an Orthodox Jewish officer — a psychiatrist stationed in a state-side hospital — from wearing his yarmulke with his uniform. The Court's opinion deferred to the military's asserted need for uniformity for the sake of uniformity, and it was impossible to identify any more substantial interest. The case may be of little precedential value outside the military. But the government's brief and three concurring justices took the possibly broader ground that yarmulkes could not be distinguished from turbans, saffron robes, and dreadlocks without invidiously discriminating among minority religions.[111] These justices were unwilling to draw such lines, and they were unwilling to exempt all religious garments. They did not explain why the lines they refused to draw among minority religious prac-

---

107. 461 U.S. 574, 602-04 (1983). For an argument that the free exercise claim should have prevailed, see Douglas Laycock, *Tax Exemptions for Racially Discriminatory Religious Schools,* 60 Tex. L. Rev. 259 (1982).

108. 472 U.S. 478 (1985).

109. Quaring v. Peterson, 728 F.2d 1121 (8th Cir. 1984).

110. 475 U.S. 503 (1986).

111. *Id.* at 512 (Stevens, J., concurring).

tices were more objectionable than the line the military had already drawn between majority and minority religious practice. There were four dissents.

Bowen v. Roy[112] involved an applicant for welfare benefits who conscientiously refused to request or provide a social security number. Three justices thought it important that the government merely withheld welfare benefits and did not impose criminal penalties on individuals without social security numbers. They would uphold a statute denying benefits without any effort to accommodate conscientious objectors if the rule is facially neutral, is not motivated by any intent to discriminate on religious grounds, and is "a reasonable means of promoting a legitimate public interest."[113] The statute requiring social security numbers easily passed that deferential test. They distinguished application of the compelling state interest test in earlier public benefit cases[114] on the ground that the statutes in those cases provided for individualized determinations of eligibility and the Social Security Act did not.[115] Much of this analysis was derived from the government's brief.

The Court's judgment was simply to vacate and remand for further proceedings.[116] The lead opinion represented neither a majority nor a plurality, and five justices rejected its proposed test.[117] These five failed to write an opinion for the Court because Justice Blackmun thought the case was probably moot and announced his view of the merits only in dictum, and Justice White refused to join Justice O'Connor's opinion for the other three.[118] If the trial court's findings on remand persuade Blackmun that the case is not moot, there appear to be five votes to apply the compelling interest test and invalidate the requirement that conscientious objectors personally apply for and use their social security number.

---

112. 476 U.S. 693 (1986).

113. *Id.* at 708 (opinion for three justices).

114. Thomas v. Review Bd. of the Ind. Employment Sec. Div., 450 U.S. 707 (1981); Sherbert v. Verner, 374 U.S. 398 (1963).

115. *Bowen,* 476 U.S. at 708 (opinion for three justices).

116. *Id.* at 712.

117. *Id.* at 715-16 (Blackmun, J., concurring in part); *id.* at 724-33 (O'Connor, J., joined by Brennan and Marshall, JJ., dissenting in part); *id.* at 733 (White, J., dissenting).

118. Justice Stevens also thought the case was probably moot. *Id.* at 717-22 (Stevens, J., concurring in part). He expressed no view on the merits, but his announced view is that almost no conscientious objection claims should be recognized. United States v. Lee, 455 U.S. 252, 261-64 (1982) (Stevens, J., concurring); *see also* Goldman v. Weinberger, 475 U.S. 503, 510-13 (1986) (Stevens, J., concurring).

3. *The Current Status of Conscientious Objection*

Collectively, these cases reveal judicial ambivalence about a constitutional right to conscientious objection. Conscientious objectors won in *Sherbert, Yoder,* and *Thomas;* they lost in *Gillette, Lee, Bob Jones,* and *Goldman; Bowen* remains unsettled. One way to reconcile these cases is to note that conscientious objectors to state statutes have won; conscientious objectors to federal statutes have lost, although *Bowen* may eventually break that pattern. The Court is generally more deferential to federal statutes, but that cannot be the whole explanation.

Another way to reconcile most of the cases is to say that the government's interests in raising armies in *Gillette,* in collecting taxes in *Lee,* and in racial integration in *Bob Jones,* are more compelling than its interests in preserving unemployment compensation funds or forcing Amish children to get two more years of formal education. But that formulation conceals a deeper difference in the cases. The Court has defined the government interests at inconsistent levels of generality.

The state interest in educating children is surely compelling, but that is not how the Court posed the question in *Yoder.* Rather, it assessed the state's interest in requiring ninth and tenth grade for Amish children who would reside in an agricultural community that eschewed modern technology and trained its own youth in skills important to that community. The comparable formulation in *Bob Jones* would not be the interest in eliminating racial discrimination in education, but rather the interest in protecting interracial dating among students at a small, private, and pervasively religious school that restricted student conduct in many other ways. The comparable formulation in *Lee* would not be the interest in collecting taxes, but the interest in collecting social security taxes for Amish employees of Amish employers, all of whom lived in a tight-knit community that, as a matter of religious belief, took care of its own needy members. A broad or narrow formulation of the governmental interest virtually determines the result.

The appearance of inconsistency is reinforced by the Court's continued citation of pre-1963 cases that rejected conscientious objection claims without applying the compelling government interest standard. These include *Braunfeld v. Brown,*[119] allowing states to enforce Sunday closing laws against Sabbatarian merchants, *Prince v. Massachusetts,*[120] enforcing child labor laws against a Jehovah's Witness whose niece helped her sell religious literature,

---

119. 366 U.S. 599 (1961).
120. 321 U.S. 158 (1944).

and *Reynolds v. United States,*[121] enforcing polygamy laws against a Mormon polygamist. The Court explicitly refused to apply the compelling interest test to the military in *Goldman;*[122] three justices would not have applied it to government benefit programs in *Bowen;*[123] and Justice Stevens would not apply it at all.[124]

Professors Freed and Polsby have suggested another consideration that might reconcile the modern conscientious objection cases.[125] Recognizing conscientious objection in *Gillette, Lee,* or *Bob Jones* might invite large numbers of false claims from those who fear combat, begrudge taxes, or hate racial minorities. Such persons might see much personal gain and no cost in exemption from a burdensome legal duty. A court or an agency would have to determine the sincerity of each claim, trying to separate the true conscientious objectors from the opportunists. These determinations would be difficult; in large numbers they could be extraordinarily burdensome. Certainly this was the experience with thousands of statutory conscientious objection hearings during the Vietnam War. Freed and Polsby suggest that avoiding such hearings is sometimes a substantial reason to refuse to recognize a right to conscientious objection. They might have said that the government interest in avoiding these hearings is compelling, but they avoid using the phrase.[126]

This problem is absent, or at least greatly attenuated, in *Sherbert, Thomas,* and *Yoder.* Sherbert and Thomas lost their jobs; Yoder gave up free public education for his children. Unemployment compensation would be only a temporary and partial substitute for Sherbert and Thomas; immunity from truancy prosecutions would offset none of Yoder's loss. Each claimant bore substantial costs even after his claim of conscientious objection was allowed. Those costs provide a substantial check on the claimant's sincerity, greatly reducing the number of claims and the state's need to litigate the sincerity of those claims that are filed. Perhaps this difference in the temptation to false claims explains the cases, although the Court has not focused on that. There is little temptation to abuse in *Goldman* and *Bowen,* but *Goldman* may be explained as a military case, and the conscientious objector may yet prevail in *Bowen.*

---

121. 98 U.S. 145 (1878).

122. *Goldman,* 475 U.S. at 506-08.

123. Bowen v. Roy, 476 U.S. 693, 706-08 (1986) (opinion of Burger, C.J., Powell, and Rehnquist, JJ.).

124. United States v. Lee, 455 U.S. 252, 261-64 (1982) (Stevens, J., concurring).

125. Mayer Freed & Dan Polsby, *Race, Religion, and Public Policy: Bob Jones University v. United States,* 1983 Sup. Ct. Rev. 1, 20-30.

126. *Id.* at 23.

Freed and Polsby suggested the explanation, but they do not think it quite fits the cases. They see substantial risk of false claims in *Sherbert* and *Thomas*. Many people would like to quit their jobs, and unemployment compensation can help cushion the blow.[127] None of these theories can explain four votes to require pictures on driver's licenses in *Jensen v. Quaring*.[128] The state's interest in pictures on driver's license is largely a matter of administrative convenience. There is no economic or other self-interested incentive to falsely claim conscientious objection to driver's license photographs. If the right to conscientious objection amounts to anything, *Jensen v. Quaring* should have been an easy case. But the Court could not decide it.

The United States filed an amicus brief in *Jensen*, arguing that the government's interest should be measured by the cost of removing pictures from the licenses of all the drivers in the state and not by the much smaller cost of exempting conscientious objectors.[129] Under that standard, few claims of conscientious objection would ever be allowed. The government took a similar position in *Bowen*,[130] and in *Goldman* it argued that the claim should be measured by the disruptive impact of saffron robes instead of the yarmulke at issue.[131]

These government briefs cast important light on the Reagan Administration position. It has been quite vocal in its minimalist view of the Establishment Clause. But in these cases it took an equally minimalist view of the Free Exercise Clause. Its position in these briefs is not proreligion, but simply statist. The Administration does not believe that minorities should have many rights that are judicially enforceable against majorities.[132]

4. Exempting Conscientious Objectors as Discrimination Against Others

The problem of fairness to others has troubled the Court ever since it worried that exempting Sabbatarian merchants from the Sunday closing laws

---

127. *Id.* at 30.

128. 472 U.S. 478 (1985).

129. *Id.*, Brief for the United States as Amicus Curiae 3, 5-6.

130. Brief for the Appellants 35.

131. *See* Goldman v. Weinberger, 485 U.S. 503, 512 (Stevens, J., concurring); *id.* at 519 (Brennan, J., dissenting).

132. Some of the government's positions may have been dictated by the Justice Department's duty to defend its clients in the other agencies. The United States did not oppose the free exercise claim in Dayton Christian Schools, Inc. v. Ohio Civil Rights Comm'n, 766 F.2d 932 (6th Cir. 1985), *rev'd on other grounds*, 477 U.S. 619 (1986).

would give them an unfair advantage over other merchants.[133] Any exemption for conscientious objectors can be viewed as discrimination against people who do not qualify for the exemption.[134] The Court has dismissed the problem in some cases and grappled with it in others.

There are two quite different aspects to the discrimination problem. One issue is whether the state can exempt some conscientious objectors and not others. Surely the state can not explicitly exempt conscientious objectors from some denominations and exclude conscientious objectors from other denominations, as in the World War I draft statute that exempted members of the historic peace churches.[135] But in 1971 the Court did permit Congress to exempt objectors to all wars without exempting objectors to unjust wars.[136]

A variation on the problem of equal treatment of conscientious objectors is whether the state can grant exemption to objectors whose claims are based in religion and deny exemption to those whose claims are based in secular moral philosophy. It was to avoid that problem in the Vietnam draft cases that the Court interpreted the requirement of religious training and belief in a way quite different from what Congress intended.[137]

The second aspect of the problem is that any conscientious objector exemption appears to discriminate against those who are burdened by the state's policy or who object to it for reasons unrelated to conscience. The problem of the merchants closed on Sunday is just one example. If Sabbatarian airline clerks are given Saturdays off, other workers who would like to spend Saturday with their families will be unable to do so.[138] If ten

133. *See Goldman,* 475 U.S. at 512-13 (Stevens, J., concurring); *id.* at 521-22 (Brennan, J., dissenting); Estate of Thornton v. Calder, Inc., 472 U.S. 703 (1985); United States v. Lee, 455 U.S. 252, 261-64 (1982) (Stevens, J., concurring). Earlier opinions grappling with this problem are collected in Laycock, *General Theory, supra* note 4, at 1414-16 (text at notes 306-17).

134. Laycock, *General Theory, supra* note 4, at 1414-16 (text at notes 306-17); Mansfield, *supra* note 73, at 849-50, 898-99. Other commentators have made a similar point in somewhat different terms: that any exemption for conscientious objectors may be a forbidden aid to religion. Jesse Choper, *The Religion Clauses of the First Amendment: Reconciling the Conflict,* 41 U. PITT. L. REV. 673, 688-701 (1980); Kurland, *supra* note 2, at 17. For a thorough response, see Michael McConnell, *Accommodation of Religion,* 1985 SUP. CT. REV. 1.

135. See *supra* note 87 and accompanying text.

136. Gillette v. United States, 401 U.S. 437 (1971).

137. Welsh v. United States, 398 U.S. 333 (1970); Seeger v. United States, 380 U.S. 163 (1965).

138. This was the problem in Trans World Airlines, Inc. v. Hardison, 432 U.S. 63 (1977), a case decided under the religious discrimination provision of the Civil Rights Act of 1964. On those facts, the Court rejected Hardison's claim that requiring him to work on his Sabbath violated the statute.

thousand conscientious objectors are exempt from the military draft, ten thousand others must serve in their place. Some of the substitutes may be killed. In a sense, these other workers and other draftees are discriminated against because of their religion. If only they would adopt religious beliefs that made them conscientious objectors, they too would be exempt from the draft and from working on Saturday.

The Court acted on these concerns in *Estate of Thornton v. Calder, Inc.*[139] A Connecticut statute allowed every employee to designate his Sabbath and refuse to work on that day. An employee designating a Sabbath did not have to claim that his conscience compelled him to abstain from work. In a narrow opinion, the Court held that the statute supported religion by granting an absolute preference for religious interests over the competing interests of employers and fellow employees. Consequently, the statute violated the Establishment Clause.

Thornton was an extreme case that highlights the problem. It does not follow that conscientious objectors can never be exempted from governmentally imposed requirements, even if the result is to shift the burden of the requirement to someone else. Professors Galanter and Pepper have each offered an explanation for the Court's intuitive judgment that most exemptions for conscientious objectors do not impermissibly discriminate against others.[140] They independently argue that exemption for conscientious objectors assures that religious minorities will be treated equally with adherents of mainstream religions. The political process provides substantial protection against government policies that violate the consciences of large numbers of believers in mainstream religions. Democratic governments do not feel free to trample on conscience when more than small numbers of idiosyncratic believers are affected. Thus, Galanter and Pepper argue, constitutionally mandated exemption for conscientious objectors redresses a form of discrimination: it gives small numbers of idiosyncratic believers the same protection that the political process affords to large numbers of mainstream believers.

It is also important to note that not every exemption for conscientious objectors shifts a burden to someone else. If Frances Quaring is issued a driver's license without a picture, no one else has to carry two pictures to make up for her exemption. Merchants who are afraid to take her checks can refuse

---

139. 472 U.S. 703 (1985). For a criticism of the case, see McConnell, *supra* note 134, at 50-58.

140. Marc Galanter, *Religious Freedom in the United States: A Turning Point?*, 1966 WIS. L. REV. 217, 291; Stephen Pepper, *Quaring May Help Supreme Court Clarify Religious Freedom Doctrine*, NAT'L L.J. April 8, 1985, at 24.

to take them; the inconvenience will fall on her. In this fairly common kind of conscientious objection case, fairness to others is not seriously at issue.[141]

B. Church Autonomy

The extent to which the Constitution protects church autonomy is an increasingly important issue. Church autonomy claims are distinct from conscientious objection claims. If a church entity conscientiously objects to some requirement placed on it by the government, the church entity will be protected under the same standards that would apply to an individual conscientious objector.[142] But, more often, churches object to government interference not on grounds of conscience, but on the ground that the government is interfering with the church's control of its own affairs. Such claims arise in many forms; I will refer to them collectively as church autonomy claims.

I have argued elsewhere that the right to church autonomy is guaranteed by the Free Exercise Clause, because interference with church autonomy hampers the exercise of religion.[143] Professor Esbeck has argued that church autonomy is part of the structural relationship between church and state guaranteed by the Establishment Clause.[144] The courts have protected church autonomy sporadically; the right is well established only in certain contexts.

1. Internal Church Disputes

Unfortunately, churches and their members continue to take internal disputes to the secular courts. Most of these cases involve disputes over the right to a church building claimed by a denomination and also by a local church, or claimed by two factions within a local church. Sometimes they involve

141. This distinction is developed in Laycock, *General Theory, supra* note 4, at 1416 (text at notes 316-17).

142. Examples are Madsen v. Erwin, 481 N.E.2d 1160 (Mass. 1985), and Walker v. First Orthodox Presbyterian Church, 22 Fair Empl. Prac. Cas. (BNA) 762 (Cal. Super. Ct. 1980), each holding that a church that believed homosexuality was a sin could not be liable for discharging homosexual employees.

143. Laycock, *General Theory, supra* note 4.

144. Carl Esbeck, *Towards a General Theory of Church-State Relations and the First Amendment*, 4 PUB. L.F. 325 (1985); Carl Esbeck, *Establishment Clause Limits on Governmental Interference with Religious Organizations*, 41 WASH. & LEE L. REV. 347 (1984).

even more sensitive questions. For example, in 1975 the Illinois Supreme Court undertook to decide which of two competing claimants should be the North American Bishop of the Serbian Eastern Orthodox Church.[145]

By 1963 the Supreme Court had apparently constitutionalized the rule that secular courts faced with internal church disputes were bound by the decision of the highest church authority to consider the matter.[146] However, subsequent decisions, less protective of the autonomy of churches, have created a choice of rules. Secular courts may defer to the highest church authority if they choose. Or, they may decide the case themselves, construing deeds, contracts, and church constitutions under "neutral principles of law."[147] "Neutral principles" must treat these church documents as ordinary legal instruments, construing them without regard to religious doctrine. The Court continues to hold that secular courts are constitutionally forbidden to resolve questions of religious doctrine. It has forbidden the once widespread rule that disputed church property should be awarded to the faction that, in the view of the secular court, adhered to the original teaching of the church.[148]

Proponents of the neutral principles rule argue that it gives churches freedom to structure their relationships in a variety of ways; local churches can affiliate with a hierarchical church without being subject to unreviewable decisions by the hierarchical tribunals.[149] Opponents respond that this freedom-of-contract protection for churches is of little value because there are hardly any occasions on which affiliating churches might want their future decisions reviewed by secular courts.[150] But, they argue, the neutral principles approach

---

145. Serbian E. Orthodox Diocese v. Milivojevich, 328 N.E.2d 268 (Ill. 1975), *rev'd*, 426 U.S. 696 (1976).

146. Kreshik v. Saint Nicholas Cathedral of the Russian Orthodox Church, 363 U.S. 190 (1960); Kedroff v. Saint Nicholas Cathedral of the Russian Orthodox Church, 344 U.S. 94 (1952). Compare Watson v. Jones, 80 U.S. (13 Wall.) 679 (1871) (decided under federal common law).

147. Jones v. Wolf, 443 U.S. 595, 602 (1979).

148. For an apparent defense of that rule, and an argument against both of the alternatives permitted by the Court, see Mansfield, *supra* note 73, at 858-68.

149. Jones v. Wolf, 443 U.S. 595, 604-06 (1979); Arlin Adams & Hanlon, *Jones v. Wolf: Church Autonomy and the Religion Clauses of the First Amendment*, 128 U. PA. L. REV. 1291, 1317-18, 1325, 1338 (1980); Ira Ellman, *Driven from the Tribunal: Judicial Resolution of Internal Church Disputes*, 69 CAL. L. REV. 1378 (1981).

150. See Laycock, *General Theory, supra* note 4, 1403-05 (text at notes 235-43). This point was made much more forcefully by the church officials with whom I worked in my consultations with the Presbyterian Church (U.S.A.). They report that it is quite rare for independent local churches to affiliate with national denominations. In the great bulk of cases, the national denomination creates the local church and subsidizes it until it can become self-supporting.

does substantial harm because it authorizes secular courts to review the decision of church authorities in every internal church dispute.

So far, the Supreme Court has permitted the neutral principles approach only in church property disputes. In *Serbian Eastern Orthodox Diocese v. Milivojevich,*[151] the Court required deference to the highest church tribunal. *Serbian Diocese* involved two internal church questions, neither of which was characterized as a property dispute. One was which of two competing claimants should be the Bishop. The other was whether North America should be one diocese or three.

2. The Entanglement Precedents

The Supreme Court's entanglement doctrine also suggests constitutional protection for church autonomy. The Court has repeatedly said that a major purpose of the Religion Clauses was to prevent excessive entanglement between church and state. But "entanglement" has been a vague term with changeable meaning.[152] Sometimes it seems to mean contact, or the opposite of separation. Sometimes it seems to mean church regulation. Sometimes it seems to mean government surveillance of churches.

A restriction on entanglement in any of these senses supports a right to church autonomy. But that implication has not been developed. The entanglement doctrine has mainly been developed in cases on financial aid to religious institutions. In that context, entanglement doctrine is not used to protect resisting churches from government interference, but to forbid certain kinds of government aid to church institutions. The litigants complaining about entanglement are not churches, but organizations defending a no-aid-of-any-kind view of the Establishment Clause.

One cannot confidently predict that the Court will use the entanglement doctrine to protect churches from objectionable government regulation. But the doctrine is well established in the financial aid cases, and it is even more appropriate in cases that do not involve financial aid. It cannot fairly or logically be that churches are protected from entanglement when the government wants to help, but not when the government wants to regulate. The Supreme Court implicitly recognized as much in two cases in which religious organizations challenged government regulation as an excessive entanglement.[153] The

151. 426 U.S. 696 (1976).

152. For a review of the Court's many uses of the term, see Laycock, *General Theory, supra* note 4, at 1392-93 (text at notes 152-63).

153. Tony and Susan Alamo Found. v. Secretary of Labor, 471 U.S. 290 (1985); NLRB v. Catholic Bishop, 440 U.S. 490 (1979).

Court decided each case on the merits, without raising any questions about standing or the relevance of entanglement doctrine.

3. Government Regulation of Churches

Government regulatory agencies have been increasingly unwilling to exempt church activities from the scope of regulation and churches have been increasingly unwilling to submit to burdensome regulations. The result has been a series of clashes over the right of churches to be exempted from regulation. Some of these cases involve claims of conscientious objection, but more often the church is claiming a right to autonomy.

The case most squarely presenting an autonomy claim in the Supreme Court is *NLRB v. Catholic Bishop*.[154] *Catholic Bishop* involved the attempt to form a teacher's union in Roman Catholic schools in the Archdiocese of Chicago. It was one of many similar cases in Catholic dioceses around the country. The church claimed exemption from the National Labor Relations Act. This claim was not based on conscientious objection, because Catholic doctrine has long affirmed the moral right of workers to organize.[155] Rather, the claim was based on a right to church autonomy. Catholic schools are religious institutions and the church asserted its right to control them. It refused to share control with a government agency, the National Labor Relations Board, or with a secular private organization, a union. The Seventh Circuit held that the church schools were constitutionally exempt from the Act.[156]

The Supreme Court affirmed, but on statutory grounds. The Court found that collective bargaining under the supervision of the Board posed a serious risk of excessive government entanglement with religion. Without resolving the constitutional question, the Court held the Act inapplicable to church schools. It believed that Congress did not intend such an arguably unconstitutional application of the Act. Four dissenters thought the Act applied, although they agreed that to apply it would raise a serious constitutional question.

The constitutional issue arose again when New York applied its State Labor Relations Act to Catholic schools. In 1985 the Second Circuit upheld the law.[157] That court plainly did not take the right to church autonomy seri-

---

154. 440 U.S. 490 (1979).

155. Pope Leo XIII, Rerum Novarum (1891).

156. Catholic Bishop v. NLRB, 559 F.2d 1112 (7th Cir. 1977), *aff'd on other grounds*, 440 U.S. 490 (1979).

157. Catholic High School Ass'n v. Culvert, 753 F.2d 1161 (2d Cir. 1985).

ously. Most of the opinion was devoted to attenuated conscientious objection claims. And the court commented that the Framers were more motivated "to prevent the establishment of an authoritarian state church like, for the example, the Church of England, than with state regulation" of churches.[158] Conceding that the Act might chill the narrow free exercise rights acknowledged by the court, the court found a compelling state interest in "the preservation of industrial peace and a sound economic order."[159]

This is the tactic of asserting the state's interest at the highest level of generality; the court did not explain why the state had any interest at all in industrial peace or economic order inside a religious institution. This opinion also reflects a watering down of the compelling interest test in another way. In 1944, the first time the Supreme Court found a compelling government interest that required it to uphold a statute that infringed what would otherwise have been constitutional rights, it relied on the government's interest in defending against a feared invasion of the Pacific coast.[160] That was the only compelling interest the Court found for decades. The Court's critics suggested that it would never find another one.[161] But the test has gradually been weakened; every bureaucracy now argues that its program serves a compelling interest. The casual acceptance of that argument in the New York collective bargaining case suggests an increasing danger that any reasonable government program will be held to serve a compelling interest.

The state courts and the lower federal courts have decided many other church autonomy claims. Courts generally have refused to exempt churches from the employment discrimination laws,[162] but they have done so with respect to the employment of ministers[163] and in cases where compliance

158. *Id.* at 1170.

159. *Id.* at 1171.

160. Korematsu v. United States, 323 U.S. 214 (1944).

161. Dunn v. Blumstein, 405 U.S. 330, 363-64 (1972) (Burger, C.J., dissenting); see Gerald Gunther, *Foreword: In Search of Evolving Doctrine on a Changing Court: A Model for a Newer Equal Protection,* 86 HARV. L. REV. 1, 8 (1972) ("scrutiny that was 'strict' in theory and fatal in fact").

162. EEOC v. Fremont Christian School, 781 F.2d 1362 (9th Cir. 1986); EEOC v. Pacific Press Publishing Ass'n, 482 F. Supp. 1291 (N.D. Cal. 1979); Marshall v. Pacific Union Conf. of Seventh-Day Adventists, 14 Empl. Prac. Dec. (CCH) 5956 (C.D. Cal. 1977); Whitney v. Greater N.Y. Corp. of Seventh-Day Adventists, 401 F. Supp. 1363 (S.D.N.Y. 1975); National Org. for Women v. President of Santa Clara College, 16 Fair Empl. Prac. Cas. (BNA) 1152 (N.D. Cal. 1975).

163. EEOC v. Southwestern Baptist Theological Seminary, 651 F.2d 277 (5th Cir. 1981); EEOC v. Mississippi College, 626 F.2d 477 (5th Cir. 1980); McClure v. Salvation Army, 460 F.2d 553 (5th Cir. 1972); Maguire v. Marquette Univ., 627 F. Supp. 1499 (E.D. Wis. 1986).

would violate church teachings.[164] There have been dozens of cases in which religious schools challenged state licensing, curriculum, and teacher certification requirements. The regulatory authorities have won most of those cases,[165] but some state supreme courts have protected substantial autonomy rights in religious schools.[166] One state has recognized that burdensome and unnecessary building code enforcement against church schools can violate constitutional rights.[167]

There has also been litigation over government regulation and Internal Revenue Service monitoring of church day care centers,[168] orphanages,[169] social service agencies,[170] and other church agencies. In many of these cases the government argues that the church agency is not performing a religious function because secular agencies could and sometimes do provide similar services. This position implicitly asserts that the government can define the scope of the church's mission.

C. Proselytizing, Religious Speech, New Religions, and the Right to Conversion

The Jehovah's Witness cases of the 1940s established that religious speech is constitutionally protected on the same terms as secular speech. The Supreme Court has continued to take that approach. The constitutional equivalence of religious and secular speech was the basis for the Supreme Court's holding

164. Dayton Christian Schools, Inc. v. Ohio Civil Rights Comm'n, 766 F.2d 932 (6th Cir. 1985), *rev'd on other grounds*, 477 U.S. 619 (1986); Dolter v. Wahlert High School, 483 F. Supp. 266 (N.D. Iowa 1980) (employment of unwed mother); Walker v. First Orthodox Presbyterian Church, 22 Fair Empl. Prac. Cas. (BNA) 762 (Cal. Super. Ct. 1980) (employment of homosexual).

165. Some examples include State v. Andrews, 651 P.2d 473 (Haw. 1982); Attorney General v. Bailey, 436 N.E.2d 139 (Mass. 1982); State ex rel. Douglas v. Faith Baptist Church, 301 N.W.2d 571 (Neb. 1981); State Bd. of Higher Educ. v. Directors of Shelton College, 448 A.2d 988 (N.J. 1982); State v. Rivinius, 328 N.W. 2d 220 (N.D. 1982); State ex rel. McElmore v. Clarksville School of Theology, 636 S.W.2d 706 (Tenn. 1982).

166. Kentucky State Bd. for Elementary & Secondary Educ. v. Rudasill, 589 S.W.2d 877 (Ky. 1979); State v. Whisner, 351 N.E.2d 750 (Ohio 1976).

167. City of Sumner v. First Baptist Church, 639 P.2d 1358 (Wash. 1982).

168. State v. Corpus Christi People's Baptist Church, Inc., 683 S.W.2d 692 (Tex. 1984).

169. Tennessee Baptist Children's Home, Inc. v. United States, 790 F.2d 534 (6th Cir. 1986).

170. Volunteers of America v. NLRB, 777 F.2d 1386 (9th Cir. 1985); Lutheran Social Serv. v. United States, 758 F.2d 1283 (8th Cir. 1985).

that college students cannot be prevented from discussing religion on campus.[171] Congress and the lower courts have disagreed on whether high school students receive the same protection.[172]

The contemporary equivalent of the Jehovah's Witnesses are the new proselytizing sects, especially the Hare Krishnas. There have been dozens of lower court cases involving the Hare Krishnas' right to solicit in various public places. Only one of these cases has reached the Supreme Court. In *International Society for Krishna Consciousness v. Heffron*,[173] the Court upheld a rule that required solicitors and exhibitors at the state fair to remain in a booth. The Court has always permitted reasonable restrictions on the time, place, and manner of speech when the state's purpose is traffic control or some other legitimate goal unrelated to censorship. The Court thought the booth rule was reasonable in light of the congestion at state fairs.

Reasonable restrictions on speech must be applied in an evenhanded way. Thus, the Court struck down a charitable solicitation ordinance that applied to some churches but not others;[174] the state is not permitted to discriminate between religions. The scope of permissible nondiscriminatory regulation of charitable solicitation, by churches or secular charities, remains unsettled.[175]

The most serious issues about the new religions have not yet reached the Supreme Court. These issues relate to allegations that some of the new religions convert new adherents by brainwashing, and to efforts by parents and others to forcibly withdraw converts from these religions. Parents have physically abducted adult converts and held them against their will until they agreed to leave their new religion. Other parents have held their adult children under guardianship orders during efforts to turn them away from a new religion. Parents often hire persons who specialize in persuading or coercing abducted converts to renounce their new religion. These persons, who call themselves "deprogrammers," say that some "deprogrammed" converts leave their new religion and express gratitude at being rescued. Others return to

171. Widmar v. Vincent, 454 U.S. 263 (1981).

172. *Compare* The Equal Access Act, 20 U.S.C. §§ 4071-4074 (Supp. II 1984), *with* Bender v. Williamsport Area School Dist., 741 F.2d 538 (3d Cir. 1984), *vacated on other grounds*, 475 U.S. 534 (1986). See Laycock, *Equal Access, supra* note 4; Ruti Teitel, *The Unconstitutionality of Equal Access Policies and Legislation Allowing Organized Student-Initiated Religious Activities in the Public High Schools: A Proposal for a Unitary First Amendment Forum Analysis*, 12 Hastings Const. L.Q. 529 (1985).

173. 452 U.S. 640 (1981).

174. Larson v. Valente, 456 U.S. 228 (1982).

175. Those questions are explored in *Secretary of State v. Joseph H. Munson Co.*, 467 U.S. 947 (1984), and *Village of Schaumburg v. Citizens for a Better Environment*, 444 U.S. 620 (1980).

their new religion at the first opportunity and sue their parents and the "deprogrammers."

The resulting litigation has produced mixed results. Most appellate courts have recognized the threat to free exercise rights and have been reluctant to legitimize abduction, involuntary "deprogramming," or guardianship orders against adults not proven to be mentally incompetent.[176] But some courts have assumed that brainwashing by religions is a serious threat and have tolerated, or even assisted, parental intervention by force and threats of force.[177] Even in cases where the "deprogrammed" converts won, juries rarely have returned substantial verdicts.

The right to convert to a new religion deserves better protection than this. The right to choose one's own religious beliefs is the very essence of religious liberty. Courts and families might legitimately intervene when a conversion is truly involuntary. But the importance of the right to convert, and the likelihood that the majority's perceptions of new religions will be distorted by hostility, require a strong presumption that conversions are voluntary. Such a presumption is not rebutted by evidence of an intense emotional experience and a sharp break with the past; these often accompany wholly voluntary religious conversions. Little more than that has been offered in most of the reported cases. In most of these cases there has been no evidence that proselytizers for the new religion used physical force, and little evidence of brainwashing, but there has been largely undisputed evidence of physical force by the parents and "deprogrammers."

It is easy to exaggerate the threat posed by new and unorthodox religions, and fears of exaggerated or imaginary threats can quickly lead to persecution. The history of the Mormons, Catholics, and Jehovah's Witnesses illustrates as much.[178] If we are to avoid repeating those mistakes with today's new religions, we must insist on clear proof when the new religions are charged with wrongdoing, and especially clear proof when the right to religious conversion is at risk.[179]

---

176. *See, e.g.,* Colombrito v. Kelly, 764 F.2d 122 (2d Cir. 1985); Taylor v. Gilmartin, 686 F.2d 1346 (10th Cir. 1983); Ward v. Connor, 657 F.2d 45 (4th Cir. 1981). Additional cases are collected in Annot., 11 A.L.R.4th 228 (1982 and Supp. 1985).

177. *See, e.g.,* Peterson v. Sorlien, 299 N.W.2d 123 (Minn. 1980). For additional examples, see the actions of the trial courts in the cases cited *supra* note 176 and the annotation cited *supra* note 176.

178. See notes 37-72 and accompanying text.

179. For a vigorous debate on these issues, see Richard Delgado, *When Religious Exercise Is Not Free: Deprogramming and the Constitutional Status of Coercively Induced Belief,* 37 VAND. L. REV. 1071 (1984); Richard Delgado, *Religious Totalism: Gentle and Ungentle Persua-*

D. Religious Participation in Public Life

Because religiously motivated speech is protected by the Free Speech and Free Exercise Clauses, there can be no doubt that churches and believers are entitled to participate in political affairs. Those who attack the right of churches to participate in politics simply misunderstand the First Amendment; they have been misled by the metaphor of separation of church and state. The word "separation" does not appear in the First Amendment. That amendment forbids the state from trying to influence the church, either by helping (the Establishment Clause) or hindering (the Free Exercise Clause). But it does not restrict church efforts to influence the state. Those efforts are constitutionally protected, just like any other private efforts to influence the state in a democracy. The Supreme Court has not equivocated on these points. In 1978 it struck down a clause of the Tennessee constitution that precluded clergy from serving in the legislature.[180] In 1961 and again in 1980 it rejected claims that legislation supported by religious groups violates the Establishment Clause merely because of its religious support.[181]

The only serious restriction on the right of churches to participate in political affairs appears in section 501(c)(3) of the Internal Revenue Code, which limits the political activities of tax exempt organizations. That statute is discussed in the next section of this Article.

E. Church Tax Exemption

1. The Right to Exemption

Churches have traditionally been tax exempt, and there has been little constitutional litigation about that exemption. Most litigation is in state courts and involves details of applying the exemption to auxiliary church facilities. There is no decision holding that churches are entitled to a general tax exemption. *Murdock v. Pennsylvania* holds that the state cannot tax religious solicitation.[182] That supports a more general argument that the state cannot tax religious exercise as such. Arguably, it follows that the state cannot tax

---

sion Under the First Amendment, 51 S. CAL. L. REV. 1 (1977); Robert N. Shapiro, *Of Robots, Persons, and the Protection of Religious Beliefs,* 56 S. CAL. L. REV. 1277 (1983).

180. McDaniel v. Paty, 435 U.S. 618 (1978).

181. Harris v. McRae, 448 U.S. 297, 319-20 (1980); McGowan v. Maryland, 366 U.S. 420, 442 (1961).

182. 319 U.S. 105 (1943).

church property essential to religious exercise. Selling a church sanctuary at a tax foreclosure sale surely raises a serious free exercise issue. But the Court explicitly reserved that issue in *Murdock*.[183]

There has also been litigation attacking the property tax exemption as an establishment of religion. The Supreme Court dealt with that claim in *Walz v. Tax Commission*,[184] holding that churches constitutionally may be included in a broad tax exemption for charitable organizations generally. Undoubtedly, the Court would decide the same way with respect to the exemption from federal income tax. Exemptions available solely to religion, and not to secular charities, such as the income tax exemption for housing allowances for ministers,[185] would be much harder to defend under the *Walz* rationale.

As a purely political matter it is easy to predict that the Supreme Court would uphold the income tax deduction for gifts to churches.[186] But that opinion would be much harder to write. The deduction resembles the property tax exemption in *Walz* in only one way: it is available to a wide range of charities, many of which are secular. But the deduction for gifts to churches is not a case of the state refraining from taxing the churches. Rather, it reduces the taxes that would otherwise be due on secular income to ordinary taxpayers. Economically, it is very much like a matching grant in the same proportions as the taxpayer's marginal tax bracket.

2. Exemption as a Means of Regulation

The Internal Revenue Service increasingly views tax exemption as a means of regulating tax exempt entities, including churches. In *Bob Jones University v. United States*, for example, the Supreme Court held that tax exempt entities must comply with public policy.[187] The IRS has just given up its long and unsuccessful effort to force church entities providing services that it considers to be secular, such as orphanages and social service agencies, to file informational tax returns.[188]

Undoubtedly the most serious regulatory use of tax exemption is section 501(c)(3) of the Internal Revenue Code. That section provides that tax ex-

183. *Id.* at 112.
184. 397 U.S. 664 (1970).
185. 26 U.S.C. § 107 (1982).
186. *Cf.* Mueller v. Allen, 463 U.S. 388 (1983). See *infra* note 243 and accompanying text.
187. 461 U.S. 574 (1983).
188. Rev. Proc. 86-23, 1986-20 I.R.B. 17. The new procedure followed two adverse court decisions. Tennessee Baptist Children's Home, Inc. v. United States, 790 F.2d 534 (6th Cir. 1986); Lutheran Social Serv. v. United States, 758 F.2d 1283 (8th Cir. 1985).

empt entities cannot endorse candidates for public office or devote any substantial part of their funds to influencing legislation. The Supreme Court has never passed on the constitutionality of this provision as applied to churches. The Court has upheld the restriction as applied to secular organizations' efforts to educate the public about political issues.[189] Several justices in that case relied on the availability of section 501(c)(4) to save the constitutionality of the restrictions in section 501(c)(3). An organization that wishes to receive tax deductible contributions and also influence legislation or elections can divide itself into two organizations, one created under section 501(c)(3) and one under section 501(c)(4). The (c)(4) affiliate must do all the political work, and contributions to it are not tax deductible. But that is not a viable solution for a church whose religious faith compels it to speak through its religious leaders on the moral aspects of political issues.[190]

F. Religious Expression in Public Places

The Supreme Court has adhered to its decisions in the school prayer cases despite continued political attack. But it has not enforced the principle of those cases in other contexts. The school cases that have reached the Court since 1963 have involved efforts to attenuate the state's relationship with the prayer or religious observance at issue. Thus, a Kentucky statute provided that if private donors would provide copies of the Ten Commandments, the public schools would post them in classrooms. The Court invalidated the practice under the Establishment Clause; Kentucky was endorsing the scriptures of a particular religious tradition.[191]

A Louisiana statute authorized school teachers to ask if any student wanted to lead a prayer. If none volunteered, the teacher could lead the prayer, but did not have to. The state argued that this left school prayer to the voluntary actions of teachers and students. But the teacher — the state's employee — plainly was sponsoring the prayer. The court of appeals invalidated the statute, and the Supreme Court summarily affirmed.[192]

Most recently, in *Wallace v. Jaffree*,[193] the Court invalidated an Alabama statute authorizing teachers to announce "that a period of silence not to ex-

189. Regan v. Taxation with Representation, 461 U.S. 540 (1983).

190. *See generally* Wilfred Caron & Deirdre Dessigue, *IRC § 501(c)(3): Practical and Constitutional Implications of "Political" Activity Restrictions,* 2 J.L. & POL. 169 (1985).

191. Stone v. Graham, 449 U.S. 39 (1980).

192. Karen B. v. Treen, 653 F.2d 897 (5th Cir. 1981), *aff'd mem.,* 455 U.S. 913 (1982).

193. 472 U.S. 38 (1985).

ceed one minute in duration shall be observed for meditation or voluntary prayer."[194] The Court found that the purpose of the statute was to endorse prayer, a purpose that violates the heart of the Establishment Clause.

A distinct but related issue is whether schools can accommodate students who wish to pray privately during the school day. In *Wallace v. Jaffree,* the Court hinted broadly that public schools could observe a moment of silence to provide an opportunity for prayer by students so inclined, so long as the state did not encourage or endorse prayer when it announced the moment of silence. A divided panel of the Third Circuit has rejected that reading, holding that any legislative intention to accommodate religion is a religious purpose forbidden by earlier Supreme Court precedents.[195]

Another way to accommodate those students would be to allow voluntary student prayer groups to meet in classrooms before or after school, on the same basis as other extracurricular groups but without school sponsorship. The Supreme Court approved meetings for college students, holding that the Free Speech Clause requires universities to give student religious organizations the same privileges accorded other student organizations.[196] But three courts of appeals have distinguished high school students from college students. Two of the cases held that high school prayer groups are not entitled to meet on campus;[197] one held that schools could not permit meetings without violating the Establishment Clause.[198] These courts believed that high school students were impressionable, unaccustomed to academic freedom, and that they would mistake toleration of religious speech on campus for government endorsement of religion. Congress responded to these decisions with the Equal Access Act,[199] forbidding schools to discriminate among extracurricular groups. The Supreme Court has failed to resolve the controversy because of standing problems.[200]

194. ALA. CODE § 16-1-20.1 (Supp. 1985).

195. May v. Cooperman, 780 F.2d 240 (3d Cir. 1985). The court relied on the secular purpose requirement of Lemon v. Kurtzman, 403 U.S. 602 (1971), discussed in text, *infra* notes 251-52. For a refutation of that reading of the purpose requirement, see Laycock, *Equal Access, supra* note 4, at 21-24, 61-63 (text at notes 102-15, 293-307). [An appeal in *May* was later dismissed on other grounds. Karcher v. May, 484 U.S. 72 (1987).]

196. Widmar v. Vincent, 454 U.S. 263 (1981).

197. Bender v. Williamsport Area School Dist., 741 F.2d 538 (3d Cir. 1984), *vacated on other grounds,* 475 U.S. 534 (1986); Brandon v. Board of Educ., 635 F.2d 971 (2d Cir. 1980).

198. Lubbock Civil Liberties Union v. Lubbock Indep. School Dist., 669 F.2d 1038 (5th Cir. 1982).

199. 20 U.S.C. §§ 4071-4074 (Supp. II 1984). For analyses of the Act and a debate over its validity, *compare* Laycock, *Equal Access, supra* note 4, *with* Teitel, *supra* note 172.

200. Bender v. Williamsport Area School Dist., 475 U.S. 534 (1986).

The Court has avoided passing on other common religious observances in the public schools. Baccalaureate services and Christmas assemblies remain common, although they appear irreconcilable with the school prayer decisions. One court of appeals approved Christmas programs with religious symbols and Christmas carols, but it forbade more intensely religious parts of the school's program, such as a set of questions and answers about the baby Jesus.[201]

The Supreme Court has permitted state-sponsored prayer or religious observance in contexts other than schools. Thus, it allowed states to hire legislative chaplains to open each legislative session with prayer.[202] And it permitted a municipal Nativity display that was part of a larger display that included Santa Claus, reindeer, and other nonreligious symbols.[203]

The Court made no serious attempt to reconcile its decisions in these cases with those in the school prayer cases. In the legislative prayer case it noted that the First Congress had both proposed the Establishment Clause and appointed a chaplain; long historical usage suggested that legislative prayer was permissible. In the Nativity display case the Court invoked a variety of rationales, not all of them entirely consistent. It said that the history of legislative chaplains and of Thanksgiving proclamations showed that some government support for religion was permissible.[204] Then it said there could be no single test for deciding what support of religion was permitted and what was forbidden.[205] Then it said that the crèche display was not an attempt to express a religious message, but that it "principally" depicted "the historical origins of this traditional event" and that to do so was a "secular purpose."[206] The Court also seemed to assume that Christmas carols in the public schools were permissible.[207]

G. Government Aid to Religious Schools

Government aid to religious schools has been on the Supreme Court's docket almost continuously since 1968. The Court has been unwilling either to ban all such aid or to permit all such aid. Instead, it has groped for a compromise

---

201. Florey v. Sioux Falls School Dist. 49-5, 619 F.2d 1311 (8th Cir. 1981).
202. Marsh v. Chambers, 463 U.S. 783 (1983).
203. Lynch v. Donnelly, 465 U.S. 668 (1984).
204. *Id.* at 673-78.
205. *Id.* at 678-79.
206. *Id.* at 680-81.
207. *Id.* at 686.

formulation that would permit some aid but not too much. At least six inconsistent theories have been endorsed by one or more justices. The majority has switched from one theory to another more than once. At least four of these theories are plausible. The result has been a series of inconsistent and almost inexplicable decisions.

1. The Possible Theories

The no-aid theory One plausible view is the no-aid theory: that any state money paid to a religious school or its students expands the school's budget and thereby aids religion. Even if the state's money is used to buy math books, that frees some of the school's money to spend on religion, or it enables the school to lower tuition and make it easier for children to attend a religious school. That appears to have been the view of the dissenters in *Everson v. Board of Education,*[208] the 1947 case upholding public bus transportation to religious schools. The majority saw bus rides as a secular public service; the dissenters thought free bus rides made it easier to attend religious schools. The dissenters' approach in *Everson* became the majority's approach with respect to instructional materials in *Wolman v. Walter.*[209]

The purchase-of-services theory A second plausible view is the purchase-of-services theory: that state money paid to a religious school is simply a purchase of educational services. The state is obligated to provide a free education for all its children; it can do so directly or through independent contractors. As long as the state does not pay more than the costs of the secular education provided, it is simply paying for services rendered and not subsidizing religion. Thus, to talk about these programs as "aid" is to beg the question.[210]

The Court applied the purchase-of-services theory to government payments to religious hospitals that cared for indigents in *Bradfield v. Roberts,*[211] an 1899 decision that has never been questioned. The Court appeared to take the same view of payments for Indians' education in *Quick Bear v. Leupp,*[212] but it has not done so in any of its modern education cases.

---

208. 330 U.S. 1 (1947).

209. 433 U.S. 229, 248-51 (1977).

210. Dean Choper's view resembles the purchase-of-services theory, although he does not use the phrase. Jesse Choper, *The Establishment Clause and Aid to Parochial Schools,* 56 CAL. L. REV. 260 (1968).

211. 175 U.S. 291 (1899).

212. 210 U.S. 50 (1908).

The equal-treatment theory A third plausible view is the equal-treatment theory. In its strong form, it holds that the government is obligated to pay for the secular aspects of education in religious schools; in its weak form, it holds that government is free to make such payments if it wishes.

Children have a constitutional right to attend religious schools.[213] If they do not exercise that right and attend public schools instead, the state will be required to spend substantial sums on their education. If they do exercise their constitutional right, they forfeit the state subsidy of their education. This can plausibly be viewed as a penalty on the exercise of their constitutional right. Chief Justice Burger took that view with respect to the Court's holding that the state could not provide on-site remedial and therapeutic services to children in religious schools.[214]

The equal-treatment theory relies on the principle that government cannot discriminate against religion, which is as basic as the principle that the government cannot support religion.[215] The discrimination against religion would be clear if any state adopted a voucher plan, issuing education vouchers that could be spent at any public or private school except religious schools. *Witters v. Washington Department of Services for the Blind*[216] was equally clear. The state provided scholarships for vocational training for the blind, but it refused to let Witters use his scholarship to be trained as a pastor or church youth director. Because he apparently could have used the scholarship to learn any secular occupation, the Supreme Court held that it would not violate the Establishment Clause to let him use the scholarship for religious training.

The Court has applied the strong form of the equal-treatment theory to religious speech, requiring colleges to allow student prayer groups to meet on campus.[217] It has applied the weak form of the equal-treatment theory to religious school aid, arguing that the Constitution does not require states to discriminate against children in religious schools.[218] But in these school aid cases, equal treatment was merely a justification for the state's program; the Court did not suggest that states are required to spend as much money to educate students in religious schools as they spend to educate students in public schools.

213. Pierce v. Society of Sisters of the Holy Names of Jesus and Mary, 268 U.S. 510 (1925).

214. Meek v. Pittenger, 421 U.S. 349, 387 (1975) (Burger, C.J., dissenting).

215. The tension between the two principles is discussed in Johnson, *supra* note 56, at 822-24; Mansfield, *supra* note 73, at 879-81.

216. 474 U.S. 481 (1986).

217. Widmar v. Vincent, 454 U.S. 263 (1981).

218. Witters v. Washington Dept. of Servs. for the Blind, 474 U.S. 481 (1986); Mueller v. Allen, 463 U.S. 388 (1983); Everson v. Board of Educ., 330 U.S. 1, 16 (1947).

The child-benefit theory A fourth plausible view of the school aid issue is the child-benefit theory: that the state can provide educational benefits directly to children or their parents, even if the benefits are used at or in connection with a religious school. But the state cannot provide the same aid directly to the school. The majority of the Court has relied on the child-benefit theory to uphold bus rides in *Everson*, textbook loans in *Board of Education v. Allen*,[219] and state income tax deductions in *Mueller v. Allen*.[220]

Proponents of the no-aid theory note that aid to a school and aid to the students in that school are economically equivalent: either makes it less expensive for students to attend the school. But others have found it symbolically important that the aid goes to the child rather than to the school. Directing the aid to the child may be seen as a symbolic affirmation of the purchase-of-services or equal-treatment theory, emphasizing that these programs provide education as well as religion. In *Witters v. Washington Department of Services for the Blind*, the Court said, in the alternative, that the student's independent choice to use his scholarship at a religious school meant that the payment to the school was not state action.[221]

The tracing theory A fifth view of the school aid issue has attracted the Court, but it is only superficially plausible. Under the tracing theory the Court tries to divide all the activities of a religious school into components that are wholly secular and components that are, or might be, affected by religion. Then it tries to trace each dollar of government money to see what the school spent it on. The Court approves aid if, and only if, the money can be traced to a wholly secular expenditure.[222] This was part of its approach to bus rides in *Everson*,[223] and to secular textbooks in *Board of Education v. Allen*.[224] But this approach cannot be applied consistently. The task of dividing school activities into secular and religious components is conceptually impossible; the whole purpose of such schools is to integrate secular and religious education.

In applying the tracing theory, the Court has distinguished primary and secondary education from higher education. The Court has concluded that religious primary and secondary schools are pervasively religious, but that religious colleges and universities are not. Consequently, aid to primary and secondary schools must be traced to uses that cannot possibly be diverted to

219. 392 U.S. 236 (1968).
220. 463 U.S. 388 (1983).
221. 474 U.S. 481, 488-89 (1986).
222. For an analysis and colorable rationale, see Mansfield, *supra* note 73, at 882-84.
223. 330 U.S. 1 (1947).
224. 392 U.S. 236 (1968).

serve religion. For those schools, the Court assumes that any teacher in any subject might also teach religious values. But the Court assumes that most instruction at the university level is secular, or at least conducted in an atmosphere of academic freedom. Consequently, aid to colleges and universities is permissible as long as it cannot be diverted to chapel services, explicit religious instruction, and the like.[225]

The little-bit theory The Court occasionally alludes to a sixth theory, which may explain more of the Court's results than the theories it relies on more often.[226] This is the theory that a little bit of aid to religious schools is permissible, but it must be structured in a way that keeps it from becoming too much. Indeed, this theory may be generalizable in ways that explain other Establishment Clause conundrums, such as the Court's approval of legislative chaplains and municipal Nativity scenes: perhaps, in general, the Court believes that a little bit of government support for religion is unobjectionable.

2. The Court's Results

It is hardly a surprise that this mix of theories has not produced coherent results. The variety of theories and the attempt to distinguish the indistinguishable in the tracing theory have produced distinctions that do not commend themselves to common sense. Thus, bus transportation to and from school is permitted,[227] but bus transportation on field trips is forbidden.[228] Why? Because the teacher might discuss religion on the field trip. Thus, under the tracing theory, the bus ride to school is wholly secular, but the field trip might not be.

The state can loan secular textbooks to students in religious schools,[229] but it cannot loan maps, projectors, or other instructional materials.[230] The child-benefit theory might have reconciled these holdings, because each child needs his own textbook but only the school needs maps and projectors.

225. Roemer v. Maryland Pub. Works Bd., 426 U.S. 736 (1976); Hunt v. McNair, 413 U.S. 734 (1973); Tilton v. Richardson, 403 U.S. 672 (1971).

226. Witters v. Washington Dept. of Servs. for the Blind, 474 U.S. 481, 488 (1986); Grand Rapids School Dist. v. Ball, 473 U.S. 373, 397 (1985); Meek v. Pittenger, 421 U.S. 349, 364 (1975).

227. Everson v. Board of Educ., 330 U.S. 1 (1947).

228. Wolman v. Walter, 433 U.S. 229, 252-55 (1977).

229. *Id.* at 236-38 (plurality opinion); Meek v. Pittenger, 421 U.S. 349, 359-62 (1975) (plurality opinion); Board of Educ. v. Allen, 392 U.S. 236 (1968).

230. Wolman v. Walter, 433 U.S. 229, 248-51 (1977); Meek v. Pittenger, 421 U.S. 349, 362-66 (1975).

But that is not what the Court said. Rather, it decided the first textbook case on a combination of child-benefit and tracing theories; then it decided the instructional materials case on the theory that any aid to the school helps religion. The Court noted that its approach to books was inconsistent with its approach to other instructional materials, but it declined to reconcile the cases.[231] Even more strange, in the very opinion in which it adopted the no-aid theory for instructional materials, it used the tracing theory to allow state-administered tests in religious schools.[232]

The Court also used the tracing theory to hold that guidance counseling, remedial instruction, and other therapeutic services are permissible if provided by public school teachers away from the religious school campus,[233] but not if provided by public school teachers on the religious school campus.[234] Why? Because the public school teachers might be influenced by the religious environment and inadvertently discuss religion with their students; that danger is insubstantial away from the religious school. However, diagnostic services are permissible even on the religious school campus because the diagnostician will not spend enough time with any one student to develop a relationship. Without a relationship he is unlikely to talk religion.[235]

Grand Rapids School District v. Ball[236] offered two additional reasons why supplemental public instruction cannot be offered on religious school campuses. First, public instruction at the religious school creates a symbolic union of church and state. Second, in an explicit application of the little-bit theory, the Court said that public instruction might gradually displace the entire secular part of the religious school curriculum, resulting in too much aid.

The tracing theory also produced paradoxical results with respect to teacher salaries and testing expenses. The state cannot pay fifteen percent of the salary of teachers who teach secular subjects in religious schools.[237] It cannot pay religious schools for the cost of conducting state-mandated testing if the religious school teachers design and grade the test.[238] In neither case could the money be traced to wholly secular uses, because the teachers might include religious material in their classes or on the exams, even in sec-

---

231. *Wolman,* 433 U.S. at 251-52 n.18.

232. *Id.* at 238-41.

233. *Id.* at 244-48.

234. Aguilar v. Felton, 473 U.S. 402 (1985); Grand Rapids School Dist. v. Ball, 473 U.S. 373 (1985); Meek v. Pittenger, 421 U.S. 349, 367-73 (1975).

235. *Wolman,* 433 U.S. at 241-44.

236. 473 U.S. 373, 389-97 (1985).

237. Lemon v. Kurtzman, 403 U.S. 602 (1971).

238. Levitt v. Committee for Pub. Educ. & Religious Liberty, 413 U.S. 472 (1973).

ular subjects. But the state is permitted to administer required tests to religious school students and grade the tests itself.[239] State designed and administered tests present no danger of religious content; they are wholly secular.

Does it follow that the state can pay the school to administer objective secular tests designed by the state? The Court said yes.[240] There was no risk of testing religious content, and paying the school to administer the tests was no more a subsidy than having the state administer the tests directly. Either approach relieved the school of the expense. On the same rationale, the state could require religious schools to take attendance and pay for the expense of doing so.[241] In each case the expense consisted of part of the teachers' time; the state paid as much as 5.4% of faculty payroll under this program.[242] So it turns out that, with enough red tape, the state can pay part of the salaries of teachers in religious schools after all. The state need only identify wholly secular job components and the time required to perform them, and pay the school for that time. This carried the tracing theory to its fictional extreme. And this decision came after the Court rejected the tracing theory with respect to instructional materials.

In 1983, *Mueller v. Allen* held that state income tax deductions for the expenses of sending children to religious schools are permissible.[243] But ten years earlier, *Committee for Public Education and Religious Liberty v. Nyquist* held that state income tax credits for the expenses of sending children to religious schools are forbidden.[244] What is the difference? The Court said that the tax credits in *Nyquist* were dovetailed with a scholarship program for low income students, making it clear that the tax credits were themselves a thinly disguised scholarship. In addition, the credit applied to private school tuition only. The tax deduction in *Mueller* also applied to transportation and supply expenses, which could be claimed by parents of public school children, and to tuition payments by the handful of children attending public schools outside their own district.

Those were real differences, but they were not very significant. Again, a theory shift was more important. *Nyquist* was written on the tracing theory, or perhaps on the no-aid theory. Scholarships and tax credits were invalid under either theory because once the students paid the money to the school it went into general revenues and could not be traced. But in *Mueller* the

239. *Wolman*, 433 U.S. 229, 239-41 (1977).
240. Committee for Pub. Educ. & Religious Liberty v. Regan, 444 U.S. 646 (1980).
241. *Id.*
242. *Id.* at 665 (Blackmun, J., dissenting).
243. 463 U.S. 388 (1983).
244. 413 U.S. 756 (1973).

Court emphasized the child-benefit theory and the equal-treatment theory. The Court thought it important that the tax savings went to parents instead of religious schools, and that parents decided independently whether to send their children to public or private schools. The state was not required to discriminate against religion by denying a deduction available to parents of public school children. It was irrelevant that ninety-six percent of the deductions were in fact claimed by parents of children in Catholic and Lutheran schools. This was a break with earlier cases in which the Court had thought it significant that most private schools were religious.[245] *Mueller* obviously rejected the no-aid theory, and did not mention the tracing theory.

Whatever the Court said, a comparison of tax deductions and tax credits suggests consistent application of the little-bit theory. There is no structural limit on a tax credit; a state could allow a credit for 100% of private school tuition. But a deduction can never be worth more than the private school's tuition multiplied by the state's marginal tax rate; and most state income tax rates are quite low. This inherent limit on the aid that could be channeled through a tax deduction may have influenced some justices to vote for the *Mueller* result without being committed to new theoretical directions in the opinion.

These tax deduction and tax credit cases also highlight an inconsistency in public perception of the issues, and probably in judicial perception as well. Tax deductions for tuition paid to religious schools are widely perceived as a form of aid that at least raises serious questions under the Establishment Clause. Yet tax deductions for gifts to the same schools, or to churches themselves for purely religious purposes, are widely perceived as raising no problem.[246] It is hard to believe that both perceptions can be correct. The breadth of the charitable contribution deduction offers weak ground for distinction, because a tuition tax deduction is always a small part of a state's efforts to finance, encourage, and subsidize education.[247] The long-standing familiarity of the charitable contribution deduction, and the novelty of tuition deductions, explain but do not justify the differences in constitutional perception.

Many commentators thought that *Mueller's* approval of tuition tax deductions indicated a substantial shift in direction — that the Burger Court would now allow much more aid. But in 1985, in *Grand Rapids v. Ball*[248] and *Aguilar v. Felton*,[249] the Court returned to the tracing theory to strike down

245. Meek v. Pittenger, 421 U.S. 349, 363 (1975) (75% of private schools in Pennsylvania).

246. Federal income tax law makes these contributions deductible from income, 26 U.S.C. § 501(c)(3)(1982), and many state income tax laws incorporate federal deductions.

247. *Cf.* Walz v. Tax Comm'n, 397 U.S. 664 (1970).

248. 473 U.S. 373 (1985).

249. 473 U.S. 402 (1985).

supplemental courses in religious schools. The political context highlights the majority's aversion to substantial aid: *Aguilar* struck down federally funded remedial instruction for impoverished children. The Court again thought it significant that most private schools receiving the aid were religious schools.[250] If *Mueller* were intended to be a new beginning, that new beginning was erased in *Grand Rapids* and *Aguilar.*

H. The Three-Part Test for Establishment

In 1971 the Court distilled from its earlier cases a three-part test to identify Establishment Clause violations. The Court said: "First, the statute must have a secular legislative purpose; second, its principal or primary effect must be one that neither advances nor inhibits religion; finally, the statute must not foster 'an excessive government entanglement with religion.'"[251]

The Court generally has adhered to this verbal formulation ever since. In cases involving prayer or religious teaching in the public schools, the Court has generally found no secular purpose. In the cases on financial aid to religious institutions, the Court has held that states are pursuing the secular purpose of educating children. But it has generally found a dilemma in the second and third parts of its test. Under the tracing theory, if aid cannot be traced to a wholly secular function it has a primary effect of advancing religion. But if the state imposes substantial controls to insure that the aid is not diverted to religious purposes, that creates too much entanglement between church and state. One way or the other, most aid to religious schools fails the three-part test.

The Court's three-part test has been subject to intense scholarly criticism.[252] Some scholars have argued that the ban on excessive entanglement in the third part of the test, and on effects that inhibit religion in the second

---

250. *Id.* at 406; 473 U.S. at 385.

251. Lemon v. Kurtzman, 403 U.S. 602, 612-13 (1971) (quoting Walz v. Tax Comm'n, 397 U.S. 664, 674 (1970)).

252. All three parts of the test are criticized in Johnson, *supra* note 56, at 825-31; Kurland, *supra* note 2, at 17-20. For criticism of the entanglement doctrine, see Choper, *supra* note 134, at 681-85; Edward Gaffney, *Political Divisiveness Along Religious Lines: The Entanglement of the Court in Sloppy History and Bad Public Policy,* 24 St. Louis U.L.J. 205 (1980); Donald Giannella, *Lemon and Tilton: The Bitter and the Sweet of Church-State Entanglement,* 1971 Sup. Ct. Rev. 147, 148, 170-76; Laycock, *General Theory, supra* note 4, at 1392-94 (text at notes 152-65); Kenneth Ripple, *The Entanglement Test of the Religion Clauses — A Ten Year Assessment,* 27 U.C.L.A. L. Rev. 1195, 1216-24 (1980).

part of the test, are free exercise concepts that have nothing to do with the Establishment Clause.[253] The dispute is more than academic. Only the affected churches or believers can sue to prevent inhibition of religion or entanglement with religion under the Free Exercise Clause. But, by making these problems Establishment Clause violations, the Court permits nonbelievers to file taxpayer suits to save the churches from "inhibition" and "entanglement," whether or not the churches want to be saved.

In addition to this expansion of the usual understanding of establishment, the three-part test has been so elastic in its application that it means everything and nothing. The meaning of entanglement has been especially slippery.[254] All of the financial aid cases summarized in the previous section were decided under the three-part test; the Court modified the three parts as necessary to accommodate all the different results and all the different theories. The Court upheld municipal Nativity scenes under the three-part test, finding that depictions of the Holy Family had a secular purpose and effect(!) and did not cause excessive entanglement between government and religion.[255] I have described the prayer cases and the financial aid cases, the two pre-eminent Establishment Clause issues, without ever mentioning the three-part test. I have done so because I think the three-part test does not help explain the Court's results and actually hampers understanding of the real issues.

IV. Conclusion

This Article has emphasized the kinds of religious liberty issues that reach the Supreme Court of the United States. Those tend to be the most difficult issues. Some of them are difficult in principle; others are clear in principle but seem difficult when applied to benefit religions that seem strange, unpopular, or threatening, or when applied to the seeming disadvantage of religions that are familiar and comfortable to the majority.

These difficulties demand our sustained attention precisely because they are difficult. But we should not lose sight of the religious liberty issues that are not difficult. Free choice of religious belief is unquestioned in this country. The right to basic religious observance is unquestioned in this country.

253. Laycock, *General Theory, supra* note 4, at 1378-88 (text at notes 57-121); Robert E. Riggs, *Judicial Doublethink and the Establishment Clause: The Fallacy of Establishment by Inhibition,* 18 VAL. U.L. REV. 285 (1984).

254. See Laycock, *General Theory, supra* note 4, at 1392-94 (text at notes 152-65).

255. Lynch v. Donnelly, 465 U.S. 668 (1984).

Religious tolerance and pluralism are our political and societal norm. We do not perfectly achieve that norm, and intolerance has not been eliminated, but it is not respectable and it is often muted. Even those who attempt to forcibly dissuade recent converts to new religions do not claim any right to interfere with free choice of religious belief. Rather, they claim that the original conversion was involuntary and that they are, in fact, protecting the convert's right to free choice. Our societal commitment to religious freedom is strong enough that no other justification for their activities could even become the subject of debate.

When the Constitution's Framers wrote the Religion Clauses they hoped to end the history of religious persecution and civil war that had plagued humankind for so long. Their effort has largely, but not perfectly, succeeded. That success is partly a direct result of the rules established by the Religion Clauses. It is partly the result of the strong societal commitment to tolerance symbolized by those clauses and now shared by most of the major religions in this country.

The constitutional clauses and the societal commitment reinforce each other in important ways. The constitutional guarantee of religious liberty provides a legal mechanism by which any individual who thinks his religious liberty is violated may call the government to account judicially, and a rhetorical mechanism by which he may call the society to account politically. But efforts to invoke the Constitution would ultimately be futile if the society became sufficiently hostile to religious liberty. Once established, religious intolerance tends to be self-sustaining, as illustrated by the cycle of religious violence and counter-violence in Northern Ireland and the Middle East. So every generation must nurture and pass on the commitment to religious liberty. Grappling with the difficult and controversial issues of religious liberty is part of that responsibility.

Religious Liberty: The Legal Rights
of Religious Belief and Ministry

30 Concern No. 1, at 16 (Jan. 1988)

Concern *was a publication of United Presbyterian Women, directed principally to female members of the Presbyterian Church (U.S.A.). This brief survey assumes no legal background.*

*   *   *

Religious liberty and religious pluralism are among America's great contributions to the world. The principal legal guarantees of this liberty are in the First Amendment to the federal Constitution, which forbids any law "respecting an establishment of religion or prohibiting the free exercise thereof."

The Free Exercise Clause protects the right of every individual to choose and practice her own religious beliefs. The government cannot ban minority faiths or penalize their members. The clause also protects the right of every religious community to build churches, schools, hospitals, and other facilities, to hold services, to prescribe its own creed and order of worship, to proselytize, and to conduct ministries. We have come to take these things for granted. But these rights do not exist in some parts of the world, and they were often violated in the American colonies. They are constitutionally guaranteed because the Framers did not take them for granted.

The Establishment Clause prevents the government from requiring people to support religions other than their own. The government cannot sponsor an official state religion. It cannot require people to attend religious services, espouse religious beliefs, or pay taxes to support religion. It cannot lend its prestige and endorsement to one religion over others, to religion over nonbelief, or to nonbelief over religion.

Together, the two clauses make religion a matter of private choice. Government cannot interfere either with your practice of your own religion or your refusal to practice someone else's. It cannot interfere coercively by punishing you or by withholding government benefits. Nor can it interfere noncoercively by persuasion or endorsement.

The History of the Religion Clauses

To the Framers of the Constitution, widespread religious persecution was recent history. But, by the time of the American Revolution, Americans had reached consensus in support of free exercise. The Establishment Clause was more controversial. The Anglicans were established in most of the southern colonies; the Congregationalists were established in most of New England. Religious minorities paid taxes for the established churches. The established churches and their clergy were reluctant to give up their tax support. And many in the Revolutionary generation feared that religion could not flourish without the aid of the state. The lengthy debates in Virginia have been the most influential in our understanding of what it means to establish religion.

The Anglicans in Virginia proposed a compromise called the general assessment. Every citizen would pay a tax to support a pastor, but each taxpayer could designate the pastor to receive his tax. Non-believers could pay their tax to a school. Supporters of the established church argued that this was fair to everybody. But the general assessment was overwhelmingly defeated. In its place, the legislature enacted Thomas Jefferson's Statute for Religious Liberty, providing that no person should ever be compelled to support any religion.

The Historic Role of Presbyterians

Presbyterians played a critical role in defeating the general assessment. The Calvinist tradition included government support for the church, and some Presbyterians were initially attracted to the seeming security of tax support. But, after study and reflection, Hanover Presbytery opposed the general assessment. Presbyterians and Baptists were the largest religious minorities in Virginia, and their combined opposition defeated the bill.

Presbyterians opposed the bill partly from principle and partly from self-interest. The seemingly fair general assessment was not fair, because it could not accommodate the different theologies and polities even of the largest Protestant denominations. Baptists believed that the church must be supported voluntarily; they refused on principle to pay taxes even to their own church. A statute that required Baptists to violate their consciences was not consistent with religious liberty.

The general assessment would also have interfered with Presbyterian polity. Then, as now, Presbyterians carefully allocated authority between clergy and laity. Lay Presbyterians realized that, if the clergy were supported by tax money collected by the state, the laity would lose any financial control over the clergy.

The Baptists and Presbyterians also realized that they were flourishing with voluntary financial support and would continue to do so. Only the Anglicans had become dependent on coerced support, and only they had reason to fear they could not function with voluntary support. They survived as the Episcopalians, but in much smaller numbers. There were many reasons for the Anglican decline, but their traditional dependence on the state was surely one of the reasons.

Some Lessons from History

The lessons of this long-ago debate in Virginia are still current. Government efforts to aid the church inevitably interfere; the aid is as likely to hurt as to help. Some churches may benefit, but others will be hurt; "nonpreferential" aid to religion is never nonpreferential in fact. This was true even when religious pluralism consisted only of variations among Protestants. It is vastly more true today. Sometimes all religions will be hurt, as when public schools try to teach about a generic least-common-denominator God who offends no one. And always, government aid saps the spirit of voluntarism that makes religion flourish.

Like the Virginia Anglicans of the 1780s, some Americans still fear that religion cannot survive without government aid, and that the Establishment Clause is bad for religion. But our national experience is different. The Free Exercise and Establishment Clauses are essential companions; both protect religious liberty.

Threats to Religious Liberty

The two great threats to religious liberty are intolerance and indifference. Our traditions of religious tolerance break down in the face of religions that seem strange or threatening. Catholic immigrants, Mormons, Jehovah's Witnesses and other new faiths have been persecuted in their turn, here in the United States.

Today a new set of high demand religions — the so-called cults — are the object of great hostility. Parents are understandably alarmed when their adult children reject their families and join such strange faiths. I imagine that Pharisee parents were equally upset with children who followed the itinerant preacher from Nazareth. But the right to choose one's faith is the most fundamental religious right, and the right to preach one's faith to potential converts is the most fundamental ministry. We must be most solicitous of the rights of unpopular faiths, for they are the most likely to be persecuted.

Fundamentalist Christians have also encountered hostility. Many people fear the political agendas of some prominent fundamentalist ministers — fear them so much that they view fundamentalists as a dangerous faction. The result is that legitimate grievances and illegitimate demands get equally hostile responses.

The much publicized lawsuits over textbooks in Alabama and Tennessee illustrate the problem. In the Alabama case, fundamentalists sought to ban books from the public schools. A broad coalition opposed this effort to conform the schools to sectarian teachings.

The Tennessee case was quite different, but it was hard to learn that from the newspapers. Fundamentalist parents in that case sought to exempt their children from reading books that would undermine their children's faith. The exemption would not have changed the school's curriculum. The parents agreed to teach their children the same reading skills with other books and submit the children to testing. The case was a simple attempt to exempt a religious minority from a requirement that violated its conscience. The Supreme Court had already approved a similar exemption for Amish children.

Civil libertarians generally, and people committed to religious liberty in particular, should have supported the fundamentalist parents in the Tennessee case. Some did; the National Council of Churches filed a brief on their behalf. But the entire civil liberties establishment lined up against them, and many religious citizens opposed what they thought was another fundamentalist attempt to take over the schools. This misperception was fueled largely by hostility to fundamentalism.

The threat to religious liberty for mainstream faiths is indifference. Presbyterians are not likely to be persecuted, but they may be regulated to death. A Presbyterian church in Missouri was recently ordered to close its day care center; a Presbyterian church in Virginia was ordered to close its mission for the homeless. In each case, the problem was the zoning laws.

Many religious people see no religious liberty issue in these cases. The zoning laws are reasonable and neutral regulations; why should the church get special treatment?

In fact these cases strike at an important part of religious liberty. Once they zone the property for churches, the zoning commissions should not be allowed to limit the ministry of the churches that locate there. In each of these cases, the zoning commission overruled the church's definition of its mission. There are scores of similar cases involving all forms of modern regulation — labor, education, civil rights, and many others. Lawsuits now pending in Chicago and Washington ask secular courts to decide who should teach theology in Catholic seminaries!

Most government regulations serve some useful purpose, and there is a widespread tendency to assume that churches should comply. Often they should. But regulation of churches always expands government control over religious ministries. Creeping regulation can be devastating to religious liberty. Churches in the Communist nations report that they are not actively persecuted; rather, they are strangled by red tape.

Red tape can be equally strangling here if indifferent bureaucrats and complacent believers continue to think that churches are no different from other institutions. The free exercise of religion is constitutionally guaranteed; the free exercise of most other things is not. An essential part of free exercise is that religious communities should control their own ministries. This part of religious liberty is endangered because we have come to take religious liberty for granted.

Religious Freedom and International Human Rights in the United States Today

12 Emory International Law Review 951 (1998)

This was a talk at a conference at the Emory Center for the Study of Law and Religion. The audience included the United Nations Special Rapporteur on Human Rights, who was working on a report on human rights in the United States. I described what, in my view, the United States was doing right, and reviewed in some detail the ways in which we were falling short of our own ideals, even if we were doing better than most other countries in the world. I spoke from notes, not a formal text, and the article is a very lightly edited version of the talk.

*   *   *

I spend most of my career in this part of the law pointing to defects in the scheme for protecting religious liberty in the United States. I am often trying to persuade the courts, Congress, and readers of law reviews that religious liberty is seriously threatened, and that we do not do nearly enough to protect it. I believe what I say. But context clearly matters.

The religious liberty glass in the United States is half empty, or a quarter empty, but it is also half or three-quarters full. From a domestic perspective, from which I usually work, the United States has not lived up to my understanding of its ideals and aspirations. From an international perspective — and subject to the fact that my knowledge of the rest of the world is very limited — I think that the United States is doing better than most countries. The problems we have are minor, compared to problems in many parts of the world.

The problem we are having the most difficulty with has also confounded most other countries that have confronted it: when and under what circumstances must religiously-motivated practices be exempted from generally applicable laws? I think that on that issue, the United States is not in compliance with its international treaty obligations. But I do not know of any nation that is in compliance.

One other thing that I should say, by way of introduction, is that the remarkably decentralized structure of government in the United States is both part of the solution and part of the problem. Federalism means that the United States has the power to govern and also that each of the fifty states has power to govern. State government is also decentralized. Cities have power to govern. Counties have power to govern. All sorts of single-issue regulatory agencies and administrative boards at each of these levels have power to govern.

In our classic political theory, decentralization of government protects liberty; no one body has too much power. In the worst case, a group that feels oppressed can move to another state that is more sympathetic to its needs. But there is a down side to that decentralization: we have vastly multiplied the number of governmental bodies. A religious minority in the United States loses if it is regulated at any level of government. It is not enough to get an exemption at the federal level and at the state level if the city enacts a regulatory ordinance with no exemption.

Decentralization aggravates the risk that the most serious religious liberty problems will occur somewhere, if only locally. Consider the overt desire to suppress a particular religious group. This problem does not arise often here, but when it does arise, decentralization increases the risk of governmental action based on that desire. A set of bigots can take over one agency or one local government; they are much less likely to take over a state or the Congress.

Against that background, I want to briefly survey the kinds of religious liberty issues that arise, give some examples, and give some sense of the frequency of significant problems in the United States. Let me start with the most serious problems and work down to the less egregious but more common problems.

The prototype of religious persecution — and the most serious religious liberty problem — is deliberate persecution of small faith groups, with the persecution motivated by larger faith groups, using legal force and the power of the government to oppress their religious opponents. That's what the great religious persecutions of history were about. That's what the great religious persecutions that persist in some countries are mostly about. It is very rare for that to happen in this country, but it does happen.

I think that the Santeria litigation that I was involved in in the early 1990s was such a case. Santeria is an Afro-Caribbean religion that still practices the sacrifice of animals. Much of the effort to suppress Santeria was the product of the animal rights movement. But plainly, in Hialeah, the city in Florida that produced the case that went to the Supreme Court,[1] part of the coalition that enacted those ordinances was conservative Christians who believed that this religion was simply blasphemous. At the city council meetings, people said that God would punish the city if it tolerated this religion, and many similar things.[2] One of the striking things about that litigation was that Santeria had been present in the United States for a long time. As long as it stayed out of public view, people didn't like it, but neither did they try to suppress it. What triggered the Hialeah litigation was that this highly unpopular underground religion attempted to go public and build a church and practice like any other faith. That the city was unprepared to tolerate. To its great credit, the Supreme Court, which has not been helpful lately on religious liberty issues, said unanimously that what Hialeah was doing to Santeria was a violation of religious liberty, even as the Supreme Court understands it. That is one example of what looks like an old-fashioned religious persecution.

The so-called cults that the Special Rapporteur mentioned — the Hare Krishnas, the Scientologists, the Unification Church, and others — have had similar problems. Organized movements, afraid that their children would be lured off into these groups, worked systematically to suppress or restrict their influence. The worst two episodes of that effort seem to be behind us: (1) the deprogramming episode that peaked in the 1970s, when members of these groups were physically abducted and held for thought reform to bring them back to the faith of their parents, or at least to bring them out of the cults,[3] and (2) the episode of tort judgments in the 1980s, when disaffected members of the cult would sue the cult for not delivering on its promise of greater happiness, and juries would bring in $30 million verdicts.[4] At one point, every temple and monastery of the Hare Krishnas was in the hands of a receiver to be sold to pay one of those judgments. Execution was stayed, and the judgment was eventually reduced.[5]

As I said, the worst of those episodes seems to be behind us. The lead per-

1. Church of the Lukumi Babalu Aye, Inc. v. City of Hialeah, 508 U.S. 520 (1993).

2. Some of these remarks are quoted *id.* at 541-42.

3. *See, e.g.,* Gilmartin v. Taylor, 686 F.2d 1346 (10th Cir. 1982); ANSON SHUPE & DAVID BROMLEY, THE NEW VIGILANTES: DEPROGRAMMERS, ANTI-CULTISTS, AND THE NEW RELIGIONS (1980).

4. *See* Molko v. Holy Spirit Ass'n, 762 P.2d 46 (Cal. 1988) (reinstating tort suit in part); George v. International Soc'y for Krishna Consciousness, 262 Cal. Rptr. 217 (Cal. Ct. App. 1989) (reducing $32 million verdict), *vacated,* 499 U.S. 914 (1991); Wollersheim v. Church of Scientology, 260 Cal. Rptr. 331 (Cal. Ct. App. 1989) (reducing $30 million verdict), *vacated,* 499 U.S. 914 (1991).

5. *See* George v. International Soc'y of Krishna Consciousness, 4 Cal. Rptr. 2d 473 (Cal. Ct. App. 1992).

secuting organization is now itself the subject of a big judgment in one of the deprogramming cases. The Cult Awareness Network has filed for bankruptcy.[6]

These examples involve religions that are deviant in the purely sociological sense of practicing something far removed from the broader norms of society. The examples show that even in this country, such religions can trigger a hostile religious response that will use the power of government to try to suppress the small and deviant religion. Even so, the closest that any of those episodes came to recurring violence was the deprogramming episode. It has been a very long time since this country has suffered the sort of religiously motivated violence against small groups that plagues some other parts of the world. There was a wave of private violence against the Jehovah's Witnesses in the 1940s,[7] and of private and even some governmental violence against the Mormons in the nineteenth century,[8] and there was intermittent Protestant-Catholic violence in the nineteenth century.[9] But those events are not recent, and such cases are now very rare in this country.

Second, there are clear cases of sustained hostility and rivalry between private groups divided in part by religious belief. These are groups that do not like each other, groups that do not trust each other, groups that think it is very bad for the country when the other exercises political influence. But this is mostly private, not governmental. It is not manifested in violence or in overtly religious governmental restrictions. Most obviously, this is what sociologist James Davidson Hunter called "the culture wars."[10]

The culture wars are partly just the left-right political split in the country, but they plainly have a religious dimension. The conservative evangelical wing of Christianity has become a political force in the country, and it has produced fear and hostility among many groups on the other side of its political issues. Many people in the United States think that evangelical Christianity is a terrible danger to American freedom, and that all possible political steps should be taken to reduce its influence. For their part, many of the evangelical Christians believe with equal fervor that the secular left is a terri-

6. *See* In re Cult Awareness Network, 205 B.R. 575 (Bankr. N.D. Ill. 1997).

7. *See* PETER IRONS, THE COURAGE OF THEIR CONVICTIONS 22-35 (1988).

8. For a history that emphasizes the role of the legal system in the Mormon persecutions, see EDWIN BROWN FIRMAGE & RICHARD COLLIN MANGRUM, ZION IN THE COURTS: A LEGAL HISTORY OF THE CHURCH OF JESUS CHRIST OF LATTER-DAY SAINTS, 1830-1900 (1988).

9. *See* CARL F. KAESTLE, PILLARS OF THE REPUBLIC: COMMON SCHOOLS AND AMERICAN SOCIETY 1760-1860, at 170 (1983); DIANE RAVITCH, THE GREAT SCHOOL WARS 36, 66, 75 (1974); ANSON PHELPS STOKES, 1 CHURCH AND STATE IN THE UNITED STATES 830-31 (1950).

10. JAMES DAVISON HUNTER, THE CULTURE WARS (1991).

ble danger to American freedom, and that all possible political steps should be taken to reduce *its* influence.

One flashpoint for these battles is the sexual revolution and the resulting conflict between groups promoting greater sexual freedom and groups promoting traditional religious teachings on sexual morality. Religious believers on the conservative side are not only evangelical Protestants, but also traditional Catholics, Orthodox Jews, most Muslims, and any other faith or tradition that adheres to traditional moral positions. The more radical elements on each side occasionally burst out into explicitly anti-religious or anti-secular statements. We had the episode a few years ago when a gay rights organization disrupted a Mass at St. Patrick's Cathedral, and we occasionally get statements from radical feminist or gay rights groups that religion and religious liberty are a fraud and oppressive and the like.[11] But these extreme acts and arguments come from a small group of people. It is not the government, and it is not the bulk of the people in any of these movements. This is the hostility of people with extreme views on each side of these issues.

At a less active level, the hostility is more widespread. There is a Gallup Poll from 1993 in which 45% of the American people said they have a "mostly unfavorable" or "very unfavorable" opinion of "religious fundamentalists" — a term not defined.[12] Eighty-six percent said they had a mostly or very unfavorable opinion of "members of religious cults or sects" — also not defined. In a 1989 poll, 30% admitted that they would not like to have "religious fundamentalists" as neighbors, and 62% said they would not like "members of minority religious sects or cults" as neighbors; only 12% admitted that they would not like to have "blacks" as neighbors.[13]

These kinds of attitudes rarely produce overt persecution. They produce instead a low-level hostility and a hostile insensitivity to religious need. This low-level hostility becomes especially important when someone from one of these churches or sects needs a discretionary decision from a low-level government official. They need a zoning variance, a special use permit, a license of some sort that is discretionary; they need the school board to accommodate the religious belief of their child in a public school. All these are things they are not clearly entitled to under any governing law, but which may be available, with more or less frequency and difficulty, on a discretionary basis. If 45% of the population is hostile to religious fundamentalists, it is a reason-

---

11. *See* Richard F. Duncan, *Who Wants to Stop the Church: Homosexual Rights Legislation, Public Policy, and Religious Freedom,* 69 Notre Dame L. Rev. 393, 440-41 (1994).

12. George Gallup, Jr., The Gallup Poll: Public Opinion 1993 at 75-76, 78 (1994).

13. George Gallup, Jr., The Gallup Poll: Public Opinion 1989 at 63, 67, 76-77 (1990).

able inference that at least 45% of governmental officials share that hostility. Most of these hostile officials understand that they cannot act on these attitudes overtly, but these attitudes inevitably affect exercises of discretion. These discretionary decisions will be harder to get for applicants asserting religious needs.

There are pockets of deeper ignorance among the population, and very occasionally among governmental officials. There are remnants of old style anti-Catholicism, anti-Mormonism, anti-Semitism, anti-Muslimism expressed on occasion in the private sector. It is rare for government to overtly act on these attitudes, but it can happen, especially on occasions of high stress. The Arab and Muslim communities experienced some difficulty during the Gulf War for example, and they continue to suffer grossly overbroad suspicions associated with fear of terrorism. But in my experience, the sheer bigotry against particular faith traditions, which used to plague Western society, has become rare.

The biggest problem has little to do with traditional religious rivalries and hostilities and everything to do with secularism and the growth of governmental regulation. The biggest problem is the pervasiveness of regulation in all aspects of our lives, and the widespread expectation that everyone will comply with secular norms. These forces conflict directly with the enormous plurality of religious views in the country to produce a whole series of conflicts between particular religious practices and particular regulations. Some of these conflicts arise in recurring patterns that we can identify and label — there is a real problem with land regulation, a real problem with American Indian religions.

Many of these conflicts do not recur in patterns. There is one unexpected conflict after another. No one in Washington could have predicted that a Jehovah's Witness would lose her job in a restaurant because she would not sing "Happy Birthday" to diners. That is a religious belief I did not know about before it emerged in litigation, and it is a safe bet that most of the rest of the non–Jehovah's-Witness world didn't know about it either. That case led to a favorable settlement for the employee and a new policy for the restaurant.[14] There has not been an epidemic of happy birthday cases, but there are at least two similar cases elsewhere in the country.[15] These odd little cases

14. For the settlement, see Philip P. Pan, *EEOC Suit Settled by Restaurant*, Washington Post at B7 (Dec. 11, 1997). For the original dispute, between Cora Miller and a Chi-Chi's in suburban Maryland, see Scott Higham, *Jehovah's Witness Says Bias Prompted Firing*, Baltimore Sun at 1A (Oct. 15, 1996).

15. *Happy Birthday Waitress Sings Blues*, Miami Herald at 5B (Dec. 8, 1994) (describing dispute between Lois Gorman and a Shoney's in St. Petersburg, Florida); Eric Miller, *Faith*

are typical in the sense that there are hundreds of different isolated conflicts between secular norms, governmental regulations, religious views, and practices that from the dominant secular perspective seem idiosyncratic.

The regulator responsible for enforcing the law in such a conflict may or may not be hostile to the religious view involved. More often, he would say that he is not hostile. But he is systematically committed to his own single-issue regulatory agenda. He is responsible for zoning this town. He is responsible for enforcing employment discrimination laws. He is responsible for whatever his issue is, his issue is not religious liberty, and he does not want to make any exceptions. He is hostile to the idea of diverse religious practice; he assumes that everyone will conform to his secular norms. That is the standard source of the conflict here, and I think in Western Europe as well.

Let me give some examples in no particular order. These are all real cases from the last few years.

There is a remarkable case in Oregon where the prison authorities arranged to tape the conversation between a murder suspect and the priest who came to hear his confession. The authorities got the confession on tape and wanted to introduce it in court; the Ninth Circuit barred any use of the tape and any further eavesdropping on confessions.[16]

There are cases of the children of Sikhs trying to attend public school. Every Sikh male is required to carry a knife, but the knife can be ceremonial. In the most widely reported case, the knife was only a few inches long, was not sharp, and was sewn into its sheath. In open court, the judge attempted to remove the knife from the sheath and could not do so. But the school board said it had an absolute rule; it would not let the student in with a knife.[17]

I mentioned the cases of the American Indians, which raise a remarkable range of issues — whether they can gather or possess eagle feathers,[18] whether they can build a bonfire for a sweat lodge,[19] though bonfires are ille-

---

Led to Firing Suit Says, Arizona Republic at A1 (Feb. 20, 1998) (describing dispute between Geoffrey Carranza and Aunt Chilada's restaurant in Phoenix).

16. *See* Mockaitis v. Harcleroad, 104 F.3d 1522 (9th Cir. 1997).

17. *See* Cheema v. Thompson, 67 F.3d 883 (9th Cir. 1995) (affirming preliminary injunction ordering school to admit child with short, dulled, and sheathed knife).

18. *Compare* United States v. Hugs, 109 F.3d 1375 (9th Cir. 1997) (holding that system of requiring government permit for religious taking of bald and golden eagles serves compelling interest by least restrictive means); *with* United States v. Abeyta, 632 F. Supp. 1301 (D.N.M. 1986) (permitting religious taking of eagles and holding that the permit system was not necessary to their protection).

19. *See* Neb. Atty. Gen'l Op. No. 94049, 1997 Neb AG Lexis 47.

gal in Nebraska because of the worry about prairie fires. There was the peyote case a few years ago.[20] The most frequently recurring conflict is over sacred places in lands in the west, lands typically owned by the federal government, no longer owned by the tribes to which they are sacred.[21]

We have had conflicts about distribution of religious literature in school, and religious meetings in school, where two principles of religious liberty come into potential conflict. On the one hand, we are very concerned that the government not use the public school to teach religion, or a particular religion; on the other hand, the individual children who attend that school retain their own right to freedom of speech and freedom of religion. The Supreme Court has said that an individual child or student group acting on its own can meet and speak and publish about religion,[22] but conflict over this issue requires frequent litigation and threats of litigation to get full compliance from the schools.

More difficult and less settled are cases where parents have religious objections to parts of the curriculum in the public school, particularly with respect to sexual matters — the school is teaching sex education, or an AIDS curriculum, or distributing condoms to high school students without parental consent.[23] But this issue also arises in other parts of the curriculum.[24] There is a remarkable casualness in the American public schools about teaching competing theories of the supernatural. The school says this topic is not religion; this is just fun, or this is meditation, and therapeutic. People who take their religion more seriously or more literally view some of these things as alternate religious schemes.[25]

---

20. *See* Employment Division v. Smith, 494 U.S. 872 (1990) (holding that government need have no reason for enforcing neutral and generally applicable law as applied to prohibit the free exercise of religion).

21. *See, e.g.,* Lyng v. Northwest Indian Cemetery Protective Association, 485 U.S. 439 (1988) (holding that government's development of its own land imposes no cognizable burden on religious activity conducted there).

22. *See* Mergens v. Board of Education, 496 U.S. 226 (1990) (upholding the Equal Access Act, 20 U.S.C. §4071 et seq. (1994), and interpreting it in manner that made it effective).

23. *See* Brown v. Hot, Sexy, and Safer Prods., Inc., 68 F.3d 525 (1st Cir. 1995) (rejecting challenge to sexually explicit school assembly); Curtis v. School Comm., 652 N.E.2d 580 (Mass. 1995) (requiring parental consent for condom distribution); Alfonso v. Fernandez, 606 N.Y.S.2d 259 (App. Div. 1993) (upholding condom distribution without parental consent).

24. *See, e.g.,* Fleischfresser v. Directors of School Dist. 200, 15 F.3d 680 (7th Cir. 1994) (rejecting claim of right to opt-out of religiously offensive reading assignments); Mozert v. Hawkins County Bd. of Educ., 827 F.2d 1058 (6th Cir. 1987) (same).

25. *See* Cowan v. Strafford R-VI School Dist., 140 F.3d 1153 (8th Cir. 1998) (holding that school board engaged in religious discrimination when it discharged a teacher for giving

This is a good place to note that much of the line of conflict is religious intensity. The conflict in the United States is not principally between Christians and Jews, certainly not between Protestants and Catholics. It is between the religiously intense and the religiously unintense, and between the religiously intense and the intensely non-theist. If there is a dominant religion in the United States, it is low-intensity theism. Those of any faith who are intense about their religion have more in common with each other than with low-intensity believers or non-believers. Muslims, Jews, Catholics, and Protestants, who are intense in their faith, have much more in common with each other than with the 80% who answer on surveys that they are Christians but seem to be only moderately intense or not intense at all.

We have conflicts over photographs on drivers' licenses[26] and over social security numbers.[27] A small but determined group of Americans have become convinced that the social security number is the mark of the beast described in the Book of Revelation: "And he causeth all, both small and great, rich and poor, free and bond, to receive a mark in their right hand, or in their foreheads; And that no man might buy or sell, save he that had the mark, or the name of the beast, or the number of his name."[28]

Obviously, we have many prison cases. In part this is because prisoners are chronic litigants. They have little to do with their time, so filing lawsuits is recreational. If they really get lucky, they get a trip out of the prison to go to the courthouse. But prison litigation also arises because prison authorities are accustomed to having near absolute power over their charges, and they rarely stop to think about the reasonableness of their rules. My favorite example of frivolous prison litigation is a case one of my former students litigated in Colorado.

Plaintiff was a 64-year-old forger in a work-release program. The prison authorities obviously did not view him as dangerous; they let him out to go to work five days a week. They let him out on Sunday to go to church, and he

---

each of her students "their very own magic rock"); Alvarado v. City of San Jose, 94 F.3d 1223 (9th Cir. 1996) (holding that city could erect statue of an Aztec god); Malnak v. Yogi, 592 F.2d 197 (3d Cir. 1979) (ordering school not to teach Transcendental Meditation with worship of a deity).

26. *See* Quaring v. Peterson, 728 F.2d 1121 (8th Cir. 1984) (finding no compelling interest in requiring every driver to have a photograph on driver's license), *aff'd by equally divided Court,* 472 U.S. 478 (1985).

27. *See* Bowen v. Roy, 476 U.S. 693 (1986) (holding that government's internal use of social security number imposed no cognizable burden on plaintiff's religion, and remanding for determination whether plaintiff's objection to using the number herself had become moot).

28. Revelation 13:16–17 (King James Version).

was the organist at the Episcopal Church in Craig, Colorado. He was a 64-year-old *Episcopalian* forger. But, they said, if you take communion under both species, you are back in the general population. The reason is that we have an absolute rule: no drugs or alcohol for prisoners, and we don't make exceptions. Under *Employment Division v. Smith*,[29] we don't have to make exceptions. The prison authorities settled.[30]

They settled not because their position was doctrinally wrong; under *Smith*, it was probably unassailable. They settled because their position was politically ridiculous, and they did not want to defend it in the newspapers. They settled on the reasonable ground that they were going to look foolish trying to defend this in front of a judge.

There are prison cases about hair and beards,[31] and about religious symbols, about whether prisoners can wear a cross or a Star of David on their clothing.[32] There are conflicts over scheduling, in prisons but also in the civilian population. A calendar has to be set up some way, and ours is set up for Sunday-observing Christians and secondarily for Saturday-observing Christians and Jews. Friday-observing Muslims are just out of luck. Small religious groups with holidays that fall in the middle of the week are also out of luck. Of course the most severe example is in the prison context. In *O'Lone v. Estate of Shabazz*,[33] the Supreme Court held that if Muslim prisoners are working when their Friday service is held, that is just too bad. The prison does not have to bring them in from the work site to attend services.

Conflict over sexuality spills out into religious liberty litigation. There have been a flurry of cases from around the country with inconsistent results involving suits against landlords for marital status discrimination when they refuse to rent their apartments to unmarried couples, and both sides have treated these cases as proxies for claims of sexual orientation discrimination when landlords refuse to rent to gay or lesbian couples.[34]

---

29. 494 U.S. 872 (1990).

30. McClellan v. Keen (D. Colo. 1994).

31. *See, e.g.*, Hines v. South Carolina Dept. of Corrections, 148 F.3d 353 (4th Cir. 1998) (upholding prison rule forbidding beards and long hair); Diaz v. Collins, 114 F.3d 69 (5th Cir. 1997) (upholding prison rule forbidding long hair); Prins v. Coughlin, 76 F.3d 504 (2d Cir. 1996) (refusing to consider prison rule forbidding beards longer than one inch).

32. *See* Sasnett v. Sullivan, 91 F.3d 1018 (7th Cir. 1996) (ordering prison authorities to permit religious jewelry under RFRA), *vacated*, 521 U.S. 1114 (1997).

33. 482 U.S. 342 (1987).

34. Swanner v. Anchorage Equal Rights Comm'n, 874 P.2d 274 (Alaska 1994) (finding compelling interest in prohibiting discrimination against unmarried couples); Smith v. Fair Empl. & Hsg. Comm'n, 913 P.2d 909 (Cal. 1996) (finding no substantial burden on religion in forcing owner of duplex to rent to unmarried couples, in violation of her belief that she

There is a huge flurry of cases that no one saw coming. When Congress passed the Religious Freedom Restoration Act (RFRA) in 1993, no one had ever heard of these cases. Now there are dozens of them. They are bankruptcy suits against churches. They arise when a church member who has been contributing a share of his income falls on financial difficulty. Eventually, he files for bankruptcy, and creditors sue the church to recover all of his contributions. First they said they wanted all the contributions for the last year before bankruptcy, because that's the most obvious theory that the Bankruptcy Code provides. Then they began to realize that under state law they could go back further. I just filed an appeal for a Texas church that is on the losing end of a $45,000 judgment for contributions that were made from 1988 to 1992, by a member who has tithed his income to that church for 43 years.[35]

Tithing and excessive spending had nothing to do with why he went bankrupt. He went bankrupt because of a business dispute. The laws that are being invoked here have been part of Anglo-American law since the sixteenth century. Someone in the mid-1980s had the bright idea that these laws could be applied to religious contributions.

Once one person thought of it, the idea caught on quickly. The first judgment against a church was in 1992,[36] and as I say, now there are dozens of those cases pending around the country. But when we held hearings on RFRA in 1992, no one in Washington had heard of these cases. Congress has responded with specific legislation to solve the problem.[37]

The employment discrimination laws as applied to churches themselves are a source of some conflict. Some churches have limitations on what women can be appointed to do. Some churches have religious requirements for employment and apply those requirements across the board, even where the secu-

---

would be assisting sinful conduct); Jasniowski v. Rushing, 678 N.E.2d 743 (Ill. App.) (finding compelling interest in prohibiting discrimination against unmarried couples), *vacated,* 685 N.E.2d 622 (Ill. 1997); Attorney Gen'l v. Desilets, 636 N.E.2d 233 (Mass. 1994) (holding that requiring landlord to rent to unmarried couples burdened his exercise of religion, and remanding for determination whether state had compelling government interest); State by Cooper v. French, 460 N.W.2d 2 (Minn. 1990) (holding that state constitution protects landlord who refuses, on religious grounds, to rent to unmarried couples); Maureen E. Markey, *The Landlord/Tenant Free Exercise Conflict in a Post-RFRA World,* 29 RUTGERS L.J. 487 (1998).

35. Cedar Bayou Baptist Church v. Gregory-Edwards, Inc., 987 S.W.2d 156 (Tex. App. — Hou. [14th Dist.] 1999).

36. In re Young, 148 B.R. 886 (Bankr. D. Minn. 1992), *aff'd,* 152 B.R. 939 (D. Minn. 1993), *rev'd,* 82 F.3d 1407 (8th Cir. 1996), *vacated sub nom.* Christians v. Crystal Evangelical Free Church, 521 U.S. 1114 (1997), *on remand,* 141 F.3d 854 (8th Cir. 1998).

37. Religious Liberty and Charitable Donation Protection Act of 1998, Pub. L. 105-183, 112 Stat. 517 (1998), codified in scattered sections of the Bankruptcy Code.

lar observer does not see the religious significance of the job. There was a case in the Supreme Court about whether the janitor in a Mormon gymnasium had to be a Mormon in good standing.[38] As a matter of federal statutory law, the church won that case, but under state statutes the answer is often less clear.

The most extreme argument in these cases is revealing for what it says about a widespread secular mind-set. In all the contexts I have mentioned, it is sometimes argued that it is improper, or even unconstitutional, to exempt religious practices from burdensome regulation. This argument says that all human purposes are the same, and that religion is just another human purpose. Government should not single out religious practice for persecution, but neither should it give religious practice any special privileges. The church is just like a secular business. The extreme version of that attitude is the employment discrimination suits against religious universities by would-be professors of theology or canon law. In some of these cases, faculty were terminated or denied tenure after using the authority of their position with a religious institution to attack the teachings of the church.[39] I do not know that anyone used the word heresy, but these faculty were teaching views on sexual relations and abortion that the church did not want taught in theology departments at church universities. In others, the dispute was over the quality of the professor's scholarship, but judicial assessment of that scholarship inevitably required judgments that were religious as well as academic.[40] From the professors' perspective, they thought they had the same rights as if they were at The University of Texas or any other public university. They thought they had exactly the same right against the Catholic University of America as they would have against the government.

There is a remarkable range of these cases of conflict between regulation and religious practice. I could give more examples, but the point is the sheer diversity of the kinds of conflicts that can arise between religious practices and pervasive regulation. Some of them are recurring, and some of them are utterly unpredictable. But that is the level of problem that we are mostly dealing with in the United States. It is usually not intended as persecution, and it is usually not religious in its motivation. It is a conflict between diverse and pervasive regulations and very diverse and pluralistic religious practices.

From the religious perspective, it feels like persecution. The government says that a church cannot build a place of worship. A lawsuit says that a reli-

38. Corporation of the Presiding Bishop v. Amos, 482 U.S. 327 (1987).

39. Maguire v. Marquette Univ., 814 F.2d 1213 (7th Cir. 1987) (rejecting claim by dissident theologian); Curran v. Catholic Univ., No. 1562-87 (D.C. Super. 1987) (same).

40. EEOC v. Catholic Univ., 83 F.3d 455 (D.C. Cir. 1996) (holding that University was protected by Constitution and by RFRA).

gious university cannot control what is taught in its theology department. So it feels exactly like persecution. But from the secular side, that is often not the motivation. Sometimes the motivation is hostility to the religious views, or to moral views associated with the religious views, and this anti-religious motivation is especially important when the government makes discretionary decisions. But often the government's rigidity has nothing to do with hostility to a religious movement. Rather, it flows from the triumph of secularism, from the view that everyone has to comply with the same regulatory rules as everybody else. In this view, what the church is asking for is not religious liberty at all; it is a special privilege.

Finally, the one important example I did not mention yet may be the most pervasive, which is land use regulations. Land use regulation is enormously intrusive in this country. It is thoroughly localized; it is thoroughly individualized. Zoning commissions and planning commissions make decisions about individual parcels of land. They decide what an owner can build on his property. The owner must have complete architectural drawings, and these must be approved in advance by the government. Land use regulation becomes a means by which anything that the neighbors don't like can be prevented. There are enormous numbers of conflicts between churches and zoning commissions, and more recently between churches and landmarking authorities. These are both forms of land use regulation, but the sources of the conflicts are very different.

The historic preservation movement and the landmarking authorities make it their task to preserve interesting buildings of the past. Unlike in the case of the great European cathedrals, here the government cannot pay to help preserve a church, however interesting or historically significant it might be. And so the decision to designate a church as a landmark and require its preservation imposes enormous costs on the church, costs that the government cannot help with. The landmark movement tends to believe that any building more than a few years old is potentially a landmark, and certainly that any church is a landmark. Religious congregations build distinctive buildings. They build them for their own internal religious purposes; they build them for the glory of God as they understand it, but their buildings often do not look like an ordinary house or a storefront sitting next door. And so in the City of New York, where we have data, churches are forty-two times more likely to be landmarked than any other property.[41] Churches can be landmarked even when they are not particularly distinctive. *City of*

---

41. N. J. L'Heureux, Jr., *Ministry v. Mortar: A Landmark Conflict,* in 2 GOVERNMENT INTERVENTION IN RELIGIOUS AFFAIRS 164, 168 (Dean M. Kelley, ed., 1986).

Boerne v. Flores[42] involved landmarking of a church that was built in 1923 and is largely invisible from the street. Passersby on the street can see little but the front wall of the church itself, and the front wall was never in controversy. The church had agreed from the beginning to preserve that.[43] These disputes over landmarking are serious and recurring.[44]

Zoning disputes are a little different, and they come at two stages in the life of a church. One issue is the location of the churches. A religious organization church buys a piece of land and wants to build a church on it, or it rents an existing building and wants to meet there. The zoning authority says churches are not permitted at that site. That site is reserved for residential, or that is reserved for commercial, or the neighbors say they do not want a church. The most common regulatory technique is that churches require special use permits, which means the zoning board has very broad discretion to grant the permit, or not grant the permit, or attach conditions that make the permit unworkable for the church.[45]

The second problem is permitted uses within existing churches. The city gives the zoning for a church, but then it wants to look at each aspect of the church's mission. The church wants to put a day care there. The city does not think that daycare is a religious function. The church has to get separate zoning for that.

The church wants to feed the poor. The city says it certainly needs separate zoning for that, and it refuses the conditional use permit. The neighbors want to exclude anything that would give poor people a reason to enter the neighborhood. Does the church have a right to carry out its mission to the poor, to do what Catholics call corporal works of mercy? Or is the church's definition of mission subject to review by the neighbors and by the zoning board? The church can feed the poor, the city often says, but only if it can afford to buy a second site somewhere else in a poor neighborhood where the neighbors won't complain. In the city's view, socioeconomic segregation trumps religious liberty.[46]

---

42. 521 U.S. 507 (1997).

43. For a more detailed description of the facts in *Boerne,* see Douglas Laycock, *Conceptual Gulfs in City of Boerne v. Flores,* 39 WM. & MARY L. REV. 743, 780-91 (1998) (text at notes 202-61).

44. *See* Angela Carmella, *Houses of Worship and Religious Liberty: Constitutional Limits to Landmark Preservation and Architectural Review,* 36 VILL. L. REV. 401 (1991).

45. I am indebted to John Mauck, an attorney in Chicago, Illinois, who specializes in church zoning cases, for explanations of the mechanics and many other details of the zoning process.

46. *See* Stuart Circle Parish v. Board of Zoning Appeals, 946 F. Supp. 1225 (E.D. Va. 1996)

Zoning authorities seem to understand that sermons and hymns and sacraments come within the initial church zoning. Everything else is up for grabs. And, again, we have the same conflict of worldviews. On the regulator side, they are accustomed to telling every land owner in the city what he can do and what he can not do with his land. From their perspective, why should the church be different?

There is substantial evidence of genuine religious discrimination in land use decisions. This is not surprising, because these zoning decisions are so individualized and discretionary. Within broad limits, the zoning authority can do whatever it wants. Whether or not zoning officials have any conscious religious motive, it would not be surprising if those churches that seem safe or familiar to the zoning board, or those with political connections to the zoning board, do better than non-mainstream faiths. This is a context where we can actually document the effect of governmental discretion and low-grade hostility toward certain religions.

Some of the evidence comes from reported zoning cases, which are the tip of a very large iceberg. These are cases where the zoning conflict was not resolved informally, where it was not resolved with the zoning board, where it went to court, where it was not resolved at the trial court, where it was appealed, and where the appeal produced a reported opinion. In a few states, trial court decisions are reported, and these are included. If we look at all these reported cases, it turns out that small faiths account for a grossly disproportionate share of the cases. Jews are about 2% of the population and about 20% of the church zoning cases. Jews plus very small Christian denominations — denominations with less than 1.5% of the population each — total about 9% of the population but account for about 50% of the church zoning cases. So here is a clear example where the larger pattern shows governmental discrimination against smaller faiths.[47]

In any individual case, it is enormously difficult to prove discrimination. When one zoning board in one small town says that Jehovah Witnesses cannot put a church where they want it, maybe the Witnesses just wanted to put their church in an inappropriate place or maybe the city just does not want any Jehovah's Witnesses around. Viewing one case at a time, it is hard to tell. But, if we look at the reported cases over a long period, it is clear that there is a significant pattern of religious discrimination.

(protecting church under RFRA); Western Presbyterian Church v. Board of Zoning Adjustment, 862 F. Supp. 538 (D.D.C. 1994) (protecting church under RFRA).

47. The study is described and the data are reported in Von G. Keetch & Matthew K. Richards, *The Need for Legislation to Enshrine Free Exercise in the Land Use Context,* 32 U.C. DAVIS L. REV. 725 (1999).

The legal and doctrinal framework for dealing with these problems is in a state of great confusion. The Free Exercise doctrine under the federal constitution is that laws must be neutral and generally applicable; that if government burdens religion with a law that is not neutral and generally applicable, then government must justify that burden under the compelling interest standard, which is the most stringent standard of justification known to U.S. law. The great ambiguity is that no one knows what is a neutral and general applicable law. There are only two cases at the Supreme Court level. There is some reason to believe that the Court thinks that nearly all laws are neutral and generally applicable, that they meant to get rid of these free exercise cases and tell churches to quit asking for exemptions.

On the other hand, there is some evidence in the first opinion,[48] and much evidence in the second opinion,[49] that religious practices are entitled to exceptions from regulatory laws in any situation where some secular practice also gets an exception. If that is the rule, then many laws fail the test of neutrality and general applicability. The way American legislatures work — and I assume the way legislatures in most of the world work — is that the way to pass a bill is to create exceptions for everybody that complains and might have the power to stop the bill if refused an exception. American laws are riddled with secular exceptions. There are hardly any laws that actually apply to everybody. If that is what generally applicable means, then what the Supreme Court has done is to vastly complicate the litigation, but at the end of the day, the exercise of religion is still entitled to exemptions in a large proportion of cases.

If I had to guess, I would say the resolution will be somewhere between the polar positions but closer to the end of the continuum that fails to protect religious liberty. That is mostly a political prediction, based not on what the Supreme Court has said, or on the logic of its doctrine, but on the widespread hostility to claims for exemption. If the Court refuses to enforce its new requirement of general applicability, then laws will be declared generally applicable even though they do not apply to everybody, and quite possibly, most of what government does will be declared neutral and generally applicable.

48. *See* Employment Div. v. Smith, 494 U.S. 872, 884 (1990) ("where the State has in place a system of individual exemptions, it may not refuse to extend that system to cases of 'religious hardship' without compelling reason.").

49. Church of the Lukumi Babalu Aye, Inc. v. City of Hialeah, 508 U.S. 520 (1993) (striking down ordinances that regulated religious practice but did not regulate secular practices that caused the same harms, and explicitly refusing to rely on governmental motive as the basis for decision).

The second level of protection is in state constitutions, which is an undeveloped body of law. At least five state supreme courts have expressly rejected the *Smith* test, and said that any burden on religion has to be justified by a compelling interest;[50] most states remain to be heard from. Traditionally there is less vigorous enforcement of constitutional rights in the state courts. Many of the state judges are elected. They have less political independence. State constitutions may develop as an important source of protection for religious liberty, but that would be a substantial new development. It has not happened in the past.

Third, there is the Religious Freedom Restoration Act, in which Congress said any law that substantially burdens religion has to be justified.[51] The Supreme Court struck that law down on federalism grounds in the *Boerne* case last term.[52] There is an attempt to pass a Religious Liberty Protection Act of 1998 that would enact the same standards insofar as Congress can do so, under other sources of congressional power in Article I.[53] These bills would protect any religious practice that affects interstate commerce. That is an odd formulation, but building a church clearly affects commerce, and hiring employees affects commerce. However far Congress can reach under the power to regulate commerce, it would protect religious liberty to that extent. Under the Spending Clause, Congress would protect religious liberty in programs that get federal money. It remains to be seen whether that will be enacted. Even if enacted, it will leave gaps. Plainly, not everything falls within the Commerce Clause or the Spending Clause. [This bill was never enacted. But parts of the bill that had political support became the Religious Land Use and Institutionalized Persons Act.]

The most severe problem is that any such legislation must be drafted in quite general terms. Religious liberty is enormously popular in principle in the United States, but as my list of examples suggests, it immediately becomes controversial in specific applications. There is always some interest group on

50. *See* Attorney Gen'l v. Desilets, 636 N.E.2d 233 (Mass. 1994); State v. Hershberger, 462 N.W.2d 393 (Minn. 1990); Hunt v. Hunt, 648 A.2d 843 (Vt. 1994); Muns v. Martin, 930 P.2d 318 (Wash. 1997); State v. Miller, 549 N.W.2d 235 (Wis. 1996) (all rejecting *Smith*); State v. Evans, 796 P.2d 178 (Kan. App. 1990) (ignoring *Smith* and adhering to pre-*Smith* law); Rupert v. City of Portland, 605 A.2d 63 (Me. 1992) (applying pre-*Smith* law but reserving issue of whether to change in light of *Smith*); *see also* Kentucky State Bd. for Elem. & Secondary Educ. v. Rudasill, 589 S.W.2d 877 (Ky. 1979); In re Brown, 478 So.2d 1033 (Miss. 1985); State v. Whisner, 351 N.E.2d 750 (Ohio 1976); State ex rel. Swann v. Pack, 527 S.W.2d 99 (Tenn. 1975) (all pre-*Smith*).

51. 42 U.S.C. § 2000bb *et seq* (1994).

52. 521 U.S. 507 (1997).

53. H.R. 4019 and S.2148 in the 105th Congress.

the other side that wants each regulation enforced without exception. So Congress drafts at a very high level of generality, staying away from the specific conflicts. Congress says that any substantial burden on religion has to be justified by a compelling interest, and then each secular interest can expect that the things that it most cares about will be held compelling.

The experience in the courts under the Religious Freedom Restoration Act was not good. On the other hand, neither was it terrible. The Religious Freedom Restoration Act protected a number of people who would not have been protected otherwise. But the win/loss rate was very poor. A survey in the law review literature reports that about 20% of RFRA claims were successful and about 80% were not.[54] [A later survey using a source that included unreported decisions as well as reported ones found a success rate above 40%.*]

The most common reason for rejecting RFRA claims was to find that there was no substantial burden on the religion. There was a burden on the religion that bothered the believers so much that they were willing to spend the time and the money to go to court, but the court said that the burden was not substantial. This is a way of getting rid of cases. There are reports that the European judges are doing the same thing with the International Covenant on Civil and Political Rights, finding no burden in many of the cases, so that they never have to deal with the hard issue of deciding whether the burden is justified.[55] I think that this judicial reaction is mostly a function of the secular view that religion should not get any special treatment, and partly a function of the view that these are hard cases, and the courts would rather not be bothered with them.

So on this question of how to protect religious liberty from generally applicable laws that burden unusual religious practices, we in the United States are not doing very well. But we are at least struggling with it. We seem to have very large majorities in both houses of Congress committed to the view that religion should be protected from regulatory burdens. The President and the Vice President are committed to that view. A number of state legislatures seem willing to enact that view.

Finally, let me return to the international human rights context. One reason Congress might choose to enact a statute like RFRA is to bring the United States into compliance with its treaty obligations. The International Cove-

---

54. *See* Ira C. Lupu, *The Failure of RFRA*, 20 UALR L. REV. 575 (1998).

[* See Amy Adamczyk, John Wybraniec, & Roger Finke, *Religious Regulation and the Courts: Documenting the Effects of Smith and RFRA*, 46 J. CHURCH & STATE 237 (2004).]

55. *See* Stephanos Stavros, *Freedom of Religion and Claims for Exemption from Generally Applicable, Neutral Laws: Lessons from Across the Pond?* 1997 EUROPEAN HUMAN RIGHTS L. REV. 607.

nant on Civil and Political Rights protects the right to manifest one's religion in observance, subject to a standard of justification that sounds similar to the compelling interest test in RFRA, although it uses a different phrase. That is a reason for Congress to enact RFRA, and it is also a source of constitutional power for Congress to enact RFRA. One basis on which Congress can regulate is to implement the treaties of the United States.[56]

Whatever the legal power of that argument, I must tell you that politically it is worse than a non-starter. It is harmful in Washington to make that argument. People who might otherwise vote to protect religious liberty threaten to vote against it if anyone tells them that the international treaties have anything to do with the bill, or that international human rights law has anything to do with it. That partly reflects the isolationist tradition that still survives to some extent in the United States. It partly reflects concerns over sovereignty and international tribunals that have been highlighted by the conflict between environmental and safety regulations and the free trade treaties. It partly reflects a view among one slice of evangelical Christianity — I think a small slice but a highly intense slice — that one-world government is a sign of the end times, and that Armageddon is coming if we start doing things because international treaties tell us to. It partly reflects the American sense of superiority on human rights issues. Congress thinks we do just fine on religious liberty issues, and that the rest of the world should not be telling us how to get it right.

I once made the mistake of testifying about human rights treaties as a source of Congressional authority to legislate. I explained in very simple terms that the Senate had made these treaties non-self-executing. No international tribunal anywhere in the world could tell Congress it had to enact RFRA, or do anything at all, to implement our treaty obligations on religious liberty. But if Congress wanted to reenact RFRA, the treaties and the Treaty Clause were a source of power to do what Congress wanted to do anyway.[57] The word came back from the Chairman to "Quit talking about that; you are hurting your case."

In terms of dealing with Congress, I am not sure that the international human rights community can make much progress or do much good, but on the substance of what we are trying to accomplish here, there does indeed seem to be a large majority in Congress to protect religious liberty from the

56. *See* Missouri v. Holland, 252 U.S. 416 (1920) (upholding legislation to implement the Migratory Bird Treaty).

57. Statement of Douglas Laycock, House Subcomm. on the Constitution (July 14, 1997).

incidental burden of pervasive regulation. In the judiciary there is great reluctance to take that mandate seriously. That is where we stand at the moment on what seems to be the most difficult problem here and in other developed countries around the world.

Round Table Discussion on International Human Rights Standards in the United States: The Case of Religion or Belief

12 Emory International Law Review 973 (1998)

Abdullahi A. An-Na'im (ed.)

This discussion concluded the conference at Emory University described in the introductory note to the preceding article. Eleven experts made opening statements, followed by less formal discussion among the panelists and responses to questions and comments from the audience. Presentations and portions of the discussion in which I took no active part have been omitted.

Two issues discussed prominently in the early opening statements were the reluctance of the United States to ratify international human rights treaties, even when the United States would generally be in compliance, and whether international guarantees of religious liberty should include any form of an establishment clause.

*   *   *

Douglas Laycock: If I can capitalize on what a couple of people have said about the record of the United States, the U.S. record is generally very good on political and religious matters. It is the international law record of the United States that is terrible. The United States often refuses to ratify, and when it does ratify, it qualifies its ratification with so many reservations, declarations, and understandings, as if to say it is not going to comply with the ratified treaty, and it sometimes refuses to submit to the jurisdiction of international tribunals. All of that has very little to do with the religious and political human rights record of the United States.

There are other areas of the international human rights agenda where the record of the United States is much worse. Besides the question of capital punishment, we obviously do not subscribe to the economic, social, and cultural rights specified by some human rights documents. There are also issues in the area of criminal procedure where the American record is very bad, although my guess is that the United States is not worse than most other places in the world. But the essential point here is that religious and political human rights are relatively well protected in the United States even though we do not submit to international mechanisms for their protection.

There is one additional reason no one has mentioned why the Senate of the United States is afraid to ratify human rights treaties. If we ratify a treaty in this country, it might actually be enforced. We are the only country in the world with an independent judiciary that has the power to strike down acts of Congress and acts of state legislatures and a long tradition of actively doing so. The American position is that, if these fuzzy ideals are written into law, they will be actually enforced. It is true that the courts do not always enforce; we have constitutional clauses that are ignored and never enforced, and other clauses that are enforced quite vigorously. But separation of powers and judicial review in the United States mean that we do not have the option that a lot of countries have of ratifying treaties on paper and ignoring them in practice. I assume that Iraq has ratified a lot of international treaties, but there are no independent enforcement mechanisms in that country that would make ratification meaningful.

If we are not willing to turn the vague language of human rights treaties over to be enforced by 700 life-appointed federal judges, why not withdraw and let the rest of the world protect human rights in its own way? That is a fair question, but part of the answer is that the premise of the question is not entirely true. There are multiple political factions within the United States on these issues. The international human rights community within the United States is strong enough to get the government to send delegations to these conventions. That faction attempts to take these treaties seriously enough, and sometimes eventually succeeds in badgering the Senate into ratifying some treaties, though subject to numerous reservations, understandings, and declarations. But the human rights community in the United States is not strong enough to defeat the reservations, understandings, and declarations, or to make the treaties self-executing, or to submit the United States to international enforcement. There are people, particularly on the right but some on the left as well, who really do want to have it both ways, who want to tell the rest of the world how to run their human rights affairs while being totally independent on our side. But much of this apparent hypocrisy is a product of different political factions who can succeed in controlling different organs of governments because of the doctrine of separation of powers.

A couple of things to add, very quickly. Adding an establishment clause to international human rights documents would not help with the attitudes

of the United States regarding ratification. A few people are strong supporters of the Establishment Clause. But the fact is, this clause is very controversial in the United States, too.

Earlier this morning I said that the real conflict in the United States is between high intensity and low intensity attitudes toward religion, and I related
that characterization to matters of assimilation to the mainstream culture.
Conflicts between Protestants and Catholics diminished with the lowering of
the intensity of attitudes on both sides, especially after Vatican II. Obviously,
negative attitudes persist toward Muslims, as colored by international politics, events in the Middle East, and so forth. But a lot of these issues have to
do with lack of assimilation and with intensity of belief. Many Americans can
deal with the idea of a Muslim in the abstract, but can not deal with Muslims
when they show up for work in robes and scarf. These are cases which religious individuals ought to win in court, but they have to be litigated, because
failure to assimilate provokes reaction.

Finally, we are not going to solve the problem of exemption from regulatory laws here today. I would just say that in a pervasively regulated society
such as this one, one can always draft an ordinance in neutral terms, without
mentioning religion, and yet be able to use it against any religious body one
wishes to attack. Neutrality of language is not sufficient protection in a society that is so heavily pluralistic and pervasively regulated.

*   *   *

Jason Waite (Emory University law graduate): My question is directed to
Professor Laycock and relates to the issue of the possible need for an establishment clause in international law. I would disagree with those who argue
for an establishment clause in international law for two reasons, both the
pragmatic reason of the type of uncertainty we find in U.S. Establishment
Clause jurisprudence, and also because I believe that the Establishment
Clause is designed as a means to an end — the end being religious liberty
which is already protected under international law. I am asking you for some
wisdom on this subject, and maybe your answer could combine reference to
where U.S. Establishment Clause jurisprudence is and where it should be, as
well as addressing whether there is a unified principle of religious liberty embodied in the U.S. religious clauses which is protected by international law.

Douglas Laycock: I agree that both clauses are a means to the end of religious
liberty. But that statement is often used as a code phrase for something else
which you may not have intended; so I had better give you the long answer

instead of the short one. The Establishment Clause and the Free Exercise Clause appear in the same sentence in the Constitution of the United States. The founders were not confused or contradicting themselves, and it was not a case of two contending factions each getting its own clause included. Rather, the same political faction demanded both clauses, and most of the political support came from evangelical churches.

So, yes, these two clauses combine to protect religious liberty. But, I think the Establishment Clause adds important things that the Free Exercise Clause does not capture by itself.[1] I agree with Jeremy Gunn's point that religious liberty would be better protected in other countries with different traditions if they had an establishment clause. But that is obviously far too controversial a claim to pose as an international norm. If we are unable to get consensus on an international norm protecting a person's freedom to change his or her religion, which is one of the most fundamental religious rights for an individual person to have, then it seems to me that we are light years away from consensus on an international establishment clause to be realized under international law.

When I say the way the speaker has formulated the question is a code phrase for some people, I mean this: some folks in the United States say that because the Establishment Clause and the Free Exercise Clause were designed with the joint purpose of protecting religious liberty, we can therefore ignore the Establishment Clause, since all the work is done by the Free Exercise Clause. I think that is a mistake. There are genuine disagreements about what the Establishment Clause means, but that is not the primary focus of today's conference. My thoughts on the big picture level can be found in a recent issue of the Emory Law Journal[2] just last year, if you are curious. But internationally, I think consensus on an establishment clause is a nonstarter. Just consider telling the Israelis to get rid of their established religion.

Jason Waite: Couldn't (or might not) the real meaning of the Establishment Clause be implicit in international instruments protecting religious liberty?

Douglas Laycock: No, absolutely not. People are paying taxes to support churches in a lot of countries.

Thomas Berg (then at Cumberland School of Law, Samford University, later at St. Thomas University (Minnesota)): Tax payments are also something that

---

1. See Douglas Laycock, *The Benefits of the Establishment Clause,* 42 DEPAUL L. REV. 373 (1992).

2. See Douglas Laycock, *The Underlying Unity of Separation and Neutrality,* 46 EMORY L.J. 43 (1997).

can be challenged under the religious liberty analysis. I guess the problem is that what the Establishment Clause adds to the Free Exercise Clause, while I think it is important, is also the most controversial aspect of it. Part of it has to do with how broadly one interprets the Free Exercise Clause. But when the Establishment Clause already adds the more problematic aspects of church-state rules, to try to elevate that up to the international level is really difficult.

*   *   *

Thomas Berg: As a teacher of intellectual property, I am familiar with the fact that for decades the United States refused to join international treaties on intellectual property, partly out of the same reasons of chauvinism, assuming that our system for the protection of intellectual property was the best and the right way to go. But in recent years, we have joined some of those international conferences and conventions out of the feeling that it is in our self-interest to do so. In order to have our own intellectual property protected in other nations, we had to join international agreements. In this light, I am wondering whether there are arguments that can be made to convince the United States that it is in our interest to join international human rights treaties that have binding force. Is that a potential line of argument, and what sort of outcome can one expect from that sort of discussion?

Johan van der Vyver (Emory University School of Law): The Law of the Sea Convention is an example of how perceptions of United States interests can influence decisions to accede to international treaties. The United States signed the Convention so that it could become part of its implementation structures.

Douglas Laycock: There are self-interested reasons to ratify economic treaties. U.S. businesses have money at stake in other countries, and so in order to be able to enforce our rights there, we have to ratify a treaty and make it enforceable here. It is hard to see the parallel in the human rights movement where we don't have self-interest at stake, but only a moral stake in how other countries are treating their citizens.

Jeremy Gunn (National Committee for Public Education and Religious Liberty): One area in which there may be interest in the United States in joining with the international community is on the question of persecution of Christians abroad. There has been a growing interest in this issue in the U.S. during the past year. Although this is only one issue, it is something in which even isolationists within the United States are interested. It is an issue that Americans who generally are opponents of overseas involvements may adopt. It offers an avenue for making the international realm more important to Middle America.

*   *   *

Rosalind Hackett (University of Tennessee, Knoxville): Speaking as an anthropologist and historian of religion, I would like to respond to some of the discussion about how we can generate consensus. It seems to me that the education sector is so vital here. I think that one of the problems in this country is that young people are not exposed to basic knowledge of other people's religious traditions. Very few of the students who come into my classes have any of that basic knowledge. So, I think that education is a very important way for building consensus and interest — it can be used to develop a sense of internationalism. The new South African constitution realizes the importance of the education sector, not least for teaching about different religious traditions, as being a way of healing past wounds and creating new nationalism. Having grown up in Britain, I have seen religious education there turned around from being mono-confessional to being very multicultural, and that is indeed making a difference in terms of tolerance of diversity in society. So if education has the power to do that, to develop a strong sense of nationalism, which is often done in this country, then why couldn't it also be used to develop a strong sense of internationalism? But I don't see that happening for many of the students who come into my classes from various high schools — if I ask them how many keep up with the world news and following international events, it is continually a minority. I do my level best to change that, but it should start much earlier than at college level.

*   *   *

Douglas Laycock: I want to comment briefly on the question of the role of education in public schools. There is some constituency in the United States for international multicultural education, although it tends to be overwhelmed by all of the other demands on the public school. If schools are finding it difficult to teach kids to read and write, how can they teach them about Malaysia and the other 197 countries in the world today? Which countries should schools cover, and what and how should they teach about them? Though it is clear that this is difficult to do well, there is some constituency for multicultural education. But I think there is no constituency whatever for teaching comparative religion in the public schools. There ought to be one, in my view. But in view of the two-generation-long fight over school prayer, and confusion about whether any mention of religion should be allowed, coupled with the fact that each side is paranoid that its views will be unfairly portrayed, public school administrators will probably be strongly opposed to teaching any comparative religion. Although the courts have always said throughout the school prayer debate that it is possible to teach comparative religion, it has never happened. Nobody actually wants it.

Rosalind Hackett: I am more familiar with issues of religious education in Britain and parts of Africa, than the United States in general, but I do know that California is perhaps leading the way in developing a multicultural religious education curriculum. I think that they are doing this in an intelligent way, instead of teaching about Malaysia or about Iran, it is rather about Iranians in the United States. So the curriculum at a place like the University of California Santa Barbara as well as in the local schools reflects that concern, namely, to study the religious geography of the local communities of the university or school. I think that these efforts are going to be propelled forward by recent developments, such as the CD-Rom by Professor Diana Eck from the Harvard Divinity School, a well-funded project to document world religions in the United States. It is called *On Common Ground.* This CD-Rom has its problems, of course. For example, she privileges Eastern religions because those are the ones she knows best, while African religions, unfortunately, feature very low down the list. She also did not include anything on what is for most people a major characteristic of the American religious landscape, namely, the whole scene of new religious movements — sects and cults. This whole field is, of course, one of the biggest challenges to the issues we are discussing here. Perhaps the reason Professor Eck decided not to include these new religious movements even though she talks about religious diversity in the United States is that they are too problematic.

Douglas Laycock: It is certainly is a step forward that someone has produced good material. There is another good project at Vanderbilt, actually, a joint effort with Vanderbilt and North Carolina, called *Living with Our Deepest Differences.* This project worked with some of the California schools; they found it to be an enormously labor-intensive process to try to negotiate a curriculum people were willing to live with, but it has had some important successes.

Michael Roan (Tandem Project, Minneapolis): Part of the problem, too, is who is teaching the religions themselves. We are talking about the lack of constituencies, and I think that this is true. But when I was a young kid, I went to Lutheran Sunday School, and they taught me: "Jesus Loves Me, This I know, Because the Bible Tells Me So." Every religion worth its salt started with that, with studies in the Qur'an, or the Talmud, throughout school age instructing children in their own religion. That is the natural urge; it is only human nature for the religious leadership to protect and promote their own religion by educating new leadership within the framework of the same religion. Tolerance may be a low priority, and the highest level of priority will be given to teaching youth about their own tradition. When will the National Council of Churches, the National Conference of Catholic Bishops, and so forth, say to all the local religious leadership to teach in Sunday School, along side, with equal emphasis and in tandem with "Jesus Loves Me," that "Human Rights Are Good for All," or something like that.

Douglas Laycock: Many denominations are not even doing their own texts any more. Sunday schools are reduced to making collages; they seem to fear that they will lose kids if they make any demand for serious study. The amount of watering down of religious education in the last generation is truly extraordinary in some denominations.

Azizah al-Hibri (University of Richmond School of Law): Let me speak on the question of teaching comparative religion in schools. It seems that a lot is actually being taught in schools today about the various religions, though maybe not in formal ways. This is a fact that a group of Muslims discovered when they visited various state school systems. They discovered a great deal of negative stereotyping of Islam. The group began a campaign to correct this situation. It started in California by helping develop better, fairer school books. They are now using that experience as a model in the other states. My point is this: while we may be reluctant to deal with the issue of teaching religion in schools, the fact of the matter is that religion is being taught in schools anyway. In fact, it is being taught in ways that may not be quite consistent with our objectives. As to Diana Eck's CD-ROM, I think it is excellent, and I am also sure that she would like very much to hear the criticism voiced by the speaker from the floor earlier.

Rosalind Hackett: Regarding negative stereotyping and related problems, this is happening not only in religion courses alone, but also world history courses.

∗   ∗   ∗

The Supreme Court and Religious Liberty

40 Catholic Lawyer 25 (2000)

This is an expanded version of an address to a conference of lawyers who represent individual Catholic bishops and their dioceses, first published in volume 40 of Catholic Lawyer. *It surveys the field from the perspective of what those lawyers need to know about recent cases in order to represent their clients. This is my most extensive treatment of how to make the most effective argument for constitutional exemptions from regulation that burdens the exercise of religion. This article also treats the Supreme Court's federalism revolution and the increased importance of arguments based on state law.*

*   *   *

In this article, I review recent developments in the Supreme Court, and closely related developments elsewhere, with respect to the free exercise of religion, the establishment of religion, and federalism. I highlight the current rules to the extent they can be identified, the deep ambiguities in some of those rules, and the most promising arguments for lawyers asserting religious liberty claims. I give extra attention to free exercise, where recent developments are most subject to misunderstanding. I speak from dual experience as an academic who studies the Court and as an advocate who has appeared in several of the cases discussed, on behalf of parties or amici.

This article originated in a presentation to the National Meeting of Diocesan Attorneys, April 19, 1998. It has been revised and updated to take account of subsequent developments through the end of the Supreme Court's term in June 2000.

I. Remaining Protections for Free Exercise of Religion

It is by now familiar history that *Employment Division v. Smith*[1] sharply cut back on free exercise protections. Under *Smith*, a regulatory burden on religious exercise requires no justification if it is imposed by a neutral and generally applicable law. There appear to be three votes to overrule *Smith*,[2] and four votes to reaffirm it.[3] Justices Ginsburg and Thomas have given no public hint of what they think, although they have had ample opportunity to criticize *Smith* if they are so inclined. No one has squarely asked the Court to overrule *Smith*, and probably someone should, but there is no obvious and attractive strategy for doing so. Certainly litigants should urge narrow interpretations of *Smith*. It may be much easier to get five votes to expand *Smith's* exceptions or interpret it more generously to religious liberty than to get five votes to squarely overrule it.

The key concept in *Smith* is "neutral and generally applicable law," and the Court gave some content to that requirement in *Church of the Lukumi Babalu Aye, Inc. v. City of Hialeah*.[4] So now we have the *Smith/Lukumi* test, but we have considerable disagreement over what exactly that test means. Perhaps the most important point about *Smith/Lukumi* is that lawyers for religious claimants should not despair prematurely.

In the effort to explain *Smith's* problems to Congress and to the public, proponents of free exercise have given it a worst-case interpretation and quite likely exaggerated its harmful consequences.[5] Sometimes worst-case interpretations are right, and *Smith* may be as bad as its strongest critics made it out to be. There are certainly lower court decisions that give it a worst-case interpretation, especially in the period from 1990 to 1993, after *Smith* and before *Lukumi*. But there are also much more promising interpretations that would greatly complicate the litigation but give free exercise claimants a plausible claim more often than not. Call the pessimistic scenario the Religious Bigotry Interpretation; claimants might have to prove that the law resulted from religious bigotry. Call the optimistic scenario the General Appli-

---

1. 494 U.S. 872 (1990).

2. *See* City of Boerne v. Flores, 521 U.S. 507, 544-65 (O'Connor, J., dissenting); *id.* at 565-66 (Souter, J., dissenting); *id.* at 566 (Breyer, J., dissenting).

3. Chief Justice Rehnquist, and Justices Stevens, Scalia, and Kennedy, were part of the *Smith* majority.

4. 508 U.S. 520 (1993).

5. *See* Douglas Laycock, *Conceptual Gulfs in City of Boerne v. Flores,* 39 WM. & MARY L. REV. 743, 771-80 (1998) (text at notes 155-201) (reviewing and analyzing the arguments made in support of the Religious Freedom Restoration Act).

cability Interpretation; claimants would have to prove only that the law is not generally applicable. The word "bigotry" does not appear either in *Smith* or in *Lukumi*, but the bad news is that in *Boerne*, Justice Kennedy used that word to summarize the *Smith* test.[6]

The requirement that *Smith* actually lays down is general applicability. If a law burdens the exercise of religion, it requires compelling justification unless it is neutral and generally applicable.[7] Taking "generally applicable" at its literal English meaning, the law has to apply to everyone, or nearly everyone, or else the burden on religious exercise must be justified under the compelling interest test.

Government lawyers routinely adopt some version of the Religious Bigotry Interpretation. They argue that under *Smith* and *Lukumi*, religious claimants must prove that government officials acted out of an anti-religious motive. If that is the standard, provable free exercise violations do not happen very often. Officials do sometimes act out of anti-religious motives; hostility to religious fundamentalists and minority religions is very widespread. But when officials act on such motives, and certainly in the more common case of anti-religious motives mixed in with a range of other motives, it is almost impossible to prove the anti-religious motive to the satisfaction of a judge. The Religious Bigotry Interpretation makes *Smith* and *Lukumi* close to worthless as a protection for free exercise. If that interpretation prevails, then we really do have the worst case.

There are lower court opinions that read *Smith* that way. *Cornerstone Bible Church v. City of Hastings*[8] involved a zoning ordinance with explicit rules about churches. Churches were expressly permitted in residential zones, and by unambiguous omission from a list of permitted uses, churches were excluded from commercial zones. The court said that the exclusion of churches from commercial zones was a generally applicable law, even though it was a special rule about churches, because there was no evidence of anti-religious motive.[9]

6. *See Boerne*, 521 U.S. at 535 ("In most cases, the state laws to which RFRA applies are not ones which will have been motivated by religious bigotry.").

7. *See* Church of the Lukumi Babalu Aye, Inc. v. City of Hialeah, 508 U.S. 520, 542 (1993) ("laws burdening religious practice must be of general applicability"); Employment Div. v. Smith, 494 U.S. 872, 878 (1990) (holding that no free exercise issue arises if burden on religious exercise is "merely the incidental effect of a generally applicable and otherwise valid provision"). For further analysis, see Richard F. Duncan, *Free Exercise Is Dead, Long Live Free Exercise: Smith, Lukumi and the General Applicability Requirement*, 3 U. PA. J. CONST. L. 850 (2001) (arguing that death of Free Exercise Clause has been greatly exaggerated).

8. 948 F.2d 464 (8th Cir. 1991).

9. *Id.* at 472 ("There is no evidence that the City has an anti-religious purpose in enforcing the ordinance. Absent evidence of the City's intent to regulate religious worship, the

A more recent example is *Swanson v. Guthrie Independent School District*.[10] The case had not been very well briefed, and the RFRA claims and the free exercise claims had been jumbled together. The best thing that happened in that case was a holding that plaintiff had waived her free exercise claim;[11] otherwise the court would have rejected that claim on the merits. That was plainly a court that, without the benefit of good briefing, instinctively read the Religious Bigotry Interpretation into *Lukumi* and *Smith*.

Such opinions are indefensible after *Lukumi*. Whatever else it may be, *Lukumi* is not a motive case. The lead opinion explicitly relies on the city's motive to exclude a particular religious group — and that part of the opinion has only two votes. So whatever the holding is, it is not a holding about motive. We have two votes for motive;[12] we have three votes with no need to consider motive because they think that *Smith* was wrongly decided;[13] we have two votes that say *Smith* was right, but motive is irrelevant to *Smith*;[14] and we have two votes that said nothing about motive one way or the other.[15] Seven Justices failed to find bad motive, but nine voted to strike down the ordinances.

If a religious claimant has evidence of bad motive, it should offer that evidence. Such evidence tends to discredit the government, and it makes the judge more sympathetic. But religious claimants should never, ever concede that they have to prove bad motive in order to make out a free exercise claim.

Lukumi, as extreme as the facts are, is a case about objectively unequal treatment.[16] The city had one rule for the religiously-motivated killing of animals, a different rule for nearly all the other reasons for killing animals, and different rules for other activities that generated the same kinds of harms. The ordinances that prohibited religious killings of animals were not gener-

---

ordinance is properly viewed as a neutral law of general applicability"). The court did subject the discrimination against churches to rational basis scrutiny under the Equal Protection Clause, and found no rational basis in the City's motion for summary judgment. *Id.* at 471-72 & n.13.

10. 135 F.3d 694 (10th Cir. 1998).

11. *See id.* at 698 ("Since the argument now advanced by Plaintiffs was not made below or ruled on by the district court, we will not address it for the first time on appeal.").

12. *See Lukumi*, 508 U.S. at 522, 540-42 (Kennedy, J., announcing the judgment).

13. *Id.* at 565-77 (Souter, J., concurring); *id.* at 577-80 (Blackmun, J., joined by O'Connor, J., concurring).

14. *Id.* at 557-59 (Scalia, J., joined by Rehnquist, CJ., concurring).

15. *Id.* at 522 (noting that White and Thomas, JJ., joined the opinion of the Court but did not join part II-A-2 (on motive), and did not write separately).

16. *Id.* at 542 ("The Free Exercise Clause 'protect[s] religious observers against unequal treatment'") (quoting Hobbie v. Unemployment Appeals Comm'n, 480 U.S. 136, 148 (Stevens, J., concurring)).

ally applicable. Whatever the reasons for the lines the city drew, the unequal treatment of religious and secular killings required compelling justification. The fallback position for the government side is this: even if *Lukumi* means the religious claimant does not have to prove bad motive, she still has to prove that religion is uniquely singled out for a burden that applies to no one else, because those were the facts of *Lukumi*. The ordinances did not affect any other significant reasons for killing an animal. The city's effort to show other possible applications was reduced to weird hypotheticals. So governments argue that laws are valid unless they are as extreme as the laws in *Lukumi*. Even if the test is not bad motive, even if the test is objectively differential treatment, governments say that religion has to be *uniquely* burdened.

Religious claimants have an answer there, too. The Court expressly says that it does not know how general the law has to be before it is generally applicable, but that the Hialeah laws did not even come close. "[T]hese ordinances fall well below the minimum standard necessary to protect First Amendment rights."[17] *Lukumi* was an extreme case, but burdensome laws do not have to be that extreme before there is a plausible free exercise claim. The minimum standard of generality required by the Free Exercise Clause is much higher than what Hialeah did in *Lukumi*.

Lukumi also talks about different ways in which one can prove lack of general applicability. They are jumbled together; it is not a good CLE [continuing legal education] opinion, but it offers much ammunition to those who read carefully. The most important thing to understand is that regulatory categories are not self-defining. The government likes to focus on the narrow law under challenge, and claim that the law is generally applicable to everything that it applies to. The city in *Lukumi* said that nobody could sacrifice; it had enacted a generally applicable law against sacrifice.[18] Plaintiffs said that sacrifice was not a relevant category. Killing animals was the relevant conduct, and there was nothing even close to a generally applicable law against killing animals.

The wave of bankruptcy cases against churches provide a less obvious illustration of the General Applicability Interpretation. There were hundreds of these lawsuits in which trustees in bankruptcy sued to recover contributions that a member made to the church before the contributor went bankrupt.[19]

---

17. 508 U.S. at 543.

18. *See id.* at 544 (summarizing the city's argument).

19. The leading and most intensively litigated case was *In re Young*, 148 B.R. 886 (Bankr. D. Minn. 1992) (entering judgment against church), *aff'd*, 152 B.R. 939 (D. Minn. 1993), *rev'd*, 82 F.3d 1407 (8th Cir. 1996) (holding that RFRA overrode the trustee's claim), *reh'g en banc denied*, 89 F.3d 494 (8th Cir. 1996), *vacated sub nom.* Christians v. Crystal Evangelical

Congress has solved the problem with a statutory amendment,[20] but the contrast between the truly general rule of the Bankruptcy Code, and the assertedly general rule of one narrow subsection of the Bankruptcy Code, still makes a good example of the battle over categorization.

Under the Bankruptcy Code as it existed prior to June 1998, the trustee would sue the church for an amount equal to the contributed funds. The contributed money had long since been spent; these were really demands that the church divert current contributions to pay the creditors of a bankrupt member. These cases were brought under §548(a)(2) of the Bankruptcy Code, and the government, as intervenor in one of these cases, argued that §548(a)(2) was generally applicable to everything it applied to.[21] In any case that fell within §548(a)(2), the creditors won and the transferee lost. The government also appeared to argue that under *Smith* and *Lukumi,* the category defined by the challenged statute did not even have to be rational.[22]

Churches responded that the court had to consider the whole Bankruptcy Code. The general rule in bankruptcy is that creditors lose: the trustee can not reach any money and the creditors do not get paid. There are thousands of transactions in the economic life of a typical debtor in the last year before bankruptcy, and nearly all these transactions dissipate funds that could have been used to pay creditors. Only a tiny handful of those transactions are ever set aside under §548(a)(2) or any other section; in most of these cases, only gifts to the church were set aside. Churches were becoming the principal source of funds available for distribution in consumer bankrupt-

---

Free Church, 521 U.S. 1114 (1997) (remanding for consideration in light of *Boerne*), *on remand,* 141 F.3d 854 (8th Cir. 1998) (upholding constitutionality of RFRA as applied to federal law), *cert. denied,* 525 U.S. 811 (1998). Other examples include In re Hodge, 220 B.R. 386 (D. Idaho 1998); In re Newman, 203 B.R. 468 (D. Kan. 1996); In re Rivera, 214 B.R. 101 (Bankr. S.D.N.Y. 1997); In re Bloch, 207 B.R. 944 (D. Colo. 1997); In re Moses, 59 B.R. 815 (Bankr. N.D. Ga. 1986); In re Missionary Baptist Found., 24 B.R. 973 (N.D. Tex. 1982). Variations on these claims include *In re Tessier,* 190 B.R. 396 (D. Idaho 1995), *appeal dis'd,* 127 F.3d 1106 (9th Cir. 1997) (trustee challenged contributions to church included in chapter 13 plan), and *Cedar Bayou Baptist Church v. Gregory-Edwards, Inc.,* 987 S.W.2d 156 (Tex. App. — Hou.[14th Dist.] 1999) (claim brought by individual creditor after trustee refused to assert it).

20. Religious Liberty and Charitable Donation Protection Act of 1998, Pub. L. 105-183, 112 Stat. 517 (1998) (principally codified in 11 U.S.C. §§ 544, 548, and 1325 (Supp. IV 1998)).

21. *See* Supplemental Brief for Intervenor United States of America 12, In re Young, 141 F.3d 854 (8th Cir. 1998) (arguing that "the statute establishes a defined category of contributions" and "operates to void all such transfers"). Usually the government is not a party in private bankruptcy cases, but trustees in bankruptcy made similar arguments.

22. *See id.* at 20 ("the rational basis for this statutory distinction is not at issue here").

cies. That is not a generally applicable law. Gifts to the church were singled out from all the debtor's money-losing transactions.[23]

The government's argument, both in *Lukumi* and in the bankruptcy cases, was entirely circular. It insisted that the challenged law defined the relevant category, and that the challenged law was generally applicable to that category. *Lukumi* rejected this argument in multiple ways. First, *Lukumi* said that if the prohibition is narrow in scope, that is evidence that the law is not neutral (a separate requirement that overlaps with general applicability).[24] Second, the Court in *Lukumi* refused to confine its analysis to the challenged ordinances; it considered the whole body of Hialeah and Florida law on killing of animals and on cruelty to animals.[25]

Most important, *Lukumi* said that if there are other activities that cause comparable harms to the same governmental interests, and those activities are not regulated, the law is not generally applicable.[26] The unregulated activity does not even have to be the same activity with a secular motive; it can be a different activity with the same effect. One of the great pieces of evidence in *Lukumi* was when the city's public health expert said that the garbage bins outside of restaurants were a much bigger health problem than people leaving sacrificed chickens in the street. Of course the city did not ban restaurants to avoid the problem of restaurant garbage, but it banned sacrifice to avoid sacrifice garbage. So the sacrifice ordinances were not generally applicable laws.[27]

Sometimes the government responds to this kind of argument by emphasizing *Smith's* language about "individualized exceptions." Government concedes arguendo that if it makes *individualized* secular exceptions, then maybe it has to make religious exceptions, but it insists that *categorical* exceptions do not trigger serious judicial review. That distinction makes no sense. Wholesale secular exceptions make the law even less generally applicable than individualized secular exceptions.[28] But *Smith* did talk about individualized exceptions when it explained the unemployment compensation

23. *See* Brief of Appellant on Remand from the Supreme Court of the United States 24-31, In re Young, 141 F.3d 1354 (8th Cir. 1998).

24. *See* Church of the Lukumi Babalu Aye, Inc. v. City of Hialeah, 508 U.S. 520, 537 (1993) ("A pattern of exemptions parallels the pattern of narrow prohibitions. Each contributes to the gerrymander.").

25. *See id.* at 537, 539, 543-45.

26. *See id.* at 543 ("The ordinances . . . fail to prohibit nonreligious conduct that endangers these interests in a similar or greater degree").

27. *Id.* at 544-45.

28. *See* Fraternal Order of Police v. City of Newark, 170 F.3d 359, 365 (3d Cir. 1999).

cases.[29] *Lukumi* did not explicitly clarify that language, but it plainly relied on categorical exceptions to show that the rule against killing animals was not neutral and generally applicable. The city allowed fishing in the city; the animal cruelty laws had an exception for medical experiments; they had an exception for pest control and exterminators. The Court relied on these and other categorical exceptions.[30] The Court said that "categories of selection are of paramount concern when a law has the incidental effect of burdening religious practice."[31]

Evidence of uneven enforcement can also be very helpful. Religious claimants should show that the government is granting exceptions under the table, or enforcing the rule only or disproportionately against churches or religiously motivated violators, or enforcing the law unevenly in some other way — if those facts are available. Such evidence shows that the law is not generally applicable in fact.

I want to note some of the more promising lower court examples. *Fraternal Order of Police v. City of Newark*[32] is the leading case at the moment. Muslim police officers, required by their faith to wear beards, challenged the city's requirement that police officers be clean shaven. The rule had two exceptions — one for medical conditions that made shaving difficult, and one for undercover officers. The court held that the medical exception undermined the city's interest in uniformity in the same way as a religious exception, and that the existence of this single secular exception made the rule not generally applicable.

> [T]he medical exemption raises concern because it indicates that the Department has made a value judgment that secular (i.e., medical) motivations for wearing a beard are important enough to overcome its general interest in uniformity but that religious motivations are not.[33]

The court said that the exception for undercover officers would not trigger heightened scrutiny. That exception was entirely outside the scope of the rule — undercover officers were not supposed to be recognized as officers — and so it reflected no willingness to sacrifice the interest in uniformity to the needs of individual officers, and thus no comparative judgment about the

---

29. *See* Employment Div. v. Smith, 494 U.S. 872, 884 (1990) ("where the state has in place a system of individual exemptions, it may not refuse to extend that system to cases of 'religious hardship' without compelling reason.")

30. *See Lukumi,* 508 U.S. at 543-44 (listing such exceptions).

31. *Id.* at 542.

32. 170 F.3d 359 (3d Cir. 1999).

33. *Id.* at 366.

relative importance of undercover operations and the free exercise of religion. But the contrast between the medical exception and the refusal of religious exceptions did reflect a judgment — that an officer's free exercise of religion was less important than other important individual needs.

Keeler v. Mayor of Cumberland[34] is a landmarking case involving an old building owned by a Catholic church in Cumberland, Maryland. In that case, there were three exceptions on the face of the landmark ordinance — for substantial benefit to city, undue financial hardship to owner, and best interests of a majority of the community.[35] It is not clear that these exceptions had ever been applied, but they were part of the law, and that was enough. The court held that the Free Exercise Clause requires a religious exception if the city recognizes secular exceptions.[36] The court might also have noted that these exceptions were so vague that they effectively required individualized decisions to grant or withhold exceptions. Indeed, if such vague exceptions are actually used, they are a virtual invitation for uneven enforcement, in which government grants exceptions to the politically powerful or well connected, or to projects that happen to appeal to key members of the city council, but not to other claimants with fewer connections or less appeal.

Rader v. Johnston[37] shows how relevant exceptions can be found in the history of implementation as well as on the face of the rule. *Rader* involved the University of Nebraska at Kearney, and a rule that said all freshmen had to live in the dorm. Doug Rader was a freshman. He was an evangelical Protestant, and he wanted to live in the religious group house across the street from campus. In discovery, he found data on the high rate of alcohol and drug abuse in the dorms. He said that living in the dorm was a near occasion of sin and that other dorm residents ridiculed his religious beliefs. He wanted to live in the religious group house where there was no record of any resident ever having a problem with alcohol, drugs, or sexual irresponsibility. There were very strict rules, and no one had ever been kicked out, because people complied with the rules.

Historically, freshmen had been allowed to live in the group house. Then the University got a new Vice-President for Student Affairs, and she apparently ordered that there be no more religious exceptions. She actually testified that "students who did not wish to live in the residence halls for religious reasons should not attend UNK."[38]

---

34. 940 F. Supp. 879 (D. Md. 1996).
35. *See id.* at 886.
36. *See id.* at 886-87.
37. 924 F. Supp. 1540 (D. Neb. 1996).
38. *Id.* at 1549. The quotation is the court's paraphrase of her testimony.

The trial lawyer did his homework and discovered the facts, and here is what he proved. First, there were some open and categorical exceptions. Freshmen over nineteen did not have to live in the dorm. Freshmen who were married did not have to live in the dorm. Freshmen living with their family in the Kearney community did not have to live in the dorm. There was an open, individualized exception: freshmen with hardship situations did not have to live in the dorm. It turned out that hardship was liberally interpreted. Mothers of small children, freshmen with medical problems, and a freshman who was needed to drive his pregnant sister to and from campus had all gotten hardship exceptions. They did not have to live in the dorm. Then it turned out there were some hidden exceptions, completely unwritten. If your parents knew a regent or development officer well enough to ask for a favor, you did not have to live in the dorm. By the time plaintiff rested, it turned out that about a third of the freshmen had been exempted, and only two-thirds actually had to live in the dorm.[39] The court held that the university's rule was not generally applicable, and that the refusal of an exception for the religiously motivated student required a compelling interest.[40]

These cases are a very far cry from *Lukumi*. In *Lukumi*, religion was singled out. Religion was the only thing that was burdened. In *Rader*, two-thirds of the freshmen were burdened. Only one-third were exempted, but that was enough. In *FOP* and *Keeler*, the court did not even note how many people fit within the secular exceptions. It seems likely that the medical exception in *FOP* exempted only a small minority of police officers, and it is entirely possible that the exceptions in *Keeler* existed only in theory. Yet each of these courts held that if government had secular exceptions for some, it could not refuse exceptions for the free exercise of religion. That is the General Applicability Interpretation of *Smith* and *Lukumi*, and it is the right interpretation. If *Smith* and *Lukumi* mean that, then religious claimants can often prevail, because the way the American legislative process works is to cut special deals and make exceptions for squeaky wheels. If you let out the interest group that complains the most, you have to let out the religious claimant as well.

It is very important that religious liberty claimants not give away the argument from the General Applicability Interpretation. If there are exceptions for secular interests, the religious claimant has to be treated as favorably as those who benefit from the secular exceptions. The logic of this argument is two-fold. First, the legislature cannot place a higher value on some well-

39. *See id.* at 1546-47 (summarizing these exceptions).
40. *Id.* at 1553.

connected secular interest group with no particular constitutional claim than it places on the free exercise of religion.[41] Second, part of the logic of *Smith* and *Lukumi* is that if burdensome laws must be applied to everyone, religious minorities will get substantial protection from the political process. The Court noted that the Hialeah ordinances appeared to be "a prohibition that society is prepared to impose upon [Santeria worshipers] but not upon itself."[42] And it continued: "This precise evil is what the requirement of general applicability is designed to prevent."[43] If a burdensome proposed law is generally applicable, other interest groups will oppose it, and it will not be enacted unless the benefits are sufficient to justify the costs. But this vicarious political protection breaks down very rapidly if the legislature is free to exempt any group that might have enough political power to prevent enactment, leaving a law applicable only to small religions with unusual practices and other groups too weak to prevent enactment.

There are also some other free exercise claims, not dependent on the General Applicability Interpretation, that survive *Smith* and *Lukumi*. These are simply outside the scope of the new rules. They could be forced into the new rules, but the Court plainly was not thinking about them in those terms. *Smith* reaffirms the line of cases holding that government may not "lend its power to one or the other side in controversies over religious authority or dogma."[44] These cases have not affected Catholics much, because even non-Catholic lawyers understand that the Roman Catholic Church is hierarchical. But all those cases remain good law, and they have their uses. Secular courts cannot resolve an internal religious dispute, and especially not a doctrinal re-

---

41. *See Lukumi*, 508 U.S. at 537-38 ("Respondent's application of the ordinance's test of necessity devalues religious reasons for killing by judging them to be of lesser import than nonreligious reasons."); Fraternal Order of Police v. City of Newark, 170 F.3d 359, 366 (3d Cir. 1999) ("When the government makes a value judgment in favor of secular motivations, but not religious motivations, the government's actions must survive heightened scrutiny.").

42. *Lukumi*, 508 U.S. at 545 (quoting Florida Star v. B.J.F., 491 U.S. 524, 542 (1989) (Scalia, J., concurring)).

43. *Lukumi*, 508 U.S. at 545-46. *See also* Railway Express Agency, Inc. v. New York, 336 U.S. 106 (1949): "There is no more effective practical guaranty against arbitrary and unreasonable government than to require that the principles of law which officials would impose upon a minority must be imposed generally. Conversely, nothing opens the door to arbitrary action so effectively as to allow those officials to pick and choose only a few to whom they will apply legislation and thus to escape the political retribution that might be visited upon them if larger numbers were affected." *Id.* at 112-13 (Jackson, J., concurring), quoted with approval by the Court, with respect to discrimination among religious faiths, in Larson v. Valente, 456 U.S. 228, 245-46 (1982).

44. *Smith*, 494 U.S. at 877.

ligious dispute, even in the guise of sorting out who owns a parcel of church property.[45]

Disputes between churches and their ministers have also been treated as outside the scope of *Smith* and *Lukumi*. So if a priest sues for employment discrimination, most courts are still refusing to hear those cases.[46] But even that rule is under attack, and exceptions are beginning to appear.[47]

Catholics do get caught up in those cases sometimes, usually not with respect to the parish church, but with respect to other organizations — social service organizations, hospitals, orphanages — places where the hierarchical lines may not be so clearly understood. This argument figured prominently in a recent Texas case in which the Catholic Conference escaped vicarious liability in a major pedophile case. We tried to explain to the Supreme Court of Texas that the National Conference of Catholic Bishops was not really in the hierarchy — that bishops report to Rome, and that the national conferences are membership organizations off to the side of the chain of command — that the Conferences did not have operational responsibility or supervisory authority over individual priests, and that an attempt to hold the Conferences liable was an attempt to reallocate religious authority among different religious organizations. Plaintiffs' claim was an attempt to say that some of

45. For the difference between the formulation that courts should not resolve internal church disputes (thus guaranteeing each church's freedom to resolve such disputes internally), and the formulation that courts should not resolve disputes over religious doctrine (thus encouraging courts and litigants to ignore such issues and resolve the dispute on the basis of some allegedly non-doctrinal issue) see Patrick Schiltz & Douglas Laycock, *Employment in Religious Organizations,* in RELIGIOUS ORGANIZATIONS IN THE UNITED STATES: A STUDY OF IDENTITY, LIBERTY, AND THE LAW 527 (James A. Seritella, *et al.*, eds., 2006). [In 2000, I cited this as forthcoming. The chapter was written, but the volume suffered extraordinary publication delays. No time travel involved.]

46. *See, e.g.,* Serbian E. Orthodox Diocese v. Milivojevich, 426 U.S. 696 (1976); Gellington v. Christian Methodist Episcopal Church, Inc., 203 F.3d 1299 (11th Cir. 2000); Combs v. Central Tex. Annual Conference, 173 F.3d 343 (5th Cir. 1999); EEOC v. Catholic Univ., 83 F.3d 455 (D.C. Cir. 1996); Young v. Northern Ill. Conference, 21 F.3d 184 (7th Cir. 1994); Scharon v. St. Luke's Episcopal Presbyterian Hosps., 929 F.2d 360 (8th Cir. 1991); Lewis v. Seventh Day Adventists Lake Region Conference, 978 F.2d 940 (6th Cir. 1992); Rayburn v. General Conf. of Seventh-Day Adventists, 772 F.2d 1164 (4th Cir. 1985).

47. *See* Bollard v. California Province of the Society of Jesus, 196 F.3d 940 (9th Cir. 1999) (holding that plaintiff had stated a claim that unremedied sexual harassment caused his constructive discharge as a Jesuit novice); *see also Religion in the Workplace: Proceedings of the 2000 Annual Meeting of the Association of American Law Schools Section on Law and Religion,* 4 EMPLOYEE RIGHTS & EMPLOYMENT POL'Y J. 87, 101-09 (remarks of Joanne Brant, appearing to argue that it is often unconstitutional for courts *not* to decide disputes between churches and their clergy).

the authority that belongs to the individual bishops also belongs to the Conferences, whether or not Catholics think it belongs there. And that was a reallocation of religious authority that could not be permitted.[48]

Weaver v. Wood[49] is an interesting illustration from Massachusetts. Plaintiffs and the trial court sought to reallocate authority inside the Christian Science Church, even though there was no schism and the church governance structure was functioning. In effect, the lawsuit attempted to use the court to create a schism. Without announcing a very clear rule, the Supreme Judicial Court of Massachusetts refused to take the bait. The principle that civil courts cannot interfere with the allocation of religious authority survives *Smith*. That principle has many applications, not all of which are obvious, and religious claimants should be alert for those applications.

The application of this principle is clearest when a church employee or a subordinate church entity is suing a supervisory entity. It is less clear, and judges have more trouble and the results are more divided, in cases where an individual member sues and the claim is that plaintiff is suing the wrong entity or suing in a way that would force a church to change the way it relates to its clergy. When plaintiff is an individual member suing, courts often do not view the case as an internal church dispute. They should, but they do not; they are much more likely to view that individual member as an outsider. So there are very mixed results in these cases about allocation of religious authority, but the important point is that they are not directly affected by *Smith*.

Fraud claims against churches can be maintained if the fraud is temporal — if you take money to build a church and spend it to stay at the Ritz-Carlton. But if the church is sued for fraud because it promised eternal salvation and the plaintiff has decided she is not going to get it, there can be no fraud claim for that. The rule that courts cannot pass on the truth of religious teaching continues after *Smith*.[50]

---

48. The case is unreported; plaintiffs dismissed their claims against the Conference when the Supreme Court of Texas granted oral argument on a petition for mandamus to prevent discovery in the case. United States Catholic Conference v. Ashby, No. 95-0250 (Tex. 1996). The underlying claims resulted in a large settlement between plaintiffs and the Diocese of Dallas. See Ed Housewright & Brooks Egerton, *Diocese, Kos Victims Settle for $23.4 Million; Bishop Apologizes, Vows to Prevent Abuse*, DALLAS MORNING NEWS 1A, July 11, 1998.

49. 680 N.E.2d 918 (Mass. 1997).

50. *See, e.g.*, United States v. Ballard, 322 U.S. 78 (1944); Tilton v. Marshall, 925 S.W.2d 672 (Tex. 1996).

II. The Recent Federalism Decisions and the Growing Importance of State Law

As everyone knows by now, the Supreme Court in *City of Boerne v. Flores*[51] case struck down the Religious Freedom Restoration Act[52] as it applied to state and local governments.[53] *Boerne* is a remarkable opinion that is not limited to religious liberty; it rolls back congressional power to enforce the Civil War Amendments quite generally.[54] At the oral argument, it was as though the Civil War had never happened. The Solicitor of Ohio asked the Court to restore the Jeffersonian vision of the states as the guardians of liberty — in a Fourteenth Amendment case![55] The Civil War and the Fourteenth Amendment were precisely about establishing federal power to protect liberty in the states; whatever the reach of that change, "the states as the guardians of liberty" is emphatically not the vision of the Fourteenth Amendment.

The most striking thing about the opinion is how the logic of *Boerne* parallels the logic of *Lochner v. New York*.[56] The Court said that there are two reasons Congress might have passed RFRA. Congress might have done it to enforce the Court's understanding of free exercise. That would be a legitimate reason. Or Congress might have done it to enact Congress's own understanding of free exercise. That would be an illegitimate reason, according to the Court.[57] And to police that boundary, the Court said that it will decide *whether the statute was factually necessary* to enforce the judicial interpretation of free exercise.[58] The Court will decide for itself, without benefit of briefing or record, how many free exercise violations are out there. The Court thought that there were not very many, so that RFRA was not necessary for its legitimate purpose, and therefore, must have been enacted for its illegitimate purpose.

Similarly in *Lochner*, the Court said that New York might have limited

---

51. 521 U.S. 507 (1997).

52. 42 U.S.C. §§ 2000bb to 2000bb-4 (1994).

53. City of Boerne v. Flores, 521 U.S. 507 (1997).

54. *See generally* Laycock, *supra* note 5 (elaborating on this theme).

55. *See* Transcript of Oral Argument, City of Boerne v. Flores, 521 U.S. 507 (1997) (No. 95-2074), *available in* U.S. Trans. LEXIS 17, at *27.

56. 198 U.S. 45 (1905). *Lochner* is the best-known symbol of activist judicial review of economic substantive due process claims.

57. *See Boerne*, 521 U.S. at 519-20 (distinguishing permitted remedial legislation to enforce the Fourteenth Amendment from forbidden substantive legislation expanding the terms of the Amendment).

58. *See id.* at 529-32 (reviewing the need for RFRA and finding it unjustified as a remedial measure).

the working hours of bakers for reasons of health or safety, which would be legitimate, or to protect bakers from economic exploitation, which would be illegitimate. The only way to prevent New York from dissembling about its motive was for the Court to decide for itself whether bakers need protection of their health and safety.[59]

RFRA remains valid as applied to federal law.[60] That is the position of the Clinton Administration,[61] and that seems clearly right. Congress's decision to limit the reach of its own statutes, to avoid unintended burdens on religious liberty, is in no way dependent on power to enforce the Fourteenth Amendment — the only power at issue in *Boerne*. Not every United States Attorney has gotten the word, but if the federal government or a private litigant challenges RFRA as applied to federal law, the Justice Department will intervene to defend the statute. It takes a narrow view of what RFRA means, but it is quite convinced that RFRA is constitutional.

On remand in light of *Boerne*, the Eighth Circuit upheld RFRA as applied to federal bankruptcy law.[62] The opinion deals with all the arguments — separation of powers, the source of congressional power under Article I, and the Establishment Clause. The dissent proceeds on the view that Congress can protect religious liberty against federal burdens — but only if it proceeds one statute at a time.[63] Congress could amend the Bankruptcy Code and amend the employment discrimination laws and then amend the labor laws. But the dissent claims that Congress can not protect religious liberty in a general statute like RFRA, because that is a disguised amendment to the

59. See *Lochner*, 198 U.S. at 61 ("The act is not, within any fair meaning of the term, a health law, but is an illegal interference with the rights of individuals, both employers and employees, to make contracts regarding labor upon such terms as they may think best.").

60. See In re Young, 141 F.3d 854 (8th Cir. 1998); EEOC v. Catholic Univ., 83 F.3d 455 (D.C. Cir. 1996). Other courts have assumed RFRA's validity without deciding the issue, rejecting the RFRA claim on other grounds. Sutton v. Providence St. Joseph Medical Center, 192 F.3d 826, 831-34 (9th Cir. 1999); Adams v. Commissioner, 170 F.3d 173, 175 (3d Cir. 1999); Alamo v. Clay, 137 F.3d 1366, 1368 (D.C. Cir. 1998); Jackson v. District of Columbia, 89 F.Supp.2d 48, 64 (D.D.C. 2000).

61. See United States v. Sandia, 188 F.3d 1215, 1217 (10th Cir. 1999) (government argued that RFRA was constitutional and applicable); *Adams*, 170 F.3d at 175 (government conceded that RFRA was constitutional and applicable); *Alamo*, 137 F.3d at 1368 (same); *Jackson*, 89 F.Supp.2d at 64 (District of Columbia defendants challenged constitutionality of RFRA, but federal Bureau of Prisons did not); Brief for Intervenor United States of America, In re Young, 141 F.3d 854 (8th Cir. 1998) (vigorously defending constitutionality of RFRA against challenge by trustee in bankruptcy).

62. In re Young, 141 F.3d 854 (8th Cir. 1998).

63. See *id.* at 865-66 (Bogue, J., dissenting).

Free Exercise Clause. This argument got a vote, which tells you that there is some judicial hostility to what Congress is trying to do.[64]

The decision in *Boerne* is part of a general invigoration and extension of doctrines to limit federal power. The Court has vigorously applied *Boerne* to other Enforcement Clause legislation, repeatedly finding that Congressional legislation to enforce the Fourteenth Amendment was unnecessary to solve any real problem.[65]

Another new federalism doctrine is that Congress cannot require the states to help enforce federal law. The lead decision here is *Printz v. United States*,[66] striking down a requirement that local law enforcement officials help screen gun-buyers for criminal records. *Printz* says that Congress can ask New York to help, just as it can ask Ontario to help, and it might get a co-operative answer. But the relationship is the same in either case. If New York chooses not to help, it has no obligation to help.

There are ways around *Printz*. Congress can use the spending power, which so far the Court has not cut back. Congress can ask the states to do something and give them money if they do it, and attach conditions to the grant of federal money.[67] There are those in the secular conservative movement who want to limit the spending power and especially limit the right to attach conditions to federal grants, in order to complete a sweep of shrinking congressional power to implement federal policy in the states.[68]

For the first time since 1936 the Court is striking down statutes as beyond

---

64. For commentary on the constitutionality of RFRA as applied to the federal government, *compare* Thomas C. Berg, *The Constitutional Future of Religious Freedom Legislation*, 20 U. ARK. LITTLE ROCK L.J. 715, 727-47 (1998) (arguing that RFRA is valid); *with* Marci Hamilton, *The Religious Freedom Restoration Act Is Unconstitutional, Period*, 1 U. PA. J. CONST. L. 1 (1998); Edward J. W. Blatnik, *Note, No RFRA Allowed: The Status of the Religious Freedom Restoration Act's Federal Application in the Wake of City of Boerne v. Flores*, 98 COLUM. L. REV. 1410 (1998).

65. *See* United States v. Morrison, 529 U.S. 598 (2000) (invalidating private cause of action under Violence Against Women Act); Kimel v. Florida Bd. of Regents, 528 U.S. 62 (2000) (invalidating Age Discrimination in Employment Act, as applied to create monetary remedies against states); Florida Prepaid Postsecondary Educ. Expense Bd. v. College Sav. Bank, 527 U.S. 627 (1999) (invalidating Patent Remedy Act, as applied to create monetary remedies against states); *but see* Lopez v. Monterey County, 525 U.S. 266 (1999) (upholding application of Voting Rights Act to non-covered jurisdiction in a covered state, describing legislation as remedial without considering whether it was necessary).

66. 521 U.S. 898 (1997).

67. *See* South Dakota v. Dole, 483 U.S. 203 (1987) (upholding requirement that states accepting federal highway funds raise drinking age to twenty-one).

68. *See* Lynn A. Baker, *Conditional Federal Spending After Lopez*, 95 COLUM. L. REV. 1911 (1995).

the reach of the commerce power. The Court struck down the Gun Free Schools Act in *United States v. Lopez*,[69] and the Violence Against Women Act in *United States v. Morrison*,[70] and it construed the federal arson act narrowly in *Jones v. United States*,[71] in part to avoid asserted constitutional problems. Each of these cases involved regulation of noncommercial activity with economic consequences; these cases are less about what commerce is interstate than about what counts as commerce in the first place. If they are confined to that, they draw an important line, but they do not limit Congressional power over commercial transactions. The opinions seem to reaffirm the traditional doctrine that Congress can regulate even small and local economic transactions if in the aggregate those transactions would affect interstate commerce.

There have been numerous recent decisions reinvigorating sovereign immunity doctrines, particularly state sovereign immunity. In *Seminole Tribe v. Florida*[72] the Court eliminated congressional power to override Eleventh Amendment immunity, except in statutes to enforce the Fourteenth Amendment. So now we are getting a round of litigation to determine which Congressional power underlies each attempted override of state immunity.[73] Statutes that impose federal-court liability on the states are invalid if passed under Article I powers (with the possible exception of the spending power[74]), but are valid if passed under Fourteenth Amendment powers. That rule obvi-

---

69. 514 U.S. 549 (1995).

70. 529 U.S. 598 (2000).

71. 529 U.S. 848 (2000).

72. 517 U.S. 44 (1996). This rule was extended to state-owned commercial enterprises in *College Sav. Bank v. Florida Prepaid Postsecondary Educ. Expense Bd.*, 527 U.S. 666 (1999), and to state courts in *Alden v. Maine*, 527 U.S. 706 (1999).

73. *See* Kimel v. Florida Bd. of Regents, 528 U.S. 62 (2000) (holding that Age Discrimination in Employment Act is not valid legislation to enforce Fourteenth Amendment); Florida Prepaid Postsecondary Educ. Expense Bd. v. College Sav. Bank, 527 U.S. 627 (1999) (holding that Patent Remedy Act is not valid legislation to enforce Fourteenth Amendment); University of Ala. v. Garrett, 193 F.3d 1214 (11th Cir. 1999) (holding that Americans with Disabilities Act is valid legislation to enforce Fourteenth Amendment and overrides state sovereign immunity), [*rev'd*, 531 U.S. 356 (2001)]; Lesage v. Texas, 158 F.3d 213 (5th Cir. 1998) (holding that Title VI of Civil Rights Act of 1964, or its implementing legislation, is valid legislation to enforce Fourteenth Amendment and overrides state sovereign immunity), *rev'd on other grounds*, 528 U.S. 18 (1999). [The Supreme Court's decision in University of Alabama v. Garrett, holding that the employment provisions of the Americans with Disabilities Act is not valid legislation to enforce the Fourteenth Amendment, was released after this article appeared in print.]

74. *See* Pederson v. Louisiana State Univ., 213 F.3d 858, 875-76 (5th Cir. 2000) (holding that state waived its immunity when it accepted federal higher education funds); Litman v. George Mason Univ., 186 F.3d 544, 548-51 (4th Cir. 1999) (same).

ously intersects with *Boerne.* The Fourteenth Amendment powers were sharply narrowed in *Boerne,* so fewer laws can be passed overriding Eleventh Amendment immunity.

So far there are limits to the federalism counter-revolution. The fundamental case that makes it possible to bring free exercise and other civil liberties litigation in federal court is *Ex parte Young,*[75] which held that a suit to enjoin constitutional violations by state officials is not a suit against the state, and thus not barred by sovereign immunity. This is a fiction, but an essential one if constitutional limits are to have much meaning. A government that cannot be sued can make a bill of rights meaningless; it can act lawlessly, not resorting to the courts in cases where citizens might raise a constitutional defense. Or it can set penalties so high that few citizens would dare violate a law to test its constitutionality. In *Idaho v. Coeur d'Alene Tribe,*[76] Justice Kennedy and Chief Justice Rehnquist wanted to rip the heart out of *Ex parte Young,*[77] but they got only their own votes.[78] So even for Justices Scalia, Thomas, and O'Connor, there are limits in this campaign to roll back federal authority. It is not clear what those limits are or where they originated, but they seem to exist.

It is equally unclear how far the rollback of federal power will go, but even as far as it has gone already, state law is assuming a much greater importance, particularly for the protection of free exercise of religion. State constitutions and state statutes matter; it is malpractice not to plead, brief, and fully develop your state constitutional free exercise claim. What often happens is that lawyers overlook the state constitution. We think federal constitutional law first. Or we tack the state claim on at the end of the complaint, but we do not spend the time to really develop it. There are few state cases, and it is so much easier to cite the cases on the federal Free Exercise Clause — even if those cases are wrong and adverse to the interests of the client. Lawyers know how to argue from cases.

How do you make an argument when no cases have been decided yet? To really develop a state constitutional claim, you have to invest some time in it.

---

75. 209 U.S. 123 (1908) (holding that suit to enjoin state official from enforcing invalid state law is not a suit against the state for purposes of sovereign immunity).

76. 521 U.S. 261 (1997).

77. *Id.* at 270-80 (arguing that *Young* should apply only after case-by-case balancing of plaintiff's need for federal forum and state's interest in state forum) (Kennedy, J., announcing the judgment).

78. *See id.* at 288-97 (O'Connor, J., joined by Scalia and Thomas, J.J., concurring) (rejecting Justice Kennedy's proposed changes in *Young,* but agreeing that the case fell within an exception to *Young*); *id.* at 297-319 (Souter, J., joined by Stevens, Ginsburg, and Breyer, J.J., dissenting).

You have to develop it in the trial court and fully brief it on appeal, and you have to argue from constitutional text, history, and first principles. The Supreme Court of Texas has said that it will not decide state constitutional claims that are just tacked on at the end. If you want that court to decide a state constitutional claim, you have to fully brief it, give the court the history of the state constitutional provision, and give the court a reason for interpreting the state clause differently from the corresponding federal clause.[79] I would not be surprised if other state courts reacted the same way. But it is worth spending the time to make that argument. Six states have now expressly rejected *Employment Division v. Smith*[80] as a matter of state constitutional law;[81] five more have decisions inconsistent with it;[82] another has held the issue open in the face of conflicting precedents.[83] Most other state supreme courts have not had occasion to pass on the question. So it is essential to make the state constitutional argument and make it independently.

Eleven other states have enacted state Religious Freedom Restoration Acts,[84] and other states are actively considering such acts. Churches and civil

79. *See* Tilton v. Marshall, 925 S.W.2d 672, 677 n.6 (Tex. 1996).

80. 494 U.S. 872 (1990).

81. Attorney Gen'l v. Desilets, 636 N.E.2d 233 (Mass. 1994); State v. Hershberger, 462 N.W.2d 393 (Minn. 1990); Humphrey v. Lane, 728 N.E.2d 1039 (Ohio 2000); Hunt v. Hunt, 648 A.2d 843 (Vt. 1994); Muns v. Martin, 930 P.2d 318 (Wash. 1997); State v. Miller, 549 N.W.2d 235 (Wis. 1996).

82. *See* State v. Evans, 796 P.2d 178 (Kan. App. 1990) (ignoring *Smith* and adhering to pre-*Smith* law); Rupert v. City of Portland, 605 A.2d 63 (Me. 1992) (applying pre-*Smith* law but reserving issue of whether to change in light of *Smith*); *see also* Kentucky State Bd. for Elem. & Secondary Educ. v. Rudasill, 589 S.W.2d 877 (Ky. 1979); In re Brown, 478 So.2d 1033 (Miss. 1985); State ex rel. Swann v. Pack, 527 S.W.2d 99 (Tenn. 1975) (all pre-*Smith*).

83. *See* Smith v. Fair Empl. & Hsg. Comm'n, 913 P.2d 909, 929-31 (Cal. 1996).

84. Ala. Const., amend. 622; Ariz. Rev. Stat. Ann. §§ 41-1493.01 to 41-1493.02 (Supp. 1999); Conn. Gen. Stat. Ann. § 52-571b (Supp. 2000); Fla. Stat. Ann. §§ 761.01 to 761.05 (Supp. 2000); An Act Relating to the Free Exercise of Religion, 2000 Idaho Laws ch. 133 (to be codified at Idaho Stat. §§ 73-401 to 73-404); 775 Ill. Comp. Stat. Ann. §§ 35/1 to 35/99 (Supp. 2000); An Act Relating to Religious Freedom, N.M. Stat. ch. 17 (2d Special Session 2000); An Act Relating to Religious Freedom, 2000 Okla. Sess. Law Serv. ch. 272 (to be codified at Okla. Stat. §§ 51-251 to 51-258); R.I. Gen. Laws §§ 42-80.1-1 to 42-80.1-4 (1999); S.C. Stat. §§ 1-32-10 to 1-32-60; Tex. Civ. Prac. & Remedies Code §§ 110.001 to 110.012 (Supp. 2000).

Educating judges and lawyers about these statutes is a major task. The first reported decisions under the Florida RFRA completely misinterpreted the statute. The state court wholly failed to understand the difference between the RFRA standard and its alternatives. *See* First Baptist Church v. Miami-Dade County, 768 So.2d 1114 (Fla. App. 2000) (equating Florida RFRA with *Lukumi* and with *Grosz v. City of Miami Beach*, 721 F.2d 729 (11th Cir. 1983), a case that (unlike *Lukumi*) applied a balancing test to any burden on religion, but liberties organizations should be actively supporting those bills, and lawyers for churches and religious claimants should be informed about the laws that already exist. The eleven states with RFRAs do not overlap the twelve states with protective interpretations of the state free exercise clauses. The bottom line here is that in at least twenty-three states, state law is plausibly read to require government to justify substantial burdens on religious exercise, without regard to whether the law is generally applicable or was motivated by religious bigotry. Some of these state RFRAs have exceptions, but most have none and all offer broad coverage. This body of state law gives much better protection to religious exercise than federal law does.

Even under the new federalism, Congress has some power to protect religious liberty under the Commerce Clause and the Spending Clause, and under the Fourteenth Amendment where Congress can make a sufficient record. There will be lots of cases that such legislation simply cannot reach, so state law will remain important, but Congress can do much if it will. Congress has just passed the Religious Land Use and Institutionalized Persons Act,[85] which would address the two largest sources of cases — prisons and land use regulation of churches. The bill would also help enforce the Free Exercise Clause by providing generally — not just in prison and land use cases — that if a claimant proves a prima facie case of a free exercise violation, the burden of persuasion shifts to the government on all elements of the claim except burden on religious exercise. So on questions such as whether unregulated secular activities are sufficiently analogous to make the law less than generally applicable, or whether the law was enacted with discriminatory or anti-religious motive, a prima facie case shifts the burden of persuasion to the government.

(unlike RFRA) did not require the city to show a compelling interest). The federal court understood the difference perfectly well and deliberately evaded the statute. *See* Warner v. City of Boca Raton, 64 F. Supp. 1272, 1281-87 (S.D. Fla. 1999) (holding that vertical grave markers were an unprotected religious preference not sufficiently connected to a protected religious tenet — despite express statutory language that religious exercise need not be required by a larger system of religious belief), [*aff'd*, 420 F.3d 1308 (11th Cir. 2005).] The first Illinois decision understood the statute but applied a much weakened version of the compelling interest test. City of Chicago Heights v. Living Word Outreach Full Gospel Church and Ministries, Inc., 707 N.E.2d 53 (Ill. App. 1998), [*rev'd in part*, 749 N.E. 2d 916 (Ill. 2001). The appellate decisions in *Warner* and *Living Word* were released after this article appeared in print.]

85. S.2869 in the 106th Congress, available in Thomas, the Congressional website, http://thomas.loc.gov (visited Sept. 17, 2000), [subsequently codified at 42 U.S.C. § 2000cc *et seq.*].

III. Explaining Religion to Courts

Lots of lawyers do not understand what religion does. A judge is a lawyer who knew a politician; lots of judges do not understand what religion does either. There are many people, including many lawyers and judges, whose image of religion is of a great schoolmarm in the sky who makes rules, and believers have to obey the rules, and that is religion. It follows in this view that you do not have a religious liberty claim unless you can point to a particular religious rule and say that you are being required to violate that rule.

It is remarkable how often this kind of argument arises in free exercise cases. Landmarking authorities in Boston told the Jesuits that they had no religious liberty right to re-orient the altar so that priests could face the people, because facing the people was only recommended — it was not required.[86] And there is actually some support for that view in the Supreme Court's opinion in *Jimmy Swaggart Ministries v. Board of Equalization*.[87]

So religious claimants often have to begin by getting over the concept of religion as compulsory rules. They have to explain to the court why religiously motivated conduct is part of the exercise of religion even if the conduct is not required. The legislative history of federal RFRA was good on that. Examples help make the point. No one is required to become a priest or a minister, but from any common sense perspective, doing so is part of the exercise of religion.[88]

Never be conclusory in your litigation of the burden issue. It may be obvious to you why the religious claimant has been burdened, but it is quite likely not obvious to the judge. Build your factual record. Think about all the possible ways to explain how religious liberty is burdened in your client's case. In the bankruptcy cases, creditors were reaching into the collection plate and taking back a thousand, ten thousand, and in one of the Texas cases, fifty thousand dollars.[89] Some judges did not see a burden there. Some of the judges that did see a burden thought it was only a burden on the donor. If the donor had anticipated the bankruptcy claim taking the money back from the church, he might have been deterred from giving. Judges had a hard problem with the most obvious point — there was a bur-

---

86. *See* Boston Landmarks Comm'n v. Society of Jesus, 564 N.E.2d 571 (Mass. 1990)

87. 493 U.S. 378 (1990).

88. *See* McDaniel v. Paty, 435 U.S. 618 (1978) (protecting the right to become a minister).

89. *See* Cedar Bayou Baptist Church v. Gregory-Edwards, Inc., 987 S.W.2d 156 (Tex. App. — Hou.[14th Dist.] 1999). The trial court entered judgment for $23,428 for contributions beginning October 15, 1988. *Id.* at 157. With accrued interest, the judgment was about $50,000 when it was reversed in 1999.

den on the church that had to divert current contributions to pay a member's old debts.

In the *Boerne* case, the Court never reached the burden issue, but the city repeatedly claimed that there was no burden in that case. It was just money. No one said the bishop could not build a church. No one said the parishioners could not worship. If they would just spend an extra $750,000, they could solve this problem. That would be no burden. Or maybe it would be an economic burden, like what happens to General Motors, but it would not be a religious burden. This is a very widespread view, and lawyers for churches have to think about ways to explain and make comprehensible how the burden reaches religious exercise. These "mere" financial burdens divert funds from religious to secular purposes, they defeat the religious purposes of the donor of the funds, and they lead directly to reduced religious functioning. In effect the City of Boerne said that the first call on St. Peter's resources was secular — that it must spend its first money to create what amounted to an architectural museum, and then if there was anything left over, it could build a place to worship. Building and maintaining the architectural museum was a prior condition on its right to build a place of worship.

Another way of thinking about this issue of compulsion versus motivation is to categorize different types of claims. Some religious liberty claims are claims of conscientious objection. The claimant's religion teaches that she just cannot do what the government is telling her to do, or that she must do some of what the government is telling her not to do. Catholic priests are not going to reveal what went on in the confessional, no matter what the government says.

Other kinds of religious liberty claims do not involve that kind of teaching. I call them church autonomy claims.[90] The Church says that this is the Catholic Church, and Catholics will decide how it should be run, and the government should not be regulating the internal operations of the Church. A church should not have to show a particular doctrinal basis for every internal management decision. The faithful or the hierarchy, depending on church polity, ought to be entitled to run their own religious organization.

---

90. *See* Douglas Laycock, *Towards a General Theory of the Religion Clauses: The Case of Church Labor Relations and the Right to Church Autonomy*, 81 COLUM. L. REV. 1373, 1388-402 (1981) (text at notes 122-227).

IV. The Establishment Clause and State Funding of Religious Organizations

A. *Funding of Secular Services by Religious Organizations*

I can offer a quicker overview of Establishment Clause issues. The Supreme Court has struggled for fifty years now with the basic idea that government should be neutral towards religion. But there are two fundamentally inconsistent understandings of what it means to be neutral. For a long time, the Court never quite saw the difference. I think it sees the difference now, but key votes at the center of the Court are still hoping not to have to choose between the two models.[91]

One side — the no-aid side — says the base line for measuring neutrality is the government doing nothing. Zero going to the church is neutral. So any money that does go to the church is a departure from neutrality and is forbidden aid, forbidden endorsement, and so forth. That version of neutrality has dramatically affected the financing of Catholic schools.

But there is another way to measure neutrality, which also has strong support in the cases, but most clearly in cases from other contexts. The alternate base line for measuring neutrality is the government's treatment of a secular organization that is providing the same service as a religious organization. That base line is highly controversial in the school cases, but we take it for granted in the hospital cases. The secular hospital and the Catholic hospital get the very same Medicare and Medicaid reimbursement, because it does not matter that one is religious and one is secular. The important point is that they are delivering medical care to people. Treatment of comparable secular providers is a very different base line that also measures a way of talking about neutrality.

In the very first modern case, *Everson v. Board of Education*,[92] Justice Black blithely endorsed both definitions of neutrality, in adjacent paragraphs. He seems not to have understood the conflict between them. The confusion has continued ever since.

For a time the Court tried to carve out different spheres of influence for these two different versions of neutrality. In the free speech cases, the law for a long time has been to treat religious speech just like high-value secular speech.[93] In social services cases — hospitals, welfare agencies, drug abuse

---

91. This overview is elaborated in Douglas Laycock, *The Underlying Unity of Separation and Neutrality*, 46 EMORY L.J. 43 (1997).

92. 330 U.S. 1 (1947).

93. *See* Capitol Square Review & Advisory Bd. v. Pinette, 515 U.S. 753 (1995); Lamb's

treatment — in general and without much litigation or debate, the rule has been to treat the religious provider just like the secular provider.[94] The recent charitable choice legislation has formalized that and raised it to a higher profile, at least in certain federal spending programs. Charitable choice laws say that when government contracts for social services with the private sector, it cannot discriminate on the basis of religion.[95] A state that contracts out must include religious providers on a nondiscriminatory basis, and it must do so without restricting their religious liberty. It cannot tell the church-run drug abuse center to take the crucifix off the wall. The combination of nondiscriminatory funding and preservation of religious liberty has provoked litigation. Some of my friends who claim to be ardent supporters of separation of church and state now claim that it is critically important to regulate the religious practices of agencies that accept federal money for their charitable functions.[96]

With respect to elementary and secondary education, the main tradition has not been nondiscrimination, but no aid. The Court's starting point has been to say that no aid is neutral and that any money is suspect. But the Court never fully committed to that. Everyone has heard the litany making fun of the odd distinctions the Court made — books but not maps, tax deductions but not tax credits, buses from home to school but not buses on field trips. The underlying cause of those silly distinctions was the Court's continuing attempt to have it both ways. The Court is pulled to the notion of no aid. But it is also pulled to this idea of no discrimination, of treating the secular provider just like the religious provider.

The most recent cases show a sharp but not yet decisive move toward nondiscrimination. The effort to maintain separate spheres of influence for the two conceptions of neutrality may have collapsed in *Rosenberger v. Rector of University of Virginia.*[97] *Rosenberger* was both a free speech case and a

---

Chapel v. Center Moriches Union Free School Dist., 508 U.S. 384 (1993); Widmar v. Vincent, 454 U.S. 263 (1981).

94. *See* Bowen v. Kendrick, 487 U.S. 589 (1988); Bradfield v. Roberts, 175 U.S. 291 (1899).

95. The enacted law is 42 U.S.C. § 604a (Supp. III 1997) (§ 104 of the Personal Responsibility and Work Opportunity Act of 1996 (more commonly known as the Welfare Reform Act)). The pending bills are the proposed Charitable Choice Expansion Act of 1999, part of S.2046 and H.R. 1607 in the 106th Congress.

96. *See generally Debate 2: Should the Government Provide Financial Support for Religious Institutions That Offer Faith-Based Social Services*, 1 RUTGERS J.L. & RELIGION, *available at* http://org.law.rutgers.edu/publications/law-religion/articles/RJLR_1_1_5.pdf (featuring The Honorable Louis H. Pollack, Glen A. Tobias, Erwin Chemerinsky, Barry W. Lynn, Douglas Laycock, and Nathan Diament).

97. 515 U.S. 819 (1995).

funding case: the Court held that if the state university funds student magazines, it has to fund a student religious magazine. *Rosenberger* was not a K-12 case, and one magazine is less important than whole systems of church-affiliated schools. But in one important way *Rosenberger* is much more difficult than the school cases. There was really no secular content in the magazine that was being funded. In the school cases, the children learn math and science and reading; the state gets full secular value for its money. But in *Rosenberger,* the only secular value was the sheer concept of neutrality and non-discrimination.

Agostini v. Felton[98] held that federal Title I money, which is used to pay public school teachers to go into private schools and deliver remedial educational services, is valid. The Court said the services no longer have to be confined to so-called neutral sites; they no longer have to be delivered in trailers on street corners. That is a huge victory for the nondiscrimination view of neutrality. The Court largely abandoned its presumption that all aid would be diverted to religious purposes. It is going to make plaintiffs prove diversion instead of presuming diversion. That too is a huge step forward for the nondiscrimination version of neutrality.

Most recently, *Mitchell v. Helms*[99] upheld federal Chapter 2 money, which is used to buy books and equipment that are loaned to private schools. The plurality opinion for four justices clearly committed to the nondiscrimination understanding of neutrality: if the aid is secular in content, and if it is distributed on a per capita basis to all kinds of schools, it does not violate the Establishment Clause.[100] Excluding religious schools from such a program would raise serious questions under the Free Exercise Clause, because it would overtly discriminate against religion.[101] The plurality opinion formally reserves the questions whether direct cash payments would be different,[102] or whether aid that supplanted the school's own spending would be different.[103] But given the nondiscrimination logic of the opinion, there is little reason to think that these differences would change the result in the view of these four justices.

Justice O'Connor, who has long been the swing vote, concurred separately. Justice Breyer joined her opinion. He had dissented in both *Rosenberger* and *Agostini,* so this may be a significant change. As usual, she

98. 521 U.S. 203 (1997).
99. 530 U.S. 793 (2000).
100. *Id.* at 809-25.
101. *Id.* at 835 n.19.
102. *Id.* at 818-20.
103. *Id.* at 814 n.7.

wrote a narrow, fact-based opinion that reserved all questions not essential to the result. She sharply criticized the plurality for making nondiscrimination dispositive, but she agreed that it was very important.[104] She identified a number of other factors that had supported the result in *Agostini* and that were also satisfied here. It was unnecessary to decide if any of these were constitutionally required; taken together, they were certainly constitutionally sufficient.[105]

Even so, there are important indications of what Justice O'Connor and Breyer think is important. The cases from the 1970s insisted that aid be delivered in forms that could not be diverted to religious uses. Government funds or equipment could not be used for religious purposes, the Court presumed that religious school teachers would violate that rule, and close monitoring to prevent diversion was a forbidden entanglement. The result was that aid had to be delivered in forms that were incapable of diversion.

The Court has now decisively broken out of this Catch-22. The *Mitchell* plurality says diversion to religious use does not matter.[106] If a computer is delivered for secular purposes and used for secular purposes, it is irrelevant if it is sometimes also used to access religious websites. Justices O'Connor and Breyer disagree. They say that diversion still matters, but they trust the good faith of teachers and officials in religious schools. They will not presume diversion; hence they will not require elaborate monitoring procedures.[107] Evidence of diversion in certain schools does not invalidate the whole program.[108] In effect, they have put the burden on opponents of aid to conduct their own investigation of religious schools — not simply to ask in discovery what the state has already found — and to prove up widespread diversion to religious uses if that is happening.

Agostini and *Mitchell* overruled large portions of four cases.[109] This eliminates many of the inconsistencies in the Court's cases; the distinction between books and equipment is gone (and thus the distinction between books

104. *Id.* at 837-40 (O'Connor, J., concurring).

105. *Id.* at 868.

106. *Id.* at 820 (plurality opinion).

107. *Id.* at 857-66 (O'Connor, J., concurring).

108. *Id.* at 865-66.

109. *See id.* at 835 (overruling Wolman v. Walter, 433 U.S. 229 (1977), and Meek v. Pittenger, 421 U.S. 349 (1975), "to the extent that [they] conflict with this holding" (plurality opinion); *id.* at 837 (O'Connor, J., concurring) ("To the extent that [they] are inconsistent with the Court's judgment today, I agree that those cases should be overruled."); Agostini v. Felton, 521 U.S. 203, 235 (1997) (overruling Aguilar v. Felton, 473 U.S. 402 (1985), and the invalidation of the Shared Time program in School Dist. of Grand Rapids v. Ball, 473 U.S. 373 (1985)).

and maps and the puzzle over atlases). Of the cases that survive, far more uphold aid than strike it down. But the cases invalidating state subsidies for teacher pay have not been overruled,[110] and *Committee for Public Education v. Nyquist*,[111] invalidating tax credits for the middle class and scholarships for the poor, has not been overruled. So despite the fireworks, and the important holding on loaning equipment to religious schools, we are left pretty much where we were with respect to vouchers and other forms of cash assistance. There are four reasonably sure votes to uphold almost any form of nondiscriminatory aid to religious schools, and the big questions are up to Justice O'Connor or new appointees. It is now possible that Justice Breyer would provide the fifth vote instead of Justice O'Connor, but past voting patterns make that seem unlikely.

These cases have crystallized the conflict between the two understandings of neutrality and focused the Court's attention on the conflict. The Court is divided four to two to three, and there may be further subdivisions within each group. If you take *Rosenberger, Agostini,* and *Mitchell* to their logical conclusion, vouchers are constitutional — but no one should assume the cases will be carried to their logical conclusion. *Rosenberger* and *Agostini* and O'Connor's opinion in *Mitchell* left lots of lines of retreat — some plausible and some just silly. In *Rosenberger* the Court said it mattered that the university did not send the check to the magazine, but rather that it sent the check to the copy shop.[112] More important, in *Agostini,* the line of retreat was that Title I money cannot be used to displace money that the school is already spending.[113] That is a real limit that would constrain what could be done with any sort of voucher programs. In Justice O'Connor's opinion in *Mitchell,* no-supplanting has become a factor to be considered, not necessarily a requirement.[114] But none of the justices clearly said that government can give aid that supplants the school's own spending.

---

110. Levitt v. Committee for Pub. Educ., 413 U.S. 472 (1973); Lemon v. Kurtzman, 403 U.S. 602 (1971). The Court has not overruled the invalidation of the Community Education program in *School Dist. of Grand Rapids v. Ball,* 473 U.S. 373 (1985). The difference between the Community Education program and the Shared Time program was that the Community Education program was taught by religious-school teachers paid with public funds; the Shared Time program was taught by public-school teachers. *But compare* Committee for Pub. Educ. v. Regan, 444 U.S. 646 (1980) (upholding payment for portion of teacher's time spent administering and grading state-prepared examinations, because state-prepared examinations were free of religious content).

111. 413 U.S. 756 (1973).

112. *See* Rosenberger v. Rector of Univ. of Va., 515 U.S. 819, 825, 842 (1995).

113. *See Agostini,* 521 U.S. at 228-29.

114. *See Mitchell,* at 867 (O'Connor, J., concurring).

The O'Connor-Breyer rule against diversion of aid to religious uses would also be a problem for vouchers. Justices O'Connor and Breyer assume that religious school teachers will not divert secular books and equipment to religious uses; they are at least much more open to the assumption that religious school teachers will teach religious concepts and values throughout the curriculum.[115] They may think that cash that can be used to pay teachers is inherently for religious purposes, automatically diverted, or perhaps more accurately, not secular in the first place.

Variations on the voucher issue have been presented to state and federal courts around the country, often with both state and federal establishment clause claims, with mixed results and repeated denials of certiorari.[116] The Supreme Court so far has avoided the issue, perhaps because neither block of four will vote to grant certiorari until Justice O'Connor tips her hand. This battle is very much far from over.

The battle will not be over even if the Supreme Court squarely upholds vouchers against federal constitutional attack. At least three-fourths of the states have state constitutional provisions on funding sectarian schools that are much more explicit, and at first glance more stringent, than the federal Establishment Clause. Perhaps the most important development in the recent cases is that the Supreme Courts of Wisconsin and Ohio interpreted such clauses in the state constitution to mean basically the same thing as the federal

---

115. *Id.* at 858-59.

116. *Compare* Kotterman v. Killian, 972 P.2d 606 (Ariz.) (upholding state tax credit for contributions to scholarship fund for private schools); Simmons-Harris v. Goff, 711 N.E.2d 203 (Ohio 1999) (rejecting state and federal establishment clause attacks on vouchers for low income students, but invalidating program on narrow and correctable state ground); Jackson v. Benson, 578 N.W.2d 602 (Wis. 1998) (rejecting state and federal establishment clause attacks on vouchers for low income students); *with* Simmons-Harris v. Zelman, 72 F. Supp. 834 (N.D. Ohio 1999) (invalidating the Ohio program upheld in *Simmons-Harris v. Goff*), *appeal pending;* Chittenden Town Sch. Dist. v. Department of Educ., 738 A.2d 539 (Vt. 1999) (invalidating unrestricted tuition reimbursement to religious schools, indicating that state could pay for secular instruction in religious school but not for religious instruction); Holmes v. Bush, 2000 WL 526364 (Fla. Cir. Ct. 2000) (invalidating vouchers for certain low-income students under Florida constitution); *with* Strout v. Albanese, 178 F.3d 57 (1st Cir. 1999) (upholding statute authorizing tuition reimbursement to secular private schools but excluding religious private schools); Bagley v. Raymond Sch. Dept., 728 A.2d 127 (Me.) (same). [*Simmons-Harris v. Zelman* was affirmed in the court of appeals, 234 F.3d 945 (6th Cir. 2001), but reversed by the Supreme Court, 536 U.S. 639 (2002). *Holmes v. Bush* was reversed by the Florida District Court of Appeals, 767 So.2d 68 (Fla. App. 2000), and after a remand, that reversal was affirmed on other grounds by the Florida Supreme Court, 919 So.2d 392 (Fla. 2006). These decisions came down after this article appeared in print.]

Establishment Clause, and not to prohibit vouchers.[117] The Supreme Court of Vermont expressly rejected this reasoning with respect to its state constitution.[118] The meaning of state constitutions will have to be litigated separately in every state, and state courts are likely to continue going both ways.

This means that religious schools face three independent hurdles: they have to win the political issue, they have to win the federal Establishment Clause issue, and they have to win the state constitutional issue or amend the state constitution in each state. Or alternatively, they have to persuade the U.S. Supreme Court that refusal to fund religious schools violates the federal Free Exercise Clause. That is a quite plausible claim in those states that fund secular private schools but not religious private schools; it seems quite implausible in states that fund only public schools and refuse to fund any private schools.

B. *Government-Sponsored Religious Speech*

The longstanding desire for prayer in public schools and at government events has been principally an evangelical Protestant issue. Catholics opposed prayers and Bible reading in the schools in the nineteenth century, when liturgical differences were more sharply felt and Catholics were more sensitive to the Protestant establishment in the schools.[119] In our time, when evangelicals and Catholics alike feel threatened by secularism, Catholics have tended to support government's right to sponsor religious observances.[120] My own view is that Catholics were right the first time; government-sponsored prayer is bad for religious minorities and nonbelievers, and equally bad for the majority whose religion is politicized, diluted, and sometimes corrupted. The demand for such government sponsorship seems to be much stronger in evangelical communities than in Catholic communities; this is principally an issue in the Deep South.

117. *See* Simmons-Harris v. Goff, 711 N.E.2d 203, 211-12 (Ohio 1999); Jackson v. Benson, 578 N.W.2d 602, 620-23 (Wis. 1998).

118. Chittenden Town Sch. Dist. v. Department of Educ., 738 A.2d 539, 559-60 (Vt. 1999).

119. For a summary of the nineteenth-century controversy over "the Protestant Bible," with citations to multiple sources, see Laycock, *supra* note 91, at 50-52 (text at notes 38-50).

120. The United States Catholic Conference filed a brief supporting the school officials in *Lee v. Weisman*, 505 U.S. 577 (1992), the case on prayer at graduation. The Conference filed no brief in *Santa Fe Indep. Sch. Dist. v. Doe*, 530 U.S. 290 (2000), the case on student elections to include prayer at school events. *Lee* squarely presented the issue of whether public schools may sponsor prayers; *Santa Fe* did not, because the school denied its sponsorship.

The Supreme Court has been remarkably consistent for nearly forty years. Private religious speech, including prayers and worship services, is protected in public places, including on government property and in public schools.[121] Government-sponsored speech that takes a position on religious questions, including prayers and worship services, is generally forbidden, and especially in public schools.[122] No case has approved government religious speech in public schools, and no case has restricted private religious speech, because of its religious content, anywhere.

With the basic principles clearly settled, litigators have been forced to press on the line between governmental and private speech. *Santa Fe Independent School District v. Doe*[123] illustrates the pattern. Both sides agreed that school-sponsored prayer was forbidden by the Establishment Clause, and that prayers of students in their private capacity were protected by the Free Speech and Free Exercise Clauses. The whole argument was whether these prayers were school-sponsored.

The Court did not think that was a close argument. The prayers in Santa Fe were delivered by a single student, elected by majority vote, given exclusive access to the microphone at an official school event. The majority found this obviously school-sponsored. The three dissenters did not really disagree. They invoked their earlier position that schools should be allowed to sponsor prayer after all, and they said the majority was premature in assuming that Santa Fe's election procedure would consistently lead to prayer. They did not give any comfort to the school's position that the elected speaker was not school-sponsored.

The opinion seems broad enough to dispose of elected student prayer leaders at athletic events, graduation, and any other official school event. The

---

121. *See, e.g.,* Santa Fe Indep. Sch. Dist. v. Doe, 530 U.S. 290 (2000); Rosenberger v. Rector of Univ. of Va., 515 U.S. 819 (1995); Capitol Square Rev. & Advisory Bd. v. Pinette, 515 U.S. 753 (1995); Lamb's Chapel v. Center Moriches Union Free Sch. Dist., 508 U.S. 384 (1993); Board of Educ. v. Mergens, 496 U.S. 226 (1990); Widmar v. Vincent, 454 U.S. 263 (1981); Fowler v. Rhode Island, 345 U.S. 67 (1953); Kunz v. New York, 340 U.S. 290 (1951); Niemotko v. Maryland, 340 U.S. 268 (1951); Saia v. New York, 334 U.S. 558 (1948); Marsh v. Alabama, 326 U.S. 501 (1946); Jamison v. Texas, 318 U.S. 413 (1943); Cantwell v. Connecticut, 310 U.S. 296 (1940).

122. *See* Lee v. Weisman, 505 U.S. 577 (1992); County of Allegheny v. ACLU, 492 U.S. 573 (1989); Stone v. Graham, 449 U.S. 39 (1980); Abington Sch. Dist. v. Schempp, 374 U.S. 203 (1963); Engel v. Vitale, 370 U.S. 421 (1962). The only exceptions are *Lynch v. Donnelly,* 465 U.S. 668 (1984) (upholding municipal Christmas display with crèche, Santa Claus, and reindeer), and *Marsh v. Chambers,* 463 U.S. 783 (1983) (upholding prayer to open each meeting of legislature).

123. 530 U.S. 290 (2000).

next round of litigation is likely to be over prayers and religious messages from valedictorians, who (unlike the winners of elections) are selected by religiously neutral means. In some districts this would lead to a healthy diversity of views over time; other districts have such a large majority of one faith, or cluster of similar faiths, that the valedictorian will usually represent the dominant religious view and any exceptions will be under enormous pressure to conform. This issue too is not likely to go away.

V. Conclusion

The Court is closely divided on all these issues: five-four on federalism, four-two-three on funding religious schools, six-three on school prayer, four-three with two undeclared on free exercise. The votes in the middle are potentially movable in response to new variations on old issues. New appointments are up for grabs.

Especially on free exercise and funding religious schools, there are deep ambiguities in present doctrine. Effective lawyers will make the most of those ambiguities; other lawyers will miss the opportunity. Just as it is better to light a candle than to curse the darkness, so it is better to develop the exceptions than to curse the adverse holdings.

Vouching towards Bethlehem

Religion in the News 2 (Summer 2002)

Religion in the News *is a publication of the Program on Religion and the News Media, of the Leonard E. Greenberg Center for the Study of Public Life, at Trinity College in Hartford, Connecticut. Most of its articles review press coverage of recent events involving religion. This article goes through the motions of reviewing the press coverage of two court opinions, one on the Pledge of Allegiance and one on vouchers for tuition at private schools. But mostly, it tries to explain what reporters need to know to cover future developments in those two controversies. An editor wrote the title, and I have no idea what it is supposed to mean.*

*   *   *

On June 26, a federal court of appeals in California decided, two to one, that it is unconstitutional for teachers to lead public school children in reciting "one nation, under God." Most of the country, and most of the press, was outraged.

The next day, the U.S. Supreme Court decided, five to four, that it is constitutional for Ohio to give Cleveland parents educational vouchers that can be spent at any school willing to accept their children, including religious schools. The country, and the press, were as deeply divided as the Court.

The one-day attention span of the news media mostly kept the two stories apart, but a few editorials and opinion columns noted a connection. The dominant reaction, in the press and among the public, was that here was one decision opposed to religion, one decision favoring religion — one decision upholding the wall of separation but carrying the idea to absurd extremes, one decision tearing down the wall of separation.

In Virginia, the *Roanoke Times and World News* said the Pledge decision "reduces to parody the bedrock principle of church-state separation," while the voucher decision "takes a battering ram to this fundamental safeguard of religious freedom, but from the opposite extreme." Among the papers that approved the voucher decision, the *San Diego Union-Tribune* contrasted that decision's "common sense" to the "loopy logic on the Pledge of Allegiance." On CNBC, Mike Barnicle said that this had been "for many people sort of a good news, bad news couple of days in terms of the way we look at the law."

Steve Chapman in the *Chicago Tribune* was the only commentator who clearly saw the two decisions as reflecting the same sound constitutional principle: "official neutrality," meaning that "in dealing with religion, the government should be neither ally nor adversary."

The great virtue of official neutrality is that it protects private choice. With prayer in public schools, or even "under God," the government decides to introduce religion into the classroom, how and to what extent, and from which religious traditions. With vouchers, parents decide whether their children will go to secular or religious schools — and if religious, then from which religious tradition and of what intensity. The Pledge decision, protecting families from a government-composed affirmation of faith, can be seen as perfectly consistent with the voucher decision, which also gives religious choices to families.

Of course, this characterization of the cases is contestable. In the Pledge case, *Newdow v. US Congress,* the dissenter said that "under God" is a minimal statement that does no real harm. That seemed to be the general view even among the minority of Americans who oppose school-sponsored prayer. Critics of the voucher decision, *Zelman v. Simmons-Harris,* called the private choice illusory. Real alternatives were limited, the Cleveland public schools were failing, and many parents must have been driven to swallow the religious element in their new schools as the price of getting a decent education for their children. Even if we could agree on private choice as the general principle, we would argue over how and when it applies.

Although few Americans saw how private choice might unite these two decisions, it is the principle embraced by the controlling swing votes on the Supreme Court, Sandra Day O'Connor and Anthony Kennedy. Kennedy and O'Connor have voted to strike down school-sponsored prayer at graduation (*Lee v. Weisman* in 1992) and a student-elected speaker who gave prayers at football games (*Santa Fe Independent School District v. Doe* in 2000). They have also voted to uphold many forms of government aid to religious private schools.

This is not just a matter of deciding how far to go in pursuit of separation of church and state. Rather, the principle of private choice means that constitutionally, vouchers and the Pledge represent fundamentally different ways of government interacting with religion.

The story begins in the mid-19th century with Horace Mann and the movement for a general system of public schools. Earlier schools had been private — free to deal with religion as they chose. Public schools required some method of dealing with denominational differences within the overwhelmingly Protestant population. Mann's solution was to teach only the basics of Christianity on which all denominations agreed, and to read the Bible "without note or comment," thus avoiding disagreements about interpretation.

Some conservative Protestants accused him of establishing his own Unitarianism, but that intra-Protestant battle was cut short by waves of Catholic immigration. Catholics objected to teaching generic Protestantism, they objected to reading the King James translation ("the Protestant Bible"), and they objected to reading it "without note or comment" — that is, without official church teaching to help students reach the right interpretation. Although they attacked the public school religious observances as an establishment of Protestantism, what they really wanted was government support for schools they could use in good conscience: their own parochial schools. The school prayer issue and the aid-to-religious-schools issue both originate in this controversy.

The issue heated up at intervals, depending on what else was going on politically. In the 1830s and 1840s, there were riots in the streets, churches burned, and people killed. In the 1850s, the Know Nothings swept elections in eight states with an anti-Catholic, anti-immigrant platform.

The Protestant position crystallized in 1876 with the proposed Blaine Amendment to the Constitution. It declared that no public money could be spent to support any sectarian school (while carefully stating that this did not preclude Bible reading in the public schools). By "sectarian" school, it meant Catholic school.

Democratic senators, responding to their immigrant constituencies in northeastern cities, defeated the Blaine Amendment. But similar provisions, called "Little Blaine Amendments" by their detractors, were written into state constitutions in nearly three-quarters of the states, where they remain in force today. These amendments generally prohibit the appropriation of funds for the support of any sectarian school, sometimes any private school. Most of them do not expressly authorize Bible reading in the public schools.

As Catholics and Jews were accepted into full membership in the American community, and as adherents of many other faiths arrived from around the world, it became harder and harder to compose religious observances that stripped out everything believers disagreed on. In 1962 and 1963, the Supreme Court struck down prayer and Bible reading in the public schools, and despite changes on the Court, it has not wavered from those decisions in 40 years.

The flap over the Pledge is the last vestige of the old Protestant stripping-out strategy. "Under God" doesn't specify which God or say anything about God's characteristics. The court of appeals thought that "under God" teaches monotheism in preference to either polytheism (Hindus and others) or nontheism (many Buddhists, and of course atheists and agnostics). But the popular reaction was that even if government is supposed to be neutral, "under God" is neutral enough.

The aid-to-religious-schools issue remained a Catholic issue until the early 1980s. Catholics sought money for their schools. Protestants and Jews were overwhelmingly opposed, and among Protestants the evangelicals and fundamentalists were the most opposed.

The issue acquired a racial dimension in the late 1960s, when many private schools were created as refuges from desegregation, especially in the Deep South. In 1971, the Supreme Court decided *Lemon v. Kurtzman,* the granddaddy modern case on aid to religious schools (and the source of the famous, or infamous, *Lemon* test for detecting establishments of religion). The plaintiff, Alton Lemon, was a black man, and he alleged that Pennsylvania's plan to subsidize teacher salaries in private schools not only gave unconstitutional aid to religion but also unconstitutionally aggravated racial segregation in the public schools. The Court did not decide the racial claim, but every Justice took note of it.

Lemon was pending at the Court simultaneously with *Swann v. Charlotte-Mecklenburg Board of Education,* the first school busing case and the first case on desegregation in a major urban school district. In *Norwood v. Harrison* in 1973, the Court struck down a program under which Mississippi supplied textbooks to segregated private schools, without questioning its earlier decisions approving state-supplied textbooks at religious schools where segregation was not alleged.

The civil rights community thus joined the coalition against aid to religious schools, which now included Protestants, Jews, public school officials and their supporters, and the teachers unions, which grew larger and stronger in the late 20th century. The anti-voucher coalition has also grown to include people opposed to new taxes, opposed to new entitlements, or worried about low-income students with vouchers showing up in suburban schools.

The dramatic rise of evangelical Protestant schools did not at first shake this coalition. In their first two decades, these schools were more concerned with avoiding intrusive government regulation than with seeking government financial assistance. At least as late as 1980, Jerry Falwell was taking the historic evangelical position that not one penny of public funds should go to any private school.

But then, in the 1980s, the evangelical Protestants switched sides. Increasingly alienated from the public schools, they chafed under the burden of paying taxes for public education and tuition for their own schools. This was a huge move, numerically, politically, and historically. Press coverage shows little awareness of this shift, either implicitly treating the present political alignments as timeless or attributing all change to the Supreme Court's general swing to the right.

The swing to the right did fuel the increasing popularity of free-market solutions to difficult problems. Many secular conservatives came to attribute public school failures to their monopoly status and argued for vouchers as a way of funding private solutions and spurring competition. Rank-and-file black parents trapped in failing inner city schools latched on to the idea; black respondents to opinion polls now generally support vouchers, despite the opposition of the civil rights leadership.

So the pro-voucher forces have also become a coalition: Catholics, evangelical Protestants, free marketeers, black parents, and people desperate to try anything that might help educate those American children who are not learning in the current system.

This shift in political balance has not proceeded far enough to enable supporters to enact widespread voucher programs. But it has made vouchers a live political issue in many states, and not just in states with large Catholic populations. It has also changed attitudes at the Supreme Court, which does, as Mr. Dooley said more than a century ago, follow the election returns. Aid to religious schools looked one way when it was only a Catholic issue and before the rapid decline in Catholic-Protestant hostility after the election of John F. Kennedy and the Second Vatican Council. It looks very different, even to the Court, when it is supported by a broad coalition that is interfaith, religious and secular, and black and white.

So where are we now? What did the voucher opinion really decide, and what issues will now emerge more prominently?

As most of the press recognized, *Zelman* is a substantial consolidating win for the pro-voucher side. The biggest news may be that the majority had five unqualified votes. O'Connor did not attempt to qualify the majority opinion as she has in most other recent religion cases.

The majority relies on parental choice to uphold the program, and that is not new. What is somewhat new is an extended inquiry into the meaning of choice. A voucher plan that steered parents toward religious schools would still be unconstitutional. But the majority's definition of "true choice" is generous, and it should be easy for legislatures to meet.

In *Zelman,* secular private schools, charter schools, magnet schools, and tutorial programs in public schools all counted as relevant choices. At times, Rehnquist's majority opinion seems to suggest that the ordinary curriculum in the regular public schools is itself an alternate choice. That argument would be stronger, and might play a bigger role, in districts where the regular public schools had not been found to be failing.

Related to this broad conception of choice, the Court looks at the voucher plan in the context of the state's entire educational system. Always in the past it has considered the program of aid to private schools in isolation. This is a huge shift in perspective, with dramatic implications.

If the voucher plan is considered in isolation, nearly all the money goes to religious schools. But when the educational system is considered as a whole (or even just private schools and the unconventional parts of the public schools), nearly all the money goes to secular schools. Most legislatures so inclined should be able to design a voucher program that will satisfy this opinion.

Unlike earlier opinions, this one does not seem concerned about government money funding too much of the religious school's budget. The limit on funding through vouchers may be what the state is willing to spend, what the public schools are spending, or, possibly, a fraction of what the private school is spending based on an estimate of the percentage of the program that is secular and the percentage that is religious.

These principles will also apply to other social services. To the extent that the President's charitable choice plan can be implemented through vouchers, this opinion eliminates the basic constitutional objections. But there will be issues about the reality of choice if secular providers cannot meet the demand for secular services. This is more of a problem in social services such as drug abuse programs, which, unlike public schools, turn people away when they are full.

The Court's majority emphasizes that vouchers pay for education in all the basic subjects, and treats as secondary the environment in which that education is offered and the possibility that religion might be taught alongside math and reading. The dissent treats the religious and secular education in religious schools as inseparable. Thus the majority says that parents can choose where they want to get their children's education while the dissent says the problem is tax money supporting religious instruction. This is not a new disagreement among the public or on the Court, but for the first time there are five solid votes for the pro-voucher side of the argument.

Direct payments to religious schools or other service providers are probably still subject to judicially imposed limits. Earlier opinions (most recently, *Mitchell v. Helms* in 2000) have upheld neutral programs of providing services or equipment to religious and secular providers, but O'Connor wrote narrow concurrences for the fifth vote, limiting the scope of what is permissible.

The battle now shifts to legislatures and to the initiative and referendum process in states that have it. The political reality is that so far voucher supporters have not been able to enact a general program anywhere. Existing programs are focused on failing schools and mostly on low-income students.

Supporters expect the Court's decision to influence public opinion and change the political balance; whether that happens is the next big question. Many legislators may continue to believe that vouchers are unconstitutional, or at least bad church-state policy, no matter what the Court says.

There remains a huge debate about educational policy, with the same strong coalitions still in place on both sides. Both sides trumpet claims that studies confirm their side of the educational policy debate, but there are not enough good studies to definitively answer the question. The truth is likely to be that some schools work and some schools don't, both public and private, and that the success of voucher programs depends heavily on how they are designed and funded.

In legislatures where opponents cannot defeat vouchers outright, they may be able to kill them indirectly by regulating employment, admissions, and curriculum in schools that accept the vouchers. Similar tactics have been highly effective in the congressional battles over the President's charitable choice proposals. There is powerful appeal to the argument that no one should be able to discriminate with public funds, but many religious providers insist they must be able to hire employees who support their religious mission and live their moral code. Bans on religious discrimination or sexual orientation discrimination can be poison pills that render these programs unacceptable to their supporters.

Many religious schools are willing to accept children of all faiths, and many will be willing to take children with disabilities, academic problems, or behavioral problems. But some will resist such requirements, and many will resist surrendering all control over admissions. Some children have problems beyond the capacity of a small private school to handle; some schools can educate a few troubled children but not a whole roomful. The state must at least satisfy itself that schools accepting vouchers are teaching the essential subjects in the curriculum, but there is a range of opinion about what is essential, and intrusive curriculum regulation may be another way to make voucher bills unacceptable to some schools.

Assuming some additional voucher plans pass, the battle will move on to state courts. There are all those "Little Blaine Amendments," many of which have not been interpreted in modern times and which state supreme courts, not federal courts, will authoritatively interpret. Voucher opponents note that many of these clauses are much more specific than the federal Establishment Clause, yet the supreme courts of Ohio and Wisconsin have shown that even quite specific clauses can be interpreted to apply only to direct payments to schools, not to vouchers. By contrast, the supreme court of Washington has interpreted its clause to forbid a student from using his state scholarship for the blind to attend a seminary.

Bear in mind that most state constitutions are much easier to amend than the federal constitution. If a majority can be persuaded to support vouchers, many state constitutions could be amended to permit them. And voucher supporters claim that these state constitutional provisions themselves violate the federal constitution because they discriminate against religion or because they were motivated by open anti-Catholicism. Lawsuits interpreting and lawsuits challenging these state constitutional provisions will both be part of the future story.

Indeed, on July 18, a federal court of appeals struck down the most stringent applications of Washington State's establishment clause. Washington had created a program of college scholarships broadly available to any student with moderate income and good grades, but unavailable to theology majors. In *Davey v. Locke,* the court held that this prohibition discriminated against religion in violation of the federal constitution. One judge dissented, and further appeals are likely. [The Supreme Court reversed this decision in *Locke v. Davey* in 2004, a decision that is closely analyzed in *Theology Scholarships, the Pledge of Allegiance, and Religious Liberty: Avoiding the Extremes but Missing the Liberty.* That article also reviews what the Supreme Court ultimately said about the Pledge of Allegiance.]

And on August 5, a state trial judge in Florida threw out Jeb Bush's voucher program for failing schools. The *New York Times* reported that Judge P. Kevin Davey ruled that "the Florida Constitution was 'clear and unambiguous' in prohibiting public money from being used in any sectarian institution." [The Florida Supreme Court later affirmed this ruling, but it relied on a different provision of the state constitution.]

Some states may offer vouchers good only at secular schools. That is hardly anyone's policy preference, but politics and circumstance could make it happen. Maine has such a program, enacted because some of its rural school districts cannot afford to maintain a modern high school, but excluding religious schools because of concerns about separation of church and state. That program is now highly vulnerable to a claim that it discriminates against religion: Maine may have to either include the religious schools or exclude the secular private schools.

Finally, some voucher plans are likely to be enacted with regulations that violate the religious commitments of some schools. Many such schools will refuse the money, but some will take the money and challenge the regulations in court. Those lawsuits may allege violations of state and federal guarantees of religious liberty and of parental rights. Courts may be inclined to say that the state can regulate what it pays for, but especially intrusive or discriminatory regulations may be struck down.

Vouchers will not serve the goal of private choice if schools accepting them are forced into the public school model. But the first story about a voucher school teaching some religious or ideological view that seems radical or out of bounds to ordinary Americans will provoke an outraged response in public opinion — probably not as widespread as the reaction to the Pledge decision, but widespread enough to be politically effective.

Leaving religion to private choice has been a great way to reduce religious conflict and to let each American pursue his or her own religious beliefs. But some Americans have always worried that other Americans would make harmful choices. And in a mixed economy, where federal, state, and local governments together spend more than a third of gross domestic product, the whole concept of private choice is contested.

What other Americans choose to do with their own money may be none of our business, but as taxpayers we take a stronger interest in how they choose to spend public funds. Sensitivities are increased when the subject is the education of the young. The intensely religious and the intensely secular each worry that the other side will somehow control the minds of the next generation. And so we fight over what children should recite in the public schools and whether the state should offer any help to parents who opt out of those schools.

This policy war has been going on for roughly 160 years now. The pro-voucher side just won a very major battle. But the war is not about to end, and there will be many future battles for the press to cover.

Church and State in the United States: Competing Conceptions and Historic Changes

13 Indiana Journal of Global Legal Studies 503 (2006)

As more fully explained in the introduction, this article summarizes the American law of religious liberty for readers with no previous knowledge of American constitutional law. It tries to assume nothing and to explain everything. It reviews history, basic concepts, and the principal disputes over the meaning of the Religion Clauses.

*　　　　*　　　　*

This article, originally written for a French audience and published in French,[1] attempts to explain the American law of church and state from the ground up, assuming no background information of any kind. That turned out to be a useful exercise; explaining the underlying assumptions we generally take for granted revealed insights and connections previously overlooked. I hope English-speaking readers will also find it useful.

Except for rewriting the introduction and updating the treatment of the most recent developments, I have changed very little from the version I submitted to the French translators. I retain the comparisons of what I knew in depth on the American side to what I think I understand superficially on the French side. I am pleased to report that my cautious observations on French law in this article passed through the hands of French editors without pro-

---

1. Douglas Laycock, *La religion et l'État aux États-Unis: affrontement des théories et changements historiques,* in LA CONCEPTION AMÉRICAINE DE LAW LAÏCITÉ 35 (Elisabeth Zoller ed., 2005). I know what I said in English; I have to take the French translation as a matter of faith.

voking argument or corrections. But no reader should make the mistake of thinking me an expert on the French system.

It is revealing to compare how two modern democratic societies, each proclaiming commitment to liberty and equality, have come to fundamentally different resolutions of these issues on nearly every point. France and the United States share a commitment to religious liberty. But different histories and different distributions of religious opinion have led to different understandings of what religious liberty means in practice.

The one-word label for the French system is *laïcité;* American scholars were invited to Paris to explain the American conception of *laïcité.* But I am not sure there *is* a relevant American conception of *laïcité.* To fully understand *laïcité,* I suspect that one must be immersed in French law and French social and political practice. In French-English dictionaries, *laïcité* is often omitted; when it appears, it is commonly translated as "secularism." This is probably a simplification, but let us accept it as a starting point. Many Americans would say that the United States has a secular government, or that it aspires to a secular government. A minority of Americans would like to see a wholly secular society. But no one in the United States would use a word like "secularism" to summarize the American understanding of church-state relations.

There is no widely accepted single word to summarize the American system. Several such words have been suggested, but none of them is universally accepted. Probably the nearest equivalent in American usage is "separation of church and state," often shortened to "separation." This is a troublesome phrase even before translation; Americans dispute its meaning, and even dispute whether it describes one of our governing principles. But separation of church and state is probably the most common phrase for summarizing American church-state relations; again, let us accept it as a starting point.

Separation of church and state requires that government be separated from religion, and thus that government itself be secular. Separation means that government is not to sponsor religion, and also, although this point gets less emphasis in the rhetoric of separation, government is not to interfere with religion. Many religious believers support separation in part because they believe that religion will flourish best without government sponsorship, and that all sponsorship is a form of interference. So separation need not lead to secularism in civil society. To the contrary, many Americans believe that separation is one important reason why religious faith persists in the United States to a far greater extent than in most other industrialized democracies. Separation does not imply that religion is best kept out of public view, or even that private religious expression should be kept out of government institutions. I do not know the French system well enough to be sure, but I think that any correspondence between separation and *laïcité* is very inexact.

Other attempts to summarize the American system are that religion must be voluntary, and that government must be neutral as between religions and as between religion and religious disbelief. Each of these principles has applications that are highly controversial in the United States. Americans dispute the meaning of neutrality just as they dispute the meaning of separation. And of course, all such explanations are mere paraphrases of the operative language of the numerous constitutional and statutory provisions protecting religious liberty.

There may be no simple explanations of our system to citizens familiar with the French system, and no clearly equivalent words or phrases in our two languages for the central concepts. My only course is to explain the American system as simply and clearly as I can, with emphasis on answers to specific practical questions. I will necessarily have to generalize in places and omit important variations. I will try not to assume background information that is familiar to Americans but might be unfamiliar in France.

Keep in mind that on many important issues of religious liberty, there are at least two sides in the United States, with intense and sustained political and legal conflict. Our adversarial legal system, and our active system of judicial review of the constitutional validity of government practices, often enable the opposing sides in political and even religious arguments to translate their claims into legal arguments. At different times in American history, very different understandings of religious liberty have prevailed. The American conception of church-state relations is disputed, and it changes over time.

I. The Basic Legal Provisions

The United States has many constitutional and statutory guarantees of religious liberty. Most important are two sentences in the Constitution of the United States. The first is the Test Oath Clause, in Article VI, clause 3, which provides: "[N]o religious Test shall ever be required as a Qualification to any Office or public Trust under the United States." England had historically required office holders to swear an oath that they believed in essential doctrines of the Church of England, or of Protestantism more generally; several of the early American states had similar provisions. The Test Oath Clause prohibits any such requirement for federal office holders. Persons of any faith or of none may freely compete for federal office and hold the office if selected. But nothing prevents voters from considering religion when they vote, and nothing prevents the President from considering religion when he makes political appointments.

The more famous provision appears in the First Amendment to the Constitution: "Congress shall make no law respecting an establishment of religion or prohibiting the free exercise thereof." "Establishment" is a word that may not translate very well. I believe it is a cognate, and that in its general sense it means roughly the same thing in French and English. But as applied to religion, "establish" and "establishment" have a special sense in English. Early in the sixteenth century, King Henry VIII of England rejected the authority of the Pope, seized control of the structure and property of the Catholic Church in England, and had his Parliament enact a law making the King the head of the church. Later English legislation referred to this new church as "the Church of England by law established." From this statutory phrase came a new English usage: An established church, or an established religion, is one supported and sponsored by the government.

To say that "Congress shall make no law respecting an establishment of religion" is thus to say that Congress shall not support or sponsor religion. This provision is commonly called the Establishment Clause. To say that Congress shall make no law "prohibiting the free exercise" of religion is more straightforward; Congress shall not prevent churches or individuals from exercising, or actively practicing, the religion of their choice. This provision is commonly called the Free Exercise Clause. The Establishment and Free Exercise Clauses together are called the Religion Clauses.

By their terms, these guarantees apply only to federal offices and to the federal Congress. But constitutional amendments after the American Civil War (1861-65) are now understood to equally protect these rights from interference by state and local governments. This is called "incorporation"; the early constitutional provisions protecting rights against the federal government are said to be "incorporated" into the Fourteenth Amendment, which protects rights against states and against local governments, which are created by states. So the Test Oath Clause, the Establishment Clause, and the Free Exercise Clause are now fully applicable to state and local governments.[2]

In addition, and even before the Civil War, states guaranteed religious liberty in their own constitutions. (American states have much more autonomy than French provinces, and before the Civil War, states had far more autonomy than they do now. Each state has its own constitution and its own bill

2. Torcaso v. Watkins, 367 U.S. 488 (1961); Cantwell v. Connecticut, 310 U.S. 296, 303 (1940).

of rights.) These state constitutional provisions tend to be more detailed than the federal provisions. They are generally, but not always, similar in meaning.

Increasingly in recent years, there are state and federal statutes to protect religious liberty. Many of these statutes exempt religious practices from government regulation; they attempt to protect religious practice more effectively than the federal Free Exercise Clause.

The American legal system relies heavily on judicial precedent arising from the decision of individual cases. So these constitutional and statutory provisions are repeatedly interpreted by courts. In a process based on common law methods, these judicial opinions themselves become part of the law. The differences between state and federal Religion Clauses, or between statutes and the federal Free Exercise Clause, are only partly reflected in different constitutional and statutory text. To a great extent, these differences have emerged as differences in judicial interpretation. Judicial interpretation can change over time, in response to legal, political, social, or even religious developments. Judges can modify or overrule earlier judicial opinions; legislatures can amend the text of statutes. Constitutions can also be amended, but that is much more difficult.

II. Some Essential History: Three Alignments of Religious Conflict

A. Protestant-Protestant Conflict: The Founding and Its Consequences

The United States never had a dominant national church that exercised great power and provoked great reaction. No church in the United States has ever occupied anything like the place of the Catholic Church in France.

The story of church-state relations in the United States begins with the thirteen English colonies that later became the thirteen original states. Most of these colonies had an established church — a church sponsored and supported by the colonial government. In each case, the established church was a particular Protestant denomination.

The Church of England was established in five southern colonies and in parts of New York. In three New England colonies, the established church was chosen by local elections, which were nearly always won by the Congregational Church (the eighteenth-century descendants of the Puritans). These established churches did *not* have centuries of accumulated wealth. They did have a dominant social and political position; they were supported by taxes collected by the government; and they provoked substantial resentment. But their story has a very different ending from the story of the Catholic Church in France.

The dominant regional position of these two established churches was threatened by continued immigration of Protestants of many denominations. Members of the churches that were not established were called "dissenters," because they dissented from the teachings of the established church. Beginning in the 1740s, Baptists, Presbyterians, and other dissenters greatly increased their numbers in a surge of religious enthusiasm known as The Great Awakening. Members of these dissenting churches were evangelical Protestants, more enthusiastic and less formal in their worship than the established churches, more intense in their faith. They were the direct religious ancestors of the evangelical movement in the United States today.

In the wake of the American Revolution, each state and the new federal government wrote a constitution. The evangelical dissenters insisted that these new constitutions address issues of religious liberty. Immediately in most states, eventually in all states, the established churches were disestablished — deprived of government sponsorship and deprived of tax support. The details varied from state to state, but disestablishment was not the work of secular revolutionaries. It was mostly the work of evangelical religious dissenters.

In the free competition for religious adherents that followed, the formerly established churches did not fare well. The Congregational Church and the Episcopal Church (the new name for what was formerly the American branch of the Church of England), today retain a membership that is affluent and politically influential but small in numbers. Together, these formerly established churches are now only 2.4% of the population.[3] The remaining 97.6% include a remarkable diversity of other Christian denominations and also a diverse array of non-Christian faiths, nonbelievers, and other secularists.

The dominant issue in the founding-era debate over disestablishment was government financial support for churches. Churches that received tax support did not want to give it up; many citizens, and especially dissenters and the unchurched, did not want to pay the taxes. Defenders of the established churches proposed as a compromise that dissenters be allowed to pay their church tax to their own church, so that tax money would be equally available to all denominations. But in the end, every state rejected this compromise. This high profile debate over tax support for churches has played a large role in the development of American understandings of religious liberty.

3. Barry A. Kosmin, Egon Mayer, & Ariela Keysar, *American Religious Identification Survey 2001*, Exhibit 1 at 13, *available at* http://www.gc.cuny.edu/research_studies/aris.pdf. [An expanded report of this research was later published as Barry A. Kosmin & Ariela Keysar, Religion in a Free Market (2006).]

B. Protestant-Catholic Conflict: The Nineteenth and Early Twentieth Centuries

The Catholic Church had a very small presence in the English colonies in what became the United States. Even so, Americans inherited a fear of Catholicism from the English experience of Protestant-Catholic conflict. Beginning in the second quarter of the nineteenth century, and continuing until World War I, there was massive Catholic immigration to the United States, resulting in serious Protestant-Catholic conflict. This conflict raised two principal issues, closely related but distinct.

Both issues grew out of the treatment of religion in the public schools. Public schools in the United States are organized and operated by local governments and funded by state and local taxes; only since the 1960s has there been modest financial aid from the federal government. Creation of public schools was mostly a nineteenth-century development, largely coinciding with the Catholic immigration.

Most of these public schools in the nineteenth century attempted to teach the Bible and the basic principles of Christianity, and to do so in a way that avoided disagreements among Christian denominations. They did not wholly succeed in avoiding disagreements among Protestants, but Protestants suppressed their disagreements in the face of what they viewed as the Catholic threat. From a Catholic perspective, the religious teaching in the schools was clearly Protestant in its scriptural translations, in its ritual practices, and in its theological presuppositions.

Catholics responded with two demands. One was to eliminate Protestant teaching in the public schools; the other was that government pay for privately run Catholic schools. In the Catholic view, they were simply demanding equality. Government paid for public schools that were Protestant; it should also pay for schools that were Catholic.

Protestants denied that the public schools were Protestant. They said that the religious exercises in the public schools were "nonsectarian," by which they meant neutral as among Christians, but that Catholic schools were "sectarian," teaching the doctrines of a particular sect. Protestants also refused to provide government funding for the small number of schools run by Protestant denominations; these schools too were sectarian. But everyone understood that Catholics were the principal target of this distinction between sectarian and nonsectarian schools.

Protestants argued that the principle from the founding — that government should not financially support churches — also meant that government should not financially support sectarian schools. Applying this principle to schools was in fact a significant extension. Catholic schools taught religion, but they also taught reading, writing, mathematics, and other secular subjects. Government could have paid for instruction in secular subjects and let the church add its own funds to pay for religious instruction. But Protestants were numerically dominant, so solutions that would permit partial funding of Catholic schools were not seriously considered. Moreover, political parties found it in their interest to agitate this issue from time to time. A majority of state constitutions were amended to forbid government financial support for sectarian schools; in 1876, a similar proposed amendment to the federal Constitution was narrowly defeated in Congress.

There was also a large Jewish immigration to the United States in the late-nineteenth and early-twentieth centuries. Of course Jewish students also objected to Christian religious instruction in the public schools. The Jewish community's principal response, then and now, was to urge that the public schools be secularized. Most American Jews did not start their own schools, and those who did start schools did not seek government financial support.

World War I cut off the great flow of European immigration, and after the war, the United States restricted its resumption. Each succeeding generation of Catholics and Jews was more assimilated than its parents, and Protestant-Catholic tension gradually eased. In 1960, John Kennedy was the first Catholic to be elected President, and he and his family were personally attractive and widely popular. Shortly thereafter, the Second Vatican Council committed the Catholic Church to freedom of conscience. After these two events, lingering anti-Catholicism in the United States collapsed with remarkable speed. Even earlier, in 1955, a well-received book argued that Protestants, Catholics, and Jews were three great branches of a common civil religion in the United States.[4]

C. Religious-Secular and Left-Right Conflict: The Late-Twentieth Century and Today

Other fault lines were emerging even as Protestant-Catholic conflict dwindled. The 1960s were a decade of great social change in the United States and elsewhere. The civil rights movement, the anti-war movement, and the sexual revolution were concentrated in the 1960s. There were race riots in many American cities. The Supreme Court delivered libertarian decisions expand-

---

4. WILL HERBERG, PROTESTANT, CATHOLIC, JEW: AN ESSAY IN AMERICAN RELIGIOUS SOCIOLOGY (1955).

ing the rights of free speech, of religious and racial minorities, and of criminal defendants. In 1973, the Court announced a constitutional right to abortion.[5]

These developments provoked a backlash, and part of that backlash was religious. Culturally conservative religious believers of all faiths — evangelical Protestants, conservative Catholics, Orthodox Jews — resisted the sexual revolution, the general attitude of permissiveness, and the sense of social disorder associated with demonstrations, crime, and riots; they were especially horrified by the right to abortion. What came to be known as the Religious Right is part of the political coalition that has elected a series of increasingly conservative American Presidents, beginning with Ronald Reagan in 1980.

This backlash had consequences for competing views of religious liberty. For most of American history, the most theologically conservative Protestants had been the most anti-Catholic, and therefore, evangelical Protestants had been among the most vigorous opponents of government funding for religious schools. But beginning in the 1960s, these conservative Protestants began building religious schools of their own. This movement began in response to racial desegregation in the public schools, but that issue eventually faded. Conservative Protestant schools have grown dramatically in numbers and show every sign of permanence, sustained by parents who view the public schools as secularized and hostile to religious faith.

At first the leaders of these Protestant schools were more concerned with avoiding government regulation than with attracting government funding. But after the regulatory issues were mostly resolved, parents in these schools increasingly resented paying taxes for public schools they felt they could not use, while also paying the full cost of creating a private alternative. Their situation was exactly that of Catholic parents a century before. And in the 1980s, evangelical Protestants changed their minds about government funding for religious schools. Since then, government funding for private schools has drawn the support of a coalition of Catholics, evangelical Protestants, secular conservatives arguing the benefits of competition in a free market, and a minority of black parents seeking alternatives to inner-city public schools that are often of low quality. As we shall see, the Supreme Court has responded; it has changed its interpretation of constitutional law about funding religious schools.

In the 1980s and later, the religious division in the United States began to look more parallel to the historic religious division in France, with intense believers arrayed against secularists.[6] But each side is a diverse coalition, dif-

---

5. Roe v. Wade, 410 U.S. 113 (1973).
6. *See* PHILLIP E. JOHNSON, REASON IN THE BALANCE: THE CASE AGAINST NATURAL-

ficult to accurately summarize. Both sides include people of many different faiths; the United States is further than ever from having a single dominant church. On one side are intensely religious, culturally conservative believers of all faiths. Conservative Protestants, Catholics, and Jews often find they have more in common with each other than with liberal adherents of their own religious tradition. These religious conservatives make effective alliances with secular conservatives in electoral politics and on issues of mutual interest. Occasionally Muslims join in this coalition of the religiously conservative, but that collaboration was never well developed, and the tensions growing out of terrorist attacks and the invasion of Iraq have made Christian-Muslim cooperation more difficult for both sides.

On the left is a small but increasingly vocal population of nonbelievers, a large group of serious religious believers who are politically and theologically liberal, and a large group that I will call nominal believers. In opinion polls, 95% percent of Americans say they believe in "God or a universal Spirit." But many of those 95% rarely attend church and appear to act on a thoroughly naturalistic worldview in their daily life. This is the group I am calling "nominal believers"; for them, God appears to be a very remote being, a metaphor, or perhaps a polite fiction. The religious affiliations of these liberal believers and nominal believers also cross the traditional divides among Protestants, Catholics, and Jews.

There has emerged among this secular and religious-left coalition a new form of anti-Catholicism. Historic anti-Catholicism in the United States was based in Protestantism, in theological disagreements, and in hostility to the papacy. This historic Protestant anti-Catholicism is now confined to a barely visible fringe. The new anti-Catholicism is based on resentment of the Church's efforts to enact certain Catholic moral teachings into law — especially on sexual behavior and abortion — and it is just as hostile to conservative Protestants as it is to conservative Catholics.

There are many smaller religious groups that do not neatly fit on either side of the main line of religious conflict. The United States once again has high immigration rates, and most of this immigration comes from places outside Europe. Many of these immigrants are Christian, but in the United States, they are so far distinguished more by their ethnic identity than by their religious identity. Many are Muslim; some are Buddhist, Hindu, or adherents of smaller religions from around the world.

Unusual variations of Christianity and Judaism have survived and some-

ISM IN SCIENCE, LAW, AND EDUCATION (1995); JAMES DAVISON HUNTER, CULTURE WARS: THE STRUGGLE TO DEFINE AMERICA (1991).

times flourished in the United States. A few of these preserve nineteenth-century lifestyles (the Amish for example); some are highly insular communities with unusual dress and customs (Hasidic Jews for example); some live in quite conventional ways but have distinctive theologies (the Mormons for example). There are groups such as the Hare Krishnas, the Scientologists, and the Unification Church, pejoratively called "cults" and euphemistically called "New Religious Movements." Perhaps a more neutral description is that they seem very strange to most Americans and they make high demands on their members.

These unusual religious groups, including the recent immigrants, produce a greatly disproportionate share of litigation about the free exercise of religion. The more mainstream groups, on either side of the division between religious conservatives and secularized liberals, produce most of the litigation about government support for religion.[7]

III. Some Frequently Heard Concepts

There have been many attempts to capture the essence of the American understanding of religious liberty in a word or a phrase. Some of these efforts have been used as political slogans; most of them have been analyzed and elaborated by academics. But there is no authoritative definition of these concepts, and no authoritative hierarchy among them, because the Supreme Court has not used them in any systematic way.

These phrases appear in Supreme Court opinions when convenient or helpful, and the Court has given some of them inconsistent meanings over time. These words indicate broad approaches rather than precise principles for deductive reasoning, and on many issues, each side tries to claim that its position is consistent with most of these approaches. Some of these terms attempt to distinguish conflicting positions, but many of them describe different aspects of the same reality. Do not exaggerate the importance of these terms. Still, I think it useful to introduce them before turning to more specific controversies.

---

7. For a more detailed account of the constitutional effects of religious change, see John C. Jeffries, Jr. and James E. Ryan, *A Political History of the Establishment Clause*, 100 MICH. L. REV. 279 (2001).

A. Separation

Separation of church and state has a range of meanings.[8] The narrowest meaning is institutional separation: nearly all Americans agree that the institutions of the church should be separate from the institutions of the state. By general law the state provides legal structures under which churches can organize themselves; most churches are not-for-profit corporations, but some have trustees to hold their property, and some are unincorporated associations. Any church can organize itself under these structures; no form of license or advance permission is required, and the state has no voice in deciding which churches can exist, in appointing church personnel, or in developing religious doctrine. Conversely, no governmental powers can be delegated to a religious organization.[9]

Perhaps the most fundamental point of separation is that questions of religion are separated from the coercive power of government. Government cannot use its coercive power for religious purposes, either on its own initiative or at the request of a church.

Financial separation was established at the founding. Government does not financially support churches, and churches generally do not pay taxes. Church tax exemption is a legislative policy; it is constitutionally permitted[10] but not constitutionally required.[11] The remaining controversy over government financial support concerns whether and to what extent the ban on financial support applies to religious schools and social service providers.

The most intense controversies are about the extent to which government functions must be separated from religious observance and ritual. For example, can government meetings open with prayer?

A longstanding minority in the United States interprets separation in a way that seeks to minimize the influence of religion. This minority sees any influence of religion on government as a contact that violates separation; they would exclude religious meetings from public places and religious arguments from political debate. This view has never attracted a majority of the Supreme Court; it is not a mainstream meaning of separation. But neither does it fade away.

8. Douglas Laycock, *The Many Meanings of Separation*, 70 U. CHI. L. REV. 1667 (2003).

9. Bd. of Educ. v. Grumet, 512 U.S. 687 (1994); Larkin v. Grendel's Den, 459 U.S. 116 (1982).

10. Walz v. Tax Comm'n, 397 U.S. 664 (1970).

11. Jimmy Swaggart Ministries v. Bd. of Equalization, 493 U.S. 378 (1990).

B. Voluntarism

Nearly all Americans believe that religious belief and activity should be voluntary, and thus that government should not coerce it. A majority of the Supreme Court, and a minority of public opinion, believe that government should not encourage or discourage religious belief or practice even if it refrains from coercion. Voluntarism is closely related to separation. Separation is the more common phrase, but voluntarism is the older of the two ideas.

The dissenting Protestants in the founding era insisted on voluntarism as part of their attack on the established church. It is obvious why voluntarism appeals to dissenters and nonbelievers; if one does not wish to go to church (or to the established church), it is important for the state to recognize that religion should be voluntary. Less obviously, the idea of voluntarism originated with devout Protestants who concluded that coerced religious faith is ineffectual, so that it did no good to coerce people into church attendance. The religious rationale for voluntarism is that only voluntary religious commitments can please God or save souls.

C. Equality

The legal equality of all faiths was settled in the founding era, as a corollary of disestablishment. The established church was deprived of its preferred status, and all churches were guaranteed the same liberties. Those who accomplished this change were thinking mostly of the different Protestant denominations, but the principle has been extended to Catholics, Jews, and all the remarkably diverse faiths that have since appeared in the United States. In principle, and to a great extent in practice, this equal status for all faiths includes those high demand religions that have drawn special regulation in some other countries, such as the Hare Krishnas and Scientologists. These small and unusual religions have the same rights as any other religious group. These groups have encountered some legal difficulties, mostly in the form of private lawsuits initiated by disgruntled former members. But they are not subject to any special regulation or supervision.

D. Neutrality

Religious neutrality is the appropriate government response to religious equality. The Supreme Court says that government should be neutral as between religious faiths, and that it should be neutral as between religion and religious disbelief. (The Court's usual phrase is neutral between "religion and non-religion," but I think that "religious disbelief" better explains what the Court means by nonreligion.) There is very broad support for these propositions with respect to the coercive powers of government; Americans overwhelmingly agree that government should not penalize either believers or nonbelievers.

There is more controversy about neutrality with respect to government subsidies. Some Americans oppose any subsidy to any organization with a religious affiliation. Other Americans support subsidies to religious schools or social service providers, but tend to think that subsidies should be confined to religions that are not too different from their own. The Supreme Court's position is that subsidies to religious organizations are sometimes forbidden, but that when they are permitted, they must be equally available to all faiths, however unfamiliar.

The most controversial application of the Supreme Court's neutrality principle is to government expressions of opinion. The Court often says that government should express no views on religious questions — it should express no preference as between different faiths or between religion and religious disbelief. This rule is settled law with narrow exceptions, but a majority of Americans are unpersuaded.

Neutrality has also generated substantial arguments about what it means to be neutral. The Supreme Court usually speaks of neutrality without specifying a definition, and sometimes it shifts from one meaning to the other. Two principal meanings have been recognized.[12]

1. Formal Neutrality.

Formal neutrality means government that is blind to religious differences. A law is formally neutral if it makes no distinctions on the basis of religion. Such a law applies equally to religious institutions and secular institutions, and it applies equally to the same conduct whether that conduct was done for religious reasons or secular reasons.

2. Substantive Neutrality.

Substantive neutrality means that government seeks to govern in such a way that it neither encourages nor discourages religious belief or practice. Some-

---

12. *See* Church of the Lukumi Babalu Aye, Inc. v. City of Hialeah, 508 U.S. 520, 559-64 (1993) (Souter, J., concurring).

times formal neutrality is also substantively neutral: if secular and religious speakers have equal rights to speak in the city park, government will treat them exactly the same (formal neutrality) and no one will be encouraged to make his message more or less religious (substantive neutrality). But supporters of substantive neutrality believe that sometimes, neutrality requires government to take account of religious differences. A law that prohibits sex discrimination in employment, in most of its applications, regulates an unfair employment practice that has little or no commercial justification. But as applied to the employment of Catholic priests or Orthodox Jewish rabbis, such a law prohibits a religious practice, strongly discouraging that practice with threats of legal penalties. Exempting the employment of clergy permits the religious practice to continue, but it does not encourage anyone to become Catholic or to become an Orthodox Jew, and it does not encourage other churches to stop ordaining and employing women clergy. Exempting the religious practice may be more neutral in its effects than regulating religious and secular practices equally.

E. Liberty

Some American commentators say that the fundamental point of religious liberty is liberty, and that all the other concepts I have mentioned are instrumental at most, distractions at worst. The goal of guaranteeing religious liberty is to ensure that each American has as much liberty as possible to choose and act on his own religious commitments or his own rejection of religion. And some would say we should pose that question directly.

F. Toleration

In the early years in some American colonies, as in Europe at the same time, the established church suppressed all other churches. This suppression of other faiths gave way to "toleration," in which one church was established and others were tolerated. "Toleration" implied subordinate status and toleration by the grace of the established church; these connotations soon became unacceptable. Disestablishment and the equality of all faiths marked the end of toleration as an acceptable account of religious liberty, and the word fell into disuse. In 1689, England's "Toleration Act" guaranteed toleration to all Protestants; a century later, America's First Amendment guaranteed "free exercise" of religion to all faiths, without limitation to Protestants. Although the word "toleration" is no longer used, we shall see that the idea lingers in disputes over government expression of religious opinion.

G. State Action

State action is a general constitutional concept, not specific to religious liberty, but it has special relevance to religious liberty. American constitutions create and regulate the branches of government, defining the powers of each. Constitutional rights limit what the government can do to the people; these rights do not limit what the people can do to the government, or to each other. Constitutional rights apply only to actions done by the government, or by someone exercising governmental authority; the usual phrase is that constitutional rights protect only against state action.

It is sometimes said that separation of church and state prevents churches from taking over the government, or even from unduly influencing the government. But the state action requirement means that the Constitution does not restrict the efforts of churches or religious individuals to influence the government. The Constitution applies only when the government itself takes action, whether on its own initiative or at the request of a church. Moreover, state action is the difference between protected free exercise and prohibited establishment. Religious conduct by private citizens is free exercise of religion; religious conduct by government is, in most cases, an establishment of religion.

IV. Principal Disputes Over the Meaning of Religious Liberty

Three great sets of practical issues produce persistent controversy over the meaning of religious liberty in the United States. Two of these controversies grow directly out of the nineteenth-century Protestant-Catholic conflict over schools: funding of religious schools, now generalized to funding of any religiously affiliated activity, and religious observances in public schools, now generalized to all religious speech with government sponsorship. The third great controversy, less publicized but in my view more fundamental, is over regulation of religious practice. Organized interest groups on both sides support lawsuits seeking to advance their views on each of these disputed issues, so there is a remarkable volume of litigation. I will try to keep jargon to a minimum, but it is impossible to explain legal developments in the United States without reference to the names of cases.

A. Funding of Religiously Affiliated Activities

The founding-era principle that government should not directly fund the religious functions of churches has survived with little disagreement for more than two hundred years. The nineteenth-century controversy over the funding of religious schools has continued unabated to the present, and is actually expanding in scope. To the extent that any funding is permitted, it is subject to the principle of equality of all faiths; government money must be available on equal terms to all. These settled principles — that government should not fund churches and that any funding of other religious organizations must be distributed on equal terms — distinguish the United States from much of Western Europe.

The political fight over government money for religious schools continued for more than a century before it reached the Supreme Court. In most places the opponents of funding won politically, so there were no funding programs to challenge in court. And it was not plausible to file a lawsuit challenging the absence of such programs; no one thought that government might be *required* to fund religious schools.

In the mid-twentieth century, as Protestant-Catholic conflict declined, a few states and localities began to enact modest programs of aid to private schools. Then in the 1960s, economic and social forces — especially the decline of central cities — threw the Catholic school system into financial crisis. Public education officials feared that Catholic schools might close in large numbers, returning many thousands of students to the public schools and causing a financial crisis there. The states most affected began searching for ways to give money to private schools, and the pace of litigation greatly accelerated.

The relevant law has changed dramatically over time as the Supreme Court responded first to one, then to the other, of two conflicting principles. In 1947, the Court announced these conflicting principles in consecutive paragraphs in the first modern Establishment Clause case, *Everson v. Board of Education.*[13] On one hand was the no-aid principle: "No tax in any amount, large or small, can be levied to support any religious activities or institutions, whatever they may be called, or whatever form they may adopt to teach or practice religion."[14] On the other was the nondiscrimination principle: government "cannot exclude individual Catholics, Lutherans, Mohammedans, Baptists, Jews, Methodists, Nonbelievers, Presbyterians, or the members of

13. 330 U.S. 1, 16 (1947).
14. *Id.* at 16.

any other faith, because of their faith, or lack of it, from receiving the benefits of public welfare legislation."[15]

In the beginning, these two principles had been consistent. The eighteenth-century debates involved earmarked taxes levied exclusively for the funding of churches. In an era with few public welfare benefits, these taxes funded purely religious programs and funded those programs preferentially. As applied to that dispute, the no-aid and nondiscrimination principles did not conflict, and the no-aid principle served religious liberty. No-aid protected citizens from being forced to contribute to churches involuntarily; it protected the churches from financial dependence on government, and thus from government control. It prevented discrimination in favor of religion, and it did not discriminate against religion. As I have said, there is still substantial consensus that government should not fund the religious functions of churches.

The modern cases are very different. In all the modern cases, government is funding some secular service — usually education, but sometimes medical care, care of neglected children, or some other social service. Government offers the money on equal terms to religious and secular providers alike. In that context, the Court had to choose between its two principles. Either government money would flow through to religious institutions, or else students in religious schools, and patients in religious hospitals, would forfeit instruction or services that the state would have paid for if they had chosen a secular school or hospital.

The nondiscrimination principle prevailed in *Everson,* which upheld government-funded bus rides to a Catholic high school — but by a 5-4 vote. Two decades later, the Court allowed states to provide secular textbooks for use in religious schools.[16] Then the Court changed direction. In *Lemon v. Kurtzman*[17] in 1971, the Court struck down a funding program for the first time, holding that states could not subsidize teachers' salaries in religious schools. The no-aid principle predominated from then until 1985.

But even in this period, the no-aid principle never completely triumphed. Instead, the Court made many fine distinctions. It permitted government support for most religious colleges,[18] but restricted aid to religious elementary and secondary schools. In the elementary and secondary cases, the Court drew distinctions that few observers would defend. The state could

---

15. *Id.* (emphasis omitted).

16. Bd. of Educ. v. Allen, 392 U.S. 236 (1968).

17. 403 U.S. 602 (1971).

18. Roemer v. Bd. of Pub. Works, 426 U.S. 736 (1976); Hunt v. McNair, 413 U.S. 734 (1973); Tilton v. Richardson, 403 U.S. 672 (1971).

provide books,[19] but not maps;[20] it could provide bus rides to school,[21] but not bus rides on field trips.[22] Perhaps most absurd, the Court prohibited government-funded remedial instruction to low-income students in religious schools,[23] but permitted that same instruction in vans parked nearby.[24] The cost of vans, and of dressing children to go back and forth in all weather between the school building and the vans, was a deadweight economic and educational loss, with benefits that were at most symbolic. This symbolism irritated the supporters of religious schools and completely failed to satisfy the objections of those who thought there should be no funding at all.

Few Justices really believed in these awkward distinctions. They emerged in part because the Supreme Court has nine Justices who cast independent votes and often have difficulty agreeing.[25] Some Justices opposed nearly all aid to religious schools; some Justices would have permitted nearly all aid to religious schools. And some Justices searched for compromise, trying to permit some aid but not too much. Some of these Justices in the middle were unwilling to overrule the earlier cases, preferring instead to draw artificial distinctions. And some of them were still trying to preserve each of the two competing principles of no-aid and nondiscrimination.

Lemon v. Kurtzman, the case that prohibited state subsidies for teacher salaries, is famous for announcing a three-part legal test that is often quoted but rarely decisive. The Court said that for a statute to comply with the Establishment Clause, three things must be true:

> First, the statute must have a secular legislative purpose; second, its principal or primary effect must be one that neither advances nor inhibits religion; finally, the statute must not foster "an excessive government entanglement with religion."[26]

19. *Allen,* 392 U.S. 236 (1968).

20. Meek v. Pittenger, 421 U.S. 349, 362-66 (1975), *overruled by* Mitchell v. Helms, 530 U.S. 793, 835-37 (2000) (plurality opinion with O'Connor, J., concurring in the overruling).

21. Everson v. Bd. of Educ., 330 U.S. 1 (1947).

22. Wolman v. Walter, 433 U.S. 229, 252-55 (1977), *overruled by Mitchell,* 530 U.S. at 835-37 (plurality opinion with O'Connor, J., concurring in the overruling).

23. Aguilar v. Felton, 473 U.S. 402 (1985), *overruled by* Agostini v. Felton, 521 U.S. 203, 235-36 (1997).

24. *Wolman,* 433 U.S. at 244-48; Walker v. San Francisco Unified Sch. Dist., 46 F.3d 1449 (9th Cir. 1995). *Wolman* has not been overruled on this point.

25. For analysis of why it is so difficult for the Court to render consistent decisions over time, see Frank H. Easterbrook, *Ways of Criticizing the Court,* 95 HARV. L. REV. 802 (1982).

26. Lemon v. Kurtzman, 403 U.S. 602, 612-13 (1971), quoting Walz v. Tax Comm'n, 397 U.S. 664, 674 (1970).

This test embodies the conflict between the no-aid and nondiscrimination principles. Its first two elements are taken almost verbatim from the Court's earlier explanations of "wholesome neutrality" toward religion.[27] Its second element, prohibiting government actions that either advance or inhibit religion, is a statement of nondiscrimination and substantive neutrality. But in practice, Justices invoking the *Lemon* test were much more concerned about government advancing religion than about government inhibiting religion. Through the 1970s and early 1980s, the Court struck down most new forms of financial aid to religious schools. The Court used the second and third elements of the *Lemon* test to create a dilemma for legislators: any aid diverted to religious uses advanced religion, and any government monitoring to prevent such diversion caused excessive entanglement. The aid the Court permitted was generally said to be incapable of religious uses, such as secular textbooks, standardized testing,[28] and diagnostic services.[29] With respect to the remedial instruction for low income students, and other services provided by government employees to students in religious schools, the Court implausibly said that the government employees providing these services were less likely to be drawn into religious discussions with the children if they were isolated in vans instead of working in a classroom of the religious school.[30]

Beginning in 1986, the Court progressively elevated the nondiscrimination principle and subordinated the no-aid principle. Since 1986, the Court has upheld six programs that permitted government funds to reach religious institutions;[31] it has invalidated none. Four decisions from the *Lemon* era have been overruled in whole or in part.[32] The most important of the new

27. Sch. Dist. v. Schempp, 374 U.S. 203, 222 (1963).

28. Comm. for Pub. Educ. & Religious Liberty v. Regan, 444 U.S. 646 (1980); *Wolman,* 433 U.S. at 238-41.

29. *Wolman,* 433 U.S. at 241-44.

30. *Id.* at 247.

31. Zelman v. Simmons-Harris, 536 U.S. 639 (2002) (school voucher program); Mitchell v. Helms, 530 U.S. 793 (2000) (federal funded equipment distributed to public and private schools on per student basis); Agostini v. Felton, 521 U.S. 203 (1997) (public school teachers providing remedial education to low-income students in public and private schools in low-income neighborhoods); Zobrest v. Catalina Foothills Sch. Dist., 509 U.S. 1 (1993) (interpreter for the deaf at Catholic high school); Bowen v. Kendrick, 487 U.S. 589 (1988) (grants for teenage sexual counseling); Witters v. Wash. Dep't of Servs. for the Blind, 474 U.S. 481 (1986) (state scholarship for vocational training for the blind, where blind student wished to attend seminary).

32. See cases cited *supra* 20, 22, & 23. The fourth case is *School District of Grand Rapids v. Ball,* 473 U.S. 373 (1985), *overruled in part by Agostini,* 521 U.S. 203.

decisions is *Zelman v. Simmons-Harris*,[33] which upheld vouchers that can be used to pay tuition at any public or private school, including religious schools. These vouchers represent a right to draw on government funds for the exclusive purpose of paying educational expenses. Government issues the voucher to individual students or their parents, who spend them at the school of their choice; the school then redeems the voucher and collects the government money. *Zelman* reasons that the government is not responsible for any resulting benefit to religion. The government supports the student; the student and his parents decide where to spend the money, and there is no state action in their choice of a school. If they choose a religious school, that is a private decision. The Court has also upheld long-term loans of equipment to private schools, including religious schools, if the equipment is distributed to all schools on the basis of enrollment.[34]

Lemon's ban on direct cash grants to religious institutions remains in effect. And the Court would be much more cautious about programs in which government exercises discretion in deciding which private schools get government money. American law tends to presume that such discretion will be abused where sensitive constitutional rights are at stake — that favored religions will get money and minority religions will not. But at least in the school context, there is no reason for legislatures to authorize either direct cash grants or discretion in distributing funds. They can deliver as much money as they are willing to spend in the form of vouchers to students and their families.

The voucher decision means that a long political tradition of no government aid to religious schools has given way to a constitutional rule that permits such aid in essentially unlimited amounts, so long as certain formalities are observed. But courts do not enact programs or appropriate funds; *Zelman* gives voucher supporters only the chance to fight further battles in Congress and in the states. They face a broad coalition of voucher opponents: church-state separationists, teachers' unions and others who fear that resources will be diverted from public schools, fiscal conservatives who oppose new entitlements and the taxes to pay for them, and suburban parents who fear that voucher programs will open suburban public schools to low-income students who might be disruptive. No state has enacted a general voucher program for all students in elementary and secondary schools. Voucher programs remain mostly experimental and concentrated on low-income students or students in schools that fail to meet educational standards.

33. 536 U.S. 639 (2002).
34. Mitchell v. Helms, 530 U.S. 793 (2000).

Even these narrow programs are routinely challenged under the relevant state constitution. Many state constitutions have detailed restrictions on financial aid to sectarian schools. Some state courts have upheld such programs, generally following the reasoning of the United States Supreme Court;[35] other state courts have held that such programs violate the state constitution.[36]

Supporters of aid programs have tried to achieve one more step in the federal courts. In a variety of specialized circumstances, some states aid secular private education but not religious private education. It was once thought that extending these programs to include religious education would violate the federal Establishment Clause, but after *Zelman,* that is clearly not true. And the Supreme Court generally says that government cannot discriminate against religion. So voucher supporters have begun to argue that states violate the Free Exercise Clause when they fund secular education but refuse to fund similarly situated religious education.

The Supreme Court rejected that claim in the first case to present the question, *Locke v. Davey.*[37] The federal constitutional rule now appears to be that government funding of religious schools is permitted but not required, and that with respect to funding, government is permitted to discriminate against religion. Despite the traditional suspicion of government discretion in American constitutional law, government now has substantial discretion to fund religious education, or not to fund it, or even to fund it on condition that the student or the school comply with special regulations that apply only to those who accept government money. In part the Court deferred to the long American tradition of not funding religious institutions, treating that tradition as legitimate although not constitutionally required. In part the Court deferred to the legislature's primary responsibility for allocation of government funds. Parts of the opinion suggest that its rule is confined to programs for the training of clergy; other parts of the opinion suggest that it will apply generally to any exclusion of religious institutions from state funding programs. New cases are already pending that present questions about the scope of *Locke v. Davey.*

For most of the twentieth century, this dispute over funding religious institutions was confined to schools. Religious hospitals and social service agencies received government funds with little controversy. That has changed

35. Kotterman v. Killian, 972 P.2d 606 (Ariz. 1999); Simmons-Harris v. Goff, 711 N.E.2d 203, 211-12 (Ohio 1999); Jackson v. Benson, 578 N.W.2d 602 (Wis. 1998).

36. Bush v. Holmes, 919 So.2d 392 (Fla. 2004); Witters v. State Comm'n for the Blind, 771 P.2d 1119 (Wash. 1989).

37. 540 U.S. 712 (2004).

with recent proposals for what is sometimes called "charitable choice," or in the Bush Administration, its "faith-based initiative." These proposals, only some of which have been enacted, increased the visibility of government grants to religious charities, and they introduced new protections for the autonomy of religious charities accepting government funds. Agencies making grants would be forbidden to discriminate against religious charities; religious charities would not have to be separately incorporated from their sponsoring churches; and religious charities could retain their right to hire employees of their own faith even if they accepted government funds. Some of these protections are significant changes from traditional practice; some appear to be mostly symbolic; the proposed employment rules resolve an existing ambiguity in favor of the religious charities. Each of these proposed changes has been politically controversial; there are continuing fights in Congress, and there is pending litigation.

Zelman and other recent cases on funding schools suggest that there is no constitutional barrier to government funding of religious charities. But some social services may require direct grants to agencies instead of vouchers to the intended beneficiaries, because legislators will be reluctant to give vouchers to neglected children, the mentally ill, or the drug addicted, and tell them to choose their own service providers. And these programs are not so well funded that government can support all providers of services; government has to choose which agencies to support. So these programs may present questions of discretionary direct grants to religious charities, questions that can be avoided in the school cases. And there will certainly be litigation over the right of the religious charity to hire persons of its own faith for government-funded positions.[38]

In short, the long-running American dispute over government funding of religiously affiliated activities continues. New issues continue to emerge, and issues that are settled in one forum become the subject of renewed dispute in other forums. It is settled that government cannot fund the core reli-

---

38. The most complete descriptions and analysis of these programs and pending proposals appear in Ira C. Lupu & Robert W. Tuttle, *The State of the Law — 2005: Legal Developments Affecting Partnerships Between Government and Faith-Based Organizations* (2005); Ira C. Lupu & Robert W. Tuttle, *The State of the Law — 2004: Partnerships Between Government and Faith-Based Organizations* (2004); Ira C. Lupu and Robert W. Tuttle, *The State of the Law — 2003: Developments in the Law Concerning Partnerships with Religious Organizations* (2003); Ira C. Lupu & Robert W. Tuttle, *Government Partnerships with Faith-Based Service Providers: State of the Law* (2002). These books are all available at The Roundtable on Religious and Social Welfare Policy, Roundtable Legal Publications, http://www.religionandsocialpolicy.org/legal/legal_publications.cfm.

gious functions of the church; how far that principle extends to other functions is the subject of continuing dispute.

B. Religious Speech With Government Sponsorship

Prayer and other religious observances at government functions, and government displays of religious symbols, have given rise to an intense and peculiarly American set of controversies. This dispute began with Protestant-Catholic conflict over religious instruction in the public schools, and schools are still at the heart of it, but the dispute has spread to prayer at government meetings and to religious displays in city parks and courthouse lawns.

No such issues were debated in the founding period. There was probably more religious rhetoric in government affairs then, and many government meetings were opened with prayer. On the other hand, gratuitous government displays of religious symbols were probably rare, and public schools did not exist. The nation was overwhelmingly Protestant, and the disagreements among Protestant denominations were not great enough to make prayers by the established clergy seriously objectionable to evangelical dissenters.

In the nineteenth century, as we have seen, Protestant religious observances in public schools gave rise to bitter controversy between Protestants and Catholics. Late in the nineteenth century, a small but vocal group of secularists sought to eliminate all government support for religion, including prayer and Bible reading.[39] Recognizing that religious observances in the schools had become divisive, a few state courts and local school boards began to restrict them.[40] Religious instruction in the public schools very slowly declined over a period of decades.

In a pair of famous decisions in 1962 and 1963, the Supreme Court held that public schools violate the Establishment Clause when they lead students in prayer or Bible reading.[41] These decisions coincided with increasing acceptance of Catholics and Jews as fully equal and welcomed citizens, and perhaps — this is much harder to measure — with more of the population drifting toward secularism or nominal belief. But by 1962, Protestant-Catholic tension had declined so far that Catholics no longer objected to prayer and Bible reading in public schools.

---

39. *See* Laycock, *supra* note 8, at 1683-84 (text at notes 26-28).

40. Early court decisions are collected in *School District of Abington Township v. Schempp*, 374 U.S. 203, 276 n.51 (1963) (Brennan, J., concurring).

41. *Schempp*, 374 U.S. 203; Engel v. Vitale, 370 U.S. 421 (1962).

The school prayer decisions were unpopular and difficult to enforce. The decisions outraged evangelical Protestants, who feel called to teach the Christian gospel to all humans, and who feel the need to seek God's blessing and guidance for any important activity, including education and government meetings. The school prayer decisions were a prime contributor to the religious backlash in the 1960s and later, and to the growth of private evangelical schools. At the same time, these decisions raised expectations among Jews and other non-Christian religious minorities, and among nonbelievers and other secularists, that they would no longer be subjected to government-sponsored Christian religious observances.

The result has been an escalating series of provocations and legal claims from both sides. There have been innumerable proposals to amend the Constitution to permit school-sponsored prayer, none of which has passed the Congress, and endless efforts to restore school-sponsored prayer while disguising and denying government sponsorship. The Supreme Court has held that teachers cannot invite students to lead the prayer,[42] and that school boards cannot conduct student elections to decide whether to have a prayer.[43] The original cases involved prayer in classrooms, but more recently the Court has invalidated prayer at graduation and at athletic events.[44] The Court refused to invalidate prayer at legislative sessions,[45] principally because of long tradition: Congress had always opened its sessions with prayer, even in the First Congress, which had proposed the Establishment Clause.

The secular side opened a second front when it began challenging government-sponsored religious displays. The Supreme Court has held that public schools cannot display the Ten Commandments in classrooms,[46] and that a county cannot display a Nativity scene (a three-dimensional depiction of the events immediately following the birth of Christ) at a central location in its courthouse.[47] But it permitted a Nativity scene displayed alongside "secular" symbols of Christmas, such as Santa Claus, reindeer, and candy canes,[48] and it permitted a menorah (the principal symbol of the Jewish celebration of Hanukkah), next to a Christmas tree and a salute-to-liberty sign.[49]

---

42. Karen B. v. Treen, 455 U.S. 913 (1982), *summarily affirming* 653 F.2d 897 (5th Cir. 1981).

43. Santa Fe Indep. Sch. Dis. v. Doe, 530 U.S. 290 (2000).

44. *Id.;* Lee v. Weisman, 505 U.S. 577 (1992).

45. Marsh v. Chambers, 463 U.S. 783 (1983).

46. Stone v. Graham, 449 U.S. 39 (1980).

47. County of Allegheny v. American Civil Liberties Union, 492 U.S. 573 (1989).

48. Lynch v. Donnelly, 465 U.S. 668 (1984).

49. *Allegheny County,* 492 U.S. 573.

Most recently, the Court decided that Texas can maintain a large granite monument displaying the Ten Commandments on the lawn of its state capitol,[50] but that two Kentucky counties cannot display the Ten Commandments on courthouse walls, surrounded by patriotic documents and a statement claiming that the Commandments are the foundation of the western legal tradition.[51] Both decisions were 5-4; only Justice Breyer supported both results. He approved the Texas display mostly because it had been in place for forty years before it first aroused controversy; this suggested, at least to him, that the display contained both a religious and a secular message and that the secular message had predominated in public perception. He joined in the Court's opinion rejecting the much more recent Kentucky displays, in substantial part because local politicians had clearly stated their purpose to promote Christianity.

As the facts of these cases suggest, this legal and cultural battle is beginning to appear absurd. Each side aggressively pushes its position as far as logic will take it; each side takes advantage of every ambiguity in the Court's opinions. The ambiguities result from the Court's unwillingness to enforce an absolute rule. The Court has said that government cannot endorse religion or any religious teaching, but the Court will not carry that rule to its logical conclusion. The results would be too unpopular, do too much damage to the Court's credibility, and do too little good for religious minorities and nonbelievers. The Court will not order Presidents to stop issuing Thanksgiving proclamations; it will not order the government to remove "In God We Trust" from the coins and the currency; it certainly will not order changes to all the religious place names that Spanish friars scattered across the American Southwest, from San Francisco to Santa Fe to Corpus Christi. The Court will not entirely ban government participation in the nation's celebration of Christmas. But the Court cannot draw a principled line between the modest religious statements it permits government to make and the longer or more sectarian statements that it will not permit government to make.

To avoid ordering an end to government celebration of Christmas, the Supreme Court said that Christmas is both a religious and a secular holiday.[52] The Court said that government can celebrate the secular aspects of the holiday, and that it would be discriminatory for government to celebrate *only* the secular aspects, so government can mix religious and secular sym-

50. Van Orden v. Perry, 545 U.S. 677 (2005).

51. McCreary County v. American Civil Liberties Union, 545 U.S. 844 (2005).

52. *Lynch*, 465 U.S. 668.

bols of Christmas. But it cannot display religious symbols alone.[53] Nobody likes that compromise, but to the Court, the alternatives seemed worse.

You can now begin to see why the two Kentucky counties claimed that the Ten Commandments are the foundation of the western legal tradition. The counties claimed they had displayed the Commandments for their secular legal significance, not their religious significance. And they claimed that their display, like the Christmas displays the Court upheld, combined religious and secular documents. The claim that the Commandments were displayed for their secular legal significance and not for religious reasons was undoubtedly a lie, and it was based on an absurd reading of legal history. But the counties' real hope was that the Court would accept their rationalizations because the Commandments hanging on a courthouse wall might seem insignificant, not worth the inevitable cost of hostile public reaction to a decision ordering them removed. There were people on both sides who wished this lawsuit had never been brought — but who also thought, once it was in the Supreme Court, that it was important for their side to win.

The underlying conceptual disputes in these cases are about the scope of the government's obligation to be neutral. Opponents of government-sponsored prayers and religious displays say that government must be neutral as between religion and disbelief, and that government must be neutral in all that it says, even if no one is coerced. Some supporters of government prayers and religious displays concede that government should be neutral as between religions, so that government prayers and displays should refer to God only in general terms, and should avoid the specifics of different faiths. But they deny that government has any obligation to be neutral as between religion and disbelief. This is a modern version of the nineteenth-century position that government should teach "nonsectarian" religion in the public schools.

But of course many of these prayers and religious displays are not neutral as between religions. They are mostly Christian, and they tend to reflect evangelical Protestant beliefs and sensibilities. The deeper position of people who support government prayers and religious displays is that government need be neutral only when it exercises its coercive powers; government need not be neutral in what it says. Supporters of government expressions of religious belief say that government can promote religious belief so long as it does not punish people who decline to participate.

The Supreme Court has rejected this position at two levels. First, the Court says that if there is a public event that many people wish to attend for

53. *Allegheny County,* 492 U.S. 573.

secular reasons, and then someone offers a prayer at that event, persons who attend are effectively coerced to participate in the prayer.[54] But that argument goes only so far; it is hard to find coercion in the case of a passive religious display. Whether or not there is coercion, the Court says government may not "endorse" a religious viewpoint.[55] Government must be neutral even in what it says about religion. This argument — whether the Establishment Clause restricts government endorsement or only government coercion — is at the heart of the dispute over government-sponsored prayer and religious displays. It is mostly irrelevant to other religious liberty issues.

Those who support government prayers and religious displays are essentially urging a return to toleration as the measure of religious liberty, although they rarely argue the point in those terms. The dominant view among evangelical Christians is that minority religions and nonbelievers should be fully protected from penalties and civil disabilities, with full protection for the free exercise of minority religions. But evangelicals also think that religion should be included in all important government functions, that of course the religion included will be broadly consistent with the majority's religious beliefs, and that no one could reasonably expect otherwise. Religious dissenters do not have to attend formal worship services, but if they want to attend public meetings, or send their children to public schools, supporters of government prayer say that of course they should have to sit through brief observances of the majority religion. In that sense, the majority religion would be preferred and supported by government, and all other religions would be tolerated.

Although the Supreme Court tightly restricts government-sponsored religious speech, it vigorously protects religious speech by private citizens. Religious speakers have full rights of free speech, even in public schools or on government property, so long as they act voluntarily and without government sponsorship. "No government sponsorship" means they must be treated the same as other speakers; they cannot be given special access to facilities or to audiences assembled by the government. This right to religious free speech means that student prayer clubs can meet in empty classrooms on the same terms as secular student clubs,[56] that students can urge their classmates to attend church or accept Christianity, and that religious groups — even the Pope — can hold services or offer Mass in public parks to the same

54. Lee v. Weisman, 505 U.S. 577 (1992).

55. Santa Fe Indep. Sch. Dist. v. Doe, 530 U.S. 290, 308 (2000); *Allegheny County,* 492 U.S. at 592-94 (1989); Wallace v. Jaffree, 472 U.S. 38, 56 (1985).

56. Good News Club v. Milford Cent. Sch., 533 U.S. 98 (2001); Bd. of Educ. v. Mergens, 496 U.S. 226 (1990).

extent that secular groups can hold meetings or rallies.[57] The Court has never held, in any context, that religious speech by private persons is subject to greater censorship or restriction because of its religious content.

The Court's restriction of government speech about religion, and its protection of private speech about religion, have been remarkably stable and persistent. But from 1994 to 2005, these two rules actually had the support of only two Justices, Kennedy and O'Connor. Justices Rehnquist, Scalia, and Thomas would have permitted significant government sponsorship of religious speech, and Justices Stevens, Souter, Ginsburg, and Breyer would have imposed significant restrictions on private religious speech in public places. This persistent division on the Court has enabled Kennedy and O'Connor to prevail; they generally had six votes to prohibit government sponsorship of religious speech, and at least five votes to invalidate government discrimination against private religious speech. But now of course, Rehnquist and O'Connor are gone. If President Bush has accomplished what he hopes with his first two appointments, Kennedy may be the new swing vote on these issues. And Kennedy had one important disagreement with O'Connor: He distinguished government-sponsored religious displays, which passers-by may just ignore, from government-sponsored religious exercises, which often trap a captive audience and which he generally voted to strike down. Eventually there will be more new Justices, and these rules may change in more dramatic ways, just as the rules on funding of religious activities changed.

Many of the same political forces that support government funding of religious schools also support government-sponsored prayers and religious displays. In each of these disputes, much of the religious and conservative coalition is aligned against the secular and liberal coalition. Why has the Court changed its mind on funding, but not on prayers and religious displays?

The explanation again lies with Justices Kennedy and O'Connor, who see these two sets of cases as very different. The difference is best explained in terms of individual choice. In the funding cases, each family gets a voucher and each family can decide where to spend that voucher. Each family can choose a religious school or a secular school. In the private religious speech cases, each speaker can decide what to say and each person around him can decide whether to listen. Each student can decide whether to attend the meetings of the student prayer club.

But prayer at a government meeting, or a religious display in a government building, requires a collective decision. Either there will be prayer for

---

57. Fowler v. Rhode Island, 345 U.S. 67 (1953); O'Hair v. Andrus, 613 F.2d 931 (D.C. Cir. 1979).

everyone present, or a prayer for no one present. If there is a prayer, there will be only one, and it will be in a form more consistent with some religious traditions than with others. Either some government official must decide, or he must appoint someone to decide, and the person appointed will become a temporary agent of the government for that limited purpose. Everyone at the meeting will participate in, or at least politely sit through, the prayer that some government agent wrote or selected. No one gets to make an individual choice about whether to pray or how to pray.

Protecting individual choices about religion, and precluding government choices about religion, is consistent with nearly all the concepts used to describe religious liberty in the United States — with separation, voluntarism, equality, neutrality, and liberty. I think Justices Kennedy and O'Connor have best implemented the American conception of religious liberty by permitting vouchers, protecting religious free speech, and restricting government prayers and religious displays. But in the current alignment of religious conflict in America, Kennedy and O'Connor have few supporters among politicians and interest groups. One side wants funding for private religious schools and prayer in public schools; the other side wants neither.

C. Regulation of Religious Practice

The final set of important and contested religious liberty issues is regulation of religious practice. In my view, this is the most fundamental and the least understood of the three sets of issues. It is most fundamental because it is only in these cases that individuals can be threatened with civil or criminal penalties for practicing their religion. It is least understood because the cases come in far greater factual variety than the funding cases or the government-sponsored religious speech cases, because many of the cases arise from non-recurring conflicts between odd religious practices and odd regulations, because many of the victims are from small and little known religious groups and many of the burdensome regulations are equally obscure. The press finds these cases harder to report; the public finds it harder to take sides. But for fifteen years now, intense disagreement over these cases has divided the Supreme Court, divided the Court from Congress, and divided state legislatures. I will try to say enough about the facts of each case to give you a more concrete sense of these varied disputes.

From 1963 to 1990, the Supreme Court said that when a government regulation burdens a religious practice, government must either exempt the religious practice from the regulation, or show that applying the regulation to the religious practice is necessary to serve a compelling government interest. The first such case in the modern era was *Sherbert v. Verner,*[58] which held that a state could not refuse unemployment compensation to a Sabbatarian who lost her job because she was unavailable for work on Saturdays. In *Wisconsin v. Yoder,*[59] the Court held that a state could not require Amish children to attend high school when their parents preferred to educate them on Amish farms. Educating children might reasonably have been thought to be a compelling government interest, but the Amish were willing to send their children to public school through eighth grade, and Wisconsin required attendance only to age sixteen, which most children reach in the middle of tenth grade. The Court found no compelling advantage in that marginal increment to academic education as compared to Amish vocational education.

Despite these decisions, the Court did not actually exempt many religious practices from regulation. Prison and military regulations were subject to much more deferential standards. Deferring to prison authorities, the Court held that state prisons need not exempt Muslims from work assignments scheduled at the same time as a weekly Muslim worship service.[60] Deferring to military authorities, the Court held that the Air Force did not have to allow a Jewish officer to wear a yarmulke with his uniform.[61] The Court found a compelling interest in enforcing the military draft, so it allowed Congress to define the scope of conscientious objection, exempting those who objected to war in any form but not those who distinguished between just and unjust wars.[62] The Court found a compelling interest in collecting taxes, so it refused to exempt Amish employers and employees from the social security tax, even though they objected to social insurance schemes and refused to accept social security benefits.[63] The Court found a compelling interest in prohibiting racial discrimination in education, so it upheld a law refusing tax exemptions to private religious schools that discriminated against black students.[64]

I think these findings of compelling interest were entirely plausible; in each of these cases, there were reasons of secular self-interest to falsely claim the religious exemption, or even to genuinely convert to the religious belief that was entitled to the exemption. An exemption in these circumstances would thus encourage other citizens to join the exempted religion, and it

58. 374 U.S. 398 (1963).
59. 406 U.S. 205 (1972).
60. O'Lone v. Estate of Shabazz, 482 U.S. 342 (1987).
61. Goldman v. Weinberger, 475 U.S. 503 (1986).
62. Gillette v. United States, 401 U.S. 437 (1971).
63. United States v. Lee, 455 U.S. 252 (1982).
64. Bob Jones Univ. v. United States, 461 U.S. 574 (1983).

would tend to greatly inflate the number of claims to exemption. But some commentators think these interests were not compelling, and that these cases suggest that the Court was not really serious about exempting religious behavior from nonessential regulation.

In 1990, in *Employment Division v. Smith*,[65] the Court changed the rule. In *Smith*, the state had refused unemployment compensation to two workers who were discharged for consuming peyote, a hallucinogenic drug, at an American Indian religious ceremony. This ceremony, and the religion organized around it, has been part of American Indian practice in western North America since before the European settlement. The drug is relatively safe but not absolutely so; it has little recreational market; its religious use is associated with a decline in abuse of alcohol and other drugs among American Indians.[66] These facts cast doubt on the government's claim of compelling interest in prohibiting the peyote religion. But in the Court's new view, none of those facts mattered.

Smith introduced an additional requirement for litigants seeking religious exemptions: is the law that burdens religious exercise "neutral" and "generally applicable"? If so, the burden on religion apparently requires no justification whatever. If not, the burden on religion is subject to the compelling interest test as before. The Court said that Oregon's ban on peyote was neutral and generally applicable, so it could be enforced against the Indian religious ceremony without regard to the religious importance of the ceremony or the regulatory importance of the law.

For convenience, call the rule from 1963 to 1990 the *Sherbert* rule, and call the new rule, announced in 1990, the *Smith* rule. Under the *Sherbert* rule, the religious claimant must prove a burden on his religion; government must then prove that it has a compelling interest in imposing that burden. Under the *Smith* rule, there is a third element. The religious claimant still must prove a burden on his religion; the court must decide whether the law imposing the burden is neutral and generally applicable; and only if the law is not neutral, or not generally applicable, must the government prove that it has a compelling interest in burdening the religious practice.

Since *Smith*, the Supreme Court has decided only one case under the *Smith* rule — a case called *Church of the Lukumi Babalu Aye, Inc. v. City of Hialeah*.[67] *Lukumi* involved an Afro-Caribbean religion that sacrifices small

---

65. 494 U.S. 872 (1990).

66. See Douglas Laycock, *The Remnants of Free Exercise*, 1990 Sup. Ct. Rev. 1, 7-8 (text at notes 32-40).

67. 508 U.S. 520 (1993).

animals, mostly goats and chickens, to its gods. Hialeah, a Florida city near Miami, prohibited the "sacrifice" of animals. The city argued that it had enacted a generally applicable ban on sacrifice. The church argued that the ordinances were a ban on killing animals for religious reasons, carefully drafted so as not to prohibit any killings of animals for secular reasons. The Court unanimously agreed with the church, holding that the ordinances were neither neutral nor generally applicable, and that they served no compelling government interest. *Lukumi* gives substance to *Smith's* requirements of neutrality and general applicability, but the meaning of those requirements remains sharply disputed.

Government lawyers claim that nearly every law is neutral and generally applicable, and that the only exceptions are laws deliberately designed to single out a religious practice. This argument has some support in the facts of *Lukumi,* and some support in the language of the *Smith* and *Lukumi* opinions. Lawyers for religious claimants say that to be "generally applicable," a law must apply to all examples of the regulated conduct, without exceptions — or at least, with very few exceptions. On this view, many laws fail the requirement of general applicability, and thus are subject to the requirement of compelling government interest. This argument has some support in the facts of *Smith,* more support in the language of the *Smith* and *Lukumi* opinions, and much support in the way those opinions explain *Sherbert* and other earlier cases that have not been overruled. The Court in *Smith* and *Lukumi* distinguished these earlier cases, which means it gave them new explanations to show that their results were consistent with the *Smith* rule.

If the government lawyers are right, the *Smith* rule provides very little protection for religious liberty. Unless government is both hostile and clumsy, it can find a way to prohibit religious practices without openly singling out religion for special regulation, and thus without getting caught under the government understanding of the *Smith* rule. If the lawyers for religious organizations are right, the *Smith* rule provides substantial protection for religious liberty, but that protection is less inclusive, more complicated, and harder to invoke than the protection of the *Sherbert* rule. Either way, religious liberty is less protected under *Smith* than under *Sherbert.*

This reduction in protection for religious liberty provoked widespread disagreement among other branches and levels of government. Congress enacted the Religious Freedom Restoration Act[68] (RFRA) in an attempt to restore the *Sherbert* rule as a matter of statutory right.

The Supreme Court held RFRA, as applied to the states, invalid as be-

---

68. 42 U.S.C. § 2000bb *et seq* (2000).

yond the powers delegated to Congress.[69] But RFRA remains in effect as applied to the federal government,[70] and Congress has actually strengthened it.[71] The first Supreme Court case interpreting RFRA gave the statute full and vigorous scope.[72] The case involved religious use of *hoasca,* a tea brewed from two Brazilian plants and containing small quantities of a hallucinogenic drug prohibited by the Controlled Substances Act. The tea has effects similar to those of peyote. RFRA expressly puts on government the burden of proving its compelling interest in individual applications of federal law to religious practice. The Court unanimously held that the government had not carried its burden, and it unanimously rejected the government's claim that it need only point to Congressional fact finding in the course of enacting the Controlled Substances Act. The government's interpretation would have nullified RFRA's allocation of the burden of proof; the Court's holding makes RFRA an important protection for religious liberty. Thirteen states have adopted state RFRAs, and at least another twelve states — arguably as many as seventeen states — have interpreted their state constitutions in ways more consistent with the *Sherbert* rule than with the *Smith* rule.[73] So in one way or another, a majority of states have rejected the *Smith* rule. But there has been remarkably little state-court litigation under these provisions, so the seriousness of state commitment to the *Sherbert* rule has not yet been tested.

Most recently, Congress enacted the Religious Land Use and Institutionalized Persons Act (RLUIPA).[74] RLUIPA protects churches against local zoning laws that often make it difficult for new churches to buy or rent a place of worship. It applies only when the real estate transaction would affect interstate commerce, or when the zoning law is administered in an individualized rather than a generally applicable way. These restrictions on the application of RLUIPA are designed to confine the law's scope to specific delegations of power to Congress, and thus to avoid the excessive scope of regulation that led to invalidation of RFRA. RLUIPA also protects the free exercise rights of

---

69. City of Boerne v. Flores, 521 U.S. 507 (1997).

70. Christians v. Crystal Evangelical Free Church (*In re Young*), 141 F.3d 854 (8th Cir. 1998).

71. The exercise of religion protected by RFRA is defined to include "any exercise of religion, whether or not compelled by, or central to, a system of religious belief." 42 U.S.C. § 2000cc-5(7) (2000); *see also* 42 U.S.C. § 2000bb-2(4) (2000).

72. Gonzales v. O Centro Espirita Beneficente Uniao do Vegetal, 546 U.S. 418 (2006).

73. These state laws and decisions are collected in Douglas Laycock, *Theology Scholarships, the Pledge of Allegiance, and Religious Liberty: Avoiding the Extremes but Missing the Liberty,* 118 Harv. L. Rev. 155, 211-12 (2004) (text at notes 368-73).

74. 42 U.S.C. § 2000cc *et seq* (2000).

prisoners in state prisons that accept federal funds. State officials have bitterly resisted RLUIPA. The Supreme Court has unanimously rejected a claim that the prison provisions violate the Establishment Clause by giving preferred treatment to religion;[75] states are also arguing in the lower courts, mostly unsuccessfully, that both the prison and the land use provisions exceed the scope of powers delegated to Congress. RFRA, RLUIPA, and other legislative enactments to protect the free exercise of religion[76] reveal the depth of disagreement on issues of regulating religious practice.

I have emphasized the ambiguity of *Smith*'s requirement that laws regulating religion be "generally applicable," but in some applications, the meaning of that phrase is clear. A recent French example makes a helpful illustration. My point here is not to evaluate the French law, but to use this much-publicized French example to illustrate the relevant American concepts.

The new French law that prohibits students from wearing conspicuous religious items in public schools would *not* be a generally applicable law in the United States, even though it applies to all religions. It does not single out Muslims, or scarves or veils. But it singles out religious behavior and regulates that behavior because it is religious, without regulating equivalent secular behavior. If I understand the law correctly, a student can wear conspicuous secular jewelry but not conspicuous religious jewelry; a student can wear a scarf as a fashion statement but not as a religious statement. Despite intense disagreement on regulation of religious practice in the United States, this law is beyond the range of the American debate. I think that all informed American lawyers would say this law singles out religion and is not generally applicable.

Such a law might still be justified as serving a compelling government interest, but when a law openly discriminates against religion, the compelling interest test is hard to satisfy. A compelling interest in regulating only religion would normally mean the need to prevent some imminent and tangible harm. Creating or preserving a more secular environment would not be a compelling interest; probably, in the American view of these issues, it is not even a legitimate interest. Accelerating the assimilation of Muslims might be compelling if assimilation is essential to addressing the problem of terrorism. But the usual response of American constitutional law to such problems is to punish individuals who violate the law, and not try to control large groups

75. Cutter v. Wilkinson, 544 U.S. 709 (2005).

76. See American Indian Religious Freedom Act Amendments of 1994, 42 U.S.C. § 1996a (2000); Religious Liberty and Charitable Donation Protection Act of 1998, Pub. L. No. 105-183 (codified as amended at 11 U.S.C. §§ 544, 546, 548, 707, 1325) (protecting churches and other charities from most claims of creditors of persons who contributed to the charity and subsequently went bankrupt).

that contain some terrorists and many innocent people. And certainly courts would doubt whether the law will actually accelerate assimilation; it may just drive Muslim girls out of public schools. Protecting young Muslim women from coercion by their parents is an interest of doubtful legitimacy for minors; for adult women, it would require clear evidence that coercion is a widespread problem. I think the law would not serve compelling interests by American standards. But the compelling interest test is malleable and poorly defined; an American judge inclined to uphold such a law might persuade himself that one or more of these interests is compelling.

Finally, some American lawyers would argue that the law does not substantially burden religion, because it permits students to wear religious symbols that are inconspicuous. Some American judges seem to believe that government does not burden religion unless it interferes with a religious practice that is compulsory in the claimant's faith tradition. A Christian student wearing a large cross might be viewed as having made an individual choice, not mandated by her religion, so that limiting her to a small cross would not be a burden on her religion.[77] This is a minority view in the United States; the Supreme Court's cases tend to the view that any religiously motivated behavior is an exercise of religion.[78] But this disagreement would likely not matter with respect to yarmulkes or Muslim scarves; most students who wear one of these would say that their religion requires it, and that any interference with this religious obligation is a substantial burden on their exercise of religion.

The underlying American argument over regulating religious behavior involves multiple issues, and the two sides only partly correspond to the two sides in the cases on government funding and government-sponsored religious speech. Supporters of the *Smith* rule tend to think that neutrality is the fundamental principle in religious liberty cases, and by neutrality, they mean formal neutrality. Supporters of the *Sherbert* rule tend to think that liberty is the fundamental principle, or that neutrality should be understood as substantive neutrality, which brings neutrality more in line with liberty. From the perspective of the claimants in *Smith* and *Lukumi*, whose central religious ritual was subject to criminal penalties, it matters little whether the law was neutral and generally applicable. What matters is that it suppressed their religious liberty, and supporters of the *Sherbert* rule think that government should not do that without a very good reason.

Religious conservatives tend to support the *Sherbert* rule, because it better protects religious liberty. Secular conservatives tend to support the

---

77. Warner v. City of Boca Raton, 887 So.2d 1023 (Fla. 2004).
78. Thomas v. Review Board, 450 U.S. 707 (1981).

Smith rule, because it better preserves social order, it reduces the occasions for judges to invalidate laws on behalf of dissenters and minorities, and it saves judges from having to balance competing interests. Many secular liberals support the *Sherbert* rule, because it better protects individual liberty. But some support the *Smith* rule, because they see religion as a generally conservative cause in the United States, and because they think the *Sherbert* rule discriminates against nonbelievers. A religious conscientious objector to a law may get exempted under the *Sherbert* rule; a secular conscientious objector usually will not. During the Vietnam War, the Court interpreted the military conscientious objection statute to protect deeply held conscientious beliefs that lacked a conventional religious basis,[79] and that approach goes far to solve the problem of discriminating against secular conscience. But it aggravates the fears of disorder, of excessive judicial intervention, and of difficult judicial decision making. Current American judges are unlikely to protect secular conscience under statutes or constitutional provisions protecting the free exercise of religion. Realistically, the current struggle is over whether and to what extent they will protect the exercise of religion as religion has traditionally been understood.

V. Conclusion

Americans agree that government should not penalize any belief about religion, and that government should not pay for core religious functions. Beyond that, the United States has competing conceptions of religious liberty. Simplifying very greatly in order to summarize, one broad coalition would have government give nondiscriminatory financial support to religious schools and charities, give verbal support to mainstream religious faith, and regulate religiously motivated behavior only when absolutely necessary. An opposing coalition would permit no government money for any religiously affiliated activity, would permit no government statements for or against religion, and would regulate religious behavior on substantially the same terms as nonreligious behavior. Each side is winning on some issues, losing on others. These coalitions are shifting and overlapping; important allies on one of these issues are often opponents on another. I examine all three sets of issues in greater depth in a recent article.[80]

79. Welsh v. United States, 398 U.S. 333 (1970); United States v. Seeger, 380 U.S. 163 (1965).

80. Laycock, *supra* note 73.

I have emphasized the arguments in American law, and not just the rules. The arguments will persist; the rules are not so stable. Justices of the Supreme Court age, retire, and die; new Justices will be appointed. The Court is deeply divided on all three sets of contested issues. The rules on funding religious institutions and regulating religious practice have changed in important ways in the last twenty years. The rules on religious speech have been more stable, but as I explained, those rules had the support of only two justices and now face an uncertain future.

American judges are not career employees in a specially trained branch of the civil service; federal judges are appointed by the President and confirmed by the Senate. In the short run, the American judiciary is insulated from politics. But in the long run, if an issue arouses intense and sustained public interest, the Supreme Court eventually responds to large changes in public opinion. So the arguments will continue, and the rules may change. If you understand the arguments, you will be able to understand the changes in the rules.

Religious Liberty in America: A Rapid Fire Overview

33 Human Rights No. 3, at 3 (Summer 2006)

Human Rights *is a publication of the Section on Individual Rights and Responsibilities of the American Bar Association. They asked me to summarize the law of religious liberty in 2500 words or less. I couldn't do it; this is just over 3000 words. The essential points are all here, but often unelaborated, unexplained, and undocumented; readers have to take my word for things. This is the executive summary.*

*   *   *

Three great sets of issues produce persistent controversy over the meaning of religious liberty in America: the funding of religiously affiliated activities; religious speech, with the allegation or reality of government sponsorship; and the regulation of religious practice.

Funding

The law on government funding of religiously affiliated activities has changed dramatically as the Supreme Court has struggled with two conflicting principles, announced in consecutive paragraphs in *Everson v. Board of Education,* 330 U.S. 1 (1947). First, the no-aid principle: "No tax in any amount, large or small, can be levied to support any religious activities or institutions." *Id.* at 16. And, second, the nondiscrimination principle: Government "cannot exclude individual Catholics, Lutherans, Mohammedans, Baptists, Jews, Methodists, Nonbelievers, Presbyterians, or the members of any other faith, because of their faith, or lack of it, from receiving the benefits of public welfare legislation." *Id.*

In the beginning, the no-aid and nondiscrimination principles did not conflict; earmarked taxes for the support of colonial-era churches violated both principles. There is still consensus that government should not fund the religious functions of churches. But the modern cases are very different. Today, government is funding some secular service, and it offers the money on equal terms to religious and secular providers alike. In that context, the Court has to choose. Either government money will flow through to religious institutions, or students in religious schools and patients in religious hospitals will forfeit instruction or services that the state would have paid for if the students and patients had chosen secular schools or hospitals.

The nondiscrimination principle prevailed until 1971, when the Court changed direction. In *Lemon v. Kurtzman,* 403 U.S. 602 (1971), the Court for the first time struck down a funding program, holding that states could not subsidize teachers' salaries in religious schools. This no-aid principle predominated until 1985. But even in this period, it never completely triumphed. The Court restricted government aid to elementary and secondary schools but permitted aid to religious colleges. In K-12, states could provide books, but not maps; bus rides to school, but not for field trips. Perhaps most absurd, the Court prohibited government-funded remedial instruction to low-income students in religious schools but permitted that same instruction in vans parked nearby. Few of the justices really believed in these distinctions, but some were unwilling to overrule earlier cases and some were still trying to preserve something of both competing principles: no aid and no discrimination.

Beginning in 1986, the Court progressively elevated the nondiscrimination principle and subordinated the no-aid principle. Since then, the Court has upheld six programs that permitted government funds to reach religious institutions; it has invalidated none. Four *Lemon*-era decisions have been overruled in whole or in part.

The most important of the decisions since 1986 is *Zelman v. Simmons-Harris,* 536 U.S. 639 (2002), which upheld the use of vouchers to pay tuition at any public or private school, including religious schools. *Zelman* reasons that the government funding supports the student; the student and his parents decide where to spend the money, and there is no state action in their choice of school. The Court also upheld long-term loans of equipment to religious schools if the equipment is distributed to all schools on the basis of enrollment. *Mitchell v. Helms,* 530 U.S. 793 (2000). *Lemon's* ban on direct cash grants to religious institutions is still good law, but in the school context, legislatures can deliver as much money as they are willing to spend in the form of vouchers.

Although *Zelman* largely eliminates federal constitutional barriers to voucher plans, these plans remain difficult to enact politically and are subject to state-law challenges. Most state constitutions have detailed restrictions on financial aid to sectarian schools. Conflicting decisions of state supreme courts have shown that these clauses can be interpreted either way.

Some states aid secular private education but not religious education. It had been thought that extending these programs to religious schools would violate the federal Establishment Clause, but after *Zelman,* that is clearly not true. And the Supreme Court generally says that government cannot discriminate against religion. Voucher supporters thought it followed that states violate the Free Exercise Clause when they fund private secular education but refuse to fund similarly situated religious education.

The Supreme Court rejected such a claim in *Locke v. Davey,* 540 U.S. 712 (2004). Under *Davey,* government funding of religious schools is permitted but not required, and with respect to funding, government is permitted to discriminate against religion. Despite the traditional suspicion of government discretion in constitutional law, government now can fund religious education, or not fund it, or fund it on condition that the student or the school comply with special regulations that apply only to those who accept government money. Parts of the opinion suggest that its rule is confined to programs for the training of clergy; other parts suggest that it will apply generally to any exclusion of religious institutions from state funding programs.

For most of the twentieth century, this dispute over funding religious institutions was confined to schools. Religious hospitals and social service agencies received government funds with little controversy. That has changed with the Bush administration's Faith-Based Initiative. These proposals increased the visibility of government grants to religious charities and they introduced new protections for the autonomy of religious charities accepting government funds.

Zelman suggests that there is no constitutional barrier to government funding of religious charities. But some social services may require direct grants to agencies instead of vouchers to the intended beneficiaries, because legislators will be reluctant to give vouchers to such vulnerable groups as neglected children, mentally ill persons, or drug addicts. And these programs are not so well funded that government can support all providers of services; government has to choose which agencies to support. So these programs may present questions of discretionary direct grants to religious charities, with the resulting risks of favoritism and religious discrimination. And there certainly will be litigation over the right of religious charities to hire persons of their own faiths for government-funded positions.

Speech

In *Engel v. Vitale,* 370 U.S. 421 (1962), and *School District v. Schempp,* 374 U.S. 203 (1963), the Supreme Court held that public schools violate the Establishment Clause when school officials lead students in prayer or Bible reading. These cases provoked a religious backlash while simultaneously raising expectations that non-Christians no longer would be subjected to government-sponsored Christian religious observances. The result has been an escalating series of claims from both sides.

There have been endless efforts to disguise government sponsorship of school prayer. In *Santa Fe Independent School District v. Doe,* 530 U.S. 290 (2000), the Court held that school boards cannot conduct student elections to decide whether to have a prayer. *Engel* and *Schempp* involved prayer in classrooms, but more recently the Court has invalidated prayer at graduation in *Lee v. Weisman,* 505 U.S. 577 (1992), and at athletic events in *Santa Fe.* But in *Marsh v. Chambers,* 463 U.S. 783 (1983), the Court refused to invalidate prayer at legislative sessions, principally because of long tradition.

The secular side opened a second front when it began challenging government-sponsored religious displays. The Court held that public schools cannot display the Ten Commandments in classrooms in *Stone v. Graham,* 449 U.S. 39 (1980), and that a county cannot display a Nativity scene at a central location in its courthouse in *Allegheny County v. ACLU,* 492 U.S. 573 (1989). But it permitted a government-sponsored Nativity scene displayed alongside "secular" symbols of Christmas, such as Santa Claus and reindeer, in *Lynch v. Donnelly,* 465 U.S. 668 (1985). It similarly permitted a Christmas tree next to a menorah and a salute-to-liberty sign in *Allegheny County.*

Most recently, the Court decided that Texas can maintain a large granite monument displaying the Ten Commandments on the lawn of its state capitol, *Van Orden v. Perry,* 545 U.S. 677 (2005), but that two Kentucky counties cannot display the Ten Commandments on courthouse walls, surrounded by patriotic documents and a statement claiming that the Ten Commandments are the foundation of the Western legal tradition. *McCreary County v. ACLU,* 545 U.S. 844 (2005). Only Justice Stephen Breyer supported both results. He approved the Texas display because it had been in place for forty years before it aroused controversy, which suggested, at least to him, that the display contained both a religious and a secular message and that the secular message predominated in public perception. He rejected the more recently installed Kentucky displays because county officials had stated clearly that their purpose in installing them was to promote Christianity.

The underlying conceptual dispute in these cases is about the scope of the government's obligation to be neutral. Must government be neutral toward religion only when it coerces someone's religious belief or behavior, or must government also be neutral in what it says about religion? The Court has found this distinction irrelevant to prayer. It has said that if there is a public event that many people attend for secular reasons, and someone offers a prayer at that event, government impermissibly is coercing persons who attend to participate in prayer. But that argument goes only so far; it is hard to find coercion in a passive display. So the Court also says government may not "endorse" a religious viewpoint; government must be neutral even in what it says about religion. This argument over endorsement, while at the heart of the dispute over government-sponsored religious speech, is largely irrelevant in other religious liberty contexts.

Although the Supreme Court tightly restricts government-sponsored religious speech, it vigorously protects religious speech by private citizens. Religious speakers have full rights of free speech on government property as long as they speak without government sponsorship. They must be treated the same as other speakers, with no special access to facilities or to government-assembled audiences. This right to religious free speech extends even to elementary schools. *Good News Club v. Milford Central School*, 533 U.S. 98 (2001). The Court never has held, in any context, that religious speech by private actors is subject to restriction because of its religious content.

The Court's rules on religious speech have been remarkably stable for half a century. Yet from 1994 to 2005, these rules had the support of only two justices, Anthony Kennedy and Sandra Day O'Connor. Because the others were divided, Kennedy and O'Connor generally had six votes to prohibit government sponsorship of religious speech and at least five votes to invalidate government discrimination against private religious speech. But now O'Connor is gone. If President George W. Bush has accomplished what he hoped with his first two Court appointments, Kennedy is the new swing vote on these issues. And Kennedy had one important disagreement with O'Connor: he distinguished religious displays, which passersby may ignore, from religious exercises, which often trap a captive audience.

Many of the same political forces that support government funding of religious schools also support government-sponsored prayers. Why has the Court changed its mind on funding but not on prayers? The explanation again lies with Kennedy and O'Connor, who see these two sets of cases as very different. In the funding cases, each family gets a voucher, and each family can choose a religious or secular school. In the private religious speech cases, each speaker can decide what to say, and each person around him can decide whether to listen. But prayer at a government function requires a collective decision. Either there will be prayer for everyone, or there will be prayer for no one. If there is a prayer, there will be only one, and it will be in a form more consistent with some religious traditions than with others. No one gets to make an individual choice. By permitting vouchers and protecting religious free speech but restricting government-sponsored prayers, Kennedy and O'Connor protected the right of individual choice.

Practice

Regulation of religious practice is the most fundamental and least understood of the three sets of issues. Only in these cases can persons be threatened with civil or criminal penalties for practicing their religion.

From 1963 to 1990, the Supreme Court's position was that when a regulation burdens a religious practice, government must either exempt the religious practice from the regulation or show that applying the regulation to the religious practice is necessary to serve a compelling government interest. In *Sherbert v. Verner*, 374 U.S. 398 (1963), the leading case, the Court held that a state could not refuse unemployment compensation to a Sabbatarian who lost her job because she was unavailable for work on Saturdays.

Despite this rule, the Court did not actually exempt many religious practices from regulation. Prison and military regulations restricting religious practices in those settings were given much deference. And the Court found compelling interests in enforcing the draft, collecting taxes, and prohibiting racial discrimination in education. These findings of compelling interest were entirely plausible; in each of these cases, there were reasons of secular self-interest to adopt, or falsely claim, the religious belief that led to the exemption. But some commentators think that these interests were not compelling and that the Court was never serious about exempting religious practice from nonessential regulation.

In *Employment Division v. Smith*, 494 U.S. 872 (1990), involving a Native American employee fired and subsequently denied unemployment benefits because of his use of peyote in a religious ritual, the Court changed the rules. *Smith* introduced an additional requirement for litigants seeking religious exemptions: Is the law that burdens religious exercise "neutral" and "generally applicable"? If so, the burden on religion requires no justification. If not, the burden on religion is subject to the compelling interest test.

The Supreme Court has decided only one subsequent case under *Smith*. *Church of the Lukumi Babalu Aye v. City of Hialeah*, 508 U.S. 520 (1993), involved an Afro-Caribbean religion that sacrifices small animals to its gods.

Hialeah argued that it had enacted a generally applicable ban on sacrifice. The church argued that the ordinances were a ban on killing animals for religious reasons, carefully drafted not to prohibit any killings of animals for secular reasons. The Court unanimously agreed with the church, holding that the ordinances were neither neutral nor generally applicable and that they served no compelling government interest.

Lukumi gives substance to *Smith*'s requirements of neutrality and general applicability, but the meaning of those requirements remains sharply disputed. Government lawyers claim that nearly every law is neutral and generally applicable, and that the only exceptions are laws designed deliberately to single out a religious practice. This argument has some support in *Lukumi*'s facts and in the *Smith* and *Lukumi* opinions. Lawyers for religious claimants say that to be generally applicable, a law must apply to *all* examples of the regulated conduct, with no, or very few, exceptions. This argument has some support in *Smith*'s facts, more support in the *Smith* and *Lukumi* opinions, and much support in the way those opinions distinguish *Sherbert* and other earlier cases that have not been overruled.

If the government lawyers are right, *Smith* provides very little protection for religious liberty. If the religious organizations are right, *Smith* provides substantial protection for religious liberty, but that protection is less inclusive, more complicated, and harder to invoke than the protection of *Sherbert*.

Smith provoked widespread disagreement among other branches and levels of government. In 1993, Congress enacted the Religious Freedom Restoration Act (RFRA) in an attempt to restore the *Sherbert* rule as a matter of statutory right. In *City of Boerne v. Flores*, 521 U.S. 507 (1997), the Court held RFRA, as applied to the states, beyond Congress's power to enact under Section 5 of the Fourteenth Amendment. But RFRA remains in effect as applied to the federal government. In *Gonzales v. O Centro Espirita Beneficente Uniao do Vegetal*, 546 U.S. 418 (2006), the Court gave RFRA full and vigorous scope. In that case, involving religious use of a mild hallucinogen prohibited by the federal Controlled Substances Act, the Court unanimously held that the government had failed to prove its claim of compelling interest, and it unanimously rejected the government's claim that it need only point to congressional fact finding in the course of enacting the Controlled Substances Act. The government's interpretation would have nullified RFRA's allocation of the burden of proof; the Court's holding makes RFRA an important protection for religious liberty.

Since 1992, thirteen states have adopted state RFRAs, and at least twelve states — arguably as many as seventeen — have interpreted their state constitutions in ways more consistent with *Sherbert* than with *Smith*. So, in one way or another, a majority of states have rejected *Smith*. But there has been remarkably little state court litigation under these provisions.

Most recently, in 2000, Congress enacted the Religious Land Use and Institutionalized Persons Act (RLUIPA). RLUIPA protects churches against local zoning laws that often make it difficult to buy or rent a place of worship. It applies only when the burden on religion would affect interstate commerce or when the zoning law is administered in an individualized rather than a generally applicable way. These restrictions are designed to ensure that RLUIPA fits within specific congressional powers, thus avoiding a charge of excessive scope that led to RFRA's invalidation. RLUIPA also protects the free exercise rights of prisoners in state prisons that accept federal funds. State officials have bitterly resisted RLUIPA. In *Cutter v. Wilkinson* 544 U.S. 709 (2005), the Supreme Court unanimously rejected a claim that the prison provisions violate the Establishment Clause. States also are arguing in the lower courts, mostly unsuccessfully, that both the prison and the land use provisions exceed the scope of powers delegated to Congress.

Continuing Controversy

Deeply inconsistent constitutional visions make this area of law especially susceptible to the effect of new Supreme Court appointments. The cases on government religious displays are in jeopardy; another Republican appointment could roll back some of the school prayer cases. Another Democratic appointment could overrule *Zelman* and invalidate vouchers again. *Smith* is more likely to be eroded than overruled; the disagreement there does not yet track party lines. Especially on the Establishment Clause issues, too many justices are interested in promoting or restricting religion. Not enough are interested in protecting liberty for believers and nonbelievers alike.

A Conscripted Prophet's Guesses about the Future of Religious Liberty in America

October 25, 2007

This was a talk at the conference celebrating the 25th Anniversary of the Emory Center for the Study of Law and Religion. As explained in the introduction, I was assigned the task of predicting the future of religious liberty over the next 25 years. The predictions are not worth much, but here they are. There is also a bibliography of articles that project future trends on particular issues.

The talk was delivered in October 2007, and the predictions speak as of that date. This written version was prepared for publication in summer 2008. The original publication plans were eventually abandoned, and the written version appears for the first time here.

*   *   *

This is written on the occasion of the 25th anniversary of the Emory Center for Law and Religion, and I understood that we were especially asked to foresee its second 25 years. Perhaps I took the instructions more literally than other speakers; I am known to be a literal-minded guy. I took the question to be: What will the world of religious liberty look like in 2032?

Damned if I know. If I could foretell the future, I would have made a fortune in the stock market by now. This is not a topic I ever would have volunteered to address.

All I can do is examine the past, look at current trends, look at what caused changes in past trends, and try to extrapolate a little bit into the future. But I can't see around the next curve, or even know how soon we will reach the next curve.

I. Religious Changes Drive Changes in Law of Religious Liberty

A. *Changes in the Past*

Throughout American history, changes in the religious beliefs and behavior of the American people have caused changes in the alignment of religious conflict, and these changes have driven much of the law of religious liberty.[1] Thus the first Great Awakening, beginning in the 1740s, led to disestablishment in the states and to guarantees of free exercise and disestablishment in the federal Constitution.

The large Catholic immigration, beginning in the second quarter of the nineteenth century, led to intense political conflict over religious observances in public schools and over demands for funding of private schools. The modern legal issues over school prayer, and government-sponsored religious observances more generally, and over financial aid to religious schools, and to religious institutions more generally, are directly descended from those nineteenth-century conflicts.

The assimilation of Catholics and Jews into the American mainstream, and into its governing elite, and the increased acceptance of religious pluralism more generally, led to the school prayer decisions in 1962 and 1963 and to the rule, generally observed but subject to exceptions, that government should not endorse any position on a religious question.[2]

We have for some time been in the midst of a great outpouring of evangelical religious fervor, which I will call the Fourth Great Awakening, although that characterization is apparently a matter of some dispute among religion scholars. This Great Awakening, which began in the 1970s and continues today, led evangelical Christians to build a set of private schools, and that led them to switch sides on government aid to religious schools. That change of position contributed powerfully to a reframing of the constitutional issues surrounding such aid. Aid to private schools was no longer just a Catholic issue; it had the support of a broad coalition that included Catholics, evangelicals, free marketeers, and black parents frustrated with failing public schools. This reframing of the issue helped lead the swing votes on the Court to change their position from banning most such aid in the 1970s to

---

1. I review these periodic realignments of religious conflict in somewhat more detail in Douglas Laycock, *Church and State in the United States: Competing Conceptions and Historic Changes*, 13 IND. J. GLOBAL LEGAL STUD. 503, 507-13 (2006) (text at notes 3-7).

2. Sch. Dist. v. Schempp, 374 U.S. 203 (1963); Engel v. Vitale, 370 U.S. 421 (1962). For the no-endorsement rule, see, *e.g.*, Santa Fe Indep. Sch. Dist. v. Doe, 530 U.S. 290, 306–08 (2000).

explaining a constitutional method to deliver as much such aid as a legislature chooses by the early 2000s.[3]

In this Fourth Great Awakening, evangelical religion grew dramatically in activism, visibility, and influence. It probably grew somewhat in numbers as well, but the most important things about this Great Awakening were the evangelical decisions to enter politics and to form litigating organizations to protect religious liberty. This evangelical activism was a reaction to perceived secularization, and of course it provoked a secular counter reaction. The conflict between these two movements has led to a much higher rate of religious liberty litigation, in the courts generally and in the Supreme Court in particular. Evangelical activism was necessary but not sufficient — the support of secular civil libertarians was usually also necessary — to the enactment of the Religious Freedom Restoration Act, the Religious Land Use and Institutionalized Persons Act, the Religious Liberty and Charitable Donations Protection Act, and thirteen state Religious Freedom Restoration Acts.[4] This evangelical activism has powerfully resisted the Court's view that government should take no position on questions of religion.

In addition to these broad-based changes, we know that a single group can make a large difference. This is most vividly illustrated by the Jehovah's Witness litigation from the late 1930s to the early 1950s.[5]

---

3. *Compare* Zelman v. Simmons-Harris, 536 U.S. 639 (2002), with Lemon v. Kurtzman, 403 U.S. 602 (1971). For explanations of how and why this change came about, see Thomas C. Berg, *Anti-Catholicism and Modern Church-State Relations*, 33 Loy. U. Chi. L.J. 121 (2001); Douglas Laycock, *Why the Supreme Court Changed Its Mind About Government Aid to Religious Institutions: It's a Lot More than Just Republican Appointments*, 2008 B.Y.U. L. Rev. 275; Ira C. Lupu, *The Increasingly Anachronistic Case Against School Vouchers*, 13 Notre Dame J.L. Ethics & Pub. Pol'y 375 (1999).

4. See Religious Freedom Restoration Act, 42 U.S.C. § 2000bb *et seq* (2000) (protecting exercise of religion from federal regulation); Religious Land Use and Institutionalized Persons Act, 42 U.S.C. § 2000cc *et seq* (2000) (protecting use of real property for religious purposes and protecting religious exercise of inmates of prisons, mental hospitals, and similar institutions); Religious Liberty and Charitable Donation Protection Act, Pub. L. No. 105-183, 112 Stat. 517 (1998) (amending 11 U.S.C. §§ 544, 546, 548, 707, 1325 (1994)) (protecting charities from claims of creditors of bankrupt contributors). Citations to state Religious Freedom Restoration Acts are collected in Douglas Laycock, *Theology Scholarships, the Pledge of Allegiance, and Religious Liberty: Avoiding the Extremes but Missing the Liberty*, 118 Harv. L. Rev. 155, 211 n.368 (2004).

5. Citations to these cases are collected in Douglas Laycock, *A Survey of Religious Liberty in the United States*, 47 Ohio St. L.J. 409, 419-20 nn. 60-72 (1986). For a more recent example of successful Jehovah's Witness litigation, see Watchtower Bible and Tract Soc'y v. Vill. of Stratton, 536 U.S. 150 (2002).

B. The Remarkable Persistence of These Issues

The details change; the alignment of factions changes; who's winning changes. But the issues remain. Americans have been fighting over religion in public schools, and over financial aid to religious private schools, since the 1820s.[6] The intensity of these fights has waxed and waned, and sometimes — especially in time of major wars — the issues faded away as attention was focused elsewhere, but the issues have always returned. Even the arguments haven't changed all that much. One side says the public schools are neutral and acceptable to all, and somewhat inconsistently, that the public schools are essential to socializing children and preserving American values, that government should not support the teaching of religion, and that religious schools are separatist and divisive. The other side says the public schools are not neutral and are unacceptable to important religious minorities, that they instill a politically dominant view about religion, that private schools teach the whole curriculum and not just religion, and that families should not be forced to choose between their faith and their children's right to a free education. We have been fighting over these issues for 180 years now, and I feel fairly confident in saying we will still be fighting over them in 2032.

The battles over free exercise have been more intermittent, but have continued for even longer. Here the central issue is whether and to what extent religiously motivated behavior should be exempted from government regulation. This issue goes back at least to 1669, when the Carolina Colony exempted conscientious objectors from swearing oaths.[7] There were major and long running political battles over exemption from military service in the colonial period and during the American Revolution.[8] There has been constitu-

---

6. *See* PHILIP HAMBURGER, SEPARATION OF CHURCH AND STATE 220-21 (2002). I rely on Hamburger for his gathering of facts, but not for his analysis, which is often implausible or tendentious. *See* Kent Greenawalt, *History as Ideology: Philip Hamburger's Separation of Church and State,* 93 CAL. L. REV. 367 (2005) (reviewing Hamburger); Douglas Laycock, *The Many Meanings of Separation,* 70 U. CHI. L. REV. 1667 (2003) (same).

7. Fundamental Constitutions of Carolina § 100 (1669), *reprinted in* 5 THE FEDERAL AND STATE CONSTITUTIONS, COLONIAL CHARTERS AND OTHER ORGANIC LAWS OF THE STATES, TERRITORIES, AND COLONIES NOW OR HERETOFORE FORMING THE UNITED STATES OF AMERICA 2772, 2784 (Francis Newton Thorpe ed., 1909).

8. *Compare* Douglas Laycock, *Regulatory Exemptions of Religious Behavior and the Original Understanding of the Establishment Clause,* 81 NOTRE DAME L. REV. 1793, 1808-25 (2006) (text at notes 70-168) (arguing that this debate ended in a legislative win for religious exemptions, subject to a requirement of contributing to the war effort in other ways less burdensome to conscience), *with* Philip Hamburger, *Religious Freedom in Philadelphia,* 54 EMORY L.J. 1603 (2005) (arguing that this debate ended in a legislative defeat for religious ex-

tional litigation over claims to exemption at least since 1813.[9] And that 1813 case was argued and publicized as a test case, which shows awareness of the issue as one that would recur.[10] I expect we will still be arguing over these issues in 2032 as well.

II. Emerging Trends and Foreseeable Changes

The basic legal issues are persistent. Changes in religious belief and behavior yield changes in how these issues are treated. So can we foresee any changes in religious belief and behavior?

A. The Fourth Great Awakening Will Come to an End

The Fourth Great Awakening will gradually fade away and come to an end. It will likely leave important changes behind it — new universities, new megachurches, new statutes on religious liberty, new litigating organizations — but the religious intensity of the last generation will not continue. I base this prediction on little more than the fact that the first three Great Awakenings all ended. These Awakenings seem to have a life span, and this one is getting long in the tooth. To this outside and theologically unsophisticated observer, the movement seems to be diffusing. The lack of a viable socially conservative candidate in the 2008 Republican primaries is one example; other examples lie in the emergence of a variety of theologies and political commitments.[11] We have controversy over evangelical environmentalists; we have Rick Warren and *The Purpose Driven Life;* we have *The Prayer of Jabez* and other versions of prosperity theology. Of course diffusion does not necessarily indicate lack of energy, and politics are collateral to a religious move-

---

emptions, because pacifist groups did not get the wholly unconditional exemption they sought).

9. People v. Phillips (N.Y. Ct. of Gen'l Sessions, June 14, 1813), *excerpted in* Michael W. McConnell, John H. Garvey, & Thomas C. Berg, Religion and the Constitution 103 (2d ed. 2006). *See also* Stansbury v. Marks, 2 U.S. (2 Dall.) 213 (Pa. 1793) (reporting litigation over whether Jewish witness could be compelled to testify on his Sabbath; the case apparently settled and the basis for the claim is not reported).

10. *See* William Sampson, The Catholic Question in America (photo reprint 1974) (1813).

11. For a journalistic assessment, see David D. Kirkpatrick, *The Evangelical Crackup,* N.Y. Times Magazine 38 (Oct. 28, 2007).

ment; conservative religious political activism could diffuse or even end without the religious awakening ending. But this Awakening has been distinguished by its political activism, and more fundamentally, there is the experience that all past religious awakenings ended.

The Fourth Great Awakening will end unless, of course, this time it's different. This Awakening arose in reaction to very specific political and moral threats, and perhaps those threats can serve as a focal point that sustains the movement. It was the threat to take away the tax exemption of segregation academies that first roused the evangelicals to political action,[12] but other, more respectable issues soon replaced that one. The most obvious and important is abortion, now joined by same-sex marriage. There is always evolution, but evolution was around for the Third Great Awakening and didn't sustain it. There are issues of sexual morality more generally, and secularism in the public schools, but those are more diffuse. There are the end-of-life issues, but on those, the right-to-life movement will mostly lose; Americans in overwhelming numbers fear being tortured by the medical establishment in their final days on earth.[13] I will come back to same-sex marriage, but in the long run, I think abortion is the principal candidate for a galvanizing opponent for conservative religious activism.

My guess is that abortion will not sustain the Fourth Great Awakening at its current level of intensity, and that quite probably the abortion issue itself will look significantly different by 2032. If *Roe v. Wade* is overruled, or whittled into insignificance, the issue will be returned to legislatures, the present Republican coalition will be destroyed, and in most states, abortion will remain generally legal but somewhat more restricted than it has been. Conversely, new appointments to the Supreme Court may reaffirm *Roe* by a wide margin and put its overruling out of reach. This outcome seems considerably less likely, but if it happens, the right-to-life movement will be harder to sustain. The intensity of the conflict over abortion for the past 35 years has been sustained partly by the profound moral stakes on both sides of the issue, but

12. H. W. Perry, Jr. & L. A. Powe, Jr., *The Political Battle for the Constitution*, 21 CONST. COMMENT. 641 (2004).

13. *See* James Lindgren, *Death by Default*, 56 L. & CONTEMP. PROBS. 185, 197-207, 231-54 (No. 3, 1993) (collecting polling data). *See also* Kathryn L. Tucker, *In the Laboratory of the States: The Progress of Glucksberg's Invitation to States to Address End-of-Life Choices*, 106 MICH. L. REV. 1593, 1607-08 (2008) (collecting polls showing super-majority support for a right to assisted suicide); Peter A. Singer, Douglas K. Martin, Merrijoy Kelner, *Quality End-of-Life Care: Patients' Perspectives*, 281 JAMA 163, 165-66 (No. 2, Jan. 13, 1999) (reporting a small-scale study of seriously ill Canadian patients). The senior author of this study is a physician at the University of Toronto, not the bioethicist at Princeton.

also by the sense that dramatic change was within reach — often just one Supreme Court appointment away — and the potential or threat of that change motivated both sides to intense effort.

Technological change could also transform the abortion issue. If medical advances make it possible to sustain early term fetuses outside the womb, abortion will no longer be necessary to preserve women's control of their bodies, but taxpayers will be quite unwilling to pay the cost of preserving all those fetuses, and both parties' coalitions will be under intense new pressures. If pharmaceutical advances move abortion into the home or into the offices of ordinary gynecologists and internists, effective regulation will be impossible.

Of course one can overpredict dramatic changes just as one can totally fail to see them coming. It is possible that abortion will be one of those persistent issues, still galvanizing religious conservatives in 2032, still performed in clinics surrounded by protestors. I would not be astonished at that outcome, but I would bet against it.

B. Religious Conflict Between Americans Will Subside

What it means for the Fourth Great Awakening to come to an end is that religious intensity will subside. It follows that religious conflict will also subside, because religious intensity is the principal line of religious conflict in the country.

The dominant religion in the country is low-intensity theism. The middle of the theological spectrum is filled by nominal believers and by serious believers without much fervor. This vast middle tends to be suspicious of — somewhat fearful of and hostile to — both the nonbelievers on one end and the intense and outspoken believers on the other. The sharpest religious conflict is between the two ends of the spectrum — between the intensely religious and the intensely secular. When the intensity is reduced on one end of the spectrum, the resulting religious conflict will also be reduced. I do not say eliminated; just reduced. The Center's second 25 years should be quieter than its first 25 years.

C. Gay Rights Will Present Serious Religious Liberty Issues

Even though religious conflict should ameliorate in general, on some specific issues it is likely to intensify. For one, the gay rights movement will continue to make progress. It has momentum, and it has demography: Hostility to same-sex relationships is declining, and young people are more tolerant of same-sex relationships than older people.[14]

Differences between young adults and older adults are sometimes age or life-cycle effects and sometimes cohort effects. If the difference is an age or life-cycle effect, the older generation once looked like the younger generation does now, and the younger generation will eventually look like the older generation does now. If it is a cohort effect, the younger generation is genuinely different from the older generation and the difference will persist as the younger generation ages. Distinguishing the two requires sophisticated statistical analysis of data over time or just waiting to see.

It is possible that today's young people will become less tolerant of gays as they get older, but my guess is that they will not; I think this is a genuine cohort difference. The older generation grew up in a time when hostility to gays was endemic. People absorbed those attitudes and often became hardened in them before they were even exposed to the gay rights movement and to the argument that sexual orientation is generally immutable. More gays and lesbians stayed in the closet, so many fewer Americans ever knew that they had gay friends or gay relatives. It seems unlikely that today's older generation ever held the views of today's younger generation. Today's young people are being socialized very differently in many relevant ways. The future should lead to greater tolerance for gays and lesbians and even for same-sex marriage, with ever increasing pressure to conform to the new mores applied to a shrinking pool of religious dissenters.

1. The Exemption Issues

There is no very good reason for there to be conflict between religious liberty and gay rights.[15] The only consistent civil libertarian perspective is to support both. Both movements are based on the view that some features of human identity and commitment are so personal and so fundamental that the state should not interfere. I have supported both gay rights and religious liberty throughout my career. What we need are strong gay rights laws with strong religious exemptions.

But almost no relevant political actor thinks that way. The leaders of the

---

14. *See* Karlyn Bowman, *Attitudes about Homosexuality and Gay Marriage* (2008), *available at* http://www.aei.org/publications/filter.all,pubID.14882/pub_detail.asp (last visited August 2, 2008) (collecting polls over time).

15. The argument in this section is elaborated in Douglas Laycock, *Afterword,* in SAME-SEX MARRIAGE AND RELIGIOUS LIBERTY: EMERGING CONFLICTS 189, 189-201 (Douglas Laycock, Anthony R. Picarello, Jr., & Robin Fretwell Wilson, eds., 2008) (text at notes 1-27).

gay rights movement, and the leaders of the evangelical religious movement, both want a total win. They don't want to have to litigate over exceptions; they don't want to risk an occasional loss. It was the gay rights movement that rallied the broader civil rights movement to kill the proposed Religious Liberty Protection Act. There, religious groups offered far more in search of compromise than gay groups offered, but still the religious groups could not pass a bill guaranteeing religious liberty. That experience, and experience in state legislatures, leads me to predict with considerable confidence that there will be gay rights laws with absurdly narrow religious exemptions — perhaps eventually with no religious exemptions at all — and there will be conservative believers who oppose enactment, resist compliance, and seek exemptions. As the gay rights movement continues to make progress, we are likely to see more and more serious religious liberty issues arising out of its success.

2. The Marriage Issues

The problem with marriage is that this is the one major institution of society in which we make absolutely no pretense of separation of church and state — not even institutional separation, which is generally uncontroversial in all other contexts.[16] But with respect to marriage, there is not even a pretense of institutional separation.

Marriage is both a religious institution and a legal institution, but we do not separate the two. Marriage is jointly administered by the state and by religious organizations. The state has delegated to clergy the power to solemnize legal marriages; most Protestant churches have de facto delegated to the state the power to dissolve religious marriages. Catholics and Orthodox Jews persist in refusing to give religious effect to secular divorce, thus showing that it is possible to separate religious marital status from legal marital status if we have the will. But most Americans never distinguish religious marriage from legal marriage; the two institutions are entirely combined in our thought.

This means that the rise of same-sex marriage will be much more difficult than it needs to be. If we properly distinguished the religious and legal relationships, it would be perfectly clear that the state can authorize legal marriages between persons of the same sex, but that it can say nothing about religious marriages. Clergy do not have to perform same-sex marriage ceremonies, and religious organizations do not have to give religious recognition to same-sex marriages. Similarly where the disagreement is reversed: states

16. I elaborate this argument *id.* at 201-07 (text at notes 28-52).

do not have to recognize religious marriages between same-sex partners, but neither can they prohibit or penalize religious marriages that lack legal effect.

All this should be clear, but none of it appears to be clear. Already there have been conflicts in both directions and on a vast range of collateral issues involving private citizens who do not want to aid and abet same-sex relationships by renting an apartment, photographing the wedding, artificially inseminating one of the spouses, providing fringe benefits to same-sex spouses, and on and on.[17] The nature of marriage, and the relationship between religious and legal marriage, will be important issues for the Center's second 25 years, provoked by increasing acceptance of same-sex marriage. The only solution will be to begin separating the two statuses, and recognizing the rights of both church and state to make their own rules. But that solution is so contrary to tradition that it may be impossible to implement.[18]

D. The Muslim Population Will Grow

The Muslim population in the United States will continue to grow, unless we shut down immigration persistently and effectively. Effectively shutting down immigration seems wholly impossible for Latin Americans; it seems possible but unlikely for Muslims. With Muslims worried about active persecution arising from the war on terrorism, they have not been especially active in free exercise litigation. But some such cases have been filed,[19] and more are readily foreseeable: litigation over veils and head coverings in employment, in airports, on driver's licenses and identification cards, perhaps in public schools; litigation over regulation of Islamic schools, and if voucher programs get off the ground (which doesn't seem likely at the moment), over more intense regulation of Islamic schools that take government money. There may be litigation over sacrifice at Eid-ul-Adha; fifteen years after the Supreme Court protected animal sacrifice from discriminatory regulation, we have renewed litigation over Santeria sacrifice pending in the Fifth Circuit.[20]

17. *See* Marc D. Stern, *Same-Sex Marriage and the Churches,* in SAME-SEX MARRIAGE AND RELIGIOUS LIBERTY, *supra* note 15, at 1.

18. *See* Charles J. Reid, Jr., *Marriage: Its Relationship to Religion, Law, and the State,* in SAME-SEX MARRIAGE AND RELIGIOUS LIBERTY, *supra* note 15, at 157.

19. *See, e.g.,* Freeman v. Dept. of Highway Safety & Motor Vehicles, 924 So.2d 48 (Fla. Dist. Ct. App. 2006) (rejecting Muslim woman's claim to veiled photo on driver's license); Ahmad v. Dept. of Correction, 845 N.E.2d 289 (Mass. 2006) (rejecting Muslim prisoner's claims of right to prayer rug and halal diet).

20. *Compare* Church of the Lukumi Babalu Aye, Inc. v. City of Hialeah, 508 U.S. 520 (1993), *with* Merced v. City of Euless, 577 F.3d 578 (5th Cir. 2009).

E. Voucher Programs Will Grow Only Slightly, and the Fight Will Be in the States

The Supreme Court has largely returned the question of vouchers to the states. But no general voucher program has been implemented in any jurisdiction. All existing voucher programs are tied to failing schools or to particular cities known to have many failing schools. There are also charter school programs; these differ from vouchers in a variety of ways, but perhaps most importantly in that they create no entitlement. There is political resistance to vouchers; no voucher plan has yet won approval in a referendum. In November 2007, Utah voters defeated a voucher plan with universal coverage and small payments by 62-38 percent, and an official of the National School Boards Association claimed that this was the eleventh referendum defeat for vouchers in eleven tries.[21] Where legislatures enact vouchers or similar programs, there is litigation under state constitutions.[22]

I think that this will probably not change. As I said, there is a large coalition in support of vouchers — many Catholics, evangelicals, free marketeers, and black parents. But there is a larger coalition on the other side — the public school lobby, teachers' unions, opponents of taxes and government spending, suburban parents happy with their schools and fearful that choice programs might disrupt the status quo with children who are difficult to educate. Republican support for vouchers is half-hearted, because Republicans support vouchers but oppose the means of paying for vouchers. If the Fourth Great Awakening fades away as I have predicted, the evangelical component of the pro-voucher coalition will lose its intensity, and the number of evangelical schools will likely decline, further eroding support for vouchers. Voucher supporters will return to the strategy of trying to enact pilot pro-

21. For the Utah proposal, see *Utah Voter Information Pamphlet, 2007 Special Election November 6*, § 1 at 4 (2007), *available at* http://elections.utah.gov/Voter%20Information%20Pamphlet_2007.pdf (last visited Aug. 2, 2008). For the election results, see *2007 Special Election November 6, 2007, available at* http://elections.utah.gov/2007.Election.Results.pdf (last visited Aug. 2, 2008). For the claim of eleven straight defeats, *see* Erik W. Robelen, *Utah's Vote Raises Bar on Choice: Voucher Program's Defeat May Lead to Strategy Shifts,* EDUC. WEEK, Nov. 14, 2007, at 1.

22. *Compare* Kotterman v. Killian, 972 P.2d 606, 616-25 (Ariz. 1999) (upholding tax credits for gifts to scholarship funds for private schools), Simmons-Harris v. Goff, 711 N.E.2d 203, 211-12 (Ohio 1999) (concluding that Cleveland voucher plan could include religious schools), and Jackson v. Benson, 578 N.W.2d 602, 620-23 (Wis. 1998) (upholding Milwaukee voucher plan), *with* Bush v. Holmes, 919 So.2d 392, 399-412 (Fla. 2006) (invalidating Florida voucher plan), and Witters v. State Comm'n for the Blind, 771 P.2d 1119, 1121-22 (Wash. 1989) (upholding state's refusal to grant scholarship for the blind to student attending seminary).

grams and expanding from there, but that strategy has been around since the beginnings of the Milwaukee program in the early 1990s, and it has not led to much in the way of expansion.

Voucher programs would raise many difficult issues if widely enacted. How intrusively can the state regulate once it is paying the bills? Can some schools be excluded all together, because their curriculum is incomplete (think of schools that teach only or mostly religion, and teach little of the secular subjects), or because they teach intolerance or anti-Americanism or other ideologies that undermine constitutional commitments? If taken seriously, these issues would force courts and legislators to think about a question they have studiously ignored: what are those few things the state has a compelling interest in insisting that every child learn?[23]

These issues will arise sporadically with respect to the small programs in place, but they will not arise in the sustained and focused way that would follow if a populous state enacted a state-wide voucher program of general applicability. We are likely to continue to duck these questions.

III. The Court

Who will be deciding these cases? Let's start with the easy part. In 2032, Chief Justice Roberts will be 77. Justice Alito will be 82; Justice Thomas will be 84. The average age at which Justices retired or died in office in the last 25 years is just under 82, so it is highly likely that one or two of them, and quite possibly all three of them, will still be sitting in the Court's center seats. Barring some accident or early health failure, all three will be on the Court for all or most of the Center's second 25 years. Who will be serving with them, and with what predilections? That depends on politics, and politics are even harder to predict than religion.

A. Presidential Elections

When I made these remarks orally in the fall of 2007, it was widely assumed that the disasters the nation suffered in the Bush Administration would lead to a Democratic President and to Democratic gains in the House and Senate

23. *See* Mozert v. Hawkins County Bd. of Educ., 827 F.2d 1058, 1071-73 (6th Cir. 1987) (Kennedy, J., concurring) (concluding that state has compelling interest in insisting that every student study every part of the curriculum).

in 2008. As I finished the written version in the late summer of 2008, the Presidential polls were very close, Iraq seemed much less of a disaster than it had seemed a year before, Afghanistan was beginning to look like a potential disaster that few saw coming, and problems in the subprime mortgage market had caused a rising foreclosure rate and had brought down one investment bank, Bear Stearns. As I revised this paragraph in the week after the election, the economy is facing its greatest crisis since the Great Depression and the United States has elected an African-American Democrat to the Presidency with large Democratic majorities in both houses of Congress. I doubt that anyone predicted all of these developments; certainly I did not. I am not foolish enough to predict political developments in the longer term; I will only note some possibilities.

One possibility is that the conservative movement will be so discredited by the bungling in Iraq and Afghanistan and New Orleans and the economy that a long period of Democratic dominance lies ahead. But voters have supported the Republican Party for many reasons, and those reasons will remain. The Republicans seemed totally discredited after Watergate, yet they regained the Presidency and the Senate only six years later. In exceptional situations, a political party can be punished for up to a century — if it bears responsibility for invading a state, destroying or redistributing that state's physical capital, destroying its social system, and killing and maiming its young men. That is the story of Republicans in the South after the Civil War. Short of that, political memories are short. Politics is partly about what you have done for me lately, and mostly about what will you do for me next, and long-term punishment for serious blunders is not all that likely.

There is also a very different scenario. It is entirely possible that the victorious Democrats will overreach politically, or that they will also turn out to be bunglers, or that one or more of the problems they inherit — in Iraq or Afghanistan or the economy or energy policy — will be so insoluble that disaster ensues no matter how skilled the new Adminstration is. Any such disaster will happen in a Democratic Administration, and in 2012, Republicans will blame the Democrats for it. The Democrats will have lost Iraq, or presided over the final collapse of the financial markets, or whatever. The Republicans will say that they would have avoided this; they would have stayed the course; they were on the brink of victory, or of a free-market solution, before the Democrats cut and ran, or imposed socialism. As bizarre as it may seem in the wake of the Bush Administration's bungling, it is entirely possible that the Democrats will be the ones worried about long-term punishment for some foreign or domestic disaster.

Longer term, Republicans predict future dominance because conservatives have larger families than liberals, because the Electoral College over-represents rural states, and because the population keeps moving south and west. Democrats predict future dominance because the knowledge occupations are the fastest growing part of the economy and racial minorities are the fastest growing part of the population. Neither side knows.

I need not venture a guess about which scenario is most likely, because only one outcome would change control of the Court. With Roberts, Thomas, and Alito in place, the liberals need five of the remaining six seats to make a majority. So long as the current ideological division holds, Democrats need long-term dominance to turn the Court around. The other way they could do it is to get very lucky on the timing of deaths and resignations. But under most plausible political outcomes, with each party winning some share of presidential elections, conservatives will probably continue to control the Court for most of the next 25 years.

B. Party Perspectives

Of course the current ideological alignment may not hold. Suppose we knew who would control the White House and the Senate. Would we then know what kinds of Justices will be appointed?

We would certainly have a better idea, but that idea would still be far from a sure thing. The two political parties have competing visions of the Constitution with respect to many issues and with respect to religious liberty in particular.[24] This alignment is unusual in our political history, and it has already lasted 40 years, which is in itself unusual for a political alignment. The current party divide on constitutional issues may last for 25 years more, but of course it may break up. Parties shift positions; they sometimes trade positions. Parties realign; coalitions break up; components of coalitions shift allegiances.

The Republican Party is commonly said to be a coalition of economic conservatives, social conservatives, and national security hawks. That is diverse enough, but in fact it is more fractured than that. The economic conservatives include big business, small business, affluent individuals, libertarians, and the tax phobic. The social conservatives' central demand is regulation of abortion and other personal moral decisions — regulation that would be anathema to many of the economic conservatives, especially including libertarians and many affluent women. Both social conservatives and

---

24. *See* Perry & Powe, *supra* note 12, at 678-88.

national security hawks have expensive agendas that conflict with the resistance to taxes that is central to the economic conservatives. Some commentators think that all the disparate threads are united by a theory of strict-father morality.[25] That theory explains much, but it seems to me to work much better for the social conservatives than for the other elements in the Republican coalition. In addition, within each wing of the coalition, there is conflict between more moderate adherents and the more extreme views of much of the base. This unlikely coalition plainly showed signs of strain in the 2008 Presidential primary season. Every element in the coalition has grievances against the others. The current Republican coalition is not as strange as the old coalition of blacks and Southern segregationists in the Democratic Party, but it has some analogous problems.

The Democratic coalition is so fragmented it is hard to describe, with tension between its secular affluent whites and its deeply religious blacks, between all its identity politics groups and its working class whites and all its other moderate voters who resent identity politics, between its populist base and its dependence on financial contributions from business, between its anti-war base and its need to prove it will protect the country, and as with the Republicans, between its moderate adherents in general and the more extreme views of much of its base. Some Democratic voters don't like the Democrats so much as they fear and despise the current version of Republicans; if part of the Republican coalition breaks off, some of those Democratic voters will be up for grabs. Some of these differences were on vivid display in the late primaries between Barack Obama and Hillary Clinton in the spring of 2008. Those differences turned out not to matter in the Democratic sweep in the fall, but they have not gone away.

With respect to religious liberty issues, Republicans for a generation have taken a dim view of the Establishment Clause, but they have been divided on the Free Exercise Clause. Religious conservatives condemned *Employment Division v. Smith*[26] and supported RFRA and RLUIPA; secular conservatives generally took the opposite positions. The Reagan Administration quietly hammered at the Free Exercise Clause for most of its time in office, offering a variety of theories to reduce the Clause to insignificance,[27] and got away with

25. *See* GEORGE LAKOFF, MORAL POLITICS 65–107 2d ed. (2002).

26. 494 U.S. 872 (1990) (holding that the Free Exercise Clause provides no protection against "neutral" and "generally applicable" laws that prohibit exercises of religion).

27. *See* Brief for the United States as Amicus Curiae Supporting Petitioners 12-26, O'Lone v. Estate of Shabazz, 482 U.S. 342 (1987) (No. 85-1722) (arguing that any restriction on the constitutional rights of prisoners, including free exercise rights, should be upheld if it bears a reasonable relation to a legitimate penological interest); Brief for the United States as

it with its base. The Reagan Justice Department is the intellectual godfather of *Smith,* even though it did not hit upon the precise formulation adopted in *Smith.* It was conservatives on the Court who delivered most of the votes for *Smith* and most of the votes to strike down RFRA.[28]

Democrats have taken an expansive view of the Establishment Clause, and they have supported Free Exercise in principle, but much of the Democratic base views free exercise as a right that benefits only conservative believers, and Democratic legislators are quick to make exceptions to free exercise for civil rights and other more favored causes. By 1998, the coalition that enacted RFRA had broken up and the House was polarized on party lines in its unsuccessful efforts to enact a replacement.

So anything could happen. Probably Republican Presidents will keep appointing judges inclined to shrink the Establishment Clause, and probably Democratic Presidents will keep appointing judges inclined to expand it. Probably views on the Free Exercise Clause will get less publicity, will not affect the appointment process, and will emerge as a surprise after confirmation. If as I have predicted the fourth Great Awakening comes to an end and religious intensity abates, the Establishment Clause may not loom so large in Supreme Court appointments either. But none of this is at all certain. And we don't know which party is going to be doing most of the appointing.

IV. Conclusion

Predictions like these are a fool's errand; it's no wonder the other speakers ignored their instructions and refused to address these questions. If I am right, I will get only an old man's bragging rights. I have one thing in common with

---

Amicus Curiae Supporting Appellees 6-19, Hobbie v. Unemployment Appeals Comm'n, 480 U.S. 136 (1987) (No. 85-993) (distinguishing outright prohibitions of religious practice from burdens on religious practice, and arguing that the Free Exercise Clause protects only against the former); Brief for the Appellants 27-41, Bowen v. Roy, 476 U.S. 693 (1986) (No. 84-780) (arguing that government's interest should be measured by its interest in maintaining the whole program and not by its interest in refusing a few exceptions); Brief for the Respondents 47-50, Goldman v. Weinberger, 475 U.S. 503 (1986) (No. 84-1097) (arguing that absolutely no exceptions of any kind could be permitted in the military); Brief for the United States as Amicus Curiae 4-15, Jensen v. Quaring, 472 U.S. 478 (1985) (No. 83-1944) (arguing for the standard urged in *Bowen v. Roy*); *compare* Brief for the United States, United States v. Lee, 455 U.S. 252 (1982) (No. 80-767) (opposing exemption from social security tax on grounds that did not threaten to undermine exemptions more generally, in brief filed by Wade McCree, the Carter Administration's Solicitor General, who had not yet been replaced).

28. City of Boerne v. Flores, 521 U.S. 507 (1997).

Justice Thomas; I too will be 84 in 2032. Unlike him, I will be retired. So who would I brag to? My grandchildren will not be impressed if I tell them what a great prophet I was back in aught seven.

If I am wrong, I risk being cited as an example of foolishness; if I am spectacularly wrong (and if anyone remembers what I said), ridicule is inevitable. We have all heard of the nineteenth-century Commissioner of the Patent Office who said the office should be closed because everything important had already been invented. We have all heard of him — but the story turns out to be entirely false.[29] At any rate, I hope and believe that I have done better than that apocryphal Commissioner. If not, remember that I didn't volunteer for the task.

BIBLIOGRAPHY

Thomas C. Berg, *Anti-Catholicism and Modern Church-State Relations,* 33 Loy. U. Chi. L.J. 121 (2001).

Thomas C. Berg, *Race Relations and Modern Church-State Relations,* 43 B.C. L. Rev. 1009 (2002).

Daniel O. Conkle, *The Path of American Religious Liberty: From the Original Theology to Formal Neutrality and an Uncertain Future,* 75 Ind. L.J. 1 (2000).

Steven G. Gey, *Life After the Establishment Clause,* 110 W. Va. L. Rev. 1 (2007).

John C. Jeffries, Jr., & James E. Ryan, *A Political History of the Establishment Clause,* 100 Mich. L. Rev. 279 (2001).

David D. Kirkpatrick, *The Evangelical Crackup,* N.Y. Times Magazine 38 (Oct. 28, 2007).

George Lakoff, *Moral Politics* (2002).

Douglas Laycock, *Church and State in the United States: Competing Conceptions and Historic Changes,* 13 Ind. J. Global Legal Stud. 503 (2006).

Douglas Laycock, *Theology Scholarships, the Pledge of Allegiance, and Religious Liberty: Avoiding the Extremes but Missing the Liberty,* 118 Harv. L. Rev. 155 (2004).

Douglas Laycock, *Why the Supreme Court Changed Its Mind About Government Aid to Religious Institutions: It's a Lot More than Just Republican Appointments,* 2008 B.Y.U. L. Rev. 275.

Douglas Laycock, Anthony M. Picarello, Jr., & Robin Fretwell Wilson, eds., *Same-Sex Marriage and Religious Liberty: Emerging Conflicts* (2008).

---

29. Samuel Sass, *A Patently False Patent Myth Still!,* SKEPTICAL INQUIRER (May-June 2003).

461

Ira C. Lupu, *The Increasingly Anachronistic Case Against School Vouchers*, 13 Notre Dame J.L. Ethics & Pub. Pol'y 375 (1999).

Ira C. Lupu, *The Lingering Death of Separationism*, 62 Geo. Wash. L. Rev. 230 (1993).

Ira C. Lupu & Robert W. Tuttle, *Ball on a Needle: Hein v. Freedom from Religion Foundation, Inc. and the Future of Establishment Clause Adjudication*, 2008 B.Y.U. L. Rev. 115.

Ira C. Lupu & Robert W. Tuttle, *Zelman's Future: Vouchers, Sectarian Providers, and the Next Round of Constitutional Battles*, 78 Notre Dame L. Rev. 917 (2003).

H. W. Perry, Jr. & L. A. Powe, Jr., *The Political Battle for the Constitution*, 21 Const. Comment. 641 (2004).

C. Book Reviews

This Section contains three book reviews, reviewing three books that are themselves overviews of the field. One appeared in a law review; law reviews publish essay-length and even article-length book reviews. The other two are very brief book notes on the model of many other disciplines. Other book reviews, focused on particular issues, will appear elsewhere in this work.

The Somewhat Long . . .

Reflections on Two Themes: Teaching Religious Liberty and Evolutionary Changes in Casebooks (1988) reviews an innovative casebook on religious liberty, *The Believer and the Powers That Are* by Judge John Noonan. The review reflects more on teaching than on the substance of religious liberty.

. . . and the Super Short

The first *Book Note* (1989) reviews Mark Tushnet's *Red, White, and Blue: A Critical Analysis of Constitutional Law,* and finds it too utopian and too political.

The second *Book Note* (1996) reviews Jesse Choper's *Securing Religious Liberty: Principles for Judicial Interpretation of the Religion Clauses,* and finds it much too formalist. Good constitutional law is somewhere in between these two extremes.

Cross References

Robert Bork's *The Tempting of America* is reviewed in Part One, Section D, of this volume, on Judicial Nominations.

Thomas Curry's *The First Freedoms,* and Leonard Levy's *The Establishment Clause,* two important histories of the treatment of religious liberty in the colonial and founding periods, are reviewed in Part Two of this volume, on History.

A Syllabus of Errors (2007), and *God vs. The Gavel: A Brief Rejoinder* (2007), both to appear in volume 2, review Marci Hamilton's *God vs. The Gavel* and extend the debate over regulatory exemptions for religiously motivated conduct.

The Many Meanings of Separation (2003), which will appear in volume 4, reviews Philip Hamburger's *Separation of Church and State,* a history of how that concept has been used and misused through American history.

Reflections on Two Themes: Teaching Religious Liberty and Evolutionary Changes in Casebooks

101 Harvard Law Review 1642 (1988)[1]

Reviewing John T. Noonan, Jr., The Believer and the Powers That Are: Cases, History, and Other Data Bearing on the Relation of Religion and Government (1987)[2]

Law professors teach mostly from casebooks, which consist principally of judicial opinions in real cases, usually heavily edited, together with comments and questions written by the editor of the casebook and sometimes excerpts from books and articles. This is a review of one of the first casebooks on religious liberty. It laments the widespread neglect of the field in available law school teaching materials, and it laments some of the pedagogical difficulties associated with the casebook genre. The first problem has largely been resolved; now there are several casebooks devoted to religious liberty, and there is expanded coverage in the general constitutional law casebooks. The second problem, in my view, is worse than ever. There is good reason for reading real cases, but there are also serious costs to relying on them too exclusively.

*   *   *

The Believer and the Powers That Are is a casebook on religious liberty. Its unusual origins seemed to promise something different — few casebooks are

1. I am grateful to Sanford Levinson, William Powers, Teresa Sullivan, and Jay Westbrook for helpful comments on earlier drafts, to Robert Bartlett, William Kibler, Ernest Kaulbach, and Peter White for helping to find and translate Middle French and Latin testimony from the rehabilitation of Joan of Arc, and to Susan Waelbroeck for research assistance.

2. Judge, United States Court of Appeals for the Ninth Circuit, and Milo Robbins Professor of Law and Legal Ethics, Emeritus, University of California at Berkeley.

published by Macmillan, supported by a grant from the Lilly Endowment, or commissioned as part of a multi-volume project by distinguished scholars at Princeton.[3] The book innovates in important ways, most notably in its extensive attention to history. Yet it is still essentially a casebook, with the usual strengths and weaknesses of the genre.

Reviewing a casebook is notoriously difficult, more so when the reviewer has had no opportunity to teach from the book. I especially feel the need to try this book in the classroom, because my reactions run as much to pedagogy as to religious liberty.

I.

Judge Noonan's book is a welcome addition to the limited selection of teaching materials on religious liberty. I know of only one competing casebook, Miller and Flowers' *Toward Benevolent Neutrality.*[4] That book was also subsidized by a charitable endowment;[5] the major commercial casebook publishers have judged that the market will not support a casebook on religious liberty.

The pedagogical styles of the two available casebooks contrast sharply. Miller and Flowers has more principal cases and reprints the opinions at greater length, but it has vastly less explanatory text, few notes on lower court decisions, and almost no critical questions or commentary. Noonan offers fewer words from the Supreme Court, but much more of everything else: text, history, lower court decisions, nonlegal materials, critical questions, and original ideas. I would prefer still more, especially of Noonan's own ideas.

General constitutional law casebooks give religious liberty only a small fraction of the attention lavished on free speech or equal protection.[6] Most of

---

3. The book's origins are summarized in a Prefatory Note (p. xi).

4. ROBERT T. MILLER & RONALD B. FLOWERS, TOWARD BENEVOLENT NEUTRALITY: CHURCH, STATE, AND THE SUPREME COURT (rev. ed. 1982).

5. Miller and Flowers was subsidized by the Markham Press Fund of Baylor University Press. *See id.* at vii, xi.

6. *Compare* GERALD GUNTHER, CONSTITUTIONAL LAW 972-1463 (11th ed. 1985) (491 pages on free speech) *with id.* at 1463-1531 (69 pages on religious liberty); *compare* WILLIAM B. LOCKHART, YALE KAMISAR, JESSE H. CHOPER, & STEVEN H. SHIFFRIN, CONSTITUTIONAL LAW: CASES, COMMENTS, QUESTIONS 629-1026 (6th ed. 1986) [hereinafter Lockhart] (398 pages on free speech) *with id.* at 1027-1129 (103 pages on religious liberty); *compare* GEOFFREY R. STONE, LOUIS MICHAEL SEIDMAN, CASS R. SUNSTEIN & MARK V. TUSHNET, CONSTITUTIONAL LAW 925-1360 (1986) [hereinafter Stone] (436 pages on free speech) *with id.* at 1361-1426 (66 pages on religious liberty). The equal protection coverage in these three books is also lavish. Another leading casebook omits the Religion Clauses en-

this limited coverage goes to the Establishment Clause; the four leading books devote zero, seventeen, twenty-three and thirty-five pages to the Free Exercise Clause.[7] This scanty treatment is ameliorated only slightly by the appearance of Jehovah's Witnesses and other religious speakers in the four to five hundred pages that each book devotes to freedom of speech. Two of these books have slightly more coverage of free exercise than of the Takings and Contracts Clauses;[8] one has slightly less.[9] Could it be that these three clauses are in equal disrepute?

One reason for the neglect of religious liberty in the major constitutional law casebooks is sheer coverage pressure. The survey course in constitutional law has grown to impossible scope; not everything important can be covered. Yet this is only a partial explanation, because the necessity of choice does not explain the choices that are made. The same casebook editors who chose to cover every doctrinal nook and cranny of free speech, equal protection, and sexual privacy have chosen to survey religious liberty quickly and to treat disestablishment as the more important religious liberty problem.

The choice to neglect religious liberty is inexplicable. Twenty-five years ago it might have been said that few Supreme Court cases construed the Establishment Clause, and that fewer still construed free exercise. That is no longer true. The Court now hears several Religion Clause cases each Term,[10]

---

tirely, *see* PAUL BREST AND SANFORD LEVINSON, PROCESSES OF CONSTITUTIONAL DECISIONMAKING: CASES AND MATERIALS (2d ed. 1983), but Professor Levinson says they may correct that in the next edition.

The slightly greater attention to religious liberty in Lockhart, Kamisar, Choper & Shiffrin is a product of Dean Choper's interest and expertise in the field. *See, e.g.,* Jesse H. Choper, *Church, State and the Supreme Court: Current Controversy,* 29 ARIZ. L. REV. 551 (1987); Jesse H. Choper, *Defining "Religion" in the First Amendment,* 1982 U. ILL. L. REV. 579; Jesse H. Choper, *The Establishment Clause and Aid to Parochial Schools — An Update,* 75 CAL. L. REV. 5 (1987); Jesse H. Choper, *The Free Exercise Clause: A Structural Overview and an Appraisal of Recent Developments,* 27 WM. & MARY L. REV. 943 (1986); Jesse H. Choper, *The Religion Clauses of the First Amendment: Reconciling the Conflict,* 41 U. PITT. L. REV. 673 (1980).

7. *See supra* note 6; *infra* notes 8-9.

8. *Compare* GUNTHER, *supra* note 6, at 475-87 (takings) *and id.* at 487-501 (contracts) *with id.* at 1509-31 (free exercise); *compare* LOCKHART, *supra* note 6, at 404-19 (takings) *and id.* at 420-30 (contracts) *with id.* at 1095-118 (free exercise); *see also id.* at 1118-29 (integrating free exercise and establishment cases in the treatment of preference among religions).

9. *Compare* STONE, *supra* note 6, at 1445-65 (takings) *and id.* at 1427-45 (contracts) *with id.* at 1410-26 (free exercise).

10. *See, e.g.,* Employment Div. v. Smith, 485 U.S. 660 (1988) (unemployment benefits for drug counselor discharged for ingesting peyote at religious service at Native American church); Lyng v. Northwest Indian Cemetery Protective Ass'n, 485 U.S. 439 (1988) (land development on ground sacred to American Indians); U.S. Catholic Conf. v. Abortion Rights

and the country is in the midst of one of its periodic revivals of religious fervor.[11] Scholarly literature on religious liberty flourishes,[12] with important contributions by some of the major casebook editors.[13] Yet except for

Mobilization, Inc., 484 U.S. 975 (1988) (granting certiorari) (political speech by tax exempt churches); Karcher v. May, 484 U.S. 72 (1987) (moment of silence in public schools); Bowen v. Kendrick, 484 U.S. 942 (1987) (noting probable jurisdiction) (government grants to religious organizations to counsel teenagers on sexual behavior); Edwards v. Aguillard, 482 U.S. 578 (1987) (creation science in public schools); Corp. of the Presiding Bishop v. Amos, 483 U.S. 327 (1987) (religious discrimination in employment by religious organizations); Bd. of Airport Comm'rs v. Jews for Jesus, Inc., 482 U.S. 569 (1987) (religious proselytizing on public property); O'Lone v. Estate of Shabazz, 482 U.S. 342 (1987) (prisoners denied opportunity to attend religious services); Hobbie v. Unemployment Appeals Comm'n, 480 U.S. 136 (1987) (unemployment benefits for Sabbath observers); Ansonia Bd. of Educ. v. Philbrook, 479 U.S. 60 (1986) (employee's use of "personal business days" to attend religious services); Ohio Civil Rights Comm'n v. Dayton Christian Sch., Inc., 477 U.S. 619 (1986) (sex discrimination in employment by religious schools); Bowen v. Roy, 476 U.S. 693 (1986) (conscientious objection to social security number); Bender v. Williamsport Area Sch. Dist., 475 U.S. 534 (1986) (religious clubs in public schools); Goldman v. Weinberger, 475 U.S. 503 (1986) (military personnel forbidden to wear yarmulkes); Witters v. Wash. Dep't of Servs. for the Blind, 474 U.S. 481 (1986) (scholarship for the blind used to attend seminary); Aguilar v. Felton, 473 U.S. 402 (1985) (publicly funded remedial education for disadvantaged children in religious schools); Sch. Dist. v. Ball, 473 U.S. 373 (1985) (public school classes offered to students in religious schools); Estate of Thornton v. Caldor, Inc., 472 U.S. 703 (1985) (right of employees not to work on their Sabbath); Jensen v. Quaring, 472 U.S. 478 (1985) (per curiam) (conscientious objection to photograph on driver's license); Wallace v. Jaffree, 472 U.S. 38 (1985) (moment of silence in public schools); Tony & Susan Alamo Found. v. Sec'y of Labor, 471 U.S. 290 (1985) (regulation of wages and hours of employees of religious organization); Bd. of Trustees v. McCreary, 471 U.S. 83 (1985) (per curiam) (private display of creche on public property).

11. *See* A. James Reichley, Religion in American Public Life 243-339 (1985); Kenneth D. Wald, Religion and Politics in the United States 182-219 (1987).

12. *See, e.g.,* Robert Cord, Separation of Church and State: Historical Fact and Current Fiction (1982); Thomas J. Curry, The First Freedoms: Church and State in America to the Passage of the First Amendment (1986); Leonard W. Levy, The Establishment Clause (1986); William Miller, The First Liberty: Religion and the American Republic (1986); *Religion and the Law Symposium,* 18 Conn. L. Rev. 697 (1986); Special Issue, *Religion and the State,* 27 Wm. & Mary L. Rev. 833 (1986); Symposium, *The Tension Between the Free Exercise Clause and the Establishment Clause of the First Amendment,* 47 Ohio St. L.J. 288 (1986); *Developments in the Law — Religion and the State,* 100 Harv. L. Rev. 1606 (1987).

13. For example, see the articles by Dean Choper cited in note 6 above; Geoffrey R. Stone, *The Equal Access Controversy: The Religion Clauses and the Meaning of "Neutrality,"* 81 Nw. U.L. Rev. 168 (1986); Geoffrey R. Stone, *Constitutionally Compelled Exemptions and the Free Exercise Clause,* 27 Wm. & Mary L. Rev. 985 (1986); Mark V. Tushnet, *The Constitution of Religion,* 18 Conn. L. Rev. 701 (1986); Mark V. Tushnet, *The Origins of the Establishment*

Schauer's supplement to Gunther,[14] these editors have not expanded the coverage in their casebooks.

Noonan's book may fill this void, at least for a while. It offers reasonably comprehensive coverage for those law schools that can afford a separate course in religious liberty. For other law schools, chapters 11 to 15 cover the modern cases under the Religion Clauses in two hundred thirty pages. These chapters would support a manageable unit in a survey course, but only for instructors willing to require their students to buy an extra book. A paperback edition would make that easier.

However, the book will continue to serve these purposes only if it is supplemented in the same way as conventional casebooks from the major casebook publishers. It remains to be seen whether Noonan, Macmillan, Princeton, and the Lilly Endowment will publish annual supplements. If they do not, the book will soon become a collection of historical documents, useful to scholars and occasionally to judges and practitioners, but inadequate in the classroom.

II.

Noonan's introduction quotes Justice Holmes: "A page of history is worth a volume of logic." (p. xiii). After noting that law schools give only lip service to this epigram, Noonan takes it seriously. He devotes nearly half the book to history, starting with the Ten Commandments (p. 3) and continuing chronologically to *United States v. McIntosh*[15] in 1931 (p. 229). The first Supreme Court opinion appears on page 184.[16] The second half of the book, on "Contemporary Controversies," is organized more doctrinally. Noonan integrates questions of free exercise and establishment, and he gives them equal attention.

The historical section contains wonderful material. There are accounts of important martyrs: Thomas à Becket (pp. 22-27), Joan of Arc (pp. 45-51), Thomas More (pp. 51-56), and Hugh Latimer (pp. 57-60).[17] Excerpts from

---

Clause, 75 GEO. L.J. 1509 (1987); Mark V. Tushnet, *Reflections on the Role of Purpose in the Jurisprudence of the Religion Clauses,* 27 WM. & MARY L. REV. 997 (1986); Mark V. Tushnet, *Religion and Theories of Constitutional Interpretation,* 33 LOY. L. REV. 221 (1987).

14. *See* GERALD GUNTHER & FREDERICK SCHAUER, INDIVIDUAL RIGHTS IN CONSTITUTIONAL LAW 220-60 (Supp. 1987) (41 pages on religious liberty).

15. 283 U.S. 605 (1931).

16. This opinion is *Watson v. Jones,* 80 U.S. (13 Wall.) 679 (1871).

17. Latimer, a prominent Protestant victim of Bloody Mary, is less well known today, perhaps because no one wrote a play about him. *Cf.* JEAN ANOUILH, THE LARK (1953) (Joan

Augustine (pp. 11-20), Thomas Aquinas (pp. 36-45), Roger Williams (pp. 65-71), Spinoza (pp. 71-75), John Locke (pp. 76-90), James Madison (pp. 93-97, 106-12), Pope Pius IX (p. 192), and many others trace the slow progress toward religious tolerance in Western thought. Saint Augustine advises a Roman governor to deal gently with heretics, "not by stretching on the rack, not by tearing on hooks, not by burning in fire, but by the blows of rods. This form of coercion is used by teachers of the liberal arts. . . ." (p. 13). Obviously, the liberal arts have changed along with religious liberty.

There is an excellent chapter on the key role of the churches in the abolition movement (pp. 168-93). This chapter includes a Senate speech by Stephen A. Douglas denouncing ministers who preached sermons against his bill to permit slavery in Kansas and Nebraska.[18] Douglas expressed a pernicious view that is still widespread: that churches should attend to the saving of souls and confine their moral teachings to the private sector:

> I say, sir, that the purity of the Christian church, the purity of our holy religion, and the preservation of our free institutions, require that Church and State shall be separated; that the preacher on the Sabbath day shall find his text in the Bible; shall preach "Jesus Christ and him crucified," shall preach from the Holy Scriptures, and not attempt to control the political organizations and political parties of the day (p. 175).[19]

Noonan provides similar material on the central role of the black churches in the civil rights movement of the 1950s and 1960s (pp. 449-53). Today, Douglas and his slaveholding allies, or Bull Connor and his segregationists, might sue the meddling churches to revoke their tax exemptions.[20]

---

of Arc); ROBERT BOLT, A MAN FOR ALL SEASONS (1960) (More); T. S. ELIOT, MURDER IN THE CATHEDRAL (1935) (Becket); GEORGE BERNARD SHAW, ST. JOAN (1924).

18. The bill authorized the creation of slave states in territories north of the Missouri Compromise line at the option of voters in each newly organized state (p. 174). It passed. *See* An Act to Organize the Territories of Nebraska and Kansas, ch. 59, §§ 1, 14, 19, 32, 10 Stat. 277, 277, 283, 284, 289 (1854).

19. CONG. GLOBE, 33d Cong., 1st Sess. 656 (1854).

20. *Cf.* Abortion Rights Mobilization, Inc. v. Regan, 544 F. Supp. 471 (S.D.N.Y. 1982) (holding that pro-choice activists have standing to challenge tax exemption of the Catholic Church on ground that it has lobbied to restrict abortion). On an appeal from a collateral order, this decision was said to be at least "colorable." In re U.S. Catholic Conf., 824 F.2d 156, 166 (2d Cir.), *cert. granted as* U.S. Catholic Conf. v. Abortion Rights Mobilization, Inc., 484 U.S. 975 (1987). [The Supreme Court reversed, holding that the Catholic Conference could refuse to produce requested documents until the standing issue was resolved. The court of appeals ultimately held that the pro-choice group did not have standing to challenge the church's tax exemption. In re U.S. Catholic Conf., 885 F.2d 1020 (2d Cir. 1989).]

Noonan's sections on abolitionists and the civil rights movement should be required reading for every liberal who has ever grumbled about right-to-lifers or conservative preachers, and for every conservative who has ever grumbled about religious lobbying for peace, disarmament, social justice, or refugees. But lest religiously motivated political activists feel self-congratulatory over abolition and civil rights, they should be required to meditate on the churches' role in Prohibition (pp. 218-19).

Noonan's notes, excerpts, and historical materials are useful even to readers generally familiar with the history he chronicles. I repeatedly marked passages for future reference as I read. His historical materials should be even more valuable to students and other newcomers to the field. The stories he tells should be a part of our culture, but they are not. Our students know distressingly little history of any kind.[21] Most know even less of religious history, because the role of religion in America has been largely excluded from public school curricula.[22] Religious liberty controversies from the past often illuminate religious liberty controversies today. For example, Noonan's discussions of abolition and civil rights illustrate the historic role of churches in politics far more effectively than a conclusory classroom statement that the churches were active in most of America's major movements for social reform. Thus Noonan offers a much needed historical perspective on contemporary debates over religious liberty.

III.

Despite their obvious value, I fear that Noonan's historical materials are crippled by his adherence to the casebook format. He presents history through cases whenever possible, and through other original documents when there are no cases. Whatever is extant is what we get: for example, Douglas' speech in the Senate (p. 175), depositions from witnesses to the trial of Joan of Arc

---

21. For studies of history instruction in American schools, and of the resulting ignorance of American youth, see E. D. Hirsch, Jr., Cultural Literacy 1-26 (1987), and Diane Ravitch & Chester Finn, What Do Our 17-Year-Olds Know? (1987). Law students are an educated elite, who surely know more than young people generally, but need to know much more. Law students have not been systematically studied, but most of them have passed through the deficient educational system that Hirsch describes.

22. *See* Association for Supervision and Curriculum Development, Religion in the Curriculum (1987); O. L. Davis, *et al.*, Looking at History: A Review of Major U.S. History Textbooks 3-4, 11 (1986); Paul C. Vitz, Censorship: Evidence of Bias in Our Children's Textbooks (1986).

(pp. 46-51), Thomas More's last letter to his daughter (pp. 54-56), and an eye-witness account of the murder of Becket (pp. 26-27).

These original documents have many of the same advantages and disadvantages as cases. On the positive side, they focus our attention on specific controversies and demand that we evaluate arguments in the context of facts. Often, they vividly capture the human actors and their emotions. On the negative side, they present information in tiny bits, asking us to induce the nature of a vast forest from a small selection of individual trees. And they are sometimes written in stilted pre-modern prose that deters readers and minimizes impact.

Original documents also have disadvantages that are usually not present in modern cases. An appellate opinion tends to focus on the heart of the controversy. Teachers and scholars worry that opinions omit facts and that events in the real world were more complex than events in the opinion, but the facts that remain are likely to be central. Letters and contemporary accounts have not been through any similar process of distillation. The contemporary observer may have seen only one slice of the dispute. What she wrote, or what survives, may be peripheral. The account of Becket's martyrdom is moving, but it tells little about the underlying dispute between the bishop and the king. Moreover, the contemporary observer, writing for an audience that had its own view of the dispute, may have left out what her readers already knew. Without the common background that the writer assumed of her readers, the contemporary account may be barely comprehensible.

Noonan's notes on these excerpts provide some background, but often not enough. His notes amount to about a quarter of the book, and that ratio appears to be the same in both the historical and doctrinal sections. Unfamiliar terms and puzzling facts are often left unexplained. For example, Augustine's letters are set in the context of the Donatist heresy (pp. 12-20). Noonan apparently assumes that all readers are familiar with Donatism. Few students will know what Donatism was; indeed, two of my colleagues with classical Catholic educations could not remember.[23] We are similarly left to wonder why theologians from Paris testified for the English against Joan of Arc (p. 46).[24] What did it mean and why did it matter that Joan's body was

---

23. The Donatists taught that the efficacy of the sacraments depends on the sanctity of the priest who performs them. *See* WILLISTON WALKER, RICHARD A. NORRIS, DAVID W. LOTZ, & ROBERT T. HANDY, A HISTORY OF THE CHRISTIAN CHURCH 201-03 (4th ed. 1985). *See generally* G. WILLIS, SAINT AUGUSTINE AND THE DONATIST CONTROVERSY (1950).

24. The English occupied Paris for years, and the city's elite collaborated. *See* DESMOND SEWARD, THE HUNDRED YEARS WAR 193, 195, 219 (1978). Joan's attempt to recapture Paris failed, and she was captured the following spring. *See id.* at 219.

"whole and uncorrupted" (pp. 47, 51)? Did this refer to virginity, menstruation, deformity, or gangrene?[25]

Such minor puzzles are only petty annoyances; perhaps Noonan thought the missing information irrelevant. More fundamentally, Noonan often fails to give us information essential to understanding historic controversies and their relation to modern issues. This immensely learned man could have told us so much more if he had used his own words and not been a slave to the casebook fashion of excerpts from original documents. For example, we get five pages of repetitive depositions from the royal inquiry into the trial of Joan of Arc. If we believe these witnesses, they leave little doubt that Joan was manipulated to her death. Yet that point could be made in a fraction of the space, and I doubt that class discussion could effectively elaborate. Nor do these excerpts teach much about the procedural law of the Inquisition. Noonan uses five pages just to achieve the sense of authenticity associated with original documents. Having made that choice, he inexplicably omits the final interrogation of Joan.[26]

25. Virginity is the obvious first guess, and it turns out to be correct, but that answer proved remarkably difficult to confirm. Final confirmation came from Professor William Kibler, a distinguished scholar of medieval French literature, who examined these depositions in the original Middle French. The passages appear in 2 JULES QUICHERAT, PROCÈS DE CONDAMNATION ET DE RÉHABILITATION DE JEANNE D'ARC DITE LA PUCELLE 3, 21 (1844). Noonan might reasonably have decided that such an inquiry was more trouble than it was worth.

Witnesses had many reasons to be interested in Joan's virginity. She always referred to herself as *la Pucelle* — the Virgin. *See* JOHN H. SMITH, JOAN OF ARC 9 (1973); MARINA WARNER, JOAN OF ARC: THE IMAGE OF FEMALE HEROISM 22 (1981). Virginity was viewed as a great virtue, and virtue was relevant to the ultimate issue: was Joan an agent of God or of the devil? In addition, there was a folk belief that the devil could not make a pact with a virgin, *see* JULES MICHELET, JOAN OF ARC 107 (Albert Guerard trans. 1957); WARNER, *supra*, at 15, and there were vague reports of prophecies that a virgin would save France, *id.* at 24-27. Finally, when these depositions were offered, twenty years after Joan's death, some witnesses may have already been making a record for canonization.

26. Noonan's choice of excerpts emphasizes the evidence of manipulation and omits the evidence of Joan's courage. Her life was initially spared when she recanted her heresies, including her claim to hear the voices of saints, and renounced the men's clothing that her voices told her to wear. Her resumption of men's clothing led to renewed interrogation and to her condemnation as a relapsed heretic. Noonan quotes those witnesses who say that Joan's English jailers forced her to wear men's clothing or none at all. Yet she testified, after some equivocation, that she wore men's clothing "of her own will," that "God had sent her," that "her voices had told her that she had done great wrong to God" by recanting, and that she had recanted "only through fear of the fire." WALTER S. SCOTT, THE TRIAL OF JOAN OF ARC 169-70 (1956) (English translation of official proceedings).

Contrast this use of space with the following tantalizing passage in Noonan's notes on Bishop Cauchon, who presided over Joan's trial:

> He was a political bishop, who knew who his masters were. Defenders still assert that he was no worse than others of his time. The defense is an indictment of the institutional arrangements that put such men in the dress of pastors (p. 46).

What were those institutional arrangements? Readers can infer that the state had a role in the selection of bishops, and that the church paid a high price for being established. Readers with even a vague recollection of medieval history would know that much anyway, and these three sentences are mainly useful for invoking that recollection. Students without such a recollection will learn little from this passage. Yet Noonan appears to know much more. He appears to report in conclusory terms his informed assessment of the late medieval church and its relation to the state.

A five-page essay would have been much more useful than the five pages of depositions. Such an essay could have described the institutional arrangements Noonan condemns, illustrated their effects with Joan's trial and additional examples, and reported his assessment of the period and perhaps contrasting assessments by others. Such an essay could have provided a basis for classroom discussion and debate. How much can the state support the church before the church begins to pay a price? Do any of today's governmental supports for religion raise in attenuated form any of the dangers illustrated by the arrangements of the fifteenth century?

The difficulty of understanding historical disputes from excerpts of original documents can be illustrated with many other examples. Becket fought Henry II over suits against clergy in secular courts (p. 22).[27] That dispute has parallels in contemporary litigation over secular resolution of internal church disputes.[28] Yet the exposition of the dispute in Noonan's notes and in two letters from one of Becket's supporters is probably insufficient to support classroom analysis of Becket's dispute, let alone its parallels to modern disputes.

Another example is Noonan's treatment of the early Massachusetts deci-

---

27. For a detailed account, see HAROLD BERMAN, LAW AND REVOLUTION: THE FORMATION OF THE WESTERN LEGAL TRADITION 255-69 (1983).

28. *See, e.g.,* Jones v. Wolf, 443 U.S. 595 (1979); Crowder v. S. Baptist Convention, 828 F.2d 718 (11th Cir. 1987); Rayburn v. Gen'l Conf. of Seventh-day Adventists, 772 F.2d 1164 (4th Cir. 1985); Douglas Laycock & Susan E. Waelbroeck, *Academic Freedom and the Free Exercise of Religion,* 66 TEX. L. REV. 1455 (1988).

sions that enabled the Unitarians to take over many of the Trinitarian Congregationalist churches, and led the Congregationalists to abandon their Massachusetts establishment (pp. 140-60). These cases are closer to our own time, and they take the familiar form of appellate opinions, but they are only slightly more comprehensible. To understand these cases, students need a description of the religious demography of Massachusetts at the time, of the routine workings of the Massachusetts establishment, and of the vocabulary of the cases. These cases turned on a distinction between the parish and the church; those terms are italicized (p. 154) but not defined. A student who does not know that the parish was a geographic unit of local government will be lost. The cases assume the background facts, and Noonan's notes are skimpy. Although most students will learn what happened, I am not confident that they will understand how it happened.[29] Nor will all of them know how fundamental was the disagreement between Unitarians and Trinitarians;[30] Noonan does not explain that either.

Noonan's history also has some omissions that are too striking to be the result of oversight. Perhaps the commitment to cases and documents combined with a page limit forced the omission of other important events. Whatever the reason, there is no mention of the Thirty Years War, a general war in

29. The Unitarian takeover reveals an exquisite irony at the heart of the Massachusetts effort to combine an established church with religious liberty. Massachusetts had local option establishment; the majority in each parish could elect the minister to be supported by local taxes. *See generally* CURRY, *supra* note 12, at 163-77; LEVY, *supra* note 12, at 26-38; Douglas Laycock, *"Nonpreferential" Aid to Religion: A False Claim About Original Intent*, 27 WM. & MARY L. REV. 875, 900-01 (1986) (text at notes 136-41). Dissenters had their own churches, and, in theory and sometimes in practice, dissenters could file an exemption certificate and pay taxes to their own minister instead of to the established church. The established church then consisted of those who adhered to the minister who had been elected.

As long as religious affiliations were stable, the Trinitarian Congregationalist majority was established in nearly every parish. The Congregationalists naturally thought of the established church as *their* church. But it was theirs only so long as they could win elections. When the ministry fell open in an established Congregational church, the church could not replace its own minister. Rather, the minister established by law was a public official, elected by the general electorate of the parish. The newly elected minister took over the church building owned by the parish and used by the winners of the previous election. When the Unitarians began to win elections in the early nineteenth century, they took over more than a quarter of the Trinitarian Congregationalist churches (p. 159). The Trinitarians were forced to repeal their own establishment to gain control of their churches (pp. 159-60).

30. As the name implies, Unitarians denied the Trinity, and thus denied the divinity of Christ. *See* AN AMERICAN REFORMATION: A DOCUMENTARY HISTORY OF UNITARIAN CHRISTIANITY 6 (Sydney E. Ahlstrom & Jonathan S. Carey eds., 1985); LEVY, *supra* note 12, at 34.

Europe between Protestant and Catholic states.[31] There is no mention of the English civil war, a war that was as much about religion as about the rights of Parliament.[32] There are only passing references to Christian persecution of Jews (pp. 21, 37, 376). Equally striking, there are only two paragraphs on Catholic objections to religious instruction and the Protestant Bible in nineteenth century public schools in the United States (p. 410-11), and no mention of the mob violence and church burnings engendered by that dispute.[33] That controversy casts critical light on the modern school prayer cases,[34] on the growth of Catholic schools, and on modern disputes over public aid to those schools;[35] it is surely more relevant to modern American law than most of Noonan's European examples.

For the same reason, I would like to see some treatment of contemporary religious hatred, as in Lebanon, Iran, or Northern Ireland, and more treatment of contemporary establishment, as in Israel, the Islamic countries, England, or West Germany.[36] Once one decides to include substantial materials other than cases, useful examples from any time and place will serve the purpose. Modern examples might teach more than examples from ancient Rome and medieval Europe. Northern Ireland shows that religious civil war can arise in a modern democratic society. Israel, England, and West Germany show that established churches survive in modern democratic societies that respect a wide range of civil liberties. Their experience can help students test the claim that even gentle establishments harm both dominant and minority faiths.

IV.

I have touched on several disparate points: the general neglect of history in the law schools; the neglect of religious liberty in constitutional law case-

---

31. *See generally* Georges Pagaés, The Thirty Years War 1618-1648 (1970); The Thirty Years' War (Geoffrey Parker ed. 1984).

32. *See generally* Will Durant & Ariel Durant, The Age of Reason Begins 184-221 (1961).

33. *See* 1 Anson Phelps Stokes, Church and State in the United States 830-35 (1950).

34. *See, e.g.,* Wallace v. Jaffree, 472 U.S. 38 (1985); Sch. Dist. v. Schempp, 374 U.S. 203 (1963); Engel v. Vitale, 370 U.S. 421 (1962).

35. *See, e.g.,* Aguilar v. Felton, 473 U.S. 402 (1985); Sch. Dist. v. Ball, 473 U.S. 373 (1985); Mueller v. Allen, 463 U.S. 388 (1983); Lemon v. Kurtzman, 403 U.S. 602 (1971).

36. Noonan does offer a useful note comparing church-state relations in England to those in the United States (pp. 441-42).

books; Noonan's reliance on excerpts from original documents; the sketchiness of his notes; and his omission of examples that seem as important as any he includes. I believe these points are connected.

The law school commitment to the case method surely contributes to each of these phenomena. Noonan's documents introduce history into a casebook with minimal deviation from casebook format, and the other problems on my list are natural responses to the intense coverage pressure induced by that format. Coverage pressure does not explain why editors neglect religious liberty instead of free speech, or why Noonan covers martyrs and omits religious wars. But the casebook format requires all editors, including Noonan, to omit much that is important.

The law curriculum was expanded to three years of case-method instruction at Harvard in 1899.[37] Law school still lasts three years, and instruction is still principally by the case method. The amount of instructional time has not changed, but the quantity and complexity of law have multiplied manyfold. Equally important, we have abandoned the 1899 conception of law as a self-contained system; we bring an ever-expanding array of other disciplines to bear on legal problems. Insoluble coverage problems are inevitable.

The case method greatly aggravates these problems, and not merely through its inefficiency at conveying information. The tradition is that law students read only a few pages each day, and that substantially everything they read must be discussed in class. This is true at Texas, it was true at Chicago when I taught there, and anecdotal evidence suggests it is true at other law schools, both elite and non-elite. I doubt there is any other discipline in the humanities or the social sciences — any other discipline that works with words — where graduate students read as few pages as law students read.

Expectations about reading assignments are formed in the first year, when the emphasis is properly on skills and students really cannot read more than a few pages a day.[38] In the second and third year, when reading and analyzing cases are familiar skills, the pace increases only slightly. Class discussion cannot seriously explore more than one or two principal cases per day without losing the advantages of the case method, and the expectation that all assigned cases will be discussed holds reading assignments to the same pace.

The result is that casebook editors and classroom teachers are forced to desperate choices. They can teach some of the field well by neglecting all the

---

37. *See* ROBERT B. STEVENS, LAW SCHOOL: LEGAL EDUCATION IN AMERICA FROM THE 1850S TO THE 1980S, at 37 (1983).

38. Expanded coverage in constitutional law may be impossible when the course is taught in the first year. I teach constitutional law in the second year, which affects my perspective.

rest, or they can superficially survey a more substantial part of the field. Law teachers tend toward the first choice, with the result that, for many students, constitutional law consists of judicial review, the commerce clause, equal protection, free speech, and sexual privacy. The list varies from teacher to teacher, but few pretend to cover everything important. The Free Exercise Clause can be reduced to seventeen casebook pages without producing any significant market pressure for more adequate treatment.[39]

With so much substantive law excluded from the course, we should hardly be surprised that history gets only scant attention. Other disciplines also appear in the classroom only interstitially and superficially, except that a few devotees omit even more law to make way for their favorite other discipline. Noonan has room to take history seriously because his book is so specialized, but he does not have room for all the major historical events that directly bear on his topic.

Casebook editors have found ways to pack more information into the casebook format. Casebooks have evolved from bare anthologies of cases[40] to the familiar "Cases, Materials, and Notes" in which there may be as much original text as there are excerpts. Editors select opinions in part for their exposition of large chunks of law — exposition that goes well beyond the inductive theory of case-method instruction. These developments make the casebook format less inefficient and more tolerable, but at the cost of substantially diluting its original advantages. Especially in the second and third years, we may be moving toward a hybrid mode of instruction in which cases are read for their expository text and superficially discussed in a half-hearted imitation of the case method.

Noonan appears to have resisted this trend, letting his cases and documents speak for themselves and minimizing his own explanations. Perhaps he minimized his own notes so he could squeeze in more original documents. Whatever the reasons, much of his historical material requires more supporting text than he provides.

V.

If I am even approximately correct in my assessment of the modern casebook, it is time to rethink the format. A combination of text and case method

39. *See supra* at 1643 (text at note 7).
40. *See* E. Allen Farnsworth, *Contracts Scholarship in the Age of the Anthology*, 85 Mich. L. Rev. 1406 (1987).

has much to recommend it, but the two methods should be kept separate. They should not be mixed into a mongrel form that fails to capture the advantages of either.

It ought to be possible to select certain parts of the course for full-dress, case-method treatment, and to teach other parts of the course from a treatise or hornbook. Similarly, if history, political theory, economics, literary criticism, or Mayan glyphs are important to a course, we need not be limited to the information we can tuck into notes on the cases. We ought to assign serious readings. Noonan's extensive attention to history is a valuable step in that direction. But to get such material into the general curriculum will probably require the efficiencies of expository text.

Perhaps a new generation of teaching materials could combine cases and expository text in a single volume in a way that preserves the separate advantages of each. Such a book might give full case-method treatment to the most important or interesting legal issues, summarize large bodies of surrounding doctrine in expository text, and include substantial excerpts from books or articles in related disciplines. Casebooks generally offer some 1200 pages of cases and notes, but most faculty can teach no more than half of that in a semester, leaving casebook editors to lament that they have "some really great stuff" in the back of the book that no one ever teaches. Maybe it would make more sense to include only 500 pages of the best material in cases and notes, and devote the rest of the book to expository text on law and related disciplines. Such a book might cover more of the subject matter in greater depth, and teachers could cover more of the book.

Such changes in the quality and quantity of reading assignments would require changes in classroom technique. It is hard to imagine a case-method discussion of a hornbook chapter. Yet it is easy to imagine a lecture that complements the chapter, or a problem that requires students to apply the chapter to hypothetical facts that expose the tensions and ambiguities in hornbook doctrine.[41] Classroom discussion of such problems might combine the expository efficiencies of hornbooks with the traditional advantages of case analysis — the emphasis on analytic skills and on the real world's stubborn refusal to fit into neat doctrinal categories.

Many teachers believe that law students will not take seriously any reading other than a case or perhaps a doctrinal summary of a case. Yet that is surely the faculty's fault. If we want students to take history seriously, we must take it seriously ourselves. If we say that history is relevant to an under-

---

41. Professor Thomas Haggard of the University of South Carolina has successfully taught labor law this way. I owe the idea to him.

standing of contemporary disputes, we must visibly bring it to bear on those disputes.

Most important, we must include it in the final examination. We can assign a whole library of interdisciplinary reading, but if the examination consists of hypothetical cases requiring issue spotting and doctrinal analysis, students have every reason to study only doctrine. The grading and examination system creates an incentive structure, and we can hardly complain if students respond to it. Students are right to believe that what is important is what is on the exam. But the faculty can change what is on the exam.

Forced to choose within the extraordinary constraints imposed by the case method, most of us decide that doctrine and traditional legal analysis are the most important things we teach. We may talk a different game, but our assignment sheets and our exams reveal our choices. Within the constraints of the case method, doctrine is the right choice. I would not want to be represented by a lawyer who knows no law, however broadly educated in the liberal arts or public policy analysis. If we can teach only a little bit, we should teach the core skills and information of the profession. Yet we need not be satisfied with teaching only a little bit. If we break out of the constraints imposed by the case method, our students can surely read more and learn more.

VI.

I have digressed a long way from Noonan's book on religious liberty, and have surely committed the sin of complaining that he did not write a different book. My reflections grow from personal doubt and dissatisfaction with my own teaching and with the constraints of traditional law school pedagogy. While others doubt the need for the third year of law school,[42] I increasingly think that we teach only a tiny fraction of what lawyers need to know.

Yet these reflections are also directly stimulated by Noonan's book. I had few of these insights when I wrote my own casebook in another field.[43] Noonan's use of unconventional materials in a decidedly conventional format has been the catalyst for new insights about the format. The successes

42. *See, e.g.,* HERBERT L. PACKER & THOMAS EHRLICH, NEW DIRECTIONS IN LEGAL EDUCATION 77-85 (1972).

43. *See* DOUGLAS LAYCOCK, MODERN AMERICAN REMEDIES: CASES AND MATERIALS (1985).

and failures of his effort to deal seriously with history have altered my understanding of the problems of law school teaching and renewed my hopes. He deserves full credit for the successes; his book makes it possible to introduce both religious liberty and serious history into the curriculum. The failures may be largely inherent in the genre.

Further progress requires us to question the case method and its traditions, to identify what the case method does well, and to develop other methods for tasks at which it fails. Such methods must evolve through trial and error; I have no clear conception of a new format or how to handle such a format in the classroom. But thanks to Judge Noonan, I have some ideas for further experimentation.

Book Note

Reviewing Mark V. Tushnet's *Red, White, and Blue: A Critical Analysis of Constitutional Law*

31 Journal of Church and State 303 (1989)

"Critical" as a genre of legal scholarship, especially in the 1980s, referred to a movement that called itself Critical Legal Studies. This CLS, not to be confused with the Christian Legal Society, cannot be readily summarized in a paragraph. In general, CLS scholars saw law as a highly malleable exercise of political power. Drawing on European theories of deconstructing texts, CLS scholars tended to believe that judges interpret the law to mean what they (the judges) want it to mean, and that what they want it to mean will generally protect entrenched interests, but that of course the law could be interpreted to protect the disadvantaged instead.

This short review reacts to the book as a whole and to the chapter on religious liberty in particular.

*　　　*　　　*

Mark Tushnet is the leading constitutional scholar of the Critical Legal Studies movement, and *Red, White, and Blue* extends and integrates his work on constitutional theory. Much of his analysis is worth reading, including his chapter on church and state, but his larger claims are wildly implausible.

Tushnet's integrating theme is the liberal and republican traditions in American constitutionalism. Liberalism emphasizes individualism and self-interest; republicanism, which Tushnet believes has been forgotten, emphasizes community and the public interest. Both traditions were important to the framers, but they had few illusions about selfless individuals.

Tushnet argues that liberalism's emphasis on self-interest makes constitutional theory both necessary and impossible. It is necessary because those who govern cannot be trusted, but impossible because those who police the governors cannot be trusted either. Separation of powers, constitutional rights, and judicial review protect us from self-interested abuse by government officials and from majoritarian tyranny. But if judges have the last word, what will protect us from judicial tyranny?

Tushnet offers two answers. In the long run, the majority will appoint new judges and do whatever it wants. In the short run, life tenured judges can do whatever they want, and no theory of constitutional interpretation will restrain them. Tushnet finds every interpretive theory capable of justifying any result a judge wants to reach. He believes that the Constitution may be interpreted to require laissez faire, socialism, or anything in between.

He sees a return to republicanism as the only hope. But Tushnet's version of republicanism is far removed from American constitutional tradition. For Tushnet, republicanism requires universal employment with tenure and a substantially equal distribution of wealth. In that happy state, one would discuss issues face to face and work things out; no constitutional theory would be needed.

Whatever the merits of these positions, he should not expect us to believe they derive from the framers. Tushnet's only link to the framers is that some framers believed that economic independence is pre-requisite to political participation. Their solution was a limited franchise; Tushnet's is massive redistribution of wealth. The two proposals do not have much in common.

Tushnet's claims of radical indeterminacy are surely related to his radical politics. He believes that private property is a bad thing; without that, it is hard to see how he could convince himself that the Constitution might require socialism. Apart from the Constitution's express protections of private property, the Constitution exists within a culture, with political and economic traditions that limit the range of plausible interpretations. If you reject major elements of those traditions, other interpretations may also seem plausible. If enough Americans come to share Tushnet's politics, judges may read the Constitution his way. He is surely right that no constitutional theory will stop a large and determined majority.

But constitutional theory moderates less determined assaults on our liberties. To shift to religious persecution examples, the Constitution did little for Mormons in the nineteenth century, but much more for Jehovah's Witnesses in the twentieth. The experience of contemporary "cults" is somewhere in between.

Constitutional theory itself influences American values and reduces the risk of a sharp turn away from the values we have constitutionalized. Surely the Religion Clauses have contributed to an unmatched degree of religious liberty and pluralism in the United States. American understanding of the Religion Clauses, however, is not the wholly passive product of an independently achieved preference for tolerance. Yet that is the implication of Tushnet's claims that Americans can make the Constitution mean anything they want it to mean.

Tushnet's chapter on church and state sees in the Supreme Court's cases a tendency to reduce claims of religious liberty to claims of free speech, denying their distinctive religious element, and a tendency to protect religious liberty only to the point where it begins to have real social consequences. He attributes these tendencies to the liberal tradition, which he thinks is incapable of understanding either the nonrational or the communal aspects of religion. This is one way to read the cases, and he makes a serious case for it. But his only solution is a vague call to revitalize republicanism, so that Americans will all be more communal. Then conflicts can be resolved informally instead of legally.

Tushnet has devoted enormous energy and intellect to showing that constitutionalism is impossible in theory. Readers who find his vision of universal virtue and cooperation impossible will prefer to explore how constitutionalism might struggle along in practice.

Book Note

Reviewing Jesse H. Choper's *Securing Religious Liberty: Principles for Judicial Interpretation of the Religion Clauses*

44 Political Studies 1015 (1996)

Jesse Choper was a major scholar of religious liberty and served for ten years as Dean of the Law School at the University of California at Berkeley. The theme of this very short review is whether courts should balance interests or make firm rules for defined categories of cases.

*   *   *

This culmination of a major scholar's work offers four idiosyncratic principles of religious liberty, proposing little protection for religious minorities. Choper believes that judges should not assess questions of degree. The result is a persistent insensitivity to the relative weight of interests and the concentration of costs and benefits. In Choper's view: believers who fear "extra-temporal consequences" if they obey a law should sometimes be exempted, but only if the exemption requires no government money. Thus, he accepts fear of eternal damnation as the reason for exemptions, but subordinates that fear to each taxpayer's tiny share of any cost. Exempting conscientious objectors from military service establishes religion, because it might influence belief, but jailing these objectors does not violate the free exercise of religion (although that too influences belief). Money spent on regulatory exemptions establishes religion, but full funding of religious schools does not, because the government gets secular value from schools. A statutory Book of Common Prayer would not establish religion if no one were coerced and no money were spent. In my view, the book illustrates the inadequacy of formal categories. Whatever the difficulties of balancing interests, we cannot do good constitutional law without making the attempt.

D. Judicial Nominations

This Section contains several short pieces on the judicial nomination process and on the nominations of Robert Bork in 1987 and Michael McConnell in 2002. Nothing here is a full scholarly treatment, but if I were to write a full scholarly treatment of the confirmation process, it would elaborate what I say here.

Religious liberty issues — especially Establishment Clause issues — played a prominent role in the debate over the McConnell nomination. Religious liberty as such played little role in the Bork nomination, and he would surely have been hostile to free exercise claims, but his nomination was perceived as important to religious conservatives. More generally, the Establishment Clause has been one of the issues that persistently divides Presidents and Senators of opposite parties in judicial confirmation battles.

Some of the items included here were written for the press, some for the Senate; one is a short book review in a scholarly journal. Some address the debate over the Senate's role in the confirmation process; others address the particular nominees. The two levels of analysis are related; public attention on the particular disputed nominations made it possible to publish popular columns on the confirmation process. I opposed Bork, and supported McConnell, in part because I believe there are real differences between them, and in part because, in my view of the nomination process, the President and the Senate should each get part of what they want.

On the Process

Philosophy Is Enough To Deny Senate Consent (1987) is a co-authored op-ed column in *USA Today,* defending the Senate's right to consider Bork's understanding of the Constitution.

Forging Ideological Compromise (2002) is an op-ed in the New York *Times,* explaining the separate roles and equal responsibility of the President and the Senate in the nomination and confirmation process.

Judicial Nominations in a Divided Government (2002) is a similar op-ed for the Austin *American-Statesman.*

Injudicious is a justification for why many liberal and centrist law professors, including me, supported the McConnell nomination. So, much of it is about McConnell, but the justification is set in the context of a larger view about the process.

On the Nominees

Letter to Joseph R. Biden and Strom Thurmond (1987) is a co-authored letter, signed by 24 law professors, laying out the case against the Bork nomination in terms that sought to avoid exaggeration.

Book Review (1991) is a review of the book Bork wrote after the Senate rejected his nomination. In my view, the book more than confirmed the Senate's judgment.

Letter to Senator Patrick Leahy (2001) is a private letter supporting the McConnell nomination.

Letter to Senator Orrin G. Hatch (2002) is a public, group letter supporting the McConnell nomination. I did not write it, but I signed it, which, in my practice with respect to group letters, signifies full agreement with everything it says.

Some of the False Attacks on Michael McConnell (2002) compares quotations attacking McConnell with quotations from his writings showing what he actually said about various issues. I wrote it as a circular to be distributed in the Senate, but it was also published in the record of the confirmation hearing.

Injudicious is hard to classify; it is as much about McConnell as about the process.

Philosophy Is Enough to Deny Senate Consent

USA Today 10A (Sept. 15, 1987)

With Sanford Levinson

The nomination of Robert Bork to the Supreme Court of the United States pro-voked debates over what Bork believed and over the role of the Senate in judicial confirmations. This op-ed column addresses the latter issue. My recollection is that this was invited; USA Today *was editorializing for the position that the nominee's understanding of the Constitution was none of the Senate's business.*

*   *   *

Austin, Texas — The Senate will soon vote on Robert Bork's nomination to the Supreme Court.

The Constitution places on all senators the duty to give or withhold consent to judicial nominations.

They can legitimately withhold consent, as they have throughout our history, if they believe that the nominee is unsuitable for the office.

As members of an independent branch, judges do not work for the President any more than they work for the Senate. Neither can claim the superior role in selecting judges.

The Senate can require that a nominee's general understanding of the Constitution and the role of the judiciary be consistent with the Senate's general understanding. If a nominee's views are unacceptable, it is entirely legitimate for the Senate to so advise the President and withhold its consent.

The notion that Senators may not directly consider the nominee's views of the Constitution is of recent and uncertain vintage. It may be an overreaction to the risk that the Senate may abuse its power to withhold consent.

Senators cannot require a nominee's agreement with their views on every issue, or even every important issue. Nor could the Senate legitimately insist that nominees promise not to hold laws unconstitutional, or not to enforce some unpopular provision of the Bill of Rights. The consent power should not be used to undermine the constitutional role of an independent judiciary as a check on the other two branches.

But it is equally improper for the President to use his power of nomination in such a fashion. It is bizarre to let the President consider ideology in nominating judges but not let an equal branch consider ideology in confirming them. If the President nominates someone uncommitted to the Constitution's solicitude for the rights of individuals and minorities — or uncommitted to the judiciary's special responsibilities to enforce those rights — the Senate is obliged to withhold its consent. That obligation comes from each Senator's oath to uphold the Constitution.

In voting to confirm a Supreme Court nominee, Senators "consent" to, and therefore legitimate, his broad jurisprudential views. No Senator who votes to confirm will be able to disclaim responsibility for the career of a Justice Bork.

As President Reagan put it, referring to a different episode, the Bork nomination is occurring on this Senate's "watch."

Each Senator will properly be assessed on how vigilantly he or she lives up to the oath of constitutional fidelity.

Letter to Senators Joseph R. Biden and Strom Thurmond

in Nomination of Robert H. Bork to Be Associate Justice
of the Supreme Court of the United States 6099 (1987)

With Sanford V. Levinson

As the Senate Judiciary Committee considered the nomination of Robert Bork to the Supreme Court, a letter opposing the nomination circulated among law professors around the country. I could not sign it. I no longer remember specifics, but there were statements that in my view were exaggerated. I often have that reaction to group letters. Sanford Levinson and I drafted this letter on a more cautious model, trying to avoid all exaggeration and to consider a broader range of issues. The letter does not discuss religious liberty issues, because Bork had not committed himself on those issues, although it is safe to assume that he would have found very little meaning in the Religion Clauses. The letter was signed by twenty-four members of the Texas faculty.

*   *   *

Perhaps the single most important task of the Committee on the Judiciary in this session will be to consider the fitness of Robert H. Bork to ascend to lifetime tenure on the United States Supreme Court. The Constitution places upon the Senate the solemn duty of giving or withholding its consent to this nomination. The Senate can withhold its consent, as it has done throughout our history, if in its independent judgment it finds the nominee unfit for the office. We call upon the Senate to withhold its consent to this nomination.

Judge Bork is a man of great intellectual ability. We have no reason to challenge his personal integrity. These are not the issues on which we base our criticisms or to which we call the Senate's attention. Rather, we are concerned with, and ask the Senate to consider, the merits of Judge Bork's views of the Constitution and of the role of the Supreme Court in enforcing the Constitution. As members of an independent branch of government, judges do not work for the President any more than they work for the Senate. Thus, the Senate's voice in their selection is properly equal to the President's. The Senate can legitimately insist that the nominee's general understanding of the Constitution and the role of the judiciary be consistent with the Senate's general understanding. If Judge Bork's views are unacceptable, it is entirely legitimate for the Senate to so advise the President and to withhold its consent.

The notion that the Senate may not directly consider the nominee's views of the Constitution is of recent and uncertain vintage. It may be an overreaction to the risk that the Senate may abuse its power to withhold consent. The Senate cannot insist that the nominee agree with a majority of the Senate on every issue. Nor could the Senate legitimately insist that nominees promise never to hold laws unconstitutional, or never to enforce some unpopular provision of the Bill of Rights. The consent power should not be used to undermine the constitutional role of an independent judiciary as a check on the other two branches.

But it is equally improper for the President to use his power of nomination in such a fashion. If the Senate determines that the President has nominated someone uncommitted to the judiciary's special responsibility for the rights of individuals and minorities, it is entitled — indeed obliged — to withhold its consent. The constitutional preventive for abuse of the nomination and consent powers is that each checks the other. The constitutional system works so long as either the President or the Senate insists on judges who will protect civil liberties against occasional majoritarian excesses. If the President nominates judges who will not enforce the Constitution, and if the Senate acquiesces, the constitutional mechanism for protecting individual rights breaks down. Indeed, the very act of confirmation is a form of "consent" to the jurisprudential views of the nominee and therefore a powerful legitimation of the broad approach later taken by the judge. The Senate will not be able to disclaim responsibility for the career of a Justice Bork. As President Reagan recently put it in regard to a different important issue, the Bork nomination is occurring on the Senate's "watch," and each Senator will be properly assessed on how vigilantly he or she lives up to the oath of constitutional fidelity.

There is, of course, a legitimate range of opinion both about the meaning of the Constitution and about the role of the Supreme Court in articulating the constitutional vision. His supporters are presenting Judge Bork as the heir of Justices Frankfurter, Harlan, and other generally admired Justices who endorsed "judicial restraint" and consequent deference to other agencies of government. Yet it is vital to note that these Justices wrote or joined in many of the decisions he has publicly criticized. Judge Bork represents not what might be called a "decent respect for the opinions" of other governmental institutions, but rather a wholesale abdication of the traditional judicial duty to be the special guardians of individual and minority rights.

Much of the press commentary has focused on his strong opposition to the Supreme Court's decisions allowing affirmative action and invalidating restrictions on abortion. These issues have been singled out because they are important to well-organized political groups; moreover, the Court has been so closely divided that one vote could change the course of decision. But it would be misleading for debate to be dominated by these especially controversial issues. Judge Bork is also strongly opposed to many decisions that are not controversial, that protect isolated individuals and small or diffuse minorities who are not represented by well-organized political groups, and that are essential to any reasonable understanding of constitutional rights.

Perhaps most striking is his extraordinarily narrow notion of what speech is protected by the First Amendment. Although he claims to have recanted some of the most startling aspects of a 1971 article in the Indiana Law Review — for example, the notion that "non-political speech" is entitled to no protection whatever — he appeared to reaffirm those views as late as his 1982 confirmation hearings. At that time he conceded only that *while on the Court of Appeals,* he would be bound by contrary Supreme Court precedent. He does appear to have conceded that moral discourse and at least some novels can sufficiently relate to politics to be protected. But there is no reason to believe that he would give any protection at all to speech to which he, for whatever reason, denies "political" status.

Moreover, he has not retreated one inch from perhaps the most troubling assertion of that article: He argued that speech advocating civil disobedience is not "political" and therefore is entitled to no protection. Thus, he would apparently allow the jailing of Martin Luther King for merely *advocating* civil disobedience. This pernicious doctrine has received no serious support from a Justice of the Supreme Court for half a century. Judge Bork admitted as much even as he derided the seminal civil liberties opinions of Justices Holmes and Brandeis, opinions that are the foundation of modern free speech law. Putting fidelity to doctrine to one side, we also note the obvious fact that the inspiring success of the civil rights movement — an example of fundamental political reform achieved basically within the structures of the American political system — depended in significant measure on the effective use of what is now constitutionally protected speech, including calls for civil disobedience. A view of the Free Speech Clause that would blithely tolerate the jailing of Dr. King is itself subversive of the central purpose of the clause.

Some of Judge Bork's most severe criticism has been reserved for the "privacy" decisions. It is absolutely crucial to recognize that his antagonism to these decisions goes well beyond questioning *Roe v. Wade,* the 1973 abortion decision. He denounces them all, including *Griswold v. Connecticut,* the 1965 decision that invalidated a state law prohibiting married couples from using contraceptives. Justice Harlan joined in *Griswold. Roe* is obviously controversial; indeed, we are divided in our assessment of that decision. But none of us believes for a moment that opposition to *Roe* entails a belief that the majority may authorize limitless incursions into the most intimate aspects of personal life, as Judge Bork seems to argue. We doubt that the Senate holds that view either.

Also revealing of Judge Bork's views of judicial role is his attack on the Court's invalidation of grossly unbalanced legislative districts and the subsequent adoption of the "one person–one vote" standard. These cases are classic illustrations of the structural necessity for judicial review. Before these decisions, a majority of the legislature in many states represented only twenty percent of the population. The favored twenty percent could never be expected to relinquish control through voluntary redistricting. Incumbents do not vote themselves out of office in such large numbers. The remedy for such a wrong had to come from the courts or it would not have come at all. Yet in the name of deference to popular rule, Judge Bork would have deferred to perpetual rule by small minorities.

Judge Bork's theory of the Equal Protection Clause is revealing in several ways. First, it is extraordinarily narrow. He believes that the clause protects only against racial discrimination. In Judge Bork's Constitution, there would be no constitutional remedy for sex discrimination or any other form of discrimination, however arbitrary. And even with respect to race, Judge Bork takes a narrow view of the Equal Protection Clause. For example, he would permit judicial enforcement of restrictive racial covenants, a practice unanimously held unconstitutional forty years ago.

There is no textual warrant for the view that "equal protection of the laws" refers only to racial discrimination. The clause is written in general terms and does not mention race. Nor is there much historical warrant for that view. We know that discrimination against blacks was a central target of the clause, but we also know that discrimination against white abolitionists, Republicans, and carpet baggers were important targets of the clause. Thus, there is ample historical evidence that the general language of the Equal Protection Clause was quite deliberate, and that any form of arbitrary discrimination may be examined under the clause.

Judge Bork attempts to justify his judicial views by saying that he merely defers to legislatures and never imposes views of his own. But his views on equal protection impeach that claim. He would apparently strike down all forms of affirmative action for racial minorities, on the ground that affirmative action discriminates against whites. He would also strike down Congressional attempts to expand the protections of the Fourteenth Amendment by legislation. Thus, he would strike down the Voting Rights Act of 1965, perhaps the most important and successful civil rights act ever passed. These views cannot be explained in terms of judicial restraint or deference to the legislature. Rather, Judge Bork appears far more deferential to the political branches when they discriminate against minorities, and less deferential to the political branches when they act to protect minorities.

Opinions obviously differ both about the merits and the constitutionality of affirmative action. But whatever one thinks of affirmative action, it cannot be that affirmative action is the one significant violation of individual rights in our time. A judge who would reject nearly all individual rights claims except those of whites challenging affirmative action should not be entrusted with final authority to enforce the Constitution.

Other issues also reveal Judge Bork's unwillingness to defer to Congress when he disagrees. He takes an extraordinarily narrow view of Congressional powers and a correspondingly broad view of executive powers. He would apparently strike down the War Powers Act and any effective form of independent prosecutor law. He would not allow Senators or Representatives to challenge executive action in court, even to test purely legislative powers such as the opportunity to override a pocket veto. He takes an extraordinarily expansive view of the executive's power to withhold information from Congress and the public.

Yet another example is Judge Bork's hostility to Congressional understanding of the antitrust laws. He would construe the Clayton Act and all other twentieth-century antitrust laws as narrowly as possible, because he believes Congress was mistaken when it enacted them. He would construe the Sherman Act to serve the single goal of economic efficiency, because he believes that Congressional desire to protect small businesses was mistaken. Whatever the merits of his antitrust theories, they are not consistent with his pose of deferring to Congress and insulating judicial decisions from his personal views.

We have summarized views that Judge Bock has expressed in print, and we have so far assumed that he will act on those views if he becomes a member of the Supreme Court. He will act on these and similar views with respect to all new issues before the Court, and he will construe very narrowly those precedents with which he disagrees. He may follow precedent on some settled issues; we do not know whether he will seek to overrule all past decisions with which he disagrees. But Judge Bork will surely attempt to overturn those decisions that he considers gravely in error; it would be naive to assume otherwise.

There is nothing objectionable in principle about overruling seriously erroneous precedents. A judge would be remiss to his own oath if he adhered to decisions that he considers important departures from the Constitution. We are not committed in this country to a doctrine that precedent controls in constitutional cases even when clearly wrong. Our tradition is one of overruling past errors, and it is not a legitimate criticism of Judge Bork simply that he would deviate from precedent.

Rather, the Supreme Court's power to remake constitutional law is precisely why the Senate must examine with care the particulars of Judge Bork's constitutional views and come to its own conclusion about their merits. This Senatorial duty is even more important when, as at present, the Court is closely divided in many important areas of the law. If Judge Bork is confirmed, his vote could prove determinative in limiting or overruling many of the protections that the Supreme Court has deemed necessary to achievement of the basic constitutional vision over the past several decades. His voting record is extreme even on the Court of Appeals, where he was bound by Supreme Court precedent. To elevate this judge to the Supreme Court, where the constraints of precedent will be far weaker, is in effect to endorse future attempts to overrule the scores of decisions he has criticized.

Professor Philip Kurland, a noted proponent of judicial restraint, has nonetheless written that it is not too much "to ask of a member of the high court that he be more than a technically well-equipped lawyer, that he also display the qualities of humility and compassion and understanding — of statesmanship[.]" Professor Kurland's mentor, Justice Frankfurter, himself once noted that "the process of constitutional interpretation compels the translation of policy into judgment, and the controlling conceptions of the Justices are their 'idealized political picture' of the existing social order." Judge Bork has portrayed an "idealized political picture" that would lead to further aggrandizement of governmental (and especially executive) power and leave unpopular individuals and minorities without any significant recourse to the federal judiciary. He has a right to hold those views. What he does not have a right to is automatic elevation to the Supreme Court.

We would be pleased, both as professors of law and as concerned citizens, to elaborate further on these points should that be deemed helpful to the committee in its important deliberations. It should be clear, of course, that our opinions are only personal and in no way imply any official endorsement of our views by The University of Texas.

Respectfully,

DOUGLAS LAYCOCK
A. Dalton Cross Professor at Law

SANFORD LEVINSON
Charles McCormick Professor of Law

[And 22 additional members of the University of Texas law faculty]

Book Review

Reviewing Robert H. Bork's *The Tempting of America: The Political Seduction of the Law*

101 Ethics 661 (1991)

Shortly after the Senate rejected his nomination, Bork resigned from the court of appeals and became a fellow at the American Enterprise Institute, a conservative think tank. He wrote this book about constitutional interpretation, aimed at an educated mass audience, in part to vindicate the positions that led to the Senate's refusal to confirm him. This review was for Ethics, *a philosophy journal published at The University of Chicago.*

*   *   *

I expected Robert Bork to offer a powerful argument for a coherent position, even if we disagreed. I was disappointed. The argument is shallow, contradictory, and undeveloped.

Bork's thesis is that judicial interpretation of the Constitution is legitimate only when it is based on "the original understanding." Any other mode of interpretation requires the Court to make political or moral judgments properly left to the political branches. Bork denounces all competing approaches as tools of elite groups seeking to impose their preferences on society.

The argument is almost entirely negative, organized around what Bork conceives to be bad examples. Some of his attacks strike home; others misfire. He reviews Supreme Court opinions from the earliest times to the present, the writings of contemporary constitutional scholars, and the arguments offered against his nomination to the Supreme Court, showing how all have deviated from his conception of the original understanding. The sinners include even the most conservative justices: Rehnquist, Scalia, Kennedy, and O'Connor (pp. 236-37). Everyone is wrong but Bork.

Only one inadequate chapter attempts to affirmatively develop Bork's position (pp. 143-60). Other formulations, and unexplained exceptions, are scattered through the book. I am left quite literally not knowing what Bork's position is.

Bork says that original understanding is not "the subjective intent of the Framers but rather the objective meaning that constitutional language had when it was adopted" (pp. 144, 218). Elsewhere, he says it is the intent of the ratifiers that counts, not the intent of the drafters (p. 181). But this question of whose intent counts arises only if he means subjective intent after all. Variations in specific individual intentions are irrelevant to objective meaning.

The objective meaning of the constitutional text does not count if the text is inconsistent with Bork's theory of the proper judicial role. The Constitution "cannot be taken as sweepingly as the words alone might suggest" (p. 147). The explicit guarantee of unenumerated rights, and the guarantee of unspecified "privileges or immunities" of citizenship, do not count at all. They are like inkblots on the parchment (p. 166).

On the other hand, the relevant original understanding is "the principle or stated value that the ratifiers wanted to protect" and not the ratifiers' likely applications of their principles to specific cases (pp. 162-63). Bork offers school desegregation and constitutional limits on libel laws as applications that are correct even though the founders would have rejected them; in Bork's view, the courts in these cases applied original principles to changed circumstances (pp. 81-82, 168). But we are told that Ronald Dworkin's distinction between concepts and conceptions is a usurpation (pp. 213-14). Bork does not explain how his principles and applications differ from Dworkin's concepts and conceptions.

Bork says he would apply equal protection of the laws to "unreasonable" sex discrimination, despite his view that the original understanding of the principles was to the contrary (p. 150). He does not explain why.

Bork asserts his view of what the original understanding was on various points, but he rarely offers evidence and he never cites historians. His only advice on how to learn the original understanding is to read the Constitution and the "secondary materials" extant at the time (p. 144). But the leading judicial interpretation of privileges and immunities, well known to the framers of the Fourteenth Amendment, does not count (p. 181). The apparent reason is that Bork does not like what it says.

Bork's dominant theme is that judges must be bound by principle and not permitted to make distinctions that depend on value judgments. He sometimes carries this to extreme lengths (e.g., p. 152). But this limit on courts is also abandoned when convenient. Flag desecration laws are constitutional, because the "national flag is different from other symbols," and courts "continually" make such distinctions (p. 128).

Bork's ill-defined and shifting concept of original understanding, with its appearing and disappearing exceptions, enables him to do exactly what he accuses everyone else of: to reach the results he wants to reach. He does not appear even moderately resistant to the temptation. But this is what he most emphatically denies. Bork asserts, but never proves, that only original understanding can "confine courts to a defined sphere of authority" (p. 155).

A serious attempt to defend that claim might begin with one of Bork's favorite examples, *Dred Scott v. Sanford* (60 U.S. 393 (1857)). He cites the case sixteen times. He correctly denounces *Dred Scott* as the case that introduced the mischievous doctrine of substantive due process (pp. 28-34). What he never says is that substantive due process is mentioned only in passing, in a single sentence that is not essential to the result (60 U.S. at 450), and that the great bulk of the opinion is based on alleged original understandings. The opinion attempts to show, with far more historical evidence than Bork offers on any issue, an original understanding that blacks could never be citizens (*id.* at 403-27), and an original understanding that the clause granting Congress power over the territories applied only to territories acquired before 1787 (*id.* at 431-46).

Thus, claims of original understanding produced what Bork apparently considers one of the worst judgments in the Court's history. If originalism can do that, where is its confining power? Nothing in Bork's book provides an answer.

Letter to Senator Patrick Leahy

July 2, 2001

I sent this letter to Senator Leahy shortly after Michael McConnell was nominated to the court of appeals. It was not intended to become part of the eventual hearing record; it was written as a Democrat speaking to the Democratic chair of the Senate Judiciary Committee. It argues that the Senate should consider the nominee's views on the Constitution, but it also argues that because they could not reject all nominees or substitute their own nominees, they would have to pick and choose. In my view, McConnell was as good a nominee as they were likely to get from the Bush Administration.

*   *   *

I write to support the nomination of Michael McConnell to the United States Court of Appeals for the Tenth Circuit. McConnell is probably the most attractive of the early Bush nominees. I hope that you do not confirm them all, but I do hope that you confirm McConnell. You will not do nearly as well with the average nominee from this Administration. As always, I write only for myself; The University of Texas takes no position on this or any other nomination.

I have known McConnell well for more than twenty years. This may speak to bias on my part, but it also speaks to knowledge. He was my student at Chicago, and he is still the best student I ever had. I have litigated with him and against him; I have testified at hearings with him and against him; we have co-authored short articles; we have each reviewed drafts of the other's work; we have sparred on the same list serves. I know him well.

He is by common consent one of the most distinguished legal academics in the United States today. He was tenured at Chicago; he has had a standing offer from Harvard; Texas and other schools have tried to lure him without success. He is also an accomplished appellate litigator — a separate skill and a separate body of experience that most legal academics lack.

He is extraordinarily intelligent. He brings powerful analytic capacity to bear on problems. More important for a judicial nominee, he is restrained in his judgments, and impeccably fair to opposing arguments. He has of course provoked disagreement, and those who disagree with him attack his arguments as well as his conclusions, but these arguments have tended to stay on the merits and at a very high level.

There is simply no imaginable reason to oppose McConnell apart from ideological disagreement with him. Now as it happens, I think that ideological disagreement is a perfectly legitimate basis for the Senate to act on. Judges do not work for the President, and the Senate is the principal safeguard against a President appointing judges who would undermine the Constitution rather than enforce it. Both the President and the Senate are responsible for appointing men and women who will enforce the Constitution, and both the President and Senate must necessarily act on their own judgment of the Constitution's meaning and principal purposes. It is just as legitimate for the Senate to consider a nominee's views in deciding whether to consent as for the President to consider a nominee's views in making the nomination.

When the President and the Senate disagree, they must inevitably meet somewhere in the middle, or no judges will be appointed at all. And because the President is unified and the Senate is not, the President is likely to have disproportionate influence in the location of this compromise. That is a political prediction, not a normative judgment; a unified Senate majority could and should move the point of compromise further to the middle. But the Senate will rarely be able to force a President to submit nominees that the Senate would choose for itself; it is likely that all the Senate can accomplish is to eliminate the most extreme of the President's nominees.

McConnell is among the most moderate of the current nominees; it would be ridiculous to target him as among the most extreme. He is too conservative for my taste, but he is not an ideologue and never has been. You will see very few Bush nominees who have worked to help legal aid clinics, or environmental organizations, or the embattled black mayor of a major American city; McConnell has done all three. He has largely avoided, and sometimes criticized, the recent excesses of the Republican Right. His experience defending the rights of religious minorities has made him far more sympathetic to civil liberties than the typical Republican nominee. He supports a broad range of free speech rights. In the growing conservative split between judicial restraint and conservative judicial activism, he is firmly on the judicial restraint side, and while one can never be sure about the effects of confirmation on a human being, I think he is likely to stay on the judicial restraint side.

The biggest judicial revolution in progress is on federalism; five Justices of the current Supreme Court are restricting the powers of Congress in ways not seen since before the New Deal, and are even undoing parts of the Civil War settlement. Here McConnell is plainly a moderate. He firmly rejects the Supreme Court's exceedingly narrow interpretation of Congressional power to enforce the Fourteenth Amendment; he would allow Congress to act on its own view of the Amendment's meaning so long as that view is fairly arguable. I would expect him to hold that some things are beyond the reach of the commerce power, but I would be astonished if he went beyond Supreme Court precedent to expand any broad scale retrenchment of Congressional power.

Finally, and at the heart of the opposition, are his views on religious liberty, which I know well. McConnell supports the right of religious minorities to practice their faiths free of nonessential government regulation. He opposes school-sponsored prayer. He has said that the Supreme Court's decision upholding legislative prayer was unprincipled. On these issues, he is closer to the ACLU than to Justice Scalia.

He opposes government funding of churches. But he believes that government can purchase secular services, such as medical care or education, from anyone. If government pays only secular providers, it coerces providers to secularize themselves. If it pays any provider who can do the job, it can avoid coercing anyone. Reasonable people may disagree, but that is hardly a radical position.

In fact, both Congress and the Court have long acted on McConnell's view of the matter in some contexts, while rejecting his view in other contexts. Government sends Medicare and Medicaid payments to religious hospitals as well as secular. Government has long funded billions of dollars in social services through religious agencies; the current battle over charitable choice is about the terms of that funding, not the fact of it. Since 1965, Congress has funded computers and other equipment, and remedial instruction in low-income neighborhoods, in religious schools as well as secular. The charitable tax deduction is available for contributions to religious charities as well as secular, and is economically equivalent to a matching grant even for contributions to the religious functions of the church itself.

Americans United for Separation of Church and State believes that not a penny of government money should ever go to any religious institution under any circumstances. That is a defensible principle, but it has never been the law, and it has never been the policy of Congress. The much publicized litigation over limits on funding elementary and secondary schools is in fact the exception; in all sorts of other areas, equal treatment of religious and secular providers has been more common.

The debate here is about boundaries between competing principles. Supreme Court precedents will largely control this; to the extent that they do not, McConnell would push that boundary further in the direction of permitting funds to flow. Having started my career with the view of Americans United on these questions, I have very gradually come to believe that McConnell is closer to right. But even if I still agreed with Americans United, I would support confirmation. Intense disagreement with McConnell on this one issue is not a basis to refuse confirmation when other nominees have far worse views across a whole range of issues — and quite likely the same or more aggressive views on this issue as well.

"Distinguished" is an over-used word, but it applies to McConnell by any standard. With all respect to the many talented judges of the courts of appeals, McConnell is far more talented than the typical nominee of either party. Because of his generally conservative views, no Democratic President would ever have nominated him. But among the range of views already found and to be expected among the nominees of the current Republican President, McConnell is an island of moderation. I hope that Democrats will vote to confirm him.

Very truly yours,
DOUGLAS LAYCOCK

Letter to Senator Orrin G. Hatch

In Confirmation Hearings on Federal Appointments 707
(Senate Committee on the Judiciary 2002)

original author unknown

I signed this letter supporting Michael McConnell's nomination to the court of appeals sometime in summer 2002. So did some three hundred other law professors of all political persuasions. It is included here, even though I did not write it, because I would not have signed it if I had not agreed in full, and because I subsequently had to write a defense of it. It also has the virtue of being short. The defense is Injudicious, *dated October 30, 2002, and thus reprinted just a little further on.*

*   *   *

We enthusiastically support the nomination of Michael W. McConnell to be a judge of the United States Court of Appeals for the Tenth Circuit.

McConnell is one of America's most distinguished constitutional law scholars and one of its most distinguished lawyers. He has published more than fifty scholarly articles in the nation's leading law reviews and has argued eleven cases before the United States Supreme Court. He is currently Presidential Professor at the University of Utah College of Law and was formerly a professor for twelve years at the University of Chicago Law School. He was a law clerk to Judge J. Skelly Wright of the United States Court of Appeals for the D.C. Circuit and to Justice William J. Brennan, Jr. of the United States Supreme Court. He served as Assistant General Counsel of the Office of Management and Budget and as Assistant Solicitor General.

McConnell's scholarly work has been path-breaking and influential. It also has been characterized by care, thoroughness, and fairness to opposing viewpoints. Both in person and in his writings, McConnell exhibits respect, gentleness, concern, rigor, integrity, a willingness to listen and to consider, and an abiding commitment to fairness and the rule of law. He provides a model of the wisdom, intelligence, temperament, craftsmanship, and personal qualities that can make a judge outstanding.

Many of the signers of this letter are Democrats who did not vote for the President who nominated Professor McConnell. Some of us have disagreed with McConnell on constitutional issues and undoubtedly will disagree with him again. All of us, however, hope that the Senate will confirm Professor McConnell without greater delay than is necessary to fulfill its important constitutional responsibilities. In our view Michael McConnell is a nominee of exceptional merit whose confirmation warrants bipartisan support.

We list our institutional affiliations for purposes of identification only.

> *Sincerely yours,*
> [followed by some 300 names and affiliations, including]
> DOUGLAS LAYCOCK
> *Alice McKean Young Regents Chair and Associate Dean*
> *University of Texas School of Law*

Forging Ideological Compromise

New York Times A31 (Sept. 18, 2002); reprinted in Confirmation Hearings on Federal Appointments 736 (Senate Committee on the Judiciary 2002)

I wrote this partly to support the nomination of Michael McConnell, whom I knew and respected, and whom I thought was as good a nominee as supporters of civil liberties were likely to get from the Bush Administration, and partly to comment on the confirmation process. The Times was much more interested in the process than in McConnell; endorsing or opposing candidates is reserved to Times editorial writers and not permitted on the op-ed page. After some negotiation, I was allowed one paragraph on McConnell by way of illustrating my comments on the process. Someone later inserted it into the record of the hearing on McConnell's nomination. I have no idea who, because it does not adhere to either side's party line.

*　　　*　　　*

The Senate Judiciary Committee begins hearings today on the nomination of Michael McConnell to a seat on the United States Court of Appeals. His opponents disagree with him on substantive legal issues, especially funding for religious schools. The McConnell hearing follows the acrimonious rejection of another nominee to the federal appeals court, Justice Priscilla Owen of the Texas Supreme Court, and a political battle looms over the nomination of Miguel Estrada, a lawyer in Washington.

Republicans say that Mr. McConnell is a highly talented lawyer of good character, which is certainly true, and that this is the only question that should legitimately concern the Senate, which is not true. The central issue in this and other nominations is the nominee's view on the Constitution, federal law, and the role of the federal courts. Presidents of both parties have tried to rule questions on these views out of bounds, and the Senate has often been timorous about its right to ask. But such questions should be at the heart of the process.

The nominations of Mr. McConnell, Ms. Owen, and Mr. Estrada are contemporary illustrations of an old debate. As far back as 1801, lame-duck Federalists tried to pack the federal courts with loyalists appointed for life. Current controversies over abortion, school vouchers, and federalism show that politicians still care what judicial nominees think.

When the President and the Senate disagree about important constitutional issues, confirmation battles are inevitable. But if Senators doubt their authority to debate a nominee's legal views openly, or are reluctant to do so, we get guerilla warfare: exaggerated or trumped-up ethics charges and stubborn refusals to consider nominations at all.

Presidents certainly consider the views of their judicial nominees, modestly in some administrations and intensely in others. It is essential to constitutional checks and balances that the Senate do the same. Judges are not like cabinet officers; they do not work for the President. Instead, they independently enforce the limits on governmental power — including the President's power.

The Senate is the principal constitutional safeguard against a President appointing judges who would undermine the Constitution rather than enforce it. Political judgments cannot be avoided, and both the President and the Senate must necessarily act on their own judgment about a judicial nominee's ideology.

When the President and the Senate disagree on constitutional interpretation, they have to meet somewhere in the middle or no judges will be appointed at all. In the current political climate, appropriate judicial appointments should be to the right of the Democrats on the Senate Judiciary Committee and to the left of the President, and certainly to the left of those elements in the Republican Party that care the most about remaking the judiciary. Confining nominees to the ideological range between the President and the Judiciary Committee would push the judiciary toward the center and exclude the extremes of both left and right. It would reduce the magnitude of periodic shifts in judicial views on constitutional issues, and would reduce the number of judgeships left vacant while the President plays to his base and the Senate stalls.

Identifying this range would require serious Senate debate. It might require the President to consult the leadership of the Senate Judiciary Committee before he makes a formal nomination, instead of simply consulting with senators from his own party about nominees from their states. It would require research and sometimes expert testimony to review nominees' records on all issues, not just those issues to which lobbying groups call attention. The goal would be not merely to reject a few extremists, but to negotiate a reasonable compromise between the President's preferences and the Senate's.

Mr. McConnell is an easy case on these criteria. He is in favor of vouchers and against abortion, for example, but he would follow the law on these issues, and he is an independent thinker with a range of moderate positions on many other issues. He has said the Supreme Court should have given Florida more time to conduct a proper recount, and he opposed the impeachment of former President Bill Clinton. Within the Republican spectrum, Mr. McConnell, who once served as a law clerk to the late Justice William Brennan of the United States Supreme Court, is plainly a moderate.

Splitting the difference between the President and the Senate would have an additional benefit: It would require parties to receive greater voter support before remaking the judiciary. If a party wants to fill the federal judiciary with its own hard-liners, it must win both the presidency and the Senate. Winning the presidency and losing the Senate is not a mandate to control two of the three branches of government.

Constitutional understandings change over time, and the selection of new judges is a principal means by which such changes find their way into our law. But the Constitution gives the President and the Senate an equal voice in that process. Just as Senators have their own understandings of the Constitution, so they must make their own judgments about the ideological commitments of the President's judicial nominees.

Some of the False Attacks on Michael McConnell

In Confirmation Hearings on Federal Appointments 737
(Senate Committee on the Judiciary 2002)

The debate over the McConnell nomination became intense. Senators, staffers, and lobbyists were circulating statements, some of them inaccurate. I was known to the members of the Senate Judiciary Committee at this point because I had been a frequent witness at a long series of hearings on various religious liberty bills — bills that will be the subject of volume 3. I was talking both to the officials in the Department of Justice who were managing the nomination and to supporters of the nomination in the conservative religious community. I don't remember whose idea this was, but someone suggested — or the idea emerged from a conversation — that I should be the one to try to correct the record. This document was written in late summer or early fall as an informal circular to be distributed to all Senators; it consists mostly of quotations of what McConnell's opponents said he said and then of what he really said. Someone inserted it into the hearing record; my guess is Senator Hatch. The document starts with reapportionment and federalism, but then it turns to a series of religious liberty issues.

*   *   *

I. The One-Person, One-Vote Decisions

The Charge:
"McConnell opposes 'one person, one vote'" — People for the American Way.

The Truth:
McConnell defended the Supreme Court's decisions requiring legislative districts of reasonably equal size. What he criticized was the requirement of

"precise mathematical equality," which has led to unconstrained gerrymandering and non-competitive districts.

What McConnell Actually Said About Unequal Apportionment:
"Until the early 1960s, the federal courts played no role in legislative districting. By almost any measure of democratic legitimacy, however, the districting process was a disaster. . . .

"This style of malapportionment in Tennessee and elsewhere gave rural and agrarian interests a lock on legislative power, despite their minority status. . . . Moreover, the urban and suburban majority had no peaceful political means for redressing the electoral balance. . . .

"A districting scheme so malapportioned that a minority faction is in complete control, without regard to democratic sentiment, violates the basic norms of republican government. . . . Constitutional standards under the Republican Form of Government Clause are ill-developed, but surely a government is not 'republican' if a minority faction maintains control, and the majority has no means of overturning it."

What McConnell Actually Said About Precise Mathematical Equality:
"In order to bring districts as close to 'precise mathematical equality' as possible, states must disregard preexisting political boundaries such as cities, townships, and counties. Adherence to these traditional boundaries was, historically, the principal constraint on creative districting, popularly known as 'gerrymandering.' Once freed from these traditional constraints by the Supreme Court's 'precise mathematical equality rule,' legislative line-drawers were able to draw maps to produce the results they desired, rending elections less a reflection of popular opinion than of legislative craftsmanship. . . . The results? Protection for incumbents, a tendency toward homogenous — and hence more partisan — districts, racial and partisan gerrymandering, and ultimately, a widespread sense that elections do not matter."

The Citation:
Michael W. McConnell, *The Redistricting Cases: Original Mistakes and Current Consequences,* 24 Harvard Journal of Law and Public Policy 103, 103-04 (2000).

II. Federalism

The Charge:
McConnell "celebrates the current Supreme Court's series of 5-4 states' rights rulings, which have impaired the ability of Congress to protect the rights of ordinary Americans and threaten to dismantle many of the legal and social justice gains of the past 70 years." — People for the American Way

The Truth:
Far from celebrating these cases, McConnell has rejected the principle that underlies them. The Court has struck down laws to "protect the rights of ordinary Americans" principally under its theory that the Court has exclusive power to interpret constitutional rights and Congress has no power to interpret constitutional protections more broadly. This principle was first stated in *City of Boerne v. Flores,* 521 U.S. 507 (1997). McConnell wrote one of the most important of the many criticisms of the Court's new rule.

What McConnell Actually Said About Congressional Enforcement of Civil Liberties:
"In *Boerne,* the Court erred in assuming that congressional interpretation of the Fourteenth Amendment is illegitimate. The historical record shows that the framers of the Amendment expected Congress, not the Court, to be the primary agent of its enforcement, and that Congress would not necessarily consider itself bound by Court precedents in executing that function. . . .

"Judicial interpretations of the Constitution are often influenced by institutional considerations, such as the principle of judicial restraint, that create 'slippage' between the Constitution as enforced and the Constitution itself. . . . But when Congress engages in constitutional interpretation under the enforcement power, it is not so constrained. The democratic values underlying the doctrine of judicial restraint do not apply to Congress. . . . Congress's decision to adopt a more robust, freedom-protective interpretation of the Free Exercise Clause did not 'alter' the Constitution or create 'new' rights. Rather, RFRA merely liberated the enforcement of free exercise rights from constraints derived from judicial restraint."

The Citation:
Michael W. McConnell, *Institutions and Interpretations: A Critique of City of Boerne v. Flores,* 111 Harvard Law Review 153, 194-95 (1997).

III. School Prayer

The Charge:
McConnell "has indicated his support for public school prayer." — Americans United for Separation of Church and State. "McConnell's confirmation would threaten the right of students not to be made captive audiences to religious worship and promotion of religion in public schools." — People for the American Way.

The Truth:
McConnell supports the school prayer decisions and testified against a school prayer amendment. He has opposed prayer at public school graduations and football games.

What McConnell Actually Said About School Prayer:
"[O]fficially sponsored and led prayer in public school classrooms would be impossible to maintain today in a way that would be either spiritually valuable or noncoercive. . . .

"I do not believe that officially sponsored, vocal classroom prayer can be administered without effectively coercing those in the minority. And that should not be permitted. . . ."

What McConnell Actually Said About Prayer at Graduation:
"I would take pains to emphasize that the concept of coercion cannot, in itself, supply a standard for distinguishing between establishments and non-establishments, and that it is vital to understand the concept of coercion broadly and realistically. For example, the Court is now being urged to adopt the coercion test in a case involving a public prayer at a junior high school graduation ceremony. I would have thought that gathering a captive audience is a classic example of coercion; participation is hardly voluntary if the cost of avoiding the prayer is to miss one's graduation. Equally seriously, it appears that the content of the prayer was subject to indirect government control, which is a species of coercion. For the Court to embrace the coercion test in this form would be a small step back toward permitting the government to indoctrinate children in the favored civil religion of nondenominational theism."

What McConnell Actually Said About Prayer at Football Games:
"If officially sanctioned prayers at public events are unconstitutional, government bodies cannot evade constitutional limitations by clever stratagems. Nor do I have any serious disagreement with the Court's conclusions, based

on this record, that the Santa Fe policy had the purpose and effect of perpetuating its prior practice of beginning football games with prayer. . . . [T]he Court's conclusions were more than reasonable.

"More importantly, the Court's general approach to the Establishment Clause issue was correct."

The Citations:
First quotation: Testimony of Michael McConnell, *Religious Freedom,* Hearing Before the Senate Judiciary Committee, Oct. 20, 1995.

Second quotation: Michael W. McConnell, *Religious Freedom at a Crossroads,* 59 University of Chicago Law Review 115, 158-59 (1992).

Third quotation: Michael W. McConnell, *State Action and the Supreme Court's Emerging Consensus on the Line Between Establishment and Private Religious Expression,* 28 Pepperdine Law Review 681, 709-10 (2001).

IV. Government Religious Observance

The Charge:
"McConnell criticized several recent Supreme Court rulings that upheld church-state separation, including *Lee v. Weisman* (1992), which prohibited government-sponsored prayer at school graduation ceremonies, and *County of Allegheny v. ACLU* (1989), which limited government endorsement of religious displays on public property. He said these decisions 'have nothing to do with freedom of religion. There is not a single person in these cases who has been hindered or discouraged by government action from following a religious practice or way of life.'" (Jan.-Feb. 1993, *American Enterprise*). — Americans United for Separation of Church and State.

The Truth:
McConnell argued for the ban on school-sponsored prayer at graduation even before the case was decided. See section III (of this document).

County of Allegheny is about municipal Christmas displays, which Americans United opposes. McConnell's criticism was that the Court should either have forbidden them or permitted them, but it should not have picked the awkward compromise it did.

In the passage quoted by Americans United, McConnell's point was not to criticize the decisions mentioned, but to criticize the Court's priorities in failing to protect private religious practices with the same rigor displayed in its cases on government sponsored religious practices.

What McConnell Actually Said About These Cases:

Two sentences past where Americans United stopped quoting, McConnell said: "My point is not that *Lee v. Weisman* or any of these other cases was wrongly decided. But the Supreme Court and the news media are so preoccupied with the finer points of freedom from religion that far more important cases of genuine freedom of religion have been almost completely neglected." He then gave examples.

What McConnell Actually Said About Prayer at Graduation:

See section III.

What McConnell Actually Said About Government Christmas Displays:

After accurately describing the facts of the cases, in which the Court struck down a nativity scene accompanied by greenery and poinsettias, but upheld one accompanied by "a Santa Claus house, reindeer, candy-striped poles, a Christmas tree, carolers, cut-out figures representing such characters as a clown, an elephant, and a teddy bear, hundreds of colored lights, a banner stating 'Season's Greetings,' and a talking wishing well":

"The Court appears to have arrived at the worst of all possible outcomes. It would be better to forbid the government to have religious symbols at all than to require that they be festooned with the trappings of modern American materialism. After all, no one's religion depends on whether the government displays the symbols of the Christian and Jewish holidays. But if there are to be religious symbols, they should be treated with respect. To allow them only under the conditions approved by the Court makes everyone the loser."

The Citations:

On the two cases: Michael McConnell, *Freedom From Religion?*, American Enterprise 34, 36-37 (Jan.-Feb. 1993).

On Christmas displays: Michael McConnell, *Religious Freedom at a Crossroads*, 59 University of Chicago Law Review 115, 126-27 (1992).

V. Separation of Church and State

The Charge:

"McConnell takes issue with Jefferson's metaphor of the 'wall of separation' between church and state, calling it 'misleading.'" — People for the American Way. "McConnell has described church-state separation as never having been a 'plausible or attractive conception of proper relations between government and religion in the modern activist state.'" Americans United for Separation of Church and State.

The Truth:

This one is partly true, but badly out of context. McConnell supports much of what most people mean by separation, but he does believe the separation metaphor has misled the Court. The one real disagreement he has on this issue with Americans United and People for the American Way is that McConnell would let the government fund secular services (such as education, medical care, treatment for drug addiction, food and shelter for the poor and the homeless) from any service provider willing to provide the service, whether religious or secular. That has been the model through most of American history for higher education, medical care, and most social services. For elementary and secondary education, we have had a different model, one that sharply limited public funds to religious schools. This is a serious disagreement. But it does not mean that McConnell generally wants to unite church and state.

What McConnell Actually Said About the Separation Metaphor:

"Separation has never been a plausible or attractive conception of proper relations between government and religion in the modern activist state. [Americans United quote ends here.] To be sure, some aspects of what can be called 'separation' are essential, and essentially uncontroversial. The government should not control the institutions of the church; nor should churches have any institutional role, as such, in government. No citizen is entitled to special privileges on account of membership in a favored denomination; nor may there be special disabilities for anyone else. Moreover, the original conception of separation — that government be strictly limited so as not to invade the province of religion — remains the best means of preserving religious freedom. Government protects religious freedom best by leaving religiously sensitive matters to the private sphere. But in many areas of life, religion and government both necessarily play a role. Indeed, with the growth of the modern welfare-regulatory state, the occasions for overlap increase exponentially, as governments regulate and subsidize activities previously private and often religious. In these many areas of overlap, the idea of 'separation between church and state is [Americans United quote starts up again here] either meaningless, or (worse) is a prescription for secularization of areas of life that are properly pluralistic. [Americans United quote ends again here] That is why principles such as neutrality (with respect to government subsidies) and accommodation (with respect to government regulation) have come to replace 'separation' in most areas of constitutional conflict."

The Citation:
Michael McConnell, *Five Reasons to Reject the Claim that Religious Arguments Should be Excluded from Democratic Deliberation,* 1999 Utah Law Review 639, 640-41.

VI. Legislative Chaplains

The Charge:
No specific charge here. But McConnell's opinion on legislative chaplains is another clear counter-example to the general charges that he wants government to impose religion on people.

The Truth:
In *Marsh v. Chambers,* 463 U.S. 783 (1983), the Supreme Court upheld legislative chaplains, basically because the First Congress had them. McConnell sharply criticized this decision.

What McConnell Said About Legislative Chaplains:
"*Marsh v. Chambers* represents original intent subverting the principle of the rule of law. Unless we can articulate some principle that explains why legislative chaplains might not violate the establishment clause, and demonstrate that that principle continues to be applicable today, we cannot uphold a practice that so clearly violates fundamental principles we recognize under the clause. . . .

"The Supreme Court offered no theory whatsoever in *Marsh v. Chambers* . . . So far as one can tell from the Court's opinion, there is simply an exception from the establishment clause for legislative chaplains. It is as if the first amendment read, 'Congress shall pass no law respecting an establishment of religion, other than a legislative chaplaincy.' . . . Indeed, it can be said that *Marsh v. Chambers* does not interpret the Constitution at all."

The Citation:
Michael W. McConnell, *On Reading the Constitution,* 73 Cornell Law Review 359, 362-63 (1988).

VII. Generalized Charges of Extremism

The Charge:
"McConnell has a long record of extremism on a broad range of individual rights issues. . . . McConnell starts to make Bork look moderate. This man wants to gut the constitutional protections that Americans count on." — Barry Lynn, Americans United for Separation of Church and State.

The Truth:
This is the most absurd charge of all. McConnell has a long record of positions and activities in support of a broad range of civil liberties, activities that unmistakably mark him as intellectually honest and independent and as a moderate among the range of possible Republican nominees. In addition to the examples above, here are some more:

Bush v. Gore:
McConnell has written that in *Bush v. Gore,* the Supreme Court should have given Florida more time to finish a proper recount. "Having rested the decision on the standardless character of the recount ordered by the state court, the logical outcome was to remand under proper constitutional standards." Michael W. McConnell, *Two-and-a-Half Cheers for Bush v. Gore,* 68 University of Chicago Law Review 657, 674 (2001).

Impeachment:
McConnell publicly opposed the impeachment of President Clinton. "Those who feel the Constitution requires the House to impeach the president are misguided, according to Michael McConnell, a prominent University of Utah constitutional law professor who sent an anti-impeachment letter Saturday to House Judiciary Chairman Henry Hyde. . . .

"'The inviolability of elections may be the most important constitutional principle that we have,' McConnell wrote. 'The best test of whether presidential misconduct rises to the level of impeachment is whether members of his own party are willing to join in the motion.'" John Heilprin, *Rep. Hansen Urging Support for Impeachment,* Salt Lake Tribune (Dec. 16, 1998).

Free Speech:
McConnell vigorously supports free speech rights, whether or not he agrees with the speaker. "I think the free-speech principle used to be fairly robust. And I consider the high point of this [was] the flag burning cases, where very solid majorities of the Court, including some of the most conservative Jus-

tices, voted — correctly, in my view — that laws against flag burning are unconstitutional. I consider this to be kind of a high point where people across the spectrum were able to agree upon a way of analyzing free-speech claims. And they would stick to those principles without regard to the political complexion of the case." *Professor Michael W. McConnell's Response,* 29 Pepperdine Law Review 747, 747 (2001).

McConnell co-chairs the Emergency Committee to Defend the First Amendment, with ACLU leader Norman Dorsen.

Representing Black Democrats:
McConnell successfully represented the first black mayor of Chicago, Harold Washington, (for free), in his political and legal battle with mostly white and more conservative opponents on the Board of Aldermen. *Roti v. Washington,* 500 N.E.2d 463 (Ill. App. 1986).

Human Rights Litigation:
McConnell represented three former Democratic Attorneys General (for free) in *McNary v. Haitian Centers Council,* a high profile case challenging an order of the first President Bush authorizing deportation of certain aliens who faced persecution in their home countries.

Legal Aid for the Poor:
McConnell served on the Board of the Austin Christian Law Center, now the Austin neighborhood branch of Chicago Legal Aid, and chaired its Finance Committee.

Judicial Nominations in a Divided Government

Austin American-Statesman A15 (Oct. 9, 2002)

The editor of the Austin American-Statesman *liked my column for the New York* Times *(Forging Ideological Compromise, Sept. 18) and asked for another piece on the same theme. This was the result.*

*　　　*　　　*

The President and the Senate Judiciary Committee are again locked in battle over judicial nominations. Republicans say that Democrats are behaving irresponsibly; Democrats say Republicans did the same thing only more so to Clinton nominees. Many nominations have been delayed, and two nominees have been rejected in committee on party line votes. Such battles have occurred throughout our history, whenever the President and the Senate have disagreed about important constitutional issues.

An odd feature of recent nomination battles is the claim that only the President may consider a nominee's views on disputed legal questions. On this view, the Senate can consider a nominee's professional qualifications and moral character, but not what the nominee thinks about the Constitution. The party that wins the presidency claims the right to control the federal courts and says the Senate may not object or even inquire. Presidents of both parties have taken this position.

The remarkable thing is the extent to which the Senate has acquiesced in this claim. This timidity does not mean the Senate confirms everyone the President nominates. It means the battle is driven underground, into refusals to schedule hearings, exaggerated or trumped-up ethics charges, and phony judgments about qualifications.

Thus Tom Daschle, the Senate majority leader, suggested that Justice

519

Priscilla Owen is not "qualified" to be a federal judge. This was an absurd lie that surely fooled no one. Justice Owen has had a distinguished record at every stage of her career from law school to the Texas Supreme Court. What Daschle meant was that, in his judgment, Owen is simply too conservative. To say she is "too" conservative is not a statement of fact that can be true or false; it is a political judgment on which Republicans and Democrats are likely to disagree.

The Senate should not disguise its political judgments with false claims about qualifications. Judges are not like cabinet officers who work for the President. Judges enforce limits on governmental power, including the President's power. Senate confirmation is an essential part of constitutional checks and balances, the principal constitutional safeguard against a single official imposing his views on two of the three branches of government. Both the President and the Senate are responsible for filling the judiciary with men and women who will enforce the Constitution, and both the President and the Senate must necessarily act on their own judgment about what the Constitution means.

When the President and the Senate disagree, they must meet in the middle or no judges will be appointed at all. It would be much easier to reach sensible compromises if the President and the Senate Democrats would talk to each other before nominations are submitted. The Constitution requires the President to act "with the Advice and Consent of the Senate," not just with its consent.

In the current political division, appropriate judicial appointments should be to the right of the Democrats on the Senate Judiciary Committee and to the left of the President. Confining nominees to this ideological range would push the judiciary toward the center and exclude the extremes of both left and right. It would reduce the magnitude of periodic shifts in judicial views on constitutional issues.

Identifying this range requires consideration of many issues, not just those important to the loudest single-issue groups. Professor Michael McConnell, whose nomination is pending, draws intense opposition from groups supporting abortion rights and groups opposed to vouchers for religious schools, two issues where his views are very conservative. But on free speech, school prayer, the rights of religious minorities, and congressional power to enforce civil rights and civil liberties, his views are moderate or even somewhat liberal.

McConnell is thus an ideal compromise nominee, offering something to both sides. Most important, his diverse positions reflect habits of mind that we should want in judges — a willingness to examine issues independently, without following either side's party line. When the confirmation process focuses on a single issue, such as abortion, compromise becomes impossible. Every nominee is either pro-choice or pro-life; the only compromises are nominees with no known position on the most deeply divisive issue of our time.

Selection of new judges is the principal means by which electoral politics legitimately influences constitutional law. But the Constitution gives the President and the Senate an equal voice in that process. The Senate cannot defer to the President on the meaning of the Constitution, and thus it cannot defer on the ideological commitments of his judicial nominees.

Injudicious: Liberals Should Get Tough on Bush's Conservative Judicial Nominees — and Stop Opposing Michael McConnell

The American Prospect Online (Oct. 30, 2002)
www.prospect.org/cs/articles?article=injudicious_103002

The McConnell nomination had very broad support among law professors, including among liberal law professors who signed the group letter over the summer. American Prospect, a liberal political magazine, said that these law professors were valuing friendship, collegiality, and loyalty to the guild above the good of the country. The editor then invited this response. No doubt friendship, collegiality, and loyalty to the guild were part of the picture. In fact, McConnell had been my student. But I believed, and argued here, that McConnell was as good a nomination as liberals were likely to get from the Bush Administration. Part of the task was to establish my credentials as a liberal, which is why the piece emphasizes that the Senate should reject more Bush nominees, even though it should not reject this one. I firmly believed both of those propositions.

*   *   *

In the November 4 issue of the *American Prospect,* Chris Mooney questions why 300 law professors, many of them political liberals, would sign a letter urging Senate Democrats to confirm Michael McConnell to the United States Court of Appeals. The 300 agreed on McConnell's sheer talent and judicial temperament; they may not agree on much else. My own reasons for signing are very different from Mooney's speculations.

I believe the Constitution gives the president and the Senate an equal voice in the selection of judges. Judges do not work for the president, and the Senate is the principal constitutional check on a president using judicial nominations to undermine constitutional rights he doesn't like. This is the constitutional structure, and through the end of the 19th century, the Senate reviewed nominations much more aggressively than it does now.

When the President and a majority of the Senate disagree on constitutional law, each side must bargain for its position. They should meet somewhere in the middle, with nominees that split the difference or with some nominees that please the President and others that please the Senate. The Senate should demonstrate its good faith, but more importantly, the Senate must demonstrate its seriousness. It can do that only by rejecting many nominees and forcing the President to the middle.

By these standards, the recent Democratic performance has been pitiful. Republicans for a generation have worked systematically to move the federal courts to the right; Democrats have done much less to resist or to move the courts back to the middle. Despite all the brave talk during this presidency about the Senate's right to consider judicial philosophy, the Senate has so far confirmed 80 Bush nominees and rejected two. Republicans complain bitterly about those two, but two rejections are not nearly enough to force the president to bargain seriously over the philosophy of judicial nominees. Fifty-one nominations remain pending; citizens interested in judicial balance can only hope that many of those nominations are being allowed to slowly die of attrition or neglect.

Given this view of the nomination process, why do I support Michael McConnell? Simply because he is one of the very best of the Bush nominees. Senators should not reject half the nominees at random; they should make intelligent choices. McConnell is among the best in part for the reasons of sheer ability set out in the letter from 300 law professors. Even after a highly successful bargaining process with this President, the Senate will have to confirm some seriously conservative nominees. The country will not be better off if it confirms the dumb ones.

McConnell is also among the best when we consider his views over a range of constitutional issues. He draws intense opposition from groups supporting abortion rights and groups opposed to vouchers for religious schools, two issues where his views are very conservative. But on free speech, school prayer, the rights of religious minorities, and Congressional power to enforce civil rights and civil liberties, his views are closer to the ACLU's than to Justice Scalia's. McConnell supports a broad range of free speech rights, and he has co-chaired a committee to oppose a constitutional amendment to ban flag burning. He supports the right of religious minorities to practice their faiths free of nonessential government regulation. He opposes school-sponsored prayer whether in the classroom or at public events like football games and graduation. He has sharply criticized the Supreme Court's decision upholding legislative chaplains.

He rejects the Supreme Court's exceedingly narrow interpretation of

Congressional power to enforce constitutional rights. In the growing conservative split between judicial restraint and conservative judicial activism, he distinguishes the vigorous enforcement of express constitutional rights from creating rights and principles without basis in the constitutional text — and the Rehnquist Court has created more of these than its predecessors.

McConnell has taken many other positions over the years that depart from Republican orthodoxy. He represented Chicago's first black mayor, Democrat Harold Washington, for free, in his early battles against mostly white and mostly more conservative opponents. He represented three former Democratic attorneys general in a human rights challenge to the first President Bush's order authorizing deportation of certain aliens facing persecution in their home countries. He opposed the impeachment of President Clinton when it mattered, and he attacked the most unprincipled part of *Bush v. Gore* — the refusal to allow Florida time to complete a recount under the Supreme Court's newly announced standards. The point of these examples is not that these particular issues are likely to recur, but that even when emotions run high, he has never followed any party line.

McConnell is thus an ideal compromise nominee, offering something to both sides. Most importantly, his independent consideration of the merits of each issue shows habits of mind that we should want in judges. The Senate should aggressively force the President to nominate judges from across the range of understandings about constitutional issues. But whether or not it does that, it should confirm Michael McConnell.

McConnell was confirmed on a voice vote on November 15, 2002. He served with distinction on the United States Court of Appeals for the Tenth Circuit until he resigned, effective August 31, 2009, to join the faculty of the Stanford Law School.

PART TWO

History

As much as any part of the Constitution, and far more than most, the Religion Clauses of the First Amendment are embedded in history. The United States was founded at a time of great ferment in church-state relations. The religious wars and persecutions in the wake of the Reformation had demonstrated the need for religious liberty. The Great Awakening had swept the colonies with religious enthusiasm and greatly increased the numbers of evangelical Christians. The Enlightenment had led to a rationalist, stripped down religion, tending toward Deism, among parts of the educated elite. The sheer increase in religious diversity doomed the established churches in New England and the southern colonies; in the long run, they could not maintain their position against the ever growing numbers of dissenters. Independence and the drafting of constitutions forced the founding generation to address these issues. Most of this debate occurred in the several states, but of course it continued at the federal level.

Serious historians, judges of all persuasions, and lawyers and activists on all sides of Religion Clause issues have mined this rich history. Conservative judges and legal scholars argue that the meaning of the Constitution is determined by the meaning it had when adopted; the appointment of many such judges has given ever more prominence to this history.

In the nineteenth century, the creation of public schools and the large Catholic immigration changed the debate over religious liberty. Intense conflict over religious observances in public schools and government funding for private schools waxed and waned through most of the century. Here is the origin of two of the three sets of religious liberty issues that divide Americans today. But the judges and many of the activists have paid much less attention to the history from the nineteenth century than to the history from the eighteenth.

To do my work over the years, I have necessarily had to investigate this history and try to master it. I have tried when reasonably possible to examine the original sources myself, and I have tried to rely on serious professional historians with respect to the vast body of sources that I could not examine personally. This Part contains the fruits of that effort.

Historical work by lawyers is often denounced as "law office history," in which a lawyer looks to history to prove a preconceived answer to some present-day question. My historical work is not history for its own sake; it does indeed look to history for evidence on present-day questions. But I have tried hard to avoid the error of forcing history to fit my preconceived preferences. I have tried to acknowledge contrary evidence, and I have sometimes found that that evidence changed my views, most notably on government funding for religious institutions. Historical evidence is usually mixed; earlier generations were no more unanimous than we are. Present-day policy preferences inevitably influence judgments about how to characterize this mixed evidence, but I have tried to insulate the gathering and reporting of the evidence from the drawing of inferences with modern applications.

Part Two, History, has six scholarly articles (two of which are quite short by law review standards) and four short pieces.

The Long (and Not So Long) . . .

Three of these articles address disputed interpretations of the Establishment Clause. The Supreme Court's conservative critics, who argue that the Establishment Clause means much less than the Court has said that it means, have tried to define some coherent theory of what the clause does mean. One such theory is that the Establishment Clause permits government to aid religion so long as it does not prefer one religion over another (the nonpreferentialist theory); another such theory is that the Establishment Clause permits government to aid religion so long as it does not coerce any person with respect to religious matters (the noncoercion theory).

I agree that the Court has oversimplified the history, but these two theories also oversimplify the history. *"Nonpreferential" Aid to Religion* (1986) shows, by overwhelming evidence in my view, that the Founders did not intend the nonpreferentialist theory.

"Noncoercive" Support for Religion (1992) shows, by a considerably thinner margin of evidence, that they did not intend the noncoercion theory either. I continue the argument against the noncoercion theory with evidence from later national experience and modern judicial interpretation. Rereading

these pieces, I find the tone a bit more combative than if I had written them today, but I think their arguments stand the test of time.

Regulatory Exemptions of Religious Behavior (2006) addresses a set of the Court's liberal and secular critics. These critics argue that it is unconstitutional for government to exempt religious practices from regulation that applies to secular instances of the same conduct. I find that there is simply no originalist support for this claim.

Continuity and Change in the Threat to Religious Liberty (1996) examines the religious wars and persecutions in the wake of the Reformation and compares those conflicts to the conflicts between government and religion today. One lesson often drawn from the wars of religion is that religions persecuted. And certainly the religious groups were not innocent. But then as now, it was the state that had the power to persecute, and the state acted for its own motives. The threat to religious liberty is from the government, not from unregulated religions.

Text, Intent, and the Religion Clauses (1990) and *Original Intent and the Constitution Today* (1990) are two related pieces, each rather short, on constitutional method. How should we use this history? What is the relationship of history to the ratified text of the Constitution?

. . . And the Short

Founders Wanted Total Neutrality (1985) is an op-ed from *USA Today,* necessarily much oversimplified, but setting out the heart of the argument for why government should be neutral towards religion.

Responding to the Nonpreferentialists (1986) reviews two books on the history of religious liberty in the colonial and founding periods. Both authors shared my rejection of nonpreferentialism, but we reached that conclusion by three rather different routes.

The Declaration Is Not Law (1991) briefly responds to an obscure debate about the legal status of the Declaration of Independence. The Declaration's second paragraph is our fundamental statement of political theory, but none of the Declaration is operative law.

Religious Liberty and Free Speech: Back to the Future (2000) is a short oral summary of the Protestant-Catholic conflicts of the nineteenth century and their implications for today.

Cross References

Inevitably, significant treatments of history appear elsewhere in this work.

There is a brief review of the role of the eighteenth-century evangelicals in *Religious Liberty as Liberty* (1996), in Part One section A.

The Mormon, Catholic, and Jehovah's Witness persecutions, and the early Supreme Court cases, are reviewed in *A Survey of Religious Liberty in the United States* (1986), in Part One section B, and the rest of that piece can now be understood as a history of the law of religious liberty from 1963 to 1986.

The history of religious conflict in the United States is divided into three distinct periods in *Church and State in the United States* (2006), also in Part One section B.

The history of the drafting of the Fourteenth Amendment will be reviewed, with an eye to answering a present-day question, in *Conceptual Gulfs in City of Boerne v. Flores* (1998), and in the briefs in the *Boerne* case (1997), both to appear in volume 3.

The brief in *Cutter v. Wilkinson* (2005), also slated for volume III, contains an early version — shorter, less nuanced, and written for a different audience — of the argument in *Regulatory Exemptions of Religious Behavior,* which appears in this Part. It also addresses the argument that the Establishment Clause was just a federalism provision that reserved establishment issues to the states and embodies no substantive position about religious liberty.

The brief in *Lee v. Weisman* (1992) contains an early version of *"Non-coercive" Support for Religion,* which appears in this Part. Parts of that brief may appear in volume 4.

The Underlying Unity of Separation and Neutrality (1997) reviews the history of Protestant-Catholic conflicts and the history and social context of the litigation that culminated in *Lemon v. Kurtzman,* the case that dominated the law of the Establishment Clause for a generation. Some of this history also appears in *Why the Supreme Court Changed Its Mind About Government Aid to Religious Institutions* (2008). Each of these articles will appear in volume 4.

The Many Meanings of Separation (2003), also to appear in volume 4, reviews the many ways in which the idea of separating church and state has been used over the long course of history.

Founders Wanted Total Neutrality

USA Today 8A (Aug. 12, 1985)

This was my half of an exchange on the op-ed page with William Bennett, the Secretary of Education in Ronald Reagan's second term. The genre calls for punch and combativeness, and it imposes word limits that preclude any subtlety and nuance. Within those constraints, this lays out the basic historical argument for why the Establishment Clause does not permit government to aid religion so long as it aids all religions equally.

*   *   *

Austin, Texas. — We're in the midst of another round of Supreme Court bashing over school prayer and other government aid to religion.

The right wing claims the government can openly support religion so long as it doesn't prefer one religion over others — and that that's what the framers of the Bill of Rights intended.

But the legislative record tells a very different tale.

A lawyer drafting the right-wing view might write: "Congress shall make no law establishing any particular denomination of religion in preference to another." In fact that is exactly how it was written in 1789 by members of the first Senate.

But the Senate rejected that version and two similar versions that explicitly stated the right-wing view. Six days later, the Senate adopted an even narrower statement of the right-wing view, but that was rejected by the House.

A conference committee produced the version ultimately ratified as the First Amendment: "Congress shall make no law respecting an establishment of religion."

This is the broadest version considered by either house. It speaks generically of "religion," not "*a* religion," "a national religion," or "any particular denomination of religion."

It forbids any law "respecting" establishment of religion — that is, any law that relates to an establishment in any way. In light of the alternatives Congress considered and rejected, it is best understood as requiring the government to be entirely neutral towards religion.

The great debates over disestablishment of the state church in Virginia had already shown how that generation understood establishment. A compromise bill would have let every Virginia taxpayer designate a church to receive his church tax. That squarely posed the issue of non-preferential aid. After intense public debate, the bill was defeated.

I do not defend all Supreme Court decisions. Some are wrong, and some of the Court's distinctions are silly. But on the most fundamental question — whether the Constitution requires neutrality towards religion or merely neutrality among religions — the Court has got it right.

Here, the intent of the framers is as clear as it ever gets; the right wing distorts that intent to suit its own preferences.

"Nonpreferential" Aid to Religion: A False Claim about Original Intent

27 William & Mary Law Review 875 (1986)

This is a review of the founding-era debates on disestablishment, focusing on a single much-disputed issue: may government aid religion if it aids all religions equally (where on the most plausible interpretation, "equally" would mean proportionately to some fair measure of each faith's private support)? This theory of "nonpreferential" aid to religion was a principal basis for criticizing the Supreme Court in the decades after World War II. But it turns out that the Founders debated this very issue. Eighteenth-century defenders of tax support for churches tried to save their programs by offering tax support to all denominations on terms as nonpreferential as they could devise. Those proposals were rejected, sooner or later, in every state that considered one. Nonpreferential drafts of the Establishment Clause also appear to have been considered and rejected in the Senate.

This article also considers the forms of aid to religion that were uncontroversial in the founding era and finds the basic distinction to be that financial aid was controversial, and eventually prohibited, but nonfinancial aid did not become controversial until the nineteenth century.

This article discusses aid to the religious functions of a church and does not consider aid to secular services, such as education or medical care delivered by religious organizations.

This paper was written for a conference on the Bill of Rights at William & Mary Law School. I was invited to comment on a paper by Professor Philip Kurland, but that ostensible purpose is reflected only in the introduction. In a

---

I am grateful to the participants in the William and Mary Bill of Rights Symposium, and to Sanford Levinson, David Little, Bruce Mann, L.A. Powe, David Rabban, Teresa Sullivan, and Mark Yudof for helpful comments.

fairly common academic maneuver, I presented my own paper that was vaguely related to his.

*   *   *

Professor Kurland usefully reviews the framing of the Religion Clauses and draws some of the lessons that emerge from that review.[1] What he says about the First Amendment is so sensible and so studiously noncontroversial that one can hardly disagree with it. He greatly overstates his casual assertion that the framers of the Fourteenth Amendment did not intend to apply the Bill of Rights to the states, but I have discussed that elsewhere.[2]

Consequently, I will have little to say about his Article as such. Instead, I will build on his Article to examine a recurring controversy about the meaning of the Establishment Clause. I will draw on Professor Kurland's Article, on a useful new book by Thomas Curry,[3] and on my own review of the relevant history. This history refutes one important claim about the Establishment Clause — that the Framers specifically intended to permit government aid to religion so long as that aid does not prefer one religion over others.

The theory that the Establishment Clause forbids only preferential aid has long been a favorite of those who support government aid to religion. It does not go away despite repeated rejection by the United States Supreme Court.[4] In the round of Establishment Clause debate triggered by the political coalition that elected Ronald Reagan to the Presidency, the "no preference" argument has been stated in one form or another by Attorney General

1. Philip B. Kurland, *The Origins of the Religion Clauses of the Constitution,* 27 Wm & Mary L. Rev. 839 (1986).

2. *Compare id.* at 842-43 with Douglas Laycock, *Taking Constitutions Seriously: A Theory of Judicial Review* (Book Review), 59 Tex L. Rev. 343, 347-48, 377 (1981) [hereinafter cited as Laycock, *Constitutions*]. For analyses of the special problems of incorporating the Establishment Clause, see Leonard Levy, The Establishment Clause 167-71 (1986); Douglas Laycock, *A Survey of Religious Liberty in the United States,* 47 Ohio St. L.J. 409, 415-16 (1986) (text at notes 28-36) [hereinafter cited as Laycock, *Religious Liberty*]; Douglas Laycock, *Towards a General Theory of the Religion Clauses: The Case of Church Labor Relations and the Right to Church Autonomy,* 81 Colum. L. Rev. 1373, 1386 n.106 (1981). For evidence of express congressional intention to incorporate the Bill of Rights into the Fourteenth Amendment, see John Hart Ely, Democracy and Distrust: A Theory of Judicial Review 22-30 (1980); Cong. Globe, 39th Cong., 1st Sess. 2765-66 (1866) (remarks of Sen. Howard).

3. Thomas Curry, The First Freedoms: Church and State in America to the Passage of the First Amendment (1986).

4. *See* Wallace v. Jaffree, 472 U.S. 38, 52-55 (1985); Abington School Dist. v. Schempp, 374 U.S. 203, 216-17 (1963); Illinois ex rel. McCollum v. Board of Educ., 333 U.S. 203, 211 (1948).

Edwin Meese,[5] Chief Justice William Rehnquist,[6] political scientists Michael Malbin[7] and Robert Cord,[8] law professor Rodney Smith,[9] and my former student, Martin Nussbaum.[10] Malbin's pamphlet and Cord's book have become standard authorities for supporters of government aid to religion. Professor Tushnet's prediction that Cord would be ignored[11] was erroneous. Justice O'Connor's concurrence in *Wallace v. Jaffree* cites Cord,[12] and Justice White's dissent was receptive.[13] Justice Rehnquist's dissent drew heavily on Cord's history without citing it.[14] Justice Stevens' opinion for the majority rejected Justice Rehnquist's conclusions on the basis of precedent,[15] but it did not refute Justice Rehnquist's account of history.[16]

The prominence and longevity of the nonpreferential aid theory are remarkable in light of the weak evidence supporting it and the quite strong evidence against it. I do not mean to overstate what we know about the Establishment Clause. Neither its history nor its text offers us a single unambiguous meaning. But they can eliminate some possible meanings, and to do that is real progress.[17] So long as the debate is dominated by a false claim, it is hard to discuss the real issues.

5. Edwin Meese, *Toward a Jurisprudence of Original Intention*, 2 BENCHMARK 1, 5 (1986).

6. Wallace v. Jaffree, 472 U.S. 38, 91-114 (1985) (Rehnquist, J., dissenting).

7. MICHAEL MALBIN, RELIGION AND POLITICS: THE INTENTIONS OF THE AUTHORS OF THE FIRST AMENDMENT (1978).

8. ROBERT CORD, SEPARATION OF CHURCH AND STATE: HISTORICAL FACT AND CURRENT FICTION (1982); Robert Cord, *Church-State Separation: Restoring the "No Preference" Doctrine of the First Amendment*, 9 HARV. J.L. & PUB. POL'Y 129 (1986).

9. Rodney Smith, *Getting Off on the Wrong Foot and Back On Again: A Reexamination of the History of the Framing of the Religion Clauses of the First Amendment and a Critique of the Reynolds and Everson Decisions*, 20 WAKE FOREST L. REV. 569 (1984).

10. L. Martin Nussbaum, *A Garment for the Naked Public Square: Nurturing American Public Theology*, 16 CUM. L. REV. 53, 62, 68, 74 (1985); L. Martin Nussbaum, *Comment, Mueller v. Allen: Tuition Tax Relief and the Original Intent*, 7 HARV. J.L. PUB. POL'Y 551, 566-77 (1984).

11. Mark Tushnet, *Book Review*, 45 LA. L. REV. 175, 175, 178 (1984).

12. 472 U.S. 38, 79 (1985) (O'Connor, J., concurring).

13. *See id.* at 90-91 (White, J., dissenting).

14. *See id.* at 92-106 (Rehnquist, J., dissenting).

15. *Id.* at 52-55 (opinion of the Court).

16. While this Comment was in press, Professor Leonard Levy published a book rejecting the nonpreferentialist thesis for reasons that are only partly consistent with the reasons advanced here. LEVY, *supra* note 2. I will not attempt to fully incorporate references to his book, but I will note our most significant disagreements.

17. *See* Frederick Schauer, *An Essay on Constitutional Language*, 29 UCLA L. REV. 797, 828 (1982).

In challenging a politically important claim and labeling it as false, I am self-consciously facing the dangers Professor Kurland highlighted when he quoted Judge Hand's metaphor of Martin Luther and Erasmus.[18] The dangers are real, but the point is overstated. The force of the metaphor derives from the fallacy of the excluded middle. Scholars may contribute their knowledge or insight to public debate on important issues. They may contribute it in a form that is understandable to a policymaker, or even to the public, consistently with their duty of rigorous intellectual honesty. Scholars should not feel constrained to publish only turgid prose in obscure journals. They should not leave the public debate to those who feel no scruples whatever to conform their claims to the evidence. Even an Erasmus may speak to the press, testify to a congressional committee, or state a carefully considered claim in forceful language.

I. The Nonpreferential Aid Claim

There are several versions of the nonpreferential aid argument, but all reach substantially the same conclusion. The claim is that the framers of the Religion Clauses intended a specific meaning with respect to the problems now treated under the Establishment Clause: government may not prefer one religion over others, but it may aid all religions evenhandedly. Under this view, the Supreme Court's more expansive interpretation is a usurpation that remains illegitimate no matter how long the Court adheres to it.

This claim is false. The framers of the Religion Clauses certainly did not consciously intend to permit nonpreferential aid, and those of them who thought about the question probably intended to forbid it. In fact, substantial evidence suggests that the Framers expressly considered the question and that they believed that nonpreferential aid would establish religion. To assert the opposite as historical fact, and to charge the Supreme Court with usurpation without acknowledging the substantial evidence that supports the Court's position, is to mislead the American people.

The fact is that the First Congress repeatedly rejected versions of the Establishment Clause that would have permitted nonpreferential aid,[19] and nothing in the sparse legislative history gives much support to the view that the Framers intended to permit nonpreferential aid.[20] Proposals for

---

18. Kurland, *supra* note 1, at 839-40 (quoting LEARNED HAND, THE SPIRIT OF LIBERTY 138 (Irving Dilliard 3d ed. 1974)).

19. *See infra* notes 26-38 and accompanying text.

20. *See infra* notes 52-96 and accompanying text.

nonpreferential financial aid were squarely rejected in Maryland and Virginia in 1785 and 1786, amidst much public debate.[21] No state offered nonpreferential aid to churches, and only Maryland and Virginia seriously proposed such aid.[22] Some of the New England states provided financial aid to more than one church, but these systems were preferential in practice and were the source of bitter religious strife.[23] There is no evidence that those schemes were the model for the Establishment Clause.

The Framers also had a second, less considered intention. Both the states and the federal government openly endorsed Protestantism and provided a variety of preferential, nonfinancial aid to Protestants. This aid was wholly noncontroversial, because the nation was so uniformly Protestant and hostile to other faiths.[24] The early preference for Protestantism is not a precedent for nonpreferential aid, and it is not an attractive model for Establishment Clause interpretation. The Framers' generation thought about Establishment Clause issues in the context of financial aid; they did not think about those issues in connection with nonfinancial aid.[25] We can make better sense of the Establishment Clause if we follow what the Framers did when they were thinking about establishment. Thus, to the extent that the Framers' intent is thought to matter, the relevant intent is their analysis of financial aid to churches.

II. The Best Evidence of the Framers' Intent: The Text of the Establishment Clause

A. *The Rejected Drafts*

Professor Kurland mentions in passing the most important fact concealed by the proponents of nonpreferential aid: the First Congress considered and rejected at least four drafts of the Establishment Clause that explicitly stated the "no preference" view.[26] So far as we can tell from the legislative journal, the issue was squarely posed in the Senate and again in the Conference Committee.

---

21. *See infra* notes 101-23 and accompanying text.
22. *See infra* notes 124-35 and accompanying text.
23. *See infra* notes 136-43 and accompanying text.
24. *See infra* notes 223-28 and accompanying text.
25. *See infra* notes 220-28 and accompanying text.
26. *See* Kurland, *supra* note 1, at 855.

The House of Representatives sent to the Senate a draft of the Establishment Clause somewhat like the version ultimately ratified:

Congress shall make no law establishing religion, or prohibiting the free exercise thereof, nor shall the rights of conscience be infringed.[27]

The first motion in the Senate clearly presented the "no preference" position. The motion was to strike out "religion, or prohibiting the free exercise thereof," and to insert, "one religious sect or society in preference to others."[28] The motion was first rejected, and then passed.[29] The proposal on the floor then read:

Congress shall make no law establishing one religious sect or society in preference to others, nor shall the rights of conscience be infringed.[30]

Next, the Senate rejected two substantively similar substitutes. First, the Senate rejected language providing:

Congress shall not make any law, infringing the rights of conscience, or establishing any Religious Sect or Society.[31]

---

27. 3 DOCUMENTARY HISTORY OF THE FIRST FEDERAL CONGRESS OF THE UNITED STATES OF AMERICA 159, 166 (House Journal) (Linda de Pauw ed. 1972) [hereinafter cited as DOCUMENTARY HISTORY]; *id.* at 136 (Senate Journal). The draft quoted in text is from the House Journal for August 21, 1789 and the engrossed bill transmitted to the Senate on August 24. The version quoted in the Annals of Congress is slightly different: "Congress shall make no law establishing religion, or to prevent the free exercise thereof, or to infringe the rights of conscience." 1 ANNALS OF CONG. 766 (Joseph Gales ed. 1834) (Aug. 20, 1789). The two discrepancies, in the free exercise and rights of conscience clauses, do not appear to affect meaning. They may have resulted from a mistranscription in the Annals, from an amendment on August 21 not reported in the Annals, or from an editorial change or mistranscription in preparing the final copy of the bill. Any error occurred in the House and does not affect the significance of the motion in the Senate.

Different printings of the Annals of Congress have different pagination; the date is the surest way to find particular passages. MALBIN, *supra* note 7, at 6 n.21.

28. See 1 DOCUMENTARY HISTORY, *supra* note 27, at 151 (Senate Journal). This motion also deleted the Free Exercise Clause, but that deletion does not seriously affect the analysis. The Senate also voted on two nonpreferential drafts that included the Free Exercise Clause. *See infra* notes 32 & 34 and accompanying text. The two issues were ultimately separated, the Free Exercise Clause was adopted, and the nonpreferential drafts of the Establishment Clause were rejected. *See infra* notes 35-36 and accompanying text.

29. 1 DOCUMENTARY HISTORY, *supra* note 27, at 151 (Senate Journal).

30. *Id.*

31. *Id.*

Second, it rejected an alternative that stated:

> Congress shall make no law establishing any particular denomination of religion in preference to another, or prohibiting the free exercise thereof, nor shall the rights of conscience be infringed.[32]

The two motions to amend by substitution appear to have presented stylistic choices. But the first vote appears to have been substantive. At the very least, these three drafts show that if the First Congress intended to forbid only preferential establishments, its failure to do so explicitly was not for want of acceptable wording. The Senate had before it three very clear and felicitous ways of making the point.

Still later the same day, the Senate appears to have abandoned the "no preference" position. It adopted a draft that spoke of all religion generically:

> Congress shall make no law establishing religion, or prohibiting the free exercise thereof.[33]

A week later, the Senate again changed its mind and adopted the narrowest version of the Establishment Clause considered by either House:

> Congress shall make no law establishing articles of faith or a mode of worship, or prohibiting the free exercise of religion. . . .[34]

The House of Representatives rejected this version. James Madison and two others represented the House on the Conference Committee[35] that produced the version of the Establishment Clause ultimately ratified:

> Congress shall make no law respecting an establishment of religion, or prohibiting the free exercise thereof. . . .[36]

The Establishment Clause actually adopted is one of the broadest versions considered by either House. It forbids not only establishments, but also any law respecting or relating to an establishment.[37] Most important, it for-

---

32. *Id.*

33. *Id.*

34. *Id.* at 166.

35. *See id.* at 181.

36. U.S. CONST. amend. I; 3 DOCUMENTARY HISTORY, *supra* note 27, at 228 (House Journal). There is a mistranscription in the Annals of Congress, substituting "a" for "the" before "free exercise." 1 ANNALS OF CONG. 913 (Joseph Gales ed. 1834) (Sept. 24, 1789).

37. *See* Lemon v. Kurtzman, 403 U.S. 602, 612 (1971). One effect of forbidding any law

bids any law respecting an establishment of "religion." It does not say "a religion," "a national religion," "one sect or society," or "any particular denomination of religion." It is religion generically that may not be established.

Malbin is a major proponent of the "no preference" position. While parsing the legislative history for support of his position, he argues that there is a big difference between establishing "a religion" and establishing "religion." He notes that to forbid establishment of "a religion" would clearly state the nonpreferentialist position, but that to forbid establishment of "religion" would not.[38] On that point, he is absolutely right. The rejected drafts pose the distinction even more clearly: establishing "religion" is not the same as establishing one sect or society, any particular denomination, or articles of faith and a mode of worship. If Congress paid any attention at all to the language it fought over, it rejected the "no preference" view.

The nonpreferentialists tend not to mention the rejected drafts, or to pass over the drafts as insignificant.[39] Some nonpreferentialists rely heavily on similar resolutions from the state ratifying conventions.[40] The Virginia, North Carolina, and New York conventions proposed Establishment Clauses similar to the rejected Senate drafts.[41] James Madison's original bill in the

---

"respecting" an establishment is that a statute requiring a state to disestablish religion would have violated the Establishment Clause. I assume that the drafters understood this, but I have seen little direct evidence that anyone feared such a statute or had a specific purpose to prevent it. For textual arguments that the clause protected state establishments, see WILBUR G. KATZ, RELIGION AND AMERICAN CONSTITUTIONS 9-10 (1964); Joseph Snee, *Religious Disestablishment and the Fourteenth Amendment*, 1954 WASH. U.L.Q. 371, 379-89. For an unexplained assertion that these arguments are "historically unconvincing," see MARK DEWOLFE HOWE, THE GARDEN AND THE WILDERNESS 22-23 (1965).

38. MALBIN, *supra* note 7, at 8.

39. CORD, *supra* note 8, at 8-9; MALBIN, *supra* note 7, at 12-13. Smith speculates that the Senate drafts were rejected only because they would have permitted aid to a coalition of two or more religions in preference to the rest. Smith, *supra* note 9, at 614. Reasonable construction would have avoided that absurd result; a simple amendment would have eliminated any risk. For example, the first Senate draft could have been amended to provide: "Congress shall make no law establishing one or more religious sects or societies in preference to others." Smith's speculation does not dispel the inference that arises from rejection of all drafts written in nonpreferentialist terms.

40. *See* CORD, *supra* note 8, at 6-7; Cord, *supra* note 8, at 136-37; Nussbaum Comment, *supra* note 10, at 570-71.

41. 3 THE DEBATES IN THE SEVERAL STATE CONVENTIONS ON THE ADOPTION OF THE FEDERAL CONSTITUTION 659 (Jonathan Elliot 2d ed. 1836) (Virginia) [hereinafter cited as ELLIOT'S DEBATES]; 4 *id.* at 244 (North Carolina); 1 *id.* at 328 (New York). The similar proposal from Rhode Island, 1 *id.* at 334, came too late to influence the text of the First Amendment.

First Congress provided: "nor shall any national religion be established."[42] Like the Senate drafts, however, all of these proposals were rejected.

An approach to interpretation that disregards the ratified amendment and derives meaning exclusively from rejected proposals is strange indeed. The "no preference" position requires a premise that the Framers were extraordinarily bad drafters — that they believed one thing but adopted language that said something substantially different, and that they did so after repeatedly attending to the choice of language.

Perhaps the Framers did not understand what they were doing and viewed the textual choices as stylistic.[43] All sorts of things become possible once one begins to speculate about what the Framers might have thought instead of giving primary weight to what they enacted. But responsible constitutional interpretation does not allow us to assume a mistake of this magnitude. When the record reflects a textual choice as clear as this one, only extraordinarily clear contrary evidence should persuade us not to follow the text.[44]

This conclusion is bolstered by the Framers' own textualism. The Senate met in secret and did not record its debates;[45] obviously, future generations were not intended to look to those debates for interpretive guidance. Jefferson Powell has shown that the Framers' generation thought it illegitimate to refer to legislative history even when it was known.[46] They applied to the Constitution the prevailing common law methods of interpreting statutes, contracts, and other operative legal texts. These methods looked to the objective meaning of the words in light of the evil addressed and the remedy proposed. References to "intention" usually meant the objective intention of the document as revealed by these methods; the subjective intention of the drafter or the members of the adopting body was deemed irrelevant. These findings present an extraordinary problem for intentionalists. If the inten-

---

42. 1 ANNALS OF CONG. 434 (Joseph Gales ed. 1834) (June 8, 1789). A committee of Maryland's ratifying convention considered and rejected a similar proposal. 2 ELLIOT'S DEBATES, *supra* note 41, at 552-53. For analysis of Madison's puzzling language, see *infra* notes 85-95 and accompanying text.

43. This possibility is considered more thoroughly *infra* notes 149-65 and accompanying text.

44. For a full statement of my commitment to textualism, see Laycock, *Constitutions, supra* note 2; *see also* Schauer, *supra* note 17, at 804-12 (rejecting interpretation of constitutional language within the "intentional paradigm," focusing on the perceived intent of the drafters at the expense of clear textual meaning).

45. 1 ANNALS OF CONG. 15 (Joseph Gales ed. 1834) (ed. note).

46. Jefferson Powell, *The Original Understanding of Original Intent*, 98 HARV. L. REV. 885 (1985).

tion of the Framers is binding, we cannot look to evidence that the Framers intended us to disregard and that they considered irrelevant to a proper understanding of their intention. At the very least, the intentionalists have the burden of explaining why they can disregard the Framers' own understanding of their intention.[47]

B. The Malbin Interpretation

Some nonpreferentialists offer a fig leaf of textual argument to go with their intent argument. To Malbin and Cord, the key textual choice is that the ratified version forbids any law respecting "*an* establishment of religion," as distinguished from a hypothetical draft forbidding any law respecting "*the* establishment of religion."[48] Malbin, who invented the argument, says: "[B]y choosing '*an* establishment' over '*the* establishment,' [the Framers] were showing that they wanted to prohibit only those official activities that tended to promote the interests of one or another particular sect."[49] The only reason he offers for this claim is that "*the* establishment" "would have emphasized the generic word 'religion.'"[50]

Malbin's argument is frivolous, and Cord's repetition does not make it any stronger. The argument is wrong for at least four reasons. First, and most important, the repeated rejection of clear language that would have stated Malbin's position overwhelms the attenuated inference he draws from the choice of "an" over "the." Second, Malbin assumes that the article in front of one noun — "establishment" — critically changes the meaning of a different noun — "religion." Recall that Malbin himself argues that putting even an indefinite article in front of "religion" would have clearly made his point.[51] Third, there is no evidence whatever that anyone thought of Malbin's hypothesized alternate draft or consciously chose "an" over "the."

47. At one point, Powell quotes Madison as rejecting reliance on the Convention's rejection of an alternative draft. *Id.* at 921. Whether Madison meant that the particular inference drawn from that vote was unreliable, or that a comparison between what was adopted and what was rejected is always illegitimate, is unclear. If the latter view were widely shared, an intentionalist would have great difficulty justifying consideration of the rejected drafts. A textualist would have much less difficulty. Text that was voted on by the body empowered to act is a more reliable source of meaning than thoughts and statements of individual members.

48. CORD, *supra* note 8, at 11-12 (quoting MALBIN, *supra* note 7, at 14). For a similar argument, see Smith, *supra* note 9, at 618.

49. MALBIN, *supra* note 7, at 14 (emphasis added).

50. *Id.*

51. *See supra* text accompanying note 38.

Fourth, "an" is perfectly consistent with the view that the amendment forbids any kind of establishment, including multiple or nonpreferential establishments. "The" establishment might have connoted that only one kind of establishment is possible — perhaps the English kind. "An" establishment more clearly communicates that any establishment — any kind of establishment — is forbidden. I would not put much weight on that argument, but it is more plausible than Malbin's. My inference from "an" at least depends on the word's effect on the noun it modifies. I do not insist that the Framers used "an" for the reason I suggest. But the possibility that they used it for my reason further reduces the likelihood that they used·it for Malbin's less plausible reason.

III. The Debate in the First Congress

A. The Relevance of the Debate

The nonpreferentialists rely heavily on the debate in the First Congress,[52] but that debate adds little to current understanding. The only recorded debate occurred in the House. No verbatim record exists, the reporter's notes are incomplete and sometimes inaccurate,[53] and the notes fill slightly less than two columns in the Annals of Congress.[54] Because the Senate met in secret,[55] only the Journal entries recording its votes are available. Thus, the attempt to override the evidence of the rejected drafts depends on those two columns of notes from the House. The nonpreferentialists rely on a puzzling statement by Madison that is probably wrong and in any event does not state the nonpreferentialist understanding of the clause. They also rely on attenuated inferences from the remarks of others. These remarks must be examined in light of the preliminary draft to which they referred.

The House debate occurred on August 15, 1789, before any of the events in the Senate. The debate concerned the draft submitted by a Select Commit-

---

52. See Wallace v. Jaffree, 472 U.S. 38, 93-98 (1985) (Rehnquist, J., dissenting); CORD, *supra* note 8, at 9-10; MALBIN, *supra* note 7, at 6-11; Smith, *supra* note 9, at 608-17; Nussbaum Comment, *supra* note 10, at 572-73.

53. Marion Tinling, *Thomas Lloyd's Reports of the First Federal Congress,* 18 WM. & MARY Q. 519 (3rd ser. 1961). Madison wrote that the notes gave "*some idea* of the discussion," but that they showed "the strongest evidences of mutilation & perversion, and of the illiteracy of the Editor." *Id.* at 532-33 (emphasis in original). *See supra* notes 27 & 36.

54. 1 ANNALS OF CONG. 729-31 (Joseph Gales ed. 1834) (Aug. 15, 1789).

55. *Id.* at 15 (ed. note).

tee, a draft somewhat narrower than the amendment ultimately adopted. Two things about this draft are important. First, it was ambiguous concerning nonpreferential aid. Second, and more important, the House promptly rejected this draft and substituted a version that was not ambiguous on this issue.

The Select Committee draft provided:

[N]o religion shall be established by law, nor shall the equal rights of conscience be infringed.[56]

The reference to "no religion" is consistent with the view that many religions exist, and that no one of them may be established by law. The possibility is best illustrated by comparing the following two formulations, which are identical except for the placement of the negative:

1. No religion shall be established by law.
2. Religion shall not be established by law.

The first formulation is the Select Committee draft. It might mean that no particular religion, or no specific religion, shall be established by law. It is not plausible to read the second formulation that way; it seems clearly to mean that religion generally shall not be established by law.

Again, I do not want to make too much of this textual inference. The first formulation is not unambiguous, especially if it is not compared to the second formulation. If the Select Committee meant to say "no particular religion," it could have said so. Nothing suggests that anyone thought of the second formulation and deliberately chose the first formulation instead. Finally, what the Select Committee draft meant ultimately makes no difference, because the House did not adopt it and the subsequent Senate and Conference Committee choices are much less ambiguous. The possible meaning of the Select Committee draft matters only because of the emphasis that has been placed on the August 15 debate. Anyone who thinks that the debate concerning this draft shows an intention to ban only preferential aid must keep in mind that the draft might have been so limited, or that some of the speakers might have so understood it.

Even more important, the House rejected the Select Committee draft at the end of the August 15 debate. Instead, it adopted the sweeping substitute offered by Mr. Livermore:

56. *Id.* at 729 (Aug. 15, 1789).

Congress shall make no laws touching religion, or infringing the rights of conscience.[57]

Any law aiding religion in any way would "touch" religion. Malbin concedes that the Livermore amendment would have forbidden nonpreferential aid and even incidental religious effects of secular programs.[58] But the surviving notes of the debate do not mention that point, and nothing clearly indicates why a majority voted for the amendment. Livermore's language had been proposed by the ratifying convention in his home state of New Hampshire,[59] and he may have been the draftsman.[60] Probably no one will ever know whether he offered the amendment for a substantive reason, out of state pride, or out of personal pride of authorship.

Malbin speculates that the Antifederalists supported Livermore's amendment because it was more restrictive than the Select Committee's draft and, in their view, any restriction on federal power was good.[61] I wish I thought he were right, because that theory devastates the claim that the Framers meant to permit nonpreferential aid. Indeed, a similar claim that the Framers intended the meaning that most severely limited federal power is a principal element of Leonard Levy's attack on the nonpreferentialists.[62] Malbin's Antifederalist explanation of the Livermore amendment suggests that a substantial block of congressmen understood the restrictive implications of the Livermore amendment and supported it because of those implications. Malbin's claim that those who spoke on August 15 wanted to permit nonpreferential aid is inconsistent with his claim that the House adopted the Livermore amendment precisely because it forbade nonpreferential aid and even incidental aid.

Malbin offers his Antifederalist explanation of the Livermore amendment to show that the House was sparring on collateral issues. That is plainly true of some of the debate, and it further reduces the importance of the debate.[63] To the extent that the members were really talking about collateral issues, it is that much more difficult to infer specific intentions about the Establishment Clause from their remarks.

---

57. *Id.* at 731.

58. MALBIN, *supra* note 7, at 10.

59. *See* 1 ELLIOT'S DEBATES, *supra* note 41, at 326.

60. *See* 1 ANSON PHELPS STOKES, CHURCH AND STATE IN THE UNITED STATES 315-16 (1950).

61. MALBIN, *supra* note 7, at 9-11.

62. *See infra* notes 166-75 and accompanying text.

63. The most obvious example is Elbridge Gerry's speech. *See* MALBIN, *supra* note 7, at 10; *infra* notes 71-72 and accompanying text.

The bottom line concerning the Livermore amendment is this: If the House had the distinction between preferential and nonpreferential aid in mind, its vote for the Livermore amendment was a vote to forbid nonpreferential aid, and the "no preference" interpretation of the debate must be wrong. If the House did not have the distinction in mind, the debate cannot speak to the issue. Either way, the debate is little help.

B. The Content of the Debate

Fifty-one representatives were present to vote on the Livermore amendment.[64] Only eight of them said anything the reporter took down, and few of the eight addressed the meaning of the Select Committee draft.[65] Mr. Vining suggested transposing the two clauses.[66] Mr. Sherman said that the amendment was unnecessary because the Constitution conferred no power to establish religion.[67] Mr. Carroll responded that the amendment would reassure those with honest doubts.[68] Mr. Madison agreed with Mr. Carroll.[69] Mr. Livermore offered his substitute without explanation.[70] These remarks do not support any inference about the meaning of the amendment.

Elbridge Gerry spoke twice. His longer speech concerned a wholly collateral issue. Madison had suggested clarifying the amendment by inserting the word "national," and Gerry took the opportunity to denounce the Federalists.[71] The opponents of the Constitution had argued all along that it created a national rather than a federal government, and Madison seemed to be confirming the charge. Madison withdrew his motion.[72]

Gerry's other comment was a suggestion that the amendment "would read better if it was, that no religious doctrine shall be established by law."[73] This substitute would have stated a narrow variant of the nonpreferentialist position, but it does not show the meaning of the draft under discussion. No one spoke in support of Gerry's substitute, it was not adopted,

---

64. 1 ANNALS OF CONG. 731 (Joseph Gales ed. 1834) (Aug. 15, 1789).
65. *See id.* at 729-31.
66. *Id.* at 729.
67. *Id.* at 730.
68. *Id.*
69. *Id.*
70. *Id.* at 731.
71. *Id.*
72. *Id.*
73. *Id.* at 730.

and it closely paralleled the final Senate draft that was rejected in the Conference Committee.

That leaves three speakers for the nonpreferentialists to rely on: Mr. Sylvester and Mr. Huntington, who appeared to resist the Establishment Clause, and Madison, who sponsored it. Sylvester feared that the Select Committee draft "might . . . have a tendency to abolish religion altogether."[74] From this comment some have argued that Sylvester was friendly to religion and convinced that religion was dependent on state aid, so that he must have intended not to forbid such aid.[75] Those inferences are not unreasonable, but it does not follow that Sylvester wanted to forbid preferential aid and permit nonpreferential aid. No one knows what kind of aid Sylvester would have permitted. A fair inference is that Sylvester opposed the Establishment Clause, that he wanted it narrowed in any way possible, and that he would have supported any kind of aid he could get. Whatever he thought, no evidence indicates that a majority shared his views. The Select Committee draft was not changed to accommodate his objection.

Mr. Huntington was the only speaker who endorsed Sylvester's remarks. Specifically, Huntington feared that the amendment would render federal courts unable to enforce pledges of money to the support of churches.[76] On its face, Huntington's statement seems to say that the amendment would go too far if it rendered church contracts unenforceable. But context reveals that Huntington probably meant more than that. He offered the example of "congregations to the Eastward." These congregations were presumably in his home state of Connecticut, because Congress then met in New York. Pledges of money to churches in Connecticut were not voluntary contracts; every citizen was required to pay a church tax to the church of his choice.[77] This scheme of taxation could be viewed as a form of multiple or nonpreferential establishment, although dissenters viewed it as preferential and oppressive. However the Connecticut scheme is characterized, Huntington seems to have said that these taxes should be enforceable in federal court. Count one vote for financial aid to religion. But like Sylvester, Huntington probably opposed the clause, and there is no evidence that the majority shared his views.

The reporter's notes of Huntington's speech continue:

By the charter of Rhode Island, no religion could be established by law; he could give a history of the effects of such a regulation; indeed the people

74. *Id.* at 729.
75. MALBIN, *supra* note 7, at 6-7; Comment, *supra* note 10, at 572 n.124.
76. 1 ANNALS OF CONG. 730-31 (Joseph Gales ed. 1834) (Aug. 15, 1789).
77. *See* CURRY, *supra* note 3, at 180-81.

were now enjoying the blessed fruits of it. He hoped, therefore, the amendment would be made in such a way as to secure the rights of conscience, and a free exercise of the rights of religion, but not to patronize those who professed no religion at all.[78]

This passage may contain more than meets the eye. Perhaps Huntington was serious about the "blessed fruits" of disestablishment so long as the concept was not taken too far, but more likely his reference to Rhode Island was sarcastic[79] and his concluding remark was a request to omit the Establishment Clause altogether. Much of the country viewed Rhode Island as radical, libertine, and unsavory,[80] and supporters of establishment thought that disestablishment was an important part of that state's problems.

The remark about patronizing those who professed no religion at all appears to be a second allusion to disputes in Connecticut about collection of the church tax from nonbelievers.[81] Connecticut was willing to let each citizen pay the church of his choice, but it was not willing to exempt nonbelievers altogether. Huntington had just urged that the federal courts be available for suits to collect this tax; perhaps he thought that a refusal to collect the tax from those who did not pay voluntarily would "patronize those who professed no religion at all." References to the rights of conscience and to free exercise already had appeared in various drafts of the Religion Clauses.[82] Huntington appears to have urged Congress to adopt the rights of conscience and free exercise clauses and to reject the Establishment Clause.

Nussbaum and Smith apparently conclude that Huntington authoritatively explained the Establishment Clause.[83] But Huntington was probably an opponent of disestablishment, or at best a grudging supporter. His view that the clause should be construed narrowly is based on his preference for establishment. The clause was not changed to eliminate Huntington's fears. Fur-

---

78. 1 ANNALS OF CONG. 730-31 (Joseph Gales ed. 1834) (Aug. 15, 1789).

79. *See* CURRY, *supra* note 3, at 203.

80. *Id.* at 20-21, 91, 112, 183; FORREST MCDONALD, NOVUS ORDO SECLORUM: THE INTELLECTUAL ORIGINS OF THE CONSTITUTION 175-76 (1985).

81. CURRY, *supra* note 3, at 203.

82. The draft under debate protected "the equal rights of conscience." 1 ANNALS OF CONG. 729 (Joseph Gales ed. 1834) (Aug. 15, 1789). The Virginia Declaration of Rights contained a Free Exercise Clause, see 1 STOKES, *supra* note 60, at 303 (quoting the clause), and Virginia's ratifying convention also had proposed an amendment containing a Free Exercise Clause, see 3 ELLIOT'S DEBATES, *supra* note 41, at 659 (quoting the proposed amendment). The first recorded congressional draft containing the phrase "free exercise" appeared on Aug. 20, 1789. 1 ANNALS OF CONG. 766 (Joseph Gales ed. 1834) (Aug. 20, 1789).

83. Smith, *supra* note 9, at 611, 613; Nussbaum Comment, *supra* note 10, at 573 n.124.

ther, as Professor Kurland mentions, the Constitution already patronized nonbelievers in an important way: the Test Oath Clause made them eligible for federal office.[84] Huntington probably thought the ban on test oaths was a bad idea too, but that is no reason to construe the Test Oath Clause to require belief in God. It is no more plausible to impute Huntington's views of the Establishment Clause to the majority.

The heart of the argument is Madison's puzzling comments about a national religion and compelled worship. Madison's tactic was not to argue with Sylvester and Huntington, but to reassure them and their sympathizers by portraying the Establishment Clause in the narrowest possible light.

Madison spoke twice. The first time, he obviously was responding to Sylvester's fear that the amendment might abolish religion altogether: "Mr. Madison said, he apprehended the meaning of the words to be, that Congress should not establish a religion, and enforce the legal observation of it by law, nor compel men to worship God in any manner contrary to their conscience."[85] Huntington responded that he understood the amendment to mean what Madison had said, but he feared "that the words might be taken in such latitude as to be extremely hurtful to the cause of religion."[86] Huntington then made his speech about collecting Connecticut church taxes and the blessed fruits of disestablishment in Rhode Island.

Madison then spoke a second time. He proposed that the House insert the word "national" before the word "religion," so that the Establishment Clause would read: "No national religion shall be established by law."[87] Madison explained that

> he believed that the people feared one sect might obtain a preeminence, or two combine together, and establish a religion to which they would compel others to conform. He thought that if the word "national" was introduced, it would point the amendment directly to the object it was intended to prevent.[88]

Madison's two statements are obviously inconsistent with modern interpretations of the Establishment Clause, but they are equally inconsistent with the view that only preferential aid is forbidden. Almost everyone agrees that the Establishment Clause means more than Madison mentioned on Au-

---

84. *See* Kurland, *supra* note 1, at 845-50, 856.
85. 1 ANNALS OF CONG. 730 (Joseph Gales ed. 1834) (Aug. 15, 1789).
86. *Id.*
87. *Id.* at 731.
88. *Id.*

gust 15.[89] If Congress appropriated one million dollars for the support of the United Methodist Church, it would not be enforcing the observation of Methodism by law. Nevertheless, the appropriation would be preferential aid, unconstitutional even under the "no preference" view of the clause. If Madison's second statement described the entire meaning of the clause, the later Senate draft forbidding uniform "articles of faith or a mode of worship"[90] would have captured the meaning perfectly. But that draft also was rejected.

It is hard to know what Madison was thinking. The two statements are inconsistent with all his previous and subsequent statements concerning establishment.[91] Nevertheless, he appears to have said the same thing clearly and twice, which reduces the risk that the reporter's notes are materially inaccurate. The statements also are consistent with Madison's June 8 draft of the clause, which provided only that no "national religion be established."[92]

Perhaps Madison was willing to settle for such a narrow amendment if that were all he could get, but subsequent developments in the Senate and the Conference Committee opened the way to more. Perhaps he believed that pressure for a single establishment with compelled observance was the issue most likely to arise, so that he believed he was accurately describing the principal consequence of the amendment. Perhaps Professor McConnell is right that coercion rather than preference is the essence of the Establishment Clause,[93] and Madison was describing the classic example of coercion. Perhaps he was dissembling. We will never know. But Madison plainly did not describe a ban on preferential aid.

Madison's proposal to insert "national" before "religion" would have strengthened the implication that only a single national establishment was forbidden. But he promptly withdrew that motion in the face of Gerry's at-

89. *But compare* Wallace v. Jaffree, 472 U.S. 38, 98 (1985) (Rehnquist, J., dissenting) ("[Madison] saw the amendment as designed to prohibit . . . a national religion, and *perhaps* to prevent discrimination among sects." (emphasis added)) with *id.* at 113 (same two goals; "perhaps" omitted).

90. *See supra* note 34 and accompanying text.

91. *See* THE COMPLETE MADISON: HIS BASIC WRITINGS 298-312 (Saul K. Padover ed. 1953) [hereinafter cited as THE COMPLETE MADISON]. For Madison's reaction to a bill aiding a particular church without coercing others to conform to it, see *id.* at 308 (vetoing bill as unconstitutional).

92. 1 ANNALS OF CONG. 434 (Joseph Gales ed. 1834) (June 8, 1789).

93. Michael W. McConnell, *Coercion: The Lost Element of Establishment*, 27 WM. & MARY L. REV. 933 (1986) [hereinafter cited as McConnell, *Coercion*]; *see* Michael W. McConnell, *Accommodation of Religion*, 1985 SUP. CT. REV. 1, 20, 35-39 [hereinafter cited as McConnell, *Accommodation*].

tack on the word "national."[94] He could have substituted a less offensive adjective; "particular," "specific," or "single" would have done nicely. Either he did not think of these words or he chose not to offer them. His failure to offer such alternatives is consistent with Professor Levy's suggestion that the word "national" was intended to emphasize that the clause bound only Congress.[95] But even if Levy's suggestion explains Madison's attempt to insert "national" into the text of the clause, it does not account for Madison's narrow explanations of the meaning of the clause.

After Madison withdrew his amendment, someone called the question on Livermore's substitute, and the House adopted it.[96] The only reported debate thus ended a lot further from the "no preference" position than it began. Gerry's substitute was ignored, Madison's amendment was withdrawn, and Livermore's sweeping substitute was adopted. No one explicitly argued that preferential establishments were bad while nonpreferential establishments were acceptable. Two of the remarks most relied on by nonpreferentialists came from apparent opponents of the clause, and neither they nor Madison stated the "no preference" position. Compared to the clear textual choices made in the Senate and in the Conference Committee, nothing in this brief debate casts any useful light on the problem.

IV. The Debates in the Revolutionary States

Independence was an occasion for reviewing church-state relations in the revolutionary states.[97] In the states with established Anglican churches, the King was the head of both the church and the state, and the question of succession extended to both his secular and his religious authority.[98] Several states wrote constitutions in the wake of independence, and they addressed church-state questions in their bills of rights. The ferment concerning this is-

94. 1 ANNALS OF CONG. 731 (Joseph Gales ed. 1834) (Aug. 15, 1789).

95. LEVY, *supra* note 2, at 76, 97. The draft did not yet explicitly mention Congress. See *id.*

96. 1 ANNALS OF CONG. 731 (Joseph Gales ed. 1834) (Aug. 15, 1789).

97. *See* CURRY, *supra* note 3, at 134.

98. The situation in Virginia exemplified the turmoil that followed independence in these states. Delegates to the Revolutionary Convention of 1776 ordered all references to King George III deleted from the liturgy, and ordered prayers for the new civil magistrates instead. THOMAS E. BUCKLEY, CHURCH AND STATE IN REVOLUTIONARY VIRGINIA, 1776-1787, at 21 (1977). These changes created a serious problem of conscience for those Anglican clergy who felt bound by their ordination oaths to support the Crown and the Book of Common Prayer. *Id.* at 43.

sue affected churches as well as governments. For example, in 1788 the Presbyterians in the United States amended their Confession to renounce the Calvinist tradition of establishment.[99]

For obvious reasons, the debates in the states are not direct evidence of the meaning of the federal Religion Clauses. Nothing in these debates was offered as an explanation of those clauses, and the Framers could support one regime of church-state relations for their respective states and a quite different regime of church-state relations for the new federal government. At the very least, the framing of a federal rule required a choice among the diverse practices in the states. Moreover, as Professor Van Alstyne has pointed out with respect to the Speech Clause, the Framers' understanding of federalism predisposed them to restrict federal power more severely than state power.[100]

Thus, I do not offer the state debates as legislative history in anything like the usual sense. Instead, I offer them as intellectual history. The state debates help show how the concept of establishment was understood in the Framers' generation. Learning how that generation understood the concept may be more informative than the brief and unfocused debate in the House. If the Framers generally understood the concept in a certain way, and if nothing indicates that they used the word in an unusual sense in the First Amendment, then we can fairly assume that the Framers used the word in accordance with their general understanding of the concept.

A. Votes Against Nonpreferential Aid

For several reasons, the debates in Virginia were most important. First, the arguments were developed most fully in Virginia. Second, Madison led the winning coalition, and he played a dominant role in the adoption of the Establishment Clause three years later. Third, the debates in Virginia may have been the best known. I am not sure of that, and the subject deserves further investigation, but most of the national figures from Virginia were involved, some in leadership roles on each side.[101] Further, the debate dragged on for

99. *See* OFFICE OF THE GENERAL ASSEMBLY, THE CONSTITUTION OF THE PRESBYTE- RIAN CHURCH IN THE UNITED STATES OF AMERICA v, 83-87, 97-99 (1946). For the earlier version, see CREEDS OF THE CHURCHES 215-16, 219-20 (John H. Leith 3d ed. 1982). The evolving views of the major denominations in Virginia are carefully reviewed in BUCKLEY, *supra* note 98.

100. *See* William Van Alstyne, *Congressional Power and Free Speech: Levy's Legacy Revisited* (Book Review), 99 HARV. L. REV. 1089, 1094-99 (1986).

101. Patrick Henry was the principal proponent of financial aid to Christian minis-

ten years.[102] It would be surprising if the leading Virginians had said nothing to their correspondents in other states. Virginia's Act for Establishing Religious Freedom[103] was published widely in Europe,[104] and was the subject of at least one pamphlet published in Philadelphia.[105] Curry also notes a Connecticut clergyman discoursing on the Virginia debates in 1791.[106]

The Virginia fight came to a head in 1785 and 1786. The defenders of establishment offered a compromise known as a general assessment, under which all Christian churches could receive tax money and every taxpayer could designate a church to receive his tax. The bill would have included Catholics, and it tried to accommodate Quaker and Mennonite objections to paid clergy.[107] Any taxpayer could refuse to designate a church, with

---

ters. CURRY, *supra* note 3, at 142. George Washington and Richard Henry Lee also took that position, BUCKLEY, *supra* note 98, at 101-02, 136, but Washington eventually abandoned the measure on the ground that it had become too divisive, *id.* at 136; LEVY, *supra* note 2, at 59. John Marshall, then a young legislator, was defeated for reelection because of his support for the bill. BUCKLEY, *supra* note 98, at 117 n.11.

Thomas Jefferson and James Madison led the opponents. CURRY, *supra* note 3, at 139, 142. Edmund Randolph also was opposed to the bill. BUCKLEY, *supra* note 98, at 124, 129-30. George Mason drafted the religious liberty clause in the Virginia Declaration of Rights and the first statute suspending collection of the tax, 1 STOKES, *supra* note 60, at 303-05, and he circulated Madison's *Memorial and Remonstrance* for signatures, BUCKLEY, *supra* note 98, at 147.

Virginia's religious leaders also were actively involved in the dispute, and they attended national meetings of their denominations during this period. *Id.* at 117-19, 123, 152 (Anglicans); *id.* at 120 (Methodists); PRESBYTERIAN BOARD OF EDUCATION AND SABBATH-SCHOOL WORK, RECORDS OF THE PRESBYTERIAN CHURCH IN THE UNITED STATES OF AMERICA 1706-1788, at 514, 528, 542-43 (1969) (Presbyterians).

102. The full ten years are reviewed in BUCKLEY, *supra* note 98, and in 1 STOKES, *supra* note 60, at 366-97.

103. Ch. 34 (1786), 12 HENING'S STATUTES AT LARGE 84 (1823). The Act also may be found in Buckley, *supra* note 98, at 190-91, CORD, *supra* note 8, at 249-50, and 1 STOKES, *supra* note 60, at 392-94.

104. 3 STOKES, *supra* note 60, at 688-89 (quoting letter from Thomas Jefferson to James Madison, Dec. 16, 1786).

105. JOHN SWANWICK, CONSIDERATIONS ON AN ACT OF THE LEGISLATURE OF VIRGINIA, ENTITLED AN ACT FOR THE ESTABLISHMENT OF RELIGIOUS FREEDOM (Philadelphia 1786), cited in BUCKLEY, *supra* note 98, at 165 n.59. The pamphlet attacked the Act, and in the political practice of the times, Swanwick's attack should have produced a responsive pamphlet defending the Act.

106. CURRY, *supra* note 3, at 182; *see also id.* at 171 (Massachusetts advocate citing Virginia law in 1780-81).

107. A Bill Establishing a Provision for Teachers of the Christian Religion, *reprinted in* Everson v. Board of Educ., 330 U.S. 1, 72-74 (1947) (Appendix to opinion of Rutledge, J., dissenting). The bill also may be found in BUCKLEY, *supra* note 98, at 188-89, and CORD, *supra* note 8, at 242-43.

undesignated church taxes going to a fund for schools.[108] These provisions were substantial improvements over superficially similar systems in Massachusetts and Connecticut.[109] Supporters of the bill invoked the slogan "Equal Right and Equal Liberty," and argued that it imposed not "the smallest coercion" to contribute to the support of religion.[110]

Madison's *Memorial and Remonstrance Against Religious Assessments*[111] was published to rally the citizenry against this nonpreferential establishment. Many similar petitions also were circulated, especially by Presbyterians and Baptists,[112] and support for establishment collapsed. The assessment bill died without a vote,[113] and the legislature enacted Jefferson's Act for Establishing Religious Freedom instead. Thus, the great debate about disestablishment in Virginia culminated in a decisive vote against nonpreferential aid.

Professors Cord and Smith try to make this choice go away by showing that Madison considered the general assessment bill preferential.[114] Madison and others were able to imagine the bill's effects on Jews, Muslims, and other non-Christians,[115] and Madison also objected that Quakers and Mennonites were not the only religious groups that needed or deserved partial exemption.[116] Both of these objections tended to show that the proposal was not quite as nonpreferential as its supporters claimed. Consequently, according to Professors Cord and Smith, some of the votes against the bill may have been votes against these preferential features rather than votes against a pure system of nonpreferential aid.

108. The bill used the phrase "seminaries of learning," which almost certainly meant schools generally and not just schools for the training of ministers. *See* 9 OXFORD ENGLISH DICTIONARY 442 (1933) (definition 4 and the examples of usage). Buckley's thorough history of the controversy treated the provision as unambiguous. *See* BUCKLEY, *supra* note 98, at 108-09, 133.

109. *See infra* notes 136-42 and accompanying text.

110. *See* CURRY, *supra* note 3, at 145.

111. JAMES MADISON, A MEMORIAL AND REMONSTRANCE (circa June 20, 1785) [hereinafter cited as *Memorial and Remonstrance*]. The *Memorial and Remonstrance* has been reprinted widely. *See, e.g.,* Everson v. Board of Educ., 330 U.S. 1, 63-72 (1947) (appendix to opinion of Rutledge, J., dissenting); CORD, *supra* note 8, at 244-49; THE COMPLETE MADISON, *supra* note 91, at 299-306.

112. BUCKLEY, *supra* note 98, at 137-40, 147-52; CURRY, *supra* note 3, at 143-46.

113. *See* BUCKLEY, *supra* note 98, at 158 n.45.

114. CORD, *supra* note 8, at 20-21; Cord, *supra* note 8, at 159-60; Smith, *supra* note 9, at 587-95.

115. BUCKLEY, *supra* note 98, at 151; CURRY, *supra* note 3, at 145; *Memorial and Remonstrance, supra* note 111, §§ 3-4. An amendment to include non-Christians had been tentatively accepted and then rejected in the legislature. BUCKLEY, *supra* note 98, at 108.

116. *Memorial and Remonstrance, supra* note 111, § 4.

That is conceivable, but it is wholly unrealistic. It is anachronistic to view aid to all denominations of Christians as preferential in 1786. There were hardly any Jews in the United States at that time, and no other non-Christians to speak of.[117] Indeed, when it suits his purpose, Cord correctly states that aid to all Christians was viewed as nonpreferential in the late eighteenth century.[118] That some Virginians could imagine the effects of establishment on non-Christians only shows how far Virginians had thought through the problem. No public figure had talked that way since Roger Williams.[119]

The provision for Quakers and Mennonites in the general assessment bill was facially preferential, but it was an attempt to make the bill less preferential in its impact. The bill would have been more objectionable without this provision. Madison did not want the Quakers and Mennonites compelled to conform; he wanted everyone to be exempt.

Virginians understood the vote against the bill as a rejection of any form of financial aid to churches. The proof of that is that the ten-year-old controversy died with this bill. No one at the time perceived that only preferential aid had been rejected; no one proposed a new bill that included non-Christians and eliminated the exemptions for Quakers and Mennonites. Instead, the Act for Establishing Religious Freedom provided that "no man shall be compelled to frequent or support any religious worship, place, or ministry whatsoever"[120] — language comprehensive enough to ban taxes for either preferential or nonpreferential aid. The Act also declared that any subsequent bill narrowing its terms would be a violation of natural right.[121]

---

117. Stokes reported that the nation's Jewish population did not reach 10,000 until well after the Revolution, with that small number concentrated largely in Newport, New York City, Philadelphia, and Charleston. 1 STOKES, *supra* note 60, at 286. He did not cite a source for these data. Deism among the Framers "usually amounted to a severely stripped down version of Christianity, with all that smacked of mystery and superstition pared away." JAMES TURNER, WITHOUT GOD, WITHOUT CREED: THE ORIGINS OF UNBELIEF IN AMERICA 51-52 (1985). Most of the prominent Framers maintained membership in some Protestant church. *See* 1 STOKES, *supra* note 60, at 293, 299, 302, 306, 310, 311, 314, 333, 339, 350, 353, 507-14. The most notable exceptions were the Roman Catholic Carrolls of Maryland. *See id.* at 324.

118. *E.g.,* CORD, *supra* note 8, at 161; Cord, *supra* note 8, at 138 n.45.

119. *See* CURRY, *supra* note 3, at 145, 182. Williams had written of "papists and protestants, Jews and Turks" all on one ship, with complete and equal religious liberty. Letter to the Town of Providence, reprinted in 1 GERALD N. GROB & ROBERT N. BECK, AMERICAN IDEAS: SOURCE READINGS IN THE INTELLECTUAL HISTORY OF THE UNITED STATES 53 (1963).

120. Ch. 34, § II (1786), 12 HENING'S STATUTES AT LARGE 84, 86 (1823).

121. *Id.* § III, 12 HENING'S STATUTES AT LARGE 86.

An equally clear vote occurred in Maryland. Supporters of establishment there proposed a tax even less preferential than the tax proposed in Virginia. Non-Christians were exempt, and Christians could pay either a minister of their choice or a fund for the poor.[122] The proposal was defeated in 1785 after substantial public debate.[123]

The votes in Virginia and Maryland show that whenever a choice between nonpreferential aid and no aid was squarely posed, Americans in the 1780's voted for no aid. When they focused on the question, they concluded that nonpreferential aid was a form of establishment and inconsistent with religious liberty.

B. Developments Elsewhere

The debates in other states provide little evidence of a different understanding. Curry's thorough survey reports little support for nonpreferential establishment. Georgia did have a nonpreferential tax on the books, but the tax appears never to have been collected, and it therefore stirred little debate.[124] Such taxes were prohibited in the Georgia Constitution of 1798.[125]

The Anglican establishment in South Carolina was abolished without substantial controversy.[126] The new law was called an establishment, and its recitals endorsed Protestantism,[127] but its substantive sections merely provided for the incorporation of churches.[128] Occasional proposals for nonpreferential financial aid drew no support.[129]

The vestigial Anglican establishments in North Carolina[130] and New York[131] were abolished without major controversy. No recognized establish-

---

122. CURRY, *supra* note 3, at 155-57. The bill may have been proposed as a political diversion, but the ensuing debate was genuine and robust. *See* McDONALD, *supra* note 80, at 43-44.

123. CURRY, *supra* note 3, at 156-57.

124. *Id.* at 152-53.

125. *See* 1 STOKES, *supra* note 60, at 440 ("No person within this State shall . . . ever be obliged to pay tithes, taxes, or any other rate, for the building or repairing any place of worship, or for the maintenance of any minister or ministry, contrary to what he believes to be right, or hath voluntarily engaged to do.").

126. CURRY, *supra* note 3, at 149-51.

127. *See* 1 STOKES, *supra* note 60, at 432-34 (quoting this lengthy provision).

128. CURRY, *supra* note 3, at 150-51.

129. *See id.* at 149-51.

130. *Id.* at 151.

131. *Id.* at 161-62.

ment had ever existed in Pennsylvania,[132] Delaware,[133] New Jersey,[134] or Rhode Island,[135] and thus these states had nothing to repeal. No one seriously proposed nonpreferential establishment in any of these six states.

Massachusetts had a system that might arguably be characterized as nonpreferential aid.[136] It was written into the Constitution of 1780, amidst considerable debate. Under this system, Massachusetts imposed a tax to support the minister elected by each town, who was nearly always a Congregationalist. Dissenters could file an exemption certificate and pay the tax to their own minister, at least in theory. In practice, the Massachusetts system was preferential, and it fell especially harshly on Quakers and Baptists. Quakers had no ministers,[137] and Baptists conscientiously objected to supporting their ministers through taxes collected by the state.[138] Baptists were a substantial minority, and their property frequently was seized for unpaid church taxes.[139]

The Massachusetts statutes referred to the minister elected by the majority as the minister "established by law."[140] I think the system was regarded as a Congregational establishment, with what the Congregationalists thought was generous toleration for dissenters. It was a deliberate move in the direction of a nonpreferential multiple establishment, but it does not appear to have been seriously considered nonpreferential. Nor was it a model for the federal Establishment Clause. Neither the system nor the controversy was widely known outside New England.[141]

Connecticut's system was quite similar to the one in Massachusetts, and it engendered similar controversies with dissenters known as Separates.[142] Somewhat similar systems were on the books in Vermont and New Hampshire, but they were not well developed and a lot of local variations were tolerated in practice.[143]

Now add one more fact: Massachusetts and Connecticut did not ratify

132. *Id.* at 159-60.

133. *Id.*

134. *Id.*

135. *Id.* at 162.

136. *See id.* at 163-77.

137. *See* BUCKLEY, *supra* note 98, at 108; 1 STOKES, *supra* note 60, at 759.

138. *See* CURRY, *supra* note 3, at 89-90, 166, 171, 175.

139. *Id.* at 168. Not surprisingly, many Baptists accommodated to the system, especially when it worked to their advantage. *See* LEVY, *supra* note 2, at 30-32, 40.

140. CURRY, *supra* note 3, at 173.

141. *Id.* at 205.

142. *See id.* at 178-84.

143. *See id.* at 184-90.

the First Amendment.[144] I do not want to overstate the importance of this. Failure to ratify need not mean strong opposition; insufficient support to overcome legislative inertia is the more likely explanation.[145] Moreover, we have no theory for summing up the disparate intentions of all the Congressmen and legislators entitled to a say in the amendment process.

But one does not need a full-blown theory to show that the understanding of religious liberty in states that ratified the Religion Clauses is more important than the understanding of religious liberty in states that did not. Massachusetts and Connecticut were to the ratification process what Huntington and Sylvester were to the House debate:[146] probably opposed to disestablishment, and at least suspicious of it. The existence of systems in Massachusetts and Connecticut that arguably resembled nonpreferential multiple establishments reveals little about what the eleven ratifying states meant by the Establishment Clause. No evidence suggests that the Massachusetts and Connecticut systems generally were thought consistent with disestablishment.

This survey shows that none of the Framers had a working model of nonpreferential establishment on which to draw. Every time a nonpreferential establishment had been proposed, it had been rejected. The allegedly nonpreferential systems in New England did not work well and demonstrably caused bitter religious strife. It is unlikely that out of this background emerged a Congress and a set of state legislatures that specifically intended to forbid preferential aid and permit nonpreferential aid. A far more plausible explanation is that the textual choice in the Senate and the Conference Committee meant what it appears to mean.

V. The Curry and Levy Interpretations

The theses of the important recent books by Thomas Curry[147] and Leonard Levy[148] now can be considered. Curry, Levy, and I agree on the central point:

---

144. *Id.* at 215. Georgia also failed to ratify the amendment. *Id.* All three states ratified the amendment in 1939, LEVY, *supra* note 2, at 85, but by then their understanding of religious liberty had caught up with the rest of the country.

145. The Massachusetts legislature took some favorable votes on the amendment but failed to proceed to final passage. Part of the opposition in all three nonratifying states was based on the view that no amendments were necessary. CURRY, *supra* note 3, at 215; LEVY, *supra* note 2, at 85-86.

146. *See supra* notes 74-84 and accompanying text.

147. CURRY, *supra* note 3.

148. LEVY, *supra* note 2.

the framers of the Establishment Clause had no specific intention to permit nonpreferential aid to religion. Levy and I agree on the stronger formulation that the Framers intended to forbid such aid. But we take three different positions on important subsidiary points.

A. *The Understanding of the Rejected Drafts*

Like the nonpreferentialists,[149] Curry believes that the whole debate was over style. Unlike the nonpreferentialists, he offers a reason for that conclusion. Curry believes that the Framers simply did not understand the distinction between preferential and nonpreferential establishments.[150] Levy waffles on this issue. At one point, he argues that the First Congress made a clear choice when it rejected nonpreferentialist drafts.[151] Later, he seems to endorse Curry's judgment that the Framers did not recognize the difference.[152]

The votes in the Senate and the Conference Committee are equally devastating to the intentionalist supporters of nonpreferential aid under Curry's view or mine. If the Framers had no concept of nonpreferential establishment — if they could not understand the difference between the drafts they were debating, and if they thought it all a matter of style — they could not possibly have intended to permit nonpreferential establishments. The Framers could not have specifically intended something they had never heard of. If the various drafts all meant the same thing to them, they are as likely to have intended no aid whatever as to have intended no preferential aid. The only difference between Curry's view and mine is that I think the Framers did understand the distinction and that they rejected nonpreferential aid as firmly as they rejected preferential aid.

Curry is surely right that not all of the Framers understood the distinction or had it in mind all the time. He shows that some of the Framers used language loosely or without understanding the distinction, although not all of his examples support his point. But he is unpersuasive in his broader claim that the Framers collectively failed to understand the distinction between preferential and nonpreferential establishments.

As shown above, defenders of establishment often offered allegedly nonpreferential establishments as a compromise.[153] The Congregationalist

149. *See supra* notes 39-42 and accompanying text.
150. *See* CURRY, supra note 3, at 207-15.
151. LEVY, supra note 2, at 82-84.
152. *Id.* at 111-14.
153. *See supra* notes 107-10, 122-23 & 136-43 and accompanying text.

defenders of the New England establishments regularly contrasted them with the objectionable establishment in England — an exclusive Anglican establishment.[154] The New England establishments remained preferential in fact, and the dissenting sects were not satisfied with their treatment, but the idea had been to make establishment fair to everyone.

The Maryland and Virginia proposals would have been much more effectively nonpreferential, and they had been thoroughly and recently debated. The 1776 statute that suspended collection of the Anglican tax in Virginia drew the distinction explicitly. It recited that the question of a general assessment for all faiths had aroused a "great variety of opinions" that "cannot now be well accommodated," so that "nothing in this act . . . shall be construed to affect or influence [that] question . . . in any respect whatever."[155] From 1776 to 1786, the issue in Virginia had been whether to repeal the Anglican tax or to extend it to all denominations. It is inconceivable that Madison had forgotten that distinction. He likely had the distinction in mind when he served on the Conference Committee that rejected the narrow Senate draft and substituted the broad language that was ultimately ratified. Many others familiar with the debates of the 1780's also must have understood the distinction.

Curry refuses to draw this inference. What chiefly troubles him is the vocabulary of the debates about general assessments. Curry's argument contains three interwoven threads, each containing a different mistake.

First, Curry argues that general assessments often were debated on grounds of religious liberty rather than establishment.[156] The problem with this argument is the equation between religious liberty and free exercise. To subsume both free exercise and establishment under religious liberty is a perfectly sensible usage and, as Professor Kurland notes, it was a common usage among the Framers.[157] Further, as Curry concedes, the word "establishment" often was used in debates over general assessments. Madison used

154. CURRY, *supra* note 3, at 131-32 (quoting John Adams as an example).

155. The provision is reprinted in BUCKLEY, *supra* note 98, at 35, and 1 STOKES, *supra* note 60, at 305.

156. Curry says, for example:

> Neither side . . . attempted to show that a general assessment constituted an essentially different kind of establishment or to differentiate it from an exclusive state preference for one religion. The parties to the general assessment dispute concerned themselves with showing whether it violated or did not violate freedom of religion.

CURRY, *supra* note 3, at 210-11. For similar equations of religious liberty and free exercise, see *id.* at 146, 217.

157. Kurland, *supra* note 1, at 844.

"establish," "established," or "establishment" thirteen times in the *Memorial and Remonstrance,* and he described the general assessment bill as "the proposed establishment."[158]

Second, Curry notes that opponents of general assessment in Virginia argued that the bill would violate the Free Exercise Clause of the Virginia Declaration of Rights.[159] Curry may exaggerate this point: he is presumably reading "free exercise" every time the opponents said "religious liberty." But the opponents did invoke the Free Exercise Clause,[160] and the reason is plain. The Declaration of Rights did not contain an Establishment Clause.[161] The Declaration and the statute suspending the Anglican tax had been passed in 1776, at the very beginning of the debate about disestablishment. Together, the Declaration and the statute guaranteed free exercise and postponed decision on establishment. Advocates of religious liberty thereafter claimed as much as they could for the Free Exercise Clause; the rhetorical benefits of invoking a constitutional right were already understood. That rhetorical strategy is entirely consistent with believing that a general assessment would also and primarily be an establishment. Indeed, the 1776 agreement to postpone establishment questions would have been illusory if the parties to the compromise had understood a general assessment to violate the Free Exercise Clause.[162]

Third, Curry concedes that general assessments often were attacked as establishments, but he argues that no one "attempted to show that a general assessment constituted an essentially different kind of establishment or to differentiate it from an exclusive state preference for one religion."[163] On the opponents' side, this statement is true and entirely understandable. Their whole claim was that a tax for all churches is not essentially different from a tax for one church; they found any church tax objectionable.

On the proponents' side, Curry's statement is simply false. Their whole claim was that a tax for all churches is essentially different from a tax for one

---

158. *Memorial and Remonstrance, supra* note 111, § 9; *see also id.* § 6 ("the establishment proposed"); *id.* § 8 ("the establishment in question").

159. *See* Curry, *supra* note 3, at 146 (quoting Virginia Declaration of Rights § 16 (1776), 9 Hening's Statutes at Large 109, 111-12 (1821)).

160. *Memorial and Remonstrance, supra* note 111, §§ 4, 15; Buckley, *supra* note 98, at 115, 148-49.

161. *See* Buckley, *supra* note 98, at 19 (quoting the provision); 1 Stokes, *supra* note 60, at 303 (same).

162. For a discussion of the understanding of the relationship between free exercise and establishment in 1776, see Buckley, *supra* note 98, at 18-19, 22, 115.

163. Curry, supra note 3, at 210.

church. Curry's point apparently is that he found few statements like "We want an establishment but it will be a different kind of establishment."[164] That finding is no surprise. Establishments were unpopular, and avoiding any mention of establishment was rhetorically more effective. Thus, Curry says the proponents defended their proposals "primarily as fair, equitable, and compatible with religious freedom and concerned themselves very little with the issue of establishment."[165] That is exactly how I would make the argument if I were hired as their media consultant. Note also how Curry's formulation of this argument again depends on the false equation of religious freedom with free exercise.

In my judgment, Curry's analysis of the debates ignores the realities of political rhetoric and elevates labels over substance. That many in the Framers' generation understood the difference between exclusive and nonpreferential establishments seems as certain as can be for a proposition about what people were thinking two hundred years ago. That they understood the language of the House and Senate drafts as stating the two competing propositions is less certain. Perhaps they paid no attention to the meaning of the language, and perhaps they never thought of the most prominent religious liberty issue of the period when they drafted that language. Those things are possible, but they are not likely.

Equally important in my view, it is illegitimate to assume such things. If one assumes that the Framers paid no attention to the meaning of what they wrote and that they were oblivious to the most prominent issues of their time, the Constitution really can be read any way at all. That is not a legitimate approach to constitutional interpretation.

B. The Arguments From Federalism

Part of Curry's argument, and a much larger part of Levy's argument, turns on a mistaken inference from the Framers' concern with federalism. The starting point for Curry is the position of two Antifederalist supporters of establishment, Patrick Henry and Elbridge Gerry. Henry and Gerry are two of Curry's prime examples of Framers who did not understand the distinction between preferential and nonpreferential aid. Each of them proposed language that would have barred only preferential establishments. Curry finds

---

164. *Id.*

165. *Id.* at 217. The pro-assessment petitions are summarized in Buckley, *supra* note 98, at 113-43.

this inconsistent with their Antifederalism: a ban on all establishments would have further restricted federal power. He therefore concludes that Henry and Gerry did not understand the distinction, and that they intended to bar all establishments even though their language mentioned only preferential establishments.[166] Levy makes a similar point about Patrick Henry.[167]

This reliance on Henry and Gerry is an example of a larger background puzzle about the drafting of the Bill of Rights. The Federalists erroneously believed that the amendments were unnecessary because the government had no power to do any of these things anyway. Their error was to focus on the lack of any express power to restrict speech, establish religion, or violate other liberties, and to overlook the risk that delegated powers might be exercised in ways that would accomplish some of the same purposes.[168] Without the Establishment Clause, the power to tax and spend for the general welfare would authorize a nonpreferential subsidy to religious organizations. That specific risk probably was not in contemplation at the time, but the underlying theory that the spending power is not limited by the enumeration of other legislative powers can be traced to Alexander Hamilton's *Report on Manufactures* in 1791.[169] When he introduced the Bill of Rights, Madison explained that even limited powers could be abused, that Congress had discretion as to means, and that a bill of rights could protect against abusive measures that might otherwise be necessary and proper means of implementing delegated powers.[170]

The Federalist theory was widely believed even though erroneous. Under that theory, the amendments were of no substantive effect. A failure to bar nonpreferential aid in the Establishment Clause would not create a power to grant such aid; powers were conferred only by the original document.

It does not follow that the Framers paid no attention to the content of the amendments. Whatever the Federalists thought, the Antifederalists were demanding amendments, and many uncommitted citizens believed amendments were necessary. To build support for the new government, the Federalists indulged these fears and agreed to amendments. Thus, the Antifederalists believed, and the Federalists assumed for the sake of argument, that the Con-

166. *See* CURRY, *supra* note 3, at 209, 214.

167. LEVY, *supra* note 2, at 74, 109-10.

168. *See* ELY, *supra* note 2, at 36.

169. *See* 10 THE PAPERS OF ALEXANDER HAMILTON 302-04 (Harold C. Syrett & Jacob E. Cooke eds. 1966); *see also* United States v. Butler, 297 U.S. 1, 64-67 (1936) (adopting Hamilton's view that power to tax and spend for the general welfare is not limited by enumerated powers).

170. 1 ANNALS OF CONG. 432-33, 438 (Joseph Gales ed. 1834) (June 8, 1789).

stitution might somehow confer dangerous powers that would make the amendments necessary. The amendments were drafted on that assumption, and any effort to make sense of them must indulge the same assumption.

Once the Framers set to the task of drafting amendments, the evidence suggests that they tried to forbid only what they considered to be abuses. Thus, Huntington was concerned that the Establishment Clause not preclude federal jurisdiction over suits to collect state church taxes;[171] he did not notice the complete absence of any basis for such jurisdiction in article III. Henry and Gerry proposed language inconsistent with their antifederalism, but quite consistent with their continued support for some kind of establishment. Henry and Gerry simply proposed for the federal government the view of establishment they supported in their own states. Nothing supports the notion that they did not understand the familiar language they proposed. Rather, these examples suggest that when the Framers debated the details of the Religion Clauses, their views on religious liberty were more salient than their views on federalism.[172]

Levy derives a much broader argument from the relationship between federalism and establishment. He argues that the federal government had no power to aid religion and that no one thought the Establishment Clause created such power. He concludes that the Establishment Clause must therefore forbid any aid to religion, even nonpreferential aid. He finds it inconceivable that the Establishment Clause implicitly creates a previously nonexistent power to grant nonpreferential aid.[173]

Levy is correct that the clause creates no power, but that is not the issue. The issue is not what powers the clause creates, but what powers it forbids. Levy fallaciously assumes that the clause must forbid any power it does not create, ignoring the possibility that the clause might be neutral on some things. If no part of the Bill of Rights were necessary, as the Federalists argued and as Levy insists, then a fortiori it was unnecessary for the prohibitions in the Bill of Rights to match point for point the powers not created by the original Constitution.

As I have already argued, the Establishment Clause was debated on the assumption that the government may have some power to aid religion. The Framers fought over how much of that hypothetical, unspecified, and possibly nonexistent power to restrain. They could have agreed to forbid or not to for-

---

171. *See supra* notes 76-77 and accompanying text.

172. This attention to the merits when debating details coexisted with a willingness to support or oppose the whole Bill of Rights for the collateral purpose of increasing or reducing public support for the new Constitution. *See* LEVY, *supra* note 2, at 87, 108-09.

173. *See id.* at xii, 65-66, 74, 84, 93, 106, 109-10, 114-17.

bid nonpreferential aid to religion, without agreeing, or without having any view at all, on whether the rest of the Constitution created power to grant nonpreferential aid. The remarks of Henry, Gerry, and Huntington suggest that the Framers did exactly that. At one point, even Levy recognizes a long list of federal powers that could be used in aid of religion.[174] The Framers foresaw and even exercised some of these uses of federal power.[175] But Levy fails to see how these alternative sources of power affect his argument.

Certainly the modern nonpreferentialists are not guilty of claiming that the Establishment Clause creates power to aid religion. Under modern understandings of the spending power and of executive and legislative power to issue proclamations, resolutions, and endorsements, the federal government can aid religion unless the Establishment Clause forbids it. Moreover, Levy's argument is wholly irrelevant to the states. So far as the federal Constitution is concerned, the states have plenary power to aid religion unless the Establishment Clause, applied to the states through the Fourteenth Amendment, forbids it. It is therefore irrelevant to show that the Establishment Clause does not create a power to aid religion; Levy must show that the Establishment Clause affirmatively forbids such a power. The two are not the same.

Levy and I agree that the Establishment Clause affirmatively forbids nonpreferential aid to religion, and that the Framers so intended. But I do not think his argument from federalism supports that conclusion.

C. Levy's View of the Surviving State Establishments

Levy views the establishments in Massachusetts, Connecticut, New Hampshire, and Vermont as multiple rather than exclusive.[176] He also notes that the constitutions of Maryland, South Carolina, and Georgia authorized multiple establishments, although he concedes that they were never put into effect.[177] Finally, he argues that the establishment in colonial New York was a multiple establishment.[178] He makes these arguments to show that multiple

174. *Id.* at 172-74.

175. *Id.* (missionaries to Indians, government land set aside for support of religion, congressional chaplains, Thanksgiving proclamations); *see supra* notes 168-70 and accompanying text.

176. LEVY, *supra* note 2, at 15-20, 26-33 (Massachusetts); *id.* at 20-22, 41-44 (Connecticut); *id.* at 23-24, 38-40 (New Hampshire); *id.* at 44-46 (Vermont).

177. *Id.* at 47.

178. *Id.* at 10-15. However characterized, this establishment was abolished in 1777. *Id.* at 26.

establishments were part of the Framers' concept of establishment, and therefore that the Establishment Clause must have forbidden multiple as well as exclusive establishments.[179] This is a useful response to scholars who claim that "establishment" can only mean an exclusive establishment.[180]

Levy goes further, arguing that these multiple establishments were also nonpreferential, and therefore that the clause forbids nonpreferential establishments as well.[181] An essential part of this argument is to elide the distinction between multiple and nonpreferential establishments. An establishment can be multiple in the sense that more than one church gets state support, and also preferential in the sense that one church gets more support than others. Indeed, this is a fair characterization of the New England establishments on which Levy bases most of his case. New England dissenters who were willing to take advantage of the coercive power of the state could get some forms of state aid, through their power to collect taxes from members who filed exemption certificates and through their occasional success in electing local ministers.[182] Thus, Levy concludes, even the dissenters were established. He is right in a sense, and to that extent these were multiple rather than exclusive establishments. But they were not nonpreferential establishments. They were enacted by Congregationalist majorities for their own benefit, and the equality of Congregationalists and dissenters remained wholly theoretical.

Levy devotes two chapters to showing that multiple establishments existed in both the colonial and early national period.[183] He devotes only scattered and conclusory passages to showing that these establishments were nonpreferential.[184] Significantly, he has an index entry for multiple establishments but not for nonpreferential establishments.[185] He simply does not distinguish the two concepts on any sustained basis.

Levy and I agree that New England tried to cover establishment with a veneer of nonpreferentialism. I believe that he is fooled by that veneer and by

179. *Id.* at 6-9, 61-62.

180. Such a claim appears in JAMES M. O'NEILL, RELIGION AND EDUCATION UNDER THE CONSTITUTION 204 (1949), quoted in LEVY, *supra* note 2, at 6.

181. LEVY, *supra* note 2, at 61-62, 110.

182. *Id.* at 15-16, 21-22, 28, 30-32, 40.

183. *Id.* at 1-62.

184. *Id.* at 20, 28-30, 61-62, 110. At one point, Levy concedes that the establishment in Connecticut was preferential in fact, though not in theory. *Id.* at 41. At another point, he says the Connecticut establishment was nonpreferential. *Id.* at 22.

185. *Id.* at 231. At one point, Levy explicitly equates exclusive and preferential establishments. *Id.* at 62.

his desire to show that the Framers were familiar with nonpreferential establishments. Levy emphasizes the nonpreferential legal theory of the New England establishments, but he gives less weight to their oppressive practical operation, which he blames on unfair administration and the Congregationalist voting majority.[186] He repeatedly says that Congregationalists benefited from demography rather than law.[187] But the demography was perfectly understood when the law was enacted and, as Levy concedes in the case of Massachusetts,[188] the Congregationalists were the intended beneficiaries of the New England establishments. He agrees that dissenters were often oppressed by the system,[189] but he never reconciles this reality with his assertions that the establishment was nonpreferential. Nor does he make any effort to explain how a system could be nonpreferential when compliance violated the conscientious beliefs of the two largest minority sects. In general, he elevates form far above substance.[190]

Levy also equates local option establishments with nonpreferential establishments. In a system in which each town could elect the established minister, dissenters were able to win a few towns. Levy looks at this from a statewide perspective and proclaims it nonpreferential.[191] But from a local perspective, each town had an exclusive establishment, mitigated only by the exemption available to local dissenters. And as noted, in a state with a large Congregationalist majority, Congregationalist dominance of local elections was foreseen and intended.

Whether the New England establishments were evenhanded enough to be called nonpreferential is not crucial to either Levy's argument or mine. The effort to appear nonpreferential, in New England and elsewhere, shows that the Framers understood the concept of a nonpreferential establishment. Unlike Levy, I think an additional step is needed to complete the argument: that when the Framers squarely focused on the choice between nonprefer-

---

186. *Id.* at 19-20, 31, 40.

187. *Id.* at 19, 45, 61-62.

188. *Id.* at 15.

189. *Id.* at 20-22, 28, 31, 41-42.

190. Commentators on Levy's work on freedom of speech and of the press have criticized a similar emphasis on the legal theory of seditious libel instead of the practical reality of a free press. *See, e.g.,* David Anderson, *The Origins of the Press Clause,* 30 UCLA L. REV. 455, 509-15 (1983); David Anderson, *Levy vs. Levy* (Book Review), 84 MICH. L. REV. 777 (1986); Merrill Jensen, Book Review, 75 HARV. L. REV. 456, 456-57 (1961). For Levy's response, conceding the validity of the criticism but only in part, see LEONARD LEVY, EMERGENCE OF A FREE PRESS (1985); Levy, *The Legacy Reexamined,* 37 STAN. L. REV. 767, 767-70 (1985).

191. LEVY, *supra* note 2, at 15, 29, 38-39, 45.

ential establishment and no establishment at all, they chose no establishment at all.[192]

Without that additional step, Levy's characterization of the surviving establishments as nonpreferential can be turned against him. A nonpreferentialist could respond that the Establishment Clause reflects the views of the large number of states that, in Levy's view, had recently replaced exclusive establishments with nonpreferential establishments. That response should fail, because the more direct evidence is to the contrary, and because Levy's characterization of the New England establishments as nonpreferential is so unconvincing. Surely not even today's nonpreferentialists believe that Congress could constitutionally mandate local option establishments modeled on the Massachusetts Constitution of 1780. However they are characterized, the New England establishments were not the model for what is permitted under the Establishment Clause.

VI. The Framers' Other Intention: Nonfinancial Aid to Religion

The state debates concerning establishment centered on financial aid. Nonfinancial government support for Protestantism was rampant and largely noncontroversial. Nonpreferentialists also invoke these practices in support of their theory.[193] Supporters of government aid to religion also make the more general claim that the Establishment Clause does not forbid anything analogous to a practice that was common in 1791. The crèche case[194] and especially the legislative prayer case[195] are based on that claim.

The argument cannot be merely that anything the Framers did is constitutional. The unstated premise of that argument is that the Framers fully thought through everything they did and had every constitutional principle constantly in mind, so that all their acts fit together in a great mosaic that is absolutely consistent, even if modern observers cannot understand the organizing principle. That is not a plausible premise. Of course the state and federal Establishment Clauses did not abruptly end all customs in tension with their implications. No innovation ever does. Momentum is a powerful force in human affairs, and the Framers were busy building a nation and creating a

192. *See supra* notes 26-51 & 101-23 and accompanying text.
193. *See* Wallace v. Jaffree, 472 U.S. 38, 99-104 (1985) (Rehnquist, J., dissenting); CORD, *supra* note 8, at 23-80; Cord, *supra* note 8, at 139-48; Smith, *supra* note 9, at 620-28; Nussbaum Comment, *supra* note 10, at 573-74.
194. Lynch v. Donnelly, 465 U.S. 668, 673-78 (1984).
195. Marsh v. Chambers, 463 U.S. 783, 786-92 (1983).

government. Their failure to spend time examining every possible Establishment Clause issue is hardly surprising. The Framers did not think that everything they did was constitutional. Professor Kurland quotes Madison's 1787 observation that many of the state bills of rights were widely violated.[196] Indeed, one of the arguments against the federal Bill of Rights was that the state bills of rights had been ineffectual.[197]

Those who would rely on early government aid to religion must identify some principled distinction between the practices the Framers accepted and those they rejected. We can then consider whether we are bound by, or are willing to adopt for ourselves, the implicit principle on which they appear to have acted. The search for patterns requires a brief review of the kinds of aid to religion that the Framers supported or at least tolerated.

The Constitutional Convention did not appoint a chaplain,[198] but the First Congress appointed chaplains, and even Madison apparently acquiesced.[199] Presidents Washington, Adams, and Madison issued Thanksgiving proclamations,[200] although Madison did so only in time of war and at the request of Congress, and his proclamations merely invited citizens so disposed to unite their prayers on a single day.[201] President Jefferson refused to issue Thanksgiving proclamations, believing them to be an establishment.[202] In retirement, Madison concluded that both the congressional chaplains and the Thanksgiving proclamations had violated the Establishment Clause.[203] He said he had never approved of the decision to appoint a chaplain.[204]

Congress also subsidized missionary work among the Indians,[205] and even Jefferson signed a treaty agreeing to build a church and supply a Catho-

---

196. Kurland, *supra* note 1, at 852.

197. *See* 1 ANNALS OF CONG. 439-40 (Joseph Gales ed. 1834) (June 8, 1789) (remarks of Mr. Madison, conceding the fact but arguing that the federal judiciary would effectively enforce a federal bill of rights).

198. CORD, *supra* note 8, at 24-25.

199. *Id.* at 23.

200. *Id.* at 51-53.

201. Madison issued Thanksgiving proclamations from 1812 to 1815. *Id.* at 53 n.12. Three of these proclamations are reprinted in Cord's book, *id.* at 257-60, and Madison's later explanation of his carefully chosen language also is quoted, *id.* at 31.

202. *Id.* at 39-41. There is evidence that Jefferson drafted a Thanksgiving bill for Virginia during a revision of the Virginia statutes. *See* Cord, *supra* note 8, at 135.

203. Elizabeth Fleet, *Madison's Detached Memoranda*, 3 WM. & MARY Q. 535, 558- 62 (3d Ser. 1946).

204. Letter from James Madison to Edward Livingston (July 10, 1822), quoted in LEVY, *supra* note 2, at 97.

205. CORD, *supra* note 8, at 53-80, 261-70.

lic priest in exchange for tribal lands of the Kaskaskias.[206] Congress continued to support sectarian education on Indian reservations until 1898.[207] Commentators have alleged that the First Congress reenacted the Northwest Ordinance, with its recital that "religion, morality, and knowledge" are necessary to good government.[208] The claim is false,[209] but I do not doubt that a large majority of the First Congress would have subscribed to the sentiment.

These examples undoubtedly evidence support for religion, but they are hard to explain as nonpreferential. Supplying a Catholic priest to a tribe of Catholic Indians may be a cheap way to buy land, but it is not a form of nonpreferential aid. A missionary or a church-run school inevitably represented a particular denomination, whatever that denomination might be. So did the congressional chaplain. Congress did not hire a chaplain from every faith, or even one from every faith represented by a Congressman.[210] I assume that most of the Framers saw no constitutional problem with a chaplain, but I doubt that they rationalized the practice on the ground that it was nonpreferential.

Professor McConnell's theory that the Establishment Clause forbids only coercive aid to religion[211] comes much closer to explaining the early activities of the federal government. But sectarian education of Indians required tax money, which McConnell agrees is coercive. So noncoercion cannot explain everything the government did either.

The substantial political resistance to establishment focused on tax support for churches.[212] The Framers' generation must have seen tax support for missionaries to the Indians as different from tax support for churches. Probably they found missionaries a cheap and effective way to educate the Indians:

---

206. The treaty is reprinted in Cord's book. *Id.* at 261-63. The United States promised to pay $1000 to build a church, and to pay a priest for seven years. The priest was to "perform the duties of his office" and also to instruct the tribe's children "in the rudiments of literature." *Id.*

207. The practice was ended by the Act of June 7, 1897, ch. 3, 30 Stat. 62.

208. CORD, *supra* note 8, at 43; CURRY, *supra* note 3, at 218; LEVY, *supra* note 2, at 172; Smith, *supra* note 9, at 627-28; Nussbaum Comment, *supra* note 10, at 574.

209. All that Congress enacted were two technical amendments. Section 1 substituted "the President of the United States" for all references to "the United States in Congress assembled." Act of Aug. 7, 1789, ch. 8, § 1, 1 Stat. 50, 52-53. Section 2 provided that the secretary of the territory should perform the duties of the governor in the event of a vacancy. *Id.* § 2, 1 Stat. at 53.

210. Congress did hire two chaplains of different denominations and rotated them between the House and Senate. Cord, *supra* note 8, at 139-40.

211. *See* McConnell, *Coercion, supra* note 93.

212. *See supra* notes 107-13, 122-23 & 136-43 and accompanying text.

they were hiring churches to provide government services.[213] Even so, religious teaching was also an accepted part of the mission, and nobody talked of any accounting to separate the costs of education in secular and religious subjects.

Once again, the practice of the states helps to flesh out the pattern. The federal government had limited legislative powers; the states' general police power gave them more opportunities to act with respect to religion. Most state constitutions guaranteed religious liberty.[214] The federal religious liberty clauses did not necessarily mean the same thing as the state religious liberty clauses, but again state practices may help show how the Framers' generation understood religious liberty.

State aid to religion was both preferential and coercive. The states continued practices that no one would defend today. All but two states had religious qualifications for holding public office,[215] and at least five states denied full civil rights to Catholics.[216] Blasphemy was commonly a crime; in Vermont blasphemy against the Trinity was a capital offense,[217] although it presumably was not enforced as such. Observance of the Christian Sabbath was widely enforced,[218] with little in the way of fictitious explanations about a neutrally selected day for families to be together.[219] These laws aroused little controversy, and almost no one thought them inconsistent with constitutional guarantees of religious liberty. Yet tax support for churches was deeply controversial and widely thought inconsistent with religious liberty.

Several reasons probably contributed to the differing reactions to financial and nonfinancial aid. First, there is always opposition to taxes, whatever

---

213. For an application of this analysis to the controversy about "aid" to church-sponsored schools, see Laycock, *Religious Liberty, supra* note 2, at 443-44 (text at notes 210-12).

214. For the texts of 12 such religion clauses, see 1 STOKES, *supra* note 60, at 303 (Virginia); *id.* at 402-03 (North Carolina); *id.* at 405 (New York); *id.* at 423-24 (Massachusetts); *id.* at 429 (New Hampshire); *id.* at 432-34 (South Carolina); *id.* at 435 (New York); *id.* at 437 (Delaware); *id.* at 438 (Pennsylvania); *id.* at 440 (Georgia); *id.* at 440-41 (Vermont); *id.* at 442-43 (Rhode Island). For a summary of the Maryland provisions, see *id.* at 439. The important Connecticut provisions were statutory; for the text of one of them, see *id.* at 412.

215. CURRY, *supra* note 3, at 162-63, 221; Morton Borden, *Federalists, Anti-Federalists, and Religious Freedom,* 21 J. CHURCH & STATE 469 (1979).

216. *See* 1 STOKES, *supra* note 60, at 402 (North Carolina); *id.* at 406 (New York); *id.* at 430 (New Hampshire); *id.* at 435 (New Jersey); *id.* at 441 (Vermont).

217. CURRY, *supra* note 3, at 190.

218. *See* McGowan v. Maryland, 366 U.S. 420, 484-95 (1961) (separate opinion of Frankfurter, J.); BUCKLEY, *supra* note 98, at 181-82; Cord, *supra* note 8, at 135.

219. This and similar secular purposes were the rationale for upholding Sunday closing laws in McGowan v. Maryland, 366 U.S. 420 (1961).

their purpose. In Virginia, the general assessment was debated at a time of high taxes and low tobacco prices in a tobacco economy.[220] Second, the tax for churches was associated with earlier unitary establishments: Anglicans in the South, and Congregationalists in the North. Broadening the tax to include other denominations did not remove the taint or end the hostility.[221] The Anglican clergy were far more dependent on tax support than denominations already accustomed to voluntary support. Third, and perhaps most important, the tax for churches split the Protestant denominations. Baptists and Quakers objected even to a nonpreferential system in which every taxpayer designated the church to receive his tax. When the Virginia Presbyterians reached the same conclusion in 1786, the assessment bill was doomed.[222]

For all these reasons, there were widespread objections to tax support for churches. What is largely the same thing, there were Protestant objections. This opposition forced the Framers' generation to think about the tax issue. Once they thought about it, they concluded that any form of tax support for churches violated religious liberty. By the time of the First Amendment, church taxes were repealed or moribund outside New England, and they were not working well in the four New England states that still tried to collect them.

The other government supports of Protestantism never aroused enough controversy to trigger similar examination. The nation was overwhelmingly Protestant and hostile to other faiths.[223] Bare tolerance of other faiths was a major accomplishment, not yet safe from reaction; accepting other faiths as equals was far in the future. John Jay led an unsuccessful movement to banish Catholics from New York,[224] and John Adams boasted that Catholics and

220. BUCKLEY, *supra* note 98, at 153-55.

221. *See e.g., id.* at 137-38, 151, 175-76; CURRY, *supra* note 3, at 147; *id.* at 157 (quoting Catholic leader John Carroll).

222. *See* BUCKLEY, *supra* note 98, at 136-39, 143, 175.

223. *See, e.g., id.* at 181-82; CURRY, *supra* note 3, at 140, 166, 170, 177; McDONALD, *supra* note 80, at 42-43; Borden, *supra* note 215, at 472-73, 478, 482. Maryland was a partial exception; it had begun as a Catholic colony, although it later had an Anglican establishment, CURRY, *supra* note 3, at 153-54, and Catholics were disenfranchised for a time. *See* McDONALD, *supra* note 80, at 42-43. A Catholic, Charles Carroll of Carrollton, signed the Declaration of Independence and served in the first Senate, and his distant relative, Daniel Carroll, signed the Constitution and served in the first House of Representatives. JAMES HENNESEY, AMERICAN CATHOLICS: A HISTORY OF THE ROMAN CATHOLIC COMMUNITY IN THE UNITED STATES 58-59 (1981); *see also* 1 ANNALS OF CONG. 18 (Joseph Gales ed. 1834) (Apr. 13, 1789) (Charles Carroll seated in the Senate); 1 STOKES, *supra* note 60, at 325 (relationship between Charles and Daniel). Charles Carroll was well respected nationally, but at least some political opponents attacked his Catholicism in bigoted terms. HENNESEY, *supra*, at 58-59.

224. CURRY, *supra* note 3, at 162.

Jacobites were as rare as comets and earthquakes in his hometown of Braintree.[225] Professor Kurland quotes other examples of Protestant bigotry among political leaders.[226] Non-Protestants could practice their religion, but they often could not vote, hold public office, or publicly criticize Protestantism. Non-Protestants certainly could not expect the government to refrain from preaching Protestantism. These conditions would not change easily. Half a century later, mob violence, church burnings, and deaths would result when Catholics objected to studying the "Protestant Bible" in public schools.[227] The anti-Catholic, anti-immigrant Know Nothing Party would sweep elections in eight states.[228]

In 1791, almost no one thought that government support of Protestantism was inconsistent with religious liberty, because almost no one could imagine a more broadly pluralist state. Protestantism ran so deep among such overwhelming numbers of people that almost no one could see that his principles on church taxes might have implications for other kinds of government support for religion. The exclusion of non-Protestants from pronouncements of religious liberty was not nearly so thorough or so cruel as the exclusion of slaves from pronouncements that all men were created equal, but both blind spots were species of the same genus.

In short, the appeal to the Framers' practice of nonfinancial aid to religion is an appeal to unreflective bigotry. It does not show what the Framers meant by disestablishment; it shows what they did without thinking about establishment at all. I believe that the relevant intention of the Framers is the one they thought about. But if that view is rejected — if both the considered and the unconsidered intentions of the Framers are binding — then the result would not be to approve nonpreferential aid. The Framers' implicit distinction was between financial aid and other aid. If both their intentions are followed, all financial aid will be forbidden, whether or not preferential. But unlimited financial aid will be permitted even if it is preferential and coercive. Few nonpreferentialists would defend that.

I am not even suggesting that we modify the principle the Framers considered. I would apply uniformly the very principle the Framers considered and accepted: that aid to religion is not saved by making it nonpreferential.

225. HENNESEY, *supra* note 223, at 77 (citing 9 JOHN ADAMS, WORKS 355 (Charles Francis Adams ed. Boston 1856)); *see also id.* at 62 (quoting Adams' derisive description of a Catholic mass).

226. Kurland, *supra* note 1, at 847-48.

227. LEVY, *supra* note 2, at 170; 1 STOKES, *supra* note 60, at 830-35.

228. 1 STOKES, *supra* note 60, at 836-37.

VII. Making Sense of the Establishment Clause Today

The United States today is more religiously diverse than anything the Framers could have imagined. Waves of immigration from Europe, Asia, and Latin America have created large and influential populations of Catholics and Jews, and significant populations of Muslims, Hindus, Buddhists, Haitian voodooists, and others. Geographic concentration and residential segregation make some of these groups invisible to the majority, but they are numerous and important to many local communities.[229] The Solicitor General and Supreme Court justices worry about equal treatment of Sikhs and Rastafarians.[230] New sects as disparate as the Mormons, the Jehovah's Witnesses, and the Scientologists have developed indigenously, and imported sects such as Krishna Consciousness and the Unification Church have attracted highly visible followers. Significant numbers of atheists and agnostics have been with us since the late nineteenth century; to the Framers, they were merely a theoretical possibility.[231] What does the Establishment Clause mean in this context?

One approach would be to imitate the Framers' conduct. Under that approach, all these new religious groups would be expected to quietly endure state-sponsored Protestantism. The government would tolerate the new faiths, but they would forever be outsiders of not quite equal status. Alternatively, we can try to identify an intelligible principle that makes sense of what the Framers ratified. I believe that the task of interpretation is to apply the principle of the Establishment Clause to the situation that exists today.

A distinction between preferential and nonpreferential aid is not the principle the Framers intended. Even if it were, that distinction has become illusory. No aid is nonpreferential. Differences among Baptists, Quakers, Congregationalists, and Anglicans made nonpreferential aid unworkable in the eighteenth century. The vastly greater religious differences today make it vastly more unworkable.

For the issues that are most controversial, nonpreferential aid is plainly impossible. No prayer is neutral among all faiths, even if one makes the mis-

---

229. For example, the "Yellow Pages" in Honolulu list 50 Buddhist and four Shinto temples and shrines. They also list one Moslem Mosque, one Baha'i temple, one Church of Krishna Consciousness, one Church of Scientology, three institutions under the category "Churches — Cosmology, Ontology, and Metaphysics," and two under the category "Churches — Spiritualism." HAWAIIAN TELEPHONE CO., OAHU YELLOW PAGES 250-56 (1986).

230. Goldman v. Weinberger, 475 U.S. 503, 512-13 (1986) (Stevens, J., concurring); *id.* at 519-20 (Brennan, J., dissenting).

231. *See* TURNER, *supra* note 117.

take of excluding atheists and agnostics from consideration.[232] On that point, Michael Malbin and I agree.[233] Government-sponsored religious symbols or ceremonies, whether in schools, legislatures, courthouses, or parks, are inherently preferential. They nearly always support Christianity, and when implemented by their most ardent supporters, they support a particular strain of evangelical Christianity.

It is theoretically possible to award equal and nonpreferential financial aid to every religious group, or perhaps to every religious leader. But the experience of the eighteenth century again suggests that workability problems are inevitable. And if the debates of the 1780's support any proposition, it is that the Framers opposed government financial support for religion.

Professor McConnell suggests the more workable principle that the Establishment Clause bars any aid to religion that coerces nonbelievers.[234] He sensibly views taxation and school prayer as coercive,[235] although the supporters of school prayer disagree. I hope he would agree that legislative prayer is equally coercive. Adults may have greater capacity to resist, but the coercion is identical. It is easier to listen quietly to the government prayer than conspicuously walk out and back in again. I also hope he would view small expenditures in support of religion as coercive, even though the taxation required to pay for them is equally small.

Taken seriously, Professor McConnell's coercion test would eliminate all government support for religion except endorsements that cost no money. Crosses and crèches would abound on government property, perhaps paid for by private contributions. Thanksgiving proclamations, resolutions encouraging church attendance, and posters of the Ten Commandments[236] would be unobjectionable. The Great Seal of the United States could be a flaming cross with the words "in this sign conquer,"[237] so long as the government only portrayed Constantine's vision and did not emulate his persecutions.[238] Government leaders and media preachers could unite their efforts

---

232. *See* Marsh v. Chambers, 463 U.S. 783, 819-21 (1983) (Brennan, J., dissenting).

233. *See Constitutional Amendments Relating to School Prayer: Hearings Before the Subcomm. on the Constitution of the Senate Comm. on the Judiciary,* 99th Cong., 1st Sess. 11, 18-19 (1986) (statement of Dr. Michael Malbin).

234. McConnell, *Coercion, supra* note 93, at 938.

235. *Id.* at 933.

236. *Cf.* Stone v. Graham, 449 U.S. 39 (1980) (per curiam) (invalidating statute directing public schools to post the Ten Commandments in classrooms).

237. *Cf.* Friedman v. Board of County Comm'rs, 781 F.2d 777 (10th Cir. 1985) (en banc) (invalidating similar seal that was prominently displayed on police cars).

238. On the eve of a decisive battle on the banks of the Tiber, Constantine saw a vision

to persuade the populace to a particular set of political and religious views.[239] These are not happy results, but I share McConnell's view that they are not as bad as coercion, and I suspect that he would find a theory to constrain some of the most egregious examples.

I have two problems with his test. First, it allows government to endorse or prefer one religious faith over others, with the inevitable result that adherents of the others will feel their inferior status.[240] Second, it makes the two Religion Clauses redundant. Religious coercion by the government violates the Free Exercise Clause. Coercion to observe someone else's religion is as much a free exercise violation as is coercion to abandon my own. If coercion is also an element of the Establishment Clause, establishment adds nothing to free exercise.

VIII. Conclusion

The principle that best makes sense of the Establishment Clause is the principle of the most nearly perfect neutrality toward religion and among religions. I do not mean neutrality in the formal sense of a ban on religious classifications,[241] but in the substantive sense of government conduct that insofar as possible neither encourages nor discourages religious belief or practice.[242]

---

of a flaming cross and the Greek words meaning "in this sign conquer." He consequently ordered his troops to mark their shields with crosses, and he put a cross on the army's banner. WILL DURANT, CAESAR AND CHRIST 654 (1944). Constantine won the battle and became the undisputed emperor, first in the west, *id.,* and later over a reunited empire, *id.* at 655. As emperor, he established Christianity and diligently persecuted heretics. *Id.* at 658, 660, 664.

239. Government officials can do this to some extent in their individual capacity as politicians. I leave to another time the difficult task of distinguishing the personal and official speech of government officials. *See* MARK G. YUDOF, WHEN GOVERNMENT SPEAKS (1983).

240. In his article on accommodation, McConnell says that accommodations must not favor one form of religious belief over another. McConnell, *Accommodation, supra* note 93, at 39. But he is reluctant to apply that standard to preferential displays of religious symbols, lest the public sphere be wholly secularized. *Id.* at 49-50. My understanding of these passages has been clarified by conversation and correspondence.

241. This is the principle proposed in Philip B. Kurland, *Of Church and State and the Supreme Court,* 29 U. CHI. L. REV. 1 (1961).

242. *See* Douglas Laycock, *Equal Access and Moments of Silence: The Equal Status of Religious Speech by Private Speakers,* 81 Nw. U.L. REV. 1, 3 (1986) (text at notes 10-11). This distinction is best illustrated by facially neutral laws that violate religious conscience. In Professor Kurland's view, a law prohibiting the consumption of alcohol could not contain an exception for sacramental wine. Such an exception would prefer religion. In my view, an exception would be required. A law banning wine at the Eucharist and the Seder would pro-

This is the principle that maximizes religious liberty in a pluralistic society, and this is the principle that the Framers identified in the context of tax support for churches. They did not substitute nonpreferential taxes for preferential taxes; they rejected all taxes. They did not substitute small taxes for large taxes; three pence was as bad as any larger sum.[243] The principle was what mattered. With respect to money, religion was to be wholly voluntary. Churches either would support themselves or they would not, but the government would neither help nor interfere.

That is what disestablishment meant to the Framers in the context in which they thought about it. They applied the principle only in that context — only to tax support. Their society was so homogeneous that they had no occasion to think about other kinds of support. Now that we have thought about it, we are not unfaithful to the Framers' intent when we apply their principle to analogous problems. Congress cannot impose civil disabilities on non-Protestants or ban blasphemy against the Trinity just because the Framers did so. It is no more able to endorse the predominant religion just because the Framers did it. Our task is not to perpetuate the Framers' blind spots, but to implement their vision.

---

hibit the free exercise of religion, however neutral its wording and however general its application. In this example, no compelling interest would justify the prohibition.

243. *Memorial and Remonstrance, supra* note 111, § 3.

Responding to the Nonpreferentialists

4 Journal of Law and Religion 241 (1986)

This is a review of two important histories of the debate over disestablishment in the founding era. The review focuses on a long-running debate that was particularly high profile in the 1980s: whether the Establishment Clause permits government to aid religion so long as it does so nonpreferentially. Both authors and I agreed that that is not what the Establishment Clause means, but we reached that conclusion by rather different routes. The heart of this review closely tracked part V of the article that precedes this one, and is omitted here.

*   *   *

The First Freedoms: Church and State in America to the Passage of the First Amendment. By Thomas J. Curry. New York: Oxford University Press, 1986.

The Establishment Clause: Religion and the First Amendment. By Leonard W. Levy. New York: Macmillan Publishing Co., 1986.

These two books review the history of church-state relations in the United States, with a focus on the meaning of the Establishment Clause. Both cover the colonial, revolutionary, and constitution-making periods. Curry ends with ratification of the First Amendment in 1791; Levy continues to the final disestablishment in Massachusetts in 1833. Levy also reviews and criticizes the Supreme Court's interpretations of the Establishment Clause.

Parts of this review are excerpted from the author's longer article on the same subject as the books reviewed. Douglas Laycock, *"Nonpreferential" Aid to Religion: A False Claim About Original Intent*, 27 Wm. & Mary L. Rev. 875 (1986).

Levy's book is a full-scale attack on a group that he helpfully labels the nonpreferentialists. The nonpreferentialists argue that the Constitution means only what the Framers intended it to mean, and that the Framers of the Establishment Clause intended to permit government aid to religion so long as no particular faith is preferred over others. Nonpreferentialists have been around for a long time, and they have been refuted before, but they have gotten a second wind in the intellectual climate that accompanied the Reagan administration. Robert Cord's 1982 book[1] argued nonpreferentialism at great length, and Attorney General Meese[2] and Chief Justice Rehnquist have become the two most visible nonpreferentialists.[3]

Levy brings his considerable historical and rhetorical talents to bear on the nonpreferentialists, sometimes with devastating effect. But his zeal gets in the way of good history and even of good advocacy. Indeed, his two principal arguments seem to me demonstrably incorrect, even though he deploys them in support of correct conclusions. His last two chapters are a rambling tirade against everything he dislikes in modern Establishment Clause jurisprudence. He is right more often than not, but the tone of these chapters is not likely to persuade the uncommitted.

Levy's student, the Rev. Thomas Curry, has done better than the master. Curry's history is more thorough, more dispassionate, and more useful. Levy wrote an attack on the nonpreferentialists and used history where helpful. Curry wrote a history first and then considered its implications for both the nonpreferentialists and their opponents. As it happens, I think Curry is mistaken in his analysis of what the Establishment Clause means. But that mistake does not seriously affect his historical account. I have already used Curry's book in my own work, and it will be an indispensable reference for both historians and lawyers interested in church-state relations in the period. Both of these books collect a wealth of useful information. But if you can read only one, read Curry.

In the rest of this essay, I wish to consider the two books' principal arguments about nonpreferentialism. Curry, Levy, and I agree on the central point: the Framers of the Establishment Clause had no specific intention to permit nonpreferential aid to religion. Levy and I agree on the stronger formulation that the Framers intended the Establishment Clause to forbid such

---

1. Robert Cord, Separation of Church and State: Historical Fact and Current Fiction (1982).

2. Edwin Meese, *Towards a Jurisprudence of Original Intention,* 2 Benchmark 1, 5 (1986).

3. Wallace v. Jaffree, 472 U.S. 38, 91-114 (1985) (Rehnquist, J., dissenting).

aid. Curry apparently believes that they intended the Free Exercise Clause, but not the Establishment Clause, to forbid such aid. Each of us disagrees with the other two on important subsidiary points. . . .

Text, Intent, and the Religion Clauses

4 Notre Dame Journal of Law, Ethics, and Public Policy 683 (1990)

This is a comment on the debate over original intent as a mode, or the only mode, of constitutional interpretation. The idea of original intent, which emphasized the subjective intentions of the founding generation, was just at this time morphing into original understanding, which emphasizes what the words of the Constitution would have meant to readers in the founding generation. I do not think that change enables the originalists to escape the criticisms in this paper, but that change is not considered here. I argue that constitutional text is primary, and historical evidence is secondary, relevant but not controlling. I also argue that there is better and worse historical evidence, and better and worse ways to use it, and that we should focus on the quality of historical arguments rather than all-or-nothing arguments about the controlling effect of intent.

This paper was an invited comment on a paper by Professor John Valauri, of the University of Northern Kentucky, at a conference at Notre Dame. Valauri also criticized arguments from original intent, and his thesis is summarized in the first few paragraphs.

*   *   *

I am grateful to Sanford Levinson, Frederick Schauer, and Jay Westbrook for helpful comments on an earlier draft.

I. The Valauri Thesis

John Valauri has reminded us of some things that bear frequent repetition.[1] The rhetoric of original intent is a favorite tactic of a large political movement. This movement won the last three Presidential elections, and it will probably appoint a majority of the Supreme Court. Original intent arguments invoke a strong logic and have a strong appeal to many people. So it is worthwhile periodically to remind us of their difficulties and vary the illustrations. Professor Valauri's paper does that.

But the problems he identifies are hardly news to constitutional lawyers, and I doubt that the jargon of hermeneutics adds much to the conventional legal expression of the same difficulties. Many others have also noted his "horizontal" critique — the difficulties of identifying a single original intent — and his "vertical" critique — the difficulties of applying that intent to new questions and modern conditions.[2] These are not the only problems with a jurisprudence of original intent, but they are two of the most serious. As Valauri recognizes,[3] the arguments on both sides are familiar and well developed.

The point of his paper is that the richness of the general debate on original intent has not been brought to bear on the use of original intent in debate over the Establishment Clause.[4] But he notes some exceptions in footnotes;[5] his ultimate claim is that the general debate has had less effect on the Establishment Clause than on other constitutional issues.

I doubt that Religion Clause debate is any more or less simplistic or intel-

---

1. John T. Valauri, *Everson v. Brown: Hermeneutics, Framers' Intent, and the Establishment Clause,* 4 NOTRE DAME J.L. ETHICS & PUB. POL'Y 661 (1990).

2. For a recent overview, see Daniel A. Farber, *The Originalism Debate: A Guide for the Perplexed,* 49 OHIO ST. L.J. 1085 (1989). For other statements of the difficulties of original intent, *see, e.g.,* J.M. Balkin, *Constitutional Interpretation and the Problem of History* (Book Review), 63 N.Y.U. L. REV. 911 (1988); Robert Bennett, *Originalist Theories of Constitutional Interpretation,* 73 CORNELL L. REV. 355 (1988); Robert Bennett, *Objectivity in Constitutional Law,* 132 U. PA. L. REV. 445 (1984); Paul Brest, *The Misconceived Quest for the Original Understanding,* 60 B.U.L. REV. 204 (1980); William Brennan, *The Constitution of the United States: Contemporary Ratification,* 27 S. TEX. L J. 433 (1986); Richard Fallon, *A Constructivist Coherence Theory of Constitutional Interpretation,* 100 HARV. L. REV. 1189, 1198-99, 1211-17 (1987); Douglas Laycock, *Taking Constitutions Seriously: A Theory of Judicial Review* (Book Review), 59 TEX. L. REV. 343, 343-52 (1981); Terrance Sandalow, *Constitutional Interpretation,* 79 MICH. L. REV. 1033 (1981); John Paul Stevens, *The Supreme Court of the United States: Reflections After a Summer Recess,* 27 S. TEX. L J. 447 (1986).

3. Valauri, *supra* note 1, at 662.

4. *Id.*

5. *Id.* at 662 n.6; 671 n.47.

lectually dishonest than debate over other hotly disputed constitutional issues. I doubt that the quality of debate varies systematically across well-developed areas of constitutional law.

I do think that tactics vary by subject matter, responding to the quantity and quality of evidence. The most common tactical pattern for original intent arguments is that one side says the Founders never thought the matter in dispute raised any constitutional question, and certainly did not affirmatively intend to make it unconstitutional, and so the political branches can do what they think is right. The other side responds that the evidence is unclear and times have changed, that it is a Constitution we are expounding and we can't turn back the clock, and in short, Justice Brennan must do what he thinks is right.

I exaggerate only slightly, and for a purpose. There are equal and opposite dangers here — to pretend that a simplistic account of the Founders' intent solves all our problems, or to pretend that the text and history of the Constitution tell us very little and constrain us not at all. Professor Valauri is plainly alert to one of these dangers. If he is equally alert to the other, then he and I do not disagree.

The typical pattern of argument about original intent has been applied to Religion Clause issues. This was precisely the argument in the legislative prayer case, where the majority relied principally on the practices of the Founders, and the dissenters said those practices were not controlling.[6] A few judges and commentators made similar arguments in the debates over prayer and religious instruction in the public schools.[7]

But Valauri is right that the main line of Establishment Clause debate has taken a different course, in which both sides rely on original intent. Because there is an unusual abundance of historical evidence, and because there is ample evidence to support both sides, both sides appeal to history. Those who would invalidate government action abandon their usual argument that original intent is not binding, and instead urge that this time original intent

---

6. Marsh v. Chambers, 463 U.S. 783 (1983).

7. *See, e.g.,* School Dist. v. Schempp, 374 U.S. 203, 236-37 (1963) (Brennan, J., concurring) ("I doubt that [Madison and Jefferson's] view, even if perfectly clear one way or the other, would supply a dispositive answer to the question presented by these cases. . . . A too literal quest for the advice of the Founding Fathers . . . seems to me futile and misdirected"); David Fellman, *Separation of Church and State: A Summary View,* 1950 WIS. L. REV. 427, 427-28 (it is "futile and pointless to inquire" into original intent); Paul G. Kauper, *Prayer, Public Schools and the Supreme Court,* 61 MICH. L. REV. 1031, 1066 (1963) (defending school prayer decision on ground of policy, and criticizing Court for pretending that either text or intent required the result).

is on their side. That tactical choice tells you something about the perceived legitimacy and persuasive power of original intent arguments. Despite their many problems, they have an almost irresistible appeal.

This tactical choice also creates Valauri's impression that the Establishment Clause debate has ignored the larger literature on original intent. Because both sides rely on original intent, there is less attention to its difficulties.[8] In the hands of the unsophisticated, the result-oriented, or even those who are honest and know better but are sometimes careless or tempted, those difficulties get less attention than usual. We have all sinned, and come short of full intellectual rigor. But the difficulties with original intent do not disappear from what we know, and they have not disappeared entirely from the debate over religious liberty.

We cannot invoke original intent in the simplistic way that Valauri condemns, but neither can we ignore history. If we are to get beyond broadsides for and against original intent, we must identify criteria for better and worse kinds of historical evidence and better and worse arguments from that evidence.

II. Text or Intent

The persistent appeal of originalist arguments derives from our commitment to the proposition that government officials derive their just powers from the consent of the governed. Where do judges get the power to enforce their conceptions of religious liberty against the political branches, and even against the people legislating directly by referendum? That power derives from critical votes that Americans cast in critical periods — in 1787-88 for Article III and the Test Oath Clause, in 1789-91 for the First Amendment, and in 1866-68 for the Fourteenth Amendment.

But "originalism" is fatally ambiguous at best, affirmatively misleading at worst. It conflates two quite different modes of argument. Textual arguments appeal to the authority of the constitutional text; intentionalist arguments appeal to the authority of the Founders' intent. (I use "Founders" to include both the framers and the ratifiers.) The Founders voted on the text, but each voter had some understanding of what the text meant. Thus, both textual and intentionalist arguments appeal to the authority of the votes that proposed and ratified the Constitution.

Several scholars have elaborated the choice between text and intent,[9] and

8. Valauri, *supra* note 1, at 662.
9. *See, e.g.*, Philip Bobbitt, Constitutional Fate 7, 9-38 (1982); Fallon, *supra* note 2,

I will not review that whole analysis here. But a brief excursion into text is prerequisite to anything I might say about intent. The constitutional text has meaning as a matter of language, and that meaning depends only in part on the Founders' intent. The text is superior in authority to intent, because only the text was submitted to the vote of the ratifiers. I do not mean to claim that intent is irrelevant, but simply that it is subordinate to the text.

In any event, we cannot directly know the intent of Founders who are long dead. We must rely on indirect evidence, and the text itself is the best evidence of intent. Extrinsic evidence of intent is secondary even with respect to intent; it is much more attenuated as evidence of the meaning of the text. We should examine the text first, and mine it for as much meaning as it will yield, before turning to extrinsic evidence of intent.

The most outspoken intentionalists invert these hierarchies of authority. They believe that intent controls text, and that extrinsic evidence of intent controls textual evidence of intent.[10] Justice Scalia's position is especially puzzling; he consistently insists that the Court must construe the statutory text and not Congressional intent,[11] but in constitutional interpretation he

---

at 1195-99 (1987); Laycock, *Constitutional Theory Matters*, 65 TEX. L. REV. 767, 774 (1987); Laycock, *supra* note 2, at 343-52; Jefferson Powell, *The Original Understanding of Original Intent*, 98 HARV. L. REV. 885 (1985); Jefferson Powell, *Constitutional Law as Though the Constitution Mattered* (Book Review), 1986 DUKE L.J. 915; Jefferson Powell, *Parchment Matters: A Meditation on the Constitution as Text*, 71 IOWA L. REV. 1427 (1986); Frederick Schauer, *An Essay on Constitutional Language*, 29 UCLA L. REV. 797 (1982). Philip Bobbitt draws a more radical distinction between text and intent than most of the other scholars cited in this footnote. In his view, textual arguments do not draw legitimacy from the votes of the Founders.

10. *See, e.g.*, RAOUL BERGER, GOVERNMENT BY JUDICIARY: THE TRANSFORMATION OF THE FOURTEENTH AMENDMENT 6 (1977) ("the intention of the framers being unmistakably expressed, that intention is as good as written into the text"); Robert Bork, *Neutral Principles and Some First Amendment Problems*, 47 IND. L.J. 1, 13 (1971) ("The words are general but surely that would not permit us to escape the framers' intent if it were clear"); Robert Bork, *Styles in Constitutional Theory*, 26 S. TEX. L.J. 383, 394 (1985) ("the source [of constitutional liberties] was the intent of the framers and ratifiers, and that was to be discerned from text, history, structure, and precedent"); Frank Easterbrook, *Substance and Due Process*, 1982 SUP. CT. REV. 85, 92 ("History lays down the baseline against which other arguments are measured"); Lino Graglia, *Do We Have an Unwritten Constitution? The Privileges or Immunities Clause of the Fourteenth Amendment*, 12 HARV. J.L. & PUB. POL'Y 83, 88 (1989) (text of Fourteenth Amendment conceals its intended purpose, and purpose controls).

11. Pennsylvania v. Union Gas Co., 491 U.S. 1, 29 (1989) (Scalia, J., concurring in part) (Court's task is not "to plumb the intent of the particular Congress that enacted a particular provision . . . but rather to give fair and reasonable meaning to the text of the United States Code"); Jett v. Dallas Indep. School Dist., 491 U.S. 701, 739 (1989) (Scalia, J., concurring) (joining Court's opinion except insofar as it relies on legislative history); Blanchard v. Bergeron, 489 U.S. 87, 97-100 (1989) (Scalia, J., concurring) (same).

apparently reverses himself, demanding exhaustive attention to constitutional history.[12]

Interpreters who emphasize extrinsic evidence of the Founders' intent tend to ignore the generality of the text and to substitute much narrower conceptions of intent. The Founders focused on the specific problems most salient to their lives, but they constitutionalized general principles that seem designed to cover whole classes of similar problems. What they left a record of having specifically and consciously intended is often a small subset of the text they proposed and ratified. Interpretation limited to specific and provable intentions thus tends to be fatally inconsistent with the constitutional text.

This inconsistency is a third reason to be skeptical of straightforward reliance on extrinsic evidence of original intent, and especially of claims about quite specific intentions. In my judgment, this argument is even more important than Professor Valauri's horizontal and vertical critiques.

The primacy of text is relevant to the meaning of the Religion Clauses. First, the word "exercise" is powerful textual evidence that the protection extends beyond mere belief and reaches religious conduct.

Second, the text of the Religion Clauses is absolute. It says "no law," not "no unreasonable law," or "no badly motivated law." We have learned that we cannot literally enforce the absolutism of the First Amendment, but neither should we ignore it. Implied exceptions to a textually absolute constitutional right should be an extraordinary thing; the Supreme Court's recent free exercise jurisprudence implies exceptions far too readily and gives insufficient weight to the absoluteness of the text.[13]

Third, some of the strongest evidence that the Establishment Clause precludes nonpreferential aid to religion is partly textual. As I have explained in more detail elsewhere,[14] the Senate and the Conference Committee considered and rejected four drafts of the Establishment Clause that were expressly and unambiguously nonpreferentialist. Congress instead proposed to the states one

12. Antonin Scalia, *Originalism: The Lesser Evil,* 57 U. Cin. L. Rev. 849, 856-57 (1989) (constitutional interpretation "requires the consideration of an enormous mass of material [and] immersing oneself in the political and intellectual atmosphere of the time").

13. *See, e.g.,* O'Lone v. Estate of Shabazz, 482 U.S. 342 (1987) (upholding prison's refusal to bring Muslim prisoners to religious service within the same prison); Goldman v. Weinberger, 475 U.S. 503 (1986) (upholding military rules forbidding the wearing of yarmulkes with uniform); Bob Jones Univ. v. United States, 461 U.S. 574, 602-04 (1983) (upholding revocation of tax exemption of pervasively religious university that prohibited interracial dating among its students).

14. Douglas Laycock, *"Nonpreferential" Aid to Religion: A False Claim About Original Intent,* 27 Wm. & Mary L. Rev. 875, 879-83 (1986) (text at notes 26-47).

of the most sweeping drafts considered by either House. That draft was ratified. The clause forbids any law respecting an establishment of religion, and the stark contrast with the rejected drafts greatly strengthens the textual inference that the unmodified word "religion" refers to religion generically.

This argument goes beyond the ratified text, but it looks to actual votes on proposed text and not to more remote evidence of what was in the heads of the Founders. I will further explore the strengths and weaknesses of this intermediate form of argument in a subsequent paper.[15]

III. The Uses of History

Once we go beyond the text to extrinsic evidence of intent, some evidence is more valuable than other evidence, and there are better and worse ways to argue from it. Intentionalist arguments must be alert to all the dangers highlighted by the various critiques — to Valauri's horizontal and vertical critiques and to the gap between broad text and specific intent.

The common search for evidence of what the Founders thought about the specific issue before the Court is vulnerable on all three grounds. When we pose the question at that level of specificity, we maximize the horizontal problems of finding evidence of what the Founders thought and of summing the thoughts of all the members of the twenty-eight legislative bodies entitled to vote on the First Amendment.[16] We maximize the vertical problem of applying their intent to modern conditions, because the focus on the specific practice tends to exclude consideration of changes in context. And we maximize the gap between text and other evidence of intent, because to pose the question in this way conceives intent at a level of generality far narrower than the language of the text.

15. Douglas Laycock, *Original Intent and the Constitution Today,* in THE FIRST LIBERTY: THE BICENTENNIAL OF THE FIRST AMENDMENT 87 (James E. Wood ed.) (1990). I underestimated the difficulties in my initial elaboration of this argument. *See* Laycock, *supra* note 14, at 883-84 n.47.

16. These were the two Houses of Congress, the two houses of the bicameral legislatures in twelve of the original thirteen states, and the unicameral legislatures in Pennsylvania and Vermont. For the ratifying states and the dates of ratification, see Historical Notes to U.S. Const., amend. I, in U.S.C.A. Pennsylvania ratified on March 10, 1790. Its Constitution of 1790, creating a bicameral legislature, was adopted on September 2 and took effect on December 7. *See* ROSALIND L. BRANNING, PENNSYLVANIA CONSTITUTIONAL DEVELOPMENT 19-20 (1960); BURTON A. KONKLE, GEORGE BRYAN AND THE CONSTITUTION OF PENNSYLVANIA 1731-1791, at 353-54 (1922). Vermont retained its unicameral legislature until 1836. *See* JEFFERSON B. FORDHAM, THE STATE LEGISLATIVE INSTITUTION 27-28 (1959).

An intent known to be widely held, or at least widely known, is more important than the isolated quotation so common to law office history. The isolated quotation, even from a Madison or a Hamilton, is maximally vulnerable to Valauri's horizontal critique.

An intent that was consciously subjected to constitutional scrutiny is more valuable than an intent or a practice that was not so examined. The unexamined continuation of a practice may reflect momentum, oversight, or failure of anyone to raise the issue, and almost certainly does not reflect a considered intent about the meaning of the Constitution. For similar reasons, constitutional scrutiny under the pressure of a real complaint from a significant minority that felt unfairly treated is more valuable than a hypothetical constitutional analysis of a practice that was largely uncontroversial in the social context of the times.

The unexamined intent is especially vulnerable to Valauri's vertical critique: a practice might have been harmless and therefore unexamined in the Founders' time, but now, because of changed social conditions, it may cause serious harm of a kind closely analogous to the harms they sought to avoid. An example is government religious observances of generic Protestant theology and liturgy.

The best non-textual evidence of intent is a widely debated social or political problem that a constitutional clause was intended to solve or ameliorate, considered in light of its contemporary social context. We read the Equal Protection Clause in light of the history of slavery and of race relations in the immediate aftermath of emancipation. Similarly, we should read the Fourth Amendment's protection against unreasonable searches and seizures in light of the pre-revolutionary controversy over general searches and writs of assistance,[17] and the Contract Clause in light of the controversy over debtor relief legislation in the 1780s.[18]

These controversies were widely known, widely debated, and consciously examined under political pressure that made the debate real and not just academic. They identify the core target of the resulting constitutional right. In-

17. *See, e.g.,* Boyd v. United States, 116 U.S. 616, 624-26 (1886); THOMAS COOLEY, CONSTITUTIONAL LIMITATIONS 301-03 (1868); TELFORD TAYLOR, TWO STUDIES IN CONSTITUTIONAL INTERPRETATION 29-44 (1969).

18. *See, e.g.,* Home Bldg. & Loan Ass'n v. Blaisdell, 290 U.S. 398, 427-28 (1934); *id.* at 454-65 (Sutherland, J., dissenting); THE FEDERALIST, No. 7 (Hamilton) at 65 (Clinton Rossiter ed. 1961); *id.* No. 44 (Madison) at 282-83; CHARLES A. BEARD, AN ECONOMIC INTERPRETATION OF THE CONSTITUTION OF THE UNITED STATES 178-81 (1913); RICHARD B. MORRIS, THE FORGING OF THE UNION, 1781-1789, at 154-59 (1987); BENJAMIN F. WRIGHT, THE CONTRACT CLAUSE OF THE CONSTITUTION 1-6 (1938).

terpreters can then search for a coherent principle, consistent with the text and as broad as the text, that centers on the core problem that the text was intended to resolve. An interpretation that would leave the core problem unresolved, or even marginal to the clause, is nearly as indefensible as an interpretation that is inconsistent with the text.

Because the best evidence of intent arises from major controversies, we should not expect to find a consensus that unites both supporters and opponents of a constitutional provision, or even a fully consistent view of all related issues among the supporters. The attitudes that give rise to the losing side of a controversy do not instantly disappear. It would be extraordinarily naive to expect that racist attitudes and racist practices suddenly disappeared in 1868, and it would be mistaken to assume that because they survived, the Equal Protection Clause permits government to act on them. It would be equally naïve to think that all vestiges of religious establishment and religious intolerance instantly disappeared when the Religion Clauses were ratified, or that their survival fixes the meaning of the Religion Clauses.

IV. History and the Religion Clauses

A. The History of Religious Persecution

The Religion Clauses had two great defining controversies. One was the long history of religious persecution and civil and international religious wars in Western societies. For two hundred years after the Reformation, religious conflict was a major factor in European politics in general and English politics in particular.[19] English highlights included Henry VIII's break with Rome; the Catholic succession of Mary; the Protestant succession of Elizabeth I; a Catholic heir-apparent through the first thirty years of Elizabeth's reign, until the execution of Mary Queen of Scots; the unsuccessful invasion of the Spanish Armada; the Civil War among Anglican Royalists, Puritan Parliamentarians, and Presbyterians allied with the Scots; the renewed fears of a Catholic succession, culminating in the Glorious Revolution of 1688, which replaced James II with William of Orange; and the endless problems of English rule in Catholic Ireland.

---

19. *See generally* GARRETT MATTINGLY, THE ARMADA (1959); THE OXFORD ILLUSTRATED HISTORY OF BRITAIN 237-359 (Kenneth O. Morgan ed. 1983); L.C.B. SEAMAN, A NEW HISTORY OF ENGLAND 191-301 (1981); ALBERT TUCKER, A HISTORY OF ENGLISH CIVILIZATION 259-373 (1972).

Religious conflicts were carried to the English colonies in America, and took new form with the growth of new denominations. Minor persecutions of Baptists and Quakers continued sporadically into the political lives of the Founders.[20] Catholics were rare outside Maryland, but the virulent anti-Catholicism of post-Reformation England appears to have been alive and well in the Founders' generation.[21]

Despite these remnants, the fight over religious persecution was more historical than contemporary. There was no significant sentiment for persecution among the Founders. Everyone subscribed to tolerance, at least for Protestants, and vestiges such as test oaths and tax supported churches were defended as consistent with tolerance.[22] But the history of serious religious conflict was recent and salient, and its broad outlines were widely known. The history of post-Reformation religious conflict was more recent to the Founders than the history of slavery is to us. It is surely reasonable to infer that the Founders intended the Religion Clauses of state and federal constitutions to prevent a renewal of these conflicts.

From that point we may reason further about what is necessarily entailed in that intent. What can we learn from the history of these religious conflicts that is relevant to the interpretation of the Religion Clauses? One thing we learn is that some humans are willing to die for religion, and that some are willing to kill for it. Because most Americans cannot imagine doing either, we find it hard to take seriously the uncompromising beliefs of religious minorities. We find exasperated judges demanding that religious minorities be reasonable.[23] But the Religion Clauses exist in substantial part

20. *See* DANIEL BOORSTIN, THE AMERICANS: THE COLONIAL EXPERIENCE 136 (1958) ("nearly fifty" Baptist ministers in Virginia jailed between 1768 and 1776); THOMAS CURRY, THE FIRST FREEDOMS: CHURCH AND STATE IN AMERICA TO THE PASSAGE OF THE FIRST AMENDMENT 168 (1986) (seizure of property from Massachusetts Baptists for unpaid church taxes); THE COMPLETE MADISON 298 (Saul Padover, ed. 1953) (Letter from Madison to William Bradford, Jan. 24, 1774, complaining that "5 or 6 well meaning men" were then in jail "for publishing their religious Sentiments which in the main are very orthodox"); *see also* BOORSTIN, *supra*, at 35-40 (early colonial persecutions of Quakers).

21. *See* examples collected in Laycock, *supra* note 14, at 916, 918 (text at notes 216, 223-28). *See also* DAVID H. BENNETT, THE PARTY OF FEAR: FROM NATIVIST MOVEMENTS TO THE NEW RIGHT IN AMERICAN HISTORY 12-22 (1988) (reviewing efforts to suppress overt anti-Catholicism during Revolution, to help unite against common enemy).

22. For an excellent treatment of the test oath controversy, see Edwin S. Gaustad, *Religion and Ratification*, in Wood, *supra* note 15, at 41. For a sampling of the arguments in favor of tax supported churches, see CURRY, *supra* note 20, at 131-32, 217.

23. *See, e.g.*, EEOC v. Ithaca Industries, 829 F.2d 519, 521-22 (4th Cir. 1987) (employee's "uncompromising and adamant refusal to work on Sunday . . . [and] his own absolutist po-

because believers are not always reasonable, and may be fanatical. The Religion Clauses must protect unusually intense religious commitments, just as they protect the rest of us from those who are so committed. Attempts to bend religious conscience to the will of the state can lead to suffering and persecution.

We can describe such an argument as intentionalist, because of its connection to what we have inferred about the intent of the Founders. But such arguments come from our own heads and not from any surviving record of what was in the heads of the Founders. What we get from the Founders is the broad contours of principle: do not prohibit the free exercise of religion, do not do anything respecting an establishment of religion, construe these rules in a way that avoids religious persecution and conflict of the sort that followed the Reformation. It is modern Americans, and not the Founders, who must draw the lessons from past persecutions and apply those lessons to current conditions. And because it is we who are drawing the lessons, we can also learn from the post-founding persecutions of Mormons, Jehovah's Witnesses, and contemporary "cults."

This allocation of responsibility is even clearer when we recognize that the Founders' general intent may require rejection of some of their unexamined but more specific intentions. The persistence of anti-Catholicism through the framing of the Religion Clauses was like the persistence of racism through the framing of the Fourteenth Amendment. We cannot reconcile it with any principled understanding of the Religion Clauses, and we should not try to do so.

Rejection of the Founders' anti-Catholicism is possible only because their intent is subordinate to the text. The Founders' views on slavery were even more inconsistent with the larger purposes of the Constitution than their views on Catholics. But they wrote their views on slavery into the ratified text, and so we were stuck with them until they could be eliminated by constitutional amendment. If they had written their anti-Catholicism into the text, we would be equally stuck. But they did not.

I have suggested elsewhere that we are not bound by the government's public observance of Protestantism in the Founders' time.[24] That too reflects

---

sition . . . precluded [employer] from making a reasonable accommodation for his religious practices"), *vacated en banc,* 849 F.2d 116 (4th Cir.); *In re* Reynolds, 83 B.R. 684, 685 (W.D. Mo. 1988) (unreasonable for debtors in bankruptcy to give more than three percent of gross income to church); *In re* Gaulker, 63 B.R. 224, 226 (Bankr. D.N.D. 1986) ("it seems a quite stern and uncaring religion" that would require such large contributions from debtors in bankruptcy).

24. Laycock, *supra* note 14, at 913-19 (text at notes 193-228).

an intent not written into the text, unexamined because uncontroversial in a nation with hardly any non-Protestants, in tension with the broad principles of the text as applied to our more pluralistic time, and a product of the same causes that fueled more overt anti-Catholicism. The case against overt government anti-Catholicism is obviously stronger than the case against government religious observances, because the tension with principled understandings of the text is so much sharper. But if we conclude that government-sponsored religious observances in our time tend to secularize religion, offend religious minorities and denigrate their status in the polity, and offend many of the most serious believers among the religious majority, then there is ample basis in textual and other modes of constitutional argument to override the weak argument from unexamined intent.

B. Disestablishment in the States

The second great defining controversy for the Religion Clauses was the fight over disestablishment in the states. That fight has been chronicled in recent books,[25] and I have examined its implications for the federal Establishment Clause in my earlier work.[26] It is sufficient here to note two things. First, taxation to support religion is at the core of what the opponents of establishment sought to prevent.[27]

Second, the defenders of establishment everywhere adopted the defensive strategy of nonpreferentialism. In New England, the attempts to be nonpreferential were transparently unsuccessful. The systems favored the Congregationalists, they were the source of bitter religious strife, and they were eliminated shortly after the framing. They were vestiges of the old regime, not models for the new.[28] In Virginia and Maryland, the proposals for a general assessment were as nonpreferential as eighteenth-century Americans could conceive, and after much debate, they were voted down.[29]

These state controversies are not part of the legislative history of the fed-

---

25. CURRY, *supra* note 20; LEONARD LEVY, THE ESTABLISHMENT CLAUSE: RELIGION AND THE FIRST AMENDMENT (1986). For a more detailed account of the debates in Virginia, see THOMAS E. BUCKLEY, CHURCH AND STATE IN REVOLUTIONARY VIRGINIA, 1776-1787 (1977).

26. Laycock, *supra* note 14, at 894-902 (text at notes 97-146).

27. *Compare id.* at 895-902 (debates over taxation to support churches) *with id.* at 913-19 (uncontroversial nonfinancial aid to religion).

28. *See id.* at 900-02.

29. *See id.* at 895-99.

eral Establishment Clause. But they are part of the intellectual and social history of what "establishment" meant to the Founders' generation. And because they are so focused on a theory that continues to be proposed, they are much better evidence of intent than we usually get. We can say with fewer qualifications than usual that the Founders rejected nonpreferentialism as the solution to the problem of religious establishment. And we can even more confidently reject the contrary position: whatever else they may have intended, it is historical nonsense to claim that the Founders affirmatively and specifically intended to permit government to aid religion on condition that it do so nonpreferentially.

There remains the vertical problem of applying this conclusion to changed conditions and changed questions. In this case, changed conditions strengthen the case against nonpreferentialism. The vast increase in religious pluralism makes nonpreferentialism even less practical today than in the eighteenth century.

But changed conditions have also posed new questions, and the answers of the 1780s are nonresponsive. The question in *Everson v. Board of Education*[30] was not whether government can aid religion financially, or whether it can aid religion nonpreferentially. The question in *Everson* was whether the bus rides were aid to religion. On that question, the debates of the 1780s have nothing to say. Earmarked taxes to pay ministers and build churches are unquestionably aid. In the modern social welfare state, it is very much harder to decide which government services are forbidden aid and which government services must be given to avoid discriminating against religion.

The most significant evidence of the Founders' intent with respect to these questions is that they paid for missionaries to teach the Indians.[31] Thus, despite their hostility to financial aid to churches, they apparently saw no problem in paying churches to deliver educational and social services. Even Jefferson participated in this practice.[32] The practice continued steadily for a hundred years. On the other hand, it was uncontroversial and unexamined, and it was ended when a later generation subjected it to Establishment Clause scrutiny.[33] This unexamined practice is weak evidence for the claim that the Founders specifically intended to permit government to pay churches to deliver educational and social services. But it is strong evidence against the claim that they specifically intended to forbid such payments. The

30. 330 U.S. 1 (1947).

31. *See* ROBERT CORD, SEPARATION OF CHURCH AND STATE: HISTORICAL FACT AND CURRENT FICTION 53-80, 261-70 (1982).

32. *Id.* at 261-63.

33. Act of June 7, 1897, ch. 3, 30 Stat. 62.

arguments for and against aid to church-run schools,[34] social welfare programs,[35] or chastity counseling[36] do not turn on anything specific in the intent of the Founders.

Twice now I have distinguished a proposition from its converse. I said there is strong evidence that the Founders opposed nonpreferential establishments, and overwhelming evidence that they did not specifically intend to permit them. I said there is weak evidence that the Founders intended to permit government to pay for social services delivered through churches, and strong evidence that they did not intend to forbid it.

These distinctions turn on the common understanding that those who assert a claim bear the burden of persuasion. It is always easier to show what the Founders did not intend than to show what they intended. Beware of arguments from false alternatives: when someone shows that the Founders did not intend *p,* he has not shown that they did intend *not p.* There may be a third alternative, in between or simply different, or there might have been such an alternative in 1791, or the Founders might have mistakenly thought there was such an alternative. Or the Founders might not have thought much about either *p* or *not p.*

In this formulation, *p* may be any proposition about the meaning of the Constitution, or about the constitutionality of any government act. For example, consider a state plan to finance education with tuition vouchers that could be used at any public or private school, including religious schools. If I show that the Founders did not intend to forbid education vouchers, I have not thereby shown that the Founders affirmatively intended to permit them. Similarly, if I show that the Founders did not affirmatively intend to permit vouchers, I have not thereby shown that the Founders did intend to forbid them. It is entirely possible that the Founders never thought about education vouchers, and that they never thought about anything sufficiently analogous to justify an inference of intent one way or the other.

Cases with respect to which the Founders had no knowable intent are not merely possible; they are common. They are not a cause for despair. We still have the primary source of constitutional law, which is the constitutional text. We are still capable of elaborating that text in a principled way. The text is primary even when there is secondary evidence of intent. The absence of such secondary evidence is, quite literally, a problem of secondary importance.

34. *See, e.g.,* Aguilar v. Felton, 473 U.S. 402 (1985); Grand Rapids School Dist. v. Ball, 473 U.S. 373 (1985); Mueller v. Allen, 463 U.S. 388 (1983).

35. *See, e.g.,* Bradfield v. Roberts, 175 U.S. 291 (1899).

36. *See* Bowen v. Kendrick, 487 U.S. 589 (1988).

Conclusion

Constitutional interpretation requires the identification of coherent principles in the constitutional text, reasoned elaboration of the implications of those principles, and application of the principles, including their implications, to current conditions. History can help in that task, but only if it is done right. It is nearly always helpful to ask what problem the Founders were trying to solve; it is rarely helpful to ask how the Founders would have decided a particular case on today's docket. And all inferences from history must be checked against the primary authority of the text.

Original Intent and the Constitution Today

in The First Freedom: Religion and the Bill of Rights 87
(James E. Wood, ed., 1990)

This is from the proceedings of a conference at Baylor University, in April 1989, to commemorate the bicentennial of Congressional passage of the Bill of Rights. It briefly reviews the history of the founding with respect to both Religion Clauses, and it further explores and elaborates appropriate and inappropriate uses of history. It emphasizes my view that we get little evidence of the meaning of the Constitution from things the founding generation did without controversy and without attending to any constitutional questions. This piece also reprises the evidence that the founding generation rejected nonpreferentialism.

This essay went to the printer in April or May 1990, immediately after the Supreme Court's momentous decision in Employment Division v. Smith, *which is mentioned very briefly.*

*　　　*　　　*

Arguments about original intent are of two distinct kinds. One may argue over what the framers intended, and one may argue over the proper role of original intent in contemporary judicial decisions. What the framers intended is principally an argument about history — about the most accurate account of the past. The role of intent in judicial decisions is principally an argument about law — about theories of constitutional interpretation.

This distinction between the two arguments is real, but there is no strict separation between them. Hardly anyone believes that original intent is wholly irrelevant to constitutional interpretation. But unless one takes that position, the two arguments are inevitably interdependent. This does not arise merely from the psychological fact that everyone tends to give more weight to those views of the framers that they agree with, although that is an important source of interdependence.

More important, one's theory of constitutional interpretation may shape the inquiry into history. Each theory of constitutional interpretation emphasizes different historical questions. If one asks different questions, one will get different answers. If legal theorists conclude that some intentions are more important than others, or that some evidence of intent is more important than other evidence, this will change the legal conclusions that are drawn from history. That is why, as John Wilson has observed, lawyers and historians ask different questions about history.[1]

Similarly, one's inquiry into history may shape one's theory of constitutional interpretation. Some of the most important arguments against reliance on original intent in constitutional interpretation are that collective intent did not exist or cannot be known with sufficient accuracy, and that even if known, the intentions of 1789 are not responsive to the questions of 1989.[2] If a legal theory poses questions to history and historical inquiry determines that the questions are unanswerable, then the legal theory will have to be changed.

How To Look for Original Intent

I find myself in the middle of both these debates. On the question of history, the original intent behind the Religion Clauses is more complex than either side wants to admit. If you find that the Founders always agreed with you, you should probably reexamine your history.

On the question of constitutional theory, the intent of the Founders matters, but it is not the only thing that matters, or even the most important. The most important source of constitutional meaning is the constitutional text. The people's representatives voted on the text. They did not vote on James Madison's notes, or the desultory debate in the House, or the secret debate in the Senate, or the private correspondence of the framers. They certainly did not vote on the constitutionality of everything the government did in the founding generation.

The ratified text has meaning to a language community that includes the

1. John F. Wilson, *Original Intent and the Quest for Comparable Consensus,* in James E. Wood, Jr., ed., THE FIRST FREEDOM: RELIGION AND THE BILL OF RIGHTS 113 (J. M. Dawson Institute of Church-State Studies at Baylor University 1990).

2. *See, e.g.,* Paul Brest, *The Misconceived Quest for the Original Understanding,* 60 B.U. L. REV. 204 (1980).

present generation as well as the framers' generation. The text states sweeping principles. This nation has had two hundred years of experience in applying those principles to changing conditions, in arguing about them, in thinking about their implications. It is hardly surprising that the broad principles stated in the text turn out to have implications that the Founders did not contemplate. So the search for intent is not for the Founders' specific applications, and usually not for how the Founders would have decided this case. Rather, the inquiry into original intent should proceed at the same level of generality as the text. If the framers had wanted a narrow list of specific rules with a detailed list of exceptions, they could have drafted that. They chose not to do so. They drafted broad principles that forbid whole categories of government misconduct in few words.

The search for intent must be for principles that are consistent with the text and as broad as the text, that solve the problems the Founders addressed in their time, and that also give effect to constitutional values in the social conditions of our time. The inquiry into intent should ask what recent abuses the clause was directed to eliminate. What real controversies was the clause supposed to resolve? These are the problems they were thinking about when they drafted and ratified the clause, and these controversies can provide a center point to anchor the broader principle stated in the constitutional text.[3]

By contrast, much less weight should be ascribed to how the Founders applied or failed to apply constitutional principles to cases that were not controversial in their time. Things that were not controversial received no serious scrutiny. They were not examined under the pressure of a real interest group with a real grievance. What the Founders thought about is more important than what they did not think about. Not everything the founding generation did was constitutional even in their social conditions, and certainly not in ours.

The best evidence of their intent is found in real controversies, where one should not expect to find consensus. There were two sides to these controversies; there were winners and losers. Racism and discrimination did not instantly disappear when the Fourteenth Amendment was ratified, and one should not expect religious intolerance or support for establishment to instantly disappear when the First Amendment was ratified.

Finally, little can be learned from the legislative history as such — from the records of debates and the Founders' explanations of what they meant.

---

3. These points are further developed in Douglas Laycock, *Text, Intent, and the Religion Clauses*, 4 Notre Dame J.L. Ethics & Pub. Pol'y 683 (1990).

Most of that material was not recorded. Much of what was recorded was re-corded inaccurately; shorthand was in its infancy. Both contemporary com-plaints and modern scholarship attest to these points.[4] Even if the legislative history is accepted at face value, it is remarkably unrevealing. The inferences one can draw from it are generally attenuated, lacking power to persuade. Some of the clearest statements seem inconsistent with large bodies of other evidence. This essay reviews what survives on the Religion Clauses. But it is more fruitful to examine the social, intellectual, and political history of the founding generation, and the great controversies of their time.

Original Intent about Disestablishment

Conflicting Evidence and Attempts to Reconcile It

The Founders' treatment of religious liberty does not easily fit into the mod-ern conceptions of any faction. By emphasizing different parts of the histori-cal record, different scholars and justices have created dramatically inconsis-tent accounts of original intent. Few of these accounts have dealt effectively, or at all, with the evidence that supports other accounts.

Beginning with *Everson v. Board of Education*,[5] the Supreme Court's offi-cial history was a strict separationist history. The Court emphasized the his-tory of religious persecution, the fight for disestablishment, the views of James Madison and Thomas Jefferson, and the Virginia Statute for Religious Liberty. The Court concluded that government must be neutral toward reli-gion, and not support it in any way.

The Court's critics,[6] and some of the Court's recent opinions,[7] empha-size very different aspects of history. Government in the Founders' genera-tion constantly supported religion. Congress appointed chaplains who of-fered daily prayers. Presidents proclaimed days of prayer and fasting. The government paid for missionaries to the Indians. The Northwest Ordinance set aside land to endow schools because, the statute recited, "religion, moral-

---

4. *See* James H. Hutson, *The Creation of the Constitution: The Integrity of the Documen-tary Record*, 65 Tex. L. Rev. 1, 6 (1986); Marion Tinling, *Thomas Lloyd's Reports of the First Federal Congress*, 18 Wm. & Mary Q., 3d ser., 519 (1961).

5. Everson v. Board of Education, 330 U.S. 1 (1947).

6. The most thorough of this work is Robert L. Cord, Separation of Church and State: Historical Fact and Current Fiction (New York: Lambeth Press, 1982). *See also* Wallace v. Jaffree, 472 U.S. 38, 91-114 (1985) (Rehnquist, J., dissenting).

7. Lynch v. Donnelly, 465 U.S. 668 (1984); Marsh v. Chambers, 463 U.S. 783 (1983).

ity, and knowledge" are necessary to good government.[8] That provision was a compromise,[9] but the compromise implied that Congress expected that the schools thus endowed would teach religion. Events confirmed the expectation. Some states retained established churches, and most enforced Sabbath laws and blasphemy laws. Most of the states that enforced such laws had their own constitutional guarantees of religious liberty. Even Madison and Jefferson supported some of these measures.

Neither side relies on other practices of the Founders' generation. No one relies on their widespread anti-Catholicism[10] or the test oaths that barred Catholics from holding office or even voting in several states.[11] But those are also part of the historical record.

The challenge for anyone trying to make sense of original intent is to account for all this evidence in a principled way. Is there a pattern to the Founders' treatment of church and state? Is there an implicit principle on which they acted? Or is there simply an ad hoc series of inconsistent actions? The *Everson* account ignores these problems; it follows Madison on his good days and ignores the rest.

The Court's critics have tried to account for more of the evidence. Their most common claim is that the Founders intended to permit government aid to religion so long as that aid does not prefer one religion over others. This nonpreferentialist thesis has been around for a long time, and the Supreme Court has repeatedly rejected it.[12] But it has refused to die. In this decade, it has been offered by former Attorney General Edwin Meese,[13] Chief Justice William H. Rehnquist,[14] political scientists Michael Malbin[15] and

---

8. The Northwest Ordinance is reprinted in a footnote to Act of Aug. 7, 1789, ch. 8, 1 Stat. 50.

9. Edwin S. Gaustad, *Religion and Ratification,* in James E. Wood, Jr., ed., THE FIRST FREEDOM: RELIGION AND THE BILL OF RIGHTS 113 (J.M. Dawson Institute of Church-State Studies at Baylor University 1990).

10. *See* Douglas Laycock, *"Nonpreferential" Aid to Religion: A False Claim About Original Intent,* 27 WM. & MARY L. REV. 875, 918 (1986) (text at notes 224-28).

11. Gaustad, *supra* note 9.

12. Wallace v. Jaffree, 472 U.S. 38, 52-55 (1985); Abington School District v. Schempp, 374 U.S. 203, 216-17 (1963); Illinois ex rel. McCollum v. Board of Education, 333 U.S. 203, 211 (1948).

13. Edwin Meese, III, *The Supreme Court of the United States: Bulwark of a Limited Constitution,* 27 S. TEX. L.J. 455, 464 (1986).

14. *Wallace,* 472 U.S. at 91-114 (Rehnquist, J., dissenting).

15. Michael J. Malbin, RELIGION AND POLITICS: THE INTENTIONS OF THE AUTHORS OF THE FIRST AMENDMENT (Washington, D.C.: American Enterprise Institute for Public Policy Research, 1978).

Robert Cord,[16] law professor Rodney Smith,[17] and the United States Catholic Conference.[18]

A recent article by law professor Steven Smith offers a different theory.[19] He concludes that the Founders intended the strict institutional separation of church and state. By that he means that the state should not exercise ecclesiastical power or interfere with the internal affairs of churches, and that the churches as such should not exercise government power or interfere in the internal affairs of government. But he concludes that that is all the Founders intended. He believes the Founders did not intend — indeed, could not imagine — a secular state separated from religious belief and observance.

None of these theories fit the historical data. The Supreme Court's simple account in *Everson* ignores too much data without justification. One has to try to understand how the Founders' seeming inconsistencies fit together in their time before rejecting any part of what they did. Neither side can just pick the parts it likes or assume that the whole nation agreed with Madison.

The nonpreferentialist account flies in the face of the data. Nonpreferentialism is one of the few issues the Founders clearly considered and decided. Nonpreferentialism was the last compromise offered by the defenders of establishment, and the founding generation repeatedly rejected it.

Institutional separation was surely an important part of what the Founders sought to accomplish, but their fights for disestablishment went beyond that. The opponents of establishment opposed all forms of financial aid to churches, including aid that would be delivered in ways arguably consistent with institutional separation. But my more fundamental disagreement with Steven Smith is over an issue of constitutional theory: the significance of the Founders' failure to think about an issue.

This essay will fill in the historical information to support these conclusions about nonpreferentialism and institutional separation, and then suggest a different set of principles to account for the evidence of the Founders' intent.

---

16. CORD, *supra* note 6.

17. Rodney K. Smith, *Getting Off on the Wrong Foot and Back on Again: A Reexamination of the History of the Framing of the Religion Clauses of the First Amendment and a Critique of the Reynolds and Everson Decisions*, 20 WAKE FOREST L. REV. 569 (1984).

18. Brief of the United States Catholic Conference as Amicus Curiae in Support of Appellants 10-15, in Aguilar v. Felton (No. 84-237), 473 U.S. 402 (1985).

19. Steven D. Smith, *Separation and the "Secular": Reconstructing the Disestablishment Doctrine*, 67 TEX. L. REV. 955 (1989).

The Fight Over Disestablishment in the States

The American Revolution provoked a general rethinking of church-state relations in many of the new states. Most of the states wrote constitutions, and where there was disagreement about church-state relations, the process of constitution writing focused attention on it. In the states with established Anglican churches, George III was head of the church as well as head of the state. The Revolution posed a question of succession in both capacities. The Virginia legislature's first reaction was to direct that wherever the Book of Common Prayer said to pray for the King, the people should pray for the legislature.[20] At the cost of considerable simplification, there emerged three main patterns: the southern colonies, the middle colonies, and New England.

Virginia and the Other Southern Colonies

Virginia is the best exemplar of the Southern colonies. In 1776, the Virginia Declaration of Rights guaranteed the free exercise of religion.[21] Also in 1776, Virginia suspended collection of the tax to support the Anglican clergy. But the statute recited that the legislature had made no decision concerning a more general tax to support all clergy.[22] That issue was reserved for the future, and it was debated intermittently for ten years.

In 1784 a general assessment bill passed two readings in the legislature. The bill assessed a tax to support teachers of the Christian religion.[23] But it provided that each citizen could designate the pastor to get his tax. Any Christian teacher was eligible — even Catholic priests. Taxpayers could even designate a fund for schools, so that non-Christians were provided for without being expressly mentioned. There was an exemption for Quakers and Mennonites, who had no paid clergy and conscientiously objected to such a tax. In short, the bill was as nonpreferential as Americans in the 1780s could imagine.

---

20. THOMAS E. BUCKLEY, CHURCH AND STATE IN REVOLUTIONARY VIRGINIA, 1776-1787, at 21 (Charlottesville: University Press of Virginia, 1977).

21. 9 HENING'S STATUTES AT LARGE 109, 111-12 par. 16 (1821). The clause is quoted in THOMAS J. CURRY, THE FIRST FREEDOMS: CHURCH AND STATE IN AMERICA TO THE PASSAGE OF THE FIRST AMENDMENT 146 (New York: Oxford University Press, 1986).

22. This statute is reprinted in BUCKLEY, *supra* note 20, at 35 and in 1 ANSON P. STOKES, CHURCH AND STATE IN THE UNITED STATES 305 (New York: Harper & Brothers, 1950).

23. The bill is reprinted in Everson v. Board of Education, 330 U.S. 1, 72-74 (1947) (appendix to opinion of Rutledge, J., dissenting), in BUCKLEY, *supra* note 20, at 188-89, and in CORD, *supra* note 6, at 242-43.

Madison got the final vote delayed to the next session so that legislators could consult their constituents. The bill was then defeated by a broad coalition, including the usual number of votes opposed to any tax. Madison was a part of that coalition, but he was only a part, and probably is given too much credit.[24] It was in this context that he wrote his *Memorial and Remonstrance Against Religious Establishments,* perhaps the classic short statement of the arguments for disestablishment.[25]

Religious denominations also played a critical role. The Baptists were the most vigorously opposed. Baptists believed that they should support their church voluntarily; they were conscientiously opposed to having that support coerced by the state.

The Methodists were also opposed. They were a smaller group, just then breaking off from the Anglicans. Whether out of principle, or just to distinguish themselves from the Anglicans, they were opposed.

The Presbyterians were a large minority, and they initially supported the bill. A tax for churches looked more attractive if they would benefit. But when Hanover Presbytery met and fully considered the issue, it came out opposed. Their opposition was based at least in part on self-interest. Presbyterian polity carefully balances power between clergy and laity. Part of the laity's control is financial: a church contracts with a minister and sets his salary. If the clergy were supported by a tax collected by the state, in an amount set by statute, the laity would lose that financial check, and the balance of power would be upset.

The Presbyterians were the last straw. When they joined the coalition against the bill, the bill was dead. Indeed, it never came to a vote.

The lessons most commonly drawn from this debate are that Virginians rejected an established church, which is true, and that they agreed on everything in the "Memorial and Remonstrance," which is probably not true.

Two other lessons are more important. First, the issue was nonpreferentialism. The bill was as nonpreferential as its supporters could make it, and the issue was precisely whether that feature made it acceptable. The answer was no.

Second, nonpreferentialism was impossible to implement even then in a

24. For more detailed accounts, see Buckley, *supra* note 20, at 113-43; Curry, *supra* note 21, at 140-48; William L. Miller, The First Liberty: Religion and the American Republic 24-36 (New York: Knopf, 1985).

25. The "Memorial and Remonstrance" is reprinted in *Everson,* 330 U.S. at 63-72 (appendix to opinion of Rutledge, J., dissenting); Cord, *supra* note 6, at 244-49; Saul K. Padover, ed., The Complete Madison: His Basic Writings 299-306 (New York: Harper, 1953).

state where the religious faiths were almost entirely Protestant and where religious diversity ran only from Anglicans to Baptists. Despite the efforts of leading Virginians and Virginia's relative homogeneity, it was impossible to implement the general assessment in a way that was acceptable to all denominations. The bill would have violated the consciences of the Baptists and upset the polity of the Presbyterians. If nonpreferentialism was impossible then, it is hard to see how it would work now, in a vastly more pluralistic society.

In 1786, in the wake of this debate, the legislature enacted Jefferson's Statute for Religious Liberty, with its provision that no person shall be compelled to frequent or support any place of worship whatsoever.[26] That language is broad enough to forbid both preferential and nonpreferential support for churches.

The other southern colonies followed somewhat similar paths with much less debate. Maryland defeated a similar bill in 1785 after a statewide debate.[27] Georgia enacted such a bill but never collected the tax; it was repealed by the constitution of 1798.[28] North Carolina disestablished without a significant fight.[29] South Carolina retained a vestigial establishment of Protestantism into the national period; proposals for a nonpreferential tax briefly surfaced and went nowhere.[30]

The Middle Colonies (and Rhode Island)

In the middle colonies, there is not much to report. There was no establishment in Pennsylvania, Delaware, or New Jersey, or in Rhode Island, a New England colony that was like a middle colony for this purpose.[31] The vestigial establishment in New York faded away without much debate.[32]

---

26. The statute is still in effect. VA. CODE ANN. 57-1 (1986). It is reprinted in BUCKLEY, *supra* note 20, at 190-91; CORD, *supra* note 6, at 249-50; and 1 STOKES, *supra* note 22, at 392-94.

27. CURRY, *supra* note 21, at 155-57; FORREST MCDONALD, NOVUS ORDO SECLORUM: THE INTELLECTUAL ORIGINS OF THE CONSTITUTION 43-44 (Lawrence, Kan.: University Press of Kansas, 1985).

28. CURRY, *supra* note 21, at 152-53; 1 STOKES, *supra* note 22, at 440.

29. CURRY, *supra* note 21, at 151.

30. *Id.* at 149-51. The South Carolina statute is reprinted in 1 STOKES, *supra* note 22, at 432-34.

31. CURRY, *supra* note 21, at 159-60, 162.

32. *Id.* at 161-62.

Massachusetts and the Rest of New England

The other great pattern was that of New England, and the examplar was Massachusetts.[33] The Massachusetts constitution of 1780 enacted a local option establishment. There was a tax to support the minister established by law, to be selected by local vote and settled by contract in each parish. In theory any denomination could win the election. Dissenters could file exemption certificates and pay the tax to their own church instead.

The convergence with the Virginia proposals is remarkable. The strategy was nonpreferential. John Adams said that Massachusetts had "the most mild and equitable establishment of religion that was known in the world, if indeed, it could be called an establishment."[34]

Dissenters did not find it so mild and equitable; the system was not so nonpreferential in practice. The Congregationalists won nearly all the local elections, and that was understood and intended. The Baptists and Quakers refused on grounds of conscience to file for exemption certificates — Quakers because they had no paid clergy and Baptists because they would support their clergy only with voluntary contributions. The authorities regularly levied on their property for unpaid taxes, which of course went to support the Congregationalists. Other dissenters sometimes had trouble qualifying for exemptions, either because of unsympathetic administration of the law or because their church was not incorporated.[35]

This establishment persisted until the Congregationalists began to lose elections to the Unitarians. Then the establishment looked onerous indeed. The last remnants of formal establishment were repealed in 1833.

Connecticut had a very similar system, with the same problems.[36] New Hampshire and Vermont had systems that were quite similar in theory, but in practice they were less organized and there was more local diversity.[37]

33. For a review of the New England experience see *id.* at 162-92; WILLIAM G. MCLOUGHLIN, NEW ENGLAND DISSENT 1630-1833: THE BAPTISTS AND THE SEPARATION OF CHURCH AND STATE (Cambridge, Mass.: Harvard University Press, 1971). For more on Massachusetts only, see JACOB C. MEYER, CHURCH AND STATE IN MASSACHUSETTS FROM 1740 TO 1833: A CHAPTER IN THE HISTORY OF THE DEVELOPMENT OF INDIVIDUAL FREEDOM (Cleveland: Western Reserve University, 1930).

34. CURRY, *supra* note 21, at 131.

35. *See* Barnes v. First Parish, 6 Mass. 400 (1810) (holding that minister of unincorporated religious society was not entitled to church taxes paid by his adherents). Incorporation in those days required a special act of the legislature; general incorporation laws were not enacted until much later.

36. CURRY, *supra* note 21, at 178-84.

37. *Id.* at 184-90.

Conclusions from the Debates in the States

Several conclusions may be drawn from this survey of the debates of the 1780s. First, some version of nonpreferentialism was on the agenda in every state where the debate got serious.

Second, the debates in Virginia were the fullest development of this widespread argument. That is what makes Virginia so important. It is not just that some of us like the Virginia outcome, or even that Madison and Jefferson were there. It is that the Virginians most fully developed the arguments that were going on all up and down the country.

Third, the remnants of establishment in New England did not work. They caused bitter religious strife and were repealed early in the national period. They were remnants of the old regime, not models for the new. The nonpreferentialists simply cannot account for this widespread rejection of their theory.

I do not think that Steven Smith can fully account for it either, although that is a closer case. In Virginia and Maryland, there was no clear issue of institutional separation. The issue was financial aid to churches, delivered in a way that minimized contact between church and state. The state would not interfere with the internal affairs of the churches; it would simply turn over the money to the church designated by the taxpayer.

The distinction between financial aid and institutional interference was part of the debate of 1784-85. Hanover Presbytery drew the distinction explicitly. In the fall of 1784, the Presbytery passed a resolution supporting a general assessment on condition that the state recognize full equality of religious bodies and full freedom for all faiths, and that there be no interference with creeds, forms of worship, and internal church affairs.[38] The state could provide tax support so long as it kept its hands off internal church affairs.

The Presbyterians eventually changed their mind, in part because they concluded that the issues could not be so cleanly separated. Tax support upset internal affairs in some churches, most notably in the disruption of Presbyterian polity. And perhaps Smith would say that letting the state perform the church function of collecting contributions is itself a violation of institutional separation. But it seems clear that much of the opposition was to the principle of government support for the churches, and not just to institutional combination. In Madison's words, the extraction of three pence was an establishment.[39]

---

38. MILLER, *supra* note 24, at 30.

39. "Memorial and Remonstrance Against Religious Establishments" par. 3 ("the same

The Legislative History

The Rejected Drafts

As noted earlier, the legislative history is often unhelpful. But in this case, the legislative history offers a remarkable confirmation of the rejection of nonpreferentialism. The Senate and the Conference Committee appear to have squarely considered the choice between forbidding any establishment or forbidding only nonpreferential establishments.[40] The Senate met in secret and did not record its debates, but it recorded motions and votes in a journal. The Senate considered four drafts of the Establishment Clause that unambiguously stated the nonpreferentialist theory:

> Congress shall make no law establishing one religious sect or society in preference to others. . . .

> Congress shall not make any law . . . establishing any Religious Sect or Society.

> Congress shall make no law establishing any particular denomination of religion in preference to another. . . .

> Congress shall make no law establishing articles of faith or a mode of worship. . . .

The first three of these drafts were rejected in the Senate. A week later, the Senate adopted the draft limited to "articles of faith or a mode of worship." That draft was rejected in the Conference Committee.

The Conference Committee produced the version ultimately ratified: "Congress shall make no law respecting an establishment of religion. . . ." This is one of the broadest drafts considered by either House. It forbids any law respecting an establishment of "religion." It does not say "a religion," "a

---

authority which can force a citizen to contribute three pence only of his property for the support of any one establishment, may force him to conform to any other establishment in all cases whatsoever").

40. Various drafts of the Religion Clauses are collected in Laycock, *supra* note 10, at 879-82 (text at notes 26-42). For original sources, see 1 Linda G. dePauw, ed., DOCUMENTARY HISTORY OF THE FIRST FEDERAL CONGRESS OF THE UNITED STATES OF AMERICA 135, 151, 166, 181 (Baltimore: Johns Hopkins University Press, 1972); 3 *id.* at 159, 166, 228; 1 ANNALS OF CONGRESS 434 (June 8, 1789); *id.* at 729-31 (August 15, 1789). Different printings of the ANNALS OF CONGRESS have different pagination; the date is a more reliable way to find particular passages.

national religion," "a single religion," "a particular religion," "one sect or society," or "any particular denomination of religion." It is religion generically that may not be established.

This drafting history is not quite as dispositive as it would be in the case of a statute. The assent of state legislatures was required to amend the Constitution, and one may not assume without evidence that state legislatures were familiar with the rejected Senate drafts. But the rejected drafts are important for several reasons. First, the rejection of nonpreferentialism in the First Congress is consistent with all the other rejections of nonpreferentialism in the founding generation. Second, the Virginia, New York, and North Carolina ratifying conventions had proposed nonpreferentialist amendments similar to the rejected Senate drafts, and those proposals had circulated around the country.[41] So even if state legislatures could not compare the actual amendment to the rejected Senate drafts, they could compare it to earlier state proposals and see the difference.

Third, although Congress could not unilaterally amend the Constitution, it could unilaterally prevent amendments by any procedure other than a new convention. So the Congressional rejection of nonpreferential drafts was dispositive, even though the Congressional proposal of the actual clause was only a proposal. It is accurate to say that the First Congress considered and authoritatively rejected proposals to forbid only preferential establishments. The persistence of nonpreferentialism in the face of this rejection is extraordinary.

The Legislative Debates

The legislative debates say little. They do not support any of the theories under consideration, but they do provide one startling piece of evidence for an interpretation even narrower than nonpreferentialism. The only recorded debate on the Religion Clauses occurred in the House of Representatives on August 15, 1789.[42] The reporter's notes fill slightly less than two columns in the Annals of Congress. The debate concerned the draft submitted by a Select Committee, and a substitute offered by Samuel Livermore. Both drafts were somewhat different from the amendment ultimately adopted. The Select Committee draft provided: "No religion shall be established by law, nor shall

41. Jonathan Elliot, ed., The Debates in the Several State Conventions on the Adoption of the Federal Constitution 224, 328, 659 (Philadelphia: J. B. Lippincott, 2d ed. 1836).

42. 1 Annals of Congress at 729-31 (August 15, 1789). This debate is more thoroughly analyzed in Laycock, *supra* note 10, at 885-94 (text at notes 52-96).

the equal rights of conscience be infringed." The Livermore substitute provided: "Congress shall make no laws touching religion, or infringing the rights of conscience."

Fifty-one representatives were present to vote on the Livermore amendment. Only eight of them said anything the reporter took down, and five of the eight said things that cast no light on meaning. Someone suggested transposing the order of the two clauses; another said no bill of rights was needed; another agreed but said it would do no harm and reassure doubters, and so on. They may have been an assembly of demigods, but their minutes sound like any other committee meeting.

Two speakers — Peter Sylvester and Benjamin Huntington — opposed the Establishment Clause. Some nonpreferentialists seem to think they were authoritatively describing the clause.[43] Instead, they were urging its deletion or at least a minimalist interpretation. One of them offered to explain "the blessed fruits" of disestablishment in Rhode Island, another sarcastic reference of the kind Edwin S. Gaustad has described earlier in this volume.[44] The speaker did not mean that disestablishment would provide blessed fruits if it were narrowly conceived.

The heart of the argument is Madison. Madison chose not to argue with Sylvester and Huntington, but to reassure them and their sympathizers by portraying the Establishment Clause in the narrowest possible light. He spoke twice, and both remarks are a puzzle. First he said: "He apprehended the meaning of the words to be, that Congress should not establish a religion, and enforce the legal observation of it by law, nor compel men to worship God in any manner contrary to their conscience."[45]

Later, he proposed that the House insert the word "national" before the word "religion," so that the Establishment Clause would read: "No national religion shall be established by law." Madison explained that "he believed that the people feared one sect might obtain a pre-eminence, or two combine together, and establish a religion to which they would compel others to conform. He thought that if the word 'national' was introduced, it would point the amendment directly to the object it was intended to prevent."[46]

What did he mean by that? His proposed amendment, "no national religion," is consistent with nonpreferentialism. His explanation is much nar-

---

43. *See* Smith, *supra* note 17, at 611, 613; L. Martin Nussbaum, Comment, *Muller v. Allen: Tuition Tax Relief and the Original Intent*, 7 HARV. J.L. & PUB. POL'Y 551, 573 n.124 (1984).

44. Gaustad, *supra* note 9, at 48. For other disparaging views of Rhode Island, see CURRY, *supra* note 21, at 20-21, 91, 112, 183; McDONALD, *supra* note 27, at 175-76.

45. 1 ANNALS OF CONGRESS at 730 (August 15, 1789).

46. *Id.* at 731 (August 15, 1789).

rower. If Congress appropriated one million dollars for the support of the United Methodist Church, it would not be enforcing the observation of Methodism by law. Yet the appropriation would be preferential, unconstitutional even under the nonpreferentialist interpretation of the clause. Whatever Madison described, it was not nonpreferentialism. Neither did he describe an amendment focused on institutional separation. To his credit, Steven Smith does not rely on these remarks.

It is hard to know what Madison was thinking. The two statements are inconsistent with all his previous and subsequent statements concerning establishment. Nevertheless, he appears to have said the same thing clearly and twice. Maybe the reporter garbled it both times, but it seems likely that Madison said something approximating what the reporter attributes to him. The two statements are also consistent with Madison's June 8 draft of the clause, which provided only that no "national religion be established."

My best guess is that on June 8 and August 15, this was all Madison thought he could get, but that by the time of the Conference Committee, he saw a chance to get more. Passage was not assured on August 15; Madison had spent the whole session just getting the amendments to the floor of the House. Many Federalists thought amendments were unnecessary; Anti-Federalists foresaw that passing amendments would take away their best criticism of the new Constitution. Congress was occupied with more urgent matters like organizing the other two branches and raising the revenue to run them.

If Madison had been describing the final draft, his remarks would be more important, but he was not. His proposal to insert the word "national" provoked a collateral attack by Elbridge Gerry. Gerry said that the Anti-Federalists had always known this was a national government and not a federal government, and here was Madison confirming the charge by using the word "national." Madison withdrew his suggestion. He could have substituted a less offensive word: "single," "particular," or "specific" would have done nicely; even "federal" might have worked. He offered none of these, and no more was heard of the "no national religion" language. It is not the Establishment Clause; it is yet another rejected draft.

At this point someone called the question on Livermore's substitute, and it was adopted. The only reported debate thus ended a lot further from the no-preference position than it began. Livermore's substitute was inelegant but sweeping. It forbad any law "touching" religion, which would include both preferential and nonpreferential laws, any form of aid or interference. No one in this brief debate said that preferential establishments were bad while nonpreferential ones were acceptable. Only three people spoke to the merits; two of them appear to have been in the minority; and no one on any side accepted Madison's explanation.

In the month that followed, explicitly nonpreferential drafts were fought over and rejected in the Senate and the Conference Committee. The debates were not recorded, but the choices were clearly presented. Whatever the Founders meant, it was not that preferential establishments are forbidden but nonpreferential establishments are allowed.

The Founders' Other Intent: Civil Religion

Nonfinancial Aid

Government in the founding generation actively supported religious belief in a variety of ways that required no transfer of funds from government to churches. What is one to make of the Congressional chaplains, the days of prayer and fasting, the Sabbath laws, the Northwest Ordinance, and all the rest? Is there some principle that reconciles these practices with the views expressed in the debates over disestablishment?

It is significant that the Founders saw no problem with government sponsorship and endorsement of generic Protestantism. They saw no problem with it because in their society, no one complained. It did no apparent harm, no one raised the issue, and they had no occasion to seriously think about it. Just as the framers excluded blacks from the proposition that all men are created equal, they less consciously, less pervasively, and less cruelly excluded non-Protestants from the proposition that government should not establish religion. If a practice was not controversial among Protestants, it was not controversial at all. Government support for generic Protestantism is not evidence of what the Establishment Clause means, because the Founders were not seriously thinking about the Establishment Clause when they did these things.

The heart of my disagreement with Steven Smith is the question of what inference to draw from things the Founders failed to think about. I say that they did not seriously think about it, and so they had no intent for us to follow, and we must apply for ourselves the principle stated in the constitutional text. He says that they did not think about it, and so they did not intend to forbid it, and therefore it is not forbidden. To put his point another way, he would say that we are bound by the consensus that caused them not to think about it.

My disagreement with Smith is not so much over history as over the theory of constitutional interpretation. I would *enforce* the broad principle ratified in the text, *in light of* the principal controversies that appear to have led to it. Smith would *narrow* the broad principle ratified in the text, to cover *only* the principal controversies that appear to have led to it. Both the bare text and the principles reflected in the Founders' debate over disestablishment have implications for government endorsements of generic Christianity in a nation with millions of non-Christians. One may not ignore those implications just because the social conditions of the Founders' time failed to focus attention on them. The municipal creche is divisive today just as the general assessment was divisive then, and both are forms of government support for religion. Those of us who would forbid the creche are taking the principles the Founders developed in the context of division between Anglicans and Baptists, and applying them to today's divisions between Christians, Jews, Muslims, Buddhists, agnostics, and atheists.

Missionaries to the Indians

One of the Founders' practices requires separate consideration. For a century, the government paid missionaries to educate the Indians.[47] In some cases, the government sent missionaries in exchange for Indian lands. These programs cannot be characterized as nonfinancial; money was paid out to churches. Yet it was somehow considered a different category from things like the general assessment. Madison and Jefferson participated, and no one seriously objected.

The most obvious explanation is that the government was buying secular services from churches, or paying churches to perform governmental tasks. This has profound implications for aid to parochial schools and for church delivery of social services. It is possible that the Founders did not think of the missionaries in these terms. Perhaps they placed these programs in a separate category for Indians, considered as foreign sovereigns, wards of the government, or some combination of the two. That proposition is hard to test, because the federal government did not deliver social services to white citizens. States did only a little more. It would be useful to know whether churches and local governments cooperated financially for the relief of the poor. When Virginia disestablished the Anglican church, the state took over poor relief from the church.[48] I do not know whether this reflected a conscious decision

---

47. *See* CORD, *supra* note 6, at 53-80, 261-70.

48. DANIEL J. BOORSTIN, THE AMERICANS: THE COLONIAL EXPERIENCE 130-31 (New York: Random House, 1958).

about disestablishment, or was simply a consequence of cutting off the church's tax revenue.

Like civil religion, the Founders do not appear to have thought much about missionaries to the Indians. It was not a subject of serious controversy. Support for missionaries cannot be attributed simply to the Founders' Protestant bias, because the government occasionally paid for Catholic missionaries too. Maybe it was a product of Christian bias. Maybe it was just a good way to get the job done.

To conclude that the Founders did not think about this much largely eliminates their intent as a factor. Apparently, they did not consciously intend for the Establishment Clause to permit such church-state cooperation. But even more obviously, they did not consciously intend for the Establishment Clause to forbid it. One cannot argue against aid to parochial schools on the basis of any direct evidence of the Founders' intent.

The question in modern times is to identify those government services that establish religion if given, and those that must be given to avoid discriminating against religion. In *Everson v. Board of Education,* the Court was nine to zero on the principle that government should not aid religion, but it was five to four on whether bus rides to transport children to school constituted aid. Those two divisions reflect the relative difficulty of the questions. The general assessment bill, with special taxes earmarked for the support of clergy, was clearly aid. Bus rides and many other things in the modern social welfare state are not so clear. This is a case where the answers of 1789 are not responsive to the questions of 1989.

A Brief Note on Free Exercise

There is less to say about the Free Exercise Clause. Its intellectual and legislative history has been less accessible, and it has received vastly less attention from judges and scholars. The controversies about free exercise in the founders' time received less attention than the controversies over establishment, and the Free Exercise Clause received much less debate. But there is more evidence of original intent than scholars have realized. Michael McConnell has just completed the first thorough marshalling of the evidence.[49]

There was of course a great formative controversy in the Founders' collective memory, relevant both to free exercise and to establishment. This was

49. Michael McConnell, *The Origins and Historical Understanding of Free Exercise of Religion,* 103 HARV. L. REV. 409 (1990).

the history of religious persecution and religious warfare in the wake of the Reformation. The memory of serious religious conflict was more recent to the Founders than the memory of slavery is to us, and minor persecutions continued into their political lifetimes.[50] It is surely reasonable to infer that the Founders intended the Religion Clauses to prevent such conflicts here.

One lesson of religious persecutions is that some humans will die for their faith, and others will kill for it. The Religion Clauses are designed in part to protect these unusually fervent believers, and to protect others from them. Religious minorities need not be reasonable; the Religion Clauses exist in part because religious minorities are not reasonable.

Another lesson of religious persecutions is that the Free Exercise Clause must protect religiously motivated conduct, as well as belief and speech. Conscientious objectors to government policy are willing to suffer greatly rather than violate their conscience; attempts to coerce religious conscience lead inevitably to persecution.[51]

McConnell identifies three significant controversies over exemptions for conscientious objection in the founding period: over oath-taking, over military conscription, and over payment of religious taxes.[52] In each of these cases, legislatures granted exemptions, and the prevailing understanding was that the legislature would violate religious liberty if it refused such exemptions. This understanding informs the meaning of the judicially enforceable guarantees of free exercise that appeared in state constitutions and in the First Amendment.

That inference is in turn confirmed by the frequent provisos in state constitutions, restricting religious exercise to acts that did not breach the peace or threaten the peace and safety of the state.[53] These provisos limit freedom of religious conduct; no one would have thought them necessary if free exercise clauses protected only religious belief. They tend to confirm that free "exercise" means what it says — that it includes conduct as well as belief.

A wholly uninformed Supreme Court has taken a different view. In an opinion with staggering implications, the Supreme Court has held that the Free Exercise Clause does not protect religious conduct from facially neutral laws.[54] The Court held that criminal punishment of Native American wor-

50. *See* Laycock, *supra* note 3, at 691 (text at note 20).

51. *See* Douglas Laycock, *Formal, Substantive, and Disaggregated Neutrality Toward Religion*, 39 DePaul L. Rev. 993, 1003, 1018 (1990) (text at notes 30-31, 100).

52. McConnell, *supra* note 49, at 1466-73.

53. *See e.g.*, Conn. Const. art. 1, § 3; Ga. Const. art. 1, § 4; Md. Declaration of Rights art. 36; Mass. Const. part 1 art. 2; N.H. Const. part 1, art. 5.

54. *See* Employment Division v. Smith, 494 U.S. 872 (1990).

ship services raised no issue under the Free Exercise Clause and required no government justification whatever! It was enough that the worship service used peyote and that the use of peyote was forbidden by a law that made no reference to religion. The same reasoning could be applied to communion wine in a dry jurisdiction, to ordination of women and homosexuals, to Sabbatarians seeking accommodations made necessary by the Christian calender, and to a host of other issues. At a stroke, the Court reduced the Free Exercise Clause to a redundant appendage of the Free Speech and Equal Protection Clauses.

The question was neither raised nor briefed by anyone. The majority consisted mostly of justices who claim to follow original intent, but they appeared totally unaware that there was any evidence of intent on this issue. The result is that religious minorities will suffer for conscience in America, and the federal courts are closed to them.

Conclusion

Occasionally the Founders' intent is clear and applicable, as in their conclusion that nonpreferential establishments were still establishments and still objectionable. More often, their intent is unclear, or not responsive to the questions asked in our time. Sometimes, their intent is a starting point for a line of reasoning that must be completed. Thus, when one concludes that conscientious objectors must be protected to avoid religious persecution, we start with the Founders' intention to avoid persecution, but fill in most of the rest of the argument ourselves.

We cannot escape the responsibility of self-government; we must decide for ourselves how to apply the Constitution in our time. But if self-government is to consist mostly of majority rule, and only sometimes of judicial interpretation, then constitutional interpretation must start with the text of the Constitution, and with such clear and applicable evidence of intent as can be found.

The Declaration Is Not Law

Quarterly, A Publication of the Christian Legal Society 8 (Fall 1991)

The editors invited this short article, to be paired with an article by Herbert W. Titus, then Dean of the Regent University College of Law and Government, which the editors said would argue that the Declaration of Independence is law. That is not actually what he argued, so the two pieces did not engage, but I had an occasion to reflect on the Declaration. The famous paragraph about self-evident truths is America's fundamental statement of political theory, but none of the document is law. The Quarterly *was later retitled* The Christian Lawyer.

*   *   *

The Declaration of Independence is not law. No one can file a justiciable lawsuit under the pursuit of happiness clause, or challenge capital punishment as a violation of the right to life. A constitutional amendment to criminalize flag burning could not be attacked as an attempt to alienate the unalienable right to liberty.

It is not part of our law that American Indians are "merciless Indian Savages, whose known rule of warfare is an undistinguished destruction of all ages, sexes and conditions." Nor is it part of our law that British recognition of French law and Catholic faith in Quebec created "an Arbitrary government" and a "fit instrument for introducing the same absolute rule into these Colonies."

As these examples illustrate, the Declaration is a mixed bag. Parts of it are a ringing statement of political philosophy. Parts of it are political propaganda from another age, with more power to embarrass than to inspire. Even the parts that still inspire remain in the realm of politics. They are not law unless enacted into law.

The Declaration did not purport to create a government or to enact any rule of law. The bulk of it is exactly what it claimed to be: a declaration to the world of American reasons for renouncing allegiance to Britain. New Governments and new laws were created in other documents — in state constitutions and the Articles of Confederation.

Political Remedies

The present Constitution depends on the Declaration's theory that the People may alter their form of government. The Constitution was not ratified under the procedures for amending the Articles of Confederation but instead by a new and independent act of the People. The People today could again abandon their Constitution and adopt an entirely new constitution. They need not use the amendment procedures of Article V unless they leave the present Constitution in effect. Eleven states invoked the Declaration in support of secession, but the deliberative processes of Gettysburg and Appomattox vested the power to alter the federal government in the whole People of the United States and not in the People of each state severally.

The Declaration is also a statement of ideals to which political argument can appeal. Lincoln said that slavery was inconsistent with the self-evident truth "that all men are created equal." He never said the Declaration made slavery illegal but only that it showed slavery to be wrong and that eventually our law must be changed to match our ideals.

The Declaration may sometimes aid in constitutional interpretation, but this use is limited. Between the Declaration and the Constitution came twelve years of intense political debate. The successful rebels of 1776 were the targets of Shays' Rebellion in 1786. If we find tensions between the Constitution and the Declaration, it may be because new views had come to prevail. The Declaration cannot change the meaning of the Constitution; at most it can make proposed interpretations seem more or less plausible.

Natural Law

The Declaration may be most helpful in construing the Ninth Amendment and the Privileges or Immunities Clause, which guarantee unenumerated rights that are not further specified in the constitutional text. These clauses are controversial, but the Declaration is some evidence that they meant what they say. These clauses write the Declaration's philosophy of unalienable natural law rights into positive law, but the Declaration is not much help in defining the content of these unenumerated rights.

What then of the Declaration's repeated references to God? Does the Declaration found our political system on the belief that rights come from God? Does it mean that our governments are also theistic and free to act on their belief in God? Is this an aid to interpreting the Establishment Clause?

I think not, for reasons having more to do with the Constitution than with the Declaration. I read the Religion Clauses as leaving religion wholly to the private sector. This is the best protection for religious liberty, and I believe it is the best interpretation of the constitutional text, the debates in the First Congress, and the extensive post-Declaration debates on disestablishment in the states. Of course the evidence does not all point in the same direction. The references to God in the Declaration are part of the contrary evidence, rather like Presidential Thanksgiving proclamations. But finding such evidence in the Declaration does not trump other arguments about the meaning of the Religion Clauses.

Nor is it clear that the Declaration taken as a whole is at odds with government neutrality toward religion. "We hold these truths to be self-evident" is the secular argument for natural law rights; that men "are endowed by their Creator with certain unalienable rights" is the religious argument. The Declaration invokes "the Laws of Nature" as well as the Laws "of Nature's God." Just as the Religion Clauses provide for people of all faiths and of none to live together with equal rights and status, so the argument of the Declaration appeals to both religious and secular audiences. The Declaration prefigures both the religious neutrality of the Religion Clauses and the political reality that most of our people are religious.

"Noncoercive" Support for Religion:
Another False Claim about the Establishment Clause

26 Valparaiso University Law Review 37 (1992)

This article considers the claim that government may aid or support religion, or particular religions, so long as no one is coerced. This has been a common argument for narrowing the Establishment Clause. I review the founding-era debates on disestablishment, where the argument seems to have been rejected, but there is not nearly so much evidence as for the rejection of nonpreferentialism. I also carefully review the Supreme Court's cases, which up to this time had rejected any requirement of coercion.

This article was part of a symposium for the Bicentennial of the Bill of Rights, which was ratified in 1791. The article closely tracks an amicus brief I filed in a case then pending in the Supreme Court, Lee v. Weisman. *The defendant school officials and the first Bush Administration argued that coercion was an essential element of any Establishment Clause violation, and that prayer at public school graduations coerced no one. The "Bush Administration" repeatedly referred to is the administration of George H. W. Bush — Bush Sr., or Bush 41.*

*   *   *

One of the fundamental and recurring controversies about the meaning of the First Amendment's Religion Clauses is whether government must be neutral between religion and nonreligion. The Supreme Court has always said yes in modern times, but persistent critics have always said no.

The Court's critics have offered two major alternatives to neutrality. The

---

This article discusses *Lee v. Weisman,* a case in which I wrote a brief amicus curiae on behalf of several religious organizations and one secular civil liberties organization.

older alternative is nonpreferentialism: that government may aid religion so long as it does not prefer one religion over another.[1] The more recently proposed alternative is noncoercion: that government may aid or endorse all religions or particular religions so long as it does not coerce anyone to religious practice or belief. The fullest development of the noncoercion theory is in the briefs in *Lee v. Weisman*.[2] Michael McConnell proposed an academic version of the theory, arguing that coercion must at least be an element of any Establishment Clause analysis.[3] McConnell's position was always more sensitive to the needs of religious minorities than the position in the *Lee* briefs, and in a more recent work, he has further moderated his position.[4] Justice Kennedy has proposed a theory in which noncoercion is a prominent element, but he also adds a requirement that government refrain from proselytizing.[5]

In earlier work, I have explored the possible meanings of neutrality,[6] argued against nonpreferentialism,[7] and sketched the beginnings of an argument against the noncoercion theory.[8] In this article, I wish to clarify the relationship among the three theories, and then further develop the argument for neutrality, this time concentrating on noncoercion.

Lee v. Weisman is pending as I write, but the noncoercion issue should remain after the case is decided. There is no reason for the Court to decide the case on so broad and ill-fitting a ground. And at the oral argument, the Justices expressed skepticism or even hostility toward a pure coercion theory.[9]

Lee involves the constitutionality of invocations and benedictions at high school graduation ceremonies and middle school promotion ceremonies in Providence, Rhode Island. The case was litigated in the lower courts as a sim-

---

1. *See, e.g.,* Wallace v. Jaffree, 472 U.S. 38, 106 (1985) (Rehnquist, J., dissenting); ROBERT CORD, SEPARATION OF CHURCH AND STATE: HISTORICAL FACT AND CURRENT FICTION (1982).

2. *See* Brief for the Petitioners; Brief for the United States as Amicus Curiae Supporting Petitioners, in the Supreme Court of the United States (No. 90-1014).

3. Michael W. McConnell, *Coercion: The Lost Element of Establishment,* 27 WM. & MARY L. REV. 933 (1986).

4. Michael W. McConnell, *Religious Freedom at a Crossroads,* 59 U. CHI. L. REV. 115, 157-65 (1992).

5. County of Allegheny v. ACLU, 492 U.S. 573, 659, 661 (Kennedy, J., dissenting).

6. Douglas Laycock, *Formal, Substantive, and Disaggregated Neutrality Toward Religion,* 39 DEPAUL L. REV. 993 (1990).

7. Douglas Laycock, *"Nonpreferential" Aid to Religion: A False Claim About Original Intent,* 27 WM. & MARY L. REV. 875 (1986).

8. *Id.* at 915-16, 921-22 (text at notes 211, 234-40).

9. Linda Greenhouse, *Justices Appear Wary in Argument over Prayer at School Graduations,* N.Y. TIMES, Nov. 7, 1991, at A14.

ple dispute about the application of settled precedents to stipulated facts.[10] Plaintiff argued that it was controlled by the school prayer cases,[11] because the prayers were school-sponsored, at a school function, with children present.[12] The Providence School Committee argued that the case was controlled by a decision upholding prayers to open sessions of the legislature,[13] because the relevant category was prayer at civic ceremonies.[14] In the School Committee's view, the fact that this was a school ceremony was incidental.

The district court and court of appeals held the prayer unconstitutional. The Supreme Court may affirm in a straightforward application of the school prayer cases. Or it may reverse, holding that one minute of prayer a year is *de minimis*. There is no need to render a sweeping decision on the noncoercion theory. There is good reason not to do so, because the noncoercion theory should not affect the result in *Lee* itself. Children desiring to attend their graduation are coerced to participate in prayer.

Even so, new counsel in the Supreme Court urged a decision based on the noncoercion theory. The School Committee argued that "government coercion of religious conformity is a necessary element of an Establishment Clause violation."[15] The Bush Administration agreed, in an amicus brief filed on behalf of the United States.[16] As argued, *Lee* presents the Court with a sweeping choice between two theories of the Religion Clauses — between neutrality, and noncoercion. This article examines that choice.

I. Neutrality, Nonpreferentialism, and Noncoercion

Nonpreferentialism and noncoercion have common political origins, and Justice Rehnquist has endorsed them both.[17] Each theory originates with the political desire for government support of religion, and each relies on the his-

---

10. Weisman v. Lee, 728 F. Supp. 68 (D.R.I.), *aff'd*, 908 F.2d 1090 (1st Cir. 1990), *cert. granted*, 499 U.S. 918 (1991).

11. Abington School Dist. v. Schempp, 374 U.S. 203 (1963).

12. Appellee's Brief, Weisman v. Lee, 908 F.2d 1090 (1st Cir. 1990) (No. 90-1151), *cert. granted*, 499 U.S. 918 (1991).

13. Marsh v. Chambers, 463 U.S. 783 (1963).

14. Brief for Appellant's (sic), Weisman v. Lee, 908 F.2d 1090 (1st Cir. 1990) (No. 90-1151), *cert. granted*, 499 U.S. 918 (1991).

15. Brief for Petitioners, *supra* note 2, at 14.

16. Brief for U.S., *supra* note 2.

17. *Compare* Wallace v. Jaffree, 472 U.S. 38, 106 (1985) (Rehnquist, J., dissenting) (nonpreferentialism); with County of Allegheny v. ACLU, 492 U.S. 573, 659, 661 (1989) (Kennedy, J., dissenting, joined by Rehnquist and others) (noncoercion).

torical observation that government in the founding era did support religion in a variety of ways. Each theory is an attempt to state a principle that will distinguish permissible and impermissible forms of government support for religion. But neither theory produces acceptable results for a pluralistic society, and neither theory captures the practices of the Founders.

It is important to clearly distinguish the two theories. They are not the same, and they have very different implications. Under nonpreferentialism, government must be neutral among religions, but it need not be neutral as between religion and disbelief. The essence of nonpreferentialism is the claim that government should be free to encourage or subsidize religious belief and practice so long as it encourages or subsidizes all religions equally. Nonpreferentialists do not urge the point, but their theory would permit government to require all persons to attend some church, so long as it let each individual choose which church to attend.

Under noncoercion theory, the Religion Clauses are not violated unless government coerces an individual to religious practice or belief. Neither neutrality nor nonpreferentialism is part of the noncoercion standard; government need not be neutral between religion and nonreligion, and it need not be neutral among competing religions. Government may endorse generic theism, generic Protestantism, Roman Catholicism, Seventh-day Adventism, or the Twelfth Street Pentecostal Holiness Church. Congress could charter The Church of the United States, so long as it did not coerce anyone to join.

Under noncoercion theory, government at all levels could take sides in debates about the nature of Christ, salvation by works or by faith, scriptural inerrancy, the authority of the Book of Mormon, or any other religious matter. The President, the Congress, or the Providence School Committee could adopt and promulgate creeds. Noncoercionists believe that "government may participate as a speaker in moral debates, including religious ones."[18]

In theory we might combine the two alternatives to neutrality. That is, we might permit government to aid religion only in ways that are both noncoercive and nonpreferential, if anyone can think of such a way. But so far as I am aware, no one has proposed that, and neither theory leaves room for that.

Thus, nonpreferentialists endorse tax support for church-affiliated schools, on the ground that any church could start schools and so such aid is nonpreferential. I think it is common ground that taxation is coercive,[19] so

---

18. American Jewish Congress v. City of Chicago, 827 F.2d 120, 132 (7th Cir. 1987) (Easterbrook, J., dissenting).

19. *See* McConnell, *supra* note 3, at 938.

nonpreferentialists would permit coercion. I doubt that many nonpreferentialists would really permit government to coerce nonbelievers to pick some church and attend it. But to avoid that result, they would have to supplement their theory of the Establishment Clause, or they would have to resort to the Free Exercise Clause.

It is equally clear that noncoercionists would not require nonpreferentialism. One of the more visible issues that noncoercionists seek to resolve is the government-sponsored creche, or nativity scene. The creche symbolizes the alleged miracle of Christ's Incarnation, a claim that is central to Christianity, heretical or blasphemous to Judaism and Islam, and largely irrelevant to the world's other great religions. If noncoercionists mean to permit government creches, they plainly mean to permit government to endorse particular religions. One can imagine a practice of noncoercive, nonpreferential religious displays, in which a government gave equal prominence to displays symbolizing central events of all religions. But no government has such a practice, and no defenders of the government-sponsored religious observances have proposed that government must observe all religions or none.[20]

Certainly the Bush Administration's argument in *Lee* did not propose any combination of noncoercion and nonpreferentialism. The Administration's argument did not at all depend on the brevity or content of the prayers in that case. The claim that no one was coerced would be equally true or false if the Providence School Committee awarded diplomas at a Solemn High Mass, or at a full-length worship service of any other faith.

The most obvious observation about the proposed noncoercion standard is that it leaves no independent meaning to the Establishment Clause. Even after *Employment Division v. Smith*,[21] government would violate the Free Exercise Clause if it coerced persons to attend or participate in religious observances against their will. The noncoercion test is also inconsistent with precedent and with sound policy toward religion, and its claimed basis in original intent is dubious at best. I begin with history.

---

20. *But cf.* Weisman v. Lee, 908 F.2d 1090, 1099 (1st Cir. 1990) (Campbell, J., dissenting) (proposing that Providence rotate the graduation prayer among all faiths and philosophies), *cert. granted*, 499 U.S. 918 (1991).

21. 494 U.S. 872 (1990)

II. The Historical Meaning of the Establishment Clause

A. Endorsement in the Time of the Founders

Neither nonpreferentialism nor noncoercion explains the practices of the Founders. As I have argued elsewhere, government supported religion in the Founders' time in those contexts in which no significant group of Protestants complained.[22] But when a Protestant complaint focused the founding generation's attention on a practice, they rejected both nonpreferentialism and noncoercion.

The classic religious establishments known to the Founders consisted of several elements in varying combinations. In the worst cases, government had endorsed an official religion, interfered with that religion's self-governance, suppressed all other religions, and required everyone to adhere to the official religion, support it with taxes, and participate in its worship. This extreme case roughly describes most sixteenth-century European establishments and seventeenth-century Massachusetts.[23]

One by one these elements were relaxed or eliminated. Dissenters were first exempted from attending the established worship services,[24] then allowed to practice their own faith,[25] then exempted from paying taxes to support the established church.[26] Eventually defenders of establishment proposed to make tax support available to minority religions as well as to the preferred religion,[27] and then government relaxed its control over the official religion.[28] The strategy of defenders of establishment in the United States was to make the establishment less coercive and less preferential. But the one element that they could never give up short of total surrender was state endorsement of the preferred religion. The only universal element of every establishment was government endorsement of one or more religions.

What happened when a state eliminated all the coercive elements of the establishment and was left with a bare endorsement of a preferred religion? Would that alone be considered an establishment in the Founders' generation? There is not as much evidence on this issue as on the issue of non-

22. Laycock, *supra* note 7, at 917-19 (text at notes 222-28).
23. See THOMAS J. CURRY, THE FIRST FREEDOMS, CHURCH AND STATE IN AMERICA TO THE PASSAGE OF THE FIRST AMENDMENT 1-28 (1986).
24. *See, e.g., id.* at 25.
25. *See, e.g., id.* at 25-27.
26. *Id.* at 89-90.
27. *Id.* at 136-48, 153-54, 164; *infra* notes 46-54 and accompanying text.
28. *See infra* note 37 and accompanying text.

preferentialism. But the preponderance of evidence is that opponents of establishment were unwilling to accept even a bare endorsement of the established churches.

The point is most clearly illustrated by the experience of Virginia and South Carolina between 1776 and 1790.[29] Before independence, the Church of England was the established church in these states. Each of these states initially responded to independence by attempting to eliminate coercion and preference while preserving establishment. Each state created an establishment by endorsement: it designated an established religion while eliminating all tax support and all coercion to believe or to attend services. These reforms proved insufficient to satisfy the American demand for disestablishment, and the endorsements were subsequently repealed. It is possible to point to arguable remnants of coercion in these schemes; preferred churches were permitted to incorporate, and that may have had some advantages over operating as a trust or an association. But the principal surviving element of these establishments was endorsement of a preferred religion, and those endorsements were unacceptable to opponents of establishment. Endorsement of a religion established that religion in the political understanding of the Founders' generation, at least when their suspicions were aroused and their attention focused on the issue.

The path to disestablishment in Virginia began in 1776, when the legislature exempted dissenters from the tax to support the Anglican Church. A tax on Anglicans remained on the books, but the legislature suspended collection. The legislature suspended this tax annually until 1779, when the tax was permanently repealed.[30] "[N]o taxes for religious purposes were ever paid in Virginia after January 1, 1777."[31]

The legislature in 1776 also repealed English laws restricting freedom of worship. Some provisions for licensing clergy remained in effect but were not enforced.[32] As the leading historian of disestablishment in Virginia summarizes the situation, "Religion in Virginia had become voluntary, and a man could believe what he wished and contribute as much or as little as he thought fit to whichever church or minister pleased him."[33]

---

29. For histories of these events, see THOMAS E. BUCKLEY, CHURCH AND STATE IN REVOLUTIONARY VIRGINIA, 1776-1787 (1977); CURRY, *supra* note 23; HAMILTON ECKENRODE, SEPARATION OF CHURCH AND STATE IN VIRGINIA (1910); ANSON PHELPS STOKES, 1 CHURCH AND STATE IN THE UNITED STATES 366-97, 432-34 (1950).

30. CURRY, *supra* note 23, at 135-36.

31. ECKENRODE, *supra* note 29, at 53.

32. BUCKLEY, *supra* note 29, at 36.

33. *Id.*

But it was equally clear that the legislature "had not disestablished the Church of England."[34] The American branch of the Church of England, soon to be known as the Protestant Episcopal Church, was still the official church in Virginia. This designation had no coercive effect on dissenters; no one was required to attend or support the Episcopal Church. The principal effect of the establishment was simply an endorsement.

The Episcopal clergy retained one vestige of coercive power: only they could perform legally recognized marriage ceremonies. The other denominations condemned this monopoly, but no one then or now would contend that the coercive effect of this monopoly was the only vestige of establishment. The legislature repealed this monopoly in 1780,[35] and residual licensing rules were eliminated in 1783 and 1784.[36]

The Episcopal Church found that its establishment carried the disadvantage of legislative supervision. The church sought to escape this supervision through an act incorporating the church and empowering it to govern itself. Such an act was passed in 1784, repealing all prior laws regulating the relationship between the state and the established church.[37] This made the established church independent of the state, but it did not satisfy the opponents of establishment.

The opponents insisted that the law incorporating the Episcopal Church still gave it special recognition and a preferred status. A Presbyterian resolution condemned the act as giving the Episcopal Church "Peculiar distinctions and the Honour of an important name," and making it "the Church of the State."[38] A Baptist committee denounced it as "inconsistent with American Freedom."[39] Other petitions said the legislature had given Episcopalians "the particular sanction of and Direction of your Honourable House."[40]

These objections go to endorsement and nothing more. It is hard to identify any residual coercive effect of the Episcopal incorporation act; its effect was to give the Episcopal Church special recognition not given to other churches. If other churches desired to incorporate, Episcopal incorporation was preferential. But it was not coercive, because the state did not tell other churches that they could incorporate if they complied with certain conditions. If there were any residual coercive effect, it fell on Episcopalians; per-

34. *Id.* at 37.
35. ECKENRODE, *supra* note 29, at 67-69.
36. *Id.* at 80, 100; BUCKLEY, *supra* note 29, at 111-12; 1 STOKES, *supra* note 29, at 383-84.
37. BUCKLEY, *supra* note 29, at 106; 1 STOKES, *supra* note 29, at 384-87.
38. BUCKLEY, *supra* note 29, at 165.
39. *Id.* at 140.
40. ECKENRODE, *supra* note 29, at 121, 122.

haps their self-government was in some way affected by the terms of the incorporation act. But they were not complaining; the act had been designed to solve that problem.

Thus, the structure of the act supports the point of the quoted objections: the objection was that other faiths perceived an endorsement. Note too that the state's endorsement was implicit rather than explicit; the opponents' objection was not limited to open and formal declarations of establishment.

Finally, in 1787, the legislature repealed the Episcopal incorporation act, repealed all laws that prevented any religious society from regulating its own discipline, confirmed all churches in their existing property, and authorized all churches to appoint trustees to manage their property.[41] This act finally repealed the last vestige of state endorsement of the Episcopal Church in Virginia.

The one remaining issue in Virginia was disposition of church property acquired with public funds before 1777. That was finally resolved in 1802, with the Episcopal Church retaining its churches but giving up its glebes, or land for the support of clergy.[42] Continuing resentment of the glebes certainly helped motivate the continued attention to the vestiges of establishment in Virginia. But with its attention focused on the issue, the founding generation in Virginia was not content to eliminate coercion, tax support, and the glebes. It also insisted on eliminating symbolic endorsements of a particular faith.

An even broader attempt at noncoercive establishment appeared in article 38 of the South Carolina Constitution of 1778.[43] The first sentence guaranteed religious toleration to all monotheists who believed in public worship and a future state of rewards and punishments; this would have included substantially the whole population. The second sentence provided that "The Christian Protestant religion shall be deemed, and is hereby constituted and declared to be, the established religion of this State." The third sentence from the end forbad any tax for the support of churches.

The one coercive element was that only established churches could obtain a corporate charter. Other churches apparently were organized as trusts or unincorporated associations; there was a synagogue in Charleston.[44]

---

41. BUCKLEY, *supra* note 29, at 170; 1 STOKES, *supra* note 29, at 394.

42. BUCKLEY, *supra* note 29, at 171-72.

43. S.C. CONST. of 1778, art. XXXVIII, in 6 FRANCIS N. THORPE, THE FEDERAL AND STATE CONSTITUTIONS, COLONIAL CHARTERS, AND OTHER ORGANIC LAWS OF THE STATES, TERRITORIES, AND COLONIES NOW OR HERETOFORE FORMING THE UNITED STATES OF AMERICA 3255-57 (1906). The provision is discussed and reprinted in 1 STOKES, *supra* note 29, at 432-34. It is also discussed in CURRY, *supra* note 23, at 149-51.

44. CURRY, *supra* note 23, at 151.

Churches desiring to incorporate were required to subscribe to five Protestant tenets set out in Article 38, their ministers were required to swear an oath set out in Article 38, and churches were required to select their ministers by majoritarian processes. Unlike the Virginia situation, these provisions may have had some tendency to coerce churches toward the prescribed tenets. But it would be myopic to say that incorporation rather than endorsement was the essence of this establishment. If non-established churches had been allowed to incorporate, and if free exercise had been extended beyond monotheists to include absolutely everybody, but the rest of Article 38 had been retained, Protestantism would still have been the established religion of South Carolina. The establishment inhered in the official endorsement of Protestantism. This establishment by endorsement was abolished by Article 8 of the Constitution of 1790.[45]

The bare endorsements of South Carolina's Constitution and Virginia's Episcopal incorporation act were the extreme instances of the strategy of making establishments more inclusive, less preferential, and less coercive. Other proposals pursued the same strategy less aggressively and with correspondingly less success.

The point is illustrated by unsuccessful proposals for general assessments to support the clergy in Virginia and Maryland. In each state, the supporters of establishment proposed a tax for the support of clergy, in which each taxpayer could designate the clergyman to receive his tax.[46] It allowed taxpayers to refuse to designate any clergyman, in which case their tax would be paid to support local schools.[47]

The element of choice in the taxpayers was said to make the establishment nonpreferential and noncoercive. The law did not require anyone to support any religion other than his own. Even more dramatic, the option to support schools meant that the law did not require anyone to support religion at all. Baptists would not be required to violate conscience by support-

---

45. S.C. Const. of 1790, art. VIII, in Thorpe, *supra* note 43, at 3264. The provision is discussed and reprinted in 1 Stokes, *supra* note 29, at 434. It is also described in Curry, *supra* note 23, at 151. Other provisions of the South Carolina Constitution of 1778 restricted voting rights to monotheists. Eleven of the thirteen states had religious qualifications for voting, Curry, *supra* note 23, at 162-63, 221, including states that otherwise guaranteed free exercise and disestablishment. The issues were viewed as separate, and repeal of voting qualification did not require repeal of the endorsement of Protestantism in Article 38.

46. The Virginia bill is reprinted in the Appendix to Justice Rutledge's dissent in *Everson v. Board of Education*, 330 U.S. 1, 72-74 (1947).

47. *Id.* at 74. The bill's reference to "seminaries of learning" meant secular schools. *See* Buckley, *supra* note 29, at 108-09, 133; Laycock, *supra* note 7, at 897 n.108.

ing their own clergy through the instruments of government.[48] Supporters of the Virginia bill invoked the slogan "Equal Right and Equal Liberty," and argued that "assessment imposed *not 'the smallest coercion'* to contribute to the support of religion."[49]

In fact the bill would have been coercive. Citizens desiring to support an unpopular religion, or desiring to support no religion at all, would have had to declare their unusual preference on the public record. Surely in many Virginia communities there was considerable social pressure to support the dominant religious leader, and the state-imposed occasion for publicly recording one's dissent would have aggravated that pressure. But school children experience intense social pressure to attend their graduation and promotion ceremonies and to conform their posture and behavior to that of all the others joining in the prayers that are offered. The position of the School Committee[50] and the Bush Administration[51] in *Lee v. Weisman* is that this sort of social pressure does not count, even when government sponsors both the religious observance and the civic event that give rise to the social pressure. Under the noncoercion rule proposed to the Supreme Court, social pressure to designate one's tax in acceptable ways would not have made the Virginia general assessment coercive.

There remained one irreducible element of coercion in the Virginia bill. Those who paid their religion tax to a school instead of to a minister would eventually wind up paying more than their share of the expense of schools. This would presumably be coercive even under the Bush Administration's definition. The sponsors of the Virginia bill had attempted to eliminate all coercion, but they had not quite succeeded.

The Maryland bill came closer. Each taxpayer could pay his tax to the minister of his choice, or to a fund for the poor.[52] In addition, any taxpayer who declared "that he does not believe in the Christian religion . . . shall not be liable to pay any tax for himself in virtue of this act."[53] So no one would be forced to support a church, and non-Christians would not be forced to support anything. Again there would be a state-created occasion for expressing one's religious dissent and exposing oneself to the social coercion of the community, but again, that same problem faces students at graduation, and the Bush Administration says that is not coercion. But the Maryland bill would

48. For the Baptist objection, see CURRY, *supra* note 23, at 89.
49. *Id.* at 145, quoting petitions to the legislature in 1784 and 1785 (emphasis added).
50. Brief for Petitioners, *supra* note 2, at 35-44.
51. Brief for U.S., *supra* note 2, at 24-28.
52. CURRY, *supra* note 23, at 155.
53. *Id.*

have coerced Christians either to support their own ministers through taxation (violating the conscience of Baptists) or to file false declarations of nonbelief; I hope the Bush Administration would recognize that as coercive. So the Maryland bill too fell short of being completely noncoercive.

Both the Maryland and Virginia assessment bills were the subject of great public debate, and each was soundly defeated. The Virginia bill was the occasion for Madison's *Memorial and Remonstrance Against Religious Assessments,* and for many similar memorials by Presbyterians, Baptists, and other religious dissenters.[54] State assistance to churches was rejected as an establishment, even with the right to designate the recipient of the tax, to pay the tax to secular uses instead of religious ones, and in Maryland, to escape the tax altogether by declaring nonbelief.

Each of these bills retained elements of coercion, despite the sponsors' best efforts to eliminate them. But it would be a mistake to focus only on coercion. Dramatically reducing the coercive elements had not satisfied the opponents of establishment, and no one at the time appears to have thought that further steps to eliminate the remnants of coercion would have made any difference. No one suggested that the state enact an assessment with unconditional exemption, in which the state would calculate a fair share contribution, serve as keeper of records and agent for collection and distribution, and collect only from those unconditionally willing to pay. Reducing or eliminating coercion did not affect the essence of what made these bills establishments. The essence of establishment, then as now, was state support for religion.

These debates in the states are directly relevant to the original meaning of the federal Establishment Clause. In sweeping terms, the Constitution prohibits any law respecting an "establishment." "Establishment" is not defined. Unavoidably, the word would have been understood in light of the recent debates over disestablishment in the states. These debates are the principal evidence of "how the words used in the Constitution would have been understood at the time."[55] As Justice Rutledge observed, "the Congressional debates on consideration of the Amendment reveal only sparse discussion, reflecting the fact that the essential issues had been settled."[56] The Court's long-standing rule that government may not aid or endorse religion is soundly based in the Founding generation's principle that government may not aid or support religion, even by bare endorsements in toothless laws.

---

54. *See* BUCKLEY, *supra* note 29, at 113-43; ECKENRODE, *supra* note 29, at 103-11.
55. ROBERT H. BORK, THE TEMPTING OF AMERICA 144 (1990).
56. Everson v. Board of Educ., 330 U.S. 1, 42 (Rutledge, J., dissenting).

B. A Note on Interpretive Method

A second thread to the argument for government-sponsored prayer is that government prayer must be constitutional because the Founders did it.[57] The premise of this argument is that anything the Founders did is constitutional. In fact Justice Kennedy has gone further, claiming that the Constitution permits anything the Founders did and "any other practices with no greater potential for an establishment of religion."[58]

The Supreme Court has squarely rejected this argument, and properly so.[59] The argument proves far too much. Equally important, it ignores the political origin of constitutional rights.

Constitutional rights are designed to prevent the recurrence of historic abuses. Eliminating such abuses often requires major political battles. The People create constitutional rights when the winners of one of these political battles believe the issue to be so important, and the danger of regression so great, that the issue must be put beyond reach of the usual political processes. Because constitutional rights emerge from major controversies, we should not expect to find a consensus that unites both supporters and opponents of a constitutional provision, or even a fully consistent view of all related issues among the supporters. The winners muster a super-majority for a broad statement of principle, but they do not achieve unanimity on the principle or even consensus on the details of its application. Every constitutional amendment has bitter opponents, and in a system of federalism and separated powers, those opponents may control whole states or branches of government. The attitudes that gave rise to the losing side of the controversy do not instantly disappear, and neither do the abusive practices that made the amendment necessary.

It ignores political reality to remove from the scope of constitutional rights any practices that survived ratification.[60] By that principle, the Alien and Sedition Acts are an authoritative interpretation of the Free Speech and Press Clauses, *de jure* segregation of schools in the District of Columbia is an authoritative interpretation of the Equal Protection Clause, and the many devices that led to near total disenfranchisement of black voters for most of a century are an authoritative interpretation of the Fifteenth Amendment. Moreover, these abuses would become the standard for further interpreta-

57. *See* Marsh v. Chambers, 463 U.S. 783 (1983).
58. County of Allegheny v. ACLU, 492 U.S. 573, 670 (1989) (Kennedy, J., dissenting).
59. *Id.* at 604-05.
60. *See* Douglas Laycock, *Text, Intent, and the Religion Clauses*, 4 Notre Dame J.L. Ethics & Pub. Pol'y 683, 688-91 (1990) (text at notes 16-18).

tion: government could engage in any other practice no more restrictive of constitutional rights than the Alien and Sedition Acts, school segregation, and disenfranchisement of black voters. Reliance on post-ratification practice leads to such absurd consequences because it proceeds backwards. It lets the behavior of government officials control the meaning of the Constitution, when the whole point is for the Constitution to control the behavior of government officials.

The relevant original understanding is not determined by every specific act of the Founders. The nation's "heritage of official discrimination against non-Christians has no place in the jurisprudence of the Establishment Clause."[61] Rather, as Robert Bork has said, the original understanding of a constitutional clause consists not of a conclusion but of a major premise. The "major premise is a principle or stated value that the ratifiers wanted to protect against hostile legislation or executive action."[62]

Another leading originalist has also explained that original intent depends on identifiable principles and not on every unexamined practice of the Founders:

> Unless we can articulate some *principle* that explains *why* legislative chaplains might not violate the Establishment Clause, and demonstrate that that principle continues to be applicable today, we cannot uphold a practice that so clearly violates fundamental principles we recognize under the Clause. . . . The insistence on a principle, and not just historical fact, follows from the function of interpretation as enforcing the Constitution as law. If the Constitution is law, it must embody *principles* so that we can ensure that like cases are treated alike, and that those governed by the Constitution can understand what is required of them.[63]

The basic principle of a constitutional clause is best identified from the controversies that gave rise to it. These controversies were consciously examined under political pressure that made the debate real and not just academic. These controversies identify the core target of the constitutional right. Interpreters can then search for a coherent principle, consistent with the constitutional text and as broad as the text, that centers on the core problem the text was intended to resolve.[64]

61. *County of Allegheny,* 492 U.S. at 604-05.

62. Bork, *supra* note 55, at 162-63.

63. Michael W. McConnell, *On Reading the Constitution,* 73 Cornell L. Rev. 359, 362-63 (1988) (emphasis in original).

64. *See* Laycock, *supra* note 60, at 690 (text at notes 17-18).

The Religion Clauses had two great defining controversies. One was the long Protestant-Catholic conflict in the wake of the Reformation. The other was the battle over disestablishment in the states. These are the contexts in which the Founders thought about the meaning of establishment, and we should look to these controversies to learn what they meant by establishment. I have already discussed the battle over disestablishment in the states. It is also revealing to examine the American continuation of Protestant-Catholic battles in the nineteenth century.

C. The Protestant Bible Controversy

Government prayer and religious proclamations, and the role of religion in public education, were not real controversies in the Founders' time. There were multiple reasons for this lack of controversy, but the most important was simply that the nation was overwhelmingly Protestant, and no significant group of Protestants was victimized by these practices. If a religious practice was not controversial among Protestants, it was not sufficiently controversial to attract political attention.

Theological and liturgical differences among Protestants were large, but for a variety of reasons, these differences appear to have been bridgeable in the rudimentary schools of the time.[65] Most schools were small, and many served a relatively homogenous local population. Some were run by local governments, some by associations of neighbors, some by entrepreneurial teachers, some by churches. Some of these schools defied characterization as public or private. In some urban areas, parents had many choices.

The historian Carl Kaestle describes the movement for a more organized system of state-supported schools as growing out of a "Native Protestant ideology" that was comprehensive in its scope, including religious, political, and social reform principles.[66] This ideology naturally incorporated religious instruction into the new common schools. The common school movement attempted to bridge the religious gaps among Americans with an unmistakably Protestant solution: by confining instruction to the most basic concepts of Christianity, and by reading the Bible "without note or comment." The Protestant leaders of the common school movement assumed that no one could object to reading the Bible, and by forbidding teachers to explain the

---

65. *See* CARL F. KAESTLE, PILLARS OF THE REPUBLIC: COMMON SCHOOLS AND AMERICAN SOCIETY 1780-1860 at 13-61 (1983).

66. *Id.* at 75-103.

passages read, they thought they had avoided sectarian disagreements about interpretation.

That solution was not entirely satisfactory even among Protestants. Conservative and evangelical Protestants accused Unitarians like Horace Mann of secularizing the public schools; stripped-down, least-common-denominator religion was not acceptable to them.[67] One spokesman for the critics charged Horace Mann's Massachusetts schools of teaching "nothing more than Deism, bald and blank."[68] But Protestants largely abandoned their disagreements to unite against the wave of Catholic immigration in the mid-nineteenth century.[69]

Catholics fundamentally challenged what seemed to them Protestant religious instruction in the public schools.[70] For one thing, Catholics used the Douay translation of the Bible, and objected to reading the King James translation, which they called "the Protestant Bible."

More important, Catholics condemned the "solution" of reading the Bible without note or comment as a fundamentally Protestant practice.[71] Protestants taught the primary authority of scripture and the accessibility of scripture to every human. Catholics taught that scripture must be understood in light of centuries of accumulated church teaching. For Catholic children to read the Bible without note or comment was to risk misunderstanding. Protestant practices were being forced on Catholic children.

The controversy over the Protestant Bible in public schools produced mob violence and church burnings in Eastern cities.[72] The resulting controversies were major political issues for decades. The anti-Catholic, anti-immigrant Know Nothing Party swept elections in eight states in the 1850s.[73] Among other things, these issues gave rise to the proposed Blaine Amendment to the Constitution, which would have codified the Protestant position by permitting Bible reading but forbidding "sectarian" instruction in any publicly-funded school. This amendment was defeated by Democrats in the Senate.[74] In Senator

---

67. CHARLES GLENN, THE MYTH OF THE COMMON SCHOOL 131-32, 179-96 (1988); *see also* KAESTLE, *supra* note 65, at 98-99.

68. Matthew Hale Smith, quoted in GLENN, *supra* note 67, at 189.

69. GLENN, *supra* note 67, at 179; KAESTLE, *supra* note 65, at 98.

70. GLENN, *supra* note 67, at 196-204; DIANE RAVITCH, THE GREAT SCHOOL WARS 3-76 (1974).

71. GLENN, *supra* note 67, at 199; RAVITCH, *supra* note 70, at 45.

72. KAESTLE, *supra* note 65, at 170; RAVITCH, *supra* note 70, at 36, 66, 75; 1 STOKES, *supra* note 29, at 830-31.

73. 1 STOKES, *supra* note 29, at 836-37.

74. 2 *id.* at 68-69.

Blaine's subsequent campaign for the Presidency, these issues gave rise to one of the most famous gaffes in American politics, the jibe that Democrats were "the party of Rum, Romanism, and Rebellion."[75]

Thus, in the wake of Catholic immigration, religion in the public schools produced exactly the sort of violent religious confrontation the Founders had sought to avoid. Religion in schools initially had been a nonproblem that raised no concern. Under changed social conditions, religion in schools became a serious violation of the disestablishment principle, which inflicted precisely "those consequences which the Framers deeply feared."[76] The principle of disestablishment did not change, but the nation was forced to confront a previously ignored application of the principle. Just as government could not endorse religion in statutes or state constitutions, neither could it endorse religion in public schools.

The first cases forbidding religious observances in public schools date from the latter part of this period.[77] On the other hand, some schools whipped or expelled Catholic children who refused to participate in Protestant observances, and some courts upheld such actions.[78] Neither side drew the line between coercion and noncoercion. Those who understood the grievance of religious minorities abandoned the offending practice; those who saw no grievance saw no reason not to coerce compliance.

The dispute over the Protestant Bible revealed the impossibility of conducting "neutral" religious observances even among diverse groups of Christians. Protestant education leaders did not set out to victimize Catholics; they genuinely thought that reading the Bible without note or comment was fair to all and harmful to none. What seemed harmless from their perspective was not harmless when applied across the full range of American pluralism.

Today, the range of religious pluralism in America is vastly greater. Immigration has brought Jews, Muslims, Buddhists, Hindus, Sikhs, Taoists, animists, and many others. Significant numbers of atheists and agnostics have been with us since the late nineteenth century; they were little more than a

75. HISTORY OF AMERICAN PRESIDENTIAL ELECTIONS 1789-1968 at 1606 (Arthur Schlesinger ed. 1971).

76. Abington School Dist. v. Schempp, 374 U.S. 203, 236 (1963) (Brennan, J., concurring).

77. State ex rel. Weiss v. District Board, 44 N.W. 967 (Wis. 1890) (mandamus against Bible reading); Board of Educ. v. Minor, 23 Ohio St. 211 (1872) (upholding and defending school board's decision to eliminate Bible reading and hymns).

78. Commonwealth v. Cooke, 7 Am. L. Reg. 417 (Boston Police Ct. 1859); KAESTLE, *supra* note 65, at 171; 1 STOKES, *supra* note 29, at 829.

theoretical possibility to the Founders.[79] The possibility of "neutral" religious observance remains a fiction.

III. The Supreme Court Precedent

The Providence School Committee and the Bush Administration acknowledge that their new rule will require modification of the familiar test of *Lemon v. Kurtzman.*[80] The *Lemon* test has been the subject of widespread academic criticism,[81] and I have been one of the critics.[82] But the Bush Administration's attack is not aimed at the unworkable or misguided parts of the *Lemon* test. The Administration rejects the sensible core of the *Lemon* test, and the whole line of pre-*Lemon* cases requiring government neutrality toward religion.

The neutrality requirement did not originate in *Lemon.* The familiar three-part *Lemon* test is simply a convenient formulation of "the cumulative criteria developed by the Court over many years."[83] The third prong, excessive entanglement, came from *Walz v. Tax Commission.*[84] The first two prongs — the proposition that government conduct should not have a primary purpose or effect of either advancing or inhibiting religion — came verbatim from one of the school prayer cases, *Abington School District v. Schempp.*[85] It is these two prongs, the *Schempp-Lemon* test, that drew the Bush Administration's principal attack.

The Bush Administration says simply that "The problem is *Lemon.*"[86] But the Administration's "problem" is not *Lemon.* The Administration's problem is nearly the whole history of Establishment Clause jurisprudence in

---

79. *See* JAMES TURNER, WITHOUT GOD, WITHOUT CREED: THE ORIGINS OF UNBELIEF IN AMERICA (1985).

80. 403 U.S. 602 (1971).

81. *See, e.g.,* Phillip Johnson, *Concepts and Compromise in First Amendment Religious Doctrine,* 72 CAL. L. REV. 817, 825-31 (1984); Philip Kurland, *The Irrelevance of the Constitution: The Religion Clauses of the First Amendment and the Supreme Court,* 24 VILL. L. REV. 3, 17-20 (1978).

82. Douglas Laycock, *Equal Access and Moments of Silence: The Equal Status of Religious Speech by Private Speakers,* 81 Nw. U.L. REV. 1, 20-28 (1986) (text at notes 100-39); Douglas Laycock, *A Survey of Religious Liberty in the United States,* 47 OHIO ST. L. REV. 409, 449-50 (1986) (text at notes 251-55).

83. Lemon v. Kurtzman, 403 U.S. 602, 612 (1971).

84. 397 U.S. 664, 674 (1970).

85. 374 U.S. 203, 222 (1963).

86. Brief for U.S., *supra* note 2, at 20.

the Supreme Court. The *Schempp-Lemon* formulation was simply an elaboration of the fundamental rule that government must be neutral with respect to religion.[87] The Court stated that rule in global terms in its first modern Establishment Clause decision, *Everson v. Board of Education:* the First Amendment "requires the state to be a neutral in its relations with groups of religious believers and nonbelievers."[88]

The Court has never abandoned *Everson's* neutrality requirement, although it has sometimes interpreted neutrality in inconsistent ways,[89] and it has twice rationalized failure to enforce rigorous neutrality against religious observances that it apparently considered harmless.[90] The Court has never suggested that government may comply with the Establishment Clause merely by refraining from coercion. The Court rejected the proposed noncoercion test at its first opportunity and at every opportunity since. A majority of a full Court firmly and explicitly rejected it just two years ago.[91] It is true that many opinions have mentioned the evil of coercing persons to participate in religious observances. That is the most egregious case of establishment, and any form of government support for religion readily slides into coercion by imperceptible degrees. But none of the Court's opinions have distinguished coercion from mere government persuasion, condemning one and approving the other. Rather, the early opinions treated coercion and government persuasion interchangeably, condemning either as unconstitutional. Because the misimpression seems widespread that "the problem is *Lemon,*" it is worthwhile reviewing in some detail the full line of cases on government-sponsored religious observance.

Justice Black wrote for the majority in *Everson:*

> Neither a state nor the Federal Government can set up a church. Neither can pass laws which aid one religion, *aid all religions,* or prefer one religion over another. Neither can force *nor influence* a person to go to or remain away from church against his will or force him to profess a belief or disbelief in any religion.[92]

This passage treats force and influence in matters of religion as equally objectionable. It treats aid to religion as the essence of establishment. And the

---

87. *Schempp,* 374 U.S. at 222.
88. 330 U.S. 1, 18 (1947).
89. See Laycock, *supra* note 6, at 1007-11 (text at notes 41-64).
90. Lynch v. Donnelly, 465 U.S. 668 (1984); Marsh v. Chambers, 463 U.S. 783 (1983).
91. County of Allegheny v. ACLU, 492 U.S. 573 (1989).
92. 330 U.S. at 15 (emphasis added).

Court certainly did not suppose that government could "set up a church" if no one were coerced to support it.

Justice Rutledge for the four dissenters in *Everson* was even more explicit about noncoercive violations of the Establishment Clause. He listed coercive violations of the Establishment Clause, and he contrasted these with "the serious surviving threat[s]" of financial aid to religious institutions and "efforts to inject religious training or exercises and sectarian issues into the public schools."[93] Thus, none of the nine Justices in *Everson* believed that coercion was an element of every Establishment Clause violation.

The Court again equated coercion and persuasion in *Zorach v. Clausen*,[94] upholding programs under which schools released students to attend private religious instruction. The Court said:

> . . . if it were established that any one or more teachers were using their office *to persuade* or force students to take the religious instruction, a wholly different case would be presented.[95]

The Court distinguished the released time program in *Zorach* from the similar program in *Illinois ex rel. McCollum v. Board of Education*,[96] on grounds that had nothing to do with coercion. The charge of coercion in both cases rested on the claim that limiting students to study hall or religious instruction coerced them to choose religious instruction.[97] *Zorach* rejected that claim, finding neither coercion nor persuasion. Thus, *Zorach*'s explanation of *McCollum*, essential to the holding in both cases, is that there was no coercion in *McCollum*, but there was an Establishment Clause violation in *McCollum* — necessarily an Establishment Clause violation without coercion. This coercion-free violation was adjudicated in 1948.

The Court distinguished the cases on the ground that religious instruction was off campus in *Zorach*, but on campus in *McCollum*.[98] The key to an Establishment Clause violation was not coercion, but use of school property. Justice Brennan believed that the use of school property mattered because it augmented the persuasive powers of the religious teachers:

> To be sure, a religious teacher presumably commands substantial respect and merits attention in his own right. But *the Constitution does not permit*

---

93. *Id.* at 44 (Rutledge, J., dissenting).
94. 343 U.S. 306 (1952).
95. *Id.* at 311.
96. 333 U.S. 203 (1948).
97. *Zorach*, 343 U.S. at 309-10.
98. *Id.* at 309.

that prestige and capacity for influence to be augmented by the investiture of all the symbols of authority at the command of the lay teacher for the enhancement of secular instruction.[99]

In *McGowan v. Maryland,*[100] the Court quoted *Everson's* explanation of establishment, permitting "neither force nor influence,"[101] and it quoted and italicized Justice Rutledge's identification of religious exercises in public schools as a noncoercive threat to disestablishment.[102]

Thus it was no innovation when the Court squarely rejected a non-coercion test in the first school prayer case, *Engel v. Vitale.*[103] Nor did the Court announce a distinction between direct and indirect coercion, as Justice Kennedy has suggested.[104] The *Engel* Court said that the Establishment Clause went far beyond even indirect coercion:

> When the power, *prestige* and financial support of government is placed behind a particular religious belief, the indirect coercive pressure upon religious minorities to conform to the prevailing officially approved religion is plain. *But the purposes underlying the Establishment Clause go much further than that.* Its first and most immediate purpose rested on the belief that a union of government and religion tends to destroy government and to degrade religion.[105]

The language elsewhere in the opinion confirms the depth of the Court's belief that coercion is no essential part of Establishment Clause analysis. It was unconstitutional for New York "to *encourage* recitation of the Regents' prayer,"[106] to place "its official stamp of *approval*" on any religion,[107] or to use its *"prestige"* to *"support or influence* the kinds of prayer the American people can say."[108]

The Court reaffirmed its commitment to government neutrality toward religion in the second school prayer case, *Abington School District v. Schempp.*[109] The Court said that the purpose of the First Amendment was "to

---

99. Abington School Dist. v. Schempp, 374 U.S. 203, 263 (Brennan, J., concurring) (emphasis added).

100. 366 U.S. 420 (1961).

101. *Id.* at 443.

102. *Id.* at 444 n.18.

103. 370 U.S. 421, 430-31 (1962).

104. County of Allegheny v. ACLU, 492 U.S. 573, 655 (1989) (Kennedy, J., dissenting).

105. *Engel,* 370 U.S. at 431 (emphasis added).

106. *Id.* at 424 (emphasis added).

107. *Id.* at 429 (emphasis added).

108. *Id.* (emphasis added).

109. 374 U.S. 203, 215, 218, 222, 225-26 (1963).

take *every form of propagation of religion* out of the realm of things which could directly or indirectly be made public business. . . ."[110] And the Court said, the state cannot "perform or *aid in performing the religious function.*"[111]

The Court first quoted the entirety of *Engel's* holding that coercion is not an element of an Establishment Clause violation,[112] and then for emphasis paraphrased it more succinctly.[113] And elaborating on "the wholesome 'neutrality' of which this Court's cases speak," the Court formulated what became the first two prongs of the *Lemon* test: "there must be a secular legislative purpose and a primary effect that neither advances nor inhibits religion."[114]

Justice Stewart in dissent suggested that coercion should be the key,[115] so the issue was squarely presented. He attracted no vote but his own. But his sensitive understanding of coercion makes clear that he would find coercion in *Lee v. Weisman.* He recognized the dangers of "psychological compulsion to participate,"[116] and he thought it would be coercive if students who failed to attend religious exercises had to forgo "the morning announcements."[117] Graduation is a far more important event than morning announcements; if requiring students to miss the morning announcements is coercive, a fortiori requiring them to miss their graduation is coercive. All nine justices in *Schempp* rejected the Bush Administration's position in *Lee v. Weisman.*

In 1968, the Court applied the *Schempp* test in *Epperson v. Arkansas,*[118] and reaffirmed the government's duty to "be neutral in matters of religious theory, doctrine, and practice."[119] That same year brought the first of the long series of cases on financial aid to church-affiliated schools. These cases are largely irrelevant to the proposed noncoercion test. Financial aid is always coercive, because it requires taxation. Distinctions in financial aid cases turn on other factors, and the real argument should center on whether the dominant aspect of the state's conduct is its aid to religion or its aid to compulsory education in secular subjects. But the financial aid cases were the occasion for

110. *Id.* at 216, *quoting* Everson v. Board of Educ., 330 U.S. 1, 26 (1947) (Jackson, J., dissenting) (emphasis added).

111. 374 U.S. at 219, *quoting Everson,* 330 U.S. at 52 (Rutledge, J., dissenting) (emphasis added).

112. 374 U.S. at 221.

113. *Id.* at 223 (". . . a violation of the Free Exercise Clause is predicated on coercion while the Establishment Clause violation need not be so attended.").

114. *Id.* at 222.

115. *Id.* at 316-20.

116. *Id.* at 318.

117. *Id.* at 320 n.8.

118. 393 U.S. 97, 107 (1968).

119. *Id.* at 103-04.

incorporation of the two-part *Schempp* test into the three-part *Lemon* test, and the resulting *Lemon* test was quoted and applied in case after case.

The real issue for the proposed noncoercion test is government-sponsored religious observances. In cases arising in the public schools, the Court has struck down every such observance it has considered. In *Stone v. Graham*,[120] Kentucky posted the Ten Commandments on the walls of school-rooms. If ever it were plausible to say there is no coercion in a school case, *Stone* would have been the case. But the Court summarily invalidated the Kentucky practice, citing state "auspices" and "official support" for religion as unconstitutional.[121]

Two years later, the Court unanimously invalidated a statute that authorized students and teachers to volunteer to lead the class in prayer.[122] The statute ineffectually provided that "no student or teacher could be compelled to pray," but that did not save the statute or even require full argument.

The following term the Court decided *Marsh v. Chambers*,[123] upholding prayer in the Nebraska legislature. The opinion announced no new standard, and it did not question the general rule of government neutrality toward religion, although the result was inconsistent with that rule. Chief Justice Burger wrote a narrow opinion, relying on the "unique history" of legislative prayer,[124] and the fact that the person claiming injury was an adult.[125] Legislative prayer appeared to be an unprincipled exception to the general rule of neutrality toward religion. In the same term, another opinion by Chief Justice Burger quoted and reaffirmed the *Schempp-Lemon* test,[126] and condemned a "symbolic benefit" to religion.[127] Eight justices joined this opinion.

The following Term suggested that *Marsh* did not apply to schools, and perhaps did not apply to anything other than the "unique" case of legislative prayer. The Court unanimously affirmed invalidation of a statute authorizing public school teachers to lead willing students in prayer.[128] And all nine Justices claimed to apply the *Schempp-Lemon* test to the municipal Christmas display

---

120. 449 U.S. 39 (1980).

121. *Id.* at 42, quoting *Schempp*, 374 U.S. at 222.

122. Karen B. v. Treen, 653 F.2d 897, 899 (5th Cir. 1981), *aff'd mem.*, 455 U.S. 913 (1982).

123. 463 U.S. 783 (1983).

124. *Id.* at 791.

125. *Id.* at 792.

126. Larkin v. Grendel's Den, Inc., 459 U.S. 116, 123 (1982).

127. *Id.* at 125.

128. Jaffree v. Wallace, 705 F.2d 1526, 1535-36 (11th Cir. 1983), *aff'd mem.*, 466 U.S. 924 (1984).

in *Lynch v. Donnelly*.[129] But the majority created another exception, finding the display sufficiently secular to justify a finding of secular purpose and effect.[130] This time the majority created an exception without admitting that it was doing so, and the resulting opinion is an intellectual embarrassment. *Marsh* and *Lynch* showed that the Court would not enforce neutrality with any rigor, but the Court did not threaten to wholly abandon the principle.

It was in *Lynch* that Justice O'Connor offered her endorsement test to clarify the first two prongs of the *Lemon* test.[131] The Court incorporated Justice O'Connor's endorsement test into its analysis the following year in *Wallace v. Jaffree*.[132] The Court quoted and applied the *Schempp-Lemon* test, but it also accepted the endorsement test as an authoritative elaboration:

> The purpose prong of the *Lemon* test asks whether government's actual purpose is to endorse or disapprove of religion. The effect prong asks whether, irrespective of government's actual purpose, the practice under review in fact conveys a message of endorsement or disapproval.[133]

Wallace was also the occasion for Justice Powell's emphatic defense of the *Lemon* test as the settled law of the Supreme Court.[134]

The endorsement test was so readily assimilated to the *Schempp-Lemon* test in this context because government-sponsored religious observances rarely present the ambiguities that the endorsement test was designed to clarify. The endorsement was offered as a way of explaining that it is not a forbidden benefit to religion to exempt conscientious objectors or otherwise remove burdens from religious practice.[135] In the context of religious observances, which do not remove burdens and rarely have plausible secular purposes, it was immediately clear that the endorsement test and the *Schempp-Lemon* test were compatible.

Two years later, in *Edwards v. Aguillard*,[136] the Court again applied the

129. 465 U.S. 668 (1984).

130. *Id.* at 681-82.

131. *Id.* at 690.

132. 472 U.S. 38 (1985).

133. *Id.* at 56 n.42, *quoting* Lynch v. Donnelly, 465 U.S. 668, 690 (1984) (O'Connor, J., concurring). For similar statements by the Court, see *Wallace*, 472 U.S. at 58 n.45, 59, 61 & n.52.

134. 472 U.S. at 63 & n.5 (Powell, J., concurring).

135. *Id.* at 83 (O'Connor, J., concurring). *See also* Laycock, *supra* note 82, at 21-22 (purpose to avoid discrimination against religion is a legitimate purpose, whether considered secular or religious). I have been persuaded that even the endorsement test does not communicate this distinction without further elaboration. See McConnell, *supra* note 4.

136. 482 U.S. 578 (1987).

Schempp-Lemon test,[137] as clarified by the endorsement test,[138] to strike down a statute requiring balanced treatment of evolution and "creation science." The Court noted that *Marsh v. Chambers* had been the only case in which the Court failed to apply the *Schempp-Lemon* test.[139]

Most recently, the Court applied the *Schempp-Lemon* test, as clarified by the endorsement test, to prohibit display of a creche in a county courthouse.[140] The Court did not say that the display was coercive; rather, it said that the display "has the effect of *endorsing* a patently Christian message."[141] The Court continued:

> Whether the key word is "endorsement," "favoritism," or "promotion," the essential principle remains the same. The Establishment Clause, at the very least, prohibits government from *appearing to take a position* on questions of religious belief. . . .[142]

The Court explained *Lynch v. Donnelly* as holding "that government may celebrate Christmas in some manner and form, but not in a way that *endorses* Christian doctrine."[143] Celebrating Christmas without endorsing Christianity would seem to be an obvious impossibility, but the *Allegheny* majority took the *Lynch* majority at its word. *Lynch* had implausibly said that Pawtucket's creche was principally secular; *Allegheny* more accurately said that Pittsburgh's creche was not.

Justice Kennedy's dissent in *Allegheny* proposed a fundamentally different standard: that "government may not coerce anyone to support or participate in any religion or its exercise,"[144] and that government may not "proselytize on behalf of a particular religion."[145]

The majority emphatically rejected this standard: *"Justice Kennedy's reading of Marsh would gut the core of the Establishment Clause, as this Court understands it."*[146] And, the Court might have added, as the Court has long and all but unanimously understood it. The *Schempp* test was adopted eight to one, and the dissenter, Justice Stewart, understood coercion much more expan-

137. *Id.* at 582-83.
138. *Id.* at 585.
139. *Id.* at 583 n.4.
140. County of Allegheny v. ACLU, 492 U.S. 573, 592 (1989).
141. *Id.* at 601 (emphasis added).
142. *Id.* at 593-94 (emphasis added).
143. *Id.* at 601 (emphasis added).
144. *Id.* at 659.
145. *Id.* at 661.
146. *Id.* at 604 (emphasis added).

sively than the Bush Administration in *Lee v. Weisman.* The *Lemon* test was adopted seven to one — eight to one with Justice Brennan's concurrence. The dissenter, Justice White, has never voted to uphold school-sponsored religious observances in a public elementary or secondary school. [Actually, it was six to one and seven to one. I forgot that Justice Marshall recused himself.]

The opinions reviewed here, committing the government to neutrality between religion and nonreligion, and forbidding government persuasion or influence in religious matters, have been joined by nearly every Justice appointed since the issues first reached the Supreme Court: by Chief Justices Vinson, Warren, and Burger, by Justices Black, Reed (in *Everson*[147] although not in *McCollum*[148]), Frankfurter, Douglas, Murphy, Jackson, Rutledge, Burton, Clark, Minton, Harlan, Stewart (in *Lemon*[149] although not in *Schempp*[150]), Brennan, White (in *Wallace,*[151] *Stone,*[152] *Epperson,*[153] and *Schempp,* although not in *Lemon*), Goldberg, Fortas, Marshall, Blackmun, Powell, Stevens, and O'Connor. If the new majority abandons the requirement of government neutrality toward religion, it will not be to correct the excesses of a few extreme liberals. It will be the work of one political faction rejecting the nearly unanimous view of all modern justices. As Justice Scalia once said, when he did not have five votes, "It is not right — it is not constitutionally healthy — that this Court should feel authorized to refashion anew our civil society's relationship with religion. . . ."[154]

IV. The Harm to Religion

It is common to assume that the objection to government-sponsored religious observances comes only from non-believers who are hostile to religion. It is easy to see that non-believers might object when government adds a prayer service to a secular function. A requirement that government be neutral as between religious belief and disbelief is designed to protect non-believers.

But a ban on government-sponsored religious observance is also necessary to neutrality among believers, and it is important to understand that. A

147. Everson v. Board of Educ., 330 U.S. 1 (1947).
148. Illinois *ex rel.* McCollum v. Board of Educ., 333 U.S. 203 (1948).
149. Lemon v. Kurtzman, 403 U.S. 602 (1971).
150. Abington School Dist. v. Schempp, 374 U.S. 203 (1963).
151. Wallace v. Jaffree, 472 U.S. 38 (1985).
152. Stone v. Graham, 449 U.S. 39 (1980).
153. Epperson v. Arkansas, 393 U.S. 97 (1968).
154. Texas Monthly, Inc. v. Bullock, 489 U.S. 1, 45 (1989) (Scalia, J., dissenting).

nonpreferentialist instinct informs much of the popular reaction to *Lee v. Weisman:* who besides an atheist could object to a short and simple prayer? That question deserves an answer.

The relevance of nonpreferentialism is political rather than doctrinal. As noted above, nonpreferentialism is no part of the proposed noncoercion test in *Lee v. Weisman.* The Bush Administration's brief would let government be as sectarian as it likes, so long as it refrains from coercion. But even if government attempts to sponsor religious observances that are neutral among believers, it will fail. Government-sponsored religious observances hurt believers as well as nonbelievers.

Such observances hurt all religions by imposing government's preferred form of religion on public occasions. It is not possible for government to sponsor a generic prayer; government inevitably sponsors a particular form of prayer. Whatever form government chooses, it imposes that form on all believers who would prefer a different form.

In some communities, government-sponsored prayer unabashedly follows the liturgy of the locally dominant faith in the community.[155] "Sensitive" communities such as Providence attempt to delete from public prayer all indicia of any particular faith, leaving only the least common denominator of majoritarian religion. But these stripped-down prayers to an anonymous deity are as much a particular form of prayer as any other prayer.

The school teachers who plan the ceremony decide what prayers are acceptable and what not, and what clergy are acceptable and what not. In this process, the schools establish a religion of mushy ecumenism. The clergy for these prayers are determined by the limits of acceptability to the mainstream. In Providence and many other cities, the guidelines for these prayers are supplied by the National Conference of Christians and Jews. The NCCJ's guidelines implement its commitment to minimizing religious and ethnic conflict. The guidelines emphasize "inclusiveness and sensitivity," and they offer a specific list of "universal, inclusive terms for deity."[156] Government adoption of these guidelines establishes an uncodified but generally accepted book of common prayer. This least-common-denominator strategy is the same strategy followed by the Protestant school reformers of the nineteenth century, and it fails for similar reasons. By removing from religious observance all those things on which different faiths overtly disagree, the school is left with

155. *See, e.g.,* Jager v. Douglas County School Dist., 862 F.2d 824, 826 (11th Cir. 1989) (frequent references to Christ); Lubbock Civil Liberties Union v. Lubbock Indep. School Dist., 669 F.2d 1038, 1039 (5th Cir. 1982) (evangelical Protestant school assemblies).

156. National Conference of Christians and Jews, Public Prayer in a Pluralistic Society 2 (undated pamphlet).

an abstract impersonal God that nearly all faiths reject. What is left is unacceptable to many believers who take their own faith seriously.

The problem is as fundamental and intractable as the question of Whom to pray to. To pray to or in the name of Christ is a blasphemy to most Jews; not to do so is theologically and liturgically incorrect to most Christians. Is it better to silently affront the Christian majority by leaving Christ out of prayer, or to overtly offend the Jewish minority by praying in Christ's name? Given the sad history of Christian-Jewish relations, leaving Christ out is probably the lesser of the evils. The Supreme Court once said that leaving Christ out is constitutionally required.[157] But leaving Christ out of prayer is not a solution; it is at the core of the problem.

Whichever choice government makes, it endorses that choice. Government-sponsored prayer on public occasions lends the weight of government practice to a preferred form of prayer. By their example, schools that leave Christ out of prayer endorse that practice as more tolerant, as more enlightened, as government approved. They lend the authority of government to a desacralized, watered-down religion that demands little of its adherents and offers few benefits in return.

The attempt to be inclusive amplifies the message of exclusion to those left out. Because such prayers are carefully orchestrated not to offend anyone who counts in the community, the message to those who are offended is that they do *not* count — that they are not important enough to avoid offending. The message is: We go out of our way to avoid offending people we care about, but we don't mind offending you. If you have a problem with this, you are too marginal to care about. This is our graduation, not yours.

It is not just nonbelievers who may be offended or excluded by prayers like those in *Lee v. Weisman*. Such prayers also exclude serious particularistic believers, those who take their own form of prayer seriously enough that they do not want to participate in someone else's form of prayer. There are still millions of Americans who believe that all religions are not equal, that their own religion is better, or even that their own religion is the one true faith, and that their faith should not be conglomerated into something that will not offend the great majority.

Those who would not pray at all, those who would pray only in private, those who would pray only after ritual purification, those who would pray only to Jesus, or Mary, or some other intermediary, those who would pray in Hebrew, or Arabic, or some other sacred tongue, are all excluded or offended by the prayers in *Lee v. Weisman*. Those who object to the political or

---

157. County of Allegheny v. ACLU, 492 U.S. 573, 603 (1989).

theological content of those prayers are similarly excluded — those whose vision of God is not the government's vision, those whose concept of God does not track the National Anthem, whose God is not "the God of the Free and Hope of the Brave," but perhaps the God of the oppressed and the Hope of the fearful.[158]

On occasion, religious observances in public schools still produce ugly confrontations between those who object to least-common-denominator prayer and those who support it. A detailed account of such an incident appears in *Walter v. West Virginia Board of Education*,[159] where an eleven-year-old Jewish child was condemned as a Christ killer because he did not appear to pray during a moment of silence. Most contemporary religious dissenters in public schools suffer in silence, and we have had no recent repetitions of the mob violence of the nineteenth century. But reduction of violence is not a reason to relax constitutional protections. Religious dissenters should not have to provoke violence to call attention to their constitutional rights.

The political content of the prayer in *Lee* illustrates another core danger of established religion. When government sponsors religious observances, it appropriates religion to its own uses and unites religious and governmental authority. The message of the invocation in *Lee v. Weisman* was an essentially political message — that American government is good, that freedom is secure, that courts protect minority rights, that America is the land of the free and the home of the brave, et cetera.

The invocation's political message is popular but not uncontroversial. The school can deliver that political message if it chooses. The rabbi can deliver that message if he chooses. But the school and the rabbi cannot unite the authority and prestige of church and state in support of that message. The school cannot recruit a rabbi to wrap that political message in religious au-

---

158. The invocation in *Lee* read as follows:

> God of the Free, Hope of the Brave: For the legacy of America where diversity is celebrated and the rights of minorities are protected, we thank You. May these young men and women grow up to enrich it. For the liberty of America, we thank You. May these new graduates grow up to guard it. For the political process of America in which all its citizens may participate, for its court system where all can seek justice we thank You. May those we honor this morning always turn to it in trust. For the destiny of America we thank You. May the graduates of Nathan Bishop Middle School so live that they help to share it. May our aspirations for our country and for these young people, who are our hope for the future, be richly fulfilled. AMEN.

Weisman v. Lee, 990 F.2d 1090, 1098 n.* (Campbell, J., dissenting).

159. 610 F. Supp. 1169, 1172-73 (S.D. W. Va. 1985).

thority. The school cannot misappropriate the authority of the church to prop up the authority of the state.

It has long been a common observation that religion has thrived in America without an establishment, and declined in Western Europe with an establishment.[160] It is less commonly observed that the established Congregationalist and Episcopalian churches of colonial America declined in numbers and influence, while the dissenting Baptists and Presbyterians, who insisted on rigorous disestablishment, grew and flourished.[161]

These long-term religious trends reflect in part the baleful effects of government sponsorship. Religion does not benefit from public prayer that "degenerates into a scanty attendance, and a tiresome formality."[162] The Providence School Committee actually quoted this description of prayer in the First Congress, apparently to show that nonbelievers need not fear being persuaded to belief.[163] But the Constitution is equally violated if government makes religion less attractive rather than more so. Government sponsorship of religion is always clumsy, and usually motivated more by political concerns than religious ones. In intolerant communities it tends inevitably toward persecution; in tolerant communities it tends inevitably toward desacralization. One function of the Establishment Clause is to avoid this dilemma.

V. Justice Kennedy's Alternative

In his dissent in the Pittsburgh creche case, Justice Kennedy proposed that the Establishment Clause might be satisfied if government refrained either from coercion or from proselytizing.[164] The Court squarely rejected Kennedy's proselytizing test,[165] and no one urged it in *Lee v. Weisman*. But it seems more likely that if the Court sharply reinterprets the Establishment Clause, it will move to Kennedy's test, which has already received four votes, instead of to the Justice Department's more extreme proposal that would let government proselytize as long as it does not coerce.

160. *See, e.g.*, Alexis de Tocqueville, Democracy in America 308-14 (Phillips Bradley ed., 1945).

161. *See* Andrew M. Greeley & Michael Hout, *Musical Chairs: Patterns of Denominational Change*, 72 Sociology & Social Research 75, 81 Table 3 (1988).

162. *Madison's "Detached Memoranda*," 3 Wm. & Mary Q. 534, 539 (3d Ser. 1946) (Elizabeth Fleet ed.).

163. Brief for Petitioners, *supra* note 2, at 32 n.33.

164. County of Allegheny v. ACLU, 492 U.S. 573, 659, 661 (1989).

165. *Id.* at 602-13.

I have only the vaguest idea which endorsements of religion would count as proselytizing. Apparently, proselytizing is a matter of degree. Some government endorsements of religion would be permitted, but persistent endorsements would be forbidden proselytizing,[166] and presumably insistent endorsements or explicit calls to conversion would be forbidden proselytizing.

Much prayer would be proselytizing, which may be why no one urged the proselytizing test in *Lee*. Prayers are an important, powerful, and frequent means of proselytizing. Evangelists lead their audience in prayer; proselytizers pray privately with individuals. No one would doubt the proselytizing intent of a pastor at commencement who prayed "that the Holy Spirit pass through this class, and touch every heart, and lead these graduates to Jesus." There are endless variations of proselytizing more subtle than this example. Unless courts and school boards are to parse the content of prayers, the only way to avoid proselytizing at commencement is to avoid prayer at commencement.

More fundamentally, the proselytizing test violates the Establishment Clause for most of the same reasons a coercion test would violate the Establishment Clause. First, the proselytizing test is inconsistent with the original meaning of the clause. The bare endorsements of the South Carolina Constitution and the Virginia Episcopal incorporation act presumably did not amount to proselytizing, but they were establishments in the understanding of the founding generation.

Second, the proselytizing test is inconsistent with historical applications of the original principle. Reading the Bible "without note or comment" was an attempt to avoid proselytizing as well as sectarian division. But as shown above, this program was the source of bitter religious strife. Religious observances in the public schools, with or without overt proselytizing, led to the very evils the Establishment Clause was designed to prevent.

Third, the proselytizing test is inconsistent with the Supreme Court's modern precedents. From the beginning, the Court has properly insisted that government be neutral toward religion. Government was not to refrain merely from coercion, or from proselytizing, but from "persuasion," from "influence," from any "stamp of approval," from any departure from "neutrality."

Fourth, government-sponsored religious observances inflict the same harms on religion whether or not government proselytizes. The vagueness of a proselytizing test may steer some governmental units away from the specific liturgy of any particular faith, but this will only reinforce the tendency to desacralization. There is no avoiding the central dilemma: when government

---

166. *Id.* at 661 (Kennedy, J., dissenting) (year-round cross on city hall would be proselytizing).

conducts religious rituals, it must conduct them in some concrete form, and whatever form it chooses is endorsed and tendered to the community as a model. For all these reasons, the proselytizing test is an inadequate protection for religious liberty.

VI. The Bush Administration's Conception of Coercion

An essential feature of *Lee* is a captive audience of young children. It is not merely that children are in attendance, or that children want to be in attendance. It is also that the event is planned especially for children, to honor children on one of the major accomplishments of their young lives. Providence says to its high school graduates, and to its middle school promotees: if you wish to be honored on your promotion, you must first be "compelled to listen to the prayers" of others.[167]

The children have no realistic choice but to sit through the prayers attentively and respectfully. They must give every outward appearance of joining in the prayers. This is not like a passive display, where people can "turn their backs."[168] Nor is it like a legislature, where adults come and go at will, and can avoid the invocation by the simple expedient of arriving late.

The Providence School Committee seemed to assume there is no coercion unless children are compelled to *believe in* the religious premises of the prayers.[169] But that is absurd. That standard would permit the state to compel church attendance, or any other religious behavior. It is impossible to compel belief; outward manifestations of belief are all that the state can ever hope to compel. When the state compels children to give respectful attention to prayers, it has violated even the coercion test.

The prayers in *Lee* are also especially problematic because of the state's role in planning and supervising the content of the prayers. School teachers plan the ceremony. They decide whether to include prayers, how many prayers, and at what point. They select the clergy to offer the prayers. They give the clergy "guidelines" to acceptable prayer. They call to make sure the clergy understand the guidelines.[170] Participating clergy cannot avoid the inference that they are unlikely to be invited again if they depart from the guidelines. Government and religion are hopelessly entangled in this process.

167. Wallace v. Jaffree, 472 U.S. 38, 72 (1985) (O'Connor, J., concurring).

168. *Cf. County of Allegheny*, 492 U.S. at 664 (Kennedy, J., dissenting).

169. *See* Brief for Petitioners, *supra* note 2, at 41 (heading 3).

170. Joint Appendix in *Lee v. Weisman*, No. 90-1014 in the Supreme Court of the United States, at 12-13.

Just as "it is no part of the business of government to compose official prayers,"[171] so it is no part of the business of government to prescribe official guidelines for prayer.

The teachers' central role in planning and supervising these prayers negates any claim that the clergyman they select is simply a private speaker. *Lee* is wholly unlike *Board of Education v. Mergens,*[172] where there was no school sponsorship and a wholly voluntary audience. It is wholly unlike religious imagery in a commencement address by Martin Luther King, where a prominent public figure was invited to speak on any topic of his choice. In *Lee,* carefully selected clergy are invited solely to pray, at times designated by the school and in accordance with liturgical guidelines imposed by the school.

Lee is not a free speech case or an equal access case. It is a school prayer case, plain and simple. In terms of school sponsorship, government entanglement, and coercion of children, *Lee* is indistinguishable from *Engel* and *Schempp.* It differs from those cases only in the frequency of the constitutional violation. If the Court holds that school prayer is permitted occasionally but not daily, it will be faced with a long series of cases asking how often is too often, and which occasions are special enough. If commencement is exempt from the school prayer cases, what about holidays, student assemblies, athletic events, pep rallies, and any other day on which an "occasion" can be identified?

School-sponsored and school-supervised prayer is not the only way to take religious note of graduation. A private baccalaureate service, sponsored by the local association of churches and synagogues, is the obvious constitutional alternative. Unsponsored student groups exercising their rights under *Mergens* might organize religious observances of the occasion. Either of these alternatives would leave religious worship in religious hands, either would avoid coercion of young children, and either would avoid government sponsorship.

VII. Conclusion

It is too often forgotten that the Establishment Clause and the Free Exercise Clause both protect religious liberty. They both protect religious believers as well as nonbelievers. In the words of the Presbyterian Church (U.S.A.):

171. Engel v. Vitale, 370 U.S. 421, 425 (1962).
172. 496 U.S. 226 (1990).

Together the two clauses guarantee that the people will have the fullest possible religious liberty. The state may not interfere with the private choice of religious faith *either by coercion or by persuasion.* It may not interfere with the expression of faith either by inducing people to abandon the religious faith and practice of their choice, or by inducing them to adopt the religious faith and practice of the government's choice.[173]

The noncoercion standard would abandon the goal of government neutrality toward and among religions. It would encourage government to denigrate, embarrass, and discomfit nonbelievers. But it would also leave America's many religions exposed to the corrupting intrusions of government. Government could sponsor preferred churches, preferred theologies, preferred liturgies, preferred forms of worship, and preferred forms of prayer. All this is entailed when government undertakes to sponsor a "civil religion."

Government by its sheer size, visibility, authority, and pervasiveness could profoundly affect the future of religion in America. For government to affect religion in this way is for government to change religion, to distort religion, to interfere with religion. Government's preferred form of religion is theologically and liturgically thin. It is politically compliant, and supportive of incumbent administrations. One function of the Establishment Clause is to protect religion against such interference. To government's clumsy efforts to assist religion, several religious amici said "No thanks. Too much of such" assistance "and we are undone; the Constitution protects us from assistance such as this."[174]

173. *God Alone Is Lord of the Conscience: A Policy Statement Adopted by the 200th General Assembly of the Presbyterian Church (U.S.A.)* (1988) at 7, reprinted in 8 J.L. & RELIGION 331, 332 (1990).

174. Amicus Curiae Brief of the American Jewish Congress, *et al.,* in Support of Respondents 8.

Continuity and Change in the Threat to Religious Liberty: The Reformation Era and the Late Twentieth Century

80 Minnesota Law Review 1047 (1996)

This article reviews religious conflict in the wake of the Reformation, on the Continent and in England, but with more attention to England. Treating that conflict as formative for American guarantees of religious liberty, I seek to specify more precisely the nature and source of the threat to religious liberty in the Reformation era, and then to compare and contrast that threat with the nature and source of the threat to religious liberty in our own time. This article is based on the Lockhart Lecture at the University of Minnesota.

*   *   *

Introduction

What is the source of threats to religious liberty? One might also ask the question the other way around: what is the problem that religious liberty is designed to solve?

This paper was originally given as the 1994 Lockhart Lecture at the University of Minnesota Law School. I have added footnotes and expanded on the text, but I have tried to retain some of the scope and style of the original lecture. Many volumes of history have been written on the Reformation; I have resisted the illusion that I can do any more than summarize broad themes and illustrate with selected examples. I am grateful to the students and faculty at Minnesota for insightful questions and comments, to Edward McGlynn Gaffney, Andrew M. Greeley, Sanford Levinson, Michael McConnell, L.A. Powe, and John Witte for helpful comments on an earlier draft, and to Nathan Adams and Christine Burgess for research assistance. The seed for this paper was planted in conversation at a conference sponsored by the Liberty Fund; the papers from that conference appeared in RELIGIOUS LIBERTY IN WESTERN THOUGHT (Noel B. Reynolds & W. Cole Durham, Jr., eds., 1996).

For nearly five hundred years in Western thought, the dominant model of the problem to be solved has been the religious conflict in the wake of the Reformation. The Reformation is important to American constitutional law because it was salient recent history to those who wrote our Religion Clauses, and because for most Americans who learned anything about religion in their history courses, the problem of religious liberty is typified by the persecutions that drove Pilgrims, Puritans, Quakers, and Catholics to found colonies in Plymouth, Massachusetts Bay, Pennsylvania, and Maryland.

The Reformation-era conflict was in some ways similar to religious conflict before and since. But like all great events, it was in some ways unique. As Justice Black summarized it in *Everson v. Board of Education:*

> Catholics had persecuted Protestants, Protestants had persecuted Catholics, Protestant sects had persecuted other Protestant sects, Catholics of one shade of belief had persecuted Catholics of another shade of belief, and all of these had from time to time persecuted Jews. Men and women had been fined, cast in jail, cruelly tortured, and killed.[1]

We can all agree that these events should not be repeated. These events were so obviously evil that the lessons to be learned may seem equally obvious — so obvious that there is little need to discuss them.

The relative dearth of explicit discussion has been a mistake. I have gradually come to realize that different commentators have drawn quite different lessons from this history. Americans do not agree on what was wrong with the Reformation-era conflicts, and consequently we do not agree on what lessons to draw for our own time. In part we can disagree about what lessons to draw because we have only the vaguest idea what actually happened. Just what was the Diet of Worms, and who forced whom to live on it?

More important, what was the dominant evil of these conflicts? Was it that people suffered for religion, or that religions imposed suffering? Is the dominant lesson that religion has a "dark side" that is "inherently intolerant and persecutory,"[2] or that efforts to coerce religious belief or practice cause great human suffering?

Any answer must begin with historical facts, not vague impressions or religious or secular prejudices. I therefore begin with some basic history. Nothing in this historical review is original or sophisticated, and none of the facts are controversial. I am summarizing from standard sources in very broad strokes. But there is a theme to my summary: the role of the State in

1. 330 U.S. 1, 9 (1947).
2. William P. Marshall, *The Other Side of Religion*, 44 HASTINGS L.J. 843 (1993).

the religious persecutions that gave rise to our Religion Clauses. I follow with an equally broad overview of contemporary religious conflict; then I compare and contrast the two periods. Much has changed since the Reformation, but one constant is that the State punishes people for disapproved religious practices.

I. The Reformation Era

A. *The Continent*

The beginning of the Reformation is conventionally dated to 1517, when Martin Luther circulated his Ninety-Five Theses on indulgences.[3] Of course Luther had predecessors, such as Wycliffe and Hus more than a century before.[4] But it was Luther and then Calvin who first launched successful religious movements, perhaps because they had the enormous advantage of the printing press.[5]

The Ninety-Five Theses circulated widely, although historians now doubt the legend that Luther nailed them to the church door in Wittenberg.[6] The Theses provoked immediate accusations of heresy,[7] but only dilatory action. There followed more than three years of political maneuvering, during which time Luther issued a series of books, sermons, and public statements that escalated his quarrel with Rome from an attack on indulgences to a denial of the authority of Popes and church councils and a redefinition of the sacraments and the means of salvation.[8]

The reasons for the delay in pursuing Luther lay in secular politics and

---

3. *See* Lewis W. Spitz, The Protestant Reformation 1517-1559 at 1 (1985).

4. John M. Todd, Reformation 84-93 (1971) (hereinafter cited as Todd, Reformation).

5. *See* H. G. Haile, Luther: An Experimental Biography 165-74 (1980) (describing the explosive distribution of Luther's works); Spitz, *supra* note 3, at 88-93 ("[T]he Reformation was the first historical movement in the post-Gutenberg era and the printing press made it possible.").

6. Haile, *supra* note 5, at 177 & n.8; Erwin Iserloh, The Theses Were Not Posted: Luther Between Reform and Reformation 46-97 (1968).

7. *See* Spitz, *supra* note 3, at 66-69 (noting that the Theses promulgated October 31, 1517, and that by mid-December, Luther's bishop had sent them to Rome with a request for heresy proceedings).

8. For detailed accounts of this period, see Roland H. Bainton, Here I Stand: A Life of Martin Luther 84-166 (1950) (hereinafter Bainton, Luther); John M. Todd, Luther 120-86 (1982) (hereinafter Todd, Luther).

power relations. The Church had to line up its temporal support, because only the State could execute heretics. And the Pope had to deal with the rulers of the German states on other issues — including revenue, a proposed Crusade, and the election of a new Holy Roman Emperor — that seemed more important than one heretic monk.[9] Eventually, Pope Leo X declared Luther to be a heretic and excommunicated him,[10] although even then he continued to delay the effective date of the decree.[11]

Charles V, the new Emperor, summoned Luther before the Diet — the imperial council — meeting in the City of Worms, and demanded that he recant.[12] It was here, before this secular body, that Luther made his famous reply: "Here I stand; I can do no other."[13] It was an innovation that the Diet exercised independent judgment on a question of heresy, but it was no innovation that only "the secular arm" could execute a heretic.[14]

Luther had come to Worms under a guarantee of safe conduct, which the Emperor honored.[15] The Edict of Worms gave Luther twenty-one days in which to flee, at the end of which he was "to be regarded as a convicted heretic," his followers "condemned," and his books "eradicated from the memory of man."[16] But the decree could not be enforced; Luther had too much support, and the Empire was little more than a loose confederation.[17] At first Frederick of Saxony offered Luther refuge and protection;[18] later, Luther re-

9. For summaries of the political considerations, see ROLAND H. BAINTON, THE REFORMATION OF THE SIXTEENTH CENTURY 54-55 (1952) (hereinafter BAINTON, REFORMATION); TODD, LUTHER, *supra* note 8, at 129-31; BARBARA W. TUCHMAN, THE MARCH OF FOLLY 115-16 (1984).

10. The papal bull is quoted in BAINTON, LUTHER, *supra* note 8, at 147.

11. *See id.* at 170, 177 (reporting that the Pope's representative to the Emperor returned the bull of excommunication to Rome for modification); BAINTON, REFORMATION, *supra* note 9, at 58-59 (reporting an earlier delay for delivery of the bull to Luther, plus sixty days in which Luther could recant, plus further delay for "political considerations").

12. BAINTON, LUTHER, *supra* note 8, at 178-86; SPITZ, *supra* note 3, at 74-75.

13. There is some doubt whether he said those words, but there was no doubt of his meaning. *See* BAINTON, LUTHER, *supra* note 8, at 185 (quoting a similar statement from the transcript, and the famous quotation from the earliest printed version); SPITZ, *supra* note 3, at 75 (quoting the printed version and stating that "[p]andemonium broke loose in the hall" after Luther spoke).

14. J.D. MACKIE, THE EARLIER TUDORS 1485-1558, at 549 (1952); EDWARD PETERS, INQUISITION 67, 94 (1958).

15. SPITZ, *supra* note 3, at 74-75.

16. BAINTON, LUTHER, *supra* note 8, at 189 (quoting the Edict of Worms).

17. *See* TODD, LUTHER, *supra* note 8, at 215 ("It began to seem that much of the established structure of society was a paper construction.").

18. BAINTON, REFORMATION, *supra* note 9, at 62; SPITZ, *supra* note 3, at 76.

turned to Wittenberg and gradually concluded that the authorities were afraid to try to arrest him.[19] In 1524, the Diet of Nurnberg decreed only that "the Edict of Worms should be enforced in so far as might be possible."[20]

Protestantism spread rapidly, quickly splitting into its most basic branches.[21] Lutheranism spread through much of Germany and all of Scandinavia;[22] Calvinism spread from Geneva to the French Huguenots, the Dutch Reformers, the English Puritans, the Scots Presbyterians, and the American colonies in New England.[23] The Anabaptists (today's Mennonites, Amish, Quakers, and the like), the radical wing of the Reformation, spread across Europe but dominated nowhere.[24] Some scholars would add the Anglicans as a fourth distinct branch, a unique combination of Lutheran, Calvinist, Catholic, and nationalist elements.[25] Protestantism spread in part for religious reasons — charismatic evangelizers offered an attractive alternative, in vernacular languages, to a Church that had grown visibly corrupt.[26] But Protestantism also spread for political reasons — it offered princes a legitimate excuse to repudiate bishops, to eliminate a competing source of authority in their domain, and to consolidate their power.[27] It spread for eco-

19. *See* TODD, LUTHER, *supra* note 8, at 228-41 (describing Luther's return to Wittenberg and authorities' fear that to arrest him might "spark off an uprising").

20. BAINTON, REFORMATION, *supra* note 9, at 147-48.

21. *Compare id.* at 77-79 (describing Lutherans, Calvinists, and Anabaptists as the three main types) *with* SPITZ, *supra* note 3, at 173-74 (denying that Anabaptists were "a significant third force in the Reformation," although conceding their "long-term importance").

22. On the spread of Lutheranism, see BAINTON, REFORMATION, *supra* note 9, at 141-59. For a succinct introduction to Luther's teachings, see SPITZ, *supra* note 3, at 76-88.

23. For the spread of Calvinism, see BAINTON, REFORMATION, *supra* note 9, at 160-82. For Calvin's teachings, see SPITZ, *supra* note 3, at 223-27.

24. On the Anabaptists, see generally BAINTON, REFORMATION, *supra* note 9, at 95-109; WILLIAM ESTEP, THE ANABAPTIST STORY (rev. ed. 1975); SPITZ, *supra* note 3, at 166-74; GEORGE HUNTSTON WILLIAMS, THE RADICAL REFORMATION (1962). For a collection of Anabaptist and other radical writings from the 1520s, see THE RADICAL REFORMATION (Michael G. Baylor, ed., 1991).

25. On Anglicanism as a "middle way" or compromise, see BAINTON, REFORMATION, *supra* note 9, at 183-210; SPITZ, *supra* note 3, at 262-67.

26. *See* BAINTON, REFORMATION, *supra* note 9, at 12-21 (summarizing the secularization and corruption of the Church); TODD, REFORMATION, *supra* note 4, at 244 (arguing that the Reformation was "primarily a religious event, something which happened because large numbers of men entertained or did not entertain particular religious beliefs," and that various secular causes were merely the non-essential occasions for religious change); TUCHMAN, *supra* note 9, at 51-126 (reviewing the papal follies from 1470 to 1530). On the emotional appeal of Protestantism, see STEVEN OZMENT, THE REFORMATION IN THE CITIES 47-120 (1975).

27. *See* BAINTON, REFORMATION, *supra* note 9, at 156 (concluding that the spread of

nomic reasons — local money would not have to be sent to Rome, and local princes could seize the lands of monasteries, convents, and bishops.[28] It spread for dynastic and sexual reasons — Henry VIII in England needed a legitimate male heir, and he wanted to marry his mistress, but the Pope would not cooperate.[29]

In the Peace of Augsburg, Catholics and Lutherans reached an accommodation within the Holy Roman Empire.[30] Each ruler in the empire would choose the religion of his realm; all his subjects would have to conform or emigrate. The historian Will Durant has written that "Protestantism was nationalism extended to religion."[31] Protestantism was more than that, but that is surely part of what it was. The same nationalist forces were at work in countries that remained Catholic, and Catholic Kings established large measures of control over national churches with significant independence from Rome.[32] It is revealing of the relative importance of religious and secular loyalties that in 1527 an army of the Catholic Emperor Charles V sacked Rome, looted the Vatican, and held the Pope for ransom.[33]

The principle of Augsburg, and the de facto rule throughout Europe, was *"cuius regio, eius religio"* — whose the rule, his the religion.[34] This principle made the State supreme over fundamental religious choices, and to the extent it could be enforced, it required State suppression of minority faiths and made the population of each state religiously uniform. The logical extreme of this principle was Erastianism, or State supremacy over the established Church,[35] and England and some of the Lutheran states in Germany reached

Lutheranism to Scandinavia was primarily motivated by politics); WILL DURANT, THE REFORMATION 438-41 (1957) (summarizing the political and economic forces that propelled Protestantism).

28. For accounts of seizures of property, see DURANT, *supra* note 27, at 439-40 (seizures of church buildings and land in Germany), 563-78 (seizures of English monasteries), 625 (seizures of monastic lands in Sweden); G. R. ELTON, REFORM AND REFORMATION: ENGLAND, 1509-1558, at 230-49 (1977) (detailing seizure of the English monasteries). Luther's lieutenant, Philip Melanchthon, complained that "[u]nder cover of the Gospel the princes were only intent on the plunder of the churches." DURANT, *supra* note 27, at 440.

29. BAINTON, REFORMATION, *supra* note 9, at 185-91; *see also* SPITZ, *supra* note 3, at 119-20 (reporting that Luther secretly authorized a bigamous marriage for a Lutheran prince); DURANT, *supra* note 27, at 449 (telling the same story with somewhat different emphasis).

30. BAINTON, REFORMATION, *supra* note 9, at 155; SPITZ, *supra* note 3, at 122-23.

31. DURANT, *supra* note 27, at 457.

32. *See id.* at 141-42.

33. SPITZ, *supra* note 3, at 116; TUCHMAN, *supra* note 9, at 121-24.

34. SPITZ, *supra* note 3, at 122.

35. *See* BAINTON, REFORMATION, *supra* note 9, at 236-38 (outlining the extent of Erastianism in England). The name comes from the Swiss theologian Thomas Erastus.

this extreme.[36] But ruler's choice did not inevitably lead to Erastianism; the State might give more or less independence to the Church that it established. Calvinists avoided Erastianism; Calvin developed a theory of Church and State as separate and independent entities with separate responsibilities, and no individual could hold both religious and political positions.[37] But this was hardly separation of church and state:[38] the State enforced religious uniformity,[39] and when the Puritans developed their democratic version of this model, only members of the established church could vote or hold political office.[40]

Of course, religious uniformity could not always be enforced. Success depended on the number of religious dissenters, the strength of the government, the relative determination of government and dissenters, and the ease or difficulty of emigration. German states remained religiously uniform into the nineteenth century,[41] perhaps because emigration to another German state was relatively easy. In France, the Edict of Nantes proclaimed toleration for Calvinists in 1598, ending a generation of civil war, executions, and reciprocal assassinations in the failed pursuit of uniformity.[42] But in 1685 Louis XIV revoked the Edict and actively persecuted Protestants, driving many of them out of France and many more into real or feigned conversions.[43] Political and religious developments fueled a demand for persecution at that time; the increased power of the central government made it possible.

In Spain and Italy, reform movements flourished briefly before the Inqui-

36. *See* SPITZ, *supra* note 3, at 362-63 (describing arrangements such as city council control of local churches in Germany and royal control of the church in England). For more on England, see *infra* text accompanying notes 57-60.

37. *See* WILLIAM J. BOUWSMA, JOHN CALVIN: A SIXTEENTH-CENTURY PORTRAIT 204 (1988); SPITZ, *supra* note 3, at 363; John Witte, Jr., *How to Govern a City on a Hill: The Early Puritan Contribution to American Constitutionalism*, 39 EMORY L.J. 41, 55 (1990).

38. *See* John Witte, Jr., *Moderate Religious Liberty in the Theology of John Calvin*, in RELIGIOUS LIBERTY IN WESTERN THOUGHT, *supra* unnumbered note at the start of this article (explaining that Calvin's approach differed vastly from the modern American idea of separation of church and state).

39. BOUWSMA, *supra* note 37, at 211-13; *see* Witte, *supra* note 37, at 56 (describing Massachusetts laws requiring Sabbath observance and church attendance, and forbidding blasphemy and idolatry).

40. Witte, *supra* note 37, at 59, 62.

41. *See* SPITZ, *supra* note 3, at 122.

42. For a summary of incidents preceding the Edict, see BAINTON, REFORMATION, *supra* note 9, at 162-72. On the French experience to the mid-1550s, see SPITZ, *supra* note 3, at 192-203.

43. BAINTON, REFORMATION, *supra* note 9, at 172; ANDREW LOSSKEY, LOUIS XIV AND THE FRENCH MONARCHY 217-28 (1994).

sitions vigorously and effectively suppressed them.[44] But neither the Inquisition nor thousands of death sentences from the Duke of Alba's irregular secular tribunal could stop reform in the Low Countries, where Calvinism and Dutch nationalism united in resistance to Catholicism and Spanish rule.[45] The ultimate solution in the Low Countries was territorial division, the creation of what is now the Netherlands (Protestant) and Belgium (Catholic).[46]

In Germany, the Peace of Augsburg lasted more or less from 1555 to 1618, finally collapsing at the outbreak of the Thirty Years War.[47] The war began with a wonderfully named incident, the Defenestration of Prague (from "fenestra," meaning "window"[48]), the throwing-out-the-window of Prague.[49] Local representatives threw two emissaries of the Emperor out a second story window; with religious and political tensions already high, that act sparked a war that lasted thirty years and eventually involved most of Europe. In general, subject to the conflicting political interests of each ruler, the war pitted Catholic states against Protestant states.[50] But the decisive intervention came when Catholic France allied with Protestant Sweden against the Catholic Emperor, thereby fatally weakening France's traditional enemy Spain, and illustrating once again that the needs of the State were more important than the needs of the Church.[51]

B. England

Of course to the American Founders, the English experience was most salient, and I want to review that experience in greater detail. An exhaustive French history of the Reformation concludes a nation-by-nation account with the statement that "[a]mong all the countries that were divided by the Reformation, . . . England comes in last so far as tolerance is concerned."[52] It

44. *See* BAINTON, REFORMATION, *supra* note 9, at 131-40; PETERS, *supra* note 14, at 95, 107, 110-11; SPITZ, *supra* note 3, at 233-35.

45. *See* WILLIAM S. MALTBY, ALBA: A BIOGRAPHY OF FERNANDO ALVAREZ DE TOLEDO, THIRD DUKE OF ALBA, 1507-1582 at 153-58 (1983) (concluding that the Council of Troubles condemned nearly 9000 to death, but executed only 1083, the rest having fled the country).

46. BAINTON, REFORMATION, *supra* note 9, at 173-78.

47. *See id.* at 155.

48. OXFORD ENGLISH DICTIONARY 670 (compact ed. 1971).

49. *See* GEOFFREY PARKER, THE THIRTY YEARS' WAR 48-49 (1984).

50. *Id.* at 82.

51. *See id.* at 148-61. For a table showing the participation of 17 European states, and the side or sides they fought on from time to time, see *id.* at 155.

52. JOSEPH LECLER, TOLERATION AND THE REFORMATION 493 (1960). The formula-

is far beyond the scope of my research to accept or reject this claim, but certainly it is plausible. Another fact seems relatively clear: the State dominated the Reformation in England to a greater extent than anywhere else in Europe. Causation is speculative, but it seems reasonable to believe that the State's dominance at least contributed to the duration and severity of religious conflict in England.

Henry VIII authored a pamphlet refuting Luther, and in 1521, the Pope rewarded him with the title Defender of the Faith.[53] Elizabeth II claims that title still. But by the later 1520s, Henry was in an escalating feud with the Catholic Church over the Pope's refusal to annul his marriage to Catherine of Aragon.[54] That marriage had produced no son who survived infancy, Catherine was at the limits of child-bearing age, and Henry had long since abandoned her bed.[55] The Pope would likely have bent doctrine to accommodate Henry and save England for the Church, but for the inconvenient fact that Catherine was the aunt of Charles V — Emperor and King of Spain, with the military power to sack Rome — and Charles loomed much larger than Henry in the Pope's political calculations.[56]

By a series of statutes in the 1530s, Parliament gave Henry sole power to appoint bishops,[57] enacted that Henry was sovereign over Church and State in England,[58] required all bishops to swear oaths acknowledging his supremacy,[59] and gave civil commissioners jurisdiction over heresy trials.[60] Royal advisers and popular pamphleteers contended to push Henry and England to-

---

tion seems designed to exclude those countries where the Reformation never became a substantial force, such as Spain and Italy.

53. BAINTON, REFORMATION, *supra* note 9, at 192; SPITZ, *supra* note 3, at 246.

54. BAINTON, REFORMATION, *supra* note 9, at 185-91.

55. *Id.* at 186; ANTONIA FRASER, THE WIVES OF KING HENRY VIII 92-93, 151-52 (1992). On the strongly felt need for a son and not just daughters, see ELTON, *supra* note 28, at 104-05, 178-79; MACKIE, *supra* note 14, at 325.

56. BAINTON, REFORMATION, *supra* note 9, at 187-88; ELTON, *supra* note 28, at 107; TUCHMAN, *supra* note 9, at 120.

57. Ecclesiastical Appointments Act (The Absolute Restraint of Annates, Election of Bishops, and Letters Missive Act), 1534, 25 Hen. 8, ch. 20 (Eng.), *reprinted in* DOCUMENTS ILLUSTRATIVE OF ENGLISH CHURCH HISTORY 201, 204-06 (Henry Gee & William J. Hardy eds., 1896) [hereinafter DOCUMENTS ILLUSTRATIVE].

58. Supremacy Act, 1534, 26 Hen. 8, ch. 1 (Eng.), *reprinted in* DOCUMENTS ILLUSTRATIVE, *supra* note 57, at 243, 243-44.

59. Ecclesiastical Appointments Act, 1534, 25 Hen. 8, ch. 20 (Eng.), *reprinted in* DOCUMENTS ILLUSTRATIVE, *supra* note 57, at 207.

60. Six Articles Act, 1539, 31 Hen. 8, ch. 14 (Eng.), *reprinted in* DOCUMENTS ILLUSTRATIVE, *supra* note 57, at 303, 307-14. For summaries of these and related statutes, see MACKIE, *supra* note 14, at 349-60.

ward or away from genuine Protestantism.[61] The Protestants made some progress, but Henry's theology remained predominantly Catholic except for papal supremacy.[62] His break with Rome was not based on religious differences; he persecuted those who challenged his takeover of the Church or the validity of his second marriage and also those who challenged Catholic doctrine on other grounds.[63] Many victims were executed, Thomas More the most famous among them.[64]

The Pope proclaimed Henry a heretic, placed England under interdict, released all English subjects from their allegiance to the Crown, and commanded them and all Christian princes to depose Henry.[65] It had little effect; power was in the State and not in the Church. Catholic sovereigns on the continent refused to let the Church promulgate the interdict in their realms.[66] The claimed power of Popes to interfere with Kings was a dangerous doctrine indeed, and Catholic Kings would not publicize it to their subjects.

Henry had quickly and successfully established the Erastian model in England; State dominance in religious matters was thereafter widely assumed. But religious battles for control of the State were just beginning. Few on either side had yet grasped the idea of tolerance.[67] Equally important, if the State controls religion, then religions must fight for control of the State. Protestant-Catholic conflict was a major part of English politics for two hundred years, and even today, economic and political conflict in Ulster largely follows Protestant-Catholic lines.[68]

61. For a summary, see SPITZ, *supra* note 3, at 236-49, 262-67. For a detailed account of every ebb and flow of the Protestant tide, *see generally* ELTON, *supra* note 28.

62. *See* Six Articles Act, 1539, 31 Hen. 8, ch. 14 (Eng.), *reprinted* in DOCUMENTS ILLUSTRATIVE, *supra* note 57, at 303 (giving firmly Catholic answers to six disputed questions of faith, and declaring contrary answers heretical). For analysis, see ELTON, *supra* note 28, at 287-88.

63. BAINTON, REFORMATION, *supra* note 9, at 198-99.

64. *See* ELTON, *supra* note 28, at 128-29, 180-81, 191-94, 293 (recounting executions of both leaders and followers from both the Protestant and Catholic factions); MACKIE, *supra* note 14, at 361-63 (describing the executions of Sir Thomas More, Cardinal Fisher, a charismatic woman who prophesied the King's death if he divorced Catherine, and the followers of this woman).

65. DURANT, *supra* note 27, at 558.

66. *Id.*

67. For the exceptions, see HENRY KAMEN, THE RISE OF TOLERATION (1967) (recounting the history of this period with emphasis on those individuals and groups who urged toleration).

68. *See generally* J. BOWYER BELL, THE IRISH TROUBLES: A GENERATION OF VIOLENCE 1967-1992, at 1-57 (1993) (surveying the social divisions in Northern Ireland on the eve of the current "Troubles"); BRENDAN O'LEARY & JOHN MCGARRY, THE POLITICS OF ANTAGO-

Under Henry's son Edward VI, and Thomas Cranmer as Archbishop of Canterbury, the Church of England became more theologically Protestant.[69] Cranmer promulgated the Book of Common Prayer, and the Acts of Uniformity required all persons to worship at services conducted in that form and no other.[70] Only two heretics were burned in Edward's reign, but many Catholics were imprisoned, and priests who adhered to the old forms or doctrines were removed from office.[71]

Edward died in 1553 at the age of fifteen.[72] His regents attempted to crown Henry's Protestant great niece, Lady Jane Grey;[73] but Parliament, the people, and a large majority of those with troops to command rallied round Edward's half-sister Mary Tudor, Catherine's daughter, a Catholic and the rightful heir.[74] She initially proclaimed toleration,[75] but within a year, she had forbidden the Protestant worship service[76] and ordered the suppression of heresy.[77] After her plans to marry Philip of Spain provoked an unsuccessful insurrection,[78] or perhaps merely as soon as she had the means at hand,[79]

NISM: UNDERSTANDING NORTHERN IRELAND 54-180 (1993) (tracing the religious and ethnic basis for the conflict from British colonization in the seventeenth century to the renewed violence following the breakdown of British hegemony in the 1960s).

69. *See* BAINTON, REFORMATION, *supra* note 9, at 199-203; MACKIE, *supra* note 14, at 507-22; TODD, REFORMATION, *supra* note 4, at 329-37.

70. First Edwardine Act of Uniformity, 1549, 2 & 3 Ed. 6, ch. 1 (Eng.), *reprinted in* DOCUMENTS ILLUSTRATIVE, *supra* note 57, at 358; Second Edwardine Act of Uniformity, 1552, 5 & 6 Ed. 6, ch. 1 (Eng.), *reprinted in* DOCUMENTS ILLUSTRATIVE, *supra* note 57, at 369.

71. DURANT, *supra* note 27, at 585.

72. MACKIE, *supra* note 14, at 526.

73. For a full account, *see generally* MARY LUKE, THE NINE DAYS QUEEN: A PORTRAIT OF LADY JANE GREY (1986).

74. *See* MACKIE, *supra* note 14, at 526-30 (describing Mary's ascension to the throne). For an account of Mary's reign, *see generally* D. M. LOADES, THE REIGN OF MARY TUDOR: POLITICS, GOVERNMENT, AND RELIGION IN ENGLAND, 1553-1558 (1979).

75. *See* Queen Mary's First Proclamation About Religion, 1553, *reprinted in* DOCUMENTS ILLUSTRATIVE, *supra* note 57, at 373, 373-74 (proclaiming that, though she would prefer all of her subjects to be Catholic, she would not compel them to be so at this time).

76. Mary's First Act of Repeal, 1553, 1 Mary, stat. 2, ch. 2 (Eng.), *reprinted in* DOCUMENTS ILLUSTRATIVE, *supra* note 57, at 377, 379 (forbidding any form of worship service other than that "most commonly used, ministered, and frequented in the said last year of the reign of the said late King Henry VIII").

77. Injunctions of Queen Mary, 1554, *reprinted in* DOCUMENTS ILLUSTRATIVE, *supra* note 57, at 380, 381.

78. MACKIE, *supra* note 14, at 536-40. The causal connection is asserted in DURANT, *supra* note 27, at 593.

79. *See* MACKIE, *supra* note 14, at 540-42, 549 ("[F]rom the very first she took it to be her

she became a far more vigorous persecutor than Henry had ever been; she is remembered as Bloody Mary.[80] Some three hundred Protestants were executed in her five years on the throne, including Cranmer and the other Protestant leaders.[81] But the persecutions appear to have alienated far more people than they intimidated.[82]

Mary was succeeded by her half-sister Elizabeth, a Protestant, in 1558.[83] Elizabeth's first Parliament reinstated the Book of Common Prayer and the Act of Uniformity.[84] Failure to attend the Anglican worship was punishable by fine, attendance at the Catholic Mass by fine and imprisonment.[85] Any person who converted to Catholicism committed a capital offense, as did any Catholic priest who remained in England.[86] Enforcement waxed and waned with political circumstance through Elizabeth's reign and through most of the next century.[87] For their part, Catholics produced a large body

---

duty to restore England to the bosom of Rome."); *see also* ELTON, *supra* note 28, at 383 ("Mary's desire to do away at once with the abominations of heresy and schism had to bow before the legal and political difficulties.").

80. DURANT, *supra* note 27, at 600.

81. *See* BAINTON, REFORMATION, *supra* note 9, at 204-06 (reporting 288 burnings and numerous Protestant deaths in prison during Mary's reign); ELTON, *supra* note 28, at 382-89 (describing the "exceptionally bloody" persecution under Mary); MACKIE, *supra* note 14, at 549-53 (reviewing the persecution with special attention to the more famous martyrs); SPITZ, *supra* note 3, at 275-76 (emphasizing Cranmer's martyrdom). For the classic account, *see generally* JOHN FOXE, FOXE'S BOOK OF MARTYRS (G. A. Williamson ed., 1965) (originally published in 1563 as ACTS AND MONUMENTS OF MATTERS MOST SPECIAL AND MEMORABLE HAPPENING IN THE CHURCH, ESPECIALLY IN THE REALM OF ENGLAND).

82. *See* ELTON, *supra* note 28, at 387-89 (describing the persecutions as a "monumentally disastrous mistake"); LOADES, *supra* note 74, at 333-34 ("[T]he persecutions failed, and could be seen by contemporaries to be failing."); MACKIE, *supra* note 14, at 560 ("Mary left . . . people disgusted with the faith that had kindled the fires of Smithfield.").

83. BAINTON, REFORMATION, *supra* note 9, at 206. For an account of Elizabeth's reign, *see generally* J. B. BLACK, THE REIGN OF ELIZABETH 1558-1603 (2d ed. 1959).

84. Act of Uniformity, 1559, 1 Eliz., ch. 2 (Eng.), *reprinted in* DOCUMENTS ILLUSTRATIVE, *supra* note 57, at 458.

85. BLACK, *supra* note 83, at 184.

86. *See* Act Against Jesuits and Seminarists, 1585, 27 Eliz., ch. 2 (Eng.), *reprinted in* DOCUMENTS ILLUSTRATIVE, *supra* note 57, at 485 (ordering all priests to leave England within 40 days of the Act's proclamation); *see also* BLACK, *supra* note 83, at 185 (detailing the severe sanctions against Catholic priests during Elizabeth's reign).

87. *See* BLACK, *supra* note 83, at 185-86 (summarizing the scope and motives of anti-Catholic persecution by Elizabeth's government); GODFREY DAVIES, THE EARLY STUARTS 1603-1660, at 204-14 (2d ed. 1959) (describing "fitful" and "intermittent" enforcement of anti-Catholic laws under James I, Charles I, and Cromwell, with fewer than 60 executions in 57 years).

of teaching about how far one could feign Protestantism without committing sin.[88]

Elizabeth never married. For the first thirty years of her reign, the heir to the throne was her cousin Mary Stuart, Mary Queen of Scots.[89] This Mary too was Catholic, the youthful widow of a King of France, and Queen in her own right of Protestant Scotland; she had abdicated her throne and fled to England in 1568, throwing herself on Elizabeth's mercy.[90] Elizabeth held Mary as a prisoner, under gentle conditions in country estates, unwilling to kill her and afraid to set her free.[91] Mary's continued life was a threat to Elizabeth's, because the assassination of Elizabeth would restore a Catholic to the throne, and any Catholic in Europe might be tempted to act on the knowledge.[92] Finally, in 1587, Elizabeth had Mary executed for treason, on charges of plotting against the life of the Queen.[93] Now the heir to the throne was Mary's son James, who had been separated from his mother in infancy and raised as a Scots Calvinist.[94]

Philip II, King of Spain and widower of Mary Tudor, responded to Mary Stuart's execution by finally launching the Spanish Armada.[95] If England could not be restored to the Church by succession, it must be restored by force. Besides, England was a rich prize, and Philip would have the King of France surrounded.[96] But bad weather and English sailing skill destroyed the Armada.[97] It is revealing that many English Catholics fought valiantly for their

---

88. *See* ROBERT E. RODES, LAW AND MODERNIZATION IN THE CHURCH OF ENGLAND: CHARLES II TO THE WELFARE STATE 81-85 (1991) (summarizing these casuistry books).

89. GARRETT MATTINGLY, THE ARMADA 6 (1959).

90. *See* BAINTON, REFORMATION, *supra* note 9, at 181-82 (discussing the Protestant opposition to Mary in Scotland); BLACK, *supra* note 83, at 108-10 (noting Elizabeth's support of Mary's right to the Scottish throne); WILL DURANT & ARIEL DURANT, THE AGE OF REASON BEGINS 110-24 (1961) (reviewing Mary's arrival, reign, and flight from Scotland).

91. *See* BLACK, *supra* note 83, at 374-75 (discussing the reasons for and conditions of Mary's imprisonment).

92. *See id.* at 376-77 (noting that the Pope had authorized assassination of heretic rulers); MATTINGLY, *supra* note 89, at 6-7 (noting public demand for Mary's death).

93. *See* BLACK, *supra* note 83, at 379-87 (reviewing the "overwhelming, irrefutable" evidence of Mary's guilt); MATTINGLY, *supra* note 89, at 1-5 (telling the story of Mary's execution).

94. BLACK, *supra* note 83, at 389.

95. *See* MATTINGLY, *supra* note 89, at 69, 80-81 (noting that news of Mary's death reached Philip on March 23, 1587, and that a flurry of orders and correspondence for the Armada was issued on March 31).

96. On Philip's mixed motives, see BLACK, *supra* note 83, at 389-91; MATTINGLY, *supra* note 89, at 79-81.

97. The best account is MATTINGLY, *supra* note 89, and a summary can be found in BLACK, *supra* note 83, at 389-405.

Protestant Queen, despite her suppression of their worship.[98] They might have preferred an English Catholic on the throne, and a Catholic majority in Parliament, but they were Englishmen, with no desire for a Spanish conquest.

By the time of Elizabeth's death in 1603, England was irretrievably Protestant, and most Catholics accepted the fact.[99] But some on both sides continued to believe that to control the religion of the Crown would be to control the religion of the country, and the Catholic population contained extremists who had not given up. In 1605, five Catholics dug a tunnel and placed thirty tons of gunpowder under the Houses of Parliament, planning to blow it up on opening day, when the King and all his ministers would be in attendance.[100] The plot was revealed and the plotters were executed. The plotter actually found in the chamber with the gunpowder was Guy Fawkes, and England still celebrates Guy Fawkes Day on November 5.[101]

But the Catholics were no longer the most serious threat to Anglican dominance. There were also the Puritans, English Calvinists who viewed the Church of England as far too Catholic. They too rejected the Uniformity Acts and the Book of Common Prayer. In 1593, Parliament enacted two parallel statutes, the Act Against Puritans[102] and the Act Against Recusants[103] (the term for Catholics who refused to attend the Anglican service). Throughout the reigns of James I and Charles I, intra-Protestant conflict steadily escalated, culminating in civil war.[104]

---

98. BLACK, *supra* note 83, at 389.

99. *See id.* at 451-57 (reviewing the growth among Catholic priests of a movement to make some accommodation with the government); CHRISTOPHER HILL, GOD'S ENGLISHMAN: OLIVER CROMWELL AND THE ENGLISH REVOLUTION 14-15 (1970) (arguing that the security of Protestant dominance was prerequisite to the intra-Protestant conflict of the next century).

100. *See* DAVIES, *supra* note 87, at 8; TRIAL OF GUY FAWKES AND OTHERS (1991) (Donald Carswell, ed., 1934) [hereinafter TRIAL] (reprinting the extant records of the trial of the conspirators, with an introduction that summarizes the known and disputed facts).

101. *Guy Fawkes,* in ACADEMIC AMERICAN ENCYCLOPEDIA (Grolier Electronic Publishing 1991). My English friends assure me that the holiday has lost any serious content; it has become the equivalent of Halloween. Trial, *supra* note 100, at 1. That is not the case with annual commemorations of the Battle of the Boyne, a 1690 battle between Protestant and Catholic armies in Ireland. See GEORGE CLARK, THE LATER STUARTS 1660-1714, at 306-08 (2d ed. 1965) (discussing the battle). The Battle of the Boyne is still enthusiastically celebrated in Northern Ireland. Bell, *supra* note 68, at 50-51.

102. Act Against Puritans, 1593, 35 Eliz., ch. 1 (Eng.), *reprinted in* DOCUMENTS ILLUSTRATIVE, *supra* note 57, at 492.

103. Act Against Recusants, 1593, 35 Eliz., ch. 2, *reprinted in* DOCUMENTS ILLUSTRATIVE, *supra* note 57, at 498.

104. *See generally* ROBERT ASHTON, THE ENGLISH CIVIL WAR: CONSERVATISM AND REVOLUTION 1603-1649 (2d ed. 1989) (assessing the Civil War and its causes); DAVIES, *supra*

The English Civil War of the 1640s was partly political and economic, partly religious. It was for the rights of Parliament and the middle class against Stuart absolutism and the hereditary aristocracy, but it was also Puritans against Anglicans, Catholics, and Scots Presbyterians. The religious causes were inextricably linked with the others;[105] arguably the religious causes dominated.[106] One of the royalist slogans was "No bishop, no king," the point being that Puritan demands for abolition of bishops would lead in time to abolition of the monarchy as well.[107] Charles I was married to a Catholic daughter of the King of France, because pursuit of strategic alliances through royal intermarriage had outweighed religious considerations for his Protestant father. But a Catholic Queen rendered the royal family suspect just as the high church Anglicans were retreating from some Calvinist doctrines, especially predestination. Puritans accused the royal family and the leading bishops of reintroducing "popery."[108] And in the end, when the victorious Puritans attempted to negotiate a settlement with their captured King, it was the religious issues that could not be resolved.[109]

Charles I lost his head,[110] and Oliver Cromwell ruled England for a decade.[111] Under Cromwell the Puritan worship service was established, but the laws requiring attendance were repealed, and at least in England the Puritans made only limited efforts to enforce the prohibitions on Catholic and Anglican services.[112] But they vigorously enforced their Sabbath laws and other moral legislation, alienating the populace in the attempt.[113] Catholics fared

---

note 87, at 1-156 (tracing English history from the accession of James I to the execution of Charles I).

105. *See generally* HILL, *supra* note 99, at 13-34 (summarizing the 40 years prior to the Civil War).

106. *See* John Morrill, *The Religious Context of the English Civil War,* 34 ROYAL HIST. SOC'Y TRANS. (5th Series) 155, 178 (1984) ("The English Civil War was not the first European Revolution; it was the last of the Wars of Religion."); *see also* ASHTON, *supra* note 104, at 98-99 (accepting Morrill's conclusion).

107. THOMAS J. CURRY, THE FIRST FREEDOMS: CHURCH AND STATE IN AMERICA TO THE PASSAGE OF THE FIRST AMENDMENT 2 (1986); DAVIES, *supra* note 87, at 70-71.

108. *See* DAVIES, *supra* note 87, at 57-60, 68-74 ("[M]ost Englishmen continued to believe that the restoration of popery was an ever present threat."); HILL, *supra* note 99, at 26-27, 32 (noting Charles's unwillingness to intervene in the Thirty Years War, and the Catholicizing influence of Archbishop Laud, Queen Henrietta, and other Catholics at court).

109. ASHTON, *supra* note 104, at 337-39.

110. *Id.* at 3; DAVIES, *supra* note 87, at 156-59.

111. *See generally* DAVIES, *supra* note 87, at 160-236.

112. *Id.* at 198-204, 210-13; *see* HILL, *supra* note 99, at 121.

113. *See* DAVIES, *supra* note 87, at 304-15 (stating that the measures "imposed a yoke heavier than most Englishmen would bear").

much worse in Ireland, where Cromwell slaughtered priests and massacred the inhabitants of two cities in his vicious reconquest.[114] One of his biographers attributes the different treatment of English and Irish Catholics to the fact that Catholicism no longer seemed a political threat in England, but that it was obviously associated with political rebellion in Ireland.[115]

The Puritan victory was only a military victory by a highly motivated minority, and England never became Puritan.[116] Charles II was restored to the throne shortly after Cromwell's death, after some military maneuvering but without bloodshed, and to general popular acclaim.[117] Charles entered into a secret treaty with Louis XIV, promising to announce his own Catholicism and "reconcile himself with the Church of Rome as soon as the welfare of the kingdom would permit," in exchange for cash payments from France.[118] This Charles, son of Charles I and his Catholic wife, may have been a secret Catholic;[119] more important, he desperately needed the money.[120] But he never performed his end of the bargain; perhaps he rightly judged that the welfare of the kingdom would not permit it.

Parliament and not the King was making religious policy, and Parliament restricted religious liberty in this reign. Quakers were imprisoned in large numbers for violating new restrictions on non-conforming services, and the Test Act of 1672 barred from public office all but Anglicans.[121]

The most bizarre outbreak of persecution was in response to the so-called Popish Plot.[122] The real plot originated with two informants who made wholly fictitious allegations of a Catholic plot to assassinate the King. There is ample evidence that the King himself did not believe the charges, and the principal accuser was convicted of perjury after public opinion subsided. But in the meantime, some thirty-five Catholics were executed for treason and similar crimes. The incident is noteworthy for its use of wholly neutral and secular laws to accomplish a religious persecution.

114. DAVIES, *supra* note 87, at 161-63; HILL, *supra* note 99, at 116-17, 121-22.

115. HILL, *supra* note 99, at 121-22.

116. DAVIES, *supra* note 87, at 314.

117. *Id.* at 251-60.

118. *See* CLARK, *supra* note 101, at 76 (summarizing the treaty of Dover); ANTONIA FRASER, ROYAL CHARLES: CHARLES II AND THE RESTORATION 275-76 (1979) (quoting the treaty).

119. A biographer concludes that any conversion happened late in life, perhaps on his deathbed, FRASER, *supra* note 118, at 149-52, 451-55, although some of her evidence is consistent with the view that Charles's need for secrecy precluded any overt Catholic practice, even in private. What he believed and when he believed it cannot be known.

120. *See* CLARK, *supra* note 101, at 76.

121. *Id.* at 17-27, 80.

122. *See id.* at 93-95.

When Charles died in 1685, the crown passed to his brother James. James was openly Catholic,[123] but the Protestant Parliament acquiesced in his ascension to the throne. England had just been through civil war and regicide; few were eager to repeat the experience. James's daughter Mary was a Protestant married to another Protestant, William of Orange;[124] one Catholic reign could be endured.

James appointed Catholics to high office, raised a royal army with mostly Catholic officers, supported Catholic bishops with royal funds, permitted the founding of new Catholic institutions, and proclaimed toleration by royal decree.[125] His Declaration of Indulgence purported to authorize public worship for all sects and to abolish all test oaths and religious penalties.[126] But this was suspect in its motives (was he really for tolerance, or only for Catholicism?) and unpopular in its policy — Protestants were not ready for tolerance.[127] Perhaps most important, the Declaration asserted an unacceptable claim of royal prerogative to override Acts of Parliament.[128] James prosecuted seven Anglican bishops for refusing to order the Declaration of Indulgence read in the churches, and a jury acquitted.[129] By now King and country were wholly at odds. The last straw came in 1688, when the Queen gave birth to a son who would be raised as a Catholic and would take the crown ahead of Mary.[130]

Leading Englishmen invited William to invade England, and William's army drove James from the throne without a battle.[131] William and Mary were crowned jointly, with William exercising the powers of the office;[132] the

---

123. *Id.* at 117.

124. Lois G. Schwoerer, The Declaration of Rights, 1689, at 108 (1981); see Clark, *supra* note 101, at 126-27. William was nephew and son-in-law to James II, first cousin and husband to Mary. For the Stuart family tree, see Fraser, *supra* note 118, at 6-7.

125. Clark, *supra* note 101, at 121-25.

126. The Declaration of Indulgence, 1687, Patent Roll, 3 James 2, part 3, No. 18, *reprinted in* Documents Illustrative, *supra* note 57, at 641.

127. *See* Clark, *supra* note 101, at 117 ("The attempts of Charles II to bring in general toleration had shown that nothing was more likely to divide the nation."); Will Durant & Ariel Durant, The Age of Louis XIV 291-92 (1963) (summarizing a successful Protestant pamphlet that argued that there could be no lasting tolerance from a Catholic king).

128. *See* Durant and Durant, *supra* note 127, at 291-93.

129. *Id.* at 291-94.

130. Clark, *supra* note 101, at 126-27; Schwoerer, *supra* note 124, at 109.

131. *See* Clark, *supra* note 101, at 133-43 (summarizing the revolution); Stuart E. Prall, The Bloodless Revolution: England 1688, at 89-242 (1972) (describing the reign and overthrow of James II).

132. Bill of Rights, *reprinted in* Documents Illustrative, *supra* note 57, at 645.

winners called it the Glorious Revolution. Parliament enacted a Bill of Rights, which set out a range of civil liberties and parliamentary rights and also provided that no Catholic and no one married to a Catholic could ever inherit the throne of England.[133] Liberty and anti-Catholicism were thus inextricably linked.

The same Parliament enacted full toleration for all Protestants, redeeming a promise to the Protestant dissenters that if they spurned James's Declaration of Indulgence, they would be granted toleration when James was gone.[134] But the Act specifically excluded "any papist or popish recusant whatsoever, or any person that shall deny in his preaching or writing the doctrine of the blessed Trinity."[135] The exclusion of those who denied the Trinity was aimed at Unitarians[136] and was not enforced against the Jews. Cromwell had readmitted the Jews to England,[137] and there have been synagogues in London continuously since 1662.[138]

By 1700, it appeared that the Protestant branch of the Stuart line would die without heirs and that the Catholic branch would again succeed to the throne. Parliament anticipated the impending crisis with the Act of Settlement, naming a German granddaughter of James I, and her Protestant heirs, as the next heirs to the throne of England.[139] Thus did England acquire George I, Elector of Hanover and King of England, a German who rarely spoke English.[140] Better that than a Catholic.

In 1745, the Stuart pretender Bonnie Prince Charlie landed in Scotland and raised the clans to invade England and claim his throne.[141] This doomed venture was a mix of Catholicism, Scots nationalism, and personal ambition for the throne. The last Catholic claimant to the throne of England was defeated, and his army slaughtered on the field at Culloden Moor,[142] 215 years

133. *Id.* at 652-53. *See generally* SCHWOERER, *supra* note 124 (discussing the development and passage of the Declaration of Rights and the Bill of Rights).

134. PRALL, *supra* note 131, at 147, 154.

135. The Toleration Act, 1689, 1 Wm. & Mary ch. 18, *reprinted in* DOCUMENTS ILLUSTRATIVE, *supra* note 57, at 654, 663.

136. *See* KAMEN, *supra* note 67, at 211 (noting that "the penal laws were held to be in force, particularly against Catholics and Unitarians").

137. DAVIES, *supra* note 87, at 214.

138. CLARK, *supra* note 101, at 36.

139. Act of Settlement, 1700, 12 & 13 William 3, ch. 2 (Eng.), *reprinted in* DOCUMENTS ILLUSTRATIVE, *supra* note 57, at 664, 666-67.

140. *See* RAGNHILD HATTON, GEORGE I: ELECTOR AND KING 129-31 (1978).

141. For a full account, *see generally* DAVID DAICHES, CHARLES EDWARD STUART: THE LIFE AND TIMES OF BONNIE PRINCE CHARLIE (1973).

142. *Id.* at 193-219.

after Henry's break with Rome, and within the living memory of the American Founders.

C. The United States

The story of religious conflict in the American colonies, and the emergence of constitutional guarantees of religious liberty, is much better known in the American legal literature,[143] and there is little need to rehearse it here. Suffice it to say that the American colonies repeated European mistakes on a smaller scale. There were established churches in New England and the southern colonies.[144] In New England, religious dissidents such as Roger Williams were expelled. Those who returned, such as Quaker missionaries, were occasionally executed.[145] As late as the 1770s, Virginia imprisoned Baptist preachers for preaching without a license.[146] In both New England and the south, religious minorities were taxed to support the established church.[147]

America also inherited England's fear of Catholicism. Colonists took the occasion of the Glorious Revolution to overthrow royal governors in New England and New York, and Lord Baltimore's Catholic government in Maryland, alleging as part of the justification in each case a fantastic international plot to Catholicize the continent.[148] In 1746, when the news of Culloden Moor reached America, the famous Methodist evangelist George Whitefield preached a sermon of thanksgiving for God's delivering Britain and her colonies from the "abominations of the whore of Babylon."[149] The Declaration of Independence cites the Quebec Act as one of England's dangerous assaults on American liberties;[150] what the Act had done was to protect Catholicism in a

---

143. *See, e.g.,* CURRY, *supra* note 107; LEONARD W. LEVY, THE ESTABLISHMENT CLAUSE (1986); Douglas Laycock, *"Noncoercive" Support for Religion: Another False Claim About the Establishment Clause,* 26 VAL. U.L. Rev. 37 (1991) [hereinafter Laycock, *Noncoercion*]; Douglas Laycock, *"Nonpreferential" Aid to Religion: A False Claim About Original Intent,* 27 WM. & MARY L. REV. 875 (1986); Michael W. McConnell, *The Origins and Historical Understanding of Free Exercise of Religion,* 103 HARV. L. REV. 1409 (1990) [hereinafter McConnell, *Origins*].

144. *See* CURRY, *supra* note 107, at 105-07.

145. *Id.* at 19.

146. *See id.* at 102, 135.

147. *Id.* at 105-07.

148. *See* DAVID S. LOVEJOY, THE GLORIOUS REVOLUTION IN AMERICA 235-88 (1972).

149. George Whitefield, *Sermon VI: Britain's Mercies, and Britain's Duty,* in GEORGE WHITEFIELD, SERMONS ON IMPORTANT SUBJECTS 87, 91 (1832).

150. *See* THE DECLARATION OF INDEPENDENCE para. 22 (U.S. 1776) ("... For abolishing the free System of English Laws in a Neighboring Province, establishing therein an arbitrary

conquered Catholic province.[151] John Jay unsuccessfully proposed to banish Catholics from New York.[152] When Catholics did arrive in large numbers, in the mid-nineteenth century, serious religious conflict ensued. The Protestant Bible controversy led to mob violence and church burnings,[153] a wave of state constitutional amendments forbidding the grant of public funds to sectarian schools,[154] and a failed attempt to amend the federal Constitution.[155] Anti-Catholic bigotry was pervasive for much of American history;[156] an equally vigorous anti-Protestantism was at the core of Catholic teaching.[157]

As late as 1960, John Kennedy's Catholicism was still a serious issue in a Presidential election, but that election also seemed to put the issue to rest.[158] Kennedy successfully addressed the religious issue in a speech to the Greater Houston Ministerial Association, a speech that was filmed and shown repeat-

---

Government, and enlarging its Boundaries, so as to render it at once an Example and fit Instrument for introducing the same absolute Rule into these Colonies. . . ."); *see also* CURRY, *supra* note 107, at 133 (noting that American colonists "reacted to the Quebec Act with frenzied accusations that it imposed tyranny and an establishment of Catholicism and endangered the entire continent").

151. An Act for Making More Effectual Provision for the Government of the Province of Quebec in North America, 1774, 14 Geo. 3, ch. 83, § 5 (Eng.), *reprinted in* 30 PICKERING'S STATS. at 549, 551 (1773) (providing that Quebec citizens may enjoy the "free exercise of religion" of the church of Rome subject to the King's supremacy).

152. CURRY, *supra* note 107, at 162.

153. For a highly condensed account of the Protestant Bible controversy, which collects multiple historical sources, see Laycock, *Noncoercion, supra* note 143, at 50-52 (text at notes 65-78).

154. For a list of these amendments, see CARL ZOLLMAN, AMERICAN CHURCH LAW §§ 65-66, at 78-80 (2d ed. 1933).

155. *See* ANSON P. STOKES, 2 CHURCH AND STATE IN THE UNITED STATES 68-69 (1950) (quoting the Blaine Amendment, which would have codified the Protestant position by authorizing Bible reading in public schools but forbidding public funding of sectarian schools).

156. *See, e.g.,* DAVID H. BENNETT, THE PARTY OF FEAR: FROM NATIVIST MOVEMENTS TO THE NEW RIGHT IN AMERICAN HISTORY *passim* (1988) (providing a detailed index entry for "anti-Catholicism"); Barbara Welter, *From Maria Monk to Paul Blanshard: A Century of Protestant Anti-Catholicism,* in UNCIVIL RELIGION: INTERRELIGIOUS HOSTILITY IN AMERICA 43 (Robert N. Bellah & Frederick E. Greenspahn, eds., 1987) [hereinafter UNCIVIL RELIGION].

157. See Jay P. Dolan, *Catholic Attitudes Toward Protestants,* in UNCIVIL RELIGION, *supra* note 156, at 72 ("[T]he very definition of Catholicism included rejection of Protestantism as an erroneous and thus inferior religion.").

158. *See* Mark A. Noll, *The Eclipse of Old Hostilities Between and the Potential for New Strife Among Catholics and Protestants Since Vatican II,* in UNCIVIL RELIGION, *supra* note 156, at 86, 88.

edly through the campaign.[159] Kennedy won the election, even though 25 percent of Americans had said in a 1958 poll that they opposed a Catholic nominee for President.[160] Kennedy got fewer Protestant votes than a Democrat should have expected, but more Catholic votes;[161] the net effect was to prove that a Catholic was electable. By 1987, the percentage saying they opposed a Catholic nominee for President was down to 8 percent.[162]

Soon after the Kennedy election came the Second Vatican Council, an even bigger turning point in Protestant-Catholic relations. The Council attributed the Reformation and the other great schisms of history to sin on both sides,[163] accepted non-Catholics as fellow Christians with a relationship to the Church and the prospect of salvation,[164] and "exhort[ed] all the Catholic faithful to . . . participate skillfully in the work of ecumenism."[165] Anti-Protestantism largely disappeared from Catholic rhetoric; anti-Catholicism became disreputable on the Protestant side. After nearly five hundred years, the fierce conflicts of the Reformation seemed to have finally played out in the United States.[166]

159. THEODORE H. WHITE, THE MAKING OF THE PRESIDENT 1960, at 259-61, 391-93 (1961) (describing the speech and reprinting the text). The speech is still a powerful statement on behalf of religious liberty and against religious tests for public office. Whether out of conviction or expediency, he committed himself to the "absolute" separation of church and state, to an absolute ban on government funds for religious institutions, and to restrictions on political statements by clergy. *Id.* at 391. Debate whether religious liberty entails these positions of course provokes very different divisions today than it did in 1960.

160. JAMES DAVISON HUNTER, CULTURE WARS 40 (1991).

161. PAUL LOPATTO, RELIGION AND THE PRESIDENTIAL ELECTION 54-59 (1985).

162. *Id.*

163. *Decree on Ecumenism,* in THE DOCUMENTS OF VATICAN II 341, 345 (Walter M. Abbott, S.J., ed., 1966).

164. *Id.; see also Dogmatic Constitution on the Church,* in THE DOCUMENTS OF VATICAN II, *supra* note 163, at 33-34 (acknowledging that Christians not in union with Rome are, even so, "joined with us in the Holy Spirit"). It is perhaps more remarkable that the Council acknowledged the prospect of salvation for Jews, Muslims, and other non-Christian believers in God, and even for "those who, without blame on their part, have not yet arrived at an explicit knowledge of God, but who strive to live a good life, thanks to His grace." *Id.* at 35. This doctrine has become a point of controversy with conservative Protestants who insist that salvation requires faith in Christ. See Resolutions for Roman Catholic and Evangelical Dialogue, reprinted in J. I. Packer, *Crosscurrents Among Evangelicals,* in EVANGELICALS AND CATHOLICS TOGETHER: TOWARDS A COMMON MISSION 147, 158 (Charles Colson & Richard John Neuhaus, eds., 1995) [hereinafter EVANGELICALS AND CATHOLICS TOGETHER].

165. *Decree on Ecumenism, supra* note 163, at 347.

166. *Compare* TODD, REFORMATION, *supra* note 4, at 346 ("Towards the end of the nineteenth century the Reformation gale [in Europe] seemed at last to be blowing itself out.") In Latin America, the conflict may be just beginning.

II. Contemporary Religious Conflict

The pattern of religious conflict in the United States today is in some ways very different from that of the Reformation era. But in some ways the core of the problem remains the same. I begin with an overview of the current situation, even broader than my overview of the Reformation, and then turn to comparisons between the two periods. Not everything in this overview of the present can be proved or even cited to conventional sources; some characterizations are based on personal impressions after working closely for nearly twenty years with people from all points of the spectrum on these issues.

Will Herberg's classic 1955 book, *Protestant, Catholic, Jew,* suggested that the United States had solved the problem of religious conflict, and that it had achieved substantial consensus on religious matters.[167] Herberg saw a "civil religion" with the three principal branches named in his title.[168] His analysis of Protestant-Catholic and Christian-Jewish conflict was right, as the Kennedy election and consequences of Vatican II dramatically confirmed. But he missed another fault line, just below the surface and ready to erupt.

The 1960s introduced a period of dramatic reaction against some of the traditional values of all three faiths: the sexual revolution, the pornography decisions and the emergence of a sexual entertainment industry, the women's movement, the abortion decisions, the gay rights movement, the school-prayer decisions, the drug scene, hippies, the counter-culture, dramatic increases in divorce and illegitimacy, and a general reaction against authority. Mass demonstrations, the civil rights movement, the anti-war movement, and the criminal procedure decisions were less religiously salient, but were equally alienating to many of the social conservatives who were also among the traditionally religious.

All of these developments contributed to the political activation of evangelical Christians and eventually to their successful alliance with other elements of the Reagan coalition;[169] this movement in turn led to a counter reaction by civil liberties organizations, some Jewish organizations, and others

---

167. *See generally* WILL HERBERG, PROTESTANT-CATHOLIC-JEW (rev. ed. 1960).

168. *Id.* at 263. Herberg described the "three equi-legitimate religious communities grounded in the common culture-religion of America" as America's "civic religion." *Id.* at 259.

169. For political science accounts of the religious right's eventual rise to prominence and influence, see MATTHEW C. MOEN, THE TRANSFORMATION OF THE CHRISTIAN RIGHT (1992); MATTHEW C. MOEN, THE CHRISTIAN RIGHT AND CONGRESS (1989); KENNETH D. WALD, RELIGION AND POLITICS IN THE UNITED STATES 182-219 (1987).

who thought that the evangelicals were a serious political threat. The bitter national debates over abortion and gay rights reactivated anti-Catholic feeling, but the basis was no longer Protestantism. The new anti-Catholics were feminists, gay activists, and civil libertarians, and their open hostility was equally directed at evangelical Protestants.[170]

The result is a polarized debate that extends to a wide range of religious liberty issues and also to social issues such as pornography, abortion, feminism, and gay rights.[171] Both sides have mastered the techniques of fundraising and constitutional litigation. Secular civil liberties organizations and Jewish organizations repeatedly line up against evangelical organizations in litigation and in legislative lobbying. Each group attempts to enlist the educational system on its side, so that controversies over education have been one of the most prolific sources of religious liberty litigation. These controversies include religious observance[172] and curricu-

---

170. For examples of anti-Catholicism, see Edward McGlynn Gaffney, Jr., *Hostility to Religion, American Style,* 42 DePaul L. Rev. 263, 279-93 (1992); for a book-length anti-Baptist hate tract, see Arthur Frederick Ide, Evangelical Terrorism: Censorship, Falwell, Robertson and the Seamy Side of Christian Fundamentalism (1986). Fundraising appeals provide frequent examples. *See, e.g.,* Contribution Memorandum from Americans United for Separation of Church and State (1995) ("I agree that we must stop the Christian Coalition, the Roman Catholic hierarchy, and their allies from destroying public education and demolishing the church/state wall.") (on file with the Minnesota Law Review); Edd Doerr, Executive Director, Americans for Religious Liberty, to members and supporters (Oct. 1995) ("Televangelist Pat Robertson's so-called Christian Coalition and its sectarian special interest allies are growing in strength and posing increasingly serious threats to religious freedom, public education, interfaith harmony, and democratic government.") (on file with the Minnesota Law Review). For a much more careful and nuanced argument that religion is a negative force on balance, see Mary Becker, *The Politics of Women's Wrongs and the Bill of "Rights": A Bicentennial Perspective,* 59 U. Chi. L. Rev. 453, 458-86 (1992) ("[R]eligion perpetuates and reinforces women's subordination, and religious freedom impedes reform."). For examination of the theoretical underpinnings of hostility to religion, see Frederick Mark Gedicks, *Public Life and Hostility to Religion,* 78 Va. L. Rev. 671 (1992) (arguing that liberal theory excludes religion from public life); Michael W. McConnell, *"God is Dead and We Have Killed Him!": Freedom of Religion in the Post-modern Age,* 1993 B.Y.U. L. Rev. 163 (arguing that liberalism and post-modernism both exclude religion from public life, reducing religious liberty to a Nietzschean right to "sing, weep, laugh, and mumble" in private).

171. *See generally* Hunter, *supra* note 160 (assessing the contemporary "culture wars").

172. *See, e.g.* Lee v. Weisman, 505 U.S. 577 (1992) (holding that public schools may not offer prayers as part of official high school graduation exercises); Board of Education v. Mergens, 496 U.S. 226 (1990) (holding that student religious clubs may meet on school premises); School Dist. of Abington v. Schempp, 374 U.S. 203 (1963) (holding that public schools may not offer religious exercises in classroom).

lum[173] in the public schools, and financing[174] and regulation[175] of private schools.

There have been important examples of cooperation and compromise, including the Williamsburg Charter,[176] a Joint Statement on Religion in the Public Schools,[177] and the spectacularly successful Coalition for the Free Exercise of Religion, in which religious and civil liberties organizations and liberals and conservatives worked together to enact the Religious Freedom Res-

173. *See generally* WARREN A. NORD, RELIGION AND AMERICAN EDUCATION: RETHINKING A NATIONAL DILEMMA (1995) (reviewing the widespread conflict over how religion should be treated in the public school curriculum, and showing that it is rarely treated at all); George Dent, *Of God and Caesar: The Free Exercise Rights of Public School Students,* 43 CASE W. RES. L. REV. 707 (1993) (arguing for the free exercise right to exempt students from public-school instruction inconsistent with religious beliefs). *See, e.g.,* Brown v. Woodlawn Joint Unified Sch. Dist., 27 F.3d 1373 (9th Cir. 1994) (holding that the Impressions reading series does not establish a religion of witchcraft); Fleischfresser v. Director of Sch. Dist. 200, 15 F.3d 680 (7th Cir. 1994) (rejecting a similar Establishment Clause challenge to the Impressions series); Mozert v. Hawkins County Bd. of Educ., 827 F.2d 1058 (6th Cir. 1987) (holding that parents have no free exercise right to remove their children from elements of public school curriculum that are in conflict with their faith); Coleman v. Caddo Parish Sch. Bd., 635 So.2d 1238 (La. App. 1994) (holding that sex education curriculum can make no moral or ethical judgments).

174. *See, e.g.,* Zobrest v. Catalina Foothills School Dist., 509 U.S. 1 (1993) (holding that deaf student entitled to a sign-language interpreter at public expense may use that interpreter at a church-affiliated private school); Aguilar v. Felton, 473 U.S. 402 (1985) (holding that federally funded remedial instruction cannot be offered on the premises of church-affiliated schools); Lemon v. Kurtzman, 403 U.S. 602 (1971) (holding that public funds may not be used to pay teachers at church-affiliated schools); Miller v. Benson, 68 F.2d 13 (7th Cir. 1995) (per curiam) (deferring issues arising out of voucher plan for education to pending state-court litigation).

175. *See, e.g.,* EEOC v. Kamehameha Schools, 990 F.2d 458 (9th Cir. 1993) (holding that school that hired only Protestant teachers was not sufficiently religious to qualify for exemption from laws against religious discrimination in employment); New Life Baptist Church Academy v. East Longmeadow, 885 F.2d 940, 950-51 (1st Cir. 1989) (collecting cases upholding state regulation to assure minimum educational quality); Kentucky State Bd. for Elem. & Sec. Educ. v. Rudasill, 589 S.W.2d 877 (Ky. 1979) (holding that intrusive state regulation of private schools violated state constitution); State v. Whisner, 351 N.E.2d 750 (Ohio 1976) (holding that pervasive regulation of private schools violated the U.S. Constitution).

176. THE WILLIAMSBURG CHARTER, *reprinted in* 8 J.L. & RELIGION 5 (1990).

177. AMERICAN JEWISH CONGRESS, *et al.,* RELIGION IN THE PUBLIC SCHOOLS: A JOINT STATEMENT OF CURRENT LAW (Apr. 1995). Drafting and endorsing organizations include the American Civil Liberties Union, the Christian Legal Society, the National Association of Evangelicals, the National Council of Churches, People for the American Way, numerous Jewish organizations, numerous denominational Christian organizations, and Muslim and Sikh organizations. *Id.*

toration Act.[178] The Coalition worked because in principle the civil liberties organizations support regulatory exemptions for religiously motivated behavior, and because the Coalition took no position on specific applications of the Act, which would inevitably have provoked disagreement over exempting religious minorities from regulation in pursuit of other issues on the civil liberties agenda. Cooperation on selected issues is important and politically healthy, but polarization has been the more common alignment.

James Davison Hunter's book *Culture Wars*[179] accurately captures much of the new divide. The principal fight is no longer between Catholics and Protestants, or between Christians and Jews, or even between believers and nonbelievers; rather it is between what Hunter calls "orthodox" and "progressive" elements of all these groups.[180] This may just be relabeling of the political split between left and right on social issues, but it has important religious dimensions. In Hunter's terminology, the orthodox remain committed "to an external, definable, and transcendent authority."[181] Usually this transcendent authority is religious, but for culturally conservative nonbelievers, it may be natural law or some other source of moral absolutes.[182] The progressives tend to view truth "as a process, as a reality that is ever unfolding."[183] Religious progressives thus tend to "resymbolize historic faiths according to the prevailing assumptions of contemporary life."[184]

On the "orthodox" side, a clear illustration of Hunter's point is that Catholics and evangelicals are on the same side of many moral issues, and some of them are exploring a more formal alliance,[185] despite deep disagreements and suspicions over theology, liturgy, and church authority[186] and less recognized but measurable differences in ways of thinking about the world.[187] The lead-

178. *See* Douglas Laycock & Oliver S. Thomas, *Interpreting the Religious Freedom Restoration Act,* 73 TEX. L. REV. 209, 210-11 & n.9 (1994) (describing the Coalition and listing its member organizations).

179. HUNTER, *supra* note 160.

180. *Id.* at 42-66; see also Noll, *supra* note 158, at 91-101 (distinguishing "New" and "Old" Protestants and Catholics, roughly corresponding to Hunter's progressives and orthodox within those faiths).

181. HUNTER, *supra* note 160, at 44.

182. *Id.* at 45-46.

183. *Id.* at 44.

184. *Id.* at 44-45.

185. *See generally* EVANGELICALS AND CATHOLICS TOGETHER, *supra* note 164.

186. For the depth of the theological differences, see Packer, *supra* note 164.

187. *See generally* Andrew M. Greeley, *Protestant and Catholic: Is the Analogical Imagination Extinct?,* 54 AM. SOC. REV. 485 (1989) (using survey data to identify a broad array of differences between Catholic and Protestant world views).

ing proponents of the current alliance come from the theologically and socially conservative wings of both Catholicism and Protestantism; with important exceptions, these are the groups who were most suspicious of the Protestant-Catholic rapprochement in the sixties and who attach the greatest importance to theological differences today. But today's alliance between Protestant and Catholic conservatives may not have been possible if the liberals on each side had not made peace a generation ago.

I think that Hunter accurately describes the two principal sides in the culture wars, although he may give insufficient attention to the moderates in the middle. The activists on each side, and the audiences for whom their fundraising letters are tailored, are far more polarized than the bulk of the population; there is substantial diversity both in the middle and within each broadly defined "side."[188] There are even moderate activists; groups such as the National Council of Churches and the Baptist Joint Committee on Public Affairs file briefs first on one side and then on the other.[189]

188. *See* Andrew M. Greeley, *With God on Their Sides,* N.Y. Times Book Rev., Nov. 24, 1991, at 13 (reviewing JAMES D. HUNTER, CULTURE WARS (1991), and concluding that "the American people's reaction to cultural conflicts is much more complex, nuanced, ambiguous and ambivalent than any two-category typology might suggest"). I do not disagree with Greeley's analysis, but I think that Hunter captures *one* important divide of special relevance to the law of religious liberty.

189. *Compare* Brief of National Council of Churches of Christ in the U.S.A. and James E. Andrews as Stated Clerk of the General Assembly of the Presbyterian Church (U.S.A.) as Amici Curiae in Support of Respondents, Board of Education v. Grumet, 512 U.S. 687 (1994) (No. 93-517) (arguing that Establishment Clause precludes deliberate creation of public school district with population all of the same religion) and Brief Amici Curiae of the American Jewish Congress, *et al.,* Lee v. Weisman, 505 U.S. 577 (1992) (No. 90-1014) (arguing that Establishment Clause precludes prayer as part of official program at public school graduation) (joined by Baptist Joint Committee on Public Affairs, National Council of Churches of Christ in the U.S.A., and James E. Andrews as Stated Clerk of the General Assembly of the Presbyterian Church (U.S.A.)); *with* Brief Amicus Curiae of the Christian Legal Society, *et al.,* Zobrest v. Catalina Foothills Sch. Dist., 509 U.S. 1 (1993) (No. 92-94) (arguing that Free Exercise requires, and Establishment Clause does not forbid, public school district to pay for deaf student's sign language interpreter on equal terms at either public or religiously affiliated high school) (joined by National Council of Churches of Christ in the U.S.A.); Brief of Baptist Joint Committee on Public Affairs *et al.,* Board of Education v. Mergens, 496 U.S. 226 (1990) (No. 88-1597) (arguing that Equal Access Act protects, and Establishment Clause does not preclude, right of student prayer club to meet in classrooms at public high school) (joined by National Council of Churches of Christ in the U.S.A., and James E. Andrews as Stated Clerk of the General Assembly of the Presbyterian Church (U.S.A.); Brief of National Council of Churches of Christ in the U.S.A. as Amicus Curiae in Support of Appellant, Jimmy Swaggart Ministries v. Board of Equalization, 493 U.S. 378 (1990) (No. 88-1374) (arguing that Free Exercise Clause precludes taxation of not-for-profit

An important part of the new situation is significant numbers of avowed nonbelievers and of believers whose belief is subordinated to a largely secular view of the world. The historian James Turner has shown that true atheism did not become intellectually possible until the 19th century.[190] The political effects of this development were delayed much longer, but they eventually came. Freud and Dewey gave skeptical foundations to whole disciplines,[191] and evolution and its skeptical interpretations became the subject of popular debate, legislation, litigation, plays, and movies.[192] Modernist versions of Christianity sought to reconcile religious faith with the new developments in science, philosophy, and public values, and eventually came to emphasize good works more than faith.[193] Phillip Johnson is surely right that "millions of people who consider themselves theists . . . have to some extent adopted modernist ways of thinking," by which he means a naturalistic and rationalist worldview that dominates public discourse and excludes or marginalizes supernatural explanations.[194] Johnson argues that this worldview is ultimately

---

sales of books, records, and other media that convey religious messages); Brief of National Council of Churches of Christ in the U.S.A., *et al.,* United States Catholic Conference v. Abortion Rights Mobilization, Inc., 487 U.S. 72 (1988) (No. 87-416) (defending Catholic organizations against penalties for contempt of court, invasive discovery, and attempts to revoke their tax exemptions by private litigation) (joined by Baptist Joint Committee on Public Affairs). I should disclose that I wrote or signed each of these briefs except the one in *Zobrest.*

190. *See generally* James Turner, Without God, Without Creed (1985) (tracing social, religious, and intellectual trends that set the stage for modern atheism).

191. *See generally* John Dewey, A Common Faith (1934) (rejecting all religious claims of supernatural reality, and proposing a religion based on faith in the accumulated values of human civilization); Sigmund Freud, The Future of an Illusion (James Strachey trans., 1961) (first published 1927) (arguing that all religious ideas are creations of human imagination).

192. *See generally* Charles Darwin, On the Origin of Species (1859) (setting out the theory of evolution). *See also* Edwards v. Aguillard, 482 U.S. 578 (1987) (striking down a statute that required the balanced treatment of creation and evolution science in public schools); Epperson v. Arkansas, 393 U.S. 67 (1968) (striking down a statute that forbad teaching of evolution in public schools and universities); Scopes v. State, 289 S.W. 363 (Tenn. 1927) (upholding a statute that forbad the teaching of evolution in public schools). A play based on the Scopes trial, Jerome Lawrence & Robert E. Lee, Inherit the Wind (1955), was made into a movie in 1960 with Spencer Tracy and Gene Kelly, and again in 1988 with Kirk Douglas and Jason Robards. Leonard Maltin's Movie and Video Guide 610 (Leonard Maltin, ed., 1994 ed.).

193. *See* Turner, *supra* note 190, at 141-202.

194. Phillip E. Johnson, Reason in the Balance: The Case Against Naturalism in Science, Law & Education 45 (1995).

inconsistent with theism;[195] it at least makes God a remote abstraction with little relevance to practical affairs.

Johnson's modernists and Hunter's progressives are overlapping but far from identical groups. There are religious progressives for whom God is a real and immediate presence in their lives. They are as committed as the orthodox to carrying out God's will, but they interpret that will differently. Their God may put more emphasis on feeding the hungry, sheltering the homeless, and correcting injustice, and they may conclude (or understand God to now reveal), that the traditional sexual morality of orthodox religion is itself a source of injustice to gays and lesbians, or that the absolute right to life is a source of injustice to women and of unnecessary suffering among the terminally ill. And of course there are devout believers who understand their God to command large elements of both the progressive and orthodox agendas — both the traditional religious concern for the poor and the traditional sexual morality and commitment to life at all stages. There are as many permutations and gradations of belief as there are persons in the population, but it can still be useful to identify and label important sources of agreement and disagreement. Hunter's progressives are identified by the belief that the moral rules of religious tradition are changeable; Johnson's modernists are identified by a worldview in which supernatural interventions are remote or nonexistent.

The more militant progressive secularists are the functional equivalent of a new religious movement, and sometimes the legal equivalent as well. For constitutional purposes, important elements of secularism must be considered religious, because any answer to religious questions must be "religion" within the meaning of the First Amendment. Is there a God? Does He or She care about human beings? Is there an afterlife? Are there supernatural forces at work in the universe? The believer says yes, the humanist manifestos quite explicitly say no,[196] the agnostic says it is impossible to say, and the indiffer-

---

195. *Id.* at 37-38.

196. *See* Paul Kurtz, *et al.,* A Secular Humanist Declaration 18 (1980) ("[W]e find that traditional views of the existence of God either are meaningless, have not yet been demonstrated to be true, or are tyrannically exploitative. . . . In spite of the fact that human beings have found religions to be uplifting and a source of solace, we do not find their theological claims to be true."); *Humanist Manifesto I, reprinted in* Corliss Lamont, The Philosophy of Humanism 285, 286 (7th ed. 1990) ("Humanism asserts that the nature of the universe depicted by modern science makes unacceptable any supernatural or cosmic guarantees of human values."); *Humanist Manifesto II, reprinted in* Lamont, *supra,* at 290, 292-93 ("We find insufficient evidence for belief in the existence of a supernatural. . . . [W]e can discover no divine purpose or providence for the human species. . . . No deity will save us; we must save ourselves. . . . Promises of immortal salvation or fear of eternal damnation are both illusory and harmful.").

ent dismiss the question as utterly irrelevant to anything that matters. The State cannot persecute any of these answers; neither can it establish any of them. State-imposed atheism on the Soviet model would violate any sensible interpretation of the Establishment Clause; persecution of atheists would violate any sensible interpretation of the Free Exercise Clause.

Religious progressives and secular progressives disagree about most matters of theology, but they agree on one important point that can be put in theological terms: no God handed down in eternally unchanging form all of the moral rules associated with traditional religion. On the issue of divine authority for traditional moral values, religious and secular progressives are on the same side.

Characterizing the dispute in religious terms also fits the sociological reality. The culture wars of the last thirty years are very like the battles of the Reformation with a substantial reduction in levels of force. In the Reformation and in our time, a new set of answers to eternal questions became sufficiently widespread to destabilize social arrangements. Then the new answers were the various versions of Protestantism; today the new answers are the various versions of secularism and progressive or modernist religion.

The claim of a culture war is in seeming tension with survey data, which overwhelmingly indicate that overall levels of religious belief and participation are not much changed from earlier generations.[197] So why do so many believers feel under siege? Part of the explanation is that Hunter's religious progressives and Johnson's theistic modernists show up as believers in opinion polls, but are often on the secular side of culture war issues. Part of the explanation is that nonbelievers are disproportionately in elite positions, where they have disproportionate influence on public discourse.

Certainly nonbelief has become respectable among elites; indeed, I have the subjective sense that the burden of justification has shifted, and now the question is whether it is intellectually respectable to believe.[198] I remember reading newspaper stories (before I was in the job market myself, so this was probably in the early sixties) about how it was bad for your corporate career not to attend church — preferably a mainline Protestant church. Today the

---

197. The most systematic collection of data is ANDREW M. GREELEY, RELIGIOUS CHANGE IN AMERICA (1989). For an overview that includes more recent data, see R. Stephen Warner, *Work in Progress toward a New Paradigm for the Sociological Study of Religion in the United States,* 98 AM. J. SOC. 1044, 1048-50 (1993). Some of this data is summarized *infra* at notes 232-245.

198. For a similar view, see Michael Novak, *The Conservative Mood,* 31 SOCIETY 13 (Jan. 1994) ("Increasingly, religion and those who take religion seriously are ridiculed by sophisticated elites.").

career incentives appear to have switched; it is conventional wisdom among believing lawyers that church-affiliated volunteer work should be omitted from resumes, although it appears still to be true that mainline Protestant churches are more acceptable on resumes than evangelical or Catholic churches.[199]

I share Stephen Carter's sense that many in the elite view religion as trivial.[200] Data are hard to come by, but anecdotal evidence abounds.[201] I have heard several colleagues say that religious claims are absurd, ridiculous, irrational, or unworthy of respect. I have never heard a colleague, at any of the three law schools where I have taught, make a religious claim in an academic context. When the student chapter of the Christian Legal Society at The University of Texas needed a speaker, I knew of only three or four church-attending colleagues on a faculty of sixty-five, none in the evangelical mode the students were seeking.

There may well be others; James Lindgren has survey data showing that a substantial majority of law professors profess conventional Christian or Jewish religious views.[202] These numbers are much higher than either he or I would have guessed based on personal experience in several law schools. One inference is that the believers feel obliged to be quiet about it. Toleration and even respect for nonbelievers is a great advance for human liberty. But disrespect and even intolerance of religious belief is an offsetting loss of equal importance.

Commenting on an earlier draft of this article, Michael McConnell suggested that the historical model for this conflict is not the Reformation at all, but the French Revolution. Among the many commitments of the revolu-

199. *See, e.g.,* STEPHEN L. CARTER, THE CULTURE OF DISBELIEF: HOW AMERICAN LAW AND POLITICS TRIVIALIZES RELIGIOUS DEVOTION 7 (1993) (reporting that an executive search firm advised a client to remove such information from his resume). Professor Robert Destro of Catholic University told a similar story at a conference at Marquette University in March 1994.

200. CARTER, *supra* note 199, at 3-15.

201. *See, e.g.,* George M. Marsden, *Religious Professors Are the Last Taboo,* WALL ST. J., Dec. 22, 1993, at A10 (arguing that it is "unacceptable" in many American universities for faculty to state religious views).

202. Lindgren mentioned these data in personal conversation in January, 1996. Publication arrangements are pending. [He apparently never published the data. There is a citation to James Lindgren, *Measuring Diversity* (Nov. 7, 2001) (unpublished manuscript, on file with author), in James Lindgren, *Conceptualizing Diversity in Empirical Terms,* 23 YALE L. & POL'Y REV. 5, 8 n.11 (2005). Some of his data are summarized *id.* at 8-9. For anyone interested in the unpublished manuscript, as of 2009, Lindgren is Professor of Law at Northwestern University.]

tionaries were science, rationalism, naturalistic explanations, intense anti-clericalism, and a short-lived but vigorous and often violent attempt to de-Christianize France.[203] A permanent anti-clerical faction in France was among the Revolution's legacies.[204] The commitment to naturalistic explanations has grown and spread ever since, at least among elites, and modern secularism is often affirmatively hostile to traditional religious belief. I am skeptical of any direct historical connection between the French Revolution and American secularism, but it does seem clear that they share common ancestry in the Enlightenment. Whatever its origins, the conflict between traditional religious believers and those who are fearful of or hostile to traditional belief is one of the central social divides of our time.

The growing influence of secularism does not mean that religion will fade away. This conflict is not likely to end with only secularists, progressives, and theistic modernists remaining; the human need for spiritual explanations runs too deep. Even among those who turn away from traditional faiths, some significant portion turn to a new wave of religions outside the Judeo-Christian tradition. These faiths represent a small fraction of all Americans, but they produce a disproportionate share of all religious liberty litigation, because the larger society has not accommodated their beliefs and practices and because they are often fervent about asserting them. These include so-called cults, such as the Unification Church,[205] the Hare Krishnas,[206] and the Scientologists;[207]

---

203. *See* Emmet Kennedy, A Cultural History of the French Revolution xxiv, 59-76, 145-55, 338-53 (1989) (tracing the sources of the revolutionaries' antipathy to religion and describing the de-Christianizing campaign); *see also* Christopher Hibbert, The Days of the French Revolution 230-33 (1980) (describing the de-Christianizing campaign).

204. *See* Kennedy, *supra* note 203, at 376-77, 379, 384-92 (describing nineteenth-century conflicts between this faction and the Catholic Church).

205. *See, e.g.,* Larson v. Valente, 456 U.S. 228 (1982) (striking down a Minnesota law that used a percentage of contributions from members and non-members to target the Unification Church for special regulation of fund solicitation); Molko v. Holy Spirit Ass'n, 762 P.2d 46 (Cal. 1988) (upholding judgment for fraud and intentional infliction of emotional distress, but not for false imprisonment based on a claim that religious teaching persuaded plaintiffs to remain in Unification Church).

206. *See, e.g.,* International Soc'y for Krishna Consciousness v. Lee, 505 U.S. 672 (1992) (upholding restrictions on solicitation in airport, but striking down restrictions on distribution of leaflets in airport); Heffron v. International Soc'y for Krishna Consciousness, Inc., 452 U.S. 640 (1981) (upholding restrictions on solicitation at state fair).

207. *See, e.g.,* Hernandez v. Commissioner, 490 U.S. 680 (1989) (holding that payments for Scientology auditing are not deductible as charitable contributions absent proof that the IRS discriminated among faiths that charge for religious benefits); Church of Scientology Int'l v. United States Dept. of Justice, 30 F.3d 224 (1st Cir. 1994) (holding that Justice Depart-

the Black Muslims;[208] a new religious assertiveness by American Indians;[209] and the great variety of unorganized spiritualism that goes under the label New Age.

Significant sections of bookstores are devoted to claims of Divine Forces in every human, of multiple planes of existence, and similar claims that are as supernatural and miraculous as anything in traditional religions. On the eve of this lecture, an affiliate of the Book-of-the-Month Club was promoting *The Art of Dreaming* by Carlos Castaneda. This is the latest in a series of books claiming "that ours is just one world in a vast cluster of realities — and that we all have the ability, by using body energy and the 'four gates' of dreams, to cross the boundaries and visit these incredible places."[210] Castaneda has reportedly sold eight million books, and a New York Times columnist has written that he "must be taken seriously as one of the important intellectual forces of our time."[211] Only a trivial number of Americans say that their religion is "New Age,"[212] but that must be because they do not think of it as a religion, or because they syncretically combine their interest in New Age mysticism with elements of more traditional religion. A fifth to nearly half the population reports belief in various supernatural claims associated with New Age — reincarnation, astrology, witchcraft, magical powers, and extrasensory perception.[213]

At least some humanists understand the persistence of spiritual longings; they have been busily trying to fill the functions of religion. Paul Kurtz has

---

ment had not sufficiently justified its refusal to disclose records of investigation of fraud against the Church); Church of Scientology Flag Service Org., Inc. v. City of Clearwater, 2 F.3d 1514 (11th Cir. 1993) (striking down parts of a charitable solicitation ordinance); Wollersheim v. Church of Scientology, 6 Cal. Rptr. 2d 532 (Cal. App. 1992) (remitting part of a judgment for intentional infliction of emotional distress).

208. *See, e.g.,* O'Lone v. Shabazz, 482 U.S. 342 (1987) (upholding prison work schedule that made it impossible for Muslim inmates to attend Friday services).

209. *See, e.g.,* Employment Division v. Smith, 494 U.S. 872 (1990) (refusing to protect right to participate in peyote worship services); Lyng v. Northwest Indian Cemetery Protective Ass'n, 485 U.S. 439 (1988) (refusing to enjoin construction of road through sacred site on public land); Bowen v. Roy, 476 U.S. 693 (1986) (refusing to order government not to use social security number to identify recipient of Aid to Families with Dependent Children).

210. Quality Paperback Club, *Visions of the Spirit* (1994).

211. Ray Walters, *Paperback Talk,* N.Y. TIMES, Jan. 11, 1981, at 35. For the sales figures, see Benjamin Epstein, *The Mystical Man,* L.A. TIMES, Dec. 26, 1995, at E1.

212. See BARRY A. KOSMIN & SEYMOUR P. LACHMAN, ONE NATION UNDER GOD: RELIGION IN CONTEMPORARY AMERICAN SOCIETY 17 (1993) (reporting 12 respondents in a survey of 113,000).

213. Nord, *supra* note 173, at 193 (collecting survey data).

written a secular humanist ethics.[214] Corliss Lamont wrote humanist services for weddings and funerals, with readings from poetry and from carefully selected passages from the Jewish and Christian scriptures.[215] These efforts are entirely appropriate developments of their position; my point is not that the humanists are inconsistent. My point is that they offer express answers to the central questions of religion, directly attacking more traditional answers, and they seek to perform the traditional social functions of religion. The humanists cannot claim a legal status different from any other group answering the same questions, debating the same issues, and performing the same functions.

The Christian right has been claiming unsuccessfully that the schools have established secular humanism.[216] They have lost those suits, and in general that is the right result, but not for the reason most commonly offered. The schools have been winning on the ground that secular humanism is not a religion, which is wrong. They should win on the ground that the schools have not taught secular humanist theology. They have not taught that there is no God and that human reason is all we can rely on.[217] What the schools have taught is moral and social values associated with secular humanism, and also with modernist versions of other religions: reasoned inquiry, individual judgment, tolerance, sexual permissiveness, etc. Schools in a democracy are entitled to teach these values, if that is what the majority wants, just as they are entitled to teach more traditional values if a majority wants that. Church and State have both spoken to morals throughout our history. On moral questions, we argue and we vote; no other solution is possible in a democracy, even though some moral positions turn out to be inconsistent with some theological positions. We can exempt those with religious reasons for noncompliance with particular laws, but general public policy and the operation of public institutions must inevitably be based on the moral decisions of political bodies.

The principle here is that of *Harris v. McRae:* a law that coincides with the moral teachings of some religion does not establish that religion.[218] This

---

214. PAUL KURTZ, FORBIDDEN FRUIT: THE ETHICS OF HUMANISM (1988).

215. CORLISS LAMONT, A HUMANIST FUNERAL SERVICE (2d ed. 1977); CORLISS LAMONT, A HUMANIST WEDDING SERVICE (3d ed. rev. 1972).

216. *See, e.g.,* Smith v. Board of Sch. Comm'rs, 827 F.2d 684 (11th Cir. 1987) (rejecting such a claim); Mary H. Mitchell, *Secularism in Public Education: The Constitutional Issues,* 67 B.U.L. REV. 603 (1987) (analyzing these claims and concluding that secular humanism is a religion but that in most cases, it has not been established).

217. *See supra* note 196 (quoting secular humanist answers to theological questions).

218. 448 U.S. 297, 318-20 (1980) (holding that government policy that accords with the moral teaching of one or more religions does not establish those religions).

is equally true of Catholic moral teaching and secular humanist moral teaching. Constitutional limits on State enforcement of morals are to be found, if at all, in unenumerated rights to autonomy in certain personal decisions.[219] They are not to be found in the Establishment Clause, or in barring certain kinds of political arguments. The First Amendment does not privilege either side in the culture wars.

Yet the idea is seriously afoot that religious arguments are excluded, limited, or at least somehow suspect, in the political process. Bruce Ackerman,[220] Robert Audi,[221] Christopher Eisgruber,[222] Kent Greenawalt,[223] Abner Greene,[224] Wil-

219. *See, e.g.,* Roe v. Wade, 410 U.S. 113, 152-53 (1973) (locating the right to an abortion in the Due Process Clause); Griswold v. Connecticut, 381 U.S. 479, 482-85 (1965) (locating the right to use contraceptives in the penumbras of the Free Speech Clause and the Third, Fourth, and Fifth Amendments, without alluding to the Establishment Clause).

220. *See generally* BRUCE ACKERMAN, SOCIAL JUSTICE IN THE LIBERAL STATE (1980) (arguing that political arguments may not presuppose any theory of the good or claim to give any privileged answers). For a powerful debate over the application of this principle to religious arguments, hear Bruce Ackerman, Kent Greenawalt, and Michael McConnell, *The Religious Voice in the Public Square,* Oral Presentation at Association of American Law Schools (Jan. 1996) (recording in collection of Jamail Research Center, The University of Texas School of Law).

221. *See* Robert Audi, *The Place of Religious Arguments in a Free and Democratic Society,* 30 SAN DIEGO L. REV. 677 (1993) (arguing that coercive public policy should be based only on accessible reasons, and that religious reasons are not accessible) [hereinafter Audi, *Argument*]; Robert Audi, *The Separation of Church and State and the Obligations of Citizenship,* 18 PHIL. & PUB. AFFAIRS 259, 274-96 (1989) (arguing that individuals have a duty not to support legislation unless they are actually motivated by secular reasons).

222. *See* Christopher L. Eisgruber, *Madison's Wager: Religious Liberty in the Constitutional Order,* 89 NW. U.L. REV. 347, 362-64 (1995) (arguing that political actors must give publicly accessible reasons for their positions, and that most religious reasons are not publicly accessible).

223. *See* KENT GREENAWALT, PRIVATE CONSCIENCES AND PUBLIC REASONS (1995) [hereinafter Greenawalt, *Consciences*] (arguing that citizens should not base political positions exclusively on religious reasons, and that public figures should make political arguments in exclusively secular terms) (hereinafter cited as GREENAWALT, CONSCIENCES); KENT GREENAWALT, RELIGIOUS CONVICTIONS AND POLITICAL CHOICE (1988) (similar arguments); Kent Greenawalt, *Grounds for Political Judgment: The Status of Personal Experience and the Autonomy and Generality of Principles of Restraint,* 30 SAN DIEGO L. REV. 647 (1993) (similar arguments).

224. *See* Abner S. Greene, *The Political Balance of the Religion Clauses,* 102 YALE L.J. 1611, 1622-23 (1993) (arguing that the Establishment Clause prohibits legislators from making religious arguments in public political debate, and that it prohibits legislation motivated by a religious reason unless the reason can be translated into a secular argument that the nonbeliever views as made in good faith). For further debate, *compare* Scott C. Idleman, *Ideology as Interpretation: A Reply to Professor Greene's Theory of the Religion*

liam Marshall,[225] Michael Perry,[226] Lawrence Solum,[227] and Kathleen Sullivan[228] have all offered versions of this argument. Fortunately, their proposals are generally far more moderate than their rhetoric. Mostly they wind up conceding that religious arguments in politics are protected by the text of the Free Speech and Free Exercise Clauses, and by the constitutional structure of democracy.[229] I would add that the evidence from the original understanding is equally strong. The evangelical sects who successfully demanded the Establishment Clause certainly were not silencing or disfranchising their members.[230]

Clauses, 1994 U. ILL. L. REV. 337, *with* Abner S. Greene, *Is Religion Special? A Rejoinder to Scott Idleman,* 1994 U. ILL. L. REV. 535.

225. *See* Marshall, *supra* note 2, at 844-45 (arguing for special constraints on religion's role in public decision-making).

226. *See* MICHAEL J. PERRY, LOVE AND POWER: THE ROLE OF RELIGION AND MORALITY IN AMERICAN POLITICS (1991) (arguing that political arguments should be excluded if they claim infallibility or if they are inaccessible to others, and that sectarian religious argument tends to fall in these categories); Michael J. Perry, *Toward an Ecumenical Politics,* 60 GEO. WASH. L. REV. 599, 603-08 (1992) [hereinafter Perry, *Politics*] (similar arguments); Michael J. Perry, *Religious Morality and Political Choice: Further Thoughts — and Second Thoughts — on Love and Power,* 30 SAN DIEGO L. REV. 703 (1993) (modifying earlier positions and appearing to argue that religious arguments are fully admissible in political debate and may be the basis of political decisions); Michael J. Perry, *Religion in Politics,* 29 U. CAL. DAVIS L. REV. 729 (1996) (modifying position again and arguing that religious arguments cannot be the basis of coercive regulation unless supported by at least one secular argument, except that the argument that all humans are sacred is always admissible).

227. *See* Lawrence B. Solum, *Constructing an Ideal of Public Reason,* 30 SAN DIEGO L. REV. 729 (1993) (arguing that only public reasons can be the basis of coercive regulation, and that religious reasons are not public).

228. Kathleen M. Sullivan, *Religion and Liberal Democracy,* 59 U. CHI. L. REV. 195, 222 (1992) (arguing that the Constitution requires the "banishment of religion from the public square").

229. *See e.g.,* GREENAWALT, CONSCIENCES, *supra* note 223 (formulating his proposals as principles of self-restraint, not as rules of law); Audi, *Argument, supra* note 221, at 700 (stating that his proposed restrictions on political argument describe "an aspect of civic virtue, not a limitation of civil (or other) rights"); Eisgruber, *supra* note 222, at 378-81 (arguing that laws enacted in response to religious arguments are not for that reason unconstitutional); Marshall, *supra* note 2, at 862-63 (conceding free speech rights but concluding that religion in the public square can be constrained by a "prevailing social norm" that religion is "off-limits" in politics); Perry, *Politics, supra* note 226, at 617 (stressing that the requirement of public accessibility is not a legal prescription and that it is not an "insurmountable obstacle" to making appropriate religious arguments in public debate); Sullivan, *supra* note 228, at 197, 201 (conceding that religious arguments in public debate are protected speech, and that such views may influence the debate, provided that public moral disputes are resolved on grounds "articulable" in secular terms).

230. On the critical role of evangelicals in demanding an Establishment Clause, see

On most religious issues today, there is no majority. All the principal antagonists perceive themselves as minorities who have been mistreated on at least some issues. This is true in my experience even of the Catholics and liberal Protestants. The evangelicals, Jews, secular humanists, civil libertarians, and the so-called cults all appear to perceive themselves as threatened minorities, whose values may be overwhelmed and their liberty curtailed by a majority that ranges from indifferent to hostile. Few of these people genuinely fear that their worship will be forbidden, or that they will be forced to worship against their will. But many on both sides fear that pervasive regulation in pursuit of the other side's moral and political values will make their lives intolerable.[231]

Each side in the culture wars tends to impute the moderates to the other side, exaggerating its own sense of being outnumbered and victimized. The nonbeliever sees polls that show a population overwhelmingly religious and almost as overwhelmingly Christian, and he feels badly threatened. In the largest-ever survey ever of religious affiliation, conducted in 1990 with a sample size of 113,000, 86.2% of respondents described themselves as some variety of Christian, and 3.3 percent claimed some other religion.[232] Agnostics, humanists, and "no religion" totaled 8.2 percent; the remaining 2.3 percent refused to answer.[233] When the question is phrased as whether the respon-

---

CURRY, *supra* note 107, at 134-37, 141, 143-46, 148-51, 156-57, 163-77, 179-83, 185-89, 195, 198-99, 216-17; McConnell, *Origins, supra* note 143, at 1436-43. For defenses of the equal right to make either religious or secular arguments in political debate, see Larry Alexander, *Liberalism, Religion, and the Unity of Epistemology,* 30 SAN DIEGO L. REV. 763 (1993) (rejecting claims of epistemological distinctions between faith and reason or religion and secular arguments); Edward McGlynn Gaffney, Jr., *Politics Without Brackets on Religious Convictions: Michael Perry and Bruce Ackerman on Neutrality,* 64 TULANE L. REV. 1143 (1990) (reviewing the role of religion in debates over slavery, civil rights, and immigration, and arguing that "[r]eligious bodies . . . surely enjoy at least the same rights as other persons and groups to participate fully in the political process"); Maimon Schwarzschild, *Religion and Public Debate in a Liberal Society: Always Oil and Water or Sometimes More Like Rum and Coca-Cola?,* 30 SAN DIEGO L. REV. 903 (1993) (arguing that although it may have been rational to view Christianity as a prime threat to liberalism in eighteenth-century Europe, it is erroneous to view religion in this way today); David Smolin, *Regulating Religious and Cultural Conflict in Postmodern America: A Response to Professor Perry,* 76 IOWA L. REV. 1067 (1991) (arguing that "fairness requires that either side of America's contemporary cultural conflict be allowed to win"); Jeremy Waldron, *Religious Contributions in Public Deliberation,* 30 SAN DIEGO L. REV. 817 (1993) (using the example of the Catholic bishops' letter on economic justice to argue for the relevance and accessibility of religious arguments in political debate).

231. *See* Smolin, *supra* note 230, at 1097 ("The loser will live in a society that is hostile to the continuance of their ways of life, even if force is not literally used to destroy them.").

232. KOSMIN & LACHMAN, *supra* note 212, at 2-3, 15-17.

233. *Id.*

dent believes in "God or a Universal Spirit," the percentage of affirmative answers rises to the mid-nineties, and this result has been remarkably stable over decades.[234] As surprising as it may be to academics, confessed nonbelievers are a single-digit minority.

These numbers are real, but they are also misleading. Only about three-quarters believe in life after death,[235] and only about two-thirds believe that God is "the all-powerful, all-knowing Creator of the universe who rules the world today."[236] These are still lopsided majorities, but now we begin to see huge minorities: Nearly 30 percent of theists and 20 percent of self-declared Christians apparently have unorthodox views on fundamental points. Only 60 to 70 percent of the population report that they are members of a church or religious organization.[237] Only about 40 percent report attending church or synagogue in any given week,[238] and a recent study based on actually counting people at services suggests that the real number is only about 20 percent.[239] That is, people appear to report going to church about twice as often as they actually go. The conservative Christian whose values are regularly rejected in public policy decisions[240] sees much of the Christian majority as only nominally Christian — as effectively on the other side. In his view, most Christians have accommodated their religious belief to the secular values of the modern age. He too feels outnumbered and threatened.

The evangelical pollster George Barna strikingly illustrates this view. His polls confirm the standard result that 95 percent of American adults profess

234. *See* George Barna, Virtual America 107 (1994) (1993-94 data; 95% believe in "God or universal force"); Greeley, *supra* note 197, at 14 (citing Gallup and General Social Survey data from 1944, 1954, 1967, and 1981; 95-97% believe in "God or universal spirit").

235. Greeley, *supra* note 197, at 14.

236. Barna, *supra* note 234, at 109.

237. Warner, *supra* note 197, at 1049 (citing Gallup poll data from 1990 (69%) and General Social Survey data from 1991 (61%); reporting peak of 73% in 1960s); *see also* Kosmin & Lachman, *supra* note 212, at 6, 9 (citing church surveys from 1890 to 1936, and Gallup poll data after World War II, with estimates of church membership ranging from 45% in 1890 to 62% in 1990s).

238. See Greeley, *supra* note 197, at 43 (citing Gallup poll data from 1939 (41%) to 1984 (40%), with low of 37% in 1940 and high of 49% in 1955). Similarly consistent polling data from multiple sources extending into more recent years is collected in C. Kirk Haddaway, *et al., What the Polls Don't Show: A Closer Look at U.S. Church Attendance,* 58 Am. Soc. Rev. 741 (1993).

239. *See* Haddaway *et al., supra* note 238 (estimating 19.6% attendance among Protestants in a typical Ohio county and 25% attendance among Catholics in 18 dioceses).

240. *See* David Frum, *Dead Wrong,* New Republic, Sept. 12, 1994, at 17 (arguing that the Christian Right has little power in imposing its policy preferences).

belief "in God or a universal force."[241] But on the basis of answers to questions about specific religious beliefs, he concludes that only 67 percent "have an orthodox Judeo-Christian view of God."[242] He further concludes that 7 percent of the population is "evangelical," 28 percent is "born-again" but not evangelical, and 65 percent is "non-Christian."[243] He explains that according to the Bible, those who are not born again are not Christian.[244] Christians with a different theology may reasonably feel that his definitions have excluded them for heresy. I do not endorse his definitions, but I report them for what they show about perceptions: both the nonbeliever and the evangelical can see themselves as part of a single-digit minority.

Barna also says, based on his general impressions and not a specific survey question, that "most Americans merely dabble in spirituality. They use it as a quick fix during crisis points, as a sedative to assuage their guilt or as a means to a worldly end."[245]

Because each group perceives itself as a mistreated minority, each appeals to the American tradition of protecting minority rights from the majority. The duality of the Religion Clauses makes it easier to structure the debate in this way. The religious groups generally appeal to the Free Exercise Clause, and their opponents to the Establishment Clause. The perception has become widespread that the Free Exercise Clause is pro-religion and the Establishment Clause is anti-religion. On this view, the two clauses are in serious conflict. Each side tends to believe that its own preferred clause should be broadly construed and vigorously enforced, and that it should prevail in any conflict with the other clause. The distilled essence of this argument appears

---

241. BARNA, *supra* note 234, at 109.

242. *Id.* at 107. The criterion was the question quoted in text at note 236 *supra*, whether God is "the all-powerful, all-knowing Creator of the universe who rules the world today."

243. *Id.* Barna counted as Christians those who claimed "a personal commitment to Christ that is still important in their lives today," and who believe they "will go to heaven because they have confessed their sins and accepted Jesus Christ as their Savior." *Id.* at 18. Gallup poll data report that about 70% of the population believes that "there is a heaven where people who have led good lives are eternally rewarded." GREELEY, *supra* note 197, at 14 (citing data from 1952, 1965, and 1980). Barna, following Calvin (and also Luther), rejects this reliance on works rather than faith. Barna defined evangelicals as Christians who say "religion is important in their lives," agree with his "orthodox Judeo-Christian concept of God," reject the view that one can get to heaven by doing good works, believe "that the Bible is accurate in all that it teaches," believe that Satan "is a living force" and not a mere "symbol of evil," and acknowledge a personal responsibility "to tell other people their religious beliefs." *Id.* at 17-18.

244. BARNA, *supra* note 234, at 18.

245. *Id.* at 108.

in Suzanna Sherry's article, *Paradox Redux*,[246] which argues that the two clauses are inherently inconsistent and that the basic and perhaps only important choice is deciding which one to subordinate to the other.[247]

This is a mistake at the most fundamental level, and not just because it imputes incoherence to the Founders. The Religion Clauses were no compromise of conflicting interests, but the unified demand of the most vigorous advocates of religious liberty.

More fundamentally, this interpretation inverts an essential purpose of the clauses: to enable people of fundamentally different religious views to live together in peace and equality, cooperating in the task of self-governance, with no one forced to suffer for their faith. Under the widespread interpretation that Professor Sherry has crystallized, the clauses can only mean that one side wins and the other side is subordinated. This interpretation abandons the goal of equality, it guarantees conflict over who will win and who will be subordinated, and it greatly increases the risk that those who are subordinated will suffer for their faith.

We think of the Reformation as principally a bipolar conflict between Protestants and Catholics, even though there were many internal conflicts on each side, and cross-cutting issues of comparable importance, such as the rise of nationalism, capitalism, and representative parliaments. We are much more aware of the subdivisions and cross-cutting issues in our own time, and it is harder to identify or precisely describe the most fundamental lines of division. But at least one of the fundamental divisions is religious, and the line of division is approximately between those who believe that God has laid down eternal and inflexible moral laws that govern both their public and private behavior, and those who do not — those who do not believe in God, or do not experience their God as so inflexible, or experience God as relevant only to their private life.

This division has replaced Protestant-Catholic and Christian-Jewish divisions as the fundamental source of religious conflict, and mediation of this conflict must therefore be a core purpose of the Religion Clauses. The question for the Religion Clauses in our time is not whether progressives and secular modernists should triumph over orthodox and traditionalists (or vice versa), but how all these groups can live together in peace and equality, cooperating in the task of self-governance, with no one forced to suffer for their faith.

---

246. *See* Suzanna Sherry, *Lee v. Weisman: Paradox Redux,* 1992 SUP. CT. REV. 123.
247. *Id.* at 124.

III. Comparing the Two Eras

A. *The Source of Persecution*

What was the central evil of the Reformation-era religious conflicts? Correspondingly, what is the central evil against which the Religion Clauses were aimed? There are two very different and widely held answers to these questions. *Either:*

1. Human beings suffered for their religious beliefs and practices; *or*
2. Religions imposed suffering on human beings.

On the first account, the fundamental purpose of the Religion Clauses is to protect the religious choices of human beings. Or as Michael McConnell has put it, "The great evil against which the Religion Clauses are directed is government-induced homogeneity" in religion.[248] On the second account, the fundamental purpose is to prevent religion from ever causing such trouble again. On the first account, the principal threat to religious liberty is the State; on the second account, the principal threat is religions.

There is some truth in both accounts; religions were both persecutors and persecutees in the Reformation era. But there is far more truth in the first account; it was the State that had the power to persecute. Religious pronouncements had no effect without the temporal power of the State. Interdicts and excommunication had no effect on those who had already repudiated the interdicting or excommunicating authority.

Even under the various Inquisitions, where the Church may have been most culpable, power to inflict temporal punishment was reserved to the State. This reservation of State power was often a bare formality,[249] but it left ultimate authority in the State, so that the Inquisition "was effective where the secular ruler proved cooperative."[250] The form and vigor of the Inquisi-

---

248. Michael W. McConnell, *Religious Freedom at a Crossroads*, 59 U. CHI. L. REV. 115, 168 (1992).

249. *See* 3 HENRY CHARLES LEA, A HISTORY OF THE INQUISITION OF SPAIN 183-90 (1907) (reviewing the practice of abandoning convicted heretics to "the secular arm," and noting that execution generally followed without any independent judgment by the State).

250. SPITZ, *supra* note 3, at 302 (speaking of the Roman Inquisition during the Counter Reformation); *see also* 1 Lea, *supra* note 249, at 289 ("[T]hroughout Christendom the relations between Church and State were too often antagonistic for [the Inquisition's] commands always to receive obedience."). For examples, see WILL DURANT, THE RENAISSANCE 527-28 (1952) (reporting that the Signory of Brescia refused to execute witches condemned

tions varied sharply over time and place, often in response to local law and politics.[251] Sometimes the State took the lead and the restraining influence came from the Church. For example, it was Ferdinand and Isabella, and not a Pope, bishop, or religious order, who invigorated the Spanish Inquisition and appointed Tomas de Torquemada, the most infamous of the Inquisitors General.[252] The Spanish Inquisition was always subject to the Crown, and only secondarily to the Pope; the Kings of Spain always appointed the Inquisitors General and had effective power to secure their resignation.[253] More generally, studies of court records have revealed that the religious judges of the Inquisitions were more lenient on average, and responsible for many fewer executions, than secular judges conducting heresy trials in other countries at the same time.[254]

Steven Carter argues that the purpose of the Religion Clauses was to protect religion from the State.[255] That is close, but not quite right; the purpose

---

by the Inquisition, despite papal excommunication of secular officials who refused to carry out the religious judgments without further inquiry); PETERS, *supra* note 14, at 110 (reporting that Italian city-states successfully insisted that local representatives sit with Roman Inquisition and that secular authorities review severe sentences).

251. *See* PETERS, *supra* note 14, at 71-74 (comparing operation of Inquisitions in different countries in the late middle ages and early modern period).

252. On Ferdinand's personal role, and on the relation of the Inquisition to the Spanish Crown, see 1 LEA, *supra* note 249, at 157-58, 172-77, 230-33, 289-98, 322-25; PETERS, *supra* note 14, at 85. The Spanish Inquisition "happened thanks to its architect and builder, who was, without question, King Ferdinand of Aragon." BENZION NETANYAHU, THE ORIGINS OF THE INQUISITION IN FIFTEENTH CENTURY SPAIN 1005 (1995). For an account of Torquemada, see ROLAND H. BAINTON, THE TRAVAIL OF RELIGIOUS LIBERTY 33-53 (1951). The Spanish Inquisition was unique, although not in ways that make it any less horrifying. Its primary target was the *conversos*, Jews who had converted (or whose ancestors had converted) to Christianity, most of them to escape murderous mobs in 1391, oppressive legislation of 1412, or expulsion from the country in 1492. HENRY KAMEN, INQUISITION AND SOCIETY IN SPAIN IN THE SIXTEENTH AND SEVENTEENTH CENTURIES 7-13, 18 (1985). Many *conversos* held prominent positions in government, finance, and even the church hierarchy; many were married into noble families. *Id.* at 18-19, 42. Their Christianity was always suspect; forced conversions did not spare them from anti-Semitism. The Spanish Inquisition lasted 300 years, but three-quarters of its victims were executed in the first 20 years, and well over 90% of the victims in that early period were *conversos*. *Id.* at 41-42. A major new history argues that most of the *conversos* were genuinely Christian, and that the underlying causes of the campaign against them were economic, racist, and nationalist, and not religious. NETANYAHU, *supra*. For a summary of this very lengthy argument, see *id.* at 1041-47.

253. 3 LEA, *supra* note 249, at 302-05.

254. *See* PETERS, *supra* note 14, at 87; *see also id.* at 111-12 (noting that secular tribunals in Italy complained that Roman Inquisition was too lenient on witchcraft).

255. CARTER, *supra* note 199, at 115-16.

was to protect religious choice from the State, and religious choice includes the choice of disbelief. Robert Alley says that Carter has it backwards, that the purpose was to protect the State from religion.[256] And, Alley says, "church and religion must first corrupt government before that state, in turn oppresses."[257] As a historical claim this is simply not true, and it is most clearly not true in the case of England, the most relevant precedent. Henry's motives were entirely secular. No Church took over his government; he took over the Church. To get his way, he had to execute the leading bishop and intimidate the rest.

The second view has been stated with more sophistication by Kathleen Sullivan, who repeatedly says the purpose of the Religion Clauses was to end "the war of all sects against all."[258] In her view, the State has imposed a truce on the warring religious sects.

The war of all against all does not accurately describe the Reformation-era conflicts. In almost every case, a better description would be that it was a war of one against all — of the State and its chosen religion against all the others. And the State was an active participant with independent motivations of its own. Even the four-cornered English conflict mostly fit the pattern of one-against-all. It was the Anglican Royalists against everyone else until the Puritans took over the State; then the Puritans turned on the Scots Presbyterians and the Irish Catholics. Shifting fortunes dictated temporary alliances; for example, Catholics supported the Royalists during the Civil War because they feared the Puritans and Presbyterians more.[259] The Catholic James II tried to save his throne by offering concessions to the dissenting Protestants, but this was one-against-all again: a desperate attempt to create an alliance of religious minorities against the Anglican majority and an Anglican Parliament more powerful than the King.[260] For most of the long period of religious conflict, one faith at a time controlled the government, and the government determined policy toward the other faiths.

256. Robert S. Alley, *The Culture of Disbelief: Trivial Pursuit,* CHURCH & STATE, Dec. 1993, at 19, 20.

257. *Id.* Despite the breadth of this statement, it is possible that in context, he is asserting that this would be true only of democratic governments. This more limited claim is belied by *Employment Division v. Smith,* 494 U.S. 872 (1990), and all other cases of democratic regulation of religion for secular reasons. Alley apparently agrees that *Smith* oppresses religion; he calls the decision "infamous." *Id.* With respect to both democratic and non-democratic governments, Alley has not thought through the implications of secular motivations for restricting religious liberty.

258. Sullivan, *supra* note 228, at 197.

259. DAVIES, *supra* note 87, at 210-11.

260. *See* PRALL, *supra* note 131, at 143-46 (explaining why a Catholic-dissenter alliance could not succeed against an Anglican majority).

The pattern of one-against-all continued in this country: Baptists, Quakers, Presbyterians, Mennonites, and Methodists united in their opposition to the Congregational establishment in New England and to the Episcopal establishment in the South. It was these evangelical sects that successfully demanded both the Free Exercise Clause and the Establishment Clause.[261]

One-against-all broke down when no one religion was strong enough to dominate. Among the first religious minorities to gain toleration were those too large to be suppressed: recall that Luther was safe in Wittenberg because the Emperor was afraid to arrest him there.[262] The Anglicans promised toleration to the Protestant dissenters because they feared a Catholic-Dissenter alliance.[263] When the dominant religion made concessions out of weakness, this was the first step on the road to religious pluralism. When there are so many religions that no one of them can hope to dominate, religious liberty is largely safe from other religions. This was Madison's insight in Federalist 51.[264] The multiplicity of religious factions competing in the marketplace of ideas — what Sullivan condemns as the war of all sects against all — is in fact an important structural protection for religious liberty.[265]

The protection provided by religious pluralism is not foolproof, even as against other religions. A coalition of similar religions can unite to oppress a dissimilar religion, or a coalition of religious and secular interest groups can unite to suppress a religion that they dislike for quite independent reasons.[266] Moreover, experience and public choice theory have revealed what Madison

261. *See* sources cited *supra* note 230.

262. *See supra* note 18 and accompanying text.

263. *See supra* text accompanying note 134 *supra*.

264. THE FEDERALIST No. 51, at 324 (Clinton Rossiter ed. 1961) ("In a free government the security for civil rights must be the same as that for religious rights. It consists in the one case in the multiplicity of interests, and in the other in the multiplicity of sects. The degree of security in both cases will depend on the number of interests and sects.").

265. Sociologists of religion seem to be discovering the marketplace model of religious competition that legal doctrine on religious liberty has long taken for granted. *See generally* Warner, *supra* note 197, at 1045 (offering a "new paradigm," based on "the idea that religious institutions in the United States operate within an open market"). Sociologists and social historians are now offering evidence to support the lawyers' claim that disestablishment explains much of the greater vitality of religion in this country as compared to Europe. *See id.* at 1048-58; GREELEY, *supra* note 197, at 126-27 (reporting survey data showing no difference in religiosity between United States and Great Britain among Catholics and non-Anglican Protestants; "lower levels of religiousness in Great Britain are purely an Anglican phenomenon."); Warner, *supra* note 197 at 1048-58.

266. *See* Douglas Laycock, *The Remnants of Free Exercise,* 1990 SUP. CT. REV. 1, 67 (describing "the anti-Santeria coalition — animal rights activists, Christian fundamentalists, and people who just seem to find animal sacrifice disgusting") (text at note 274).

failed to recognize:[267] that a well-organized political minority can do the same things if its victims are smaller in number, or not well-organized, or lacking political influence for some other reason.

Although religions work to suppress other religions in these scenarios, they do so through the ordinary political process and through the coercive power of the State. The mechanisms by which a religious minority might be suppressed in a religiously pluralist state are identical whether the political faction demanding suppression is a coalition of other religions, or a secular interest group demanding activist regulation without exceptions for religious dissenters. And in our time, one religion attempting to suppress another is a rare event compared to the far more common case of a secular interest group attempting to suppress a religious practice.[268]

It is emphatically not my claim that the churches have been innocent, either in the Reformation era or today. But I do emphasize two points about the State: 1) in general, it was only the State that had the *power* to persecute, and 2) either the State or the Church could provide the *motive* to persecute.

Persecutions depend on the coercive power of the State. Churches could persecute only when the religious authority of the Church was combined with the governing authority of the State, or when the Church usurped the State's monopoly of legitimate violence. Occasional private persecutions, as in civil wars, pogroms, and deprogramming, usually depend on the instigation or at least the acquiescence of State; they always depend on usurping the monopoly of legitimate violence.

Either Church or State could provide the motive for persecution. The Church could urge or request the State to persecute, or the State could persecute for its own reasons. The evil was the same in either case: human beings suffered for their religious belief and practice.

The central meaning of separation of Church and State is to separate these two sources of authority, depriving religion of the State's power to coerce, *and* depriving the State of power over religion. That separation accomplished, the State still has its monopoly of legitimate violence. It has the power to regulate and punish, to seize the property of individuals and groups, to imprison them or execute them. The State, as always, remains a direct threat to liberty.

267. *See* THE FEDERALIST, *supra* note 264, No. 10 at 80 ("If a faction consists of less than a majority, relief is supplied by the republican principle, which enables the majority to defeat its sinister views by regular vote.").

268. *See* Laycock, *supra* note 266, at 57-58 (analyzing why secular interest groups resist religious exemptions, illustrating with examples of landmarking and gay rights lobbies) (text at notes 221-25).

The Church has only the power to persuade. Its members have the power to compete for votes with all other citizens. And while I would fear a government dominated by activists from the Christian Coalition, I would equally fear a government dominated by activists from the Environmental Defense Fund, the National Organization of Women, the National Taxpayers League, the Humane Society, the National Historic Trust, the American Civil Liberties Union, or any other group with a strong commitment to one or a few issues. The twentieth century has produced Hitler, Stalin, Mao, and Pol Pot, and in our own country terrorist bombs on behalf of peace, environmentalism, the right to bear arms, and the liberation of Puerto Rico. It is not that "religion" is "inherently intolerant and persecutory"; rather, the risk of intolerance and persecution is a risk of any human movement organized for a common purpose. I see no reason to believe that religion presents a risk different in kind or degree from the risk of secular ideologies.[269]

B. Reductions in Force and in the Stakes of Competition

Two obvious differences between Reformation-era conflicts and our own are the levels of force and the stakes of the conflict. Kathleen Sullivan's notion of the war of all against all provides a useful point of departure. Criticizing Michael McConnell's view that the evil is government-imposed religious homogeneity, she says, "In other words, the war of all sects against all is to continue by other means after the truce."[270]

I do not know exactly what Sullivan means by this, although she cannot mean the apparent implication that McConnell's view brings little improvement over the previous situation. Even if she were right that the war of all against all continues "by other means," the change in means would be one of the great advances of human history. Instead of guns, burning stakes, and chopping blocks, we use political organization, voting, litigation, free debate, and attempts to structure rules of debate to exclude the other side. This change is not complete; we also still use criminal punishment and the threat of criminal punishment against religiously motivated behavior.[271] But we

269. *See* Schwarzschild, *supra* note 230, at 910-15 ("Religion seems an odd choice as prime threat to liberalism at the end of a century that has been so greatly dominated by struggles over Communism, fascism, and extreme nationalism").

270. Sullivan, *supra* note 228, at 198.

271. *See, e.g.,* Church of the Lukumi Babalu Aye, Inc. v. City of Hialeah, 508 U.S. 520 (1993) (striking down laws against religious sacrifice of animals); Employment Division v. Smith, 494 U.S. 872 (1990) (upholding application of drug laws to religious use of peyote).

have made great progress toward channeling the conflict into legal, political, and social means, and away from violent means.

Equally important is a change that Sullivan does not acknowledge, a reduction in the stakes of competition. The war of all sects continues in the sense that sects may compete for adherents and for their views of proper government policy. But they may not compete to impose theology or forms of worship. They may not admit to the goal of suppressing other faiths, and in fact they rarely attempt it. The competition among sects is no longer total war; it is no longer for the right to exist and practice one's faith. These basic rights are largely conceded to all, and serious believers have a much greater interest in uniting against the secularism that threatens them all.

The circle of toleration has expanded manyfold since the Reformation, and indeed, since the American founding. Catholics, Jews, Mormons, Protestants of all types, humanists, atheists, and agnostics are all within the circle. Hostility and suspicion continue in some quarters, but tolerance is proclaimed all around and the goal of suppression is repudiated.

The circle of toleration does not yet include the entire population. Some groups are subjected to mistreatment that readily fits the popular image of the Reformation-era model — attempted suppression because of overt religious hostility. A clear example is deprogramming of so-called cult members: kidnapping and physical coercion to force the victim to recant unacceptable religious beliefs and practices.[272] Another example is the ruinous jury verdicts against some of these unfamiliar religions, mostly for torts committed by religious communications.[273] Another example was the Hialeah City Council meeting to consider the Church of the Lukumi Babalu Aye's attempt to open a church at which it would practice animal sacrifice. Among the reasons offered for prohibiting the church was that animal sacrifice was sinful, "an abomination to the Lord," and the worship of demons.[274] But these examples of overt hostility to minority religions as such are far removed from the principal lines of conflict today.

---

272. For an account, see J. Thomas Ungerleider & David K. Wellisch, *Deprogramming (Involuntary Departure), Coercion, and Cults, in* CULTS AND NEW RELIGIOUS MOVEMENTS 239, 239-42 (Mark Galanter, ed., 1989).

273. *See, e.g.,* Wollersheim v. Church of Scientology, 6 Cal. Rptr. 2d 532 (Cal. App. 1992) ($30 million verdict, of which $2.5 million affirmed; in this case, the judgment was not based just on religious communications); George v. International Soc'y for Krisha Consciousness, 4 Cal. Rptr. 2d 473 (Cal. App. 1992) ($32.6 million verdict, of which $1.5 million affirmed and punitive damage claims remanded for retrial) (unpublished opinion).

274. Church of the Lukumi Babalu Aye, Inc. v. City of Hialeah, 508 U.S. 520, 541 (1993) (plurality opinion). The record contains more in the same vein. I represented the Church on appeal.

C. The Changing Motives and Expanded Role of Government

Today's religious conflicts are much more likely to be secular versus religious instead of religious versus religious. The typical oppressive measure directed at a religious group results from the demands of some secular interest group and from the vastly expanded role of government. As government regulation and government benefits become more pervasive, and as religion becomes ever more pluralistic, government and religion interact more often and in more complex ways.

Government burdens on religious exercise arise as incidents of secular regulation or from eligibility requirements of benefit programs, and rarely from one religion trying to suppress another. Illustrative issues are whether the State must pay unemployment compensation to a conscientious objector who quit his job in a defense plant,[275] whether historical landmark laws can control the architecture of churches,[276] or whether Catholic teaching hospitals must perform and teach the techniques of abortion.[277] Establishment Clause controversies arise from private religious exercise in public places,[278] or from religious participation in the distribution of government social services,[279] and only occasionally from direct government attempts to support

275. *See* Thomas v. Review Bd., 450 U.S. 707 (1981) (holding such a worker constitutionally entitled to unemployment compensation).

276. *See* Flores v. City of Boerne, 73 F.3d 1352 (5th Cir. 1996) (reinstating one count of complaint alleging that historic zoning made it impossible to expand church and thus forced church to turn worshipers away from mass); Rector of St. Bartholomew's Church v. City of New York, 914 F.2d 348 (1990) (upholding New York's refusal to allow the church to replace a landmarked building). [After publication of this article, the decision in *Flores v. City of Boerne* was reversed on other grounds. 521 U.S. 507 (1997).]

277. St. Agnes Hosp. v. Riddick, 748 F. Supp. 319, 320-32 (D. Md. 1990) (holding that the state may require a Catholic hospital to teach abortion techniques if it has residents in obstetrics and gynecology).

278. *See, e.g.,* Capitol Square Rev. & Advisory Bd. v. Pinette, 515 U.S. 753 (1995) (holding that a state that permits unattended displays in public forum must permit unattended religious displays); Widmar v. Vincent, 454 U.S. 263 (1981) (holding that a state university that makes its facilities generally available to student groups may not deny use of those facilities to a student group desiring to use them for religious purposes).

279. *See, e.g.,* Rosenberger v. Rector of the Univ. of Va., 515 U.S. 819 (1995) (holding that state university that funds wide range of student publications from student activity fees must fund student religious publications); Zobrest v. Catalina Foothills School Dist., 509 U.S. 1 (1993) (holding that the Establishment Clause is not violated by a public school district paying the salary of a sign language interpreter in a parochial school); Everson v. Board of Educ., 330 U.S. 1 (1947) (holding that the state could reimburse parents for the cost of transporting their children to parochial school).

religion. Today's controversies are more complex and harder to decide, and it is harder to treat the range of disputes with theoretical consistency.

In addition, all sides are more prone to assert their alleged rights than in the past. The culture wars make interest groups and regulators less receptive to pleas of religious liberty, less willing to exempt religious minorities from regulation even when the cost to the regulatory scheme is mostly symbolic.[280] Many secularists see little reason to accommodate an incomprehensible superstition that has lingered beyond its time, and many modernist believers see no reason why anyone's religious belief should affect the pursuit of public policy. Secular movements on both left and right exhibit the same tendency to excess and absolutism that we see in some religious movements.

The Supreme Court seems confident that it can distinguish deliberate suppression of religious exercise from general laws that suppress religious exercise only incidentally. In the Court's view, only deliberate suppression raises a constitutional question.[281]

Suzanna Sherry has defended that distinction in originalist terms that are directly relevant to my review of the Reformation:

> [T]he founding generation had no idea that government might be so involved in the lives of the people as to prohibit ordinary, everyday practices that affect religion. Advocates of the religion clauses feared deliberate persecution, not unforeseen general government growth with a negative impact on religion.[282]

The originalist question, as Justice Brennan once said, should be whether a practice threatens those "consequences which the Framers deeply feared."[283] The evil of the Reformation-era conflict was that the State with its coercive power made human beings suffer for their religious belief and practice; that

---

280. *See* Swanner v. Anchorage Equal Rights Comm'n, 874 P.2d 274, 282-83 (Alaska 1994) (asserting a "transactional" compelling interest in eliminating marital status discrimination in every housing transaction, without evidence that unmarried couples had difficulty finding housing).

281. *Compare* Church of Lukumi Babalu Aye, Inc. v. City of Hialeah, 508 U.S. 520 (1993) (holding that regulation that targets religion or discriminates against religion must be justified by compelling interest) *with* Employment Div. v. Smith, 494 U.S. 872 (1990) (holding that neutral and generally applicable laws may be applied to suppress core religious practices, and that such application requires no justification).

282. Sherry, *supra* note 246, at 148. I will not repeat here all the reasons for thinking that the Court was wrong. *See generally* Laycock, *supra* note 266; Michael W. McConnell, *Free Exercise Revisionism and the Smith Decision,* 57 U. CHI. L. REV. 1109 (1990).

283. School Dist. of Abington v. Schempp, 374 U.S. 203, 236 (1963).

was the consequence the Founders feared. The evil is the same, whatever the State's motive. *Employment Division v. Smith*[284] threatens that consequence; the Religious Freedom Restoration Act[285] attempts to avoid it. My disagreement with Professor Sherry illustrates the familiar problem of the level of generality at which to state a principle. When the evil is human suffering, and the sufferer is penalized because of his religious practice, focusing on the motive of those inflicting the suffering seems to miss the point.

In addition, more than one inference can be drawn from Professor Sherry's historical assumption. She is largely right that the Founders "had no idea that government might be so involved in the lives of the people as to prohibit ordinary, everyday practices that affect religion." The Founders encountered this problem, and granted legislative exemptions, but the issue arose only occasionally.[286] The Founders knew about governments that would prevent a disfavored faith from building a church at all; they presumably could not imagine a government that would prevent a mainstream church from adding needed worship space because architecture buffs liked the old building.[287] But I doubt they would have thought one of these governments less tyrannical than the other, or that they would have thought that only one of these governments had prohibited the free exercise of religion.

Professor Sherry reasons that the Founders would not have thought to forbid something they could not anticipate — suppression of religious practice by an activist government acting for secular reasons. But it is equally clear that the Founders did not think to authorize this thing they could not anticipate. The question is whether a novel threat to religious liberty falls within the principle of the Religion Clauses; the Founders' failure to anticipate the novel threat does not answer that question. To assume that it does is an error analogous to excluding Mormons and Jehovah's Witnesses from the Free Exercise Clause, television from the Free Press Clause, and wire taps from the Search and Seizure Clause.

Finally, recall that the Reformation-era governments often acted for their own secular reasons, even in religious matters. That is, part of the evil known to the Founders was religious persecution for secular motives, which is not so

---

284. 494 U.S. 872 (1990).

285. 42 U.S.C. § 2000bb to § 2000bb-4 (1994).

286. *See* McConnell, *Origins, supra* note 143, at 1466-73.

287. These are the facts of Flores v. City of Boerne, 73 F.3d 1352 (5th Cir. 1996) (upholding the constitutionality of the Religious Freedom Restoration Act, 42 U.S.C. § 2000bb to § 2000bb-4 (1994)). I should disclose that I represented Archbishop Flores on appeal. [After this article was published, the Supreme Court reversed, holding the Act unconstitutional as applied to state and local governments.]

different from today's "neutral and generally applicable laws" — enacted for secular reasons but with the effect of suppressing a religious practice.[288]

One of the most famous Reformation examples might itself be described as a neutral and generally applicable law if adjudicated today under the Free Exercise Clause. In Henry's England, it was treason to question the validity of his second marriage.[289] This prohibition was based on the strongest reasons of national security. If his second marriage were invalid, the children of that marriage would be illegitimate; the claim of illegitimacy would challenge their right to the throne and threaten civil war over the succession. This particular form of treason was committed by stating a core Catholic belief, but the law applied to everyone and was stated in religiously neutral terms. Perhaps the example goes away because if it were litigated today, the law would be struck down under the Free Speech Clause or the Treason Clause.[290] Even so, I think the example further undermines the claim that neutral and generally applicable laws were no part of the problem the Founders sought to solve.

Disagreement over the validity of Henry's marriage turned on an underlying religious disagreement, but the underlying religious basis for the law would probably not keep it from being neutral and generally applicable under current doctrine. *Employment Division v. Smith*[291] relied on *Braunfeld v. Brown*,[292] which upheld the conviction of an Orthodox Jewish merchant for selling retail goods on Sunday. Plainly an underlying religious disagreement over the proper designation of the Sabbath was at the heart of this prosecution. But the Court separated the rather modest secular functions of the Sunday closing law from its religious origins; the secular functions assertedly made it neutral and generally applicable. Similarly, a court could easily separate the underlying religious dispute from the critical secular function of Henry's marriage and of the law commanding respect for that marriage.

Another contemporary example of allegedly neutral laws with religious underpinnings is the landmarking of churches. In the wake of *Smith*, lower courts have held that landmarking laws are neutral and generally applica-

---

288. Employment Div. v. Smith, 494 U.S. 872, 879 (1990).

289. The First Act of Succession, 1534, 25 Henry 8, ch. 22 (Eng.), *reprinted in* Documents Illustrative, *supra* note 57, at 232, 238-39.

290. U.S. Const., Art. III, § 3, cl. 1 ("Treason against the United States, shall consist only in levying War against them, or in adhering to their Enemies, giving them Aid and Comfort. No person shall be convicted of Treason unless on the Testimony of two Witnesses to the same overt act, or on Confession in open Court.").

291. 494 U.S. 872, 880 (1990).

292. 366 U.S. 599 (1961) (plurality opinion).

ble,[293] even though they apply only to certain properties and thus affected property owners do not get the protection that the political process provides against oppression by laws that burden everybody. One study found that churches are landmarked at a rate more than forty-two times higher than any other kind of property.[294] Why? Because the landmark lobby appears to like sacred architecture. As Emily Hartigan has said in conversation, they want "the faint after-aroma of religion," but not the real thing. I do not believe that landmark laws are neutral and generally applicable, but if the courts say they are, Henry's treason law would be so a fortiori.

A religious disagreement underlies all neutral and generally applicable laws that burden religion, at least in the sense that the State rejects the minority's religious belief. Just as Henry rejected the Catholic belief that only the Pope could annul his marriage to Catherine, so Oregon rejected the belief that one can directly experience the presence of God through peyote intoxication,[295] and Wisconsin rejected the belief that a simple life without a high school education better conforms to God's will.[296] The law would have been different if a sufficient block of voters had been peyote worshipers or Old Order Amish, just as the treason law would have been different if Henry had remained Catholic. The fundamental split between secular and religious worldviews informs all disputes about exempting religious minorities from regulation.

I do not mean to impute any of these thoughts to the Founders except the most basic one: they did not want people to suffer for their religious beliefs and practices. The suggestions in this section are not offered as original intent in the sense that the Founders consciously thought about these things. Rather, they are offered as part of the related practice of interpreting a provision in light of the evil it was intended to remedy. The religious conflict in the wake of the Reformation was the most salient example of the evil to be avoided, and a major part of that example was government dominating religion, persecuting religious dissenters, and interfering in religious matters for reasons of state.

---

293. Rector of St. Bartholomew's Church v. City of New York, 914 F.2d 348, 354-55 (2d Cir. 1990).

294. N.J. L'Heureux, Jr., *Ministry v Mortar: A Landmark Conflict*, in GOVERNMENT INTERVENTION IN RELIGIOUS AFFAIRS 2, at 164, 168 (DEAN M. KELLEY, ed., 1986).

295. *See* Employment Div. v. Smith, 494 U.S. 872 (1990).

296. *See* Wisconsin v. Yoder, 406 U.S. 205 (1972).

IV. Conclusion

My view of the central lesson to be drawn from the Reformation should not be a surprise; it is consistent with our basic constitutional theory. The Constitution was written on the assumption that the concentration of powers necessary to an effective government is a threat to human liberty, and that those powers must be divided and constrained. The Bill of Rights protects the people from the government, not the other way around. The state-action distinction is drawn with special sharpness in the Religion Clauses: religious belief and practice by private persons is specially protected; the same religious belief or practice by government is specifically prohibited. The puzzle is why the opposite assumption — that the Religion Clauses protect the government from religious citizens — has become so widespread.

In part it is because those who hold that view have misread history. They have blamed too much on the Church and too little on the State. In part it is because they have thought that their preferred secular ideologies were inherently different from religion, and that religion is uniquely susceptible to the temptation to intolerance and absolutism. I think that they are wrong on each of these points.

The First Amendment constrains Congress, not churches, and this is no accident. The amendment was aimed squarely at the problem that the Founders sought to solve. During the Reformation and today, it was and is governments that punish people for religious beliefs and practices. The most common motives have changed, the alignment of factions has changed, but the central evil has remained the same.

Religious Liberty and Free Speech:
Back to the Future — What 21st Century Legal Culture
Can Learn from the 19th Century's First Amendment

1 Engage 132 (2000)

This was one of four brief presentations to the annual convention of the Federalist Society, the well-known association of conservative lawyers, judges, and law students. We were each asked to speak about First Amendment issues in the nineteenth century and any modern lessons that might be drawn from those issues. The oral presentations were printed with minimal editing.

I talked about the Mormon persecutions, which began under neutral and generally applicable laws; today the Supreme Court says that such laws are not judicially reviewable under the Free Exercise Clause. And I talked about Protestant-Catholic conflict over schools, which was the origin of modern controversies over school prayer and over government funds for private religious schools.

I also referred to the two speakers who preceded me, Michael Curtis of Wake Forest Law School and Gerard Bradley of Notre Dame Law School. Professor Curtis spoke about suppression of anti-slavery speech before the Civil War. Professor Bradley spoke about Bible reading in public schools, Protestant-Catholic conflict, and the proposed Blaine Amendment to the Constitution, which would have forbidden the use of public funds for private religious schools while explicitly protecting Bible reading in the public schools.

∗   ∗   ∗

Let me say in passing that there is a religious strand to the story Michael Curtis just told — suppression and control of religion among the slaves was also part of the Republican grievances against the South and also part of the reason for incorporating the Bill of Rights into the Fourteenth Amendment. I do not have time to tell you about that today, but it parallels what we have just heard from Professor Curtis.

My view of the nineteenth century on church/state is that there were two formative controversies that are more important than the Court realizes to modern church/ state doctrine. One was the Protestant/Catholic conflict and one was the hatred of the Mormons by just about everybody. Today we think of it as mostly about polygamy, but that issue actually arose fairly late.

The Mormons were driven out of every place in which they ever tried to live, by force and violence, even before polygamy became a public issue. The reasons are not entirely clear. One of the more memorable episodes was when the Governor of Missouri issued an extermination order — that if they do not leave the state, exterminate them — and he sent the National Guard out to execute it. It is not clear how serious the National Guard was, and it was not all that much stronger than the Mormons, but there were a couple of battles and the Mormons did, indeed, leave the state. They eventually went to the furthest regions of Mexico in 1846. Unfortunately, that part of Mexico was ceded to the United States in 1848 and they were back in the soup. Eventually, in a case that the Court has been relying on recently, *Reynolds v. United States* (1878), one of the second-tier leaders of the Mormon Church was prosecuted and convicted of polygamy. That was the case that went to the Supreme Court. There were hundreds of these prosecutions in the District of Utah.

Today, the Supreme Court says with respect to regulation of religious practices that the important thing is that the law has to be neutral and generally applicable. If it is generally applicable, then it can be applied to religiously motivated practices and there is no need to make exceptions or to justify the refusal to make exceptions. They sometimes cite *Reynolds v. United States* for that proposition, although that is not what *Reynolds* says. In *Reynolds* the Court really did not care whether the law was generally applicable or not. I suppose it was generally applicable in the most obvious sense, because bigamy had been a crime at common law and polygamy was forbidden generally, not just when it was religiously motivated. On the other hand, there was something decidedly unusual about legislating family law in the Congress of the United States, instead of the territorial legislature. In that sense, this was a unique law enacted only for the purpose of reaching the Mormons, because Congress did not like what the territorial legislature in Utah would have done with the issue.

But none of that was at issue. The Court did not care whether it was generally applicable or not. The Court simply said that belief is protected, but conduct is not protected and it does not matter that it's religious — religious conduct is still conduct that can be regulated. Then they went on to say that polygamy is not religion. Europeans do not do this. Only Africans and Asians do this and it is not civilized. Just because you call it religion, we do not have to treat it as religion — it is, in fact, abhorrent, and it is not really a religion.

The Court got in a few other shots, but it was not an opinion about neutrality and general applicability. It also turned out that the distinction between belief and conduct did not hold. The Court was not content merely to let the government regulate Mormon conduct. In later cases, such as *Davis v. Beason* (1890), which was essentially a test oath case, you had to swear you were not a Mormon. If you could not take that oath, you could not vote in the territory of Idaho. They upheld that. The Court has relied on that case recently too, although it is almost certainly implicitly overruled in numerous cases [and that implicit overruling was finally recognized in *Romer v. Evans* (1996)].

Finally, in *Late Corporation v. United States* (1890), Congress forfeited the corporate charter of the Church and forfeited all its property, except actual places of worship. The Court upheld that, principally because of the Church's speech. The case was not about conduct; it was about speech, and for speech you could forfeit all your property. Generally applicable laws can be used as a tool to reach unpopular religions, and once you start down that path, there turns out to be no good or logical stopping point.

The Catholic part of the story is mostly about the Establishment Clause, but it comes back into the Free Exercise Clause a bit here, and fits the theme of the Mormon persecution. The high water mark of legally enacted anti-Catholicism in the United States was probably the Oregon law to close all private schools in the 1920s, which the Supreme Court struck down in *Pierce v. Society of Sisters* (1925). That was a neutral and generally applicable law, enacted solely for the purpose of getting rid of Catholic schools.

The Court has in modern times created a category that is not adequate to protect religious minorities, and with some of these nineteenth-century examples or very early twentieth-century examples we can now look back with more distance and more objectivity and reveal the inadequacy of that framework.

Now, let me say a bit about the Establishment Clause and about the Protestant/Catholic conflict that Professor Bradley has already touched on. I draw one of the same lessons he drew and a very different lesson about the other issue.

There was widespread hostility to Catholics through most of American history. Overt conflict rose and fell all through the nineteenth century, in part for external political reasons. The popes kept issuing statements that democracy was a bad form of government, although the rank and file paid not the slightest attention to that, either here or in Europe. American Catholics were vigorously defending themselves against the charge that they were antidemocratic.

There was the Grant speech that Gerry Bradley talked about. [In 1875, President Grant condemned the forces of "superstition, ambition, and ignorance," by which he meant Catholics, and proposed that not one dollar of public funds should go to the support of any "sectarian" schools.] In 1854, the Know Nothings, who were anti-Catholic and anti-immigrant, swept elections in eight states. There was mob violence and there were church burnings. The Catholic churches in Philadelphia were burned. The Catholic churches in New York were saved because the Bishop brought out all the Irish thugs armed with pitchforks. That quasi-military force turned out to be stronger than the gang of Protestant thugs who were trying to burn down the cathedral. It was a nasty business, and the principal issue then as now was about schools and, in particular in those days, what the Catholics called the Protestant Bible in the schools. The solution of Horace Mann and the early founders of the Common School Movement was to try to go to basics, to teach only those most basic principles of Christianity on which the different denominations should not disagree, and to read the Bible without note or comment. Without note or comment meant the teacher just reads it, and if she does not explain what it means, she cannot get into any denominational controversies and everything will be fine.

Now, conservative and even some other Protestants did not much like that. They thought it was too stripped-down, too much like Unitarianism. That fight was just getting off the ground in the 1840s when the Protestants united, closed ranks, and dropped that battle to unite against the Catholic threat. The Protestant position throughout this whole controversy was to say that reading the Bible without comment is nonsectarian and who could possibly object to that? To which the Catholic response was, one, you are reading the Protestant Bible, it's the King James translation, it is not our translation; and two, without note or comment is fundamentally, unmistakably a Protestant practice.

The Protestant teaching is scripture only: all the revelation is contained in scripture and it is open to any human mind that wants to read it. The Catholic teaching is that the magisterium, the teaching authority of the Church, is the only safe guide to revelation. In response to General Grant's speech, one of the Catholic Bishops — I think in Chicago — said "to read the Bible without note or comment is as sectarian and Protestant a practice as saying the Mass is a sectarian Catholic practice." In retrospect, there can hardly be any doubt about that.

The Jewish community, which was smaller, was dealing with the same problems of Protestant instruction in the schools. But the Catholic and Jewish communities responded in very different ways. The Catholics responded by building their own school system and trying to get a share of the public money to help with that effort. The Jewish community responded by staying in the public school system and doing what it could to minimize or reduce the level of Protestant teaching and to secularize the public schools. Those two different positions, which are familiar to us today, go back to this late-nineteenth-century dispute.

The Blaine Amendment was an attempt to codify the Protestant position on both these issues. You keep the Bible reading in the public schools and you cut off forever any money to the Catholic schools. It was defeated, pretty much on party lines in the Senate, with Democrats responding to the immigrant vote in the northeastern cities and voting against it. Similar provisions were enacted in about two-thirds of the states, and they have a very unpleasant history behind them.

The first school prayer cases are not *Engel* and *Schempp* in 1963 [*Engel v. Vitale* and *Abington School District v. Schempp*]. They are from this nineteenth-century period in the Supreme Courts of Wisconsin and Ohio. In the Police Court in Boston, in a case where little Tommy Cook was whipped by his teacher for refusing to read the King James Bible, the indictment against his teacher was dismissed. The Supreme Court of Wisconsin actually held school prayer and Bible reading unconstitutional in 1890 under the State Constitution. Ohio wrote a sympathetic opinion upholding the discretion of school authorities to abandon it.

I think the lesson to draw about school prayer from this episode is not that there were a lot of people doing it and that they even proposed a constitutional amendment to say it was okay. [This is an unfriendly summary of the lesson Gerry Bradley drew from the same events.] I think the lesson is in the failed attempt to say there is a neutral form of prayer. The attempt to offer some kind of least common denominator prayer or religious instruction in the public schools is doomed. It can never be fair to minorities, even among Christians. It led to massive conflict and it led to violence. The religious minorities who are unhappy today should get their rights respected without being forced to provoke violence as their predecessors did in the nineteenth century.

With respect to the funding issues, I do agree with Gerry. Here is maybe the most revealing thing: for 110 years, the federal government paid churches and missionaries to provide schools to the American Indians. Even Jefferson did it and no one raised a shadow of a question about the Establishment Clause.

The *eighteenth*-century fight was about the funding of churches. It was not about the funding of education in secular subjects being offered in religious environments or by church-affiliated schools. Government funding to churches to educate Indians was ended by statute in 1897, in the wake of another one of these anti-Catholic political uprisings. The Protestant/Catholic debate over the Protestant Bible and the funding of Catholic schools fundamentally shifted the American tradition on funding; it took a rule that had been no funding of churches, and converted it into a rule of no funding of education associated with churches.

That tradition does not go back to the founding; it goes back to this anti-Catholic movement in the late nineteenth century. Maybe it could be justified on its own terms, but it never has been. Justices who were educated in their formative period at the tail end of this era were the Justices who wrote it into constitutional law, starting in the late 1940s and continuing into the 1970s. There is an anti-Catholic hate tract cited in Douglas's opinion in *Lemon* [*Lemon v. Kurtzman* (1971)]. I am not sure he knew what he was citing, although I think he probably did. There is similar talk in Justice Black's opinion in *Board of Education v. Allen* in 1968. We have a tradition that has come down to us with very tainted origins, and we have forgotten the origins. When we tell the story of the Religion Clauses, it goes from 1791 to today, skipping over where some of the critical developments came from. We need to take a new look at the issue of funding social services and education in religious environments.

I think that the lesson to draw from the nineteenth-century experience is that you achieve neutrality by making government funding available to a wide range of providers. You do not achieve neutrality by putting religion in the public schools and trying to figure out a way of doing it neutrally. There is no way to do it neutrally.

Regulatory Exemptions of Religious Behavior and the Original Understanding of the Establishment Clause

81 Notre Dame Law Review 1793 (2006)

The most disputed issue under the Free Exercise Clause is whether the Constitution sometimes requires that religiously motivated behavior be exempted from generally applicable laws. Even if the Constitution never requires such exemptions, most judges and scholars agree that the legislature can enact them. But a minority of judges and scholars deny even that. They say that a regulatory exemption for a religious practice is preferential treatment, a form of unconstitutional support for religion, that violates the Establishment Clause. The Supreme Court has repeatedly rejected this argument, although its decisions are sufficiently ambiguous that opponents of exemptions keep making it.

This article reviews the history of the founding era for evidence of original understanding on the Establishment Clause question. The issue of regulatory exemptions for religion arose frequently in the founding era, but the issue of whether

I wrote this article in the midst of my transition from The University of Texas to The University of Michigan, so I was able to use two great libraries. Of course I lacked the time to exhaust the resources of either. I am grateful to Jamie Richards at Texas for research assistance, to Aimee Mangan and the research staff in Michigan's law library for help finding colonial sources, and to participants in the Columbia Law School Workshop on Legal Theory for comments and questions that were both challenging and helpful. A special thank you to J. William Frost, Professor Emeritus of Religion at Swarthmore College, who volunteered to check sources at the Swarthmore library on my behalf.

I have examined original sources wherever possible, but I benefited enormously from the work of other scholars who had already examined those sources with somewhat different questions in mind — especially J. William Frost, Philip Hamburger, Richard K. MacMaster, and Ellis West. I have retained the original spelling from the sixteenth-, seventeenth-, and eighteenth-century sources except where I had to rely on a compilation or reprint that had modernized spelling.

those exemptions violated the Establishment Clause did not. After looking in all the places where the establishment argument should have been made if anybody had thought exemptions established the exempted religion, I conclude that no significant body of opinion in the founding era believed that exemptions raised any issue of establishment.

Along the way, I review some interesting but mostly forgotten episodes. The most important of these is the long debate over the militia in eighteenth-century Pennsylvania. The century was marked by frequent wars, but the pacifist Quakers were politically dominant until the eve of the American Revolution. Whether to have a militia at all and, if so, what to do about conscientious objectors were the subjects of prolonged debate.

*   *   *

The Symposium that includes this Article proclaims a "(re)turn to history" in religious-liberty law. I doubt that we were ever away from history. Church-state relations were a much contested issue at the time of the American Founding, and those debates left an unusually thick record. All sides in modern debates have mined that record, however selectively, for evidence of original understanding.

One side cites Madison and Jefferson; the other side cites the defenders of the established church. One side cites the decision to end direct financial support of churches; the other side cites congressional chaplains and religious rhetoric by politicians and government officials. At least in political and judicial debates, neither side makes much effort to take account of the evidence offered by the other side, or to craft a theory that explains why the Founders accepted government support of religion in some contexts and not in others.

The claims that nonpreferential aid is permitted, or that noncoercive aid is permitted, fit modern agendas much better than they fit eighteenth-century practice. Not all forms of government support for religion were controversial in the late eighteenth century, but once a form of support became controversial, making it nonpreferential or even noncoercive did not end the controversy.[1] A better first approximation is that the Founders prohibited

---

1. *See generally* Douglas Laycock, *"Noncoercive" Support for Religion: Another False Claim About the Establishment Clause,* 26 VAL. U. L. REV. 37 (1991) [hereinafter Laycock, *"Noncoercive" Support*] (rejecting the theory that the Founders were concerned only with coercive government support for religion); Douglas Laycock, *"Nonpreferential" Aid to Religion: A False Claim About Original Intent,* 27 WM. & MARY L. REV. 875 (1986) [hereinafter Laycock, *"Nonpreferential" Aid*] (rejecting the theory that the Founders were concerned only with support that preferred one or some denominations over others).

forms of support that were controversial among Protestants; government financial support for churches was controversial in the eighteenth century but nonfinancial support did not become controversial until the nineteenth century, when Catholic immigration expanded the range of religious pluralism and thus the range of controversy.[2]

The use of history has been selective not just in the sense that each side prefers its own half of history, but also in the sense that some prominent history is invoked repeatedly, and other history, less widely known, is largely ignored. Both sides in the Supreme Court give much attention to the late eighteenth century but very little to the nineteenth-century Protestant-Catholic battles over public schools, although those battles are the true origin of modern controversies over both financial aid to private schools and religious observance in public schools.[3] The Court has long debated Establishment Clause issues in originalist terms,[4] but it rewrote the law of free exercise without a glance at original understanding.[5] When scholars began providing the historical evidence on free exercise,[6] each side predictably adopted the evidence that supported the position it had already taken.[7] The Court endlessly

2. *See* Laycock, *"Nonpreferential" Aid, supra* note 1, at 913-19.

3. *See* John C. Jeffries, Jr. & James E. Ryan, *A Political History of the Establishment Clause,* 100 MICH. L. REV. 279, 297-305 (2001); Douglas Laycock, *Church and State in the United States: Competing Conceptions and Historic Changes,* 13 IND. J. GLOBAL LEGAL STUD. 503 (2006); Douglas Laycock, *The Many Meanings of Separation,* 70 U. CHI. L. REV. 1667, 1682 (2003) (reviewing PHILIP HAMBURGER, SEPARATION OF CHURCH AND STATE (2002)).

4. *See, e.g.,* Everson v. Bd. of Educ., 330 U.S. 1, 8-16 (1947) (relying on history of disestablishment in America, and especially in Virginia); *id.* at 33-43 (Rutledge, J., dissenting) (same); Wallace v. Jaffree, 472 U.S. 38, 91-106 (1985) (Rehnquist, J., dissenting) (relying on debates in the First Congress and the history of government support for religion).

5. *See* Employment Div. v. Smith, 494 U.S. 872 (1990).

6. *Compare* Philip A. Hamburger, *A Constitutional Right of Religious Exemption: An Historical Perspective,* 60 GEO. WASH. L. REV. 915 (1992) (arguing that the original understanding offers no support for a free exercise right to regulatory exemptions), *with* Michael W. McConnell, *The Origins and Historical Understanding of Free Exercise of Religion,* 103 HARV. L. REV. 1409 (1990) (arguing that the original understanding is somewhat supportive of such a right).

7. *Compare* City of Boerne v. Flores, 521 U.S. 507, 537-44 (1997) (Scalia, J., concurring) (arguing that historical evidence supports *Employment Division v. Smith*), and Employment Division v. Smith, 494 U.S. 872, 876-90 (Scalia, J.) (holding that government-imposed burdens on religious practice require no justification if imposed by neutral and generally applicable law), *with Boerne,* 521 U.S. at 548-64 (O'Connor, J., dissenting) (arguing that historical evidence is inconsistent with *Smith*), and *Smith,* 494 U.S. at 892-903 (O'Connor, J., concurring) (rejecting *Smith's* rule and arguing that all government-imposed burdens on religious practice require a compelling justification).

debates what the framers of the First Amendment thought about establishment, but it shows no interest in what the framers of the Fourteenth Amendment thought about establishment, although it is the Fourteenth Amendment that applies in most of its cases.[8] The Court is reasonably familiar with late-eighteenth-century evidence on funding and religious speech by government officials,[9] but often it addresses newly emerging issues with little awareness of historical evidence that might be relevant.

This Article addresses one such underexamined issue. Some opponents of regulatory exemptions for religious practice claim that exemptions prefer religion and thus violate the Establishment Clause. This claim is inconsistent with the original understanding. There is much originalist debate about whether the founding generation understood regulatory exemptions to be constitutionally required.[10] But there is virtually no evidence that anyone thought they were constitutionally prohibited or that they were part of an establishment of religion. The established church had no need for exemptions, because its teachings were in accord with government policy. Exemptions protect minority religions, and they emerged only in the wake of toleration of dissenting worship. Exemptions are subject to limits in specific cases; they cannot prefer particular faiths or particular religious practices, and they cannot impose significant costs on persons not voluntarily engaged in the exempted religious practice. But nothing in our constitutional tradition suggests that regulatory exemptions for religious practice are facially invalid.

Fortunately, the Court agrees. Three times in recent years it has unanimously rejected the claim that regulatory exemptions for religiously motivated conduct establish the unregulated religion.[11] It reached these decisions

8. For nineteenth-century developments in disestablishment, see Kurt T. Lash, *The Second Adoption of the Establishment Clause: The Rise of the Nonestablishment Principle*, 27 ARIZ. ST. L.J. 1085, 1100-54 (1995). I do not subscribe to Lash's federalism interpretation of the Establishment Clause as of 1791, but that disagreement must await another day.

9. *See, e.g.*, Van Orden v. Perry, 565 U.S. 677, 722-31 (2005) (Stevens, J., concurring) (conceding history of religious statements by federal officials and providing additional context); McCreary County v. ACLU of Ky., 545 U.S. 844, 886-89, 895-98 (2005) (Scalia, J., dissenting) (reviewing history of religious statements by federal officials); Rosenberger v. Rector of Univ. of Va., 515 U.S. 819, 852-60 (Thomas, J., concurring) (reviewing founding-era opposition to funding of churches); *id.* at 868-72 (Souter, J., dissenting) (same); *see also* cases cited *supra* note 4.

10. *See supra* notes 6-7.

11. Cutter v. Wilkinson, 544 U.S. 709, 719-26 (2005); Bd. of Educ. v. Grumet, 512 U.S. 687, 705-06 (1994); *id.* at 711-12 (Stevens, J., concurring); *id.* at 715-16 (O'Connor, J., concurring); *id.* at 722-27 (Kennedy, J., concurring in the judgment); *id.* at 743-45 (Scalia, J., dissenting); Corp. of the Presiding Bishop v. Amos, 483 U.S. 327, 334-39 (1987); *id.* at 340-46 (Brennan, J., concur-

without inquiring into original understanding. This Article argues that such evidence as we have of original understanding supports the Court's decisions.

It is no part of my claim that original understanding should be controlling. But original understanding is relevant on almost any view of constitutional interpretation, and in the view of some Justices, it should be decisive. So it is a matter of some importance to review the original understanding that supports or contradicts the Court's decisions.

I. Regulatory Exemptions and the Establishment Clause

A. The Attack on Regulatory Exemptions

Establishment Clause attacks on religious exemptions come in many variations.[12] But the core idea at the heart of all those arguments is that government can establish a religion by failing to regulate it, at least if the religion or one of its practitioners does some act that is regulated in secular contexts. Exemptions from government regulation are said to give special preference to the unregulated religious practice, and thus to establish the religion of which the practice is a part.

---

ring); *id.* at 346 (Blackmun, J., concurring); *id.* at 348-49 (O'Connor, J., concurring); *see infra* notes 254-67 and accompanying text; *see also Smith,* 494 U.S. at 890 (reaffirming legislative power to enact exemptions while holding that they are not constitutionally required); *id.* at 893-97 (O'Connor, J., concurring) (arguing that exemptions are constitutionally required).

12. This argument is made most forcefully and explicitly in the losing briefs in the cases cited *supra* note 11. *See* Brief for Respondents at 10-24, *Cutter,* 544 U.S. 709 (No. 03-9877); Brief for Respondents at 21-29, *Grumet,* 512 U.S. 687 (Nos. 93-517, 93-527, 93-539); Brief for Appellees at 25-39, *Amos,* 483 U.S. 327 (Nos. 86-179, 86-401). For academic versions of the argument, see PHILIP B. KURLAND, RELIGION AND THE LAW 17-18, 40-41, 111-12 (1962) (arguing that the Religion Clauses prohibit any government classification based on religion, either to impose a burden or confer a benefit, including religious exemptions from regulation); Steven G. Gey, *Why Is Religion Special?: Reconsidering the Accommodation of Religion Under the Religion Clauses of the First Amendment,* 52 U. PITT. L. REV. 75, 182-85 (1990) (arguing that regulatory exemptions for religion subordinate democratic control to a nondemocratic, extrahuman force); Suzanna Sherry, Lee v. Weisman: *Paradox Redux,* 1992 SUP. CT. REV. 123, 123-24 (arguing that the Establishment Clause prohibits the exemptions that the Free Exercise Clause seems to require, so that one of the clauses must be interpreted very narrowly and its values subordinated to the values of the other). For a more nuanced view, see CHRISTOPHER L. EISGRUBER & LAWRENCE G. SAGER, RELIGIOUS FREEDOM AND THE CONSTITUTION 246-52 (2006) (arguing that exemptions are unconstitutional if they exceed the authors' principle of "equal liberty," which depends on sophisticated comparisons of religious commitments to comparably important secular commitments).

The argument proceeds from the premise that the Establishment Clause, or the Establishment Clause and Free Exercise Clause together, require government neutrality toward religion, including neutrality between religion and nonreligion. That premise has been controversial, but I share it; nothing in this Article depends on rejecting the premise of government neutrality toward religion.

The second step in the modern argument that exemptions violate the Establishment Clause is to assume that neutrality means what I have called "formal neutrality" — the absence of rules that formally distinguish on the basis of religion.[13] A rule that children may consume wine at communion services and Seder dinners, but not at secular events — or any other rule permitting a thing to be done for religious purposes but not for secular purposes — violates formal neutrality. Regulatory exemptions are not formally neutral, but they are often consistent with what I have called "substantive neutrality."[14]

Formal neutrality seeks to create religiously neutral *categories;* substantive neutrality seeks to create religiously neutral *incentives,* minimizing the extent to which government either encourages or discourages religious practice.[15] Criminalizing communion wine for children is a powerful discouragement of a religious exercise; permitting children to take both the bread and wine at communion is unlikely to encourage nonbelievers to attend worship services, or to encourage believers to shift from a denomination that uses grape juice to a denomination that uses wine.

This choice between formal and substantive neutrality poses the modern conceptual argument in a nutshell, but it is relevant here only to the task of integrating original understanding with modern interpretation. My principal purpose here is to test the conclusion of the formal neutrality argument — that religious exemptions violate the Establishment Clause — against the original understanding of the Establishment Clause.

There is no significant originalist support for the core idea that exempting religion from regulation establishes religion. Exemptions from regulation were no part of the establishment of religion known to the founding generation. Exemptions emerged as an outgrowth of the state-by-state process of expanding free exercise. Some of these exemptions provoked substantial debate, and their opponents made many arguments, but I have found no one in

---

13. *See* Douglas Laycock, *Formal, Substantive, and Disaggregated Neutrality Toward Religion,* 39 DePaul L. Rev. 993, 999-1001 (1990).

14. *Id.* at 1001.

15. *See id.* at 1001-06; *see also* Church of the Lukumi Babalu Aye, Inc. v. City of Hialeah, 508 U.S. 520, 561-63 (1993) (Souter, J., concurring) (further comparing formal and substantive neutrality).

the eighteenth century who attacked them as an establishment of religion or denied that legislatures had power to enact them.

B. The Features of Establishment

The essence of establishment was government sponsorship and control of a single church or, in later years, of a group of churches, such as all Protestant denominations, or all Christian denominations. In Judge McConnell's comprehensive survey of establishment in England and the colonies, he identifies six historic "Elements of the Establishment":[16]

1. Governmental Control Over the Doctrines, Structure, and Personnel of the State Church;[17]
2. Mandatory Attendance at Religious Worship Services in the State Church;[18]
3. Public Financial Support [of the state church];[19]
4. Prohibition of Religious Worship in Other Denominations;[20]
5. Use of the State Church for Civil Functions;[21] and
6. Limitation of Political Participation to Members of the State Church.[22]

This careful listing of six distinct elements is organizationally helpful, but of course each of these elements is familiar from other descriptions of the established churches.[23] Each of these historic elements of the establishment is prohibited by modern constitutional law, sometimes with controversy about the limits of the principle and its application to analogous cases:

1. Government controlled the doctrine, structure, and personnel of the established church; today, government is not permitted to control the doctrine, structure, or personnel of religious organizations.[24]

16. Michael W. McConnell, *Establishment and Disestablishment at the Founding, Part I: Establishment of Religion*, 44 Wm. & Mary L. Rev. 2105, 2131 (2003).
17. *Id.*
18. *Id.* at 2144.
19. *Id.* at 2146.
20. *Id.* at 2159.
21. *Id.* at 2169.
22. *Id.* at 2176.
23. *See, e.g.,* Thomas J. Curry, The First Freedoms: Church and State in America to the Passage of the First Amendment 1-77 (1986).
24. *See, e.g.,* Jones v. Wolf, 443 U.S. 595, 602-06 (1979) (holding that civil courts may re-

2. Government mandated attendance at worship services of the established church; today, mandatory attendance at worship services is unconstitutional, even when judicial deference is at its maximum, as in judicial review of military regulations.[25] The contested modern counterpart to mandatory worship is prayer and other religious observances at government-sponsored events that people attend for secular reasons.[26]

3. The established church received tax support for its core religious functions; today, tax support for those functions is clearly unconstitutional, and the debated question is whether tax support of religiously sponsored schools or social services is sufficiently analogous to be an establishment.[27]

4. Government suppressed religious competition with the established church; today, restrictions on minority faiths are rarely part of any effort to establish some other religion, and such restrictions are now treated as a free exercise issue.[28] This distinction has very early roots. Both England and America reached relative consensus on free exercise long before they

---

solve church property disputes on basis of church's own documents, or by deferring to church tribunals, but not on the basis of judicial resolution of any issue of religious doctrine or practice); Serbian E. Orthodox Diocese v. Milivojevich, 426 U.S. 696, 708-25 (1976) (holding that civil courts cannot review church tribunal's decisions to remove bishop and divide diocese); Kedroff v. Saint Nicholas Cathedral, 344 U.S. 94, 106-21 (1952) (holding that a statute awarding church property and authority to dissident faction in preference to those recognized by original church authorities violates the Free Exercise Clause).

25. *See* Anderson v. Laird, 466 F.2d 283, 283-84 (D.C. Cir. 1972) (per curiam) (invalidating compulsory chapel at military academies); *id.* at 284-96 (Bazelon, J., concurring); *id.* at 296-305 (Leventhal, J., concurring).

26. *See, e.g.,* Santa Fe Indep. Sch. Dist. v. Doe, 530 U.S. 290, 301-17 (2000) (holding that student-led invocation at high-school football games violates the Establishment Clause); Lee v. Weisman, 505 U.S. 577, 586-99 (1992) (holding that clergy-led invocation at middle-school graduation violates the Establishment Clause); Sch. Dist. v. Schempp, 374 U.S. 203, 223-27 (1963) (holding that opening school day with prayer and Bible reading violates the Establishment Clause); Engel v. Vitale, 370 U.S. 421, 424-36 (1962) (holding that reciting an official prayer in public schools violates the Establishment Clause).

27. *See, e.g.,* Zelman v. Simmons-Harris, 536 U.S. 639, 648-63 (2002) (upholding program of state vouchers that could be used to pay tuition at wide range of public and private schools, including religious schools); Lemon v. Kurtzman, 403 U.S. 602, 611-25 (1971) (holding that cash grants to supplement teacher salaries at religious schools violate the Establishment Clause).

28. *See, e.g.,* Church of the Lukumi Babalu Aye, Inc. v. City of Hialeah, 508 U.S. 520, 531-47 (1993) (holding that ban on animal sacrifice violates the Free Exercise Clause); Employment Div. v. Smith, 494 U.S. 872, 876-90 (1990) (holding that Free Exercise Clause requires no justification of government-imposed burdens on religious practice if those burdens are imposed by neutral and generally applicable law).

reached anything like consensus on disestablishment. England enacted "toleration" for all Trinitarian Protestants in 1688, in the wake of the Glorious Revolution,[29] and John Locke published his influential justification for toleration the following year.[30] The core idea of "toleration" was that religious dissenters would be free to worship in their own way while the established church continued to function with little or no change for everyone else.[31]

5. Government used the established church for civil functions; today, government cannot delegate government functions to religious organizations,[32] and the point of modern controversy is whether it can contract for performance of specific services on equal terms with religious and secular organizations alike.[33]

6. Government restricted political participation to members of the estab-

29. An Act for Exempting their Majestyes Protestant Subjects Dissenting from the Church of England from the Penalties of Certaine Lawes, 1688, 1 W. & M., c. 18, *reprinted in* 6 THE STATUTES OF THE REALM 74 (photo. reprint 1993) [1810] [hereinafter Toleration Act].

30. *See* John Locke, *A Letter Concerning Toleration,* in THE SECOND TREATISE OF GOVERNMENT AND A LETTER CONCERNING TOLERATION 125 (J. W. Gough ed., Basil Blackwell 3d ed. 1966) (1690). The letter was first published in English in November 1689; a revised edition was published in 1690. *See* J. W. Gough, *Introduction* to THE SECOND TREATISE OF GOVERNMENT AND A LETTER CONCERNING TOLERATION *supra,* at xlvi-xlvii.

31. So, for example, the English statute commonly known as the "Act of Toleration" was written in terms of the rights and duties of persons "dissenting from the Church of England," as indicated in the formal title, in §§ 4, 5, and 6, and in similar formulations in § 7 ("dissenting Protestants") and § 10 ("Dissenters from the Church of England"). *See* Toleration Act, *supra* note 29. *See also* People v. Philips (N.Y. Ct. Gen. Sess. June 14, 1813), *in* WILLIAM SAMPSON, THE CATHOLIC QUESTION IN AMERICA 9 (photo. reprint 1974) (1813), *and excerpts reprinted in Privileged Communications to Clergymen,* 1 CATH. LAW. 199, 207 (1955) ("In this country there is no alliance between church and state; no established religion; no tolerated religion — for toleration results from establishment.").

32. *See, e.g.,* Bd. of Educ. v. Grumet, 512 U.S. 687, 696-702 (1994) (plurality opinion) (holding that state cannot define a school district on religious lines); *id.* at 728-30 (Kennedy, J., concurring) (providing the fifth vote on the ground that state cannot draw electoral boundaries on religious lines); Larkin v. Grendel's Den, Inc., 459 U.S. 116, 120-27 (1982) (holding that state cannot delegate to churches any portion of its power to grant or withhold liquor licenses).

33. *See, e.g.,* Zelman v. Simmons-Harris, 536 U.S. 639, 648-63 (2002) (holding that state can pay for education of children in religious and secular schools alike); Bowen v. Kendrick, 487 U.S. 589, 602-18 (1988) (holding that government can give grants to both religious and secular non-profit organizations for programs to prevent adolescent pregnancy); Bradfield v. Roberts, 175 U.S. 291, 295-300 (1899) (holding that government could contract with Providence Hospital, owned and operated by an order of nuns, for care of the indigent patients in the District of Columbia).

lished church; today, the state cannot restrict political participation on the basis of religious convictions or participation.[34]

Even the modern controversy over government endorsement of religious beliefs may readily be analogized to government designating the church or group of churches to be established.[35]

Exemptions from regulation do not appear on Judge McConnell's list or in any other description of the established church. The established church had no need of regulatory exemptions, because government rarely made laws that prevented members of the established church from practicing their religion. Laws regulating conduct were generally consistent with the moral commitments of the established church, both because the established church and its members had substantial political influence, and because government's control over the established church, generally including the power to appoint clergy, tended to prevent the emergence of religious teachings that challenged government policy.[36] The King was the supreme head of the Church of England,[37] all Anglican clergy were appointed under his authority,[38] and fundamental religious teachings were specified by statute, beginning with the wonderfully named act "abolishing diversity in Opynions."[39] In Massachusetts and the other New England establishments modeled on Massachusetts, clergy were elected by the voters of each local jurisdiction.[40]

34. *See, e.g.,* McDaniel v. Paty, 435 U.S. 618, 625-29 (1978) (plurality opinion) (holding that state constitutional provision precluding ministers from serving in the legislature violates Free Exercise Clause); *id.* at 629-42 (Brennan, J., concurring) (stating that provision violates both Free Exercise and Establishment Clauses); *id.* at 642-43 (Stewart, J., concurring) (stating that provision violates "First Amendment"); *id.* at 643-46 (White, J., concurring) (stating that provision violates Equal Protection Clause).

35. *See* Laycock, *"Noncoercive" Support, supra* note 1, at 41-48.

36. *See* McConnell, *supra* note 16, at 2131-44 (reviewing the many ways in which government controlled the established church).

37. *See* An Acte concernynge the Kynges Highnes to be supreme heed of the Churche of Englande & to have auctoryte to refourme & redresse all errours heresyes & abuses yn the same, 1534, 26 Hen. 8, c. 1 (Eng.), *reprinted in* 3 THE STATUTES OF THE REALM, *supra* note 29, at 492.

38. *See* An Acte restraynyng the payment of Annates, &c, 1534, 25 Hen. 8, c. 20 (Eng.), *reprinted in* 3 THE STATUTES OF THE REALM, *supra* note 29, at 462.

39. *See* An Acte abolishing diversity in Opynions, 1539, 31 Hen. 8, c. 14 (Eng.), *reprinted in* 3 THE STATUTES OF THE REALM, *supra* note 29, at 739.

40. *See* MASS. CONST., pt. I, art. III (1780), *reprinted in* 3 THE FEDERAL AND STATE CONSTITUTIONS, COLONIAL CHARTERS AND OTHER ORGANIC LAWS OF THE STATES, TERRITORIES, AND COLONIES NOW OR HERETOFORE FORMING THE UNITED STATES OF AMERICA, at 1888, 1889-90 (Francis Newton Thorpe ed., 1909) [hereinafter LAWS OF THE STATES].

Even a nonestablished church has no need for exemptions where its members have political control. Thus in Pennsylvania, where there was never an established church, there was no exemption from military service or oath taking so long as the Society of Friends — "the people commonly called Quakers" in the usage of the time — were politically dominant. Instead, the laws did not require military service or oath taking of anyone.[41] Exemptions were enacted only after Quakers lost control — when the Crown imposed oath requirements[42] and when a new political majority enacted conscription to raise an army for the Revolution.[43] Then the Quakers, as a faith unable to control public policy even in Pennsylvania, needed exemptions. And within the limits described in the next Part, these exemptions were enacted.[44]

II. The Origin of Regulatory Exemptions

Regulatory exemptions emerged when the majority became willing to provide for the religious liberty of minority faiths. Exemptions were never part of the establishment; they grew out of a political commitment to free exercise. The emergence of free exercise was an early step in the long process of disestablishment, but as we shall see, regulatory exemptions could and did coexist with formally established churches.

Disestablishment did not happen all at once; it emerged first in certain colonies and later state-by-state in the early Republic. The formal designation of an established and tax-supported church was abandoned over a period of about sixty years, beginning in the 1770s and ending in 1833.[45] But this

---

41. The Law About the Manner of Giving Evidence and Against Such as Lie in Conversation, c. 99, 2 PA. STAT. 133 (1700), repealed by the Queen in Council (1706).

42. An Act Prescribing the Forms of Declaration of Fidelity, Abjuration and Affirmation, Instead of the Forms Heretofore Required in Such Cases, ch. 281, 3 PA. STAT. 427 (1724). The long dispute over oaths in the early eighteenth century is described in J. WILLIAM FROST, A PERFECT FREEDOM: RELIGIOUS LIBERTY IN PENNSYLVANIA 23-25 (1990).

43. *See, e.g.,* Ellis M. West, *The Right to Religion-Based Exemptions in Early America: The Case of Conscientious Objectors to Conscription,* 10 J.L. & RELIGION 367, 388-94 (1994) (summarizing developments from a perspective hostile to exemptions).

44. *See* PA. CONST. of 1776, pt. I, art. VIII, *reprinted in* 5 LAWS OF THE STATES, at 3081, 3083 ("Nor can any man who is conscientiously scrupulous of bearing arms, be justly compelled thereto, if he will pay such equivalent. . . ."). This and other Pennsylvania provisions, and the qualification of an "equivalent," are discussed *infra* in notes 125-32 and accompanying text.

45. *See* Carl H. Esbeck, *Dissent and Disestablishment: The Church-State Settlement in the Early American Republic,* 2004 BYU L. REV. 1385, 1432-48, 1457-1540 (reviewing disestablish-

was just one stage in a longer process; the multiple elements of the classic establishment were abandoned one-by-one over a period of centuries, and the gradual abandonment of informal government support for popular religion continues, with debate and resistance, to this day.

As early as 1675, Connecticut exempted Quakers from attending the established worship — provided they did not assemble for religious purposes themselves;[46] after 1708, Connecticut permitted dissenters to worship in their own way.[47] In 1689, the Act of Toleration permitted dissenting Trinitarian Protestants to worship in England.[48] This reform spread slowly and unevenly through the colonies, although resistance persisted in Virginia up to the eve of the Revolution.[49] In 1753, the King's Attorney General issued an opinion that the Act of Toleration applied throughout the colonies.[50]

Once a state decided that minority faiths should be permitted to freely worship, the logic of toleration suggested that they should also be exempted from other laws that made their lives unnecessarily difficult. The impulse that led to toleration was that religious dissenters should be free to live in a jurisdiction and that their lives should not be made miserable because of their faith. Once a jurisdiction came around to this view, it quickly became apparent that toleration must apply not just to belief, but also to religious speech and worship, and to important religious conduct. Dissenters could not live in a state where their worship was penalized, but neither could they live in a state where any of their other important religious practices were penalized. Some legislators may have viewed these regulatory exemptions for

---

ment state-by-state). The beginning date would be much earlier if one includes the states that never had a tax-supported church.

46. Act of July 9, 1675, *reprinted in* 2 THE PUBLIC RECORDS OF THE COLONY OF CONNECTICUT, FROM 1665 TO 1678, 260, 264 (Hartford, F.A. Brown 1852). For descriptions of this and other early steps toward tolerance, see CURRY, *supra* note 23, at 25.

47. *See* An Act for securing the Rights of Conscience in matters of Religion, to Christians of every Denomination in this State, *reprinted in* ACTS AND LAWS OF THE STATE OF CONNECTICUT IN AMERICA 21 (Hartford, Elisha Babcock 1786) [hereinafter CONNECTICUT LAWS]. The cited source is an alphabetical collection of Connecticut statutes in effect in 1786, but it does not give dates of enactment. The Baptist leader John Leland gives the date of the original version of this statute as 1708. *See Extracts from Connecticut Ecclesiastical Laws,* in JOHN LELAND, THE CONNECTICUT DISSENTER'S STRONG BOX: No. 1, at 26, 28 (New London, Charles Holt 1802), *available* at Infotrac, Gale Doc. No. F3704953471.

48. Toleration Act, *supra* note 29.

49. *See* Esbeck, *supra* note 45, at 1475-76, 1485-87, 1537; McConnell, *supra* note 16, at 2161-69.

50. *See* SANFORD H. COBB, THE RISE OF RELIGIOUS LIBERTY IN AMERICA 105-06 (1902).

religious conduct as a right and others as a matter of legislative grace, but either way, regulatory exemptions quickly emerged in the wake of toleration for dissenting worship.

The first exemption from oath taking appeared in 1669 in the Carolina colony,[51] which from its charter in 1663 recruited settlers by advertising "full and free Liberty of Conscience."[52] As toleration spread through the eighteenth century, the exemption from oath taking became nearly universal.[53] Even Connecticut and Massachusetts, the colonies that had persecuted Quakers most vigorously,[54] enacted exemptions from oath taking in the eighteenth century.[55] The right to affirm instead of swear appears four times,

51. Fundamental Constitutions of Carolina § 100 (1669), *reprinted in* 5 LAWS OF THE STATES, *supra* note 40, at 2772, 2784. Subsection III says that "every church or profession shall, in their terms of communion, set down the external way whereby they witness a truth as in the presence of God. . . ." *Id.* § 100 (III), at 2784. Thomas Curry reports that Quakers "enter[ed] pledges in a book in lieu of swearing." CURRY, *supra* note 23, at 56. By the Revolution, North Carolina had adopted the common solution of allowing Quakers to affirm instead of swear. *See* An Act Concerning Oaths, ch. 108, § 4 (1777) (codifying "the manner heretofore used and accustomed"), *reprinted in* 1 LAWS OF THE STATE OF NORTH CAROLINA 269, 270 (Raleigh, Joseph Gales 1821); An Act for Establishing Courts of Law, and for Regulating the Proceedings Therein, ch. 115, § 42 (1777) (making clear that the exemption extended to criminal as well as civil trials), *reprinted in* 1 LAWS OF THE STATE OF NORTH CAROLINA, *supra*, at 281, 300.

52. CURRY, *supra* note 23, at 56.

53. *See* Arlin M. Adams & Charles J. Emmerich, *A Heritage of Religious Liberty*, 137 U. PA. L. REV. 1559, 1630-32 (1989) (collecting provisions from state and federal constitutions).

54. *See* CURRY, *supra* note 23, at 21-22. Massachusetts hanged four Quakers between 1658 and 1661, when the Crown intervened to stop the practice. *See id.* at 22; Act of May 22, 1661 (providing for multiple whippings and banishment of Quakers, and execution of those who returned repeatedly), *reprinted in* 4 RECORDS OF THE GOVERNOR AND COMPANY OF THE MASSACHUSETTS BAY IN NEW ENGLAND pt. 2, at 18, 19-20 [*379] (Nathaniel B. Shurtleff ed., Boston, William White 1854) [hereinafter MASSACHUSETTS BAY RECORDS]; Act of Nov. 27, 1661 (suspending these penalties in deference to a letter from the King), *reprinted in* 4 MASSACHUSETTS BAY RECORDS, *supra*, at 34, 34 [*390]; Act of Oct. 8, 1662 (reinstating a smaller number of whippings, and banishment), *reprinted in* 4 MASSACHUSETTS BAY RECORDS, *supra*, at 58, 59 [*407].

55. For Connecticut, see An Act for Prescribing and Establishing Forms of Oaths in This State, *reprinted in* CONNECTICUT LAWS, *supra* note 47, at 182, 187; An Act Relative to the People Commonly Called Quakers, *reprinted in* CONNECTICUT LAWS, *supra* note 47, at 196, 197. For Massachusetts, see An Act Providing that the Solemn Affirmation of the People Called Quakers Shall, in Certain Cases, Be Accepted Instead of an Oath in the Usual Form, and for Preventing Inconveniences by Means of Their Having Heretofore Acted in Some Town Offices Without Taking the oaths by Law Required for Such Offices, ch. 20 (1744), *reprinted in* 3 ACTS AND RESOLVES, PUBLIC AND PRIVATE, OF THE PROVINCE OF THE MASSACHUSETTS BAY 126 (Boston, Albert J. Wright 1878) [hereinafter MASSACHUSETTS ACTS AND RESOLVES]. For discussion, see CURRY, *supra* note 23, at 89-90.

matter-of-factly and without controversy, in the Constitution of the United States, in provisions ratified both before and simultaneously with the Establishment Clause.[56] However familiar and uncontroversial it has become, the exemption from the obligation to take oaths is in fact a religious exemption from a generally applicable law. Those who proposed and ratified the Establishment Clause do not appear to have thought that this exemption was an establishment of religion.

North Carolina and Maryland enacted exemptions from the requirement of removing hats in court.[57] This was a response to a famous incident, much denounced in America, in which an English judge had a hat placed upon the head of William Penn, and then held Penn in contempt for refusing to remove it.[58] Rhode Island exempted Jews from incest laws with respect to marriages "within the degrees of affinity or consanguinity allowed by their religion."[59]

Another common set of exemptions, more closely connected to the process of disestablishment, was exemption from paying taxes to support the established church. Beginning in the eighteenth century, exemptions from church taxes spread through the colonies that collected such taxes, although implementation was sometimes grudging.[60] The famous general assessment proposal in Virginia, in 1785, was a last attempt to preserve financial support

---

56. *See* U.S. CONST. art. I, § 3, cl. 6 (oath of Senators when sitting as court of impeachment); *id.* art. II, § 1, cl. 8 (presidential oath); *id.* art. VI, cl. 3 (oath of state and federal legislators and executive and judicial officers to support the Constitution); *id.* amend. IV (oath on application for search warrant).

57. *See* Act of Apr. 19, 1784, ch. 29, § II, 1784 N.C. SESS. LAWS 363, 363 ("[I]t shall be lawful for the people called Quakers to wear their hats as well within the several courts of judicature in this state as elsewhere, unless otherwise ordered by the court."), *microformed on* North Carolina General Assembly Acts (William S. Hein & Co.). The Maryland law, which may have been some sort of executive order, is described in ROBERT J. BRUGGER, MARYLAND: A MIDDLE TEMPERAMENT 1634-1980, at 29-30 (1988).

58. For elaboration of this incident, see McConnell, *supra* note 6, at 1471-72.

59. An Act Regulating Marriage and Divorce § 7, 1798, *reprinted in* 2 THE FIRST LAWS OF THE STATE OF RHODE ISLAND 481, 483 (John D. Cushing ed., 1983).

60. *See, e.g.,* An Act To Exempt Persons Commonly Called Anabaptists, and Those Called Quakers, Within This Province, from Being Taxed for and Towards the Support of Ministers, 1728, *reprinted in* 2 MASSACHUSETTS ACTS AND RESOLVES, *supra* note 55, at 494-96 (Boston, Wright & Potter 1874); MASS. CONST., pt. I, art. III ("And all moneys paid by the subject to the support of public worship, and of the public teachers aforesaid, shall, if he require it, be uniformly applied to the support of the public teacher or teachers of his own religious sect or denomination, provided there be any on whose instructions he attends"), *reprinted in* 3 LAWS OF THE STATES, *supra* note 40, at 1888, 1890. For additional examples and discussion, see CURRY, *supra* note 23, at 89-90; Esbeck, *supra* note 45, at 1434-36, 1440-47, 1476-77, 1479, 1489-91, 1498, 1508 n.431, 1512; McConnell, *supra* note 6, at 1469.

for churches by including all Christian denominations in the benefits and by universalizing the exemption — any taxpayer could support either the church of his choice or a fund for schools.[61] But on this issue, exemptions and multiple establishments were only a stopgap. Virginia's general assessment bill was defeated. By 1833, the last state system of tax support for churches was repealed in Massachusetts,[62] and exemptions from the church tax were no longer an issue.

The first exemption for conscientious objectors to military conscription was enacted in 1673, in famously tolerant Rhode Island.[63] It provided that no person or persons conscientiously opposed to military service

> shall at any time be compelled against his or her judgment and conscience to trayne, arm or fight, to kill any person nor persons by reason of, or at the command of any officer of this Collony, civill nor military, nor by reasons of any by-law here past or formerly enacted; nor shall suffer any punishment, fine, distraint, pennalty nor imprisonment, who cannot in conscience traine, fight, nor kill any person nor persons. . . .[64]

The act further provided that conscientious objectors should perform what would be called, in twentieth-century discussions of conscription,[65] alternative service:

61. The Virginia bill is reprinted as a supplementary appendix to Justice Rutledge's dissenting opinion in *Everson v. Board of Education*, 330 U.S. 1, 72-74 (1947) (Rutledge, J., dissenting). For analysis, see THOMAS E. BUCKLEY, CHURCH AND STATE IN REVOLUTIONARY VIRGINIA 108-09 (1977).

62. *See* MASS. CONST. amend. art. XI (repealing "the third article of the bill of rights").

63. *See* R. R. Russell, *Development of Conscientious Objector Recognition in the United States*, 20 GEO. WASH. L. REV. 409, 412-13 (1952). An earlier Massachusetts law exempted any person who would pay twelve pence. Act of Oct. 19, 1664, *reprinted in* 4 MASSACHUSETTS BAY RECORDS, *supra* note 54, at 135 [*458]. But there is no reason to assume this was for the benefit of conscientious objectors; Massachusetts had reenacted its laws for whipping and banishing Quakers only two years before. *See supra* note 54. Massachusetts finally exempted Quakers from military service in 1757. An Act to exempt the People called Quakers from the Penalty of the Law for Non-attendance on Military Matters, ch. 17 (1757) [hereinafter Massachusetts Act], *reprinted in* 4 MASSACHUSETTS ACTS & RESOLVES, *supra* note 55, at 49 (Rand, Avery & Co. 1881).

64. Act of Aug. 13, 1673, *reprinted in* 2 RECORDS OF THE COLONY OF RHODE ISLAND AND PROVIDENCE PLANTATIONS IN NEW ENGLAND 488, 498 (John Russell Bartlett ed., Providence, Crawford Green & Bro. 1857) [hereinafter RHODE ISLAND RECORDS].

65. *See* 50 U.S.C. App. § 456(j) (requiring conscientious objectors to perform "noncombatant service," or, if they conscientiously object to that as well, "such civilian work contributing to the maintenance of the national health, safety, or interest as the Director may deem appropriate"). For repeated use of the phrases "alternative service" and "alternative civilian

> Provided, nevertheless . . . that when any enemy shall approach or assault the Collony or any place thereof, that then it shall be lawfull for the civill officers for the time beinge, as civill officers (and not as martiall or military) to require such said persons as are of sufficient able bodye and of strength (though exempt from arminge and fightinge), to conduct or convey out of the danger of the enemy, weake and aged impotent persons, women and children, goods and cattle, by which the common weale may be better maintained, and works of mercy manifested to distressed, weake persons; and shall be required to watch to informe of danger (but without armes in martiall manner and matters), and to performe any other civill service by order of the civill officers for the good of the Collony, and inhabitants thereof;[66]

Exemption from military service was of course the most controversial claim to exemption.[67] This exemption is necessary to relieve an egregious burden on one of the most deeply held obligations of conscience, but it also confers a large secular benefit, relieving those exempted from essential duties that can be dangerous, unpleasant, and difficult. The secular benefit creates resentment; where the number of conscientious objectors is large, as in colonial Pennsylvania, exemption concentrates the burdens of military service on others to an extent that is significant and not just theoretical. The effect on secular benefits and burdens distorts religious incentives; it can tempt people to falsely claim the exemption, or to honestly adopt the religious belief that makes them eligible for the exemption. In cases such as this, where religious exemption confers a substantial secular benefit, it is difficult to choose the more nearly neutral course.[68]

Most colonies, and later most states, responded to this difficulty with a compromise something like that illustrated in Rhode Island: Quakers and similar conscientious objectors were exempt from military service in person, but were required to provide a substitute, pay a commutation fee, or less commonly, perform alternative service.[69] This is a real and important ex-

---

service" to describe this requirement, see Johnson v. Robison, 415 U.S. 361, 364, 365 nn.1 & 6, 367, 374, 376, 378-79, 382-83, 385 n.19 (1974); *id.* at 388-89 (Douglas, J., dissenting).

66. Act of Aug. 13, 1673, *reprinted in* RHODE ISLAND RECORDS, *supra* note 64, at 498-99.

67. *See generally* West, *supra* note 43 (reviewing the debate over military service exemptions from a perspective quite hostile to exemptions).

68. *See* Laycock, *supra* note 13, at 1016-18.

69. *See, e.g.,* N.H. CONST. OF 1784, pt. I, art. I, § XIII (amended 1964) ("No person who is conscientiously scrupulous about the lawfulness of bearing arms, shall be compelled thereto, provided he will pay an equivalent."), *reprinted in* 4 LAWS OF THE STATES, *supra* note 40, at 2453, 2455; PA. CONST. of 1776, Declaration of Rights, art. VIII, reprinted in 5 LAWS OF

emption, even though less than what the Quakers and other pacifist faiths wanted. The debates over these exemptions are a principal topic of the next Part.

III. The Founding-Era Debates

A. *Legislative Debates*

Legislatively enacted exemptions for religious practice were thus common by the time of the First Amendment. There is of course a large originalist debate about whether this practice of exemptions was embedded in the Free Exercise Clause.[70] But there is no plausible originalist debate about whether such exemptions violated the Establishment Clause or any state establishment clause. The founding generation was familiar with legislatively enacted exemptions for religious practice, and the states were busily engaged in disestablishing churches, but there is hardly a trace of anyone arguing that legislatively enacted exemptions were an establishment.

The principal subject of relevant debate was exemption from military service. Opponents argued that unconditional exemptions from military service were bad policy, but not that exemptions were unconstitutional or that they implicated any concern about establishment of religion. In the First Congress, the Select Committee proposed to include, in what became our Second Amendment, a clause providing that "no person religiously scrupulous shall be compelled to bear arms."[71] Debating this proposal in the Committee of the Whole, Elbridge Gerry feared that government would "declare who are those religiously scrupulous, and prevent them from bearing arms."[72] In this way, government might "destroy the militia, in order to raise an army upon their ruins."[73] This objection seems so implausible — among other things, it would require that "compelled" be interpreted as "permitted" — as to suggest a willingness to argue just about anything in support of a reflexive opposition. But he did not argue that the proposed exemption would establish religion; that argument was apparently too implausible and unfa-

---

THE STATES, *supra* note 40, at 3081, 3083; Massachusetts Act, *supra* note 63, at 49. For additional examples and discussion, see Adams & Emmerich, *supra* note 53, at 1632-33; McConnell, *supra* note 6, at 1468-69; Russell, *supra* note 63, at 414; West, *supra* note 43, at 389.

70. *See supra* notes 6-7 and accompanying text.

71. 1 ANNALS OF CONG. 749 (Aug. 17, 1789) (Joseph Gales ed., 1834).

72. *Id.*

73. *Id.* at 750.

miliar to occur to him. The argument would not have been unfamiliar if he had heard anyone else make it. This at least suggests that no such argument was circulating in the First Congress, or in New York City (where the First Congress met), or back home in Massachusetts.

Other opponents made a variety of more plausible arguments. Mr. Jackson thought the amendment to exempt conscientious objectors "unjust," unless those exempted were required to pay an equivalent.[74] Mr. Smith thought those exempted should find a substitute.[75] Mr. Benson moved to strike the whole clause and leave the issue to the legislature.[76] "I have no reason to believe but the Legislature will always possess humanity enough to indulge this class of citizens in a matter they are so desirous of; but they ought to be left to their discretion."[77] His motion was defeated, 24-22.[78]

Three days later, on the floor of the House, Mr. Scott also argued that this exemption should be left to the legislature. "I conceive it, said he, to be a legislative right altogether. There are many sects I know, who are religiously scrupulous in this respect; I do not mean to deprive them of any indulgence the law affords."[79] The proposal was amended to read that "no person religiously scrupulous shall be compelled to bear arms *in person*," and as amended, passed by the requisite two-thirds vote.[80] The clause was later removed in the Senate,[81] where debate was not recorded.

This debate reveals opponents who wanted a more limited exemption, requiring payment of a fee or provision of a substitute. These opponents prevailed in the House, by the addition of the words "in person." The debate reveals other opponents who wanted the whole issue left to legislatures, and these opponents appear to have prevailed in the Senate. But the recorded debate contains no suggestion that legislative exemptions were in any way con-

---

74. *Id.*

75. *Id.*

76. *Id.* at 751.

77. *Id.*

78. *Id.*

79. *Id.* at 767 (Aug. 20, 1789).

80. *Id.* (emphasis added). The only other recorded statements are those of Mr. Sherman, *id.* at 750, Mr. Vining, *id.* at 751, and Mr. Boudinot, *id.* at 767, all supporting the exemption as proposed, and Mr. Stone, who thought the text should clarify "what the words 'religiously scrupulous' had reference to," *id.* at 751.

81. *See* 1 Documentary History of the First Federal Congress of the United States of America 136, 154 (Linda Grant de Pauw ed., 1972) (showing proposed fifth Article of Amendment as received from House, with exemption from bearing arms (Aug. 25, 1789), and as passed by Senate, amended to omit exemption from bearing arms (Sept. 4, 1789)).

stitutionally suspect. There is no hint in this debate of any issue concerning establishment of religion.

Debate was far more prolonged in Pennsylvania, where Quakers and other peace churches were a substantial minority.[82] And that debate is unusually well preserved, because local political practice put so much in writing — in long petitions to the legislative Assembly and in the exchange of formal messages, elaborating each side's arguments, between the governor and the Assembly.

Quakers and their political allies, including nonpacifists who supported what came to be known as the Quaker party, controlled the Pennsylvania Assembly well into the second half of the eighteenth century.[83] Quaker refusal to create a militia was a recurring issue, because of Indian raids on the frontier and also because of the risk of invasion during Britain's intermittent wars with other European powers. The issue periodically became acute, most notably in 1739, when the Crown wanted colonial troops for the War of Jenkins' Ear;[84] in 1747, toward the end of King George's War;[85] in 1755, at the outbreak of the French and Indian War;[86] and in 1775, at the outbreak of the Revolution.[87] Quakers demanded an unconditional exemption from military ser-

---

82. *See* RICHARD K. MACMASTER, ET AL., CONSCIENCE IN CRISIS 50-55 (1979). Analyzing the available data sets, none of which is complete, MacMaster concludes that members of the peace churches were something under a quarter of Pennsylvania's population in the decade before the Revolution, *id.* at 52, and a somewhat larger percentage of voters, *id.* at 52-54.

83. *See* FROST, *supra* note 42, at 64.

84. This was a colonial war between England and Spain, fought over trade and influence in the Caribbean; the precipitating excuse was the action of Spanish privateers who seized the ship of an English smuggler, Captain Robert Jenkins, and cut off one of his ears as a warning to others. *See* MACMASTER ET AL., *supra* note 82, at 61-62; REED BROWNING, THE WAR OF THE AUSTRIAN SUCCESSION 23-24 (1993).

85. This was the American name for the colonies' part in a much larger war that historians eventually named the War of the Austrian Succession. *See* EDMUND S. MORGAN, BENJAMIN FRANKLIN 63 (2002) (equating the two names); BROWNING, *supra* note 84, at xii (noting that the modern name dates from the nineteenth century). Arising out of long-lasting strategic conflicts among the great European powers, *id.* at 26-33, the war lasted nearly eight years and is estimated to have killed half a million people, *id.* at 365, 375-77.

86. *See, e.g.,* WILLIAM M. FOWLER, JR., THE FRENCH AND INDIAN WAR AND THE STRUGGLE FOR NORTH AMERICA, 1754-1763 (2005). Fought in North America for imperial control of the eastern half of the continent, this war was also part of a larger European conflict, known in Europe as the Seven Years War. *Id.* at 1.

87. *See, e.g.,* ROBERT MIDDLEKAUFF, THE GLORIOUS CAUSE (1982). For discussion of the disputes between pacifist and non-pacifist Pennsylvanians associated with these wars, *see* FROST, *supra* note 42, at 29-30, 32, 36, 38, 41, 62; MACMASTER ET AL., *supra* note 82, at 31-

vice, and some Quakers refused to pay taxes too closely linked to the war effort.[88] The nonpacifists, long a majority of the population and a strong majority in the revolutionary Assembly, were willing to offer exemption only from military service, and only on condition that those exempted do something else instead — usually pay additional sums of cash to support the war effort. These disputes over the militia and conscription provoked a long political battle, which the Quakers finally lost in 1775 and later.

In the years before 1755, and to a declining extent thereafter, the Quaker party controlled the Assembly and refused to create any form of organized militia. Nonpacifists attacked this policy on many grounds, including one that might be understood as an argument about establishment of religion: "No governor objected to the conscientious scruples of Friends, but all insisted that Friends did not have the right to impose their practices and beliefs upon others."[89] On first encountering this argument in the secondary literature, I thought it analogous to modern arguments that laws corresponding to religious teachings violate the Establishment Clause. After finally tracking this argument down in original sources, I think that this is mostly not what the Quakers' critics were saying. Most of the time, their argument sounded much more in policy than in religion. Defense was a necessity, so Quaker peace principles were bad policy, and the whole colony was stuck with this bad policy because of the religious scruples of those in political power.[90] But at least one pamphleteer, expounding on this political theme, did implicitly accuse the Quakers of acting like an established church:

32, 61-83, 165-68, 213-23, 278-300; Philip Hamburger, *Religious Freedom in Philadelphia*, 54 EMORY L.J. 1603 (2005); West, *supra* note 43, at 385-87, 389-90.

88. *See* FROST, *supra* note 42, at 39; MACMASTER ET AL., *supra* note 82, at 29-30, 33-34, 78-81, 221, 354-64. Illustrative petitions for exemption from war taxes are reprinted *id.* at 113-15.

89. FROST, *supra* note 42, at 30; *see also id.* at 36; West, *supra* note 43, at 386-87.

90. See Message to the Assembly from Governor George Thomas (Jan. 10, 1740), in 3 PENNSYLVANIA ARCHIVES (8TH SERIES) 2535, 2535 (Gertrude McKinney ed. 1931) [hereinafter ARCHIVES] ("I must lament the unhappy Circumstances of a Country, populous indeed, extensive in its Trade, blessed with many natural Advantages, and capable of defending itself; but from a religious Principle of its Representatives against bearing of Arms, subject to become the Prey of the first Invader"); Message from Governor George Thomas (Jan. 23, 1740), in 3 ARCHIVES, *supra*, at 2547, 2551 ("The Demeanor of the People called *Quakers*, may have merited the Protection of the Crown, and the Esteem of Mankind; and I believe this is the first Instance, of a Number of them made use of Liberty of Conscience for tying up the Hands of his Majesty's Subjects, from defending a valuable Part of his Dominions"). I do not mean to imply that Professor Frost misread the sources. Rather, I misread Professor Frost; because he and I were focused on somewhat different questions, I read more into his paraphrase than he had intended. Professor West closely tracks Professor Frost on this point, and I probably misread him as well.

[Y]ou see that our Assembly are, and have always been *Quakers,* and that they are still *principled* against bearing Arms. What can be more absurd than such a Declaration from those who are in the room of our *Protectors?* That which is the chief Design of Government, they declare they can have nothing to do with! . . . [The Quakers say that] we will not provide for [the Province's] Safety, as other Provinces have done for theirs, by compulsive Methods, nor depart one Jot from our Principles, if it were to save it from Destruction. Neither will we give up the Government to others who would take Care of its Defence; for the Laws are all *ours,* the Country is *ours;* and tho' it be true that great Numbers of People, of other religious Denominations, are come among us, yet they came by our *Toleration.*

And now what more need be said to shew how unjustly this Province is swayed by a Faction, and sacrificed to their separate Interests. Our very Laws themselves breathe the Spirit, and speak the Language, of a Faction, who tell us that we are all *tolerated* only by their Grace and Favour. And yet these high and mighty Lords, who speak so loudly of *tolerating* others, can plead no Establishment in their own Behalf.[91]

Even this passage seems more concerned with faction than with establishment. But assuming it is not anachronistic to read this passage as including an argument about establishment, it is an argument that the modern courts have uniformly rejected.[92] There is an ill-defined point at which the state would be unconstitutionally compelling religious worship or observance of religious ritual,[93] but short of that, the Court's view has been that the state is simply regulating behavior within its power to regulate and that it is irrelevant if such regulation corresponds with the moral views of one or more religions. So any Establishment Clause implications of this anti-Quaker argument went well beyond modern Establishment Clause doctrine.

But more fundamentally, even if this is an Establishment Clause argument, it is not an Establishment Clause argument *about exemptions.* The refusal to

91. WILLIAM SMITH, A BRIEF VIEW OF THE CONDUCT OF PENNSYLVANIA, FOR THE YEAR 1755, at 75 (London, R. Griffiths 1756) (*available at* Infotrac, Gale Doc. No. CW3302956857). Smith was a politically active Anglican priest. *See* FROST, *supra* note 42, at 49-50.

92. *See* Harris v. McRae, 448 U.S. 297, 319-20 (1980) (holding that refusal to fund abortions is not an establishment); McGowan v. Maryland, 366 U.S. 420, 444 (1961) (holding that Sunday closing laws are not an establishment); Clayton v. Place, 884 F.2d 376, 379-81 (8th Cir. 1989) (holding that school's refusal to sponsor or permit dances is not an establishment).

93. The line between regulating behavior and mandating religious observance is briefly discussed in Douglas Laycock, *Freedom of Speech That Is Both Religious and Political,* 29 U.C. DAVIS L. REV. 793, 812-13 (1996).

create a militia was in no sense a policy of exemption; it was an enactment of Quaker policy for everyone, and this imposition of the views of one faith was precisely the point of the establishment-sounding attack on the colony's policy.

The argument against the Quakers' refusal to create a militia is more akin to an argument for exemptions — adherents of faiths that were willing to fight should be exempt from the general policy of pacifism. But this would not be a standard-form argument for exemption. It seems unlikely that many Anglicans or Presbyterians felt *religiously* compelled to fight, although people may have talked themselves into this position. The preamble to the 1755 militia law, drafted by Benjamin Franklin,[94] recites that "some" members of nonpacifist denominations "think it their Duty to fight in defense of their Country, their Wives, their Families and Estates, and such have an Equal Right to Liberty of Conscience with others."[95] In any event, no law prevented individuals from fighting back when attacked, or even from organizing themselves into voluntary militias;[96] what was wanted was an organized defense, which required affirmative government conduct and not merely an exemption from regulation.[97] So the analogy is quite imperfect. But to the ex-

94. *See* FROST, *supra* note 42, at 39.

95. An Act for the Better Ordering and Regulating Such as Are Willing and Desirous to be United for Military Purposes Within This Province, ch. 405 (1755) [hereinafter 1755 Act], *reprinted in* 5 PA. STAT., *supra* note 41, at 197 (William Stanley Ray 1898). The Act is partially reprinted in MACMASTER ET AL., *supra* note 82, at 115-17.

96. *See* FROST, *supra* note 42, at 31, 34-35 (summarizing the Quaker arguments).

97. *See* Message to the Assembly from Governor George Thomas (Jan. 10, 1740), in 3 ARCHIVES, *supra* note 90, at 2535, 2537 ("An Officer without legal Authority, and Men under no legal Obligation, may indeed exhibit a pretty piece of Pagentry for a little Time, but it can be of no real Service in the Defence of a Country"); Message to the Assembly from Governor George Thomas (Jan. 23, 1740), in 3 ARCHIVES *supra* note 90, at 2547, 2551 ("no more than two or three Hundred Men appeared under Arms in the Time of a former Governor, and . . . even that Number may not be persuaded to do it now as they see no Probability of being serviciable to their Country, for want of being put under proper Regulations by Law"); Message to the Assembly from Governor Robert Hunter Morris (Nov. 3, 1755), in 5 ARCHIVES *supra* note 90, at 4094, 4095 ("The People in the Back Counties have on this important Occasion behaved themselves with uncommon Spirit and Activity; but complain much of the Want of Order and Discipline, as well as of Arms and Ammunition."); A Representation to the General Assembly of the Province of Pennsylvania, by several of the principal Inhabitants of the City of Philadelphia, in said Province (Nov. 11, 1755), in 5 ARCHIVES *supra* note 90, at 4115, 4116 ("it would neither be adviseable for the Sake of such Men themselves, nor yet for the Sake of *Public Liberty,* to keep up an armed Force in the Country, without the Sanction and Authority of Law"); *id.* at 4117 ("no Sums of Money, however great, will answer the Purpose of Defence, without such a Law as we desire"). Each quotation is taken from a longer passage elaborating the theme.

tent the argument was that the politically dominant Quakers should not force religious minorities to conform to a Quaker policy of pacifism, that is closely akin to arguing that religious minorities should have been exempt from the existing law.

At the outbreak of the French and Indian War, Quakers still held a majority in the Assembly,[98] but the refusal to provide a militia became politically untenable.[99] It may also have been untenable for Quakers to conscript others while exempting themselves; the Franklin-drafted preamble recited that such a law would be "inconsistent and partial."[100] (Franklin was not a Quaker, but he supported the Quaker party.[101]) The Quakers' remarkable proposed solution was a voluntary militia. The act provided that it would henceforth be lawful "for the freemen of this province to form themselves into companies, as heretofore they have used in time of war without law,"[102] and went on to provide for the governance and regulation of this militia, authorizing election of officers, articles of war, and courts martial,[103] and exempting all "who are conscientiously scrupulous of bearing arms," and "any other Persons of what Persuasion or Denomination soever who have not first voluntarily signed the said articles after due consideration."[104] This voluntary militia comes considerably closer to a broadly applicable legislative exemption from the official pacifist policy.

This compromise satisfied neither the pacifists nor their opponents.[105] In 1756, after the delays incident to trans-Atlantic communication, the Crown "repealed" (that is, vetoed) the Act as ineffectual.[106] The Quaker Yearly Meeting condemned Quaker legislators for sacrificing conscience to retain power, urging them to resign.[107] After 1756, there was never again a Quaker majority in the Assembly.[108] But the Quaker party, now consisting of "political Quakers" who disregarded the Meeting's advice to withdraw, other pacifists, and their non-pacifist allies, continued to control the Assembly until the Revolution,[109] mak-

---

98. *See* FROST, *supra* note 42, at 39.

99. *See* West, *supra* note 43, at 386-87.

100. 1755 Act, *supra* note 95, at 197.

101. *See* FROST, *supra* note 42, at 38-39; SMITH, *supra* note 91, at 76.

102. 1755 Act, *supra* note 95, § 1, at 198.

103. *Id.* §§ 1-2.

104. *Id.* § 2.

105. See FROST, *supra* note 42, at 39.

106. The fact of the veto appears in a note to 1755 Act, *supra* note 95, at 201. For the veto message, see 6 ARCHIVES, *supra* note 90, at 4394-95 (Charles F Hoban ed., 1935).

107. *See* FROST, *supra* note 42, at 39.

108. *See id.*

109. *See id.* at 32, 39, 60.

ing ever greater efforts to satisfy the political pressure for an effective military defense.[110]

The Assembly tried again in 1757. This time it enacted conscription, with an exemption for conscientious objectors, provided that objectors either pay a fine of twenty shillings or perform such alternative service as extinguishing fires, suppressing slave insurrections, caring for the wounded, conveying messages, and taking women, children, the infirm, or threatened property to places of safety.[111] This time the governor vetoed the bill as ineffectual, and the provision for alternative service did not reappear in any subsequent legislation.[112]

Meanwhile, militia supporters worked to make something useful out of a legally unauthorized voluntary militia. In 1747, with French privateers raiding on the lower Delaware and reports of a French invasion planned for the following summer,[113] Benjamin Franklin had successfully urged the creation of an "Association" of persons willing to defend the colony.[114] He organized a lottery to raise funds for fortifications, and solicited artillery from other colonies.[115] The resulting Association was disbanded when King George's War ended in 1748.[116]

In the French and Indian War, there were again volunteer units modeled on the Association, and the governor commissioned officers for these troops, relying on authority granted to William Penn in the colony's original char-

110. *Id.* at 62 ("The Quaker party survived until 1976 only by repudiating the goals of the Society of Friends."). Another commentator has suggested a more complicated story — that the Quakers who left politics expanded the reach of the peace teaching while the political Quakers emphasized other Quaker teachings. Quaker teaching on pacifism conflicted with Quaker teaching on the government's duty to defend the people, and this conflict became most apparent where Quakers controlled the government. For an account of the Quakers' evolving efforts to resolve this conflict, and the deep split that emerged by the middle of the eighteenth century, see Hermann Wellenreuther, *The Political Dilemma of the Quakers in Pennsylvania, 1681-1748*, 94 PA. MAGAZINE OF HISTORY & BIOGRAPHY 135 (1970).

111. An Act for Forming and Regulating the Militia Within this Province (1757), *reprinted in* MACMASTER ET AL., *supra* note 82, at 117, 119. This legislation does not appear in the Pennsylvania Statutes at Large, presumably because the governor never signed the bill.

112. *See* MACMASTER ET AL., *supra* note 82, at 117.

113. *See* MORGAN, *supra* note 85, at 65.

114. *See Plain Truth: or, Serious Considerations On the Present State of the City of Philadelphia, and Province of Pennsylvania, By a Tradesman of Philadelphia* 19-22 (1747), *available at* Infotrac, Gale Doc. No. CW3304472384 et seq.). For discussion, see EDWIN S. GAUSTAD, BENJAMIN FRANKLIN 52-54 (2006); MACMASTER ET AL., *supra* note 82, at 68-71; MORGAN, *supra* note 85, at 65-70.

115. *See* GAUSTAD, *supra* note 114, at 53-54; MORGAN, *supra* note 85, at 67-68.

116. *See* MACMASTER ET AL., *supra* note 82, at 71.

ter.[117] The governor emphasized the limited scope of this authority, warning the Assembly: "I have neither Money, Arms or Ammunition at my Disposal; all I have therefore been able to do has been to issue Commissions to such as were willing to take them, and to encourage the People to defend themselves and their Families till the Government was enabled to protect them."[118] The Assembly now acted to provide regulations and funds for these troops,[119] but it did not enact any further militia legislation.

When the Revolution came, the issue was squarely posed. National existence was at stake; Quakers were a highly visible and affluent minority, suspected of Toryism;[120] in their resistance to war, some of them made statements supporting the Crown.[121] The British threatened Philadelphia by late 1776, and captured the city in 1777.[122] Many pacifists were disfranchised for refusing to pay taxes or affirm loyalty to the revolutionary government, effectively excluding Quakers from the Assembly.[123] There was hostility to pacifists and episodes of harsh treatment.[124] Political conditions could not have been worse for a claim of exemption from military service. Yet the basic exemption survived.

Pennsylvania's initial response was to support the Association, turning it into a de facto state-sponsored militia. On the question of who should serve, the state adopted an exemption from military service on condition of paying

117. *See* FROST, *supra* note 42, at 40 (describing the volunteers); An Act for Regulating the Officers and Soldiers Commisionated and Raised by the Governor for the Defense of this Province, ch. 409 (1756) [hereinafter 1756 Act], *reprinted in* 5 PA. STAT. (William Stanley Ray 1898), *supra* note 41, at 219. The governor's action and the source of his authority are recited in the preamble. *Id.* at 219-20.

118. Message to the Assembly from Governor Robert Hunter Morris (Nov. 3, 1755), in 5 ARCHIVES, *supra* note 90, at 4095.

119. *See, e.g.,* 1756 Act, *supra* note 117, at 219; An Act for Striking the Sum of Thirty Thousand Pounds in Bills of Credit and Giving the Same to the King's Use, and for Providing a Fund To Sink the Bills so To Be Emitted by Laying an Excise upon Wine, Rum, Brandy and Other Spirits, ch. 411 (1756), *reprinted in* 5 PA. STAT. (William Stanley Ray 1898), *supra* note 41, at 243.

120. *See* Frost, *supra* note 42, at 36, 63, 66-67; Hamburger, *supra* note 87, at 1609. The pacifist Mennonites were also seen as affluent. *See* MACMASTER ET AL., *supra* note 82, at 46-47.

121. *See* Hamburger, *supra* note 87, at 1623-24.

122. For the threat to Philadelphia in December 1776, see DAVID MCCULLOUGH, 1776, at 263-64 (2005). For the capture and occupation of the city from September 1777 to May 1778, see MIDDLEKAUFF, *supra* note 87, at 355, 389-91, 420, 541-44 (1982).

123. *See* FROST, *supra* note 42, at 67-69.

124. *See* MACMASTER ET AL., *supra* note 82, at 281, 290, 293, 397-407; West, *supra* note 43, at 393.

a monetary "equivalent."[125] The Assembly initially resolved that all white males between the ages of 16 and 50, "not scrupulous of bearing arms," should be urged "to join the said Association immediately," and that those "who shall not associate for the Defence of this Province, ought to contribute an equivalent to the Time spent by the Associators in acquiring the military Discipline."[126] Not quite three weeks later, the Assembly enacted "Rules and Regulations for the better Government of the Military Association in Pennsylvania,"[127] "Articles of Association in Pennsylvania,"[128] which the Assembly "earnestly recommend[ed]" that all "associators" sign,[129] and a special tax of two pounds and ten shillings on all white males between the ages of 16 and 50 who failed to sign the Articles of Association.[130]

In 1776, at a convention almost entirely composed of the Quakers' opponents,[131] the revolutionaries wrote the same basic solution — conscientious objection subject to payment of an equivalent — into the state constitution:

> That every member of society hath a right to be protected in the enjoyment of life, liberty and property, and therefore is bound to contribute his proportion towards the expence of that protection, and yield his personal service when necessary, or an equivalent thereto: But no part of a man's property can be justly taken from him, or applied to public uses, without his own consent, or that of his legal representatives: Nor can any man who is conscientiously scrupulous of bearing arms, be justly compelled thereto, if he will pay such equivalent. . . .[132]

Over the decades of this long political battle, supporters of a militia and opponents of an unconditional exemption made a wide variety of arguments: that pacifism was a false religion, that "justice and equity" required

125. *See* FROST, *supra* note 42, at 62-63; West, *supra* note 43, at 390-91.

126. Resolves of the Assembly (Nov. 8, 1775), *reprinted in* 8 PA. STAT., *supra* note 41, at 492 (1902). For discussion, see MACMASTER ET AL., *supra* note 82, at 222; Hamburger, *supra* note 87, at 1622-23.

127. Rules and Regulations for the Better Government of the Military Association in Pennsylvania (Nov. 25, 1775), *reprinted in* 8 PA. STAT., *supra* note 41, at 499 (1902).

128. *Id.* at 506.

129. *Id.*

130. Resolutions directing the Mode of Levying Taxes on Non-Associators in Pennsylvania § 8 (Nov. 25, 1775) [hereinafter 1775 Non-Associators Resolution], *reprinted in* 8 PA. STAT., *supra* note 41, at 512, 514 (1902).

131. *See* FROST, *supra* note 42, at 64-65.

132. PA. CONST. of 1776, Declaration of Rights, art. VIII, *reprinted in* 5 LAWS OF THE STATES, *supra* note 40, at 3081, 3083. For discussion of this provision, see FROST, *supra* note 42, at 65; Hamburger, *supra* note 87, at 1625-26.

service from all, that Quakers and their property would benefit fully from the common defense provided by others, that refusal to serve in time of war struck at "the very Existence of Civil Government," that the religious liberty guarantee in Pennsylvania's charter did not include exemption from military service, that some Quakers had paid taxes for military measures and some had even served in the military.[133] But I have found no mention of a claim that unconditional exemption for Quakers would establish their religion, support their religion, grant preference to their religion, or any other such formulation — not in the substantial original sources I have been able to examine personally and not in extensive summaries and quotations by vigorous opponents of regulatory exemptions.[134] The many petitions opposing the pacifist position did not even oppose exemptions outright. They uniformly urged that pacifists be required to provide more financial support to the military, but *not* that they be required to *serve* in the military.[135]

Because the Quakers ultimately got considerably less than they demanded, some opponents of exemptions claim the outcome in Pennsylvania as a victory that shows the founding generation's opposition to exemptions.[136] But this badly mischaracterizes the political outcome — pacifists were in fact exempted from military service. To pay a financial "equivalent" was a burden, both on conscience and on the pacifists' secular interests. But it was much less of a burden on either than actual military service with the risk of killing or of being killed. That is the commonsense understanding both in our time and in theirs. Certainly in my generation, which was draft eligible during the Vietnam War, both the government and potential draftees viewed conscientious objector status as a real exemption, worth determined litigation,[137] despite the burdens of alternative service. The Court upheld statutory provisions awarding educational benefits to military veterans but not to those who performed civilian alternative service, explaining in part that the

---

133. For summaries of these debates, see FROST, *supra* note 42, at 29-43, 60-69; Hamburger, *supra* note 87, at 1615-21; West, *supra* note 43, at 390-91.

134. *See* Hamburger, *supra* note 87, at 1608-12, 1615-26; West, *supra* note 43, at 390-91.

135. For petitions urging the pacifist position, see 8 ARCHIVES, *supra* note 90, at 7259-60, 7311-13, 7333-43, 7422-23, 7425-26 (Charles F. Hoban ed., 1935). Some of these petitions, and other similar petitions, are reprinted in MACMASTER ET AL., *supra* note 82, at 246-47, 260-66, 307-10. Some are quoted in the paragraphs that follow.

136. *See* Hamburger, *supra* note 87, at 1604-05, 1630-31; West, *supra* note 43, at 381-82.

137. *See, e.g.,* Clay v. United States, 403 U.S. 698 (1971) (reviewing conviction of Muhammad Ali for failing to report for induction after erroneous denial of conscientious objector claim). A Westlaw search for "selective service" and "conscientious objector" after 1963 and before 1976 reveals 32 cases in the Supreme Court and 1,389 in the "All Federal Cases" database.

burdens of military service were much greater.[138] And Justice Harlan, who had some sympathy with the argument that exemptions are an establishment, viewed conscientious objector status as a real exemption that squarely raised the Establishment Clause issue,[139] despite the requirement of alternative service.

The revolutionary generation took a similar view. A petition of officers of the Philadelphia Association, demanding that conscientious objectors pay an equivalent, argued that pacifists "may be exempted from actually bearing Arms; (and in such Case by paying a Fine for such Exemption, he is in a better Situation than one who risks his Life in the Service)."[140] A month earlier these officers had argued that nonpacifists would find it more attractive to pay the equivalent than to serve in person: "People *sincerely* and *religiously* scrupulous are but few in Comparison to those who upon this Occasion, as well as others, make *Conscience* a *Convenience.*"[141] A different group of officers in 1776 argued that an Associator must pay for his own equipment and "risk his Life," so that even with the equivalent, the non-Associator had such a "great Advantage . . . in Point of Interest [that it] would entirely defeat the Association, if the People in general were not actuated by a patriotic Spirit."[142] The privates of the Philadelphia Association, in a petition endorsed by their officers,[143] argued that "no Terms of Exemption, affecting Property meerely, can be deemed equal to the Risks and Dangers to which they expose themselves who are under the most solemn Engagements of Honour and Duty to lay down their Lives, if necessary, in Defence of their Country."[144]

138. *See* Johnson v. Robison, 415 U.S. 361, 378-82 (1974) (noting the rigors of military discipline and potential hazards of military duty).

139. *See* Welsh v. United States, 398 U.S. 355-61 (1970) (Harlan, J., concurring); *see also infra* notes 246-50 and accompanying text (discussing *Welsh*).

140. A Memorial of the Officers of the Military Association of the City and Liberties of Philadelphia (Oct. 31, 1775) [hereinafter Memorial of the Officers], in 8 ARCHIVES, *supra* note 90, at 7339.

141. Memorial from the Officers of the Military Association for the City and Liberties of Philadelphia (Sept. 27, 1775), in 8 ARCHIVES, *supra* note 90, at 7259 (Charles F. Hoban ed., 1935).

142. The Petition of Mark Bird, Daniel Broadhead, Balsar Geehr and Jonathan Potts, Esquires, Field-Officers in the Several battalions in Berks County, in Behalf of Said Battalions (Feb. 23, 1776), in 8 ARCHIVES, *supra* note 90, at 7399 (Charles F. Hoban ed., 1935).

143. The Memorial of the Officers of the Military Association of the City and Liberties of Philadelphia (Feb. 17, 1776), in 8 ARCHIVES, *supra* note 90, at 7407 (Charles F. Hoban ed., 1935) ("*Sheweth,* THAT your Memorialists have perused, at the Request of the private Associators of this City and Liberties, their Petition to your Honourable House, and concur with them in the Sentiments therein contained").

144. The Petition of the Privates of the Military Association of the City and Liberties of

The financial equivalent was increased in response to such concerns, first to three pounds and ten shillings per year[145] and then to double the normal rate of property tax.[146] Double property tax was imposed not just on conscientious objectors, but on "every person not subject to nor performing military duty" — thus including those who were too old or disabled to serve — with exceptions for public officials, clergy, and nuclear families with a member already serving or killed or captured.[147] These taxes were substantial, but they were not designed to stamp out sincere claims of conscience. The privates of the Philadelphia Association argued that "the Terms imposed upon Non-Associators should be such as to induce every Man of suitable Age and Strength *(not truly conscientiously scrupulous)* to join in the Association."[148] Scholars who have studied the question conclude that the vast majority of members of the peace churches refused to serve,[149] and that most of those who did serve were attracted early by the revolutionary cause, not coerced later by threats of fines.[150]

Nor did opposition to military exemptions necessarily entail opposition to all exemptions. For reasons already stated,[151] military exemption is one of the hardest cases. Opposition to exemption in the hardest case does not imply opposition in easier cases. This core of this rather obvious idea appears in a statement of Rev. Francis Alison, a mid-century Presbyterian leader. (Presbyterians tended to live on the frontier, and had much at stake in opposition to pacifism.[152]) In a 1756 sermon, Alison said that "All . . . should have a

---

Philadelphia (Feb. 17, 1776) [hereinafter Petition of the Privates], in 8 ARCHIVES, *supra* note 90, at 7402, 7403 (Charles F. Hoban ed., 1935).

145. *See* Resolutions directing the Mode of Levying Taxes on Non-Associators § 8 (Apr. 5, 1776) [hereinafter 1776 Non-Associators Resolution], reprinted in 8 PA. STAT., *supra* note 41, at 538, 540-41 (1902).

146. *See* An Act for Making More Equal the Burden of the Public Defense and for Filling the Quota of Troops to Be Raised in This State, ch. 773, § 1 (1777), *reprinted in* 9 PA. STAT., *supra* note 41, at 167 (1903).

147. *See id.* § 3.

148. Petition of the Privates, *supra* note 144, at 7404 (emphasis added).

149. *See* MACMASTER ET AL., *supra* note 82, at 300 (estimating that 95% of Mennonites and Amish refused to serve, and that all the peace churches refused to serve "with a degree of unanimity that would never be matched again in any American war"); *id.* at 525 (reporting that Quaker meetings disowned Quakers who served, and that those disowned for this cause were "an insignificant minority"); FROST, *supra* note 42, at 67 (stating that "a few Quakers" dissented from the teaching on military service).

150. *See* MACMASTER ET AL., *supra* note 82, at 525.

151. *See supra* notes 67-68 and accompanying text.

152. *See* FROST, *supra* note 42, at 51.

free use of their religion, but so as not on that score to burden or oppress others."[153] This statement does not take a clear position on regulatory exemptions either way, but it does draw the essential distinction: protect religious liberty up to the point at which it burdens or oppresses others, and no further. Some exemptions burden or oppress others; many do not. The privates of the Philadelphia Association illustrated the distinction neatly; they wanted "all Persons alledging Scruples of Conscience" to take "a Test by Oath or Affirmation" to prove their sincerity.[154] So they demanded an equivalent for exemption from military service, but were entirely comfortable with the exemption from taking oaths. Similarly, when the state's revolutionary government imposed a loyalty oath, it provided for oath or affirmation.[155] More remarkably, Pennsylvania provided for conscientious objection by tax assessors — public officials — who were subject to a fine of up to ten pounds for failing to compile lists of white males of military age, "unless such assessor's refusal proceeds from conscientious motives."[156]

Those who demanded an equivalent for military exemption in Pennsylvania had to argue that the colony's Charter of Privileges[157] did not guarantee exemption without an equivalent. Even in that context, most of their arguments focused on the special cost of exemption from military service, and not on disputing a right to exemptions more generally. A revolutionary com-

153. *Id.* (quoting Alison's 1756 "Love of Country" sermon).

154. Petition of the Privates, *supra* note 144, at 7406.

155. *See* An Act for the Further Security of the Government, ch. 796 (1778), *reprinted in* 9 PA. STAT., *supra* note 41, at 238 (1903); An Act Obliging the Male White Inhabitants of This State to Give Assurances of Allegiance to the Same and for Other Purposes Therein Mentioned, ch. 756 (1777), *reprinted in* 9 PA. STAT., *supra* note 41, at 110 (1903). The oath or affirmation required by the 1778 Act is reprinted in FROST, *supra* note 42, at 67.

156. *See* 1776 Non-Associators Resolution, *supra* note 145, § 2, at 538, 540-41; 1775 Non-Associators Resolution, *supra* note 130, § 2, at 512, 514. The county commissioners were then to appoint "some other proper person" to make out the list. See § 3 of each Resolution.

157. Charter of Privileges Granted by William Penn, Esq. to the Inhabitants of Pennsylvania and Territories, art. I (1701), *reprinted in* 5 LAWS OF THE STATES, *supra* note 40, at 3076, 3077. This guarantee stated:

> I do hereby grant and declare, That no Person or Persons, inhabiting in this Province or Territories, who shall confess and acknowledge *One* almighty God, the Creator, Upholder and Ruler of the World; and profess him or themselves obliged to live quietly under the Civil Government, shall be in any Case molested or prejudiced, in his or their Person or Estate, because of his or their conscientious Persuasion or Practice, nor be compelled to frequent or maintain any religious Worship, Place or Ministry, contrary to his or their Mind, or to do or suffer any other Act or Thing, contrary to his or their Mind, or to do or suffer any other Act or Thing, contrary to their religious Persuasion.

mittee of Philadelphia argued that "Self-preservation is the first Principle of Nature," "that the Safety of the People is the supreme law," and "that the Doctrine of Passive Obedience and Non-resistance is incompatible with our Freedom and Happiness."[158] The Philadelphia privates argued "that the great Law of Self-preservation is equally binding with the Letter of written Charters."[159] They also said:

> Liberty of Conscience is so sacred a Thing that it ought ever to be preserved inviolate, and we will always rejoice to see any Body of Men assert their Right to it. But when, under Pretence of this Liberty the very Existence of Civil Government is struck at, we beg Leave to represent that either the Liberty claimed must be given up or the Government dissolved.[160]

In modern doctrinal terms, all these arguments would fit comfortably under the rubric of asserting a compelling governmental interest in military service. The Philadelphia privates also offered a textual basis for this argument. In the paragraph following the passage just quoted, they noted that the persons protected by the charter's religious liberty clause "are by that very Clause made to 'profess themselves obliged to live quietly under the civil Government,' which cannot possibly be when they refuse to support the Measures often necessary to its very existence."[161] Professor Hamburger reads this as embracing his argument that any violation of law was a breach of peace that overrode state guarantees of religious liberty in the founding era.[162] Perhaps there were Philadelphians who would have accepted that argument, but that is not the argument the privates made. The privates' argument did not concern just any breach of peace, but only the refusal to support measures necessary to government's "very existence."

There was also a textual argument that the religious liberty provision in Pennsylvania's charter could not be read to guarantee exemption from military service when the colony's original charter authorized William Penn to "levy, muster and train all Sorts of Men, of what Condition soever, . . . and to make War," and to do these things at a time when it was anticipated that

---

158. The Petition and Remonstrance of the Committee of the City and Liberties of Philadelphia (Oct. 31, 1775) [hereinafter City Committee], in 8 ARCHIVES, *supra* note 90, at 7334, 7336 (Charles F. Hoban ed., 1935).

159. A Representation from the Committee of Privates of the Association Belonging to the City of Philadelphia, and its Districts (Oct. 31, 1775) [hereinafter Representation of the Privates], in 8 ARCHIVES, *supra* note 90, at 7339, 7341 (Charles F. Hoban ed., 1935).

160. *Id.* at 7341-42.

161. *Id.* at 7342.

162. *See* Hamburger, *supra* note 87, at 1620-21.

Quakers would be the principal settlers in the colony.[163] This too was an argument that reaches only to exemption from military service.

On the other hand, one argument attacked the claim of a right to exemptions quite generally. The Philadelphia officers argued that the charter's guarantees of religious liberty "relate only to an Exemption from any Acts of Uniformity in Worship, and from paying towards the Support of other religious Establishments — than those to which the Inhabitants of this Province respectively belong."[164] Moreover, this narrow interpretation was arguably written into the general religious liberty clause in Pennsylvania's 1776 Constitution.[165] But if we are to read the references to "religious worship" in that document as a telling restriction, we must give equal weight to the elimination of any such restrictive references in Pennsylvania's 1790 Constitution.[166]

The argument of the officers, and the subsequent evolution of the state constitution's religious liberty clause, are relevant evidence in the originalist debate about whether Pennsylvanians in the founding generation understood free exercise of religion to include a presumptive right to exemptions. But they are no evidence at all on the principal question here — did they understand the principles of disestablishment to preclude exemptions even when the political process was willing to grant them? Clearly they did not. They granted exemption from military service, on condition of a financial equivalent, and they never questioned the exemption from oath taking even

163. Representation of the Privates, *supra* note 159, at 7339, 7342-43, quoting Charter for the Province of Pennsylvania (1681), *reprinted in* 5 Laws of the States, *supra* note 40, at 3035, 3042. Substantially the same argument appears in City Committee, *supra* note 158, at 7334, 7335.

164. Memorial of the Officers, *supra* note 140, at 7338.

165. *See* Pa. Const. of 1776, Declaration of Rights, art. II ("And that no authority can or ought to be vested in, or assumed by any power whatever, that shall in any case interfere with, or in any manner controul, the right of conscience in the free exercise of religious worship."), *reprinted in* 5 Laws of the States, *supra* note 40, at 3081, 3082. Professor Hamburger reads this as a decisive rejection of a constitutional right to exemptions from regulation of any conduct other than worship. *See* Hamburger, *supra* note 87, at 1624-25. Judge McConnell finds no evidence that lawyers of the time interpreted state freedom of worship clauses more narrowly than state free exercise clauses. *See* McConnell, *supra* note 6, at 1461. This general religious liberty clause was separate from the clause granting exemption from military service subject to payment of an equivalent. See text accompanying *supra* note 132.

166. *See* Pa. Const. of 1790, art. IX, § 3 (stating "that no human authority can, in any case whatever, control or interfere with the rights of conscience"), *reprinted in* 5 Laws of the States, *supra* note 40, at 3081, 3100. The separate provision conditionally guaranteeing exemption from military service was also retained: "Those who conscientiously scruple to bear arms shall not be compelled to do so, but shall pay an equivalent for personal service." *Id.* art. VI, § 2, *reprinted in* 5 Laws of the States, *supra* note 40, at 3081, 3099.

at the height of the controversy and the resulting suspicion of those who refused to serve.

Exemptions from military service were controversial, and rightly so, because those exemptions imposed serious burdens on persons outside the exempted faiths, and especially so in Pennsylvania, where Quakers and other
pacifist sects were a large minority of the population. But if exemptions were
in principle an objectionable preference for religion, the controversy should
have extended to other exemptions as well. So far as we can tell, it did not.

States enacted other exemptions without leaving a record of similar debate. Exemptions from oath taking were not controversial by the time of the
founding. Early in Pennsylvania's history, there was substantial conflict over
whether to require oaths of anybody, and then whether to exempt Quakers
from that requirement, but that conflict was resolved by 1724.[167] The royal officials and local Anglicans insisting on oaths in those early days would not
have been concerned about establishment of religion. Elsewhere in the colonies, and certainly in the period of broad movements for disestablishment,
"oath taking never became a serious source of conflict with the authorities."[168] This absence of recorded controversy is evidence that no substantial
body of opinion thought that exemptions from oath taking raised an issue of
establishment.

With respect to the exemptions from paying taxes for the established
church, the focus of debate was on whether the tax should be continued at
all, whether members of minority faiths should have to pay taxes to their own
church, and whether the exemptions were fairly administered.[169] No one appears to have thought that exemptions made things worse, or that exemptions established a religion. The question was whether exemptions were
enough.

B. Judicial Debates

Early in the nineteenth century, there was litigation over constitutional
claims to exemptions not enacted by the legislature. Here too I have found
almost no evidence of anyone arguing that exemptions established religion.
Some lawyers argued against exemptions, and some judges ruled against
exemptions, but only one lawyer appears to have argued — briefly and un-

---

167. *See* FROST, *supra* note 42, at 23-25.
168. CURRY, *supra* note 23, at 81.
169. *See id.* at 163-92; Esbeck, *supra* note 45, at 1434-37, 1440-47.

successfully — that exemptions might violate a state or federal establishment clause.

John Gibson, Chief Justice of Pennsylvania, whose opinions are commonly cited as early rejections of any claim to a constitutional right to regulatory exemptions, said clearly that such exemptions could be allowed by legislators, or even by judges in cases properly within judicial discretion. In *Philips v. Gratz*,[170] a Jewish plaintiff sought a continuance when his case was called for trial on Saturday.[171] The motion was denied, the case was tried, and plaintiff appealed.[172] Chief Justice Gibson wrote:

> The religious scruples of persons concerned with the administration of justice will receive all the indulgence that is compatible with the business of government; and had circumstances permitted it, this cause would not have been ordered for trial on the Jewish Sabbath. But when a continuance for conscience' sake is claimed as a right, and at the expense of a term's delay, the matter assumes a different aspect.[173]

He thus held that the state constitution did not *require* exemption, but he was equally clear in his view that it did not *prohibit* exemption. He made the same point later in the opinion, criticizing a New York decision protecting the confidentiality of a Catholic confession.[174] Chief Justice Gibson said he supported "the policy of protecting the secrets of auricular confession. But considerations of policy address themselves with propriety to the legislature, and not to a magistrate."[175]

Counsel for the defendant, arguing against the exemption, did not claim otherwise. They urged that an exemption would be unworkable, and that the constitutional guarantee of religious liberty was confined to "faith and religious worship" and did not affect "performance of a civil duty."[176] But they did not suggest that an exemption would establish anyone's religion.

Similarly in other cases, to the extent we have either an opinion of the court or argument of counsel opposing a claimed exemption, there is little suggestion that the legislature could not provide exemptions or that such

170. 2 Pen. & W. 412 (Pa. 1831).

171. *Id.* at 412.

172. *Id.* at 412-13.

173. *Id.* at 416.

174. *Id.* at 417.

175. *Id.*

176. *Id.* at 415. They made this argument under the 1790 constitution, which had eliminated the language that seemed to expressly limit protection to worship. See *supra* notes 165-66 (comparing the text of Pennsylvania's 1776 and 1790 constitutions).

legislative exemptions would establish a religion. In *Commonwealth v. Wolf*,[177] the Pennsylvania Supreme Court affirmed the conviction of a Jew for working on Sunday.[178] The court rejected his claim that the conviction violated his religious liberty,[179] principally on the ground that despite his contrary representations, his religion did not require him to work on Sunday. Nothing in the opinion hints that a contrary judgment would have established a religion.

In *Commonwealth v. Drake*,[180] an early Massachusetts case, a criminal defendant sought a new trial on the ground that the state had introduced evidence of his penitential confession to members of his church.[181] The state successfully argued that the confession was voluntary and reliable, that it had not been required by any ecclesiastical rule of his faith, and that its admission in evidence violated "no legal or constitutional principle."[182] The state did not argue, and the court did not suggest, that a rule excluding the evidence would establish a religion.

In *State v. Willson*,[183] defendant refused to serve on a grand jury. The case appears to have been a test case on behalf of a Christian denomination known as Covenanters, who viewed jury service as an offense to God. We do not have the argument for the state, and there may not have been one. South Carolina's Constitutional Court of Appeals rejected defendant's claim, principally on the ground that it would be impossible to detect false claims, so that the benefit of exemptions would be "not so much for the scrupulous as for those who have no scruples."[184] There is no hint of an Establishment Clause argument, and the negation of such an argument is implied: the court spoke with apparent approval of cases in which members of the sect appeared for duty, and "were readily excused" when the court found that more than enough jurors were available.[185]

The only exception I have encountered is a brief and conclusory passage in the prosecutor's argument in *People v. Philips*.[186] This is the New York case

177. 3 Serg. & Rawle 48 (Pa. 1817).
178. *Id.* at 48-50.
179. *Id.* at 49-50.
180. 15 Mass. (14 Tyng) 161 (1818).
181. *Id.* at 161.
182. *Id.* at 162.
183. 13 S.C.L. (2 McCord) 393 (1823).
184. *Id.* at 395.
185. *Id.* at 396.
186. People v. Philips (N.Y. Ct. Gen. Sess. June 14, 1813), *reprinted in* SAMPSON, *supra* note 31, at 9; and excerpts reprinted in MICHAEL W. MCCONNELL ET AL., RELIGION AND

in which the state sought to compel a Catholic priest to testify to what he learned in the confessional.[187] Mostly the prosecutor argued that New York's guarantee of freedom of worship did not excuse the performance of civic duties.[188] But he also said, in a single passing sentence, that "whenever any one shall claim to do what may justly offend the others, he claims an unequal, and so an unconstitutional 'preference.'"[189] There it is — the heart of the modern Establishment Clause argument in a single unelaborated phrase.

The argument did not succeed. The court interpreted the New York Constitution in a quite modern way that sounds much like the compelling interest test. The state constitutional exception, permitting regulation of religion in cases of "*licentiousness, of practices inconsistent* with the *tranquillity* and *safety of the state*," "has reference to something actually, not negatively injurious. To acts committed, not to acts omitted — offences of a deep dye, and of an extensively injurious nature."[190] The court did not use the phrase "compelling government interest," but the idea is plainly similar. In the court's view, free exercise required regulatory exemptions, and the argument that the commitment to disestablishment might prohibit them did not deserve a response.

There is a similar holding, a good bit later than the other cases discussed, from a Virginia trial court in *Commonwealth v. Cronin*.[191] There the defendant, who had fatally beaten his wife, called her priest as a witness and asked if she had admitted to adultery in her final confession.[192] The court held, in a substantial opinion, that compelling the priest to testify would have the effect of suppressing a sacrament of the Catholic faith, and that constitutional guarantees of religious liberty clearly precluded such a result.[193] There is no reference to any Establishment Clause argument. But the prosecutor apparently did argue that exempting Catholic priests "would be extending to them a privilege not enjoyed by clergymen of the protestant persuasion."[194] There is no indication that this argument was rooted in the state's establishment clause; in any event, the argument of discrimination between two religions, based on the principle that all faiths must be treated equally, is very different

---

THE CONSTITUTION 103 (2nd ed. 2006). More extensive excerpts are reprinted in *Privileged Communications to Clergymen*, 1 CATH. LAW. 199 (1955).

187. McCONNELL ET AL., *supra* note 186, at 103-04.

188. *Id.* at 104-06.

189. *Id.* at 104.

190. *Id.* at 108 (emphasis added by court).

191. 1 Q.L.J. 128 (Va. Cir. Ct. 1856).

192. *Id.* at 129.

193. *See id.* at 133-42.

194. *Id.* at 140.

from the modern argument that religious exemptions discriminate against activities that are in no sense religious.[195] The court found the argument "scarcely . . . necessary to notice"; Protestants had no practice analogous to Catholic confession, and when the law deprived Protestants of one of their sacraments, they too would be exempt.[196]

Finally, and also rather late in the day, there is the litigation that culminated in the Supreme Court's decision in *Permoli v. Municipality No. 1*.[197] This was a challenge to a New Orleans ordinance prohibiting Catholic funerals except at a designated mortuary chapel. On its face, the ordinance was not generally applicable and thus did not really present an exemption issue. But the city argued that in effect it was generally applicable, because it was a health measure to prevent the spread of yellow fever,[198] and only Catholics held open-casket funerals.[199] The city argued that the ordinance was justified by "necessity,"[200] and that it did not violate Catholic conscience because the practice of holding funerals in the cathedral was merely a matter of "discipline," not of "dogma."[201] (This argument that the claimant does not understand his own religion, which appeared here and in *Commonwealth v. Wolf*,[202] is a remarkably common way of trying to duck the exemptions issue.) Finally, and decisively, the city argued that there was no federal issue, because the First Amendment did not apply to the states, and because earlier federal guarantees of religious liberty in Louisiana (in legislation incorporating the Northwest Ordinance, implementing the treaty by which the territory was acquired from France, and authorizing citizens of the territory to form a state government) had lapsed when Louisiana became a state.[203] Once again, there is no hint of anything like an argument that exempting Catholics from a general policy would raise an issue of establishment.

It is hard to prove a negative. It is hard to prove that no one believed a

195. The case of religion-like commitments with nontheistic foundations is explored *infra* in text at notes 246-52.

196. *Cronin*, 1 Q.L.J. at 140.

197. 44 U.S. (3 How.) 589 (1845).

198. *See id.* at 600.

199. *See id.* at 601. It would not be learned until the early twentieth century that yellow fever is spread by mosquitos and not by dead bodies. *See* DAVID McCULLOUGH, THE PATH BETWEEN THE SEAS 142-45, 409-15, 421-23, 465-68 (1977) (tracing progress from the filth and dead-body theories of the nineteenth century to the elimination of yellow fever from the Panama Canal project in 1905).

200. *Id.*

201. *Id.* at 603.

202. 3 Serg. & Rawle 48 (Pa. 1817); see *supra* notes 177-79 and accompanying text.

203. *Permoli*, 44 U.S. (3 How.) at 606-08.

proposition that was never advanced and thus drew no rebuttals. But these legislative and judicial debates are obvious places where the Establishment Clause argument should have appeared if anyone believed it, or if anyone had even thought of it. Except for what amounts to a throw-away line in the prosecutor's argument in *People v. Philips*,[204] the New York confessional case, the argument simply does not appear. The argument appears to have been generally unimagined in the late-eighteenth and early-nineteenth centuries.

C. Other Scholarly Treatments of Founding-Era Debates

The scholars who argue that regulatory exemptions are an establishment are not originalists.[205] There is a substantial originalist debate over whether regulatory exemptions are constitutionally *required*, in which historically-minded opponents of exemptions have argued that exemptions were not required by the original understanding. But none of those scholars has seriously argued that regulatory exemptions were *forbidden* by the original understanding, and none has cited a single instance of anyone in the founding generation arguing that regulatory exemptions were unconstitutional. Rather, their position is that exemptions were commonly granted but were thought to be a matter of legislative grace.

Ellis West acknowledges that "exemptions from conscription laws were often granted to religious conscientious objectors before, during, and after the Revolution"; he attributes this to legislative "sympathy."[206] Philip Hamburger argues: "[T]hat various state statutes (or even constitutions) expressly granted religious exemptions from military service and other specified civil obligations hardly suggests that such exemptions were rights under the United States Constitution."[207] Gerard Bradley makes an impassioned conceptual and originalist case against regulatory exemptions under the Free Exercise Clause, but insists that "[n]othing in this idea (and nothing in the Constitution) prohibits relief from neutral, generally applicable laws for conscientious objectors by *legislative accommodation*."[208]

The only historically-minded scholar who has in any way attempted to link regulatory exemptions to establishment is Philip Hamburger. In his

---

204. *See supra* notes 186-90 and accompanying text (discussing *Philips*).

205. *See supra* note 12.

206. West, *supra* note 43, at 375.

207. Hamburger, *supra* note 6, at 948.

208. Gerard V. Bradley, *Beguiled: Free Exercise Exemptions and the Siren Song of Liberalism*, 20 HOFSTRA L. REV. 245, 262 (1991).

most recent work, Hamburger concludes that religious exemptions do not generally violate the Federal Establishment Clause.[209] So perhaps his earlier work is best read as claiming only that some key participants in eighteenth-century debates argued or believed that exemptions were establishments. But even this claim would go far beyond his evidence.

Hamburger notes that religious dissenters attacking the privileges of the established church often argued for equal rights for all faiths.[210] Then he claims that this equal-rights argument "had implications for exemption,"[211] because exemptions "could create unequal civil rights."[212] But this is Hamburger talking, not anyone from the eighteenth century. He has few examples of anyone attacking exemptions on these grounds — none that do so unambiguously and none that connect such an attack to an establishment of religion. Hamburger himself acknowledges elsewhere that proponents of religious liberty often clarified broad rhetoric about equal rights and opposition to laws taking cognizance of religion, insisting that government must also protect free exercise.[213] And just as legislators could grant exemptions and support them on policy grounds without believing they were constitutionally required — Hamburger's principal point — so critics could oppose exemptions on policy grounds without believing they were constitutionally prohibited.

Hamburger's effort to link exemptions with establishment gets no support from the few examples of eighteenth-century views in his footnotes. To show that Presbyterians might have opposed exemptions, he quotes a 1777 memorial of Virginia Presbyterians stating that "the concerns of religion, are beyond the limits of civil control," and that accordingly, the church should not "receive any emoluments from any human establishments for the support of the gospel."[214] Hamburger takes this quotation out of context; the *Memorial* was opposing the proposed general assessment, a tax for the support of Christian clergy of all denominations.[215] The entire *Memorial* is devoted to the "the propriety of a general assessment, or whether every reli-

---

209. *See* Hamburger, *supra* note 87, at 1607 n.8 ("[T]he establishment clause permits at least some legislative exemptions.").

210. Hamburger, *supra* note 6, at 946.

211. *Id.*

212. *Id.* at 947.

213. Philip A. Hamburger, *Equality and Diversity: The Eighteenth-Century Debate About Equal Protection and Equal Civil Rights,* 1992 SUP. CT. REV. 295, 343-45.

214. Hamburger, *supra* note 6, at 946 n.117 (quoting Memorial of the Presbytery of Hanover to the General Assembly of Virginia (Apr. 25, 1777) [hereinafter Memorial of Virginia Presbyterians], *reprinted in* WILLIAM ADDISON BLAKELY, AMERICAN STATE PAPERS 96, 98 (photo. reprint 2000) (1911)).

215. Memorial of Virginia Presbyterians, *supra* note 214, at 96-99.

gious society shall be left to voluntary contributions for the maintenance of the ministers of the gospel who are of different persuasions."[216] Indeed, the *Memorial* says that this issue is the only reason the *Memorial* was prepared.[217] The immediate context of Hamburger's quotation is also about the assessment, as the sentences immediately proceeding that quotation make clear:

> Neither does the church of Christ stand in need of a general assessment for its support; and most certain we are that it would be of no advantage, but an injury to the society to which we belong; and as every good Christian believes that Christ has ordained a complete system of laws for the government of his kingdom, so we are persuaded that by his providence, he will support it to its final consummation. In the fixed belief of this principle, that the kingdom of Christ, and the concerns of religion, are beyond the limits of civil control, we should act a dishonest, inconsistent part, were we to receive any emoluments from any human establishments for the support of the gospel.[218]

"Emoluments" thus has its customary meaning of "[p]rofit or gain arising from station, office, or employment; dues; reward, remuneration, salary."[219] The quotation is about money; it has nothing to do with regulatory exemptions.

"Emoluments" once had a second meaning, now long obsolete, of "advantage, benefit, comfort."[220] The *Oxford English Dictionary* cites examples from 1633 to 1756, all suggesting physical comforts, not legal privileges.[221] We may see a lingering example of this usage in the other quotation Hamburger offers. He quotes the Baptist leader John Leland as the only pastor of the time to criticize the exemption of the clergy from taxation and military service.[222] Hamburger quotes the italicized portion of the following passage in Leland's most famous sermon against establishments, *The Rights of Conscience Inalienable:*[223]

216. *Id.* at 97.

217. *Id.* ("We would therefore have given our honorable Legislature no further trouble on this subject, but we are sorry to find that there yet remains a variety of opinions touching the propriety of a general assessment . . .").

218. *Id.* at 98.

219. 5 THE OXFORD ENGLISH DICTIONARY 182 (2d ed. 1989) (collecting examples from 1480 to 1881).

220. *Id.*

221. *Id.*

222. Hamburger, *supra* note 6, at 947 n.119.

223. John Leland, *The Rights of Conscience Inalienable* (1791), *in* 2 POLITICAL SERMONS OF THE AMERICAN FOUNDING ERA, 1730-1805, at 1079, 1083-99 (Ellis Sandoz ed., 2d ed. 1998).

Ministers should share the same protection of the law that other men do, and no more. To proscribe them from seats of legislation, &c. is cruel. *To indulge them with an exemption from taxes and bearing arms is a tempting emolument. The law should be silent about them; protect them as citizens (not as sacred officers) for the civil law knows no sacred religious officers.*[224]

"Emolument" here may refer to the financial benefit of tax exemption, the physical benefit of exemption from military service, or both. The important point is that these clergy exemptions were based on religious status, not on any religious belief that prevented compliance with the law. Few if any clergy conscientiously objected to taxes other than the tax for the established church, and few clergy outside the historic peace churches conscientiously objected to military service.[225] Yet all got the exemptions, simply because of their occupation.[226] As Justice O'Connor has explained, the fundamental distinction between status and belief helps reconcile regulatory exemptions with a strong principle of religious equality:

What makes accommodation permissible, even praiseworthy, is not that the government is making life easier for some particular religious group as such. Rather, it is that the government is accommodating a deeply held belief. Accommodations may thus justify treating those who share this belief differently from those who do not; but they do not justify discriminations based on sect.[227]

This distinction was not developed in the eighteenth century, but something like it may have been implicit, reconciling the common rhetoric of equal rights with the common practice of exemptions for conscientious objectors. This implicit distinction could explain why the religious minorities that demanded equal rights for all faiths did not oppose regulatory exemp-

224. *Id.* at 1094 (emphasis added).

225. The issue did not arise, because the clergy were exempt without regard to conscience. But in an era when denominational differences were much sharper than today, it would have been almost unimaginable for a pacifist clergyman to lead a nonpacifist church.

226. *See, e.g.,* An Act for Forming, Regulating, and Conducting the Military Force of This State, *reprinted in* CONNECTICUT LAWS, *supra* note 47, at 144, 144 (exempting "Ministers of the Gospel"); An Act to Regulate the Militia of the Commonwealth of Pennsylvania, ch. 750, § 2 (1777) (exempting "ministers of the gospel (or clergy)"), *reprinted in* 9 PA. STAT., *supra* note 41, at 75, 77 (1903). Despite the difficulty of answering Leland's objection, clergy are still exempt from military service in the existing stand-by draft legislation. *See* 50 U.S.C. App. § 456(g) (2000).

227. Bd. of Educ. v. Grumet, 512 U.S. 687, 715 (1994) (O'Connor, J., concurring in part and concurring in judgment).

tions on that ground, and why John Leland attacked privileges for the clergy as such but did not attack exemptions for conscientious objectors.

The very sermon Hamburger quotes illustrates the distinction between exemptions based on belief and exemptions based on status. Leland attacked the Connecticut tax for the support of the clergy as an establishment.[228] Protestant dissenters were exempt from paying this tax, and Leland also attacked that exemption.[229] But he did not attack the *exemption* as an establishment; he attacked it as not going far enough.[230] It presumed the power to tax,[231] it treated the exemption as an indulgence rather than a right,[232] and it required the dissenters claiming the exemption to submit certificates to examination by the Justice of the Peace, thus submitting a religious matter to civil authority.[233] He attacked the failure to exempt Jews, Catholics, Turks, and "heathens."[234] And he proposed that the consciences of both sides could be satisfied by reversing the burden of registering one's belief — by taxing all those who submitted their names as believing in the tax, and exempting all those who expressed their conscientious objection by doing nothing:

> It is likely that one part of the people in Connecticut believe in conscience that gospel preachers should be supported by the force of law; and the other part believe that it is not in the province of civil law to interfere or any ways meddle with religious matters. How are both parties to be protected by law in their conscientious belief?
>
> Very easily. Let all those whose consciences dictate that they ought to be taxed by law to maintain their preachers bring in their names to the society-clerk by a certain day, and then assess them all, according to their estates, to raise the sum stipulated in the contract [between each church and its pastor]; and all others go free. Both parties by this method would enjoy the full liberty of conscience without oppressing one another, the law use no force in matters of conscience, the evil of Rhode-Island [where contracts to pay the clergy were widely believed to be unenforceable] law be escaped, and no persons could find fault with it (in a political point of view) but those who fear the consciences of too many would lie dormant, and therefore wish to force them to pay.[235]

228. Leland, *supra* note 223, at 1092-98.
229. *Id.* at 1092-95.
230. *Id.*
231. *Id.* at 1094.
232. *Id.*
233. *Id.* at 1094.
234. *Id.* at 1092.
235. *Id.* at 1097.

This is unambiguously a proposal for a tax with an exemption based on conscientious belief, although implemented in a way that maximizes both the liberty of the religious dissenters and the opportunity for false claims. Perhaps it was sarcastic, meant to illustrate the unworkability of any defensible scheme of taxation to support religion. But whether serious or sarcastic, neither this proposal nor Leland's undoubtedly serious attack on the narrowness of the then-existing exemption is consistent with a view that exemptions impermissibly establish the exempted religion.

Hamburger would dismiss the exemption from the church tax as irrelevant. He would distinguish exemption from a law that was religious in purpose and effect, from the perspective of majority and dissenters alike, from a law that — at least from the perspective of the majority — was wholly secular and religiously neutral.[236] It is true that Americans eventually rejected the tax for the established church as illegitimate. But for much of the eighteenth century, Americans in states with established churches viewed those taxes as wholly legitimate, and simultaneously enacted exemptions for religious dissenters.[237] These exemptions may have been the most attractive case, or the most easily understood, but it is anachronistic not to view them as genuine exemptions.

The exemption question was not near the center of Leland's concerns, because Baptists had no need of exemptions beyond exemption from the tax for the established church and exemption from laws licensing the clergy.[238] These laws could be repealed entirely — and eventually were. Leland apparently believed, consistent with a focus on laws such as these, that human affairs could be divided into a domain of conscience and a domain of civil society, with no overlap. In such a world, exemptions would not be needed to protect conscience, and should not be allowed from laws in the proper domain of civil society.[239] He did not define the two domains. In one sermon he

236. Hamburger, *supra* note 6, at 930-31.

237. *See supra* notes 60-62 and accompanying text.

238. *See* RALPH KETCHAM, JAMES MADISON 54-58 (1971) (describing James Madison's complaints about these laws shortly before the Revolution); ANSON PHELPS STOKES, 1 CHURCH AND STATE IN THE UNITED STATES 369 (1950) (describing the effect on Baptists of Virginia's licensing laws); McConnell, *supra* note 16, at 2165-66 (same).

239. JACK NIPS [JOHN LELAND], THE YANKEE SPY 19 (Boston, John Asplund 1794).

> It is often the case, that laws are made which prevent the liberty of conscience; and because men cannot stretch their consciences, like a nose of wax, these nonconformists are punished as vagrants that disturb the peace. The complaint is, "These men, being Jews, do exceedingly trouble the city." Let any man read the laws that were made about *Daniel* and the three children, and see who were the aggressors,

said that a person's conscience governs "all his actions,"[240] but in another he arguably equated conscience with worship.[241] Of course, even worship falls on the action side of the belief/action distinction; the three most recent free exercise cases in the Supreme Court all involved prohibited acts of worship.[242] We know that he opposed exemptions from laws on murder and battery,[243] but those are easy cases then and now. We do not know whether he thought that religious liberty for Quakers should include exemptions from serving in the military, taking oaths, or removing their hats in court.

Leland's statements about freedom of conscience, like many similar statements on both sides from the same era, are ultimately ambiguous on the difference between protecting only belief and worship, or protecting other religiously motivated conduct as well. So I do not claim that Leland affirmatively supported a right to religious exemptions from laws regulating conduct, even where the exempted conduct would do little or no harm to others. I do claim that there is not the slightest evidence that he opposed such exemptions as unconstitutional, and that his opposition to exemptions based on one's status as a clergyman, which may well have been grounded in his opposition to establishments, is no evidence of a similarly grounded opposition to exemption based on conscience. Hamburger's quotations simply do not support his claim that eighteenth-century advocates of religious liberty thought that exemptions for conscience' sake raised issues of establishment.

There were nearly four million Americans alive in the 1780s. Somewhere, sometime, someone might have said something condemning regulatory exemptions as an establishment — something more than a passing reference from a single prosecutor who lost his case a quarter century after ratification.

---

the law makers or the law breakers. The rights of conscience should always be considered inalienable — religious opinions as not the objects of civil government, nor any ways under its jurisdiction; laws should only respect civil society; then if men are disturbers they ought to be punished. *Id.*

240. Leland, *supra* note 223, at 1085.

241. LELAND, *supra* note 239, at 19 ("[W]hen a man is a peaceable subject of state, he should be protected in worshiping the Deity according to the dictates of his own conscience").

242. Gonzales v. O Centro Espirita Beneficente Uniao Do Vegetal, 546 U.S. 418, 424-27 (2006) (protecting consumption of *hoasca,* an herbal tea that contains a controlled substance, in a worship service); Church of the Lukumi Babalu Aye, Inc. v. City of Hialeah, 508 U.S. 520, 524-25 (1993) (protecting sacrifice of animals in a worship service); Employment Div. v. Smith, 494 U.S. 872, 874-76 (1990) (refusing to protect consumption of peyote, a controlled substance, in a worship service).

243. LELAND, *supra* note 239, at 18.

Another such quote might surface, or even more than one. But it is clear that such views were no significant part of the Founding-era debate on religious liberty.

IV. From Original Understanding to the Present

This original understanding helps explain and confirm both American practice and Supreme Court precedent. From the late seventeenth century to the present, there is an unbroken tradition of legislatively enacted regulatory exemptions. James Ryan, using a Lexis search and sampling techniques, estimated that there were 2000 religious exemptions on state and federal statute books in 1992.[244] The idea that these exemptions may violate the Establishment Clause is of modern origin, perhaps first seriously suggested by Philip Kurland in 1962.[245]

244. James E. Ryan, *Smith and the Religious Freedom Restoration Act: An Iconoclastic Assessment,* 78 VA. L. REV. 1407, 1445 & n.215 (1992). His search method appears to have included tax exemptions as well as regulatory exemptions.

245. *See* KURLAND, *supra* note 12, at 17-18, 40-41, 111-12. The argument also appears in highly conclusory fashion — in a single phrase — in the unsuccessful argument of the prosecutor in *People v. Philips* (N.Y. Ct. Gen. Sess. June 14, 1813). *See supra* note 189 and accompanying text.

A related, but different argument appeared in the World War I draft cases. In World War I, the exemption from military service was limited to members "of any well-recognized religious sect or organization at present organized and existing and whose existing creed or principles forbid its members to participate in war in any form" and who personally shared that tenet of the organization's creed. Selective Draft Act of 1917, ch. 15, § 4, 40 Stat. 76, 78. The famous anarchist Emma Goldman, prosecuted for giving speeches and distributing literature that allegedly induced men not to register for the draft, argued that the exemption provision discriminated on the basis of denomination and established the preferred denominations. Brief on Behalf of Plaintiffs in Error at 33-40, Goldman v. United States, 245 U.S. 474 (1918) (No. 702). An amicus brief argued that the provision denied free exercise of religion to conscientious objectors in unexempted denominations or with nontheistic moral commitments. Brief of Walter Nelles, Ruthenberg v. United States, 245 U.S. 480 (1918) (No. 656). These arguments would have to be taken quite seriously today under cases rigorously enforcing the constitutional ban on denominational discrimination. *See* Larson v. Valente, 456 U.S. 228, 244 (1982) ("The clearest command of the Establishment Clause is that one religious denomination cannot be officially preferred over another."); Bd. of Educ. v. Grumet, 512 U.S. 687, 702-05 (1994) (invalidating statute that relieved burden on one religious group with no mechanism to assure similar relief to any other religious group similarly situated); *see also* Welsh v. United States, 398 U.S. 333, 335-44 (1970) (plurality opinion) (construing statutory exemption from military service to include nontheistic objectors); United States v. Seeger, 380 U.S. 163, 173-85 (1965) (same). But in 1918, the Court summarily

Justice Harlan adopted a version of the argument in his concurring opinion in *Welsh v. United States*.[246] He would have permitted Congress to exempt men with deeply held conscientious objection to military service, but he would not have permitted Congress to exempt objectors who based their moral objection on some form of traditional religion without also exempting those who based their equally deep moral objection on some form of secular philosophy.[247] But where Congress attempted to exempt only the former, his remedy would have been to extend the exemption to include the latter as well.[248]

I have no fundamental quarrel with Harlan's position on this issue, although I would prefer a different explanation for his result. I have long urged that given the current distribution of religious opinion, exemptions should extend to the deep-seated moral objections of those who reject traditional religious teachings.[249] This result is most easily reached by taking a broadly inclusive view of what counts as religion, including both affirmative and negative answers to the great religious questions — essentially by the plurality's route in *Welsh*[250] rather than by Justice Harlan's, although either route will suffice. Persons with sufficiently deep moral objections to a law are similarly situated with traditional religious objectors; persons with other kinds of objections to a law are not.

My disagreement is with those who would interpret religion narrowly and traditionally, and who would also reject Harlan's remedy for too-narrow exemption laws, and who would then invalidate religious exemptions as discriminatory. Judges and others who combine these three positions would deny religious liberty to the overwhelming majority of conscientious objectors because of such judges' own refusal to protect the small minority of equally conscientious objectors whose objection is based on a belief that

---

rejected both the establishment and free exercise arguments as unworthy of discussion. *Goldman*, 245 U.S. at 476; Selective Draft Law Cases, 245 U.S. 366, 389-90 (1918). For brief accounts of Emma Goldman and the *Selective Draft Law Cases*, see DAVID M. RABBAN, FREE SPEECH IN ITS FORGOTTEN YEARS 65-67, 270-71 (1997).

246. 398 U.S. 333, 356-67 (1970) (Harlan, J., concurring).

247. *See id.* at 356-61.

248. *See id.* at 361-67.

249. *See* Laycock, *supra* note 13, at 1002; Douglas Laycock, *Religious Liberty as Liberty*, 7 J. CONTEMP. LEGAL ISSUES 313, 326-37 (1996).

250. *Welsh*, 398 U.S. at 335-44 (plurality opinion) (concluding, despite restrictive statutory language, that Welsh's deeply held moral convictions were religious). To similar effect, see *United States v. Seeger*, 380 U.S. 163, 173-85 (1965) (treating as religious those beliefs that occupy, in the life of a nontheist, a place parallel to that occupied by God in the life of a traditional believer).

doesn't seem to fit traditional or conventional understandings of religion.[251] The best solution is to exempt all conscientious objectors (always subject to the compelling interest exception), whether religious or nonreligious by traditional theistic conceptions. The second-best solution is to protect at least the great majority of conscientious objectors who are traditionally religious; this "majority" is a diffuse and disparate majority of a generally small minority holding deep moral objections to laws with majority support. The worst outcome is to deny protection to all conscientious objectors because legislators and judges find it difficult to explicitly extend protection to a small number of the hardest cases.

Some readers may find this a surprise ending. What is the difference between my saying that the right to religious exemptions should be extended to nontheists with deep-seated moral objections, and others saying that exemptions exclusively for religious believers violate the Establishment Clause? Both positions have some basis in the principle of neutrality between different religious beliefs. But they differ in two important ways. The Establishment Clause argument, at least as it has been presented in recent litigation, tends to take a much broader view of who is discriminated against. Some proponents of the Establishment Clause argument — not all — appear to believe that an exemption for Sabbath observers establishes religion because there is no exemption for football fans or for parents having trouble finding child care. But I would extend exemptions only to persons whose claim is sufficiently analogous to what all would agree is a religion. In the absence of a theistic belief or a nontheistic organization or tradition that is functioning like a religion (such as Buddhism), that analogy can be made out only by a deep-seated moral commitment — not by just any other highly desired Saturday activity.

More fundamentally, the opponents of exemptions let the principle of formal neutrality toward religion swallow a second principle practiced at the founding: that legislators could exempt religious objectors from regulation. The problem of the secular conscientious objector did not exist in the Founders' time. Now that such objectors exist, the solution is to extend the exemption principle to include them, not to repeal the exemption principle because neutrality has become more difficult to implement. I have made the normative argument for regulatory exemptions elsewhere and will not repeat it here.[252] But the claim that the emergence of a significant secular minority

251. *See* Laycock, *supra* note 249, at 336-37.
252. *See, e.g., id.* at 316-26, 347-48; Douglas Laycock, *The Remnants of Free Exercise*, 1990 SUP. CT. REV. 1, 10-68.

makes it unconstitutional for legislatures to exempt religious practices from regulation would turn the Religion Clauses on their head, treating increased opposition to religious belief and believers as in itself a reason that requires government to restrict legislative protection for the religious liberty of those believers — when increased opposition to a group should more properly be a reason for vigilance in protecting the liberties of that group.

Conclusion

The Supreme Court is deeply divided on the question of whether regulatory exemptions are sometimes constitutionally required.[253] But since the retirement of Justice Harlan, the Court has repeatedly been unanimous in support of the general view that regulatory exemptions are constitutionally permitted.[254] The Court first seriously addressed the issue in *Corporation of the Presiding Bishop v. Amos,*[255] unanimously upholding a provision exempting religious organizations from a federal prohibition on religious discrimination in employment.[256] The most recent example is *Cutter v. Wilkinson,*[257] unanimously rejecting Establishment Clause challenges to

253. *Compare* City of Boerne v. Flores, 521 U.S. 507, 537-44 (Scalia, J., concurring), *with id.* at 544-65 (1997) (O'Connor, J., dissenting).

254. *See* Cutter v. Wilkinson, 544 U.S. 709, 719-26 (2005); Bd. of Educ. v. Grumet, 512 U.S. 687, 705-06 (1994); *id.* at 711-12 (Stevens, J., concurring); *id.* at 715-16 (O'Connor, J., concurring); *id.* at 722-24 (Kennedy, J., concurring in the judgment); *id.* at 743-45 (Scalia, J., dissenting); Employment Div. v. Smith, 494 U.S. 872, 890 (1990); *id.* at 893-97 (O'Connor, J., concurring); Corp. of the Presiding Bishop v. Amos, 483 U.S. 327, 334-39 (1987); *id.* at 340-46 (Brennan, J., concurring); *id.* at 346 (Blackmun, J., concurring); *id.* at 348-49 (O'Connor, J., concurring). *But see Boerne,* 521 U.S. at 536-37 (Stevens, J., concurring) (arguing, without mention of his opinion in *Grumet* or the opinions he joined in *Amos* and *Smith,* that the Religious Freedom Restoration Act, 42 U.S.C. § 2000bb-1 (2000), establishes religion by preferring churches to art galleries).

255. 483 U.S. 327 (1987).

256. *See id.* at 334 ("This Court has long recognized that the government may (and sometimes must) accommodate religious practices and that it may do so without violating the Establishment Clause," quoting Hobbie v. Unemployment Appeals Comm'n, 480 U.S. 136, 144-45 (1987)); *id.* at 345 (Brennan, J., concurring) ("substantial potential for chilling religious activity . . . justifies a categorical exemption for nonprofit activities" of religious organizations); *id.* at 346 (Blackmun, J., concurring) (upholding the exemption "essentially for the reasons" stated by Justice O'Connor); *id.* at 349 (O'Connor, J., concurring) ("the objective observer should perceive the Government [exemption] as an accommodation of the exercise of religion rather than as a Government endorsement of religion").

257. 544 U.S. 709 (2005).

the prison provisions of the Religious Land Use and Institutionalized Persons Act (RLUIPA).[258]

Of course there are limits to this rule. Regulatory exemptions are invalid if they are "absolute" and "take[] no account" of burdens on others in particular applications,[259] or if they are confined to a single sect,[260] or to a single religious practice in a context where other religious practices are equally relevant to the exemption.[261] The Court invalidated a tax exemption because in the plurality's view there was no burden on religious exercise to be relieved and the cost of the exemption burdened other taxpayers,[262] or because, in the more convincing view of a concurring opinion, the exemption created a content-discriminatory tax on the press.[263] But nothing in these cases supports any version of the claim that regulatory exemptions are facially, generally, or usually invalid. To the contrary, in two of these cases limiting the reach of exemptions, large majorities made a point of reaffirming the constitutionality of legislation exempting religious practices from burdensome regulation — eight justices in *Texas Monthly v. Bullock*[264] and nine justices in *Board of Education v. Grumet*[265] (perhaps more commonly known as *Kiryas Joel*). Every Justice said it again in *Employment Division v. Smith*,[266] the case

258. *See id.* at 719-26 (holding that RLUIPA § 3, 42 U.S.C. § 2000cc-1 (2000), appropriately lifts burdens on the free exercise of religion without unduly burdening others and without discriminating among faiths).

259. Estate of Thornton v. Caldor, Inc., 472 U.S. 703, 709 (1985).

260. *See* Bd. of Educ. v. Grumet, 512 U.S. 687, 702-05 (1994).

261. *See Thornton,* 472 U.S. at 711-12 (O'Connor, J., concurring).

262. Tex. Monthly, Inc. v. Bullock, 489 U.S. 1, 18-19 & n.8 (1989) (plurality opinion).

263. *Id.* at 25-26 (White, J., concurring); *see id.* at 27-28 (Blackmun, J., concurring).

264. *See id.* at 18 n.8 (plurality opinion) (approving *Amos*); *id.* at 28 (Blackmun, J., concurring) (approving *Amos*); *id.* at 38-40 (Scalia, J., dissenting) (arguing that regulatory and tax exemptions are generally permitted and sometimes required). Justice White's brief concurrence said nothing about the exemption issue one way or the other. *See id.* at 25-26 (White, J., concurring).

265. *See* 512 U.S. 687, 705 (1994) ("the Constitution allows the state to accommodate religious needs by alleviating special burdens"; reaffirming *Amos*); *id.* at 711-12 (Stevens, J., concurring) (distinguishing facts of *Grumet* from "a decision to grant an exemption from a burdensome general rule"); *id.* at 716 (O'Connor, J., concurring) ("The Constitution permits '*nondiscriminatory* religious-practice exemption[s],'" quoting Employment Division v. Smith, 494 U.S. 872, 890 (1990) (emphasis by Justice O'Connor)); *id.* at 723-24 (Kennedy, J., concurring) (approving *Amos* and similar cases); *id.* at 744 (Scalia, J., dissenting) ("The Court has . . . long acknowledged the permissibility of legislative accommodation.").

266. *See* 494 U.S. at 890 ("a nondiscriminatory religious-practice exemption is permitted"); *id.* at 893-97 (O'Connor, J., concurring) (arguing that regulatory exemptions for religious exercise are constitutionally required).

that limited free exercise claims to exemptions. And as already noted,[267] they unanimously so held in *Amos* and *Cutter*.

The argument that regulatory exemptions implicate the Establishment Clause is relatively new. It grows from misapplication of attempts to summarize the principles of disestablishment and free exercise in the broad language of neutrality. But if ripped from context and historical roots, such broad language can suggest results inconsistent with those underlying principles.

As understood by those in the founding generation who labored in the states on behalf of disestablishment, there was a material difference between support for organized religion (establishment, and a threat to religious liberty) and exemption for religious practice (liberty enhancing, whether or not required by free exercise). Exemptions are not a way of expanding the power of the dominant religion; they are a way of protecting religions that lack the political power to prevent legislation that imposes substantial burdens on their religious practice. Government support makes a religion better off than it would have been if government had done nothing; regulatory exemptions relieve burdens imposed by government and leave the religion's adherents no better off than if government had not imposed the burden in the first place. Government does not establish a religion by leaving it alone. And there is no evidence the Founders thought otherwise.

267. *See supra* notes 255-58 and accompanying text.

PART THREE

Appendices

"God Alone Is Lord of the Conscience":
Policy Statement and Recommendations
Regarding Religious Liberty

Committee on Religious Liberty and Church/State Relations, Presbyterian Church (U.S.A) (1988) (reprinted in 8 Journal of Law & Religion 331 [1990])

This Statement is presented in an Appendix because it does not speak in my own voice and is only partly my work, yet it is too important to omit. From 1983 to 1988, I served on the Committee on Religious Liberty and Church/State Relations of the Presbyterian Church (U.S.A.). I was the only law professor on the Committee, and the principal legal expert, although the Rev. Dean Kelley, a Methodist minister and long-time point person on religious liberty for the National Council of Churches, brought enormous self-taught erudition on religious liberty issues to the Committee's work. The remaining members were a diverse and talented group of Presbyterian clergy and laypeople, identified at the end of this Appendix. The Committee produced this wide-ranging Statement on religious liberty, which was ultimately adopted by the General Assembly, the highest governing body of the church.

Much of the legal analysis in this Statement derives from my work, and many passages are recognizably mine. The many passages that place this work in the context of Reformed faith and Presbyterian history clearly are not mine. And I deferred to the views of the rest of the Committee on all questions of policy; I was acutely aware that this was a Presbyterian Statement, and that I was not a Presbyterian. A related background paper, which I authored individually and which describes the development of the relevant law from the founding to the mid-1980s, appears in Part One, Section B (Analytic and Descriptive Overviews), under the title A Survey of Religious Liberty in the United States.

*   *   *

For two hundred years, General Assemblies of the Presbyterian Church have been concerned with religious liberty and the relationship of church and state. The first General Assembly might well have heard the echo of Hanover

Presbytery's mighty Memorial to the Virginia legislature: "We ask no ecclesiastical establishments for ourselves; neither can we approve of them when granted to others." Since 1788, our basic Principles of Church Order have placed in the first position the powerful commitment of our Reformed faith to religious liberty: "God alone is Lord of the conscience. . . . We do not even wish to see any religious constitution aided by the civil power, further than may be necessary for protection and security, and at the same time be equal and common to all others."

The Bill of Rights in the Constitution of our civil order also accords the first position to this same commitment: "Congress shall make no law respecting an establishment of religion, or prohibiting the free exercise thereof. . . ." These clauses have been remarkably successful in guaranteeing religious liberty and assuring religious peace in a nation of extraordinary religious vitality and pluralism. As we deal with the difficult and controversial issues of religious liberty, we must not lose sight of its many aspects that are not controversial. Freedom of religious belief is unquestioned in this country. The right to basic religious observance is unquestioned. It is unthinkable that civil and political rights might be conditioned on adherence to a particular religious faith. In many countries of the world, none of these things are true.

Religious tolerance and pluralism are our political and societal norm. We do not perfectly achieve that norm and intolerance has not been eliminated, but it is not respectable and it is often muted. We have not had serious outbreaks of religious violence in nearly a century. In many countries of the world these things are not true either.

We believe that the rights to free exercise and nonestablishment are of equal importance in guaranteeing religious liberty. It is frequently said that there is a tension between the clauses, because one forbids government to harm religion and the other forbids government to support religion. It is true that there is sometimes a tension with respect to particular applications. But the great purposes of the two clauses are in harmony. Together the two clauses guarantee that the people will have the fullest possible religious liberty. The state may not interfere with the private choice of religious faith either by coercion or by persuasion. It may not interfere with the expression of faith either by inducing people to abandon the religious faith and practice of their choice, or by inducing them to adopt the religious faith and practice of the government's choice.

We believe that the establishment clause requires government to be wholly neutral in matters of religion. Government may not require adherence to a particular religious belief, designate an official state church, or endorse a religion. Government may not sponsor religious observances or grant financial aid to religion. Nor may government support religion in some generic fashion that is allegedly nonpreferential. No support of religion could be nonpreferential in a society as religiously diverse as ours. At best the government would support a broad group of somewhat similar majority religions, with the inevitable result that nonbelievers and members of religious minorities are excluded. Actual or symbolic exclusion of such minorities is inconsistent with one great purpose of the establishment clause: to affirm that every individual can be a full member of the civil polity whatever his or her religious belief.

We believe that the free exercise clause protects religious exercise in all its manifestations. It protects religious belief and basic religious observance. It protects religious proselytizing, the religious teaching of moral values, and the churches' invocation of those values in the political process. It protects the right of churches and individual believers to exercise religious conscience in the face of laws that would force them to violate that conscience. It protects the right to build religious institutions and to manage those institutions autonomously with a minimum of interference from government regulation. Some of these rights may on occasion be overridden by a compelling government interest, but such interests must be truly compelling, involving intolerable threats to public health and safety or serious impositions on persons not affiliated with the church.

The application of such sweeping guarantees to such an important dimension of public and private life is always complex and often controversial, particularly since adoption of the Fourteenth Amendment and subsequent Supreme Court decisions brought the Bill of Rights to bear on actions by state and local governments as well as the federal; and more particularly in the past fifty years as the Supreme Court made clear that the religion clauses were included in the reach of the Fourteenth Amendment.

In each historical era the General Assembly of the Presbyterian Church has addressed the problems that seemed important at that time. In the period from World War II to the 1970s, much of the attention was devoted to establishment clause issues. There were vigorous and continuing debates over religious instruction during public school hours, prayer and Bible reading in public schools, diplomatic representation at the Vatican, and financial aid to religious schools. Free exercise issues were not ignored, but establishment clause issues dominated.

Recently, a different kind of problem has become apparent: governmental intrusions into religious institutions and activities, and restrictions on the free exercise of religion. In 1976 the General Assembly of the Presbyterian

Church in the United States protested the use of missionaries as informants by federal intelligence agencies. In 1981, the church adopted changes in the Form of Government in response to the use by civil courts of the concept of "neutral principles of law" to permit congregations to withdraw from Presbyterian and other presbyterial and hierarchical denominations and to take the church property with them, in effect reducing these churches to a congregational polity by judicial fiat.

Amicus filings led the 1982 General Assembly of the United Presbyterian Church in the United States of America to wrestle painfully with the implications of the Internal Revenue Service's revocation of the tax exemption of Bob Jones University for "violation of public policy" with respect to racial discrimination; and led the 1984 General Assembly to debate issues arising from the firing of a bank teller because he refused to resign from the leadership of an organization of his church advocating for the civil rights of homosexual persons. In 1985, the Stated Clerk of the General Assembly entered suit against the United States government for hiring persons with criminal records to infiltrate churches and tape religious meetings, seeking evidence against church leaders and workers active in the "sanctuary movement."

Other troubling developments suggest increasing impairments of the free exercise of religion and the right of churches to control their own affairs. Some examples:

Local governments have used zoning regulations to restrict the mission of local churches, such as feeding or sheltering the homeless, to prohibit prayer meetings in private homes, to bar new churches from residential areas, and even to bar any church at all from an entire municipality.

Church buildings have been designated as landmarks without the consent of the religious groups that own them, thus obligating the churches to maintain the facade at their own expense or face criminal penalties.

The highest court of Massachusetts has authorized a trial court to entertain an invasion of privacy suit by a clergyman against his bishop, and to examine the deliberations of church tribunals that resulted in the clergyman's involuntary retirement in order to determine whether the church tribunals relied on information allegedly obtained from the clergyman's psychiatrist, and to award damages accordingly.

More than a dozen state statutes that require the reporting of suspected abuse make an exception for the attorney-client privilege but not for the priest-penitent privilege.

A judge issued an order barring a divorced father from taking his children to a Presbyterian Sunday School while he had legal custody of them.

California courts allowed the attorney general to place an entire church in receivership on the complaint of disgruntled members, alleging that member contributions created a charitable trust that the state was permitted to supervise.

Tennessee courts held that churches which openly opposed a liquor-by-the-drink referendum had to register as political action committees and file financial reports.

In several states, courts have awarded punitive damages to members or disaffected former members of churches who have received church discipline or alleged that the religion held out promises to them which were not fulfilled.

The Internal Revenue Service has applied the section of the tax code that prohibits religious and charitable organizations from intervening in political campaigns to religious efforts to influence public opinion and public policy on moral issues, even to the extent of questioning the distribution of voting records of incumbent legislators.

The Internal Revenue Code exempts churches and their "integrated auxiliaries" from filing annual information returns. The Internal Revenue Service defined "integrated auxiliaries" in a way that excluded church-owned hospitals, orphanages, and social service agencies, even when the church defined these agencies as integral to its mission.

Judges have signed orders permitting adults to be seized and held against their will for the purpose of reversing religious commitments of which their parents disapproved.

An appellate court in California ruled that a church and its leaders can be sued for punitive damages because of the suicide of a young man who was being counselled.

Such new problems illustrate the need to reexamine church-state relations with a special concern for the free exercise of religion. This does not mean that the earlier concern to prevent the establishment of religion is less important, for the prohibition against establishment is under attack today as perhaps never before in modern times. But it is essential to give equal attention to the free exercise of religion, and particularly to the corporate free exercise of religion. If the free exercise clause does not apply fully to religious bodies, then the religious liberty of individuals will also in time be curtailed, for the very continuity and perpetuation of religious life depends on religious movements, organizations, and institutions. In a day when institutions of all kinds are not held in high esteem, it is important to reaffirm their essential role in carrying vital patterns of human commitment beyond the passing moment.

Since the time of Calvin, Reformed Protestants have felt called to share their vision of God's intended order for the human community, and

Presbyterians have recognized and acted on the responsibility to seek social justice and peace and to promote the biblical values of freedom and liberty as well as corporate responsibility within the political order. The church itself must consider what conditions of the civil society are necessary to the effective conduct of the church's mission and ministry, and seek the recognition of those needs by society and state. If the church does not do so, no one else will do it for us. Many of the troubling encroachments listed above result from a lack of comprehension on the part of judges, legislators, and administrators of the proper scope, intensity, and importance of religious commitment and activity, and of its value for religious adherents and for the whole society.

The rules established by the religion clauses of the First Amendment have served us well. But the continuing vitality and clarity of religious liberty rest also, in a very important way, on the strong societal commitment to tolerance symbolized by these clauses and now taken for granted by most of the citizens and major religions in this country. The constitutional clauses and the societal commitment reinforce each other in important ways. The constitutional guarantee of religious freedom provides a legal mechanism through which government can be called to account judicially. But efforts to invoke the Constitution will falter and may ultimately fail if the society is sufficiently insensitive, indifferent, or hostile to the need for tolerance and the value and meaning of religious liberty. So the constitutional guarantee of religious liberty is also an important symbolic mechanism through which the church and others must seek to keep the societal understanding of and commitment to religious liberty vital and clear from generation to generation.

Our struggle with difficult and controversial issues dealt with in this report and our necessary endeavor to articulate the conditions of the civil society necessary to the free and effective conduct of the church's mission and ministry, then, are not dictated simply by institutional self-interest. They are also a vital dimension of Presbyterian witness and responsibility for the fundamental importance of religious liberty in and to the civil commonwealth. As a contemporary foundation for both tasks, we reaffirm the great historic principle of 1788, cited earlier, that "God alone is Lord of the conscience"; and the words of a proposed amendment to the Westminster Confession of Faith adopted by the General Assembly of the Presbyterian Church U.S.A. in 1938, the 150th anniversary of the adoption of that principle. Although more than sixty-eight percent of the presbyteries that voted approved the amendment, it narrowly failed because a few presbyteries did not vote. The words still ring true and relevant as a classic statement of Reformed understanding of relations between church and state, commitment to religious liberty, and the rights and duties of Presbyterians and the Presbyterian Church in the civil order:

> Civil government . . . may not assume the functions of religion. It must grant equal rights to every religious group showing no favor and granting no power to one above another. . . . Civil government has the right to require loyalty and obedience of its citizens, but may not require of them that allegiance which belongs to God alone. It must recognize the inherent liberty of the church to determine its faith and creed, to maintain public and private worship, preaching and teaching, and to hold public and private religious and ecclesiastical assemblies. It must recognize the right of the church to determine the nature of its government and the qualifications of its ministers and members; to render Christian service and to carry on missionary activity at home and abroad. For the attainment of all such ends, the church has the right to employ the facilities guaranteed to all citizens and associations: but it must not use violent or coercive measures for its spiritual ends, nor allow their use on its behalf. (Minutes, PCUSA, 1938, Part I, pp. 46-47).

The following analysis and affirmations regarding contemporary religious liberty issues considers them under seven general headings:

The Right of Church Autonomy and Government Regulation of Church
    Activity
Conduct Motivated by Conscience
Government Support for Religious Institutions
Taxation and Religious Organizations
New Religions and Threats to Conversion
Religious Expression in Public Places
Religious Participation in Public Life

A. The Right of Church Autonomy and Government Regulation of Church Activity

The extent to which the Constitution protects the autonomy of churches has become an increasingly important legal issue, with profound theological implications, as both the scope of church activity and the scope of government regulatory effort have expanded. The right of individuals freely to hold and express faith is widely understood to be at the heart of the First Amendment rights to freedom of religion and freedom of speech. The right of church autonomy — that is, the right of the corporate worshipping community to order itself and carry on its activities free from government intervention — is less well understood and documented, but no less clear and vital.

The individual's right to believe cannot be divorced from the right to exercise that belief in the company and community of others. For nearly every human being, the right to practice religion only as a solitary individual is virtually no right at all. The constitutional right to the free exercise of religion must protect not only the right to hold faith and speak freely of it to others but also the right freely to practice it through a worshipping body at work in the world.

We begin, therefore, with the principle that each worshipping community has the right to govern itself and order its life and activity free of government intervention. Churches must be free of government regulation of any kind and at any level in all but the most compelling circumstances. This right of church autonomy is protected by the free exercise clause of the First Amendment, but it is not the same as the right to conscientious objection discussed below. That right involves a claim of exemption from a statute of general application on the grounds that enforcement would result in a violation of individual conscience. The right of the church to control its own life and activity should not depend upon a showing that a governmental regulation violates a central tenet of church doctrine or even that other bodies of the same faith claim exemption from the regulation at issue.

The definitional question of what constitutes a "religion" or an "exercise of religion" is at the threshold of the issues of government regulation. We recognize that in the most rudimentary legal sense courts and public agencies must often make a determination of whether a particular group is a "religion" entitled to First Amendment protection as matters apparently related to religious bodies come before them. In such instances, great latitude must be given to the self-understanding of the group in question, since it is for the religious group — not the government — to state whether it is a "church." Government may inquire into the sincerity with which beliefs are held but may not rule upon their authenticity. On those occasions when determination of First Amendment applicability is necessary, the court or agency must of course bring some criteria to bear, but we reject the notion of a single, formal objective definition based on traditional forms of religion.

Many claims of the power to regulate arise from attempts to divide church activities into a protected "religious" category and nonprotected "nonreligious" ones, based on the nature of the activity or the organizational form it takes. There is a profoundly disturbing apparent misperception about the nature of the church and its mission at the root of most such attempts. The liturgical, sacramental, doctrinal "core functions" are identified as the "religious" dimension. The program activity of the church and the structures that administer and support it are categorized as "integrated auxiliaries" and "secular functions." The scope of First Amendment protection is effectively narrowed to the four walls of the sanctuary and within them extended only to the cultic practices absolutely unique to the church.

Programs of service and charity are as vital to the life and mission of most churches as acts of worship and evangelism. The church's pension agency is no less "church" because business corporations also have pension agencies. Church activities and affiliates should not be subject to regulation merely because they are doing things that are also done by secular charities and others. Nor should it matter whether such affiliates are separately incorporated. How a church structures itself and how it allocates authority should be irrelevant to the state. Churches may be hierarchical or congregational, episcopal or democratic, clerical or lay, incorporated or informally associated, a single entity or a network of subsidiaries and affiliates — all are entitled to autonomy by the free exercise clause. We oppose regulations based on governmental distinctions among the church's activities and organizational structure, such as the Internal Revenue Service regulations on integrated auxiliaries, and will continue to seek their defeat or repeal.

As a general matter, then, churches should be left alone except when there is a compelling reason for government interference or regulation, or when they voluntarily seek government assistance in the form of police or fire protection. However, the right of church autonomy is not absolute; it must be balanced against governmental interests in protecting the public health and safety. We claim no right for human sacrifice or mass suicide. But not every building code is essential to safety, and nonessential building codes or zoning regulations should not be applied to prevent the use of existing religious buildings for additional religious purposes. As with any other constitutionally protected activity, the government must first show a genuinely compelling state interest in order to justify any intrusion into religious activity at all. Even when such an interest is demonstrated, such as the need to enforce the criminal laws, government must be limited to the least intrusive means by which to accomplish the stated purpose.

There is a tendency for governmental agencies to define every regulatory activity as serving a compelling purpose, and governments often assert interests that are wholly inadequate to justify restrictions on church activity. For example, we reject the use of zoning authority to prevent church members from gathering to pray in private homes, or in an attempt to close a shelter for the homeless, and the use of the license and inspection power to require permits for church suppers. Similarly, while the state may have an interest in preserving historic buildings, it may not reorder the funding priorities of the congregation by insisting that the church devote significant sums to the maintenance of a church structure, without regard to whether it has money left for its mission, nor may the government exercise its powers of eminent domain to operate the building as a state-run museum.

A church's claim to autonomy is strongest with respect to its own internal affairs. Religious bodies are entitled to autonomy in determining the terms and conditions of membership, doctrine, and polity; the selection, supervision and discipline of employees; the confidentiality of records and communications within the church; and the use and control of church property.

Disputes among church members about the handling of church funds or property should be decided by the highest ecclesiastical authority recognized by both sides to the dispute before the disagreement arose. Submission of such disputes to the civil courts is improper. If they are brought before a civil court, any judgment other than that which affirms the jurisdiction of the highest ecclesiastical authority is a violation of church autonomy. We reject the application of so-called "neutral principles" of law to internal church property disputes. Such an approach is an unwarranted intrusion into the internal affairs of any church and, we believe, an unconstitutional usurpation of the authority of churches with hierarchical and connectional polities. Similarly, individual members who have become disaffected from a religious group or chafe under its discipline are not entitled to seek redress in the courts. Those who have affiliated themselves with a church have consented to its authority. If they become dissatisfied with the church they can leave it, but the government has no right to respond to their appeals to regulate their relationship with their church.

Statutes regarding the solicitation and handling of funds may be applied where charges of fraud are made, but great care must be taken to avoid unnecessary interference with church activities and records in adjudicating such claims. While we do not claim charitable immunity for personal injuries caused by the negligence of church employees, we reject the notion that the state may place a church in receivership or otherwise dictate its day-to-day affairs, even in the presence of a bona fide claim of criminal fraud.

The church's claim to autonomy is less strong when a governmental regulation purports to protect those outside the church who may come in contact with it. Those who have affiliated themselves with a church have not only consented to its authority; they also constitute a private association. Where such consent or associational character is lacking or suspect, the state has a greater right and responsibility to regulate to protect public health and safety. Thus, because children lack full power to consent, state regulation of the activities of church day schools and child care centers may be looked at differently than regulation of adult Bible study groups. However, regulation of church schools and day care centers should take account of the need for religious freedom, and such schools should not be required to use the same methods and personnel as public schools. It should be sufficient if students in a church school are performing at roughly the same grade level as those in public schools.

Labor regulations and employment discrimination laws often come in conflict with a church's constitutional right to autonomy. We recognize and affirm the duty of the church to be a just and compassionate employer. As Presbyterians, we oppose employment discrimination based on religion, race, sex, national origin, or sexual orientation, both inside and outside the church except where these are bona fide qualifications for church leadership. Similarly, we believe that the church has a moral duty to provide adequate compensation and working conditions for its employees. We reject, however, the notion that the government may impose such regulations on employment in all church activities. Any consideration of the degree of permissible regulation must depend upon the type of employment involved.

Church employees may cover the spectrum from "insiders," such as the clergy, to "outsiders," such as those who work in church-owned businesses like wineries or publishing houses. The appropriateness of government regulation concerning these employees depends upon the terms under which they undertook employment. If they entered employment with full knowledge of the church's employment practices or with the understanding that their employment was an exercise of faith, the government should not attempt to regulate their relationship with the church employer. If, however, they work in a primarily technical activity or one that principally serves a public clientele, such as a church-run hospital or publishing house; and if the church contracted with them on essentially secular terms, the argument for government interest in regulating the terms of their employment is more persuasive, provided that it not interfere with religious activities. Where church employees have given informed consent to special terms or practices of employment, little if any justification exists for regulation of the employment relationship beyond protection of the basic health and safety of employees in the workplace. An employee's commitment to work long hours for low pay and a church's decision to fire an unwed parent are free exercises of religion that should not be regulated or reviewed by the state.

771

A church has an absolute right to be free of government infiltration. Because government infiltration destroys the fabric of trust and fellowship essential to a worshipping community, it strikes at the very heart of church autonomy. If the government has reasonable cause to believe that certain church members are involved in criminal activity, it may take appropriate steps within the law to investigate the activities of those members, not the overall activities of the church. The government should never be permitted to conduct wiretaps of church telephones, monitor church services and meetings electronically, or otherwise search church premises without a warrant based on a strong showing of good cause to believe that evidence of criminal activity will be removed or destroyed if the warrant does not issue. Nor should the government use or seek to enlist church missionaries or employees in covert activities, either against fellow church members or against foreign governments.

In summary, churches have a First Amendment right to order their life and carry on their activities free of government intervention. Government assertions of the right to regulate cannot be allowed to intrude upon protected religious activity. Neither interest — that of the government to regulate or of the church to be autonomous — is absolute. The rights of the church are strongest and most in need of First Amendment protection when the issue is internal to the church and the activity is intensely religious in nature. In such situations, the government can assert little or no permissible interest and should be prohibited from intruding at all. In other areas, such as those involving persons not members of the church or where the activity is less intensely religious, government intrusion may be justifiable, assuming a compelling state interest and means carefully tailored to accomplishing the state's legitimate goal in a manner least intrusive upon First Amendment freedoms.

In view of the foregoing considerations, the 200th General Assembly (1988) adopts the following affirmations:
1. Churches have a right of autonomy protected by the free exercise clause of the First Amendment. Each worshipping community has the right to govern itself and order its life and activity free of government intervention.
2. The government must assert a compelling interest and demonstrate an imminent threat to public safety before the right of autonomy may be set aside in specific instances and government permitted to interfere with internal church activities. The need to separate business activity from residential areas is not sufficient to justify use of zoning regulations to

prevent prayer meetings in private homes or to prohibit the use of the church building as a shelter for the homeless.

3. Churches have a fundamental right to be free of government infiltration. Court-approved wiretaps and searches of church premises can only be made on a showing that evidence of crime endangering public health or safety will be removed or destroyed and that no other less intrusive means exist to satisfy the need to preserve such evidence.

4. We concede the appropriateness of some governmental regulation of church activities in the interests of public health and safety. Fire and earthquake regulations, sanitary and building codes may properly be made applicable to churches, provided that they do not entail unreasonable cost, are genuinely health and safety related, and are appropriate to the pattern of church activity rather than a supposed secular analog. A church kitchen used a few hours a month for church groups is not the same as a public restaurant.

5. The government may not require a congregation to maintain a church structure because of its historical significance or subject it to proceedings in eminent domain in order to preserve a church structure. The church should make every effort to cooperate with efforts to preserve esthetic and architectural character but must finally itself be the judge of what religious life and mission require concerning property and its use.

6. Internal disputes within churches, including disputes over church property, should be decided by the highest ecclesiastical authority recognized by both sides before the dispute arose. The application of so-called "neutral principles of law" by civil courts violates the right to autonomy of hierarchical and connectional churches.

7. Those who consent to be governed by a church, including its employees, should not be subject to governmental regulation. We reject the notion that minimum wage laws or other labor regulations may properly be applied to church organizations.

8. As a matter of faith and witness, the church has a moral duty to provide adequate compensation and safe working conditions for its employees and to offer employment without discrimination. The church should voluntarily meet or exceed the standards and practices required by law for nonreligious employers.

9. Courts and public agencies called upon to assess the bona fides of a claim to protection under the First Amendment should not base their decision on traditional notions of religion but should give substantial deference to the self-understanding of that group, looking to the three considerations described in this statement.

B. Conduct Motivated by Conscience

The exercise of individual and corporate conscience must be affirmed as an integral aspect of religious liberty. The church is always obliged to respect claims of conscience, lest it frustrate efforts to obey the will of God. We need not agree with the specific dictates of another's conscience to respect and support the right to exercise that conscience. Paul told Christians that they were freed from Jewish dietary laws, but if the conscience of another is offended by eating certain foods, "for conscience' sake — I mean his conscience, not yours — do not eat it" (I Corinthians 10:28-29). The obligation to respect the exercise of conscience is not only a dynamic of life within the church; it is both a demand and a dilemma of the First Amendment's protection of religious freedom.

The demand, of course, arises from the basic structure of the First Amendment: no prohibition on the free exercise of religion, on activity flowing from religious faith. The dilemma arises when an individual or group claims exemption from laws or regulations that on their face do not seem to concern religion, on the grounds that compliance would require conduct contrary to religious conscience and thus unconstitutionally burden free exercise.

In regard to churches, as noted in the discussion of the right of church autonomy, many laws governing the behavior of corporate bodies in this nation contain specific exemptions for "churches, conventions or associations of churches and their integrated auxiliaries." These exemptions arise from the appropriate recognition of church autonomy; they nevertheless forestall any objection of conscience.

The broad form exemption on the grounds of conscience rarely occurs in legislation primarily affecting individual conduct. Some exemptions have been recognized by special legislation: Amish people do not have to pay Social Security taxes, pacifists do not have to serve in the military, and Jewish officers in the army may wear yarmulkes. But the dilemmas surrounding response to conduct motivated by religious conscience are most often worked out in the courts as individuals raise claims of conscience as grounds for exemption from laws of general application. The values of religious liberty are so paramount that such claims should be accorded the greatest deference.

Claims of conscience, however, are not self-validating. The mere assertion of a conscientious objection cannot automatically ensure exemption. Society through government is justified in appropriate examination to test sincerity of conscientious belief, though not to judge its validity. As with church autonomy, claims of conscience cannot be absolute; they may sometimes need to be overridden. The burden of proof should be powerfully upon those who would deny the exercise of conscience in any given situation. The courts have said that the governmental interest must be "compelling" before overriding a claim of conscience, but that term lacks definition. Every governmental bureaucracy believes that its program serves a compelling interest. More helpfully, the Supreme Court has said that government can infringe the claims of conscience only when "the gravest abuses endangering paramount interests give occasion for permissible limitation" (*Sherbert v. Verner,* 1963).

We therefore believe that individuals should be excused from the obligation to obey laws of general application that violate their conscience unless an exemption threatens an intolerable risk to public health or safety or a serious imposition on specific individuals who have not consented to the imposition.

The formation of conscience occurs in community, but its exercise is very often finally an individual matter. Because the individual is the bearer of conscience, it does not matter whether others of the same faith make the same conscientious claim, a point now recognized in constitutional interpretation (*Thomas v. Review Board,* 1981). Nor should it be determinative whether the corporate body has defined the matter as a central point of doctrine or requirement of piety. The legal protection of idiosyncratic individual beliefs should be equal to the protection of the most traditional orthodoxies.

The exercise of religious conscience has come in conflict with governmental policies in a variety of contexts. Some of the most significant and troublesome areas are examined briefly in the following sections.

1. Military Service and Other Civic Duties

The very term "conscientious objection" has come to be applied in popular usage almost exclusively to those who refuse military service on grounds of conscience. Though we have here appropriately applied the term to a far wider range of conduct motivated by conscience, issues of conscience and war deserve first discussion since exemption for conscience has been recognized in both legislation and court decisions. Present selective service laws grant exemption from military service to those who by "religious training and belief are conscientiously opposed to participation in war in any form." (The military draft ended in 1972, but registration was resumed in 1980.) The basis for conscientious objection to military service was broadened beyond traditional religious grounds to individual moral grounds in 1965 and 1970 (*Seeger v. United States*), but the limitation of the exemption to those who oppose war in any form has remained and been deemed permissible (*Gillette v. United States,* 1971). This effectively excludes from the exemption those whose conscience conforms to the position of the Presbyterian Church and others in the just war tradition, who say that in good conscience they could fight in a just war but could not fight in an unjust war. Given the long history of theological reflection about just war and the incorporation of just war criteria in common political discourse and international law, it would be rational and consistent to extend the exemption to conduct informed by such conscience. The refusal to do so undoubtedly stems from prudential rather than principled reasons. There are far more Christians in the just war tradition than pacifists, and more and more people are coming to believe that opposition to policies predicated on the permissibility of nuclear war is an act of conscience since nuclear war violates just war criteria. The General Assembly of the Presbyterian Church (U.S.A.) maintains a register of Presbyterians who object to participation either to all war or to unjust wars on the grounds of conscience and continues to seek changes in Selective Service law and regulations to recognize these claims of conscience. Persons exercising religious conscience may also refuse to work on the production of munitions, to perform certain civic obligations such as jury duty, or may even engage in civil disobedience rather than acquiesce in conduct that violates conscience. A nineteenth-century example of the latter is the transportation of escaped slaves to Canada in violation of the fugitive slave laws. The protection of political refugees from Central America may eventually be construed as civil disobedience on grounds of religious conscience. Some forms of conscientious civil disobedience are undertaken to induce government to fulfill its legal responsibilities in such areas as civil rights or environmental protection.

2. *Conscientious Objection and Civil Disobedience*

There is an important distinction between conscientious objection and civil disobedience, though the two concepts are frequently confused. One may conscientiously object to disfavored acts of government without engaging in specific acts of disobedience to law, particularly if one is not immediately affected personally, as white people were not barred from restaurants under Jim Crow laws. Likewise, one may, for the sake of publicity, group solidarity, or tactical advantage, engage in acts of civil disobedience without necessarily invoking the dictates of conscience. Often what is properly to be understood as legal may be in doubt. Local laws may be challenged in the name of a higher constitutional law, as happened in the civil rights protests of the 1960s. The claims of moral law attach to the higher constitutional law, but the claims are not "only" moral. Sanctuary workers are asserting the rights of conscience but are also challenging the interpretations of existing federal law by the Immigration and Naturalization Service, claiming to obey laws being flouted by government officials. Despite the many acts that are loosely called "civil disobedience," it is probably quite rare in the American legal system for what is established as settled constitutional law to be explicitly violated on the grounds of a countervailing moral law. More typically, the objectors seek to introduce their understanding of the moral law into the realm of constitutional protections.

The usual distinction between "civil" disobedience and ordinary criminal disobedience rests not only on the appeal to law as the source of motivation but also on the willingness of the civil disobedient to accept the penalty normally imposed for the infraction. Criminals do not announce their intentions in advance as civil disobedients do. So conceived, such acts of civil disobedience may be an exercise of conscience whether explicitly religious or not. They should be respected by the church as fully as acts of explicitly religious conscience.

3. Medical Treatment

Jehovah's Witnesses have refused blood transfusions, and others have refused medical treatment on the grounds of religious conscience. The courts have at times overridden that right, especially when a child's life is at stake and parental objections to medical treatment are based upon the parents' religious beliefs. Most often, the courts have allowed competent adults to refuse medical treatment on religious grounds. We believe that this strikes the right balance. Denial of the right to refuse medical treatment exemplifies the conflict between the freedom of religious expression and the need to protect the innocent from direct harm not of their own choosing.

Holistic medicine has been growing as a field, and many have a new awareness of ancient truths about the spiritual dimension of healing. In addition, we are confronted in new ways with ethical issues relating conception, abortion, euthanasia, and the rationing of costly medical technologies. Facing these issues has enlarged our understanding of or at least heightened our concern for the complex intersection between religion and medicine. Religious liberty bears on medical practice in new ways as personal decisions based on religious convictions confront the traditional and legal commitments of medical practitioners and both confront the capacities of new technologies. Courts will, of course, decide many cases in this area; but the church should not leave such issues to the courts. Sensitive to the demands of conscience and committed to their protection, the church should be prepared to offer independent counsel and support to those facing difficult medical choices.

4. Conditions of Employment, Sabbath Observance, Nondiscrimination

The right to observe the Sabbath according to the tenets of one's religion despite conflicting work schedules has been tested on numerous occasions in the courts. The Supreme Court has held that unemployment compensation benefits could not be withheld from a Seventh-day Adventist discharged because she would not work on Saturday, and in *Hobbie v. Unemployment Appeals Commission,* 1987, resoundingly reaffirmed that position. The Civil Rights Act of 1964 gave statutory acknowledgement to the right of religious conscience in employment situations and a certain amount of protection, though courts have held the required accommodation to conduct motivated by religious conscience to be de minimis.

If Sabbath observance is regarded as protected religious expression, this does not mean that in employment cases the protection can extend to the point of discriminating against other workers. An airline was required to make only "reasonable" adjustments of work schedules to accommodate a Seventh-day Adventist *(TWA v. Hardison).* A recent case (involving a Presbyterian) held that if time off for Sabbath observance has the effect of imposing greater burdens on workers with higher seniority than on the Sabbath observant, this would be a violation of the establishment clause *(Thornton v. Calder).*

In a rather different recent discrimination case *(Dorr v. First Kentucky National Corp.),* a bank manager was forced out of his job when he would not resign as president of an Episcopal-Catholic organization advocating the rights of gays and lesbians. He claimed that the office was an expression of his religious conviction. The federal district court, however, held that this discrimination was not on the basis of religion and therefore not covered by the Civil Rights Act of 1964, largely on the grounds that such activity was not required by the doctrine or discipline of his church. The court's willingness to blank out individual conscience if not a required tenet of organizational creed and to substitute its own judgment of what constitutes religious motivation for that of the claimant is most disturbing.

5. Use of Illegal Drugs for Religious Purposes

The California Supreme Court in *People v. Woody* in 1964 found that the application of the state criminal statutes to American Indians using peyote in a traditional religious ceremony was unconstitutional. The finding that the use of peyote was central to their faith influenced the court in distinguishing between that case and the prohibition of polygamy as applied to the Mormons in 1878. The prosecution in *Woody* contrasts sharply with the exclusion of sacramental wine from anti-alcohol laws during Prohibition. The religious exercise of majorities, or influential minorities, will often be protected by the legislative process. These cases also illustrate the difficulty of drawing the line between protecting public health and safety and protecting religious conscience.

6. Sanctuary for Political Refugees

Some Presbyterians are deeply involved in the issue of providing sanctuary for political refugees, especially those from Central America. While sanctuary advocates claim that United States statutory law and international law support their position, those openly providing shelter for refugees also realize the potential risk that they will ultimately be held to have violated immigration laws. The claims of conscience should be respected with regard to those in the sanctuary movement who struggle to provide a refuge for victims of repression and violence in light of civil laws that may hinder such refuge.

Summary

The exercise of conscientious objection should not be seen primarily as a negative legal right, but as a positive moral virtue. "Conscientious objection" has often come to signify merely a negative right to object. It should also signify acts of affirmation, the affirmation of fundamental values of justice and of equal dignity and respect for all humans. Ultimately, we are called to "obey God rather than men" (Acts 5:29). The legal right is itself positive; it is grounded not in grudging governmental concession to conscience but in the positive protection of religious conscience as a fundamental civic value.

The courts have been wisely reluctant to assume the task of defining what constitutes "religious" convictions, though they have not always been steady in their resolve to prevent other governmental officials from doing so. There was a time when periodicals that editorialized against war lost their second class mailing privileges and ministers who preached against war were prosecuted. At least one socialist was sentenced to three years in federal prison for saying that the draft law was unconstitutional.

The protection of conduct motivated by religious conscience is fundamental to the vitality of the free exercise clause. In seeking to maintain it, we are grateful for the words of Justice Jackson in the *Barnette* case, "If there is any fixed star in our constitutional constellation, it is that no official, high or petty, can prescribe what shall be orthodox in politics, nationalism, religion, other matters of opinion, or force citizens to confess by word or act their faith therein."

779

In view of the foregoing considerations, the 200th General Assembly (1988) adopts the following affirmations:

1. Individuals should be excused from obeying laws of general application which violate their conscience except when "the gravest abuses endangering paramount interests give occasion for permissible limitation."

2. The legal defense of freedom of conscience must be conceived broadly enough to include freedom for the nonreligious conscience.

3. The protection of religious conscience should not be limited to actions stemming from beliefs shared by all members of one religious group or to what is required by the creed or order of one religious group. It includes practice that may be regarded as voluntary by one's religion as well as that which is individually derived.

4. The right of adults to refuse medical treatment for themselves on religious grounds should be upheld but not their right to withhold medical care for their minor children when such treatment is deemed necessary to prevent death or permanent injury.

5. The diversity of understandings of different religious groups as to what constitutes health should be respected.

6. The right to observe the Sabbath and other days of religious obligation should be protected, but not to the significant material disadvantage of co-workers whose days of religious obligation are different or those who are not religiously affiliated.

7. The present selective service law, which requires that conscientious objectors be opposed to all wars, should be changed to allow exemption as well for those opposed only to participation in particular wars on the ground that they are unjust.

8. Not all employment discrimination can be reached by laws. The church should be prepared to expose, analyze and confront cases of discrimination in public or private employment based on religious conviction or status, as well as on grounds of race, religion, nationality, sex, or sexual orientation, and to provide aid and comfort to the victims.

9. Claims of Christian conscience should not be lightly or cynically made, and should be tested to the maximum extent possible by the counsel of the Christian community.

C. Government Support for Religious Institutions

Religious organizations in the United States have almost invariably understood activities in education, welfare, health, and other social services to be part of religious commitment and mission, sometimes focused on those in their own faith group but very often extended to serve the needs of the public community. Over the course of our history as a nation, the society has increasingly recognized a public responsibility to meet such needs through the use of public funds. In some instances, governmental agencies provide such programs directly (public schools, veterans' hospitals, unemployment benefits, public welfare, etc.); in others, public funds are made available to individuals (through grants or vouchers, education loans, GI Bill, food stamps, Medicare, etc.); in a third pattern, private institutions receive loans or grants of public funds to provide the defined service to the public (student and elderly housing, hospital construction, job training, halfway houses, feeding programs, hotels for the homeless, etc.).

In the past forty years there has been a great expansion in the scope of governmental social service, health, and education programs in this third pattern, through which public funds are available for a wide range of privately sponsored and administered social service activities. These programs exist at every governmental level, and government often actively seeks the participation of religious organizations in many of them. There is continuing controversy within both the religious and secular community about both the constitutionality and the propriety of such government assistance and church participation.

These are not new issues. When the General Assembly of the United Presbyterian Church adopted the landmark 1963 report on "Relations Between Church and State" and the guidelines it contained, there was no guideline relating to church use of public funds. Those who drafted the report were not unaware of the issue but noted that it was a problem "so complex as to deny responsible consideration within the limited time and space available." Shortly thereafter a new process was initiated, resulting in a report and recommendations on "Church Participation in Public Programs" approved by the 181st General Assembly (1969). This analysis is based on that report and, we believe, consistent with it.

In these developments, the distinction between purely private and purely public agencies has become blurred as national need demanded and public policy permitted vastly expanded cooperation between voluntary organizations and government. The provisions of the First Amendment create a unique context and tension for church-government cooperation in this regard. On the one hand, churches should not have to abandon needed social services traditionally part of their life in an era when cooperation between government and private agencies has become both common and productive. Indeed, to exclude them from eligibility alone among voluntary agencies would seem to be arbitrary and discriminatory and a possible infringement on the free exercise of religion. On the other hand, government may not use its influence and funds to support or advance religion, requiring that substantive religious character and purpose be divorced from the activity. Government in the United States is not only required by the Constitution to safeguard the freedom of religious exercise; it is also expressly forbidden to take any measures that establish religion. The 1969 General Assembly recognized this tension:

> Applied literally, "organic separation of church and state" would forbid not only churches but their representatives, clergy or laymen, even to organize enabling bodies, entirely independent of church control, to set public programs afoot in local communities. But this would refuse minimal cooperation with a legitimate activity of government and would disbar church-associated citizens from exercising their civil rights. Yet if the wisdom of the separationist tradition is ignored, initial activity by churches may well evolve into uncritical acceptance of government policy at the expense of the church's prophetic function. The church must not sell itself to any government elite. . . . "Separation of church and state" does not mean the divorce of religion from social and political concern, nor silence the church's social witness, nor forbid loyalty to and support of just government; it warns against the legal establishment of religion, restrictions on its free exercise, and the gradual development of organic institutional ties that fix public obligations on churches and thus erode religious liberty and tend to bring government under the influence of any or all religious groups to the disadvantage of other Americans. . . .
>
> The churches cannot afford to assume a position that will impede effective welfare work by church or state or limit the liberty of the state to meet fairly the diversity of demands made upon it in a pluralistic society, or systematically refuse cooperation with government in meeting this human need. On the other hand, the church cannot consent for itself or for other religious bodies to measures of cooperation with government which endanger the freedom of the church to witness as it sees fit, or which tend toward an establishment of religion, or which present the church to public view in any way inconsistent with its primary character as witness to God's reconciliation of the world in Christ.

As these citations make clear, the General Assembly has recognized for many years that, apart from questions of constitutionality, the church faces serious issues related to its own liberty of faith and action when it receives government funds. The 1969 General Assembly noted the distinction between "church-controlled" and "church-related" and urged that "temporary or permanent community agencies qualified to receive public funds" be established at church initiative to maintain such programs; and, if church control was temporarily necessary for start up or experimental programs, that any permanent program resulting . . . be removed from church control and put under the control of independent community-based bodies." Holding that "in the conduct of social services church agencies should accept necessary and proper governmental regulation and supervision," the Assembly noted:

> The church must decide from its own point of view whether or not it will enter into cooperative arrangements with government. The church's overriding problem is whether or not God's work in Christ is obscured by its cooperation in a particular governmental program and the acceptance of the legal structures attendant upon it.

In the section on church autonomy, we noted that under the free exercise clause the church should be free of both government interference and government regulation in ordering its life and activity, except where truly compelling government interests are at stake. When government appropriates funds for a constitutionally permitted social service to citizens and structures the service in such a way that private agencies are permitted to act as agents for government in the delivery of the service, we believe that churches should be eligible to receive such funds, but with significant conditions that modify the understanding noted above. In short, the area of permissible government regulation of the church's activity is widened; and the church's right to structure its activity to reflect its religious character and purpose is narrowed. Public funds require public accountability and may not be used in ways that advance or support religion, whether or not in the context of charitable service.

The church is not obligated to accept public funds to support its works of humanitarian service and indeed may deem the necessary conditions too harsh to meet. There is no constitutional right to receive such public funds; their denial in order to avoid palpable infringement of the establishment prohibition does not itself constitute a burden on the free exercise of religion. The church may initiate service ministries and operate service agencies, either for its own adherents or for the public, without governmental intervention and regulation when it uses its own resources to do so. When it wishes to use public funds for serving public needs, the church should understand that it gives implied consent to necessary and proper governmental regulation and supervision, and to the civil compact concerning the organic relationship between church and state.

It is useful to repeat that public funding for specific social service activities does not permit government regulation in a way that compromises the autonomy or leads to entanglement with the more central religious functions of the religious body. To facilitate the proper relationship, we strongly recommend that churches and church agencies adopt organizational structures for conducting social service activities open to the public that keep them distinct from other aspects of church life, though not necessarily separate, if any use of public funds is contemplated.

1. Education

Constitutional and public policy doctrines have evolved to permit and regulate substantial use of public funds by religious organizations in the areas of health and welfare, social service, and higher education, though there are still areas of tension and controversy. Religiously controlled elementary and secondary education, however, remains a source of unsettled legal interpretation and unresolved policy conflict. For that reason, it requires a brief separate analysis.

Some religious faiths believe that the general education of children and young people should occur in an explicitly religious context — that religious and secular education should be thoroughly integrated. Public education cannot accommodate their belief. Those who hold such belief have a right under the Constitution to create and attend such schools, and many have done so, most notably the Roman Catholic Church and conservative Christian groups who operate "Christian academies." In providing general education, these schools are helping to achieve a highly valued public purpose — the education of the public — and many have long contended that they should in some way be aided by public funds.

Those who have argued for such support point out that the cost of executing and maintaining the physical facilities for these schools, quite apart from the cost of instruction, saves the state from financing identical facilities for public schools. They further contend that such schools provide substantial instruction in secular subjects and that public funds could be allocated to those subjects without violating the prohibition on state support for religion. It is also argued that requiring students who attend church-sponsored schools to forfeit public support that would have been available if they had attended public schools penalizes the exercise of their religious liberty and unfairly discriminates against religious members of the public in the expenditure or administration of public funds.

Those who have argued against such support point out that those who create such schools openly acknowledge that they do so in order to achieve the pervasive and thorough integration of secular and religious education. The pervasive religious character and purpose of the school means that all education in such schools is religious so that aid to such schools aids religious instruction. There is, in short, no secular function that the state can permissibly aid, since government may not sponsor or support religion or religious education. It is acknowledged that persons who pay tuition for religious schools also pay taxes for public education, but the payment of taxes by religious persons does not create any right whatsoever to a proportionate distribution of the total tax fund for their religious enterprises. Neither does the Constitution require reimbursement for such expense as the state may have been spared by the free exercise of religion.

At the level of constitutional interpretation, government aid to religious schools has been on the Supreme Court's docket almost continuously for twenty years. The Court has been unwilling either to ban all aid or to permit all forms of aid that have been proposed. It has to all appearances searched for a formulation that would validate some aid, but not too much, relying principally on the "child benefit" approach or the "secular component" approach. The former holds that the state can constitutionally fund educational benefits directly to children or their parents, even if used at or in connection with a religious school, though it cannot provide the same aid directly to the school. The latter relies on an attempt to divide the activities of a religious school into components that are wholly secular and components that clearly are or might be affected by religion, approving aid only if it can be traced to a wholly secular expenditure. Since the whole purpose of such schools is to integrate secular and religious education, such an approach seems well nigh conceptually impossible. A third approach, "purchase of services," in which the state provides services through independent contractors, was upheld in regard to religious hospitals that cared for indigents (*Bradfield v. Roberts,* 1899) and to religious schools providing Indian education (*Quick Bear v. Leupp,* 1908) but does not seem to enter into court consideration of modem religious schools cases.

The result of the Supreme Court's search for a coherent formulation is a series of inconsistent and finely distinguished decisions that have permitted the state to fund bus transportation to and from school, lend secular textbooks to students, provide on-site diagnostic services by state employees to students, pay religious schools to administer objective secular tests designed by the state and to take attendance; but have prohibited the state from funding bus transportation for field trips, providing maps or projectors, providing counseling or remedial instruction by state employees on-site, or paying a proportion of teacher's salaries for the time spent teaching secular subjects.

In *Mueller v. Allen* in 1983, the Supreme Court held that state income tax deductions for the expenses of sending children to religious schools were constitutionally permissible, at least in some circumstances. It was significant to the Court that the deduction applied to expenses for transportation and supplies which could be claimed by parents of public school children and to tuition payments by a small number of children attending public schools outside their own districts. Here was an apparent use of an "equal treatment" approach. The state was not required to discriminate against religion by denying a deduction available to parents of public school children.

Thus, it would appear that income tax deductions for private school tuition would be constitutionally permissible; and, if so, it would be discriminatory to deny the deduction to parents who sent their children to religious private schools. Such a deduction tailored only to religious school tuition would be unconstitutional; but in the affirmative, it would appear that if the deductibility of contributions to charitable organizations can constitutionally be extended to churches, then a similar deduction for private schools could extend also to religious schools.

Alternatively, it has been proposed the state could give the parents of every school-age child a voucher with which to purchase education in any accredited institution of their choice. In such a policy scenario, it would certainly appear constitutional for the voucher to be spent for tuition at a religious school. To deny that, we note again, would be discriminatory. The Supreme Court articulated this principle in *Witters* recently (1986), though it has been accepted at the policy level at least since the GI Bill was used for seminary training following World War II. *Witters* concerned the refusal of the State of Washington to allow Witters to use a state scholarship for vocational training for the blind to be trained as a pastor or church youth director. Since he could have used the scholarship to learn any secular occupation, the Court held that it did not violate the First Amendment for him to use it for religious training.

The search for a legal formulation that will permit direct state aid to religious schools will most likely continue to occur within very narrow limits, frustrated by the pervasive religious character and purpose of the schools and the constitutional barrier to government support of religion.

The opposition of Presbyterian General Assemblies to tuition tax credits and vouchers does not rest on constitutional arguments or interpretation but on the long-standing commitment to free and universal public education of the highest possible quality. That opposition was vigorously restated in 1982: ". . . on record as opposing all forms of tuition tax credits and vouchers at levels lower than the college level." The introduction to that action provides a succinct restatement of the historic rationale for it:

Whereas universal public education has its roots in the Presbyterian Church, and pronouncements of The United Presbyterian Church in the United States of America, historically, have sought to undergird public education and have opposed use of public funds for private or parochial schools; and

Whereas free public education has been a cornerstone of American democratic society, playing an important role in building an educated and freedom-loving nation and teaching children of many different national origins, languages, cultures, and religions how to live together; and

Whereas many powerful voices favor tuition tax credits, which would offer substantial rewards to parents for withdrawing their children from public schools and enrolling them in private schools, or a voucher system by which public funds would be channeled by parents directly to private schools; and

Whereas such methods would stimulate development of schools for separate races, religions, languages, cultures, political groups, and social and economic classes, and would cause a decline of the public schools; and

Whereas many private schools thus obtaining public funds would either be remote from public control or would find increasing control damaging to their reason for existence; and

Whereas many private schools could operate largely or entirely lacking licensed teachers, racial equality, sexual equality, and a commitment to religious freedom and our traditional democratic ideals. (Minutes, 1982 UPC, Part I, pp. 520-521)

Conclusion

As Presbyterians continue to struggle with the theological, legal, and public policy issues of government aid to religious institutions, they should take thought about three matters. First, we must take care that our particular institutional history and interests do not distort our constitutional and public policy views. Presbyterians have social service agencies but no parochial schools. Second, we must take care that our theological and ecclesiastical history of hostility to Roman Catholicism does not unconsciously continue to affect our constitutional and public policy views. Third, we must take care that the integrity of the faith and mission of the church is not slowly and subtly compromised by the relationship with government that comes with financial support. Religious liberty can be put at risk by our own decisions to mute witness and trim behavior so as not to give offense quite as readily as by overt governmental restrictions.

The 1969 General Assembly spoke to all three of these concerns:

> The greatest danger is that the church will misunderstand itself. The United Presbyterian Church intends to be and always become a fellowship of the servants of Christ. It does not intend to become a hostage of government. It does intend to join with public and private bodies in continuing service to humankind and thus bear witness to God's own reconciliation of the world in Christ. It does not intend to support programs of cooperation between church and state that may be fairly regarded by other Americans as inconsistent with the First Amendment as understood by the Supreme Court. It does intend to reserve the right at all times to judge proposals and programs of cooperation with government from two points of view that answer to its own double character: Do such programs of cooperation enable the church both to manifest and witness effectively to God's own reconciling action in Jesus Christ? Do such programs of cooperation make for equal justice to all citizens and religious groups in the American constitutional framework?
>
> The United Presbyterian Church asks nothing for itself that it does not willingly grant others. The General Assembly recommends to its agencies, judicatories, and institutions of the Church the following criterion: If our own proposals were substantively adopted as the official position of the Roman Catholic hierarchy, the Jewish community agencies, and others, would United Presbyterians be satisfied with the consequent evolution of church-state relations in the United States?

In view of the foregoing considerations, the 200th General Assembly (1988) adopts the following affirmations:

1. Government payments on behalf of individuals, under programs such as Medicare, Medicaid, and scholarship assistance, should without exception be available to clients and students at church-sponsored agencies and institutions on exactly the same terms as if those patients or clients were receiving their services from secular entities.

2. Government should not discriminate against religious institutions and agencies in the expenditure or administration of public funds when the public purpose can be achieved by the religious group in a way that does not support or advance religion. When public funds are made available to private agencies to meet welfare and social service needs, religious programs and agencies should not be excluded provided that:
   (a) the service is open to the public without discrimination on the basis of race, age, sex, religion or national origin;

(b) the service is administered without religious emphasis or content, or religious preference or other discrimination in employment or purchase of services;

(c) no public funds are used by religiously controlled organizations to acquire permanent title to real property (where existing religiously owned property requires minor modifications to meet specific requirements of the particular program and there are public funds expressly available for such purpose, they may be used by the church also);

(d) the religious organization or agency is subject to the same provisions for safety, general standards and licensing, qualifications of personnel, and financial accountability as other private agencies.

3. Since each state guarantees the right to a free public elementary and secondary education and maintains universally accessible institutions for that purpose, we oppose as a matter of public policy the use of substantial public funds to support private educational systems, including tax deductions or credits and use of educational vouchers.

4. Where government provides noncurricular services to both public and private schools that involve the itineration of public employees to the institutions, schools sponsored by religious organizations should not be excluded.

5. Tax deductions for contributions to religious agencies, or for payments to religious schools should they be enacted, should not be viewed as support or aid for religion. A policy decision by the state to refrain from taxing is not equivalent to a decision to appropriate public revenues.

6. Service ministries operated by or related to Presbyterian governing bodies, whether or not they receive public funds, should offer all services without restriction based on race, sex, religion, ethnic origin, or sexual orientation, and should conform to requisite health and safety requirements and standards regarding licensing and personnel qualifications. Where such programs are expected to continue for considerable time, placing them under the control of independent community-based bodies should be carefully considered. In light of the division within the religious and public life of this nation concerning government aid for religious schools and the great significance of quality education for all our children, we urge continuing study and reflection on the whole subject at every level of the church. The child benefit, purchase of service, and equal treatment approaches in particular merit careful analysis, both in ongoing constitutional interpretation and in public policy considerations.

D. *Taxation and Religious Organizations*

Questions concerning the tax status and tax liability of religious property, persons, income, and activity continue to arise at every level of political and religious life. The taxing power is the lifeblood of society from neighborhood to nation. But the power to tax is the power to reward and regulate, and sometimes to destroy. By taxing some things and refraining from taxing others, or by making tax benefits conditional on certain behavior, governing authority can reward, punish, or induce conformity to its purposes.

Issues surrounding taxation and religion are older than the First Amendment, which frames American consideration of them. The power to tax citizens to pay clergy salaries was a prominent aspect of the debate leading to the adoption of the Bill of Rights. Variations of that question continue to arise, joined by new issues arising from the expanded activity and wealth of both government and religion since the eighteenth century: property, income, and sales tax exemptions for religious organizations; clergy housing allowances and Social Security participation; the tax status of religious organizations that engage in lobbying on political issues; the taxation of "activities income" of religious organizations; loss of tax exemption because of "nonconformity to public policy"; taxation of church-sponsored and controlled activities because they are deemed by the state to be "nonreligious"; etc.

"No establishment" and "free exercise" interests are intertwined in such issues. The two First Amendment clauses are closely related, often simply different perspectives on a given issue. There is very nearly always tension between the two clauses; and court decisions move narrowly along the line of tension, with particular solutions determined by whether free exercise or no-establishment interests are seen to dominate.

The threshold constitutional issue is whether the state is required to exempt religious organizations from taxation in order to avoid infringing the right of free exercise, or prohibited from exempting religious organizations to avoid establishing religion. For example, there is a plausible constitutional claim to property tax exemption for houses of worship. For if a church could not afford to pay, it might have to abandon its house of worship or see it sold at auction. Surely, that is an intolerable burden on free exercise. On the other hand, if the church does not pay tax on its land and building, others must pay a bit more to support public services that benefit all property owners, including the church. These others, nonbelievers and all, are arguably being required to support the church and that sounds like an establishment.

In the *Walz* case in 1970, the Supreme Court held that giving churches the same property tax exemption available to other charitable organizations does not violate the establishment clause. In 1943, in the *Murdock* case, states had been told that they may not collect a peddler's tax from proselytizers who distribute religious literature and request contributions in return, seemingly embracing the broad principle that the state may not tax specifically religious exercise; it could not tax sermons, or prayers, or distribution of the Sacrament. But the Court said that these sorts of taxes were different from taxes on property and income, and it has never decided whether the free exercise clause requires tax exemption for church property or income.

However, it is increasingly common at the lower levels for courts to hold that the exemption of religious organizations from taxation is a matter of "sovereign grace" and not a matter of constitutional right. Most cases stating this doctrine arise at the boundaries of state exemption statutes; they tend to involve property such as church camps and parking lots. Courts tend to say that because the exemption is a matter of grace, the legislature can decide which property is exempt and which property is taxable. The Supreme Court, in the *Bob Jones* decision in 1983, itself commented that tax exemption was a matter of legislative grace, but since the university's free exercise claims were rejected on the grounds of a compelling state interest in racial equality in education, it is unclear whether the Court would deny tax exemption to religious organizations for violating "public policy" where the government interest is less than compelling.

When the tension between no-establishment and free-exercise is resolved in a way that leaves legislatures some discretion to tax or exempt from tax, a second and wholly different question arises. May the legislature grant a conditional tax exemption, exempting only those churches that conform to government policy? If government were free to grant or withhold tax exemptions as different churches pleased or displeased it, government could control all but the most resolute of the churches. Recent court decisions appear to lean in this direction, with potentially very serious implications for both establishment clause and free exercise clause interpretation. These implications are discussed more fully below and in the background material.

Thus, the constitutional situation in general seems to be: The state may grant tax exemptions to religion without violating the establishment clause; the State may not tax specifically religious exercise, but may tax some religious property or activity or place conditions on a grant of tax exemption without violating the free exercise clause.

The church's position on these issues is not dictated by court decisions. We believe that government cannot constitutionally tax the core exercise of religion, and that it therefore cannot constitutionally tax the property integral to those functions. Sacred location and space, a place to meet for prayer, praise, instruction, and celebration, are intrinsic to communities of faith. Such property is currently exempt in all states, so despite the loose language of court opinions, there is no square holding that states or municipalities could constitutionally tax such property. Where the costs of general community services such as fire and police protection, street lights, highway maintenance, education, and culture are met by taxes based on the assessed value of property and buildings, churches should vigorously resist any attempt to repeal the existing exemptions for core religious property, even if courts hold such taxes constitutional. Such taxes would strike at the heart of religious exercise and fall with devastating force on economically marginal congregations whose land and property might be assessed at very high levels.

On the other hand, where service is provided directly and billed separately, such as water and sewer service or sidewalk construction, the church should pay, even for that part of the cost pertaining to core religious property. When a community decides to bill individual users for a service, the church cannot plausibly claim the same service for free. The distinction is between services provided on a fee-for-service basis, with charges approximating the cost of providing the service, and services provided to the public as needed and funded by general taxation.

We recognize that the definition of "core religious property" will be varied and controverted. It may be a large cathedral or a tiny storefront, a mountain or a mesa. It may include ornate altars or plain classrooms. When and if definitional questions arise, a religious organization's sincere judgment that property is essential to its core cultic exercise is entitled to substantial deference.

Some congregations have made voluntary contributions to government "in lieu of tax." Such contributions should be viewed as truly a matter of grace, not as an obligation or a quid pro quo for tax exemption. We do not generally recommend them, though in particular circumstances other governing bodies may find them appropriate.

Regardless of what property is tax exempt, it is even more critical that any tax exemptions for churches not be conditional on the church's belief or behavior. The Supreme Court has held in other contexts that the government may not penalize constitutionally protected conduct by withholding a tax exemption (*Speiser v. Randall*, 1958). This protection surely applies to churches, but the Court has never had occasion to say so. Some lower courts have thought that if tax exemption is a matter of governmental grace, the government can condition tax exemption on waiver of constitutional rights. In 1972, the *Christian Echoes* decision denied tax exemption to a religious organization that had violated the restriction on influencing legislation in section

501(c)(3) of the Internal Revenue Code. The court of appeals said bluntly that churches could speak on political issues and pay taxes or remain silent and be tax exempt, but that they had no constitutional right to free speech and tax exemption at the same time.

The Supreme Court did not review the *Christian Echoes* decision, so it did not set a national precedent. However, two important decisions in 1983 seemed to move the Court in the direction of the *Christian Echoes* position, though a careful reading indicates that it has not fully embraced it. In *Bob Jones*, as noted above, the Court held that the Internal Revenue Service may deny tax exemption to religious institutions that violate "public policy" where a compelling government interest is at stake. The principal factor operating was not "conformity to public policy" but "compelling state interest." As we have recognized in other sections, a truly compelling government interest may override religious free exercise interests that would otherwise rise to the level of constitutional rights.

The other 1983 decision, *Taxation With Representation (TWR)*, did not involve religion but is analogous in potentially important ways. TWR argued that the 501(c)(3) restriction on influencing legislation violated its rights to free speech. The Court agreed that "the government may not deny a benefit to a person because he exercises a constitutional right." But it held that this rule did not apply to TWR's case because it could organize a 501(c)(4) affiliate, completely under its control, to carry on its political activities. Contributors to the 501(c)(4) could not claim a deduction, but the Court found no constitutional right to a tax deduction for contributions to influence legislation. Tax exemption for influencing legislation was a matter of grace. The Court agreed that government could not penalize TWR's exercise of constitutional rights but found no penalty on the basis of the particular facts in the case.

The matter is quite different for the church, but there is no certainty that the Court would so construe it. In "attempting to influence legislation" churches speak to the moral aspects of political issues. Such witness flows directly from fundamental faith and is integral to its free exercise. It is essential to the church's identity and mission, and to the moral authority of its pronouncements, that it speak as "church" through its religious structures and leaders. No church can be restricted to speaking on political issues solely through functionaries employed by a political affiliate without violating its faith and calling. Any attempt to segregate a church's political speech from its moral and religious speech fundamentally misunderstands the nature of church speech on political issues. A later section of this statement analyzes why speaking on the moral implications of political issues is a core religious function, protected by the free exercise clause, though it is also political speech, protected by the free speech and free press clauses.

We hold that the restrictions in section 501(c)(3) when applied to the speech of the church and its leaders are unconstitutional as a limitation on a core religious function. Religious organizations must be permitted to express their religious and moral perspective on political issues directly without forfeiting their tax exemption or the deductibility of contributions to them. This constitutional protection is extended to those religious organizations whose participation in public political debate is in the context of their overall religious witness. Religious organizations are not and should not be structured for the main purpose of supporting particular candidates or influencing particular legislation. If it is alleged that an organization has claimed religious character to shelter a principally political purpose, evaluation of such organizations must be made on the same considerations outlined elsewhere in this statement for determining what is or is not a religious organization.

More generally, we deny the legitimacy of government attempts to regulate churches by granting or withholding tax exemptions. Regulations attached to tax exemption must be justified by a compelling government interest. As affirmed in the sections on conscientious objection and church autonomy, "compelling interest" must be narrowly defined.

When the state grants exemption from taxes to religious organizations, the basic definition of what constitutes religious activity must be made by those organizations. With increasing frequency, taxing jurisdictions seek to collect taxes from religious organizations on particular property or activity in the face of statutory provisions exempting "churches, conventions, or councils of churches and their integrated auxiliaries" from tax liability. In such instances, the justification is most often that the property or activity is not sufficiently "religious" to qualify, although wholly owned, operated, controlled, and defined by the religious organization as a part of its life and work. We urge Presbyterians, when dealing with such situations, to recognize that the issue is not "whether the church should pay taxes." The issue is: "Who defines the church's nature and ministry?" The church need not argue that it is constitutionally entitled to a part exemption; it need not necessarily press for exemptions defined in past times to be retained, except for those related to core religious functions. But where the law contains the broad-form exemption for religious and charitable organizations and activities, Presbyterians must resist any attempt by taxing authorities to define some of the properties and activities wholly controlled and defined by the church as nonreligious.

These considerations, of course, do not apply to what is generally known as the "unrelated business income" of religious organizations and the property used to produce it. The Presbyterian Church and others have long affirmed both the constitutionality and appropriateness of such taxation. Indeed, most of the so-called mainline religious bodies requested the legislation covering such income and property in sections 501(b), 511, 512, and 513 of the Internal Revenue Code.

Subject to the foregoing, particular taxes or exclusions from taxes should treat religious organizations equally with charitable and non-profit organizations; or put another way, religious organizations should not be singled out for either penalty or privilege.

Some have argued that the church should pay taxes whether or not similar charitable and nonprofit organizations do. This argument may be based on a conviction that tax exemption for churches is an unconstitutional establishment of religion. That argument has been rejected by the Supreme Court. The argument may also be based on a conviction that the church compromises its potential for prophetic witness if it "accepts favors" from the state. Unless the church has sought or defended privileged tax status only for religious organizations, which Presbyterians should certainly oppose except for property essential to the core functions of religion, we do not believe this argument has weight. Indeed, if churches were excluded from tax provisions, either exemptions or liabilities, applicable to general charitable and non-profit organizations, that would discriminate against them simply because of their status as religious bodies. That could well be unconstitutional but should be opposed in any case.

Two existing provisions of the Internal Revenue Code violate the principle of no special benefit — no special burden for religious organizations. Under one section, clergy are permitted to exclude from taxable income a housing allowance or value of the free use of a manse provided to them. The exclusion applies to ordained persons who are educators, administrators, and other church functionaries as well as to retired clergy. Another section of the code permits employees of other organizations to exclude the value of housing furnished to them for the convenience of their employer at the place of employment, but the exclusion for clergy applies whether or not the manse meets the standards specified in that section. Such a provision available only to clergy raises establishment of religion questions and is inappropriate under the principle noted above. The tax status of the value of clergy housing should be determined by the same provisions that apply to employees of other organizations.

Sections 1401 and following of the Internal Revenue Code require clergy to pay Social Security taxes as "self-employed persons" imposing a special burden on these religious employees relative to the employees of other organizations. The rationale for this legal fiction was that a requirement that the religious organization pay the tax would constitute a free exercise burden on the religious body itself. Since the funds in either case come from the same source, the believing contributors, free exercise is no more or no less burdened by either method of payment. The pattern of Social Security tax payments for clergy should be the same as for employees of other organizations.

The 1970 General Assembly (PCUS) approved several criteria regarding taxation and tax exemption of religious bodies. The criteria are generally consistent with the analysis and recommendations of this report, with the exception of "voluntary contributions in lieu of taxation."

In view of the foregoing considerations, the 200th General Assembly (1988) adopts the following affirmations:

1. The state may not use its power to tax or to exempt from taxation, to restrict, or place conditions on the exercise of religion.
2. The state may not tax the central exercise of religion or property essential to the core functions of religion. We hold that the application of the restrictions in Section 501(c)(3) of the Internal Revenue Code to the speech of the church and its leaders is an unconstitutional limitation on a central exercise of religion.
3. We support exemption of other church property and income as a matter of legislative policy. Such exemptions do not "establish" religion.
4. We concede that some properties and operations of religious organizations may be subjected to taxation by legislative act but we will resist all efforts to do so by administrative determination, in the face of statutes that exempt churches from taxation, that some properties or activities wholly controlled and operated by the church as part of its mission are "nonreligious."
5. We affirm the legitimacy of taxing unrelated business income and property used to generate such income.
6. Particular taxes or exclusions from tax should treat religious organizations equally with charitable and nonprofit organizations; religious organizations should not be singled out for either penalty or privilege except for the exemption of property essential to the core functions of religion.
7. Special tax exemptions or burdens for the property and income of ministers or other church employees are inappropriate. They should be phased out over a period long enough to accommodate the reliance of many churches on existing exemptions.

8. Payments to government for specific services billed separately to all property owners are not "taxes" and may legitimately be required of religious organizations at the same rate as for other property owners.

9. Churches should feel no obligation to make voluntary contributions in lieu of taxes, and all such contributions should be truly voluntary. They are not a quid pro quo for tax exemption.

E. New Religions and Threats to Conversion

When the First Amendment to the Constitution was written two hundred years ago there were thirty-six religious bodies or denominations serving a population of approximately five million. Now there are over fifteen hundred religious bodies in the United States. Two hundred years of religious freedom, immigration, and cultural evolution have created a far more pluralistic religious climate. In the nineteenth century there were large immigrations of Catholics and Jews. New denominations emerged, as diverse as Jehovah's Witnesses and Mormons. More recently, Buddhists and others have come from the Far East, and Moslems from the Middle East. Eastern religions have won converts here, and new indigenous religions have developed. Finally, urbanization and increasing mobility have led to the geographical dispersion and greater visibility of once relatively isolated groups and, consequently, much more interaction with religions once on the edge of society.

These new religions, often indiscriminately branded as "cults," compete with the interests of the more traditional religions in the society. They often have charismatic leaders and rigorous pieties that demand much more of their followers than is demanded by older religions that have become less militant and more comfortable. New religions may deviate in other ways from the cultural and religious norms of the society in which they exist. They are often feared and disliked, and their success engenders hostility. The conflicts and persecutions associated with the spread of Christianity, the spread of Islam, and the Protestant Reformation illustrate that at times there can be no greater danger to religious liberty than the conflict between new and traditional religions.

Some people have resorted to extraordinary means in the attempt to control "cults" and "rescue" their converts. Unwilling to believe that a loved one would convert to a strange religion that demands great personal sacrifice, distraught relatives and friends are quick to conclude that the "cult" must have "brainwashed" the convert. Relatives of converts have fought "brainwashing" with "deprogramming," a process in which individuals who are members of a religious group are abducted and held captive during efforts to persuade them to recant their beliefs. Some courts have held that such deprogramming is false imprisonment, a civil wrong for which the victim can recover damages. A few deprogrammers have been criminally prosecuted for kidnapping.

Deprogrammers have sought to avoid these risks by finding legal authority for their actions. In several states, legislation has been introduced that would allow parents to seize adult children from religious groups and initiate deprogramming. Other deprogrammers have invoked statutes providing for guardians or conservators of incompetents. A few courts have appointed parents as guardians over their adult children, with authority to hold the "ward" for deprogramming. In vacating such an order, the California Appellate Court noted that guardianship of adults who experienced religious conversion would violate religious liberty and license "therapy" for purposes of thought control.

We can be sympathetic to the fears and anxieties engendered when family members or friends become deeply involved with strange and demanding religious groups, but the charge of brainwashing is rarely justified and the response of deprogramming under physical restraint is indefensible. Some new religions do win converts through emotional manipulation. So do some traditional religions. It is undoubtedly true that television evangelists manipulate more people's emotions in our society than do proselytizing cults. Nearly all religions make unverifiable promises of spiritual benefits; some religions, both old and new, make more or less specific promises of material benefit as well. The essence of Christianity is the miracle of Christ's death and resurrection and the promise of eternal life through God's grace. These are not "provable propositions," and we have no right to insist that the claims of new religions be subjected to empirical verification. As the Supreme Court recognized in *United States v. Ballard* (1943), people "may believe what they cannot prove. . . . Religious experiences which are as real as life to some may be incomprehensible to others."

The law cannot question claims of faith, nor can it fairly distinguish among external environmental influences and "the inner testimony of the Spirit" to judge the authenticity of conversion. Mystery and emotion are vital elements in the life and expression of nearly all religions. Incense and invitation hymn, ritual of friendship and mourner's bench — by what standards can courts differentiate the great variety of ways by which religion "manipulates" the emotional environment of potential converts? Neither courts nor other private parties are in a position to evaluate the subjective experience of someone converted or introduced to a new religious faith. Government intrusion into the embrace of faith violates the First Amendment guarantee of free exercise in the most fundamental way.

The law must confine itself to clearly defined and identifiable abuses. Most fundamentally, physical coercion must be forbidden whether engaged in by proselytizers or deprogrammers. To legalize any form of physical coercion or restraint for purposes of deprogramming strikes at the heart of the right to choose one's own religion. The law can provide remedies for fraudulent claims about empirical facts in this world, not dependent on any claim of faith, whether engaged in by proselytizers or deprogrammers. A religious leader cannot solicit money for relief of the poor or construction of a shrine when he intends to spend it on luxuries for himself. For better or worse, he can solicit money on the promise that God will bless the giver. Proper enforcement of existing laws would provide adequate remedies for physical coercion and secular fraud.

Several cases are in the courts now in which former members of new religious groups seek damages on various grounds, usually some form of fraud. In most instances, the persons had been active and satisfied adherents for a considerable period of time before becoming disaffected. They are ordinarily backed by organizations known principally for their anti-cult stance and activity. Some extremely punitive damage verdicts (in the millions of dollars) have been awarded by lower courts. Some of these have been reversed, but several cases are still in the trial or appeals process. We view such litigation with the same perspective outlined above. It is no more appropriate for the courts to judge the authenticity of faith and conversion retrospectively than at its initiation. The prospect of government assessing financial penalties on religious bodies to compensate disillusioned lapsed members is so fundamentally offensive to the First Amendment as to appear incomprehensible. The possibility of disillusionment with faith is part of the freedom to embrace it in the first place. The law should not attempt to preclude the latter or protect us from the former.

Finally, we recognize the rights of parents to control their unemancipated children and the pain of parents when children at any age leave the family's religion. Greater attention and education must be provided to families whose members have become involved in a new religion. The church community should be encouraged to assist family members, parents and friends attempting to cope with the seemingly "alien" religious experience of a loved one. Likewise the church community must always be supportive and compassionate toward individuals attempting to grow in their conversions and religious experiences, remembering that life in faith is also a developing and changing reality for those embracing new religions.

In view of the foregoing considerations, the 200th General Assembly adopts the following affirmations:

1. The right to choose one's own religion, and to change that choice, is the most fundamental religious liberty. This right must be vigorously protected from governmental intrusion or physical coercion, either by those seeking to convert or those seeking to prevent conversion. This right should also be protected from fraud, but courts cannot evaluate claims of religious faith.

2. The church should be tolerant of other religions and respect their right to proselytize and practice their beliefs in accordance with the tenets of their faith.

3. We oppose judicial and legislative efforts to interfere with freely chosen and maintained religious commitments by legal adults, whether based on attempts to define legally undesirable "cult" religion, the use of conservator and guardian procedures, or reversal through legally authorized deprogramming.

4. We further oppose the use of civil law by persons disaffected or disenchanted with their religious experience, unless plausible allegations of physical coercion or fraudulent claims related to empirical facts are present. The right of religious freedom carries responsibility for its exercise and the risk of disenchantment.

5. The church should provide counsel, education, and support for the family members and friends of those who have converted to a new faith or undergone a powerful religious experience, and indicate understanding and continued openness to those who have converted.

F. Religious Expression in Public Places

Prayer and other religious expression in public places have been the subject of continuing controversy. Some have sought to eliminate all religious expression from public places; others have aggressively promoted it with the stated intent to imply governmental approval, if not sponsorship, of Christianity. In between are those who simply want, for instance, to gather on a university campus for Bible study just as other students gather to seek a ban on nuclear testing and find themselves in court instead. Most of these controversies can be resolved by maintaining a clear distinction between government-sponsored expression and private expression. Religious expression by the government itself or sponsored by the government threatens religious liberty and is forbidden by the establishment clause. On the other hand, religious expression by private citizens and organizations, initiated by private citizens and organizations, is protected by both the free speech and free exercise clauses and cannot be banned from public places. Like political speech, religious speech in public places can constitutionally be subjected to neutral regulations of time, place, and manner. But it may not be restricted because of its content by either prior restraint or subsequent penalty.

Religious expression takes different forms, of course. An Easter sunrise service in the city park or a papal mass in the plaza is clearly appropriate and constitutional on the principle stated above. The proposal to erect a large lighted cross in a public park overlooking the city is another matter. Such a prominent and permanent display of religious symbolism can hardly avoid the color of religious establishment. The initiative and the funds to implement it may be private but the "speech" is governmental.

Government should be absolutely neutral in matters of religion, and the religion clauses commit the nation to that posture. Much of the controversy over school prayer and other public religious expression arises from the conviction that government may support one religion if it tolerates other religions, or that it may support religion generically if it does so nonpreferentially and noncoercively. The drafters of the First Amendment repeatedly rejected language that would have allowed such a stance. Such convictions, then, do not pass constitutional muster and would in any event be bad public policy; they do not keep the government sufficiently out of religion. The establishment clause prohibits government preference for one religion over others or of religion over nonreligion. This does not mean that the clause prefers nonreligion; indeed, it prevents governmental indoctrination against religion. Neither government programs nor public school curricula may be shaped to any theological view, whether theistic, agnostic, or atheistic.

The ban on religious expression by government protects religious choice from government intrusion. It also protects religion from trivialization by government. Of necessity, seeking not to offend, not to exclude, and not to particularize, government religious expression would be a vague and syncretistic civil religion. The inevitable tendency would be to endorse a pale version of the predominant beliefs in the locality, offending not only those who hold other beliefs but also those who take seriously the predominant beliefs. The Supreme Court recognized these problems in its 1963 decisions prohibiting state-sponsored or teacher-initiated religious expression in public schools. It is regrettable that the Court has departed from this rule in other contexts, as in its decisions permitting legislative prayers, *Marsh v. Chambers* (1983), and municipal nativity scenes, *Lynch v. Donnelly* (1984). The Court's emphasis on the secular nature of Christmas in concluding that a crèche does not sponsor or endorse religion is offensive to Christians and transparently false to non-Christians.

Although government may not sponsor religious expression, it does not follow that private citizens cannot pray or speak of religion in public places. To forbid religious speech in a public place where nonreligious speech is permitted would violate the free speech, free exercise, and equal protection guarantees of the Constitution. That would convert the required governmental neutrality toward religion into governmental hostility. The Supreme Court properly applied this principle in *Widmar v. Vincent* (1981), holding that student religious groups are entitled to meet on college campuses on the same terms as nonreligious extracurricular groups.

There has been controversy and litigation over whether high school students are entitled to this right to conduct religious activities on school grounds. There are clear differences in the context. In most instances, high school students are in school under compulsory attendance laws; that is, their presence is more a matter of government requirement than private choice. In many instances, clubs and activities are structured during the instructional day and are viewed explicitly as part of the instructional curriculum, making them more "curricular" than "extracurricular" and more "government-sponsored" than private. And it has been argued by courts that high school students are more impressionable than college students, and therefore more likely to take school permission as school sponsorship.

Nevertheless, we believe that the principle noted above can be applied equally to high school students. That is, if the high school has created an "open forum," allowing genuinely extracurricular and privately initiated student groups to meet in the school building, it should grant the same rights to student religious groups. There is no requirement that schools establish such an open forum, though we are persuaded that it is a sound policy, subject to reasonable time, place, and manner regulations. The fear that such equal treatment of religious speech will permit evasion of the school prayer decisions arises from failure to distinguish government-sponsored speech from private speech that happens to occur in a public place. To preserve that distinction and avoid abuses, school officials must not be allowed to create and sponsor student religious groups.

The controversy over "moments of silence" in public schools illustrates another failure to distinguish private from public religious speech. Most courts that have considered the matter have held "moment of silence" legislation or policies to be unconstitutional, discovering that the expressed intent and classroom implementation make it a "silent prayer" sponsored by the school. Experience confirms that such abuse has been widespread where the "moment of silence" has been instituted. Prayer should remain a private religious expression without government sponsorship or endorsement. A "moment of silence" is not inherently unconstitutional, of course, but we do not believe that such statutes should be enacted. The pressure to enact them comes from those who openly acknowledge the intent to "get prayer back in the schools"; thus it is improbable that the "moment of silence" would be implemented in a wholly neutral way.

The public school does not have to pretend that religion does not exist or is not to be mentioned in public, though it may neither endorse or oppose religious beliefs nor observe or belittle religious rituals. Public schools are constitutionally permitted and should be strongly encouraged to teach about the role religious faith and religious persons and groups have played in history, politics, social life, literature, and art; so long as the treatment is comprehensive, objective, and treats different religions with complete neutrality. The exclusion of the role of religion tragically distorts the curriculum and the educational experience. The distortion is widespread, as recent textbook evaluation studies have demonstrated. In the interests of authentic education, this situation must be remedied.

There are difficulties in this "objective inclusion of the role of religion"; and it is largely those difficulties, rather than hostility to religion, that deter textbook publishers and school administrators and teachers. There are those in the community who see "endorsement" in any mention of religion in the school curriculum. There are those who want any mention of religion to be tailored to essentially evangelistic ends. And there are those for whom "objectivity" precludes the mention of unflattering things about their particular religion or any mention at all of the role of religions of which they disapprove. However, between the endorsement of religion and the exclusion of religion, there is a wide range of possibilities, some of which come close to the ideals of neutrality and objectivity. This particular form of "religious expression in public places" is so important and so neglected that Presbyterians should give particular attention to the efforts to find that neutral and objective middle.

Public schools do have a responsibility to teach general moral values around which there is substantial social consensus. This teaching must not depend upon theological justification or invoke theological sanctions. The duty to teach the religious basis for moral values rests with the home and the church. When the state recognizes a compelling need to deal with controversial moral issues such as sexuality, it may constitutionally hold and teach values based on nontheological considerations but would be wise to acknowledge competing views and treat them with respect and encourage students to think through moral questions for themselves. Students holding minority views are bound to be offended when the government adopts one position on a controversial moral question without reference to other views.

Religious expression also often asserts views on controversial matters, such as the origin of the universe and the forms of life. Religious views of these matters may sometimes conflict with views from scientific or other perspectives. The right of public expression for religious views does not carry a guarantee that they will not be challenged. The state is entitled to express views on these matters from nonreligious perspectives, even though it is obligated to remain neutral on questions of religion. Thus, for example, the state is free to teach the scientific evidence in favor of evolution and to require students to achieve basic literacy in science. But it cannot require students to accept the premise that science is the only way to answer these questions. If some students believe that the scientific evidence is irrelevant because religion provides a different answer, the state must respect that belief.

Religion in its many forms and expressions is a vital force in the lives of people in this nation and thus in the society in the largest sense. Arguments and efforts that tend toward the total exclusion of religious expression from the public life of the people are mischievous and mistaken and must be resisted. However, public expression must not be confused with official sponsorship, which is both unconstitutional and bad policy. The line is not always clear, of course. In those instances, commitment to freedom of expression deserves at least equal weight to concern about establishment, particularly as close cases are considered.

Christianity is the historic and familiar majority religious faith in the United States. Our stories of civic origin, whether flowing from New England or New Spain, are inseparably intertwined with Christian energy and expression. The Presbyterian Church is a well-known and highly respected expression of Christian religion, deeply rooted in American life and history and enjoying both political and social access and influence in most places. Because of these things, Presbyterians have particular responsibility for community leadership in safeguarding the legal and responsible public expression of religion and for modeling such expression in their own life.

Presbyterians should, first, be careful of the constitutional limits and legal requirements when considering or planning public services or acts of witness, either for themselves or with other religious groups. Majority status and political access can lead us or others unconsciously to forget the limits and bypass the requirements.

Presbyterians should, second, be alert to the barriers encountered by religious minorities, particularly new and unfamiliar ones, in exercising rights to constitutional and legal public expression. Remembering our own early history as Protestants, we should be quick to advocate and defend their rights, no matter how "wrong" their faith or how strange their practice may seem. Their liberty is of a piece with our own.

Presbyterians should, third, be sensitive to the faith and feeling of others in planning public religious expression. "Appropriateness" should not be simply a legal question. Such consideration for others is right in itself; it is also important in keeping the civil compact of tolerance strong. We should give careful thought as to whether the "time, place, and manner" we contemplate will give unnecessary offense to those of other faiths or no faith, not simply if they conform to legal requirements.

In view of the foregoing considerations, the 200th General Assembly (1988) adopts the following affirmations:

1. Government must be neutral in matters of religion. It may not show preference of one religion over others, for religion in general, or for religion over nonreligion. While contact and conversation between public officials and religious leaders on public policy issues are certainly appropriate, official institutional ties between government and religion are not. For that reason, we continue to oppose the appointment of ambassadors to the Holy See of the Roman Catholic Church.

2. Government may not engage in, sponsor, or lend its authority to religious expression or religious observance. We continue to oppose any constitutional amendment to permit public schools to sponsor prayer.

3. Religious speech and assembly by private citizens and organizations, initiated by them, is protected both by the free exercise of religion and free speech clauses of the Constitution and cannot be excluded from public places.

4. The display of religious symbols in connection with private speech and assembly in public places is appropriate and legal. We oppose the permanent or unattended display of religious symbols on public property as a violation of the religious neutrality required of government.

5. Religious speech and assembly in public places may be regulated by government as to time, place, and manner, but only in a neutral manner and not to any greater extent than nonreligious expression.

6. Statutes permitting "moments of silence" in public schools are not inherently unconstitutional but should not be enacted because they are subject to abuse through pressures to allow state-sponsored prayer or endorse religion.

7. If a public secondary school permits genuinely extracurricular student-

initiated group activities in noninstructional time, religious expression should be permitted, subject to the same regulations and restrictions.

8. Public schools may constitutionally teach their students about religion in a neutral way. The incorporation of factual and objective references to the role of religion when teaching history, social studies, art, and literature is essential to a comprehensive and balanced education and should be encouraged and assisted in every possible way.
9. Presbyterians should be particularly vigilant to protect the right to public religious expression for new and unpopular minority faiths, and be sensitive to the faith and feelings of others in their own public expressions of faith.

G. Religious Participation in Public Life

The metaphor of a "wall of separation between church and state" is particularly misleading when used to advocate the separation of religion from politics or from any other dimension of the public order. The First Amendment has never meant separation of religion from community or separation of the church from public life. On their face, the religion clauses constitute an absolute prohibition on government participation in religious life; there is no hint that barrier was even thought to isolate religion from the life of the republic.

For Reformed Christians, there is a happy coincidence between the legal and the theological. Participation by individuals and groups in public life — including its political, economic, and social dimensions — is not only a constitutional right but also a religious responsibility. From 1788, in the same Basic Principles that placed a commitment to liberty of conscience at the heart of the church's faith and governance, the Presbyterian Church in this nation has articulated "an inseparable connection between faith and practice, truth and duty" (FG-1.0304). We assert that "the promotion of social righteousness" is one of the great ends of the church (FG-1.0200); and that "the recognition of the human tendency to idolatry and tyranny calls the people of God to work for the transformation of society by seeking justice and living in obedience to the Word of God" (FG 2.500). The church is called to share "with Christ in the establishing of his just, peaceable, and loving rule in the world" (G-3.0300). What is articulated in order has been made central in confession: "To be reconciled to God is to be sent into the world as God's reconciling community. This community, the church universal, is entrusted with God's message of reconciliation and shares God's labor of healing the enmities which separate people from God and from each other. . . . The church gathers to praise God . . . and to speak and act in the world's affairs as may be appropriate to the needs of the time" (BC-9.31,9.36).

According to the Reformed tradition and the standards of the Presbyterian Church (U.S.A.), then, it is a limitation and denial of faith not to seek its expression in both a personal and a public manner, in such ways as will not only influence but transform the social order. Faith demands engagement in the secular order and involvement in the political realm.

Participation in public life implies both support for and criticism of the public order. Religious bodies and people of faith hold to a wide variety of convictions, ideas, and values that make important contributions to the shape and strength of public life. That life has been shaped by individuals and groups that have sought to create new forms, sustain traditional ones, challenge existing ideologies and reform or resist unjust institutions. Participation is thus viewed by the government sometimes as a blessing and at other times as a threat. It is not surprising that many, particularly those who hold power, often prefer less participation by citizens and groups in the public arena, including those motivated by religious convictions, or at least wish that such participation be limited to a supportive role.

The participation of church bodies and believers in public life has seldom gone uncriticized or unchallenged and that is perhaps more true today than ever. Religious groups have participated vigorously on both sides of public policy debates on Central America and abortion, in the face of internal criticism and public challenges, both legal and rhetorical. In each major political party, ordained clergy candidates for the presidency have developed impressive strength, based in large part on the support of coreligionists who have moved into local and state politics as organized religious groups, in a direct way. In 1984, the stance of the candidate for Vice President on abortion was publicly criticized by leaders of her own church which occasioned widespread analysis and debate within the Catholic Church and the public media. In all these and similar developments, there were frequent charges that such activity was in violation of the "separation of church and state" allegedly required by the First Amendment. However, the Supreme Court has properly rejected claims that legislation violates the establishment clause if it embodies the moral teachings of a religious group or has been advocated by religious groups (*Harris v. McRae*, 1980; *McGowan v. Maryland*, 1961). The Court has struck down a clause in the Tennessee constitution that disqualified clergy from serving in the state legislature (*McDaniel v. Paty*, 1978). Such victories on behalf of religious participation in the political realm should not tempt us to relax our vigilance. Attempts to deny and reduce the full expression of religious convictions within the public order, whether by churches or their adherents, are not likely to diminish.

Some of the most serious pressures on religious participation in public life have come through the provisions of the Internal Revenue Code that a tax exempt religious organization is not to devote a "substantial" part of its activity to attempts to influence legislation nor participate or intervene in political campaigns on behalf of any candidate for public office. In 1976 the IRS held that an organization that had asked candidates for public office to endorse a code of campaign ethics had engaged in prohibited activity, though the organization had not endorsed any candidate or published the response to its request. In 1978, the IRS denied tax exemption to an organization that had sent a questionnaire to candidates and published the responses without comment in its newsletter. That created such an uproar that it was replaced by a vague ruling establishing an "all the facts and circumstances test." Two 1980 rulings seemed to relax the IRS limitations to some degree. A "private letter ruling" held that the reporting of votes on proposed legislation and the presentation of testimony to the platform committees of the two major political parties did not constitute participation in a political campaign. Revenue Ruling 80-282 held that publishing congressional voting records on a number of issues after the close of the session would not jeopardize exempt status, though the publication would show whether the votes were in accord with the organization's positions on the issues. The Internal Revenue Service does not seem to be able to distinguish between discussion of issues and candidates, on one hand, and intervention in campaigns on behalf of specific candidates, on the other, though the Supreme Court emphasized the necessity of this distinction in interpreting laws dealing with political expression (*Buckley v. Valeo*, 1976).

The Supreme Court has never had opportunity to rule squarely on the restrictions on political activity by churches contained in the Internal Revenue Code. We believe that the right of religious bodies and individuals to participate in public political life is not only an imperative of faith but is grounded in the guarantees of the First Amendment. Religious groups and people of faith enjoy freedom of speech and assembly, petition for redress of grievances, and all the other liberties accorded other groups and individuals under the Constitution. In the case of religious groups, however, these are the instruments of the transcendent guarantee of religious liberty. The right to petition and the right to speak freely are in service to the even more fundamental right to free exercise of religion, which government may not infringe. The First Amendment does not and could not compel religious participation in public life; but it stands sentry over all attempts to ban or burden it.

For these reasons, limitations upon the freedom of religious bodies to participate in public life are illegitimate and unconstitutional. The church is bound to reject any regulations limiting church advocacy of particular legislation or endorsement of candidates, or establishing religious qualifications for office holders. We acknowledge that some campaign finance laws and similar regulations applicable to all could also be applicable to churches, though not in any fashion that suggests that political activity is the major purpose of churches or that requires excessive governmental entanglement in the overall affairs of the church. But we deny the legitimacy of special restrictions on religious bodies or clergy, whether imposed on the basis of religion or as a condition of tax exempt status. And we deny the legitimacy of any restrictions on the church's own speech on social or political issues. Specifically, the political activity provisions of 501(c)(3) of the Internal Revenue Code, which limit the right of tax exempt churches to influence legislation or political campaigns, abridge religious liberty. As affirmed in the section on the church and taxation, they should be repealed or held unconstitutional.

We recognize the tendency of governments, political parties, and candidates to invoke the support of religion and religious bodies to legitimate their policies and power, and to seek the blessing of religious authority for partisan purposes. We must also recognize that churches can be tempted to seek political authority and control of the political process in the effort to make their vision of society mandatory for the society. It is easy to step from advocating our vision to seeking to enforce it, from protecting religious liberty to requiring "right" belief and action.

The church must advocate its positions on public issues, but it should not seek to exercise political authority in its own right. We venture no opinion on whether explicitly religious political parties would be held to be a constitutional form of participation in public life. We do assert that we are opposed to such participation on both theological and public policy grounds and that any such party that might win election would be barred by the First Amendment from implementing an explicitly religious platform.

For the same reasons of policy, we believe that the church's advocacy of public policy goals should not draw heavily on the specific theological language and symbols that animate our vision of public life. We should translate our vision into the language of public discourse. When we support job training programs for the homeless poor, we draw motivation from the Old Testament witness of God's care for the sojourner and Jesus' infinite love for the excluded, but we should not advocate the policy on the ground that God wills it, whether or not such advocacy is constitutional. We should translate our advocacy into the language of the common civic vision, the language of justice, equality, and opportunity.

Presbyterian Elder Thomas Wiseman, Chief Judge of the United States District Court for the Middle District of Tennessee, speaks of religious participation in public life as "evangelizing Caesar" and admirably summarizes the issues of public participation, after noting that some attempts are both unwise and unconstitutional:

> Not that churches and individual Christian Americans should not evangelize Caesar to observe what Christ has commanded. Urging an end to the arms race, or advocating greater emphasis on social programs to aid the poor and oppressed, are advancing Christian precepts but not the Christian religion. . . .
>
> As a Reformed Christian, I am dedicated to the continuing effort to reform the world and its institutions. Political participation is where much of the action is in this effort.
>
> In my own Presbyterian church today there are those who believe the immigration laws are contrary to the law of God and, therefore, they are participating in the sanctuary movement. Putting this kind of belief into action is in the highest tradition of the faith, as when the apostles told the high priest they must obey the law of God rather than man. It is another way of evangelizing Caesar and has proved effective as in the civil disobedience of the Civil Rights movement and opposition to the war in Vietnam.
>
> We can insist upon maintaining the wall of separation between church and state while still exercising the church's prophetic role of calling Caesar to task when he commits error. I have suggested to you that there is no inconsistency between maintenance of that wall and evangelical advocacy that Caesar exercise his functions according to the teachings of Christ, so long as we don't ask Caesar to put on the trappings of religion. I have suggested that it is constitutionally acceptable, but often prudentially unwise, to attempt to evangelize others to moral conduct through Caesar: it violates both the Establishment Clause, and its historical and ideological reason for being, to attempt to evangelize others through Caesar in any matter relating to worship or religious practice, or inculcation of belief.

In view of the foregoing considerations, the 200th General Assembly (1988) adopts the following affirmations:

1. The corporate entities and individual members of the Presbyterian Church (U.S.A.) are obliged by the religious faith and order they profess to participate in public life and become involved in the realm of politics.
2. Pastors and officials of the church, as well as lay members, have the right

and responsibility to stand for and hold public office when they feel called to do so.

3. The "free exercise of religion" must be understood to include and protect the right to practice faith in public and private as well as the right to believe and thus to include participation in public affairs by the individuals and church bodies for which such participation is an element of faith.

4. As part of the church participation in public life, governing bodies of the Presbyterian Church (U.S.A.) at every level should speak out on public and political issues, taking care to articulate the moral and ethical implications of public policies and practices.

5. We recognize that speaking out on issues will sometimes constitute implicit support or opposition to particular candidates or parties, where policy and platform differences are clearly drawn. Since such differences are the vital core of the political process, church participation should not be curtailed on that account; but we believe that it is generally unwise and imprudent for the church explicitly to support or oppose specific candidates, except in unusual circumstances.

6. We reject and oppose any attempts on the part of the church to exercise political authority or to use the political process to achieve governmental sponsorship of worship or religious practice.

7. We oppose attempts by government to limit or deny religious participation in public life by statute or regulation, including Internal Revenue Service regulations on the amount or percentage of money used to influence legislation, and prohibition of church intervention in political campaigns. We will join with others, as occasion permits, to seek repeal of such regulations and statutes, or a definitive ruling by the Supreme Court on their constitutionality.

The Committee that co-authored this report was comprised as follows:

MEMBERS

Rev. Gregory Gibson, Esq., Convenor
Dayton, OH

Rev. John C. Bennett
Claremont, CA

Ms. Alice Bonner, Esq.
Atlanta, GA

Mr. Braxton Epps, Esq.
Camden, NJ

Ms. Doris Haywood
New York, NY

Rev. Elenora Ivory
Washington, DC

Ms. Robin Johansen, Esq.
San Francisco, CA

Prof. Douglas Laycock
School of Law
University of Texas at Austin

Prof. David Little
Department of Religious Studies
University of Virginia at Charlottesville

Prof. Lee McDonald
Department of Government
Pomona College

Mr. William Scheu, Esq.
Jacksonville, FL

Rev. Richard Symes
Palo Alto, CA

CONSULTANTS

Rev. Charles Casper, Esq.
Philadelphia, PA

Rev. Dean M. Kelley
National Council of Churches
New York, NY

Mr. William P. Thompson, Esq.
Princeton, NJ

STAFF

Rev. Dean H. Lewis
Presbyterian Church (U.S.A.)
Louisville, KY

Gail Hastings Benfield
Presbyterian Church (U.S.A.)
Louisville, KY

Reading Legal Citations for Nonlegal Readers

As I said in the Preface, readers so inclined can skip the footnotes without missing much. I try to avoid adding more text in the footnotes; nearly all of what you will find in the footnotes is citations to other scholars and to operative sources of law — court opinions, constitutions, statutes, and regulations. Still, even readers generally inclined to skip footnotes may sometimes wonder where some surprising or important statement came from. What does he cite for that? Is he talking about the Supreme Court of the United States, or some other court?

The answers to such questions are in the footnotes. Sometimes the answers are encoded in succinct abbreviations, but the code is not hard to decipher. Here is the key. Readers so inclined can read the whole Appendix for a fairly simple introduction to legal citations. Or, they can skim through until they see a centered citation that looks like the one they are trying to decipher; the explanation of that citation form will be immediately above and below.

The Basic Pattern

The basic pattern of legal citations is an author's name, if any; a title or the name of a case or statute, a volume number, an abbreviation for the book or periodical that contains what is being cited, a page number or section number, and a date of publication in parenthesis. Additional information can be tacked on at the end or tucked into the parenthesis, or tucked in elsewhere and separated by commas. Putting the volume number before the periodical may initially seem odd to readers from other disciplines; putting it at the end seems odd to lawyers.

In the abbreviation for the book or periodical, and in the parenthesis at the end, there is much useful information about the source being cited and the extent of its authority. These codes are not complicated, and they are explained below.

Courts

One code appears in text. "The Court," with a capital C and no further identification, refers to the Supreme Court of the United States. "The court," with a lowercase c, means some other court — anything from a United States Court of Appeals or a state supreme court to an assistant magistrate in the city court of Smalltown, USA, to courts in general. This is always true in articles. But in briefs, there is an obsequious exception: I always capitalize the Court when referring to the court to which the brief was submitted.

Court Opinions

The largest amount of encoded information occurs in citations to court opinions, more commonly known as cases. Usually, but not absolutely, you can recognize a case citation because it will begin with two names, separated by a "v." Here is a typical case citation:

Lee v. Weisman, 505 U.S. 577 (1992)

The two names are the names of the lead plaintiff (the person or persons who are suing) and the lead defendant (the person or persons being sued). The "v." stands for versus. So this is Lee versus Weisman. Lee was a middle-school principal in Providence, Rhode Island; Weisman was a parent complaining about prayers at graduation. Weisman was the plaintiff; in the lower courts, this case was *Weisman v. Lee*. But in the Supreme Court (and also in some state supreme courts), the first-named party is the petitioner, the party who lost in the highest lower court. So about half the time, the order of the names gets reversed in the Supreme Court. Case names are usually italicized in text, but not in citations in footnotes. When the name of a person in a case appears in roman type in text, it refers to the person; when italicized, it refers to the case.

Names of companies, government agencies, and institutions are often tightly abbreviated in the footnotes, but these abbreviations usually make reasonable sense in ordinary English. So you might see:

Santa Fe Indep. Sch. Dist. v. Doe, 530 U.S. 290 (2000)

This would be Santa Fe Independent School District versus Doe.

Occasionally, for procedural reasons that need not concern readers, a case is identified by the name of only one side. In these cases, there is usually a prefatory phrase, often in Latin. So you will occasionally see case names that look like this:

Ex parte Young
In re Young
In the Matter of Young

However the name is formulated, the real information is in what follows the name. The basic pattern is number, abbreviation, number, which indicates the volume, the series of books (known as a reporter) in which the opinion appears, and the page number. So *Lee v. Weisman* is reported in volume 505, of the United States Reports, at page 577. The number in parentheses is the date of the decision. The Court decided this case in 1992. *Santa Fe Independent School District v. Doe* is in volume 530 at page 290, and was decided in 2000.

If the citation is to a particular passage inside the opinion, the page number (or numbers) of that passage will be identified. So you will often see something like this:

Lee v. Weisman, 505 U.S. 577, 598-99 (1992)
or
Lee v. Weisman, 505 U.S. 577, 579 n.* (1992)

In the first example, the specific passage cited appears at pages 598-99; in the second, it appears in the footnote marked *, which begins at page 579.

A second parenthesis following the date may give information about who wrote the opinion, especially if the opinion was not supported by a majority of the Court. So you might see:

Lee v. Weisman, 505 U.S. 577, 607 (1992) (Blackmun, J., concurring)
or
Lee v. Weisman, 505 U.S. 577, 643 (1992) (Scalia, J., dissenting)

These citations are to specific pages in a concurring opinion by Justice Blackmun, or in a dissenting opinion by Justice Scalia. A concurring opinion agrees with the judgment of the Court, but offers additional or different reasons or explanations. A dissenting opinion disagrees with the judgment of the Court and explains why. Sometimes an opinion will be labeled "plurality," like this:

> Mitchell v. Helms, 530 U.S. 793 (2000) (plurality opinion)

This typically means the opinion is the lead opinion and announces the judgment of the Court, but that less than a majority of the Court signed the opinion. Such an opinion has much less authority than an opinion by a majority (often called an "opinion of the Court"). Lawyers then look to concurring opinions to see if they can count a majority of the whole Court for particular propositions that appear both in the plurality opinion and in one or more of the concurring opinions. This need to distinguish majorities from pluralities applies to any multi-member court, not just the Supreme Court of the United States.

The volume and page numbers in a citation are useful only if you want to find the full opinion. But the abbreviation between the volume and the page number is useful for other purposes. It identifies the reporter, and that is the first step in identifying the court that decided the case. And the court that decided the case tells you much about how important or authoritative the decision is.

U.S. Supreme Court

The Supreme Court of the United States is cited to U.S. (United States Reports). From the reader's perspective, the abbreviation U.S. tells you that all the examples so far were decided in the Supreme Court of the United States. The United States Reports are slow to publish, so in the interim, Supreme Court cases may be cited to S.Ct., U.S.L.W., or Westlaw (abbreviated WL). But nearly all of those variant citations have been eliminated from this work.

U.S. Courts of Appeals

One step below the Supreme Court, there are thirteen federal courts of appeals. Eleven of them sit in numbered geographic circuits; one sits in the District of Columbia (the D.C. Circuit), and one specialized court (rarely or never cited in this work) is called the Federal Circuit. Their opinions are cited to the Federal Reporter, which is now in its third series of volume numbers. The three series of the Federal Reporter are cited as F., F.2d, and F.3d. The particular court is specified in the parenthesis by number, D.C., or Fed. So a typical citation for a court of appeals case is:

Weisman v. Lee, 908 F.2d 1090 (1st Cir. 1990)

This case is reported in volume 908 of Federal Reporter, Second Series, at page 1090, and it was decided by the United States Court of Appeals for the First Circuit in 1990.

The circuit that decided a case tells you something about geography, and that may tell you something about the political makeup of the court or the social conditions that led to the litigation. Here are the states and territories in each circuit:

First Circuit:	Maine, New Hampshire, Massachusetts, Rhode Island, Puerto Rico
Second Circuit:	New York, Connecticut, Vermont
Third Circuit:	Pennsylvania, New Jersey, Delaware, Virgin Islands
Fourth Circuit:	Maryland, Virginia, West Virginia, North Carolina, South Carolina
Fifth Circuit:	Texas, Louisiana, Mississippi
Sixth Circuit:	Michigan, Ohio, Kentucky, Tennessee
Seventh Circuit:	Wisconsin, Illinois, Indiana
Eighth Circuit:	Minnesota, Iowa, Missouri, Arkansas, North Dakota, South Dakota, Nebraska
Ninth Circuit:	California, Oregon, Washington, Idaho, Montana, Nevada, Arizona, Alaska, Hawaii, Guam, American Samoa, Northern Marianas
Tenth Circuit:	Wyoming, Colorado, Utah, New Mexico, Kansas, Oklahoma
Eleventh Circuit:	Florida, Georgia, Alabama
D.C. Circuit:	District of Columbia
Federal Circuit:	Patent cases and federal government contract cases from anywhere

U.S. District Courts

Below the courts of appeals are the eighty-nine federal district courts, which are the federal trial courts. They are organized by districts, and each district is one state or part of one state. Within states, districts are named by direction: the northern, southern, eastern, western, middle, or central district of the state. District court opinions are reported in the Federal Supplement, which is now in its second series, and abbreviated F. Supp. or F. Supp. 2d. So a typical district court citation looks like this:

Weisman v. Lee, 728 F. Supp. 68 (D.R.I. 1990)

This *Weisman v. Lee* was decided in the United States District Court for the District of Rhode Island in 1990, and it is reported in volume 728 of the Federal Supplement, at page 68. A citation to a case from a state divided into multiple districts would look like this:

Good News Club v. Milford Central School,
21 F. Supp. 2d 147 (N.D.N.Y. 1998)

The abbreviation in the parenthesis tells you that this case was decided in the United States District Court for the Northern District of New York.

U.S. Bankruptcy Courts

Adjunct to the federal district courts are the federal bankruptcy courts, and their decisions are occasionally cited in this work. These decisions are reported in the Bankruptcy Reporter, abbreviated B.R., and the courts are identified by Bankr. plus the abbreviation for their district. So a typical Bankruptcy Court citation looks like this:

In re Young, 148 B.R. 886 (Bankr. D. Minn. 1992)

State Supreme Courts

Most state court opinions are published in a set of regional reporters, organized by geography. These are the Atlantic (A. and A.2d), Northeastern (N.E. and N.E.2d), Northwestern (N.W. and N.W.2d), Pacific (P., P.2d, and P.3d),

Southeastern (S.E. and S.E.2d), Southern (So. and So.2d), and Southwestern (S.W., S.W.2d, and S.W.3d) reporters. More helpfully, the name of the state is always indicated in the parenthesis with the date. So a typical citation to a state court looks like this:

Westbrook v. Penley, 231 S.W.3d 389 (Tex. 2007)

If the name of the state appears with no further elaboration, the case was decided by the state supreme court.

State Courts of Appeal

Each state has one or more courts of appeal (sometimes described as intermediate courts of appeals) below its supreme court. Their decisions are generally in the same regional reporters with the state supreme court cases, and while they have a variety of names, for simplicity in this work they are generally indicated by the addition of "App." after the name of the state. So a typical citation to a state court of appeal looks like this:

Penley v. Westbrook, 146 S.W.3d 220 (Tex. App. 2004)

Because New York and California are so big, they have their own reporters. New York's intermediate court of appeals is called the Appellate Division, and its decisions are reported in the New York Supplement (N.Y.S. and N.Y.S.2d). So a typical New York Appellate Division citation looks like this:

Catholic Charities v. Serio, 808 N.Y.S.2d 447 (App. Div. 2006)

California's intermediate court of appeals cases appear in the California Reporter (Cal. Rptr., Cal. Rptr. 2d, and Cal. Rptr. 3d). A typical citation looks like this:

Smith v. Fair Empl. & Hsg. Comm'n, 30 Cal. Rptr. 2d 395
(Cal. App. 1994)

A few state courts have sufficiently distinctive names that they get special abbreviations. Pennsylvania has a Commonwealth Court (Pa. Commw.) and a Superior Court (Pa. Super.); Texas and Oklahoma have courts of criminal appeals (Crim. App.) that are each state's highest court in criminal matters; and

Texas used to have courts of civil appeals (Civ. App.) There are probably others that I am not thinking of right now, but the legal reader will recognize them and the general reader rarely need worry about the distinctions between these and other intermediate courts.

State Trial Courts

In most states, trial court decisions are not reported. The principal exceptions are New York and Pennsylvania. New York trial court decisions are reported in the New York Supplement (N.Y.S. and N.Y.S.2d) and in the Miscellaneous Reports (Misc., Misc. 2d, and Misc. 3d). Miscellaneous Reports are cited only when the case is not reported in New York Supplement. And to confuse everyone who is not a New York lawyer, the principal New York trial court is called the Supreme Court; New York's highest court is the Court of Appeal. So a typical New York trial court decision looks like this:

Church of Our Lady of Vilna v. Archbishopric of New York,
841 N.Y.S.2d 818 (Sup. 2007)

The abbreviation N.Y.S. tells you it's a New York case, and the Sup. tells you it's a Supreme Court case, which in New York means a trial court case.

Pennsylvania trial court decisions are reported in the Pennsylvania District and County Reports (Pa. D. & C., Pa. D. &. C. 2d, Pa. D.& C. 3d, and Pa. D.& C. 4th). So a typical Pennsylvania trial court decision would look like this:

Bonson v. Diocese of Altoona-Johnstown, 67 Pa. D. & C. 4th 419
(Com. Pl. 2004)

This case is reported in volume 67 of the fourth series of District and County Reports, and it was decided in the Court of Common Pleas.

Administrative Agencies

Administrative agencies often issue quasi-judicial decisions. These are usually reported in a reporter that bears the same name as the agency, and they are cited on the same pattern as court decisions. There is no need to work through all the agencies here, because the pattern should be familiar by now.

One agency whose decisions are cited in this work is the National Labor Relations Board. Because the Board itself is a party to every case in that agency, the cases are referred to by the name of the other party only. So a typical citation to an NLRB case would look like this:

Diocese of Ft. Wayne-South Bend, Inc., 224 N.L.R.B. 1226 (1976)

State administrative agencies have fewer reported decisions, but the citations generally follow an analogous pattern.

Subsequent History

If a decision of a lower court is appealed, or a decision of an agency is reviewed by a court, the authority of the decision in the lower court or agency depends on what happened in the higher court. Where the authority of a case is affected by its subsequent history, that history is indicated with a verb or verb phrase that indicates what happened and a citation to the higher court case where it happened. Common indications of subsequent history are affirmed *(aff'd)*, reversed *(rev'd)*, vacated *(vacated)*, appeal dismissed *(appeal dis'd)*, certiorari granted *(cert. granted)* (which means that the Supreme Court of the United States has agreed to hear the case). For very recent decisions, there may be an indication of certiorari denied *(cert. denied)*, to show that the judgment is final and there will be no further review. Sometimes these verbs are modified with a phrase such as "on other grounds," which means that the affirmance or reversal has nothing to do with the point for which the case is being cited. Some of these phrases are technical, but most of them make reasonable sense in ordinary English. A citation of a trial court decision with a complete subsequent history might look like this:

Weisman v. Lee, 728 F. Supp. 68 (D.R.I.), *aff'd*, 908 F. 2d 1090
(1st Cir. 1990), *aff'd*, 505 U.S. 577 (1992)

In this example, the decision of the United States District Court for the District of Rhode Island was affirmed by the United States Court of Appeals for the First Circuit, and that decision was affirmed in turn by the Supreme Court of the United States. The omission of a date in the parenthesis with "D.R.I." means that that court's decision was in the same year as the next decision in the subsequent history — that the district court and court of appeals both decided the case in 1990.

Federal Statutes

Most citations to statutes follow the familiar pattern of number-abbreviation-number, but the references are somewhat different. A typical citation to a federal statute looks like this:

42 U.S.C. § 2000e-(1)(k) (2006)

The abbreviation U.S.C. indicates the United States Code, where all federal statutes are compiled and arranged by subject matter. The number before the abbreviation refers to the "title" rather than to the volume. The United States Code is divided into fifty titles, which are very large subject matter groupings of statutes. Each title is further divided into chapters, sections, subsections, subsubsections, and sometimes even finer subdivisions. The symbol § means section, and the number after the abbreviation is the section number, including any further subdivisions that might be needed. So this citation is to a part of an Act of Congress codified in Title 42 of the United States Code, section 2000e-(1)(k), as it appeared in the 2006 version of the code. Of course such a section might be amended from time to time, so the 2006 version might be different from the 2000 version. The items in this work were written over a period of thirty years, so the statutory citations are to the statutes as they existed and as they were published at the time of each item's original publication. Consequently, there are citations to every publication of the United States Code since 1970.

Statutes are enacted more or less continuously. Between compilations they are published in supplements, generally indicated by "Supp." in the parenthesis with the date. So an amendment enacted in 2003 would be cited like this:

42 U.S.C. § 2000e-(1)(k) (Supp. III 2003)

Occasionally, usually where the enacting history is important or the citation is to a version of the statute that has been amended or repealed, statutes are cited to Statutes at Large (Stat.), a chronological compilation of every Act of Congress since 1789. Because it has no subject matter organization, Statutes at Large has no titles. Instead, each Act of Congress has either a Public Law number or a chapter number. These citations generally contain the name of the Act and its Public Law or chapter number, a volume number and a page number in Statutes at Large, the date of enactment, and where relevant, a section number and page number within the Act. So a typical citation looks like this:

Religious Freedom Restoration Act, Pub. L. No. 103-141, § 6(a),
107 Stat. 1488, 1489 (1993)

This would be the original section 6(a) of Religious Freedom Restoration Act, which was Public Law No. 103-141 (the 141st public law enacted by the 103rd Congress), and which begins at page 1488 of volume 107 of Statutes at Large. Section 6(a) appears at page 1489.

Federal Regulations

Federal regulations are cited on the same pattern to the Code of Federal Regulations, cited as:

Equal Participation of Religious Organizations, 29 C.F.R. § 2.32 (2007)

This would be title 29 of the Code of Federal Regulations at section 2.32 in the 2007 compilation.

Before they are compiled into the C.F.R. by subject matter, new and proposed regulations are published every day in the Federal Register (Fed. Reg.). A typical citation would look like this:

Participation in Department of Health and Human Services
Programs by Religious Organizations, Providing for Equal
Treatment of All Department of Health and Human Services
Program Participants, 69 Fed. Reg. 42586-01 (July 16, 2004).

State Statutes

Citations to state statutes are varied, but follow the same basic pattern. One variation is that the title number and the section numbers are often combined into a single entry after the abbreviation. The abbreviation, whether in between or at the beginning, always contains the name of the state and nearly always the term Stat. or Code or Laws. Sometimes the abbreviation, more often the parenthesis with the date, includes the name of a private publisher. So typical citations to state statutes look like this:

IDAHO CODE § 73-401 *et seq.* (Michie Supp. 2004)
or
71 PA. CONS. STAT. ANN. § 2401 (West Supp. 2004)

In the first example, the statute begins at section 401 of title 73 of the Idaho Code, and it is printed in the 2004 Supplement. In the second example, the statute is section 2401 of title 71 of the Pennsylvania Consolidated Statutes Annotated, and it is printed in the 2004 Supplement.

The chronological printings of state laws are called session laws, because they are typically printed for each session of the legislature. Typically the volume number is the year of enactment, the abbreviation includes the name of the state and the word Laws, and after the abbreviation comes a chapter number or section number, or sometimes a page number. So a typical citation to a state session law looks like this:

> An Act Relating to Government Restrictions on the Exercise of Religion, 1999 Tex. Sess. Law ch. 399 (Vernon)

Because the volume number indicates the date, it is not repeated in the parenthesis. Vernon is the private publisher authorized to publish the session laws.

State Regulations

State regulations are cited on the same model as federal regulations. Compilations by subject matter, analogous to the Code of Federal Regulations, have names such as Texas Administrative Code (Tex. Admin. Code) or Administrative Rules of South Dakota (S.D. Admin. R.). Chronological publications, analogous to the Federal Register, have names like Texas Register (Tex. Reg.) or Utah State Bulletin (Utah Bull.).

Articles

Citations to articles build on the pattern of citations to cases and statutes: Author, title, volume number, journal title, page number, date. Always remember that the volume number comes before the journal title, not after. So a typical citation to an article looks like this:

> Douglas Laycock & Oliver S. Thomas, *Interpreting the Religious Freedom Restoration Act*, 73 Tex. L. Rev. 209 (1994)

This co-authored article, with the title in italics, appeared in 1994, in volume 73 of the Texas Law Review, at page 209. In articles, but generally not in briefs, there is the curious convention that the abbreviation for the journal is printed in large and small capitals.

Some journals use the date as their volume number, and in that case there is no parenthesis with a date. So we get citations like this:

Douglas Laycock, *The Remnants of Free Exercise*, 1990 Sup. Ct. Rev. 1

This one appeared in the 1990 Supreme Court Review, at page 1.

The names of journals are tightly abbreviated, but if you keep in mind that most legal journals are published by law schools, most of the abbreviations are not hard to decipher.

Books

Books are cited by author, title, and date, usually omitting any mention of the publisher, and in large and small capitals in footnotes to articles. Citations to a particular page are inserted after the title and before the date. So a typical book citation looks like this:

Kent Greenawalt, Religion and the Constitution 266-69 (2006)

Short Forms and Cross References

Many legal sources are cited repeatedly in the same article, often with some dramatically shortened form of citation and, for books and articles, a reference to the footnote that contains the full citation. Cases are cross-referenced by the name of one party, books and articles by the name of the author. Earlier footnotes are referenced with *supra*. So a reference to page 586 of the opinion in *Lee v. Weisman* might look like this:

Lee, 505 U.S. at 586.

Full citation information will be found in an earlier footnote, usually not far away. For articles and books, we get:

Laycock, *supra* note 10, at 21.
or
Laycock, *supra* note 15, at 366.

The large and small caps in the second example indicate that the reference is to a book. The full citations would be in the referenced footnotes, and the citations in this footnote are to the particular pages referenced after "at."

If there were two Laycock articles in footnote 10, the cross-reference would include a short form of the title. In footnote 10, after the full citation, there would be a parenthetical such as "(hereinafter cited as Laycock, *Remnants*)." Then, when the cross-reference came, it would say:

Laycock, *Remnants, supra* note 10, at 21.

The occasional forward reference, always done for explanatory reasons and never as a citation shortcut, is indicated with *infra*. Typical examples would be:

See text and notes *infra* note 225.
See *infra* note 225 and accompanying text.

The compulsive citation habits of lawyers generate so many footnotes that note numbers make for a handy system of cross-reference.

References to the single citation in the immediately preceding footnote are indicated with *id*. So:

Id. at 224.

This would mean at page 224 of the source cited in the immediately preceding footnote.

Details

Of course there is more, but the rest is detail. The examples above will cover 99 percent of all the citations in this work. And nearly all the rest are variations and elaborations of these basic forms. Readers who are curious about who said or decided what can usually get the answer from the citations without much difficulty.

Index

gious organizations and, 790. *See also* Free exercise of religion

Free Exercise Clause and Establishment Clause: General Theories (2000): on Establishment Clause, 111-20; on Free Exercise Clause, 103-11; overview of, 2

Free exercise of religion: but not to burden or oppress others, 737-38; conscientious objection cases prior to 1963 under, 291-92, 293; Founders' use of 'religious liberty' and 'establishment' and, 558-59, 560; government-suppressed religious competition and, 716-17; history of exemption claims from government regulation, 448-49; participation in politics and, 811; regulatory exemptions and, 719, 720-21; RFRA and broadened definition of, 186, 186n.367; use of phrase in Constitution, 81

Free Press Clause, 629-30

Free Speech Clause: Alien and Sedition Acts as authoritative interpretation of, 629-30; Bork's views on, 492; evangelicals interweaving patriotism and religion and, 52; excluding nontheists from Free Exercise Clause and, 74; general constitutional law casebooks' coverage of, 467; *Locke v. Davey* (2004) and, 164-68; Mormon forfeiture of property and, 705; protection from being forced to affirm atheistic beliefs, 73; *Rosenberger* compared to *Velasquez* and, 147; tax deductions for influencing legislation, 792-93. *See also* Religious speech

French and Indian War, 727, 731, 732-33

French Revolution, 680-81. *See also* France

Freud, Sigmund, 677

Frost, J. William, 728n.90

Fundamentalist Christians. *See* Evangelical Christians

Funding religious organizations: burden rights and neutrality rights in, 149-50; charitable choice options and, 420-21; discriminatory cases, 146-47; discriminatory refusal in *Davey*, 222; doctrinal context of, 134-39; establishment and, 715, 716; federal government schools for American Indians, 567, 591, 610-11, 707-8; Feldman on funding for, 258; Founders' rejection of for religious

functions, 85, 259-60; Gey on no-aid for, 258-59; hazards of governmental discretion in, 169-74; history of dispute over, 415-22; *Locke v. Davey* (2004) on, 127, 129, 143-46, 189-90, 193; nonpreferentialism of Establishment Clause and, 115; O'Connor-Breyer rule on diversion of aid to religious uses, 383-86; other limits to *Davey*, 156-68; overview of what the state must fund, 143-46; penalties vs. refusal to fund, 148-56; preferential, 93-94; and protecting religious liberty, 221; religious intensity of program where funds are used, 157-60; religious liberty issues with, 132-33; with secular programs, 93-94; with secular programs, substantive neutrality and, 95; separating funded and unfunded activities in, 151-56; what state may fund, 139-43. *See also* Financial aid; Religious schools

Galanter, Marc, 302

Garvey, John H., 57, 65

Gay rights movement: anti-Catholic feelings and, 335, 673; extracurricular school clubs, 256; political activism of evangelical Christians and, 450, 672; religious liberty issues and, 451-54

General Applicability Interpretation, of Free Exercise Clause: bankruptcy suits against churches and, 363-65; claims under, 368-69; college dormitory residence requirements, 367-68; individualized vs. categorical exceptions and, 365-66; landmarking case exceptions, 367; medical exceptions and, 366-67; as optimistic result of *Smith-Lukumi*, 360-61; other free exercise claims not dependent on, 369-71

General assessment bill (Virginia, 1785): as coercive, 626-28; Curry's account of, 559-60; endorsement test and, 628; exemptions and, 722-23; Hamburger's account of, 747-48; as nonpreferential, 551-53, 558; opponents of, 89-90, 275, 601; Presbyterian opposition to, 90, 327-28, 570, 601, 747, 761-62; reasons for defeat of, 570. *See also* Virginia

Generally applicable laws: *Am. Family Ass'n. v. FCC* (D.C. Cir. 2004) on,